Moral Philosophy

A COMPREHENSIVE INTRODUCTION

Moral Philosophy

A COMPREHENSIVE INTRODUCTION

Brooke Noel Moore • Robert Michael Stewart
California State University, Chico

Mayfield Publishing Company
Mountain View, California
London • Toronto

Library of Congress Cataloging-in-Publication Data

Moore, Brooke Noel.
Moral philosophy : a comprehensive introduction / by Brooke Noel Moore and Robert Michael Stewart.
p. cm.
Includes index.
ISBN 1-55934-037-1
1. Ethics. I. Stewart, Robert. II. Title.
BJ1012.M6267 1993
170—dc20 93-11106
CIP

Manufactured in the United States of America
10 9 8 7 6 5 4 3 2 1

Mayfield Publishing Company
1280 Villa Street
Mountain View, CA 94041

Sponsoring editor, James Bull; production editor, April Wells-Hayes; copyeditor, Sally Peyrefitte; text and cover designer, Gary A. Head; art director, Jeanne M. Schreiber; manufacturing manager, Martha Branch. The text was set in 10-1/2 / 11-1/2 Garamond by TypeLink, Inc. and printed on 45# New Era Matte by Arcata Graphics.

Acknowledgments and copyrights continue at the back of the book on pages 653–654, which constitute an extension of the copyright page.

PREFACE

We admit that the title is a bit bold. Still, the distinctive feature of this volume is its comprehensiveness. The first part of the book explains the fundamental theories, concepts, distinctions, and issues of ethics. The second part contains reading selections, arranged chronologically, from the most important Western moral philosophers. For every selection we provide a brief introduction in which we explain the theory of the selection's author. Accordingly, Part II is a historical survey of ethics from the Greeks through the twentieth century, with readings. The third and final part of the book is an introduction to applied ethics; it, too, contains selected readings.

Because Part I explains the fundamental issues and concepts of ethics, it lays the foundation for Parts II and III, helping readers understand the material in those later parts. Those parts, in turn, give life and substance to the issues and concepts discussed in Part I. Students will find in Part I frequent references to material in the other parts. Instructors may choose to integrate assignments from Part I and Part II, as well as from Part III.

We believe this book offers conspicuous advantages to instructors of different types of ethics courses. Those instructors who favor a historical approach to ethics can provide their students with a solid theoretical framework within which to survey the history of ethics. Those who favor a conceptual approach will have at hand a brief history of the subject, with readings, to enrich their students' understanding of the subject. Both types of instructors will have available material in applied ethics, which is of widespread current interest among philosophers and which tends to strike students as especially important. And finally, instructors who teach applied ethics or who approach general ethics via applied ethics will have readily available a fertile source of historical and conceptual background material.

Certainly there are many important moral philosophers whose works are not represented in Parts II and III. We have been disinclined to assume that a comprehensive introduction must be an all-inclusive catalogue. Nevertheless, the selections in Part II include works from writers whose influence on Western moral thought has been the most profound. The selections in Part III provide a good introductory survey of applied ethics—a survey that covers both problems of social policy and problems of individual moral choice. We have also been selective in Part I; still, we think that it will familiarize readers with most of the issues, concepts, and theories that concern moral philosophers today.

Many philosophical essays are technical, and we have tried to keep to a minimum the number of selections that university undergraduates are apt to find horribly taxing. But to deserve our claim to have provided a comprehensive introduction, we couldn't omit all difficult readings, and some of those found in this collection will challenge even the ablest students. Among the classical selections, those from Aquinas and Kant are probably the most difficult; among the more demanding contemporary pieces we'd list those by Hare, Harman, and Capaldi, and the first essay by Foot. We have tried to help students with difficult selections by providing fairly detailed introductory comments. Also, we have included study questions at the end of each selection to help readers understand the essays they have read.

At the end of the book you'll find a fairly extensive and current list of suggested readings.

Finally, we'd defeat the purpose of our book if we didn't provide some way for our readers to find their way around its three parts; it's especially important for readers of Parts II and III to be able to refer back to the conceptual material in Part I. So we have included a fairly detailed index, and we think students will find it more than routinely useful. Instructors should encourage them to make frequent use of it, we think.

Several individuals have helped us in creating this volume, and we'd now like to thank them. Naturally, we don't blame them for any errors or other problems we've failed to detect. You shouldn't blame them either. They are Philippa Foot, Richard Brandt, Dan Barnett, Jim Oates, Tom Imhoff, and Eric Gampel. We are also grateful to Linda Bomstad, California Polytechnic State University, San Luis Obispo; Karen Hanson, Indiana University; Sterling Harwood, San Jose State University; Anita Silvers, San Francisco State University; and Becky White, California State University, Chico, for their thoughtful review of the manuscript.

CONTENTS

PART

CONCEPTS AND PROBLEMS OF ETHICS

This book consists of three parts. In Part I, we explain the fundamental theories, concepts, distinctions, and issues of ethics. Its six chapters give you the theoretical framework you need to understand the selections in Parts II and III.

In Chapter 1, we aim to give you a reasonable sense of what ethics is, what it isn't, and what relationship it bears to other subjects. In Chapter 2, we explain some of the fundamental distinctions moral philosophers make. In Chapter 3, we explore another fundamental ethical distinction: the distinction between fact and value. In addition, Chapter 3 addresses the issue of whether moral knowledge is possible in the first place.

Ethical theories embody various conceptions of well-being. In Chapter 4, we examine the most significant of these conceptions. Since ethics is concerned with how we should live and what kind of people we should be, in Chapter 5 we explain the fundamental theories of moral conduct. In Chapter 6, we discuss some considerations related to agency (that is, the power of acting for an end), such as free will and weakness of will.

Thus our intention in Part I is to familiarize you with most of the issues, concepts, and theories that interest moral philosophers today. When you read the selections in Parts II and III, we recommend that you refer back to this part whenever you encounter a concept or distinction you don't feel you fully understand. Don't forget to use the index to help you locate things.

CHAPTER 1

PHILOSOPHY, ETHICS, AND PRACTICE

Religion, Social Science, and Philosophy

What is it that moral philosophers do? How does moral philosophy differ from moral theology and social scientific accounts of morality?

Many people answer ethical questions by looking to the moral codes found in sacred scriptures or the edicts of religious authorities. Some people hold that conscience is our only guide when it comes to applying these moral rules or principles to what we say and do. Conscience, they believe, gives us objective knowledge about what we ought to do in particular circumstances, perhaps because God gave it to us. Yet, we should realize, religious texts and authorities can conflict on matters of morality, and the same uncertainties and conflicts can arise among the consciences of human beings.

Moral theologians attempt to understand, interpret, and resolve ethical questions within the context of assumptions about God's will, the soul, salvation, and the afterlife. Moral philosophers, by contrast, often challenge such assumptions and ask to what extent moral inquiry can be done independently of theological beliefs. Of course, many moral philosophers have made religious beliefs central to their theories, and moral theology and moral philosophy can overlap. But modern moral philosophers tend to approach ethical questions from a basically secular standpoint, to look for rational or natural explanations of moral phenomena. After all, we need moral concepts and rules whether God exists or not, and it would be interesting to know whether morality can stand apart from religion.

Theology, philosophy, and science have historically depended on each other in various ways even when at odds. To distinguish these realms of inquiry from one another, we need to determine what kind of knowledge each aims at attaining and how it pursues that knowledge. Here are some preliminary suggestions. Science describes and explains natural phenomena in natural terms, using empirical evidence in accordance with the principles of logic. Theology attempts to describe and explain the whole of nature in supernatural terms, to reveal causes and levels of reality behind our ordinary experience that are beyond the scope of scientific methods. Philosophy aims to understand our concepts and practices of explanation, justification, description, knowledge, experience, and reality. Doing philosophy involves criticizing these ideas as well as proposing better ways of thinking about life and the world.

Two aims of this chapter are to locate the more specialized field of moral philosophy, or philosophical ethics, within the broader discipline of philosophy and to show how it differs from the ways in which social scientists—especially psychologists—approach the study of morality and values. The first objective is relatively easy and straightforward; the latter will take more time and effort.

The Divine Command Theory of Morality

Can morality be identified with God's commands to human beings? Or is morality in some way independent of divine will? Can God command what is morally evil or wrong? If he did so, would that make it right for us?

These and related questions have puzzled theologians and philosophers since at least the time of Socrates (see, for example, the famous discussion of piety or holiness in Plato's dialogue *Euthyphro*). William of Ockham, a prominent medieval philosopher, held that moral rightness and wrongness are defined by God's will, in contrast to Saint Augustine's position that God cannot will evil. Saint Thomas Aquinas argued that given our divinely created capabilities, nature, and circumstances, it would be logically impossible for God to command a different morality. Ralph Cudworth, an eighteenth-century British moralist, asserted that God cannot make what is immoral morally right, for much the same reason as he cannot make a four-sided triangle. Other philosophers have put forth a weaker view than Cudworth's—that some moral truths are necessary and unchangeable even by God, but others are contingent and alterable. Quite apart from the question of whether an omnipotent Being could make morality anything he chose, there are questions about how we could know his will and why we ought to obey it (if God commanded you to kill a member of your family, as in the story of Abraham and Isaac, should you obey?).

One thing is clear: We would need morality even if we gave up belief in God, so morality ought to have another foundation. Finding this ground, if it exists, is one of the central tasks of secular moral philosophy.

Traditionally, philosophy has been divided into four or five major areas: Metaphysics is the study of our basic concepts of reality—existence, mind, matter, substance, property, causation, and so forth. Epistemology is the philosophical study of knowledge itself, dealing with issues about what, if anything, we can know and how we can know it. (Logic is sometimes regarded as a part of philosophy, too, but many classify it as a separate discipline comparable to mathematics.) Ethics, social-political philosophy, and aesthetics, finally, deal with matters of value—what sorts of personal choices, sociopolitical systems, and artistic endeavors are good, right, or just.

Philosophical ethics, then, deals mainly with the personal choices we make about how to live our lives, what things to pursue, and how to act toward others. It involves the attempt to provide theoretical standards for evaluating our decisions, actions, characters, and practices or policies. Moral philosophers also are often interested in how we apply such general criteria to specific practices (for example, whether abortion or capital punishment is right) or to concrete instances of these practices (that is, whether a given case of abortion or execution is right). Finally, ethics or moral philosophy, like philosophy generally, is concerned with analyzing, defining, or clarifying our basic ideas and beliefs—specifically, ideas and beliefs about good and evil, motives and actions, right and wrong, and the acceptability of our ways of reasoning about what we ought or ought not to do.

Of course, anthropologists, sociologists, and psychologists sometimes study moral beliefs, codes, institutions, and practices, too. Yet their intentions are primarily explanatory—this is what essentially distinguishes social science from moral philosophy, where the central concern is to *evaluate, assess,* or *justify* moral views. Before proceeding, we need to clarify this distinction.

Explanation and Justification

We often talk about the *reasons* why people do things; we say, for example, "Sam swerved his car in order to avoid hitting the child." We also offer reasons why people have certain beliefs, attitudes, and feelings: "Sandy believes that Clinton will be reelected because the economy is strong"; "Seymour feels guilty because he lied." The reasons why we act, believe, and feel the way we do are central to our understanding of ourselves and our relations to others.

These reasons fall into two broad categories—*explanatory* reasons and *justifying* reasons. In other words, when we give or demand reasons for people's actions, beliefs, feelings, and so forth, we are looking either (a) to explain why people have the feelings or beliefs they have or why they do what they do, or (b) to find out what justification—what *good* reason—they have, if any, for feeling, believing, or acting as they do. Often we are looking for both.

When people give a reason for doing something, it is sometimes unclear whether they intend to explain why it was done or to show that it was a good or rational thing to do. Consider the first of the examples at the beginning of this section: "Sam swerved his car in order to avoid hitting the child" gives a reason that is *both* explanatory and justifying. But if the reason were "because he was drunk," that would be *only* an explanatory reason, since drunkenness is usually not considered a good reason for erratic driving. These cases are quite clear. By contrast, consider this claim: "Sam drove over the speed limit in order to get his injured child to the hospital." Some people would argue that Sam's reason not only explains (in part) why he acted criminally, but also *justifies* him (at least partially). Often only further questioning of the speaker will clarify whether he or she means to explain, justify, or both.

Both explanatory and justifying reasons can be either prima facie or conclusive. A *prima facie* reason for doing (or believing or feeling) something is a reason "other things equal"; that is, a prima facie reason explains and/or justifies *in the absence of contrary considerations.* Whether there are in fact such contrary considerations is a question that is left open. A detective might ascribe a motive that explains why a suspect would commit a crime, constructing a prima facie case for believing that the suspect is guilty (for example, the suspect is the sole beneficiary of a recent insurance policy on the victim's life). Whether the suspect has a *conclusive* reason to commit the crime depends on the presence of prima facie reasons *against* doing it (for example, the likelihood of getting caught and punished) and whether these reasons outweigh the reasons for doing it. *Conclusive* implies "all things considered."

We consider people to be rational or reasonable when they believe, act, and feel in accordance with good reasons. But we should not assume that there is always one rational or reasonable choice and never more than one. Some philosophers have denied furthermore that—strictly speaking—it makes sense to say that choices, actions, desires, and emotions can be rational or irrational. The most famous advocate of this position is the eighteenth-century philosopher David Hume. In his early masterpiece, *A Treatise of Human Nature* (first published anonymously in 1739), Hume makes his point vividly: It is not contrary to reason to prefer my total misery to a small amount of pain for a complete stranger, nor the world's destruction to a scratch on my little finger.

Hume's view is that our attempts to justify actions, desires, and feelings rationally must rest on assumptions about their relationships to rational beliefs (which can be true or false, since they represent the world as being so-and-so). If a want, feeling, or act is the result of false or unreasonable beliefs—for example, if I mistakenly believe that I will be happy or healthy if I get what I want, or that my act will bring about my intended aim in the most efficient way—then my desire or action is open to criticism from a rational standpoint. But if I know all the relevant facts and have chosen the most effective means to my ends, then I am beyond rational criticism as far as that desire or action is concerned.

Other major figures in the history of moral philosophy, most notably Plato, Aristotle, and Immanuel Kant, take positions sharply opposed to Hume's. Their conceptions of rationality and of what is good for human beings are more objective than Hume's: These thinkers believe that practical reasons are (at least in moral contexts) independent of the agent's actual desires and attitudes. Kant, for example, insists that we can have a moral reason for doing something that is contrary to our inclinations. Kant's theory of practical reason differs in important ways from the accounts of Plato and Aristotle, as we will see later. But all three philosophers were rationalists in a sense that Hume was not, and they maintained that moral judgments have an objectivity grounded in human reason and human nature.

Judging people and their actions to be rational or irrational, reasonable or unreasonable, and so forth, is—whatever theory of practical rationality we accept—inescapable in our social lives. Rationality is a concept that bridges the notions of explanation and justification; we rely on rationality both to understand why people do what they do (as well as predict their actions) and to evaluate them and their acts.

Sometimes we're cautioned not to be judgmental about the behavior of others, that if we only understand better their points of view—they might have different beliefs or needs and interests than we do, for example—we wouldn't be so quick to criticize or condemn. This is often good advice, of course. Isn't it often necessary to "put ourselves in others' positions" (as hard as this can be) if we're to be fair and accurate in our moral assessments?

Yet we mustn't confuse this wise advice with the more extreme and dubious claim that nobody ever has a right to judge other people morally. The fact that moral judgment is occasionally inappropriate doesn't mean that it always or usually has to be. For instance, we tend to label as hypocrites people who condemn others for doing what they do themselves. But this is not to say that these "hypocrites" are mistaken or wholly out of place in their judgments of others. They can be blind in their own case, weak-willed, or in some other way inconsistent and still be justified in their moral judgments about other people. Think, for instance, about smokers who tell others not to smoke; their advice is sound, even if they don't follow it themselves.

Again, it is true that we should sometimes refrain from judging other people or their acts morally. However, we would go too far to conclude that we would always forgive wrongdoers once we fully understood their perspectives and circumstances. No one, after all, makes a comparable claim about good actions and persons, only bad ones. If we accepted the general principle, shouldn't we also be prepared to say that complete understanding would keep us from praising the positive? More to the point, this view could rest on several assumptions: that human beings lack free will (a controversial belief we will discuss in Chapter 6), that people's characters and actions therefore cannot be truly bad or wrong, and that consequently these actions *must* be excused or forgiven. But that is a dubious inference, as we will see more clearly later on.

Nevertheless, we still need to face a question that many people, particularly those who have some background in psychology or other social sciences, might ask: Why do we justify or evaluate behavior at all? Shouldn't we just try to understand and perhaps help people to change?

We can begin to answer this very reasonable question by remarking that most of us, most of the time, feel called upon to justify, assess, and criticize ourselves and others. We are often almost compelled—inwardly, if not outwardly—to do this so that we can satisfy what seem to be urgent needs. Of course, this feeling might be wholly the result of socialization processes rather than an innate tendency. And it's frequently a self-serving parody, what we call "rationalization," instead of true justification.

Let's assume that our common need or desire to justify and evaluate persons and their actions is entirely the product of the moral training we receive from society, beginning in our earliest years. Certainly this desire is useful, indeed indispensable, to society. How could a community exist without it? We must have ways of restraining, guiding, and otherwise influencing people's actions if we are to live together in secure, orderly, mutually beneficial arrangements. Law serves this function coercively. But we also need moral rules and standards to shape social behavior in areas where legal reinforcement would be ineffective or too costly.

But that is only part of the answer. More fundamentally, we all have *ideals,* and we use the language of justification and assessment to express these value conceptions and invite others to share them or measure up to them when the ideals are common. (Needless to say, we often do this to ourselves as well; we try to motivate ourselves to change bad habits or in some other manner live up to the goals we have set for ourselves.) Without ideals we would hardly be human.

Suppose we didn't talk about good and bad or right and wrong at all, but only tried to limit ourselves to finding out why people do what they do, predict what they will do, and reinforce or change their behavior without recourse to praising, blaming, judging, evaluating, advocating, prescribing, or condemning. Social life as we know it would not exist! We would be much the poorer, not only because we would lose a very effective means of motivating people without using physical force, but also because we would have no conceptual or linguistic means to formulate, express, and promulgate our values and social ideals.

But, we might now ask, if we justify and evaluate all the time, what do we need moral philosophy for? What use do ordinary people in real life have for the kind of theory philosophers engage in? To help answer these questions, let's take a brief look at the evolution of moral philosophy over the centuries. We will, of course, consider the history of ethics more carefully in Part II.

Theory, Practice, and the History of Ethics

In ancient Athens during the time of the great philosophers, ethical and political questions were the major subjects of discussion and debate among the educated, free male citizens, many of whom aspired to public office in that democratic city-state. The Sophists, wandering teachers of many disciplines, mainly rhetoric, were known for their denial that moral matters are objective matters. From their travels, the Sophists came to see the diversity of moral codes and values found in different societies. Typically, the Sophists concluded that morality was essentially conventional, as opposed to natural; in the famous words of Protagoras, "Man is the measure of all things."

Against this view stands Socrates. As portrayed by his student Plato, he believes in the existence of moral truths that transcend the customs, laws, and other conventions of societies. The latter are but reflections of public opinion, which is often wrong, the product of ignorance, prejudice, and selfish interest. What most people think, therefore, Socrates considers to be of little importance. For this stance he finally paid with his life. Prosecuted and convicted on charges of impiety and corrupting the youth, Socrates chose death by poison instead of exile from Athens.

Whether we share the convictions of Socrates and Plato or not, it is certainly the case that we can criticize the beliefs of our society, as well as those of other cultures, on a rational basis. How far we can go in this rational criticism of norms and values is one of the central questions running through the history of Western moral philosophy. Most philosophers would agree, however, that we cannot take the views of our society on moral matters as the final authority (simple relativism); nor is the individual's own opinion the final court of appeal in ethics (simple subjectivism). Reason and argument, involving appeal to principles and acknowledged goods, have a place in disputes about values.

We can understand the history of moral philosophy as a succession of theories about what is good, right, and just, each philosopher responding to the theories of his predecessors and contemporaries. With few exceptions, the major moral philosophies are attempts to get beyond simple appeals to what we ourselves feel or think, uncritically, about moral matters. Our prephilosophical views about ethics are often inconsistent, based on factual error and ignorance, bias, or narrow self-interest. The accidents of birth, upbringing, and cultural background tend to determine much of what we think and feel about right and wrong. Philosophers as different as Plato and Hume, Kant and Mill have all tried to show that reason can, at least to some degree, take us to a more objective standpoint. From that standpoint we can examine the common moral beliefs we have been taught and make some of the hard moral decisions that are an inescapable part of life.

Socrates challenges the common conceptions of piety in Plato's *Euthyphro,* of virtue in the *Meno,* of justice in the *Republic.* He shows the contradictions in ordinary people's beliefs about ethics and points out that these beliefs often depend on falsehoods and ignorance of the facts. Socrates tries to give a more systematic account of ethical ideas—one that will stand the test of reason and motivate those who understand it. Indeed, some recent research indicates that persons who have reflected rationally about moral beliefs are more likely to act in accordance with their professed convictions than are those who simply accept uncritically whatever they think is the prevailing opinion.

In the Christian philosophical tradition, which is much influenced by Plato, Aristotle, and the Stoics (who, like the Epicureans, were most concerned about giving practical ethical advice), we find profound attempts to balance the claims of reason and faith. Saint Augustine and Saint Thomas Aquinas are the two salient thinkers in this tradition prior to the rise of Protestantism. Their philosophical investigations of morality reveal how reason can expose error in commonly held beliefs and remove confusions and misunderstandings. They offer practical counsel that is valuable to Christians and non-Christians alike.

The first major philosopher of the modern period was the great English materialist and rationalist Thomas Hobbes. His moral and social philosophy is a rigorous attempt to base morality on a social contract between self-interested, rational individuals. Without theological premises, Hobbes develops a scientific model for understanding society, ethics, and politics that remains influential today. By contrast, the later British philosopher David Hume, more skeptical about the power of reason in human affairs and opposed to the egoism of Hobbes, bases his moral theory partly on what he takes to be the capacity for sympathy and benevolence in human nature. His empiricism and agnosticism, while limiting his reliance on rationality, nevertheless are consistent with his aim of "overturning the vulgar systems of morality"—the unsophisticated beliefs of the common man as interpreted by second-rate philosophers and theological moralists.

From the late eighteenth century through the nineteenth, the two most important moral theories were utilitarianism, which follows Hume in its emphasis on benevolence and posits the maximization of social happiness as the aim of morality, and the duty-based theory of Immanuel Kant, an ethic of respect for persons grounded in abstract conceptions of rationality and freedom, that is, the human capacity for autonomous choice. These theories—which are philosophical variations on central values of Judeo-Christian morality as expressed in the Ten Commandments and the Sermon on the Mount—remain central to contemporary philosophy.

Friedrich Nietzsche's philosophy of value represents a radical departure from the utilitarian and Kantian theories. He rejects wholesale the idea that Christian morality should—in any of its aspects—be defended by philosophy. Instead he advocates a new order of values according to which the superior members of the human species are entitled to reject the claims and disregard the interests of the "common herd." Thus, in a more radical way than any of his predecessors, Nietzsche challenges our ordinary moral beliefs, forcing us to rethink many of our most basic convictions.

Recent moral philosophy, however, is largely concerned with the criticism and development of ideas and perspectives associated with Aristotle, Hume, the utilitarians, and Kant. Twentieth-century ethical theory is preoccupied with questions about meaning and knowledge in evaluative contexts as well. The last twenty years have also seen a growing interest in problems of applied ethics—how we can interpret theories to help us solve real-life, concrete moral quandaries. Abortion, euthanasia, health care distribution, and other issues in medical ethics have received extensive treatment by contemporary moral philosophers, as have many problems in business ethics, such as preferential treatment and the morality of advertising. The philosophical literature on issues in professional ethics, environmental ethics, agricultural ethics, and several other fields has grown remarkably.

Although the tasks of moral philosophy can't be reduced to scientific ones, the findings of the social sciences are highly relevant to philosophical research. Sociobiology, anthropology, and social psychology are especially pertinent fields for ethics, and in recent years some important work has been done in the study of moral development. We will conclude this chapter with a summary of some of this research, in the hope that it might further illuminate some of the relationships between philosophical and psychological studies of morality.

Psychology and Moral Development

Following in the footsteps of the French child psychologist Jean Piaget, whose book *The Moral Judgement of the Child* is considered the seminal work in its field, the late Lawrence Kohlberg attempted to establish the existence of a series of stages through which people pass as they develop their abilities to reason about morality. In his *Essays on Moral Development,* Kohlberg distinguishes three levels of moral development, each divided into two stages:

1. Preconventional:
   a. punishment and obedience (avoid/submit)
   b. egoism (satisfy one's own desires)
2. Conventional:
   a. good/nice (please others)
   b. uphold society (respect rules/authority)
3. Postconventional:
   a. social contract (obey useful rules)
   b. conscience and universal principles (autonomous assent to universal rules)

Kohlberg believes that these stages are common to all cultures and that to reach the highest stage—something most of us do not manage—we must pass through the earlier ones. The three levels characterize moral growth in terms of progress from a conception of right action as self-rewarding, to the view that right action is a matter of loyalty and conformity to social rules, and finally to the idea that right acts are those permitted by principles that are autonomously adopted.

Carol Gilligan, a former student of Kohlberg, has challenged his theory, noting that his use of male subjects may have resulted in a biased conclusion. Kohlberg claims, for instance, that fewer women than men reach the highest stage in his schema. In *In a Different Voice: Psychological Theory and Women's Development,* Gilligan distinguishes two approaches to ethical thinking: (1) the *justice perspective,* according to which morality is understood primarily in terms of rules that specify rights and order them by relative importance when they conflict; and (2) the *caring perspective,* which emphasizes kindness and beneficence, maintaining personal relationships, and sensitivity to one's own needs and those of others in particular circumstances. She discusses Kohlberg's example of a man who can save the life of his wife only by stealing an expensive drug that he cannot afford to buy. One taking the justice perspective would likely justify the act on the basis of a right to life having priority over property rights, at least in this type of case. Someone who had the care perspective, in contrast, would focus on what could be done to sustain relationships and meet urgent needs of everyone, if that is possible. The conclusion might be the same, but the approaches are different—especially regarding the centrality of general rules. Obligations and rights, in fact, might depend on a climate in which trust is normal and reasonable, as the philosopher Annette Baier has argued in her article "What Do Women Want in a Moral Theory?" The nurturing of relationships of trust might be a more fundamental moral concern than the imposition of obligations and the recognition of rights.

Gilligan found that more women than men approach moral issues from the care perspective, perhaps because of innate differences, perhaps because of socialization. She summarizes the levels of moral growth from the care perspective thus:

1. Preconventional: self-centered (one's own needs are the sole focus of concern)
2. Conventional: self-sacrificing (the needs of others are of greater concern)
3. Postconventional: mature ethic of caring (can balance one's own needs and those of others)

Kohlberg admitted the significance of Gilligan's findings and modified his own theory in response; he came to see that the care perspective is an equally valid alternative. Gilligan similarly acknowledges the value of both perspectives in her recent work. Gilligan's research has given inspiration and direction to many women philosophers, particularly feminists, who are developing convincing alternatives to rationalistic, obligation-centered approaches to ethical theory often associated with a masculine perspective. We encourage you to investigate some of this recent literature, a sampling of which we provide in our Suggested Further Reading at the end of this text.

CHAPTER 2

Some Basic Distinctions

Morality and Law

Morality and legal institutions serve some of the same broad functions in societies such as ours. We can look to both morality and the law when we make judgments about people's obligations, rights, and responsibilities; both provide reasons for acting that motivate and justify. For example, when we say that Jones has a right to do so-and-so, we can be making either a moral or a legal claim. Also, we can study morality as a social phenomenon or institution, just as we study legal practices and structures and how they have evolved in a culture. And like law, morality can be understood, at least in part, as a means by which societies exert control over their members to promote such ends as stability, security, and the general welfare. But despite these important similarities, we should not identify morality with law. What, then, are the important differences?

We might begin by remarking on one obvious difference: Laws are codified and enforced by official authorities. They are promulgated by a central authority of some type, such as a judge, dictator, legislature, or administrative agency. Like the laws of a church or other private organization, civil and criminal laws constrain and guide behavior in accordance with commonly acknowledged rules that limit or increase people's opportunities to do various things. Usually, laws that define crimes are backed by penalties to be imposed on violators who are apprehended and convicted. Civil courts award damages to parties whose rights are judged to have been infringed by the state or by private parties.

Moral wrongdoers, in constrast, do not generally face specified punishments, such as prison or fines, if they are discovered. Nor can we bring people suspected of moral wrongdoing before an ethical court to determine whether they are indeed guilty of breaking "moral law." And although it's certainly sometimes possible to express moral rules in overly simple, unqualified ways (for example, telling children, "Do not lie, cheat, or steal"), there are many reasonable qualifications and exceptions implicit in moral rules—qualifications and exceptions that cannot be stated in the ways the law generally requires. The innumerable volumes of rules and doctrines written by practical moralists do not have the status of positive law. Even in our predominantly Judeo-Christian culture, the Mosaic Ten Commandments do not have the role that books of humanly made statutes do.

It is true that private corporations and even our federal government today have official committees and departments charged with the responsibilities of enforcing ethical behavior on the part of employees. But we should not confuse such quasi-legal institutional ethics with morality per se. When making moral judgments about people's actions, we must consult our own consciences or reflective principles, not those of an official or political authority. We may, of course, habitually defer to the moral judgment of a religious or political leadership, but that is a choice we are ultimately morally responsible for as individuals. Moreover, the penalties we impose on people we consider guilty of moral (but not legal) wrongdoing are typically less severe than those the law imposes on criminals. We can refuse to acknowledge or associate with moral miscreants, at least sometimes; we can publicly condemn them or inform others in more discreet ways of their transgressions. Sometimes we are justified in doing to them what they did to their victims. But (apart from cases of parental authority or its equivalents) we cannot inflict bodily harm, deny liberty, or take the property of moral wrongdoers who have committed no criminal offense.

There is a less obvious difference between morality and law. Whereas laws resolve conflicts of interest only among persons and groups in society, moral principles and ideals also guide individuals in harmonizing their inner conflicts. Traditionally, one of the central aims of ethics has been to help us determine what things in life are worth pursuing and what things are most worth choosing when we cannot have everything we want—or when our desires rest on false beliefs or unfortunate experiences. True, some people might contend that these intrapersonal conflicts are outside the scope of morality proper, as the term "moral" is used in our culture today. Still, these intrapersonal conflicts, like the more obvious interpersonal ones, have traditionally been a central concern of moral philosophers. They are not, however, generally a concern of law.

The relationships between law and morality are many and varied. Philosophers and legal theorists disagree about precisely what these relationships are. Of course, a society's laws tend to be in part determined by widespread moral beliefs and ideals. In fact, one central tradition in Western thought, natural law theory (as represented, for example, by Saint Thomas Aquinas) goes so far as to assert that a law is valid only if it meets certain standards of moral acceptability. Another tradition, known as legal positivism, denies that valid laws must be moral ones in any degree.

Rather than attempting to resolve these questions here, let's instead conclude by reminding ourselves that many laws are not based on morality and sometimes conflict with it (for example, many laws concerning civil and criminal liability). For most of us, morality is a higher and more comprehensive standard by which to judge laws. This is perhaps the best reason to avoid confusing morality with law.

Metaethics, Normative Ethics, and Applied Ethics

Within the field of moral philosophy we can distinguish three levels of inquiry: *metaethics*, sometimes called *analytical ethics; normative ethics*, also known as *substantive ethics;* and *applied* or *practical ethics*. The first two are theoretical, whereas the third basically deals with interpreting theories or principles in particular contexts.

Metaethics concerns the nature of moral judgment and reasoning. It deals with such questions as "What does 'good' mean?" and "How can we rationally support moral positions?" Conceptual analysis is thus a major part of metaethical inquiry—it tries to clarify what people mean by words such as *right, ought, duty, virtue, justice*, and so forth (or at least, what the best or clearest way of using these terms would be). Metaethics attempts to show in broad terms how we might rationally approach those questions, but not to settle them. Metaethicists are concerned with whether morality is objective or subjective, whether moral knowledge is possible, and, if so, how it is possible. Chapter 3 surveys some of these metaethical topics.

Normative ethics deals with matters of good and evil, right and wrong, justice and injustice. Instead of attempting to explain the meanings of these terms, which is the task of metaethics, normative ethics presupposes some understanding of the relevant conceptions, at least provisionally, and seeks to arrive at principles or rules that tell us what things are good, right, and just. When we do normative ethics, we make moral judgments; in doing metaethics, we make judgments *about* moral judgments, and these metaethical judgments need not be based on moral criteria. Normative ethics is the theory of ethics proper; that is, normative ethics is a philosophical attempt to give a systematic account of what makes actions right or wrong, morally speaking; of what makes persons and their motives good or bad; and of what makes practices and institutions just or unjust, fair or not fair, beneficial or harmful. Normative ethics tries to show when and why things have these moral characteristics. Chapters 4 and 5 consider some traditional theories of normative ethics.

Applied ethics covers such subfields as business ethics, medical ethics, engineering ethics, journalistic ethics, and other branches of professional ethics. It can also include environmental ethics, the ethics of intimate relationships, and the ethical dimensions of particular public policy areas, such as race relations and famine relief. Generally speaking, this part of moral philosophy—which has flourished over the past two decades—attempts to show the implications of normative theory for specific moral issues or particular decisions in concrete circumstances. Part III deals with how to apply, interpret, and qualify the principles we arrive at in normative theory.

Our brief discussion of the three levels or divisions of moral philosophy stops short of taking up such complex and controversial questions as these: Is metaethics really "neutral" between different normative ethical theories? If not, can we do metaethics without bringing in substantive moral positions? Is applied ethics (or practical ethics) always a matter of applying general principles or rules to cases? Or do we have specific intuitions about some cases that need not be justified in any general terms? These are important problems, and you should keep them in mind when you read and think about the selections in Parts II and III.

Value, Obligation, and Virtue

The distinction between the concepts of *value* and *obligation* is comparatively straightforward, yet, as we will see, there are unsettled questions about the relationship between the two ideas. By *value* we refer to a family of concepts, such as goodness, worth, merit, desert, benefit, well-being, and so on. *Obligation* concepts, in contrast, express ideas about what we owe, what we ought to do, what we must do, what we are bound to do, our duty—as well as what is right and what is just. Philosophers often use the term *axiological* to refer to value concepts, and the term *deontic* to refer to obligation concepts.

Just and *dutiful*, among other terms, can also designate good traits of character, or *virtues*. Virtue is thus a third category that overlaps the categories of value and obligation.

As we noted earlier, both value and obligation concepts can be used in moral as well as legal and other nonmoral contexts. Value concepts apply mostly to things,

Aristotle on Friendship

Friendliness is, according to Aristotle, one of the moral virtues, and having friends is essential to living a good life. Aristotle distinguishes three major forms or levels of friendship. The first is friendship of utility or advantage; in this relationship, both parties derive tangible benefits from the association (a business partnership is one example). A friendship of pleasure, in contrast, need not offer mutual advantage in that sense; rather, the friends simply enjoy each other's company (drinking buddies, for instance, have this sort of friendship). The third and highest form is the friendship of virtue or esteem. This type can include the first and second types, but it goes beyond them. In a friendship of virtue, regard for one's friend is based on shared values and good qualities of character. The reciprocity of this best of all friendships involves a mutual desire to help the other become a better person and live a happier life. Aristotle says that a friend of this kind is like another self. One cannot have such a friendship with a bad person.

Aristotle's concept of *philia,* which we translate as "friendship," is actually broader in meaning than our English word; it covers any relationship with mutual liking, where one friend wishes the other well and is disposed to help him or her. Thus friendships include parental and sibling relationships, marriages and business relationships, relationships between members of clubs and organizations, and so forth. Civic friendship, the most general advantage-friendship, is the basis for a good society, on Aristotle's theory.

persons (their characters, especially), motives, intentions, results, and lives. Obligation concepts tend to apply to actions and institutional arrangements that are sustained by actions; sometimes they apply to feelings and thoughts as well.

Normative ethicists fall into three categories, according to how they view the relationship between value and obligation: consequentialists, deontologists, and proponents of virtue ethics. The consequentialist believes that moral obligation is entirely a matter of bringing about valuable results. The deontologist thinks that at least some moral obligations are *not* a matter of producing good consequences. Advocates of virtue ethics try to explain both valuable outcomes and right action in terms of good qualities of human character. In Chapter 5 we take a more thorough look at these three positions.

Whatever theoretical path we take, it is plain that the distinction between value concepts and obligation concepts is a part of common ways of thinking—the difference, very roughly, between saying that something is good and saying that something ought to be done. Now we turn to another distinction: moral versus nonmoral.

Moral and Nonmoral

As we have already pointed out, there are moral uses of words such as *ought* and *good* as well as uses that do not have anything to do with morality. How do we distinguish moral from nonmoral judgments?

One obvious answer, which seems correct as far as it goes, is that we examine the *reasons* we use to support our value judgments. If these reasons are moral reasons—

that is, if they refer to moral principles—then the original judgment about what is good, right, or obligatory is a moral one, as opposed to a judgment about what is in one's self-interest, or what is instrumentally useful, or legally required, and so on. Thus, "He did the right thing" is a moral judgment if it is supported by a reason such as "By doing so he kept his promise, and people ought to keep their promises."

The problem, of course, is that we need to explain in turn what makes a principle a moral principle. "People ought to keep their promises" could be a principle of prudence, telling us what people should do if they want to promote their own good. Business people, for instance, will profit from a reputation for being true to their word and might therefore be advised to earn such a good reputation by doing what they promise, at least most of the time.

Kant distinguishes moral imperatives from nonmoral ones in part by emphasizing the apparent *categorical* nature of the requirements of morality. Our prudential imperative example ("People ought to keep their promises so that they can gain a good reputation and profit thereby") is *conditional* on an agent's *wanting* to benefit from a good reputation. A moral "ought," by contrast, applies to the agent without any such condition, independently of what he or she wants or does not want. For example, we wouldn't morally justify breaking a promise on the grounds that we didn't care about the advantages of keeping it.

According to Kant, having rationality and free will are the only requirements a being must meet in order to be subject to moral principles. Animals, the insane, and those suffering from certain other mental disorders are not morally responsible; the rest of us are, whether we like it or not. We can therefore say that on Kant's view, a moral principle of conduct is one that applies to all free, rational beings, and only to them.

A contemporary philosopher much influenced by Kant, R. M. Hare suggests a related criterion for a principle's being a moral one: *universality.* This is a difficult concept to explain, partly because there are stronger and weaker forms of it, and these are easily confused. The basic idea is that if something is right for one person to do in a certain situation, then it is right for anyone in a similar situation. The same standards of moral right and wrong apply to everyone, we think. A related intuition is conveyed in the so-called Golden Rule: Do unto others as you would have them do unto you. Taking these two notions together, Hare defends a strong version of universality—that if our stance is a moral one, then we must be willing to accept its being applied in all possible cases that fall under a general principle, including those in which we ourselves are "on the receiving end." A principle that is universal will apply to everyone, including oneself, in similar circumstances. Thus, if I advocate on moral grounds that murderers be given capital punishment, I imply that if I am a murderer, I ought to receive that same penalty.

We might also consider *overridingness* as a criterion for moral principles: that is, we can identify a person's moral principles by finding out which principle, among all the principles that person accepts, is most important to him. In cases of conflict, the moral principle is the one that is weightier or gets priority over the other principles the person holds. A person's morality is, on this criterion, that principle or ordered set of principles by which he ultimately guides his choices and actions—in other words, by which he lives. Suppose, for instance, that whenever she is faced with a choice between her own interests and those of her family, a woman always or usually acts to promote the latter. On the criterion we are discussing—a simple version of overridingness—the woman's belief that she ought to give priority to her family's good is a moral principle for her.

The criteria of universality and overridingness are *formal*; that is, they don't say anything about what the content of moral principles must be. Some naturalist critics argue that these conditions are not sufficient to distinguish moral principles from other types of action-guiding principles. They point out that a principle such as "Everyone ought to avoid stepping on cracks in the sidewalk" is hardly a moral principle, though it is universal and could be overriding for some very eccentric individuals. Also, what about the obvious fact that moral principles can override other moral principles? Indeed, overridingness might not even be a necessary criterion for a moral principle, for reasons we'll consider later in this chapter.

These critics of Hare, most notably Philippa Foot (see Chapter 11) and G. J. Warnock, insist that moral principles cannot be about just anything. They must have a certain content, broadly speaking, or at least a certain general point or purpose. This general object of morality might be to realize an ideal of personal excellence, for instance, or to promote human flourishing and well-being. Warnock characterizes it in his book *The Object of Morality* as the betterment of the human condition in certain respects; moral principles and virtues correct for some common selfish tendencies in human nature, making social life possible and desirable. By nature, we are too limited in our sympathies, mostly favoring ourselves and people we like or are close to; by acquiring a sense of morality, we avoid some kinds of behavior contrary to the general good. This partial "amelioration of the human predicament" is the general point or purpose of moral principles and the character traits that exemplify them, Warnock asserts.

Which of these general views about the definition of *morality* and the nature of moral principles is correct? Perhaps neither is simply and straightforwardly true. It might well be that formal properties such as universality and overridingness (in various interpretations) do not distinguish moral from nonmoral principles. Yet it's not clear that a reference to essential content will either. First of all, there is considerable disagreement over what the content of morality is, and no apparent agreement about how to resolve that. Utilitarians would likely define moral considerations as those that promote societal happiness; Kantians would emphasize respect for persons as self-governing individuals, in addition to the formal criteria we already mentioned. The words *moral* and *ethical* have no very precise ordinary meanings, and a look into their respective Latin and Greek origins doesn't really help here. What separates the moral from the nonmoral thus seems to be a matter of one's substantive moral theory; in other words, we can't answer the metaethical question of what *moral* means or should mean apart from answering normative ethical questions.

A second point is that there seems to be no clear-cut distinction between what we commonly count as moral and as nonmoral considerations. Some people consider certain ideals of human character to be moral ideals appropriate for everyone, whereas others see these ideals as a matter of personal preference or taste. These groups would disagree about whether someone who makes a living as an exotic dancer is acting immorally, for example. What counts as morally degrading or demeaning to oneself is a question that will probably never be answered to everyone's agreement. Indeed, the very idea that we might have moral obligations to ourselves is controversial. Although it's true that Judeo-Christian and other religious moral systems include such duties, some philosophers insist that morality concerns only our actions toward others. On the latter view, there is no moral issue when the agent is the only person seriously affected.

Of course, the fact that we may disagree about the boundaries of the moral and nonmoral realms, as in the previous example, does not show that the categories overlap. But consider the case of enlightened self-interest, or *prudence*: It is obviously a virtue in the sense that it is good for its possessor; but is it a *moral* virtue? Traditionally it has been regarded as such, particularly by religious moralists, as well as by the Greeks. Needless to say, prudent persons are less of a burden on their fellows and more able to help others in distress. If morality has to do merely with responsibilities to others, prudence can still be a morally desirable quality in people. But its primarily self-regarding nature suggests that prudence would be valued most by egoists. Some philosophers maintain that ethical egoism is not a *moral* perspective at all, since it focuses ultimately on oneself and does not take into account the good of others except as a means to one's own ends.

These and other difficulties have led some philosophers to abandon the question of the definition of morality, because it is objectively unanswerable and, moreover, unimportant. Charles Stevenson, in his influential book *Ethics and Language*, asserts that the difference between moral and nonmoral considerations is basically psychological, in that one's moral attitudes are usually marked by a special sense of urgency or importance. In *A Theory of the Good and the Right*, Richard Brandt stresses the fact that moral failure is often accompanied by a sense of guilt, in contrast to the disappointment and regret of imprudence. (Yet can't I feel guilty for not having lived up to my potential as a scholar or athlete or artist—at having let myself down?) Peter Singer, in his article "The Triviality of the Debate Over 'Is'-'Ought' and the Definition of 'Moral,'" argues that by specifying factual or objective criteria for morality, we are only pushing the debate to another level: that of what motives or justifications we have, if any, for caring about morality so defined—in other words, why we should be moral.

It is evident that the questions of what makes a principle, reason, or judgment a moral (as opposed to nonmoral) one and of what makes something a *valid* moral principle, reason, or judgment are closely related. Neither seems answerable apart from the standpoint of a particular normative theory or conception that gives *content*. This is suggested not only by the history of moral philosophy but also by anthropological studies and historical inquiry. Because moral conceptions among varied cultures and time periods have been so diverse, we might doubt whether there is any timeless, transcultural standard of morality that captures a common set of features. There don't seem to be any properties that all conceptions share. Perhaps some definitions are useful for certain purposes but not others—for example, philosophical as opposed to sociological investigation—and there is no "correct definition."

In any event, analysis of the concept of morality (or should we say of various concepts of morality?) is worthwhile because it leads us to insights about other matters and raises interesting, intriguing questions. This is true quite often in philosophy. After sustained attention, perhaps over centuries and by the greatest of minds, some philosophical questions that once seemed very important—and appeared to have a true answer—fade away in the light of new questions and realizations, often more careful and subtle, which now occupy our thought. Progress in philosophy, and sometimes in science, too, can be like this — not so much finding answers to specific questions, but rather discovering new, more discriminating or fruitful ways of looking at things. The puzzles and questions never end in philosophy; answers that satisfy us for very long are the exception.

Supererogation and Admirable Immorality

Before we move on to the substantive questions of ethics, we need to examine one more important distinction: the difference between obligation and supererogation. An obligatory act is one that we ought to do or must do, either other things being equal, or all things considered. A supererogatory act is one that is commendable — good — but "beyond the call of duty," as we often put it. Heroic acts are common examples of supererogation, as when a bystander rushes into a burning building to rescue a child, at considerable risk to his own life. Since he isn't a firefighter or police officer, that kind of morally praiseworthy conduct isn't expected of him.

This distinction has a long history in Western moral philosophy, going at least back to Medieval ethics, if not to Aristotle. Recently (about thirty-five years ago, that is), there was a renewal of interest in supererogation among American and British philosophers, sparked by the publication of J. O. Urmson's article "Saints and Heroes," which we include in Chapter 13. Although the obligation/supererogation distinction might seem fairly clear and uncontroversial to you, some have challenged it. Certain ethical theorists (see Peter Singer's essay following Urmson's) seem reluctant or unable to recognize it, a problem we discuss in Chapter 5.

For now, let's discuss instead a kind of puzzle that can arise in our ordinary ethical thinking, once we just begin to get theoretical. We sometimes hear people say, "It's always better to be morally better" or "We should be as morally good as possible." These might strike us, at first glance, as almost obviously true statements. Who could doubt that we ought to be the best moral agents we can be and that all of us should be dedicated moral agents?

However, if we assent to these sorts of statements, we have a problem. Supererogatory action would disappear as a meaningful category: If we ought always to be the best moral agents we can be, and assuming that *ought* implies "have an obligation" in this context, then the extraordinary, morally valuable acts we call "supererogatory" are really obligatory. There would then be no meaningful distinction between what we are morally required (obligated, duty-bound) to do, on the one hand, and what is morally good but not required on the other hand — that is, supererogatory.

How do we get out of this puzzle? Let's look at the assertion "We ought always to be the best moral agents we can be." This suggests three interpretations: (1) We are morally required always to do whatever we can that is most valuable from a moral point of view; (2) we are morally better to the degree that we do the best we morally can; and (3) we are in some nonmoral respect better or more dutiful insofar as we act as best we can from the moral point of view.

Now it should be apparent that (1) simply rules out a meaningful distinction between the morally obligatory and the supererogatory. There is no obvious reason to accept (1), and there are good reasons not to; without further argument, then, we should deny (1). Interpretations (2) and (3) do not create any conceptual puzzle: (2) is trivially true and says nothing about obligation or duty, whereas (3) is a statement about what we ought to do from a nonmoral point of view, be the best we can morally speaking, for nonmoral reasons. We will have more to say about statements such as (3) shortly. All we need to see right now is that (3) doesn't say anything about what we are morally bound or required to do, so it creates no problem for the idea of morally supererogatory acts.

What this bit of analysis suggests is that people are confused when they say things like "We ought to be as morally good as possible," if they don't keep our three interpretations distinct. Conflating them can lead to the counterintuitive conclusion that moral supererogation is impossible. While (2) and (3) might be true or acceptable, (1)—which implies that we have a conclusive moral duty to morally perfect ourselves in every way—probably is not. But only (1) or something like it rules out supererogatory action.

Before we consider another problem about the relationship between moral and nonmoral points of view as expressed in (3), let's conclude our brief discussion of supererogation by citing the definition David Heyd offers*:

An act is supererogatory if and only if

1. It is neither obligatory nor forbidden.
2. Its omission is not wrong and does not deserve sanction or criticism—either formal or informal.
3. It is morally good, both by virtue of its (intended) consequences and by virtue of its intrinsic value (being beyond duty).
4. It is done voluntarily for the sake of someone else's good and is thus meritorious.

Supererogatory acts are, in other words, truly optional, morally valuable, and voluntarily altruistic in intent.

There are other interesting problems concerning supererogation (for instance, within the context of friendships and love relationships). But let's mention one that has to do with the possibility of nonmoral considerations overriding moral ones—the idea of an immoral act being admirable. Does this make sense? Surely not, if moral considerations are always, by definition, final or overriding. But we've seen reason to doubt that they are.

Consider the case of someone like Paul Gauguin, the French artist, who left his family to live and paint in Tahiti. His wife and children were destitute and suffered greatly after he abandoned them. Still, some would say, we should admire Gauguin for following his artistic mission, despite his failure to carry out his moral responsibilities. He did produce some great works of art. (Bernard Williams in his article "Moral Luck" raises more complicated questions. For example, suppose Gauguin, for one reason or another, had failed to produce masterpieces—how would this affect our assessment of him?)

What would you say? It's hard to see how Gauguin's decision to sacrifice the good of his wife and children to his art could be justified morally. If it is immoral,

*David Heyd, *Supererogation: Its Status in Ethical Theory* (New York: Cambridge University Press, 1982), 115.

all things considered, then how could we admire him for having made it? If we did, we would be responding to values outside morality—values, moreover, that are more important than moral values. But even if we don't share this admiration, it does seem to make sense. Without going so far as Nietzsche (who, you will recall from our discussion in Chapter 1, wanted to replace conventional moral values with others expressing human excellence of other sorts), we must concede that morality does not always have the final word in our judgments of people.

CHAPTER 3

Facts, Values, and Moral Knowledge

Are There Knowable Moral Facts?

Before we can talk about the substantive questions of moral theory and applied ethics, we need to look at some fundamental problems about the nature of moral reality and whether we can know about it. These problems have vexed philosophers at least since the time of Socrates. Of course, we won't attempt to solve them here—only to explain what the questions are and to survey the important positions philosophers have taken trying to answer them over the centuries.

The two most basic questions can be stated thus: Are there facts about what is moral and immoral? If there are such facts, can we know what they are? How could we gain this knowledge? The first question is metaphysical (it has to do with ultimate reality), the second epistemological (it concerns what we can know). Both are also metaethical questions.

It is often hard to separate these two sorts of questions. Obviously, we will tend to be uninterested in moral facts that are unknowable, and it hardly makes sense to posit such facts. Here we'll survey four historically significant positions that answer both questions in the affirmative; later in this chapter, we'll consider some negative positions.

Objective Naturalism

Objective naturalism is the view that there are moral facts we can know in the same way we know other facts about the natural world—that is, by observation, commonsense reasoning, and the methods of science. Objective naturalists can be either reductivist or nonreductivist. Reductive naturalists attempt to reduce ethical facts to empirical facts. For example, the claim that "goodness" can be defined as "pleasantness" is a reductivist claim, because it involves the assertion that goodness is the same thing as the empirical property of being pleasant. Nonreductive naturalists, by contrast, deny that such definitions are useful or correct. Indeed, it's hard to find convincing examples of successful reductions in metaethics, and it's also difficult to name very many philosophers of major importance who have held a reductivist form of ethical naturalism.

What about nonreductive naturalists? Aristotle, Saint Thomas Aquinas, David Hume, and John Stuart Mill are among the major figures in the history of moral philosophy who could be considered to belong in this camp. Philippa Foot is a present-day member of the group, as you will see when you read her article, "Moral

Conscience as a Moral Authority

Many people take their consciences to be their guide in moral matters, especially when they are unsure what they ought to do or when they feel strongly tempted to do wrong. Conscience has both epistemic (knowledge-giving) and motivating roles in civilized behavior, and there is nothing objectionable in relying on it in many circumstances. In fact, we probably could not have a viable moral community without it. But does conscience give us objective moral knowledge? Some prominent philosophers and theologians have thought that it does. One important example is the eighteenth-century British moral philosopher and Anglican bishop Joseph Butler. Butler believed that God gives us consciences in order to lead us to do what will, if generally practiced, produce good results for society. Lying, for instance, is wrong—and our conscience tells us so—even when it would probably create more benefits on a specific occasion; if people generally lied whenever they thought lying would be beneficial, the overall consequences for society would be terrible. Yet how can we know that conscience is a God-given faculty for discerning moral truth? Moreover, how are we to judge and act when conscience is silent or gives conflicting dictates? Furthermore, people's consciences conflict with one another and can, it seems, often be mistaken. (For a discussion of the latter problem, see the selection from Aquinas in Chapter 9.) Empirical naturalism offers an alternative, nontheistic, view of conscience according to which we acquire it through moral education. Conscience is not innate on this conception, and its content (what it tells us) is a matter of what we learn from society, which might not be objective truth.

Beliefs" (Chapter 11). While these philosophers avoid simple definitions of ethical terms (such as "morally right" means "productive of happiness"), they generally maintain that there are empirical criteria—standards of judgment—for applying ethical terms to acts, agents, and motives. These criteria are not just a matter of opinion or subjective preference; they are objective, because they reflect a true conception of human nature and human needs, especially the needs that social life imposes.

A nonreductive naturalist might argue, for instance, that a person's good is determined by certain universal needs that have a biological basis or that normally develop in social interaction. Someone who is courageous and possesses self-control, generally speaking, is more likely to do well in life than is someone who lacks these virtues. And a person who lives and chooses virtuously acts rightly from a moral standpoint. One's own good, moral virtue, and morally right action can be linked in these ways with empirical facts. These facts about human nature and society determine moral facts even though the moral facts cannot be reduced to empirical facts by any definitions.

Some philosophers, as well as many people who have no background in philosophy, would still deny that there are objective criteria for applying moral terms correctly, if we take *objective* to mean something like "determined by nature and not by individual preferences or those of society." This denial is common in our time, just as it was among the Sophists and those they influenced in Socrates' Athens thousands of years ago. The two major forms of this denial are subjectivism and relativism. Let's see how they can be best expressed and what can be said for them.

Subjectivism

Subjectivism is the position that moral judgments simply describe individual desires and attitudes. We will consider only the first-person form. For example, when I say that murder is wrong, I'm merely saying that I don't want people to murder or that I disapprove of it strongly. We can say that my preferences or attitudes are rationally based, in the sense that they reflect that I know what murder is and what its effects are. But my own desires or attitudes, not any objective standard, are the final court of appeal in judging whether murder is wrong. My judgment would be wrong only if it were not fully informed and consistent—subjectivists deny that there is any other ground for criticizing a person's moral judgments and beliefs. On a subjectivist view, ethical judgments, like judgments of taste, vary from person to person and don't have any factual basis outside of an individual's own mind.

Why do many people hold a subjectivist position about ethics? Because of the difficulty in rationally resolving many of the ethical disagreements we encounter in everyday life, and (at a more theoretical level) because of the general failure of objective naturalists to give a satisfactory account of moral knowledge. To elaborate the first point: We all experience, from time to time, the frustration of being unable to convince someone to share what we think is an obviously correct ethical position. Yet we are at a loss to show our opponents to be inconsistent, and we still seem to disagree about the ethical issue even when we agree (or would agree) about all the empirical facts of the situation. As C. L. Stevenson argues in "The Nature of Ethical Disagreement" (see Chapter 11), there is disagreement in belief and disagreement in attitude; ethical disagreement—with its emotional aspects—often involves the latter. When it does, and no nonmoral facts or logical points lead people to change their attitudes of approval or disapproval, then we have a rationally unresolvable disagreement in attitude.

But besides the problem of resolving ethical disagreement, no one has been able to show that any position stronger than the subjectivists' is true. Keep in mind that subjectivists admit there are knowable moral facts; they deny only that these moral facts are objective in the sense that they are independent of personal attitudes and preferences. The objective naturalistic position, despite the efforts of major proponents over the entire history of moral philosophy, has yet to be developed in a systematic way that meets the challenges of subjectivism. Exactly how do we know objective moral facts? If these are natural facts, why don't we have a science of morality? Of course, the fact that objective naturalists haven't answered these questions so far doesn't mean they will never succeed in doing so. But until they are able to explain what natural moral facts are and how we can know them generally, the subjectivist position will continue to attract followers.

What can be said against subjectivism? Well, for one thing, it certainly doesn't seem to most of us that when we make moral judgments, we are just expressing beliefs about our own attitudes and preferences. On the simple first-person version of ethical subjectivism that we are considering, my statement that stealing is wrong would mean only that I disapprove of stealing or don't want people to steal. If that is truly what my attitude or desire is, then the ethical judgment is true; otherwise it is not. But these don't seem to be the real truth conditions for the judgment that stealing is wrong. We tend to think—unless we are committed subjectivists—that the truth of "Stealing is wrong" doesn't depend on the speaker's desires or attitudes about stealing. It appears to be an objective moral fact.

A related point is that moral judgments appear to have a kind of *authority* that first-person statements about attitudes or desires lack. Many people think that judgments such as "Slavery is unjust"—when they are true—are a standard by which to assess our attitudes and preferences and to modify or change them if necessary. They don't simply describe the preferences we currently have. Our present attitudes and desires can be mistaken, incorrect, or irrational.

This consideration has led some subjectivists to hold that what moral judgments describe are not our actual, current attitudes or desires but, instead, those we *would have* were we more knowledgeable, rational, consistent, and so forth. To assert that slavery is morally wrong or unjust, on this version of the theory, would be equivalent to asserting that I (the speaker) would disapprove of it were I fully informed, consistent, and so on. Moral judgments thus are a sort of prediction about what the speaker's attitudes and preferences would be under more ideal circumstances, if this type of subjectivism is valid.

Is this more sophisticated subjectivism acceptable as a metaethical theory? It depends partly on whether you think it would make sense to say, "I would disapprove of slavery were I fully informed about it and also consistent in my beliefs and reasoning, and so on, but slavery is not unjust." If this statement does make sense, then *unjust* cannot mean "what I would disapprove of if I were fully informed and consistent." This test is one proposed by the British philosopher G. E. Moore, called the "Open Question Argument." For this to be a relevant objection to a metaethical theory, however, we'd have to assume that the theory is offered as an analysis of what we ordinarily mean when we make ethical claims. If it is, then clearly the sentence "Slavery is unjust" does not mean the same as "I would disapprove of slavery were I fully knowledgeable and consistent." If the two sentences did mean the same thing, as do "John is a bachelor" and "John is an unmarried male adult," then it would be nonsensical—a contradiction—to deny one and affirm the other sentence. We cannot consistently say "John is a bachelor, but John is not an unmarried adult male." But we can affirm one of the propositions and consistently deny the other in the example about the injustice of slavery. So they cannot mean the same thing.

However, subjectivists can avoid this line of objection by saying that they offer this theory, not as an analysis of what we commonly mean by ethical terms and judgments, but rather as a proposal about what we *should* mean by them. J. L. Mackie, in his book *Ethics: Inventing Right and Wrong,* takes this position. He argues that we are commonly confused or mistaken when we use ethical language. We falsely think we are talking about objective moral properties of people, their actions, and so forth, when in fact there are no such properties at all. When we realize this, all we are left with to express in ethical utterances are our desires and attitudes, likes and dislikes—or, at least, those we would have were we more informed and consistent. We will consider a similar view at the end of this chapter, when we discuss R. B. Brandt's approach to moral justification.

The debate between subjective and objective naturalism is very much alive in moral philosophy today, and it is not our purpose here to try to resolve it. But we should mention some other theories about moral facts and knowledge that are also viable alternatives in this great debate.

Relativism

Relativism has many different forms. It can be an anthropological theory about the fundamental differences between the values and moral ideals of different cultures, that is, a descriptive theory which says only that there are such differences ("The basic moral beliefs of the Maori allowed cannibalism under certain conditions, but those of contemporary Europeans did not"). We will call this "cultural (or descriptive) relativism about morality." Or it can be a theory about what moral rules, conventions, norms, and so on, are binding on people, namely, those of their own culture or society and time ("The moral code of our society currently prohibits infanticide, so it is wrong for us to commit it"). We call this "normative relativism about morality." One can accept both of these types of relativism about morality, or neither, or one but not the other. To accept normative relativism about morality, however, is to identify moral facts with facts about what is required or valued by a society or culture; moral knowledge would then be knowledge about those conventions and ideals.

We can note immediately some interesting similarities and contrasts between normative relativism and ethical subjectivism. Both are forms of naturalism opposed

Two Forms of Relativism About Morality

Relativism about values is a very hard concept to define at the most abstract level. What we are calling subjectivism is even a kind of relativity of value to individual persons. But we are using *relativism* to express the idea that values are relative to groups, communities, societies, or cultures as they exist during periods of time. Two important forms of relativism about moral values are these:

Cultural (descriptive) relativism is an anthropological thesis that the basic values of a culture often oppose those of others. In its most extreme form, cultural relativism is the assertion that there are no common moral beliefs or ideals among all societies at all times.

Normative relativism is a philosophical claim about morality. It is the position that the prevailing moral values, beliefs, norms, and so on, of a person's time and place are those that truly apply to him or her. That is to say, what your society agrees is good or bad, right or wrong is the final standard for your moral decisions and the only relevant basis for moral argument with your fellow citizens. This theory is sometimes called *moral conventionalism.* Normative relativists typically assert as well the distinct claim that there are no valid standards by which to judge the moral values, beliefs, or ideals of fundamentally different cultures—that is, to say that some are objectively superior to others.

to objective naturalism. Whereas subjectivism makes the individual the final court of moral judgments' truth, normative relativism accords this right to society or culture. Sometimes, in fact, normative relativism is called "intersubjectivism" for these reasons. Normative relativists hold that moral authority rests in the collective beliefs and habits of a population related in historical, cultural, and political terms, or in other ways that would need to be explained. They deny that the individual's moral attitudes or values determine what is right or wrong, but they also deny that there are standards of morality apart from the norms and values of a given community or culture.

What are some of the reasons for adopting normative relativism? We can begin by remarking on the apparent diversity of moral beliefs among people of different societies and cultures, not to mention over different historical periods. Indeed, we find considerable variety in pluralistic societies such as ours when we compare the moral views of people of diverse ethnic and economic backgrounds. Differences of religious belief and even—if Gilligan is correct—of gender might create opposing ethical perspectives.

Of course, it's quite possible that these differences are not *fundamental* ones. Cultural relativism claims that they are; normative relativism infers from this that there are no standards of moral truth that transcend culture or the norms of a community. But cultural relativism could be false. The differences we observe might only be differences of nonmoral belief, or they might be due to circumstantial variety. They need not reflect basic differences of moral principle, values, or ideals. For example, the attitudes or norms prevalent in various cultures about infanticide, euthanasia for the elderly, or even slavery might not be differences of principle. They could be explained, perhaps, as different *applications* of the *same* basic principles common to all humanity in all epochs. It's simply that when societies find themselves in harsh conditions (of near subsistence or constant danger from other tribes, for instance), or when their beliefs about religion (God's will), metaphysics (immortality of the soul) or empirical facts (circumstances and consequences) differ, they are likely to apply universally accepted principles or common human values to reach divergent conclusions from those of other societies.

It would be very difficult to determine whether cultural or descriptive relativism is true. For one thing, it's hard to define what a *basic* moral value or principle is, in addition to the problem discussed earlier of what counts as a *moral* value or principle (is there a universal definition?). But let's assume for the sake of argument that cultural relativism *is* true: Does normative relativism about morality follow?

No, it is false that normative relativism logically follows. Even if we assume that fundamental moral values differ among societies (another term very hard to define: what makes a population a society?) and that individuals get their moral values from their societies or cultures (not always uncritically, of course), we cannot conclude that moral facts and moral knowledge are relative. This is an example of the difficulty of inferring a conclusion about what ought to be from premises about what is.

What other premises would we need to conclude that normative relativism is true? One consideration that can be invoked in arguing for metaethical relativity is that terms such as *obligation, duty, just,* and so forth would appear to have no meaning apart from conceptions of what is normal, lawful, expected in a social practice, or in accordance with a socially accepted rule. The obligation to keep a promise, for example, presupposes the institution of promising, an overall background of trust, and a generally understood rule that we must, other things equal, keep our commitments. Similar things can be said about our duties to our parents and the justness of respecting the property of others.

In other words, morality—or moralities—are social phenomena. Their existence requires a complex web of social practices, beliefs, habits, responses, and motivations. Moral facts are determined by the norms and practices of actual societies, the relativist concludes, because those societies would not be what they are without those norms and practices. Normative relativists thus insist that moral reality is social reality. And because moralities—like legal systems—belong to societies or cultures, they will ultimately tend to differ to the extent that societies have fundamental differences. There is no super-societal, intercultural basis for judging the values or ideals of radically different societies, they conclude.

But although this is a plausible and relevant argument for one kind of ethical relativism, much more would need to be said to prove it's truth, and we can't pursue the question here. However, we should mention one other argument that is mistakenly thought to support a kind of moral relativism, and we'll conclude with a survey of some of the major shortcomings and problems of that theory.

People sometimes think that there is a connection between normative relativism and toleration—that the conviction that morality is relative requires an attitude of "hands off" and respect for the values of other cultures. Many believe that this attitude, furthermore, is a good thing, because it shows a liberal and non-ethnocentric awareness of human diversity. Toleration might not presuppose relativism, they might say, but relativism demands toleration, so normative relativism is good. Or does it really have these implications?

That it does not should be plain if we think a bit more deeply and clearly. Moreover, even if normative relativism did entail toleration of other societies' morals, it's not so certain that it would always be a good policy. Recall that we have described normative relativism as belief in two theses, roughly stated: (1) Moral facts are determined by the norms of particular societies (or other collectives); (2) these norms are often fundamentally different among societies, so there are no common grounds outside a society for saying what moral views are correct and what are not. Now suppose that it's a basic norm of *your* society to impose its values on other societies. If normative relativism is true, then people in your society morally ought to be intolerant. Were it a basic value in your society to avoid imposition of this sort on other societies, then toleration would follow. Thus toleration is neither supported nor ruled out, logically, by the truth of normative relativism by itself.

Still, it might be that if we accepted normative relativism, we'd be more reluctant to impose our values on other peoples because we'd know we had no rational basis for saying our values are more correct. But normative relativism itself does not require toleration. Further, it's debatable whether toleration is always morally right—consider present-day cultures that oppress women and punish sexual deviations, adultery, and even premarital sex with death. The liberalism of our culture involves some kinds of toleration, but not necessarily the toleration of the intolerant, the ignorant, and the vicious, whether in our own society or others with which we have dealings.

This leads us to our first major objection to normative relativism. It is not hard to find examples of past and present societies that permit—or even consider virtuous—practices that we consider shocking and terrible. Honor codes, for instance, that mandate the stoning of women thought guilty of adultery or the exile of rape victims are not unknown in the world even now. Normative relativism seems to imply that, at least for people living in societies with that conception of honor, those practices are morally right, honorable, and obligatory. They do not seem so to us because we have different cultural norms and traditions, perhaps due to different religious beliefs and historical experiences. But aren't our values—at least in this instance—better? Aren't we also entitled to say with some objective basis, moreover, that such societies are wrong or mistaken, perhaps morally less advanced than we are? Normative relativism, if true, appears to deny us a basis for saying either of these things. If it is true that our values are better or that their norms are objectively mistaken—and by that we mean not just that theirs are not compatible with ours—then normative relativism must be false or unacceptable.

A second objection points out the difficulty of explaining moral reform within a society in the context of normative relativism. If right and wrong, and all other moral distinctions, are determined by what the society's prevailing moral norms and ideals permit, prohibit, encourage, or discourage, then how could moral reformers radically opposed to those values correctly use moral language to condemn them and persuade fellow citizens to reject them? Of course, when the current norms and values are vague or contradictory, there is room for such critical use of moral language within a society; that much relativism allows. But radical challenges to clear, precise, consistent norms is another matter. We can imagine a society in which slavery or racial persecution is sanctioned by clear and consistent norms, for example—how could an abolitionist say that those practices are morally wrong?

Neither of these objections is conclusive, and perhaps there are ways of rebutting them or other forms of ethical relativism that can avoid them. (We have considered only one very general formulation of the theory here. Gilbert Harman's relativistic conception is different in some respects; see his essay in Chapter 11.) Our discussion, brief as it is, can only introduce some of the issues. Whether ethical relativism is a better theory than objective naturalism or subjectivism, and why it is or isn't, are complicated questions.

But let's examine one more theory about the status of moral facts and moral knowledge. This theory has a long philosophical tradition, and it was especially influential among English-speaking philosophers in the eighteenth and early twentieth centuries.

Intuitionism

Intuitionism is opposed to objective naturalism in that it denies that moral properties are empirical. It also rejects subjectivism and relativism, insisting that moral right and wrong have an objective foundation independent of the attitudes of individuals and norms of social groups. Intuitionists believe that normal human beings have a moral faculty or capacity—sometimes identified with conscience—that gives insight into a moral reality that lies beyond the empirical world of science and sense experience. These objective moral intuitions could be about general moral truths or about what to do in particular cases.

Although intuitionism is not as widely held by moral philosophers as it once was, some elements of the theory can be found in the writings of contemporary exponents of moral realism and objectivism. The most important intuitionists of the early part of this century were the British philosophers G. E. Moore, H. A. Prichard, and W. D. Ross. Moore is best remembered for his "Open Question Argument," mentioned previously, which is intended to show that reductive naturalistic definitions of *good* are always false. All definitions of the form "Goodness is *X*" are mistaken, he thought, because we can always sensibly ask of whatever is assumed to have the property *X* whether it is good or not. If so, then goodness cannot be the same thing as property *X*. (You might want to try this test yourself with your favorite naturalistic definition—would whether something is good remain an open question if it has the property you identify with goodness?)

Moore believes that goodness is the primary ethical property; he defines rightness in terms of what promotes the good. Others, such as Prichard and Ross, thought rightness to be primary, and hundreds of years earlier Samuel Clarke asserted that *fittingness* was the basic moral predicate. But these intuited moral properties will seem obscure and mysterious to many of us, even otherworldly, once we realize that they are not part of the empirical realm. Take goodness as Moore described it, for example: a simple, indefinable, non-natural property. It belongs to pleasure, knowledge, virtue, friendship, and many other things too numerous to list. But we still don't really know what goodness is, how to tell what things have it, and why we should care about it.

In short, intuitionism avoids many of the problems with rival theories, but only by avoiding the hard questions. It makes assumptions about reality and knowledge that are largely untenable in the minds of most philosophers today. We have little reason to believe in such intuited, objective, but not empirical moral properties; we cannot explain how we come to know them if they do exist. Subjectivism and relativism give accounts of moral convictions and ethical language which at least make sense and can account for why we tend to think (erroneously, in their view) that morality has an objective status. And it is far from clear that all types of objective naturalism—especially of the nonreductive sort—are false.

Varieties of Moral Skepticism

Before we look at the idea of objectivity in more detail, we need to consider the position that there are no moral properties of things and no moral knowledge in the most standard sense. We'll also discuss two other types of moral skepticism—about the power of moral knowledge to motivate us to act and about the possibility of rationally justifying acting morally.

Noncognitivism

Noncognitivism denies that there are moral facts or knowledge. All four of the views considered earlier in this chapter are forms of cognitivism; that is, they assert that moral judgments express beliefs—they differ only in their conception of what moral beliefs are about (what sort of facts moral facts are). But noncognitivists maintain that moral judgments don't have as their main purpose the expression of beliefs at all. Rather, we use them to express attitudes or to perform some kind of speech act other than stating facts and expressing our beliefs (though that might be *part* of what we do in making ethical judgments).

One type of noncognitivism is the *emotive theory of ethics.* This theory was developed in the 1930s and 1940s by several philosophers who were influenced by the moral philosophy of Hume as well as by the advances in the philosophy of language that were being made in their own time. Sir Alfred Ayer and Charles Stevenson were the two best known emotivists. Stevenson, in particular, works out this theory in the most detail. Its central idea is that moral judgments, besides describing things, serve to express the emotions—or, better, attitudes—of the people who utter them; they also invite others to share those emotions or attitudes (pro or con). Early, crude versions of emotivism liken moral claims to either commands and imperatives ("You ought to do this" equals "Do this") or to verbal ejaculations, such as "Boo!" and "Hurray!" Stevenson's more refined theory is in some respects like subjectivism, with one exception: On his theory, moral claims *express* rather than describe attitudes for or against something, and they attempt to bring about a similar attitude in the audience.

Stevenson argues in great detail that moral reasoning consists in getting clear, first, about all of the empirical facts of the matter and making sure one hasn't committed any logical errors. But when it comes to moving from factual premises to a moral conclusion, Hume's problem about inferring an "ought" from statements about what "is" arises. Stevenson insists that no such inference is logically permissible because of the emotive meaning of ethical judgments. The emotive meaning is that part of their meaning which makes them expressive of the speaker's pro and con attitudes as well as suitable for creating those same attitudes in other people. Factual language is descriptive in meaning, he contends, whereas ethical language is both descriptive and emotive. Thus purely factual premises in a deductive argument cannot validly lead to an ethical conclusion, since the emotive meaning of ethical terms goes beyond mere description. Reasons in ethics are psychologically—not logically—related to ethical conclusions. What counts as a good reason for an ethical view is itself a matter of one's attitudes and not something objective. Persuasive reasons, those effective in getting others to adopt one's own attitudes, are what we ultimately look for.

Emotivism is an interesting alternative to the descriptive metaethical theories discussed in the last section. With its emphasis on the dynamic uses of moral language—expressing feelings and attitudes, trying to get others to share them—the emotive theory opens up an important dimension of moral discourse to philosophical study. But further developments in the philosophy of language during the mid-twentieth century led to a different type of noncognitive theory—prescriptivism, which focuses on the speech acts we perform in making moral judgments.

Hare's prescriptivism is the most influential of these recent noncognitive theories. As Stevenson does, Hare recognizes a distinction between two types of meaning: evaluative (like emotive meaning) and descriptive. Genuine, sincere ethical utterances have both types of meaning. When I say that John is rude, for instance, I'm both describing him (the descriptive meaning of *rude*) and condemning or criticizing him (the evaluative meaning). Hare argues that the most general and common ethical terms, *good* and *ought* especially, are used to commend and prescribe choices and actions, whatever their descriptive meanings are. Descriptive meaning is important in ethics mainly because it imposes the requirement of universalizability on ethical prescriptions. As we discussed in Chapter 2, this is the requirement that if we say, for example, that John ought in the present circumstances to keep his promise to pay Joan $100, then we're committed to the position that anyone like John who has promised anyone like Joan $100, in any circumstances relevantly similar to the present, ought to pay it. Words such as *ought* and *good* must be applied consistently: Whatever one's descriptive criteria, one must stick to them in similar cases, commending or prescribing the same things if the same reasons (descriptive criteria) are present.

To illustrate this again, let's consider Hare's famous example of the Nazi who is conscientious in the sense that he realizes he must universalize his particular ethical judgments about Jews and be prepared to act accordingly when similar circumstances arise (the prescriptive aspect). If the Nazi says that some Jews ought to be put to death, then he is committed by universalization to the position that anyone who is a Jew ought to be put to death, the reason being that Jews ought to be put to death because they are Jews (and thus supposedly have other characteristics in common as well). Now suppose he discovers that he, the Nazi, is himself Jewish. The universal and prescriptive nature of his original ethical judgment commits him to the view that *he* ought to be put to death. If Hare's reasoning is sound, this certainly imposes some rational limits on moral judgment, even though there are no moral facts and there is no moral knowledge.

We said that noncognitivism of either the emotivist or prescriptivist type represents a kind of moral skepticism, since they deny the possibility of moral knowledge. Objective naturalists and intuitionists have often been quite emotional in their positions in response to noncognitivism, sometimes claiming that it weakens the moral fiber of society. We will talk about this worry later, when we consider the importance of moral knowledge for theory and practice. There are other, more serious problems for noncognitivism, some of them also difficulties of subjectivist theories. For the most part, they are somewhat technical and concern the inadequacies of noncognitivism as a theory about what we ordinarily mean when we use moral language. Let's suppose the objections are sound—we won't try to examine them here. Stevenson and others who hold to an emotivist or prescriptivist position could readily concede that noncognitivism does not explicate the common meanings of ethical terms. Perhaps, they can reply, we don't have any clear or precise meanings for our moral expressions, and we have false beliefs about moral objectivity. Noncognitive theories explain what we are *doing* when we use moral language in dynamic contexts of argument, and so on, and that's what's important. Think of emotivist and prescriptivist analyses as themselves prescriptions for how we should understand a revised moral language, they might say, adding that what matters in ethics is ultimately getting people to share our attitudes and act on them. Their view captures this fact best.

Rational Skepticism and Motivational Skepticism

Rather than pursue these questions further, let's move on to consider two other types of moral skepticism: *rational skepticism* and *motivational skepticism*. They have to do with the relation between moral judgments that are accepted (or believed to be true) and the two kinds of reasons we distinguished in Chapter 2, moral and prudential.

To understand rational and motivational skepticism, let's begin by asking a question: Why should I be moral? That is a question we sometimes ask ourselves or expect others to answer. It arises when we believe that we are morally required to do something we don't really want to do. What sort of answer would be likely to satisfy us in those circumstances? Let's consider three possibilities: (1) Being moral is to my advantage; (2) being moral will help support the kind of society in which people flourish; (3) being moral will help me become the kind of person I want to be.

The first reply is that, contrary to what we think, doing the morally right act would be in our interest or at least get us something we want. Of course, this sort of reason probably isn't a *moral* reason. But if we're looking for a prudential justification or a motivating reason, then we would be satisfied with the answer, assuming we're convinced it is true. When doing what is moral coincides with doing what is good for ourselves or what we want (or gets us what we want), we're usually satisfied with our situation. When morality and self-interest don't coincide, however, we often decide not to do what is morally right. The second type of moral skepticism makes much of this fact.

Philosophers as different as Plato, Aristotle, Epicurus, and Hobbes all attempted to demonstrate that morality and one's own true good always, in the end, coincide (as you'll see when you read the selections from their works that follow in Part II). Without trying to explain or judge these varied arguments here, we'll briefly sketch two other kinds of answers that differ notably from the self-interested one. These answers and the interpretations of "Why should I be moral?" to which they respond can be found in the writings of some of the ancient philosophers we've mentioned as well as their modern descendants. Each kind of answer has its skeptical critics.

We can also understand "Why should I be moral?" to mean "What social purposes does morality serve?" A satisfactory answer, accordingly, would explain the preconditions for a stable and prosperous society in which people can flourish and be happy and values can pass from one generation to the next. Among these requirements, we can reasonably suppose, are the public acceptance of and general conformity to a range of rules of conduct that enjoin people to keep commitments, respect the lives and property of others, and be honest, loyal, law-abiding, and so on — in short, the conventional rules of morality as we know them. In acting morally, then, I am doing my part in upholding norms of behavior that promote social well-being in various ways.

A third interpretation of "Why should I be moral?" emphasizes the idea of a personal ideal, that is, a conception of the kind of person I want to be or aspire to become. Instead of the general question, let's focus for a minute on the question of why I ought to be moral in a particular case, for example, why I ought to turn in a wallet with some money that I found today. On the one hand, I certainly might enjoy keeping and spending the money. On the other hand, I want to be an honest and conscientious person, one who respects others' property and acts on principles that I expect others to follow with regard to me. If the latter motivation is stronger, I'll return the wallet and money to its owner. In general, we could say, we should be moral because we want to be the sort of person who has the traits or characteristics of the moral person, period.

The three answers and interpretations of "Why should I be moral?" do, of course, overlap somewhat; they can complement and reinforce one another. But we need to ask two questions: (1) Do they rationally justify morality to everyone always? and (2) will they always motivate people to act morally even if they accept them as rational justifications? Rational skeptics doubt or deny that everyone has a good reason to be moral; motivational skeptics question or reject the belief that reasons that justify will necessarily motivate us.

To get clearer about these forms of skepticism, let's see how their proponents might reply to the three responses to "Why should I be moral?" A skeptic about rational justification could appeal to common experience, as we already remarked, in challenging the first argument—it simply isn't true that everyone in every situation will find that, on due reflection and in the final analysis, acting morally will be best for him, be to his advantage, or get him what he wants. If this is the *only* kind of rational justification there is for acting, then this skeptic is probably correct that morality cannot be rationally justified.

But what about the other two arguments? The proponent of rational skepticism can concede that at least some of the moral rules most societies recognize are socially beneficial, if not absolutely necessary. But what is necessary is that most people follow them most of the time—not that all of us do all of the time. I just might decide to be a frequent exception, a free rider on the morality upheld by others. This will be especially easy if I can become rich and powerful, or at least clever enough, to avoid getting caught in immoral acts and chastised or punished. Plato tells in the *Republic* the story of a shepherd named Gyges who finds a magic ring that renders him invisible. He commits many immoral acts without penalty of discovery, eventually assuming the throne as a tyrant. Of course, it's good even for most criminals that most people are basically moral. But why should we ourselves do our part when we can avoid getting caught?

The third answer is also very weak. What about those of us who just don't want to be the sort of person who is honest, kind, principled, and otherwise conventionally moral? Maybe we don't care. Or maybe we have a different, "higher" conception—as did Nietzsche—of the kind of person we aspire to be, believing that conventional ideals of the moral self are suited only for the inferior, common folk. (This skeptic might also add that for those who do aspire to be moral, the third answer seems to come down to the first.)

The proponent of rational skepticism has put forth pretty strong replies. There are, of course, still other arguments for the rationality of morality—Kant presents one that you will study when you read Part II. But it could be that this skeptic is on solid ground in asserting that morality cannot be rationally justified to everyone, at least if rational justification depends on what individuals want, need, or care about. In fact, Prichard, from his intuitionist point of view, believes that the entire attempt to justify morality rests on a mistake, as you will see if you read his essay included in Part II.

Finally, skeptics about motivation argue that whatever the rational justification for morality we might find, it won't move us to act accordingly unless we have, or come to have, certain desires or concerns. They point out that even a sound case that doing something will be best for me, in terms of my future good, won't motivate me unless I have a present desire to promote my good in the future. (Think of smoking or dieting, for example.) It should be even more apparent that unless I want to be moral or care about moral values, I just *will not act* morally, whatever rational case there is for it. The motivational skeptic concludes, typically, by observing that many people don't have the relevant wants, won't ever acquire them, and perhaps aren't even *capable* of doing so. Isn't morality, then, irrelevant to such people?

Perhaps the motivational skeptic is at least partly correct. Kant, and more recently Thomas Nagel, have argued that desires are not necessary to motivate—that mere beliefs, such as the belief that something is morally obligatory, can by themselves lead to action. But this is very hard to see. Many philosophers are convinced of Hume's position on this matter: Beliefs alone cannot produce actions; only desires or passions can do so. You can see the force of Hume's view by imagining a being—a biological organism or a robot created in a laboratory—that only has cognitive states (beliefs, knowledge, opinions, and so on), no affective ones (wants, desires, emotions, and so on). Would this being *do* anything? If you had only beliefs, would *you* do anything? *What* would you do, and why?

Yet even if we are Humeans about motivation and also concede that some people have a definite lack of desires or cares pertaining to morality, what is the importance of this for ethics? These sorts of people are not, generally, worth arguing with; in practice we try to avoid them or force them to avoid doing bad things to us. Most of us do have some moral concerns, so morality can often motivate us to act or refrain from doing things. Some deep issues arise at this point, the question of free will in particular. And there are psychological and other scientific questions about motivation and action that philosophers will never be able to answer by themselves. In Chapter 6 we make some observations about freedom and determinism, but now we must move on to one final problem about motivation and ethical convictions.

So far in our presentation of skeptical arguments about morality, we've assumed a stance about the relationship between ethical convictions and reasons for action. That stance is known as *externalism.* Many philosophers, especially noncognitivists, are committed to an alternative view of this relation, known as *internalism.* What can be said about these two opposing positions that would lead us to adopt one over the other?

Externalists about moral convictions or judgments assert that it makes sense to say, for example, that Smith knows he ought to help the needy but doesn't have any inclination to do so. In other words, externalists hold that there is no necessary connection between believing on the one hand that something is morally good, right, or obligatory and, on the other hand, being motivated to choose or do it. Internalists claim that there *is* such a connection, that it doesn't make sense to assert that someone has a moral conviction but has no motivation to act accordingly. To put their view more technically, internalists maintain that part of what it means to judge sincerely that something is good or right, bad or wrong, is that we have some motivation (even if it's not always a strong one) to choose it if it's good, avoid it if it's bad. We would presumably also encourage others to do things we believe right, discourage and even punish them for doing what we think wrong.

Why would some philosophers believe in this "internal" relation between sincere moral judgment and motivation? We find it odd to say, for example, that Sally believes abortion is morally wrong but has no qualms about having one herself or encouraging others to do so. Certainly, there are hypocrites—people who don't practice what they preach—but we tend to think they don't *really* believe what they say. There are also weak-willed people (most of us!), who seem unable to live up to their own standards. Yet weakness of will, about which we'll say more in Chapter 6, might be understood as involving a battle among our inclinations, those that pull us toward doing what we believe best or right and those temptations pulling us away.

We won't try to resolve the internalist/externalist debate here, though we should note a serious problem for internalists. In contrast to the externalist position, which can make perfect sense of a certain type of amoralism—the belief that one *does* have moral obligations but no inclination to act accordingly—the internalist appears bound to deny that there are any such cases. This denial is very doubtful. Don't we know of people who sincerely (for all we can tell) admit that morality generally requires them to act very differently from the ways that they do, yet who say they just don't care at all? Internalism implies that no one, logically, can be like this. True, in many contexts there is some oddity in saying, "This is the right thing to do, but I have no motivation to do it, and I don't care if others do either." But this oddity, the externalist could point out, doesn't mean a contradiction. Perhaps it's just that we normally are entitled to assume that people's avowed moral beliefs go together with some degree of care or concern to act on them, but that nevertheless sometimes they don't.

There is also a kind of internalism that has to do with reasons for acting, asserting that justifying reasons always must be motivating as well. But can't we properly say, for example, "Steve is totally unconcerned about the well-being of his ex-wife and children, but their needs are a good moral reason for him to pay some of their expenses?" If you think so, you're an externalist about good reasons.

We'll let you decide between these positions. To conclude our discussion of moral skepticism, we'll simply remark that internalism doesn't really help us avoid the possibility of having to admit that some people don't have a sufficient motivation, sometimes, to do the morally right thing. Internalism implies only that *some* motivation is part of sincere belief that an act is right—not *enough* motivation to get the person to do it. Some forms of moral skepticism might well be correct. But even then it would be debatable how this would or should affect our moral practice. After all, just because we might not be able to justify being moral in a self-interested way or to motivate everybody *always* to be moral, most people have good reasons to act morally most of the time. Perhaps, in much the same way that some philosophers deal with skepticism concerning our factual beliefs (that there is a material world independent of our minds, for example), we can allow that some forms of moral skepticism are true and yet proceed to live our lives in much the same way as before. Touching a hot stove would still cause us pain, for example, even if the stove did not exist apart from our perceptions of it. Similarly, even if we were convinced that moral considerations did not rationally motivate everyone all of the time, most of us would still have reasons to act morally in a great many cases. Perhaps objective moral knowledge is not so crucial to real life.

The Idea of Objectivity

So far in this chapter we've used the term *objective* without any detailed discussion of what it could mean. What would count as objective moral truth and knowledge? Is it possible? To what extent might ethics be subjective?

Our culture's current model of objective inquiry is, of course, natural science. But two lines of questioning immediately come to mind. First, what makes science objective, assuming that it is? And second, is even science totally objective—might it not have some aspects that, in some sense, are not objective?

Are Ethical and Scientific Objectivity Comparable?

In one respect, we think of science as objective because it (supposedly) requires interpersonal confirmation or disconfirmation and unbiased observation and interpretation. These requirements are closely related in that the former is one guarantee of the latter. Because the conclusions reached in scientific investigation are accepted only if there is a consensus among scientists and because this depends on different investigators obtaining similar results when performing similar experiments, the biases of individual scientists will tend to be corrected. What we want to know for present purposes is whether the same conception of objectivity makes sense for ethics. And if it does not, is there another understanding of what it means to be objective that does make sense?

Some philosophers maintain that the same general standard of objective truth can, so far as we know, be applied to both science and ethics. Objectivity, one suggests, depends "on our best efforts to think well about a subject matter, relying on each other for correction and stimulation. Put crudely and without needed qualification, a belief is objectively true if conscientious and intelligent investigators with access to all the relevant data and argument would, in the end, accept it."*

This conception of objectivity is closely tied to one of the methods of moral inquiry we'll examine later in this chapter. In this case, we should ask a number of questions: Might not the natural sciences be objective in some stronger sense than this? For example, what would be the equivalents in ethical theory to observational data in the sciences? Further, what is the likelihood of convergence of belief in moral philosophy, even in the ideal, long-run circumstances imagined? Couldn't it be that differences of cultural background, life experiences, and interests would prevent the kind of convergence among moral investigators that we would find among scientists?

The last question brings us back to the notion of bias. In some sense we can probably agree that ethical as well as scientific thinking should be unbiased. For example, we commonly believe that looking at a situation from the moral point of view requires impartiality. At the very least, this means that we don't just consult our own self-interest or favor those we like when we make moral judgments. Like a judge in a court of law, a competent moral judge must, among other things, avoid partiality of that sort. But perhaps complete impartiality would demand even more—that we disregard or prevent the influence of our gender, our upbringing, our cultural norms, our class interests or perspectives, our religious beliefs, and our ideals and aspirations on our moral judgments. That might be impossible in ethics (and maybe also in science, though for somewhat different reasons).

How Could We Account for Objectivity in Ethics?

Let's try to bring our discussion down to a more concrete level, setting aside for now the matter of whether ethical and scientific objectivity are comparable. And instead

*Warren Quinn, "Reflection and the Loss of Moral Knowledge: Williams on Objectivity," *Philosophy and Public Affairs* 16 (1987): 199.

of talking about ethics, for the moment, let's talk about another area in which we make value judgments—aesthetics. Suppose we say that Beethoven's Ninth Symphony is a better composition than "Me So Horny." If anyone were to dispute this, we could back up our value judgment with reasons, pointing to the complexity, emotional depth and expressiveness, originality, and other features of the symphony, together with its near-universal acceptance as a masterpiece among authorities and audiences. Isn't it an objective matter of fact that the Beethoven symphony is better?

Now, let's try a similar example of moral evaluation. In fact, here are two: "Slavery is morally unjust" and "Saddam Hussein is an evil man." How could anyone disagree with these statements? Well, some people do. Slavery in one form or another has been accepted in many societies throughout history, including ours. Of course, it's difficult to find anyone who will defend it today, and so far as we know no society officially sanctions it as such. Yet we do know that there are numerous countries in which ordinary citizens have fewer rights and less liberty than many slaves had in previous times; there are also people who will defend these regimes as just—indeed, even as moral models for other societies. Likewise, there are those who assert, with apparent sincerity, that Saddam Hussein is not evil. We might dismiss such people as moral idiots, but how can we prove that they're wrong?

A normative relativist would explain our sense that the two moral statements are obvious facts by observing that within our culture or society, they are objectively true—relative, that is, to the norms and values we generally share. We have some widely held beliefs about injustice that imply that slavery is unjust, at least under circumstances found in our society and time. Similarly, we have a conception about goodness that derives largely from the Judaic and Christian traditions, according to which tyrants such as Saddam Hussein are clearly evil. Much the same can be said about our aesthetic judgment. Within the community of those interested in serious music, obviously it's true that Beethoven's symphonies are better than pop songs.

The problem, as we saw earlier, is that our ethical and other evaluations seem to make claims to truth that go beyond the norms, ideals, standards, and conventions of our own society or of some particular group of aficionados or experts among us. Relativists don't seem able to explain this—or to explain it away, either. Neither can avowed subjectivists, who make evaluations relative to their own individual interests and principles. Many of our ethical and aesthetic judgments seem to be objectively true, in much the same sense that many nonevaluative judgments are objectively true.

Maybe some value judgments are "just a matter of opinion," whereas others are objectively true or false. In other words, maybe there is no absolute fact-value gap—some, but not all, values *are* facts. This is a plausible position, but it leads us to further questions. *Which* ethical judgments are factually or objectively true, and how do we know this? If it's just a matter of agreeing on certain criteria and if there's no rational basis for defending the criteria themselves, we seem to be back in a relativistic position. Our society's standards of excellence in music and our criteria for moral excellence must have some rational support beyond the fact of general acceptance, it seems.

So let's approach the problem from the other direction.. Are there any matters that are just matters of opinion? Whether Bach or Beethoven is the better composer might be an example. We could note that there are no agreed criteria of excellence among devotees of classical music that would provide a basis for ranking one of these great musicians over the other. Analogously, in moral contexts, there are cases in which it is a matter of opinion whether one obligation is more stringent than (gets priority over) another, when both clearly exist according to accepted norms and practices. There just isn't any agreed rule about which is the more important obligation in such circumstances of conflict. So although there do seem to be genuine matters of opinion in ethics and aesthetics, they exist in the context of broader areas of agreement. There is probably no basis for saying that Beethoven is better than Bach, but we do know that the Chicago Symphony plays their music better than does the Chico Symphony. That's objectively true, whatever the explanation. And though it would be idle to argue whether Saint Francis is morally superior to Mother Teresa, we know that both are far better human beings than Hitler or Stalin.

Again, the central problem of metaethics is the question of how to explain or account for this seeming objectivity of some value judgments, while at the same time allowing for the apparent subjectivity of others (for example, the judgment that abortion is morally wrong or that capital punishment is right). Our purpose here is, of course, only to introduce problems — not solve them. We have tried to show that objectivity admits of different forms and degrees and also that simply identifying empirical facts with objectivity and evaluations with subjectivity won't do. The distinction between descriptive and evaluative judgments seems to cut across the distinction between objective and subjective matters.

Does Skepticism Undercut Moral Philosophy?

One final question needs some attention. Suppose that all or most moral questions don't have objectively true answers that we can know. How disturbed should we be about this possibility? To focus our thoughts more precisely, suppose that there are no moral facts apart from facts about the beliefs that individuals or groups have about moral matters. Science, we can imagine, is able to explain those beliefs without postulating any moral facts. Would this undercut or render irrelevant the kind of inquiry that moral philosophers engage in?

Not necessarily. For one thing, moral knowledge might not have the objectivity of scientific knowledge, but the comparison itself is arguably irrelevant. Moral knowledge is not so much a matter of knowing *that* as knowing *how* (to live, choose, and act). There are better and worse ways of doing things given our aims, purposes, desires, needs, and interests. Although we might not be able to evaluate objectively the "given" — that is, the aims and interests we have individually or collectively — this isn't always necessary. Our basic moral ideals and principles might be expressions of such aims and interests, nothing more. Yet we will want to know how we could be more consistent in our advocacy and pursuit of our moral ideals, how we might change or modify our principles in light of fuller information about other things. In the next section, we consider two ways to do this.

Two Methods of Moral Inquiry

The two methods of moral inquiry we'll examine — *reflective equilibrium* and *rational desire* — are intended to clarify and guide our moral thinking at its most fundamental levels; they are worth using whether some form of objectivism is true or not, for they make no assumptions about objective truth.

Reflective Equilibrium

The first method for determining the acceptability of moral judgments and principles is similar to the second in some important ways. But one central difference is its reliance on the idea of a considered moral judgment. John Rawls, the leading proponent of this first approach, defines a considered moral judgment (sometimes the word *intuition* is used, but we will avoid it) as a judgment that a person makes with confidence under conditions that render errors of judgment less likely. An example is the moral conviction that slavery as it existed in the American South was unjust. Most of us would make that judgment with confidence and on the basis of adequate knowledge of what that slavery was like; moreover, we would have the conviction even when we had nothing to gain personally and were in a calm state of mind. In contrast, we sometimes make moral judgments of which we are not confident or that are the result of bias, ignorance, or emotional upset; those are *not* considered moral judgments. Considered moral judgments can be of any level of generality, Rawls states, so that (to return to our example) we can make them about all cases of slavery as well as about a particular case or range of cases.

When we take stock of the range of considered moral convictions or judgments we have about all sorts of things, we want to know what underlying principles we accept (or would accept) to support those moral beliefs consistently. You will recall that when we give reasons for our moral judgments, we appeal to such principles. Thus, we can support our moral judgment about slavery by appealing to the principle that it is unjust to take away an innocent human being's basic liberty, forcing him or her to be a servant. The principle is always more general than the particular moral judgment it supports. (Perhaps principles are themselves very general moral judgments.)

Rawls calls the process of bringing our considered moral judgments into harmony with one another and with the principles supporting them the attempt to achieve *reflective equilibrium.* It is an attempt to reflect on the reasons why we make the considered judgments about moral matters we do and to make those judgments and supporting principles consistent with each other — in other words, to arrive at a unified, coherent body of moral positions: an equilibrium.

Narrow reflective equilibrium must be distinguished from *wide reflective equilibrium.* When we achieve narrow reflective equilibrium, we achieve only a consistent set of moral positions based on what we now know. Wide reflective equilibrium, by contrast, is what we would attain if our moral positions not only formed a consistent, integrated body, but also resulted from reflection on all of the possible theories and arguments that could affect our positions one way or the other. Clearly, no one could ever achieve such a Godlike state of total moral consistency based on total awareness or knowledge of all possible moral arguments and theories. Still, we mere mortals can be closer to this ideal state or farther away. The closer we come to it, the more justified we are in holding the moral views we have. In other words, we (at least many of us) care about what moral positions we *would* take if we were completely consistent and fully aware of everything that could be argued on behalf of (and against) all possible positions, even though we can never attain that ideal state of perfect moral rationality.

To clarify further the notions we've introduced, let's apply Rawls's method of wide reflective equilibrium to an example or two. We'll see how this method formalizes generally accepted approaches to moral thought and argument that are typical of intelligent moral discourse and debate.

Suppose someone feels strongly that abortion is morally wrong. For her it would be a considered moral judgment, let's assume, because she is not only confident of it, but also sufficiently informed, unbiased, and emotionally undisturbed. So her judgment passes the first test. But there is the further test: Does it fit with her other considered judgments and principles?

She might support the judgment by citing the principle (P1): "It is wrong to kill another human being intentionally." However, this principle seems to conflict with some of her judgments about what ought to be done with murderers and the principle (P2): "Those who are guilty of murder ought to be executed." So, to be consistent, she must modify (P1) to read (P1′): "It is wrong to kill another innocent human being intentionally." But next consider a situation in which innocent people are used as shields by an aggressor, as in some wartime conditions; is it wrong to kill those people if necessary to win a battle or save oneself? If she thinks it is permissible, at least sometimes, then she needs a further change or qualification in the original principle; otherwise, she would have another inconsistency.

Knowledge of new facts and use of imagination are essential to serious moral reflection. In moral argument with others, we usually try to show an inconsistency in their moral positions, forcing them to modify or give up a judgment or principle in light of previously unappreciated information or new perspectives. That is what the attempt to reach wide reflective equilibrium involves. Note the revisability of considered moral judgments and principles—they are never infallible or certain. But they have an initial credibility that other, more hasty moral judgments don't. What we're seeking, each of us, is consistency and a well-informed basis for our moral positions; the closer we get to perfect consistency and awareness of all possible arguments and theories, the nearer we are to complete wide reflective equilibrium.

Here's one more example of how the method would work in practice. Take the case of someone contemplating the morality of an extramarital affair. Let's say that his initial considered judgment is that it would be permissible (at least in the circumstances). (We assume, perhaps too generously, that he feels confident about it, has thought about likely consequences for everyone concerned, is not biased in his own favor, and so on.) However, although he might be able to justify his judgment to some extent by invoking a principle about sexual freedom, or maybe a principle that it is never impermissible to do something that won't hurt others (he plans to be very sneaky), let's say that he holds still another principle: that it is wrong (all else being equal) to break a serious commitment. Obviously, these principles conflict. Therefore, he must either (a) give up his original judgment about the proposed affair, or (b) give up or modify the principle about commitment, or (c) show by citing another principle why the prima facie wrong is outweighed by competing moral considerations in favor of having the affair outside his marriage.

Rational Desire

We turn now to another method for moral inquiry, Richard Brandt's concept of the rational choice of a moral code. Instead of relying on considered moral judgments, this method uses the idea of a rational desire. On this view, a rational desire is a want that would persist in the face of vivid awareness of all the relevant information we could get about what we want, why, and so forth. We will say more about this idea in the next chapter. For now, simply think of the distinction between wanting something because you're ignorant and wanting something after you know all about it. Brandt argues that to determine what actions are right (and what moral judgments are correct or justified) we should consider this question: What moral code (system of rules or principles) would we want generally accepted in the society in which we expect to live our lives—and our descendants to live theirs—were we fully, vividly aware of all the relevant facts of what would happen as a result of accepting various moral codes?

To see the relevance of this very abstract question, we can look at one of Brandt's own examples, the case of someone who wonders whether homosexual relations are morally wrong and whether it is right to tolerate others' taking part in them. The answers to these two specific questions, Brandt insists, would depend on the answer to the general question: Would the ideal moral code for our society—the one we would want if we had adequate knowledge—prohibit homosexual acts and require us to condemn or prevent them?

Some of us have a strong aversion to homosexuality, of course, so we might want rules against it in our moral code—as we now think and feel. However, if we knew more about homosexuality, especially its causes and natural (as opposed to socially induced) consequences, perhaps we wouldn't be so opposed to it. After all, the ancient Athenians accepted it in some forms; it seems prevalent in certain animal species; and homosexual relationships seem as likely to be loving and committed as heterosexual ones. Moreover, maybe the many bad consequences we associate with it would not occur if it were widely accepted in our society. If we set aside purely religious objections and also worries about the spread of disease (which is not limited to homosexuals), it's not so clear that after thoughtful, informed reflection we would still be averse to homosexual behavior on the part of people who are so inclined.

Another example from the area of sexual ethics is incest. Is it always morally wrong? On Brandt's method, we would try to figure out whether the moral code we would want accepted in our society, were we fully informed, would include a rule prohibiting incest in all circumstances. We know that most societies have moral and legal rules against it, though its definition might vary (for example, how close the relative must be for the act to be considered incest). We also know that incest can involve an increased risk of genetically defective offspring. In most cases, we might think, there is good reason to morally oppose it. However, what about cases where biological siblings meet many years after separation at birth, fall in love, and want to marry but remain childless? Would we rationally want to prohibit that?

In short, Brandt's method is an alternative to Rawls's in that he gives no particular credibility to our considered moral judgments. Rather, Brandt believes, it is our informed choice of a moral code that is important for evaluating moral claims. What both have in common is their emphasis on the ways in which information can bear on our moral views; those views that are able to survive confrontation with facts and arguments and are part of a consistent set are justified, at least for the person holding them.

We won't be concerned here to debate the comparative advantages of each. They are both useful. (And, to the extent that our moral judgments and attitudes or desires go together, they are likely to lead to similar results.) When coming to the theories and problems discussed in subsequent chapters, you will have many opportunities to apply these two methods as you arrive at your own conclusions.

CHAPTER 4

THEORIES OF WELL-BEING

Three Types of Hedonism

What is the good life for human beings? What does happiness consist in? Are there many things that are good in themselves, or do they all reduce to one?

These questions about the nature of human well-being have preoccupied Western philosophers since before the time of Socrates. They are not—at least not directly—about what makes a person morally good; rather, they are about what gives a person a good life, in the sense of being well-off or flourishing. These are questions about what kind of life it is in a person's best interests to lead. Whether such a life is a morally good one is a separate matter.

One of the most common and influential theories of human well-being philosophers have put forth is hedonism—the belief that, in the final analysis, the good life consists only in pleasure and the absence of pain. In other words, hedonists assert that pleasure is the only thing (nonmorally) good in itself, pain or suffering the only thing bad in itself. Everything else is to be evaluated in terms of whether it produces pleasurable or painful results.

We will consider the three major kinds of hedonism philosophers have developed over the centuries: quantitative hedonism, qualitative hedonism, and Epicureanism. We'll also try to evaluate some of the criticisms made of each. This will lead naturally to a consideration of other theoretical conceptions of the good that have been historically important and remain viable alternatives to hedonism.

The simplest type of value hedonism is *quantitative hedonism.* The positions of the Greek philosopher Aristippus, as conveyed to us by Diogenes Laertius in his *Lives of Eminent Philosophers,* and the English philosopher Jeremy Bentham are forms of quantitative hedonism. All pleasures are good in themselves, and all painful experiences are intrinsically bad; greater pleasures are better than lesser ones, and the opposite is, of course, true of pains. But what is meant by "greater pleasures"? What would be a life of greatest pleasure?

For Aristippus, the more intense and simple pleasures of the body are best. They are more real, in a sense, and don't usually rest on false beliefs and hopes. Bentham, over two thousand years later, argues that intensity and duration (how long the pleasure lasts) are the only two criteria for determining the value of pleasures considered in themselves for one person. Thus, he asserts, the game of pushpin (similar to bowling) is as good as poetry if the pleasure the person gains is as intense and long-lasting—indeed, it might be more so for many uncultivated people, we might add. How uplifting or refined the pleasure is doesn't matter.

If one pleasure is greater in value than another (other things equal) when it is greater in intensity or duration, then what makes a life better than another? According to quantitative hedonism, the better, more valuable, happier life is the one with the greater balance of pleasure over pain. Some pains are worth enduring to get intrinsically valuable pleasures that outweigh them or to avoid greater pains (think about the dentist).

To sum up, how good or happy your life is, according to this type of hedonism, depends on how much pleasure you experience during its course and how little pain interrupts it—nothing else. Judgments about the moral character of the pleasure or about its "higher quality" are irrelevant. If you have a good time throughout your life and are able to avoid much suffering, then you're a happy individual. It doesn't matter whether you get pleasure from opera or drag racing, learning or drinking, penning poems or pigging out on pizza; whatever does it for you is what is more valuable to you, period.

What can we say for quantitative hedonism? Well, it's surely true that pleasure has a central role in the good life and that pain and suffering tend to detract from happiness (though they can have the extrinsic benefits of making us grow and appreciate things we wouldn't have otherwise). Philosophers who would deny this much, if there are any, would be clearly wrong. However, we need to address two criticisms of quantitative hedonism, which can be traced back to Plato. In the next section, we consider a general objection to hedonism of all kinds: namely, that there are intrinsically good things besides pleasure.

In his dialogue *Gorgias*, through his character Socrates, Plato compares the life of someone seeking only intense and long-lasting pleasure to the existence of some lowly organism dwelling at the bottom of the sea. A clam might experience a considerable balance of pleasant sensation over pain, but humans are more complex organisms. Why would they be satisfied with a good clam-life? Surely we must, at the very least, distinguish the higher pleasures of which humans are capable from those of lower life forms. We might get very intense pleasure from scratching an itch like a dog, but would a life of perpetual pleasure of that sort be good or happy?

Plato discusses another source of difficulty for hedonism in his late dialogue *Philebus*. This is the problem of "false pleasure." Consider one form of it: You are pleased at the prospect of your loved one arriving on the next plane, but it turns out that he missed the flight and won't arrive until the next day. Your pleasure was "false," because it was based on a false belief. There are other forms of false pleasure: mistaking the cessation of pain (a neutral state) for pleasure and distorting our memories of past experiences, so that we make false judgments about the relative magnitudes of pleasures and pains. Does the hedonist think even false pleasures in this sense are good?

We can further illustrate Plato's idea of false pleasure. Imagine someone quite naïve and unintelligent, who goes through life thinking that he has the love and respect of others, blind to the fact that they actually hate and despise him. Moreover, he is unaware of the darker side of life generally, indifferent for the most part to others' misfortunes and quite shallow, so that he never experiences the meaninglessness and futility that sometimes confront us in this life. False beliefs and plain ignorance shield him, so that he usually feels very good, pleased with his life, and able to enjoy a small range of rather simple things. Is this person truly happy, in the sense of living a good life for a human being? What about the character in the novel *Flowers for Algernon* (made into the film *Charly*)—a seriously retarded man who enjoys life much less after a drug raises his IQ to a high level? Was he living a better life before?

The point of Plato's criticisms is not to deny value to all pleasures, only to convince us that some are not valuable in themselves or are objectively of lesser value than others, regardless of what is subjectively felt. The hedonist can reply that false pleasures are still pleasant to those who have them and therefore intrinsically preferable to pain. If you were a cancer patient, wouldn't it be better to anticipate recovery joyously, experiencing false pleasure instead of great suffering—which is what you would experience if you knew that in fact you were terminal? At least sometimes, ignorance is indeed bliss. Even so, how can a simple hedonist explain the lesser value, other things equal, of false pleasures compared to "true" ones? They can be equally intense and long-lasting, and these are the only standards of value offered.

But let's say something more about the first line of objection, since it takes us directly to consideration of the second type of hedonism. Since we're talking about the good life for *human* beings—not lower animals or some higher but radically different creatures—our idea of human good or happiness must reflect a view of human nature. Perhaps Aristippus and Bentham had too simple a conception of our nature, limited by too narrow a sense of human potentiality. Human beings are capable of growth; they tend to change for better or worse over time; and they can experience pleasures and pains that no other animal can. Is it unreasonable to infer that human good or well-being—true happiness as opposed to mere contentment—requires higher, uniquely human pleasures, those involving the exercise of capacities only humans have?

John Stuart Mill, rejecting the simple hedonism of his teacher, Bentham, developed a *qualitative hedonistic theory of value*, based on a dynamic conception of the human self as a being capable of improvement. We shouldn't think of people as static entities with fixed tastes and preferences, none any better than any others. As does Aristotle, Mill thinks we are capable of development, and through cultivation and education we can realize our potentialities for higher experiences and activities. The best life for humans involves a large share of the higher pleasures, that is, those we feel when exercising thought, artistic creativity, noble abilities, and so forth.

How do we know that pleasures connected with higher, distinctively human capacities of certain sorts are intrinsically better? As you will see (in Chapter 10) when you read Chapter 2 of his essay *Utilitarianism*, Mill argues that a competent judge, someone who has experienced both higher and lower pleasures, will tend to prefer the former (an idea which we find also in Plato's *Republic*). Since we judge most other things in terms not just of quantity but also of quality, Mill insists, surely pleasure should not be any different. Though intensity and duration often characterize higher pleasures—and, Mill thinks, are an adequate basis for preferring them—the fact that they are of higher quality provides a better reason.

A person whose life includes a greater share of the higher pleasures will live a better life, a happier life, than someone who has a much lesser share, Mill believes. This is generally so despite the fact that the more developed person is more susceptible to experience a kind of misery of which the less developed are unaware. Mill himself experienced enough of this "higher" suffering to force us to respect his conclusion, whether or not we think it true of most people. Note that he is arguing, not that lower pleasant experiences are not valuable, but rather that people whose lives consist mainly or exclusively of such pleasures will be at most merely content, like satisfied animals—not happy.

Is Pleasure Just the Absence of Pain?

Plato and Epicurus offer two opposing views of the relationship between pleasure and pain. Plato holds that there is a neutral state of being neither in pleasure nor in pain, a state that is sometimes mistaken for one of them but is actually distinct. If intense pain suddenly ceases, we can easily think that we are experiencing pleasure; Plato, however, would argue that it is likely only "false pleasure." (See his discussion in the *Philebus.*) Epicurus, in contrast, would insist that if we feel or think we are experiencing true pleasure, then we really are. How could we be mistaken about that? As Epicurus conceives of the relationship, there is no neutral state between pleasure and pain. A person is always feeling one or the other, because pleasure is just the absence of pain. Plato's view is perhaps closer to our commonsense way of thinking—and probably accepted by a greater number of philosophers. The Epicurean view, however, has its proponents, too, among them the nineteenth-century German philosopher Arthur Schopenhauer, whose pessimism was reinforced by the thought that pleasure is just the temporary cessation of pain or frustration. Which position do you think is correct and why do you believe so?

Before looking at some problems with Mill's qualitative hedonism, we should discuss a third view of the good life, that of the Greek philosopher Epicurus. Although Mill cites him as a forebear in *Utilitarianism,* Epicurus's often misunderstood conception is actually rather different from Mill's. When we hear the term *Epicurean* these days, we think of someone who seeks sensual pleasures—an epicure is someone who enjoys fine food and wine. Some vulgar and uneducated contemporaries of Epicurus thought that members of his school held orgies on a regular basis. (In contrast to the earlier schools of Plato and Aristotle, the Epicurean school admitted women and accorded them status in proportion to their philosophical ability.)

In fact, what Epicurus recommends is a life of simple pleasures—those natural and necessary—and otherwise an avoidance of pain, especially of mental suffering or disturbance. His ideal was a state of *ataraxia,* untroubledness. You will recall Plato's idea that one kind of false pleasures involved confusing absence of pain with actual pleasure. For Epicurus, this was not a confusion at all: pleasure essentially *is* the absence of pain, discomfort, frustration, and worry. Even if we agree with Plato on this point, we should see the attractiveness of the Epicurean ideal, especially for people living in very uncertain and troubled times.

Epicurus counsels withdrawal from public or political involvement, and he believes that the gods are indifferent to human actions, so we need not fear any punishment in an afterlife. Once having attained wisdom about life, a goatskin of wine and a piece of cheese would be enough for a person's happiness. There is no reason to fear death, he maintains, because when we are alive death does not touch us, and when we are dead we cannot experience anything. Whatever we think of this argument, it's evident from surviving accounts of his life that Epicurus lived as he taught. He was a good and wise man who cheerfully endured the long and painful illness that eventually took his life.

Only a few of Epicurus's works have survived to our time; you will read one of his letters in Chapter 8. But we might raise one point now. Some people will say that the Epicurean conception of the good life involves settling for too little. It is too cautious, unengaged. By being more involved and seeking a richer range of experiences, including many sensual pleasures, as well as developing abilities and talents besides the philosophical, a person might lead a better type of life. Perhaps the Epicurean variety of happiness is appropriate only for certain kinds of people.

Mill, in fact, advocates a life that includes the pleasures of excitement as well as the calmer, more reflective enjoyments. He was very much involved in public affairs, even serving for a time in the British Parliament. His championing of women's rights was remarkable considering his time and position. For Mill, as for Aristotle, living the good life is a matter of developing our abilities in many different areas, thereby experiencing the pleasures involved in exercising our faculties and skills. Women are just as capable as men, Mill thinks, of living this kind of life. Mill goes so far as to assert that it is much better to be a Socrates dissatisfied than a fool satisfied, just as it is preferable to be a dissatisfied human than to be a contented pig.

This brings us to a serious problem for Mill's theory. He puts forth his standard of the competent judge as a kind of independent perspective enabling a person, at least theoretically, to make a rational choice between different kinds of life—apparently even across species, if we take the pig remark seriously. Does this standard really do this, or is it merely a question-begging argumentative device? Is it possible or meaningful to make comparisons of this radical sort?

Certainly many of us are strongly tempted to say that Socrates lived a better life than did a useless simpleton and that on the whole it's better to be a human being than even a fortunate pig. But why do we think this? Is it perhaps just a bias on our part? After all, the simpleton and the swine experience their pleasures *as* the sorts of creatures they are—not as Mill's qualified judge would experience them. The judge is essentially a higher being himself, not a neutral referee (otherwise he couldn't experience the higher pleasures). Maybe there is no impartial, objective, rational basis for asserting that one life is better or happier than others, apart from the quantitative criteria (intensity and duration) that earlier seemed inadequate.

A different, but not unrelated, problem for Mill is that in attempting to defend hedonism he comes very close to abandoning it entirely. He argues in Chapter 4 of *Utilitarianism* that such things as knowledge, friendship, and moral virtue—often cited along with pleasure as examples of intrinsic goods—are not mere means to happiness, but neither are they distinct from it. Rather, they are in some sense part of happiness. If a happy life, in Mill's terms, is a life in which higher pleasures predominate, then a person can't experience the pleasures of knowledge, friendship, and virtue without pursuing knowledge, friendship and virtue. But some would argue that they are goods even when they don't bring pleasure; often they bring more pain than pleasure. Mill's optimism might have blinded him to the need to come down on one side of the fence or the other: either knowledge and other such goods are good only to the extent that they bring pleasure, or they are desirable for their own sake.

The problem is clear. If we take the first alternative, then knowledge and so on are not good in themselves; they won't even be extrinsic goods (goods that are valuable because of what they produce) when they bring no pleasure or cause more pain. That position is hedonistic. But if we take the second alternative, then we give up hedonism entirely, because we would be admitting there are intrinsic goods other than pleasure.

These points are not intended as decisive objections to Mill's theory of the good. But they focus our attention on genuine difficulties in his arguments. Hedonism, in its various forms, still represents a plausible theory of human well-being or happiness. You might have some ideas of your own about how Mill's theory can be developed and better defended, or you might want to defend some other version of hedonism. As you reflect on your own life and the things you seek, we hope that these theories will become meaningful to you.

Pluralism, Desires, and Needs

One of the most common criticisms of hedonism, as we noted earlier, is simply that there are things besides pleasure, however broadly defined, that are good in themselves—that make up a happy life. We've avoided the difficult question of what pleasure is, using the term in its broadest extension, so that we could include everything from ordinary sensual delights to the feelings of self-satisfaction a person gets from knowingly doing a good deed. But whether we think of pleasure, enjoyment, and related concepts as mental states or attitudes, it's plain to many people that these ideas do not cover all of what is intrinsically good.

Pluralism in Value

We observed earlier that it is possible to have false pleasure. Robert Nozick offers an example that might help us focus our discussion at this stage (see his essay "Happiness" in Chapter 11). He asks us to consider the possibility of an Experience Machine. This science-fiction contraption is a sort of VCR for the brain, allowing us to program our lives for an indefinite period into the future. Once the connections are complete and the machine is turned on, Nozick imagines, we would lose any recollection of the process of being connected; our pseudo-experiences on the machine would seem completely real to us, indistinguishable from what really happened to us before. The advantage of hooking into the Experience Machine is, of course, that we can program experiences that we want—our dreams and ambitions can all be "fulfilled," our desires "satisfied," and our pleasures "experienced" (perhaps with just a little pain or frustration to heighten the pleasure). Why not connect ourselves to the Experience Machine instead of living out our real lives, with all the pain and disappointment, misery and depression, sadness and failure that come to almost all of us? Would you? Why or why not?

Nozick believes that most of us would not trade our real lives for an imitation life of preprogrammed experiences. We want to really do certain things, to really be persons of certain qualities—not merely to think and feel, falsely, that we are. There are things we want, quite rationally, besides pleasure or any other kind of subjective experience or mere mental state, if Nozick is right.

What are some of these things? We've already mentioned a few: knowledge, friendship, moral virtue; others could be personal growth, achievement of many kinds, appreciation of art, self-expression, a sense of meaning. Many people would think of power, status, and the respect and admiration of others as very valuable in themselves, essential components in a life that is good or the best. (That they are extrinsically good—valuable because of what they can produce—is less disputable.) Love is perhaps the most common example of an intrinsic good that ordinary people would mention. Expanding on Nozick's argument, we might say that we want truly to be loved, not just to think we are and have the subjective feelings associated with it. The insane, the drug addicted, and the characters in Huxley's novel *Brave New World* might subjectively feel quite good most of the time, but they are out of touch with reality, and their lives lack goods of the sort we've just listed. They are not, we might conclude, living well.

The thesis that there are many things good in themselves is called *pluralism in value theory*. Pluralism can, however, have objective and subjective forms. Subjective pluralism typically interprets the idea of intrinsic goodness as a capacity to satisfy or fulfill a desire, either an actual want or an informed want for something in itself (for its own sake, not as a means). Things are good, that is, because people want or would desire them. Objective pluralism is harder to define, but involves the idea that people want things because they are good. Keeping in mind our earlier conclusion that objectivity and subjectivity admit of degrees, we can understand absolute subjectivism and absolute objectivism as opposite ends of a spectrum. On an objective pluralistic theory of value, we might say, goodness for someone is a property relatively independent of the person's desires—compared to what subjective theories claim, that is. Unless we are talking about the extreme or pure forms of each theory, then, we ought to speak about relative objectivity and relative subjectivity.

Let's first consider a simple and extreme subjective theory, the idea that something that is good for someone is merely something that the person actually wants. Hobbes seems to have held this kind of theory. An objectivist would, of course, immediately reply, "You're saying that things are good if someone desires them; in fact, we desire things because they're good (independently of our desiring them)." The subjectivist might reply that this is confused thinking—wanting something is what makes it good for us, though it's true that we desire things because of their objective properties (of which goodness is not one). What comes first, desiring or thinking good, might seem like the question about the chicken and the egg, and the question of whether we desire things because they are good or things are good because we desire them seems similarly unfruitful. We'll therefore consider some other, more straightforward objections to extreme subjectivism about value.

One objection is that we sometimes want things because we're ignorant. Past deprivation or emotional turmoil (or depression) can also influence our desires in ways that make them rationally suspect. We have, then, a problem of what we might call "false desire" akin to Plato's idea of false pleasure. Let's look at some examples. Suppose I want to be a rock star; being convinced that this life would have certain features that would fulfill a range of wants, I sacrifice everything else for it. But on achieving my objective I find that it's not at all what I thought the life of a star would be like, and I'm very unhappy. I was ignorant, or had false beliefs, about it. Or take a second example. Because of a lack of love from a stern and distant father, a woman seeks relationships with similar men; she is always disappointed with these involvements. Clearly, her desire to relate intimately with emotionally cold men is an attempt to compensate for her childhood deprivation, and it leads her to act in ways that are contrary to her true interests.

What these examples suggest is that satisfying desires may not be a good or valuable thing for people—it can even be bad for them. (An extreme version of this point is expressed in the ancient saying that when the gods want to punish us, they give us everything we want.) Wants based on false beliefs or lack of adequate information, past deprivation (another example of which might be a miser's wants), or transient and irrational emotions and moods are often not good to fulfill.

A second objection is that some things people want are simply senseless, particularly if they sacrifice other good things to get them. Wanting posthumous fame might be an example of this—how could it be good for you to have it, since you will be dead if and when it comes? Another example is dedicating yourself to getting into the *Guinness Book of World Records* by means of some useless achievement, for example, accumulating the largest ball of string in existence.

Informed Desires

For these and other reasons, it looks as if we must give up the simple, extreme form of the subjective pluralistic theory. A more widely accepted view these days is that goodness or value, what makes up a person's well-being, consists in fulfilling his or her informed desires. On one version of this view, to say that something is good for me is to assert that I *would* want it if I were fully informed about it. Realistically, this is too strong—we should say not "full information," but perhaps "available information" that is in some sense "relevant," that is, likely to affect the person's motivations one way or the other. Brandt has worked out a view of this kind, insisting that we use this definition: Something that is good in itself for someone is something that person desires for its own sake once he or she has been maximally influenced by available information about it. The intuitive idea is that if somebody still desires something after knowing all that can be known about it, then that thing is valuable for that person. Satisfaction of that desire would contribute to the person's well-being, other things equal.

A number of objections and puzzles arise when we consider this view. For one thing, is it our *actual* present or future informed desires that we ought to satisfy? Or is it the desires that we *would* have, hypothetically, if we were informed in a way that in fact we never will be? Presumably it's the former, for it hardly makes sense to say that what is good for us is the fulfillment of a range of desires we'll never have, because we'll never get or appreciate the relevant information. But the first interpretation seems to rule out the possibility that there are things good for us that we will never want; still, one could insist that those are things that *would* be good for us but aren't good for us as we are now or as we will in fact become. Listening to all of Wagner's *Ring Cycle,* for example, would be a good experience for me were I to become sufficiently knowledgeable and sensitive in matters musical. But I never will, let's suppose, so it isn't and won't ever be a good experience for me.

How much and what sort of information would be necessary to "validate" a desire as one that would be good to satisfy? This is also problematic. We noted Brandt's position that we must adequately appreciate all relevant available information, that is, all the facts we could find out that might move us to seek or avoid something. There might be facts that aren't in any realistic sense available to us prior to fulfilling the desire but that would make a difference; for example, there is no way I can know that a certain food is toxic for me (toxic only for me, not for anyone else) until I satisfy my desire to eat it and suffer the bad consequences. It seems that unavailable information sometimes is relevant to the goodness of something.

Here's another problem. Some desires seem to disappear as we get fuller information about what we want, but their fulfillment is nevertheless a good thing. Curiosity is one kind of case—a desire to learn about something is one I wouldn't have if I knew all that could be known about it. Another kind of example is the appetite for food and sex. We could be repelled by the idea of sex or eating if we knew all that went on at a physiological level when we did these things, at least if we're very squeamish. But that wouldn't make them bad for us or our desire to satisfy them not rational.

We should mention one more problem. People's desires change over time, for many different reasons. What I want or most desire now might be totally unappealing to me a few years from now. If the aim is to maximize desire-satisfaction over my lifetime, let's assume, should I give longer-lasting desires priority over less enduring ones? Why, or why not? Should I treat later desires as more important than earlier ones? Again, this needs justification. There is also the matter of intensity—should I give priority to more intense wants (other things equal) over those less strong? For what reason? A theory of the kind we're considering has to address these questions and many others if it's to be acceptable. Perhaps the idea of a life plan, as invoked by John Rawls and James Griffin, would be helpful here. We tend to structure our desires and aims into more or less coherent patterns, extending into the indefinite future. We could understand well-being as the achievement of goals and fulfillment of desires that are parts of an overall well-informed plan of life. But it remains uncertain how to deal with major changes of people's life plans, especially when promoting the good of others.

Needs

These worries and objections might be overcome by a fuller development of the informed desire theory. But let's now briefly turn to what some philosophers would regard as a better alternative—a more objective type of pluralism. This view sets aside our desires and instead centers on the idea of *needs*. Something is good for us, according to this position, if it fulfills a need. We are in a state of general well-being to the extent that our needs are satisfied. We have needs for many different things (hence pluralism), but our needs are usually fewer than our desires, and often they don't over-lap. In general, needs seem, perhaps by definition, to be more urgent than desires.

But what exactly is the definition of *need*? Something is a need if it's necessary for something else assumed to be of value. Thus food, shelter, clothing, health care, and so on are basic needs for human life. Less basic might be needs for intellectual growth, love and affection, recreation, and so forth. But our definition of *need* doesn't help us much in determining whether to extend this list further, to know what other things belong on it and what things don't. After making countless efforts to come up with an objective criterion of humans' needs, we might go so far as to concede that one person's need is another's wish or desire.

Griffin makes two interesting points about the idea of a need.* First, he notes that informed desires are sometimes more urgent than needs. For example, some

*James Griffin, *Well-Being* (Oxford: Clarendon Press, 1986), chapter 3.

scholars would rather have more books than the exercise equipment they need to promote their health. Arguably, their desire for the additions to their library should have priority for them. A second point Griffin makes is that the urgency of needs is a function of (among other things) the extent to which they are met, especially in relation to other needs and desires. Good health might matter much less to someone who has no liberty, for example. Griffin asserts that it's unclear how we can assess the relative importance of needs apart from informed desires. (He also maintains that informed desires are more independent of social expectations and contingent circumstances than uninformed desires.) He believes that an informed desire theory of well-being, with some modifications, is the most reasonable account; on his view, it is *not* even essential that we experience the satisfaction of our desire.

If Griffin is correct, therefore, it seems that any interpretation of well-being in terms of need satisfaction is not only hard to distinguish from, but also seems to depend on, a desire satisfaction theory. Perhaps some version of the informed desire theory is the best way of interpreting the idea of human well-being, if we are pluralists about value. But we should consider another kind of objective theory of the good life for human beings: perfectionism.

Excellence of Self

Both hedonistic and desire satisfaction theories can be regarded as interpretations of what happiness is, as we commonly think of it in our culture. But the goal of happiness, in this way of understanding it, is to some people not the highest aim of mankind. Some have indeed contemptuously dismissed it, especially when the happy life is understood as one of enjoyment, comfort, ease, self-concern, and the pursuit of one's personal interests in a mundane sense. Albert Einstein (echoing Nietzsche) saw it as a pigsty philosophy of life—what really matters, he thought, is the quest for truth and greatness. Richard Nixon said much the same thing in an interview once, insisting that happiness is unimportant compared to accomplishing great things in the public arena.

To do great deeds requires great human beings. The idea that what we should seek in our lives is not pleasurable or desired outcomes for ourselves but rather to acquire good traits of character is often called (somewhat misleadingly) *perfectionism.* On this view, our life's supreme goal is not so much perfection (which is usually unattainable) but improvement. We should make ourselves better, in the sense of "more excellent." Becoming a better person includes what we think of as moral improvement, but more than that. We should strive to be smarter and more pleasant socially, some would say, but those qualities aren't moral virtues to us. Generally, the ideal of perfectionism tells us to try to acquire the abilities and character traits that enable us to attain excellence in ourselves.

The idea of cultivating the self, of developing one's potential for excellence, is prominent in Greek ethics, most importantly in Aristotle's theory of the human good. We translate the word *eudaimonia* into English as "happiness"—literally, it means "good spirits"—and among the ancient Greeks it seems to have had the same vague meaning that our word does. But in Aristotle's theory, the term is defined technically to mean "activity in accordance with virtue." In other words, Aristotle acknowledges the common view that happiness is the goal of life for rational men, but he attempts to resolve the widespread disagreement about what it is by giving his own special definition. Aristotle's definition makes some sense in the context of his overall theory, but it might strike us as implausible at first. After all, can't we act in virtuous — that is, excellent — ways without being happy?

Underlying Aristotle's theory of human well-being or happiness is a conception of human nature, one that is both descriptive and normative. (You might recall our earlier discussion of ethical naturalism in Chapter 3.) The descriptive part of Aristotle's theory of human nature is metaphysical and biological, whereas the normative aspect can be seen as an ideal. Perfectionists, as we have said, think that human beings have the potential for various excellences; the aim of life is to develop and exercise these potentials. For Aristotle, humans are essentially rational beings; that is what distinguishes us from animals of other species. He argues that we have an *ergon*, that is, a function or characteristic work, just as our bodily organs do (the eyes have the function to see, and so on). Our function is to reason, and we are thus excellent humans to the degree that we reason well, both theoretically and practically. What we are metaphysically and biologically, in other words, determines what we ought to do. Aristotle is clearly an ethical naturalist.

We are most fully human, then, when we actualize our potential for virtuous or excellent action. Aristotle distinguishes excellence of body, of character, and of intellect. Needless to say, the first of these would be discussed in a treatise on medicine or biology; only the latter two are treated in the *Nicomachean Ethics* (see Chapter 7). In this book, we find what appear to be two different ideals of life, one that has to do with excellent character, the other with intellectual excellence. The first ideal is that of the person of public affairs, the politician who has the good of the community uppermost in his hierarchy of goals. This individual needs the good traits of character that will enable him to be effective in promoting the good of his state: justice, courage, truthfulness, and so on. The other ideal is that of the contemplative philosopher — the theoretically wise man who experiences the pleasure of apprehending unchanging truths. How to reconcile these different conceptions of the best life is a difficult matter of interpretation. Perhaps all that we can say is that the contemplative ideal is most suitable for what Aristotle saw as the highest kind of man (like himself), whereas the ideal of public service is best for able and well-positioned men who are less philosophical. (It is also a puzzle how Aristotle can hold that the best life is the most fully human but at the same time compare the contemplative life to that of God.)

In any event, these remarks on Aristotle's conception of human nature help us better appreciate his theory of happiness. His untutored contemporaries, we noted, would define *eudaimonia* as "living and doing well." In what does that consist? They might have said that it was a matter of getting pleasure, honor, and so on. But Aristotle rejects such answers; pleasure, for example, is a supreme purpose only for nonhuman animals. Like Plato, Aristotle insists that pleasure cannot be the sole good for human beings, since wisdom added to pleasure is much better than pleasure alone. Rather, he argues, happiness is activity of the soul that expresses the highest, most complete virtue (excellence) within a life that is complete. Such a life (either of the ideals we discussed in the previous paragraph) would be pleasant because it is valuable, though with some qualifications.

Aristotle notes that things such as pleasure, friendship, and theoretical knowledge are or should be chosen for their own sake and not merely as means. But we can also say that they are parts (constituents) of the final supreme end of happiness: They make up *eudaimonia* rather than being mere means to it. (Mill takes a similar position in *Utilitarianism.*) Gaining or participating in these goods requires having and exercising excellent traits of character and intellect, the virtues. We cannot choose happiness for the sake of anything else; it is complete in itself.

But just as a virtue like truthfulness, justice, or courage can in unfortunate circumstances bring a person to a bad end, possessing the full range of virtues does not guarantee happiness by itself. We must presuppose certain favorable conditions if we are to infer that the individual is truly happy. Among these prerequisites are being well-born, reasonably affluent, good-looking, healthy, free, and an accepted member of a community. In Aristotle's culture, moreover, being male was necessary to have a chance at complete happiness—women could not acquire the full range of virtues. (Aristotle would have, in fact, insisted that this limitation was not due purely to cultural restrictions.) A childless person can't be fully happy, either, nor can someone whose children shame him after his death! (Aristotle seems to have subscribed to the view of some Greek thinkers that happiness not only implies goodness of life as a whole, but also can be affected after the person ceases to exist. We can't be certain someone's happy until he's dead, and maybe not even then.)

Whether Aristotle's beliefs about the conditions of happiness are true or not, we certainly can't accuse him of ignoring its dependence on fortune. In this regard his position differs from that of Epicurus (and those of some of the Stoics), who thought that a good man could be happy under torture. Indeed, if we take the arguments of the *Republic* seriously, Plato was closer to Stoic and Epicurean views than was Aristotle. Happiness is not, then, according to Aristotle, just a matter of having a virtuous soul. One must also possess excellences of birth (social class), physical appearance (beauty or handsomeness), and health—things we have at most limited control over, if any.

In Aristotle's pluralistic perfectionism we thus find a very reasonable theory of what the good life of human beings is. He tells us, in effect, that our reason can show us what things are worth doing in life, and our happiness consists in doing them well.

Some people object that Aristotle's notion of what things are excellences is conditioned by his cultural and class surroundings, that his account lacks universality and (as a result) true objectivity. But perhaps it is impossible for any theory to escape these limitations. To point out that Aristotle's doesn't is hardly a major objection. After all, hedonism is subject to the same limits: What people take pleasure in is heavily influenced by their culture and circumstances; desires, even informed ones, are also relative to expectations and social conditions. The criticism that standards of excellence could be similarly relative, therefore, might not be serious.

Still, Aristotle's theory has one major difficulty. Even within the context of classical Greek culture, there were many opposing ideals of the person and conceptions of the best life, particularly during different periods. Epicurus, as we discussed earlier, has a conception of the ideal life that is in many ways the exact opposite of Aristotle's ideal of the political life. Epicurus teaches that we should avoid entangling ourselves in public concerns and not let our happiness depend on the success of such projects. Instead we should live very simply, doing our best to avoid pain and worry. Epictetus also takes a position very antithetical to Aristotle's; he thinks that even a slave can live and fare well. We might conclude that Aristotle's two

Happiness and Objective Reality

Is happiness an objective state—a matter, say, of living by certain interpersonally valid standards? Or is it more subjective, a matter of enjoying or being satisfied with one's life? In this chapter, we have discussed happiness mostly in terms of well-being or a person's good, which are somewhat broader concepts. But Aristotle's *eudaimonia* is equally comprehensive, and it posits objective conditions that lives must meet if they are to be truly "happy." Robert Nozick (in his essay "Happiness"; see Chapter 11) and Lynne McFall (in her book *Happiness*) also put forth accounts of this idea that lean heavily toward the objective side of the spectrum. Aristippus and Bentham represent, of course, the extreme subjective approach, whereas Mill and Brandt take a modified subjectivist stance, as does Richard Kraut in his article "Two Conceptions of Happiness."

At issue between subjectivists and objectivists on happiness are questions such as these: Can a person believe he or she is happy and be mistaken? How much knowledge of oneself and one's situation are needed to be happy? Are there certain general features which any human life must have to be truly happy, or do these vary widely among persons? What you decide about these questions will depend, in part, on what you would say about some standard problem cases: the insane, drug addicts, people who live by serious misconceptions, hedonists who waste their potentials for self-development, and so forth. It is important that we arrive at some conclusions for ourselves, since—consciously or not—what we think will determine what we strive for in life.

ideals of life are really best only for certain well-positioned men with certain interests who live in one kind of society, yet even some of them could find the Epicurean or Stoic ideas of how to live one's life more congenial.

To sum up this point, cultures usually recognize more than one ideal of human life, and different (sometimes incompatible) excellences or virtues correspond to these various ideals. Unless we're convinced by an Aristotelian account of human nature, we seem to have no objective basis for saying that everyone should make the choice of one particular ideal and acquire a specific set of virtues. But Aristotle's view that people have an essential function, and that rationality determines a particular scale of values, is very hard to accept. It is reasonable to go along with his prescription to choose the mean between extremes (for example, be neither cowardly or foolhardy, but courageous), an ideal sometimes oversimplified as "Be moderate in all things." However, what count as the extremes or limits is often a matter of fundamental disagreement, especially in questions of justice. In this regard it would be interesting to contrast the ideals of Aristotle and Nietzsche, both of whom understand human good in terms of excellence.*

Hedonists offer a different line of criticism, insisting that the apparent plurality of goods that constitute the good life are really reducible to one: pleasure, albeit of

*On this point, see Alasdair MacIntyre, *After Virtue*, 2d ed. (South Bend, Ind.: University of Notre Dame Press, 1984).

many sorts. Aristotle clearly recognizes some importance of pleasure to the good life, but does he fully accord it the central significance due to it? Sometimes he speaks of it as a mere accompaniment to virtue, like bloom on a youthful cheek. In other passages, he states that it is essential to virtuous action that one take pleasure in doing it. It seems to be his position that we ought to seek excellence for its own sake, however, not because it gives us pleasure. In this respect he differs with Mill, who shares his concern to rank pleasures according to their quality. Mill also understands the good for human beings in terms of the development of individual potential; but for him the good is a matter of cultivating a wide range of capacities to experience higher pleasures. Mill thus combines the most important features of perfectionism and hedonism, without clearly abandoning the latter view (though some critics accuse him of adopting pluralism). In any event, Mill's qualitative perfectionist hedonism seems a serious alternative to Aristotle's conception. You might even consider it an improvement, if you place central importance on the role of pleasure in the ideal life.

Thus far we've considered several conceptions of what constitutes the good life. Human well-being—what makes life worth living—has been interpreted in terms of pleasure, the satisfaction of informed desires and needs, and the development of our potential for excellent activity. Which of these types of theories best explains the range of things we consider good to have in our lives? That's something you'll want to think through for yourself as you read the selections in Part II.

Value and Meaning

Before concluding this chapter, we should say something about a concept that is easily confused with value or goodness, but that on further analysis seems distinct. This is the idea of meaning in life.

"What is the meaning of life?" is commonly thought to be the paradigmatic example of a philosophical question. But we're here concerned with a different, though related question: "What gives an individual life meaning?" We'll proceed on the assumption that there is no one, general meaning of life over and above the meanings that persons individually give to or find in their lives. Even if these meanings are subjective and nonrational, they are obviously important to the lives of many of us. We need to arrive at some understanding of them, however preliminary, in order to begin to see their relation to value and the good life.

The word *meaning* has importantly different meanings. The sentence "Smoke means there's a fire" uses the word in a very different sense from the sentence " 'No Smoking' means we may not smoke." The philosopher Paul Grice labeled the first use "natural meaning," the second "communicational meaning."* Consider another use: "He means to get even with his former colleagues." Here the word has the sense of "intends" or "plans." In the sentence "His gesture of kindness means a lot to me," we seem to have yet another sense, perhaps the one in which we are now interested.

Most of us want to do or experience things in our lives that mean something to us. They are what make our lives meaningful. Something may be very enjoyable

*H. P. Grice, "Meaning," *Philosophical Review* 66 (1957): 377–88.

and even an exercise of an excellence without being meaningful. (Think of good sex without love, or an accomplished athletic performance devoid of any special significance for the athlete.) It seems that enjoyable and excellent activities are valuable, as far as they go. But for an activity to be meaningful, something more seems necessary. Some jobs may be pleasant and draw on the skills of employees yet not give them a sense of meaning in their work. They might find that meaning in their personal lives—through family, friends, religion, and so on—or they might feel totally alienated from what they do.

We can find some clues to what meaningful activity or experience is if we look more carefully at some of these examples. Let's fill out one of them a bit more. A baseball star hits his 231st home run; he's happy, the crowd is pleased, and he's exercised a great skill. He's brought his team a bit closer to winning the game, let's suppose. But that run doesn't by itself win the game, or even make a difference in the end; it's not a World Series game, either. So he doesn't see it as a meaningful act or event. Now let's change things. Suppose that this home run breaks the all-time record or wins the Series. Now it will seem meaningful to the player (and many fans of baseball). It has special significance; it is important; it represents the achievement of a goal he's had for most of his life and for which he's worked hard.

Take another example. Employees of a large corporation, treated indifferently by their superiors, produce goods of low quality for a mass consumer market. The goods might sell well, and the employees might be well paid for their labor. But although they're not treated badly, the indifference of management to their perspectives and concerns, the lack of a sense of community within the firm (something the Japanese take pains to create), and the lack of quality in their products (and hence the lack of any pride they take in producing them) leaves many of the employees with a sense that their work is meaningless, however pleasant and remunerative it may be. This would not be the case if the employees produced goods of high quality they could be proud of and if they were able to feel they were part of a "family" and a tradition, people whose special skills are not only valued economically but also admired by others. If their own names were on the product itself (or a label), they might have additional pride and a sense of doing meaningful work. Some people would insist that a role in the firm's decisions would contribute even more to that end.

Meaning seems to be related therefore to significant, especially important events or activities—those that seem to make a difference, to matter. Meaningful life and activity also appear to have something to do with connecting—becoming a part of some larger group, project, cause, institution, or tradition. Seeing oneself, for example, as a part of baseball history, one's accomplishments as a player take on a special meaning; the same can be true of one's products as a worker, if the employment setting is conducive to it. (Think not only of the Japanese model of corporate responsibility and organization, but also of the idea of a tradition of craftsmanship that we find in other countries.)

Our question "What gives an individual life meaning?" shouldn't be confused with "What gives an individual life value (that is, makes it worth living)?" We can live a good life, overall, without having a sense of meaning—at least many people can. But meaning is nevertheless something we tend to seek in our lives, whether we succeed in finding it or not. It might even be that "finding it" is in some sense an illusion. We need a better philosophical understanding of this idea. So far we've said that notions such as significance, importance, and mattering have something to do

Limits and Meaning

Is a meaningful human life possible without death? Bernard Williams raises this question in his essay "The Makropulos Case: Reflections on the Tedium of Immortality." The essay concerns a story by Czech science-fiction writer Karel Capek. Elina Makropulos (as she is now named) is a woman who began taking a potion 342 years ago that prolongs life as long as one wants. She lives many different lives over the centuries, seeing and experiencing the full spectrum of human happiness and misery, triumph and degradation. Finally, unable to find any reason to continue living, she chooses death. Williams concludes, "Immortality, or a state without death, would be meaningless . . . so, in a sense, death gives the meaning to life" (*Problems of the Self: Philosophical Papers 1956–1972* [Cambridge: Cambridge University Press, 1973], 82). A human life without suffering and struggle would be similarly devoid of meaning. As Schopenhauer (who holds that life is meaningless in any event) expresses the idea, "Life presents itself chiefly as a task—the task, I mean, of subsisting at all. . . . If this is accomplished, life is a burden, and then there comes the second task of doing something with that which has been won—of warding off boredom, which, like a bird of prey, hovers over us, ready to fall wherever it sees a life secure from need." What is boredom, Schopenhauer asks, "but the feeling of the emptiness of life?" As things are, "we take no delight in existence except when we are struggling for something . . ." ("On the Vanity of Existence," in *The Will to Live: Selected Writings of Arthur Schopenhauer*, ed. Richard Taylor, trans. T. Bailey Saunders [New York: Ungar, 1967]). Thus deprivation, hardship, disappointment, and finally death—usually considered great evils—appear to be necessary conditions of a meaningful life.

with meaning in life; they seem to connect value with meaning. We also suggested that the individual's connection with a thing greater than himself or herself seems to be characteristic of meaningful life.

At least one other idea seems essential to begin to understand this concept of meaning in a person's life. People who feel that they have meaningful lives have a perspective on themselves and what they do that is different from those who don't feel this way. They interpret what they do in the light of some image or conception of human life and the universe as a whole. Very often this is a religious interpretation—but it doesn't have to be, at least in the strict sense. Seeing one's life as an opportunity, a gift from God, for the purpose of carrying out his will is a moral and metaphysical interpretation of human existence that gives it a point. A purely biological perspective, in contrast, which emphasizes evolution of the species and survival does not seem to give us a sense of meaning. Thinking about the differences between these two common pictures of human life should give us more clues to what meaning is. (Why do some interpretations give meaning, and others not?)

Thomas Nagel has observed that too distant and objective a perspective on our lives seems to rob them of meaning.* Caught up in our plans, projects, and daily concerns—to write and publish a book, earn a promotion, gain recognition or a

*Thomas Nagel, "The Absurd," in *The Meaning of Life*, ed. E. D. Klemke (New York: Oxford University Press, 1981).

higher salary—we attach an importance to what we're doing that tends to disappear to the extent that we can, in our mind's eye, look at ourselves from "the perspective of eternity." What real difference does it make, in the final analysis, what we accomplish? We will all die; our solar system—and perhaps the entire universe—will dissolve into nothingness at some future time. Does anything really matter, given the fact of our mortality and the assumption that there is no afterlife of the kinds posited by Judaism, Christianity, or Islam?

But would eternal life—even in Heaven—really give us meaning, either? It could not have any purpose beyond itself, for one thing. Moreover, perpetual life wouldn't necessarily even be happy; it could be far more miserable than we can imagine. The never-ending struggle of Sisyphus, as portrayed by Albert Camus in the selection in Chapter 11, is one form it might take. The very idea of eternal happiness, perfect in all respects, seems to be inconceivable. Might not the eventuality of death itself be a condition of meaning? Though we can't pursue these questions further here, you might want to take other philosophy courses that deal with them, perhaps a course in the philosophy of religion, and look up some of the books listed in our Suggestions for Further Reading.

CHAPTER 5

Theories of Moral Conduct

Psychological and Ethical Egoism

Now that we've looked at some theories about what makes a life good and what gives it meaning, we can consider some major theories about how people ought to make moral decisions and be motivated to act. We will survey several influential conceptions of right conduct or virtuous action, along with the views of motivation that typically underlie them.

Psychological Egoism

One common theory of motivation that is used to support more than one kind of theory of right conduct is *psychological egoism.* This can be broadly defined as the claim that everyone's actions are always (or necessarily) motivated solely by the desire to get something he or she believes is good for himself or herself. This is a view of human motives that is widely held among people generally, and we must take it seriously. Note that it is *not* a thesis about what persons ought to do; rather, it is a descriptive, psychological statement about what in fact is always the ultimate motivating desire in everyone's actions.

Psychological egoism does *not* entail that all human actions actually bring something good to the agent, let alone what is best for him or her. That would be to say that all human actions are at least to some degree rational; that we know to be false. It doesn't even entail that the agent will have good reason to believe he or she will benefit. All that is claimed is this: Whenever people do something, it is only because they think (correctly or not) something desirable for themselves will result from it.

The desirable outcome or benefit could be anything from pleasure (the position called "hedonistic psychological egoism") to a wide range of other possible intrinsic goods for people, such as we surveyed in the previous chapter. We should add to our definition, however, that humans might, according to psychological egoism, also act to avoid something that they think is bad for themselves.

Is psychological egoism true? If so, how could we prove it? We could begin by observing that egoistic motives certainly do exist behind many, if not most, human actions. This is especially true in our economic behavior; people generally work, trade, and save in order to get things they want for themselves. But is it true of everything everyone ever voluntarily does? That's a very strong claim. Let's see if we can find a clear and convincing counterexample to the thesis of the psychological egoist. If we can, the thesis is false; if we cannot, we have a good reason to accept it.

A frequent source of examples brought against psychological egoism is our ordinary conception of intimate human relationships, especially those involving deep friendship or love of one kind or another. The most persuasive examples are cases of people sacrificing for their children or giving up their lives to save the one they love. We often think that true love or friendship will sometimes require putting the other person's good above our own. To many people, it's obvious that we are capable of this altruistic behavior. However, as we have defined psychological egoism, it's far from clear that what we know about the actions of friends and lovers is inconsistent with that thesis. In cases of sacrifice of this sort, we might allow, there is always some good thing that the agents believe they will get for themselves, or at least some bad thing they will avoid. Friends and those in love relationships, whether parental or romantic, are people whose conception of their own good is intertwined with that of their loved ones. They will be happy, in general, when their beloved or friend is happy; they will suffer when the other does, too. (This is quite apart from the usual expectations of reciprocity in most such relationships.) So, benefiting friends and those we love will, at least to some degree, benefit us; at least we tend to assume this. In cases of the ultimate sacrifice—giving up one's life for another—we avoid the suffering of living on without our loved one.

Opponents of psychological egoism often cite the lives of the saintly or heroic as counterexamples. How could psychological egoism be consistent with what we know about people like Albert Schweitzer and Mother Teresa, who devote their lives to helping the poor, diseased, and wretched? And what about soldiers who throw themselves on grenades or volunteer for "suicide missions"? Aren't they giving up their lives so that their comrades or countrymen might live or remain free?

Yet isn't it possible, the psychological egoist might reply, that Dr. Schweitzer *enjoyed* doing what he did, felt his life more meaningful as a result—more satisfying in some basic respects? If so, he may have lived as a doctor helping African natives *because* of these good things he experienced for himself. The same might be true of Mother Teresa—who believes herself to be doing God's will and, as a result, anticipates a reward of eternal, perfect happiness in Heaven. As for soldiers who give up their lives in combat to save others, we should realize (the argument continues) that they have been trained to do this in some cases, strongly encouraged and rewarded at the very least. Even the actions of Japanese kamikaze pilots in World War II might be accounted for egoistically; these men received much honor (a major good in their society) during their lives, and in the event they were called upon to die (not all were), it would have been very bad for them to try to avoid their duty, probably worse than death.*

The standard counterexamples to psychological egoism seem very far from conclusive. In the absence of other, better ones, we might look at a different kind of counterargument. An eighteenth-century British moralist and Anglican bishop, Joseph Butler, offered an interesting objection in his *Sermons* (later restated by Hume in an appendix to his *Enquiry Concerning the Principles of Morals*). Butler argued that many of the things we get pleasure from are pleasurable only because we want them for their own sake; therefore, the desire for pleasure cannot be the only desire that moves us to act. This is an argument, specifically, against hedonistic psychological egoism, and it has had so much influence that we'll quote it at length:

*For a compelling account of the kamikaze, see K. Naido, *Thunder Gods* (New York: Kodansha International, 1979).

> [T]he very idea of an interested pursuit necessarily presupposes particular passions or appetites; since the very idea of interest or happiness consists in this, that an appetite or affection enjoys its object. It is not because we love ourselves that we find delight in such and such objects, but because we have particular affections towards them. Take away these affections, and you leave self-love absolutely nothing at all to employ itself about; no end or object for it to pursue, excepting only that of avoiding pain. . . . [T]he very idea of interest or happiness other than absence of pain implies particular appetites or passions; these being necessary to constitute that interest or happiness. . . . The principle we call "self-love" never seeks anything external for the sake of the thing, but only as a means of happiness or good; particular affections rest in the external things themselves. One belongs to man as a reasonable creature reflecting upon his own interest or happiness. The other, though quite distinct from reason, are as much a part of human nature.
>
> That all particular appetites and passions are towards *external things themselves*, distinct from the *pleasure arising from them*, is manifested from hence—that there could not be this pleasure, were it not for that prior suitableness between the object and the passion; there could be no enjoyment or delight for one thing more than another, from eating food more than from swallowing a stone, if there were not an affection or appetite to one thing more than another. (Butler's italics.)

Butler's argument is thought-provoking and sophisticated. But it ultimately depends on the reality of pleasurable experiences that can be had only by those who want whatever produces the pleasure for its own sake, not just because it gives pleasure. We need to find a convincing example. Henry Sidgwick, a prominent nineteenth-century English moral philosopher, suggested hunger. We desire to eat food when we are hungry; any pleasure that accompanies eating is fine, but it's not an essential object of hunger. However, the hedonistic psychological egoist could reply that we wouldn't desire to eat if the consequences of not eating were pleasant or neutral. We desire to eat because not eating is unpleasant and debilitating, whereas eating is usually pleasurable.

Another possible example is doing a good deed. We typically don't feel good about the good deed if at the time we consciously focus on the pleasure we expect to feel rather than the plight of the person we are helping. This kind of case relates to a more general phenomenon, the so-called paradox of hedonism. Often when we do something, even just for ourselves, and concentrate not so much on the activity but mainly on the pleasure we expect from it, we don't receive the pleasure. More generally still, happiness often comes not to those who always consciously seek it, but to people who aim at other, more concrete goals; happiness follows as a sort of by-product. Still, this might not be a good counterexample to the thesis of psychological egoism. The reason is that we don't need to focus on, attend to, or be conscious of our desire for pleasure in order to be motivated by it. That kind of conscious dwelling on what we ultimately want is counterproductive, just as it would be for an Olympic athlete who is seeking a gold medal.

We won't try to resolve the question of whether psychological egoism is both significant and true, for it's a very complex one. There are many different versions of it, both hedonistic and nonhedonistic. It's certainly hard to see how psychological egoism could be confirmed or disconfirmed, but this is a problem characteristic of most psychological generalizations. We should question the view of some philosophers that all forms of the thesis are either obviously false or trivially true. For all we know, it's quite possible that some version of psychological egoism, adequately and precisely formulated, will be empirically confirmed by psychological research. What concerns us now is what the implications of the thesis would be for ethical conduct.

Ethical Egoism

One theory of how we ought to act that fits very well with psychological egoism is *ethical egoism,* which tells us that we should always do what is most likely to promote our overall best interests. In other words, ethical egoism says that we ought to be rational in pursuit of good things for ourselves, to go for maximum well-being instead of just immediate gratification. Rather than acting on present impulses for what we want right now, ethical egoists look at the long-term consequences of their choices: How will doing this affect my happiness over the rest of my life, especially by affecting my health, relationships with others, and so forth? Ethical egoism does *not* presuppose the truth of psychological egoism, but the latter has traditionally been an argument for the former. After all, if psychological egoism is true, then ethical egoism seems to be the most reasonable theory about how we ought to act. As we will see, however, even that is not so certain—we might be egoistically rational and choose an ethical theory other than egoism.

It's not our purpose to evaluate ethical egoism here, but we will say a few things about how we might assess its acceptability as an ethical theory. Recall the two methods for moral reasoning we presented at the end of Chapter 3. If we consider Rawls's method of wide reflective equilibrium, it is apparent that ethical egoism, although it can be a consistent theory, does not cohere very well with the considered moral judgments that most of us make—for example, that it's wrong for someone to steal or murder even if it brings the person great benefit. This suggests that ethical egoism is not an adequate theory of morality as most of us understand it. Yet it is unclear what that proves. Most of us would say, on reflection, that lying, stealing, cheating, and even more extreme acts are morally wrong even when they would advance the agent's long-term self-interest (egoism, at least of a simple sort, would say that they are permissible on that condition). For this reason, ethical egoism seems to fail as a theory of moral rightness. But ethical egoists could reply that they don't care to justify their theory in that way—by showing that it is consistent with common moral views, even after reflection. Rather, they want to argue that ethical egoism is the most rational way to guide our choices and actions in life, regardless of what ordinary morality says to do.

If morality as commonly conceived in our society (and perhaps in most or all cultures) imposes limits on rational self-interested action—that is, requires us sometimes to sacrifice our own good out of respect for the interests of others—then how, if at all, could we rationally justify such limitations? Let's look at our other method of moral inquiry, the approach favored by Brandt. This method tells us to imagine what our society would be like if everyone acted according to a principle that says, "Whenever you are faced with a choice, do what is most likely to promote your long-term best interests." Hobbes argued centuries ago that this would be a terrible situation—a war of everyone against everyone else, in which no one is safe and there is little progress or stability. He postulates a contract among members of the human race to submit to law and its equal restraints on self-interested action, so that all of us can individually be better off in the long run. Later in this chapter we consider a contemporary contractarian moral theory, that of Rawls. The present point is merely that ethical egoism (of the kind we are discussing) appears unacceptable, paradoxical as this sounds, from a rational egoistic point of view. We just would not want people in general to live according to it, much as we might want to ourselves. The consequences of general acceptance would make most of us badly off.

What does this suggest about ethical egoism? If the consequences of its common acceptance would be disastrous (a conclusion not established here, but quite plausible), then it would be unacceptable as a general theory about how people ought to act and live their lives. This is so regardless of the relevance of our ordinary considered moral convictions. But there might be more defensible forms of ethical egoism. Or it could be that the perspective of the egoist should enter into ethics in other, less direct ways. There is much more philosophical work to be done on issues relating to egoism in its various forms.

Utilitarianism and Benevolence

The next theory we consider can be seen as an attempt to broaden the egoist's scope of concern to include not just himself or herself but all of society. This is *act-utilitarianism*, which tells us that whenever we face a choice, we should perform that action most likely to maximize the good of people generally. Some utilitarians would go even further, arguing that all sentient beings should be the focus of our moral concern. But whether the scope of moral concern is restricted to one's society, or all of humankind, or all animals capable of sensation, or even all *possible* beings of one sort or another, the utilitarian sharply opposes the egoist's sole concern with his or her own well-being. From a utilitarian perspective, all of us matter equally—everyone counts as one, and no one as more than one. My welfare or happiness and yours have the same moral importance, taken in themselves. (For a good example of utilitarian thinking, see Peter Singer's article in Chapter 13). Utilitarians believe that we ought to promote *social* well-being, in contrast to the ethical egoists' sole concern with personal (one's own) well-being.

Utilitarians use *utility* in the technical sense favored by economists and philosophers, meaning "welfare" or "happiness." Those concepts are in turn usually explained in terms of pleasure or desire satisfaction, as we discussed in the last chapter. More precisely, we should say that utility (think "usefulness for human welfare") is to be defined as the *balance* of welfare or happiness over the opposite, that is, suffering and unhappiness. In other words, the aim of the utilitarian is to find out what state of affairs would involve the most well-being for people in general, after subtracting all of the suffering it would involve, and to bring about that outcome. We should also distinguish the notion of total social utility from average social utility: Those who opt for total utility want to create as much happiness as possible, even if the average person would thereby have less of it; average utility, by contrast, is what you get by dividing total utility by the number of people who experience it. For our present purposes, let's assume we'll be dealing with average utility when we say that the utilitarian aims at maximizing social utility.

Often you'll hear the utilitarian principle explained as "Do what will produce the greatest happiness for the greatest number." Although this is partly correct, it is sloppy and misleading. This informal statement of the principle of utility won't do, because it tells us to maximize two different things: on the one hand, to produce the greatest amount of happiness; on the other hand, to produce happiness for the greatest number of people. Strictly speaking, what the utilitarian aims to do is bring about the greatest amount of general happiness (average or total social utility), period. How many people experience happiness is a different matter, though often we can assume that the more the happiness, other things equal, the greater the number of people who are likely to be happy or well-off.

Act-Utilitarianism

Act-utilitarianism directs us to do the following when confronted with a decision about what to do: (1) Find out what our options are—the range of alternative actions open to us in our circumstances; (2) determine what the probable consequences of each option are for the utility of everyone who would be affected; and (3) choose the action that would have the highest probable utility for those people collectively. If two or more possible courses of action have the same probable utility,

Bentham's Utilitarian Prison

The condition of English prisons in the late eighteenth century was abysmal; in 1784, Parliament began to deport prisoners to Australia to alleviate overcrowding. Jeremy Bentham, whose keen interest in legislative and penal reform naturally led him to tackle this problem, proposed an alternative: a circular prison administered on empiricist, utilitarian principles of rehabilitation. The Panopticon, as he named it, was based on an architectural idea of his brother Samuel. All of the prison cells would be arranged concentrically around a pavilion from which a small number of guards, who could not be seen by the inmates, would keep constant watch. The voice of the head inspector, Bentham suggested, could be piped into the individual cells, and the prisoners would come to regard it as that of an omnipotent, omniscient being. "If it were possible to find a method of becoming master of everything which might happen to a certain number of men, to dispose of everything around them so as to produce on them the desired impression, to make certain of their actions, of their connections, and of all the circumstances of their lives, so that nothing could escape, nor could oppose the desired effect, it cannot be doubted that a method of this kind would be a very powerful and a very useful instrument which governments might apply to various objects of the utmost importance," Bentham wrote in *Panopticon.* Insane asylums, hospitals, schools, and factories might benefit from the same arrangement (including contract management by private companies), Bentham boldly suggested! Although supported by members of Parliament, the Panopticon was never built, much to Bentham's disappointment.

then (if the other options have less) either may be chosen; that is, they are equally right morally.

While this apparently simple and straightforward theory of what we morally ought to do might seem quite appealing—and, indeed, we sometimes do decide what to do in this way—we need to look more closely at how it would likely be put into practice. Keep in mind that act-utilitarianism is meant to apply to all cases, not just some, in which more than one alternative is open to us.

To begin with a simple example, suppose that you promised a friend to drive him to the airport tomorrow. He is counting on you and would be seriously inconvenienced if you canceled or didn't show up tomorrow morning. But when you get up that morning, you think about some of the other things you could do instead—working on your book manuscript, doing volunteer work for a local charity, or even just doing something unproductive that you would really enjoy. Now, if you are an act-utilitarian in this situation, you must try to figure out what the expected utilities of these different actions are and see if any are higher than the probable utility that would be involved in keeping your promise. If one of the alternatives has a higher expected utility, then that is what you morally ought to do, even if it just happens to be something that benefits yourself (you might get so much fun from doing what you want that it would outweigh the negative utility your friend would experience from being stood up.) Or suppose that you have decided to keep your promise, given your present understanding of the options, but on the way to his house you come upon an auto accident and—after calculating the expected utility—stop to render assistance to a victim, with the result that your friend misses his flight.

Most of us would consider the latter case a justified breaking of the promise, depending on more detailed description of the facts. But would breaking the promise to do just anything that would have a higher expected utility be satisfactory in this sort of situation? Would a principle about promises creating an obligation be intelligible in a society of act-utilitarians? Applying Rawls's method of wide reflective equilibrium can help us to answer the first question; applying Brandt's method might help us answer the second. (These two methods are discussed in Chapter 3.) We doubt that most people approaching wide reflective equilibrium would find that the act-utilitarian attitude toward keeping promises squares with their considered moral convictions. As for the second question, it is hard to say whether promises would ever be made if people believed that they ought to be kept only when doing so would likely maximize social utility. Wouldn't it be less than fully rational to advocate such a societal norm, even if it could exist?

Critics of act-utilitarianism often choose desert-island or deathbed promises as counterexamples to that theory. (You promise Uncle Felix to administer his vast estate after his demise for the benefit of stray cats. Should you keep your commitment, or should you spend the money to benefit needy humans?) But we don't have to go to such atypical cases, with their special complications, to make our point: Act-utilitarianism has trouble accounting for the obligations arising from promises. This is in fact only one aspect of a larger problem for this theory, for it has problems with the entire range of special obligations and duties that people have in virtue of voluntary undertakings, the roles they occupy, or the social circumstances in which they find themselves. To take just one example, consider the special obligations people normally feel they have to their own relatives, friends, and loved ones. On an act-utilitarian view, these relationships morally count for nothing in themselves; only if it would maximize the general good would you be allowed to give a preference to those close to you when their interests and the good of strangers conflict. (Imagine a lifeboat situation when your ship is sinking at sea.)

Even more broadly, we should recognize the difficulty act-utilitarians have in allowing for the special personal goals and projects that most persons set as part of their long-term plans of life. These things—career success, particular achievements, a family, religious commitments, social causes, and so on—must always take a back seat if the person's time and energy or financial resources could be used differently in order to promote social utility. How many of us would be willing to make such sacrifices on a regular basis? (For an example of this, again see Peter Singer's article "Famine, Affluence and Morality" in Chapter 13.)

This brings us to the basic question of what motivates, or could motivate, us to accept and follow act-utilitarianism. That theory, as we have remarked, can demand sacrifice of our own good, the good of loved ones, and our major goals and projects. You might be surprised that some of the early utilitarians, Bentham among them, were psychological egoists. Why would creatures supposedly motivated only by a desire to get pleasure and avoid pain for themselves (humans as Bentham understands them) accept a theory of right conduct such as act-utilitarianism? Only if society were arranged so that the good of all or most people would depend heavily on everyone else's. This can be achieved, Bentham thinks, through law, political reform, and moral education. Perhaps he's too optimistic.

John Stuart Mill is also quite optimistic about the progress of humankind in moral matters. But in addition to the legal, religious, social, and educational sanctions that utilitarians can employ to get compliance with their principle, Mill (as you will see when you read the third chapter of his *Utilitarianism*) believes that a natural sense of human sympathy and solidarity would support utilitarianism—indeed, more so than other moral positions. Yet are we really as benevolent and altruistic as act-utilitarianism—or even less direct forms of utilitarianism—demand?

In addition to the motivational demands of act-utilitarianism, there are significant knowledge requirements placed on agents. Individuals must not only be able to figure out what the full range of alternative actions in their situations include, but also have a grasp of the likely consequences of each alternative for the well-being of everyone affected. This can be extremely complicated, especially with large numbers of people. Moreover, it seems necessary to make interpersonal comparisons of utility—to determine what difference, if any, there is between the degree of pleasure or desire-satisfaction Jones gets from a certain state of affairs (for example, having a new car) and the degree that Smith receives from the same outcome (that is, having the new car himself). We do sometimes make these comparisons with confident sense of their rationality; for instance, we're sure that a scratch on Jones's little finger causes him less pain than a severed arm would cause Smith. However, we usually make such comparisons only in extreme cases. It is sometimes hard to know or measure mental states even in ourselves, let alone among many different people.

This burden of knowledge, especially when we view it in the context of normal human partiality and bias, would likely lead many of us to make mistakes even when we try to be conscientious act-utilitarians. Often we would fail to choose the utility-maximizing alternative. Furthermore, would we really want people to break promises or cheat or steal even in circumstances where that would maximize utility for everyone affected? Take the case of an act-utilitarian moral philosopher who forges letters of recommendation from famous colleagues in order to get his book on ethics published. Would we want most authors to act that way even when they could get away with it? Would it really benefit society in the long run? What these and related points imply is that act-utilitarianism might be self-defeating and that a more indirect appeal to utility would be a better basis for developing a utilitarian theory.

Rule-Utilitarianism

Act-utilitarianism tells people to apply the principle of utility directly (try to maximize expectable social good) to each occasion of decision and action. An alternative, indirect form of utilitarianism is *rule-utilitarianism.* Rule-utilitarians don't advocate trying to maximize social utility on each particular occasion; rather, they propose that we try first to figure out what set of more specific moral rules would—if generally accepted and followed in our society—maximize utility and then to act as the relevant rule directs us. For example, the ideal utility-maximizing moral code for a society such as ours might well include a rule telling us not to lie or forge documents, except in certain special circumstances. If the need to publish our ethics book is not among those exceptional circumstances, then the ideal moral code clearly directs us not to do so. There can, of course, be rule conflicts within the code and problems of interpretation, but often matters will be clear.

Brandt's influential rule-utilitarian theory, which he believes fully informed people might support over other ethical systems, is discussed in Chapter 11, where we include a selection from his work. Instead of presenting some of the problems facing rule-utilitarianism now, let's mention one advantage it has over act-utilitarianism: rule-utilitarianism is better able to allow for supererogation (see Chapter 2). Our earlier treatment of this idea attempted to clarify the commonsense view that there are morally required acts (duties and obligations) and also morally optional but very praiseworthy acts (saintly and heroic ones, for example). Act-utilitarians such as Singer have trouble recognizing this distinction, since for them any act likely to maximize social utility is morally mandatory; there seems to be nothing commendable morally beyond duty. Rule-utilitarians, in framing an ideal moral code, can allow for morally good but optional acts.

Acting from Duty

Utilitarianism, both direct and indirect, remains a widely accepted theory despite these problems, especially among moral philosophers in England and the United States, as well as economists and legal theorists. In recent years, however, there has been a revival of interest in the most important modern rival type of theory, deontologism. We will define deontological theories as those that do *not* make the moral rightness or obligatoriness of actions depend *entirely* on the (nonmoral) value of their consequences. Recall that both ethical egoism and act-utilitarian theories make the rightness of actions solely a function of whether or not they produce the best consequences, either from the standpoint of the agent's good (egoism) or society's (utilitarianism). That is to say, they are axiological, or value-based, moral theories. Deontologists reject the idea that rightness can be completely a matter of maximizing value or good consequences. Sometimes it is, but usually it is a matter of other considerations, too.

What, then, do deontologists base rightness and related moral properties on? The answer varies according to the particular type of deontological theory we are discussing. But let's try to give a very general reply. Often it is said that deontologists believe that some actions are morally right or wrong because of what they are in themselves, apart from any good or bad consequences for people's well-being. For example, lying is wrong even when it might bring about more happiness than telling the truth. Although lying sometimes might, all things considered, be morally justified in terms of good consequences (saving many innocent lives, for instance, by lying to evildoers), this is not generally so. Similar things can be said about the acts of keeping promises, treating people equally, refraining from theft, and so on. Deontologists maintain that there are certain things we must or must not do, period (unless they conflict with a more stringent duty, as we will see later). The root of the term *deontologism* is a Greek word meaning roughly "what must be done."

Monistic Deontology: Kant

A key concept in deontological theories of the kind developed by Kant is the idea of respect for persons. Kantians insist that utilitarian theories lump people together and treat them only as possible experiencers of pleasure and pain, satisfaction and frustration. It's as if all of society or humanity were one giant person whose only concern was to have as much utility as possible. This collectivism is repugnant to Kantians, who insist on recognizing the moral separateness of persons and their dignity as autonomous individuals. It is not morally acceptable, for example, to enslave, mistreat, or deceive some people in order to create maximum good for society (the majority). Related to this is an emphasis on individual responsibility, something we discuss in Chapter 6. Kant expresses this fundamental moral insight in the second formulation of his categorical imperative: Act always so as to treat humanity (whether in your own person or that of others) as an end in itself, never as a means only.

A feature common to deontological theories is that they allow more individual freedom of choice than does act-utilitarianism. Remember that the latter theory requires that we always, every time we have any choice of alternatives, try to maximize the well-being of everyone whose situation might be affected by what we do. In principle, whether you cut your hair one way or another or what you have for dessert would be a moral issue. After all, your utility level, and possibly that of other people, will probably be affected (however slightly) by what you choose. Deontological theories, in contrast, direct us to perform or refrain from certain kinds of acts. When there is no relevant moral rule of obligation or duty, we are free to do what we want. Thus deontologists have no problem accounting for supererogatory acts. Unusually generous or heroically self-sacrificing deeds, if they do not violate a duty to oneself, are praiseworthy and good but nevertheless a personal option.

Deontologists, then, insist that moral rightness and related concepts cannot be reduced to maximizing nonmoral value (good consequences for people). What would motivate persons to act as utilitarianism directs, you will recall, are considerations of self-interest and sympathy with others, a sense of solidarity, benevolence. How would deontologists understand moral motivation?

Typically, deontologists assert that acting from a sense of duty, obligation, or justice —doing the right thing because it is right and for no other reason—is the most (if not the only) morally appropriate motive. We discussed earlier Hume's contention that only passions and desires can lead or cause a person to act. If this is so, then how can a belief that something is right, by itself, move an agent to do that? Maybe moral beliefs are not regular beliefs, but more like noncognitive attitudes, involving desires and aversions. Or we might say that, strictly speaking, the desire to do what is right for its own sake is what motivates us to act as deontologists would have us do.

Kant maintains that our feelings and desires, subjective and variable as they are, do not provide a solid enough foundation for morality. He distinguishes morally right acts from morally good or worthy acts. You can do the right thing, morally speaking, for the wrong reason—out of self-interest, for example. (You are nevertheless following the relevant moral rule, in the sense that you're doing what it says to do). But performing a morally good act involves having the proper intention or motivation, doing what is right because you respect the moral law—that is, because it's right. Feelings of concern or love for others may serve as additional impetus to act rightly, but they cannot make a right act a good act. Only acting from duty itself can do that. Kant argues, further, that an agent who struggles against his feelings and inclinations and succeeds in doing what is morally right just because he believes it is right represents the best example of someone doing a morally good act.

Some critics of Kant's deontologism reject the idea that only an action done from duty is morally good. Why shouldn't an act that is intentionally done out of love or concern for the welfare of others be seen as morally worthy? Kant might be correct to focus on intentions rather than outcomes of action, but he is mistaken, they argue, in maintaining that the only morally valuable motive is the sense of duty. Not all deontologists go so far as Kant in this regard; some recognize the moral worth of both benevolence and acting from duty.

Pluralistic Deontology: Ross

A more detailed discussion of Kant's theory precedes the selections in Chapter 10 from his *Foundations of the Metaphysics of Morals.* Kant's deontologism is monistic: He attempts to reduce all of morality to one fundamental principle, the categorical imperative. A different kind of deontological theory is W. D. Ross's pluralistic account of moral rightness and obligation. In contrast to Kant and utilitarianism, Ross's theory stipulates that there are a number of separate, irreducible moral principles, not just one very general one.

We earlier introduced Ross's concept of a prima facie duty or obligation, that is, what we ought to do in the absence of a more stringent duty. Ross presents a list of basic principles of prima facie duty in his book *The Right and the Good.* Let's survey these principles to get a better idea of what a pluralistic deontological theory looks like.

Two duties that Ross believes are basic to morality are (1) nonmaleficence and (2) beneficence: not harming others intentionally and doing good for others, respectively. In general, though not always, we would say that doing no harm is the more stringent duty of the two. Note that by recognizing beneficence as a duty—one among others—Ross in effect concedes that there is some validity in utilitarianism. It is simply that the latter doctrine takes things too far by making beneficence the whole of morality instead of only one important part.

Other prima facie duties include (3) fidelity, by which Ross primarily means keeping promises and being truthful; (4) reparation, making up to someone for an injury one has done to that person; (5) gratitude, repaying a benefit or kindness;

and (6) self-improvement (like Aristotle and Kant, Ross believes this is a moral duty, not just a matter of personal choice). Finally, Ross includes (7) justice as an important moral duty. He understands it in somewhat Aristotelian terms; essentially, justice is a question of making sure that good things go to those who merit or deserve them.

Ross does not claim that his list is exhaustive, only that these are among the moral duties that reflective, mature adults will find reasonable. (Are there others that you would include? Why?) When these duties conflict, as we said earlier, we must rely on our intuitive judgment to tell us which gets priority or represents the more urgent moral requirement in the particular case. There is no simple (or even complex) formula that will solve that kind of problem for us. It seems to be a matter of judgment.

Where Kant is an absolutist about certain duties (for example, truth-telling and promise-keeping), Ross is not. Sometimes deontological ethics is mistakenly thought to be absolutist, but in fact we can be deontologists and allow for exceptions to moral rules. What deontologists oppose is the utilitarian position that, as a general moral policy, only consequences matter, that we can break a promise or lie or steal if that brings about more social utility than would keeping the promise, telling the truth, or respecting ownership. The special relationships between individuals, especially due to past ties and commitments, are important to deontologists.

Deontological theories bring out what Ross describes as "the highly personal character of duty." What I do is crucial and, generally speaking, more relevant morally than focusing on the total effect of different courses of action on human happiness or welfare. Deontologists bring the agent-centered aspects of morality to the forefront. I must not do wrong, either out of concern for the general utility or on the basis of a belief that since other people are going to shirk their duty, I may too. What others do is largely out of my control most of the time, as is the total outcome for everyone's well-being in the long run (there are too many complications to let any one person determine that). What I can do, once my duty is clear to me, is try my utmost to act accordingly.

This is not to say that what others are likely to do is always irrelevant to determining my moral duty, or that the happiness of others is always irrelevant either. But these considerations, by themselves, do not in general excuse me from keeping promises, avoiding injury to others, repaying debts, and so forth. The overall balance of well-being over unhappiness is not my direct concern if I am viewing morality as a deontologist. Nor is it necessarily an indirect concern, as it would be for a rule-utilitarian. Kant, for instance, rejects explicitly the idea that morality has a purpose of maximizing social happiness or individual happiness. Rather, on his view, being morally good is to be *deserving* of happiness, which we can only hope will come to the virtuous in the next life if not in this one. The happiness of evildoers is obviously a bad thing, Kant would insist, and another fault of utilitarianism is that it seems to give moral consideration to the happiness or pleasure of killers, rapists, and thieves. (Would we really consider it morally relevant or appropriate to include the satisfaction of sadistic desires in the determination of moral rightness?)

Some see a weakness in deontological theories: that they don't make enough allowance for doing good or preventing harm. Axiological (value-based) theories such as egoism and utilitarianism have two noteworthy strengths: (1) they appeal to our feeling that, in the final analysis, nothing really matters other than happiness or good consequences; (2) because they are concerned with maximizing the good, they always entail that a better outcome is morally to be preferred over a worse outcome. Since deontologists reject both of these theses, certain kinds of moral cases are problematic for them.

Let's consider two examples, for which we are indebted to Bernard Williams and Philippa Foot. First, suppose you're visiting a Third World country governed by a vicious dictator. He has just rounded up a dozen of his political opponents, and he makes you (his honored guest) the following offer: If you shoot one of them yourself, he will let the other eleven go free; if you do not, he will have all of them shot. What would you do? An act-utilitarian would tell you to kill the one innocent person so as to save the lives of the other eleven. But Kant and Ross would insist that killing an innocent person is a violation of your duty, period. If the dictator kills all of them, the guilt is his, not yours. For a second example, imagine that you're in charge of a trolley car system, guiding trains onto tracks by a set of controls. You suddenly see a train car heading for a group of workers who are unaware that they are in imminent danger. Unless you move the car onto another track, most of them will probably be killed. However, the only available alternative track has a man standing on it, who would certainly be killed if you diverted the car. What should you do? What would you do? If you did divert the car, sacrificing one innocent life to save several others, you would be doing what act-utilitarianism directs you to do. A deontologist might insist that you should not divert the car from its course.

Whether deontological theories could recognize or permit a larger role for maximizing consequentialist moral considerations is an open question. It should, at least, be clear where some of the battle lines are drawn between existing theories. There is, furthermore, a third type of theory—one that shares features both with value-based, consequentialist ethical views such as egoism and utilitarianism and with deontological theories. We are speaking of virtue-based ethics.

Virtue Ethics

The conception that ethics centers on good character traits of individuals is predominant among the ancient Greeks, particularly Plato and Aristotle. We find it in Medieval moral thought, as you will see when you read the selections in Part II from Abelard and Aquinas. And it is characteristic of eighteenth-century British moral philosophy as well; Hume's theory is an outstanding example. Lately there has been a resurgence of interest among Anglo-American moral philosophers in this type of theory. The works of neonaturalists such as Philippa Foot, P. T. Geach, and G. J. Warnock are good examples, as are the writings of Alasdair MacIntyre.

Among Socrates' contemporaries it was commonly thought that a virtue (confining ourselves to moral virtues) is a trait of character known to be beneficial, in general, to the person who has it. It could also be good for others, but it must benefit this person first and foremost. The belief that something is a virtue only if it is good for its possessor—which works well for traits such as cleverness and courage, temperance and wit—obviously leads to problems if we want to list honesty, justice, and similar traits as moral virtues. These are not always, or perhaps even usually, good things to have from one's own point of view; they seem to conflict with self-interest too often. (Consider a related question: Is it a good thing to be able to feel guilty?)

Moral virtues as we would think of them today, within a Judeo-Christian tradition, need not be good things to possess from a self-interested point of view. (At least not in this life, that is. A religious belief in an afterlife for the virtuous, and punishment for the vicious obviously keeps the link between moral virtue and self-interest.) Let's broaden and secularize the concept of moral virtue to say that it includes the traits of character that are good for their possessor *as a member* of a good society, one in which people get along with a reasonable degree of harmony, peace, and order and in which they are able to flourish and have some chance of living well and carrying out their projects. We could go further still in a utilitarian vein and say simply that moral virtues are character traits that contribute to the society's well-being (whether or not they are good for each person.) But for now let's stay with the former, more Aristotelian conception, which links social good with a certain understanding of individual good.

In the previous chapter we discussed the idea that the good life consists in the development of the self's capacities for excellence. Within the context of the ethical theory developed by Aristotle, which we examine in Chapter 7, this conception of human good serves as the basis for asserting that the traits of courage, temperance, friendliness, magnanimity, justice, and other qualities of character are good for us to have as well as good for society. Aristotle does not himself fill out the argument, which has to be made for each supposed virtue individually. But if *eudaimonia* (or happiness) is identified with activity in accordance with virtues, intellectual and moral, then we at least have a foundation for virtue, whether the approach can be successfully carried out or not.

But we don't need to accept Aristotle's idea of the good to be virtue ethicists. A theory of goodness that is pluralistic might furnish a basis for the belief that justice and most of the other traits we think are moral virtues are indeed good for people to have, both for their own sakes and for others'. Let's focus now on two of the hardest cases: honesty and justice. Later on we will examine integrity. There are certain real benefits, we can argue, that persons will obtain only if they cooperate with others in an open, honest, and just manner, at least most of the time. These objective goods include the security that comes from mutual trust, the likelihood of reciprocity, and the respect and affections of others. Vicious people might not understand what they lose by their way of relating to others, or they might think that power and cunning are more than adequate substitutes for good will and decency. But they are probably wrong, the virtue ethicist will usually argue. The cost of always being on one's guard and of maintaining a pattern of deception can be great.

What distinguishes virtue ethics from its utilitarian and deontological rivals? Its center of attention is character traits, not a general rule or set of rules and actions, either in respect of their motives or consequences. Utilitarians are primarily concerned with the likely results of acts; deontologists focus on the intentions behind particular acts. Both have conceptions of what it is to be morally virtuous, but virtue ethicists give this concept a fundamental role in their theory. For virtue ethicists, the primary question is not "What ought I to do?" but instead, "What kind of person ought I to be?" On the one hand, virtue ethics, like ethical egoism and rule-utilitarianism, is axiological, taking goodness or value as primary, but it has a different understanding of what goodness consists in. On the other hand, virtue ethics shares with deontological theories an emphasis on the individual person and his or her integrity; they reject expediency aimed at bringing about some general outcome.

A reasonable virtue-based ethics will accord general rules a place in morality (how else can we understand virtues such as justice?), but a virtuous agent is not someone always trying to consciously apply them. Rather, he or she will act habitually in the right way, without stopping to calculate probable consequences in most cases or struggle with conscience.

Virtue-based ethics is also sometimes called "aretaic," from the Greek word *arete*, which we translate as "virtue." Although we're not considering a specific theory of this type right now—and so have nothing we can evaluate by means of the methods presented at the end of Chapter 3—we will mention two problems confronting aretaic moral theories.

One problem is that these theories can be relativistic, a feature many critics find to be a serious weakness. The traits of character that allow a person to flourish and get along well in a society that is backward by modern Western liberal standards would be virtues to people in that society but may seem like vices to us. (Think of the submissiveness expected of women in some Middle Eastern societies.) We want some objective basis for evaluating social rules, norms, and conventions of different cultures. At least, it seems, we need such a basis to avoid the relativity toward which an ethics of virtue might lead us. Proponents of this kind of theory do not address this problem adequately.

Another problem for a virtue-based ethics, insofar as it maintains a close connection between a person's well-being and his or her possession of the moral virtues, is to establish that there is such a connection without defining *well-being* trivially in terms of virtue itself. Happiness would have to be understood in terms not identical with morally virtuous action. In fact, for aretaic ethics to avoid this and the previous problem, it needs a universally, objectively valid conception of human well-being.

We should say a few things about the moral psychology presupposed by virtue-centered ethics. Most of these points could be accepted by many having deontological theories, too.

The sense of self-esteem is an important source of motivation for an aretaic ethical theory. Thinking oneself worthy overall, being proud of oneself, is a basic ingredient of happiness, at least for most of us. Knowing that one is acting viciously can cause shame, guilt, regret, or remorse. Having these feelings often is obviously contrary to a state of well-being. Like self-respect (the moral attitude that has to do with not permitting abuse or humiliation of ourselves), self-esteem is often based on virtues that are widespread and traditional within our society. Our socialization, which involves emotional conditioning, can reflect values that we might later—maybe after philosophical reflection—come to question, if not reject outright. Outdated codes of honor furnish many examples (what one is supposed to do if insulted, for example). When we reject old values or standards, we go through a difficult period of emotional adjustment as old reactions and attitudes fail to match our new principles. Changing attitudes toward people of other races and adopting liberal sexual ethics are common examples.

One of the most important virtues, not only from a moral viewpoint, is integrity. We commonly attribute integrity to people who are truthful, honest, conscientious about keeping their commitments, and fair to others. But integrity is not the same as any of these virtues. A person who is fundamentally evil might have some integrity, yet a good person cannot be without a large measure of it. Integrity is a kind of wholeness and consistency of the self in which "inner" values do not undercut each other or contradict "outer" words and behavior. Lack of integrity typically goes along with hypocrisy, self-deception, or weakness of will, a topic we discuss in Chapter 6. People who are devoid of integrity tend not to respect themselves or others.

In *Pride, Shame, and Guilt: Emotions of Self-Assessment*, Gabriele Taylor observes that the person without integrity is corrupt in the straightforward sense that he or she does not "hold together" or have an identity, because of a lack of consistent values. She notes that if integrity and self-respect are necessarily related and if a self-respecting person cannot deny respect to others, then (as some philosophers have argued recently) we have some basis to conclude that someone who has integrity must acknowledge rights and legitimate interests of others.

We now turn to the topic of rights and the virtue of justice. We will look at some deontological theories and compare them with utilitarian and aretaic interpretations of justice and rights.

Rights and Justice

While we don't want to go too far into the field of social and political philosophy in our short discussion of rights and justice, it is impossible to separate that field from moral philosophy completely. Philosophers and legal theorists commonly define "P has a right to X" as "P has no obligation not to X." Rights can be negative (a person's right not to have something done to him or her) or positive (a person's right to have or be given something). But we should also add that a right imposes corresponding obligations or duties on others and that we are usually justified in enforcing them through legal institutions, when possible, or on one's own.

We should interpret narrowly the fact that having a right to do something entails not having any obligation not to do that action. A person can have a right to do something that is morally wrong or reflects badly on his or her character. An example is the right to speak freely. (In this case, a right is more than a constitutional or legal right; it has a moral basis.) We have a right to say things that are offensive, indecent, or prejudiced, though it is usually not right to exercise our right to free speech that way. We would say it is wrong to do so, though it violates no obligation of a kind that ought to be enforced.

Rule-utilitarians can recognize rights in a derivative manner, as Mill does in the last part of *Utilitarianism.* He believes that justice is a matter of respecting individual rights, which are things society ought to defend in the interests of the general welfare. There is a problem with maintaining that rights depend on calculations of social utility: Sometimes it may not be in the interests of society to allow for basic freedoms, equal treatment, or due process. Even slavery might be justified on that basis. It is entirely possible that during the history of certain societies—perhaps including our own—there were periods when the utility of having slaves outweighed their suffering, especially if the enslaved were not much better off free. But would that make slavery not a violation of rights?

Deontologists can recognize rights as fundamental; indeed, their theory is perfectly suited to this. The natural rights tradition, as represented by John Locke and some of the American Founding Fathers, is essentially deontological, at least when separated from earlier natural law conceptions. Kant is clearly a proponent of the position that rights are fundamental, as is Robert Nozick, who states: "Individuals have rights and there are things no person or group may do to them [without vio-

Positive Rights and Social Justice

Philosophers and legal theorists commonly distinguish two general kinds of rights, negative and positive. Negative rights are rights *not* to do certain things or to have them *not* done by others; positive rights are rights to do specific things or to have others do them. Many rights can be classified in either category, depending on how we describe what it is that one has a right to (for example, is the right to free speech negative or positive?) Negative and positive obligations often correlate with negative and positive rights — my right to life entails that others have an obligation not to kill me.

Some purported rights are best thought of as positive. Rights of recipience are a good example. These rights are claims to receive something, such as assistance or payment. They can arise in various ways, most commonly perhaps through some form of voluntary agreement. Welfare rights are a kind of recipience rights, a type obviously not arising from the voluntary agreement of most of those who have to fulfill the supposed obligations corresponding to them. Many who question or deny the validity of welfare rights point to this fact as an argument against them — how could people have a right to be supported by others who are not responsible for their situation? The recent concept of social justice is based on the assumption that there are welfare rights, together with the belief that in some sense these rights are equal for all citizens. It implies more than an obligation to be beneficent or humane, since it demands greater equality of material circumstances and not merely alleviation of hardship.

lating their rights]."* Sometimes it is said that rights (or the most basic ones) are inalienable; that is, we cannot give them up or lose them. However we evaluate that claim, it's plain that on a foundational interpretation of rights, rights function as what Nozick terms "side-constraints" on action. They don't tell us what to aim at; rather, they tell us what we must or must not do to others in the process of pursuing our personal objectives.

Although the idea of justice as we understand it can reasonably be analyzed as a matter of enforcing rights, that does not apply to the concept as it's found in the philosophies of Plato and Aristotle, even allowing for problems of translation. For Plato, justice is a master virtue of persons and even whole societies or states; it is the proper ordering of the parts, each doing its proper function in light of a rational understanding of the Good. For Aristotle, justice is a matter of according people the goods (honors, wealth, and so on) that they deserve, so that there is a proportional equality of merit and benefits. For the ordinary Athenian of their time, the word we translate as "justice" is essentially a matter of giving people their due.

What will seem to us a particularly narrow use of *justice* is Hume's. He restricts the term largely to matters of property rights and international relations. In his moral theory, other virtues take up much of the territory justice covers in the theories of Kant and the rationalists. Hume's restricted use of *justice* is perhaps indicative of his close relationship to earlier aretaic and later utilitarian theories of morality.

**Anarchy, State, and Utopia* (New York: Basic Books, 1974), ix.

Similarly, his conservatism could partly explain why Hume makes less of the idea of rights than would his liberal—especially French and American—contemporaries.

The broad scope of justice and rights as we understand them today in the West is a product of our intellectual and political history. We should nevertheless draw a distinction between two areas or types of justice: distributive and retributive. Distributive justice concerns the allocation of social benefits and burdens to individuals—the protection of basic liberties, property rights, powers and opportunities, and so forth, as well as the responsibilities involved in respecting and providing for these things. Retributive justice is primarily a matter of punishing and rectifying wrongs, a topic discussed in Chapter 6. We'll conclude this chapter with a look at John Rawls's influential theory of distributive justice.

Moral Contractualism

The attempt to elaborate and ground a theory of justice by referring to an actual or imaginary social agreement is nothing new. Plato considers and criticizes this approach in his *Republic.* Epicurus later put forth a theory of this type himself. Rawls takes his inspiration from the modern social contract tradition in political philosophy, especially as represented by Locke, Rousseau, and Kant. But in contrast to Hobbes, Locke, and Rousseau, Rawls is not merely offering a theory of the obligation to obey government. He attempts to derive an entire morality—principles of distributive justice as well as natural duties of personal morality—from a hypothetical contract among rational beings. In this respect he is closest to Kant, and Rawls in fact maintains that his theory can be given a Kantian interpretation, as we'll see. Contract theories of morality are usually deontological.

Rawls's theory first appeared in his early article "Justice as Fairness," which we have included in Part II. A series of longer articles led to his highly influential book *A Theory of Justice*, which has in turn been followed by further articles developing and defending its main points. In our brief exposition here we'll focus on the mature theory presented in his book as typical of current forms; for other recent versions, see the works of David Gauthier and Thomas Scanlon cited in the Suggestions for Further Reading.

The distinction between actual and hypothetical agreement needs to be explained at the outset. Rawls does not hold the view that Gilbert Harman proposes in his article "Relativistic Ethics: Morality as Politics" (see Chapter 11)—that morality rests on an actual, though implicit, contract or understanding among real people in a particular society. Instead Rawls holds that justice and other parts of morality are the outcome of a contract that is hypothetical, one that never has and never will actually take place. How can an imaginary agreement be a basis for moral justification? We will try to explain Rawls's answer to this question after we have gone over some of the main aspects of his theory.

The imaginary, initial contract situation in Rawls's theory is called "the original position." It corresponds in some respects to the state of nature in traditional contract theories such as Hobbes's and Locke's. It is a premoral situation in which we can place all human beings who ever will have lived. They are faced with the challenge to agree on a set of moral principles to regulate their lives in real societies in the real world. You might think it impossible to get any agreement about ethics in these circumstances, but Rawls believes he has a way around this problem.

The device he proposes is "the veil of ignorance." Everyone in the original position would be denied knowledge of who he or she is—including whether one is male or female, of a particular faith or none, of one race or another, and so on. Hypothetical contractors would not even know their own society or social class, IQ, physical traits, moral outlooks, or plans of life. Tastes, preferences, interests, and all of the things that set humans at odds would be cloaked from view by the veil of ignorance. However, there is some compensation: The contractors would be completely aware of all the general facts of psychology, economics, politics, and sociology—far more than we now know or are ever likely to know.

What would motivate the imaginary contractors in their choice of a conception of justice and other moral principles? Rawls stipulates that they're rationally self-interested and mutually disinterested (that is, they're moved neither by benevolence nor envy). Since they don't know who they are—indeed, they're all the same as far as they can tell—the aim of the contractors is to maximize their stock of primary social goods once they enter real-life societies. These goods are the basic fruits of social cooperation: liberty, opportunity, wealth and income, and the social bases of self-respect. They are general means to other desirable things.

The strategy that Rawls believes his contractors would adopt is the "maximin strategy," a conservative, nonrisky approach to getting agreement on a moral conception. In other words, what they would do is to seek to avoid ending up in a bad position (to minimize the chances of being a slave in their society, for instance) rather than gamble on a very advantageous position for themselves. There is no real bargaining in the original position because of the veil of ignorance, which precludes knowledge of one's natural and social advantages over others. Indeed, because the veil renders everyone equal in knowledge, motivation, risk aversion, and so on, there need be only *one* person in the original position, a fact that has caused some critics to question whether Rawls's theory is properly termed a contract theory at all.

Ethical egoism would be the result of no agreement on moral principles in the original position, Rawls suggests. But if the maximin strategy were followed, he believes, the parties would unanimously agree on certain broad principles that we'll discuss shortly. What they wouldn't accept, he argues, is utilitarianism, because that conception allows for the sacrifice of the interests of some for the greater good of others. The principle of utility does not guarantee a minimum of liberty, wealth, and so forth, for everyone; as we noted earlier, it seems to ignore the essential separateness of persons. As Rawls puts it, "Each person possesses an inviolability founded on justice that even the welfare of society as a whole cannot override."* Not that the parties in the original position have a view about justice, of course; rather, because none of them would want to risk being a sacrificial victim, they would *choose* a conception of justice that protects everyone. Rawls thinks the contractors would also reject a system of natural liberty rights, such as Nozick's, or a perfectionist conception, such as Aristotle's. The former would leave the worse-off at the mercy of the better-endowed and more fortunate members of society (those

---

**A Theory of Justice* (Cambridge, Mass.: Harvard University Press, 1971), 3.

who can take care of themselves or who inherit property). The latter would be illiberal and involve an imposition on everyone of the same conception of human good or excellence.

The egalitarian, deontological principles that Rawls believes to be the most likely terms of agreement would include personal ones specifying the obligations a person incurs as a result of voluntary acts (for example, fairness and promise-keeping) and the natural duties of individuals (for example, mutual aid and support for just institutions). The hypothetical agreement would also state that a society whose basic structure or network of fundamental institutions (especially political and economic) is just will (if it is an advanced society) embody the following principles: "(1) Each person is to have an equal right to the most extensive total system of equal basic liberties compatible with a similar system of liberty for all. (2) Social and economic inequalities are to be arranged so that they are both: (a) to the greatest benefit of the least advantaged, consistent with the just savings principle, and (b) attached to offices and positions open to all under conditions of fair equality of opportunity."* Rawls takes the position that in a developed society such as our own, the principles should be lexically ordered so that liberties come first, while equal opportunity is ranked second, and benefit to the least advantaged in terms of economic shares is third, if it is not possible to implement all of these things. Equal liberty, for example, shouldn't be sacrificed to greater economic opportunity or equality of income.

Rawls's theory of distributive justice is a philosophical defense of contemporary American welfarist, democratic liberalism. Why should anyone who questions those political values accept it? Basically, Rawls would answer that many of us accept the moral conditions expressed in the idea of the original position: impartiality, fairness, and the appropriate circumstances for arriving at a conception of right. If he is correct that we would agree on a set of principles similar to those above—and many critics have cast doubt on that—then we could be committed to those principles. But if we don't accept the original position with its egalitarian features, Rawls hopes we might eventually do so when we approach wide reflective equilibrium in our own moral thinking. Hypothetical choice in the original position is just a useful way of representing our basic moral beliefs and showing what might follow from them; that is its justifying force.

If we are sympathetic to a Kantian moral perspective, Rawls's theory offers us a reinterpretation of some of Kant's ideas. The parties in the original position are free and equal rational beings who autonomously legislate morality for themselves in the spirit of the third formulation of the Categorical Imperative (the so-called Kingdom of Ends interpretation that you'll study in Chapter 10). The result is a theory that Rawls believes expresses equal respect and consideration for all persons, according them a dignity that utilitarianism cannot recognize.

Even though criticism of Rawls's theory has been extensive, many have used his approach to deal with problems of public policy and applied personal ethics. Our aim in this chapter has been to give a broad overview of the major types of ethical theories still current in mainstream moral philosophy. Each of these might be true or acceptable in part but not its entirety. What they represent are different ways of systematizing central themes from our Judeo-Christian moral heritage. We might

---

**A Theory of Justice*, 302.

feel that all of them (except perhaps for Ross's) are too complex and systematic—that they try to impose too great an order and coherence on our moral attitudes, making them more "rational" and theoretical than it is reasonable to expect. Just how abstract and systematic ethics should be is a hotly debated issue among moral philosophers today; a number of feminist philosophers, in particular, have challenged what they see as too great a preoccupation with rational system-building. Perhaps you'll have a view of your own by the time you complete Part III.

CHAPTER 6

Problems of Agency

Moral Standing

In the last three chapters we dealt with some very general problems of moral philosophy: Are there knowable moral facts? What is human well-being? What principles make actions right or virtuous? Most of this chapter focuses on somewhat narrower questions having to do with various aspects of responsibility and agent-centered concerns. But we begin with a basic problem facing any philosophical theory of morality: What makes a being morally significant in its own right; that is, what gives moral standing?

Most of us agree that all human beings have moral standing, although we might believe that the severely retarded, the insane, and those in a "persistent vegetative state," as physicians say, have a lesser or diminished moral standing compared to the rest of us. At the other extreme, few would argue that rocks and bodies of water have moral standing, though it can be morally wrong to harm or destroy parts of the environment, either because we and other animals depend on it for survival or because we have an aesthetic or recreational interest in it. "Moral standing," as we here use the phrase, expresses the idea that whatever possesses it is either a moral agent or a moral patient.

Let's look at these two concepts in detail. A moral agent is morally responsible, in general (not in every case), for what he or she does. An agent is a being to whom we usually ascribe rights. Other animals lacking some of the important attributes of humans—which would be all or nearly all of the other creatures on our planet—are not moral agents. What these important features are we'll consider shortly. A moral patient, by contrast, doesn't have to be the kind of being responsible for its actions. If we believe that nonhuman animals are moral patients, then we are committed to the view that it is wrong to do certain things to them (or not to do some things for them), independently of any particular interest we might have in them. The last clause is important here: A moral patient (even if not also a moral agent) is a being that must be treated in certain ways even if we don't care about it or like it (for example, it's not a pet or cute and cuddly). Torturing insects is morally wrong in itself, regardless.

Normal adult humans are both moral patients and moral agents. We see the scope of moral concern as protecting all people in certain ways but also as holding most of them generally responsible for what they do or don't do. That humans, like virtually all living things, have a good and can be harmed is what makes us moral patients. What about other things that can be damaged or destroyed, especially human artifacts? Buildings, automobiles, works of art, and jewelry can belong to people, and to destroy them is wrong because they are protected by the owners' right to property. It would also be wrong in virtue of the fact (let's assume) that oth-

What Is a Person?

What makes a living being a person? Plants are not persons, and most of us do not regard nonhuman animals on our planet as persons, though some would argue that gorillas and dolphins come close. It's also arguable that some living human beings are not persons—unborn children, neonates, the severely retarded or permanently comatose. We can imagine persons who are not human, furthermore; angels and demons or life forms from other galaxies might qualify. "Person" carries a moral significance greater than that of "human," since it implies a certain level of dignity and a right to respect that not all human beings are obviously entitled to. We award the status of personhood to individuals meeting certain criteria, for example, rationality, self-control, and the ability to interact with others at a suitably complex level. These criteria overlap (and might even be identical with) the conditions that define what it is to be a moral agent.

Philosophers have for centuries been very much concerned with questions about what gives persons identity over time. John Locke's theory of personal identity emphasizes memory as the essential link between our previous and later selves. Other theories stress bodily continuity or other features as what makes us "the same person." The possibility of multiple personalities in the same body is a problem for any theory that would identify persons with bodies. It is also of considerable ethical interest, as in the case of an alleged rape victim who claimed that not all of her personalities consented to sex. Personhood is a very complex idea, another example of a concept that is both descriptive and evaluative.

ers have an interest in them or could benefit from their preservation. The same might be true of social institutions. But this isn't to say they have moral standing, in our sense—if no one were ever to care about the existence or condition of the Mona Lisa or the crown jewels of England, then there would be no wrong in destroying them. They have no moral significance in their own right, apart from how beings with moral standing would feel about them, that is.

Still, we need to give some good argument for this view. Although a car and a piece of jewelry can certainly be damaged and although some things are good for them, they don't really have *a good* in the sense that living beings do. That's why they should probably not be regarded as moral patients. They can't flourish or suffer, in a literal sense of experiencing pain and misery. This suggests at least one condition or set of conditions for being a moral patient: life, sentience, and consciousness. But do all living, conscious things that can experience pleasure and/or pain (as many microorganisms, such as amoebae, cannot) have the status of moral patienthood? To answer that would involve us in complicated questions about the moral status of animals, and it's not our purpose to settle these matters here. Philosophers have differed on these issues; some take the strong view that animals have rights, but most only ascribe rights to beings that are morally responsible.

Even if we concede that all living, conscious, sentient beings are moral patients, we might still want to maintain a distinction between the moral status of humans (not all of whom are moral agents) and other animals. For example, a severely mentally impaired or physically paralyzed human is arguably not a moral agent, but only a moral patient, as is a normal, healthy monkey. We might insist that the monkey is "less" of a moral patient than is the human, though some people would be of the opposite opinion. In any event, it is not necessary to assume that all moral patients are equal, regardless of their species or individual condition. It should be plain that these questions are not of purely abstract, theoretical interest; think about cases in which human flourishing conflicts with animal welfare, for example, developing wilderness areas or performing organ transplants from baboons to human babies.

What are some reasons that people, especially philosophers, have given for thinking humans have a higher moral status than do animals? Apart from attributes that have to do with moral agency — or at least the potential for it — it's hard to find good reasons. Some people would cite the evolutionary position of humans relative to other species; others would talk about our position in the "food chain." But it is hard to evaluate these things, which are too vaguely stated and not obviously morally relevant. Perhaps the best reason is that normal humans are in some sense capable, on the average, of a higher quality of life than are any other animals on earth. Humans are self-conscious, can experience the "higher" emotions, create artistic and intellectual products, plan for the remote future and understand their own mortality, seek meaning, and so on.

This answer, if broadly acceptable, still doesn't help us much with a case in which the well-being of a monkey, baboon, or dolphin conflicts with that of a "defective" human. Moreover, at least some of these attributes that make possible a supposedly higher quality of life for humans are also relevant to moral responsibility, because they have to do with rationality and related ideas, among them freedom. Let's therefore take up the topic of human freedom and the traditional problem of free will and determinism, which will lead us into a discussion of responsibility and its bases.

Free Will and Determinism

We ordinarily believe that most of the acts people perform are done of their own free will. But what is it to act of our own free will? Might our beliefs about free will be largely false? If they are, do our convictions about moral responsibility have to be abandoned as a result? These are very difficult and very important questions. We can't, of course, answer them here. But we can offer a clearer understanding of what is involved in different positions philosophers have taken on them, especially the strong and weak points in each view.

The commonsense view about human agency and freedom consists of beliefs that at least some of our actions are "up to us," that we choose them from among several options, and that our decisions and their realization in action are "voluntary." There are circumstances in which this is not the case: a person who is coerced or compelled, not in possession of his or her faculties because of drugs or mental illness, or perhaps manipulated in certain ways by others' influences on his or her emotions and knowledge. Otherwise we generally do the things we do "of our own free choice" and bear responsibility for those acts.

Note that this common, unphilosophical view of free agency does not necessarily involve the commitment that there is a human faculty of will or mental states of willing (often termed *volitions*). But this view does appear to include the belief that often or most of the time agents can do otherwise—that there is more than one action within their power or capability to choose and do. The conviction that people can often choose and act differently is very hard to analyze, however, and it seems to conflict with some other beliefs that seem to follow from a scientific understanding of our world and our place in it.

Modern science has had remarkable success in constructing theories that explain, predict, and sometimes give us the ability to control events in the physical realm. More modest achievements have been credited to the behavioral sciences, psychology and psychiatry. But the more we learn about the physical processes underlying the behavior of humans and other animals, the more tempting it is to adopt the view that the actions of living, conscious organisms, including humans, obey the same kinds of general causal laws that (with the possible exception of subatomic particles) physical entities do. This view is known as *determinism.*

Determinism about human agency implies that there are general laws (psychological, physiological, or at some other level of explanation) that express causal relationships between mental or physical states and actions of certain types. If determinism is true and if we come to know enough about those laws and about the properties of individual agents and their circumstances, then it should be possible to predict with fair accuracy what they will do under those conditions and perhaps to shape or control their actions as well. We stress that those are two very big "ifs." But despite the best efforts of many philosophical and scientific critics of determinism, no one has yet come up with a sound argument to undercut its plausibility, let alone rule out its possibility.

Returning to the commonsense level for a moment, we should be aware of the extent to which our usual ways of dealing with and understanding people come close to assuming causal determination of their behavior. We often know just what to do in order to get others to act in certain ways, based on a general familiarity with human behavior patterns. When we know a particular individual well, our predictive and controlling powers tend to increase to the extent we know the person's character, habits, likes and dislikes, and personality traits. Furthermore, wouldn't we find it hard to attribute responsibility to people if we thought of their free acts as uncaused in the sense of being random? Both of these points give some support—though by no means conclusive—to determinism.

However, we might doubt the truth of determinism when we think about how surprising human beings can sometimes be, how they can often overcome adverse circumstances and resist strong internal and external pressures to do what they believe is good or right. Kant, for one, was impressed by this, and he posits a contracausal human freedom of will. For Kant, a requirement of morality is that we have such free choice, that at least some of our decisions are not determined by factors outside of our control, including events that happened even before our birth. This notion of free will is mysterious and obscure, however; Kant has to locate this freedom outside the empirical world of science, placing it in the metaphysical realm of things-in-themselves. As pure intellects, he claims, we must be free, though as subjects of scientific study our acts are causally determined by our beliefs and inclinations. This dualism is hard to understand.

Other philosophers, influenced by Aristotle, have proposed that human beings cause their own actions, originating them without determination by any external influences. This idea of free choice is also hard to understand. We tend to think that

Four Positions on the Free Will Problem

The four responses we present to the problem of freedom and determinism are briefly stated as follows. Note that the first two stances are forms of incompatibilism (determinism would leave no room for human freedom), whereas the latter two are types of compatibilism (determinism allows for meaningful freedom).

1. Hard determinism
   a. Determinism is true; and
   b. We are not free or responsible for anything we do.
2. Strong (contracausal) "libertarianism"
   a. Determinism is false; and
   b. We are free and responsible for many things we do.
3. Soft determinism
   a. Determinism is true; and
   b. We are still free and responsible for many things we do.
4. Agnostic compatibilism
   a. Determinism might or might not be true; but
   b. We are still free and responsible for many things we do.

what people do is a function, in some sense, of their beliefs and desires, and we know that these are what they are in large part because of external influences that appear to be causes. This seems to conflict with the idea of free action as entirely self-caused, which is hard to grasp anyway. Because we cannot really comprehend the concept of uncaused or self-caused action, it is tempting to dismiss it out of hand, but that would be unwarranted. We have such a poor understanding of human agency at the theoretical level that we ought to leave open many possible positions.

At the opposite extreme is the philosophical position William James labeled "hard determinism." Like the contracausal free will position, it involves a denial that determinism and free will (in a sense allowing for moral responsibility) are compatible. But it sharply differs with that view in that it affirms determinism and rejects freedom and responsibility. Our choices and actions are all predetermined by causes outside our control, hard determinists say, whether we like it or not; so we should just give up any ideas about human freedom, responsibility, and (in one sense) dignity. When someone acts, there is no relevant sense in which he or she could have done otherwise. Therefore, there is no freedom and, in turn, no genuine moral responsibility. Blaming and praising might often be effective, but they are not deserved.

Some determinists challenge that last chain of inferences. They are known as "soft determinists." In contrast to the other two positions, the soft determinist attempts to show that determinism and meaningful freedom of action are actually (contrary to what most suppose) consistent with one another. This position has been taken by a long line of modern philosophers, mainly British, from Hobbes through Hume and Mill to Ayer and others in this century.

Soft determinists have expressed their attempts to reconcile free will with determinism in different ways. We will simply try to state the common points. First, soft determinists emphasize that causation is not compulsion; because my action is causally determined doesn't mean that I couldn't have helped doing it in the sense I was forced to do it, and that I am perhaps excused from responsibility on that ground. Second, on the assumption that our beliefs and desires causally determine what we do, it remains true that in the absence of compulsion and ignorance we still act freely, in the sense that we do what we want to do. Though we do not directly choose most of our beliefs and desires, for we acquire or form them in complex causal processes, we can certainly give up or modify many of them through reflection and education or therapy. So even the causes of our actions can often be acted on themselves by our own choice; this decision to change our beliefs or desires would itself be determined, of course, by other beliefs and desires. Third, the sense in which I could not have acted otherwise if my action were causally determined does not appear to rule out my having had the *capacity* (capability, power) to have done otherwise. Because my act is causally necessitated, it must be the case that I will do it. But I still have the power to do other things I won't do. (My car has the power to go 140 mph even though it never will.) It does not follow that I must do it. Fourth, the capacity to respond to praise, blame, and punishment is all that is needed for free and responsible action; in other words, responsibility is linked to responsiveness. We will say more about this later.

Philosophers who accept soft determinism frequently ally themselves with the commonsense view that we outlined at the beginning of this section. On their interpretation of our ordinary way of thinking about free action and responsibility, there is no conflict with determinism. We are simply misled by some philosophers, scientists, or other confused people into thinking that there is an inconsistency. Closer analysis, they insist, shows that determinism allows for freedom (here, freedom equals absence of compulsion), doing what we really want to do, and having the capacity to do otherwise. We can continue to blame and punish people as before, allowing for excuse from responsibility on the usual grounds; determinism does *not* change anything, in other words.

The truth of determinism is not the main issue for us. What we are mainly interested in right now is what *would* follow *were* determinism true for our views about responsibility, blame, and punishment. Soft determinism is appealing because it says, "It makes no real difference whether determinism is true (though we think it is) — we are still free and responsible beings."

However, the soft determinist has to face some serious problems and objections. Consider an example Richard Taylor devised. A mad scientist is able to cause you to have whatever beliefs, desires, or intentions he chooses by stimulating your brain; he causes you to have a strong desire to shoot Jones, and you act on that desire. Are you free and responsible for shooting Jones? Though your desire was admittedly not caused in the usual ways, you were not compelled to act. You did what you wanted, and you have the general capacity to act otherwise in the sense that *if* you wanted to act differently, you would. This counterexample to soft determinism implies that, at the very least, more needs to be said about the notions of capacity, free choice, and responsibility to make the position convincing. The subject in Taylor's example does not seem to be free and responsible for his or her action. What we need to know is whether that conclusion is correct, and why or why not.

Personal Responsibility

Since it is very difficult to analyze the notion of freedom in this context, perhaps a better approach would be to look at the concept of responsibility. It might be that responsibility does not require freedom of will in any strong sense or that if it did we could change our conception of it without serious moral repercussions.

Responsibility, legal or moral, is a normative concept. For subjectivists, relativists, and noncognitivists, this implies that the concept of moral responsibility assumes standards or criteria that are humanly created and changeable. To say that people are responsible for what they do, in this sense, is just to assert that they deserve or ought to have moral credit or discredit for their acts—to be held accountable for it—these philosophers might claim. Our principles or standards of desert and accountability will be part of our theory of moral conduct. It is, in a way, up to us to decide when people are responsible and when they are not. "Free" and "capable of doing otherwise" are not normative concepts, by comparison, but we must decide whether they are (in any senses we could assign to them) morally relevant to responsibility.

There is, of course, a sense of "responsible" that is not normative (unless one thinks of causal laws as norms). For example, we say that a clog in a carburetor is responsible for a car's poor performance. The subject in Taylor's example is responsible, in that sense, for killing Jones. But it is doubtful that he is morally or legally responsible. That would depend on what we think morality or the law requires.

It seems a mistake to think that our beliefs about moral responsibility must depend on the truth about metaphysical questions concerning free will, capacities for action, and so on. We might never have those questions satisfactorily answered. Or it could turn out that we don't have free will and the power to do otherwise than we do, in some sense. But we must continue to praise and reward, blame and punish—to hold people accountable for their acts, to judge them responsible or not for what they do. Some have suggested instead that therapy would be a substitute for these things, for example, regarding criminals and other wrongdoers as sim-

The Incompatibilist Argument

Incompatibilists believe that determinism rules out the possibility that we have free will in any sense that would allow for responsibility. One way of stating their common pattern of argument is this:

1. If determinism is true, then we can never do otherwise than what we are caused to do by factors outside our control.
2. If we can never do otherwise, then our will is not free in any meaningful sense.
3. If our will is not free, then we cannot justifiably be held responsible for what we do; that is, we are not truly responsible and do not deserve anything.
4. If we never deserve anything, then we cannot justifiably be praised or blamed, punished or rewarded.
5. If we cannot justifiably be praised or blamed for anything, then moral judgments are never appropriate.

ply diseased and in need of professional (often medical) help. (It's not clear what would replace praise and reward for good deeds, on that position.) It is doubtful that most of us would find this acceptable as a substitute for responsibility.

Why wouldn't we be able to give up the idea of responsibility in that way? For one thing, it's unlikely that the therapeutic substitute would be generally very effective. But quite apart from the consequences, we tend to feel a need to express certain feelings and make certain distinctions with respect to people and their acts. The language of responsibility allows us to mark what we think are important differences among agents and actions. You would be very upset if a heavy equipment operator sent his wrecking ball into your living room as you sat there watching TV. But compare how you would react when you found out what caused him to do it: (a) a stroke, or (b) a malicious sense of humor. You would think and feel differently in these two cases, and you would believe yourself to be justified in taking differing courses of action in response. Of course, if you are a hard determinist who practices what you preach, you could say that in neither case was the operator responsible for his act, but if (b) is the cause, then he is a bad man, as opposed to blameworthy. Yet it's doubtful that hard determinists could even consistently use "bad man," because that term also seems to presuppose desert, responsibility, and so on — the notions they reject.

Whatever their metaphysical differences, it could be that both the hard determinist and the believer in contracausal free will err in assuming too high or too strict standards of accountability. (Skeptics in epistemology often do the same in using expressions such as "fully justified" and "could not be mistaken.") That is, a philosopher such as Arthur Schopenhauer or a psychologist such as B. F. Skinner (both hard determinists), as well as philosophers such as Kant and Sartre (their contracausal opponents), might be guilty of assuming that more is required for responsibility than we normally expect or need to expect if we are to be enlightened and consistent.

Our suggestion, in other words, is that praising and rewarding, blaming and punishing might not depend on the agent's having the radical freedom that the hard determinists and their polar opposites think it does. We are going to continue holding people responsible, most of the time, for what they do, regardless. The belief that this would be unreasonable or inconsistent of us if we admitted determinism appears to rely on a conception of the responsible human agent — a moral concept — that we need not accept. For lack of a better term, let's call this position "agnostic compatibilism."

But how could we reject or give up the idea of human agents as beings whose choices are "up to them," who often can do otherwise, and still keep our beliefs and attitudes about responsibility? Doesn't "ought" imply "can"? If someone deserves praise or blame, mustn't he or she have initiated the act, that is, been the original or "first cause" of the act? Wouldn't determinism make us see human agents as just complicated biological machines programmed by their genes and environments, without dignity?

Let's briefly take up the last question first. If determinism is true, then perhaps we are more like machines than we now believe. But that would not change the fact that we are (unlike any machines we have created) conscious and capable of desire, feeling, emotion, and perception. Our hopes and aspirations for our lives wouldn't change. As a species, we would still be capable of all of the creative achievements that have marked human history and of all of the moral good and evil. There would be no reason, so far as we can see, to treat one another differently. Since dignity is grounded in these kinds of uniquely human attributes—and what else could it be based on?—our human dignity would survive the truth of determinism. We are not unthinking, unfeeling, uncreative machines, nor are we akin to puppets directly subject to others' will, as in Taylor's example. The fact that we can, if determinism is true, trace the causes of our actions back to events that took place before we were born should not affect our dignity.

The possibility that we are not "first causes" of our actions also gives no good reason to question whether we ever deserve anything, including praise and blame, for what we do. The worry might be expressed something like this: "If people only do good because they were caused to by things outside their control, how can they take any credit?" or "If the acts of evil people are due to a character that they could not help but have, given their genetic makeup and environment, how can we really blame them?" The answer to this challenge is, according to the position we are presenting, that we decide who deserves credit or blame and for what reasons. There is nothing about the meanings of *desert* and *blameworthy* that would keep us from using them in their original senses if we accepted determinism.

There is also the worry that if we didn't have the capability or power to do anything other than one specific predetermined action in a set of circumstances, we could not appropriately evaluate people's actions at all, at least not using moral terms such as *deserve* and *ought.* The problem here seems to depend on an assumption about the logical relations between those moral terms and words expressing the power to act in more than one way. "*Ought* implies *can*" is the way philosophers often express it. If it is causally predetermined that I will do *x* at a certain time and place, then it doesn't seem to make sense to say that I ought to do anything else or that I deserve praise if I act otherwise.

Several points can be made on behalf of the agnostic compatibilist position we are discussing. (1) It is not clear that determinism rules out having the capability or power to act otherwise than a person does or will act. Soft determinists (the other compatibilist position we presented) believe that an agent can be determined in his or her actions yet (in some sense needing to be explained) have the capability to act differently. (2) As soft determinists would also point out, there can be a reason to address "oughts" to people even if their actions are predetermined: The moral judgment can have a causal efficacy itself, sometimes motivating them to act differently than if the judgment had not been made. (3) Finally, there is no simple connection between, for example, "John ought to do *x*" and either "John can do *x*" or "John can do something other than *x*." The latter should be obvious: It remains the case that John ought to tell the truth, let's say, even if he can't do otherwise, for example, because he is too unimaginative to lie. But it is also common to assert that people ought to be in places they cannot now be or that they ought to feel a certain emotion they cannot feel at will. The statement "John ought to visit his grandmother right now" certainly doesn't seem sensible if John cannot now physically do that; however, we can say "John ought to *be* visiting his grandmother right now" on the assumption that it wasn't physically impossible for him to go there in the recent past.

Thus far we've been discussing the responsibility of individuals for their own actions. Although it might be unreasonable or unjust to hold persons accountable for doing things they couldn't help, it is sometimes done, especially by those in authority, often for utilitarian reasons. The agnostic compatibilist theory about responsibility, like soft determinism, denies the claim of hard determinists and proponents of contracausal freedom that it is *illogical* to do so. But in contrast to soft determinism, the present compatibilist position makes no assumption about the truth of determinism in fact, nor does it try to show that determinism is consistent with the capability of agents to act otherwise than they do. (This is an open question.) All that the present position claims is that responsibility and related concepts could still be used in their current significance were we to find out that determinism is true. We might look at or think of human agents somewhat differently, but we would not need to stop attributing responsibility, praising, and blaming.

If we come to believe that determinism is true at some future time, then people might be regarded as more like cars and computers. We could still evaluate them much as we do now; the praise and blame directed at them would just be more causally effective than praise and blame directed at machines. Bad, irresponsible people would be like badly built or designed (or programmed) computers. Of course, in a world in which machines did respond to praise and blame, we would hold them responsible, too, and if people did not have the capacity to respond to these things, it would be inappropriate to apply them to people.

Before we explore ideas about blame and punishment, however, we should say something further about responsibility. In addition to our notions of individual responsibility, ideas of collective responsibility are found both in ordinary moral thought and in discussions by philosophers. We speak, for instance, of the responsibilities of national and state governments, of universities, and of voluntary associations; even unorganized groups and crowds are sometimes said to be responsible or to blame for their actions.

Where philosophers disagree are on the questions of whether collective "entities" such as nations and corporations are something over and above the individuals who compose them and their relations to one another and, if so, whether and how they can be held responsible as such. The position that statements about institutions and other collectives can be reduced to a set of statements about some or all of their members and their relationships to each other is called *methodological individualism.* Methodological holists or collectivists deny that such reduction is possible. A simple example might help illustrate the disagreement. Is a college chess club something more than its members and their understandings of how they are to act toward one another? Certainly it can endure beyond the periods of the current members' participation, maybe even lasting for generations. But if it had no members, wouldn't it cease to exist? If the club is supposed to be something more than its members and their relationships, what could it be?

Methodological individualists would also hold the view, naturally, that in the final analysis only individual human beings can be responsible for their actions, because (strictly speaking) only individuals act. Groups, they might say, do not literally act anymore than they eat and digest. Their holist opponents resist this view, asserting that responsibility can be sometimes assigned to groups as such, even random collections of people (for example, some bystanders at an accident scene). They hold different views about how the responsibility and blame are to be apportioned to members of collectives, if at all.

Why is this theoretical disagreement important? Because we are sometimes forced to face this issue in deciding whether citizens of a government that committed war crimes are responsible and should have to pay compensation; whether citizens of a country with a history of racial discrimination going back to slavery owe victims and their descendants restitution through affirmative action; or if investors in a corporation whose management behaves unethically or illegally are responsible for the actions of those managers. (The last, and perhaps the first, of these cases are examples of what is called "vicarious responsibility" where authorized agents commit wrongs when in the employ of others.) The My Lai massacre of Vietnamese villagers by some American troops on March 16, 1968, is another case in which issues of collective responsibility arise.

However we stand on the question of the reducibility of social institutions and other collectives, it seems that effective judgments of responsibility and the praise or blame that typically follow require that they be directed ultimately at individuals—even if the initial attribution of blame, for example, is directed at a group. The remaining task is to develop an account of responsibility for persons who act in the name of a group or organization, that is, office holders. That account of responsibility must include a rationale for allocating different degrees or amounts of responsibility, for example, in proportion to decision-making power. Philosophers and others who are working on corporate and governmental responsibility issues continue to contribute to our understanding of this question.

Blame and Punishment

Despite what appears to be a political trend toward blaming groups (even "society") for undesirable situations, we'll continue to focus on the responsibility of individuals for their own acts. We'll set aside the more complicated cases, however, in which people act as organization members. Responsibility, we've noted, is closely related to praise and blame, reward and punishment. But what exactly is the relationship? We said that an agent is responsible in general or for a particular act if he or she ought to be held accountable. What rules or principles of law or morality determine accountability depends on what is accepted. The rule, for instance, that an agent must (in some sense) have been able to do otherwise in order to be accountable is a rule widely but not always accepted, as we said earlier. Praise and blame, which are positive and negative expressions of attitude, respectively, are one level of response to agents who are accountable for their acts. Reward and punishment are a more extreme level, for they involve greater cost.

As we remarked in connection with the word *responsible, blame* has a purely causal sense as well. (In that respect, it differs from *praise.*) We blame the weather for the loss of this year's citrus crop, even though we don't think of meteorological forces as responsible moral agents. Moral blame is directed at those we deem morally responsible for their acts, and it involves the belief that they did not meet some standard or norm when they acted (for example, caused an undesirable event). Similarly, a person is thought praiseworthy if he or she acts better than the standard or normal expectation, for example, brings about a very good outcome. The standard itself is in part fixed by our beliefs about what most people in similar circumstances manage to do or avoid doing.

Blameworthiness, then, is being deserving of blame on account of falling below an accepted standard in behavior or, in some instances, character (as when we blame someone for being lazy or insensitive). But when we say that someone is blameworthy, we also imply that there are no excuses for his or her subpar conduct or character. In the case of praiseworthiness, by contrast, we don't seem to have an exact analogue of excuses, although we do sometimes refrain from praise if, for example, we find out that the agent had a great deal to gain from his or her action anyway and little to lose. The British philosopher J. L. Austin, in his famous essay "A Plea for Excuses,"* notes that some excuses—perhaps even most—are only partial, mitigating to a degree but not completely the blame we think is due. He also stresses the difference between an excuse and a justification. We sometimes confuse the two in actual cases, but there is a real difference between saying "What I did was wrong, but . . ." and "What I did was not wrong at all, because . . .". The former is the typical pattern of excuse.

Excuses tend to fall into three major categories, notwithstanding the subtle complexities Austin reveals in his essay. Involuntariness is one category that has received considerable attention from philosophers at least since Aristotle's important treatment of responsibility in his *Nicomachean Ethics.* To show that what we did was not a voluntary act in some sense or that we did not voluntarily omit to do something is a very common way of excusing our action or omission. Because of either a lack of capability or a lack of opportunity, we might fail to act as morally required but not deserve blame. A second category covers unintentional acts and omissions: when we do or omit something because of a mistake, accident, or inadvertence. If our unintentional wrong act or omission is due to negligence, however, blame and even punishment might be still in order. The third category covers excusable acts that, while intentional, were done or omitted in what could be considered at least partly excusing circumstances—for example, threats, coercion, pain, or dire need. There are other cases, such as acting while intoxicated or under hypnosis, that are not easily classified, though they arguably belong in the category of involuntary acts and omissions.

A theory of responsibility would lay out in detail the kinds of considerations that excuse various types of wrong actions and to what extent. It would explicate the concepts of "voluntariness," "avoidable ignorance," "negligence," and their contradictories. Moreover, it would give a general explanation of why certain excuses are adequate and when.

Sometimes we hear it said that "to understand all is to excuse all." The apparent meaning of such a statement is that if we knew all of the reasons why someone did any wrong act, in any circumstances, we would see that he or she didn't really deserve any blame or punishment. Some people hold this view about the responsibility of even those criminals thought to be guilty of the most heinous acts. In our discussion of punishment, we will assume that this position is false or unacceptable. It seems to rest on assumptions of a hard determinist sort, which we have questioned, and perhaps also on a kind of misguided softheartedness, ignoring in some cases the feelings of victims or their survivors as well as the practical necessity of making distinctions between conditions that excuse and those that merely explain actions.

Since punishment usually involves inflicting greater pain or discomfort on wrongdoers than does expressing blame, we should look at some of the traditional

*In his *Philosophical Papers* (Oxford: Clarendon Press, 1961).

justifications offered for the practice of meting punishment out. Five or six traditional grounds or aims of punishment deserve discussion; some of them tied to particular types of ethical theories. A full treatment would take us far into the philosophy of law, but we believe that our brief survey should be helpful as a first glance at some of the moral underpinnings of retributive justice.

One common justification, which can be traced at least back to Socrates and Plato, is that punishment, when properly administered, can serve to reform or rehabilitate the wrongdoer. On this theory, it's important that the people who are to be punished understand why they are being punished, to see that they truly deserve it. Certainly it is true that in our legal system we try to avoid punishing those who, perhaps because of a form of mental illness, do not and cannot understand why what they did was wrong and therefore why they deserve punishment. This is especially true in the case of capital punishment, where there are at best very limited opportunities for a positive effect on the person's character (in this life, anyhow). Punishment, on this view, should aim at making the wrongdoers morally better, either for their own sake or for that of society; this is unlikely if they do not see a connection between what they did, their character, and what is necessary to lead a better life.

Some criminals or wrongdoers do feel they merit punishment; however atypical, these individuals (because of guilt feelings or whatever) may actively seek or demand to be punished, sometimes even with death. This would seem a necessary first stage for reform-based punishment to be effective, yet how often can we count on it or bring it about? In a small number of cases, it is useful to confront criminals with not only a detailed account of what they did but also with their victims and the victims' suffering. But it's unrealistic to think that our present penal system makes most criminals better people or that any other feasible arrangement we know about would rehabilitate them.

If reform of the wrongdoer cannot be the sole or most fundamental aim of punishment, what are some other legitimate grounds or purposes for it? For some crimes, it is possible to compel wrongdoers to compensate their victims. When restitution is made, however, it is not clear that we can say that anyone is thereby punished. In any event, for most crimes it is probably impossible to force wrongdoers to compensate their victims in financial terms. But victims and survivors might feel that prison or execution is a kind of nonmonetary compensation they're entitled to, perhaps the only thing that would satisfy them emotionally. We can raise several questions here: Is this revenge? Is revenge always wrong? Is revenge the most common motive for punishment generally?

A theory of just punishment that is sometimes accused of legitimizing revenge is the retributive theory. Kant and other deontologists typically are retributivists. They hold that the primary, if not sole, justification for punishing someone is that he or she deserves it on account of an inexcusable wrong action, period. Further advantages, such as reforming the wrongdoer's character or protecting society, are incidental. On a strict retributivist view, they are not justifications in themselves. Kant would insist that punishing wrongdoers is what the categorical imperative requires: treating them as rational, autonomous agents responsible for their deeds. He goes so far as to assert that if a society were to dissolve itself, it would first have to execute all of the convicted murderers in order to do justice. But he would oppose punishment on utilitarian grounds, since that could involve treating some people as mere means to the good of others, for example, the security of the majority. The central idea of retributivism, again, is that punishing is a response to wrongdoing, not a way of getting certain good consequences or preventing bad results. To the extent that it is just, punishment is thus backward-looking, a matter of "balancing the scales" again.

It should be taken for granted that guilt is a necessary condition for punishment. It's wrong to punish innocent persons in order to bring about some social benefit if we know that's what we're doing. But is inexcusable guilt a sufficient condition of justifiable punishment, as the retributivists assert? Consequentialist or value-based ethical theorists would insist, to the contrary, that some good must result from punishment or some harm be prevented, at least as a general practice. Of course, we could count the emotional satisfaction of victims or their loved ones as a good to be achieved by punishment, unless there's some objection to this, as our questions about revenge suggest. What should be clear, in any case, is that the strict retributive theory makes just punishment independent of such consequences. Accordingly, retributive theorists cannot offer a value-based account of proportionality, that is, how much punishment is appropriate for such-and-such an offense. What basis would serve to make the punishments fit the crime is therefore a difficult problem for pure retributivism. The Old Testament formula of "an eye for an eye, a tooth for a tooth," often too cruel to carry out in practice, would not always give us guidance anyway.

Another traditional justification for punishment—sometimes combined with retributivist considerations (as in John Locke's theory)—is the deterrence theory. Utilitarians tend to hold this position, unless they oppose punishment entirely. The general system of legal punishment, we tend to think, serves to deter many people (not all, of course) from committing crimes. More effective apprehension and conviction procedures, along with more severe penalties, might even increase the deterrence value of punishment, although considerations of humanity and due process set limits to any moves our society could make in that direction. In addition to the discouragement of convicted persons, their punishment, we think, has some tendency to discourage others from similar courses of wrong action. If the penalty in question is incarceration or execution, there is the obvious further benefit of actually preventing (not just deterring) the person who is punished from committing further crimes against the public. A deterrence theory, its proponents argue, has an objective, nonarbitrary basis for determining what punishment is appropriate for a given offense: Penalties should be severe enough to produce an acceptable level of deterrence, given the other social values to be promoted and protected, such as liberty and due process. (Utilitarians can simply reduce this to setting penalties at the level that would produce the highest expectable social utility.)

Although a pure deterrence theory seems unacceptable—it would permit the punishment of the innocent—perhaps a mixed theory that combines retributive and deterrence considerations in some manner would be the most adequate. This does, in fact, appear to be the commonsense position that supports our actual legal system of punishment, however imperfect. But there are two other rationales for punishing wrongdoers that don't quite fit under the standard formulations of the theories we have discussed, so we should mention them briefly before concluding this section.

It is sometimes argued that without a system of legal punishment, we would have chaos, anarchy, or some form of vigilante "justice." Hobbes's idea of what the state of nature prior to society and government would be like represents one possible scenario. Locke's comparatively more benign conception of life without civil society and its criminal law would still allow for much unjust and excessive punishment meted out by individuals who felt wronged and lacked impartiality. Our system of legal punishment, despite its many shortcomings, is clearly better than either of these alternatives. We thus have a kind of justification for our practice and institutions of punishment that is more fundamental than the deterrence theory—as well as more comprehensive—and that includes the deontological concern of preventing injustice. (However, in contrast to the strict deontologism of Kant, this rationale for punishment aims at minimizing certain kinds of injustice; it is to that extent consequentialist in logical structure.)

Another common justification for punishment is that it serves to express the outrage of society at the act of the criminal. This expressivist position is interesting in that it suggests a kind of legitimate need for revenge, but at the societal rather than the individual victim's level. It comes close to the retributivist theory, since what is being expressed could be understood as genuine, justified moral indignation. But the outrage or condemnation that society is supposed to express through official punishment might not, depending on the theory, have moral import or status. Some argue that the position seems to collapse into either a deterrence or retributivist view; or they object to it on the ground that there are other ways society could express its feelings against crime. But would they be as powerful?

A complete account of the moral basis of punishment would attempt to answer a wide range of important questions: What methods of punishment are acceptable for any kind of crime? Is capital punishment ever just? Why would it be or not be? How far does mental illness in some forms affect the voluntariness of wrongful acts and thus the culpability of the agent? Is it just to make the dependents of criminals suffer from their punishment? A complete theory would also show us the relative weight and relationships of the different considerations we have discussed.

Weakness of Will

When discussing moral responsibility, we can't avoid the question of its relationship to free will, which we have examined in some detail. But there is another problem concerning will that needs to be mentioned: the phenomenon of weakness of will and how we can explain or understand it.

Weakness of will (called *akrasia* by the Greeks) is of considerable interest to Socrates, Plato, and Aristotle, and philosophical interest in this phenomenon has revived over the last few decades, primarily among British and American philosophers. In the *Meno*, the *Protagoras*, and other Platonic dialogues, Socrates raises the question in different forms. For our purposes, we can simply say that Socrates is puzzled how anyone could know what is good and yet do evil voluntarily. We have, then, a paradox—two beliefs both of which seem to be true separately but when conjoined appear to yield a contradiction. We know that people sometimes are aware of what is good, right, or ought to be done; we also believe it is true that people sometimes act voluntarily in evil ways. But how could anyone knowingly choose to do evil?

Saint Paul expressed his consternation thus: "The good that I would, I do not; the evil that I would not, that I do" (Romans 7:15). Later Saint Augustine wrote of this weakness in similar terms. But it is important to realize that they were using a conception of will that the ancient Greeks did not possess; that conception was essentially a product of the Judeo-Christian religious tradition. We, of course, are quite at home with this idea; the point is only that we don't need to think in terms of willing ourselves to see a puzzle or paradox here. Furthermore, weakness of will is more general than moral weakness, as we would understand the latter notion. We could be weak-willed about doing something we think is in our best interests (what we consider a prudential matter); moral weakness, in contrast, seems to do with not acting on moral principles we supposedly accept.

Let's focus for the moment on ordinary, nonmoral weakness of will by offering a simple example. I want to lose ten pounds right now; I think that would be in my best interests, both healthwise and romantically. Yet almost everytime I have the chance to eat something I like, I give in and so choose what is bad for me. I know that I am choosing what is bad for me when I do so; is my choice a voluntary one? Well, it's not done in ignorance, and no one is forcing me. Moreover, I seem to have control over my choice—I believe I could do otherwise, refraining and sticking to my diet, but I just don't. I fail to exercise the ability I think that I have, acting against "my better judgment."

Now for an example of moral weakness. Consider the case of Seymour, who has promised to visit his aging Aunt Zelda the next time he's in town. His visits mean a lot to her, and she is counting on him coming now that he's back in the city. But Seymour finds the visits painfully boring and depressing, taxing his powers of trivial conversation. He knows that he should go this time, since he promised her. But he would really rather do something else (attend the exciting stamp collectors' conventions going on at the same time), and that's exactly what he does, perhaps after some internal struggle in true Kantian fashion.

How are we to understand what is going on in these cases? Isn't it hard to see, at least in the first example, how I could voluntarily act against what I believe to be best, against what I ought to do? In some sense, we think, what I really want most is to lose weight. How then do I manage to choose what I know to be incompatible with achieving that aim, time after time? We know that people do act this way; those who do so frequently over a range of different temptations we classify (perhaps with an attitude of superiority) as generally weak-willed.

One straightforward explanation of what is going on in the first case is that I'm just acting impulsively out of a strong desire for immediate gratification, losing sight of my longer-term and in some sense more important goal. Some people have more self-control or self-discipline ("will-power") than I do, at least with respect to food, and they are more successful with diets. Exactly what is involved in having that kind of control is not clear, however. Is it something I can choose to develop? Can I be weak-willed about overcoming my weak will? Being less prone than average to giving in to immediate prospects of pleasure (or avoiding immediate pain) needs explanation itself, whether or not it can in turn account for many cases of weakness of will and strength of will.

It's not hard to see how someone (Seymour, in our example) can do what he knows to be morally wrong (breaking his promise) voluntarily, unless we make certain dubious assumptions about what it means to know or believe that something is morally good or bad, right or wrong. We often do decide what people's accepted moral principles are by seeing what they do in critical situations; if they have a habit of breaking promises, for instance, we tend to think that they don't really believe that breaking a promise is morally wrong. But we don't have to conclude that—unless, that is, we are internalists about moral judgments (see Chapter 3). Hare, as we noted earlier, holds the position that to assent to a real value judgment (as he uses this term) sincerely, we must have some motivation to act in the appropriate way. He also takes the position that a moral principle is one that someone regards as overriding in the sense that he or she gives it priority in choosing among other concerns and interests. If we consider these two theses together, it is apparent that Hare has a problem allowing for and explaining weakness of will, or what he calls "backsliding" in moral contexts.

In all or most examples of weakness of will, moral or prudential, we seem to find a psychological conflict between (a) what an agent believes is the most reasonable, prudent, or important thing to do—what is most worthwhile or honorable, in his eyes—and (b) what he thinks would give him pleasure or immediate benefit, what he most wants in the sense of most intensely wants (as opposed to "really wants," which is on the other side of the conflict). A more detailed explanation is not within our grasp, though philosophers continue to do important work on this problem, often in connection with questions of rationality and self-deception. A theory of responsibility would clearly have to deal with this issue.

Intentions, Acts, and Omissions

We have already remarked on the importance of the agent's intentions in assessing the morality of persons and what they do, particularly in a deontological theory. There are a number of difficult philosophical issues concerning intentions that have a bearing on morality. One is of special importance for determining responsibility: Is there a moral difference between doing something that you know or believe will have certain undesirable consequences and doing that action with the intention of producing those consequences? This question is related to and sometimes conflated with another basic question: Is it morally important to distinguish acts from omissions?

According to the so-called doctrine of the double effect, a part of traditional Catholic moral theology, what we strictly intend are our ends and the means we choose to realize them; we can foresee bad side effects of our chosen means without thereby strictly intending those effects, in which case we are not morally responsible for them. The doctrine thus states that at least part of the time there is an objective and morally relevant difference between the strictly intended ends and means of an agent, on the one hand, and the effects he or she foresees but does not strictly (but only obliquely) intend, on the other hand.

This doctrine has received considerable criticism from philosophers outside the Catholic Church, though others have defended it. While its applications are not always clear in a given case—a problem for most moral principles, needless to say—a simple case might illustrate how it could be applied. Suppose that a pregnant woman is diagnosed with uterine cancer; only a hysterectomy will save her life. The doctrine could be interpreted as sanctioning this operation; although it will involve the death of the fetus, that is an unintended but merely foreseen side effect. Next, consider a different case: The unborn child itself is threatening the life of the mother, and she is expected to die (though the child will be delivered and survive) if nothing is done. The doctrine we are considering seems to provide no justification for an abortion to save the expectant mother's life, since that would involve directly intending the death of the unborn child as a means.

Rather than trying to assess the doctrine of the double effect and weigh the objections made against it—a major undertaking beyond the scope of this introductory treatment—let's consider another thesis with which the doctrine is sometimes confused. Philippa Foot, in her article "Abortion and the Doctrine of the Double Effect,"* argues that the purported distinction between strictly intended and unintended but foreseen effects seems to be conflated by some of its philosophical defenders with a quite different distinction: the distinction between what we do and what we allow. (*Allowing* is here to be understood as not intervening in some ongoing process so as to prevent a bad result; this is different from enabling something to occur by removing some obstacle.) The doing of something requires bodily movement, whereas mere allowing in this sense is a matter of omission, of not acting. The thesis implicit in the use of this distinction is that there is, at least in some contexts, a morally relevant difference between doing and allowing. For example, allowing people to starve in a foreign country is not as morally objectionable as sending them poisoned food.

Foot goes on to point out that our laws and our common morality distinguish positive rights and duties from negative ones. The former require action, whereas the latter are a matter of allowing (negative duties) or being allowed (negative rights). Generally speaking—there are definite exceptions—we tend to regard negative duties as more stringent or to be given priority over positive ones. To borrow another of her examples, it would be wrong to murder someone even if that were necessary to feed one's own children (a positive duty). She proceeds to show how various hard cases might be resolved on the basis of the distinction between positive and negative duties and our beliefs about their relative stringency, an approach she finds superior to reliance on the double effect doctrine.

We should remark that act-utilitarians have no use for the positive/negative distinction between duties. For them it has no moral significance as such, because all that matters, they maintain, is the maximization of good consequences. James Rachels's essay in Chapter 12 is representative of the view that the distinction is of no moral significance. We should also note, however, that rule-utilitarians can and often do recognize a moral distinction here, though not in the fundamental way that a deontologist might. Ross, for example, would insist that the prima facie duty not to kill an innocent human being is more stringent than is the duty to help someone who would otherwise die, and this priority of negative over positive prima facie moral duties has nothing to do with the general happiness of society. The rule-utilitarian, in contrast, can take the position that the long-term best interests of society are served by making a distinction between these two classes of duties and giving priority to the negative ones more often in the moral code. Utilitarians who advocate an ideal moral code theory, such as Brandt does, thus have an option denied to direct (act-) utilitarians. But would it maximize expectable utility for a

*In her *Virtues and Vices* (Oxford: Basil Blackwell, 1978).

given society over a given time period to assign greater priority, usually, to negative duties and/or rights? That would be, of course, an empirical question.

Apart from the rule-utilitarian approach, what other way might there be to explain and also justify our tendency to give greater priority to negative duties and rights? Two points can be made: (1) Negative rights often seem to protect more central interests of all human beings, for example, the right not to be killed, deprived of liberty, or assaulted. (2) Positive duties tend to be more burdensome than negative ones, although (again) there are plenty of exceptions. (We will also want to distinguish positive duties that are voluntarily accepted, as in an uncoerced promise or contract, from those that are simply imposed by one's social circumstances, for example, duties to one's parents.) It seems that the negative rights and duties form a sort of core morality that consists of the most essential moral rules or principles, the ones we would most want to have recognized and imposed on us and our fellows. Most of us would generally rather not be harmed or overburdened, even at the risk of not being aided. Gilbert Harman offers a theory that morality is relative to a given society's understandings, conventions, and contracts. It is a virtue of his theory, he observes, that it allows and accounts for the generally greater importance of negative rights and duties, because those are the ones that self-interested parties to a social contract would tend to agree weigh more heavily.

The distinction between positive and negative rights or duties and the moral significance of doing as opposed to allowing remain controversial issues in contemporary ethical theory. How to explain and justify these views, if possible, is something a complete account of moral responsibility must show.

Moral Dilemmas

A final topic we should raise is the concept of moral dilemma and the matter of whether there are irresolvable dilemmas in ethics. In the philosophers' special sense, a moral dilemma is not just any problem of moral decision or judgment where the answer is not obvious. (This is the common meaning of the term.) Rather, a moral dilemma in the technical sense is a case in which a person is morally required to do *x*, all things considered, and at the same time do something incompatible (logically or physically) with doing *x*, all things considered. In other words, a moral dilemma in this narrow sense is a situation in which an agent is actually required by morality to do two or more things that he or she cannot all do.

Here's a possible example of a moral dilemma. John promises to help Jeanne move her furniture to a new apartment at 9:00 A.M. next Sunday and also forgetfully promises Jeff to drive him to the airport at that same time. It's impossible for John to do both things promised. If we conclude—as some moral philosophers would not—that John must do both, then we have a genuine moral dilemma. (How could it be resolved in a rational, nonarbitrary way?)

Some philosophers would resist the position that there are irresolvable moral dilemmas. Among them we could list Aristotle (who thinks the virtues form a unified, consistent whole), Aquinas, Kant, and all utilitarians. Sartre, by contrast, seems to allow for this position in his doctrine of moral commitment, at least insofar as he believes there is no rational necessity of making one basic moral choice instead of another. His famous example of the World War II Frenchman torn between a sense of duty to his aged mother and to his country—he must decide whether to stay home and care for her or join the Resistance—seems to be a moral dilemma.

It's not hard to see how moral dilemmas could arise within commonsense morality as we know it. Our Judeo-Christian heritage, as we said before, consists of diverse values and principles that—even if they don't conflict logically—are likely to require courses of action that are incompatible in some situations. The range of moral terms we use to express our judgments (*obligatory, ought, must, best choice*) suggests the possibility of such conflicts. (What we're obligated to do might not be our best course of action, morally speaking, for example.) Thomas Nagel, in his essay "The Incommensurability of Value,"* argues that five different categories of moral considerations are bound to conflict sometimes: obligations, rights, utility, perfectionist ideals, and personal commitments. We shouldn't assume that our preferred moral system will be consistent in all possible circumstances. Yet that coherence is the ideal of many philosophers, for how could there be moral truth or rationality without it?

Bernard Williams offers a different line of argument for the reality of moral dilemmas in his article "Ethical Consistency."† He suggests that moral conflicts are more like conflicts of our own desires than of our own beliefs. When you must choose which of two incompatible wants to satisfy, the unsatisfied want doesn't usually just go away; you can feel regret at not having fulfilled it. But when you have a conflict of beliefs, the one you give up isn't normally a source of regret. (You now think you have the truth, or what is more probably the truth, so why feel any loss at the rejection of your previous belief?) In a moral conflict, when you cannot meet all of what you see as your moral commitments, you tend to feel regret, remorse, or even guilt.

But can we infer from this that there are moral dilemmas, genuine conflicts of moral requirements, all things considered? It doesn't seem so. As Foot and other critics have pointed out, feeling regret can be explained in a number of ways that do not involve an irresolvable conflict of moral requirements. For example, you can know that you did do the right thing, on balance, and still feel regret that it was necessary to cause someone pain by doing so. Remorse and guilt are more complicated emotions. If someone feels remorse or guilt after doing what he or she believes was morally required, we would ask whether those feelings are rational or justified. In any event, this argument for moral dilemmas seems very inconclusive.

One argument that denies the existence of moral dilemmas is based on the idea that there are values within morality that cannot be measured on some common scale, for example, obligations versus perfectionist considerations. This is more promising, but more needs to be said. Clearly we sometimes confidently make such judgments about the priority of conflicting moral considerations of different types. For instance, we judge that protecting an individual's right to free speech is more important than a small increase in social utility. Yet it is not plausible to assume that an adequate morality would have priority rules to deal with all cases of moral considerations conflicting among themselves. Ross insists that a kind of perception allows us to resolve such conflicts, but that is an obscure notion.

---

*In his *Mortal Questions* (Cambridge: Cambridge University Press, 1979).

†In his *Moral Luck* (New York: Cambridge University Press, 1981).

As we see it, it's an open question whether or not there are irresolvable moral dilemmas, situations where an agent cannot do right without doing wrong, all things considered. We find examples in literature (Melville's Billy Budd might be one), and we appear to find them in real life, fortunately not too often. In the final analysis, the question about moral dilemmas seems to depend on more basic questions about what moral theory is true or most acceptable. You will explore these questions in more depth as you study the historical and contemporary philosophical readings in Part II.

PART

II

HISTORY OF WESTERN MORAL PHILOSOPHY

Part II of this book is a collection of representative readings, ordered chronologically, from the most important moral philosophers. As we said in the Preface, we do not assume that a comprehensive introduction to moral philosophy, such as this book, must be an all-inclusive collection of readings; so, not all philosophers are represented. But those whose works appear are fairly widely regarded as having exerted the most profound influence on contemporary moral philosophy.

Mostly we let these philosophers speak for themselves, limiting our own comments mainly to introductory remarks. We encourage you to refer to the material in Part I if you have difficulty with the ideas and theories you find here in Part II.

CHAPTER 7

Greek Moral Philosophy

Let's distinguish moral philosophy from an ethic. An ethic is just a set of principles of conduct that govern a person or a group. Moral philosophy is somewhat different; it is the critical consideration of what principles *ought* to govern people and of the nature, sources, and justification of these principles.

Principles of conduct—ethics—are as old as society itself. But moral philosophy is comparatively recent. It was a by-product of *sophistry*, which was practiced by a group of Greek thinkers who lived around the fifth century B.C. The Sophists made their living by teaching the art of how to win arguments. At this time, the Near East was governed by the Athenian democracy, and as in any democracy, power and influence was held primarily by those who had mastered the tactics of persuasion. The Sophists were experts at devising clever arguments to support any claim, and they shared their expertise with others—for a fee.

To demonstrate their abilities, these Greek experts of persuasion were fond of disproving accepted opinion, including accepted opinion about principles of proper conduct. A few took a measure of pride in "proving" that what seemed the worst thing to do was actually the best thing to do. A result, naturally, was that people began critically to consider the nature and justification of moral principles. Moral philosophy had begun.

Socrates

At this time there lived in Athens a stonemason named Socrates (469–399 B.C.), who also was exceptionally adept at argumentation.

Socrates spent his time enticing Athenians to philosophize with him, mainly about supposed moral virtues such as bravery and piety. Usually, by the end of these discussions Socrates had made his victims look foolish. Eventually, enough of them suffered this misfortune to have Socrates brought to trial on trumped-up charges of corrupting youth and promoting worship of new deities. He was found guilty and executed, an event that tempered the fondness of his followers for democracy.

Unlike Socrates, most of the Sophists wanted to win arguments but were not especially concerned with learning the truth. This was not true of all of them, and some, such as Protagoras (ca. 490–ca. 421 B.C.) and Gorgias (ca. 485–ca. 380 B.C.) were respected as wise thinkers. Indeed, *sophia* means "wisdom," and originally the title "Sophist" was a token of respect. But many of the Sophists were merely clever persuaders who favored captivating argument over sound reasoning.

Socrates, by contrast, really wanted to know the truth. When he lured an unsuspecting Athenian into a discussion of justice, for instance, his aim wasn't to demonstrate his own mental agility or to demolish his opponent—though usually both resulted—but to discover *what justice is.* Socrates was engaged in a critical consideration of moral concepts and principles. Moral philosophy is therefore often said to have begun with Socrates.

Socrates himself left no writings. The specific conclusions he drew about the issues with which he concerned himself we can only infer from the writings of others, most notably his pupil, Plato. For this reason, Socrates' main contributions to moral philosophy lie not in his findings, but in his interests and methodology.

His primary interest, as Aristotle said of him, was "to find the universal" in ethical matters. He was not content with the traditional and accepted views of courage, justice, piety, virtue, and the greatest good; instead, he wanted to know the *ultimate nature* of these things. He insisted, in addition, that the correct understanding of ethical concepts must rest on sound reasoning (rather than on, say, faith, or intuition, or popular wisdom). His methodology emphasized "dialectic," the procedure by which truth is elicited from the mind itself and not through empirical study. Socrates changed the main focus of philosophy from metaphysics to moral philosophy.

Socrates, as we said, left no writings. Nevertheless, the following excerpt from Plato's *Republic* gives a good example of Socrates' interests. The specific views Plato attributes to "Socrates" in this dialogue are Plato's own but nonetheless reflect the influence of Socrates on Plato. In addition, the dialogue offers a vivid portrayal of Socrates' method of philosophizing.

In this excerpt, Socrates (who is the speaker in the dialogue) has just been discussing the nature of justice with some of his friends when he is interrupted by Thrasymachus (who in real life was a famous Sophist). Thrasymachus denounces Socrates as a simpleton and dismisses the discussion as childish drivel. Justice, he announces, is nothing other than the advantage of the stronger. He elaborates this to mean that all states are set up to the advantage of the ruling party. Socrates then traps Thrasymachus into an apparent self-contradiction: namely, that on Thrasymachus's theory it is just to do both what is to the advantage of the ruling party and what is not to its advantage.

Thrasymachus responds that Socrates has gained his point only by assuming that a ruler makes mistakes. A *true* ruler, he says, doesn't make mistakes; so, it is just to do what is to the advantage of the ruler, insofar as he is truly a ruler.

Socrates then argues that just as physicians and pilots do not seek their own advantage but instead seek the advantage of their subjects, so likewise a true ruler does not seek his own advantage but instead seeks the advantage of his subjects.

The main speaker in the selection is Socrates, who refers to himself as "I" and to Thrasymachus as "he."

from the *Republic*

Plato

Plato lived from around 427 B.C. to 347 B.C. This is Book I of his *Republic*, translated by Benjamin Jowett.

Book I
Of Wealth, Justice, Moderation, and Their Opposites

PERSONS OF THE DIALOGUE

SOCRATES, *who is the narrator.*	CEPHALUS.
GLAUCON.	THRASYMACHUS.
ADEIMANTUS.	CLEITOPHON.
POLEMARCHUS.	

And others who are mute auditors.

The scene is laid in the house of Cephalus at the Piræus; and the whole dialogue is narrated by Socrates the day after it actually took place to Timæus Hermocrates, Critias, and a nameless person, who are introduced in the Timæus.

I went down yesterday to the Piræus with Glaucon, the son of Ariston, that I might offer up my prayers to the goddess; and also because I wanted to see in what manner they would celebrate the festival, which was a new thing. I was delighted with the procession of the inhabitants; but that of the Thracians was equally, if not more, beautiful. When we had finished our prayers and viewed the spectacle, we turned in the direction of the city; and at that instant Polemarchus, the son of Cephalus, chanced to catch sight of us from a distance as we were starting on our way home, and told his servant to run and bid us wait for him. The servant took hold of me by the cloak behind, and said, Polemarchus desires you to wait.

I turned round, and asked him where his master was.

There he is, said the youth, coming after you, if you will only wait.

Certainly we will, said Glaucon; and in a few minutes Polemarchus appeared, and with him Adeimantus, Glaucon's brother, Niceratus, the son of Nicias, and several others who had been at the procession.

Polemarchus said to me, I perceive, Socrates, that you and your companion are already on your way to the city.

You are not far wrong, I said.

But do you see, he rejoined, how many we are?

Of course.

And are you stronger than all these? for if not, you will have to remain where you are.

May there not be the alternative, I said, that we may persuade you to let us go?

But can you persuade us, if we refuse to listen to you? he said.

Certainly not, replied Glaucon.

Then we are not going to listen; of that you may be assured.

Adeimantus added: Has no one told you of the torch-race on horseback in honor of the goddess which will take place in the evening?

With horses! I replied. That is a novelty. Will horsemen carry torches and pass them one to another during the race?

Yes, said Polemarchus; and not only so, but a festival will be celebrated at night, which you certainly ought to see. Let us rise soon after supper and see this festival; there will be a gathering of young men, and we will have a good talk. Stay then, and do not be perverse.

Glaucon said, I suppose, since you insist, that we must.

Very good, I replied.

Accordingly we went with Polemarchus to his house; and there we found his brothers Lysias and Euthydemus, and with them Thrasymachus the Chalcedonian, Charmantides the Pæanian, and Cleitophon, the son of Aristonymus. There too was Cephalus, the father of Polemarchus, whom I had not seen for a long time, and I thought him very much aged. He was seated on a cushioned chair, and had a garland on his head, for he had been sacrificing in the court; and there were some other chairs in the room arranged in a semicircle, upon which we sat down by him. He saluted me eagerly, and then he said:

You don't come to see me, Socrates, as often as you ought: If I were still able to go and see you I would not ask you to come to me. But at my age I can hardly get to the city, and therefore you should come oftener to the Piræus. For, let me tell you that the more the pleasures of the body fade away, the greater to me are the pleasure and charm of conversation. Do not, then, deny my request, but make our house your resort and keep company with these young men; we are old friends, and you will be quite at home with us.

I replied: There is nothing which for my part I like better, Cephalus, than conversing with aged men; for I regard them as travellers who have gone a journey which I too may have to go, and of whom I ought to inquire whether the way is smooth and easy or rugged and difficult. And this is a question which I should like to ask of you, who have arrived at that time which the poets call the "threshold of old age": Is life harder toward the end, or what report do you give of it?

I will tell you, Socrates, he said, what my own feeling is. Men of my age flock together; we are birds of a feather, as the old proverb says; and at our meetings the tale of my acquaintance commonly is: I cannot eat, I cannot drink; the pleasures of youth and love are fled away; there was a good time once, but now that is gone, and life is no longer life. Some complain of the slights which are put upon them by relations, and they will tell you sadly of how many evils their old age is the cause. But to me, Socrates, these complainers seem to blame that which is not really in fault. For if old age were the cause, I too, being old, and every other old man would have felt as they do. But this is not my own experience, nor that of others whom I have known. How well I remember the aged poet Sophocles, when in answer to the question, How does love suit with age, Sophocles—are you still the man you were? Peace, he replied; most gladly have I escaped the thing of which you speak; I feel as if I had escaped from a mad and furious master. His words have often occurred to my mind since, and they seem as good to me now as at the time when he uttered them. For certainly old age has a great sense of calm and freedom; when the passions relax their hold, then, as Sophocles says, we are freed from the grasp not of one mad master only, but of many. The truth is, Socrates, that these regrets, and also the complaints about relations, are to be attributed to the same cause, which is not old age, but men's characters and tempers; for he who is of a calm and happy nature will hardly feel the pressure of age, but to him who is of an opposite disposition youth and age are equally a burden.

I listened in admiration, and wanting to draw him out, that he might go on—Yes, Cephalus, I said; but I rather suspect that people in general are not convinced by you when you speak thus; they think that old age sits lightly upon you, not because of your happy disposition, but because you are rich, and wealth is well known to be a great comforter.

You are right, he replied; they are not convinced: and there is something in what they say; not, however, so much as they imagine. I might answer them as Themistocles answered the Seriphian who was abusing him and saying that he was famous, not for his own merits but because he was an Athenian: "If you had been a native of my country or I of yours, neither of us would have been famous." And to those who are not rich and are impatient of old age, the same reply may be made; for to the good poor man old age cannot be a light burden, nor can a bad rich man ever have peace with himself.

May I ask, Cephalus, whether your fortune was for the most part inherited or acquired by you?

Acquired! Socrates; do you want to know how much I acquired? In the art of making money I have been midway between my father and grandfather: for my grandfather, whose name I bear, doubled and trebled the value of his patrimony, that which he inherited being much what I possess now; but my father, Lysanias, reduced the property below what it is at present; and I shall be satisfied if I leave to these my sons not less, but a little more, than I received.

That was why I asked you the question, I replied, because I see that you are indifferent about money, which is a characteristic rather of those who have inherited their fortunes than of those who have acquired them; the makers of fortunes have a second love of money as a creation of their own, resembling the affection of authors for their own poems, or of parents for their children, besides that natural love of it for the sake of use and profit which is common to them and all men. And hence they are very bad company, for they can talk about nothing but the praises of wealth.

That is true, he said.

Yes, that is very true, but may I ask another question?—What do you consider to be the greatest blessing which you have reaped from your wealth?

One, he said, of which I could not expect easily to convince others. For let me tell you, Socrates, that when a man thinks himself to be near death, fears and cares enter into his mind which he never had before; the tales of a world below and the punishment which is exacted there of deeds done here were once a laughing matter to him, but now he is tormented with the thought that they may be true: either from the weakness of age, or because he is now drawing nearer to that other place, he has a clearer view of these things; suspicions and alarms crowd thickly upon him, and he begins to reflect and consider what wrongs he has done to others. And when he finds that the sum of his transgressions is great he will many a time like a child start up in his sleep for fear, and he is filled with dark forebodings. But to him who is conscious of no sin, sweet hope, as Pindar charmingly says, is the kind nurse of his age:

> "Hope," he says, "cherishes the soul of him who lives in justice and holiness, and is the nurse of his age and the companion of his journey—hope which is mightiest to sway the restless soul of man."

How admirable are his words! And the great blessing of riches, I do not say to every man, but to a good man, is, that he has had no occasion to deceive or to defraud others, either intentionally or unintentionally; and when he departs to the world below he is not in any apprehension about offerings due to the gods or debts which he owes to men. Now to this peace of mind the possession of wealth greatly contributes; and therefore I say, that, setting one thing against another, of the many advantages which wealth has to give, to a man of sense this is in my opinion the greatest.

Well said, Cephalus, I replied; but as concerning justice, what is it?—to speak the truth and to pay your debts—no more than this? And even to this are there not exceptions? Suppose that a friend when in his right mind has deposited arms with me and he asks for them when he is not in his right mind, ought I to give them back to him? No one would say that I ought or that I should be right in doing so, any more than they would say that I ought always to speak the truth to one who is in his condition.

You are quite right, he replied.

But then, I said, speaking the truth and paying your debts is not a correct definition of justice.

Quite correct, Socrates, if Simonides is to be believed, said Polemarchus, interposing.

I fear, said Cephalus, that I must go now, for I have to look after the sacrifices, and I hand over the argument to Polemarchus and the company.

Is not Polemarchus your heir? I said.

To be sure, he answered, and went away laughing to the sacrifices.

Tell me then, O thou heir of the argument, what did Simonides say, and according to you, truly say, about justice?

He said that the repayment of a debt is just, and in saying so he appears to me to be right.

I shall be sorry to doubt the word of such a wise and inspired man, but his meaning, though probably clear to you, is the reverse of clear to me. For he certainly does not mean, as we were just now saying, that I ought to return a deposit of arms or of anything else to one who asks for it when he is not in his right senses; and yet a deposit cannot be denied to be a debt.

True.

Then when the person who asks me is not in his right mind I am by no means to make the return?

Certainly not.

When Simonides said that the repayment of a debt was justice, he did not mean to include that case?

Certainly not; for he thinks that a friend ought always to do good to a friend, and never evil.

You mean that the return of a deposit of gold which is to the injury of the receiver, if the two parties are friends, is not the repayment of a debt —that is what you would imagine him to say?

Yes.

And are enemies also to receive what we owe to them?

To be sure, he said, they are to receive what we owe them; and an enemy, as I take it, owes to an enemy that which is due or proper to him—that is to say, evil.

Simonides, then, after the manner of poets, would seem to have spoken darkly of the nature of justice; for he really meant to say that justice is the giving to each man what is proper to him, and this he termed a debt.

That must have been his meaning, he said.

By heaven! I replied; and if we asked him what due or proper thing is given by medicine, and to whom, what answer do you think that he would make to us?

He would surely reply that medicine gives drugs and meat and drink to human bodies.

And what due or proper thing is given by cookery, and to what?

Seasoning to food.

And what is that which justice gives, and to whom?

If, Socrates, we are to be guided at all by the analogy of the preceding instances, then justice is the art which gives good to friends and evil to enemies.

That is his meaning, then?

I think so.

And who is best able to do good to his friends and evil to his enemies in time of sickness?

The physician.

Or when they are on a voyage, amid the perils of the sea?

The pilot.

And in what sort of actions or with a view to what result is the just man most able to do harm to his enemy and good to his friend?

In going to war against the one and in making alliances with the other.

But when a man is well, my dear Polemarchus, there is no need of a physician?

No.

And he who is not on a voyage has no need of a pilot?

No.

Then in time of peace justice will be of no use?

I am very far from thinking so.

You think that justice may be of use in peace as well as in war?

Yes.

Like husbandry for the acquisition of corn?

Yes.

Or like shoemaking for the acquisition of shoes —that is what you mean?

Yes.

And what similar use or power of acquisition has justice in time of peace?

In contracts, Socrates, justice is of use.

And by contracts you mean partnerships?

Exactly.

But is the just man or the skilful player a more useful and better partner at a game of draughts?

The skilful player.

And in the laying of bricks and stones is the just man a more useful or better partner than the builder?

Quite the reverse.

Then in what sort of partnership is the just man a better partner than the harp-player, as in playing the harp the harp-player is certainly a better partner than the just man?

In a money partnership.

Yes, Polemarchus, but surely not in the use of money; for you do not want a just man to be your counsellor in the purchase or sale of a horse; a man who is knowing about horses would be better for that, would he not?

Certainly.

And when you want to buy a ship, the shipwright or the pilot would be better?

True.

Then what is that joint use of silver or gold in which the just man is to be preferred?

When you want a deposit to be kept safely.

You mean when money is not wanted, but allowed to lie?

Precisely.

That is to say, justice is useful when money is useless?

That is the inference.

And when you want to keep a pruning-hook safe, then justice is useful to the individual and to the State; but when you want to use it, then the art of the vine-dresser?

Clearly.

And when you want to keep a shield or a lyre, and not to use them, you would say that justice is useful; but when you want to use them, then the art of the soldier or of the musician?

Certainly.

And so of all other things—justice is useful when they are useless, and useless when they are useful?

That is the inference.

Then justice is not good for much. But let us consider this further point: Is not he who can best strike a blow in a boxing match or in any kind of fighting best able to ward off a blow?

Certainly.

And he who is most skilful in preventing or escaping from a disease is best able to create one?

True.

And he is the best guard of a camp who is best able to steal a march upon the enemy?

Certainly.

Then he who is a good keeper of anything is also a good thief?

That, I suppose, is to be inferred.

Then if the just man is good at keeping money, he is good at stealing it.

That is implied in the argument.

Then after all, the just man has turned out to be a thief. And this is a lesson which I suspect you must have learnt out of Homer; for he, speaking of Autolycus, the maternal grandfather of Odysseus, who is a favorite of his, affirms that

> "He was excellent above all men in theft and perjury."

And so, you and Homer and Simonides are agreed that justice is an art of theft; to be practised, however, "for the good of friends and for the harm of enemies"—that was what you were saying?

No, certainly not that, though I do not now know what I did say; but I still stand by the latter words.

Well, there is another question: By friends and enemies do we mean those who are so really, or only in seeming?

Surely, he said, a man may be expected to love those whom he thinks good, and to hate those whom he thinks evil.

Yes, but do not persons often err about good and evil: many who are not good seem to be so, and conversely?

That is true.

Then to them the good will be enemies and the evil will be their friends?

True.

And in that case they will be right in doing good to the evil and evil to the good?

Clearly.

But the good are just and would not do an injustice?

True.

Then according to your argument it is just to injure those who do no wrong?

Nay, Socrates; the doctrine is immoral.

Then I suppose that we ought to do good to the just and harm to the unjust?

I like that better.

But see the consequence: Many a man who is ignorant of human nature has friends who are bad friends, and in that case he ought to do harm to them; and he has good enemies whom he ought to benefit; but, if so, we shall be saying the very opposite of that which we affirmed to be the meaning of Simonides.

Very true, he said; and I think that we had better correct an error into which we seem to have fallen in the use of the words "friend" and "enemy."

What was the error, Polemarchus? I asked.

We assumed that he is a friend who seems to be or who is thought good.

And how is the error to be corrected?

We should rather say that he is a friend who is, as well as seems, good; and that he who seems only and is not good, only seems to be and is not a friend; and of an enemy the same may be said.

You would argue that the good are our friends and the bad our enemies?

Yes.

And instead of saying simply as we did at first, that it is just to do good to our friends and harm to our enemies, we should further say: It is just to do good to our friends when they are good, and harm to our enemies when they are evil?

Yes, that appears to me to be the truth.

But ought the just to injure anyone at all?

Undoubtedly he ought to injure those who are both wicked and his enemies.

When horses are injured, are they improved or deteriorated?

The latter.

Deteriorated, that is to say, in the good qualities of horses, not of dogs?

Yes, of horses.

And dogs are deteriorated in the good qualities of dogs, and not of horses?

Of course.

And will not men who are injured be deteriorated in that which is the proper virtue of man?

Certainly.

And that human virtue is justice?

To be sure.

Then men who are injured are of necessity made unjust?

That is the result.

But can the musician by his art make men unmusical?

Certainly not.

Or the horseman by his art make them bad horsemen?

Impossible.

And can the just by justice make men unjust, or speaking generally, can the good by virtue make them bad?

Assuredly not.

Any more than heat can produce cold?

It cannot.

Or drought moisture?

Clearly not.

Nor can the good harm anyone?

Impossible.

And the just is the good?

Certainly.

Then to injure a friend or anyone else is not the act of a just man, but of the opposite, who is the unjust?

I think that what you say is quite true, Socrates.

Then if a man says that justice consists in the repayment of debts, and that good is the debt which a just man owes to his friends, and evil the debt which he owes to his enemies—to say this is not wise; for it is not true, if, as has been clearly shown, the injuring of another can be in no case just.

I agree with you, said Polemarchus.

Then you and I are prepared to take up arms against anyone who attributes such a saying to Simonides or Bias or Pittacus, or any other wise man or seer?

I am quite ready to do battle at your side, he said.

Shall I tell you whose I believe the saying to be?

Whose?

I believe that Periander or Perdiccas or Xerxes or Ismenias the Theban, or some other rich and mighty man, who had a great opinion of his own power, was the first to say that justice is "doing good to your friends and harm to your enemies."

Most true, he said.

Yes, I said; but if this definition of justice also breaks down, what other can be offered?

Several times in the course of the discussion Thrasymachus had made an attempt to get the argument into his own hands, and had been put down by the rest of the company, who wanted to hear the end. But when Polemarchus and I had done speaking and there was a pause, he could no longer hold his peace; and, gathering himself up, he came at us like a wild beast, seeking to devour us. We were quite panic-stricken at the sight of him.

He roared out to the whole company: What folly, Socrates, has taken possession of you all? And why, sillybillies, do you knock under to one another? I say that if you want really to know what justice is, you should not only ask but answer, and you should not seek honor to yourself from the refutation of an opponent, but have your own answer; for there is many a one who can ask and cannot answer. And now I will not have you say that justice is duty or advantage or profit or gain or interest, for this sort of nonsense will not do for me; I must have clearness and accuracy.

I was panic-stricken at his words, and could not look at him without trembling. Indeed I believe that if I had not fixed my eye upon him, I should have been struck dumb: but when I saw his fury rising, I looked at him first, and was therefore able to reply to him.

Thrasymachus, I said, with a quiver, don't be hard upon us. Polemarchus and I may have been guilty of a little mistake in the argument, but I can assure you that the error was not intentional. If we were seeking for a piece of gold, you would not imagine that we were "knocking under to one another," and so losing our chance of finding it. And why, when we are seeking for justice, a thing more precious than many pieces of gold, do you say that we are weakly yielding to one another and not doing our utmost to get at the truth? Nay, my good friend, we are most willing and anxious to do so, but the fact is that we cannot. And if so, you people who know all things should pity us and not be angry with us.

How characteristic of Socrates! he replied, with a bitter laugh; that's your ironical style! Did I not foresee — have I not already told you, that whatever he was asked he would refuse to answer, and try irony or any other shuffle, in order that he might avoid answering?

You are a philosopher, Thrasymachus, I replied, and well know that if you ask a person what numbers make up twelve, taking care to prohibit him whom you ask from answering twice six, or three times four, or six times two, or four times three, "for this sort of nonsense will not do for me" — then obviously, if that is your way of putting the question, no one can answer you. But suppose that he were to retort: "Thrasymachus, what do you mean? If one of these numbers which you interdict be the true answer to the question, am I falsely to say some other number which is not the right one? — is that your meaning?" — How would you answer him?

Just as if the two cases were at all alike! he said.

Why should they not be? I replied; and even if they are not, but only appear to be so to the person who is asked, ought he not to say what he thinks, whether you and I forbid him or not?

I presume then that you are going to make one of the interdicted answers?

I dare say that I may, notwithstanding the danger, if upon reflection I approve of any of them.

But what if I give you an answer about justice other and better, he said, than any of these? What do you deserve to have done to you?

Done to me! — as becomes the ignorant, I must learn from the wise — that is what I deserve to have done to me.

What, and no payment! A pleasant notion!

I will pay when I have the money, I replied.

But you have, Socrates, said Glaucon: and you, Thrasymachus, need be under no anxiety about money, for we will all make a contribution for Socrates.

Yes, he replied, and then Socrates will do as he always does — refuse to answer himself, but take and pull to pieces the answer of someone else.

Why, my good friend, I said, how can anyone answer who knows, and says that he knows, just nothing; and who, even if he has some faint notions of his own, is told by a man of authority not to utter them? The natural thing is, that the speaker should be someone like yourself who professes to know and can tell what he knows. Will you then kindly answer, for the edification of the company and of myself?

Glaucon and the rest of the company joined in my request, and Thrasymachus, as anyone might see, was in reality eager to speak; for he thought that he had an excellent answer, and would distinguish himself. But at first he affected to insist on my answering; at length he consented to begin. Behold, he said, the wisdom of Socrates; he refuses to teach himself, and goes about learning of others, to whom he never even says, Thank you.

That I learn of others, I replied, is quite true; but that I am ungrateful I wholly deny. Money I have none, and therefore I pay in praise, which is all I have; and how ready I am to praise anyone who appears to me to speak well you will very soon find out when you answer; for I expect that you will answer well.

Listen, then, he said; I proclaim that justice is nothing else than the interest of the stronger. And now why do you not praise me? But of course you won't.

Let me first understand you, I replied. Justice, as you say, is the interest of the stronger. What, Thrasymachus, is the meaning of this? You cannot mean to say that because Polydamas, the pancratiast, is stronger than we are, and finds the eating of beef conducive to his bodily strength, that to eat beef is therefore equally for our good who are weaker than he is, and right and just for us?

That's abominable of you, Socrates; you take the words in the sense which is most damaging to the argument.

Not at all, my good sir, I said; I am trying to understand them; and I wish that you would be a little clearer.

Well, he said, have you never heard that forms of government differ — there are tyrannies, and there are democracies, and there are aristocracies?

Yes, I know.

And the government is the ruling power in each State?

Certainly.

And the different forms of government make laws democratical, aristocratical, tyrannical, with a view to their several interests; and these laws, which are made by them for their own interests, are the justice which they deliver to their subjects, and him who transgresses them they punish as a breaker of the law, and unjust. And that is what I mean when I say that in all States there is the same principle of justice, which is the interest of the government; and as the government must be supposed to have power, the only reasonable conclusion is that everywhere there is one principle of justice, which is the interest of the stronger.

Now I understand you, I said; and whether you are right or not I will try to discover. But let me remark that in defining justice you have yourself used the word "interest," which you forbade me to use. It is true, however, that in your definition the words "of the stronger" are added.

A small addition, you must allow, he said.

Great or small, never mind about that: we must first inquire whether what you are saying is the truth. Now we are both agreed that justice is interest of some sort, but you go on to say "of the stronger"; about this addition I am not so sure, and must therefore consider further.

Proceed.

I will; and first tell me, Do you admit that it is just for subjects to obey their rulers?

I do.

But are the rulers of States absolutely infallible, or are they sometimes liable to err?

To be sure, he replied, they are liable to err.

Then in making their laws they may sometimes make them rightly, and sometimes not?

True.

When they make them rightly, they make them agreeably to their interest; when they are mistaken, contrary to their interest; you admit that?

Yes.

And the laws which they make must be obeyed by their subjects—and that is what you call justice?

Doubtless.

Then justice, according to your argument, is not only obedience to the interest of the stronger, but the reverse?

What is that you are saying? he asked.

I am only repeating what you are saying, I believe. But let us consider: Have we not admitted that the rulers may be mistaken about their own interest in what they command, and also that to obey them is justice? Has not that been admitted?

Yes.

Then you must also have acknowledged justice not to be for the interest of the stronger, when the rulers unintentionally command things to be done which are to their own injury. For if, as you say, justice is the obedience which the subject renders to their commands, in that case, O wisest of men, is there any escape from the conclusion that the weaker are commanded to do, not what is for the interest, but what is for the injury of the stronger?

Nothing can be clearer, Socrates, said Polemarchus.

Yes, said Cleitophon, interposing, if you are allowed to be his witness.

But there is no need of any witness, said Polemarchus, for Thrasymachus himself acknowledges that rulers may sometime command what is not for their own interest, and that for subjects to obey them is justice.

Yes, Polemarchus—Thrasymachus said that for subjects to do what was commanded by their rulers is just.

Yes, Cleitophon, but he also said that justice is the interest of the stronger, and, while admitting both these propositions, he further acknowledged that the stronger may command the weaker who are his subjects to do what is not for his own interest; whence follows that justice is the injury quite as much as the interest of the stronger.

But, said Cleitophon, he meant by the interest of the stronger what the stronger thought to be his interest—this was what the weaker had to do; and this was affirmed by him to be justice.

Those were not his words, rejoined Polemarchus.

Never mind, I replied, if he now says that they are, let us accept his statement. Tell me, Thrasymachus, I said, did you mean by justice what the stronger thought to be his interest, whether really so or not?

Certainly not, he said. Do you suppose that I call him who is mistaken the stronger at the time when he is mistaken?

Yes, I said, my impression was that you did so, when you admitted that the ruler was not infallible, but might be sometimes mistaken.

You argue like an informer, Socrates. Do you mean, for example, that he who is mistaken about the sick is a physician in that he is mistaken? or that he who errs in arithmetic or grammar is an arithmetician or grammarian at the time when he is making the mistake, in respect of the mistake? True, we say that the physician or arithmetician or grammarian has made a mistake, but this is only a way of speaking; for the fact is that neither the grammarian nor any other person of skill ever makes a mistake in so far as he is what his name implies; they none of them err unless their skill fails them, and then they cease to be skilled artists. No artist or sage or ruler errs at the time when he is what his name implies; though he is commonly said to err, and I adopted the common mode of speaking. But to be perfectly accurate, since you are such a lover of accuracy, we should say that the ruler, in so far as he is a ruler, is unerring, and, being unerring, always commands that which is for his own interest; and the subject is required to execute his commands; and therefore, as I said at first and now repeat, justice is the interest of the stronger.

Indeed, Thrasymachus, and do I really appear to you to argue like an informer?

Certainly, he replied.

And do you suppose that I ask these questions with any design of injuring you in the argument?

Nay, he replied, "suppose" is not the word—I know it; but you will be found out, and by sheer force of argument you will never prevail.

I shall not make the attempt, my dear man; but to avoid any misunderstanding occurring between us in future, let me ask, in what sense do you speak of a ruler or stronger whose interest, as you were saying, he being the superior, it is just that the inferior should execute—is he a ruler in the popular or in the strict sense of the term?

In the strictest of all senses, he said. And now cheat and play the informer if you can; I ask no quarter at your hands. But you never will be able, never.

And do you imagine, I said, that I am such a madman as to try and cheat Thrasymachus? I might as well shave a lion.

Why, he said, you made the attempt a minute ago, and you failed.

Enough, I said, of these civilities. It will be better that I should ask you a question: Is the physician, taken in that strict sense of which you are speaking, a healer of the sick or a maker of money? And remember that I am now speaking of the true physician.

A healer of the sick, he replied.

And the pilot—that is to say, the true pilot—is he a captain of sailors or a mere sailor?

A captain of sailors.

The circumstance that he sails in the ship is not to be taken into account; neither is he to be called a sailor; the name pilot by which he is distinguished has nothing to do with sailing, but is significant of his skill and of his authority over the sailors.

Very true, he said.

Now, I said, every art has an interest?

Certainly.

For which the art has to consider and provide?

Yes, that is the aim of art.

And the interest of any art is the perfection of it—this and nothing else?

What do you mean?

I mean what I may illustrate negatively by the example of the body. Suppose you were to ask me whether the body is self-sufficing or has wants, I should reply: Certainly the body has wants; for the body may be ill and require to be cured, and has therefore interests to which the art of medicine ministers; and this is the origin and intention of medicine, as you will acknowledge. Am I not right?

Quite right, he replied.

But is the art of medicine or any other art faulty or deficient in any quality in the same way that the eye may be deficient in sight or the ear fail of hearing, and therefore requires another art to provide for the interests of seeing and hearing—has art in itself, I say, any similar liability to fault or defect, and does every art require another supplementary art to provide for its interests, and that another and another without end? Or have the arts to look only after their own interests? Or have they no need either of themselves or of another?—having no faults or defects, they have no need to correct them, either by the exercise of their own art or of any other; they have only to consider the interest of their subject-matter. For every art remains pure and faultless while remaining true—that is to say, while perfect and unimpaired. Take the words in your precise sense, and tell me whether I am not right.

Yes, clearly.

Then medicine does not consider the interest of medicine, but the interest of the body?

True, he said.

Nor does the art of horsemanship consider the interests of the art of horsemanship, but the interests of the horse; neither do any other arts care for themselves, for they have no needs; they care only for that which is the subject of their art?

True, he said.

But surely, Thrasymachus, the arts are the superiors and rulers of their own subjects?

To this he assented with a good deal of reluctance.

Then, I said, no science or art considers or enjoins the interest of the stronger or superior, but only the interest of the subject and weaker?

He made an attempt to contest this proposition also, but finally acquiesced.

Then, I continued, no physician, in so far as he is a physician, considers his own good in what he prescribes, but the good of his patient; for the true physician is also a ruler having the human body as a subject, and is not a mere money-maker; that has been admitted?

Yes.

And the pilot likewise, in the strict sense of the term, is a ruler of sailors, and not a mere sailor?

That has been admitted.

And such a pilot and ruler will provide and prescribe for the interest of the sailor who is under him, and not for his own or the ruler's interest?

He gave a reluctant "Yes."

Then, I said, Thrasymachus, there is no one in any rule who, in so far as he is a ruler, considers or enjoins what is for his own interest, but always what is for the interest of his subject or suitable to his art; to that he looks, and that alone he considers in everything which he says and does.

When we had got to this point in the argument, and everyone saw that the definition of justice had been completely upset, Thrasymachus, instead of replying to me, said, Tell me, Socrates, have you got a nurse?

Why do you ask such a question, I said, when you ought rather to be answering?

Because she leaves you to snivel, and never wipes your nose: she has not even taught you to know the shepherd from the sheep.

What makes you say that? I replied.

Because you fancy that the shepherd or neatherd fattens or tends the sheep or oxen with a view to their own good and not to the good of himself or his master; and you further imagine that the rulers of States, if they are true rulers, never think of their subjects as sheep, and that they are not studying their own advantage day and night. Oh, no; and so entirely astray are you in your ideas about the just and unjust as not even to know that justice and the just are in reality another's good; that is to say, the interest of the ruler and stronger, and the loss of the subject and servant; and injustice the opposite; for the unjust is lord over the truly simple and just: he is the stronger, and his subjects do what is for his interest, and minister to his happiness, which is very far from being their own. Consider further, most foolish Socrates, that the just is always a loser in comparison with the unjust. First of all, in private contracts: wherever the unjust is the partner of the just you will find that, when the partnership is dissolved, the unjust man has always more and the just less. Secondly, in their dealings with the State: when there is an income-tax, the just man will pay more and the unjust less on the same amount of income; and when there is anything to be received the one gains nothing and the other much. Observe also what happens when they take an office; there is the just man neglecting his affairs and perhaps suffering other losses, and getting nothing out of the public, because he is just; moreover he is hated by his friends and acquaintance for refusing to serve them in unlawful ways. But all this is reversed in the case of the unjust man. I am speaking, as before, of injustice on a large scale in which the advantage of the unjust is most apparent; and my meaning will be most clearly seen if we turn to that highest form of injustice in which the criminal is the happiest of men, and the sufferers or those who refuse to do injustice are the most miserable — that is to say tyranny, which by fraud and force takes away the property of others, not little by little but wholesale; comprehending in one, things sacred as well as profane, private and public; for which acts of wrong, if he were detected perpetrating any one of them singly, he would be punished and incur great disgrace — they who do such wrong in particular cases are called robbers of temples, and man-stealers and burglars and swindlers and thieves. But when a man besides taking away the money of the citizens has made slaves of them, then, instead of these names of reproach, he is termed happy and blessed, not only by the citizens but by all who hear of his having achieved the consummation of injustice. For mankind censure injustice, fearing that they may be the victims of it and not because they shrink from committing it. And thus, as I have shown, Socrates, injustice, when on a sufficient scale, has more strength and freedom and mastery than justice; and, as I said at first, justice is the interest of the stronger, whereas injustice is a man's own profit and interest.

Thrasymachus, when he had thus spoken, having, like a bathman, deluged our ears with his words, had a mind to go away. But the company would not let him; they insisted that he should remain and defend his position; and I myself added my own humble request that he would not leave us. Thrasymachus, I said to him, excellent man, how suggestive are your remarks! And are you going to run away before you have fairly taught or learned whether they are true or not? Is the attempt to determine the way of man's life so small a matter in your eyes — to determine how life may be passed by each one of us to the greatest advantage?

And do I differ from you, he said, as to the importance of the inquiry?

You appear rather, I replied, to have no care or thought about us, Thrasymachus — whether we live better or worse from not knowing what you say you know, is to you a matter of indifference. Prithee, friend, do not keep your knowledge to yourself; we are a large party; and any benefit which you confer upon us will be amply rewarded. For my own part I openly declare that I am not convinced, and that I do not believe injustice to be more gainful than justice, even if uncontrolled and allowed to have free play. For, granting that there may be an unjust man who is able to commit injustice either by fraud or force, still this does not convince me of the superior advantage of injustice, and there may be others who are in the same predicament with myself. Perhaps we may be wrong; if so, you in your wisdom should convince us that we are mistaken in preferring justice to injustice.

And how am I to convince you, he said, if you are not already convinced by what I have just said; what more can I do for you? Would you have me put the proof bodily into your souls?

Heaven forbid! I said; I would only ask you to be consistent; or, if you change, change openly and let there be no deception. For I must remark, Thrasymachus, if you will recall what was previously said, that although you began by defining the true physician in an exact sense, you did not observe a like exactness when speaking of the shepherd; you thought that the shepherd as a shepherd tends the sheep not with a view to their own good, but like a mere diner or banqueter with a view to the pleasures of the table; or, again, as a trader for sale in the market, and not as a shepherd. Yet surely the art of the shepherd is concerned only with the good of his subjects; he has only to provide the best for them, since the perfection of the art is already insured whenever all the requirements of it are satisfied. And that was what I was saying just now about the ruler. I conceived that the art of the ruler, considered as a ruler, whether in a State or in private life, could only regard the good of his flock or subjects; whereas you seem to think that the rulers in States, that is to say, the true rulers, like being in authority.

Think! Nay, I am sure of it.

Then why in the case of lesser offices do men never take them willingly without payment, unless under the idea that they govern for the advantage not of themselves but of others? Let me ask you a question: Are not the several arts different, by reason of their each having a separate function? And, my dear illustrious friend, do say what you think, that we may make a little progress.

Yes, that is the difference, he replied.

And each art gives us a particular good and not merely a general one—medicine, for example, gives us health; navigation, safety at sea, and so on?

Yes, he said.

And the art of payment has the special function of giving pay: but we do not confuse this with other arts, any more than the art of the pilot is to be confused with the art of medicine, because the health of the pilot may be improved by a sea voyage. You would not be inclined to say, would you? that navigation is the art of medicine, at least if we are to adopt your exact use of language?

Certainly not.

Or because a man is in good health when he receives pay you would not say that the art of payment is medicine?

I should not.

Nor would you say that medicine is the art of receiving pay because a man takes fees when he is engaged in healing?

Certainly not.

And we have admitted, I said, that the good of each art is specially confined to the art?

Yes.

Then, if there be any good which all artists have in common, that is to be attributed to something of which they all have the common use?

True, he replied.

And when the artist is benefited by receiving pay the advantage is gained by an additional use of the art of pay, which is not the art professed by him?

He gave a reluctant assent to this.

Then the pay is not derived by the several artists from their respective arts. But the truth is, that while the art of medicine gives health, and the art of the builder builds a house, another art attends them which is the art of pay. The various arts may be doing their own business and benefiting that over which they preside, but would the artist receive any benefit from his art unless he were paid as well?

I suppose not.

But does he therefore confer no benefit when he works for nothing?

Certainly, he confers a benefit.

Then now, Thrasymachus, there is no longer any doubt that neither arts nor governments provide for their own interests; but, as we were before saying, they rule and provide for the interests of their subjects who are the weaker and not the stronger—to their good they attend and not to the good of the superior. And this is the reason, my dear Thrasymachus, why, as I was just now saying, no one is willing to govern; because no one likes to take in hand the reformation of evils which are not his concern, without remuneration. For, in the execution of his work, and in giving his orders to another, the true artist does not regard his own interest, but always that of his subjects; and therefore in order that rulers may be willing to rule, they must be paid in one of three modes of payment, money, or honor, or a penalty for refusing.

What do you mean, Socrates? said Glaucon. The first two modes of payment are intelligible enough, but what the penalty is I do not understand, or how a penalty can be a payment.

You mean that you do not understand the nature of this payment which to the best men is the great inducement to rule? Of course you know that ambition and avarice are held to be, as indeed, they are, a disgrace?

Very true.

And for this reason, I said, money and honor have no attraction for them; good men do not wish to be openly demanding payment for governing and so to get the name of hirelings, nor by secretly helping themselves out of the public revenues to get the name of thieves. And not being ambitious they do not care about honor. Wherefore necessity must be laid upon them, and they must be induced to serve from the fear of punishment. And this, as I imagine, is the reason why the forwardness to take office, instead of waiting to be compelled, has been deemed dishonorable. Now the worst part of the punishment is that he who refuses to rule is liable to be ruled by one who is worse than himself. And the fear of this, as I conceive, induces the good to take office, not because they would, but because they cannot help — not under the idea that they are going to have any benefit or enjoyment themselves, but as a necessity, and because they are not able to commit the task of ruling to anyone who is better than themselves, or indeed as good. For there is reason to think that if a city were composed entirely of good men, then to avoid office would be as much an object of contention as to obtain office is at present; then we should have plain proof that the true ruler is not meant by nature to regard his own interest, but that of his subjects; and everyone who knew this would choose rather to receive a benefit from another than to have the trouble of conferring one. So far am I from agreeing with Thrasymachus that justice is the interest of the stronger. This latter question need not be further discussed at present; but when Thrasymachus says that the life of the unjust is more advantageous than that of the just, his new statement appears to me to be of a far more serious character. Which of us has spoken truly? And which sort of life, Glaucon, do you prefer?

I for my part deem the life of the just to be the more advantageous, he answered.

Did you hear all the advantages of the unjust which Thrasymachus was rehearsing?

Yes, I heard him, he replied, but he has not convinced me.

Then shall we try to find some way of convincing him, if we can, that he is saying what is not true?

Most certainly, he replied.

If, I said, he makes a set speech and we make another recounting all the advantages of being just, and he answers and we rejoin, there must be a numbering and measuring of the goods which are claimed on either side, and in the end we shall want judges to decide; but if we proceed in our inquiry as we lately did, by making admissions to one another, we shall unite the offices of judge and advocate in our own persons.

Very good, he said.

And which method do I understand you to prefer? I said.

That which you propose.

Well, then, Thrasymachus, I said, suppose you begin at the beginning and answer me. You say that perfect injustice is more gainful than perfect justice?

Yes, that is what I say, and I have given you my reasons.

And what is your view about them? Would you call one of them virtue and the other vice?

Certainly.

I suppose that you would call justice virtue and injustice vice?

What a charming notion! So likely too, seeing that I affirm injustice to be profitable and justice not.

What else then would you say?

The opposite, he replied.

And would you call justice vice?

No, I would rather say sublime simplicity.

Then would you call injustice malignity?

No; I would rather say discretion.

And do the unjust appear to you to be wise and good?

Yes, he said; at any rate those of them who are able to be perfectly unjust, and who have the power of subduing States and nations; but perhaps you imagine me to be talking of cut-purses. Even this profession, if undetected, has advantages, though they are not to be compared with those of which I was just now speaking.

I do not think that I misapprehend your meaning, Thrasymachus, I replied; but still I cannot hear without amazement that you class injustice with wisdom and virtue, and justice with the opposite.

Certainly I do so class them.

Now, I said, you are on more substantial and almost unanswerable ground; for if the injustice which you were maintaining to be profitable had been admitted by you as by others to be vice and deformity, an answer might have been given to you on received principles; but now I perceive that you will call injustice honorable and strong, and to the unjust you will attribute all the qualities which were attributed by us before to the just, seeing that you do not hesitate to rank injustice with wisdom and virtue.

You have guessed most infallibly, he replied.

Then I certainly ought not to shrink from going through with the argument so long as I have reason to think that you, Thrasymachus, are speaking your real mind; for I do believe that you are now in earnest and are not amusing yourself at our expense.

I may be in earnest or not, but what is that to you?—to refute the argument is your business.

Very true, I said; that is what I have to do: But will you be so good as answer yet one more question? Does the just man try to gain any advantage over the just?

Far otherwise; if he did he would not be the simple amusing creature which he is.

And would he try to go beyond just action?

He would not.

And how would he regard the attempt to gain an advantage over the unjust; would that be considered by him as just or unjust?

He would think it just, and would try to gain the advantage; but he would not be able.

Whether he would or would not be able, I said, is not to the point. My question is only whether the just man, while refusing to have more than another just man, would wish and claim to have more than the unjust?

Yes, he would.

And what of the unjust—does he claim to have more than the just man and to do more than is just?

Of course, he said, for he claims to have more than all men.

And the unjust man will strive and struggle to obtain more than the just man or action, in order that he may have more than all?

True.

We may put the matter thus, I said—the just does not desire more than his like, but more than his unlike, whereas the unjust desires more than both his like and his unlike?

Nothing, he said, can be better than that statement.

And the unjust is good and wise, and the just is neither?

Good again, he said.

And is not the unjust like the wise and good, and the just unlike them?

Of course, he said, he who is of a certain nature, is like those who are of a certain nature; he who is not, not.

Each of them, I said, is such as his like is?

Certainly, he replied.

Very good, Thrasymachus, I said; and now to take the case of the arts: you would admit that one man is a musician and another not a musician?

Yes.

And which is wise and which is foolish?

Clearly the musician is wise, and he who is not a musician is foolish.

And he is good in as far as he is wise, and bad in as far as he is foolish?

Yes.

And you would say the same sort of thing of the physician?

Yes.

And do you think, my excellent friend, that a musician when he adjusts the lyre would desire or claim to exceed or go beyond a musician in the tightening and loosening the strings?

I do not think that he would.

But he would claim to exceed the non-musician?

Of course.

And what would you say of the physician? In prescribing meats and drinks would he wish to go beyond another physician or beyond the practice of medicine?

He would not.

But he would wish to go beyond the non-physician?

Yes.

And about knowledge and ignorance in general; see whether you think that any man who has knowledge ever would wish to have the choice of saying or doing more than another man who has knowledge. Would he not rather say or do the same as his like in the same case?

That, I suppose, can hardly be denied.

And what of the ignorant? would he not desire to have more than either the knowing or the ignorant?

I dare say.

And the knowing is wise?

Yes.

And the wise is good?

True.

Then the wise and good will not desire to gain more than his like, but more than his unlike and opposite?

I suppose so.

Whereas the bad and ignorant will desire to gain more than both?

Yes.

But did we not say, Thrasymachus, that the unjust goes beyond both his like and unlike? Were not these your words?

They were.

And you also said that the just will not go beyond his like, but his unlike?

Yes.

Then the just is like the wise and good, and the unjust like the evil and ignorant?

That is the inference.

And each of them is such as his like is?

That was admitted.

Then the just has turned out to be wise and good, and the unjust evil and ignorant.

Thrasymachus made all these admissions, not fluently, as I repeat them, but with extreme reluctance; it was a hot summer's day, and the perspiration poured from him in torrents; and then I saw what I had never seen before, Thrasymachus blushing. As we were now agreed that justice was virtue and wisdom, and injustice vice and ignorance, I proceeded to another point:

Well, I said, Thrasymachus, that matter is now settled; but were we not also saying that injustice had strength — do you remember?

Yes, I remember, he said, but do not suppose that I approve of what you are saying or have no answer; if, however, I were to answer, you would be quite certain to accuse me of haranguing; therefore either permit me to have my say out, or if you would rather ask, do so, and I will answer "Very good," as they say to story-telling old women, and will nod "Yes" and "No."

Certainly not, I said, if contrary to your real opinion.

Yes, he said, I will, to please you, since you will not let me speak. What else would you have?

Nothing in the world, I said; and if you are so disposed I will ask and you shall answer.

Proceed.

Then I will repeat the question which I asked before, in order that our examination of the relative nature of justice and injustice may be carried on regularly. A statement was made that injustice is stronger and more powerful than justice, but now justice, having been identified with wisdom and virtue, is easily shown to be stronger than injustice, if injustice is ignorance; this can no longer be questioned by anyone. But I want to view the matter, Thrasymachus, in a different way: You would not deny that a State may be unjust and may be unjustly attempting to enslave other States, or may have already enslaved them, and may be holding many of them in subjection?

True, he replied; and I will add that the best and most perfectly unjust State will be most likely to do so.

I know, I said, that such was your position; but what I would further consider is, whether this power which is possessed by the superior State can exist or be exercised without justice or only with justice.

If you are right in your view, and justice is wisdom, then only with justice; but if I am right, then without justice.

I am delighted, Thrasymachus, to see you not only nodding assent and dissent, but making answers which are quite excellent.

That is out of civility to you, he replied.

You are very kind, I said; and would you have the goodness also to inform me, whether you think that a State, or an army, or a band of robbers and thieves, or any other gang of evildoers could act at all if they injured one another?

No, indeed, he said, they could not.

But if they abstained from injuring one another, then they might act together better?

Yes.

And this is because injustice creates divisions and hatreds and fighting, and justice imparts harmony and friendship; is not that true, Thrasymachus?

I agree, he said, because I do not wish to quarrel with you.

How good of you, I said; but I should like to know also whether injustice, having this tendency to arouse hatred, wherever existing, among slaves or among freemen, will not make them hate one another and set them at variance and render them incapable of common action?

Certainly.

And even if injustice be found in two only, will they not quarrel and fight, and become enemies to one another and to the just?

They will.

And suppose injustice abiding in a single person, would your wisdom say that she loses or that she retains her natural power?

Let us assume that she retains her power.

Yet is not the power which injustice exercises of such a nature that wherever she takes up her abode, whether in a city, in an army, in a family, or in any other body, that body is, to begin with, rendered incapable of united action by reason of sedition and distraction? and does it not become its own enemy and at variance with all that opposes it, and with the just? Is not this the case?

Yes, certainly.

And is not injustice equally fatal when existing in a single person—in the first place rendering him incapable of action because he is not at unity with himself, and in the second place making him an enemy to himself and the just? Is not that true, Thrasymachus?

Yes.

And, O my friend, I said, surely the gods are just?

Granted that they are.

But, if so, the unjust will be the enemy of the gods, and the just will be their friends?

Feast away in triumph, and take your fill of the argument; I will not oppose you, lest I should displease the company.

Well, then, proceed with your answers, and let me have the remainder of my repast. For we have already shown that the just are clearly wiser and better and abler than the unjust, and that the unjust are incapable of common action; nay, more, that to speak as we did of men who are evil acting at any time vigorously together, is not strictly true, for, if they had been perfectly evil, they would have laid hands upon one another; but it is evident that there must have been some remnant of justice in them, which enabled them to combine; if there had not been they would have injured one another as well as their victims; they were but half-villains in their enterprises; for had they been whole villains, and utterly unjust, they would have been utterly incapable of action. That, as I believe, is the truth of the matter, and not what you said at first. But whether the just have a better and happier life than the unjust is a further question which we also proposed to consider. I think that they have, and for the reasons which I have given; but still I should like to examine further, for no light matter is at stake, nothing less than the rule of human life.

Proceed.

I will proceed by asking a question: Would you not say that a horse has some end?

I should.

And the end or use of a horse or of anything would be that which could not be accomplished, or not so well accomplished, by any other thing?

I do not understand, he said.

Let me explain: Can you see, except with the eye?

Certainly not.

Or hear, except with the ear?

No.

These, then, may be truly said to be the ends of these organs?

They may.

But you can cut off a vine-branch with a dagger or with a chisel, and in many other ways?

Of course.

And yet not so well as with a pruning-hook made for the purpose?

True.

May we not say that this is the end of a pruning-hook?

We may.

Then now I think you will have no difficulty in understanding my meaning when I asked the question whether the end of anything would be that which could not be accomplished, or not so well accomplished, by any other thing?

I understand your meaning, he said, and assent.

And that to which an end is appointed has also an excellence? Need I ask again whether the eye has an end?

It has.

And has not the eye an excellence?

Yes.

And the ear has an end and an excellence also?

True.

And the same is true of all other things; they have each of them an end and a special excellence?

That is so.

Well, and can the eyes fulfil their end if they are wanting in their own proper excellence and have a defect instead?

How can they, he said, if they are blind and cannot see?

You mean to say, if they have lost their proper excellence, which is sight; but I have not arrived at that point yet. I would rather ask the question more generally, and only inquire whether the things which fulfil their ends fulfil them by their own proper excellence, and fail of fulfilling them by their own defect?

Certainly, he replied.

I might say the same of the ears; when deprived of their own proper excellence they cannot fulfil their end?

True.

And the same observation will apply to all other things?

I agree.

Well; and has not the soul an end which nothing else can fulfil? for example, to superintend and command and deliberate and the like. And are these functions proper to the soul, and can they rightly be assigned to any other?

To no other.

And is not life to be reckoned among the ends of the soul?

Assuredly, he said.

And has not the soul an excellence also?

Yes.

And can she or can she not fulfil her own ends when deprived of that excellence?

She cannot.

Then an evil soul must necessarily be an evil ruler and superintendent, and the good soul a good ruler?

Yes, necessarily.

And we have admitted that justice is the excellence of the soul, and injustice the defect of the soul?

That has been admitted.

Then the just soul and the just man will live well, and the unjust man will live ill?

That is what your argument proves.

And he who lives well is blessed and happy, and he who lives ill the reverse of happy?

Certainly.

Then the just is happy, and the unjust miserable?

So be it.

But happiness, and not misery, is profitable?

Of course.

Then, my blessed Thrasymachus, injustice can never be more profitable than justice.

Let this, Socrates, he said, be your entertainment at the Bendidea.

For which I am indebted to you, I said, now that you have grown gentle toward me and have left off scolding. Nevertheless, I have not been well entertained; but that was my own fault and not yours. As an epicure snatches a taste of every dish which is successively brought to table, he not having allowed himself time to enjoy the one before, so have I gone from one subject to another without having discovered what I sought at first, the nature of justice. I left that inquiry and turned away to consider whether justice is virtue and wisdom, or evil and folly; and when there arose a further question about the comparative advantages of justice and injustice, I could not refrain from passing on to that. And the result of the whole discussion has been that I know nothing at all. For I know not what justice is, and therefore I am not likely to know whether it is or is not a virtue, nor can I say whether the just man is happy or unhappy.

Study Questions

1. What, according to Cephalus, are the main advantages of wealth?
2. What is the definition of justice offered by Polemarchus, and what interpretation of this definition do Socrates and Polemarchus agree on?

3. Can it be the function of the just man to harm or do evil to anyone, according to Socrates? Explain.
4. What is Thrasymachus's original definition of justice, and to whose advantage, according to Thrasymachus, are the laws in all states?
5. How does Socrates argue against the idea that the just is to do what is for the advantage of the stronger? How does Socrates defend the idea that true rulers seek the advantage of the people they rule?
6. Explain Socrates' rejoinder to Thrasymachus's belief that the just are the most unhappy and the unjust the most happy, and that the life of the unjust man is better than that of the just.
7. Explain Socrates' response to Thrasymachus's idea that the just person is a simpleton and a fool.
8. How does Socrates refute the theory that injustice is a strong and potent thing?
9. Do the just have a better and happier life, according to Socrates? Explain why or why not.

Plato

Socrates' most famous pupil was Plato (427–347 B.C.), and Plato's most famous contribution to philosophy was his *theory of Forms*. Plato's theory of Forms is a metaphysical theory, a theory about the ultimate nature of reality.

The theory of Forms is subtle. If you're new to philosophy, you're apt to have trouble with it, unless you keep yourself open to the possibility that what exists—what is real—is *not* limited to *particulars*, things such as tables, chairs, trees, amoebas, atoms, planets, or (if you believe in them) ghosts or angels.

Let's consider two round plates. Each plate is a particular thing. But the two plates have *something in common*: roundness. The roundness, Plato said, is not some third particular. It is a Form.

The Form *roundness*, then, is what qualifies a plate, or anything else that has it, as being round. It is that which all round things have in common. Likewise the Form *beauty* is that which all beautiful things have in common, and the Form *generosity* is what all generous people have in common.

Now note again that a Form is not particular. A particular can be in only one place at a given time. You, for example, are a particular thing, and you can be only in one place at a given time. But the Form *beauty*, that which all beautiful things have in common, is present in a beautiful waterfall in Colorado and in a beautiful painting in New Haven and in a beautiful skyscraper in downtown Seattle. The Form *beauty*, therefore, is not like you or a space alien or your car. The Form *beauty* is not a particular thing, although it may be found in all things that qualify as beautiful.

Forms—The Ultimate Reality

Notice further that a particular thing is beautiful only if beauty is present in it—or, as Plato often says, only if the particular "partakes" of the Form *beauty*. The shiny red BMW in the parking lot is beautiful only to the extent that it partakes of the Form *beauty*. The reason is that the Form *beauty* is what qualifies the BMW as a beautiful thing.

According to Plato, then, this means that every beautiful particular *owes its existence as a beautiful particular* to the Form *beauty*. Thus, he concludes, the Form *beauty* has more reality than the particulars that exemplify it or partake of it.

But let's not stop here. The BMW is a car; thus, it also partakes of the Form *car* because the Form *car*, of course, is what a thing must have in order to qualify as a car. The BMW owes its existence as a beautiful car, and in fact owes its existence *as anything at all*, to the assortment of Forms that it partakes of: the Form *car*, the Form *beauty*, the Form *red*, and so forth.

Thus, according to Plato, what is *truly* real is not the particular objects we experience around us, but the various Forms that these objects exemplify, or of which they "partake." What *ultimately* is real is the Forms, not the particular objects that we encounter and that partake of the Forms.

Forms—Timeless and Unchanging

Be aware too that Plato's Forms are unchanging and hence timeless. Why? Well, the BMW may change. With sufficient change, it may indeed cease to be beautiful. But *Beauty itself* cannot cease to be beautiful. Beauty itself, the Form, cannot ever change, since to change it would cease to be what it is. And since it cannot cease to be and cannot change, it cannot grow older: It is timeless, Plato argues.

True, the BMW probably became beautiful at some point in time, probably when paint was first applied to it. But when it became beautiful, Beauty itself did not come into existence: What came into existence was the paint job that gave it beauty.

Forms—Unperceivable

Notice finally that Plato's Forms are not perceptible to the senses. At first this seems a mistake; if the BMW's beauty could not be perceived by the eye, who would be willing to buy one at the going prices? But consider the matter more carefully. What you see is not the Form *beauty*, but *that* the car is beautiful. The beauty is something you apprehend with your mind, Plato would say. Similarly, you may think you see the roundness of the plate, but what you really see is *that* the plate is round; you see *that* the plate partakes of roundness.

So a grasp of true reality, an understanding of the Forms, according to Plato, requires reason and the intellect. Indeed, according to Plato "sensible knowledge" is an oxymoron, a combination of incongruous words. What sensory experiences presents to us is mere instances of the various Forms, the mere *shadow-images* of the true reality which belongs only to the Forms and which can be apprehended only by the mind. True knowledge must have as its object true reality, and true reality—the Forms—cannot be grasped through the senses.

The Forms and Moral Philosophy

What does this have to do with moral philosophy?

According to Plato, the various Forms make up a hierarchy. (For example, the Form *beauty* is of a higher order than the Form *smelly*.) And the top Form of all, the apex of the hierarchy, is the Form *Good*, that is, pure goodness, or the Good.

Now actions and laws are ethically proper, Plato holds, only to the extent that they conform to the Form *Good*. In practice this means that we should govern ourselves by reason and the intellect (these come to the same thing, for Plato), since it is only through reason and the intellect that we gain access to the realm of Forms and the Form *Good*.

As a practical matter, then, Plato's moral philosophy enjoins us to be governed by reason, by the intellect.

It may perhaps have occurred to you to wonder, why the fuss? If Plato thinks we ought to be rational, why not just say so and spare us the metaphysics? And anyway, what specifically does it amount to, telling us to be "ruled by reason"? Does this really tell us anything *specific* about what we should and should not do?

In answer to the first question, it is his metaphysical "speculation" that marks Plato as a moral philosopher. For Plato, it isn't enough just to put forth ideas about what people should do: The Sophists and Socrates had shown that moral principles require justification. By specifying the ultimate source of all reality and value (the Form *Good*), Plato attempts to provide a justification for his moral philosophy. When we understand that ultimate reality belongs to the Forms and that the Form *Good* is the highest Form, then we must accept the ruling authority of reason, because access to the Forms is gained only through reason.

To determine what it means to be governed by reason, we have to take a brief look at Plato's psychological theory. Plato distinguishes three different elements in the human soul: raw appetites, drives, and the intellect. In the properly functioning person, the intellect is in charge and the person is, accordingly, ruled by reason. To each of the three elements there corresponds a virtue that manifests itself when each element is functioning as it should, that is, when each element is governed by reason. When reason rules our appetites, we display the virtue temperance; when it rules our drives, we display courage; and when it rules the intellect, we exhibit wisdom.

Thus, when you are ruled by reason, you will be temperate, courageous, and wise. In addition, you will be just, for justice is the virtue that results when all the elements of the soul function as they are supposed to — that is, in obedience to reason. What Plato calls "justice," therefore, is the key virtue. Indeed, in Plato's terminology, *just* and *virtuous* can be used interchangeably.

What Plato's cardinal moral principle, "Be governed by reason," dictates, therefore, is that you must possess temperance, courage, wisdom, and "justice." Only by being virtuous (that is, by being "just"), he holds, can you have a well-ordered soul and obtain psychological health and true happiness. To be virtuous is to be happy, in the theory of Plato.

Plato is very aware of the objections that might be raised to the idea that true happiness lies in being virtuous. At the end of the first book of the *Republic*, Thrasymachus challenges Socrates to explain how a virtuous ("just") life can possibly be preferable to a life of calculated self-indulgence. Thrasymachus's challenge to Socrates is then taken up in the second book of the *Republic* by the characters Glaucon and Adeimantus (in real life Plato's older brothers). Glaucon and Adeimantus make it tough for Socrates. First, Glaucon gives a powerful statement of the advantages that are enjoyed by the person who is not virtuous. (A defense of the benefits of vice over virtue more convincing than that given by Glaucon in Book II of the *Republic* has never been devised.) Next, they ask Socrates to suppose two things. Suppose, they say, that the virtuous person is not seen as virtuous by others and thus receives no recognition or praise for being virtuous. Suppose also, they say, that the *nonvir-*

tuous person completely disguises the fact that he is a base and self-serving creature and thus enjoys the benefits of selfishness without suffering the disapproval of society. Can Socrates demonstrate to them that virtue is better than vice even under these suppositions? Plato, you can see, does not want his spokesperson to be accused of having an easy target to shoot down.

Can Plato rise to the task he has set for himself? Can Socrates answer the challenge to Glaucon and Adeimantus? To do so, Socrates argues that the principles that pertain to the individual person are analogous to those that pertain to a "larger" person, namely, the state. He then considers (at some length) the principles that pertain to the state and applies them to the individual. His answer to Glaucon and Adeimantus is a long time in coming and, in fact, is not fully disclosed until Book IX of the *Republic* (although a summary version of the answer is revealed in Book IV).

In Book IX, Plato (Socrates) offers three proofs that true happiness goes hand in hand with virtue. Remember that according to Plato the individual mirrors the state. It has been established earlier in the dialogue that the best form of government is aristocracy, or "royalty"—a state governed by rational philosopher-kings. It has also been established that the most degenerate form of government is tyranny, and that tyranny emerges from what Plato calls "democracy" (by "democracy" Plato means government by an unrestrained mob). Analogously, the most virtuous individual is the person whose soul is governed by the intellect, whereas the least virtuous of individuals is the person who has a tyrannical nature. Socrates begins by considering this least virtuous of all persons and how miserable he must really be, *especially* if he actually occupies a position of power.

The third proof is a little more difficult than the first two. To understand it, recall that for Plato true reality belongs to the Forms, which are eternal and unchanging and can be apprehended only by the intellect. And don't be confused by Socrates' references to the rank order of the various forms of government. The best, as we have explained, is aristocracy or royalty, followed, in order, by timocracy (in which the ruling class is motivated by love of honor), plutocracy or oligarchy (in which the rulers primarily desire riches), democracy, and finally—at the bottom of the list—tyranny.

At the beginning of the excerpt, Socrates ("I") is speaking to Adeimantus ("he").

from the *Republic*

Plato

The *Republic*, considered one of Plato's greatest dialogues, is certainly his most famous dialogue. This is Book IX of Benjamin Jowett's translation.

Book IX
On Wrong or Right Government, and the Pleasures of Each

SOCRATES, ADEIMANTUS

Last of all comes the tyrannical man; about whom we have once more to ask, how is he formed out of the democratical? and how does he live, in happiness or in misery?

Yes, he said, he is the only one remaining.

There is, however, I said, a previous question which remains unanswered.

What question?

I do not think that we have adequately determined the nature and number of the appetites, and until this is accomplished the inquiry will always be confused.

Well, he said, it is not too late to supply the omission.

Very true, I said; and observe the point which I want to understand: Certain of the unnecessary pleasures and appetites I conceive to be unlawful; everyone appears to have them, but in some persons they are controlled by the laws and by reason, and the better desires prevail over them—either they are wholly banished or they become few and weak; while in the case of others they are stronger, and there are more of them.

Which appetites do you mean?

I mean those which are awake when the reasoning and human and ruling power is asleep; then the wild beast within us, gorged with meat or drink, starts up and, having shaken off sleep, goes forth to satisfy his desires; and there is no conceivable folly or crime—not excepting incest or any other unnatural union, or parricide, or the eating of forbidden food—which at such a time, when he has parted company with all shame and sense, a man may not be ready to commit.

Most true, he said.

But when a man's pulse is healthy and temperate, and when before going to sleep he has awakened his rational powers, and fed them on noble thoughts and inquiries, collecting himself in meditation; after having first indulged his appetites neither too much nor too little, but just enough to lay them to sleep, and prevent them and their enjoyments and pains from interfering with the higher principle—which he leaves in the solitude of pure abstraction, free to contemplate and aspire to the knowledge of the unknown, whether in past, present, or future: when again he has allayed the passionate element, if he has a quarrel against anyone—I say, when, after pacifying the two irrational principles, he rouses up the third, which is reason, before he takes his rest, then, as you know, he attains truth most nearly, and is least likely to be the sport of fantastic and lawless visions.

I quite agree.

In saying this I have been running into a digression; but the point which I desire to note is that in all of us, even in good men, there is a lawless wild-beast nature, which peers out in sleep. Pray, consider whether I am right, and you agree with me.

Yes, I agree.

And now remember the character which we attributed to the democratic man. He was supposed from his youth upward to have been trained under a miserly parent, who encouraged the saving appetites in him, but discountenanced the unnecessary, which aim only at amusement and ornament?

True.

And then he got into the company of a more refined, licentious sort of people, and taking to all their wanton ways rushed into the opposite extreme from an abhorrence of his father's meanness.

At last, being a better man than his corruptors, he was drawn in both directions until he halted midway and led a life, not of vulgar and slavish passion, but of what he deemed moderate indulgence in various pleasures. After this manner the democrat was generated out of the oligarch?

Yes, he said; that was our view of him, and is so still.

And now, I said, years will have passed away, and you must conceive this man, such as he is, to have a son, who is brought up in his father's principles.

I can imagine him.

Then you must further imagine the same thing to happen to the son which has already happened to the father: he is drawn into a perfectly lawless life, which by his seducers is termed perfect liberty; and his father and friends take part with his moderate desires, and the opposite party assist the opposite ones. As soon as these dire magicians and tyrant-makers find that they are losing their hold on him, they contrive to implant in him a master-passion, to be lord over his idle and spendthrift lusts — a sort of monstrous winged drone — that is the only image which will adequately describe him.

Yes, he said, that is the only adequate image of him.

And when his other lusts, amid clouds of incense and perfumes and garlands and wines, and all the pleasures of a dissolute life, now let loose, coming buzzing around him, nourishing to the utmost the sting of desire which they implant in his drone-like nature, then at last this lord of the soul, having Madness for the captain of his guard, breaks out into a frenzy; and if he finds in himself any good opinions or appetites in process of formation, and there is in him any sense of shame remaining, to these better principles he puts an end, and casts them forth until he has purged away temperance and brought in madness to the full.

Yes, he said, that is the way in which the tyrannical man is generated.

And is not this the reason why, of old, love has been called a tyrant?

I should not wonder.

Further, I said, has not a drunken man also the spirit of a tyrant?

He has.

And you know that a man who is deranged, and not right in his mind, will fancy that he is able to rule, not only over men, but also over the gods?

That he will.

And the tyrannical man in the true sense of the word comes into being when, either under the influence of nature or habit, or both, he becomes drunken, lustful, passionate? Of my friend, is not that so?

Assuredly.

Such is the man and such is his origin. And next, how does he live?

Suppose, as people facetiously say, you were to tell me.

I imagine, I said, at the next step in his progress, that there will be feasts and carousals and revellings and courtesans, and all that sort of thing; Love is the lord of the house within him, and orders all the concerns of his soul.

That is certain.

Yes; and every day and every night desires grow up many and formidable, and their demands are many.

They are indeed, he said.

His revenues, if he has any, are soon spent.

True.

Then come debt and the cutting down of his property.

Of course.

When he has nothing left, must not his desires, crowding in the nest like young ravens, be crying aloud for food; and he, goaded on by them, and especially by love himself, who is in a manner the captain of them, is in a frenzy, and would fain discover whom he can defraud or despoil of his property, in order that he may gratify them?

Yes, that is sure to be the case.

He must have money, no matter how, if he is to escape horrid pains and pangs.

He must.

And as in himself there was a succession of pleasures, and the new got the better of the old and took away their rights, so he being younger will claim to have more than his father and his mother, and if he has spent his own share of the property, he will take a slice of theirs.

No doubt he will.

And if his parents will not give way, then he will try first of all to cheat and deceive them.

Very true.

And if he fails, then he will use force and plunder them.

Yes, probably.

And if the old man and woman fight for their own, what then, my friend? Will the creature feel any compunction at tyrannizing over them?

Nay, he said, I should not feel at all comfortable about his parents.

But, O heavens! Adeimantus, on account of some new-fangled love of a harlot, who is anything but a necessary connection, can you believe that he would strike the mother who is his ancient friend and necessary to his very existence, and would place her under the authority of the other, when she is brought under the same roof with her; or that, under like circumstances, he would do the same to his withered old father, first and most indispensable of friends, for the sake of some newly found blooming youth who is the reverse of indispensable?

Yes, indeed, he said; I believe that he would.

Truly, then, I said, a tyrannical son is a blessing to his father and mother.

He is indeed, he replied.

He first takes their property, and when that fails, and pleasures are beginning to swarm in the hive of his soul, then he breaks into a house, or steals the garments of some nightly wayfarer; next he proceeds to clear a temple. Meanwhile the old opinions which he had when a child, and which gave judgment about good and evil, are overthrown by those others which have just been emancipated, and are now the body-guard of love and share his empire. These in his democratic days, when he was still subject to the laws and to his father, were only let loose in the dreams of sleep. But now that he is under the dominion of Love, he becomes always and in waking reality what he was then very rarely and in a dream only; he will commit the foulest murder, or eat forbidden food, or be guilty of any other horrid act. Love is his tyrant, and lives lordly in him and lawlessly, and being himself a king, leads him on, as a tyrant leads a State, to the performance of any reckless deed by which he can maintain himself and the rabble of his associates, whether those whom evil communications have brought in from without, or those whom he himself has allowed to break loose within him by reason of a similar evil nature in himself. Have we not here a picture of his way of life?

Yes, indeed, he said.

And if there are only a few of them in the State, and the rest of the people are well disposed, they go away and become the body-guard of mercenary soldiers of some other tyrant who may probably want them for a war; and if there is no war, they stay at home and do many little pieces of mischief in the city.

What sort of mischief?

For example, they are the thieves, burglars, cutpurses, foot-pads, robbers of temples, man-stealers of the community; or if they are able to speak, they turn informers and bear false witness and take bribes.

A small catalogue of evils, even if the perpetrators of them are few in number.

Yes, I said; but small and great are comparative terms, and all these things, in the misery and evil which they inflict upon a State, do not come within a thousand miles of the tyrant; when this noxious class and their followers grow numerous and become conscious of their strength, assisted by the infatuation of the people, they choose from among themselves the one who has most of the tyrant in his own soul, and him they create their tyrant.

Yes, he said, and he will be the most fit to be a tyrant.

If the people yield, well and good; but if they resist him, as he began by beating his own father and mother, so now, if he has the power, he beats them, and will keep his dear old fatherland or motherland, as the Cretans say, in subjection to his young retainers whom he has introduced to be their rulers and masters. This is the end of his passions and desires.

Exactly.

When such men are only private individuals and before they get power, this is their character; they associate entirely with their own flatterers or ready tools; or if they want anything from anybody, they in their turn are equally ready to bow down before them: they profess every sort of affection for them; but when they have gained their point they know them no more.

Yes, truly.

They are always either the masters or servants and never the friends of anybody; the tyrant never tastes of true freedom or friendship.

Certainly not.

And may we not rightly call such men treacherous?

No question.

Also they are utterly unjust, if we were right in our notion of justice?

Yes, he said, and we were perfectly right.

Let us, then, sum up in a word, I said, the character of the worst man: he is the waking reality of what we dreamed.

Most true.

And this is he who being by nature most of a tyrant bears rule, and the longer he lives the more of a tyrant he becomes.

That is certain, said Glaucon, taking his turn to answer.

And will not he who has been shown to be the wickedest, be also the most miserable? and he who has tyrannized longest and most, most continually and truly miserable; although this may not be the opinion of men in general?

Yes, he said, inevitably.

And must not the tyrannical man be like the tyrannical State, and the democratical man like the democratical State; and the same of the others?

Certainly.

And as State is to State in virtue and happiness, so is man in relation to man?

To be sure.

Then comparing our original city, which was under a king, and the city which is under a tyrant, how do they stand as to virtue?

They are the opposite extremes, he said, for one is the very best and the other is the very worst.

There can be no mistake, I said, as to which is which, and therefore I will at once inquire whether you would arrive at a similar decision about their relative happiness and misery. And here we must not allow ourselves to be panic-stricken at the apparition of the tyrant, who is only a unit and may perhaps have a few retainers about him; but let us go as we ought into every corner of the city and look all about, and then we will give our opinion.

A fair invitation, he replied; and I see, as everyone must, that a tyranny is the wretchedest form of government, and the rule of a king the happiest.

And in estimating the men, too, may I not fairly make a like request, that I should have a judge whose mind can enter into and see through human nature? he must not be like a child who looks at the outside and is dazzled at the pompous aspect which the tyrannical nature assumes to the beholder, but let him be one who has a clear insight. May I suppose that the judgment is given in the hearing of us all by one who is able to judge, and has dwelt in the same place with him, and been present at his daily life and known him in his family relations, where he may be seen stripped of his tragedy attire, and again in the hour of public danger—he shall tell us about the happiness and misery of the tyrant when compared with other men?

That again, he said, is a very fair proposal.

Shall I assume that we ourselves are able and experienced judges and have before now met with such a person? We shall then have someone who will answer our inquiries.

By all means.

Let me ask you not to forget the parallel of the individual and the State; bearing this in mind, and glancing in turn from one to the other of them, will you tell me their respective conditions?

What do you mean? he asked.

Beginning with the State, I replied, would you say that a city which is governed by a tyrant is free or enslaved?

No city, he said, can be more completely enslaved.

And yet, as you see, there are freemen as well as masters in such a State?

Yes, he said, I see that there are—a few; but the people, speaking generally, and the best of them are miserably degraded and enslaved.

Then if the man is like the State, I said, must not the same rule prevail? His soul is full of meanness and vulgarity—the best elements in him are enslaved; and there is a small ruling part, which is also the worst and maddest.

Inevitably.

And would you say that the soul of such a one is the soul of a freeman or of a slave?

He has the soul of a slave, in my opinion.

And the State which is enslaved under a tyrant is utterly incapable of acting voluntarily?

Utterly incapable.

And also the soul which is under a tyrant (I am speaking of the soul taken as a whole) is least capable of doing what she desires; there is a gadfly which goads her, and she is full of trouble and remorse?

Certainly.

And is the city which is under a tyrant rich or poor?

Poor.

And the tyrannical soul must be always poor and insatiable?

True.

And must not such a State and such a man be always full of fear?

Yes, indeed.

Is there any State in which you will find more of lamentation and sorrow and groaning and pain?

Certainly not.

And is there any man in whom you will find more of this sort of misery than in the tyrannical man, who is in a fury of passions and desires?

Impossible.

Reflecting upon these and similar evils, you held the tyrannical State to be the most miserable of States?

And I was right, he said.

Certainly, I said. And when you see the same evils in the tyrannical man, what do you say of him?

I say that he is by far the most miserable of all men.

There, I said, I think that you are beginning to go wrong.

What do you mean?

I do not think that he has as yet reached the utmost extreme of misery.

Then who is more miserable?

One of whom I am about to speak.

Who is that?

He who is of a tyrannical nature, and instead of leading a private life has been cursed with the further misfortune of being a public tyrant.

From what has been said, I gathered that you are right.

Yes, I replied, but in this high argument you should be a little more certain, and should not conjecture only; for of all questions, this respecting good and evil is the greatest.

Very true, he said.

Let me then offer you an illustration, which may, I think, throw a light upon this subject.

What is your illustration?

The case of rich individuals in cities who possess many slaves: from them you may form an idea of the tyrant's condition, for they both have slaves; the only difference is that he has more slaves.

Yes, that is the difference.

You know that they live securely and have nothing to apprehend from their servants?

What should they fear?

Nothing. But do you observe the reason of this?

Yes; the reason is, that the whole city is leagued together for the protection of each individual.

Very true, I said. But imagine one of these owners, the master say of some fifty slaves, together with his family and property and slaves, carried off by a god into the wilderness, where there are no freemen to help him—will he not be in an agony of fear lest he and his wife and children should be put to death by his slaves?

Yes, he said, he will be in the utmost fear.

The time has arrived when he will be compelled to flatter divers of his slaves, and make many promises to them of freedom and other things, much against his will—he will have to cajole his own servants.

Yes, he said, that will be the only way of saving himself.

And suppose the same god, who carried him away, to surround him with neighbors who will not suffer one man to be the master of another, and who, if they could catch the offender, would take his life?

His case will be still worse, if you suppose him to be everywhere surrounded and watched by enemies.

And is not this the sort of prison in which the tyrant will be bound—he who being by nature such as we have described, is full of all sorts of fears and lusts? His soul is dainty and greedy, and yet alone, of all men in the city, he is never allowed to go on a journey, or to see the things which other freemen desire to see, but he lives in his hole like a woman hidden in the house, and is jealous of any other citizen who goes into foreign parts and sees anything of interest.

Very true, he said.

And amid evils such as these will not he who is ill-governed in his own person—the tyrannical man, I mean—whom you just now decided to be the most miserable of all—will not he be yet more miserable when, instead of leaving a private life, he is constrained by fortune to be a public tyrant? He has to be master of others when he is not master of himself: he is like a diseased or paralytic man who is compelled to pass his life, not in retirement, but fighting and combating with other men.

Yes, he said, the similitude is most exact.

Is not his case utterly miserable? and does not the actual tyrant lead a worse life than he whose life you determined to be the worst?

Certainly.

He who is the real tyrant, whatever men may think, is the real slave, and is obliged to practise the greatest adulation and servility, and to be the flatterer of the vilest of mankind. He has desires which he is utterly unable to satisfy, and has more wants than anyone, and is truly poor, if you know how to inspect the whole soul of him: all his life long he is beset with fear and is full of convulsions and distractions, even as the State which he resembles: and surely the resemblance holds?

Very true, he said.

Moreover, as we were saying before, he grows worse from having power: he becomes and is of necessity more jealous, more faithless, more unjust, more friendless, more impious, than he was at first; he is the purveyor and cherisher of every sort of vice, and the consequence is that he is supremely miserable, and that he makes everybody else as miserable as himself.

No man of any sense will dispute your words.

Come, then, I said, and as the general umpire in theatrical contests proclaims the result, do you also decide who in your opinion is first in the scale of happiness, and who second, and in what order the others follow: there are five of them in all—they are the royal, timocratical, oligarchial, democratical, tyrannical.

The decision will be easily given, he replied; they shall be choruses coming on the stage, and I must judge them in the order in which they enter, by the criterion of virtue and vice, happiness and misery.

Need we hire a herald, or shall I announce that the son of Ariston (the best) has decided that the best and justest is also the happiest, and that this is he who is the most royal man and king over himself; and that the worst and most unjust man is also the most miserable, and that this is he who being the greatest tyrant of himself is also the greatest tyrant of his State?

Make the proclamation yourself, he said.

And shall I add, "whether seen or unseen by gods and men"?

Let the words be added.

Then this, I said, will be our first proof; and there is another, which may also have some weight.

What is that?

The second proof is derived from the nature of the soul: seeing that the individual soul, like the State, has been divided by us into three principles, the division may, I think, furnish a new demonstration.

Of what nature?

It seems to me that to these three principles three pleasures correspond; also three desires and governing powers.

How do you mean? he said.

There is one principle with which, as we were saying, a man learns, another with which he is angry; the third, having many forms, has no special name, but is denoted by the general term appetitive, from the extraordinary strength and vehemence of the desires of eating and drinking and the other sensual appetites which are the main elements of it; also money-loving, because such desires are generally satisfied by the help of money.

That is true, he said.

If we were to say that the loves and pleasures of this third part were concerned with gain, we should then be able to fall back on a single notion; and might truly and intelligibly describe this part of the soul as loving gain or money.

I agree with you.

Again, is not the passionate element wholly set on ruling and conquering and getting fame?

True.

Suppose we call it the contentious or ambitious—would the term be suitable?

Extremely suitable.

On the other hand, everyone sees that the principle of knowledge is wholly directed to the truth, and cares less than either of the others for gain or fame.

Far less.

"Lover of wisdom," "lover of knowledge," are titles which we may fitly apply to that part of the soul?

Certainly.

One principle prevails in the souls of one class of men, another in others, as may happen?

Yes.

Then we may begin by assuming that there are three classes of men—lovers of wisdom, lovers of honor, lovers of gain?

Exactly.

And there are three kinds of pleasure, which are their several objects?

Very true.

Now, if you examine the three classes of men, and ask of them in turn which of their lives is pleasantest, each will be found praising his own and depreciating that of others: the money-maker will contrast the vanity of honor or of learning if they bring no money with the solid advantages of gold and silver?

True, he said.

And the lover of honor—what will be his opinion? Will he not think that the pleasure of riches is vulgar, while the pleasure of learning, if it brings no distinction, is all smoke and nonsense to him?

Very true.

And are we to suppose, I said, that the philosopher sets any value on other pleasures in comparison with the pleasure of knowing the truth, and in that pursuit abiding, ever learning, not so far indeed from the heaven of pleasure? Does he not call the other pleasures necessary, under the idea that if there were no necessity for them, he would rather not have them?

There can be no doubt of that, he replied.

Since, then, the pleasures of each class and the life of each are in dispute, and the question is not which life is more or less honorable, or better or worse, but which is the more pleasant or painless—how shall we know who speaks truly?

I cannot myself tell, he said.

Well, but what ought to be the criterion? Is any better than experience, and wisdom, and reason?

There cannot be a better, he said.

Then, I said, reflect. Of the three individuals, which has the greatest experience of all the pleasures which we enumerated? Has the lover of gain, in learning the nature of essential truth, greater experience of the pleasure of knowledge than the philosopher has of the pleasure of gain?

The philosopher, he replied, has greatly the advantage; for he has of necessity always known the taste of the other pleasures from his childhood upward: but the lover of gain in all his experience has not of necessity tasted—or, I should rather say, even had he desired, could hardly have tasted—the sweetness of learning and knowing truth.

Then the lover of wisdom has a great advantage over the lover of gain, for he has a double experience?

Yes, very great.

Again, has he greater experience of the pleasures of honor, or the lover of honor of the pleasures of wisdom?

Nay, he said, all three are honored in proportion as they attain their object; for the rich man and the brave man and the wise man alike have their crowd of admirers, and as they all receive honor they all have experience of the pleasures of honor; but the delight which is to be found in the knowledge of true being is known to the philosopher only.

His experience, then, will enable him to judge better than anyone?

Far better.

And he is the only one who has wisdom as well as experience?

Certainly.

Further, the very faculty which is the instrument of judgment is not possessed by the covetous or ambitious man, but only by the philosopher?

What faculty?

Reason, with whom, as we were saying, the decision ought to rest.

Yes.

And reasoning is peculiarly his instrument?

Certainly.

If wealth and gain were the criterion, then the praise or blame of the lover of gain would surely be the most trustworthy?

Assuredly.

Of if honor, or victory, or courage, in that case the judgment of the ambitious or pugnacious would be the truest?

Clearly.

But since experience and wisdom and reason are the judges—

The only inference possible, he replied, is that pleasures which are approved by the lover of wisdom and reason are the truest.

And so we arrive at the result, that the pleasure of the intelligent part of the soul is the pleasantest of the three, and that he of us in whom this is the ruling principle has the pleasantest life.

Unquestionably, he said, the wise man speaks with authority when he approves of his own life.

And what does the judge affirm to be the life which is next, and the pleasure which is next?

Clearly that of the soldier and lover of honor; who is nearer to himself than the money-maker.

Last comes the lover of gain?

Very true, he said.

Twice in succession, then, has the just man overthrown the unjust in this conflict; and now comes the third trial, which is dedicated to Olympian Zeus the saviour: a sage whispers in my ear that no pleasure except that of the wise is quite true and pure—all others are a shadow only; and surely this will prove the greatest and most decisive of falls?

Yes, the greatest; but will you explain yourself?

I will work out the subject and you shall answer my questions.

Proceed.

Say, then, is not pleasure opposed to pain?

True.

And there is a neutral state which is neither pleasure nor pain?

There is.

A state which is intermediate, and a sort of repose of the soul about either—that is what you mean?

Yes.

You remember what people say when they are sick?

What do they say?

That after all nothing is pleasanter than health. But then they never knew this to be the greatest of pleasures until they were ill.

Yes, I know, he said.

And when persons are suffering from acute pain, you must have heard them say that there is nothing pleasanter than to get rid of their pain?

I have.

And there are many other cases of suffering in which the mere rest and cessation of pain, and not any positive enjoyment, are extolled by them as the greatest pleasure?

Yes, he said; at the time they are pleased and well content to be at rest.

Again, when pleasure ceases, that sort of rest or cessation will be painful?

Doubtless, he said.

Then the intermediate state of rest will be pleasure and will also be pain?

So it would seem.

But can that which is neither become both?

I should say not.

And both pleasure and pain are motions of the soul, are they not?

Yes.

But that which is neither was just now shown to be rest and not motion, and in a mean between them?

Yes.

How, then, can we be right in supposing that the absence of pain is pleasure, or that the absence of pleasure is pain?

Impossible.

This, then, is an appearance only, and not a reality; that is to say, the rest is pleasure at the moment and in comparison of what is painful, and painful in comparison of what is pleasant; but all these representations, when tried by the test of true pleasure, are not real, but a sort of imposition?

That is the inference.

Look at the other class of pleasures which have no antecedent pains and you will no longer suppose, as you perhaps may at present, that pleasure is only the cessation of pain, or pain of pleasure.

What are they, he said, and where shall I find them?

There are many of them: take as an example, the pleasures of smell, which are very great and have no antecedent pains; they come in a moment, and when they depart leave no pain behind them.

Most true, he said.

Let us not, then, be induced to believe that pure pleasure is the cessation of pain, or pain of pleasure.

No.

Still, the more numerous and violent pleasures which reach the soul through the body are generally of this sort—they are reliefs of pain.

That is true.

And the anticipations of future pleasures and pains are of a like nature?

Yes.

Shall I give you an illustration of them?

Let me hear.

You would allow, I said, that there is in nature an upper and lower and middle region?

I should.

And if a person were to go from the lower to the middle region, would he not imagine that he is going up; and he who is standing in the middle and sees whence he has come, would imagine that he is already in the upper region, if he has never seen the true upper world?

To be sure, he said; how can he think otherwise?

But if he were taken back again he would imagine, and truly imagine, that he was descending?

No doubt.

All that would arise out of his ignorance of the true upper and middle and lower regions?

Yes.

Then can you wonder that persons who are inexperienced in the truth, as they have wrong ideas about many other things, should also have wrong ideas about pleasure and pain and the intermediate state; so that when they are only being drawn toward the painful they feel pain and think the pain which they experience to be real, and in like manner, when drawn away from pain to the neutral or intermediate state, they firmly believe that they have reached the goal of satiety and pleasure; they, not knowing pleasure, err in contrasting pain with the absence of pain, which is like contrasting black with gray instead of white—can you wonder, I say, at this?

No, indeed; I should be much more disposed to wonder at the opposite.

Look at the matter thus: Hunger, thirst, and the like, are inanitions of the bodily state?

Yes.

And ignorance and folly are inanitions of the soul?

True.

And food and wisdom are the corresponding satisfactions of either?

Certainly.

And is the satisfaction derived from that which has less or from that which has more existence the truer?

Clearly, from that which has more.

What classes of things have a greater share of pure existence, in your judgment—those of which food and drink and condiments and all kinds of sustenance are examples, or the class which contains true opinion and knowledge and mind and all the different kinds of virtue? Put the question in this way: Which has a more pure being—that which is concerned with the invariable, the immortal, and the true, and is of such a nature, and is found in such natures; or that which is concerned with and found in the variable and mortal, and is itself variable and mortal?

Far purer, he replied, is the being of that which is concerned with the invariable.

And does the essence of the invariable partake of knowledge in the same degree as of essence?

Yes, of knowledge in the same degree.

And of truth in the same degree?

Yes.

And, conversely, that which has less of truth will also have less of essence?

Necessarily.

Then, in general, those kinds of things which are in the service of the body have less of truth and essence than those which are in the service of the soul?

Far less.

And has not the body itself less of truth and essence than the soul?

Yes.

What is filled with more real existence, and actually has a more real existence, is more really filled than which is filled with less existence and is less real?

Of course.

And if there be a pleasure in being filled with that which is according to nature, that which is more really filled with more real being will more really and truly enjoy true pleasure; whereas that which participates in less real being will be less truly and surely satisfied, and will participate in an illusory and less real pleasure?

Unquestionably.

Those, then, who know not wisdom and virtue, and are always busy with gluttony and sensuality, go down and up again as far as the mean; and in this region they move at random throughout life, but they never pass into the true upper world; thither they neither look, nor do they ever find their way, neither are they truly filled with true being, nor do they taste of pure and abiding pleasure. Like cattle, with their eyes always looking down and their heads stooping to the earth, that is, to the dining-table, they fatten and feed and breed, and, in their excessive love of these delights, they kick and butt at one another with horns and hoofs which are made of iron; and they kill one another by reason of their insatiable lust. For they fill themselves with that which is not substantial, and the part of themselves which they fill is also unsubstantial and incontinent.

Verily, Socrates, said Glaucon, you describe the life of the many like an oracle.

Their pleasures are mixed with pains—how can they be otherwise? For they are mere shadows and pictures of the true, and are colored by contrast, which exaggerates both light and shade, and so they implant in the minds of fools insane desires of themselves; and they are fought about as Stesichorus says that the Greeks fought about the shadow of Helen at Troy, in ignorance of the truth.

Something of that sort must inevitably happen.

And must not the like happen with the spirited or passionate element of the soul? Will not the passionate man who carries his passion into action, be in the like case, whether he is envious and ambitious, or violent and contentious, or angry and discontented, if he be seeking to attain honor and victory and the satisfaction of his anger without reason or sense?

Yes, he said, the same will happen with the spirited element also.

Then may we not confidently assert that the lovers of money and honor, when they seek their pleasures under the guidance and in the company of reason and knowledge, and pursue after and win the pleasures which wisdom shows them, will also have the truest pleasures in the highest degree which is attainable to them, inasmuch as they follow truth; and they will have the pleasures which are natural to them, if that which is best for each one is also most natural to him?

Yes, certainly; the best is the most natural.

And when the whole soul follows the philosophical principle, and there is no division, the several parts are just, and do each of them their own business, and enjoy severally the best and truest pleasures of which they are capable?

Exactly.

But when either of the two other principles prevails, it fails in attaining its own pleasure, and compels the rest to pursue after a pleasure which is a shadow only and which is not their own?

True.

And the greater the interval which separates them from philosophy and reason, the more strange and illusive will be the pleasure?

Yes.

And is not that farthest from reason which is at the greatest distance from law and order?

Clearly.

And the lustful and tyrannical desires are, as we saw, at the greatest distance?

Yes.

And the royal and orderly desires are nearest?

Yes.

Then the tyrant will live at the greatest distance from true or natural pleasure, and the king at the least?

Certainly.

But if so, the tyrant will live most unpleasantly, and the king most pleasantly?

Inevitably.

Would you know the measure of the interval which separates them?

Will you tell me?

There appear to be three pleasures, one genuine and two spurious: now the transgression of the tyrant reaches a point beyond the spurious; he has run away from the region of law and reason, and taken up his abode with certain slave pleasures which are his satellites, and the measure of his inferiority can only be expressed in a figure.

How do you mean?

I assume, I said, that the tyrant is in the third place from the oligarch; the democrat was in the middle?

Yes.

And if there is truth in what has preceded, he will be wedded to an image of pleasure which is thrice removed as to truth from the pleasure of the oligarch?

He will.

And the oligarch is third from the royal; since we count as one royal and aristocratical?

Yes, he is third.

Then the tyrant is removed from true pleasure by the space of a number which is three times three?

Manifestly.

The shadow, then, of tyrannical pleasure determined by the number of length will be a plane figure.

Certainly.

And if you raise the power and make the plane a solid, there is no difficulty in seeing how vast is the interval by which the tyrant is parted from the king.

Yes; the arithmetician will easily do the sum.

Or if some person begins at the other end and measures the interval by which the king is parted from the tyrant in truth of pleasure, he will find him, when the multiplication is completed, living 729 times more pleasantly, and the tyrant more painfully by this same interval.

What a wonderful calculation! And how enormous is the distance which separates the just from the unjust in regard to pleasure and pain!

Yet a true calculation, I said, and a number which nearly concerns human life, if human beings are concerned with days and nights and months and years.

Yes, he said, human life is certainly concerned with them.

Then if the good and just man be thus superior in pleasure to the evil and unjust, his superiority will be infinitely greater in propriety of life and in beauty and virtue?

Immeasurably greater.

Well, I said, and now having arrived at this stage of the argument, we may revert to the words which brought us hither: Was not someone saying that injustice was a gain to the perfectly unjust who was reputed to be just?

Yes, that was said.

Now, then, having determined the power and quality of justice and injustice, let us have a little conversation with him.

What shall we say to him?

Let us make an image of the soul, that he may have his own words presented before his eyes.

Of what sort?

An ideal image of the soul, like the composite creations of ancient mythology, such as the Chimera, or Scylla, or Cerberus, and there are many others in which two or more different natures are said to grow into one.

There are said to have been such unions.

Then do you now model the form of a multitudinous, many-headed monster, having a ring of heads of all manner of beasts, tame and wild, which he is able to generate and metamorphose at will.

You suppose marvellous powers in the artist; but, as language is more pliable than wax or any similar substance, let there be such a model as you propose.

Suppose now that you make a second form as of a lion, and a third of a man, the second smaller than the first, and the third smaller than the second.

That, he said, is an easier task; and I have made them as you say.

And now join them, and let the three grow into one.

That has been accomplished.

Next fashion the outside of them into a single image, as of a man, so that he who is not able to look within, and sees only the outer hull, may believe the beast to be a single human creature.

I have done so, he said.

And now, to him who maintains that it is profitable for the human creature to be unjust, and unprofitable to be just, let us reply that, if he be right, it is profitable for this creature to feast the multitudinous monster and strengthen the lion and the lion-like qualities, but to starve and weaken the man, who is consequently liable to be dragged about at the mercy of either of the other two; and he is not to attempt to familiarize or harmonize them with one another—he ought rather to suffer them to fight, and bite and devour one another.

Certainly, he said; that is what the approver of injustice says.

To him the supporter of justice makes answer that he should ever so speak and act as to give the man within him in some way or other the most complete mastery over the entire human creature. He should watch over the many-headed monster like a good husbandman, fostering and cultivating the gentle qualities, and preventing the wild ones from growing; he should be making the lion-heart his ally, and in common care of them all should be uniting the several parts with one another and with himself.

Yes, he said, that is quite what the maintainer of justice will say.

And so from every point of view, whether of pleasure, honor, or advantage, the approver of justice is right and speaks the truth, and the disapprover is wrong and false and ignorant?

Yes, from every point of view.

Come, now, and let us gently reason with the unjust, who is not intentionally in error. "Sweet sir," we will say to him, "what think you of things esteemed noble and ignoble? Is not the noble that which subjects the beast to the man, or rather to the god in man? and the ignoble that which subjects the man to the beast?" He can hardly avoid saying, Yes—can he, now?

Not if he has any regard for my opinion.

But, if he agree so far, we may ask him to answer another question: "Then how would a man profit if he received gold and silver on the condition that he was to enslave the noblest part of him to the worst? Who can imagine that a man who sold his son or daughter into slavery for money, especially if he sold them into the hands of fierce and evil men, would be the gainer, however large might be the sum which he received? And will anyone say that he is not a miserable caitiff who remorselessly sells his own divine being to that which is most godless and detestable? Eriphyle took the necklace as the price of her husband's life, but he is taking a bribe in order to compass a worse ruin."

Yes, said Glaucon, far worse—I will answer for him.

Has not the intemperate been censured of old, because in him the huge multiform monster is allowed to be too much at large?

Clearly.

And men are blamed for pride and bad temper when the lion and serpent element in them disproportionately grows and gains strength?

Yes.

And luxury and softness are blamed, because they relax and weaken this same creature, and make a coward of him?

Very true.

And is not a man reproached for flattery and meanness who subordinates the spirited animal to the unruly monster, and, for the sake of money, of which he can never have enough, habituates him in the days of his youth to be trampled in the mire, and from being a lion to become a monkey?

True, he said.

And why are mean employments and manual arts a reproach? Only because they imply a natural weakness of the higher principle; the individual is unable to control the creatures within him, but has to court them, and his great study is how to flatter them.

Such appears to be the reason.

And therefore, being desirous of placing him under a rule like that of the best, we say that he ought to be the servant of the best, in whom the Divine rules; not, as Thrasymachus supposed, to the injury of the servant, but because everyone had better be ruled by divine wisdom dwelling within him; or, if this be impossible, then by an external authority, in order that we may be all, as far as possible, under the same government, friends and equals.

True, he said.

And this is clearly seen to be the intention of the law, which is the ally of the whole city; and is seen also in the authority which we exercise over children, and the refusal to let them be free until we have established in them a principle analogous to the constitution of a State, and by cultivation of this higher element have set up in their hearts a guardian and ruler like our own, and when this is done they may go their ways.

Yes, he said, the purpose of the law is manifest.

From what point of view, then, and on what ground can we say that a man is profited by injustice or intemperance or other baseness, which will make him a worse man, even though he acquire money or power by his wickedness?

From no point of view at all.

What shall he profit, if his injustice be undetected and unpunished? He who is undetected only gets worse, whereas he who is detected and punished has the brutal part of his nature silenced and humanized; the gentler element in him is liberated, and his whole soul is perfected and ennobled by the acquirement of justice and temperance and wisdom, more than the body ever is by receiving gifts of beauty, strength, and health, in proportion as the soul is more honorable than the body.

Certainly, he said.

To this nobler purpose the man of understanding will devote the energies of his life. And in the first place, he will honor studies which impress these qualities on his soul, and will disregard others?

Clearly, he said.

In the next place, he will regulate his bodily habit and training, and so far will he be from yielding to brutal and irrational pleasures, that he will regard even health as quite a secondary matter; his first object will be not that he may be fair or strong or well, unless he is likely thereby to gain temperance, but he will always desire so to attemper the body as to preserve the harmony of the soul?

Certainly he will, if he has true music in him.

And in the acquisition of wealth there is a principle of order and harmony which he will also observe; he will not allow himself to be dazzled by the foolish applause of the world, and heap up riches to his own infinite harm?

Certainly not, he said.

He will look at the city which is within him, and take heed that no disorder occur in it, such as might arise either from superfluity or from want; and upon this principle he will regulate his property and gain or spend according to his means.

Very true.

And, for the same reason, he will gladly accept and enjoy such honors as he deems likely to make him a better man; but those, whether private or public, which are likely to disorder his life, he will avoid?

Then, if that is his motive, he will not be a statesman.

By the dog of Egypt, he will! in the city which is his own he certainly will, though in the land of his birth perhaps not, unless he have a divine call.

I understand; you mean that he will be a ruler in the city of which we are the founders, and which exists in idea only; for I do not believe that there is such a one anywhere on earth?

In heaven, I replied, there is laid up a pattern of it, methinks, which he who desires may behold, and beholding, may set his own house in order. But whether such a one exists, or ever will exist in fact, is no matter; for he will live after the manner of that city, having nothing to do with any other.

I think so, he said.

Study Questions

1. Explain why Socrates maintains that the person who is most evil will be the most miserable, and why the person who is the tyrant the longest time is the longest in misery.
2. What are the three forms of pleasure, according to Socrates? Why is the philosopher's opinion about pleasure the most reliable?
3. Explain why Socrates believes that people whose souls are governed by their intellect are the happiest.

Aristotle

According to Plato, you'll recall, human activity is morally praiseworthy to the extent that it exemplies or partakes of goodness, that is, partakes of the Form *Good.* Likewise, the human soul or psyche is well-ordered (good) to the extent that it exemplifies or partakes of the Form *Good*, which it does when it is governed by reason. Thus, what defines all moral value, for Plato, is a single Form, something that is distinct from and apart from the world and its inhabitants. Aristotle was Plato's student, but his moral philosophy is different from his teacher's, especially in its theoretical underpinnings.

Our Highest Good: Happiness

Aristotle's moral philosophy, like Plato's, is closely related to his metaphysics. Think back to Plato's Forms, ideal entities that exist separately from this world. Aristotle lays heavy criticism on Plato's theory. There is no separate realm of forms, Aristotle maintains. What is real is individual things—plants, people, rocks, and so forth—and each individual thing is a combination of matter and some particular form. Robert Stewart, for example, is matter in the form of a man. If this matter had an entirely different form, then Stewart would not be a man but something else—a spider, maybe. But neither Stewart's form nor his matter are found in separation from one another or in isolation, according to Aristotle.

According to Aristotle, what determines a thing's form is its objective, or what Aristotle refers to as its "final cause." Why is this thing here before us a screwdriver? Well, it is a screwdriver because it has the form of a screwdriver and not the form of (say) a chisel, and it has that form because its objective is to screw and unscrew screws and not to chisel. Likewise, what is good for a thing depends on its objective. Given what a screwdriver is supposed to do, it isn't good to chisel with it.

The same principle applies to the human being. What is good for the human animal depends on the fundamental objective of human existence. What is the human animal's fundamental objective, or good? According to Aristotle, it is that which we desire for its own sake and not as a means to something else. And, he claims, there is in fact only one thing we seek for its own sake: happiness. True, we do seem to seek other things for their own sake, such as pleasure, for example. But pleasure, Aristotle figures, is really just an ingredient of happiness. Happiness is our highest good.

Let's be more specific about what Aristotle believes happiness consists in. Since humans are rational organisms, human happiness consists in two things, one belonging to the organism side and one belonging to the rational side. First, as living organisms we have biological needs whose fulfillment brings us pleasure or enjoyment. So, our happiness consists in part in enjoyment or pleasure—but only in part. For we are also rational; indeed, our *ergon*, or basic function, is to reason. Consequently, our happiness also consists in part in developing and exercising our capacity to reason.

Since our capacity to reason distinguishes us from other animals, it is especially important to develop and exercise it, Aristotle holds. When we exercise our capacity to reason, we may be said to be virtuous. Thus, happiness is (in effect) "activity in accordance with virtue." When we use our capacity to reason to acquire understanding and enlightenment, we are intellectually virtuous; when we use our capacity to reason to moderate and temper our drives and appetites—that is, to find the mean between extremes—we are morally virtuous.

The bulk of Aristotle's most important work in ethics, the *Nicomachean Ethics*, is dedicated to analyzing specific moral virtues as the mean between extremes. For instance, courage is the mean between fearing nothing (foolhardiness) and fearing everything (cowardice).

In a way, Aristotle's findings do not seem very different from Plato's, until you look carefully at the underlying philosophy. Aristotle and Plato both are less concerned with the question "What ought one do?" than with the question "What kind of person ought one be?" Both, that is to say, emphasize the importance of traits of character, the importance of being virtuous. And both would agree on the nature of many virtues; certainly both favor the intellectual life. But Plato grounds his moral philosophy on the idea that there exists an ideal Form *Good*, which exists apart from the natural world in a realm of external and unchanging Forms. Aristotle grounds his moral philosophy simply on human nature: What is goodness for us is fixed by our natural highest objective.

Aristotle also emphasizes (more so than Plato) that virtue is a matter of habit. A chisel that is sometimes sharp and sometimes dull does not achieve its objective very well; similarly, if we are rational only sporadically, we don't fill our human objective very well. Connected with this idea that the virtuous person acts in the right way as a matter of habit is another observation Aristotle makes: that a person's character is revealed by what he or she finds pleasure in. "He who faces danger with pleasure, or, at any rate, without pain, is courageous," Aristotle notes.

But even more important, Aristotle (again unlike Plato), believes that having a virtuous soul does not guarantee that you will have happiness. According to Aristotle, happiness requires that certain conditions be met, including being well-born, good-looking, healthy, free, reasonably well-to-do, and accepted by your community. We must also note that another prerequisite to happiness, according to Aristotle, is being a male.

The following selection consists of excerpts from Aristotle's *Nicomachean Ethics.* In Book I, Aristotle explains what goodness for humans consists in; in Book II, he addresses the moral virtues.

from the *Nicomachean Ethics*

Aristotle

Aristotle, Plato's most famous student, lived from 384 B.C. to 322 B.C. Reprinted here are Books I and II of Aristotle's *Nicomachean Ethics*, translated by F. H. Peters.

Book I. The End.

1. Every art and every kind of inquiry, and likewise every act and purpose, seems to aim at some good: and so it has been well said that the good is that at which everything aims.

But a difference is observable among these aims or ends. What is aimed at is sometimes the exercise of a faculty, sometimes a certain result beyond that exercise. And where there is an end beyond the act, there the result is better than the exercise of the faculty.

Now since there are many kinds of actions and many arts and sciences, it follows that there are many ends also; *e.g.* health is the end of medicine, ships of shipbuilding, victory of the art of war, and wealth of economy.

But when several of these are subordinated to some one art or science, — as the making of bridles and other trappings to the art of horsemanship, and this in turn, along with all else that the soldier does, to the art of war, and so on, — then the end of the master-art is always more desired than the ends of the subordinate arts, since these are pursued for its sake. And this is equally true whether the end in view be the mere exercise of a faculty or something beyond that, as in the above instances.

2. If then in what we do there be some end which we wish for on its own account, choosing all the others as means to this, but not every end without exception as a means to something else (for so we should go on *ad infinitum*, and desire would be left void and objectless), — this evidently will be the good or the best of all things. And surely from a practical point of view it much concerns us to know this good; for then, like archers shooting at a definite mark, we shall be more likely to attain what we want.

If this be so, we must try to indicate roughly what it is, and first of all to which the arts or sciences it belongs.

It would seem to belong to the supreme art or science, that one which most of all deserves the name of master-art or master-science.

Now Politics seems to answer to this description. For it prescribes which of the sciences a state needs, and which each man shall study, and up to what point; and to it we see subordinated even the highest arts, such as economy, rhetoric, and the art of war.

Since then it makes use of the other practical sciences, and since it further ordains what men are to do and from what to refrain, its end must include the ends of the others, and must be the proper good of man.

For though this good is the same for the individual and the state, yet the good of the state seems a grander and more perfect thing both to attain and to secure; and glad as one would be to do this service for a single individual, to do it for a people and for a number of states is nobler and more divine.

This then is the aim of the present inquiry, which is a sort of political inquiry.

3. We must be content if we can attain to so much precision in our statement as the subject before us admits of; for the same degree of accuracy is no more to be expected in all kinds of reasoning than in all kinds of handicraft.

Now the things that are noble and just (with which Politics deals) are so various and so uncertain, that some think these are merely conventional and not natural distinctions.

There is a similar uncertainty also about what is good, because good things often do people harm: men have before now been ruined by wealth, and have lost their lives through courage.

Our subject, then, and our data being of this nature, we must be content if we can indicate the truth roughly and in outline, and if, in dealing with matters that are not amenable to immutable laws, and reasoning from premises that are but probable, we can arrive at probable conclusions.

The reader, on his part, should take each of my statements in the same spirit; for it is the mark of an educated man to require, in each kind of inquiry, just so much exactness as the subject admits of: it is equally absurd to accept probable reasoning from a mathematician, and to demand scientific proof from an orator.

But each man can form a judgment about what he knows, and is called "a good judge" of that—of any special matter when he has received a special education therein, "a good judge" (without any qualifying epithet) when he has received a universal education. And hence a young man is not qualified to be a student of Politics; for he lacks experience of the affairs of life, which form the data and the subject-matter of Politics.

Further, since he is apt to be swayed by his feelings, he will derive no benefit from a study whose aim is not speculative but practical.

But in this respect young in character counts the same as young in years; for the young man's disqualification is not a matter of time, but is due to the fact that feeling rules his life and directs all his desires. Men of this character turn the knowledge they get to no account in practice, as we see with those we call incontinent; but those who direct their desires and actions by reason will gain much profit from the knowledge of these matters.

So much then by way of preface as to the student, and the spirit in which he must accept what we say, and the object which we propose to ourselves.

4. Since—to resume—all knowledge and all purpose aims at some good, what is this which we say is the aim of Politics; or, in other words, what is the highest of all realizable goods?

As to its name, I suppose nearly all men are agreed; for the masses and the men of culture alike declare that it is happiness, and hold that to "live well" or to "do well" is the same as to be "happy."

But they differ as to what this happiness is, and the masses do not give the same account of it as the philosophers.

The former take it to be something palpable and plain, as pleasure or wealth or fame; one man holds it to be this, and another that, and often the same man is of different minds at different times,—after sickness it is health, and in poverty it is wealth; while when they are impressed with the consciousness of their ignorance, they admire most those who say grand things that are above their comprehension.

Some philosophers, on the other hand, have thought that, beside these several good things, there is an "absolute" good which is the cause of their goodness.

As it would hardly be worth while to review all the opinions that have been held, we will confine ourselves to those which are most popular, or which seem to have some foundation in reason.

But we must not omit to notice the distinction that is drawn between the method of proceeding from your starting-points or principles, and the method of working up to them. Plato used with fitness to raise this question, and to ask whether the right way is from or to your starting-points, as in the race-course you may run from the judges to the boundary, or *vice versa.*

Well, we must start from what is known.

But "what is known" may mean two things: "what is known to us," which is one thing, or "what is known" simply, which is another.

I think it is safe to say that *we* must start from what is known to *us.*

And on this account nothing but a good moral training can qualify a man to study what is noble and just—in a word, to study questions of Politics. For the undemonstrated fact is here the starting point, and if this undemonstrated fact be sufficiently evident to a man, he will not require a "reason why." Now the man who has had a good moral training either has already arrived at starting-points or principles of action, or will easily accept them when pointed out. But he who neither has them nor will accept them may hear what Hesiod says—

> "The best is he who of himself doth know;
> Good too is he who listens to the wise;
> But he who neither knows himself nor heeds
> The words of others, is a useless man."

5. Let us now take up the discussion at the point from which we digressed.

It seems that men not unreasonably take their notions of the good or happiness from the lives actually led, and that the masses who are the least refined suppose it to be pleasure, which is the reason why they aim at nothing higher than the life of enjoyment.

For the most conspicuous kinds of life are three: this life of enjoyment, the life of the statesman, and, thirdly, the contemplative life.

The mass of men show themselves utterly slavish in their preference for the life of brute beasts, but their views receive consideration because many of those in high places have the tastes of Sardanapalus.

Men of refinement with a practical turn prefer honour; for I suppose we may say that honour is the aim of the statesman's life.

But this seems too superficial to be the good we are seeking: for it appears to depend upon those who give rather than upon those who receive it; while we have a presentiment that the good is something that is peculiarly a man's own and can scarce be taken away from him.

Moreover, these men seem to pursue honour in order that they may be assured of their own excellence—at least, they wish to be honoured by men of sense, and by those who know them, and on the ground of their virtue or excellence. It is plain, then, that in their view, at any rate, virtue or excellence is better than honour; and perhaps we should take this to be the end of the statesman's life, rather than honour.

But virtue or excellence also appears too incomplete to be what we want; for it seems that a man might have virtue and yet be asleep or be inactive all his life, and, moreover, might meet with the greatest disasters and misfortunes; and no one would maintain that such a man is happy, except for argument's sake. But we will not dwell on these matters now, for they are sufficiently discussed in the popular treatises.

The third kind of life is the life of contemplation: we will treat of it further on.

As for the money-making life, it is something quite contrary to nature; and wealth evidently is not the good of which we are in search, for it is merely useful as a means to something else. So we might rather take pleasure and virtue or excellence to be ends than wealth; for they are chosen on their own account. But it seems that not even they are the end, though much breath has been wasted in attempts to show that they are.

6. Dismissing these views, then, we have now to consider the "universal good," and to state the difficulties which it presents; though such an inquiry is not a pleasant task in view of our friendship for the authors of the doctrine of ideas. But we venture to think that this is the right course, and that in the interests of truth we ought to sacrifice even what is nearest to us, especially as we call ourselves philosophers. Both are dear to us, but it is a sacred duty to give the preference to truth.

In the first place, the authors of this theory themselves did not assert a common idea in the case of things of which one is prior to the other; and for this reason they did not hold one common idea of numbers. Now the predicate good is applied to substances and also to qualities and relations. But that which has independent existence, what we call "substance," is logically prior to that which is relative; for the latter is an offshoot as it were, or [in logical language] an accident of a thing or substance. So [by their own showing] there cannot be one common idea of these goods.

Secondly, the term good is used in as many different ways as the term "is" or "being:" we apply the term to substances or independent existences, as God, reason; to qualities, as the virtues; to quantity, as the moderate or due amount; to relatives, as the useful; to time, as opportunity; to place, as habitation, and so on. It is evident, therefore, that the word good cannot stand for one and the same notion in all these various applications; for if it did, the term could not be applied in all the categories, but in one only.

Thirdly, if the notion were one, since there is but one science of all the things that come under one idea, there would be but one science of all goods; but as it is, there are many sciences even of the goods that come under one category; as, for instance, the science which deals with opportunity in war is strategy, but in disease is medicine; and the science of the due amount in the matter of food is medicine, but in the matter of exercise is the science of gymnastic.

Fourthly, one might ask what they mean by the "absolute:" in "absolute man" and "man" the word "man" has one and the same sense; for in respect of manhood there will be no difference between them; and if so, neither will there be any difference in respect of goodness between "absolute good" and "good."

Fifthly, they do not make the good any more good by making it eternal; a white thing that lasts a long while is no whiter than what lasts but a day.

There seems to be more plausibility in the doctrine of the Pythagoreans, who [in their table of opposites] place the one on the same side with the good things [instead of reducing all goods to unity]; and even Speusippus* seems to follow them in this.

However, these points may be reserved for another occasion; but objection may be taken to what I have said on the ground that the Platonists do not speak in this way of all goods indiscriminately, but hold that those that are pursued and welcomed on their own account are called good by reference to one common form or type, while those things that tend to produce or preserve these goods, or to prevent their opposites, are called good only as means to these, and in a different sense.

It is evident that there will thus be two classes of goods: one good in themselves, the other good as means to the former. Let us separate then from the things that are merely useful those that are good in themselves, and inquire if they are called good by reference to one common idea or type.

Now what kind of things would one call "good in themselves"?

Surely those things that we pursue even apart from their consequences, such as wisdom and sight and certain pleasures and certain honours; for although we sometimes pursue these things as means, no one could refuse to rank them among the things that are good in themselves.

If these be excluded, nothing is good in itself except the idea; and then the type or form will be meaningless.

If however, these are ranked among the things that are good in themselves, then it must be shown that the goodness of all of them can be defined in the same terms, as white has the same meaning when applied to snow and to white lead.

But, in fact, we have to give a separate and different account of the goodness of honour and wisdom and pleasure.

Good, then, is not a term that is applied to all these things alike in the same sense or with reference to one common idea or form.

But how then do these things come to be called good? for they do not appear to have received the same name by chance merely. Perhaps it is because they all proceed from one source, or all conduce to one end; or perhaps it is rather in virtue of some analogy, just as we call the reason the eye of the soul because it bears the same relation to the soul that the eye does to the body, and so on.

But we may discuss these questions at present; for to discuss them in detail belongs more properly to another branch of philosophy.

And for the same reason we may dismiss the further consideration of the idea; for even granting that this term good, which is applied to all these different things, has one and the same meaning throughout, or that there is an absolute good apart from these particulars, it is evident that this good will not be anything that man can realize or attain: but it is a good of this kind that we are now seeking.

It might, perhaps, be thought that it would nevertheless be well to make ourselves acquainted with this universal good, with a view to the goods that are attainable and realizable. With this for a pattern, it may be said, we shall more readily discern our own good, and discerning achieve it.

There certainly is some plausibility in this argument, but it seems to be at variance with the existing sciences; for though they are all aiming at some good and striving to make up their deficiencies, they neglect to inquire about this universal good. And yet it is scarce likely that the professors of the several arts and sciences should not know, nor even look for, what would help them so much.

And indeed I am at a loss to know how the weaver or the carpenter would be furthered in his art by a knowledge of this absolute good, or how a man would be rendered more able to heal the sick or to command an army by contemplation of the pure form or idea. For it seems to me that the

*Plato's nephew and successor.

physician does not even seek for health in this abstract way, but seeks for the health of man, or rather of some particular man, for it is individuals that he has to heal.

7. Leaving these matters, then, let us return once more to the question, what this good can be of which we are in search.

It seems to be different in different kinds of action and in different arts, — one thing in medicine and another in war, and so on. What then is the good in each of these cases? Surely that for the sake of which all else is done. And that in medicine is health, in war is victory, in building is a house, — a different thing in each different case, but always, in whatever we do and in whatever we choose, the end. For it is always for the sake of the end that all else is done.

If then there be one end of all that man does, this end will be the realizable good, — or these ends, if there be more than one.

By this generalization our argument is brought to the same point as before. This point we must try to explain more clearly.

We see that there are many ends. But some of these are chosen only as means, as wealth, flutes, and the whole class of instruments. And so it is plain that not all ends are final.

But the best of all things must, we conceive, be something final.

If then there be only one final end, this will be what we are seeking, — or if there be more than one, then the most final of them.

Now that which is pursued as an end in itself is more final than that which is pursued as means to something else, and that which is never chosen as means than that which is chosen both as an end in itself and as means, and that is strictly final which is always chosen as an end in itself and never as means.

Happiness seems more than anything else to answer to this description: for we always choose it for itself, and never for the sake of something else; while honour and pleasure and reason, and all virtue or excellence, we choose partly indeed for themselves (for, apart from any result, we should choose each of them), but partly also for the sake of happiness, supposing that they will help to make us happy. But no one chooses happiness for the sake of these things, or as a means to anything else at all.

We seem to be led to the same conclusion when we start from the notion of self-sufficiency.

The final good is thought to be self-sufficing [or all-sufficing]. In applying this term we do not regard a man as an individual leading a solitary life, but we also take account of parents, children, wife, and, in short, friends and fellow-citizens generally, since man is naturally a social being. Some limit must indeed be set to this; for if you go on to parents and descendants and friends of friends, you will never come to a stop. But this we will consider further on: for the present we will take self-sufficing to mean what by itself makes life desirable and in want of nothing. And happiness is believed to answer to this description.

And further, happiness is believed to be the most desirable thing in the world, and that not merely as one among other good things: if it were merely one among other good things [so that other things could be added to it], it is plain that the addition of the least of other goods must make it more desirable; for the addition becomes a surplus of good, and of two goods the greater is always more desirable.

Thus it seems that happiness is something final and self-sufficing, and is the end of all that man does.

But perhaps the reader thinks that though no one will dispute the statement that happiness is the best thing in the world, yet a still more precise definition of it is needed.

This will best be gained, I think, by asking, What is the function of man? For as the goodness and the excellence of a piper or a sculptor, or the practiser of any art, and generally of those who have any function or business to do, lies in that function, so man's good would seem to lie in his function, if he has one.

But can we suppose that, while a carpenter and a cobbler has a function and a business of his own, man has no business and no function assigned him by nature? Nay, surely as his several members, eye and hand and foot, plainly have each his own function, so we must suppose that man also has some function over and above all these.

What then is it?

Life evidently he has in common even with the plants, but we want that which is peculiar to him. We must exclude, therefore, the life of mere nutrition and growth.

Next to this comes the life of sense; but this too he plainly shares with horses and cattle and all kinds of animals.

There remains then the life whereby he acts—the life of his rational nature, with its two sides or divisions, one rational as obeying reason, the other rational as having and exercising reason.

But as this expression is ambiguous, we must be understood to mean thereby the life that consists in the exercise of the faculties; for this seems to be more properly entitled to the name.

The function of man, then, is exercise of his vital faculties [or soul] on one side in obedience to reason, and on the other side with reason.

But what is called the function of a man of any profession and the function of a man who is good in that profession are generically the same, *e.g.* of a harper and of a good harper; and this holds in all cases without exception, only that in the case of the latter his superior excellence at his work is added; for we say a harper's function is to harp, and a good harper's to harp well.

(Man's function then being, as we say, a kind of life—that is to say, exercise of his faculties and action of various kinds with reason—the good man's function is to do this well and beautifully [or nobly]. But the function of anything is done well when it is done in accordance with the proper excellence of that thing.)

If this be so the result is that the good of man is exercise of his faculties in accordance with excellence or virtue, or, if there be more than one, in accordance with the best and most complete virtue.

But there must also be a full term of years for this exercise; for one swallow or one fine day does not make a spring, nor does one day or any small space of time make a blessed or happy man.

This, then, may be taken as a rough outline of the good; for this, I think, is the proper method,—first to sketch the outline, and then to fill in the details. But it would seem that, the outline once fairly drawn, any one can carry on the work and fit in the several items which time reveals to us or helps us to find. And this indeed is the way in which the arts and sciences have grown; for it requires no extraordinary genius to fill up the gaps.

We must bear in mind, however, what was said above, and not demand the same degree of accuracy in all branches of study, but in each case so much as the subject-matter admits of and as is proper to that kind of inquiry. The carpenter and the geometer both look for the right angle, but in different ways: The former only wants such an approximation to it as his work requires, but the latter wants to know what constitutes a right angle, or what is its special quality; his aim is to find out the truth. And so in other cases we must follow the same course, lest we spend more time on what is immaterial than on the real business in hand.

Nor must we in all cases alike demand the reason why; sometimes it is enough if the undemonstrated fact be fairly pointed out, as in the case of the starting-points or principles of a science. Undemonstrated facts always form the first step or starting-point of a science; and these starting-points or principles are arrived at some in one way, some in another—some by induction, others by perception, others again by some kind of training. But in each case we must try to apprehend them in the proper way, and do our best to define them clearly; for they have great influence upon the subsequent course of an inquiry. A good start is more than half the race, I think, and our starting-point or principle, once found, clears up a number of our difficulties.

8. We must not be satisfied, then, with examining this starting-point or principle of ours as a conclusion from our data, but must also view it in its relation to current opinions on the subject; for all experience harmonizes with a true principle, but a false one is soon found to be incompatible with the facts.

Now, good things have been divided into three classes, external goods on the one hand, and on the other goods of the soul and goods of the body; and the goods of the soul are commonly said to be goods in the fullest sense, and more good than any other.

But "actions and exercises of the vital faculties or soul" may be said to be "of the soul." So our account is confirmed by this opinion, which is both of long standing and approved by all who busy themselves with philosophy.

But, indeed, we secure the support of this opinion by the mere statement that certain actions and exercises are the end; for this implies that it is to be ranked among the goods of the soul, and not among external goods.

Our account, again, is in harmony with the common saying that the happy man lives well and does well; for we may say that happiness, according to us, is living well and doing well.

And, indeed, all the characteristics that men expect to find in happiness seem to belong to happiness as we define it.

Some hold it to be virtue or excellence, some prudence, others a kind of wisdom; others, again, hold it to be all or some of these, with the addition of pleasure, either as an ingredient or as a necessary accompaniment; and some even include external prosperity in their account of it.

Now, some of these views have the support of many voices and of old authority; others have few voices, but those of weight; but it is probable that neither the one side nor the other is entirely wrong, but that in some one point at least, if not in most, they are both right.

First, then, the view that happiness is excellence or a kind of excellence harmonizes with our account; for "exercise of faculties in accordance with excellence" belongs to excellence.

But I think we may say that it makes no small difference whether the good be conceived as the mere possession of something, or as its use — as a mere habit or trained faculty, or as the exercise of that faculty. For the habit or faculty may be present, and yet issue in no good result, as when a man is asleep, or in any other way hindered from his function; but with its exercise this is not possible, for it must show itself in acts and in good acts. And as at the Olympic games it is not the fairest and strongest who receive the crown, but those who contend (for among these are the victors), so in life, too, the winners are those who not only have the excellences, but manifest these in deed.

And, further, the life of these men is in itself pleasant. For pleasure is an affection of the soul, and each man takes pleasure in that which he is said to love, — he who loves horses in horses, he who loves sight-seeing in sight-seeing, and in the same way he who loves justice in acts of justice, and generally the lover of excellence or virtue in virtuous acts or the manifestation of excellence.

And while with most men there is a perpetual conflict between the several things in which they find pleasure, since these are not naturally pleasant, those who love what is noble take pleasure in that which is naturally pleasant. For the manifestations of excellence are naturally pleasant, so that they are both pleasant to them and pleasant in themselves.

Their life, then, does not need pleasure to be added to it as an appendage, but contains pleasure in itself.

Indeed, in addition to what we have said, a man is not good at all unless he takes pleasure in noble deeds. No one would call a man just who did not take pleasure in doing justice, nor generous who took no pleasure in acts of generosity, and so on.

If this be so, the manifestations of excellence will be pleasant in themselves. But they are also both good and noble, and that in the highest degree — at least, if the good man's judgment about them is right, for this is his judgment.

Happiness, then, is at once the best and noblest and pleasantest thing in the world, and these are not separated, as the Delian inscription would have them to be: —

> "What is most just is noblest, health is best,
> Pleasantest is to get your heart's desire."

For all these characteristics are united in the best exercises of our faculties; and these, or some one of them that is better than all the others, we identify with happiness.

But nevertheless happiness plainly requires external goods too, as we said; for it is impossible, or at least not easy, to act nobly without some furniture of fortune. There are many things that can only be done through instruments, so to speak, such as friends and wealth and political influence: and there are some things whose absence takes the bloom off our happiness, as good birth, the blessing of children, personal beauty; for a man is not very likely to be happy if he is very ugly in person, or of low birth, or alone in the world, or childless, and perhaps still less if he has worthless children or friends, or has lost good ones that he had.

As we said, then, happiness seems to stand in need of this kind of prosperity; and so some identify it with good fortune, just as others identify it with excellence.

9. This has led people to ask whether happiness is attained by learning, or the formation of habits, or any other kind of training, or comes by some divine dispensation or even by chance.

Well, if the Gods do give gifts to men, happiness is likely to be among the number, more likely, indeed, than anything else, in proportion as it is better than all other human things.

This belongs more properly to another branch of inquiry; but we may say that even if it is not heaven-sent, but comes as a consequence of virtue or some kind of learning or training, still it seems to be one of the most divine things in the world; for the prize and aim of virtue would appear to be better than anything else and something divine and blessed.

Again, if it is thus acquired it will be widely accessible; for it will then be in the power of all except those who have lost the capacity for excellence to acquire it by study and diligence.

And if it be better that men should attain happiness in this way rather than by chance, it is reasonable to suppose that it is so, since in the sphere of nature all things are arranged in the best possible way, and likewise in the sphere of art, and of each mode of causation, and most of all in the sphere of the noblest mode of causation. And indeed it would be too absurd to leave what is noblest and fairest to the dispensation of chance.

But our definition itself clears up the difficulty; for happiness was defined as a certain kind of exercise of the vital faculties in accordance with excellence or virtue. And of the remaining goods [other than happiness itself], some must be present as necessary conditions, while others are aids and useful instruments to happiness. And this agrees with what we said at starting. We then laid down that the end of the art political is the best of all ends; but the chief business of that art is to make the citizens of a certain character—that is, good and apt to do what is noble. It is not without reason, then, that we do not call an ox, or a horse, or any brute happy; for none of them is able to share in this kind of activity.

For the same reason also a child is not happy; he is as yet, because of his age, unable to do such things. If we ever call a child happy, it is because we hope he will do them. For, as we said, happiness requires not only perfect excellence or virtue, but also a full term of years for its exercise. For our circumstances are liable to many changes and to all sorts of chances, and it is possible that he who is now most prosperous will in his old age meet with great disasters, as is told of Priam in the tales of Troy; and a man who is thus used by fortune and comes to a miserable end cannot be called happy.

10. Are we, then, to call no man happy as long as he lives, but to wait for the end, as Solon said?

And, supposing we have to allow this, do we mean that he actually is happy after he is dead? Surely that is absurd, especially for us who say that happiness is a kind of activity or life.

But if we do not call the dead man happy, and if Solon meant not this, but that only then could we safely apply the term to a man, as being now beyond the reach of evil and calamity, then here too we find some ground for objection. For it is thought that both good and evil may in some sort befall a dead man (just as they may befall a living man, although he is unconscious of them), *e.g.* honours rendered to him, or the reverse of these, and again the prosperity or the misfortune of his children and all his descendants.

But this, too, has its difficulties; for after a man has lived happily to a good old age, and ended as he lived, it is possible that many changes may befall him in the persons of his descendants, and that some of them may turn out good and meet with the good fortune they deserve, and others the reverse. It is evident too that the degree in which the descendants are related to their ancestors may vary to any extent. And it would be a strange thing if the dead man were to change with these changes and become happy and miserable by turns. But it would also be strange to suppose that the dead are not affected at all, even for a limited time, by the fortunes of their posterity.

But let us return to our former question; for its solution will, perhaps, clear up this other difficulty.

The saying of Solon may mean that we ought to look for the end and then call a man happy, not because he now is, but because he once was happy.

But surely it is strange that when he is happy we should refuse to say what is true of him, because we do not like to apply the term to living men in view of the changes to which they are liable, and because we hold happiness to be something that endures and is little liable to change, while the fortunes of one and the same man often undergo many revolutions: for, it is argued, it is plain that, if we follow the changes of fortune, we shall call the same man happy and miserable many times over, making the happy man "a sort of chameleon and one who rests on no sound foundation."

We reply that it cannot be right thus to follow fortune. For it is not in this that our weal or woe lies; but, as we said, though good fortune is needed to complete man's life, yet it is the excellent employment of his powers that constitutes his happiness, as the reverse of this constitutes his misery.

But the discussion of this difficulty leads to a further confirmation of our account. For nothing human is so constant as the excellent exercise of our faculties. The sciences themselves seem to be less abiding. And the highest of these exercises are the most abiding, because the happy are occupied with them most of all and most continuously (for this seems to be the reason why we do not forget how to do them).

The happy man, then, as we define him, will have this required property of permanence, and all through life will preserve his character; for he will be occupied continually, or with the least possible interruption, in excellent deeds and excellent speculations; and, whatever his fortune be, he will take it in the noblest fashion, and bear himself always and in all things suitably, since he is truly good and "foursquare without a flaw."

But the dispensations of fortune are many, some great, some small. The small ones, whether good or evil, plainly are of no weight in the scale; but the great ones, when numerous, will make life happier if they be good; for they help to give a grace to life themselves, and their use is noble and good; but, if they be evil, will enfeeble and spoil happiness; for they bring pain, and often impede the exercise of our faculties.

But nevertheless true worth shines out even here, in the calm endurance of many great misfortunes, not through insensibility, but through nobility and greatness of soul. And if it is what a man does that determines the character of his life, as we said, then no happy man will become miserable; for he will never do what is hateful and base. For we hold that the man who is truly good and wise will bear with dignity whatever fortune sends, and will always make the best of his circumstances, as a good general will turn the forces at his command to the best account, and a good shoemaker will make the best shoe that can be made out of a given piece of leather, and so on with all other crafts.

If this be so, the happy man will never become miserable, though he will not be truly happy if he meets with the fate of Priam.

But yet he is not unstable and lightly changed: he will not be moved from his happiness easily, nor by any ordinary misfortunes, but only by many heavy ones; and after such, he will not recover his happiness again in a short time, but if at all, only in a considerable period, which has a certain completeness, and in which he attains to great and noble things.

We shall meet all objections, then, if we say that a happy man is "one who exercises his faculties in accordance with perfect excellence, being duly furnished with external goods, not for any chance time, but for a full term of years:" to which perhaps we should add, "and who shall continue to live so, and shall die as he lived," since the future is veiled to us, but happiness we take to be the end and in all ways perfectly final or complete.

If this be so, we may say that those living men are blessed or perfectly happy who both have and shall continue to have these characteristics, but happy as men only.

11. Passing now from this question to that of the fortunes of descendants and of friends generally, the doctrine that they do not affect the

departed at all seems too cold and too much opposed to popular opinion. But as the things that happen to them are many and differ in all sorts of ways, and some come home to them more and some less, so that to discuss them all separately would be a long, indeed an endless task, it will perhaps be enough to speak of them in general terms and in outline merely.

Now, as of the misfortunes that happen to a man's self, some have a certain weight and influence on his life, while others are of less moment, so is it also with what happens to any of his friends. And, again, it always makes much more difference whether those who are affected by an occurrence are alive or dead than it does whether a terrible crime in a tragedy be enacted on the stage or merely supposed to have already taken place. We must therefore take these differences into account, and still more, perhaps, the fact that it is a doubtful question whether the dead are at all accessible to good and ill. For it appears that even if anything that happens, whether good or evil, does come home to them, yet it is something unsubstantial and slight to them if not in itself; or if not that, yet at any rate its influence is not of that magnitude or nature that it can make happy those who are not, or take away their happiness from those that are.

It seems then — to conclude — that the prosperity, and likewise the adversity, of friends does affect the dead, but not in such a way or to such an extent as to make the happy unhappy, or to do anything of the kind.

12. These points being settled, we may now inquire whether happiness is to be ranked among the goods that we praise, or rather among those that we revere; for it is plainly not a mere potentiality, but an actual good.

What we praise seems always to be praised as being of a certain quality and having a certain relation to something. For instance, we praise the just and the courageous man, and generally the good man, and excellence or virtue, because of what they do or produce; and we praise also the strong or the swift-footed man, and so on, because he has a certain gift or faculty in relation to some good and admirable thing.

This is evident if we consider the praises bestowed on the Gods. The Gods are thereby made ridiculous by being made relative to man; and this happens because, as we said, a thing can only be praised in relation to something else.

If, then, praise be proper to such things as we mentioned, it is evident that to do the best things is due, not praise, but something greater and better, as our usage shows; for the Gods we call blessed and happy, and "blessed" is the term we apply to the most god-like men.

And so with good things: no one praises happiness as he praises justice, but calls it blessed, as something better and more divine.

On these grounds Eudoxus is thought to have based a strong argument for the claims of pleasure to the first prize: for he maintained that the fact that it is not praised, though it is a good thing, shows that it is higher than the goods we praise, as God and the good are higher; for these are the standards by reference to which we judge all other things, — giving praise to excellence or virtue, since it makes us apt to do what is noble, and passing encomiums on the results of virtue, whether these be bodily or psychical.

But to refine on these points belongs more properly to those who have made a study of the subject of encomiums; for us it is plain from what has been said that happiness is one of the gods which we revere and count as final.

And this further seems to follow from the fact that it is a starting-point or principle: for everything we do is always done for its sake; but the principle and cause of all good we hold to be something divine and worthy of reverence.

13. Since happiness is an exercise of the vital faculties in accordance with perfect virtue or excellence, we will now inquire about virtue or excellence; for this will probably help us in our inquiry about happiness.

And indeed the true statesman seems to be especially concerned with virtue, for he wishes to make the citizens good and obedient to the laws. Of this we have an example in the Cretan and the Lacedæmonian lawgivers, and any others who have resembled them. But if the inquiry belongs to Politics or the science of the state, it is plain that it will be in accordance with our original purpose to pursue it.

The virtue or excellence that we are to consider is, of course, the excellence of man; for it is the good of man and the happiness of man that we started to seek. And by the excellence of man I mean excellence not of body, but of soul; for happiness we take to be an activity of the soul.

If this be so, then it is evident that the statesman must have some knowledge of the soul, just as the man who is to heal the eye or the whole body must have some knowledge of them, and that the more in proportion as the science of the state is higher and better than medicine. But all educated physicians take much pains to know about the body.

As statesmen [or students of Politics], then we must inquire into the nature of the soul, but in so doing we must keep our special purpose in view and go only so far as that requires; for to go into minuter detail would be too laborious for the present undertaking.

Now, there are certain doctrines about the soul which are stated elsewhere with sufficient precision, and these we will adopt.

Two parts of the soul are distinguished, an irrational and a rational part.

Whether these are separated as are the parts of the body or any divisible thing, or whether they are only distinguishable in thought but in fact inseparable, like concave and convex in the circumference of a circle, makes no difference for our present purpose.

Of the irrational part, again, one division seems to be common to all things that live, and to be possessed by plants—I mean that which causes nutrition and growth; for we must assume that all things that take nourishment have a faculty of this kind, even when they are embryos, and have the same faculty when they are full grown; at least, this is more reasonable than to suppose that they then have a different one.

The excellence of this faculty, then, is plainly one that man shares with other beings, and not specifically human.

And this is confirmed by the fact that in sleep this part of the soul, or this faculty, is thought to be most active, while the good and the bad man are undistinguishable when they are asleep (whence the saying that for half their lives there is no difference between the happy and the miserable; which indeed is what we should expect; for sleep is the cessation of the soul from those functions in respect of which it is called good or bad), except that they are to some slight extent roused by what goes on in their bodies, with the result that the dreams of the good man are better than those of ordinary people.

However, we need not pursue this further, and may dismiss the nutritive principle, since it has no place in the excellence of man.

But there seems to be another vital principle that is irrational, and yet in some way partakes of reason. In the case of the continent and of the incontinent man alike we praise the reason or the rational part, for it exhorts them rightly and urges them to do what is best; but there is plainly present in them another principle besides the rational one, which fights and struggles against the reason. For just as a paralyzed limb, when you will to move it to the right, moves on the contrary to the left, so is it with the soul; the incontinent man's impulses run counter to his reason. Only whereas we see the refractory member in the case of the body, we do not see it in the case of the soul. But we must nevertheless, I think, hold that in the soul too there is something beside the reason, which opposes and runs counter to it (though in what sense it is distinct from the reason does not matter here).

It seems, however, to partake of reason also, as we said: at least, in the continent man it submits to the reason; while in the temperate and courageous man we may say it is still more obedient; for in him it is altogether in harmony with the reason.

The irrational part, then, it appears, is twofold. There is the vegetative faculty, which has no share of reason; and the faculty of appetite or of desire in general, which in a manner partakes of reason or is rational as listening to reason and submitting to its sway,—rational in the sense in which we speak of rational obedience to father or friends, not in the sense in which we speak of rational apprehension of mathematical truths. But all advice and all rebuke and exhortation testify that the irrational part is in some way amenable to reason.

If then we like to say that this part, too, has a share of reason, the rational part also will have two divisions: one rational in the strict sense as possessing reason in itself, the other rational as listening to reason as a man listens to his father.

Now, on this division of the faculties is based the division of excellence; for we speak of intellectual excellences and of moral excellences; wisdom and understanding and prudence we call intellectual, liberality and temperance we call moral virtues or excellences. When we are speaking of a man's moral character we do not say that he is wise or intelligent, but that he is gentle or temperate. But we praise the wise man, too, for his habit of mind or trained faculty; and a habit or trained faculty that is praiseworthy is what we call an excellence or virtue.

from the *Nicomachean Ethics*

Aristotle

Book II. Moral Virtue.

1. Excellence, then, being of these two kinds, intellectual and moral, intellectual excellence owes its birth and growth mainly to instruction, and so requires time and experience, while moral excellence is the result of habit or custom. . . .

From this it is plain that none of the moral excellences or virtues is implanted in us by nature; for that which is by nature cannot be altered by training. For instance, a stone naturally tends to fall downwards, and you could not train it to rise upwards, though you tried to do so by throwing it up ten thousand times, nor could you train fire to move downward, nor accustom anything which naturally behaves in one way to behave in any other way.

The virtues, then, come neither by nature nor against nature, but nature gives the capacity for acquiring them, and this is developed by training.

Again, where we do things by nature we get the power first, and put this power forth in act afterwards: as we plainly see in the case of the senses; for it is not by constantly seeing and hearing that we acquire those faculties, but, on the contrary, we had the power first and then used it, instead of acquiring the power by the use. But the virtues we acquire by doing the acts, as is the case with the arts too. We learn an art by doing that which we wish to do when we have learned it; we become builders by building, and harpers by harping. And so by doing just acts we become just, and by doing acts of temperance and courage we become temperate and courageous.

This is attested, too, by what occurs in states; for the legislators make their citizens good by training; *i.e.* this is the wish of all legislators, and those who do not succeed in this miss their aim, and it is this that distinguishes a good from a bad constitution.

Again, both the moral virtues and the corresponding vices result from and are formed by the same acts; and this is the case with the arts also. It is by harping that good harpers and bad harpers alike are produced: and so with builders and the rest; by building well they will become good builders, and bad builders by building badly. Indeed, if it were not so, they would not want anybody to teach them, but would all be born either good or bad at their trades. And it is just the same with the virtues also. It is by our conduct in our intercourse with other men that we become just or unjust, and by acting in circumstances of danger, and training ourselves to feel fear or confidence, that we become courageous or cowardly. So, too, with our animal appetites and the passion of anger; for by behaving in this way or in that on the occasions with which these passions are concerned, some become temperate and gentle, and others profligate and ill-tempered. In a word, acts of any kind produce habits of characters of the same kind.

Hence we ought to make sure that our acts be of a certain kind; for the resulting character varies as they vary. It makes no small difference, therefore, whether a man be trained from his youth up in this way or in that, but a great difference, or rather all the difference.

2. But our present inquiry has not, like the rest, a merely speculative aim; we are not inquiring merely in order to know what excellence or virtue is, but in order to become good; for otherwise it would profit us nothing. We must ask therefore about these acts, and see of what kind they are to be; for, as we said, it is they that determine our habits or character.

First of all, then, that they must be in accordance with right reason is a common characteristic of them, which we shall here take for granted, reserving for future discussion the question what this right reason is, and how it is related to the other excellences.

But let it be understood, before we go on, that all reasoning on matters of practice must be in outline merely, and not scientifically exact: for, as we said at starting, the kind of reasoning to be demanded varies with the subject in hand; and in practical matters and questions of expediency there are no invariable laws, any more than in questions of health.

And if our general conclusions are thus inexact, still more inexact is all reasoning about particular cases; for these fall under no system of scientifically established rules or traditional maxims, but the agent must always consider for himself what the special occasion requires, just as in medicine or navigation.

But though this is the case we must try to render what help we can.

First of all, then, we must observe that, in matters of this sort, to fall short and to exceed are alike fatal. This is plain (to illustrate what we cannot see by what we can see) in the case of strength and health. Too much and too little exercise alike destroy strength, and to take too much meat and drink, or to take too little, is equally ruinous to health, but the fitting amount produces and increases and preserves them. Just so, then, is it with temperance also, and courage, and the other virtues. The man who shuns and fears everything and never makes a stand, becomes a coward; while the man who fears nothing at all, but will face anything, becomes foolhardy. So, too, the man who takes his fill of any kind of pleasure, and abstains from none, is a profligate, but the man who shuns all (like him whom we call a "boor") is devoid of sensibility. Thus temperance and courage are destroyed both by excess and defect, but preserved by moderation.

But habits or types of character are not only produced and preserved and destroyed by the same occasions and the same means, but they will also manifest themselves in the same circumstances. This is the case with palpable things like strength. Strength is produced by taking plenty of nourishment and doing plenty of hard work, and the strong man, in turn, has the greatest capacity for these. And the case is the same with the virtues: by abstaining from pleasure we become temperate, and when we have become temperate we are best able to abstain. And so with courage: by habituating ourselves to despise danger, and to face it, we become courageous; and when we have become courageous, we are best able to face danger.

3. The pleasure or pain that accompanies the acts must be taken as a test of the formed habit or character.

He who abstains from the pleasures of the body and rejoices in the abstinence is temperate, while he who is vexed at having to abstain is profligate; and again, he who faces danger with pleasure, or, at any rate, without pain, is courageous, but he to whom this is painful is a coward.

For moral virtue or excellence is closely concerned with pleasure and pain. It is pleasure that moves us to do what is base, and pain that moves us to refrain from what is noble. And therefore, as Plato says, man needs to be so trained from his youth up as to find pleasure and pain in the right objects. This is what sound education means.

Another reason why virtue has to do with pleasure and pain, is that it has to do with actions and passions or affections; but every affection and every act is accompanied by pleasure or pain.

The fact is further attested by the employment of pleasure and pain in correction; they have a kind of curative property, and a cure is effected by administering the opposite of the disease.

Again, as we said before, every type of character [or habit or formed faculty] is essentially relative to, and concerned with, those things that form it for good or for ill; but it is through pleasure and pain that bad characters are formed — that is to say, through pursuing and avoiding the wrong pleasures and pains, or pursuing and avoiding them at the wrong time, or in the wrong manner, or in any other of the various ways of going wrong that may be distinguished.

And hence some people go so far as to define the virtues as a kind of impassive or neutral state of mind. But they err in stating this absolutely, instead of qualifying it by the addition of the right and wrong manner, time, etc.

We may lay down, therefore, that this kind of excellence [*i.e.* moral excellence] makes us do what is best in matters of pleasure and pain, while vice or badness has the contrary effect. But the following considerations will throw additional light on the point.

There are three kinds of things that move us to choose, and three that move us to avoid them: on the one hand, the beautiful or noble, the advantageous, the pleasant; on the other hand, the ugly or base, the hurtful, the painful. Now, the good man is apt to go right, and the bad man to go wrong, about them all, but especially about pleasure: for pleasure is not only common to man with animals, but also accompanies all pursuit or choice; since the noble, and the advantageous also, are pleasant in idea.

Again, the feeling of pleasure has been fostered in us all from our infancy by our training, and has thus become so engrained in our life that it can scarce be washed out. And, indeed, we all more or less make pleasure our test in judging of actions. For this reason too, then, our whole inquiry must be concerned with these matters; since to be pleased and pained in the right or the wrong way has great influence on our actions.

Again, to fight with pleasure is harder than to fight with wrath (which Heraclitus says is hard), and virtue, like art, is always more concerned with what is harder; for the harder the task the better is success. For this reason also, then, both [moral] virtue or excellence and the science of the state must always be concerned with pleasures and pains; for he that behaves rightly with regard to them will be good, and he that behaves badly will be bad.

We will take it as established, then, that [moral] excellence or virtue has to do with pleasures and pains; and that the acts which produce it develop it, and also, when differently done, destroy it; and that it manifests itself in the same acts which produced it.

4. But here we may be asked what we mean by saying that men can become just and temperate only by doing what is just and temperate: surely, it may be said, if their acts are just and temperate, they themselves are already just and temperate, as they are grammarians and musicians if they do what is grammatical and musical.

We may answer, I think, firstly, that this is not quite the case even with the arts. A man may do something grammatical [or write something correctly] by chance, or at the prompting of another person: he will not be grammatical till he not only does something grammatical, but also does it grammatically [or like a grammatical person], *i.e.* in virtue of his own knowledge of grammar.

But, secondly, the virtues are not in this point analogous to the arts. The products of art have their excellence in themselves, and so it is enough if when produced they are of a certain quality; but in the case of the virtues, a man is not said to act justly or temperately [or like a just or temperate man] if what he does merely be of a certain sort — he must also be in a certain state of mind when he does it; *i.e.,* first of all, he must know what he is doing; secondly, he must choose it, and choose it for itself; and, thirdly, his act must be the expression of a formed and stable character. Now, of these conditions, only one, the knowledge, is necessary for the possession of any art; but for the possession of the virtues knowledge is of little or no avail, while the other conditions that result from repeatedly doing what is just and temperate are not a little important, but all-important.

The thing that is done, therefore, is called just or temperate when it is such as the just or temperate man would do; but the man who does it is not just or temperate, unless he also does it in the spirit of the just or the temperate man.

It is right, then, to say that by doing what is just a man becomes just, and temperate by doing what is temperate, while without doing thus he has no chance of ever becoming good.

But most men, instead of doing thus, fly to theories, and fancy that they are philosophizing and that this will make them good, like a sick man who listens attentively to what the doctor says and then disobeys all his orders. This sort of philosophizing will no more produce a healthy habit of mind than this sort of treatment will produce a healthy habit of body.

5. We have next to inquire what excellence or virtue is.

A quality of the soul is either (1) a passion or emotion, or (2) a power or faculty, or (3) a habit or trained faculty; and so virtue must be one of these three. By (1) a passion or emotion we mean appetite, anger, fear, confidence, envy, joy, love, hate, longing, emulation, pity, or generally that which is accompanied by pleasure or pain; (2) a power or faculty is that in respect of which we are said to be capable of being affected in any of these ways, as, for instance, that in respect of which we are able to be angered or pained or to pity; and (3) a habit or trained faculty is that in respect of which we are well or ill regulated or disposed in the matter of our affections; as, for instance, in the matter of being angered, we are ill regulated if we are too violent or too slack, but if we are moderate in our anger we are well regulated. And so with the rest.

Now, the virtues are not emotions, nor are the vices — (1) because we are not called good or bad in respect of our emotions, but are called so in respect of our virtues or vices; (2) because we are neither praised nor blamed in respect of our emotions (a man is not praised for being afraid or angry, nor blamed for being angry simply, but for being angry in a particular way), but we are praised or blamed in respect of our virtues or vices; (3) because we may be angered or frightened without deliberate choice, but the virtues are a kind of deliberate choice, or at least are impossible without it; and (4) because in respect of our emotions we are said to be moved, but in respect of our virtues and vices we are not said to be moved, but to be regulated or disposed in this way or in that.

For these same reasons also they are not powers or faculties; for we are not called either good or bad for being merely capable of emotion, nor are we either praised or blamed for this. And further, while nature gives us our powers or faculties, she does not make us either good or bad. (This point, however, we have already treated.)

If, then, the virtues be neither emotions nor faculties, it only remains for them to be habits or trained faculties.

6. We have thus found the genus to which virtue belongs; but we want to know, not only that it is a trained faculty, but also what species of trained faculty it is.

We may safely assert that the virtue or excellence of a thing causes that thing both to be itself in good condition and to perform its function well. The excellence of the eye, for instance, makes both the eye and its work good; for it is by the excellence of the eye that we see well. So the proper excellence of the horse makes a horse what he should be, and makes him good at running, and carrying his rider, and standing a charge.

If, then, this holds good in all cases, the proper excellence or virtue of man will be the habit or trained faculty that makes a man good and makes him perform his function well.

How this is to be done we have already said, but we may exhibit the same conclusion in another way, by inquiring what the nature of this virtue is.

Now, if we have any quantity, whether continuous or discrete, it is possible to take either a larger [or too large], or a smaller [or too small], or an equal [or fair] amount, and that either absolutely or relatively to our own needs.

By an equal or fair amount I understand a mean amount, or one that lies between excess and deficiency.

By the absolute mean, or mean relatively to the thing itself, I understand that which is equidistant from both extremes, and this is one and the same for all.

By the mean relatively to us I understand that which is neither too much nor too little for us; and this is not one and the same for all.

For instance, if ten be larger [or too large] and two be smaller [or too small], if we take six we take the mean relatively to the thing itself [or the arithmetical mean]; for it exceeds one extreme by the same amount by which it is exceeded by the other extreme: and this is the mean in arithmetical proportion.

But the mean relatively to us cannot be found in this way. If ten pounds of food is too much for a given man to eat, and two pounds too little, it does not follow that the trainer will order him six pounds: for that also may perhaps be too much for the man in question, or too little; too little for Milo, too much for the beginner. The same holds true in running and wrestling.

And so we may say generally that a master in any art avoids what is too much and what is too little, and seeks for the mean and chooses it—not the absolute but the relative mean.

If, then, every art or science perfects its work in this way, looking to the mean and bringing its work up to this standard (so that people are wont to say of a good work that nothing could be taken from it or added to it, implying that excellence is destroyed by excess or deficiency, but secured by observing the mean; and good artists, as we say, do in fact keep their eyes fixed on this in all that they do), and if virtue, like nature, is more exact and better than any art, it follows that virtue also must aim at the mean—virtue of course meaning moral virtue or excellence; for it has to do with passions and actions, and it is these that admit of excess and deficiency and the mean. For instance, it is possible to feel fear, confidence, desire, anger, pity, and generally to be affected pleasantly and painfully, either too much or too little, in either case wrongly; but to be thus affected at the right times, and on the right occasions, and towards the right persons, and with the right object, and in the right fashion, is the mean course and the best course, and these are characteristics of virtue. And in the same way our outward acts also admit of excess and deficiency, and the mean or due amount.

Virtue, then, has to deal with feelings or passions and with outward acts, in which excess is wrong and deficiency also is blamed, but the mean amount is praised and is right—both of which are characteristics of virtue.

Virtue, then, is a kind of moderation, inasmuch as it aims at the mean or moderate amount.

Again, there are many ways of going wrong (for evil is infinite in nature, to use a Pythagorean figure, while good is finite), but only one way of going right; so that the one is easy and the other hard—easy to miss the mark and hard to hit. On this account also, then, excess and deficiency are characteristic of vice, hitting the mean is characteristic of virtue:

"Goodness is simple, ill takes any shape."

Virtue, then, is a habit or trained faculty of choice, the characteristic of which lies in moderation or observance of the mean relatively to the persons concerned, as determined by reason, *i.e.* by the reason by which the prudent man would determine it. And it is a moderation, firstly, inasmuch as it comes in the middle or mean between two vices, one on the side of excess, the other on the side of defect; and, secondly, inasmuch as, while these vices fall short of or exceed the due measure in feeling and in action, it finds and chooses the mean, middling, or moderate amount.

Regarded in its essence, therefore, or according to the definition of its nature, virtue is a moderation or middle state, but viewed in its relation to what is best and right it is the extreme of perfection.

But it is not all actions nor all passions that admit of moderation; there are some whose very names imply badness, as malevolence, shamelessness, envy, and, among acts, adultery, theft, murder. These and all other like things are blamed as being bad in themselves, and not merely in their excess or deficiency. It is impossible therefore to go right in them; they are always wrong: rightness and wrongness in such things (*e.g.* in adultery) does not depend upon whether it is the right person and occasion and manner, but the mere doing of any one of them is wrong.

It would be equally absurd to look for moderation or excess or deficiency in unjust cowardly or profligate conduct; for then there would be moderation in excess or deficiency, and excess in excess, and deficiency in deficiency.

The fact is that just as there can be no excess or deficiency in temperance or courage because the mean or moderate amount is, in a sense, an extreme, so in these kinds of conduct also there can be no moderation or excess or deficiency, but the acts are wrong however they be done. For, to put it generally, there cannot be moderation in excess or deficiency, nor excess or deficiency in moderation.

7. But it is not enough to make these general statements [about virtue and vice]: we must go on and apply them to particulars [*i.e.* to the several virtues and vices]. For in reasoning about matters of conduct general statements are too vague, and do not convey so much truth as particular propositions. It is with particulars that conduct is concerned: our statements, therefore, when applied to these particulars, should be found to hold good.

These particulars then [*i.e.* the several virtues and vices and the several acts and affections with which they deal], we will take from the following table.

Moderation in the feelings of fear and confidence is courage: of those that exceed, he that exceeds in fearlessness has no name (as often happens), but he that exceeds in confidence is foolhardy, while he that exceeds in fear, but is deficient in confidence, is cowardly.

Moderation in respect of certain pleasures and also (though to a less extent) certain pains is temperance, while excess is profligacy. But defectiveness in the matter of these pleasures is hardly ever found, and so this sort of people also have as yet received no name: let us put them down as "void of sensibility."

In the matter of giving and taking money, moderation is liberality, excess and deficiency are prodigality and illiberality. But both vices exceed and fall short in giving and taking in contrary ways: the prodigal exceeds in spending, but falls short in taking; while the illiberal man exceeds in taking, but falls short in spending. (For the present we are but giving an outline or summary, and aim at nothing more; we shall afterwards treat these points in greater detail.)

But, besides these, there are other dispositions in the matter of money: there is a moderation which is called magnificence (for the magnificent is not the same as the liberal man: the former deals with large sums, the latter with small), and an excess which is called bad taste or vulgarity, and a deficiency which is called meanness; and these vices differ from those which are opposed to liberality: how they differ will be explained later.

With respect to honour and disgrace, there is a moderation which is high-mindedness, an excess which may be called vanity, and a deficiency which is little-mindedness.

But just as we said that liberality is related to magnificence, differing only in that it deals with small sums, so here there is a virtue related to high-mindedness, and differing only in that it is concerned with small instead of great honours. A man may have a due desire for honour, and also more or less than a due desire: he that carries this desire to excess is called ambitious, he that has not enough of it is called unambitious, but he that has the due amount has no name. There are also no abstract names for the characters, except "ambition," corresponding to ambitious. And on this account those who occupy the extremes lay claim to the middle place. And in common parlance, too, the moderate man is sometimes called ambitious and sometimes unambitious, and sometimes the ambitious man is praised and sometimes the unambitious. Why this is we will explain afterwards; for the present we will follow out our plan and enumerate the other types of character.

In the matter of anger also we find excess and deficiency and moderation. The characters themselves hardly have recognized names, but as the moderate man is here called gentle, we will call his character gentleness; of those who go into extremes, we may take the term wrathful for him who exceeds, with wrathfulness for the vice, and wrathless for him who is deficient, with wrathlessness for his character.

Besides these, there are three kinds of moderation, bearing some resemblance to one another, and yet different. They all have to do with intercourse in speech and action, but they differ in that one has to do with the truthfulness of this intercourse, while the other two have to do with its pleasantness—one of the two with pleasantness in matters of amusement, the other with pleasantness in all the relations of life. We must therefore speak of these qualities also in order that we may the more plainly see how, in all cases, moderation is praiseworthy, while the extreme courses are neither right nor praiseworthy, but blamable.

In these cases also names are for the most part wanting, but we must try, here as elsewhere, to coin names ourselves, in order to make our argument clear and easy to follow.

In the matter of truth, then, let us call him who observes the mean a true [or truthful] person, and observance of the mean truth [or truthfulness]: pretence, when it exaggerates, may be called boasting, and the person a boaster; when it understates, let the names be irony and ironical.

With regard to pleasantness in amusement, he who observes the mean may be called witty, and his character wittiness; excess may be called buffoonery, and the man a buffoon; while boorish may stand for the person who is deficient, and boorishness for his character.

With regard to pleasantness in the other affairs of life, he who makes himself properly pleasant may be called friendly, and his moderation friendliness; he that exceeds may be called obsequious if he have no ulterior motive, but a flatterer if he has an eye to his own advantage; he that is deficient in this respect, and always makes himself disagreeable, may be called a quarrelsome or peevish fellow.

Moreover, in mere emotions and in our conduct with regard to them, there are ways of observing the mean; for instance, shame is not a virtue, but yet the modest man is praised. For in these matters also we speak of this man as observing the mean, of that man as going beyond it (as the shame-faced man whom the least thing makes shy), while he who is deficient in the feeling, or lacks it altogether, is called shameless; but the term modest is applied to him who observes the mean.

Righteous indignation, again, hits the mean between envy and malevolence. These have to do with feelings of pleasure and pain at what happens to our neighbours. A man is called righteously indignant when he feels pain at the sight of undeserved prosperity, but your envious man goes beyond him and is pained by the sight of any one in prosperity, while the malevolent man is so far from being pained that he actually exults in the misfortunes of his neighbours.

But we shall have another opportunity of discussing these matters.

As for justice, the term is used in more senses than one; we will, therefore, after disposing of the above questions, distinguish these various senses, and show how each of these kinds of justice is a kind of moderation.

And then we will treat of the intellectual virtues in the same way.

8. There are, as we said, three classes of disposition, viz. two kinds of vice, one marked by excess, the other by deficiency, and one kind of virtue, the observance of the mean. Now, each is in a way opposed to each, for the extreme dispositions are opposed both to the mean or moderate disposition and to one another, while the moderate disposition is opposed to both the extremes. Just as a quantity which is equal to a given quantity is also greater when compared with a less, and less when compared with a greater quantity, so the mean or moderate dispositions exceed as compared with the defective dispositions, and fall short as compared with the excessive dispositions, both in feeling and in action; *e.g.* the courageous man seems foolhardy as compared with the coward, and cowardly as compared with the foolhardy; and similarly the temperate man appears profligate in comparison with the insensible, and insensible in comparison with the profligate man; and the liberal man appears prodigal by the side of the illiberal man, and illiberal by the side of the prodigal man.

And so the extreme characters try to displace the mean or moderate character, and each represents him as falling into the opposite extreme, the coward calling the courageous man foolhardy, the foolhardy calling him coward, and so on in other cases.

But while the mean and the extremes are thus opposed to one another, the extremes are strictly contrary to each other rather than to the mean; for they are further removed from one another than from the mean, as that which is greater than a given magnitude is further from that which is less, and that which is less is further from that which is greater, than either the greater or the less is from that which is equal to the given magnitude.

Sometimes, again, an extreme, when compared with the mean, has a sort of resemblance to it, as foolhardiness to courage, or prodigality to liberality; but there is the greatest possible dissimilarity between the extremes.

Again, "things that are as far as possible removed from each other" is the accepted definition of contraries, so that the further things are removed from each other the more contrary they are.

In comparison with the mean, however, it is sometimes the deficiency that is the more opposed, and sometimes the excess; *e.g.* foolhardiness, which is excess, is not so much opposed to courage as cowardice, which is deficiency; but insensibility, which is lack of feeling, is not so much opposed to temperance as profligacy, which is excess.

The reasons for this are two. One is the reason derived from the nature of the matter itself: since one extreme is, in fact, nearer and more similar to the mean, we naturally do not oppose it to the mean so strongly as the other; *e.g.* as foolhardiness seems more similar to courage and nearer to it, and cowardice more dissimilar, we speak of cowardice as the opposite rather than the other: for that which is further removed from the mean seems to be more opposed to it.

This, then, is one reason, derived from the nature of the thing itself. Another reason lies in ourselves: and it is this—those things to which we happen to be more prone by nature appear to be more opposed to the mean: *e.g.* our natural inclination is rather towards indulgence in pleasure, and so we more easily fall into profligate than into regular habits: those courses, then, in which we are more apt to run to great lengths are spoken of as more opposed to the mean; and thus profligacy, which is an excess, is more opposed to temperance than the deficiency is.

9. We have sufficiently explained, then, that moral virtue is moderation or observance of the mean, and in what sense, viz. (1) as holding a middle position between two vices, one on the side of excess, and the other on the side of deficiency, and (2) as aiming at the mean or moderate amount both in feeling and in action.

And on this account it is a hard thing to be good; for finding the middle or the mean in each case is a hard thing, just as finding the middle or centre of a circle is a thing that is not within the power of everybody, but only of him who has the requisite knowledge.

Thus any one can be angry—that is quite easy; any one can give money away or spend it: but to do these things to the right person, to the right extent, at the right time, with the right object, and in the right manner, is not what everybody can do, and is by no means easy; and that is the reason why right doing is rare and praiseworthy and noble.

He that aims at the mean, then, should first of all strive to avoid that extreme which is more opposed to it, as Calypso* bids Ulysses—

> "Clear of these smoking breakers keep thy ship."

For of the extremes one is more dangerous, the other less. Since then it is hard to hit the mean precisely, we must "row when we cannot sail," as the proverb has it, and choose the least of two evils; and that will be best effected in the way we have described.

And secondly we must consider, each for himself, what we are most prone to—for different natures are inclined to different things—which we may learn by the pleasure or pain we feel. And then we must bend ourselves in the opposite direction; for by keeping well away from error we shall fall into the middle course, as we straighten a bent stick by bending it the other way.

But in all cases we must be especially on our guard against pleasant things, and against pleasure; for we can scarce judge her impartially. And so, in our behaviour towards her, we should imitate the behaviour of the old counsellors towards Helen,† and in all cases repeat their saying: if we dismiss her we shall be less likely to go wrong.

---

*Hom., Od., xii. 101–110, and 219–220: Calypso should be Circe.

†Hom., Il., iii. 154–164.

This then, in outline, is the course by which we shall best be able to hit the mean.

But it is a hard task, we must admit, especially in a particular case. It is not easy to determine, for instance, how and with whom one ought to be angry, and upon what grounds, and for how long; for public opinion sometimes praises those who fall short, and calls them gentle, and sometimes applies the term manly to those who show a harsh temper.

In fact, a slight error, whether on the side of excess or deficiency, is not blamed, but only a considerable error; for then there can be no mistake. But it is hardly possible to determine by reasoning how far or to what extent a man must err in order to incur blame; and indeed matters that fall within the scope of perception never can be so determined. Such matters lie within the region of particulars, and can only be determined by perception.

So much then is plain, that the middle character is in all cases to be praised, but that we ought to incline sometimes towards excess, sometimes towards deficiency; for in this way we shall most easily hit the mean and attain to right doing.

Study Questions

1. According to Aristotle, at what does all human activity aim? Give some examples to illustrate his point.
2. What science studies the chief good, according to Aristotle? Why does he hold this?
3. Why can't the investigation of what is noble and just be exact, according to Aristotle?
4. What is the chief good, according to Aristotle, and why does he maintain this?
5. What are two incorrect opinions as to the chief good, according to Aristotle. Why does he hold that they are incorrect?
6. What, according to Aristotle, is the function of a human being? What does this question have to do with happiness?
7. What are the two parts of the soul, according to Aristotle? What two kinds of virtue correspond to these parts?
8. When Aristotle says that virtues are not implanted in us by nature, what does he mean? How do we become virtuous?
9. What do deficiency and excess do to moral qualities, according to Aristotle? Why?
10. What do pleasure and pain tell us about our character, according to Aristotle?
11. Why does Aristotle regard virtues as characteristics?
12. Why does Aristotle think of virtues as means between extremes?
13. Explain what Aristotle means by saying that pleasure is a whole.
14. In what does perfect happiness consist, according to Aristotle? Explain.

CHAPTER 8

Hellenistic and Roman Ethics

Socrates' most famous student was Plato, and Plato's most famous student was Aristotle. Aristotle's most famous student, in turn, was the Macedonian king Alexander the Great. Alexander, however, preferred conquering the world to philosophizing; in fact, it is doubtful that Alexander was much influenced by Aristotle's teachings.

The period of Macedonian rule of the Greek-speaking world, which began with Alexander around 335 B.C. and lasted about a century and a half, is known as the Hellenistic Age. During this and the lengthy period of Roman pre-eminence that followed, two schools of moral philosophy flourished, Epicureanism and Stoicism. Both were products of Greek culture, not Macedonian or Roman. Even today many Westerners subscribe to the basic principles of Epicureanism or Stoicism, or both.

Epicureanism

Epicureanism started with Epicurus (341–270 B.C.) and lasted as a school of philosophy for almost four hundred years. Its principal tenet was that since by nature you seek a pleasant life above all else, that's exactly what you should do. And the way to do that, according to Epicurus, is to satisfy your desires. But Epicurus was not recommending a life of fine wine, fabulous cuisine, and resplendent luxury. He did not think that the pleasant life is best achieved by satisfying *every* desire.

Epicurus thought that our desires fall into one of three groups:

1. Those that are natural and must be satisfied if you are to have a pleasant life: the desire for food and shelter, for example
2. Those that are natural but need not be satisfied for a pleasant life: the desire for sexual gratification, for instance
3. Those that are neither natural nor necessary to satisfy (the desires for wealth and fame, for example)

To obtain the pleasant life, according to Epicurus, the best strategy to follow is always to satisfy desires of the first kind; occasionally to satisfy desires of the second kind, provided that doing so doesn't lead to pain or trouble; and never to satisfy desires of the third kind, since doing so is apt to produce trouble over the long run.

Epicurus, in short, did not think it wise to do away with all restraints. We are here *for life*. What is desirable, therefore, is not the pursuit of momentary pleasure but a prudent way of living that will maximize our chances of living relatively free from pain. Epicurus recommended a relaxed and composed mode of living, in which you cultivate your intellect, have modest needs, indulge only the basic desires, and enjoy the company of like-minded friends.

Stoicism

Let's make a distinction between a Stoic and a stoic. A stoic is someone who endures pain and suffering with indifference. A Stoic is a member of the school of philosophy that was founded by Zeno (334–262 B.C.) and whose first members met with him on his porch, or *stoa*. Stoicism spread to Rome and survived as a school until almost the third century A.D. Several famous Romans were Stoics, including Cicero (106–43 B.C.), Seneca (ca. 4 B.C.–A.D. 65), and Marcus Aurelius, the Roman emperor (A.D. 121–180). One of the most famous Stoics was Epictetus (first to second centuries A.D.), a former Roman slave who became an influential instructor of philosophy.

The Stoics, too, emphasized the importance of the pleasant life. But they were much influenced by Cynicism, a school of philosophy founded around 440 B.C. by Antisthenes, a disciple of Socrates. The Cynics proudly suppressed normal desires and displayed an almost fanatical preference for poverty as well as indifference to the people and events around them. The Stoics, influenced by the Cynics, believed that the key to the pleasant life is indifference to pleasure and pain. You really can't control what will happen to you, so the best strategy is not to become too involved with yourself or with what happens to you. Treat life as an actor in a play treats a part: Since circumstances have assigned you to a particular role, play it well, but be as indifferent to what happens to you in life as is the actor to what happens to his character.

Why can't you control what will happen to you? According to the Stoic metaphysics, events unfold themselves in accordance with natural law, which in their view is a rational force that vitalizes everything. Since all that happens is determined by the logic of the universe (that is, by natural law), whatever happens happens necessarily and is for the best. What happens is inevitable. Therefore, do not become involved emotionally in what happens: instead, accept it with passive indifference.

The Stoic concept of natural law developed into the Roman theory that there is a universal moral law that is valid for all nations and people. (Roman jurisprudence was based on this theory.) The later Stoics also believed that our fellow creatures are equals under natural law and that therefore we have a duty toward them as members of a sort of universal brotherhood. This concept of a universal natural law and the related concept of moral duty became increasingly important in Western ethical thought, and the two ideas mark perhaps the most important contributions of Stoicism to moral philosophy.

The moral philosophy of the Hellenistic and Roman periods was more practical and less theoretical than that of the classical Greeks. The Epicureans stressed leading the pleasant life through moderate living, and the Stoics emphasized leading the untroubled life through acceptance of the natural order. Whether the Stoic philosophy of emotional apathy blends harmoniously with their concept of civic duty is, however, open to question.

The following selections are from Epicurus ("Epicurus to Menoeceus") and Epictetus (*The Encheiridion*). Notice that both writings consist of practical advice for the individual. Thus, they both assume that the ethically proper thing to do is to act in one's own self-interest. In other words, they are both expressions of *ethical egoism*, which was discussed in Chapter 5 and which you might wish to refer to now. Notice too that Epicurus explicitly accepts *psychological egoism*, the doctrine that in all conscious action people seek to promote their self-interest above all else. Probably, Epictetus also assumed that people naturally seek their own self-interest as the primary good, although he does not explicitly say so.

The varieties of egoism advocated in these selections could well seem to you to be attractive moral philosophies. Accordingly, you might consider some difficulties that attach to egoistic philosophies: If, on the one hand, people naturally do seek their own self-interest, then isn't it unnecessary to tell them they should do this? And if, on the other hand, they do *not* naturally seek their own self-interest, isn't it futile to tell them they should? For that matter, if you are an ethical egoist, is it in your self-interest to tell others to seek *their* own self-interest? Wouldn't it be sounder for you to tell them that they should seek the common good?

Epicurus to Menoeceus

Epicurus

Epicurus lived from around 341 B.C. to 270 B.C. Although he is a prominent figure in the history of philosophy, most of his numerous writings have been lost. Reprinted here is "Epicurus to Menoeceus," from *Epicurus: The Extant Remains*, translated by Cyril Bailey.

Let no one when young delay to study philosophy, nor when he is old grow weary of his study. For no one can come too early or too late to secure the health of his soul. And the man who says that the age of philosophy has either not yet come or has gone by is like the man who says that the age for happiness is not yet come to him, or has passed away. Wherefore both when young and old a man must study philosophy, that as he grows old he may be young in blessings through the grateful recollection of what has been, and that in youth he may be old as well, since he will know no fear of what is to come. We must then meditate on the things that make our happiness, seeing that when this is with us we have all, but when it is absent we do all to win it.

The things which I used unceasingly to commend to you, these do and practice, considering them to be the first principles of the good life. First of all believe that god is a being immortal and blessed, even as the common idea of a god is engraved on men's minds, and do not assign to him anything alien to his immortality or ill-suited to his blessedness: but believe about him everything that can uphold his blessedness and immortality. For gods there are, since the knowledge of them is by clear vision. But they are not such as the many believe them to be: for indeed they do not consistently represent them as they believe them to be. And the impious man is not he who denies the gods of the many, but he who attaches to the gods the beliefs of the many. For the statements of the many about the gods are not conceptions derived from sensation, but false suppositions, according to which the greatest misfortunes befall the wicked and the greatest blessings the good by the gift of the gods. For men being accustomed always to their own virtues welcome those like themselves, but regard all that is not of their nature as alien.

Become accustomed to the belief that death is nothing to us. For all good and evil consists in sensation, but death is deprivation of sensation. And therefore a right understanding that death is nothing to us makes the mortality of life enjoyable, not because it adds to it an infinite span of time, but because it takes away the craving for immortality. For there is nothing terrible in life for the man who has truly comprehended that there is nothing terrible in not living. So that the man speaks but idly who says that he fears death not because it will be painful when it comes, but because it is painful in anticipation. For that which gives no trouble when it comes is but an empty pain in anticipation. So death, the most terrifying of ills, is nothing to us, since so long as we exist, death is not with us; but when death comes, then we do not exist. It does not then concern either the living or the dead, since for the former it is not, and the latter are no more.

But the many at one moment shun death as the greatest of evils, at another yearn for it as a respite from the evils in life. But the wise man neither seeks to escape life nor fears the cessation of life, for neither does life offend him nor does the absence of life seem to be any evil. And just as with food he does not seek simply the larger share and nothing else, but rather the most pleasant, so he seeks to enjoy not the longest period of time, but the most pleasant.

And he who counsels the young man to live well, but the old man to make a good end, is foolish, not merely because of the desirability of life, but also because it is the same training which teaches to live well and to die well. Yet much worse still is the man who says it is good not to be born, but "once born make haste to pass the gates of Death." For if he says this from conviction why does he not pass away out of life? For it is open to him to do so, if he had firmly made up his mind to this. But if he speaks in jest, his words are idle among men who cannot receive them.

We must then bear in mind that the future is neither ours, nor yet wholly not ours, so that we may not altogether expect it as sure to come, nor abandon hope of it, as if it will certainly not come.

We must consider that of desires some are natural, others vain, and of the natural some are necessary and others merely natural; and of the necessary some are necessary for happiness, others for the repose of the body, and others for very life. The right understanding of these facts enables us to refer all choice and avoidance to the health of the body and the soul's freedom from disturbance, since this is the aim of the life of blessedness. For it is to obtain this end that we always act, namely, to avoid pain and fear. And when this is once secured for us, all the tempest of the soul is dispersed, since the living creature has not to wander as though in search of something that is missing, and to look for some other thing by which he can fulfil the good of the soul and the good of the body. For it is then that we have need of pleasure, when we feel pain owing to the absence of pleasure; but when we do not feel pain, we no longer need pleasure. And for this cause we call pleasure the beginning and end of the blessed life. For we recognize pleasure as the first good innate in us, and from pleasure we begin every act of choice and avoidance, and to pleasure we return again, using the feeling as the standard by which we judge every good.

And since pleasure is the first good and natural to us, for this very reason we do not choose every pleasure, but sometimes we pass over many pleasures, when greater discomfort accrues to us as the result of them: and similarly we think many pains better than pleasures, since a greater pleasure comes to us when we have endured pains for a long time. Every pleasure then because of its natural kinship to us is good, yet not every pleasure is to be chosen: even as every pain also is an evil, yet not all are always of a nature to be avoided. Yet by a scale of comparison and by the consideration of advantages and disadvantages we must form our judgement on all these matters. For the good on certain occasions we treat as bad, and conversely the bad as good.

And again independence of desire we think a great good—not that we may at all times enjoy but a few things, but that, if we do not possess many, we may enjoy the few in the genuine persuasion that those have the sweetest pleasure in luxury who least need it, and that all that is natural is easy to be obtained, but that which is superfluous is hard. And so plain savours bring us a pleasure equal to a luxurious diet, when all the pain due to want is removed; and bread and water produce the highest pleasure, when one who needs them puts them to his lips. To grow accustomed therefore to simple and not luxurious diet gives us health to the full, and makes a man alert for the needful employments of life, and when after long intervals we approach luxuries disposes us better towards them, and fits us to be fearless of fortune.

When, therefore, we maintain that pleasure is the end, we do not mean the pleasures of profligates and those that consist in sensuality, as is supposed by some who are either ignorant or disagree with us or do not understand, but freedom from pain in the body and from trouble in the mind. For it is not continuous drinkings and revellings, nor the satisfaction of lusts, nor the enjoyment of fish and other luxuries of the wealthy table, which produce a pleasant life, but sober reasoning, searching out the motives for all choice and avoidance, and banishing mere opinions, to which are due the greatest disturbance of the spirit.

Of all this is the beginning and the greatest good is prudence. Wherefore prudence is a more precious thing even than philosophy: for from prudence are sprung all the other virtues, and it teaches us that it is not possible to live pleasantly without living prudently and honourably and justly, nor, again, to live a life of prudence, honour, and justice without living pleasantly. For the virtues are by nature bound up with the pleasant life, and the pleasant life is inseparable from them. For indeed who, think you, is a better man than he who holds reverent opinions concerning the gods, and is at all times free from fear of death, and has reasoned out the end ordained by nature? He understands that the limit of good things is easy to fulfil and easy to attain, whereas the course of ills is either short in time or slight in pain: he laughs at destiny, whom some have introduced as the mistress of all things. He thinks that with us lies the chief power in determining events, some of which happen by necessity and some by chance, and some are within our control; for while necessity cannot be called to account, he sees that chance is inconstant, but that which is in our control is subject to no master, and to it are naturally attached praise and blame. For indeed it were better to follow the myths about the gods than to become a slave to the destiny of the natural philosophers: for the former suggests a hope of placating the gods by worship, whereas the latter involves a necessity which knows no placation. As to chance, he does not regard it as a god as most men do (for in a god's acts there is no disorder), nor as an uncertain cause of all things: for he does not believe that good and evil are given by chance to man for the framing of a blessed life, but that opportunities for great good and great evil are afforded by it. He therefore thinks it better to be unfortunate in reasonable action than to prosper in unreason. For it is better in a man's actions that what is well chosen should fail, rather than that what is ill chosen should be successful owing to chance.

Meditate therefore on these things and things akin to them night and day by yourself, and with a companion like to yourself, and never shall you be disturbed waking or asleep, but you shall live like a god among men. For a man who lives among immortal blessings is not like to a mortal being.

Study Questions

1. Explain in your own words why death, according to Epicurus, is nothing to us.
2. For what end do we always act, according to Epicurus?
3. Is every pleasure desirable and every pain an evil, according to Epicurus? Describe the sorts of pleasure Epicurus recommends.
4. Why is independence of desire a great good, according to Epicurus?
5. What's so good about prudence, according to Epicurus?

The Encheiridion

Epictetus

Epictetus (first to second centuries A.D.) was sold into slavery as a child but was educated and eventually freed. He was the most influential of all the Stoics, though he wrote nothing. *The Encheiridion* consists of lecture notes from one of his students. From *The Discourses*, Vol. II, translated by W. A. Oldfather (Cambridge, Mass.: Harvard University Press, 1966).

1. Some things are under our control, while others are not under our control. Under our control are conception, choice, desire, aversion, and, in a word, everything that is our own doing; not under our control are our body, our property, reputation, office, and, in a word, everything that is not our own doing. Furthermore, the things under our control are by nature free, unhindered, and unimpeded; while the things not under our control are weak, servile, subject to hindrance, and not our own. Remember, therefore, that if what is naturally slavish you think to be free, and what is not your own to be your own, you will be hampered, will grieve, will be in turmoil, and will blame both gods and men; while if you think only what is your own to be your own, and what is not your own to be, as it really is, not your own, then no one will ever be able to exert compulsion upon you, no one will hinder you, you will blame no one, will find fault with no one, will do absolutely nothing against your will, you will have no personal enemy, no one will harm you, for neither is there any harm that can touch you.

With such high aims, therefore, remember that you must bestir yourself with no slight effort to lay hold of them, but you will have to give up some things entirely, and defer others for the time being. But if you wish for these things also, and at the same time for both office and wealth, it may be that you will not get even these latter, because you aim also at the former, and certainly you will fail to get the former, which alone bring freedom and happiness.

Make it, therefore, your study at the very outset to say to every harsh external impression, "You are an external impression and not at all what you appear to be." After that examine it and test it by these rules which you have, the first and most important of which is this: Whether the impression has to do with the things which are under our control, or with those which are not under our control; and, if it has to do with some one of the things not under our control, have ready to hand the answer, "It is nothing to me."

2. Remember that the promise of desire is the attainment of what you desire, that of aversion is not to fall into what is avoided, and that he who fails in his desire is unfortunate, while he who falls into what he would avoid experiences misfortune. If, then, you avoid only what is unnatural among those things which are under your control, you will fall into none of the things which you avoid; but if you try to avoid disease, or death, or poverty, you will experience misfortunate. Withdraw, therefore, your aversion from all the matters that are not under our control, and transfer it to what is unnatural among those which are under our control. But for the time being remove utterly your desire; for if you desire some one of the things that are not under our control you are bound to be unfortunate; and, at the same time, not one of the things that are under our control, which it would be excellent for you to desire, is within your grasp. But employ only choice and refusal, and these too but lightly, and with reservations, and without straining.

3. With everything which entertains you, is useful, or of which you are fond, remember to say to yourself, beginning with the very least things, "What is its nature?" If you are fond of a jug, say, "I am fond of a jug"; for when it is broken you will not be disturbed. If you kiss your own child or

wife, say to yourself that you are kissing a human being; for when it dies you will not be disturbed.

4. When you are on the point of putting your hand to some undertaking, remind yourself what the nature of that undertaking is. If you are going out of the house to bathe, put before your mind what happens at a public bath—those who splash you with water, those who jostle against you, those who vilify you and rob you. And thus you will set about your undertaking more securely if at the outset you say to yourself, "I want to take a bath, and, at the same time, to keep my moral purpose in harmony with nature." And so do in every undertaking. For thus, if anything happens to hinder you in your bathing, you will be ready to say, "Oh, well, this was not the only thing that I wanted, but I wanted also keep my moral purpose in harmony with nature; and I shall not so keep it if I am vexed at what is going on."

5. It is not the things themselves that disturb men, but their judgments about these things. For example, death is nothing dreadful, or else Socrates too would have thought so, but the judgment that death is dreadful, *this* is the dreadful thing. When, therefore, we are hindered, or disturbed, or grieved, let us never blame anyone but ourselves, that means, our own judgments. It is the part of an uneducated person to blame others where he himself fares ill; to blame himself is the part of one whose education has begun; to blame neither another nor his own self is the part of one whose education is already complete.

6. Be not elated at any excellence which is not your own. If the horse in his elation were to say, "I am beautiful," it could be endured; but when you say in your elation, "I have a beautiful horse," rest assured that you are elated at something good which belongs to a horse. What, then, is your own? The use of external impressions. Therefore, when you are in harmony with nature in the use of external impressions, then be elated; for then it will be some good of your own at which you will be elated.

7. Just as on a voyage, when your ship has anchored, if you should go on shore to get fresh water, you may pick up a small shell-fish or little bulb on the way, but you have to keep your attention fixed on the ship, and turn about frequently for fear lest the captain should call; and if he calls, you must give up all these things, if you would escape being thrown on board all tied up like the sheep. So it is also in life: If there be given you, instead of a little bulb and a small shell-fish, a little wife and child, there will be no objection to that; only, if the Captain calls, give up all these things and run to the ship, without even turning around to look back. And if you are an old man, never even get very far away from the ship, for fear that when He calls you may be missing.

8. Do not seek to have everything that happens happen as you wish, but wish for everything to happen as it actually does happen, and your life will be serene.

9. Disease is an impediment to the body, but not to the moral purpose, unless that consents. Lameness is an impediment to the leg, but not to the moral purpose. And say this to yourself at each thing that befalls you; for you will find the thing to be an impediment to something else, but not to yourself.

10. In the case of everything that befalls you, remember to turn to yourself and see what faculty you have to deal with it. If you see a handsome lad or woman, you will find continence the faculty to employ here; if hard labour is laid upon you, you will find endurance; if reviling, you will find patience to bear evil. And if you habituate yourself in this fashion, your external impressions will not run away with you.

11. Never say about anything, "I have lost it," but only "I have given it back." Is your child dead? It has been given back. Is your wife dead? She has been given back. "I have had my farm taken away." Very well, this too has been given back. "Yet it was a rascal who took it away." But what concern is it of yours by whose instrumentality the Giver called for its return? So long as He gives it to you, take care of it as of a thing that is not your own, as travellers treat their inn.

12. If you wish to make progress, dismiss all reasoning of this sort: "If I neglect my affairs, I shall have nothing to live on." "If I do not punish my slave-boy he will turn out bad." For it is better to die of hunger, but in a state of freedom from

grief and fear, than to live in plenty, but troubled in mind. And it is better for your slave-boy to be bad than for you to be unhappy. Begin, therefore, with the little things. Your paltry oil gets spilled, your miserable wine stolen; say to yourself, "This is the price paid for a calm spirit, this the price for peace of mind." Nothing is got without a price. And when you call your slave-boy, bear in mind that it is possible he may not heed you, and again, that even if he does heed, he may not do what you want done. But he is not in so happy a condition that your peace of mind depends upon him.

13. If you wish to make progress, then be content to appear senseless and foolish in externals, do not make it your wish to give the appearance of knowing anything; and if some people think you to be an important personage, distrust yourself. For be assured that it is no easy matter to keep your moral purpose in a state of conformity with nature, and, at the same time, to keep externals; but the man who devotes his attention to one of these two things must inevitably neglect the other.

14. If you make it your will that your children and your wife and your friends should live forever, you are silly; for you are making it your will that things not under your control should be under your control, and that what is not your own should be your own. In the same way, too, if you make it your will that your slave-boy be free from faults, you are a fool; for you are making it your will that vice be not vice, but something else. If, however, it is your will not to fail in what you desire, this is in your power. Wherefore, exercise yourself in that which is in your power. Each man's master is the person who has the authority over what the man wishes or does not wish, so as to secure it, or take it away. Whoever, therefore, wants to be free, let him neither wish for anything, nor avoid anything, that is under the control of others; or else he is necessarily a slave.

15. Remember that you ought to behave in life as you would at a banquet. As something is being passed around it comes to you; stretch out your hand and take a portion of it politely. It passes on; do not detain it. Or it has not come to you yet; do not project your desire to meet it, but wait until it comes in front of you. So act toward children, so toward a wife, so toward office, so toward wealth; and then some day you will be worthy of the banquets of the gods. But if you do not take these things even when they are set before you, but despise them, then you will not only share the banquet of the gods, but share also their rule. For it was by so doing that Diogenes and Heracleitus, and men like them, were deservedly divine and deservedly so called.

16. When you see someone weeping in sorrow, either because a child has gone on a journey, or because he has lost his property, beware that you be not carried away by the impression that the man is in the midst of external ills, but straightway keep before you this thought: "It is not what has happened that distresses this man (for it does not distress another), but his judgment about it." Do not, however, hesitate to sympathize with him so far as words go, and, if occasion offers, even to groan with him; but be careful not to groan also in the centre of your being.

17. Remember that you are an actor in a play, the character of which is determined by the Playwright; if He wishes the play to be short, it is short; if long, it is long; if He wishes you to play the part of a beggar, remember to act even this rôle adroitly; and so if your rôle be that of a cripple, an official, or a layman. For this is your business, to play admirably the rôle assigned you; but the selection of that rôle is Another's.

18. When a raven croaks inauspiciously, let not the external impression carry you away, but straightway draw a distinction in your mind, and say, "None of these portents are for me, but either for my paltry body, or my paltry estate, or my paltry opinion, or my children, or my wife. But for me every portent is favourable, if I so wish; for whatever be the outcome, it is within my power to derive benefit from it."

19. You can be invincible if you never enter a contest in which victory is not under your control. Beware lest, when you see some person preferred to you in honour, or possessing great power, or otherwise enjoying high repute, you are ever carried away by the external impression, and deem him happy. For if the true nature of the good is one of the things that are under our control, there

is no place for either envy or jealousy; and you yourself will not wish to be a praetor, or a senator, or a consul, but a free man. Now there is but one way that leads to this, and that is to despise the things that are not under our control.

20. Bear in mind that it is not the man who reviles or strikes you that insults you, but it is your judgment that these men are insulting you. Therefore, when someone irritates you, be assured that it is your own opinion which has irritated you. And so make it your first endeavour not to be carried away by the external impression; for if once you gain time and delay, you will more easily become master of yourself.

21. Keep before your eyes day by day death and exile, and everything that seems terrible, but most of all death; and then you will never have any abject thought, nor will you yearn for anything beyond measure.

22. If you yearn for philosophy, prepare at once to be met with ridicule, to have many people jeer at you, and say, "Here he is again, turned philosopher all of a sudden," and "Where do you suppose he got that high brow?" But do you not put on a high brow, and do you so hold fast to the things which to you seem best, as a man who has been assigned by God to this post; and remember that if you abide by the same principles, those who formerly used to laugh at you will later come to admire you, but if you are worsted by them, you will get the laugh on yourself twice.

23. If it should ever happen to you that you turn to externals with a view to pleasing someone, rest assured that you have lost your plan of life. Be content, therefore, in everything to *be* a philosopher, and if you wish also to be taken for one, show to yourself that you are one, and you will be able to accomplish it.

24. Let not these reflections oppress you: "I shall live without honour, and be nobody anywhere." For, if lack of honour is an evil, you cannot be in evil through the instrumentality of some other person, any more than you can be in shame. It is not your business, is it, to get office, or to be invited to a dinner-party? Certainly not. How, then, can this be any longer a lack of honour? And how is it that you will be "nobody anywhere," when you ought to be somebody only in those things which are under your control, wherein you are privileged to be a man of the very greatest honour? But your friends will be without assistance? What do you mean by being "without assistance"? They will not have paltry coin from you, and you will not make them Roman citizens. Well, who told you that these are some of the matters under our control, and not rather things which others do? And who is able to give another what he does not himself have? "Get money, then," says some friend, "in order that we too may have it." If I can get money and at the same time keep myself self-respecting, and faithful, and high-minded, show me the way and I will get it. But if you require me to lose the good things that belong to me, in order that you may acquire the things that are not good, you can see for yourselves how unfair and inconsiderate you are. And which do you really prefer? Money, or a faithful and self-respecting friend? Help me, therefore, rather to this end, and do not require me to do those things which will make me lose these qualities.

"But my country," says he, "so far as lies in me, will be without assistance." Again I ask, what kind of assistance do you mean? It will not have loggias or baths of your providing. And what does that signify? For neither does it have shoes provided by the blacksmith, nor has it arms provided by the cobbler; but it is sufficient if each man fulfill his own proper function. And if you secured for it another faithful and self-respecting citizen, would you not be doing it any good? "Yes." Very well, and then you also would not be useless to it. "What place, then, shall I have in the State?" says he. Whatever place you *can* have, and at the same time maintain the man of fidelity and self-respect that is in you. But if, through your desire to help the State, you lose these qualities, of what good would you become to it, when in the end you turned out to be shameless and unfaithful?

25. Has someone been honoured above you at a dinner-party, or in salutation, or in being called in to give advice? Now if these matters are good, you ought to be happy that he got them; but if evil, be not distressed because you did not get them; and bear in mind that, if you do not act the same way that others do, with a view to getting things which are not under our control, you can-

not be considered worthy to receive an equal share with others. Why, how is it possible for a person who does not haunt some man's door, to have equal shares with the man who does? For the man who does not do escort duty, with the man who does? For the man who does not praise, with the man who does? You will be unjust, therefore, and insatiable, if, while refusing to pay the price for which such things are bought, you want to obtain them for nothing. Well, what is the price for heads of lettuce? An obol, perhaps. If, then, somebody gives up his obol and gets his heads of lettuce, while you do not give up your obol, and do not get them, do not imagine that you are worse off than the man who gets his lettuce. For as he has his heads of lettuce, so you have your obol which you have not given away.

Now it is the same way also in life. You have not been invited to somebody's dinner-party? Of course not; for you didn't give the host the price at which he sells his dinner. He sells it for praise; he sells it for personal attention. Give him the price, then, for which it is sold, if it is to your interest. But if you wish both not to give up the one and yet to get the other, you are insatiable and a simpleton. Have you, then, nothing in place of the dinner? Indeed you have; you have not had to praise the man you did not want to praise; you have not had to put up with the insolence of his doorkeepers.

26. What the will of nature is may be learned from a consideration of the points in which we do not differ from one another. For example, when some other person's slave-boy breaks his drinking-cup, you are instantly ready to say "That's one of the things which happen." Rest assured, then, that when your own drinking-cup gets broken, you ought to behave in the same way that you do when the other man's cup is broken. Apply now the same principle to the matters of greater importance. Some other person's child or wife has died; no one but would say, "Such is the fate of man." Yet when a man's own child dies, immediately the cry is, "Alas! Woe is me!" But we ought to remember how we feel when we hear of the same misfortune befalling others.

27. Just as a mark is not set up in order to be missed, so neither does the nature of evil arise in the universe.

28. If someone handed over your body to any person who met you, you would be vexed; but that you hand over your mind to any person that comes along, so that, if he reviles you, it is disturbed and troubled — are you not ashamed of that?

29. In each separate thing that you do, consider the matters which come first and those which follow after, and only then approach the thing itself. Otherwise, at the start you will come to it enthusiastically, because you have never reflected upon any of the subsequent steps, but later on, when some difficulties appear, you will give up disgracefully. Do you wish to win an Olympic victory? So do I, by the gods! for it is a fine thing. But consider the matters which come before that, and those which follow after, and only when you have done that, put your hand to the task. You have to submit to discipline, follow a strict diet, give up sweet cakes, train under compulsion, at a fixed hour, in heat or in cold; you must not drink cold water, nor wine just whenever you feel like it; you must have turned yourself over to your trainer precisely as you would to a physician. Then when the contest comes on, you have to "dig in" beside your opponent, and sometimes dislocate your wrist, sprain your ankle, swallow quantities of sand, sometimes take a scourging, and along with all that get beaten. After you have considered all these points, go on into the games, if you still wish to do so; otherwise, you will be turning back like children. Sometimes they play wrestlers, again gladiators, again they blow trumpets, and then act a play. So you too are now an athlete, now a gladiator, then a rhetorician, then a philosopher, yet with your whole soul nothing; but like an ape you imitate whatever you see, and one thing after another strikes your fancy. For you have never gone out after anything with circumspection, nor after you had examined it all over, but you act at haphazard and half-heartedly.

In the same way, when some people have seen a philosopher and have heard him speaking like Euphrates (though, indeed, who can speak like him?), they wish to be philosophers themselves. Man, consider first the nature of the business, and then learn your own natural ability, if you are able to bear it. Do you wish to be a contender in the pentathlon, or a wrestler? Look to your arms, your thighs, see what your loins are like. For one man has a natural talent for one thing, another for another. Do you suppose that you can eat in the same fashion, drink in the same fashion, give way to impulse and to irritation, just as you do now? You must keep vigils, work hard, abandon your own people, be despised by a paltry slave, be laughed to scorn by those who meet you, in everything get the worst of it, in honour, in office, in court, in every paltry affair. Look these drawbacks over carefully, if you are willing at the price of these things to secure tranquillity, freedom and calm. Otherwise, do not approach philosophy; don't act like a child—now a philosopher, later on a tax-gatherer, then a rhetorician, then a procurator of Caesar. These things do not go together. You must be one person, either good or bad; you must labour to improve either your own governing principle or externals; you must work hard either on the inner man, or on things outside; that is, play either the role of a philosopher or else that of a layman.

30. Our duties are in general measured by our social relationships. He is a father. One is called upon to take care of him, to give way to him in all things, to submit when he reviles or strikes you. "But he is a bad father." Did nature, then, bring you into relationship with a *good* father? No, but simply with a father. "My brother does me wrong." Very well, then, maintain the relation that you have toward him; and do not consider what he is doing, but what you will have to do, if your moral purpose is to be in harmony with nature. For no one will harm you without your consent; you will have been harmed only when you think you are harmed. In this way, therefore, you will discover what duty to expect of your neighbor, your citizen, your commanding officer, if you acquire the habit of looking at your social relations with them.

31. In piety towards the gods, I would have you know, the chief element is this, to have right opinions about them—as existing and as administering the universe well and justly—and to have set yourself to obey them and to submit to everything that happens, and to follow it voluntarily, in the belief that it is being fulfilled by the highest intelligence. For if you act in this way, you will never blame the gods, nor find fault with them for neglecting you. But this result cannot be secured in any other way than by withdrawing your idea of the good and the evil from the things which are not under our control, and placing it in those which are under our control, and in those alone. Because, if you think any of those former things to be good or evil, then, when you fail to get what you want and fall into what you do not want, it is altogether inevitable that you will blame and hate those who are responsible for these results. For this is the nature of every living creature, to flee from and to turn aside from the things that appear harmful, and all that produces them, and to pursue after and to admire the things that are helpful, and all that produces them. Therefore, it is impossible for a man who thinks that he is being hurt to take pleasure in that which he thinks is hurting him, just as it is also impossible for him to take pleasure in the hurt itself. Hence it follows that even a father is reviled by a son when he does not give his child some share in the things that seem to be good; and this it was which made Polyneices and Eteocles enemies of one another, the thought that the royal power was a good thing. That is why the farmer reviles the gods, and so also the sailor, and the merchant, and those who have lost their wives and their children. For where a man's interest lies, there is also his piety. Wherefore, whoever is careful to exercise desire and aversion as he should is at the same time careful also about piety. But it is always appropriate to make libations, and sacrifices, and to give of the firstfruits after the manner of our fathers, and to do all this with purity, and not in a slovenly or careless fashion, nor, indeed, in a niggardly way, nor yet beyond our means.

32. When you have recourse to divination, remember that you do not know what the issue is going to be, but that you have come in order to find out from the diviner; yet if you are indeed a philosopher, you know, when you arrive, what the nature of it is. For if it is one of the things which are not under our control, it is altogether necessary that what is going to take place is neither good nor evil. Do not, therefore, bring to the diviner desire or aversion, and do not approach him with trembling, but having first made up your mind that

every issue is indifferent and nothing to you, but that, whatever it may be, it will be possible for you to turn it to good use, and that no one will prevent this. Go, then, with confidence to the gods as to counsellors; and after that, when some counsel has been given you, remember whom you have taken as counsellors, and whom you will be disregarding if you disobey. But go to divination as Socrates thought that men should go, that is, in cases where the whole inquiry has reference to the outcome, and where neither from reason nor from any other technical art are means vouchsafed for discovering the matter in question. Hence, when it is your duty to share the danger of a friend or of your country, do not ask of the diviner whether you ought to share that danger. For if the diviner forewarns you that the omens of sacrifice have been unfavourable, it is clear that death is portended, or the injury of some member of your body, or exile; yet reason requires that even at this risk you are to stand by your friend, and share the danger with your country. Wherefore, give heed to the great diviner, the Pythian Apollo, who cast out of his temple the man who had not helped his friend when he was being murdered.

33. Lay down for yourself, at the outset, a certain stamp and type of character for yourself, which you are to maintain whether you are by yourself or at a meeting with people. And be silent for the most part, or else make only the most necessary remarks, and express these in few words. But rarely, and when occasion requires you to talk, talk, indeed, but about no ordinary topics. Do not talk about gladiators, or horse-races, or athletes, or things to eat or drink — topics that arise on all occasions; but above all, do not talk about people, either blaming, or praising, or comparing them. If, then, you can, by your own conversation bring over that of your companions to what is seemly. But if you happen to be left alone in the presense of aliens, keep silence.

Do not laugh much, nor at many things, nor boisterously.

Refuse, if you can, to take an oath at all, but if that is impossible, refuse as far as circumstances allow.

Avoid entertainments given by outsiders and by persons ignorant of philosophy; but if an appropriate occasion arises for you to attend, be on the alert to avoid lapsing into the behavior of such laymen. For you may rest assured, that, if a man's companion be dirty, the person who keeps close company with him must of necessity get a share of his dirt, even though he himself happens to be clean.

In things that pertain to the body take only as much as your bare need requires, I mean such things as food, drink, clothing, shelter and household slaves; but cut down everything which is for outward show or luxury.

In your sex-life preserve purity, as far as you can, before marriage, and, if you indulge, take only those privileges which are lawful. However, do not make yourself offensive, or censorious, to those who do indulge, and do not make frequent mention of the fact that you do not yourself indulge.

If someone brings you word that So-and-so is speaking ill of you, do not defend yourself against what has been said, but answer, "Yes, indeed, for he did not know the rest of the faults that attach to me; if he had, these would not have been the only ones he mentioned."

It is not necessary, for the most part, to go to the public shows. If, however, a suitable occasion ever arises, show that your principle concern is for none other than yourself, which means, wish only for that to happen which does happen, and for him only to win who does win; for so you will suffer no hindrance. But refrain utterly from shouting, or laughter at anyone, or great excitement. And after you have left, do not talk a great deal about what took place, except in so far as it contributes to your own improvement; for such behavior indicates that the spectacle has aroused your admiration.

Do not go rashly or readily to people's public readings, but when you do go, maintain your own dignity and gravity, and at the same time be careful not to make yourself disagreeable.

When you are about to meet somebody, in particular when it is one of those men who are held in very high esteem, propose to yourself the question, "What would Socrates or Zeno have done under these circumstances?" and then you will not be at a loss to make proper use of the occasion. When you go to see one of those men who have great power, propose to yourself the thought, that you will not find him at home, that you will be shut out, that the door will be slammed in your face, that he will pay no attention to you. And if, despite all this, it is your duty to go, go and take what comes, and never say to yourself, "It was not worth all the trouble." For this is characteristic of the layman, that is, a man who is vexed at externals.

In your conversation avoid making mention at great length and excessively of your own deeds or dangers, because it is not as pleasant for others to hear about your adventures, as it is for you to call to mind your own dangers.

Avoid also raising a laugh, for this is a kind of behavior that slips easily into vulgarity, and at the same time is calculated to lessen the respect which your neighbours have of you. It is dangerous also to lapse into foul language. When, therefore, anything of the sort occurs, if the occasion be suitable, go even so far as to reprove the person who has made such a lapse; if, however, the occasion does not arise, at all events show by keeping silence, and blushing, and frowning, that you are displeased by what has been said.

34. When you get an external impression of some pleasure, guard yourself, as with impressions in general, against being carried away by it; nay, let the matter wait upon *your* leisure, and give yourself a little delay. Next think of the two periods of time, first, that in which you will enjoy your pleasure, and second, that in which, after the enjoyment is over, you will later repent and revile your own self; and set over against these two periods of time how much joy and self-satisfaction you will get if you refrain. However, if you feel that a suitable occasion has arisen to do the deed, be careful not to allow its enticement, and sweetness, and attractiveness to overcome you; but set over against all this the thought, how much better is the consciousness of having won a victory over it.

35. When you do a thing which you have made up your mind ought to be done, never try not to be seen doing it, even though most people are likely to think unfavourably about it. If, however, what you are doing is not right, avoid the deed itself altogether; but if it is right, why fear those who are going to rebuke you wrongly?

36. Just as the propositions, "It is day," and "It is night," are full of meaning when separated, but meaningless if united; so also, granted that for you to take the larger share at a dinner is good for your body, still, it is bad for the maintenance of the proper kind of social feeling. When, therefore, you are eating with another person, remember to regard, not merely the value for your body of what lies before you, but also to maintain your respect for your host.

37. If you undertake a rôle which is beyond your powers, you both disgrace yourself in that one, and at the same time neglect the rôle which you might have filled with success.

38. Just as you are careful, in walking about, not to step on a nail or to sprain your ankle, so be careful also not to hurt your governing principle. And if we observe this rule in every action, we shall be more secure in setting about it.

39. Each man's body is a measure for his property, just as the foot is a measure for his shoe. If, then, you abide by this principle, you will maintain the proper measure, but if you go beyond it, you cannot help but fall headlong over a precipice, as it were, in the end. So also in the case of your shoe; if once you go beyond the foot, you get first a gilded shoe, then a purple one, then an embroidered one. For once you go beyond the measure there is no limit.

40. Immediately after they are fourteen, women are called "ladies" by men. And so when they see that they have nothing else but only to be the bedfellows of men, they begin to beautify themselves, and put all their hopes in that. It is worth while for us to take pains, therefore, to make them understand that they are honoured for nothing else but only for appearing modest and self-respecting.

41. It is a mark of an ungifted man to spend a great deal of time in what concerns his body, as in much exercise, much eating, much drinking, much evacuating of the bowels, much copulating. But these things are to be done in passing; and let your whole attention be devoted to the mind.

42. When someone treats you ill or speaks ill of you, remember that he acts or speaks thus because he thinks it is incumbent upon him. That being the case, it is impossible for him to follow

what appears good to you, but what appears good to himself; whence it follows, that, if he gets a wrong view of things, the man that suffers is the man that has been deceived. For if a person thinks a true composite judgment to be false, the composite judgment does not suffer, but the person who has been deceived. If, therefore, you start from this point of view, you will be gentle with the man who reviles you. For you should say on each occasion, "He thought that way about it."

43. Everything has two handles, by one of which it ought to be carried and by the other not. If your brother wrongs you, do not lay hold of the matter by the handle of the wrong that he is doing, because this is the handle by which the matter ought not to be carried; but rather by the other handle—that he is your brother, that you were brought up together, and then you will be laying hold of the matter by the handle by which it ought to be carried.

44. The following statements constitute a *non sequitur*: "I am richer than you, therefore I am superior to you"; or, I am more eloquent than you are, therefore I am superior to you." But the following conclusions are better: "I am richer than you are, therefore my property is superior to yours"; or, "I am more eloquent than you are, therefore my elocution is superior to yours." But *you* are neither property nor elocution.

45. Somebody is hasty about bathing; do not say that he bathes badly, but that he is hasty about bathing. Somebody drinks a good deal of wine; do not say that he drinks badly, but that he drinks a good deal. For until you have decided what judgment prompts him, how do you know that what he is doing is bad? And thus the final result will not be that you receive convincing sense-impressions of some things, but give your assent to others.

46. On no occasion call yourself a philosopher, and do not, for the most part, talk among laymen about your philosophic principles, but do what follows from your principles. For example, at a banquet do not say how people ought to eat, but eat as a man ought. For remember how Socrates had so completely eliminated the thought of ostentation, that people came to him when they wanted him to introduce them to philosophers, and he used to bring them along. So well did he submit to being overlooked. And if talk about some philosophic principle arises among laymen, keep silence for the most part, for there is great danger that you will spew up immediately what you have not digested. So when a man tells you that you know nothing, and you, like Socrates, are not hurt, then rest assured that you are making a beginning with the business you have undertaken. For sheep too, do not bring their fodder to the shepherds and show how much they have eaten, but they digest their food within them, and on the outside produce wool and milk. And so do you, therefore, make no display to the laymen of your philosophical principles, but let them see the results which come from these principles when digested.

47. When you have become adjusted to simple living in regard to your bodily wants, do not preen yourself about the accomplishment; and so likewise, if you are a water-drinker, do not on every occasion say that you are a water-drinker. And if ever you want to train to develop physical endurance, do it by yourself and not for outsiders to behold; do not throw your arms around statues, but on occasion, when you are very thirsty, take cold water into your mouth, and then spit it out, without telling anybody.

48. This is the position and character of a layman: He never looks for either help or harm from himself, but only from externals. This is the position and character of the philosopher: He looks for all his help or harm from himself.

Signs of one who is making progress are: He censures no one, praises no one, blames no one, finds fault with no one, says nothing about himself as though he were somebody or knew something. When he is hampered or prevented, he blames himself. And if anyone compliments him, he smiles to himself at the person complimenting; while if anyone censures him, he makes no defence. He goes about like an invalid, being careful not to disturb, before it has grown firm, any part which is getting well. He has put away from himself his every desire, and has transferred his aversion to those things only, of what is under our control, which are contrary to nature. He exercises no pronounced choice in regard to anything. If he gives the appearance of being foolish or ignorant he does not care. In a word, he keeps guard against himself as though he were his own enemy lying in wait.

49. When a person gives himself airs because he can understand and interpret the books of Chrysippus, say to yourself, "If Chrysippus had not written obscurely, this man would have nothing about which to give himself airs."

But what is it I want? To learn nature and to follow her. I seek, therefore, someone to interpret her; and having heard that Chrysippus does so, I go to him. But I do not understand what he has written; I seek, therefore, the person who interprets Chrysippus. And down to this point there is nothing to justify pride. But when I find the interpreter, what remains is to put his precepts into practice; this is the only thing to be proud about. If, however, I admire the mere act of interpretation, what have I done but turned into a grammarian instead of a philosopher? The only difference, indeed, is that I interpret Chrysippus instead of Homer. Far from being proud, therefore, when somebody says to me, "Read me Chrysippus," I blush the rather, when I am unable to show him such deeds as match and harmonize with his words.

50. Whatever principles are set before you, stand fast by these like laws, feeling that it would be impiety for you to transgress them. But pay no attention to what somebody says about you, for this is, at length, not under your control.

51. How long will you still wait to think yourself worthy of the best things, and in nothing to transgress against the distinctions set up by the reason? You have received the philosophical principles which you ought to accept, and you have accepted them. What sort of a teacher, then, do you still wait for, that you should put off reforming yourself until he arrives? You are no longer a lad, but already a full-grown man. If you are now neglectful and easy-going, and always making one delay after another, and fixing first one day and then another, after which you will pay attention to yourself, then without realizing it you will make no progress, but, living and dying, will continue to be a layman throughout. Make up your mind, therefore, before it is too late, that the fitting thing for you to do is to live as a mature man who is making progress, and let everything which seems to you to be best be for you a law that must not be transgressed. And if you meet anything that is laborious, or sweet, or held in high repute, or in no repute, remember that *now* is the contest, and here before you are the Olympic games, and that it is impossible to delay any longer, and that it depends on a single day and a single action, whether progress is lost or saved. This is the way Socrates became what he was, by paying attention to nothing but his reason in everything that he encountered. And even if you are not yet a Socrates, still you ought to live as one who wishes to be a Socrates.

52. The first and most necessary division in philosophy is that which has to do with the application of the principles, as, for example, Do not lie. The second deals with the demonstrations, as, for example, How comes it that we ought not to lie? The third confirms and discriminates between these processes, as, for example, How does it come that this is a proof? For what is a proof, what is logical consequence, what contradiction, what truth, what falsehood? Therefore, the third division is necessary because of the second, and the second because of the first; while the most necessary of all, and the one in which we ought to rest, is the first. But we do the opposite; for we spend our time in the third division, and all our zeal is devoted to it, while we utterly neglect the first. Wherefore, we lie, indeed, but are ready with the arguments which prove that one ought not to lie.

53. Upon every occasion we ought to have the following thoughts at our command:

> Lead thou me on, O Zeus, and Destiny.
> To that goal long ago to me assigned.
> I'll follow and not falter; if my will
> Prove weak and craven, still I'll follow on.
> "Whoso has rightly with necessity complied,
> We count him wise, and skilled in things divine."
> "Well, O Crito, if so it is pleasing to the gods, so let it be."
> "Anytus and Meletus can kill me, but they cannot hurt me."

Study Questions

1. What things are under our control, according to Epictetus, and what does that have to do with how you should live your life?
2. What does Epictetus advise you do before each undertaking?
3. What things disturb people, according to Epictetus?
4. What should you seek to have happen, according to Epictetus?
5. What would Epictetus advise you to do if a loved one had died?
6. When you see someone in sorrow, what should you do, according to Epictetus?
7. What does Epictetus mean by saying that our duties are measured by our social relationships?
8. How should you behave in society, according to Epictetus?

EARLY CHRISTIAN ETHICS

By the end of the second century A.D., the colossus that was the Roman Empire had begun to decline. In the last part of the fifth century, the last of the West Roman emperors, Romulus Augustulus, was deposed by the Goths — an event so unremarkable at the time that, had it happened today, it would have been buried in the back pages of the *New York Times*— and the Dark Ages followed.

During the decline of Rome, and prior to the Dark Ages, Christianity had spread throughout all classes of Roman society. Vigorous and violent official persecution of Christians gradually gave way to toleration and then finally, in the fourth century, to outright support under Constantine. Church and state thus ultimately became two distinct authorities within society, living side by side through periods both of conflict and alliance.

The rise of Christianity is usually attributed to its offer of happiness in the next world, which appealed to the suffering masses (among others). Of course, happiness in the next world may hold certain attractions even for those who are fully comfortable with this life. Still, the early church fathers — Paul, for instance — held that this world is merely a proving ground for boundless reward in an afterlife. Saint Augustine (354–430), the greatest philosopher of the later period of the Roman empire, agreed.

Augustine

Augustine helped provide a philosophical framework for Christian dogma. In doing this, he was much influenced by earlier philosophical traditions, especially those flowing from Plato and from the Stoics. Augustine is sometimes said to have "Platonized" Christianity.

And for good reason. Think back for a moment to Plato. Plato invented the two-worlds philosophy. There, on the one hand, is the Light: the realm of Forms that are perfect, unchanging, timeless, and the source of all that is good and all that is real. Here, on the other hand, is the Darkness: the world of matter, of ignorance, illusion, and error — the world of shadow-things.

Augustine realized that Plato's idea of two realms was quite intelligible, and thus he made his own distinction between the natural world and a further dimension in which God exists. This is not to say that Augustine thought that God was a Platonic Form: Augustine's God is a personal deity, a living intelligence.

Augustine also found in Plato's philosophy a potential answer to what is known as the *problem of evil,* which we can state as follows: If evil exists because God cannot prevent it from existing, then God is not all-powerful. Conversely, if he is all-powerful, then he permits evil to exist, which means that he is not all-good. In short, given the existence of evil, it seems either that God is not all-powerful or is not all-good.

A lazy response to the problem is to dismiss it as "mere words," or to say, "God has his reasons, and it isn't for us to try to understand them." But deeper Christian thinkers have recognized that the problem of evil is a serious problem.

Augustine's solution borrows from Plato. Recall that for Plato, the Form *Good* is the source not merely of all goodness, but of all reality. Thus, for Plato, in effect, what lacks in goodness also lacks in reality; therefore, what is totally lacking in goodness — evil — is unreal. Augustine liked this idea. Nature is created by God, he reasoned, and hence nature is good without caveat or qualification. What *appears* to be natural evil — earthquakes, pestilence, flood, famine, and so on — is *disguised* good that really is a part of God's plan. Since true evil is unreal, Augustine could theorize, it is not created by God.

This solution to the problem of evil may seem satisfactory when applied to natural evils, such as floods and earthquakes. Floods are an absence of dryness, and famine is a lack of food, and both arguably may contribute to some long-range divine purpose. But you cannot really explain moral evil, the type of evil caused by the wrongdoing of people, this way, and Augustine was well aware of this. Moral evil, the evil of people, Augustine held, is human *sin*. To understand Augustine's concept of sin, we have to consider his idea of virtue.

Happiness, according to Augustine, lies in having what you love, but for your happiness to be complete, the object of your love must truly be without imperfection. Robert Stewart owns a car that he likes. Brooke Moore also owns a car that he likes. Thus Stewart and Moore both are happy. But Stewart's Lamborghini is vastly superior to Moore's old Plymouth, a fact that Moore himself must concede. So even Moore must admit that Stewart is better off than he is.

True happiness, however, does not come from having cars, for even the best cars have their imperfections. There is indeed only one thing that suffers no imperfections whatsoever: God. Therefore, *true* happiness, according to Augustine, lies in loving God and in "participating in His peace."

According to Augustine, therefore, our highest good, or virtue, consists in loving and having God. Sin, by contrast, is *distorted* love, loving something other than God — money, cars, fame, and so forth — as though this other thing were itself God.

Notice then that virtue and sin, according to Augustine, are thus *conditions of the soul.* What counts, for Augustine, is living out of love for God — that is, having faith. Doing supposedly good deeds is of secondary importance. When it comes to appraising someone's moral worth, what matters is not the person's accomplishments, but the *state of mind* in which or from which he or she acts.

Augustine's two-worlds theory is clearly Platonic in origin. Also recognizably Platonic is the idea that virtue is a condition of the soul, a condition in which the soul is inspired by love for the most perfect of all things. Of course, for Plato this most perfect of all things is the Form of the Good, and Plato would have said that the soul should be governed by reason, not inspired by love for the Christian God.

Augustine's concept of sin and the closely related notion of *free will*, however, certainly are not very Platonic. For Socrates and Plato, as we have seen, wrongdoing is always the result of ignorance. For Augustine, this idea is unacceptable. Adam did not eat of the forbidden fruit because he was ignorant; he did so knowingly, of his own free will. The intertwined concepts of sin and free will are essential to Christian moral philosophy. Without them, it would be difficult to maintain that God is the author only of what is good.

Another important concept in Augustine's moral philosophy that is not found in the earlier Platonic tradition is that this world is a *proving ground* for eternal reward or punishment. Implicit in this belief is the idea that proper living here and now is to be done not for its own sake, but for the sake of eternal bliss. For Augustine, true happiness is a condition of the soul; we achieve it only when we participate in God's peace, and therefore we don't achieve it completely in this life. A vision of God face to face is our reward for faith, for virtue.

The concepts of sin and free will and the theory that this world is a proving ground for the next represent departures from the Platonic tradition. However, the most important departure is at the same time the most obvious one: Augustine believed that the ultimate moral authority is a personal god.

Today, there is very wide acceptance—in Western societies, at any rate—that rightness can be established only by the decrees of a god. To many Westerners, it seems ludicrous to suppose otherwise. "Without God everything is permissible," wrote Dostoyevski. We tend to assume that if there is no God, then there is no ultimate criterion of morality; if God does not exist, then nothing is right and nothing is wrong.

Yet, the matter must be considered carefully. Is it really true that a god, or God, must *decree* that something is right and proper for it to *be* right and proper? As we proceed through the history of philosophy, we'll find several alternatives to this view. (Indeed, we already have. Plato sets forth an alternative to the Augustinian view, as do Aristotle and the Stoics and Epicureans.)

Let's summarize Augustine's views. Although Augustine accepted, with some modification, the two-realms metaphysical framework of Plato, his moral philosophy is distinctively Christian in its emphasis on sin, free will, a personal God as the ultimate moral authority, and the idea that the world is a testing ground for future reward or punishment. These are all common ideas in today's commonsense moral philosophy and are accepted by many who do not regard themselves as Christian.

In the following selection, Saint Augustine explains his views on true happiness and its relationship to God.

from *The Enchiridion* and *The City of God*

Augustine

Augustine, one of the most influential Christian philosophers, lived from 354 to 430. This selection consists of "Good and Evil" from *The Enchiridion*, translated by J. F. Shaw (Edinburgh, 1892) and "The Supreme Good Not in This Life," from *The City of God*, translated by Marcus Dods (n.p., n.d.).

Good and Evil

Chapter X
The Supremely Good Creator Made All Things Good

By the Trinity, thus supremely and equally and unchangeably good, all things were created; and these are not supremely and equally and unchangeably good, but yet they are good, even taken separately. Taken as a whole, however, they are very good, because their *ensemble* constitutes the universe in all its wonderful order and beauty.

Chapter XI
What Is Called Evil in the Universe Is But the Absence of Good

And in the universe, even that which is called evil, when it is regulated and put in its own place, only enhances our admiration of the good; for we enjoy and value the good more when we compare it with the evil. For the Almighty God, who, as even the heathen acknowledge, has supreme power over all things, being Himself supremely good, would never permit the existence of anything evil among His works, if He were not so omnipotent and good that He can bring good even out of evil. For what is that which we call evil but the absence of good? In the bodies of animals, disease and wounds mean nothing but the absence of health; for when a cure is effected, that does not mean that the evils which were present—namely, the diseases and wounds—go away from the body and dwell elsewhere: they altogether cease to exist; for the wound or disease is not a substance, but a defect in the fleshly substance—the flesh itself being a substance, and therefore something good, of which those evils—that is, privations of the good which we call health—are accidents. Just in the same way, what are called vices in the soul are nothing but privations of natural good. And when they are cured, they are not transferred elsewhere: when they cease to exist in the healthy soul, they cannot exist anywhere else.

Chapter XII
All Beings Were Made Good, But Not Being Made Perfectly Good, Are Liable to Corruption

All things that exist, therefore, seeing that the Creator of them all is supremely good, are themselves good. But because they are not, like their Creator, supremely and unchangeably good, their good may be diminished and increased. But for good to be diminished is an evil, although, however much it may be diminished, it is necessary, if the being is to continue, that some good should remain to constitute the being. For however small or of whatever kind the being may be, the good which makes it a being cannot be destroyed without destroying the being itself. An uncorrupted nature is justly held in esteem. But if, still further, it be incorruptible, it is undoubtedly considered of still higher value. When it is corrupted, however, its corruption is an evil, because it is deprived of some sort of good. For if it be deprived of no good, it receives no injury; but it does receive injury, therefore it is deprived of good. Therefore, so long as a being is in process of corruption, there is in it some good of which it is being deprived; and if a part of the being should remain which cannot be corrupted, this will certainly be an incorruptible being, and accordingly the process of corruption will result in the manifestation of this great good. But if it do not cease to be corrupted, neither can it cease to possess good of which corruption may deprive it. But if it should be thoroughly and completely consumed by corruption, there will then be no good left, because there will be no being. Wherefore corruption can consume the good only by consuming the being. Every being, therefore, is a good; a great good, if it can not be corrupted; a little good, if it can: but in any case, only the foolish or ignorant will deny that it is a good. And if it be wholly consumed by corruption, then the corruption itself must cease to exist, as there is no being left in which it can dwell.

Chapter XIII
There Can Be No Evil Where There Is No Good; and an Evil Man Is an Evil Good

Accordingly, there is nothing of what we call evil, if there be nothing good. But a good which is wholly without evil is a perfect good. A good, on the other hand, which contains evil is a faulty or imperfect good; and there can be no evil where there is no good. From all this we arrive at the curious result: that since every being, so far as it is a being, is good, when we say that a faulty being is an evil being, we just seem to say that what is good is evil, and that nothing but what is good can be evil, seeing that every being is good, and that no evil can exist except in a being. Nothing then, can be evil except something which is good. And although this, when stated, seems to be a contradiction, yet the strictness of reasoning leaves us no escape from the conclusion. We must, however, beware of incurring the prophetic condemnation: "Woe unto them that call evil good, and good evil: that put darkness for light, and light for darkness: that put bitter for sweet, and sweet for bitter." And yet our Lord says: "An evil man out of the evil treasure of his heart bringeth forth that which is evil." Now, what is an evil man but an evil being? for a man is a being. Now, if a man is a good thing because he is a being, what is an evil man but an evil good? Yet, when we accurately distinguish these two things, we find that it is not because he is a man that he is evil, or because he is wicked that he is a good; but that he is a good because he is a man, and an evil because he is wicked. Whoever, then, says, "To be a man is an evil," or, "To be wicked is a good," falls under the prophetic denunciation: "Woe unto them that call evil good and good evil!" For he condemns the work of God, which is the man, and praises the defect of man, which is the wickedness. Therefore every being, even if it be a defective one, in so far as it is a being is good, and in so far as it is defective is evil.

Chapter XIV
Good and Evil Are an Exception to the Rule that Contrary Attributes Cannot Be Predicated of the Same Subject. Evil Springs Up in What Is Good, and Cannot Exist Except in What Is Good

Accordingly, in the case of these contraries which we call good and evil, the rule of the logicians, that two contraries cannot be predicated at the same time of the same thing, does not hold. No weather is at the same time dark and bright: no food or drink is at the same time sweet and bitter: no body is at the same time and in the same place black and white: none is at the same time and in the same place deformed and beautiful. And this rule is found to hold in regard to many, indeed nearly all, contraries, that they cannot exist at the same time in any one thing. But although no one can doubt that good and evil are contraries, not only can they exist at the same time, but evil cannot exist without good, or in anything that is not good. Good, however, can exist without evil. For a man or an angel can exist without being wicked; but nothing can be wicked except a man or an angel: and so far as he is a man or an angel, he is good; so far as he is wicked, he is an evil. And these two contraries are so far co-existent, that if good did not exist in what is evil, neither could evil exist; because corruption could not have either a place to dwell in, or a source to spring from, if there were nothing that could be corrupted; and nothing can be corrupted except what is good, for corruption is nothing else but the destruction of good. From what is good, then, evils arose, and except in what is good they do not exist; nor was there any other source from which any evil nature could arise. For if there were, then, in so far as this was a being, it was certainly a good: and a being which was incorruptible would be a great good; and even one which was corruptible must be to some extent a good, for only by corrupting what was good in it could corruption do it harm.

Chapter XCVI
The Omnipotent God Does Well Even in the Permission of Evil

Nor can we doubt that God does well even in the permission of what is evil. For He permits it only in the justice of His judgment. And surely all that is just is good. Although, therefore, evil, in so far as it is evil, is not a good; yet the fact that evil as well as good exists, is a good. For if it were not a good that evil should exist, its existence would not be permitted by the omnipotent God, who without doubt can as easily refuse to permit what He does not wish, as bring about what He does wish. And if we do not believe this, the very first sentence of our creed is endangered, wherein we profess to believe in God the Father Almighty. For He is not truly called Almighty if He cannot do whatsoever He pleases, or if the power of His almighty will is hindered by the will of any creature whatsoever.

Chapter C
The Will of God Is Never Defeated, Though Much Is Done that is Contrary to His Will

These are the great works of the Lord, sought out according to all His pleasure, and so wisely sought out, that when the intelligent creation, both angelic and human, sinned, doing not His will but their own, He used the very will of the creature which was working in opposition to the Creator's will as an instrument for carrying out His will, the supremely Good thus turning to good account even what is evil, to the condemnation of those whom in His justice He has predestined to punishment, and to the salvation of those whom in His mercy He has predestined to grace. For, as far as relates to their own consciousness, these creatures did what God wished not to be done: but in view of God's omnipotence, they could in no wise effect their purpose. For in the very fact that they acted in opposition to His will, His will concerning them was fulfilled. And hence it is that "the works of the Lord are great, sought out according to all His pleasure," because in a way unspeakably strange and wonderful, even what is done in opposition to His will does not defeat His will. For it would not be done did He not permit it (and of course His permission is not unwilling, but willing); nor would a Good Being permit evil to be done only that in His omnipotence He can turn evil into good.

Chapter CI
The Will of God, Which Is Always Good, Is Sometimes Fulfilled through the Evil Will of Man

Sometimes, however, a man in the goodness of his will desires something that God does not desire, even though God's will is also good, nay, much more fully and more surely good (for His will never can be evil): for example, if a good son is anxious that his father should live, when it is God's good will that he should die. Again, it is possible for a man with evil will to desire what God wills in His goodness: for example, if a bad son wishes his father to die, when this is also the will of God. It is plain that the former wishes what God does not wish, and that the latter wishes what God does wish; and yet the filial love of the former is more in harmony with the good will of God, though its desire is different from God's than the want of filial affection of the latter, though its desire is the same as God's. So necessary is it, in determining whether a man's desire is one to be approved or disapproved, to consider what it is proper for man, and what it is proper for God, to desire, and what is in each case the real motive of the will. For God accomplishes some of His purposes, which of course are all good, through the evil desires of wicked men: for example, it was through the wicked designs of the Jews, working out the good purpose of the Father, that Christ was slain; and this event was so truly good, that when the Apostle Peter expressed his unwillingness that it should take place, he was designated Satan by Him who had come to be slain. How good seemed the intentions of the pious believers who were unwilling that Paul should go up to Jerusalem lest the evils which Agabus had foretold should there befall him! And yet it was God's purpose that he should suffer these evils for preaching the faith of Christ, and thereby become a witness for Christ. And this purpose of His, which was good, God did not fulfill through the good counsels of the Christians, but through the evil counsels of the Jews; so that those who opposed His purpose were more truly His servants than those who were the willing instruments of its accomplishment.

The Supreme Good Not in This Life

If, then, we be asked what . . . the supreme good and evil is, . . . [we] reply that life eternal is the supreme good, death eternal the supreme evil, and that to obtain the one and escape the other we must live rightly. And thus it is written, "The just lives by faith," for we do not as yet see our good, and must therefore live by faith; neither have we in ourselves power to live rightly, but can do so only if He who has given us faith to believe in His help do help us when we believe and pray. As for those who have supposed that the sovereign good and evil are to be found in this life, and have placed it either in the soul or the body, or in both, or, to speak more explicitly, either in pleasure or in virtue, or in both; in repose or in virtue, or in both; in pleasure and repose, or in virtue, or in all combined; in the primary objects of nature, or in virtue, or in both,—all these have, with a marvellous shallowness, sought to find their blessedness in this life and in themselves. Contempt has been poured upon such ideas by the Truth, saying by the prophet, "The Lord knoweth the thoughts of men" (or, as the Apostle Paul cites the passage, "The Lord knoweth the thoughts of the *wise*") "that they are vain."

For what flood of eloquence can suffice to detail the miseries of this life? Cicero, in the *Consolation* on the death of his daughter, has spent all his ability in lamentation; but how inadequate was even his ability here? For when, where, how, in this life can these primary objects of nature be possessed so that they may not be assailed by unforeseen accidents? Is the body of the wise man exempt from any pain which may dispel pleasure, from any disquietude which may banish repose? The amputation or decay of the members of the body puts an end to its integrity, deformity blights its beauty, weakness its health, lassitude its vigour, sleepiness or sluggishness its activity,—and which of these is it that may not assail the flesh of the wise man? Comely and fitting attitudes and movements of the body are numbered among the prime natural blessings; but what if some sickness makes the members tremble? what if a man suffers from curvature of the spine to such an extent that his hands reach the ground, and he goes upon all fours like a quadruped? Does not this destroy all beauty and grace in the body, whether at rest or in motion? What shall I say of the fundamental blessings of the soul, sense and intellect, of which the one is given for the perception, and the other for the comprehension of truth? But what kind of sense is it that remains when a man becomes deaf and blind? where are reason and intellect when disease makes a man delirious? We can scarcely, or not at all, refrain from tears, when we think of or see the actions and words of such frantic persons, and consider how different from and even opposed to their own sober judgment and ordinary conduct their present demeanour is. And what shall I say of those who suffer from demoniacal possession? Where is their own intelligence hidden and buried while the malignant spirit is using their body and soul according to his own will? And who is quite sure that no such thing can happen to the wise man in his life? Then, as to the perception of truth, what can we hope for even in this way while in the body, as we read in the true book of Wisdom, "The corruptible body weigheth down the soul, and the earthly tabernacle presseth down the mind that museth upon many things?" And eagerness, or desire of action . . . is also reckoned among the primary advantages of nature; and yet is it not this which produces those pitiable movements of the insane, and those actions which we shudder to see, when sense is deceived and reason deranged?

In fine, virtue itself, which is not among the primary objects of nature, but succeeds to them as the result of learning, though it holds the highest place among human good things, what is its occupation save to wage perpetual war with vices—not those that are outside of us, but within; not other men's, but our own,—a war which is waged especially by that virtue which . . . we [call] temperance, and which bridles carnal lusts, and prevents them from winning the consent of the spirit to wicked deeds? For we must not fancy that there is no vice in us, when, as the apostle says, "The flesh lusteth against the spirit;" for to this vice there is a contrary virtue, when, as the same writer says, "The spirit lusteth against the flesh." "For these two," he says, "are contrary one to the other, so that you cannot do the things which you would." But what is it we wish to do when we seek to attain the supreme good, unless that the flesh should cease to lust against the spirit, and that there be no vice in us against which the spirit may lust? And as we cannot attain to this in the present life, however ardently we desire it, let us by God's help accomplish at least this, to preserve the soul from succumbing and yielding to the flesh that lusts against it, and to refuse our consent to the perpetration of sin. Far be it from us, then, to fancy that while we are still engaged in this intestine war, we have already found the happiness which we seek to reach by victory. And who is there so wise that he has no conflict at all to maintain against his vices?

What shall I say of that virtue which is called prudence? Is not all its vigilance spent in the discernment of good from evil things, so that no mistake may be admitted about what we should desire and what avoid? And thus it is itself a proof that we are in the midst of evils, or that evils are in us; for it teaches us that it is an evil to consent to sin, and a good to refuse this consent. And yet this evil, to which prudence teaches and temperance enables us not to consent, is removed from this life neither by prudence nor by temperance. And justice, whose office it is to render to every man his due, whereby there is in man himself a certain just order of nature, so that the soul is subjected to God, and the flesh to the soul, and consequently both soul and flesh to God,—does not this virtue demonstrate that it is as yet rather labouring towards its end than resting in its finished work? For the soul is so much the less subjected to God as it is less occupied with the thought of God; and the flesh is so much the less subjected to the spirit as it lusts more vehemently against the spirit. So long, therefore, as we are beset by this weakness, this plague, this disease, how shall we dare to say that we are safe? and if not safe, then how can we be already enjoying our final beatitude? Then that virtue which goes by the name of fortitude is the plainest proof of the ills of life, for it is these ills which it is compelled to bear patiently. And this holds good, no matter though the ripest wisdom co-exists with it. And I am at a loss to understand how the Stoic philosophers can presume to say that these are no ills, though at the same time they allow the wise man to commit suicide and pass out of this life if they become so grievous that he cannot or ought not to endure them. But such is the stupid pride of these men who fancy that the supreme good can be found in this life, and that they can become happy by their own resources, that their wise man, or at least the man whom they fancifully depict as such, is always happy, even though he become blind, deaf, dumb, mutilated, racked with pains, or suffer any conceivable calamity such as may compel him to make away with himself; and they are not ashamed to call the life that is beset with these evils happy. O happy life, which seeks the aid of death to end it! If it is happy, let the wise man remain in it; but if these ills drive him out of it, in what sense is it happy? Or how can they say that these are not evils which conquer the virtue of fortitude, and force it not only to yield, but so to rave that it in one breath calls life happy and recommends it to be given up? For who is so blind as not to see that if it were happy it would not be fled from? And if they say we should flee from it on account of the infirmities that beset it, why then do they not lower their pride and acknowledge that it is miserable? Was it, I would ask, fortitude or weakness which prompted Cato to kill himself? for he would not have done so had he not been too weak to endure Caesar's victory. Where, then, is his fortitude? It has yielded, it has succumbed, it has been so thoroughly overcome as to abandon, forsake, flee this happy life. Or was it no longer happy? Then it was miserable. How, then, were these not evils which made life miserable, and a thing to be escaped from?

And therefore those who admit that these are evils, as the Peripatetics do, and the Old Academy, the sect which Varro advocates, express a more intelligible doctrine; but theirs also is a surprising mistake, for they contend that this is a happy life which is beset by these evils, even though they be so great that he who endures them should commit suicide to escape them. "Pains and anguish of body," says Varro, "are evils, and so much the worse in proportion to their severity; and to escape them you must quit this life." What life, I pray? This life, he says, which is oppressed by such evils. Then it is happy in the midst of these very evils on account of which you say we must quit it? Or do you call it happy because you are at liberty to escape these evils by death? What, then, if by some secret judgment of God you were held fast and not permitted to die, nor suffered to live without these evils? In that case, at least, you would say that such a life was miserable. It is soon relinquished, no doubt, but this does not make it not miserable; for were it eternal, you yourself would pronounce it miserable. Its brevity, therefore, does not clear it of misery; neither ought it to be called happiness because it is a brief misery. Certainly there is a mighty force in these evils which compel a man—according to them, even a wise man—to cease to be a man that he may escape them, though they say, and say truly, that it is as it were the first and strongest demand of nature that a man cherish himself, and naturally therefore avoid death, and should so stand his own friend as to wish and vehemently aim at continuing to exist as a living creature, and subsisting in this union of soul and body. There is a mighty force in these evils to overcome this natural instinct by which death is by every means and with all a man's efforts avoided, and to overcome it so completely that what was avoided is desired, sought after, and if it cannot by any other way be obtained, is inflicted by the man on himself. There is a mighty force in these evils which make fortitude a homicide,—if, indeed, that is to be called fortitude which is so thoroughly overcome by these evils, that it not only cannot preserve by patience the man whom it undertook to govern and defend, but is itself obliged to kill him. The wise man, I admit, ought to bear death with patience, but when it is inflicted by another. If, then, as these men maintain, he is obliged to inflict it on himself, certainly it must be owned that the ills which compel him to this are not only evils, but intolerable evils. The life, then, which is either subject to accidents, or environed with evils so considerable and grievous, could never have been called happy, if the men who give it this name had condescended to yield to the truth, and to be conquered by valid arguments, when they inquired after the happy life, as they yield to unhappiness, and are overcome by the overwhelming evils, when they put themselves to death, and if they had not fancied that the supreme good was to be found in this mortal life; for the very virtues of this life, which are certainly its best and most useful possessions, are all the more telling proofs of its miseries in proportion as they are helpful against the violence of its dangers, toils and woes. For if these are true virtues,—and such cannot exist save in those who have true piety,—they do not profess to be able to deliver the men who possess them from all miseries; for true virtues tell no such lies, but they profess that by the hope of the future world this life, which is miserably involved in the many and great evils of this world is happy as it is also safe. For if not yet safe, how could it be happy? And therefore the Apostle Paul, speaking not of men without prudence, temperance, fortitude and justice, but of those whose lives were regulated by true piety, and whose virtues were therefore true, says, "For we are saved by hope: now hope which is seen is not hope; for what a man seeth, why doth he yet hope for? But if we hope for that we see not, then do we with patience wait for it." As, therefore, we are saved, so we are made happy by hope. And as we do not as yet possess a present, but look for a future salvation, so is it with our happiness, and this "with patience;" for we are encompassed with evils, which we ought patiently to endure, until we come to the ineffable enjoyment of unmixed good; for there shall be no longer anything to endure. Salvation, such as it shall be in the world to come, shall itself be our final happiness. And this happiness these philosophers refuse to believe in, because they do not see it, and attempt to fabricate for themselves a happiness in this life, based upon a virtue which is as deceitful as it is proud.

Study Questions

1. Explain how Augustine absolves God of the charge of having created evil.
2. Can there be evil without there being good, according to Augustine? Explain.
3. Can one and the same thing be both evil and good, according to Augustine? Explain.
4. What is the supreme good and supreme evil, according to Augustine. What must we do to have the one and to escape the other?
5. What, according to Augustine, is the purpose of virtue?
6. What, according to Augustine, is justice?
7. What, according to Augustine, does the virtue of fortitude provide proof of?

Peter Abelard

The Dark Ages lasted from about the time Augustine died to about 1000. During this period, barbarian hordes invaded what had been the Roman Empire, hacking and maiming its once proud corpus. The drumbeat of Western progress slowed and stopped, and the march toward urbanized civilization moved in retrograde. True, the remnants of Roman culture tempered the invading tribes. And in 800, Charlemagne, the Carolingian king of the Franks, created his own replacement "Roman" empire and did his best to preserve classical literature and to halt the decline of the mind. Nevertheless, learning and literacy were rare. Artistic and intellectual achievements during the epoch were few and feeble, illuminating the grim twilight but dimly.

Nevertheless, by the end of the age of invasions (around the middle of the eleventh century), the various barbarian conquerors had been Romanized, that is, civilized and Christianized. The trend toward economic decentralization began to reverse itself. A series of states, miniscule but fairly stable and unified by Catholicism, spread across Europe. Towns grew and prospered. Forests were cleared, river valleys drained, and land reclaimed from the sea. The Church and its officials enjoyed power and prestige. Pope Urban II, fascinated with reclaiming Jerusalem, initiated the Crusades.

During the Middle Ages, as these next few centuries are called, the trend toward intellectual decline also was reversed. One important invigorating intellectual stimulus was Aristotle. In the Dark Ages, his texts had been lost to the Christian world, but not to the Arabian. Gradually, Latin translations of Arab translations of Greek texts, especially those of Aristotle, were circulated among Christian churchmen. Some, notably Albert the Great (1193–1280), regarded Aristotle as the greatest of all philosophers. Many others regarded Aristotle's thought as wholly incompatible with Christian doctrine, but on balance, the rediscovery of Aristotle helped make the medieval mind more receptive to reason. It was now possible to think that human reason is a very useful tool in understanding some of the mysteries of God and nature.

In moral philosophy, the Augustinian theory that virtue is essentially a matter of having a mind that is disposed to do right—that it isn't what you do that matters but the state of mind with which you do it—was accepted throughout the Dark Ages and into the Middle Ages. Some of the implications of this theory were worked out by Peter Abelard (1079–1142), who helped usher in the new age of (relative) enlightenment. He believed the search for truth is aided by argument and questioning. This philosophy was accepted by many *magistri*, the teachers in the universities, which were first formalized at about this time.

Abelard began his exploration of Augustine's theory by making a distinction between moral defects or imperfections, and other defects or imperfections of the mind, such as being dull-witted or having a bad memory. Moral defects are those that incline or dispose you to do what you shouldn't do or not do what you should do.

Abelard made a further distinction between moral defects and sin. Sin is "contempt of God," that is, not doing what we ought to do or not renouncing what we ought to renounce. This definition of sin enabled Abelard to maintain that sin is not real and thus is not something that can be attributed to God.

Having made these distinctions, Abelard argued that sin does not consist in having evil desires, nor in acting on them. Rather, sin consists in *consenting* to act on them. He also allowed that a sinful *act*, an act simply that ought not be done, such as killing someone, can be committed without an evil will. For Abelard, virtue consists not in having no evil desires, but in not consenting to act on them: "The evil will itself, when restrained, though it may not be quenched, procures the palm-wreath for those who resist it."

You will perhaps note that the conceptions of sin given in the preceding two paragraphs are not exactly the same, though perhaps we could restore consistency to Abelard's theories by distinguishing the sinful *act* from the sinful *person*. In any case, Abelard's general view is clear enough: To be evil is not to lack evil impulses, but to consent to act in accordance with them. In short, God "weighs the intention rather than the deed."

This theory dictates that you can be guilty of sin even though you do not do a wrongful or sinful act (if the intent is there, you sin), as well as that you need not be guilty of sin even though your act is wrongful (as, for example, if you are constrained to kill someone while not wanting to do so). It also seems to lead Abelard to the conclusion that there is greater virtue in having evil impulses and not consenting to act on them, than in not having evil impulses at all.

You should keep Abelard in mind when you read about Kant (Chapter 10), who believed that the only thing that is good in and of itself is the good will.

from Ethics

Peter Abelard

Peter Abelard (1079–1142) was a French philosopher, theologian, and composer but was perhaps best known for his love affair with Heloise. Reprinted here are the prologue and first three chapters of *Abelard's Ethics*, translated by J. R. McCallum.

Prologue

In the study of morals we deal with the defects or qualities of the mind which dispose us to bad or good actions. Defects and qualities are not only mental, but also physical. There is bodily weakness; there is also the endurance which we call strength. There is sluggishness or speed; blindness or sight. When we now speak of defects, therefore, we pre-suppose defects of the mind, so as to distinguish them from the physical ones. The defects of the mind are opposed to the qualities; injustice to justice; cowardice to constancy; intemperance to temperance.

Chapter I. The Defect of Mind Bearing upon Conduct

Certain defects or merits of mind have no connection with morals. They do not make human life a matter of praise or blame. Such are dull wits or quick insight; a good or a bad memory; ignorance or knowledge. Each of these features is found in good and bad alike. They have nothing to do with the system of morals, nor with making life base or honourable. To exclude these we safeguarded above the phrase "defects of mind" by adding "which dispose to bad actions," that is, those defects which incline the will to what least of all either should be done or should be left undone.

Chapter II. How Does Sin Differ from a Disposition to Evil?

Defect of this mental kind is not the same thing as sin. Sin, too, is not the same as a bad action. For example, to be irascible, that is, prone or easily roused to the agitation of anger is a defect and moves the mind to unpleasantly impetuous and irrational action. This defect, however, is in the mind so that the mind is liable to wrath, even when it is not actually roused to it. Similarly, lameness, by reason of which a man is said to be lame, is in the man himself even when he does not walk and reveal his lameness. For the defect is there though action be lacking. So, also, nature or constitution renders many liable to luxury. Yet they do not sin because they are like this, but from this very fact they have the material of a struggle whereby they may, in the virtue of temperance, triumph over themselves and win the crown. As Solomon says: "Better a patient than a strong man; and the Lord of his soul than he that taketh a city." (Prov. xvi, 32.) For religion does not think it degrading to be beaten by man; but it is degrading to be beaten by one's lower self. The former defeat has been the fate of good men. But, in the latter, we fall below ourselves. The Apostle commends victory of this sort; "No one shall be crowned who has not truly striven." (2 Tim. ii, 5.) This striving, I repeat, means standing less against men than against myself, so that defects may not lure me into base consent. Though men cease to oppose us, our defects do not cease. The fight with them is the more dangerous because of its repetition. And as it is the more difficult, so victory is the more glorious. Men, however much they prevail over us, do not force baseness upon us, unless by their practice of vice they turn us also to it and overcome us through our own wretched consent.

They may dominate our body; but while our mind is free, there is no danger to true freedom. We run no risk of base servitude. Subservience to vice, not to man, is degradation. It is the overlordship of defects and not physical serfdom which debases the soul.

Chapter III. Definition of "Defect" and of Sin

Defect, then, is that whereby we are disposed to sin. We are, that is, inclined to consent to what we ought not to do, or to leave undone what we ought to do. Consent of this kind we rightly call sin. Here is the reproach of the soul meriting damnation or being declared guilty by God. What is that consent but to despise God and to violate His laws? God cannot be set at enmity by injury, but by contempt. He is the highest power, and is not diminished by any injury, but He avenges contempt of Himself. Our sin, therefore, is contempt of the Creator. To sin is to despise the Creator; that is, not to do for Him what we believe we should do for Him, or, not to renounce what we think should be renounced on His behalf. We have defined sin negatively by saying that it means not doing or not renouncing what we ought to do or renounce. Clearly, then, we have shown that sin has no reality. It exists rather in *not being* than in *being*. Similarly we could define shadows by saying: The absence of light where light usually is.

Perhaps you object that sin is the desire or will to do an evil deed, and that this will or desire condemns us before God in the same way as the will to do a good deed justifies us. There is as much quality, you suggest, in the good will as there is sin in the evil will; and it is no less "in being" in the latter than in the former. By willing to do what we believe to be pleasing to God we please Him. Equally, by willing to do what we believe to be displeasing to God, we displease Him and seem either to violate or despise His nature.

But diligent attention will show that we must think far otherwise of this point. We frequently err, and from no evil will at all. Indeed, the evil will itself, when restrained, though it may not be quenched, procures the palm-wreath for those who resist it. It provides, not merely the materials for combat, but also the crown of glory. It should be spoken of rather as a certain inevitable weakness than as sin. Take, for example, the case of an innocent servant whose harsh master is moved with fury against him. He pursues the servant, drawing his sword with intent to kill him. For a while the servant flies and avoids death as best he can. At last, forced all unwillingly to it, he kills his master so as not to be killed by him. Let anyone say what sort of evil will there was in this deed. His will was only to flee from death and preserve his own life. Was this an evil will? You reply: "I do not think this was an evil will. But the will that he had to kill the master who was pursuing him was evil." Your answer would be admirable and acute if you could show that the servant really willed what you say that he did. But, as I insisted, he was unwillingly forced to his deed. He protracted his master's life as long as he could, knowing that danger also threatened his own life from such a crime. How, then was a deed done voluntarily by which he incurred danger to his own life? . . .

Sin, therefore, is sometimes committed without an evil will. Thus sin cannot be defined as "will." True, you will say, when we sin under constraint, but not when we sin willingly, for instance, when we will to do something which we know ought not to be done by us. There the evil will and sin seem to be the same thing. For example a man sees a woman; his concupiscence is aroused; his mind is enticed by fleshly lust and stirred to base desire. This wish, this lascivious longing, what else can it be, you say, than sin?

I reply: What if that wish may be bridled by the power of temperance? What if its nature is never to be entirely extinguished but to persist in struggle and not fully fail even in defeat? For where is the battle if the antagonist is away? Whence the great reward without grave endurance? When the fight is over nothing remains but to reap the reward. Here we strive in contest in order elsewhere to obtain as victors a crown. Now, for a contest, an opponent is needed who will resist, not one who simply submits. This opponent is our evil will over which we triumph when we subjugate it to the divine will. But we do not entirely destroy it. For we needs must ever expect to encounter our enemy.

What achievement before God is it if we undergo nothing contrary to our own will, but merely practice what we please? Who will be grateful to us if in what we say we do for him we merely satisfy our own fancy?

You will say, what merit have we with God in acting willingly or unwillingly? Certainly none: I reply. He weighs the intention rather than the deed in his recompense. Nor does the deed, whether it proceed from a good or an evil will, add anything to the merit, as we shall show shortly. But when we set His will before our own so as to follow His and not ours, our merit with God is magnified, in accordance with that perfect word of Truth: "I came not to do mine own will, but the will of Him that sent me." (John vi, 38.) To this end He exhorts us: "If anyone comes to me, and does not hate father, and mother . . . yea his own soul also, he is not worthy of me." (Luke xiv, 26.) That is to say, "unless a man renounces his parents' influence and his own will and submits himself to my teaching, he is not worthy of me." Thus we are bidden to hate our father, not to destroy him. Similarly with our own will. We must not be led by it; at the same time, we are not asked to root it out altogether.

When the Scripture says: "Go not after your own desires" (Eccles. xviii, 30) . . . I think that it is plain that no natural physical delight can be set down as sin, nor can it be called guilt for men to delight in what, when it is done, must involve the feeling of delight.

For example, if anyone obliged a monk, bound in chains, to lie among women, and the monk by the softness of the couch and by contact with his fair flatterers is allured into delight, though not into consent, who shall presume to designate guilt the delight which is naturally awakened?

You may urge, with some thinkers, that the carnal pleasure, even in lawful intercourse, involves sin. Thus David says: "Behold in sin was I conceived." (Ps. 1, 7.) And the Apostle, when he had said: "Ye return to it again" (I Cor. vii, 5), adds nevertheless, "This I say by way of concession, not of command." (ibid., v, 6.) Yet authority rather than reason, seems to dictate the view that we should allow simple physical delight to be sin. For, assuredly, David was conceived not in fornication, but in matrimony: and concession, that is forgiveness, does not, as this standpoint avers, condone when there is no guilt to forgive. As for what David meant when he says that he had been conceived "in iniquity" or "in sin" and does not say "whose" sin, he referred to the general curse of original sin, wherein from the guilt of our first parents each is subject to damnation, as it is elsewhere stated: "None are pure of stain, not the infant a day old, if he has life on this earth." As the blessed Jerome reminds us and as manifest reason teaches, the soul of a young child is without sin. If, then, it is pure of sin, how is it also impure by sinful corruption? We must understand the infant's purity from sin in reference to its personal guilt. But its contact with sinful corruption, its "stain," is in reference to penalty owed by mankind because of Adam's sin. He who has not yet perceived by reason what he ought to do cannot be guilty of contempt of God. Yet he is not free from the contamination of the sin of his first parents, from which he contracts the penalty, though not the guilt, and bears in penalty what they committed in guilt. When, therefore, David says that he was conceived in iniquity or sin, he sees himself subject to the general sentence of damnation from the guilt of his racial parents, and he assigns the sins, not to his father and mother but to his first parents. . . .

We come, then, to this conclusion, that no one who sets out to assert that all fleshly desire is sin may say that the sin itself is increased by the doing of it. For this would mean extending the consent of the soul into the exercise of the action. In short, one would be stained not only by consent to baseness, but also by the mire of the deed, as if what happens externally in the body could possibly soil the soul. Sin is not, therefore, increased by the doing of an action: and nothing mars the soul except what is of its own nature, namely consent. This we affirmed was alone sin, preceding action in will, or subsequent to the performance of action. Although we wish for, or do, what is unseemly, we do not therefore sin. For such deeds not uncommonly occur without there being any sin. On the other hand, there may be consent without the external effects, as we have indicated. There was wish without consent in the case of the man who was attracted by a woman whom he caught sight of, or who was tempted by his neighbour's fruit, but who was not enticed into consent. There was evil consent without evil desire in the servant who unwillingly killed his master.

Certain acts which ought not to be done often are done, and without any sin, when, for instance, they are committed under force or ignorance. No one, I think, ignores this fact. A woman under constraint of violence, lies with another's husband. A man, taken by some trick, sleeps with one whom he supposed to be his wife, or kills a man, in the belief that he himself has the right to be both judge and executioner. Thus to desire the wife of another or actually to lie with her is not sin. But to consent to that desire or to that action is sin. This consent to covetousness the law calls covetousness in saying: "Thou shalt not covet." (Deut. v, 21.) Yet that which we cannot avoid ought not to be forbidden, nor that wherein, as we said, we do not sin. But we should be cautioned about the consent to covetousness. So, too, the saying of the Lord must be understood: "Whosoever shall look upon a woman to desire her." (Matt. v, 28.) That is, whosoever shall so look upon her as a slip into consent to covetousness, "has already committed adultery with her in his heart" (Matt. v, 28), even though he may not have committed adultery in deed. He is guilty of sin, though there be no sequel to his intention. . . .

Blessed Augustine, in his careful view of this question, reduces every sin or command to terms of charity and covetousness, and not to works. "The law," he says, "inculcates nothing but charity, and forbids nothing but covetousness." The Apostle, also, asserts: "All the law is contained in one word: thou shalt love thy neighbour as thyself," (Rom. xiii, 8, 10), and again, "Love is the fulfilling of the law." (ibid.)

Whether you actually give alms to a needy person, or charity makes you ready to give, makes no difference to the merit of the deed. The will may be there when the opportunity is not. Nor does it rest entirely with you to deal with every case of need which you encounter. Actions which are right and actions which are far from right are done by good and bad men alike. The intention alone separates the two classes of men. . . .

Briefly to summarize the above argument: Four things were postulated which must be carefully distinguished from one another.

1. Imperfection of soul, making us liable to sin.
2. Sin itself, which we decided is consent to evil or contempt of God.
3. The will or desire of evil.
4. The evil deed.

To wish is not the same thing as to fulfil a wish. Equally, to sin is not the same as to carry out a sin. In the first case, we sin by consent of the soul: the second is a matter of the external effect of an action, namely, when we fulfil in deed that whereunto we have previously consented. When, therefore, temptation is said to proceed through three stages, suggestion, delight, consent, it must be understood that, like our first parents, we are frequently led along these three paths to the commission of sin. The devil's persuasion comes *first* promising from the taste of the forbidden fruit immortality. Delight follows. When the woman sees the beautiful tree, and perceives that the fruit is good, her appetite is whetted by the anticipated pleasure of tasting. This desire she ought to have repressed, so as to obey God's command. But in consenting to it, she was drawn *secondly* into sin. By penitence she should have put right this fault, and obtained pardon. Instead, she *thirdly* consummated the sin by the deed. Eve thus passed through the three stages to the commission of sin.

By the same avenues we also arrive not at sin, but at the action of sin, namely, the doing of an unseemly deed through the suggestion or prompting of something within us. If we already know that such a deed will be pleasant, our imagination is held by anticipatory delight and we are tempted thereby in thought. So long as we give consent to such delight, we sin. Lastly, we pass to the third stage, and actually commit the sin.

It is agreed by some thinkers that carnal suggestion, even though the person causing the suggestion be not present, should be included under sinful suggestion. For example, a man having seen a woman falls into a sensual desire of her. But it seems that this kind of suggestion should simply be called delight. This delight, and other delights of the like kind, arise naturally and, as we said above, they are not sinful. The Apostle calls them "human temptations." No temptation has taken you yet which was not common to men. God is faithful, and will not suffer you to be tempted above what you are able; but will, with the temptation make a way of escape, that you may be able to bear it. By temptation is meant, in general, any movement of the soul to do something unseemly, whether in wish or consent. We speak of human temptation without which it is hardly or never possible for human weakness to exist. Such are sexual desire, or the pleasures of the table. From these the Psalmist asks to be delivered when he says: "Deliver me from my wants, O Lord" (Ps. xxiv, 17); that is, from the temptations of natural and necessary appetites that they may not influence him into sinful consent. Or, he may mean: "When this life is over, grant me to be without those temptations of which life has been full."

When the Apostle says: "No temptation has taken you but what is human," his statement amounts to this: Even if the soul be stirred by that delight which is, as we said, human temptation, yet God would not lead the soul into that consent wherein sin consists. Someone may object: But by what power of our own are we able to resist those desires? We may reply: "God is faithful, who will not allow you to be tempted," as the Scripture says. In other words: We should rather trust him than rely upon ourselves. He promises help, and is true to his promises. He is faithful, so that we should have complete faith in him. Out of pity God diminishes the degree of human temptation, does not suffer us to be tempted above what we are able, in order that it may not drive us to sin at a pace we cannot endure, when, that is, we strive to resist it. Then, too, God turns the temptation to our advantage: for He trains us thereby so that the recurrence of temptation causes us less care, and we fear less the onset of a foe over whom we have already triumphed, and whom we know how to meet. . . .

Study Questions

1. Explain the difference between moral defects and other mental imperfections.
2. What is the difference between a moral defect and sin? Explain what sin is, according to Abelard.
3. Explain why, for Abelard, sin does not consist in having evil desires or in acting on them, but in consenting to act on them. Use examples, if necessary.
4. In what does virtue consist, according to Abelard? Why?

Thomas Aquinas

The greatest philosopher of the medieval period was Thomas Aquinas (ca. 1225–1274). Aquinas, who studied with Albert the Great, is credited with having reconciled Aristotle with Christianity, and his Aristotelian version of Christianity is still taught in Catholic schools as the correct philosophy.

As you would expect, Aquinas agreed with Augustine that God is the source of all that is good and is real. God's *eternal law*, Aquinas held, rules over all things at all times. This eternal law as it applies to humans on earth was equated by Aquinas with *natural law*. Aquinas's conception of natural law is one of his principal contributions to philosophy. Natural law, he maintained, prescribes the fundamental precepts of morality, and we come to understand it through conscience and reason. *Human law*, the statutory law of civilized society, ideally should conform to natural law, he believed. Aquinas thus reinterpreted the Stoic concept of natural law, which for the Stoics was the universal expression of reason and the governing principles of nature, as the eternal law of God. This law becomes evident to us through reason, and we embody its principles in our statutes.

Humans also have a spiritual dimension, Aquinas believed, and the aspect of God's eternal law that applies to this dimension he called *divine law*. We apprehend divine law not through conscience or reason, but through revelation.

Aquinas also basically agreed with Augustine that the end or goal of human existence is happiness of the soul. But Aquinas had a more profound idea of what that happiness consists in. Specifically, Aquinas distinguished our natural goal, which is happiness here and now, from happiness everlasting, which is our ultimate goal. Natural law, the law of reason, can indeed lead us to worldly happiness if we but follow it, he said. And divine law, God's gift to us, directs us to happiness everlasting.

Accordingly, Aquinas distinguished two sets of virtues: the natural virtues—such as courage, temperance, justice, and prudence—and the higher spiritual virtues of faith, love, and hope.

In the selection that follows, from his *Summa Theologica*, Aquinas explains a good part of his ethical theory. This work basically consists of a series of "articles," which are essentially brief essays. Each article typically (1) begins with a question followed by an answer that Aquinas does not agree with, together with supporting arguments. Having thus presented the "objections" to his view on the question at hand, Aquinas then (2) sets forth for his own view, together with arguments for his view. Finally, he (3) answers the objections. What you will read here is mainly the material in (2). It may be difficult to follow this reading, unless you remember that the second part of each article is here reprinted disconnected from the first and third parts.

Also, in this section, references such as *[Q1 a4]* designate question 1, article 4; references such as *[a4]* designate article 4 of the question last mentioned.

When Aquinas refers to "the philosopher," he is speaking of Aristotle.

from *Summa Theologica*

Thomas Aquinas

Thomas Aquinas lived from 1225 to 1274. Reprinted here are selections from his most influential work, *Summa Theologica*, translated by the English Dominican Fathers in twenty-two volumes (London: Benziger Publishing Company, 1912–1936).

IaIIae

Questions 1–5: Treatise on the Last End.

[Q1 a1] Of actions done by man those alone are properly called *human*, which are proper to man as man. Now man differs from irrational animals in this, that he is master of his actions. Wherefore those actions alone are properly called human, of which man is master. Now man is master of his actions through his reason and will; whence, too, the free-will is called the faculty and will of reason. Therefore those actions are properly called human which proceed from a deliberate will. And if any other actions befit man, they can be called actions *of a man*, but not properly *human* actions, since they are not proper to man as man. —Now it is clear that whatever actions proceed from a power, are caused by that power in accordance with the nature of its object. But the object of the will is the end and the good. Therefore all human actions must be for an end.

[a3] . . . [H]uman acts, whether they be considered as actions, or as passions, receive their species from the end. . . . [A]cts are called human, inasmuch as they proceed from a deliberate will. Now the object of the will is the good and the end. And hence it is clear that the principle of human acts . . . is the end. . . . And since, as Ambrose says, . . . *morality is said properly of man*, moral acts properly speaking receive their species from the end, for moral acts are the same as human acts.

Reply objection 3: One and the same act, in so far as it proceeds once from the agent, is ordained to but one proximate end, from which it has its species: but it can be ordained to several remote ends, of which one is the end of the other. It is possible, however, that an act which is one in respect to its natural species, be ordained to several ends of the will: thus this act *to kill a man*, which is but one act in respect of its natural species, can be ordained, as to an end, to the safeguarding of justice, and to the satisfying of anger: the result being that there would be several acts in different species of morality: since in one way there will be an act of virtue, in another, an act of vice. For a movement does not receive its species from that which is its terminus accidently, but only from that which is its *per se* terminus. . . . [T]here is no reason why acts which are the same considered in their natural species, should not be diverse, considered in their moral species, and conversely.

[a4] . . . Now there is to be observed a twofold order in ends,—the order of intention, and the order of execution: and in either of these orders there must be something first. For that which is first in the order of intention, is the principle, as it were, moving the appetite; consequently, if you remove this principle, there will be nothing to move the appetite. On the other hand, the principle in execution is that wherein operation has its beginning; and if this principle be taken away, no one will begin to work. Now the principle in the intention is the last end; while the principle in execution is the first of the things which are ordained to the end. Consequently, on neither side is it possible to go on to infinity; since if there were no last end, nothing would be desired, nor would any action have its term, nor would the intention of the agent be at rest; while if there is no first thing among those that are ordained to the end, none would begin to work at anything, and counsel would have no term, but would continue indefinitely.

[Q2 a4] . . . First, because, since happiness is man's supreme good, it is incompatible with any evil. Now all the foregoing can be found both in good and in evil men.—Secondly, because, since it is the nature of happiness to *satisfy of itself*, as stated in *Ethic.* i., having gained happiness, man cannot lack any needful good. But after acquiring any one of the foregoing, man may still lack many goods that are necessary to him; for instance, wisdom, bodily health, and suchlike.—Thirdly, because, since happiness is the perfect good, no evil can accrue to anyone therefrom. . . .

[Q3 a4] . . . I say, then, that as to the very essence of happiness, it is impossible for it to consist in an act of the will. For . . . happiness is the attainment of the last end. But the attainment of the end does not consist in the very act of the will. For the will is directed to the end, both absent, when it desires it; and present, when it is delighted by resting therein. Now it is evident that the desire itself of the end is not the attainment of the end, but is a movement towards the end: while delight comes to the will from the end being present; and not conversely, is a thing made present, by the fact that the will delights in it. Therefore, that the end be present to him who desires it, must be due to something else than an act of the will.

This is evidently the case in regard to sensible ends. For if the acquisition of money were through an act of the will, the covetous man would have it from the very moment that he wished for it. But at that moment it is far from him; and he attains it, by grasping it in his hand, or in some like manner; and then he delights in the money got. And so it is with an intelligible end. For at first we desire to attain an intelligible end; we attain it, through its being made present to us by an act of the intellect; and then the delighted will rests in the end when attained.

So, therefore, the essence of happiness consists in an act of the intellect: but the delight that results from happiness pertains to the will. . . .

[a5] Happiness consists in an operation of the speculative rather than of the practical intellect. . . . First, because if man's happiness is an operation, it must needs be man's highest operation. Now man's highest operation is that of his highest power in respect of its highest object: and his highest power is the intellect, whose highest object is the Divine Good, which is the object, not of the practical, but of the speculative intellect. Consequently happiness consists principally in such an operation, viz., in the contemplation of Divine things. . . .

Secondly, it is evident from the fact that contemplation is sought principally for its own sake. But the act of the practical intellect is not sought for its own sake but for the sake of action: and these very actions are ordained to some end. Consequently it is evident that the last end cannot consist in the active life, which pertains to the practical intellect. . . .

Therefore the last and perfect happiness, which we await in the life to come, consists entirely in contemplation. But imperfect happiness, such as can be had here, consists first and principally in contemplation, but secondarily, in an operation of the practical intellect directing human actions and passions, as stated in *Ethic.* x.

[a8] Final and perfect happiness can consist in nothing else than the vision of the Divine Essence. . . .

[Q4 a7] For imperfect happiness, such as can be had in this life, external goods are necessary, not as belonging to the essence of happiness, but by serving as instruments to happiness, which consists in an operation of virtue. . . . For man needs, in this life, the necessaries of the body, both for the operation of contemplative virtue, and for the operation of active virtue, for which latter he needs also many other things by means of which to perform its operations.

On the other hand, such goods as these are nowise necessary for perfect Happiness, which consists in seeing God. . . .

[Q5 a8] Happiness can be considered in two ways. First according to the general notion of happiness: and thus, of necessity, every man desires happiness. For the general notion of happiness consists in the perfect good. . . . But since good is the object of the will, the perfect good of a man is that which entirely satisfies his will. Consequently to desire happiness is nothing else than to desire that one's will be satisfied. And this everyone desires. Secondly we may speak of Happiness according to its specific notion, as to that in which it consists. And thus all do not know Happiness; because they know not in what thing the general notion of happiness is found. And consequently, in this respect, not all desire it. . . .

Questions 6–48: Treatise on Human Acts.

[Q6 a1] There must needs be something voluntary in human acts. . . . [T]he principle of some acts or movements is within the agent, or that which is moved; whereas the principle of some movements or acts is outside. For when a stone is moved upwards, the principle of this movement is outside the stone: whereas when it is moved downwards, the principle of this movement is in the stone. Now of those things that are moved by an intrinsic principle, some move themselves, some not. For since every agent or thing moved, acts or is moved for an end . . . those are perfectly moved by an intrinsic principle, whose intrinsic principle is one not only of movement but of movement for an end. Now in order for a thing to be done for an end, some knowledge of the end is necessary. Therefore, whatever so acts or is so moved by an intrinsic principle, that it has some knowledge of the end, has within itself the principle of its act, so that it not only acts, but acts for an end. . . . And consequently, since both are from an intrinsic principle, to wit, that they act and that they act for an end, the movements of such things are said to be voluntary: for the word *voluntary* implies that their movements and acts are from their own inclination. Hence it is that according to the definitions of Aristotle, Gregory of Nyssa, and Damascene, the voluntary is defined not only as having a *principle within* the agent, but also as implying *knowledge.* Therefore, since man especially knows the end of his work, and moves himself, in his acts especially is the voluntary to be found.

[a4] . . . The reason of this is that the act of the will is nothing else than an inclination proceeding from the interior principle of knowledge: just as the natural appetite is an inclination proceeding from an interior principle without knowledge. Now what is compelled or violent is from an exterior principle. Consequently it is contrary to the nature of the will's own act, that it should be subject to compulsion or violence: just as it is also contrary to the nature of a natural inclination or movement. For a stone may have an upward movement from violence, but that this violent movement be from its natural inclination is impossible. In like manner a man may be dragged by force: but it is contrary to the very notion of violence, that he be thus dragged of his own will.

[a8] If ignorance cause involuntariness, it is in so far as it deprives one of knowledge, which is a necessary condition of voluntariness, as was declared above (A.1). But it is not every ignorance that deprives one of this knowledge. Accordingly, we must take note that ignorance has a threefold relationship to the act of the will: in one way, *concomitantly*; in another, *consequently*; in a third way, *antecedently.*— *Concomitantly*, when there is ignorance of what is done; but, so that even if it were known, it would be done. For then, ignorance does not induce one to wish this to be done, but it just happens that a thing is at the same time done and not known. . . . [Consider the case of a man who kills an enemy whom he wishes to kill, but at the time he thinks he is killing a stag.] [I]gnorance of this kind . . . does not cause involuntariness, since it is not the cause of anything that is repugnant to the will; but it causes *non-voluntariness*, since that which is unknown cannot be actually willed. Ignorance is *consequent* to the act of the will, in so far as ignorance itself is voluntary: and this happens in two ways. . . . First, [when] the act of the will is brought to bear on the ignorance: as when a man wishes not to know, that he may have an excuse for sin, or that he may not be withheld from sin. . . . [T]his is called *affected ignorance.*— Secondly, ignorance is said to be voluntary, when it regards that which one can and ought to know: for in this sense *not to act* and *not to will* are said to be voluntary. . . . And ignorance of this kind happens, either when one does not actually consider what one can and ought to consider;—this is called *ignorance of evil choice*, and arises from some passion or habit: or when one does not take the trouble to acquire the knowledge which one ought to have; in which sense, ignorance of the general principles of law, which one ought to know, is voluntary, as being due to negligence.—Accordingly

if, in either of these ways, ignorance is voluntary, it cannot cause involuntariness simply. Nevertheless, it causes involuntariness in a certain respect, inasmuch as it precedes the movement of the will towards the act, which movement would not be, if there were knowledge. Ignorance is *antecedent* to the act of the will, when it is not voluntary, and yet is the cause of man's willing what he would not will otherwise. Thus a man may be ignorant of some circumstance of his act, which he was not bound to know, the result being that he does that which he would not do, if he knew of that circumstance; for instance, a man, after taking proper precaution, may not know that someone is coming along the road, so that he shoots an arrow and slays a passer-by. Such ignorance causes involuntariness simply.

[Q7 a2] Circumstances come under the consideration of the theologian. . . . First, because the theologian considers human acts, inasmuch as man is thereby directed to Happiness. Now, everything that is directed to an end should be proportionate to that end. But acts are made proportionate to an end by means of a certain commensurateness, which results from the due circumstances. Hence, the theologian has to consider the circumstances.—Secondly, because the theologian considers human acts according as they are found to be good or evil, better or worse: and this diversity depends on circumstances, as we shall see further on (Q18, AA10, 11). . . .

[a4] . . . Now, the motive and object of the will is the end. Therefore that circumstance is the most important of all which touches the act on the part of the end, viz., the circumstance *why*: and the second in importance, is that which touches the very substance of the act, viz., the circumstance *what he did.* As to the other circumstances, they are more or less important, according as they more or less approach to these.

[Q8 a1] The will is a rational appetite. Now every appetite is only of something good. The reason of this is that the appetite is nothing else than an inclination of a person desirous of a thing towards that thing. Now every inclination is to something like and suitable to the thing inclined. Since, therefore, everything, inasmuch as it is being and substance, is a good, it must needs be that every inclination is to something good. And hence it is that the Philosopher says (*Ethic* i.) that *the good is that which all desire.*

But it must be noted that, since every inclination results from a form, the natural appetite results from a form existing in the nature of things: while the sensitive appetite, as also the intellective or rational appetite, which we call the will, follows from an apprehended form. Therefore, just as the natural appetite tends to good existing in a thing; so the animal or voluntary appetite tends to a good which is apprehended. Consequently, in order that the will tend to anything, it is requisite, not that this be good in very truth, but that it be apprehended as good. Wherefore the Philosopher says (*Phys.* ii.) that *the end is a good, or an apparent good.*

[Q9 a1] A thing requires to be moved by something in so far as it is in potentiality to several things; for that which is in potentiality needs to be reduced to act by something actual; and to do this is to move. Now a power of the soul is seen to be in potentiality to different things in two ways: first, with regard to acting and not acting; secondly, with regard to this or that action. Thus the sight sometimes sees actually, and sometimes sees not: and sometimes it sees white, and sometimes black. It needs therefore a mover in two respects: viz., as to the exercise or use of the act, and as to the determination of the act. . . .

The motion of the subject itself is due to some agent. And since every agent acts for an end . . . the principle of this motion lies in the end. And hence it is that the art which is concerned with the end, by its command moves the art which is concerned with the means: just as the *art of sailing commands the art of shipbuilding* (*Phys.* ii.). Now good in general, which has the nature of an end, is the object of the will. Consequently, in this respect, the will moves the other powers of the soul to their acts: for we make use of the other powers when we will. . . .

On the other hand, the object moves, by determining the act, after the manner of a formal principle, whereby in natural things actions are specified, as heating by heat. Now the first formal principle is universal *being* and *truth*, which is the object of the intellect. And therefore by this kind of motion the intellect moves the will, as presenting its object to it.

[Q18] We must now consider the good and evil of human acts. First, how a human act is good or evil; secondly, what results from the good or evil of a human act, as merit or demerit, sin and guilt.

Under the first head there will be a threefold consideration: the first will be of the good and evil of human acts, in general; the second, of the good and evil of internal acts; the third, of the good and evil of external acts.

[a1] . . . [E]very action has goodness, in so far as it has being: whereas it is lacking in goodness, in so far as it is lacking in something that is due to its fulness of being; and thus it is said to be evil: for instance if it lacks the quantity determined by reason, or its due place, or something of the kind.

[a2] . . . Now the first thing that belongs to the fulness of being seems to be that which gives a thing its species. And just as a natural thing has its species from its form, so an action has its species from its object, as movement from its term. And therefore, just as the primary goodness of a natural thing is derived from its form, which gives it its species, so the primary goodness of a moral action is derived from its suitable object: hence some call such an action *good in its genus*; for instance, *to make use of what is one's own.* And just as, in natural things, the primary evil is when a generated thing does not realize its specific form (for instance, if instead of a man, something else be generated); so the primary evil in moral actions is that which is from the object, for instance, *to take what belongs to another.* And this action is said to be *evil in its genus,* genus here standing for species, just as we apply the term *mankind* to the whole human species.

[a3] In natural things, it is to be noted that the whole fulness of perfection due to a thing, is not from the mere substantial form, that gives it its species; since a thing derives much from supervening accidents, as man does from shape, colour, and the like; and if any one of these accidents be out of due proportion, evil is the result. So is it with action. For the plenitude of its goodness does not consist wholly in its species, but also in certain additions which accrue to it by reason of certain accidents: and such are its due circumstances. Wherefore if something be wanting that is requisite as a due circumstance the action will be evil.

[a4] The disposition of things as to goodness is the same as their disposition as to being. Now in some things the being does not depend on another, and in these it suffices to consider their being absolutely. But these are things the being of which depends on something else, and hence in their regard we must consider their being in its relation to the cause on which it depends. Now just as the being of a thing depends on the agent and the form, so the goodness of a thing depends on its end. . . . [H]uman actions . . . have a measure of goodness from the end on which they depend, besides that goodness which is in them absolutely.

Accordingly a fourfold goodness may be considered in a human action. First, that which, as an action, it derives from its genus; because as much as it has of action and being so much has it of goodness. . . . Secondly, it has goodness according to its species; which is derived from its suitable object. Thirdly, it has goodness from its circumstances, in respect, as it were, of its accidents. Fourthly, it has goodness from its end, to which it is compared as to the cause of its goodness.

Reply objection 3: Nothing hinders an action that is good in one of the ways mentioned above, from lacking goodness in another way. And thus it may happen that an action which is good in its species or in its circumstances, is ordained to an evil end, or vice versa. However, an action is not good simply, unless it is good in all those ways: since *evil results from any single defect, but good from the complete cause,* as Dionysius says. . . .

[a6] . . . [I]n a voluntary action, there is a twofold action, viz., the interior act of the will, and the external action: and each of these actions has its object. The end is properly the object of the interior act of the will: while the object of the external action, is that on which the action is brought to bear. Therefore, just as the external action takes its species from the object on which it bears: so the interior act of the will takes its species from the end, as from its own proper object.

Now that which is on the part of the will is formal in regard to that which is on the part of the external action: because the will uses the limbs to act as instruments; nor have external actions any measure of morality, save in so far as they are voluntary. Consequently the species of a human act is considered formally with regard to the end, but materially with regard to the object of the external action. Hence the Philosopher says (*Ethic.* v.) that *he who steals that he may commit adultery, is, strictly speaking, more adulterer than thief.*

[a9] It sometimes happens that an action is indifferent in its species; but considered in the individual it is good or evil. . . . [A] moral action . . . derives its goodness not only from its object, whence it takes its species; but also from the circumstances, which are its accidents, as it were. . . . And every individual action must needs have some circumstance that makes it good or bad, at least in respect of the intention of the end. For since it belongs to the reason to direct; if an action that proceeds from deliberate reason be not directed to the due end, it is, by that fact alone, repugnant to reason, and is specifically evil. But if it be directed to a due end it is in accord with reason; wherefore it is specifically good. . . . Consequently every human action that proceeds from deliberate reason, if it be considered in the individual, must be good or bad.

If, however, it does not proceed from deliberate reason, but from some act of the imagination, as when a man strokes his beard, or moves his hand or foot; such an action, properly speaking, is not moral or human; since this depends on the reason. Hence it will be indifferent, as standing apart from the genus of moral actions.

[a10] . . . [T]hat which, in one action, is taken as a circumstance added to the object that specifies the action, can again be taken by the directing reason, as the principal condition of the object that determines the action's species. Thus to appropriate another's property is specified by reason of the property being *another's,* and in this respect it is placed in the species of theft; and if we consider that action also in its bearing on place or time, then this will be an additional circumstance. But since the reason can direct as to place, time, and the like, it may happen that the condition as to place, in relation to the object, is considered as being in disaccord with reason: for instance, reason forbids damage to be done to a holy place. Consequently to steal from a holy place has an additional repugnance to the order of reason. And thus place, which was first of all considered as a circumstance, is considered here as the principal condition of the object, and as itself repugnant to reason. And in this way, whenever a circumstance has a special relation to reason, either for or against, it must needs specify the moral action whether good or bad.

[a11] . . . [I]t happens sometimes that a circumstance does not regard a special order of reason in respect of good or evil, except on the supposition of another previous circumstance, from which the moral action takes its species of good or evil. Thus to take something in a large or small quantity, does not regard the order of reason in respect of good or evil, except a certain other condition be presupposed, from which the action takes its malice or goodness; for instance, if what is taken belongs to another, which makes the action to be discordant with reason. Wherefore to take what belongs to another in a large or small quantity, does not change the species of the sin. Nevertheless it can aggravate or diminish the sin. . . .

[Q19 a5] . . . [S]ome distinguished three kinds of actions: for some are good generically; some are indifferent; some are evil generically. And they say that if reason or conscience tell us to do something which is good generically, there is no error: and in like manner if it tell us not to do something which is evil generically. . . . On the other hand if a man's reason or conscience tell him that he is bound by precept to do what is evil in itself; or that what is good in itself, is forbidden, then his reason or conscience errs. In like manner if a man's reason or conscience tell him, that what is indifferent in itself, for instance to raise a straw from the ground, is forbidden or commanded, his reason or conscience errs. They say, therefore, that reason or conscience, when erring in matters of indifference, either by commanding or by forbidding them, binds. . . . But they say that when reason or conscience errs in commanding what is evil in itself, or in forbidding what is good in itself and necessary for salvation, it does not bind; wherefore in such cases the will which is at variance with erring reason or conscience is not evil.

But this is unreasonable. For in matters of indifference, the will that is at variance with erring reason or conscience, is evil in some way on account of the object, on which the goodness or malice of the will depends; not indeed on account of the object according as it is in its own nature; but according as it is accidentally apprehended by reason as something evil to do or to avoid. . . . [F]rom the very fact that a thing is proposed by the reason as being evil, the will by tending thereto becomes evil. And this is the case not only in indifferent matters, but also in those that are good or evil in themselves. For not only indifferent matters can receive the character of goodness or malice accidentally; but also that which is good, can receive the character of evil, or that which is evil, can receive the character of goodness, on account of the reason apprehending it as such. For instance, to refrain from fornication is good: yet the will does not tend to this good except in so far as it is proposed by the reason. If, therefore, the erring reason propose it as an evil, the will tends to it as to something evil. Consequently the will is evil, because it wills evil, not indeed that which is evil in itself, but that which is evil accidentally, through being apprehended as such by the reason. . . . We must therefore conclude that, absolutely speaking, every will at variance with reason, whether right or erring, is always evil.

[a6] [The question, "whether an erring conscience excuses,"] depends on what has been said above about ignorance. For it was said (Q6 A8) that ignorance sometimes causes an act to be involuntary, and sometimes not. . . . [W]hen ignorance causes an act to be involuntary, it takes away the character of moral good and evil; but not, when it does not cause the act to be involuntary. . . . [W]hen ignorance is in any way willed, either directly or indirectly, it does not cause the act to be involuntary. And I call that ignorance *directly* voluntary, to which the act of the will tends: and that, *indirectly* voluntary, which is due to negligence, by reason of a man not wishing to know what he ought to know. . . .

If then reason or conscience err with an error that is voluntary . . . then such an error of reason or conscience does not excuse the will, that abides by that erring reason or conscience, from being evil. But if the error arise from ignorance of some circumstance, and without any negligence, so that it cause the act to be involuntary, then that error of reason or conscience excuses the will, that abides by that erring reason, from being evil. For instance, if erring reason tell a man that he should go to another man's wife, the will that abides by that erring reason is evil; since this error arises from ignorance of the Divine Law, which he is bound to know. But if a man's reason errs in mistaking another for his wife, and if he wish to give her her right when she asks for it, his will is excused from being evil: because this error arises from ignorance of a circumstance, which ignorance excuses, and causes the act to be involuntary.

[Q20 a1] External actions may be said to be good or bad in two ways. First, in regard to their genus, and the circumstances connected with them: thus the giving of alms, if the required conditions be observed, is said to be good. Secondly, a thing is said to be good or evil, from its relation to the end: thus the giving of alms for vainglory is said to be evil. Now, since the end is the will's proper object, it is evident that this aspect of good or evil, which the external action derives from its relation to the end, is to be found first of all in the act of the will, whence it passes to the external action. On the other hand, the goodness or malice which the external action has of itself, on account of its being about due matter and its being attended by due circumstances, is not derived from the will, but rather from the reason. . . .

[a2] . . . [F]or a thing to be evil, one single defect suffices, whereas, for it to be good simply, it is not enough for it to be good in one point only, it must be good in every respect. If therefore the will be good, both from its proper object and from its end, it follows that the external action is good. But if the will be good from its intention of the end, this is not enough to make the external action good: and if the will be evil either by reason of its intention of the end, or by reason of the act willed, it follows that the external action is evil.

[a5] The consequences of an action are either foreseen or not. If they are foreseen, it is evident that they increase the goodness or malice. . . .

But if the consequences are not foreseen, we must make a distinction. Because if they follow from the nature of the action, and in the majority of cases, in this respect, the consequences increase the goodness or malice of that action: for it is evident that an action is specifically better, if better results can follow from it; and specifically worse, if it is of a nature to produce worse results.—On the other hand, if the consequences follow by accident and seldom, then they do not increase the goodness or malice of the action: because we do not judge of a thing according to that which belongs to it by accident. . . .

[Q21 a1] Evil is more comprehensive than sin, as also is good than right. For every privation of good, in whatever subject, is an evil: whereas sin consists properly in an action done for a certain end, and lacking due order to that end. Now the due order to an end is measured by some rule. In things that act according to nature, this rule is the natural force that inclines them to that end. When therefore an action proceeds from a natural force, in accord with the natural inclination to an end, then the action is said to be right. . . .

Now in those things that are done by the will, the proximate rule is the human reason, while the supreme rule is the Eternal Law. When, therefore, a human action tends to the end, according to the order of reason and of the Eternal Law, then that action is right: but when it turns aside from that rectitude, then it is said to be a sin. . . . Hence it follows that a human action is right or sinful by reason of its being good or evil.

[a] Just as evil is more comprehensive than sin, so is sin more comprehensive than blame. For an action is said to deserve praise or blame, from its being imputed to the agent. . . . Now an action is imputed to an agent, when it is in his power, so that he has dominion over it: and this is the case in all voluntary acts. . . . Hence it follows that good or evil, in voluntary actions alone, renders them worthy of praise or blame: and in suchlike actions, evil, sin and guilt are one and the same thing.

[a3] We speak of merit and demerit, in relation to retribution, rendered according to justice. Now, retribution according to justice is rendered to a man, by reason of his having done something to another's advantage or hurt. . . .

It is therefore evident that a good or evil action deserves praise or blame, in so far as it is in the power of the will: that it is right or sinful, according as it is ordained to the end; and that its merit or demerit depend on the retribution of justice to another.

Questions 49–89: Treatise on Habit.

[Q49 a4] [H]abit implies a disposition in relation to a thing's nature, and to its operation or end, by reason of which disposition a thing is well or ill disposed thereto. Now for a thing to need to be disposed to something else, three conditions are necessary. . . . [First] that which is disposed should be distinct from that to which it is disposed; and so, it should be related to it as potentiality is to act. . . . [Second] that which is in a state of potentiality in regard to something else, be capable of determination in several ways and to various things. Whence if something be in a state of potentiality in regard to something else, but in regard to that only, there we find no room for disposition and habit. . . . [Third] in disposing the subject to one of those things to which it is in potentiality, several things should concur, capable of being adjusted in various ways: so as to dispose the subject well or ill to its form or to its operation. Wherefore the simple qualities of the elements which suit the natures of the elements in one single fixed way, are not called dispositions or habits, but *simple qualities*: but we call dispositions or habits, such things as health, beauty, and so forth, which imply the adjustment of several things which may vary in their relative adjustability. . . .

[Q54 a3] . . . [A] good habit is one which disposes to an act suitable to the agent's nature, while an evil habit is one which disposes to an act unsuitable to nature. Thus, acts of virtue are suitable to human nature, since they are according to reason, whereas acts of vice are discordant from human nature, since they are against reason. . . .

[Q55, a1] Virtue denotes a certain perfection of a power. Now a thing's perfection is considered chiefly in regard to its end. But the end of power is act. Wherefore power is said to be perfect, according as it is determinate to its act.

Now there are some powers which of themselves are determinate to their acts; for instance, the active natural powers. And therefore these natural powers are in themselves called virtues. But the rational powers, which are proper to man, are not determinate to one particular action, but are inclined indifferently to many: and they are determinate to acts by means of habits, as is clear from what we have said above (Q49 A4). Therefore human virtues are habits.

[Q58 a3] Human virtue is a habit perfecting man in view of his doing good deeds. Now, in man there are but two principles of human actions, viz., the intellect or reason and the appetite. . . . Consequently every human virtue must needs be a perfection of one of these principles. Accordingly if it perfects man's speculative or practical intellect in order that his deed may be good, it will be an intellectual virtue: whereas if it perfects his appetite, it will be a moral virtue. . . .

[Q57 a1] . . . [A] habit . . . may be called a virtue for two reasons: first, because it confers aptness in doing good; secondly, because besides aptness, it confers the right use of it. [It is only in the first sense that intellectual virtues are virtues.] For it does not follow that, if a man possess a habit of speculative science, he is inclined to make use of it, but he is made able to consider the truth in those matters of which he has scientific knowledge:—that he make use of the knowledge which he has, is due to the motion of his will. . . .

[a5] Prudence is a virtue most necessary for human life. For a good life consists in good deeds. Now in order to do good deeds, it matters not only what a man does, but also how he does it; to wit, that he do it from right choice and not merely from impulse or passion. And, since choice is about things in reference to the end, rectitude of choice requires two things; namely, the due end, and something suitably ordained to that due end. Now man is suitably directed to his due end by a virtue which perfects the soul in the appetitive part, the object of which is the good and the end. And to that which is suitably ordained to the due end man needs to be rightly disposed by a habit in his reason, because counsel and choice, which are about things ordained to the end, are acts of the reason. Consequently an intellectual virtue is needed in the reason, to perfect the reason, and make it suitably affected towards things ordained to the end; and this virtue is prudence. Consequently prudence is a virtue necessary to lead a good life.

[Q58 a4] Moral virtue can be without some of the intellectual virtues, viz., wisdom, science, and art; but not without understanding and prudence. Moral virtue cannot be without prudence, because it is a habit of choosing, i.e., making us choose well. Now in order that a choice be good, two things are required. First, that the intention be directed to a due end; and this is done by moral virtue, which inclines the appetitive faculty to good according to reason, which is a due end. Secondly, that man take rightly those things which have reference to the end: and this he cannot do unless his reason counsel, judge and command aright, which is the function of prudence. . . . Wherefore there can be no moral virtue without prudence: and consequently neither can there be without understanding. For it is by virtue of understanding that we know self-evident principles both in speculative and in practical matters. Consequently just as right reason in speculative matters, in so far as it proceeds from naturally known principles, presupposes the understanding of those principles, so also does prudence, which is the right reason about things to be done.

[a5] Other intellectual virtues can, but prudence cannot, be without moral virtue. The reason for this is that prudence is the right reason about things to be done (and this, not merely in general, but also in particular). . . . Now right reason demands principles from which reason proceeds to argue. And when reason argues about particular cases, it needs not only universal but also particular principles. As to universal principles of action, man is rightly disposed by the natural understanding of principles, whereby he understands that he should do no evil; or again by some practical science. But this is not enough in order that man may reason aright about particular cases. For it happens sometimes that the aforesaid universal principle, known by means of understanding or science, is destroyed in a particular case by reason

of a passion: thus to one who is swayed by concupiscence, when he is overcome thereby, the object of his desire seems good, although it is opposed to the universal judgment of his reason. Consequently, as by the habit of natural understanding or of science, man is made to be rightly disposed in regard to the universal principles of action; so, in order that he be rightly disposed with regard to the particular principles of action, viz., the ends, he needs to be perfected by certain habits, whereby it becomes connatural, as it were, to man to judge aright of the end. This is done by moral virtue: for the virtuous man judges aright of the end of virtue. . . . Consequently the right reason about things to be done, viz., prudence, requires man to have moral virtue.

[Q61 a3] [First] any virtue that causes good in reason's act of consideration, may be called prudence; every virtue that causes the good of right and due in operations, be called justice; every virtue that curbs and represses the passions, be called temperance; and every virtue that strengthens the mind against any passions whatever, be called fortitude. . . . [In the second way of speaking] prudence is the virtue which commands; justice, the virtue which is about due actions between equals; temperance, the virtue which suppresses desires for the pleasures of touch; and fortitude, the virtue which strengthens against dangers of death. . . .

Questions 90–108: Treatise on Law.

[Q90 a1] Law is a rule and measure of acts, whereby man is induced to act or is restrained from acting: for *lex* (law) is derived from *ligare* (to bind), because it binds one to act. Now the rule and measure of human acts is the reason, which is the first principle of human acts . . . ; since it belongs to the reason to direct to the end, which is the first principle in all matters of action, according to the Philosopher (*Phys.* ii). Now that which is the principle in any genus, is the rule and measure of that genus: for instance, unity in the genus of numbers, and the first movement in the genus of movements. Consequently it follows that law is something pertaining to reason.

Reply Objection 1: Since law is a kind of rule and measure, it may be in something in two ways. First, as in that which measures and rules: and since this is proper to reason, it follows that, in this way, law is in the reason alone.—Secondly, as in that which is measured and ruled. In this way, law is in all those things that are inclined to something by reason of some law: so that any inclination arising from a law, may be called a law, not essentially, but by participation as it were. . . .

[a2] . . . Now as reason is a principle of human acts, so in reason itself there is something which is the principle in respect of all the rest: wherefore to this principle chiefly and mainly law must needs be referred.—Now the first principle in practical matters, which are the object of the practical reason, is the last end: and the last end of human life is bliss or happiness. . . . Consequently the law must needs regard principally the relationship to happiness. Moreover, since every part is ordained to the whole, as imperfect to perfect; and since one man is a part of the perfect community, the law must needs regard properly the relationship to universal happiness. Wherefore the Philosopher . . . mentions both happiness and the body politic: for he says (*Ethic.* v.) that we call those legal matters *just, which are adapted to produce and preserve happiness and its parts for the body politic*: since the state is a perfect community, as he says in *Polit.* i.

Now in every genus, that which belongs to it chiefly is the principle of the others, and the others belong to that genus in subordination to that thing: thus fire, which is chief among hot things, is the cause of heat in mixed bodies, and these are said to be hot in so far as they have a share of fire. Consequently, since the law is chiefly ordained to the common good, any other precept in regard to some individual work, must needs be devoid of the nature of a law, save in so far as it regards the common good. Therefore every law is ordained to the common good.

[a3] . . . Now to order anything to the common good, belongs either to the whole people, or to someone who is the viceregent of the whole people. And therefore the making of a law belongs either to the whole people or to a public personage who has care of the whole people: since in all other

matters the directing of anything to the end concerns him to whom the end belongs.

[a4] [A] law is imposed on others by way of a rule and measure. Now a rule or measure is imposed by being applied to those who are to be ruled and measured by it. Wherefore, in order that a law obtain the binding force which is proper to a law, it must needs be applied to the men who have to be ruled by it. Such application is made by its being notified to them by promulgation. Wherefore promulgation is necessary for the law to obtain its force.

Thus from the four preceding articles, the definition of law may be gathered; and it is nothing else than an ordinance of reason for the common good, made by him who has care of the community, and promulgated.

[Q91 a1] [A] law is nothing else but a dictate of practical reason emanating from the ruler who governs a perfect community. Now it is evident, granted that the world is ruled by Divine Providence . . . that the whole community of the universe is governed by Divine Reason. Wherefore the very Idea of the government of things in God the Ruler of the universe, has the nature of a law. And since the Divine Reason's conception of things is not subject to time but is eternal, . . . therefore it is that this kind of law must be called eternal.

[Q93 a1] Just as in every artificer there pre-exists a type of the things that are made by his art, so too in every governor there must pre-exist the type of the order of those things that are to be done by those who are subject to his government. . . . Now God, by His wisdom, is the Creator of all things, in relation to which He stands as the artificer to the products of his art. . . . Moreover He governs all the acts and movements that are to be found in each single creature. . . . Wherefore as the type of the Divine Wisdom, inasmuch as by It all things are created, has the character of art, exemplar or idea; so the type of Divine Wisdom, as moving all things to their due end, bears the character of law. Accordingly the eternal law is nothing else than the type of Divine Wisdom, as directing all actions and movements.

[a3] [L]aw denotes a kind of plan directing acts towards an end. Now wherever there are movers ordained to one another, the power of the second mover must needs be derived from the power of the first mover; since the second mover does not move except in so far as it is moved by the first. Wherefore we observe the same in all those who govern, so that the plan of government is derived by secondary governors from the governor in chief: thus the plan of what is to be done in a state flows from the king's command to his inferior administrators. . . . Since then the eternal law is the plan of government in the Chief Governor, all the plans of government in the inferior governors must be derived from the eternal law. But these plans of inferior governors are all other laws besides the eternal law. Therefore all laws, in so far as they partake of right reason, are derived from the eternal law. . . .

[a5] . . . Now just as man . . . impresses a kind of inward principle of action on the man that is subject to him, so God imprints on the whole of nature the principles of its proper actions. . . . Consequently irrational creatures are subject to the eternal law, through being moved by Divine providence; but not, as rational creatures are, through understanding the Divine commandment.

[Q91 a2] . . . [I]t is evident that all things partake somewhat of the eternal law, in so far as, namely, from its being imprinted on them, they derive their respective inclinations to their proper acts and ends. Now among all others, the rational creature is subject to Divine providence in the most excellent way, in so far as it partakes of a share of providence, by being provident both for itself and for others. Wherefore it has a share of the Eternal Reason, whereby it has a natural inclination to its proper act and end: and this participation of the eternal law in the rational creature is called the natural law. . . . [T]he light of natural reason, whereby we discern what is good and what is evil, which is the function of the natural law, is nothing else than an imprint on us of the Divine light. It is therefore evident that the natural law is nothing else than the rational creature's participation of the eternal law.

[Q94 a1] . . . [T]he term habit may be applied to that which we hold by a habit: thus faith may mean that which we hold by faith. And accordingly, since the precepts of the natural law are sometimes considered by reason actually, while sometimes they are in the reason only habitually, in this way the natural law may be called a habit. . . .

[a2] [T]he precepts of the natural law are to the practical reason, what the first principles of demonstrations are to the speculative reason; because both are self-evident principles. Now a thing is said to be self-evident in two ways: first, in itself; secondly, in relation to us. Any proposition is said to be self-evident in itself, if its predicate is contained in the notion of the subject: although, to one who knows not the definition of the subject, it happens that such a proposition is not self-evident. For instance, this proposition, *Man is a rational being*, is, in its very nature, self-evident, since who says *man*, says a *rational being*: and yet to one who knows not what a man is, this proposition is not self-evident. Hence . . . certain axioms or propositions are universally self-evident to all; and such are those propositions whose terms are known to all, as, *Every whole is greater than its part,* and *Things equal to one and the same are equal to one another*. But some propositions are self-evident only to the wise, who understand the meaning of the terms of such propositions: thus to one who understands that an angel is not a body, it is self-evident that an angel is not circumscriptively in a place: but this is not evident to the unlearned, for they cannot grasp it.

Now a certain order is to be found in those things that are apprehended universally. For that which, before aught else, falls under apprehension, is *being*, the notion of which is included in all things whatsoever a man apprehends. Wherefore the first indemonstrable principle is that *the same thing cannot be affirmed and denied at the same time*, which is based on the notion of *being* and *not-being*: and on this principle all others are based. . . . Now as *being* is the first thing that falls under the apprehension simply, so *good* is the first thing that falls under the apprehension of the practical reason, which is directed to action: since every agent acts for an end under the aspect of good. Consequently the first principle in the practical reason is one founded on the notion of good, viz., that *good is that which all things seek after.* Hence this is the first precept of law, that *good is to be done and ensued, and evil is to be avoided.* All other precepts of the natural law are based upon this: so that whatever the practical reason naturally apprehends as man's good (or evil) belongs to the precepts of the natural law as something to be done or avoided.

Since, however, good has the nature of an end, and evil, the nature of a contrary, hence it is that all those things to which man has a natural inclination, are naturally apprehended by reason as being good, and consequently as objects of pursuit, and their contraries as evil, and objects of avoidance. Wherefore according to the order of natural inclination, is the order of the precepts of the natural law. Because in man there is first of all an inclination to good in accordance with the nature which he has in common with all substances: inasmuch as every substance seeks the preservation of its own being, according to its nature: and by reason of this inclination, whatever is a means of preserving human life, and of warding off its obstacles, belongs to the natural law. Secondly, there is in man an inclination to things that pertain to him more specially, according to that nature which he has in common with other animals: and in virtue of this inclination, those things are said to belong to the natural law, *which nature has taught to all animals*, such as sexual intercourse, education of offspring, and so forth. Thirdly, there is in man an inclination to good, according to the nature of his reason, which nature is proper to him: thus man has a natural inclination to know the truth about God, and to live in society: and in this respect, whatever pertains to this inclination belongs to the natural law; for instance, to shun ignorance, to avoid offending those among whom one has to live, and other such things regarding the above inclination.

[a4] [T]o the natural law belong those things to which a man is inclined naturally: and among these it is proper to man to be inclined to act according to reason. Now the process of reason is from the common to the proper. The speculative reason, however, is differently situated in this matter, from the practical reason. For, since the speculative reason is busied chiefly with necessary things, which cannot be otherwise than they are, its proper conclusions, like the universal principles, contain the truth without fail. The practical reason, on the other hand, is busied with contingent

matters, about which human actions are concerned: and consequently, although there is necessity in the general principles, the more we descend to matters of detail, the more frequently we encounter defects. Accordingly then in speculative matters truth is the same in all men, both as to principles and as to conclusions: although the truth is not known to all as regards the conclusions, but only as regards the principles which are called common notions. But in matters of action, truth or practical rectitude is not the same for all, as to matters of detail, but only as to the general principles: and where there is the same rectitude in matters of detail, it is not equally known to all.

It is therefore evident that, as regards the general principles whether of speculative or of practical reason, truth or rectitude is the same for all, and is equally known by all. As to the proper conclusions of the speculative reason, the truth is the same for all, but is not equally known to all: thus it is true for all that the three angles of a triangle are together equal to two right angles, although it is not known to all. But as to the proper conclusions of the practical reason, neither is the truth or rectitude the same for all, nor, where it is the same, is it equally known by all. Thus it is right and true for all to act according to reason: and from this principle it follows as a proper conclusion, that goods entrusted to another should be restored to their owner. Now this is true for the majority of cases: but it may happen in a particular case that it would be injurious, and therefore unreasonable, to restore goods held in trust; for instance if they are claimed for the purpose of fighting against one's country. And this principle will be found to fail the more, according as we descend further into detail, *e.g.*, if one were to say that goods held in trust should be restored with such and such a guarantee, or in such and such a way; because the greater the number of conditions added, the greater the number of ways in which the principle may fail, so that it be not right to restore or not to restore.

Consequently we must say that the natural law, as to general principles, is the same for all, both as to rectitude and as to knowledge. But as to certain matters of detail, which are conclusions, as it were, of those general principles, it is the same for all in the majority of cases, both as to rectitude and as to knowledge; and yet in some few cases it may fail, both as to rectitude, by reason of certain obstacles (just as natures subject to generation and corruption fail in some few cases on account of some obstacle), and as to knowledge, since in some the reason is perverted by passion, or evil habit, or an evil disposition of nature: thus formerly, theft, although it is expressly contrary to the natural law, was not considered wrong among the Germans, as Julius Caesar relates (*De Bello Gall.* vi.)

[a5] A change in the natural law may be understood in two ways. First, by way of addition. In this sense nothing hinders the natural law from being changed: since many things for the benefit of human life have been added over and above the natural law, both by the Divine law and by human laws.

Secondly, a change in the natural law may be understood by way of subtraction, so that what previously was according to the natural law, ceases to be so. In this sense, the natural law is altogether unchangeable in its first principles: but in its secondary principles, which . . . are certain detailed proximate conclusions drawn from the first principles, the natural law is not changed so that what it prescribes be not right in most cases. But it may be changed in some particular cases of rare occurrence, through some special causes hindering the observance of such precepts. . . .

[Q100 a1] . . . [S]ince the moral precepts are about matters which concern good morals; and since good morals are those which are in accord with reason; and since also every judgment of human reason must needs be derived in some way from natural reason; it follows, of necessity, that all the moral precepts belong to the law of nature; but not all in the same way. For there are certain things which the natural reason of every man, of its own accord and at once, judges to be done or not to be done: *e.g., Honour thy father and thy mother,* and *Thou shalt not kill, Thou shalt not steal*: and these belong to the law of natural absolutely.—And there are certain things which, after a more careful consideration, wise men deem obligatory. Such belong to the law of nature, yet so that they need to be inculcated, the wiser teaching the less wise: *e.g., Rise up before the hoary head, and honour the person of the aged man*, and the like.—And there are some things, to judge of which, human reason needs Divine instruction, whereby we are taught about the things of God: *e.g., Thou shalt not make to thyself a graven thing, nor the likeness of anything; Thou shalt not take the name of the Lord thy God in vain.*

[a3] . . . [T]wo kinds of precepts are not reckoned among the precepts of the decalogue: viz., first general principles, for they need no further promulgation after being once imprinted on the natural reason to which they are self-evident; as, for instance, that one should do evil to no man, and other similar principles: — and again those which the careful reflection of wise men shows to be in accord with reason: since the people receive these principles from God, through being taught by wise men. Nevertheless both kinds of precepts are contained in the precepts of the decalogue; yet in different ways. For the first general principles are contained in them, as principles in their proximate conclusions; while those which are known through wise men are contained, conversely, as conclusions in their principles.

[Q91 a3] . . . [J]ust as, in the speculative reason, from naturally known undemonstrable principles, we draw the conclusions of the various sciences, the knowledge of which is not imparted to us by nature, but acquired by the efforts of reason, so too it is from the precepts of the natural law, as from general and indemonstrable principles, that the human reason needs to proceed to the more particular determination of certain matters. These particular determinations, devised by human reason, are called human laws, provided the other essential conditions of law be observed, as stated above (Q 90, AA 2, 3, 4). . . .

[Q95 a1] [M]an has a natural aptitude for virtue; but the perfection of virtue must be acquired by man by means of some kind of training. . . . [A] man needs to receive this training from another, whereby to arrive at the perfection of virtue. And as to those young people who are inclined to acts of virtue, by their good natural disposition, or by custom, or rather by the gift of God, paternal training suffices, which is by admonitions. But since some are found to be depraved, and prone to vice, and not easily amenable to words, it was necessary for such to be restrained from evil by force and fear, in order that, at least, they might desist from evil-doing, and leave others in peace, and that they themselves, by being habituated in this way, might be brought to do willingly what hitherto they did from fear, and thus become virtuous. Now this kind of training, which compels through fear of punishment, is the discipline of laws. Therefore, in order that man might have peace and virtue, it was necessary for laws to be framed. . . .

[a2] As Augustine says (*De Lib. Arb.* i.), *that which is not just seems to be no law at all*: wherefore the force of a law depends on the extent of its justice. Now in human affairs a thing is said to be just, from being right, according to the rule of reason. But the first rule of reason is the law of nature. . . . Consequently every human law has just so much of the nature of law, as it is derived from the law of nature. But if in any point it deflects from the law of nature, it is no longer a law but a perversion of law.

But it must be noted that something may be derived from the natural law in two ways: first, as a conclusion from premises, secondly, by way of determination of certain generalities. The first way is like to that by which, in sciences, demonstrated conclusions are drawn from the principles: while the second mode is likened to that whereby, in the arts, general forms are particularized as to details: thus the craftsman needs to determine the general form of a house to some particular shape. Some things are therefore derived from the general principles of the natural law, by way of conclusions; *e.g.,* that *one must not kill* may be derived as a conclusion from the principle that *one should do harm to no man*: while some are derived therefrom by way of determination; *e.g.*, the law of nature has it that the evil-doer should be punished; but that he be punished in this or that way, is a determination of the law of nature.

Accordingly both modes of derivation are found in the human law. But those things which are derived in the first way, are contained in human law not as emanating therefrom exclusively, but have some force from the natural law also. But those things which are derived in the second way, have no other force than that of human law.

[a4] . . . [P]ositive law is divided into the *law of nations* and *civil law*, according to the two ways in which something may be derived from the law of nature. [T]o the law of nations belong those

things which are derived from the law of nature, as conclusions from premises, *e.g.*, just buyings and sellings, and the like, without which men cannot live together, which is a point of the law of nature, since man is by nature a social animal, as is proved in *Polit.* i. But those things which are derived from the law of nature by way of particular determination, belong to the civil law, according as each state decides on what is best for itself. . . .

Reply Objection 1: The law of nations is indeed, in some way, natural to man, in so far as he is a reasonable being, because it is derived from the natural law by way of a conclusion that is not very remote from its premises. Wherefore men easily agreed thereto. Nevertheless it is distinct from natural law, especially from the natural law which is common to all animals.

[Q96 a1] Whatever is for an end should be proportionate to that end. Now the end of law is the common good. . . . Hence human laws should be proportionate to the common good. . . .

[a2] . . . [A] measure should be homogeneous with that which it measures. . . . Wherefore laws imposed on men should also be in keeping with their condition, for, as Isidore says (*Etym.* ii.), law should be *possible both according to nature, and according to the customs of the country*. . . .

Now human law is framed for a number of human beings, the majority of whom are not perfect in virtue. Wherefore human laws do forbid all vices, from which the virtuous abstain, but only the more grievous vices, from which it is possible for the majority to abstain; and chiefly those that are to the hurt of others, without the prohibition of which human society could not be maintained: thus human law prohibits murder, theft, and suchlike.

[a3] . . . [T]here is no virtue whose acts cannot be prescribed by the law. Nevertheless human law does not prescribe concerning all the acts of every virtue: but only in regard to those that are ordainable to the common good. . . .

[a4] Laws framed by man are either just or unjust. If they be just, they have the power of binding in conscience, from the eternal law whence they are derived. . . . Now laws are said to be just, both from the end, when, to wit, they are ordained to the common good,—and from their author, that is to say, when the law that is made does not exceed the power of the lawgiver,—and from their form, when, to wit, burdens are laid on the subjects, according to an equality of proportion and with a view to the common good. For, since one man is a part of the community, each man, in all that he is and has, belongs to the community; just as a part, in all that it is, belongs to the whole; wherefore nature inflicts a loss on the part, in order to save the whole: so that on this account, such laws as these, which impose proportionate burdens, are just and binding in conscience, and are legal laws.

On the other hand, laws may be unjust in two ways: first, by being contrary to human good, through being opposed to the things mentioned above:—either in respect of the end, as when an authority imposes on his subjects burdensome laws, conducive, not to the common good, but rather to his own cupidity or vainglory;—or in respect of the author, as when a man makes a law that goes beyond the power committed to him;—or in respect of the form, as when burdens are imposed unequally on the community, although with a view to the common good. The like are rather acts of violence than laws. . . . Wherefore such laws do not bind in conscience, except perhaps in order to avoid scandal or disturbance, for which cause a man should even yield his right. . . .

Secondly, laws may be unjust through being opposed to the Divine good: such are the laws of tyrants inducing to idolatry, or to anything else contrary to the Divine law: and laws of this kind must nowise be observed, because, as stated in Acts v. 29, *we ought to obey God rather than men.*

[IIaIIae Q104 a5] . . . [A] subject is not bound to obey his superior, if the latter command him to do something wherein he is not subject to him. For Seneca says (*De Beneficiis* iii.): *It is wrong to suppose that slavery falls upon the whole man: for the better part of him is excepted. His body is subjected and assigned to his master, but his soul is his own.* Consequently in matters touching the internal movement of the will man is not bound to obey his fellow-man, but God alone.

Nevertheless man is bound to obey his fellow-man in things that have to be done externally by means of the body: and yet, since by nature all men are equal, he is not bound to obey another man in matters touching the nature of the body, for instance in those relating to the support of his body or the begetting of his children. Wherefore servants are not bound to obey their masters, nor children their parents, in the question of contracting marriage or of remaining in the state of virginity or the like. But in matters concerning the disposal of actions and human affairs, a subject is bound to obey his superior within the sphere of his authority; for instance, a soldier must obey his general in matters relating to war, a servant his master in matters touching the execution of the duties of his service, a son his father in matters relating to the conduct of his life and the care of the household; and so forth.

[IIaIIae Q42 a2] *Reply Objection 3:* A tyrannical government is not just, because it is directed, not to the common good, but to the private good of the ruler. . . . Consequently there is no sedition in disturbing a government of this kind, unless indeed the tyrant's rule be disturbed so inordinately, that his subjects suffer greater harm from the consequent disturbance than from the tyrant's government. Indeed it is the tyrant rather that is guilty of sedition, since he encourages discord and sedition among his subjects, that he may lord over them more securely; for this is tyranny, being conducive to the private good of the ruler, and to the injury of the multitude.

[Q91 a4] Besides the natural and the human law it was necessary for the directing of human conduct to have a Divine law. And this for four reasons. First, . . . since man is ordained to an end of eternal happiness which is inproportionate to man's natural faculty, . . . it was necessary that . . . man should be directed to his end by a law given by God.

Secondly, because, on account of the uncertainty of human judgment, especially on contingent and particular matters, different people form different judgments on human acts; whence also different and contrary laws result. In order, therefore, that man may know without any doubt what he ought to do and what he ought to avoid, it was necessary for man to be directed in his proper acts by a law given by God, for it is certain that such a law cannot err.

Thirdly, . . . man is not competent to judge of interior movements, that are hidden, but only of exterior acts which appear: and yet for the perfection of virtue it is necessary for man to conduct himself aright in both kinds of acts. Consequently human law could not sufficiently curb and direct interior acts; and it was necessary for this purpose that a Divine law should supervene.

Fourthly, because. . . . human law cannot punish or forbid all evil deeds: since while aiming at doing away with all evils, it would do away with many good things, and would hinder the advance of the common good, which is necessary for human intercourse. In order, therefore, that no evil might remain unforbidden and unpunished, it was necessary for the Divine law to supervene, whereby all sins are forbidden.

IIaIIae

[Q31 a2] . . . [S]ince the love of charity extends to all, beneficence also should extend to all, but according as time and place require: because all acts of virtue must be modified with a view to their due circumstances.

[a3] . . . Now one man's connexion with another may be measured in reference to the various matters in which men are engaged together; (thus the intercourse of kinsmen is in natural matters, that of fellow-citizens is in civic matters, that of the faithful is in spiritual matters, and so forth): and various benefits should be conferred in various ways according to these various connexions, because we ought in preference to bestow on each one such benefits as pertain to the matter in which, speaking simply, he is most closely connected with us. And yet this may vary according to the various requirements of time, place, or matter in hand: because in certain cases one ought, for instance, to succour a stranger, in extreme necessity, rather than one's own father, if he is not in such urgent need.

[Q40 a1] In order for a war to be just, three things are necessary. First, the authority of the sovereign by whose command the war is to be waged. For it is not the business of a private individual to declare war. . . . And as the care of the common weal is committed to those who are in authority, it is their business to watch over the common weal of the city, kingdom or province subject to them. And just as it is lawful for them to have recourse to the sword in defending that common weal against internal disturbances, when they punish evil-doers, . . . so too, it is their business to have recourse to the sword of war in defending the common weal against external enemies.

Secondly, a just cause is required, namely that those who are attacked, should be attacked because they deserve it on account of some fault. . . .

Thirdly, it is necessary that the belligerents should have a rightful intention, so that they intend the advancement of good, or the avoidance of evil. Hence Augustine says (*De Verb. Dom.*): *True religion looks upon as peaceful those wars that are waged not for motives of aggrandisement, or cruelty, but with the object of securing peace, of punishing evil-doers, and of uplifting the good.* For it may happen that the war is declared by the legitimate authority, and for a just cause, and yet be rendered unlawful through a wicked intention. Hence Augustine says (*Contra Faust.* xxii.): *The passion for inflicting harm, the cruel thirst for vengeance, an unpacific and relentless spirit, the fever of revolt, the lust of power, and suchlike things, all these are rightly condemned in war.*

[Q57 a1] It is proper to justice . . . to direct man in his relations with others: because it denotes a kind of equality, as its very name implies; indeed we are wont to say that things are adjusted when they are made equal. . . . On the other hand the other virtues perfect man in those matters only which befit him in relation to himself. . . .

[a2] [T]he *right* or the *just* is a work that is adjusted to another person according to some kind of equality. Now a thing can be adjusted to a man in two ways: first by its very nature, as when a man gives so much that he may receive equal value in return, and this is called *natural right.* In another way a thing is adjusted or commensurated to another person, by agreement, or by common consent, when, to wit, a man deems himself satisfied, if he receives so much. This can be done in two ways: first by private agreement, as that which is confirmed by an agreement between private individuals; secondly, by public agreement, as when the whole community agrees that something should be deemed as though it were adjusted and commensurated to another person, or when this is decreed by the prince who is placed over the people, and acts in its stead, and this is called *positive right.*

[Q61 a1] [P]articular justice is directed to the private individual, who is compared to the community as a part to the whole. Now a twofold order may be considered in relation to a part. In the first place there is the order of one part to another, to which corresponds the order of one private individual to another. This order is directed by commutative justice, which is concerned about the mutual dealings between two persons. In the second place there is the order of the whole towards the parts, to which corresponds the order of that which belongs to the community in relation to each single person. This order is directed by distributive justice, which distributes common goods proportionately. Hence there are two species of justice, distributive and commutative.

[Q63 a1] . . . For the equality of distributive justice consists in allotting various things to various persons in proportion to their personal dignity. Accordingly, if one considers that personal property by reason of which the thing allotted to a particular person is due to him, this is respect not of the person but of the cause. . . . For instance if you promote a man to a professorship on account of his having sufficient knowledge, you consider the due cause, not the person; but if, in conferring something on someone, you consider in him not the fact that what you give him is proportionate or due to him, but the fact that he is this particular man (e.g. Peter or Martin), then there is respect of the person, since you give him something not for some cause that renders him worthy of it, but simply because he is this person. And any circumstance that does not amount to a reason why this man be worthy of this gift, is to be referred to his person: for instance if a man promote someone to a prelacy or a professorship, because he is rich or because he is a relation of his, it is respect of persons. It may happen, however, that a circumstance of person makes a man worthy as regards one thing, but not as regards another: thus consanguinity makes a man worthy to be appointed heir to an estate, but not to be chosen for a position of ecclesiastical authority: wherefore consideration of the same circumstance of person will amount to respect of persons in one matter and not in another. It follows, accordingly, that respect of persons is opposed to distributive justice in that it fails to observe due proportion. Now nothing but sin is opposed to virtue: and therefore respect of persons is a sin.

[Q64 a1] There is no sin in using a thing for the purpose for which it is. Now the order of things is such that the imperfect are for the perfect, even as in the process of generation nature proceeds from imperfection to perfection. Hence it is that just as in the generation of a man there is first a living thing, then an animal, and lastly a man, so too things, like the plants, which merely have life, are all alike for animals, and all animals are for man. Wherefore it is not unlawful if man use plants for the good of animals, and animals for the good of man. . . .

Now the most necessary use would seem to consist in the fact that animals use plants, and men use animals, for food, and this cannot be done unless these be deprived of life: wherefore it is lawful both to take life from plants for the use of animals, and from animals for the use of men. . . .

[a2] . . . Now every part is directed to the whole, as imperfect to perfect, wherefore every part is naturally for the sake of the whole. For this reason we observe that if the health of the whole body demands the excision of a member, through its being decayed or infectious to the other members, it will be both praiseworthy and advantageous to have it cut away. Now every individual person is compared to the whole community, as part to whole. Therefore if a man be dangerous and infectious to the community, on account of some sin, it is praiseworthy and advantageous that he be killed in order to safeguard the common good. . . .

[a5] It is altogether unlawful to kill oneself, for three reasons. First, because everything naturally loves itself, the result being that everything naturally keeps itself in *being*, and resists corruption so far as it can. Wherefore suicide is contrary to the inclination of nature, and to charity whereby every man should love himself. Hence suicide is always a mortal sin, as being contrary to the natural law and to charity.

Secondly, because every part, as such, belongs to the whole. Now every man is part of the community, and so, as such, he belongs to the community. Hence by killing himself he injures the community. . . .

Thirdly, because life is God's gift to man, and is subject to His power, Who kills and makes to live. Hence whoever takes his own life, sins against God, even as he who kills another's slave, sins against that slave's master, and as he who usurps to himself judgment of a matter not entrusted to him. For it belongs to God alone to pronounce sentence of death and life. . . .

[a7] Nothing hinders one act from having two effects, only one of which is intended, while the other is beside the intention. Now moral acts take their species according to what is intended. . . . Accordingly the act of self-defence may have two effects, one is the saving of one's life, the other is the slaying of the aggressor. Therefore this act, since one's intention is to save one's own life, is not unlawful, seeing that it is natural to everything to keep itself in *being*, as far as possible. And yet, though proceeding from a good intention, an act may be rendered unlawful, if it be out of proportion to the end. Wherefore if a man, in self-defence, uses more than necessary violence, it will be unlawful: whereas if he repel force with moderation his defence will be lawful. . . . Nor is it necessary for salvation that a man omit the act of moderate self-defence in order to avoid killing the other man, since one is bound to take more care of one's own life than of another's. But . . . it is not lawful for a man to intend killing a man in self-defence, except for such as have public authority, who while intending to kill a man in self-defence, refer this to the public good, as in the case of a soldier fighting against the foe, and in the minister of the judge struggling with robbers, although even these sin if they be moved by private animosity.

[Q66 a1] External things can be considered in two ways. First, as regards their nature, and this is not subject to the power of man, but only to the power of God Whose mere will all things obey. Secondly, as regards their use, and in this way, man has a natural dominion over external things, because, by his reason and will, he is able to use them for his own profit, as they were made on his account: for the imperfect is always for the sake of the perfect. . . .

[a2] Two things are competent to man in respect of exterior things. One is the power to procure and dispense them, and in this regard it is lawful for man to possess property. Moreover this is necessary to human life for three reasons. First because every man is more careful to procure what is for himself alone than that which is common to many or to all: since each one would shirk the labour and leave to another that which concerns the community. . . . Secondly, because human affairs are conducted in more orderly fashion if each man is charged with taking care of some particular thing himself, whereas there would be confusion if everyone had to look after any one thing indeterminately. Thirdly, because a more peaceful state is ensured to man if each one is contented with his own. Hence it is to be observed that quarrels arise more frequently where there is no division of the things possessed.

The second thing that is competent to man with regard to external things is their use. In this respect man ought to possess external things, not as his own, but as common, so that, to wit, he is ready to communicate them to others in their need. . . .

Reply Objection 1: Community of goods is ascribed to the natural law, not that the natural law dictates that all things should be possessed in common, and that nothing should be possessed as one's own: but because the division of possessions is not according to the natural law, but rather arose from human agreement which belongs to positive law. . . . Hence the ownership of possessions is not contrary to the natural law, but an addition thereto devised by human reason.

[a7] Things which are of human right cannot derogate from natural right or Divine right. Now according to the natural order established by Divine providence, inferior things are ordained for the purpose of succouring man's needs by their means. Wherefore the division and appropriation of things which are based on human law, do not preclude the fact that man's needs have to be remedied by means of these very things. Hence whatever certain people have in superabundance is due, by natural law, to the purpose of succouring the poor. . . .

Since, however, there are many who are in need, while it is impossible for all to be succoured by means of the same thing, each one is entrusted with the stewardship of his own things, so that out of them he may come to the aid of those who are in need. Nevertheless, if the need be so manifest and urgent, that it is evident that the present need must be remedied by whatever means be at hand (for instance when a person is in some imminent danger, and there is no other possible remedy), then it is lawful for a man to succour his own need by means of another's property, by taking it either openly or secretly: nor is this properly speaking theft or robbery.

[Q71 a1] Since defence of the poor man's suit belongs to the works of mercy . . . no man is sufficient to bestow a work of mercy on all those who need it. Wherefore, as Augustine says (*De Doct. Christ.* i.), *since one cannot do good to all, we ought to consider those chiefly who by reason of place, time, or any other circumstance, by a kind of chance are more closely united to us.* He says *by reason of place,* because one is not bound to search throughout the world for the needy that one may succour them; and it suffices to do works of mercy to those one meets with. . . . He says also *by reason of time,* because one is not bound to provide for the future needs of others, and it suffices to succour present needs. . . . Lastly he says, *or any other circumstances,* because one ought to show kindness to those especially who are by any tie whatever united to us. . . .

It may happen however that these circumstances concur, and then we have to consider whether this particular man stands in such a need that it is not easy to see how he can be succoured otherwise, and then one is bound to bestow the work of mercy on him. If, however, it is easy to see how he can be otherwise succoured, either by himself, or by some other person still more closely united to him, or in a better position to help him, one is not bound so strictly to help the one in need that it would be a sin not to do so: although it would be praiseworthy to do so where one is not bound to. Therefore an advocate is not always bound to defend the suits of the poor, but only when the aforesaid circumstances concur, else he would have to put aside all other business, and occupy himself entirely in defending the suits of poor people. The same applies to a physician with regard to attendance on the sick.

[Q77 a1] It is altogether sinful to have recourse to deceit in order to sell a thing for more than its just price, because this is to deceive one's neighbour so as to injure him. . . . But, apart from fraud, we may speak of buying and selling in two ways. First, as considered in themselves, and from this point of view, buying and selling seem to be established for the common advantage of both parties. . . . Now whatever is established for the common advantage, should not be more of a burden to one party than to another, and consequently all contracts between them should observe equality of thing and thing. Again, the quality of a thing that comes into human use is measured by the price given for it, for which purpose money was invented. Therefore if either the price exceed the quantity of the thing's worth, or, conversely, the thing exceed the price, there is no longer the equality of justice: and consequently, to sell a thing for more than its worth, or to buy it for less than its worth, is in itself unjust and unlawful.

Secondly we may speak of buying and selling, considered as accidentally tending to the advantage of one party, and to the disadvantage of the other: for instance, when a man has great need of a certain thing, while another man will suffer if he be without it. In such a case the just price will depend not only on the thing sold, but on the loss which the sale brings on the seller. And thus it will be lawful to sell a thing for more than it is worth in itself, though the price paid be not more than it is worth to the owner. Yet if the one man derive a great advantage by becoming possessed of the other man's property, and the seller be not at a loss through being without that thing, the latter ought not to raise the price, because the advantage accruing to the buyer, is not due to the seller, but to a circumstance affecting the buyer. Now no man should sell what is not his, though he may charge for the loss he suffers.

On the other hand if a man find that he derives great advantage from something he has bought, he may, of his own accord, pay the seller something over and above: and this pertains to his honesty.

Reply Objection 1: [H]uman law is given to the people among whom there are many lacking virtue, and it is not given to the virtuous alone. Hence human law was unable to forbid all that is contrary to virtue; and it suffices for it to prohibit whatever is destructive of human intercourse, while it treats other matters as though they were lawful, not by approving of them, but by not punishing them. Accordingly, if without employing deceit the seller disposes of his goods for more than their worth, or the buyer obtains them for less than their worth, the law looks upon this as licit, and provides no punishment for so doing, unless the excess be too great, because then even human law demands restitution to be made, for instance if a man be deceived in regard to more than half the amount of the just price of a thing.

[a3] It is always unlawful to give anyone an occasion of danger or loss, although a man need not always give another the help or counsel which would be for his advantage in any way; but only in certain fixed cases, for instance when someone is subject to him, or when he is the only one who can assist him. Now the seller who offers goods for sale, gives the buyer an occasion of loss or danger, by the very fact that he offers him defective goods, if such defect may occasion loss or danger to the buyer: — loss, if, by reason of this defect, the goods are of less value, and he takes nothing off the price on that account: — danger, if this defect either hinder the use of the goods or render it hurtful, for instance, if a man sells a lame for a fleet horse, a tottering house for a safe one, rotten or poisonous food for wholesome. Wherefore if suchlike defects be hidden, and the seller does not make them known, the sale will be illicit and fraudulent, and the seller will be bound to compensation for the loss incurred.

On the other hand, if the defect be manifest, for instance if a horse have but one eye, or if the goods though useless to the buyer, be useful to someone else, provided the seller take as much as he ought from the price, he is not bound to state the defect of the goods, since perhaps, on account of that defect the buyer might want him to allow a greater rebate than he need. Wherefore the seller may look to his own indemnity, by withholding the defect of the goods.

[a4] A tradesman is one whose business consists in the exchange of things. [E]xchange of things is twofold: one, natural as it were, and necessary, whereby one commodity is exchanged for another, or money taken in exchange for a commodity, in order to satisfy the needs of life. Suchlike trading, properly speaking, does not belong to tradesmen, but rather to housekeepers or civil servants who have to provide the household or the state with the necessaries of life. The other kind of exchange is either that of money for money, or of any commodity for money, not on account of the necessities of life, but for profit, and this kind of exchange, properly speaking, regards tradesmen according to the Philosopher (*Polit.* i.). The former kind of exchange is commendable because it supplies a natural need: but the latter is justly deserving of blame, because, considered in itself, it satisfies the greed for gain, which knows no limit and tends to infinity. Hence trading, considered in itself, has a certain debasement attaching thereto, in so far as, by its very nature, it does not imply a virtuous or necessary end. Nevertheless gain which is the end of trading, though not implying, by its nature, anything virtuous or necessary, does not, in itself, connote anything sinful or contrary to virtue: wherefore nothing prevents gain from being directed to some necessary or even virtuous end, and thus trading becomes lawful. Thus, for instance, a man may intend the moderate gain which he seeks to acquire by trading for the upkeep of his household, or for the assistance of the needy: or again, a man may take to trade for some public advantage, for instance, lest his country lack the necessaries of life, and seek gain, not as an end, but as payment for his labour.

[Q78 a1] To take usury for money lent is unjust in itself, because this is to sell what does not exist, and this evidently leads to inequality which is contrary to justice.

In order to make this evident, we must observe that there are certain things the use of which consists in their consumption: thus we consume wine when we use it for drink, and we consume wheat when we use it for food. Wherefore in suchlike things the use of the thing must not be reckoned apart from the thing itself, and whoever is granted the use of the thing, is granted the thing itself; and for this reason, to lend things of this kind is to transfer the ownership. Accordingly if a man wanted to sell wine separately from the use of the wine, he would be selling the same thing twice, or he would be selling what does not exist, wherefore he would evidently commit a sin of injustice. In like manner he commits a sin of injustice who lends wine or wheat, and asks for double payment, viz., one, the return of the thing in equal measure, the other, the price of the use, which is called usury.

On the other hand there are things the use of which does not consist in their consumption: thus to use a house is to dwell in it, not to destroy it. Wherefore in such things, both may be granted: for instance, one man hand over to another the ownership of his house while reserving to himself the use of it for a time, or vice versa, he may grant the use of the house, while retaining the ownership. For this reason a man may lawfully make a charge for the use of his house, and, besides this, revendicate the house from the person to whom he has granted its use, as happens in renting and letting a house.

Now money . . . was invented chiefly for the purpose of exchange: and consequently the proper and principal use of money is its consumption or alienation whereby it is sunk in exchange. Hence it is by its very nature unlawful to take payment for the use of money lent, which payment is known as usury: and just as a man is bound to restore other ill-gotten goods, so is he bound to restore the money which he has taken in usury.

[a4] It is by no means lawful to induce a man to sin, yet it is lawful to make use of another's sin for a good end, since even God uses all sin for some good. . . .

Accordingly, . . . it is by no means lawful to induce a man to lend under a condition of usury: yet it is lawful to borrow for usury from a man who is ready to do so and is a usurer by profession; provided the borrower have a good end in view, such as the relief of his own or another's need. Thus too it is lawful for a man who has fallen among thieves to point out his property to them (which they sin in taking) in order to save his life. . . .

Study Questions

1. What are the two types of happiness, according to Aquinas? Are external goods required for the lesser kind of happiness? Why?
2. What actions are the proper subject of morality, according to Aquinas?
3. Can ignorance cause an act to be involuntary, according to Aquinas? Explain.
4. Is ignorance itself ever voluntary, according to Aquinas? Explain.
5. What are the "circumstances" of an act? What is the order of importance of the various circumstances?
6. What are the four sources of goodness in human actions, according to Aquinas?
7. In what ways might a person's conscience err or be mistaken, according to Aquinas?
8. When does an erring conscience excuse the will from moral blame, according to Aquinas?
9. Explain what Aquinas means by saving that evil is more comprehensive than sin, sin more comprehensive than blame, and good more comprehensive than right.
10. What does Aquinas mean by saying that human virtues are habits? What is the difference between an intellectual virtue and a moral virtue?
11. What, according to Aquinas, is the eternal law? In what sense are rational creatures subject to it? What is the relationship between natural law and eternal law?
12. Explain the relationship between human law and natural law. What is the end of human law? Describe two ways in which laws may be unjust.
13. According to Aquinas, is it just to overthrow a tyrannical government?
14. What are the conditions that must be met for a war to be just, according to Aquinas?
15. What does Aquinas mean by saying "respect of persons is a sin"?
16. What is wrong with suicide, according to Aquinas?
17. Is a lawyer obliged to represent the poor, according to Aquinas? Explain.

CHAPTER 10

MODERN MORAL PHILOSOPHY

The Middle Ages, whose greatest philosopher was Thomas Aquinas, ended when the Renaissance began in the fourteenth century. Renaissance intellectuals were proud of the sparkling accomplishments of their "rebirth of Rome" and spoke derisively of the cultural squalor of the previous nine centuries (it was these intellectuals who invented the term "Dark Ages"). Theirs was the age of Botticelli, Raphael, Michelangelo, and Titian; Palladio, Palestrina, and Gabrieli; Petrarch, Boccaccio, and da Vinci. Machiavelli invented *realpolitik*; Italian sovereigns invented the science of diplomacy; Renaissance painters discovered perspective; and Columbus discovered America. Guns were introduced to society, and, equally important, so was movable type. The Stoic and biblical notion that happiness comes from poverty and virtue was replaced by the idea that the ideal man cultivates all his potentialities—and, moreover, is rich.

But we'll pass over this epoch to the Modern period in Western history, which began around the seventeenth century, and to the next great figure in moral philosophy, the Englishman Thomas Hobbes (1588–1679).

Hobbes

Thomas Hobbes was a materialist. We are not using that term in its everyday sense, that is, to denote someone who is preoccupied with material possessions. We are using the term in its primary philosophical meaning, to denote someone who maintains that physical matter is the only reality and that everything that happens can be explained as the result of physical processes. It is in this sense that Hobbes was a materialist, for he believed that only matter exists and that there is no such thing as the nonphysical soul. According to Hobbes, our thoughts and our emotions, our hopes and our fears, even our reasoning and our volitions are just simply manifestations of moving particles within our brains.

What, then, of values? Hobbes said that the words *good* and *evil* merely denote what you desire and hate, and your desires and aversions are ultimately the manifestation of moving matter within your brain.

It just so happens, according to Hobbes, that one human desire is overriding: the desire to protect our own well-being. Accordingly, Hobbes maintained, it follows automatically that our primary "good" is to safeguard our welfare.

Now, either we live in a situation in which we can do this, or we do not, he reasoned. The first type of situation he called a condition of "peace." Peace prevails, Hobbes said, when people cannot harm one another. When they can harm one another, they live in a state of "war." This is the natural state of people, in Hobbes's opinion.

Observe that Hobbes defined peace as a condition in which people *cannot* harm one another, not as a condition in which people voluntarily *do not* harm one another. Hobbes believed that by nature people will harm one another unless they are *prevented* from doing so. People are really just selfish brutes, he said, who will use any means at their disposal to achieve their ends. Since, in his opinion, anything and anyone can be used to further one's ends, unless you and I are prevented from hurting each other, we will inevitably wind up doing so.

But what became of the soaring admiration for man that tended to characterize the thought of the earlier intellectuals of the Renaissance? Hobbes in fact did admire the rational capabilities of some men. He lived in the early stages of the Scientific Revolution, during which Kepler, Galileo, Boyle, Harvey, Huygens, and others made many of the most important scientific discoveries of all time. But this was also a period of acute civil chaos in England (and on the continent of Europe too, for that matter), and Hobbes saw around him ugly proof of his theory that people will take full advantage of one another if there is no strong central authority to maintain peace and order.

So the natural inclinations of people, according to Hobbes, place them in a war of each against all, a situation that really does not serve anyone's best interest. What people should do, Hobbes said, is agree to transfer their collective strength, along with their natural right to use whatever is necessary to defend themselves, to a sovereign authority who will use this power to make people abide by their agreements and live in a state of peace.

This sovereign, which Hobbes called the *Leviathan,* may be an individual, or a group. It is, in either case, an absolute dictator, since it has the strength of the many. When people transfer their power and rights to the Leviathan, they do so unconditionally and irrevocably.

Hobbes went so far as to say that this collective transfer of power to a sovereign is commanded by natural law. However, when Hobbes talked about natural law, or about natural laws (for he used the plural), he did not have in mind anything at all like Aquinas's natural law. He certainly did not have in mind some absolute moral law of God. What Hobbes called natural laws are merely rational principles of prudent behavior, prescriptions for safeguarding your own life. And what they "command" is that, for their own safety, people should submit to an absolute dictator as the best road out of the state of chaos, mistrust, and violence in which they would otherwise inevitably find themselves.

When people agree among themselves to transfer their power and rights to the central power, they in effect create a *social contract.* This social contract not only delivers people from anarchy and chaos, but also is the basis for all law and justice (in this context, Hobbes meant civil laws, not natural laws). Hobbes defined *justice* and *injustice* as the keeping and not-keeping of covenants (agreements). If Moore pays Stewart for some work Stewart did, as Moore had agreed he would, then that's "just." If Moore welshes on the agreement, that's unjust. But the point, according to Hobbes, is that agreements are mere words unless there exists a sovereign power that compels people to stand by their agreements. People have to know that they will be punished if they don't honor their covenants, otherwise, people won't honor them, Hobbes said.

Further, the social contract among people that created the Leviathan is not a contract between them and it. Because the Leviathan holds all the power, it could break any contract it made with the people, and that just means that any such contract would be mere empty words. Furthermore, because there logically cannot be a covenant between the sovereign and its subjects and because justice, according to Hobbes, is the keeping of covenants, it follows that the sovereign cannot act unjustly towards its subjects. Accordingly, the sovereign has the right to lay down any laws that it can enforce—with one exception noted below—and these laws logically cannot be unjust. Hobbes's sovereign has no legal or moral obligation to its subjects.

However, if the Leviathan fails to provide security to its subjects, they may transfer their allegiance to another sovereign. In addition, the sovereign cannot rightfully lay down some law that requires a subject to end his or her own life. (No one has the right to take his or her own life, so this right is not one of those that people transfer to the sovereign through the social contract.)

Much in Hobbes's political theorizing invites criticism, but our concern is with Hobbes's moral philosophy. Let's just summarize the main points. Good, according to Hobbes, is merely an expression of desire. Evil, similarly, is an expression of an aversion. There are natural laws, but these are simply prescriptions for ensuring personal safety, which is our fundamental desire. Finally, justice and injustice consist merely in keeping and failing to keep agreements that are enforced by the sword of the sovereign.

Perhaps Hobbes's most important contribution to moral philosophy is his theory that certain fundamental moral values, specifically justice, come to exist only when people contract among themselves to transfer their powers to a central authority. The theory that values arise, not from God or nature or the Form of the Good or some other source, but out of a social contract is known as *contractarianism* or *contractualism.* Hobbes was the first modern contractarian.

The following selection is from Hobbes's major work, *Leviathan.*

from *Leviathan*

Thomas Hobbes

Thomas Hobbes (1588–1679) was on close terms with many other great minds of his age, but his physicalistic metaphysics was deeply offensive to churchmen. Reprinted here are excerpts from his most famous work, *Leviathan*, published in 1651. Spelling and punctuation have been modernized.

Chapter VI. Of the Interior Beginnings of Voluntary Motions, commonly called the Passions, And the Speeches by which they are expressed.

There be in animals two sorts of motions peculiar to them: One called vital, begun in generation and continued without interruption through their whole life; such as are the course of the blood, the pulse, the breathing, the concoction, nutrition, excretion, &c; to which motions there need no help of imagination: The other is animal motion, otherwise called voluntary motion; as to go, to speak, to move any of our limbs, in such manner as is first fancied in our minds. That sense is motion in the organs and interior parts of man's body, caused by the action of the things we see, hear, &c; And that fancy is but the Relics of the same motion, remaining after Sense. . . . And because going, speaking, and the like voluntary motions depend always upon a precedent thought of whither, which way, and what, it is evident that the imagination is the first internal beginning of all voluntary motion. And although unstudied men, do not conceive any motion at all to be there, where the thing moved is invisible, or the space it is moved in, is (for the shortness of it) insensible, yet that doth not hinder, but that such motions are. For let a space be never so little, that which is moved over a greater space, whereof that little one is part, must first be moved over that. These small beginnings of motion, within the body of man, before they appear in walking, speaking, striking, and other visible actions, are commonly called endeavour.

This endeavour, when it is toward something which causes it, is called appetite, or desire, and the latter being the general name and the other, often-times restrained to signify the desire of food, namely hunger and thirst. And when the endeavour is fromward something, it is generally called aversion. These words *appetite* and *aversion* we have from the Latins; and they both of them signify the motions, one of approaching, the other of retiring. . . . For Nature itself does often press upon men those truths, which afterwards, when they look for somewhat beyond Nature, they stumble at. For the schools find in mere appetite to go, or move, no actual motion at all: but because some motion they must acknowledge, they call it metaphorical motion; which is but an absurd speech: for though words may be called metaphorical, bodies and motions cannot.

That which men desire, they are also said to love: and to hate those things for which they have aversion. So that desire and love are the same thing, save that by Desire, we always signify the absence of the object; by love, most commonly the presence of the same. So also by aversion, we signify the absence; and by hate, the presence of the object.

Of appetites and aversions, some are born with men; as appetite of food, appetite of excretion, and exoneration (which may also and more properly be called aversions, from somewhat they feel in their bodies), and some other appetites, not many. The rest, which are appetites of particular things, proceed from experience and trial of their effects upon themselves or other men. For of things we know not at all or believe not to be, we can have no further desire than to taste and try.

But aversion we have for things not only which we know have hurt us, but also that we do not know whether they will hurt us or not.

Those things which we neither desire nor hate we are said to contemn: contempt being nothing else but an immobility, or contumacy of the heart, in resisting the action of certain things; and proceeding from that the heart is already moved otherwise, by other more potent objects, or from want of experience of them.

And because the constitution of a man's body is in continual mutation, it is impossible that all the same things should always cause him the same appetites and aversions: much less can all men consent in the desire of almost any one and the same object.

But whatsoever is the object of any man's appetite or desire, that is it, which he for his part calleth *good*; and the object of his hate and aversion, *evil*; and of his contempt, *vile* and *inconsiderable*. For these words of good, evil, and contemptible are ever used with relation to the person that useth them: There being nothing simply and absolutely so, nor any common rule of good and evil, to be taken from the nature of the objects themselves, but from the person of the man (where there is no commonwealth) or (in a Commonwealth) from the person that representeth it; or from an arbitrator or judge, whom men disagreeing shall by consent set up and make his sentence the rule thereof.

The Latin tongue has two words whose significations approach to those of good and evil, but are not precisely the same; and those are *pulchrum* and *turpe*. Whereof the former signifies that, which by some apparent signs promiseth good; and the latter, that which promiseth evil. But in our tongue we have not so general names to express them by. But for *pulchrum*, we say in some things, *fair*; in others, *beautiful* or *handsome*, or *gallant*, or *honourable*, or *comely*, or *amiable*; and for *turpe*, *foul*, *deformed*, *ugly*, *base*, *nauseous*, and the like, as the subject shall require. All which words in their proper places signify nothing else, but the *mine*, or countenance, that promiseth good and evil. So that of good there be three kinds: good in the promise, that is *pulchrum*; Good in effect, as the end desired, which is called *jucundum*, *delightful*; and good as the means, which is called *utile*, *profitable*; and as many of evil: For evil in promise is that they call *Turpe*; evil in effect and end is *molestum*, *unpleasant*, *troublesome*; and evil in the means, *inutile*, *unprofitable*, *hurtful*. . . .

Chapter XIII. Of the Natural Condition of Mankind, as concerning their Felicity and Misery.

Nature hath made men so equal in the faculties of body and mind, as that though there be found one man sometimes manifestly stronger in body or of quicker mind than another, yet when all is reckoned together, the difference between man and man is not so considerable as that one man can thereupon claim to himself any benefit to which another may not pretend as well as he. For as to the strength of body, the weakest has strength enough to kill the strongest, either by secret machination or by confederacy with others, that are in the same danger with himself.

And as to the faculties of the mind (setting aside the arts grounded upon words, and especially that skill of proceeding upon general and infallible rules, called Science; which very few have, and but in few things; as being not a native faculty, born with us, nor attained, as prudence, while we look after somewhat else) I find yet a greater equality amongst men, than that of strength. For prudence is but experience, which equal time equally bestows on all men, in those things they equally apply themselves unto. That which may perhaps make such equality incredible is but a vain concept of one's own wisdom, which almost all men think they have in a greater degree than the vulgar; that is, than all men but themselves, and a few others, whom by fame, or for concurring with themselves, they approve. For such is the nature of men, that howsoever they may acknowledge many others to be more witty, or more eloquent, or more learned, yet they will hardly believe there be many so wise as themselves: For they see their own wit at hand, and other men's at a distance. But this proveth rather that men are in that point equal, than unequal. For there is not ordinarily a greater sign of the equal distribution of anything, than that every man is contented with his share.

From this equality of ability ariseth equality of hope in the attaining of our ends. And therefore if any two men desire the same thing, which nevertheless they cannot both enjoy, they become enemies; and in the way to their end (which is principally their own conservation, and sometimes their delectation only) endeavour to destroy or subdue one another. And from hence it comes to pass, that where an invader hath no more to fear than another man's single power; if one plant, sow, build, or possess a convenient seat, others may probably be expected to come prepared with forces united to dispossess and deprive him, not only of the fruit of his labour, but also of his life or liberty. And the invader again is in the like danger of another.

And from this diffidence of one another, there is no way for any man to secure himself, so reasonable as anticipation; that is, by force or wiles to master the persons of all men he can, so long, till he see no other power great enough to endanger him: And this is no more than his own conservation requireth and is generally allowed. Also because there be some, that taking pleasure in contemplating their own power in the acts of conquest, which they pursue farther than their security requires; if others, that otherwise would be glad to be at ease within modest bounds, should not by invasion increase their power, they would not be able, long time, by standing only on their defence to subsist. And by consequence, such augmentation of dominion over men, being necessary to a man's conservation, it ought to be allowed him.

Again, men have no pleasure (but on the contrary a great deal of grief) in keeping company where there is no power able to overawe them all. For every man looketh that his companion should value him at the same rate he sets upon himself: And upon all signs of contempt or undervaluing, naturally endeavours as far as he dares (which amongst them that have no common power to keep them in quiet, is far enough to make them destroy each other) to extort a greater value from his contemners by dommage; and from others, by the example.

So that in the nature of man, we find three principal causes of quarrel. First, competition; secondly, diffidence; thirdly, glory.

The first maketh men invade for gain; the second, for safety; and the third, for reputation. The first use violence to make themselves masters of other men's persons, wives, children, and cattle; the second, to defend them; the third, for trifles, as a word, a smile, a different opinion, and any other sign of undervalue, either direct in their persons or by reflection in their kindred, their friends, their nation, their profession, or their name.

Hereby it is manifest that during the time men live without a common power to keep them all in awe, they are in that condition which is called war, and such a war as is of every man against every man. For war consisteth not in battle only, or the act of fighting, but in a tract of time, wherein the will to contend by battle is sufficiently known: and therefore the notion of time is to be considered in the nature of war, as it is in the nature of weather. For as the nature of foul weather lieth not in a shower or two of rain, but in an inclination thereto of many days together: so the nature of war consisteth not in actual fighting, but in the known disposition thereto during all the time there is no assurance to the contrary. All other time is peace.

Whatsoever therefore is consequent to a time of war, where every man is enemy to every man, the same is consequent to the time wherein men live without other security than what their own strength and their own invention shall furnish them withal. In such condition, there is no place for industry, because the fruit thereof is uncertain: and consequently no culture of the earth, no navigation nor use of the commodities that may be imported by sea, no commodious building, no instruments of moving and removing such things as require much force, no knowledge of the face of the earth, no account of time, no arts, no letters, no society; and which is worst of all, continual fear and danger of violent death; and the life of man, solitary, poor nasty, brutish, and short.

It may seem strange to some man that has not well weighed these things that Nature should thus dissociate and render men apt to invade and destroy one another: and he may therefore, not trusting to this inference made from the passions, desire perhaps to have the same confirmed by experience. Let him therefore consider with himself when taking a journey, he arms himself and seeks to go well accompanied; when going to sleep, he locks his doors; when even in his house he locks his chests; and this when he knows there be laws and public officers armed to revenge all injuries shall be done him; what opinion he has of his fellow subjects, when he rides armed; of his fellow citizens, when he locks his doors; and of his children and servants, when he locks his chests. Does he not there as much accuse mankind by his actions, as I do by my words? But neither of us accuse man's nature in it. The desires and other passions of man are in themselves no sin. No more are the actions that proceed from those passions, till they know a law that forbids them: which till laws be made they cannot know: nor can any law be made, till they have agreed upon the person that shall make it.

It may peradventure be thought, there was never such a time, nor condition of war as this, and I believe it was never generally so over all the world, but there are many places where they live now. For the savage people in many places of *America*, except the government of small families, the concord whereof dependeth on natural lust, have no government at all and live at this day in that brutish manner, as I said before. Howsoever, it may be perceived what manner of life there would be, where there were no common power to fear, by the manner of life which men that have formerly lived under a peaceful government use to degenerate into in a civil war.

But though there had never been any time wherein particular men were in a condition of war one against another, yet in all times, kings and persons of sovereign authority, because of their independency, are in continual jealousies and in the state and posture of gladiators, having their weapons pointing and their eyes fixed on one another; that is, their forts, garrisons, and guns upon the frontiers of their kingdoms and continual spies upon their neighbours, which is a posture of war. But because they uphold thereby the industry of their subjects, there does not follow from it that misery which accompanies the Liberty of particular men.

To this war of every man against every man, this also is consequent: that nothing can be unjust. The notions of right and wrong, justice and injustice have there no place. Where there is no common power, there is no law: where no law, no injustice. Force and fraud are in war the two cardinal virtues. Justice and Injustice are none of the faculties neither of the body nor mind. If they were, they might be in a man that were alone in the world, as well as his senses and passions. They are qualities that relate to men in society, not in solitude. It is consequent also to the same condition, that there be no propriety, no dominion, no *mine* and *thine* distinct, but only that to be every man's that he can get, and for so long as he can keep it. And thus much for the ill condition, which man by mere Nature is actually placed in; though with a possibility to come out of it, consisting partly in the passions, partly in his reason.

The passions that incline men to peace are fear of death, desire of such things as are necessary to commodious living, and a hope by their industry to obtain them. And reason suggesteth convenient articles of peace upon which men may be drawn to agreement. These articles are they which otherwise are called the laws of Nature: whereof I shall speak more particularly, in the two following chapters.

Chapter XIV. Of the first and second Natural Laws, and of Contracts.

The right of Nature, which writers commonly call *jus naturale*, is the liberty each man hath to use his own power as he will himself for the preservation of his own nature; that is to say, of his own life, and consequently, of doing anything, which in his own judgment and reason he shall conceive to be the aptest means thereunto.

By liberty is understood, according to the proper signification of the word, the absence of external impediments: which impediments may oft take away part of a man's power to do what he would, but cannot hinder him from using the power left him, according as his judgment and reason shall dictate to him.

A law of Nature (*Lex Naturalis*) is a precept, of general rule, found out by reason, by which a man is forbidden to do that which is destructive of his life or taketh away the means of preserving the same, and to omit that by which he thinketh it may be best preserved. For though they that speak of this subject use to confound *jus*, and *lex, right* and *law*, yet they ought to be distinguished; because right consisteth in liberty to do or to forbear, whereas law determineth and bindeth to one of them: so that law and right differ as much as obligation and liberty, which in one and the same matter are inconsistent.

And because the condition of man (as hath been declared in the precedent Chapter) is a condition of War of everyone against everyone, in which case everyone is governed by his own reason, and there is nothing he can make use of that may not be a help unto him in preserving his life against his enemies, it followeth that in such a condition every man has a right to everything, even to one another's body. And therefore, as long as this natural right of every man to every thing endureth, there can be no security to any man, (how strong or wise soever he be) of living out the time which Nature ordinarily alloweth men to live. And consequently it is a precept, or general rule of reason, *That every man ought to endeavour peace as far as he has hope of obtaining it; and when he cannot obtain it, that he may seek, and use, all helps and advantages of war.* The first branch of which rule containeth the first and fundamental law of Nature, which is *to seek peace and follow it.* The second, the sum of the right of Nature, which is *By all means we can, to defend ourselves.*

From this fundamental law of Nature, by which men are commanded to endeavour peace, is derived this second law: *That a man be willing, when others are so too, as far forth as for peace and defence of himself he shall think it necessary, to lay down this right to all things; and be contented with so much liberty against other men as he would allow other men against himself.* For as long as every man holdeth this right, of doing anything he liketh, so long are all men in the condition of war. But if other men will not lay down their right, as well as he, then there is no reason for anyone, to divest himself of his: For that were to expose himself to prey (which no man is bound to) rather than to dispose himself to peace. This is that law of the Gospel: *Whatsoever you require that others should do to you, that do ye to them. . . .*

To lay down a man's right to anything is to divest himself of the liberty of hindering another of the benefit of his own right to the same. For he that renounceth, or passeth away his right, giveth not to any other man a right which he had not before, because there is nothing to which every man had not right by Nature: but only standeth out of his way, that he may enjoy his own original right without hindrance from him, not without hindrance from another. So that the effect which redoundeth to one man by another man's defect of right is but so much diminution of impediments to the use of his own right original.

Right is laid aside either by simply renouncing it or by transferring it to another. By simply renouncing, when he cares not to whom the benefit thereof redoundeth. By transferring, when he intendeth the benefit thereof to some certain person or persons. And when a man hath in either manner abandoned or granted away his Right, then is he said to be obliged, or bound, not to hinder those to whom such right is granted or abandoned from the benefit of it: and that he ought, and it is his duty, not to make void that voluntary act of his own: and that such hindrance is injustice and injury, as being *sine jure*; the right being before renounced or transferred. So that injury or injustice in the controversies of the world, is somewhat like to that which in the disputations of scholars is called *absurdity.* For as it is there called an absurdity to contradict what one maintained in the beginning, so in the world, it is called injustice and injury voluntarily to undo that which from the beginning he had voluntarily done. The way by which a man either simply renounceth or transferreth his right is a declaration, or signification, by some voluntary and sufficient sign or signs that he doth so renounce or transfer, or hath so renounced or transferred the same, to him that accepteth it. And these signs are either words only, or actions only, or (as it happeneth most often) both words and actions. And the same are the bonds by which men are bound and obliged: bonds that have their strength, not from their own Nature, (for nothing is more easily broken than a man's word) but from fear of some evil consequence upon the rupture.

Whensoever a man transferreth his right or renounceth it, it is either in consideration of some right reciprocally transferred to himself or for some other good he hopeth for thereby. For it is a voluntary act: and of the voluntary acts of every man, the object is some *Good to himself*. And therefore there be some rights which no man can be understood by any words, or other signs, to have abandoned or transferred. As first a man cannot lay down the right of resisting them that assault him by force to take away his life, because he cannot be understood to aim thereby at any good to himself. The same may be said of wounds and chains and imprisonment; both because there is no benefit consequent to such patience, as there is to the patience of suffering another to be wounded or imprisoned, as also because a man cannot tell when he seeth men proceed against him by violence whether they intend his death or not. And lastly the motive and end for which this renouncing and transferring of right is introduced is nothing else but the security of a man's person in his life and in the means of so preserving life, as not to be weary of it. And therefore if a man by words, or other signs, seems to despoil himself of the end for which those signs were intended; he is not to be understood as if he meant it, or that it was his will, but that he was ignorant of how such words and actions were to be interpreted.

The mutual transferring of right is that which men call *contract*.

There is difference between transferring of right to the thing and transferring, or tradition, that is, delivery of the thing itself. For the thing may be delivered together with the translation of the right, as in buying and selling with ready money or exchange of goods or lands: and it may be delivered some time after.

Again, one of the contractors may deliver the thing contracted for on his part and leave the other to perform his part at some determinate time after, and in the mean time be trusted; and then the contract on his part is called *pact*, or *covenant*. Or both parts may contract now to perform hereafter, in which cases, he that is to perform in time to come, being trusted, his performance is called *keeping of promise* or Faith; and the failing of performance (if it be voluntary) *violation of faith*.

When the transferring of right is not mutual, but one of the parties transferreth in hope to gain thereby friendship or service from another or from his friends or in hope to gain the reputation of charity or magnanimity, or to deliver his mind from the pain of compassion, or in hope of reward in heaven, this is not contract, but *gift, free-gift, grace*: which words signify one and the same thing.

Signs of contract are either *express* or *by inference*. Express are words spoken with understanding of what they signify: And such words are either of the time present or past, as *I give, I grant, I have given, I have granted, I will that this be yours*, or of the future, as *I will give, I will grant*: which words of the future are called *promise*.

Signs by inference are sometimes the consequence of words; sometimes the consequence of silence; sometimes the consequence of actions; sometimes the consequence of forbearing an action: and generally a sign by inference of any contract is whatsoever sufficiently argues the will of the contractor.

Words alone, if they be of the time to come and contain a bare promise are an insufficient sign of a Free-gift and therefore not obligatory. For if they be of the time to come, as *Tomorrow I will give*, they are a sign I have not given yet, and consequently that my right is not transferred but remaineth till I transfer it by some other act. But if the words be of the time present, or past, as *I have given, or do give to be delivered tomorrow*, then is my tomorrow's right given away today, and that by the virtue of the words, though there were no other argument of my will. And there is a great difference in the signification. . . . between *I will that this be thine tomorrow* and *I will give it thee tomorrow*: For the word *I will*, in the former manner of speech, signifies an act of the will present; but in the latter, it signifies a promise of an act of the will to come: and therefore the former words, being of the present, transfer a future right; the latter, that be of the future, transfer nothing. But if there be other signs of the will to transfer a Right, besides Words, then, though the gift be free, yet may the right be understood to pass by words of the future: as if a man propound a prize to him that comes first to the end of a race, The gift is free; and though the words be of the future, yet the right passeth: for if he would not have his words so be understood, he should not have let them run.

In contracts, the right passeth not only where the words are of the time present or past, but also where they are of the future: because all contract is mutual translation, or change of Right; and therefore he that promiseth only because he hath already received the benefit for which he promiseth is to be understood as if he intended the right should pass: for unless he had been content to have his words so understood, the other would not have performed his part first. And for that cause, in buying and selling and other acts of contract, a promise is equivalent to a covenant, and therefore obligatory.

He that performeth first in the case of a contract is said to *merit* that which he is to receive by the performance of the other; and he hath it as *due.* Also when a prize is propounded to many which is to be given to him only that winneth, or money is thrown amongst many to be enjoyed by them that catch it, though this be a free gift, yet so to win, or so to catch, is to *merit* and to have it as due. For the right is transferred in the propounding of the prize and in throwing down the money; though it be not determined to whom, but by the event of the contention. But there is between these two sorts of merit, this difference, that in contract, I merit by virtue of my own power and the contractor's need; but in this case of free gift, I am enabled to merit only by the benignity of the giver. In contract, I merit at the contractor's hand that he should depart with his right; in this case of gift, I merit not that the giver should part with his right, but that when he has parted with it, it should be mine, rather than another's. And this I think to be the meaning of that distinction of the schools, between *Meritum congrui* and *Meritum condigni.* For God Almighty, having promised Paradise to those men (hoodwinked with carnal desires) that can walk through this world according to the Precepts and Limits prescribed by him; they say, he that shall so walk shall merit Paradise *ex congruo.* But because no man can demand a right to it by his own Righteousness or any other power in himself but by the free grace of God only, they say, no man can merit Paradise *ex condigno.* This I say, I think is the meaning of that distinction; but because disputers do not agree upon the signification of their own terms of art longer than it serves their turn, I will not affirm anything of their meaning: only this I say, when a gift is given indefinitely, as a prize to be contended for, he that winneth meriteth and may claim the prize as due.

If a covenant be made wherein neither of the parties perform presently, but trust one another in the condition of mere Nature (which is a condition of war of every man against every man) upon any reasonable suspicion, it is void: But if there be a common power set over them both, with right and force sufficient to compel performance, it is not void. For he that performeth first has no assurance the other will perform after, because the bonds of words are too weak to bridle men's ambition, avarice, anger, and other passions, without the fear of some coercive power, which in the condition of mere Nature, where all men are equal, and judges of the justness of their own fears, cannot possibly be supposed. And therefore he which performeth first does but betray himself to his enemy, contrary to the right (he can never abandon) of defending his life and means of living.

But in a civil estate, where there is a power set up to constrain those that would otherwise violate their faith, that fear is no more reasonable; and for that cause, he which by the covenant is to perform first is obliged so to do.

The cause of fear which maketh such a covenant invalid must be always something arising after the Covenant made, as some new fact, or other sign of the will not to perform: else it cannot make the Covenant void. For that which could not hinder a man from promising ought not to be admitted as a hindrance of performing.

He that transferreth any right transferreth the means of enjoying it, as far as lieth in his power. As he that selleth land is understood to transfer the herbage and whatsoever grows upon it; nor can he that sells a mill turn away the stream that drives it. And they that give to a man the right of government in sovereignty are understood to give him the right of levying money to maintain soldiers and of appointing magistrates for the administration of justice.

To make covenants with brute beasts is impossible; because not understanding our speech, they understand not nor accept of any translation of right, nor can translate any Right to another: and without mutual acceptance, there is no covenant.

To make covenant with God is impossible, but by mediation of such as God speaketh to, either by revelation supernatural, or by his lieutenants that govern under him, and in his name: for otherwise we know not whether our covenants be accepted or not. And therefore they that vow anything contrary to any law of Nature vow in vain, as being a thing unjust to pay such vow. And if it be a thing commanded by the law of Nature, it is not the vow, but the law that binds them.

The matter or subject of a Covenant is always something that falleth under deliberation (for to covenant is an act of the will; that is to say, an act, and the last act, of deliberation) and is therefore always understood to be something to come; and which is judged possible for him that covenanteth, to perform.

And therefore, to promise that which is known to be impossible is no covenant. But if that prove impossible afterwards, which before was thought possible, the Covenant is valid and bindeth (though not to the thing itself) yet to the value; or, if that also be impossible, to the unfeigned endeavour of performing as much as is possible: for to more no man can be obliged.

Men are freed of their covenants two ways: by performing or by being forgiven. For performance is the natural end of obligation; and Forgiveness, the restitution of liberty, as being a re-transferring of that right in which the obligation consisted.

Covenants entered into by fear, in the condition of mere Nature, are obligatory. For example, if I covenant to pay a ransom or service for my life to an enemy, I am bound by it. For it is a contract wherein one receiveth the benefit of life; the other is to receive money or service for it; and consequently, where no other law (as in the condition, of mere Nature) forbiddeth the performance, the covenant is valid. Therefore prisoners of war if trusted with the payment of their ransom are obliged to pay it; and if a weaker prince make a disadvantageous peace with a stronger, for fear he is bound to keep it, unless (as hath been said before) there ariseth some new and just cause of fear to renew the war. And even in commonwealths, if I be forced to redeem myself from a thief by promising him money, I am bound to pay it, till the civil law discharge me. For whatsoever I may lawfully do without obligation, the same I may lawfully covenant to do through fear: and what I lawfully covenant, I cannot lawfully break.

A former covenant makes void a latter. For a man that hath passed away his right to one man today hath it not to pass tomorrow to another: and therefore the latter promise passeth no right, but is null.

A covenant not to defend myself from force, by force, is always void. For (as I have shown before) no man can transfer or lay down his right to save himself from death, wounds, and imprisonment, the avoiding whereof is the only end of laying down any right, and therefore the promise of not resisting force, in no covenant transferreth any right; nor is obliging. For though a man may covenant thus, *Unlesse I do so, or so, kill me*; he cannot covenant thus, *Unlesse I do so, or so, I will not resist you, when you come to kill me.* For man by nature chooseth the lesser evil, which is danger of death in resisting; rather than the greater, which is certain and present death in not resisting. And this is granted to be true by all men, in that they lead criminals to execution and prison with armed men, notwithstanding that such criminals have consented to the law by which they are condemned.

A covenant to accuse oneself, without assurance of pardon, is likewise invalid. For in the condition of Nature, where every man is judge, there is no place for accusation: and in the civil state, the accusation is followed with punishment, which being force, a man is not obliged not to resist. The same is also true of the accusation of those by whose condemnation a man falls into misery, as of a father, wife, or benefactor.

For the testimony of such an accuser, if it be not willingly given, is presumed to be corrupted by Nature and therefore not to be received: and where a man's testimony is not to be credited, he is not bound to give it. Also accusations upon torture are not to be reputed as testimonies. For torture is to be used but as means of conjecture, and light, in the further examination and search of truth; and what is in that case confessed, tendeth to the ease of him that is tortured, not to the informing of the torturers and therefore ought not to have the credit of a sufficient testimony: for whether he deliver himself by true or false accusation, he does it by the right of preserving his own life.

The force of words, being (as I have formerly noted) too weak to hold men to the performance of their covenants, there are in man's nature but two imaginable helps to strengthen it. And those are either a fear of the consequence of breaking their word or a glory or pride in appearing not to need to break it. This latter is a generosity too rarely found to be presumed on, especially in the pursuers of wealth, command, or sensual pleasure, which are the greatest part of Mankind. The passion to be reckoned upon is fear, whereof there be two very general objects: one, the power of spirits invisible; the other, the power of those men they shall therein offend. Of these two, though the former be the greater power, yet the fear of the latter is commonly the greater Fear. The Fear of the former is in every man his own religion, which hath place in the nature of man before civil society. The latter hath not so; at least not place enough to keep men to their promises, because in the condition of mere Nature, the inequality of power is not discerned but by the event of battle. So that before the time of civil society, or in the interruption thereof by war, there is nothing can strengthen a covenant of peace agreed on against the temptations of avarice, ambition, lust, or other strong desire, but the fear of that invisible power, which they every one worship as God, and fear as a revenger of their perfidy. All therefore that can be done between two men not subject to civil power is to put one another to swear by the God he feareth: which *swearing*, or *oath*, is a *forme of speech added to a promise, by which he that promiseth signifieth that unless he perform, he renounceth the mercy of his God or calleth to him for vengeance on himself.* Such was the heathen form, *Let Jupiter kill me else, as I kill this Beast.* So is our Form, *I shall do thus, and thus, so help me God.* And this, with the rites and ceremonies, which everyone useth in his own religion, that the fear of breaking faith might be the greater.

By this it appears that an oath taken according to any other form or rite than his that sweareth is in vain and no oath; and that there is no swearing by anything which the swearer thinks not God. For though men have sometimes used to swear by their kings for fear or flattery, yet they would have it thereby understood, they attributed to them divine honour. And that swearing unnecessarily by God is but profaning of his name: and swearing by other things, as men do in common discourse, is not swearing, but an impious custom gotten by too much vehemence of talking.

It appears also that the oath adds nothing to the obligation. For a covenant, if lawful, binds in the sight of God without the oath as much as with it; if unlawful, bindeth not at all, though it be confirmed with an Oath.

Chapter XV.
Of Other Laws of Nature.

From that law of Nature by which we are obliged to transfer to another such rights, as being retained, hinder the peace of mankind, there followeth a third, which is this, *That men perform their covenants made:* without which, covenants are in vain and but empty words; and the right of all men to all things remaining, we are still in the condition of War.

And in this law of Nature consisteth the fountain and original of justice. For where no covenant hath preceded, there hath no right been transferred, and every man has right to every thing; and consequently, no action can be unjust. But when a covenant is made, then to break it is unjust: and the definition of injustice is no other than *the not performance of covenant.* And whatsoever is not unjust is just.

But because Covenants of mutual trust, where there is a fear of not performance on either part (as hath been said in the former Chapter) are invalid; though the original of justice be the making of covenants, yet injustice actually there can be none, till the cause of such fear be taken away; which while men are in the natural condition of war cannot be done. Therefore before the names of just and unjust can have place, there must be some coercive power to compel men equally to the performance of their covenants, by the terror of some punishment greater than the benefit they expect by the breach of their covenant; and to make good that propriety, which by mutual contract men acquire in recompense of the universal right they abandon: and such power there is none before the erection of a commonwealth. And this is also to be gathered out of the ordinary definition of justice in the schools: for they say, that *Justice is the constant will of giving to every man his own.* And therefore where there is no own, that is, no propriety, there is no injustice; and where there is no coerceive power erected, that is, where there is no commonweath, there is no Propriety, all men having Right to all things: therefore where there is no commonwealth, there nothing is unjust. So that the nature of justice consisteth in keeping of valid covenants, but the validity of covenants begins not but with the constitution of a civil power, sufficient to compel men to keep them. And then it is also that Propriety begins.

The fool hath said in his heart, there is no such thing as justice; and sometimes also with his tongue, seriously alleging that every man's conservation and contentment, being committed to his own care, there could be no reason why every man might not do what he thought conduced thereunto; and therefore also to make or not make, keep or not keep Covenants was not against reason, when it conduced to one's benefit. He does not therein deny that there be covenants; and that they are sometimes broken, sometimes kept; and that such breach of them may be called injustice and the observance of them justice: but he questioneth whether injustice, taking away the fear of God (for the same fool hath said in his heart there is no God) may not sometimes stand with that reason which dictateth to every man his own good; and particularly then, when it conduceth to such a benefit, as shall put a man in a condition to neglect not only the dispraise and revilings, but also the power of other men. The Kingdom of God is gotten by violence: but what if it could be gotten by unjust violence? Were it against reason so to get it, when it is impossible to receive hurt by it? And if it be not against reason, it is not against justice, or else justice is not to be approved for good. From such reasoning as this, successful wickedness hath obtained the name of virtue: and some that in all other things have disallowed the violation of faith yet have allowed it when it is for the getting of a kingdom. And the heathen that believed that Saturn was deposed by his son Jupiter believed nevertheless the same Jupiter to be the avenger of injustice, somewhat like to a piece of law in *Cokes Commentaries on Litleton*, where he says, If the right heir of the Crown be attainted of treason, yet the Crown shall descend to him and *eo instante* the attainder be void: From which instances a man will be very prone to infer that when the heir apparent of a kingdom shall kill him that is in possession, though his father, you may call it injustice or by what other name you will; yet it can never be against reason, seeing all the voluntary actions of men tend to benefit of themselves, and those actions are most reasonable that conduce most to their ends. This specious reasoning is nevertheless false.

For the question is not of promises mutual, where there is no security of performance on either side, as when there is no civil power erected over the parties promising; for such promises are no covenants. But either where one of the parties has performed already or where there is a power to make him perform, there is the question whether it be against reason, that is, against the benefit of the other to perform, or not. And I say it is not against reason. For the manifestation whereof, we are to consider first, that when a man doth a thing, which notwithstanding anything can be foreseen, and reckoned on, tendeth to his own destruction, howsoever some accident which he could not expect, arriving may turn it to his benefit; yet such events do not make it reasonably or wisely done. Secondly, that in a condition of war, wherein every man to every man, for want of a common power to keep them all in awe, is an enemy, there is no man can hope by his own strength or wit to defend himself from destruction, without the help of confederates; where everyone expects the same defence by the Confederation that anyone else does: and therefore he which declares he thinks it reason to deceive those that help him can in reason expect no other means of safety than what can be had from his own single power. He therefore that breaketh his covenant and consequently declareth that he thinks he may with reason do so, cannot be received into any society that unite themselves for peace and defence, but by the error of them that receive him, nor when he is received, be retained in it, without seeing the danger of their error, which errors a man cannot reasonably reckon upon as the means of his security: and therefore if he be left or cast out of Society, he perisheth; and if he live in society, it is by the errors of other men, which he could not foresee nor reckon upon, and consequently against the reason of his preservation; and so, as all men that contribute not to his destruction, forbear him only out of ignorance of what is good for themselves.

As for the instance of gaining the secure and perpetual felicity of heaven, by any way, it is frivolous, there being but one way imaginable; and that is not breaking, but keeping, of covenant.

And for the other instance of attaining sovereignty by rebellion, it is manifest that though the event follow, yet because it cannot reasonably be expected, but rather the contrary, and because by gaining it so, others are taught to gain the same in like manner, the attempt thereof is against reason. Justice therefore, that is to say, keeping of covenant, is a rule of reason by which we are forbidden to do anything destructive to our life, and consequently a law of Nature.

There be some that proceed further and will not have the law of Nature to be those rules which conduce to the preservation of man's life on earth, but to the attaining of an eternal felicity after death, to which they think the breach of Covenant may conduce and consequently be just and reasonable (such are they that think it a work of merit to kill, or depose, or rebel against, the sovereign power constituted over them by their own consent). But because there is no natural knowledge of man's estate after death, much less of the reward that is then to be given to breach of faith, but only a belief grounded upon other men's saying that they know it supernaturally or that they know those that knew them, that knew others, that knew it supernaturally; breach of faith cannot be called a precept of reason or Nature.

Others that allow for a law of Nature, the keeping of faith, do nevertheless make exception of certain persons as heretics, and such as use not to perform their covenant to others: and this also is against reason. For if any fault of a man be sufficient to discharge our covenant made, the same ought in reason to have been sufficient to have hindered the making of it.

The names of just and injust, when they are attributed to men, signify one thing; and when they are attributed to actions, another. When they are attributed to men, they signify conformity or inconformity of manners to reason. But when they are attributed to actions, they signify the conformity of inconformity to reason, not of manners, or manner of life, but of particular actions. A just man therefore is he that taketh all the care he can, that his actions may be all just: and an unjust man is he that neglecteth it. And such men are more often in our language styled by the names of righteous and unrighteous than Just and Unjust, though the meaning be the same. Therefore a righteous man does not lose that title by one or a few unjust Actions that proceed from sudden passion or mistake of things or persons: nor does an unrighteous man lose his character for such actions as he does, or forbears to do, for fear, because his will is not framed by the justice, but by the apparent benefit of what he is to do. That which gives to humane actions the relish of justice is a certain nobleness or gallantness of courage (rarely found) by which a man scorns to be beholding for the contentment of his life, to fraud, or breach of promise. This justice of the manners is that which is meant where justice is called a virtue, and injustice a vice.

But the justice of actions denominates men not just, *guiltless*: and the injustice of the same (which is also called injury) gives them but the name of *guilty*.

Again, the injustice of manners is the disposition or aptitude to do injury, and is injustice before it proceed to act, and without supposing any individual person injured. But the injustice of an action (that is to say, injury) supposeth an individual person injured; namely him to whom the covenant was made. And therefore many times the injury is received by one man, when the damage redoundeth to another. As when the Master commandeth his servant to give money to a stranger, if it be not done, the injury is done to the master, whom he had before covenanted to obey; but the damage redoundeth to the stranger, to whom he had no obligation and therefore could not injure him. And so also in Commonwealths, private men may remit to one another their debts, but not robberies or other violences, whereby they are damaged; because the detaining of debt is an injury to themselves, but robbery and violence are injuries to the person of the commonwealth.

Whatsoever is done to a man, conformable to his own will signified to the doer, is no injury to him. For if he that doeth it hath not passed away his original right to do what he please by some antecedent covenant, there is no breach of covenant, and therefore no injury done him. And if he have, then his will to have it done being signified is a release of that covenant: and so again there is no Injury done him.

Justice of actions is by writers divided into *commutative,* and *distributive*: and the former they say consisteth in proportion arithmetical, the latter in proportion geometrical. Commutative therefore they place in the equality of value of the things contracted for; and distributive, in the distribution of equal benefit to men of equal merit. As if it were injustice to sell dearer than we buy or to give more to a man than he merits. The value of all things contracted for is measured by the appetite of the contractors, and therefore the just value is that which they can be contented to give. And merit (besides that which is by Covenant, where the performance on one part meriteth the performance of the other part and falls under justice commutative, not distributive) is not due by justice, but is rewarded of grace only. And therefore this distinction, in the sense wherein it useth to be expounded, is not right. To speak properly, commutative justice is the justice of a contractor, that is, a performance of covenant in buying and selling, hiring and letting to hire, lending and borrowing, exchanging, bartering, and other acts of contract.

And distributive justice, the justice of an arbitrator: that is to say, the act of defining what is Just. Wherein (being trusted by them that make him Arbitrator) if he perform his trust, he is said to distribute to every man his own: and this is indeed just distribution and may be called (though improperly) distributive justice, but more properly equity, which also is a law of Nature, as shall be shown in due place.

As *justice* dependeth on antecedent Covenant, so does gratitude depend on antecedent grace, that is to say, antecedent free-gift, and is the fourth law of Nature, which may be conceived in this form, *That a man which receiveth benefit from another of mere grace, endeavour that he which giveth it, have no reasonable cause to repent him of his good will.* For no man giveth but with intention of good to himself, because gift is voluntary; and of all voluntary acts, the object is to every man his own good, of which if men see they shall be frustrated, there will be no beginning of benevolence, or trust, nor consequently of mutual help, nor of reconciliation of one man to another; and therefore they are to remain still in the condition of war, which is contrary to the first and fundamental law of Nature, which commandeth men to *seek peace.* The breach of this law is called *ingratitude* and hath the same relation to grace that injustice hath to obligation by covenant. . . .

Study Questions

1. Explain the differences between desire and aversion, and love and hate, according to Hobbes.
2. In what way are people equal, according to Hobbes?
3. What does this equality lead to?

4. What are the three principal causes of quarrels, according to Hobbes? Explain.
5. Explain what war and peace consist in, according to Hobbes, and what life is like in Hobbes's state of nature.
6. What becomes of right and wrong, justice and injustice, in the Hobbesian state of nature?
7. What is the difference between a right of nature and a law of nature, according to Hobbes? What are the first law of nature and the right of nature?
8. What, according to Hobbes, are contracts and covenants?
9. Explain what Hobbes means by saying that covenants without swords are but words.
10. What is the third law of nature, according to Hobbes?
11. In what do justice and injustice consist, and what is required for there to be justice, according to Hobbes?

Hume

One of the most important moral philosophers of the next century (that is, the eighteenth) was David Hume (1711–1776). Hume's thought marked a crossroads in the history of moral philosophy.

First, Hume maintained that moral principles are not divine edicts. He believed that the order that is apparent in the universe is mild evidence that the universe has or once had a creative force behind it, a force that is vaguely analogous to human intelligence. But we really cannot say anything about the moral values of this creative force, he said, and any attempt to derive principles of ethical conduct by considering its nature is just idle speculation.

And second, Hume held that moral principles are not the "offspring of reason." By this he meant that reason cannot determine what is good and what is not. Consider an act of murder, he said. Turn it this way in your mind, and then turn it that way. Reason will tell you only what has happened—that one person has ended the life of another—and what the possible causes and consequences of the act might be. Reason does not disclose the moral wrongfulness of the act. That the murder is immoral, Hume held, is a verdict not of reason but of sentiment. That a man has no qualms about murdering people is a failure not of his reason—he may well be a genius, as far as that goes—but of his heart.

It is because moral judgments are not the offspring of reason, according to Hume, that moral judgments are not logically entailed by any purely empirical judgments, that is, judgments of fact. To use Hume's terminology from his *Treatise of Human Nature*, we cannot derive a judgment that something *ought to be* or *ought not to be* from assertions about what *is* or *is not*. This dictum, that you cannot deduce an "ought" from an "is," is the central premise in what later came to be known as antinaturalism (see Chapter 3), the focus of much discussion in the twentieth century.

Other, nonmoral, value judgments also are not the offspring of reason. That a statue is beautiful is a judgment based not on reason but on sentiment. True, reason can tell you something about the harmony and proportion of the statue, but the harmony and proportion must please your aesthetic sensibilities if you are to find the statue beautiful.

If we consider the qualities we depict with words that express or connote moral approval, we find that these qualities please our moral sensibilities, just as the qualities we find artistically praiseworthy are those that please our aesthetic sensibilities. But what kinds of qualities please our moral sensibilities? Primarily, according to Hume, it is benevolent qualities—qualities that exhibit a person's concern for others and humankind generally—that please our moral sensibilities and that therefore we label morally good. To see or hear about—or even just think about—someone extending a helping hand to another person pleases our moral faculty.

Why does benevolence bring us please? According to Hume, it does so because we are *sympathetic* creatures. We bestow moral praise on benevolence *not* (as some cynics would have it) because we like to imagine ourselves as receiving the benefits of benevolence, but because by our very nature we have feelings for others. So, to summarize, a judgment of moral approval is an expression of a particular kind of sentiment, a pleasurable sentiment that we experience when we are presented with behavior done out of concern for others.

In his analysis of moral language and the situations in which we employ it, Hume also discovered that when we morally praise (or condemn) an individual, we are primarily praising the individual's *character*; we find his or her actions praiseworthy (or condemnatory) mainly as indications of character: "If some *action* be either virtuous or vicious, 'tis only as a sign of some quality or character. It must depend upon durable principles of the mind, which extend over the whole conduct, and enter into the personal character."

It's important to notice how Hume's inquiries took a different tack from those taken by most previous moral philosophers. These philosophers, perhaps with the limited exception of Hobbes, were primarily concerned with normative questions: What is virtuous and right and good? What ought one do, and why? Hume, by contrast, asked such questions as these: What is a moral judgment? What do we in fact praise as morally good? What features of our psychology lead us to judge as morally good the things we do?

Hume's questions, you should observe, are non-normative. They call for factual answers, not normative answers. Of course, from Hume's perspective, moral standards are not the commands of God and are not the dictates of reason; accordingly, they are just simply the products of human thinking. From this perspective, therefore, the question "What *is* good?" ultimately does reduce to the question "What do people *call* 'good'?"

We can now see why Hume left moral philosophy at a crossroads. On the one hand, moral philosophy might assume that, despite Hume, moral principles are objectively grounded on God or reason (or on something else)—and go on to try to determine what these principles are. Alternatively, it might follow Hume and stop searching for such norms. The first alternative was the one taken by Kant; the second is pretty much the one taken by some contemporary analytic moral philosophers. A third alternative, taken by the existentialists, is to discuss the implications for human existence of the Humean idea that moral standards have no objective grounding. We'll return to these matters later in this chapter and in Chapter 11.

from *An Enquiry Concerning the Principles of Morals*

David Hume

David Hume (1711–1776) was better known among his contemporaries as a historian than as a philosopher. Reprinted here are sections I, II, III, V, VI, and IX and appendices I and III from his *Enquiry Concerning the Principles of Morals*, from the edition published in 1777. We have omitted some footnotes.

Section I
Of the General Principles of Morals

Disputes with men, pertinaciously obstinate in their principles, are, of all others, the most irksome; except, perhaps, those with persons, entirely disingenuous, who really do not believe the opinions they defend, but engage in the controversy, from affectation, from a spirit of opposition, or from a desire of showing wit and ingenuity, superior to the rest of mankind. The same blind adherence to their own arguments is to be expected in both; the same contempt of their antagonists; and the same passionate vehemence, in inforcing sophistry and falsehood. And as reasoning is not the source, whence either disputant derives his tenets; it is vain to expect, that any logic, which speaks not to the affections, will ever engage him to embrace sounder principles.

Those who have denied the reality of moral distinctions, may be ranked among the disingenuous disputants; nor is it conceivable, that any human creature could ever seriously believe, that all characters and actions were alike entitled to the affection and regard of everyone. The difference, which nature has placed between one man and another, is so wide, and this difference is still so much farther widened, by education, example, and habit, that, where the opposite extremes come at once under our apprehension, there is no scepticism so scrupulous, and scarce any assurance so determined, as absolutely to deny all distinction between them. Let a man's insensibility be ever so great, he must often be touched with the images of Right and Wrong; and let his prejudices be ever so obstinate, he must observe, that others are susceptible of like impressions. The only way, therefore, of converting an antagonist of this kind, is to leave him to himself. For, finding that nobody keeps up the controversy with him, it is probable he will, at last, of himself, from mere weariness, come over to the side of common sense and reason.

There has been a controversy started of late, much better worth examination, concerning the general foundation of Morals; whether they be derived from Reason, or from Sentiment; whether we attain the knowledge of them by a chain of argument and induction, or by an immediate feeling and finer internal sense; whether, like all sound judgement of truth and falsehood, they should be the same to every rational intelligent being; or whether, like the perception of beauty and deformity, they be founded entirely on the particular fabric and constitution of the human species.

The ancient philosophers, though they often affirm, that virtue is nothing but conformity to reason, yet, in general, seem to consider morals as deriving their existence from taste and sentiment. On the other hand, our modern enquirers, though they also talk much of the beauty of virtue, and deformity of vice, yet have commonly endeavoured to account for these distinctions by metaphysical reasonings, and by deductions from the most abstract principles of the understanding. Such confusion reigned in these subjects, that an opposition of the greatest consequence could prevail between one system and another, and even in the parts of almost each individual system; and yet nobody, till very lately, was ever sensible of it. The elegant Lord Shaftesbury, who first gave occasion to remark this distinction, and who, in general, adhered to the principles of the ancients, is not, himself, entirely free from the same confusion.

It must be acknowledged, that both sides of the question are susceptible of specious arguments.

Moral distinctions, it may be said, are discernible by pure *reason*: else, whence the many disputes that reign in common life, as well as in philosophy, with regard to this subject: the long chain of proofs often produced on both sides; the examples cited, the authorities appealed to, the analogies employed, the fallacies detected, the inferences drawn, and the several conclusions adjusted to their proper principles. Truth is disputable: not taste: what exists in the nature of things is the standard of our judgement; what each mans feel within himself is the standard of sentiment. Propositions in geometry may be proved, systems in physics may be controverted; but the harmony of verse, the tenderness of passion, the brilliancy of wit, must give immediate pleasure. No man reasons concerning another's beauty; but frequently concerning the justice or injustice of his actions. In every criminal trial the first object of the prisoner is to disprove the facts alleged, and deny the actions imputed to him: the second to prove, that, even if these actions were real, they might be justified, as innocent and lawful. It is confessedly by deductions of the understanding, that the first point is ascertained: how can we suppose that a different faculty of the mind is employed in fixing the other?

On the other hand, those who would resolve all moral determinations into *sentiment*, may endeavour to show, that it is impossible for reason ever to draw conclusions of this nature. To virtue, say they, it belongs to be *amiable* and vice *odious*. This forms their very nature or essence. But can reason or argumentation distribute these different epithets to any subjects, and pronounce beforehand, that this must produce love, and that hatred? Or what other reason can we ever assign for these affections, but the original fabric and formation of the human mind, which is naturally adapted to receive them?

The end of all moral speculations is to teach us our duty; and, by proper representations of the deformity of vice and beauty of virtue, beget correspondent habits, and engage us to avoid the one, and embrace the other. But is this ever to be expected from inferences and conclusions of the understanding, which of themselves have no hold of the affections or set in motion the active powers of men? They discover truths; but where the truths which they discover are indifferent, and beget no desire or aversion, they can have no influence on conduct and behaviour. What is honourable, what is fair, what is becoming, what is noble, what is generous, takes possession of the heart, and animates us to embrace and maintain it. What is intelligible, what is evident, what is probable, what is true, procures only the cool asset of the understanding; and gratifying a speculative curiosity, puts an end to our researches.

Extinguish all the warm feelings and prepossessions in favour of virtue, and all disgust or aversion to vice: render men totally indifferent towards these distinctions; and morality is no longer a practical study, nor has any tendency to regulate our lives and actions.

These arguments on each side (and many more might be produced) are so plausible, that I am apt to suspect, they may, the one as well as the other, be solid and satisfactory, and that *reason* and *sentiment* concur in almost all moral determinations and conclusions. The final sentence, it is probable, which pronounces characters and actions amiable or odious, praiseworthy or blameable; that which stamps on them the mark of honour or infamy, approbation or censure; that which renders morality an active principle and constitutes virtue our happiness and vice our misery; it is probable, I say, that this final sentence depends on some internal sense or feeling, which nature has made universal in the whole species. For what else can have an influence of this nature? But in order to pave the way for such a sentiment, and give a proper discernment of its object, it is often necessary, we find, that much reasoning should precede, that nice distinctions be made, just conclusions drawn, distant comparisons formed, complicated relations examined, and general facts fixed and ascertained. Some species of beauty, especially the natural kinds, on their first appearance, command our affection and approbation; and where they fail of this effect, it is impossible for any reasoning to redress their influence, or adapt them better to our taste and sentiment. But in many orders of beauty, particularly those of the finer arts, it is requisite to employ much reasoning, in order to feel the proper sentiment; and a false relish may frequently be corrected by argument and reflection. There are just grounds to conclude, that moral beauty partakes much of this latter species, and demands the assistance of our intellectual faculties, in order to give it a suitable influence on the human mind.

But though this question, concerning the general principles of morals, be curious and important, it is needless for us, at present, to employ farther care in out researches concerning it. For if we can be so happy, in the course of this enquiry, as to discover the true origin of morals, it will then easily appear how far either sentiment or reason enters into all determinations of this nature.[1] In order to attain this purpose, we shall endeavour to follow a very simple method: we shall analyse that complication of mental qualities, which form what, in common life, we call Personal Merit: we shall consider every attribute of the mind, which renders a man an object either of esteem and affection, or of hated and contempt; every habit or sentiment or faculty, which, if ascribed to any person, implies either praise or blame, and may enter into any panegyric or satire of his character and manners. The quick sensibility, which, on this head, is so universal among mankind, gives a philosopher sufficient assurance, that he can never be considerably mistaken in framing the catalogue, or incur any danger of misplacing the objects of his contemplation: he needs only enter into his own breast for a moment, and consider whether or not he should desire to have this or that quality ascribed to him, and whether such or such an imputation would proceed from a friend or enemy. The very nature of language guides us almost infallibly in forming a judgement of this nature; and as every tongue possesses one set of words which are taken in a good sense, and another in the opposite, the least acquaintance with the idiom suffices, with out any reasoning, to direct us in collecting and arranging the estimable or blameable qualities of men. The only object of reasoning is to discover the circumstances on both sides, which are common to these qualities; to observe that particular in which the estimable qualities agree on the one hand, and the blameable on the other; and thence to reach the foundation of ethics, and find those universal principles from which all censure or approbation is ultimately derived. As this is a question of fact, not of abstract science, we can only expect success, by following the experimental method, and deducing general maxims from a comparison of particular instances. The other scientific method, where a general abstract principle is first established, and is afterwards branched out into a variety of inferences and conclusions, may be more perfect in itself, but suits less the imperfection of human nature, and is a common source of illusion and mistake in this as well as in other subjects. Men are now cured of their passion for hypotheses and systems in natural philosophy, and will hearken to no arguments but those which are derived from experience. It is full time they should attempt a like reformation in all moral disquisitions; and reject every system of ethics, however subtle or ingenious, which is not founded on fact and observation.

We shall begin our enquiry on this head by the consideration of the social virtues, Benevolence and Justice. The explication of them will probably give us an opening by which the others may be accounted for.

[1]See Appendix i.

Section II
Of Benevolence

Part I

It may be esteemed, perhaps, a superfluous task to prove, that the benevolent or softer affections are estimable; and wherever they appear, engage the approbation and good-will of mankind. The epithets *sociable, good-natured, humane, merciful, grateful, friendly, generous, beneficent,* or their equivalents, are known in all languages, and universally express the highest merit, which *human nature* is capable of attaining. Where these amiable qualities are attended with birth and power and eminent abilities, and display themselves in the good government or useful instruction of mankind, they seem even to raise the possessors of them above the rank of *human nature*, and make them approach in some measure to the divine. Exalted capacity, undaunted courage, prosperous success; these may only expose a hero or politician to the envy and ill-will of the public: but as soon as the praises are added of humane and beneficent; when instances are displayed of lenity, tenderness or friendship; envy itself is silent, or joins the general voice of approbation and applause.

When Pericles, the great Athenian statesman and general, was on his death-bed, his surrounding friends, deeming him now insensible, began to indulge their sorrow for their expiring patron, by enumerating his great qualities and successes, his conquests and victories, the unusual length of his administration, and his nine trophies erected over the enemies of the republic. *You forget,* cries the dying hero, who had heard all, *you forget the most eminent of my praises, while you dwell so much on those vulgar advantages, in which fortune had a principle share. You have not observed that no citizen has ever yet worne mourning on my account.*[2]

In men of more ordinary talents and capacity, the social virtues become, if possible, still more essentially requisite; there being nothing eminent, in that case, to compensate for the want of them, or preserve the person from our severest hatred, as well as contempt. A high ambition, an elevated courage, is apt, says Cicero, in less perfect characters, to degenerate into a turbulent ferocity. The more social and softer virtues are there chiefly to be regarded. These are always good and amiable.[3]

The principal advantage, which Juvenal discovers in the extensive capacity of the human species, is that it renders our benevolence also more extensive, and gives us larger opportunities of spreading our kindly influence than what are indulged to the inferior creation.[4] It must, indeed, be confessed, that by doing good only, can a man truly enjoy the advantages of being eminent. His exalted station, of itself but the more exposes him to danger and tempest. His sole prerogative is to afford shelter to inferiors, who repose themselves under his cover and protection.

But I forget, that it is not my present business to recommend generosity and benevolence, or to paint, in their true colours, all the genuine charms of the social virtues. These, indeed, sufficiently engage every heart, on the first apprehension of them; and it is difficult to abstain from some sally of panegyric, as often as they occur in discourse or reasoning. But our object here being more the speculative, than the practical part of morals, it will suffice to remark, (what will readily, I believe, be allowed) that no qualities are more intitled to the general good-will and approbation of mankind than beneficence and humanity, friendship and gratitude, natural affection and public spirit, or whatever proceeds from a tender sympathy with others, and a generous concern for our kind and species. These wherever they appear seem to transfuse themselves, in a manner, into each beholder, and to call forth, in their own behalf, the same favourable and affectionate sentiments, which they exert on all around.

Part II

We may observe that, in displaying the praises of any humane, beneficent man, there is one circumstance which never fails to be amply insisted on, namely, the happiness and satisfaction, derived to society from his intercourse and good offices. To his parents, we are apt to say, he endears himself by his pious attachment and duteous care still more than by the connexions of nature. His children never feel his authority, but when employed for their advantage. With him, the ties of love are consolidated by beneficence and friendship. The ties of friendship approach, in a fond observance of each obliging office, to those of love and inclination. His domestics and dependants have in him a sure resource; and no longer dread the power of fortune, but so far as she exercises it over him. From him the hungry receive food, the naked clothing, the ignorant and slothful skil and industry. Like the sun, an inferior minister of providence he cheers, invigorates, and sustains the surrounding world.

If confined to private life, the sphere of his activity is narrower; but his influence is all benign and gentle. If exalted into a higher station, mankind and posterity reap the fruit of his labours.

As these topics of praise never fail to be employed, and with success, where we would inspire

[2]Plut. in Pericle.

[3]Cic. de Officiis, lib. i.

[4]Sat. xv. 139 and seq.

esteem for any one; may it not thence be concluded, that the utility, resulting from the social virtues, forms, at least, a *part* of their merit, and is one source of that approbation and regard so universally paid to them?

* * *

Upon the whole, then, it seems undeniable, *that* nothing can bestow more merit on any human creature than the sentiment of benevolence in an eminent degree; and *that* a *part,* at least, of its merit arises from its tendency to promote the interests of our species, and bestow happiness on human society. We carry our view into the salutary consequences of such a character and disposition; and what ever has so benign an influence, and forwards so desirable an end, is beheld with complacency and pleasure. The social virtues are never regarded without their beneficial tendencies, nor viewed as barren and unfruitful. The happiness of mankind, the order of society, the harmony of families, the mutual support of friends, are always considered as the result of their gentle dominion over the breasts of men.

How considerable a *part* of their merit we ought to ascribe to their utility, will better appear from future disinquisitions;[5] as well as the reason, why this circumstance has such a command over your esteem and approbation.[6]

Section III
Of Justice

Part 1

That Justice is so useful to society, and consequently that *part* of its merit, at least, must arise from that consideration, it would be a superfluous undertaking to prove. That public utility is the *sole* origin of justice, and that reflections on the beneficial consequences of this virtue are the *sole* foundation of its merit; this proposition, being more curious and important, will better deserve our examination and enquiry.

Let us suppose that nature has bestowed on the human race such profuse *abundance* of all *external* conveniences, that, without any uncertainty in the event, without any care or industry on our part, every individual finds himself fully provided with whatever his most voracious appetites can want, or luxurious imagination wish or desire. His natural beauty, we shall suppose, surpasses all acquired ornaments: the perpetual elemency of the seasons renders useless all clothes or covering; the raw herbage affords him the most delicious fare; the clear fountain, the richest beverage. No laborious occupation required: no tillage: no navigation. Music, poetry, and contemplation form his sole business: conversation, mirth, and friendship his sole amusement.

It seems evident that, in such a happy state, every other social virtue would flourish, and receive tenfold increase; but the cautious, jealous virtue of justice would never once have been dreamed of. For what purpose make a partition of goods, where every one has already more than enough? Why give rise to property, where there cannot possibly be any injury? Why call this object *mine,* when upon the seizing of it by another, I need but stretch out my hand to possess myself to what is equally valuable? Justice, in that case, being totally useless, would be an idle ceremonial, and could never possibly have place in the catalogue of virtues.

We see, even in the present necessitous condition of mankind, that, wherever any benefit is bestowed by nature in an unlimited abundance, we leave it always in common among the whole human race, and make no subdivisions of right and property. Water and air, though the most necessary of all objects, are not challenged as the property of individuals; nor can any man commit injustice by the most lavish use and enjoyment of these blessings. In fertile extensive countries, with few inhabitants, land is regarded on the same footing. And no topic is so much insisted on by those, who defend the liberty of the seas, as the unexhausted use of them in navigation. Were the advantages procured by navigation, as inexhaustible, these reasoners had never had any adversaries to refute; nor had any claims ever been advanced of a separate, exclusive dominion over the ocean.

---

[5]Sect. iii. and iv.

[6]Sect. v.

It may happen, in some countries, at some periods, that there be established a property in water, none in land;[7] if the latter be in greater abundance than can be used by the inhabitants, and the former be found, with difficulty, and in very small quantities.

Again; suppose, that, though the necessities of human race continue the same as at present, yet the mind is so enlarged, and so replete with friendship and generosity, that every man has the utmost tenderness for every man, and feels no more concern for his own interest than for that of his fellows; it seems evident, that the use of justice would, in this case, be suspended by such an extensive benevolence, nor would the divisions and barriers of property and obligation have ever been thought of. Why should I bind another, by a deed or promise, to do me any good office, when I know that he is already prompted, by the strongest inclination, to seek my happiness, and would, of himself, perform the desired service; except the hurt, he thereby receives, be greater than the benefit accruing to me? in which case, he knows, that, from my innate humanity and friendship, I should be first to oppose myself to his impudent generosity. Why raise land marks between my neighbour's field and mine, when my heart has made no division between our interests; but shares all his joys and sorrows with the same force and vivacity as if originally my own? Every man, upon this supposition, being a second self to another, would trust all his interests to the discretion of every man; without jealousy, without partition, without distinction. And the whole human race would form only one family; where all would lie in common, and be used freely, without regard to property; but cautiously too, with as entire regard to the necessities of each individual as if our own interests were most intimately concerned.

In the present disposition of the human heart, it would, perhaps, be difficult to find complete instances of such enlarged affections; but still we may observe, that the case of families approaches towards it; and the stronger the mutual benevolence is among the individuals, the nearer it approaches; till all distinction of property be, in a great measure, lost and confounded among them. Between married persons, the cement of friendship is by the laws supposed so strong as to abolish all division of possessions; and has often, in reality, the force ascribed to it. And it is observable, that, during the ardour of new enthusiasms, when every principle is inflamed into extravagance, the community of goods has been frequently attempted; and nothing but experience of its inconveniences, from the returning or disguised selfishness of men, could make the imprudent fanatics adopt anew the ideas of justice and of separate property. So true is it, that this virtue derives its existence entirely from its necessary *use* to the intercourse and social state of mankind.

To make this truth more evident, let us reverse the forgoing suppositions; and carrying everything to the opposite extreme, consider what would be the effect of these new situations. Suppose a society to fall into such want of all common necessaries, that the utmost frugality and industry cannot preserve the greater number from perishing, and the whole from extreme misery; it will readily, I believe, be admitted, that the strict laws of justice are suspended, in such a pressing emergence, and give place to the stronger motives of necessity and self-preservation. Is it any crime, after a shipwreck, to seize whatever means or instrument of safety one can lay hold of, without regard to former limitations of property? Or if a city besieged were perishing with hunger; can we imagine, that men will see any means of preservation before them, and lose their lives, from a scrupulous regard to what, in other situations, would be the rules of equity and justice? The use and tendency of that virtue is to procure happiness and security, by preserving order in society: but where the society is ready to perish from extreme necessity, no greater evil can be dreaded from violence and injustice; and every man may now provide for himself by all the means, which prudence can dictate, or humanity permit. The public, even in less urgent necessities, opens granaries, without the consent of proprietors; as justly supposing, that the authority of magistracy may, consistent with equity, extend so far: but were any number of men to assemble, without the tie of laws or civil jurisdiction; would

[7]Genesis, chaps. xiii and xxi.

an equal partition of bread in a famine, though effected by power and even violence, be regarded as criminal or injurious?

Suppose likewise, that it should be a virtuous man's fate to fall into the society of ruffians, remote from the protection of laws and government; what conduct must he embrace in that melancholy situation? He sees such a desperate rapaciousness prevail; such a disregard to equity, such contempt of order, such stupid blindness to future consequences, as must immediately have the most tragical conclusion, and must terminate in destruction to the greater number, and in a total dissolution of society to the rest. He, meanwhile, can have no other expedient than to arm himself, to whomever the sword he seizes, or the buckler may belong: To make provision of all means of defence and security: And his particular regard to justice being no longer of use to his own safety or that of others, he must consult the dictates of self-preservation alone, without concern for those who no longer merit his care and attention.

When any man, even in political society, renders himself by his crimes, obnoxious to the public, he is punished by the laws in his goods and person; that is, the ordinary rules of justice are, with regard to him, suspended for a moment, and it becomes equitable to inflict on him, for the *benefit* of society, what otherwise he could not suffer without wrong or injury.

The rage and violence of public war; what is it but a suspension of justice among the warring parties, who perceive, that this virtue is now no longer of any *use* or advantage to them? The laws of war, which then succeed to those of equity and justice, are rules calculated for the *advantage* and *utility* of that particular state, in which men are now placed. And were a civilized nation engaged with barbarians, who observed no rules even of war, the former must also suspend their observance of them, where they no longer serve to any purpose; and must render every action or recounter as bloody and pernicious as possible to the first aggressors.

Thus, the rules of equity or justice depend entirely on the particular state and condition in which men are placed, and owe their origin and existence to that utility, which results to the public from their strict and regular observance. Reverse, in any considerable circumstance, the condition of men: Produce extreme abundance or extreme necessity: Implant in the human breast perfect moderation and humanity, or perfect rapaciousness and malice: By rendering justice totally *useless*, you thereby totally destroy its essence, and suspend its obligation upon mankind.

The common situation of society is a medium amidst all these extremes. We are naturally partial to ourselves, and to our friends; but are capable of learning the advantage resulting from a more equitable conduct. Few enjoyments are given us from the open and liberal hand of nature; but by art, labour, and industry, we can extract them in great abundance. Hence the ideas of property become necessary in all civil society: Hence justice derives its usefulness to the public: And hence alone arises its merit and moral obligation.

These conclusions are so natural and obvious, that they have not escaped even the poets, in their descriptions of the felicity attending the golden age or the reign of Saturn. The seasons, in that first period of nature, were so temperate, if we credit these agreeable fictions, that there was no necessity for men to provide themselves with clothes and houses, as a security against the violence of heat and cold: The rivers flowed with wine and milk: The oaks yielded honey; and nature spontaneously produced her greatest delicacies. Nor were these the chief advantages of that happy age. Tempests were not alone removed from nature; but those more furious tempests were unknown to human breasts, which now cause such uproar, and engender such confusion. Avarice, ambition, cruelty, selfishness, were never heard of: Cordial affection, compassion, sympathy, were the only movements with which the mind was yet acquainted. Even the punctilious distinction of *mine* and *thine* was banished from among the happy race of mortals, and carried with it the very notion of property and obligation, justice and injustice.

This *poetical* fiction of the *golden age*, is in some respects, of a piece with the *philosophical* fiction of the *state of nature*; only that the former is represented as the most charming and most peaceable condition, which can possibly be imagined; whereas the latter is painted out as a state of mutual war and violence, attended with the most extreme necessity. On the first origin of mankind, we are told, their ignorance and savage nature were so prevalent, that they could give no mutual trust, but must each depend upon himself and his own force or cunning for protection and security. No law was heard of: No rule of justice known: No distinction of property regarded: Power was the only measure of right; and a perpetual war of all against all was the result of men's untamed selfishness and barbarity.[8]

Whether such a condition of human nature could ever exist, or if it did, could continue so long as to merit the appellation of a *state*, may justly be doubted. Men are necessarily born in a family-society, at least; and are trained up by their parents to some rule of conduct and behaviour. But this must be admitted, that, if such a state of mutual war and violence was ever real, the suspension of all laws of justice, from their absolute inutility, is a necessary and infallible consequence.

The more we vary our views of human life, and the newer and more unusual the lights are in which we survey it, the more shall we be convinced, that the origin here assigned for the virtue of justice is real and satisfactory.

Were there a species of creatures intermingled with men, which, though rational, were possessed of such inferior strength, both of body and mind, that they were incapable of all resistance, and could never, upon the highest provocation, make us feel the effects of their resentment; the necessary consequence, I think, is that we should be bound by the laws of humanity to give gentle usage to these creatures, but should not, properly speaking, lie under any restraint of justice with regard to them, nor could they possess any right or property, exclusive of such arbitrary lords. Our intercourse with them could not be called society, which supposes a degree of equality; but absolute command on the one side, and servile obedience on the other. What we covet, they must instantly resign: Our permission is the only tenure, by which they hold their possessions: Our compassion and kindness the only check, by which they curb our lawless will: And as no inconvenience ever results from the exercise of a power, so firmly established in nature, the restraints of justice and property, being totally *useless*, would never have place in so unequal a confederacy.

This is plainly the situation of men, with regard to animals; and how far these may be said to possess reason, I leave it to others to determine. The great superiority of civilized Europeans above barbarous Indians, tempted us to imagine ourselves on the same footing with regard to them, and made us throw off all restraints of justice, and even of humanity, in our treatment of them. In many nations, the female sex are reduced to like slavery, and are rendered incapable of all property, in opposition to their lordly masters. But though the males, when united, have in all countries bodily force sufficient to maintain this severe tyranny, yet such are the insinuation, address, and charms of their fair companions, that women are commonly able to break the confederacy, and share with the other sex in all the rights and privileges of society.

Were the human species so framed by nature as that each individual possessed within himself every faculty, requisite both for his own preservation and for the propagation of his kind: Were all society and intercourse cut off between man and man, by the primary intention of the supreme Creator: It seems evident, that so solitary a being would be as much incapable of justice, as of social justice and conversation. Where mutual regards and forebearance serve to no manner of purpose, they would never direct the conduct of any reasonable man. The headlong course of the passions would be checked by no reflection on future consequences. And as each man is here supposed to love himself alone, and to depend only on himself and his own activity for safety and happiness, he would, on every occasion, to the utmost of his power, challenge the preference above every other being, to none of which he is bound by any ties, either of nature or of interest.

But suppose the conjunction of the sexes to be established in nature, a family immediately arises; and particular rules being found requisite for its subsistence, these are immediately embraced;

[8]This fiction of a state of nature, as a state of war, was not first started by Mr. Hobbes, as is commonly imagined. Plato endeavors to refute an hypothesis very like it in the second, third, and fourth books de republica. . . .

though without comprehending the rest of mankind within their prescriptions. Suppose that several families unite together into one society, which is totally disjoined from all others, the rules, which preserve peace and order, enlarge themselves to the utmost extent of that society; but becoming then entirely useless, lose their force when carried one step farther. But again suppose, that several distinct societies maintain a kind of intercourse for mutual convenience and advantage, the boundaries of justice still grow larger, in proportion to the largeness of men's views, and the force of their mutual connexions. History, experience, reason sufficiently instruct us in this natural progress of human sentiments, and in the gradual enlargement of our regards to justice, in proportion as we become acquainted with the extensive utility of that virtue.

Part II

If we examine the *particular* laws, by which justice is directed, and property determined; we shall still be presented with the same conclusion. The good of mankind is the only object of all these laws and regulations. Not only is it requisite, for the peace and interest of society, that men's possessions should be separated; but the rules, which we follow, in making the separation, are such as can best be contrived to serve farther the interests of society.

We shall suppose that a creature, possessed of reason, but unacquainted with human nature, deliberates with himself what rules of justice or property would best promote public interest, and establish peace and security among mankind: His most obvious thought would be, to assign the largest possessions to the most extensive virtue, and give every one the power of doing good, proportioned to this inclination. In a perfect theocracy, where a being, infinitely intelligent, governs by particular volitions, this rule would certainly have place, and might serve to the wisest purposes: But were mankind to execute such a law; so great is the uncertainly of merit, both from its natural obscurity, and from the self-conceit of each individual, that no determinate rule of conduct would ever result from it; and the total dissolution of society must be the immediate consequence. Fanatics may suppose, *that dominion is founded on grace*, and *that saints alone inherit the earth*; but the civil magistrate very justly puts these sublime theorists on the same footing with common robbers, and teaches them by the severest discipline, that a rule, which, in speculation, may seem the most advantageous to society, may yet be found, in practice, totally pernicious and destructive.

That there were *religious* fanatics of this kind in England, during the civil wars, we learn from history; though it is probable, that the obvious *tendency* of these principles excited such horror in mankind, as soon obliged the dangerous enthusiasts to renounce, or at least conceal their tenets. Perhaps the *levellers*, who claimed an equal distribution of property, were a kind of *political* fanatics, which arose from the religious species, and more openly avowed their pretensions; as carrying a more plausible appearance, of being practicable in themselves, as well as useful to human society.

It must indeed, be confessed, that nature is so liberal to mankind, that, were all her presents equally divided among the species, and improved by art and industry, every individual would enjoy all the necessaries, and even most of the comforts of life; nor would ever be liable to any ills but such as might accidentally arise from the sickly frame and constitution of his body. It must also be confessed, that, wherever we depart from this equality, we rob the poor of more satisfaction than we add to the rich, and that the slight gratification of a frivilous vanity, in one individual, frequently costs more than bread to many families, and even provinces. It may appear withal, that the rule of equality, as it would be highly *useful*, is altogether not *impracticable*; but has taken place, at least in an imperfect degree, in some republics; particularly that of Sparta; where it was attended, it is said, with the most beneficial consequences. Not to mention that the Agrarian laws, so frequently claimed in Rome, and carried into execution in many Greek cities, proceeded, all of them, from a general idea of the utility of this principle.

But historians, and even common sense, may inform us, that, however specious these ideas of *perfect* equality may seem, they are really, at bottom, *impracticable*; and were they not so, would be extremely *pernicious* to human society. Render possessions ever so equal, men's different degrees of art, care, and industry will immediately break that equality. Or if you check these virtues, you reduce society to the most extreme indigence; and instead of preventing want and beggary in a few, render it unavoidable to the whole community. The most rigorous inquisition too is requisite to watch every inequality on its first appearance; and the most severe jurisdiction, to punish and redress it. But besides, that so much authority must soon degenerate into tyranny, and be exerted with great partialities; who can possibly be possessed of it, in such a situation as is here supposed? Perfect equality of possessions, destroying all subordination, weakens extremely the authority of magistracy, and must reduce all power nearly to a level, as well as property.

We may conclude, therefore, that, in order to establish laws for the regulation of property, we must be acquainted with the nature and situation of man; must reject appearances, which may be false, though specious; and must search for those rules, which are, on the whole, most *useful* and *beneficial*. Vulgar sense and slight experience are sufficient for this purpose; where men give not way to too selfish avidity, or too extensive enthusiasm.

Who sees not, for instance, that whatever is produced or improved by man's art or industry ought, for ever, to be secured to him, in order to give encouragement to such *useful* habits and accomplishments? That the property ought to also descend to children and relations, for the same *useful* purpose? That it may be alienated by consent, in order to beget that commerce and intercourse, which is so *beneficial* to human society? And that all contracts and promises ought carefully to be fulfilled, in order to secure mutual trust and confidence, by which the general *interest* of mankind is so much promoted?

Examine the writers on the laws of nature; and you will always find, that, whatever principles they set out with, they are sure to terminate here at last, and to assign, as the ultimate reason for every rule which they establish, the convenience and necessities of mankind. A concession thus extorted, in opposition to systems, has more authority than if it had been made in prosecution of them. What other reason, indeed, could writers ever give, why this must be *mine* and that *yours*; since uninstructed nature surely never made any such distinction? The objects which receive these appellations are, of themselves, foreign to us; they are totally disjoined and separated from us; and nothing but the general interests of society can form the connexion.

Sometimes the interests of society may require a rule of justice in a particular case; but may not determine any particular rule, among several, which are all equally beneficial. In that case, the slightest *analogies* are laid hold of, in order to prevent that indifference and ambiguity, which would be the source of perpetual dissension. Thus possession alone, and first possession, is supposed to convey property, where no body else has any preceding claim and pretension. Many of the reasonings of lawyers are of this analogical nature, and depend on very slight connexions of the imagination.

Does any one scruple, in extraordinary cases, to violate all regard to the private property of individuals, and sacrifice to public interest a distinction which had been established for the sake of that interest? The safety of the people is the supreme law: All other particular laws are subordinate to it, and dependent on it: And if, in the *common* course of things, they be followed and regarded; it is only because the public safety and interest *commonly* demand so equal and impartial an administration.

Sometimes both *utility* and *analogy* fail, and leave the laws of justice in total uncertainty. Thus, it is highly requisite, that prescription or long possession should convey property; but what number of days or months or years should be sufficient for that purpose, it is impossible for reason alone to determine. *Civil laws* here supply the place of the natural *code*, and assign different terms for prescription, according to the different *utilities*, proposed by the legislator. Bills of exchange and promissory notes, by the laws of most countries, prescribe sooner than bonds, and mortgages, and contracts of a more formal nature.

In general we may observe that all questions of property are subordinate to the authority of civil laws, which extend, restrain, modify, and alter the rules of natural justice, according to the particular *convenience* of each community. The laws have, or ought to have, a constant reference to the constitution of government, the manners, the climate, the religion, the commerce, the situation of each society. A late author of genius, as well as learning, has prosecuted this subject at large, and has established, from these principles, a system of political knowledge, which abounds in ingenious and brilliant thoughts, and is not wanting in solidity.[9]

What is man's property? Anything which it is lawful for him, and for him alone, to use. *But what rule have we by which we can distinguish these objects?* Here we must have recourse to statutes, customs, precedents, analogies, and a hundred other circumstances; some of which are constant and inflexible, some variable and arbitrary. But the ultimate point, in which they all professedly terminate, is the interest and happiness of human society. Where this enters not into consideration, nothing can appear more whimsical, unnatural, and even superstitious, than all or more of the laws of justice and of property.

Those who ridicule vulgar superstitions, and expose the folly of particular regards to meats, days, places, postures, apparel, have an easy task; while they consider all the qualities and relations of the objects, and discover no adequate cause for that affection or antipathy, veneration of horror, which have so mighty an influence over a considerable part of mankind. A Syrian would have starved rather than taste pigeon: an Egyptian would not have approached bacon: But if these species of food be examined by the senses of sight, smell, or taste, or scrutinized by the sciences of chemistry, medicine, or physics, no difference is ever found between them and any other species, nor can that precise circumstance be pitched on, which may afford a just foundation for the religious passion. A fowl on Thursday is lawful food; on Friday abominable: Eggs in this house and in this diocese, are permitted during Lent; a hundred paces farther, to eat them is a damnable sin. This earth or building, yesterday was profane; today, by the muttering of certain words, it has become holy and sacred. Such reflections as these, in the mouth of a philosopher, one may safely say, are too obvious to have any influence; because they must always, to every man, occur at first sight; and where they prevail not, of themselves, they are surely obstructed by education, prejudice, and passion, not by ignorance or mistake.

It may appear to a careless view, or rather a too abstracted reflection, that there enters a like superstition into all the sentiments of justice; and that, if a man expose its object, or what we call property, to the same scrutiny of sense and science, he will not, by the most accurate enquiry, find any foundation for the difference made by moral sentiment. I may lawfully nourish myself from this tree; but the fruit of another of the same species, ten paces off, it is criminal for me to touch. Had I worn this apparel an hour ago, I had merited the severest punishment; but a man, by pronouncing a few magical syllables, has now rendered it fit for my use and service. Were this house placed in a neighbouring territory, it had been immoral for me to dwell in it; but being built on this side of the river, it is subject to a different municipal law, and by its becoming mine I incur no blame or

[9]The author of *L'Esprit des Loix.* This illustrious writer, however, sets out with a different theory, and supposes all right to be founded on certain *rapports* or relations; which is a system, that, in my opinion, never will be reconciled with true philosophy. Father Malebranche, as far as I can learn, was the first that started this abstract theory of morals, which was afterwards adopted by Cudworth, Clarke, and others; and as it excludes all sentiment, and pretends to found everything on reason, it has not wanted followers in this philosophic age. See Section I, Appendix I. With regard to justice, the virtue here treated of, the inference against this theory seems short and conclusive. Property is allowed to be dependent on civil laws; civil laws are allowed to have no other object, but the interest of society: This therefore must be allowed to be the sole foundation of property and justice. Not to mention, that our obligation itself to obey the magistrate and his laws is founded on nothing but the interests of society.

If the ideas of justice, sometimes, do not follow the dispositions of civil law; we shall find, that these cases, instead of objections, are confirmations of the theory delivered above. Where a civil law is so perverse as to cross all the interests of society, it loses all its authority, and men judge by the ideas of natural justice, which are conformable to those interests. Sometimes also civil laws, for useful purposes, require a ceremony or form to any deed; and where that is wanting, their decrees run contrary to the usual tenour of justice; but one who takes advantage of such chicanes, is not commonly regarded as an honest man. Thus, the interests of society require, that contracts be fulfilled; and there is not a more material article either of natural or civil justice: But the omission of a trifling circumstance will often, by law, invalidate a contract, *in foro humano,* but not *in foro conscientiae,* as divines express themselves. In these cases, the magistrate is supposed only to withdraw his power of enforcing the right, not to have altered the right. Where his intention extends to the right, and is conformable to the interests of society; it never fails to alter the right; a clear proof of the origin of justice and of property, as assigned above.

censure. The same species of reasoning it may be thought, which so successfully exposes superstition, is also applicable to justice; nor is it possible, in the one case more than in the other, to point out, in the object, that precise quality or circumstance, which is the foundation of the sentiment.

But there is this material difference between *superstition* and *justice*, that the former is frivolous, useless, and burdensome; the latter is absolutely requisite to the well-being of mankind and existence of society. When we abstract from this circumstance (for it is too apparent ever to be overlooked) it must be confessed, that all regards to right and property, seem entirely without foundation, as much as the grossest and most vulgar superstition. Were the interests of society nowise concerned, it is as unintelligible why another's articulating certain sounds implying consent, should change the nature of my actions with regard to a particular object, as why the reciting of a liturgy by a priest, in a certain habit and posture, should dedicate a heap of brick and timber, and render it, thenceforth and for ever, sacred.[10]

These reflections are far from weakening the obligations of justice, or diminishing anything from the most sacred attention to property. On the contrary, such sentiments must acquire new force from the present reasoning. For what stronger foundation can be desired or conceived for any duty, than to observe, that human society, or even human nature, could not subsist without the establishment of it; and will still arrive at greater degrees of happiness and perfection, the more inviolable the regard is, which is paid to that duty?

The dilemma seems obvious: As justice evidently tends to promote public utility and so support civil society, the sentiment of justice is either derived from our reflecting on that tendency, or like hunger, thirst, and other appetites, resentment, love of life, attachment to offspring, and other passions, arises from a simple original instinct in the human breast, which nature has implanted for like salutary purposes. If the latter be the case, it follows, that property, which is the object of justice, is also distinguished by a simple original instinct, and is not ascertained by any

[10]It is evident, that the will or consent alone never transfers property, nor causes the obligation of a promise (for the same reasoning extends to both), but the will must be expressed by words or signs, in order to impose a tie upon any man. The expression being once brought in as subservient to the will, soon becomes the principal part of the promise; nor will a man be less bound by his word, though he secretly give a different direction to his intention, and withhold the assent of his mind. But though the expression makes, on most occasions, the whole of the promise, yet it does not always so; and one who should make use of any expression, of which he knows not the meaning, and which he uses without any sense of the consequences, would not certainly be bound by it. Nay, though he know its meaning, yet if he use it in jest only, and with such signs as evidently show, that he has no serious intention of binding himself, he would not lie under any obligation of performance; but it is necessary, that the words be a perfect expression of the will, without any contrary signs. Nay, even this we must not carry so far as to imagine, that one, whom, by our quickness of understanding, we conjecture, from certain signs, to have an intention of deceiving us, is not bound by his expression or verbal promise, if we accept of it; but must limit this conclusion to those cases where the signs are of a different nature from those of deceit. All these contradictions are easily accounted for, if justice arise entirely from its usefulness to society; but will never be explained on any other hypothesis.

It is remarkable that the moral decisions of the *Jesuits* and other relaxed casuists, were commonly formed in prosecution of some such subtilties of reasoning as are here pointed out, and proceed as much from the habit of scholastic refinement as from any corruption of the heart, if we follow the authority of Mons. Bayle. See his Dictionary, article Loyola. And why has the indignation of mankind risen so high against these causists; but because every one perceived, that human society could not subsist were such practices authorized, and that morals must always be handled with a view to public interest, more than philosophical regularity? If the secret direction of the intention, said every man of sense, could invalidate a contract; where is our security? And yet a metaphysical schoolman might think, that, where an intention was supposed to be requisite, if that intention really had not place, no consequence ought to follow, and no obligation be imposed. The casuistical subtilties may not be greater than the subtilties of lawyers, hinted at above; but as the former are *pernicious*, and the latter *innocent* and even *necessary*, this is the reason of the very different reception they meet with from the world.

It is a doctrine of the Church of Rome, that the priest, by a secret direction of his intention, can invalidate any sacrament. This position is derived from a strict and regular prosecution of the obvious truth, that empty words alone, without any meaning or intention in the speaker, can never be attended with any effect. If the same conclusion be not admitted in reasonings concerning civil contracts, where the affair is allowed to be of so much less consequence than the eternal salvation of thousands, it proceeds entirely from men's sense of the danger and inconvenience of the doctrine in the former case: And we may thence observe, that however positive, arrogant, and dogmatical any superstition may appear, it never can convey any thorough persuasion of the reality of its objects, or put them, in any degree, on a balance with the common incidents of life, which we learn from daily observation and experimental reasoning.

argument or reflection. But who is there that ever heard of such an instinct? Or is this a subject in which new discoveries can be made? We may as well expect to discover, in the body, new senses, which had before escaped the observation of all mankind.

But farther, though it seems a very simple proposition to say, that nature, by an instinctive sentiment, distinguishes property, yet in reality we shall find, that there are required for that purpose ten thousand different instincts, and these employed about objects of the greatest intricacy and nicest discernment. For when a definition of *property* is required, that relation is found to resolve itself into any possession acquired by occupation, by industry, by prescription, by inheritance, by contract, &c. Can we think that nature, by an original instinct, instructs us in all these methods of acquisition?

These words too, inheritance and contract, stand for ideas infinitely complicated; and to define them exactly, a hundred volumes of laws, and a thousand volumes of commentators, have not been sufficient. Does nature, whose instincts in men are all simple, embrace such complicated and artificial objects, and create a rational creature, without trusting anything to the operation of his reason?

But even though all this were admitted, it would not be satisfactory. Positive laws can certainly transfer property. It is by another original instinct, that we recognize the authority of kings and senates, and mark all the boundaries of their jurisdiction? Judges too, even though their sentence be erroneous and illegal, must be allowed, for the sake of peace and order, to have decisive authority, and ultimately to determine property. Have we original innate ideas of praetors and chancellors and juries? Who sees not, that all these institutions arise merely from the necessities of human society?

All birds of the same species in every age and country, built their nests alike: In this we see the force of instinct. Men, in different times and places, frame their houses differently: Here we perceive the influence of reason and custom. A like inference may be drawn from comparing the instinct of generation and the institution of property.

How great soever the variety of municipal laws, it must be confessed, that their chief outlines pretty regularly concur; because the purposes, to which they tend, are everywhere exactly similar. In like manner, all houses have a roof and walls, windows and chimneys; though diversified in their shape, figure, and materials. The purposes of the latter, directed to the conveniences of human life, discover not more plainly their origin from reason and reflection, than do those of the former, which points all to a like end.

I need not mention the variations, which all the rules of property receive from the finer turns and connexions of the imagination, and from the subtleties and abstractions of law-topics and reasonings. There is no possibility of reconciling this observation to the notion of original instincts.

What alone will beget a doubt concerning the theory, on which I insist, is the influence of education and acquired habits, by which we are so accustomed to blame injustice, that we are not, in every instance, conscious of any immediate reflection on the pernicious consequences of it. The views the most familiar to us are apt, for that very reason, to escape us; and what we have very frequently performed from certain motives, we are apt likewise to continue mechanically, without recalling, on every occasion, the reflections, which first determined us. The convenience, or rather necessity, which leads to justice is so universal, and everywhere points so much to the same rules, that the habit takes place in all societies; and it is not without some scrutiny, that we are able to ascertain its true origin. The matter, however, is not so obscure, but that even in common life we have every moment recourse to the principle of public utility, and ask, *What must become of the world, if such practices prevail? How could society subsist under such disorders?* Were the distinction or separation of possessions entirely useless, can any one conceive, that it ever should have obtained in society?

Thus we seem, upon the whole, to have attained a knowledge of the force of that principle here insisted on, and can determine what degree of esteem or moral approbation may result from reflections on public interest and utility. The necessity of justice to the support of society is the sole foundation of that virtue; and since no moral excellence is more highly esteemed, we may conclude that this circumstance of usefulness has, in general, the strongest energy, and most entire command over our sentiments. It must, therefore, be the source of a considerable part of the merit ascribed to humanity, benevolence, friendship, public spirit, and other social virtues of that stamp; as it is the sole source of the moral approbation paid to fidelity, justice, veracity, integrity, and those other estimable and other useful qualities and principles. It is entirely agreeable to the rules of philosophy, and even of common reason; where any principle has been found to have a great force and energy in one instance, to ascribe to it a like energy in all simpler instances. This indeed is Newton's chief rule of philosophizing.[11]

Section V
Why Utility Pleases

Part I

It seems so natural a thought to ascribe to their utility the praise, which we bestow on the social virtues, that one would expect to meet with this principle everywhere in moral writers, as the chief foundation of their reasoning and enquiry. In common life, we may observe, that the circumstance of utility is always appealed to; nor is it supposed, that a greater eulogy can be given to any man, than to display his usefulness to the public, and enumerate the services, which he has performed to mankind and society. What praise, even of an inanimate form, if the regularity and elegance of its parts destroy not its fitness for any useful purpose! And how satisfactory an apology for any disproportion or seeming deformity, if we can show the necessity of that particular construction for the use intended! A ship appears more beautiful to an artist, or one moderately skilled in navigation, where its prow is wide and swelling beyond its poop, than if it were framed with a precise geometrical regularity, in contradiction to all the laws of mechanics. A building, whose doors and windows were exact squares, would hurt the eye by that very proportion; as ill adapted to the figure of a human creature, for whose service the fabric was intended. What wonder then, that a man, whose habits and conduct are hurtful to society, and dangerous or pernicious to every one who has an intercourse with him, should, on that account, be an object of disapprobation, and communicate to every spectator the strongest sentiment of disgust and hatred.[12]

But perhaps the difficulty of accounting for these effects of usefulness, or its contrary, has kept philosophers from admitting them into their systems of ethics, and has induced them rather to employ any other principle, in explaining the origin of moral good and evil. But it is no just reason for rejecting any principle, confirmed by experience, that we cannot give a satisfactory account of its origin, nor are able to resolve it into other more general principles. And if we would employ a little thought on the present subject, we need be at no loss to account for the influence of utility, and to deduce it from principles, the most known and avowed in human nature.

From the apparent usefulness of the social virtues, it has readily been inferred by sceptics, both ancient and modern, that all moral distinctions arise from education, and were, at first, invented, and afterwards encouraged, by the art of politicians, in order to render men tractable, and subdue their natural ferocity and selfishness, which incapacitated them for society. This principle, indeed, of precept and education, must so far be

[11]Principia, Lib. iii.

[12]We ought not to imagine because an inanimate object may be useful as well as a man, that therefore it ought also, according to this system, to merit the appellation of *virtuous.* The sentiments, excited by utility, are, in the two cases, very different; and the one is mixed with affection, esteem, approbation, &c., and not the other. In like manner, an inanimate object may have good colour and proportions as well as a human figure. But can we ever be in love with the former? There are a numerous set of passions and sentiments, of which thinking rational beings are, by the original constitution of nature, the only proper objects; and though the very same qualities be transferred to an insensible, inanimate being, they will not excite the same sentiments. The beneficial qualities of herbs and minerals are, indeed, sometimes called their *virtues;* but this is an effect of the caprice of language, which ought not to be regarded in reasoning. For though there be a species of approbation attending even inanimate objects, when beneficial, yet this sentiment is so weak, and so different from that which is directed to beneficent magistrates or statesmen; that they ought not be ranked under the same class or appellation.

A very small variation of the object, even where the same qualities are preserved, will destroy a sentiment. Thus, the same beauty, transferred to a different sex, excites no amorous passion, where nature is not extremely perverted.

owned to have a powerful influence, that it may frequently increase or diminish, beyond their natural standard, the sentiments of approbation or dislike; and may even, in particular instances, create without any natural principle, a new sentiment of this kind; as is evident in all superstitious practices and observances: But that *all* moral affection or dislike arises from this origin, will never surely be allowed by any judicious enquirer. Had nature made no such distinction, founded on the original constitution of the mind, the words, *honourable* and *shameful, lovely* and *odious, noble* and *despicable*, had never had place in any language; nor could politicians, had they invented these terms, ever have been able to render them intelligible, or make them convey any idea to the audience. So that nothing can be more superficial than this paradox of the sceptics; and it were well, if, in the abstruser studies of logic and metaphysics, we could as easily obviate the cavils of that sect, as in the practical and more intelligible sciences of politics and morals.

The social virtues must, therefore, be allowed to have a natural beauty and amiableness, which, at first, antecedent to all precept or education, recommends them to the esteem of uninstructed mankind, and engages their affections. And as the public utility of these virtues is the chief circumstance, whence they derive their merit, it follows, that the end, which they have a tendency to promote, must be some way agreeable to us, and take hold of some natural affection. It must please, either from considerations of self-interest, or from more generous motives and regards.

It has often been asserted, that, as every man has a strong connexion with society, and perceives the impossibility of his solitary subsistence, he becomes, on that account, favourable to all those habits or principles, which promote order in society, and insure to him the quiet possession of so inestimable a blessing. As much as we value our own happiness and welfare, as much must we applaud the practice of justice and humanity, by which alone the social confederacy can be maintained, and every man reap the fruits of mutual protection and assistance.

This deduction of morals from self-love, or a regard to private interest, is an obvious thought, and has not arisen wholly from the wanton sallies and sportive assaults of the sceptics. To mention no others, Polybius, one of the gravest and most judicious, as well as most moral writers of antiquity, has assigned this selfish origin to all our sentiments of virtue. But through the solid practical sense of that author, and his aversion to all vain subtleties, render his authority on the present subject very considerable; yet is not this an affair to be decided by authority, and the voice of nature and experience seems plainly to oppose the selfish theory.

We frequently bestow praise on virtuous actions, performed in very distant ages and remote countries; where the utmost subtilty of imagination would not discover any appearance of self-interest, or find any connexion of our present happiness and security with events so widely separated from us.

A generous, a brave, a noble deed, performed by an adversary, commands our approbation; while in its consequences it may be acknowledged prejudicial to our particular interest.

Where private advantage concurs with general affection for virtue, we readily perceive and avow the mixture of these distinct sentiments, which have a very different feeling and influence on the mind. We praise, perhaps, with more alacrity, where the generous humane action contributes to our particular interest: But the topics of praise, which we insist on, are very wide of this circumstance. And we may attempt to bring over others to our sentiments, without endeavouring to convince them, that they reap any advantage from the actions which we recommend to their approbation and applause.

Frame the model of a praiseworthy character, consisting of all the most amiable moral virtues: Give instances, in which these display themselves after an eminent and extraordinary manner: You readily engage the esteem and approbation of all your audience, who never so much as enquire in what age and country the person lived, who possessed these noble qualities: A circumstance, however, of all others, the most material of self-love, or a concern for our own individual happiness.

Once on a time, a statesman, in the shock and contest of parties, prevailed so far as to procure, by his eloquence, the banishment of an able adversary; whom he secretly followed, offering him money for his support during his exile, and soothing him with topics of consolation in his misfortunes. *Alas!* cries the banished statesman, *with what regret must I leave my friends in this city, where even enemies are so generous!* Virtue, though in an enemy, here pleased him: And we also give it the just tribute or praise and approbation; nor do we retract these sentiments, when we hear, that the action passed in Athens, about two thousand years ago, and that the persons' names were Eschines and Demosthenes.

What is that to me? There are few occasions, when this question is not pertinent: And had it that universal, infallible influence supposed, it would turn into ridicule every composition, and almost every conversation, which contain any praise or censure of men and manners.

It is but a weak subterfuge, when pressed by these facts and arguments, to say, that we transport ourselves, by the force of imagination, into distant ages and countries, and consider the advantage, which we should have reaped from these characters, had we been contemporaries, and had any commerce with the persons. It is not conceivable, how a *real* sentiment or passion can ever arise from a known *imaginary* interest; especially when our *real* interest is still kept in view, and is often acknowledged to be entirely distinct from the imaginary, and even sometimes opposite to it.

A man, brought to the brink of a precipice, cannot look down without trembling; and the sentiment of *imaginary* danger actuates him, in opposition to the opinion and belief of *real* safety. But the imagination is here assisted by the presence of a striking object; and yet prevails not, except it be also aided by novelty, and the unusual appearance of the object. Custom soon reconciles us to heights and precipices, and wears off these false and delusive terrors. The reverse is observable in the estimates which we form of characters and manners; and the more we habituate ourselves to an accurate scrutiny of morals, the more delicate feeling do we acquire of the most minute distinctions between vice and virtue. Such frequent occasion, indeed, have we, in common life, to pronounce all kinds of moral determinations, that no object of this kind can be new or unusual to us; nor could any *false* views or prepossessions maintain their ground against an experience, so common and familiar. Experience being chiefly what forms the associations of ideas, it is impossible that any association could establish and support itself, in direct opposition to that principle.

Usefulness is agreeable, and engages our approbation. This is a matter of fact, confirmed by daily observation. But, *useful*? For what? For somebody's interest, surely. Whose interest then? Not our own only: For our approbation frequently extends farther. It must, therefore, be the interest of those, who are served by the character of action approved of; and these we may conclude, however remote, are not totally indifferent to us. By opening up this principle, we shall discover one great source of moral distinctions.

Part II

Self-love is a principle in human nature of such extensive energy, and the interest of each individual is, in general, so closely connected with that of the community, that those philosophers were excusable, who fancied that all our concern for the public might be resolved into a concern for our own happiness and preservation. They saw every moment, instances of approbation or blame, satisfaction or displeasure toward characters and actions; they denominated the objects of these sentiments, *virtues*, or *vices*; they observed, that the former had a tendency to increase the happiness, and the latter the misery of mankind; they asked, whether it were possible that we could have any general concern for society, or any disinterested resentment of the welfare or injury of others; they found it simpler to consider all these sentiments as modifications of self-love; and they discovered a pretence, at least, for this unity of principle, in that close union of interest, which is so observable between the public and each individual.

But notwithstanding this frequent confusion of interests, it is easy to attain what natural philosophers, after Lord Bacon, have affected to call the *experimentum crucis*, or that experiment which points out the right way in any doubt or ambiguity. We have found instances, in which private interest was separate from public; in which it was even contrary: And yet we observed the moral sentiment to continue, notwithstanding this disjunction of interests. And wherever these distinct interests sensibly concurred, we always found a sensible increase of the sentiment, and a more warm affection to virtue, and detestation of vice, or what we properly call, *gratitude* and *revenge.* Compelled by these instances, we must renounce the theory, which accounts for every moral sentiment by the principle of self-love. We must adopt a more public affection, and allow, that the interests of society are not, even on their own account, entirely indifferent to us. Usefulness is only a tendency to a certain end; and it is a contradiction in terms, that anything pleases as means to an end, where the end itself no wise affects us. If usefulness, therefore, be a source of moral sentiment, and if this usefulness be not always considered with a reference to self; it follows, that everything, which contributes to the happiness of society, recommends itself directly to our approbation and good-will. Here is a principle, which accounts, in great part, for the origin of morality: And what need we seek for abstruse and remote systems, when there occurs one so obvious and natural.[13]

Have we any difficulty to comprehend the force of humanity and benevolence? Or to conceive, that the very aspect of happiness, joy, prosperity, gives pleasure; that of pain, suffering, sorrow, communicates uneasiness? The human countenance, says Horace, borrows smiles or tears from the human countenance. Reduce a person to solitude, and he loses all enjoyment, except either of the sensual or speculative kind; and that because the movements of his heart are not forwarded by correspondent movements in his fellow-creatures. The signs of sorrow and mourning, though arbitrary, affect us with melancholy; but the natural symptoms, tears and cries and groans, never fail to infuse compassion and uneasiness. And if the effects of misery touch us in so lively a manner; can we be supposed altogether insensible or indifferent towards its causes; when a malicious or treacherous character and behaviour are presented to us?

We enter, I shall suppose, into a convenient, warm, well-contrived apartment: We necessarily receive a pleasure from its very survey; because it presents us with the pleasing ideas of ease, satisfaction, and enjoyment. The hospitable, good-humoured, humane landlord appears. This circumstance surely must embellish the whole; nor can we easily forbear reflecting, with pleasure, on the satisfaction which results to every one from his intercourse and good-offices.

His whole family, by the freedom, ease, confidence, and calm enjoyment, diffused over their countenances, sufficiently express their happiness. I have a pleasing sympathy in the prospect of so much joy, and can never consider the source of it, without the most agreeable emotions.

He tells me, that an oppressive and powerful neighbour had attempted to dispossess him of his inheritance, and had long disturbed all his innocent and social pleasures. I feel an immediate indignation arise in me against such violence and injury.

But it is no wonder, he adds, that a private wrong should proceed from a man, who had enslaved provinces, depopulated cities, and made the field and scaffold stream with human blood. I am struck with horror at the prospect of so much misery, and am actuated by the strongest antipathy against its author.

In general, it is certain, that, wherever we go, whatever we reflect on or converse about, everything still presents us with the view of human happiness or misery, and excites in our breast a sympathetic movement of pleasure or uneasiness. In our serious occupations, in our careless amusements, this principle still exerts its active energy.

* * *

If any man from a cold insensibility, or narow selfishness of temper, is unaffected with the images of human happiness or misery, he must be equally indifferent to the images of vice and virtue: As, on

[13]It is needless to push our researches so far as to ask, why we have humanity or a fellow-feeling with others. It is sufficient, that this is experienced to be a principle in human nature. We must stop somewhere in our examination of causes; and there are, in every science, some general principles, beyond which we cannot hope to find any principle more general. No man is absolutely indifferent to the happiness and misery of others. The first has a natural tendency to give pleasure; the second, pain. This every one may find in himself. It is not probable, that these principles can be resolved into principles more simple and universal, whatever attempts may have been made to that purpose. But if it were possible, it belongs not to the present subject; and we may here safely consider these principles as original; happy, if we can render all the consequences sufficiently plain and perspicuous!

the other hand, it is always found, that a warm concern for the interests of our species is attended with a delicate feeling of all moral distinctions; a strong resentment of injury done to men; a lively approbation of their welfare. In this particular, though great superiority is observable of one man above another; yet none are so entirely indifferent to the interest of their fellow-creatures, as to perceive no distinctions of moral good and evil, in consequence of the different tendencies of actions and principles. How, indeed, can we suppose it possible in any one, who wears a human heart, that if there be subjected to his censure, one character or system of conduct, which is beneficial, and another which is pernicious to his species or community, he will not so much as give a cool preference to the former, or ascribe to it the smallest merit or regard? Let us suppose such a person ever so selfish; let private interest have ingrossed ever so much his attention; yet in instances, where that is not concerned, he must unavoidably feel *some* propensity to the good of mankind, and make it an object of choice, if everything else be equal. Would any man, who is walking along, tread as willingly on another's gouty toes, whom he has no quarrel with, as on the hard flint and pavement? There is here surely a difference in the case. We surely take into consideration the happiness and misery of others, in weighing the several motives of action, and incline to the former, where no private regards draw us to seek our own promotion or advantage by the injury of our fellow-creatures. And if the principles of humanity are capable, in many instances, of influencing our actions, they must, at all times, have *some* authority over our sentiments, and give us a general approbation of what is useful to society, and blame of what is dangerous or pernicious. The degrees of these sentiments may be the subject of controversy; but the reality of their existence, one should think, must be admitted in every theory or system.

* * *

The more we converse with mankind, and the greater social intercourse we maintain, the more shall we be familiarized to these general preferences and distinctions, without which our conversation and discourse could scarcely be rendered intelligible to each other. Every man's interest is peculiar to himself, and the aversions and desires, which result from it, cannot be supposed to affect others in a like degree. General language, therefore, being formed for general use, must be moulded on some more general views, and must affix the epithets of praise or blame, in conformity to sentiments, which arise from the general interests of the community. And if these sentiments, in most men, be not so strong as those, which have a reference to private good; yet still they must make some distinction, even in persons the most depraved and selfish; and must attach the notion of good to a beneficient conduct, and of evil to the contrary. Sympathy, we shall allow, is much fainter than our concern for ourselves, and sympathy with persons remote from us much fainter than that with persons near and contiguous; but for this very reason it is necessary for us, in our calm judgments and discourse concerning the characters of men, to neglect all these differences, and render our sentiments more public and social. Besides, that we ourselves often change our situation in this particular, we every day meet with persons who are in a situation different from us, and who could never converse with us were we to remain constantly in that position and point of view, which is peculiar to ourselves. The intercourse of sentiments, therefore, in society and conversation, makes us form some general unalterable standard, by which we may approve or disapprove of characters and manners. And though the heart takes not part entirely with these general notions, nor regulates all its love and hatred by the universal abstract differences of vice and virtue, without regard to self, or the persons with whom we are more intimately connected; yet have these moral differences a considerable influence, and being sufficient, at least for discourse, serve all our purposes in company, in the pulpit, on the theatre, and in the schools.[14]

[14]It is wisely ordained by nature, that private connexions should commonly prevail over universal views and considerations; otherwise our affections and actions would be dissipated and lost, for want of a proper limited object. Thus a small benefit done to ourselves, or our near friends, excites more lively sentiments of love and approbation than a great benefit done to a distant commonwealth: But still we know here, as in all the senses, to correct these inequalities by reflection, and retain a general standard of vice and virtue, founded chiefly on general usefulness.

Thus, in whatever light we take this subject, the merit, ascribed to the social virtues, appears still uniform, and arises chiefly from that regard, which the natural sentiment of benevolence engages us to pay to the interests of mankind and society. If we consider the principles of the human make, such as they appear to daily experience and observation, we must, *a priori*, conclude it impossible for such a creature as man to be totally indifferent to the well or ill-being of his fellow-creatures, and not readily, of himself, to pronounce, where nothing gives him any particular bias, that what promotes their happiness is good, what tends to their misery is evil, without any farther regard or consideration. Here then are the faint rudiments, at least, or outlines, of a *general* distinction between actions: and in proportion as the humanity of the person is supposed to encrease, his connexion with those who are injured or benefited, and his lively conception of their misery or happiness; his consequent censure or approbation acquires proportionable vigour. There is no necessity, that a generous action, barely mentioned in an old history or remote gazette, should communicate any strong feelings of applause and admiration. Virtue, placed at such a distance, is like a fixed star, which, though to the eye of reason it may appear as luminous as the sun in his meridian, is so infinitely removed as to affect the senses, neither with light nor heat. Bring this virtue nearer, by our acquaintance or connexion with the persons, or even by an eloquent recital of the case; our hearts are immediately caught, our sympathy enlivened, and our cool approbation converted into the warmest sentiments of friendship and regard. These seem necessary and infallible consequences of the general principles of human nature, as discovered in common life and practice.

Again; reverse these views and reasonings: Consider the matter *a posteriori*; and weighing the consequences, enquire if the merit of social virtue be not, in a great measure, derived from the feelings of humanity, with which it affects the spectators. It appears to be matter of fact, that the circumstances of *utility*, in all subjects, is a source of praise and approbation: That it is constantly appealed to in all moral decisions concerning the merit and demerit of actions: That is the *sole* source of that high regard paid to justice, fidelity, honour, allegiance, and chastity: That it is inseparable from all the other social virtues, humanity, generosity, charity, affability, lenity, mercy, and moderation: And, in a word, that is a foundation of the chief part of morals, which has a reference to mankind and our fellow-creatures.

It appears also, that, in our general approbation of characters and manners, the useful tendency of the social virtues moves us not by any regards to self-interest, but as an influence much more universal and extensive. It appears that a tendency to public good, and to the promoting of peace, harmony, and order in society, does always, by affecting the benevolent principles of our frame, engage us on the side of the social virtues. And it appears, as an additional confirmation, that these principles of humanity and sympathy enter so deeply into all our sentiments, and have so powerful an influence, as may enable them to excite the strongest censure and applause. The present theory is the simple result of all these inferences, each of which seems founded on uniform experience and observation.

Were it doubtful, whether there were any such principle in our nature as humanity or a concern for others, yet when we see, in numberless instances, that whatever has a tendency to promote the interests of society, is so highly approved of, we ought thence to learn the force of the benevolent principle; since it is impossible for anything to please as means to an end, where the end is totally indifferent. On the other hand, were it doubtful, whether there were, implanted in our nature, any general principle of moral blame and approbation, yet when we see, in numberless instances, the influence of humanity, we ought hence to conclude, that it is impossible, but that everything which promotes the interest of society must communicate pleasure, and what is pernicious gives uneasiness. But when these different reflections and observations concur in establishing the same conclusion, must they not bestow an undisputed evidence upon it?

It is however hoped, that the progress of this argument will bring a farther confirmation of the present theory, by showing the rise of other sentiments of esteem and regard from the same or like principles.

Section VI
Of Qualities Useful to Ourselves

Part I

It seems evident, that where a quality or habit is subjected to our examination, if it appear in any respect prejudicial to the person possessed of it, or such as incapacitates him for business and action, it is instantly blamed, and ranked among his faults and imperfections. Indolence, negligence, want of order and method, obstinacy, fickleness, rashness, credulity; these qualities were never esteemed by any one indifferent to a character; much less, extolled as accomplishments or virtues. The prejudice, resulting from them, immediately strikes our eye, and gives us the sentiment of pain and disapprobation.

No quality, it is allowed, is absolutely either blameable or praiseworthy. It is all according to its degree: A due medium, says the Peripatetics, is the characteristic of virtue. But this medium is chiefly determined by utility. A proper celerity, for instance, and dispatch in business, is commendable. When defective, no progress is ever made in the execution of any purpose: When excessive, it engages us in precipitate and ill-concerted measures and enterprises: By such reasonings, we fix the proper and commendable mediocrity in all moral and prudential disquisitions; and never lose view of the advantages, which result from any character or habit.

Now as these disadvantages are enjoyed by the person possessed of the character, it can never be *self-love* which renders the prospect of them agreeable to us, the spectators, and prompts our esteem and approbation. No force of imagination can convert us into another person, and make us fancy, that we, being that person, reap benefit from those valuable qualities, which belong to him. Or if it did, no celerity of imagination could immediately transport us back, into ourselves, and make us love and esteem the person, as different from us. Views and sentiments, so opposite to known truth and to each other, could never have place, at the same time, in the same person. All suspicion, therefore, of selfish regards, is here totally excluded. It is a quite different principle, which actuates our bosom, and interests us in the felicity of the person whom we contemplate. Where his natural talents and acquired abilities give us the prospect of elevation, advancement, a figure in life, prosperous success, a steady command over fortune, and the execution of great or advantageous undertakings; we are struck with such agreeable images, and feel a complacency and regard immediately arise towards him. The ideas of happiness, joy, triumph, prosperity, are connected with every circumstance of his character, and diffuse over our minds a pleasing sentiment of sympathy and humanity.[15]

Let us suppose a person originally framed so as to have no manner of concern for his fellow-creatures, but to regard the happiness and misery of all sensible beings with greater indifference than even two contiguous shades of the same colour. Let us suppose, if the prosperity of nations were laid on the one hand, and their ruin on the other, and he were desired to choose; that he would stand like the schoolman's ass, irresolute and undetermined, between equal motives; or rather, like the same ass between two pieces of wood or marble, without any inclination or propensity to either side. The consequence, I believe, must be allowed just, that such a person, being absolutely unconcerned, either for the public good of a community or the private utility of others, would look on every quality, however pernicious, or however beneficial, to society, or to its possessor, with the same indifference as on the most common and uninteresting object.

---

[15]One may venture to affirm, that there is no human creature, to whom the appearance of happiness (where envy or revenge has no place) does not give pleasure, that of misery, uneasiness. This seems inseparable from our make and constitution. But they are only the more generous minds, that are thence prompted to seek zealously the good of others, and to have a real passion for their welfare. With men of narrow and ungenerous spirits, this sympathy goes not beyond a slight feeling of the imagination, which serves only to excite sentiments of complacency or censure, and makes them apply to the object either honourable or dishonourable appellations. A griping miser, for instance, praises extremely *industry* and *frugality* even in others, and sets them, in his estimation, above all the other virtues. He knows the good that results from them, and feels that species of happiness with a more lively sympathy, than any other you could represent to him; though perhaps he would not part with a shilling to make the fortune of the industrious man, whom he praises so highly.

But if, instead of this fancied monster, we suppose a *man* to form a judgment or determination in the case, there is to him a plain foundation of preference, where everything else is equal; and however cool his choice may be, if his heart be selfish, or if the persons interested be remote from him; there must still be a choice or distinction between what is useful, and what is pernicious. Now this distinction is the same in all its parts, with the *moral distinction*, whose foundation has been so often, and so much in vain, enquired after. The same endowments of the mind, in every circumstance, are agreeable to the sentiment of morals and to that of humanity; the same temper is susceptible of high degrees of the one sentiment and of the other; and the same alteration in the objects, by their nearer approach or by connexions, enlivens the one and the other. By all the rules of philosophy, therefore, we must conclude, that these sentiments are originally the same; since, in each particular, even the most minute, they are governed by the same laws, and are moved by the same objects.

* * *

In this kingdom, such continued ostentation, of late years, has prevailed among men in *active* life with regard to *public spirit*, and among those in *speculative* with regard to *benevolence*; and so many false pretentions to each have been, no doubt, detected, that men of the world are apt, without any bad intention, to discover a sullen incredulity on the head of those moral endowments, and even sometimes absolutely to deny their existence and reality. In like manner I find, that, of old, the perpetual cant of the *Stoics* and *Cynics* concerning *virtue,* their magnificent professions and slender performances, bred a disgust in mankind; and Lucian, who, though licentious with regard to pleasure, is yet in other respects a very moral writer, cannot sometimes talk of virtue, so many boasted without betraying symptoms of spleen and irony. But surely this peevish delicacy, whence-ever it arises can never be carried so far as to make us deny the existence of every species of merit, and all distinction of manners and behaviour. Besides *discretion, caution, enterprise, industry, assiduity, frugality, economy, good-sense, prudence, discernment*; besides these endowments, I say, whose very names force an avowal of their merit, there are many others, to which the most determined scepticism cannot for a moment refuse the tribute of praise and approbation. *Temperance, sobriety, patience, constancy, perseverance, forethought, considerateness, secrecy, order, insinuation, address, presence of mind, quickness of conception, facility of expression,* these, and a thousand more of the same kind, no man will ever deny to be excellencies and perfections. As their merit consists in their tendency to serve the person, possessed of them, without any magnificent claim to public and social desert, we are the less jealous of their pretensions, and readily admit them into the catalogue of laudable qualities. We are not sensible that, by this concession, we have paved the way for all the other moral excellencies, and cannot consistently hesitate any longer, with regard to disinterested benevolence, patriotism, and humanity.

It seems, indeed, certain, that first appearances are here, as usual, extremely deceitful, and that it is more difficult, in a speculative way, to resolve into self-love the merit which we ascribe to the selfish virtues above mentioned, than that even of the social virtues, justice and beneficence. For this latter purpose, we need but say, that whatever conduct promotes the good of the community is loved, praised, and esteemed by the community, on account of that utility and interest, of which every one partakes; and though this affection and regard be, in reality, gratitude, not self-love, yet a distinction, even of this obvious nature, may not readily be made by superficial reasoners; and there is room, at least, to support the cavil and dispute for a moment. But as qualities, which tend only to the utility of their possessor, without any reference to us, or to the community, are yet esteemed and valued; by what theory or system can we account for this sentiment from self-love, or deduce it from that favourite origin? There seems here to be a necessity for confessing that the happiness and misery of others are not spectacles entirely indifferent to us; but that the view of the former, whether in its causes or effects, like sunshine or the prospect of well-cultivated plains (to carry our pretensions no higher), communicates a secret joy and satisfaction; the appearance of the latter, like a lowering cloud or barren landscape, throws a melancholy damp over the imagination. And this concession being once made, the difficulty is over; and a natural unforced interpretation of the phenomena of human life will afterwards, we may hope, prevail among all speculative enquirers.

Section IX
Conclusion

Part I

It may justly appear surprising that any man in so late an age, should find it requisite to prove, by elaborate reasoning, that Personal Merit consists altogether in the possession of mental qualities, *useful* or *agreeable* to the *person himself* or to *others*. It might be expected that this principle would have occurred even to the first rude, unpractised enquirers concerning morals, and been received from its own evidence, without any argument or disputation. Whatever is valuable in any kind, so naturally classes itself under the division of *useful* or *agreeable*, the *utile* or the *dulce*, that it is not easy to imagine why we should ever seek further, or consider the question as a matter of nice research or inquiry. And as every thing useful or agreeable must possess these qualities with regard either to the *person himself* or to *others*, the complete delineation or description of merit seems to be performed as naturally as a shadow is cast by the sun, or any image is reflected upon water. If the ground, on which the shadow is cast, be not broken and uneven; nor the surface from which the image is reflected, disturbed and confused; a just figure is immediately presented, without any art or attention. And it seems a reasonable presumption, that systems and hypotheses have perverted our natural understanding, when a theory, so simple and obvious, could so long have escaped the most elaborate examination.

But however the case may have fared with philosophy, in common life these principles are still implicitly maintained; nor is any other topic of praise or blame ever recurred to, when we employ any panegyric or satire, any applause or censure of human action and behaviour. If we observe men, in every intercourse of business or pleasure, in every discourse and conversation, we shall find them nowhere, except in the schools, at any loss upon this subject. What so natural, for instance, as the following dialogue? You are very happy, we shall suppose one to say, addressing himself to another, that you have given your daughter to Cleanthes. He is a man of honour and humanity. Every one, who has any intercourse with him, is sure of *fair* and *kind* treatment.[16] I congratulate you too, says another, on the promising expectations of this son-in-law; whose assiduous application to the study of laws, whose quick penetration and early knowledge both of men and business, prognosticate the greatest honours and advancement.[17] You surprise me, replies a third, when you talk of Cleanthes as a man of business and application. I met him lately in a circle of the gayest company, and he was the very life and soul of our conversation: so much wit with good manners; so much gallantry without affectation; so much ingenious knowledge so genteelly delivered, I have never before observed in any one.[18] You would admire him still more, says a fourth, if you knew him more familiarly. That cheerfulness, which you might remark in him, is not a sudden flash struck out by company: it runs through the whole tenor of his life, and preserves a perpetual serenity on his countenance, and tranquillity in his soul. He has met with severe trials, misfortunes as well as dangers; and by his greatness of mind, was still superior to all of them.[19] The image, gentlemen, which you here have delineated of Cleanthes, cried I, is that of accomplished merit. Each of you has given a stroke of the pencil to his figure; and you have unawares exceeded all the pictures drawn by Gratian or Castiglione. A philosopher might select this character as a model of perfect virtue.

And as every quality which is useful or agreeable to ourselves or others is, in common life, allowed to be a part of personal merit; so no other will ever be received, where men judge of things by their natural, unprejudiced reason, without the delusive glosses of superstition and false religion.

[16]Qualities useful to others.

[17]Qualities useful to the person himself.

[18]Qualities immediately agreeable to others.

[19]Qualities immediately agreeable to the person himself.

Celibacy, fasting, penance, mortification, self-denial, humility, silence, solitude, and the whole train of monkish virtues; for what reason are they everywhere rejected by men of sense, but because they serve to no manner of purpose; neither advance a man's fortune in the world, nor render him a more valuable member of society; neither qualify him for the entertainment of company, nor increase his power of self-enjoyment? We observe, on the contrary, that they cross all these desirable ends; stupefy the understanding and harden the heart, obscure the fancy and sour the temper. We justly, therefore, transfer them to the opposite column, and place them in the catalogue of vices; nor has any superstition force sufficient among men of the world, to pervert entirely these natural sentiments. A gloomy, hair-brained enthusiast, after his death, may have a place in the calendar; but will scarcely ever be admitted, when alive, into intimacy and society, except by those who are as delirious and dismal as himself.

It seems a happiness in the present theory, that it enters not into that vulgar dispute concerning the *degrees* of benevolence or self-love, which prevail in human nature; a dispute which is never likely to have any issue, both because men, who have taken part, are not easily convinced, and because the phenomena, which can be produced on either side, are so dispersed, so uncertain, and subject to so many interpretations, that it is scarcely possible accurately to compare them, or draw from them any determinate inference or conclusion. It is sufficient for our present purpose, if it be allowed, what surely, without the greatest absurdity cannot be disputed, that there is some benevolence, however small, infused into our bosom; some spark of friendship for human kind; some particle of the dove kneaded into our frame, along with the elements of the wolf and serpent. Let these generous sentiments be supposed ever so weak; let them be insufficient to move even a hand or finger of our body, they must still direct the determinations of our mind, and where everything else is equal, produce a cool preference of what is useful and serviceable to mankind, above what is pernicious and dangerous. A *moral distinction*, therefore, immediately arises; a general sentiment of blame and approbation; a tendency, however faint, to the objects of the one, and a proportionable aversion to those of the other. Nor will those reasoners, who so earnestly maintain the predominant selfishness of human kind, be any wise scandalized at hearing of the weak sentiments of virtue implanted in our nature. On the contrary, they are found as ready to maintain the one tenet as the other; and their spirit of satire (for such it appears, rather than of corruption) naturally gives rise to both opinions; which have, indeed, a great and almost an indissoluble, connexion together.

Avarice, ambition, vanity, and all passions vulgarly, though improperly, comprised under the denomination of *self-love*, are here excluded from our theory concerning the origin of morals, not because they are too weak, but because they have not a proper direction for that purpose. The notion of morals implies some sentiment common to all mankind, which recommends the same object to general approbation, and makes every man, or most men, agree in the same opinion or decision concerning it. It also implies some sentiment, so universal and comprehensive as to extend to all mankind, and render the actions and conduct, even of the persons the most remote, an object of applause or censure, according as they agree or disagree with that rule of right which is established. These two requisite circumstances belong alone to the sentiment of humanity here insisted on. The other passions produce in every breast, many strong sentiments of desire and aversion, affection and hatred; but these neither are felt so much in common, nor are so comprehensive, as to be the foundation of any general system and established theory of blame or approbation.

When a man denominates another his *enemy*, his *rival*, his *antagonist*, his *adversary*, he is understood to speak the language of self-love, and to express sentiments, peculiar to himself, and arising from his particular circumstances and situation. But when he bestows on any man the epithets of *vicious* or *odious* or *depraved*, he then speaks another language and expresses sentiments, in which he expects all his audience to concur with him. He must here, therefore, depart from his private and particular situation, and must choose a point of view, common to him with others; he must move some universal principle of the human frame, and touch a string to which all mankind have an accord and symphony. If he mean, therefore, to express that this man possesses qualities, whose tendency is pernicious to society, he has chosen this common point of view, and has touched the principle of humanity, in which every man, in some degree, concurs. While the human heart is compounded of the same elements as at present, it will never be wholly indifferent to public good, nor entirely unaffected with the tendency of characters and manners. And though this affection of humanity may not generally be esteemed so strong as vanity or ambition, yet, being common to all men, it can alone be the foundation of morals, or of any general system of blame or praise. One man's ambition is not another's ambition, nor will the same event or object satisfy both; but the humanity of one man is the humanity of every one, and the same object touches this passion in all human creatures.

But the sentiments, which arise from humanity, are not only the same in all human creatures, and produce the same approbation or censure; but they also comprehend all human creatures; nor is there any one whose conduct or character is not, by their means, an object to every one of censure or approbation. On the contrary, those other passions, commonly denominated selfish, both produce different sentiments in each individual, according to his particular situation; and also contemplate the greater part of mankind with the utmost indifference and unconcern. Whoever has a high regard and esteem for me flatters my vanity; whoever expresses contempt mortifies and displeases me; but as my name is known but to a small part of mankind, there are few who come within the sphere of this passion, or excite, on its account, either my affection or disgust. But if you represent a tyrannical, insolent, or barbarous behaviour, in any country or in any age of the world, I soon carry my eye to the pernicious tendency of such a conduct, and feel the sentiment of repugnance and displeasure towards it. No character can be so remote as to be, in this light, wholly indifferent to me. What is beneficial to society or to the person himself must still be preferred. And every quality or action, of every human being, must, by this means, be ranked under some class or denomination, expressive of general censure or applause.

What more, therefore, can we ask to distinguish the sentiments, dependent on humanity, from those connected with any other passion, or to satisfy us, why the former are the origin of morals, not the latter? Whatever conduct gains my approbation, by touching my humanity, procures also the applause of all mankind, by affecting the same principle in them; by what serves my avarice or ambition pleases these passions in me alone, and affects not the avarice and ambition of the rest of mankind. There is no circumstance of conduct in any man, provided it have a beneficial tendency, that is not agreeable to my humanity, however remote the person; but every man, so far removed as neither to cross nor serve my avarice and ambition, is regarded as wholly indifferent by those passions. The distinction, therefore, between these species of sentiment being so great and evident, language must soon be moulded upon it, and must invent a peculiar set of terms, in order to express those universal sentiments of censure or approbation, which arise from humanity, or from views of general usefulness and it contrary. Virtue and Vice become then known; morals are recognized; certain general ideas are framed of human conduct and behaviour; such measures are expected from men in such situations. This action is determined to be conformable to our abstract rule; that other, contrary. And by such universal principles are the particular sentiments of self-love frequently controlled and limited.[20]

---

[20]It seems certain, both from reason and experience, that a rude, untaught savage regulates chiefly his love and hatred by the ideas of private utility and injury, and has but faint conceptions of a general rule or system of behaviour. The man who stands opposite to him in battle, he hates heartily, not only for the present moment, which is almost unavoidable, but for ever after; nor is he satisfied without the most extreme punishment and vengeance. But we, accustomed to society, and to more enlarged reflections, consider, that this man is serving his own country and community; that any man, in the same situation, would do the same; that we ourselves, in like circumstances, observe a like conduct; that, in general, human society is best supported on such maxims: and by these suppositions and views, we correct, in some measure, our ruder and narrower passions. And though much of our friendship and enmity be still regulated by private considerations of benefit and harm, we pay, at least, this homage to general rules, which we are accustomed to respect, that we commonly pervert our adversary's conduct, by imputing malice or injustice to him, in order to give vent to those passions, which arise from self-love and private interest. When the heart is full of rage, it never wants pretences of this nature; though sometimes as frivolous, as those from which Horace, being almost crushed by the fall of a tree, affects to accuse of parricide the first planter of it.

From instances of popular tumults, seditions, factions, panics, and of all passions, which are shared with a multitude, we may learn the influence of society in exciting and supporting any emotion; while the most ungovernable disorders are raised, we find, by that means, from the slightest and most frivolous occasions. Solon was no very cruel, though, perhaps an unjust legislator who punished neuters in civil wars; and few, I believe, would, in such cases, incur the penalty, were their affection and discourse allowed sufficient to absolve them. No selfishness, and scarce any philosophy, have there force sufficient to support a total coolness and indifference; and he must be more or less than man, who kindles not in the common blaze. What wonder then, that moral sentiments are found of such influence in life; though springing from principles, which may appear, at first sight, somewhat small and delicate? But these principles, we must remark, are social and universal; they form, in a manner, the *party* of humankind against vice or disorder, its common enemy. And as the benevolent concern for others is diffused, in a greater or less degree, over all men, and is the same in all, it occurs more frequently in discourse, is cherished by society and conversation, and the blame and approbation, consequent on it, are thereby roused from that lethargy into which they are probably lulled, in solitary and uncultivated nature. Other passions, though perhaps originally stronger, yet being selfish and private, are often overpowered by its force, and yield the dominion of our breast to those social and public principles.

Another spring of our constitution, that brings a great addition of force to moral sentiments, is the love of fame; which rules, with such uncontrolled authority, in all generous minds, and is often the grand object of all their designs and undertakings. By our continual and earnest pursuit of a character, a name, a reputation in the world, we bring our own deportment and conduct frequently in review, and consider how they appear in the eyes of those who approach and regard us. This constant habit of surveying ourselves, as it were, in reflection, keeps alive all the sentiments of right and wrong, and begets, in noble natures, a certain reverence for themselves as well as others, which is the surest guardian of every virtue. The animal conveniences and pleasures sink gradually in their value; while every inward beauty and moral grace is studiously acquired, and the mind is accomplished in every perfection, which can adorn or embellish a rational creature.

Here is the most perfect morality with which we are acquainted: here is displayed the force of many sympathies. Our moral sentiment is itself a feeling chiefly of that nature, and our regard to a character with others seems to arise only from a care of preserving a character with ourselves; and in order to attain this end, we find it necessary to prop our tottering judgment on the correspondent approbation of mankind.

But, that we may accommodate matters, and remove if possible every difficulty, let us allow all these reasonings to be false. Let us allow that, when we resolve the pleasure, which arises from views of utility, into the sentiments of humanity and sympathy, we have embraced a wrong hypothesis. Let us confess it necessary to find some other explication of that applause, which is paid to objects, whether inanimate, animate, or rational, if they have a tendency to promote the welfare and advantage of mankind. However difficult it be to conceive that an object is approved of on account of its tendency to a certain end, while the end itself is totally indifferent: let us swallow this absurdity, and consider what are the consequences. The preceding delineation or definition of Personal Merit must still retain its evidence and authority: it must still be allowed that every quality of the mind, which is *useful* or *agreeable* to the *person himself* or to *others*, communicates a pleasure to the spectator, engages his esteem, and is admitted under the honourable denomination of virtue or merit. Are not justice, fidelity, honour, veracity, allegiance, chastity, esteemed solely on account of their tendency to promote the good of society? Is not that tendency inseparable from humanity, benevolence, lenity, generosity, gratitude, moderation, tenderness, friendship, and all the other social virtues? Can it possibly be doubted that industry, discretion, frugality, secrecy, order, perseverance, forethought, judgement, and this whole class of virtues and accomplishments, of which many pages would not contain the catalogue;

can it be doubted, I say, that the tendency of these qualities to promote the interest and happiness of their possessor, is the sole foundation of their merit? Who can dispute that a mind, which supports a perpetual serenity and cheerfulness, a noble dignity and undaunted spirit, a tender affection and good-will to all around; as it has more enjoyment within itself, is also a more animating and rejoicing spectacle, than if dejected with melancholy, tormented with anxiety, irritated with rage, or sunk into the most abject baseness and degeneracy? And as to the qualities, immediately *agreeable to others*, they speak sufficiently for themselves; and he must be unhappy, indeed, either in his own temper, or in his situation and company, who has never perceived the charms of a facetious wit or flowing affability, of a delicate modesty or decent genteelness of address and manner.

I am sensible, that nothing can be more unphilosophical than to be positive or dogmatical on any subject; and that, even if *excessive* scepticism could be maintained, it would not be more destructive to all just reasoning and inquiry. I am convinced that, where men are the most sure and arrogant, they are commonly the most mistaken, and have there given reins to passion, without that proper deliberation and suspense, which can alone secure them from the grossest of absurdities. Yet, I must confess, that this enumeration puts the matter in so strong a light, that I cannot, *at present*, be more assured of any truth, which I learn from reasoning and argument, than that personal merit consists entirely in the usefulness or agreeableness of qualities to the person himself possessed of them, or to others, who have any intercourse with him. But when I reflect that, though the bulk and figure of the earth have been measured and delineated, though the motions of the tides have been accounted for, the order and economy of the heavenly bodies subjected to their proper laws, and Infinite itself reduced to calculation; yet men still dispute concerning the foundation of their moral duties. When I reflect on this, I say, I fall back into diffidence and scepticism, and suspect that an hypothesis, so obvious, had it been a true one, would, long ere now, have been received by the unanimous suffrage and consent of mankind.

Appendix I
Concerning Moral Sentiment

If the foregoing hypothesis be received, it will now be easy for us to determine the question first started,[21] concerning the general principles of morals; and though we postponed the decision of that question, lest it should then involve us in intricate speculations, which are unfit for moral discourses, we may resume it at present, and examine how far either *reason* or *sentiment* enters into all decisions of praise or censure.

One principal foundation of moral praise being supposed to lie in the usefulness of any quality or action, it is evident that *reason* must enter for a considerable share in all decisions of this kind; since nothing but that faculty can instruct us in the tendency of qualities and actions, and point out their beneficial consequences to society and to their possessor. In many cases this is an affair liable to great controversy: doubts may arise; opposite interests may occur; and a preference must be given to one side, from very nice views, and a small overbalance of utility. This is particularly remarkable in questions with regard to justice; as is, indeed, natural to suppose, from that species of utility which attends this virtue.[22] Were every single instance of justice, like that of benevolence, useful to society; this would be a more simple state of the case, and seldom liable to great controversy. But as single instances of justice are often pernicious in their first and immediate tendency, and as the advantage to society results only from the observance of the general rule, and from the concurrence and combination of several persons in the same equitable conduct; the case here becomes more intricate and involved. The various circumstances of society; the various consequences of any practice; the various interests which may be proposed; these, on many occasions, are doubtful, and subject to great discussion and inquiry. The object of municipal laws is to fix all the questions with regard to justice: the debates of civilians; the reflections of politicians; the precedents of history and

[21]Sect. I.

[22]See App. III.

public records, are all directed to the same purpose. And a very accurate *reason* or *judgement* is often requisite, to give the true determination, amidst such intricate doubts arising from obscure or opposite utilities.

But though reason, when fully assisted and improved, be sufficient to instruct us in the pernicious or useful tendency of qualities and actions; it is not alone sufficient to produce any moral blame or approbation. Utility is only a tendency to a certain end; and were the end totally indifferent to us, we should feel the same indifference towards the means. It is requisite a *sentiment* should here display itself, in order to give a preference to the useful above the pernicious tendencies. This sentiment can be no other than a feeling for the happiness of mankind, and a resentment of their misery; since these are the different ends which virtue and vice have a tendency to promote. Here therefore *reason* instructs us in the several tendencies of actions, and *humanity* makes a distinction in favour of those which are useful and beneficial.

This partition between the faculties of understanding and sentiment, in all moral decisions, seems clear from the preceding hypothesis. But I shall suppose that hypothesis false: it will then be requisite to look out for some other theory that may be satisfactory; and I dare venture to affirm that none such will ever be found, so long as we suppose reason to be the sole source of morals. To prove this, it will be proper to weigh the five following considerations.

I. It is easy for a false hypothesis to maintain some appearance of truth, while it keeps wholly in generals, makes use of undefined terms, and employs comparisons, instead of instances. This is particularly remarkable in that philosophy, which ascribes the discernment of all moral distinctions to reason alone, without the concurrence of sentiment. It is impossible that, in any particular instance, this hypothesis can so much as be rendered intelligible, whatever specious figure it may make in general declamations and discourses. Examine the crime of *ingratitude*, for instance; which has place, wherever we observe good-will, expressed and known, together with good-offices performed, on the other side, and a return of ill-will or indifference, with ill-offices or neglect on the other: anatomize all these circumstances, and examine, by your reason alone, in what consists the demerit or blame. You never will come to any issue or conclusion.

Reason judges either of *matter of fact* or of *relations.* Enquire then, *first,* where is that matter of fact which we here call *crime*; point it out; determine the time of its existence; describe its essence or nature; explain the sense or faculty to which it discovers itself. It resides in the mind of the person who is ungrateful. He must, therefore, feel it, and be conscious of it. But nothing is there, except the passion of ill-will or absolute indifference. You can not say that these, of themselves, always and in all circumstances, are crimes. No, they are only crimes when directed towards persons who have before expressed and displayed good-will towards us. Consequently, we may infer, that the crime of ingratitude is not any particular individual *fact*; but arises from a complication of circumstances, which, being presented to the spectator, excites the *sentiment* of blame, by the particular structure and fabric of his mind.

This representation, you say, is false. Crime, indeed, consists not in a particular *fact,* of whose reality we are assured by *reason;* but it consists in certain *moral relations,* discovered by reason, in the same manner as we discover by reason the truths of geometry or algebra. But what are the relations, I ask, of which you here talk? In the case stated above, I see first good-will and good-offices in one person; then ill-will and ill-offices in the other. Between these, there is a relation of *contrariety.* Does the crime consist in that relation? But suppose a person bore me ill-will or did me ill-offices; and I, in return, were indifferent towards him, or did him good offices. Here is the same relation of *contrariety*; and yet my conduct is often highly laudable. Twist and turn this matter as much as you will, you can never rest the morality on relations; but must have recourse to the decisions of sentiment.

When it is affirmed that two and three are equal to the half of ten, this relation of equality I understand perfectly. I conceive, that if ten be divided into two parts, of which one has as many units as the other; and if any of these parts be compared to two added to three, it will contain as many units as that compound number. But when you draw thence a comparison to moral relations,

I own that I am altogether at a loss to understand you. A moral action, a crime, such as ingratitude, is a complicated object. Does the morality consist in the relation of its parts to each other? How? After what manner? Specify the relation: be more particular and explicit in your propositions, and you will easily see their falsehood.

No, say you, the morality consists in the relation of actions to the rule of right; and they are denominated good or ill, according as they agree or disagree with it. When is this rule of right? In what does it consist? How is it determined? By reason, you say, which examines the moral relations of actions. So that moral relations are determined by the comparison of action to a rule. And that rule is determined by considering the moral relations of objects. Is not this fine reasoning?

All this is metaphysics, you cry. That is enough; there needs nothing more to give a strong presumption of falsehood. Yes, reply I, here are metaphysics surely; but they are all on your side, who advance an abtruse hypothesis, which can never be made intelligible, nor quadrate with any particular instance or illustration. The hypothesis which we embrace is plain. It maintains that morality is determined by sentiment. It defines virtue to be *whatever mental action or quality gives to a spectator the pleasing sentiment of approbation*; and vice the contrary. We then proceed to examine a plain matter of fact, to wit, what actions have this influence. We consider all the circumstances in which these actions agree, and thence endeavor to extract some general observations with regard to these sentiments. If you call this metaphysics, and find anything abstruse here, you need only conclude that your turn of mind is not suited to the moral sciences.

II. When a man, at any time, deliberates concerning his own conduct (as, whether he had better, in a particular emergence, assist a brother or a benefactor), he must consider these separate relations, with all the circumstances and situations of the persons, in order to determine the superior duty and obligation; and in order to determine the proportion of lines in any triangle, it is necessary to examine the nature of that figure, and the relation which its several parts bear to each other. But notwithstanding this appearing similarity in the two cases, there is, at bottom, an extreme difference between them. A speculative reasoner concerning triangles or circles considers the several known and given relations of the parts of these figures; and thence infers some unknown relation, which is dependent on the former. But in moral deliberations we must be acquainted beforehand with all the objects, and all their relations to each other and from a comparison of the whole, fix our choice or approbation. No new fact to be ascertained: no new relation to be discovered. All the circumstances of the case are supposed to be laid before us, ere we can fix any sentence of blame or approbation. If any material circumstance be yet unknown or doubtful, we must first employ our inquiry or intellectual faculties to assure us of it; and must suspend for a time all moral decision or sentiment. While we are ignorant whether a man were aggressor or not, how can we determine whether the person who killed him be criminal or innocent? But after every circumstance, every relation is known, the understanding has no further room to operate, nor any object on which it could employ itself. The approbation or blame which then ensues, cannot be the work of the judgement, but of the heart; and is not a speculative proposition or affirmation, but an active feeling or sentiment. In the disquisitions of the understanding, from known circumstances and relations, we infer some new and unknown. In moral decisions, all the circumstances and relations must be previously known; and the mind, from the contemplation of the whole, feels some new impression of affection or disgust, esteem or contempt, approbation or blame.

Hence the great difference between a mistake of *fact* and one of *right*; and hence the reason why the one is commonly criminal and not the other. When Oedipus killed Laius, he was ignorant of the relation, and from circumstances, innocent and involuntary, formed erroneous opinions concerning the action which he committed. But when Nero killed Agrippina, all the relations between himself and the person, and all the circumstances of the fact, were previously known to him; but the motive of revenge, or fear, or interest, prevailed in his savage heart over the sentiments of duty and humanity. And when we express that detestation against him to which he himself, in a little time, became insensible, it is not that we see any relations, of which he was ignorant; but that, for the rectitude of our disposition, we feel sentiments against which he was hardened from flattery and a long perseverance in the most enormous crimes. In these sentiments, then, not in a discovery of relations of any kind, do all moral determinations consist. Before we can pretend to form any decision of this kind, everything must be known and ascertained on the side of the object or action. Nothing remains but to feel, on our part, some sentiment of blame or approbation; whence we pronounce the action criminal or virtuous.

III. This doctrine will become still more evident, if we compare moral beauty with natural, to which in many particulars it bears so near a resemblance. It is on the proportion, relation, and position of parts, that all natural beauty depends; but it would be absurd thence to infer, that the perception of beauty, like that of truth in geometrical problems, consists wholly in the perception of relations, and was performed entirely by the understanding or intellectual faculties. In all the sciences, our mind from the known relations investigates the unknown. But in all the decisions of taste or external beauty, all the relations are beforehand obvious to the eye; and we thence proceed to feel a sentiment of complacency or disgust, according to the nature of the object, and disposition of our organs.

Euclid has fully explained all the qualities of the circle; but has not in any proposition said a word of its beauty. The reason is evident. The beauty is not a quality of the circle. It lies not in any part of the line, whose parts are equally distant from a common centre. It is only the effect which that figure produces upon the mind, whose peculiar fabric of structure renders it susceptible of such sentiments. In vain would you look for it in the circle, or seek it, either by your senses or by mathematical reasoning, in all the properties of that figure.

* * *

IV. Inanimate objects may bear to each other all the same relations which we observe in moral agents; though the former can never be the object of love or hatred, nor are consequently susceptible of merit or iniquity. A young tree, which over-tops and destroys its parent, stands in all the same relations with Nero, when he murdered Agrippina; and if morality consisted merely in relations, would no doubt be equally criminal.

V. It appears evident that the ultimate ends of human actions can never, in any case, be accounted for by *reason*, but recommend themselves entirely to the sentiments and affections of mankind, without any dependance on the intellectual facilities. Ask a man *why he uses exercise*; he will answer, *because he desires to keep his health*. If you then enquire, *why he desires health*, he will readily reply, *because sickness is painful*. If you push your enquiries farther, and desire a reason *why he hates pain*, it is impossible he can ever give any. This is an ultimate end, and is never referred to any other object.

Perhaps to your second question, *why he desires health*, he may also reply, that *it is necessary for the exercise of his calling*. If you ask, *why he is anxious on that head*, he will answer, *because he desires to get money*. If you demand *Why? It is the instrument of pleasure*, says he. And beyond this is it an absurdity to ask for a reason. It is impossible there can be a progress *in infinitum*; and that one thing can always be a reason why another is desired. Something must be desirable on its own account, and because of its immediate accord or agreement with human sentiment and affection.

Now as virtue is an end, and is desirable on its own account, without fee and reward, merely for the immediate satisfaction which it conveys; it is requisite that there should be some sentiment which it touches, some internal taste or feeling, or whatever you may please to call it, which distinguishes moral good and evil, and which embraces the one and rejects the other.

Thus the distinct boundaries and offices of *reason* and of *taste* are easily ascertained. The former conveys the knowledge of truth and falsehood: the latter gives the sentiment of beauty and deformity, vice and virtue. The one discovers objects as they really stand in nature, without addition and diminution: the other has a productive faculty, and gilding or staining all natural objects with the colours, borrowed from internal sentiment, raises in a manner a new creation. Reason being cool and disengaged, is no motive to action, and directs only the impulse received from appetite or inclination, by showing us the means of attaining happiness or avoiding misery: Taste, as it gives pleasure or pain, and thereby constitutes happiness or misery, becomes a motive to action, and is the first spring or impulse to desire and volition. From circumstances and relations, known or supposed, the former leads us to the discovery of the concealed and unknown: after all circumstances and relations are laid before us, the latter makes us feel from the whole a new sentiment of blame or approbation. The standard of the one, being founded on the nature of things, is eternal and inflexible, even by the will of the Supreme Being: the standard of the other arising from the eternal frame and constitution of animals, is ultimately derived from that Supreme Will, which bestowed on each being its peculiar nature, and arranged the several classes and orders of existence.

Appendix III Some Farther Considerations with Regard to Justice

The intention of this Appendix is to give some more particular explication of the origin and nature of Justice, and to mark some differences between it and the other virtues.

The social virtues of humanity and benevolence exert their influence immediately by a direct tendency or instinct, which chiefly keeps in view the simple object, moving the affections, and comprehends not any scheme or system, nor the consequences resulting from the concurrence, imitation, or example of others. A parent flies to the relief of his child; transported by that natural sympathy which actuates him, and which affords no leisure to reflect on the sentiments or conduct of the rest of mankind in like circumstances. A generous man cheerfully embraces an opportunity of serving his friend; because he then feels himself under the dominion of the beneficent affections, nor is he concerned whether any person in the universe were ever before actuated by such noble motives, or will ever afterwards prove their influence. In all these cases the social passions have in view a single individual object, and pursue the safety or happiness alone of the person loved and esteemed. With this they are satisfied: in this they acquiesce. And as the good, resulting from their benign influence, is in itself complete and entire, it also excites the moral sentiment of approbation, without any reflection on farther consequences, and without any more enlarged views of the concurrence or imitation of the other members of society. On the contrary, were the generous friend or disinterested patriot to stand alone in the practice of beneficence, this would rather inhance his value in our eyes, and join the praise of rarity and novelty to his other more exalted merits.

The case is not the same with the social virtues of justice and fidelity. They are highly useful, or indeed absolutely necessary to the well-being of mankind: but the benefit resulting from them is not the consequence of every individual single act; but arises from the whole scheme or system concurred in by the whole, or the greater part of the society. General peace and order are the attendants of justice or a general abstinence from the possessions of others; but a particular regard to the particular right of one individual citizen may frequently, considered in itself, be productive of pernicious consequences. The result of the individual acts is here, in many instances, directly opposite to that of the whole system of actions; and the former may be extremely hurtful, while the latter is, to the highest degree, advantageous. Riches, inherited from a parent, are, in a bad man's hand, the instrument of mischief. The right of succession may, in one instance, be hurtful. Its benefit arises only from the observance of the general rule; and it is sufficient, if compensation be thereby made for all the ills and inconveniences which flow from particular characters and situations.

Cyrus, young and unexperienced, considered only the individual case before him, and reflected on a limited fitness and convenience, when he assigned the long coat to the tall boy, and the short coat to the other of smaller size. His governor instructed him better, while he pointed out more enlarged views and consequences, and informed his pupil of the general, inflexible rules, necessary to support general peace and order in society.

The happiness and prosperity of mankind, arising from the social virtue of benevolence and its subdivisions, may be compared to a wall, built by many hands, which still rises by each stone that is heaped upon it, and receives increase proportional to the diligence and care of each workman. The same happiness, raised by the social virtue of justice and its subdivisions, may be compared to the building of a vault, where each individual stone would, of itself, fall to the ground; nor is the whole fabric supported but by the mutual assistance and combination of its corresponding parts.

All the laws of nature, which regulate property, as well as all civil laws, are general, and regard alone some essential circumstances of the case, without taking into consideration the characters, situations, and connexions of the person concerned, or any particular consequences which may result from the determination of these laws in any particular case which offers. They deprive, without scruple, a beneficent man of all his possessions, if acquired by mistake, without a good title; in order to bestow them on a selfish miser, who has already heaped up immense stores of superfluous riches. Public utility requires that property should be regulated by general inflexible rules; and though such rules are adopted as best serve the same end of public utility, it is impossible for them to prevent all particular hardships, or make beneficial consequences result from every individual case. It is sufficient, if the whole plan or scheme be necessary to the support of civil society, and if the balance of good, in the main, do thereby preponderate much above that of evil. Even the general laws of the universe, though planned by infinite wisdom, cannot exclude all evil or inconvenience in every particular operation.

It has been asserted by some, that justice arises from Human Conventions, and proceeds from the voluntary choice, consent, or combination of mankind. If by *convention* be here meant a *promise* (which is the most usual sense of the word) nothing can be more absurd than this position. The observance of promises is itself one of the most considerable parts of justice, and we are not surely bound to keep our word because we have given our word to keep it. But if by convention be meant a sense of common interest, which sense each man feels in his own breast, which he remarks in his fellows, and which carries him, in concurrence with others, into a general plan or system of actions, which tends to public utility; it must be owned, that, in this sense, justice arises from human conventions. For if it be allowed (what is, indeed, evident) that the particular consequences of a particular act of justice may be hurtful to the public as well as individuals; it follows that every man, in embracing the virtue, must have an eye to the whole plan or system, and must expect the concurrence of his fellows in the same conduct and behaviour. Did all his views terminate in the consequences of each act of his own, his benevolence and humanity, as well as his self-love, might often prescribe to him measures of conduct very different from those which are agreeable to the strict rules of right and justice.

Thus, two men pull the oars of a boat by common convention for common interest, without any promise or contract: thus gold and silver are made the measures of exchange; thus speech and words and language are fixed by human convention and agreement. Whatever is advantageous to two or more persons, if all perform their part; but what loses all advantage if only one perform, can arise from no other principle. There would otherwise be no motive for any one of them to enter into that scheme of conduct.

The word *natural* is commonly taken in so many senses and is of so loose a signification, that it seems vain to dispute whether justice be natural or not. If self-love, if benevolence be natural to man; if reason and forethought be also natural; then may the same epithet be applied to justice, order, fidelity, property, society. Men's inclination, their necessities, lead them to combine; their understanding and experience tell them that this combination is impossible where each governs himself by no rule, and pays no regard to the possessions of others: and from these passions and reflections conjoined, as soon as we observe like passions and reflections in others, the sentiment of justice, throughout all ages, has infallibly and certainly had place to some degree or other in every individual of the human species. In so sagacious an animal, what necessarily arises from the exertion of his intellectual faculties may justly be esteemed natural.[23]

Among all civilized nations it has been the constant endeavour to remove everything arbitrary and partial from the decision of property, and to fix the sentence of judges by such general views and considerations as may be equal to every member of society. For besides, that nothing could be more dangerous than to accustom the bench, even in the smallest instance, to regard private friendship or enmity; it is certain, that men, where they imagine that there was no other reason for the preference of their adversary but personal favour, are apt to entertain the strongest ill-will against the magistrates and judges. When natural reason, therefore, points out no fixed view of public utility by which a controversy of property can be decided, positive laws are often framed to supply its place, and direct the procedure of all courts of judicature. When these too fail, as often happens, precedents are called for; and a former decision, though given itself without any sufficient reason, justly becomes a sufficient reason for new decision. If direct laws and precedents be wanting, imperfect and indirect ones are brought in aid; and the controverted case is ranged under them by analogical reasonings and comparisons, and similitudes, and correspondencies, which are often more fanciful than real. In general, it may safely be affirmed that jurisprudence is, in this respect, different from all the sciences; and that in many of its nicer questions, there cannot properly be said to be truth or falsehood on either side. If one pleader bring the case under any former law or precedent, by a refined analogy or comparison; the opposite pleader is not at a loss to find an opposite analogy or comparison: and the preference given by the judge is often founded more on taste and imagination than on any solid argument. Public utility is the general object of all courts of judicature; and this utility too requires a stable rule in all controversies: but where several rules, nearly equal and indifferent, present themselves, it is a very slight turn of thought which fixes the decision in favour of either party.[24]

We may just observe, before we conclude this subject, that after the laws of justice are fixed by views of general utility, the injury, the hardship, the harm, which result to any individual from a violation of them, enter very much into consideration, and are a great source of that universal blame which attends every wrong or iniquity. By the laws

[23]Natural may be opposed, either to what is *unusual, miraculous* or *artificial.* In the two former senses, justice and property are undoubtedly natural. But as they suppose reason, forethought, design, and a social union and confederacy among men, perhaps that epithet cannot strictly, in the last sense, be applied to them. Had men lived without society, property had never been known, and neither justice nor injustice had ever existed. But society among human creatures had been impossible without reason and forethought. Inferior animals, that unite, are guided by instinct, which supplies the place of reason. But all these disputes are merely verbal.

[24]That there be a separation or distinction of possessions, and that this separation be steady and constant; this is absolutely required by the interests of society, and hence the origin of justice and property. What possessions are assigned to particular persons; this is, generally speaking, pretty indifferent; and is often determined by very frivolous views and considerations. We shall mention a few particulars.

Were a society formed among several independent members, the most obvious rule, which could be agreed on, would be to annex property to *present* possession, and leave every one a right to what he at present enjoys. The relation of possession, which takes place between a person and the object, naturally draws on the relation of property.

For a like reason, occupation or first possession becomes the foundation of property.

Where a man bestows labour and industry upon any object, which before belonged to no body; as in cutting down and shaping a tree, in cultivating a field, &c., the alterations, which he produces, causes a relation between him and the object, and naturally engages us to annex it to him by the new relation of property. This cause here concurs with the public utility, which consists in the encouragement given to industry and labour.

Perhaps too, private humanity towards the possessor concurs, in this instance, with the other motives, and engages us to leave with him what he has acquired by sweat and labour; and what he has flattered himself in the constant enjoyment of. For though private humanity can, by no means, be the origin of justice; since the latter virtue so often contradicts the former; yet when the rule of separate and constant possession is once formed by the indispensable necessities of society, private humanity, and an aversion to the doing a hardship to another, may, in a particular instance, give rise to a particular rule of property.

I am much inclined to think, that the right succession or inheritance much depends on these connexions of the imagination, and that the relation to a former proprietor begetting a relation to the object, is the cause why the property is transferred to a man after the death of his kinsman. It is true; industry is more encouraged by the transference of possession to children or neat relations: but this consideration will only have place in a cultivated society;

of society, this coat, this horse is mine, and *ought* to remain perpetually in my possession: I reckon on the secure enjoyment of it: by depriving me of it, you disappoint my expectations, and doubly displease me, and offend every bystander. It is a public wrong, so far as the rules of equity are violated: it is a private harm, so far as an individual is injured. And though the second consideration could have no place, were not the former previously established: for otherwise the distinction of *thine* and *mine* would be unknown in society: yet there is no question but the regard to general good is much enforced by the respect to particular. What injures the community, without hurting any individual, is often more lightly thought of. But where the greatest public wrong is also conjoined with a considerable private one, no wonder the highest disapprobation attends so iniquitous a behaviour.

Study Questions

1. What is the controversy concerning the general foundation of morals that Hume wishes to resolve? What is his method for resolving the controversy?
2. What qualities, according to Hume, are most approved by humankind? Explain some of the arguments he uses to establish this. What does he say is the sole source of the high regard paid to justice, and what is the foundation of morality?
3. What does Hume think of the idea that moral distinctions were invented by the rich and powerful just to make people manageable? How does Hume defend his view?
4. What does Hume think of the idea that we praise the social virtues only because it is in our selfish interest to do so? Why does he think that?
5. How does Hume respond to the charge that when we derive pleasure from a story about a generous deed done in a distant land, we do so only because we picture ourselves benefiting from the deed?
6. What happens to a person who lives in solitude, according to Hume? Why?
7. What is the point of Hume's story about what we experience when we enter into "a convenient, warm, well-contrived apartment?"

---

whereas the right of succession is regarded even among the greatest Barbarians.

Acquisition of property by *accession* can be explained no way but by having recourse to the relations and connexions of the imaginations.

The property of rivers, by the laws of most nations, and by the natural turn of our thoughts, is attributed to the proprietors of their banks, excepting such vast rivers as the Rhine or the Danube, which seem too large to follow as an accession to the property of the neighbouring fields. Yet even these rivers are considered as the property of that nation, through whose dominions they run; the idea of a nation being of a suitable bulk to correspond with them, and bear them such a relation in the fancy.

The accessions, which are made to land, bordering upon rivers, follow the land, say the civilians, provided it be made by what they call *alluvion*, that is, insensibly and imperceptibly; which are circumstances, that assist the imagination of the conjunction.

Where there is any considerable portion torn at once from one bank and added to another, it becomes not *his* property, whose land it falls on, till it unite with the land, and till the trees and plants have spread their roots into both. Before that, the thought does not sufficiently join them.

Is short, we must ever distinguish between the necessity of a separation and constancy in men's possession, and the rules, which assign particular objects to particular persons. The first necessity is obvious, strong, and invincible: the latter may depend on a public utility more light and frivilous, on the sentiment of private humanity and aversion to private hardship, on positive laws, on precedents, analogies, and very fine connexions and turns of the imagination.

8. According to Hume, is it self-love that makes us praise the qualities of another person that are beneficial to that other person—qualities such as industry, frugality, economy, and good sense? Explain.
9. What does Hume think of what he calls the monkish virtues? Why does he think this?
10. What role, according to Hume, does reason play in moral judgments? What role does sentiment play? What are the five considerations Hume discusses in appendix 1 intended to show?

Kant

Immanuel Kant (1724–1804) took the first alternative mentioned in our discussion of Hume; that is, he argued that (despite Hume) we must look to reason to find out what is morally right and wrong. Kant made four assumptions: (1) there are moral principles; (2) they are knowable; (3) a moral principle by its very nature holds universally; and (4) only reason can deliver knowledge of principles that hold universally.

The third assumption is very important for Kant's moral philosophy. Because a moral principle holds universally, or "categorically," the supreme prescription of morality is *to act always in such a way that you could, rationally, will the principle on which you act to be a universal law.* This principle is referred to by Kant as the *categorical imperative.*

Suppose, for instance, that you see a portable CD player on the front seat of someone's car and so you help yourself. The principle on which you have acted, expressed grammatically in the imperative form, is therefore something like "Take what belongs to someone else when you want it." But if it were a universal law that one should take what belongs to someone else when one wants it, the idea of something's *belonging to someone* would be meaningless. Consequently, the principle itself would be meaningless, if it were a universal law. So it would be irrational for you to want or "will" the principle to be a universal law.

It would likewise be irrational for *anyone* to want the principle to be a universal law. The supreme prescription of morality, or categorical imperative (act always in such a way that rationally you could will the principle on which you act to be a universal law), thus assumes that *all* rational agents—all persons—are *equally* legitimate legislators of the moral law. This means, according to Kant, that you should *treat rational beings never simply as a means but always at the same time as ends.* Indeed, Kant regards this dictum as an alternative formulation of the categorical imperative. Thus, a key idea in Kant's moral philosophy is the concept of respect for persons. It is morally unacceptable to enslave, mistreat, or mislead people for the sake of some "greater good," such as the well-being or happiness of the greater society. To treat people in this way would be to treat them merely as means, not as ends.

Kant contrasts moral imperatives with "hypothetical" imperatives. Hypothetical imperatives are expressed in conditional form and state that you ought to do something *if* a certain end is desired. For example, the imperative "If you want people to like you, then keep your promises," is hypothetical, or conditional. It enjoins you to do something if you want people to like you. A moral imperative, by contrast (for example, "Keep your promises") holds categorically and unconditionally. It commands obedience for no other end than its own rightness.

This means that what you morally should do, you should do simply because it is right. Doing something for any other purpose—even if the purpose is noble—is to act under the command of a hypothetical imperative, which is not a moral imperative. For Kant, therefore, you should do your moral duty just simply because it is your moral duty. Kant is philosophy's leading deontologist, one who thinks that moral obligations are not simply a matter of producing good consequences (see Chapter 5).

It follows from this that what counts morally is your intention, or "will." Did you do what you did because it is the moral thing to do or for the sake of some other end? Only if you acted for the first reason is your act morally good. Acting out of concern or love for others does not suffice to make an act morally good, even if the result of the act is noble and its consequences are entirely fortunate. Likewise, if you do something simply because it is the moral thing to do, then you acted morally—regardless of what the consequences of your act were.

The following selection is from Kant's *Foundations of the Metaphysics of Morals.* It begins with the point that the only thing that can be taken as good without qualification is a good will.

from *Grounding for the Metaphysics of Morals*

Immanuel Kant

Kant lived from 1724 to 1804 and spent his entire life within the vicinity of Königsberg. Reprinted here are the first two sections of his *Grounding for the Metaphysics of Morals,* translated by James W. Ellington (Indianapolis: Hackett Publishing Company, 1981).

First Section
Transition from the Ordinary Rational Knowledge of Morality to the Philosophical

There is no possibility of thinking of anything at all in the world, or even out of it, which can be regarded as good without qualification, except a *good will.* Intelligence, wit, judgment, and whatever talents of the mind one might want to name are doubtless in many respects good and desirable, as are such qualities of temperament as courage, resolution, perseverance. But they can also become extremely bad and harmful if the will, which is to make use of these gifts of nature and which in its special constitution is called character, is not good. The same holds with gifts of fortune; power, riches, honor, even health, and that complete well-being and contentment with one's condition which is called happiness make for pride and often hereby even arrogance, unless there is a good will to correct their influence on the mind and herewith also to rectify the whole principle of action and make it universally conformable to its end. The sight of a being who is not graced by any touch of a pure and good will but who yet enjoys an uninterrupted prosperity can never delight a rational and impartial spectator. Thus a good will seems to constitute the indispensable condition of being even worthy of happiness.

Some qualities are even conducive to this good will itself and can facilitate its work. Nevertheless, they have no intrinsic unconditional worth; but they always presuppose, rather, a good will, which restricts the high esteem in which they are otherwise rightly held, and does not permit them to be regarded as absolutely good. Moderation in emotions and passions, self-control, and calm deliberation are not only good in many respects but even seem to constitute part of the intrinsic worth of a person. But they are far from being rightly called good without qualification (however unconditionally they were commended by the ancients). For without the principles of a good will, they can become extremely bad; the coolness of a villain makes him not only much more dangerous but also immediately more abominable in our eyes than he would have been regarded by us without it.

A good will is good not because of what it effects or accomplishes, nor because of its fitness to attain some proposed end; it is good only through its willing; i.e., it is good in itself. When it is considered in itself, then it is to be esteemed very much higher than anything which it might ever bring about merely in order to favor some inclination, or even the sum total of all inclinations. Even if, by some especially unfortunate fate or by the niggardly provision of stepmotherly nature, this will should be wholly lacking in the power to accomplish its purpose; if with the greatest effort it should yet achieve nothing, and only the good will should remain (not, to be sure, as a mere wish but as the summoning of all the means in our power), yet would it, like a jewel, still shine by its own light as something which has its full value in itself. Its usefulness or fruitlessness can neither augment nor diminish this value. Its usefulness would be, as it were, only the setting to enable us to handle it in ordinary dealings or to attract to it the attention of those who are not yet experts, but not to recommend it to real experts or to determine its value.

But there is something so strange in this idea of the absolute value of a mere will, in which no account is taken of any useful results, that in spite of all the agreement received even from ordinary reason, yet there must arise the suspicion that such an idea may perhaps have as its hidden basis merely some high-flown fancy, and that we may have misunderstood the purpose of nature in assigning to reason the governing of our will. Therefore, this idea will be examined from this point of view.

In the natural constitution of an organized being, i.e., one suitably adapted to the purpose of life, let there be taken as a principle that in such a being no organ is to be found for any end unless it be the most fit and the best adapted for that end. Now if that being's preservation, welfare, or in a word its happiness, were the real end of nature in the case of a being having reason and will, then nature would have hit upon a very poor arrangement in having the reason of the creature carry out this purpose. For all the actions which such a creature has to perform with this purpose in view, and the whole rule of his conduct would have been prescribed much more exactly by instinct; and the purpose in question could have been attained much more certainly by instinct than it ever can be by reason. And if in addition reason had been imparted to this favored creature, then it would have had to serve him only to contemplate the happy constitution of his nature, to admire that nature, to rejoice in it, and to feel grateful to the cause that bestowed it; but reason would not have served him to subject his faculty of desire to its weak and delusive guidance nor would it have served him to meddle incompetently with the purpose of nature. In a word, nature would have taken care that reason did not strike out into a practical use nor presume, with its weak insight, to think out for itself a plan for happiness and the means for attaining it. Nature would have taken upon herself not only the choice of ends but also that of the means, and would with wise foresight have entrusted both to instinct alone.

And, in fact, we find that the more a cultivated reason devotes itself to the aim of enjoying life and happiness, the further does man get away from true contentment. Because of this there arises in many persons, if only they are candid enough to admit it, a certain degree of misology, i.e., hatred of reason. This is especially so in the case of those who are the most experienced in the use of reason, because after calculating all the advantages they derive, I say not from the invention of all the arts of common luxury, but even from the sciences (which in the end seem to them to be also a luxury of the understanding), they yet find that they have in fact only brought more trouble on their heads than they have gained in happiness. Therefore, they come to envy, rather than despise, the more common run of men who are closer to the guidance of mere natural instinct and who do not allow their reason much influence on their conduct. And we must admit that the judgment of those who would temper, or even reduce below zero, the boastful eulogies on behalf of the advantages which reason is supposed to provide as regards the happiness and contentment of life is by no means morose or ungrateful to the goodness with which the world is governed: There lies at the root of such judgments, rather, the idea that existence has another and much more worthy purpose, for which, and not for happiness, reason is quite properly intended, and which must, therefore, be regarded as the supreme condition to which the private purpose of men must, for the most part, defer.

Reason, however, is not competent enough to guide the will safely as regards its objects and the satisfaction of all our needs (which it in part even multiplies); to this end would an implanted natural instinct have led much more certainly. But inasmuch as reason has been imparted to us as a practical faculty, i.e., as one which is to have influence on the will, its true function must be to produce a will which is not merely good as a means to some further end, but is good in itself. To produce a will good in itself reason was absolutely necessary, inasmuch as nature in distributing her capacities has everywhere gone to work in a purposive manner. While such a will may not indeed be the sole and complete good, it must, nevertheless, be the highest good and the condition of all the rest, even of the desire for happiness. In this case there is nothing inconsistent with the wisdom of nature that the cultivation of reason, which is requisite for the first and unconditioned purpose, may in many ways restrict, at least in this life, the attainment of the second purpose, viz., happiness, which is always conditioned. Indeed happiness can even be reduced to less than nothing, without nature's failing thereby in her purpose; for reason recognizes as its highest practical function the establishment of a good will, whereby in the attainment of this end reason is capable only of its own kind of satisfaction, viz., that of fulfilling a purpose which is in turn determined only by reason, even though such fulfilment were often to interfere with the purposes of inclination.

The concept of a will estimable in itself and good without regard to any further end must now be developed. This concept already dwells in the natural sound understanding and needs not so much to be taught as merely to be elucidated. It always holds first place in estimating the total worth of our actions and constitutes the condition of all the rest. Therefore, we shall take up the concept of *duty*, which includes that of a good will, though with certain subjective restrictions and hindrances, which far from hiding a good will or rendering it unrecognizable, rather bring it out by contrast and make it shine forth more brightly.

I here omit all actions already recognized as contrary to duty, even though they may be useful for this or that end; for in the case of these the question does not arise at all as to whether they might be done from duty, since they even conflict with duty. I also set aside those actions which are really in accordance with duty, yet to which men have no immediate inclination, but perform them because they are impelled thereto by some other inclination. For in this [second] case to decide whether the action which is in accord with duty has been done from duty or from some selfish purpose is easy. This difference is far more difficult to note in the [third] case where the action accords with duty and the subject has in addition an immediate inclination to do the action. For example,[1] that a dealer should not overcharge an inexperienced purchaser certainly accords with duty; and where there is much commerce, the prudent merchant does not overcharge but keeps to a fixed price for everyone in general, so that a child may buy from him just as well as everyone else may. Thus customers are honestly served, but this is not nearly enough for making us believe that the merchant has acted this way from duty and from principles of honesty; his own advantage required him to do it. He cannot, however, be assumed to have in addition [as in the third case] an immediate inclination toward his buyers, causing him, as it were, out of love to give no one as far as price is concerned any advantage over another. Hence the action was done neither from duty nor from immediate inclination, but merely for a selfish purpose.

On the other hand,[2] to preserve one's life is a duty; and, furthermore, everyone has also an immediate inclination to do so. But on this account the often anxious care taken by most men for it has no intrinsic worth, and the maxim of their action has no moral content. They preserve their lives, to be sure, in accordance with duty, but not from duty. On the other hand,[3] if adversity and hopeless sorrow have completely taken away the taste for life, if an unfortunate man, strong in soul and more indignant at his fate than despondent or dejected, wishes for death and yet preserves his life without loving it — not from inclination or fear, but from duty — then his maxim indeed has a moral content.[4]

[1][The ensuing example provides an illustration of the second case.]

[2][This next example illustrates the third case.]

[3][The ensuing example illustrates the fourth case.]

[4][Four different cases have been distinguished in the two foregoing paragraphs. Case 1 involves those actions which are contrary to duty (lying, cheating, stealing, etc.). Case 2 involves those which accord with duty but for which a person perhaps has no immediate inclination, though he does have a mediate inclination thereto (one pays his taxes not because he likes to but in order to avoid the penalties set for delinquents, one treats his fellow well not because he really likes them but because he wants their votes when at some future time he runs for public office, etc.). A vast number of so-called "morally good" actions actually belong to this case 2 — they accord with duty because of self-seeking inclinations. Case 3 involves those which accord with duty and for which a person does have an immediate inclination (one does not commit suicide because all is going well with him, one does not commit adultery because he considers his wife to be the most desirable creature in the whole world, etc.). Case 4 involves those actions which accord with duty but are contrary to some immediate inclination (one does not commit suicide even when he is in dire distress, one does not commit adultery even though his wife has turned out to be an impossible shrew, etc.). Now case 4 is the crucial test case of the will's possible goodness — but Kant does not claim that one should lead his life in such a way as to encounter as many such cases as possible in order constantly to test his virtue (deliberately marry a shrew so as to be able to resist the temptation to commit adultery). Life itself forces enough such cases upon a

To be beneficent where one can is a duty; and besides this, there are many persons who are so sympathetically constituted that, without any further motive of vanity or self-interest, they find an inner pleasure in spreading joy around them and can rejoice in the satisfaction of others as their own work. But I maintain that in such a case an action of this kind, however dutiful and amiable it may be, has nevertheless no true moral worth.[5] It is on a level with such actions as arise from other inclinations, e.g., the inclination for honor, which if fortunately directed to what is in fact beneficial and accords with duty and is thus honorable, deserves praise and encouragement, but not esteem; for its maxim lacks the moral content of an action done not from inclination but from duty. Suppose then the mind of this friend of mankind to be clouded over with his own sorrow so that all sympathy with the lot of others is extinguished, and suppose him still to have the power to benefit others in distress, even though he is not touched by their trouble because he is sufficiently absorbed with his own; and now suppose that, even though no inclination moves him any longer, he nevertheless tears himself from this deadly insensibility and performs the action without any inclination at all, but solely from duty—then for the first time his action has genuine moral worth.[6] Further still, if nature has put little sympathy in this or that man's heart, if (while being an honest man in other respects) he is by temperament cold and indifferent to the sufferings of others, perhaps because as regards his own sufferings he is endowed with the special gift of patience and fortitude and expects or even requires that others should have the same; if such a man (who would truly not be nature's worst product) had not been exactly fashioned by her to be a philanthropist, would he not yet find in himself a source from which he might give himself a worth far higher than any that a good-natured temperament might have? By all means, because just here does the worth of the character come out; this worth is moral and incomparably the highest of all, viz., that he is beneficent, not from inclination, but from duty.[7]

To secure one's own happiness is a duty (at least indirectly); for discontent with one's condition under many pressing cares and amid unsatisfied wants might easily become a great temptation to transgress one's duties. But here also do men of themselves already have, irrespective of duty, the strongest and deepest inclination toward happiness, because just in this idea are all inclinations combined into a sum total.[8] But the precept of happiness is often so constituted as greatly to interfere with some inclinations, and yet men cannot form any definite and certain concept of the sum of satisfaction of all inclinations that is called happiness. Hence there is no wonder that a single inclination which is determinate both as to what it promises and as to the time within which it can be satisfied may outweigh a fluctuating idea; and there is no wonder that a man, e.g., a gouty patient, can choose to enjoy what he likes and to suffer what he may, since by his calculation he has here at least not sacrificed the enjoyment of the present moment to some possibly groundless expectations of the good fortune that is supposed to be found in health. But even in this case, if the universal inclination to happiness did not determine his will and if health, at least for him, did not figure as so necessary an element in his calculations; there still remains here, as in all other cases, a law, viz., that he should promote his happiness not from inclination but from duty, and thereby

person without his seeking them out. But when there is a conflict between duty and inclination, duty should always be followed. Case 3 makes for the easiest living and the greatest contentment, and anyone would wish that life might present him with far more of these cases than with cases 2 or 4. But yet one should not arrange his life in such a way as to avoid case 4 at all costs and to seek out case 3 as much as possible (become a recluse so as to avoid the possible rough and tumble involved with frequent association with one's fellows, avoid places where one might encounter the sick and the poor so as to spare oneself the pangs of sympathy and the need to exercise the virtue of benefiting those in distress, etc.). For the purpose of philosophical analysis Kant emphasizes case 4 as being the test case of the will's possible goodness, but he is not thereby advocating puritanism.]

[5][This is an example of case 3.]

[6][This is an example of case 4.]

[7][This is an even more extreme example of case 4.]

[8][This is an example of case 3.]

for the first time does his conduct have real moral worth.[9]

Undoubtedly in this way also are to be understood those passages of Scripture which command us to love our neighbor and even our enemy. For love as an inclination cannot be commanded; but beneficence from duty, when no inclination impels us[10] and even when a natural and unconquerable aversion opposes such beneficence,[11] is practical, and not pathological, love. Such love resides in the will and not in the propensities of feeling, in principles of action and not in tender sympathy; and only this practical love can be commanded.

The second proposition[12] is this: An action done from duty has its moral worth, not in the purpose that is to be attained by it, but in the maxim according to which the action is determined. The moral worth depends, therefore, not on the realization of the object of the action, but merely on the principle of volition according to which, without regard to any objects of the faculty of desire, the action has been done. From what has gone before it is clear that the purposes which we may have in our actions, as well as their effects regarded as ends and incentives of the will, cannot give to actions any unconditioned and moral worth. Where, then, can this worth lie if it is not to be found in the will's relation to the expected effect? Nowhere but in the principle of the will, with no regard to the ends that can be brought about through such action. For the will stands, as it were, at a crossroads between its a priori principle, which is formal, and its a posteriori incentive, which is material; and since it must be determined by something, it must be determined by the formal principle of volition, if the action is done from duty—and in that case every material principle is taken away from it.

The third proposition, which follows from the other two, can be expressed thus: Duty is the necessity of an action done out of respect for the law. I can indeed have an inclination for an object as the effect of my proposed action; but I can never have respect for such an object, just because it is merely an effect and is not an activity of the will. Similarly, I can have no respect for inclination as such, whether my own or that of another. I can at most, if my own inclination, approve it; and, if that of another, even love it, i.e., consider it to be favorable to my own advantage. An object of respect can only be what is connected with my will solely as ground and never as effect—something that does not serve my inclination but, rather, outweighs it, or at least excludes it from consideration when some choice is made—in other words, only the law itself can be an object of respect and hence can be a command. Now an action done from duty must altogether exclude the influence of inclination and therewith every object of the will. Hence there is nothing left which can determine the will except objectively the law and subjectively pure respect for this practical law, i.e., the will can be subjectively determined by the maxim[13] that I should follow such a law even if all my inclinations are thereby thwarted.

Thus the moral worth of an action does not lie in the effect expected from it nor in any principle of action that needs to borrow its motive from this expected effect. For all these effects (agreeableness of one's condition and even the furtherance of other people's happiness) could have been brought about also through other causes and would not have required the will of a rational being, in which the highest and unconditioned good can alone be found. Therefore, the pre-eminent good which is called moral can consist in nothing but the representation of the law in itself, and such a representation can admittedly be found only in a rational being insofar as this representation, and not some

[9][This example is a weak form of case 4; the action accords with duty but is not contrary to some immediate inclination.]

[10][This is case 4 in its weak form.]

[11][This is case 4 in its strong form.]

[12][The first proposition of morality says that an action must be done from duty in order to have any moral worth. It is implicit in the preceding examples but was never explicitly stated.]

[13]A maxim is the subjective principle of volition. The objective principle (i.e., one which would serve all rational beings also subjectively as a practical principle if reason had full control over the faculty of desire) is the practical law.

expected effect, is the determining ground of the will. This good is already present in the person who acts according to this representation, and such good need not be awaited merely from the effect.[14]

But what sort of law can that be the thought of which must determine the will without reference to any expected effect, so that the will can be called absolutely good without qualification? Since I have deprived the will of every impulse that might arise for it from obeying any particular law, there is nothing left to serve the will as principle except the universal conformity of its actions to law as such, i.e., I should never act except in such a way that I can also will that my maxim should become a universal law.[15] Here mere conformity to law as such (without having as its basis any law determining particular actions) serves the will as principle and must so serve it if duty is not to be a vain delusion and a chimerical concept. The ordinary reason of mankind in its practical judgments agrees completely with this, and always has in view the aforementioned principle.

For example, take this question. When I am in distress, may I make a promise with the intention of not keeping it? I readily distinguish here the two meanings which the question may have; whether making a false promise conforms with prudence or with duty. Doubtless the former can often be the case. Indeed I clearly see that escape from some present difficulty by means of such a promise is not enough. In addition I must carefully consider whether from this lie there may later arise far greater inconvenience for me than from what I now try to escape. Furthermore, the consequences of my false promise are not easy to foresee, even with all my supposed cunning; loss of confidence in me might prove to be far more disadvantageous than the misfortune which I now try to avoid. The more prudent way might be to act according to a universal maxim and to make it a habit not to promise anything without intending to keep it. But that such a maxim is, nevertheless, always based on nothing but a fear of consequences becomes clear to me at once. To be truthful from duty is, however, quite different from being truthful from fear of disadvantageous consequences; in the first case the concept of the action itself contains a law for me, while in the second I must first look around elsewhere to see what are the results for me that might be connected with the action. For to deviate from the principle of duty is quite certainly bad; but to abandon my maxim of prudence can often be very advantageous for me, though to abide by it is certainly safer. The most direct and infallible way, however, to answer the question as to whether a lying promise accords with duty is to ask myself whether I would really be content if my maxim (of extricating myself from difficulty by means of a false promise) were to hold as a universal law for myself as well as for others, and could I really say to myself that everyone may promise falsely when he finds himself in a difficulty from which he can find no other way to extricate himself. Then I immediately become aware that I can indeed will the lie but can not at all will a universal law to lie. For by such a law there would really be no promises at all, since in vain would my willing future actions be professed

---

[14]There might be brought against me here an objection that I take refuge behind the word "respect" in an obscure feeling, instead of giving a clear answer to the question by means of a concept of reason. But even though respect is a feeling, it is not one received through any outside influence but is, rather, one that is self-produced by means of a rational concept; hence it is specifically different from all feelings of the first kind, which can all be reduced to inclination or fear. What I recognize immediately as a law for me, I recognize with respect; this means merely the consciousness of the subordination of my will to a law without the mediation of other influences upon my sense. The immediate determination of the will by the law, and the consciousness thereof, is called respect, which is hence regarded as the effect of the law upon the subject and not as the cause of the law. Respect is properly the representation of a worth that thwarts my self-love. Hence respect is something that is regarded as an object of neither inclination nor fear, although it has at the same time something analogous to both. The object of respect is, therefore, nothing but the law—indeed that very law which we impose on ourselves and yet recognize as necessary in itself. As a law, we are subject to it without consulting self-love; as imposed on us by ourselves, it is a consequence of our will. In the former aspect, it is analogous to fear; in the latter, to inclination. All respect for a person is properly only respect for the law (of honesty, etc.) of which the person provides an example. Since we regard the development of our talents as a duty, we think of a man of talent as being also a kind of example of the law (the law of becoming like him by practice), and that is what constitutes our respect for him. All so-called moral interest consists solely in respect for the law.

[15][This is the first time in the *Grounding* that the categorical imperative is stated.]

to other people who would not believe what I professed, or if they over-hastily did believe, then they would pay me back in like coin. Therefore, my maxim would necessarily destroy itself just as soon as it was made a universal law.[16]

Therefore, I need no far-reaching acuteness to discern what I have to do in order that my will may be morally good. Inexperienced in the course of the world and incapable of being prepared for all its contingencies, I only ask myself whether I can also will that my maxim should become a universal law. If not, then the maxim must be rejected, not because of any disadvantage accruing to me or even to others, but because it cannot be fitting as a principle in a possible legislation of universal law, and reason exacts from me immediate respect for such legislation. Indeed I have as yet no insight into the grounds of such respect (which the philosopher may investigate). But I at least understand that respect is an estimation of a worth that far outweighs any worth of what is recommended by inclination, and that the necessity of acting from pure respect for the practical law is what constitutes duty, to which every other motive must give way because duty is the condition of a will good in itself, whose worth is above all else . . .

Second Section Transition from Popular Moral Philosophy to a Metaphysics of Morals

. . . Everything in nature works according to laws. Only a rational being has the power to act according to his conception of laws, i.e., according to principles, and thereby has he a will. Since the derivation of actions from laws requires reason, the will is nothing but practical reason. If reason infallibly determines the will, then in the case of such a being actions which are recognized to be objectively necessary are also subjectively necessary, i.e., the will is a faculty of choosing only that which reason, independently of inclination, recognizes as being practically necessary, i.e., as good. But if reason of itself does not sufficiently determine the will, and if the will submits also to subjective conditions (certain incentives) which do not always agree with objective conditions; in a word, if the will does not in itself completely accord with reason (as is actually the case with men), then actions which are recognized as objectively necessary are subjectively contingent, and the determination of such a will according to objective laws is necessitation. That is to say that the relation of objective laws to a will not thoroughly good is represented as the determination of the will of a rational being by principles of reason which the will does not necessarily follow because of its own nature.

The representation of an objective principle insofar as it necessitates the will is called a command (of reason), and the formula of the command is called an imperative.

All imperatives are expressed by an *ought* and thereby indicate the relation of an objective law of reason to a will that is not necessarily determined by this law because of its subjective constitution (the relation of necessitation). Imperatives say that something would be good to do or to refrain from doing, but they say it to a will that does not always therefore do something simply because it has been represented to the will as something good to do. That is practically good which determines the will by means of representations of reason and hence not by subjective causes, but objectively, i.e., on grounds valid for every rational being as such. It is distinguished from the pleasant as that which influences the will only by means of sensation from merely subjective causes, which hold only for this or that person's senses but do not hold as a principle of reason valid for everyone.[1]

[16][This means that when you tell a lie, you merely take exception to the general rule that says everyone should always tell the truth and believe that what you are saying is true. When you lie, you do not thereby will that everyone else lie and not believe that what you are saying is true, because in such a case your lie would never work to get you what you want.]

[1]The dependence of the faculty of desire on sensations is called inclination, which accordingly always indicates a need. The dependence of a contingently determinable will on principles of reason, however, is called interest. Therefore an interest is found only in a dependent will which is not of itself always in accord with reason; in the divine will no interest can be thought. But even the human will can take an interest in something without thereby acting from

A perfectly good will would thus be quite as much subject to objective laws (of the good), but could not be conceived as thereby necessitated to act in conformity with law, inasmuch as it can of itself, according to its subjective constitution, be determined only by the representation of the good. Therefore no imperatives hold for the divine will, and in general for a holy will; the *ought* is here out of place, because the *would* is already of itself necessarily in agreement with the law. Consequently, imperatives are only formulas for expressing the relation of objective laws of willing in general to the subjective imperfection of the will of this or that rational being, e.g., the human will.

Now all imperatives command either hypothetically or categorically. The former represent the practical necessity of a possible action as a means for attaining something else that one wants (or may possibly want). The categorical imperative would be one which represented an action as objectively necessary in itself, without reference to another end.

Every practical law represents a possible action as good and hence as necessary for a subject who is practically determinable by reason; therefore all imperatives are formulas for determining an action which is necessary according to the principle of a will that is good in some way. Now if the action would be good merely as a means to something else, so is the imperative hypothetical. But if the action is represented as good in itself, and hence as necessary in a will which of itself conforms to reason as the principle of the will, then the imperative is categorical.

An imperative thus says what action possible by me would be good, and it presents the practical rule in relation to a will which does not forthwith perform an action simply because it is good, partly because the subject does not always know that the action is good and partly because (even if he does know it is good) his maxims might yet be opposed to the objective principles of practical reason.

A hypothetical imperative thus says only that an action is good for some purpose, either possible or actual. In the first case it is a problematic practical principle; in the second case an assertoric one. A categorical imperative, which declares an action to be of itself objectively necessary without reference to any purpose, i.e., without any other end, holds as an apodeictic practical principle.

Whatever is possible only through the powers of some rational being can be thought of as a possible purpose of some will. Consequently, there are in fact infinitely many principles of action insofar as they are represented as necessary for attaining a possible purpose achievable by them. All sciences have a practical part consisting of problems saying that some end is possible for us and of imperatives telling us how it can be attained. These can, therefore, be called in general imperatives of skill. Here there is no question at all whether the end is reasonable and good, but there is only a question as to what must be done to attain it. The prescriptions needed by a doctor in order to make his patient thoroughly healthy and by a poisoner in order to make sure of killing his victim are of equal value so far as each serves to bring about its purpose perfectly. Since there cannot be known in early youth what ends may be presented to us in the course of life, parents especially seek to have their children learn many different kinds of things, and they provide for skill in the use of means to all sorts of arbitrary ends, among which they cannot determine whether any one of them could in the future become an actual purpose for their ward, though there is always the possibility that he might adopt it. Their concern is so great that they commonly neglect to form and correct their children's judgment regarding the worth of things which might be chosen as ends.

There is, however, one end that can be presupposed as actual for all rational beings (so far as they are dependent beings to whom imperatives apply); and thus there is one purpose which they not

interest. The former signifies practical interest in the action, while the latter signifies pathological interest in the object of the action. The former indicates only dependence of the will on principles of reason by itself, while the latter indicates the will's dependence on principles of reason for the sake of inclination, i.e., reason merely gives the practical rule for meeting the need of inclination. In the former case the action interests me, while in the latter case what interests me is the object of the action (so far as this object is pleasant for me). In the First Section we have seen that in the case of an action done from duty regard must be given not to the interest in the object, but only to interest in the action itself and in its rational principle (viz., the law).

merely can have but which can certainly be assumed to be such that they all do have by a natural necessity, and this is happiness. A hypothetical imperative which represents the practical necessity of an action as means for the promotion of happiness is assertoric. It may be expounded not simply as necessary to an uncertain, merely possible purpose, but as necessary to a purpose which can be presupposed a priori and with certainty as being present in everyone because it belongs to his essence. Now skill in the choice of means to one's own greatest well-being can be called prudence[2] in the narrowest sense. And thus the imperative that refers to the choice of means to one's own happiness, i.e., the precept of prudence, still remains hypothetical; the action is commanded not absolutely but only as a means to a further purpose.

Finally, there is one imperative which immediately commands a certain conduct without having as its condition any other purpose to be attained by it. This imperative is categorical. It is not concerned with the matter of the action and its intended result, but rather with the form of the action and the principle from which it follows; what is essentially good in the action consists in the mental disposition, let the consequences be what they may. This imperative may be called that of morality.

Willing according to these three kinds of principles is also clearly distinguished by dissimilarity in the necessitation of the will. To make this dissimilarity clear I think that they are most suitably named in their order when they are said to be either *rules of skill, counsels of prudence,* or *commands (laws) of morality.* For law alone involves the concept of a necessity that is unconditioned and indeed objective and hence universally valid, and commands are laws which must be obeyed, i.e., must be followed even in opposition to inclination. Counsel does indeed involve necessity, but involves such necessity as is valid only under a subjectively contingent condition, viz., whether this or that man counts this or that as belonging to his happiness. On the other hand, the categorical imperative is limited by no condition, and can quite properly be called a command since it is absolutely, though practically, necessary. The first kind of imperatives might also be called technical (belonging to art), the second kind pragmatic[3] (belonging to welfare), the third kind moral (belonging to free conduct as such, i.e., to morals).

The question now arises: how are all of these imperatives possible?[4] This question does not seek to know how the fulfillment of the action commanded by the imperative can be conceived, but merely how the necessitation of the will expressed by the imperative in setting a task can be conceived. How an imperative of skill is possible requires no special discussion. Whoever wills the end, wills (so far as reason has decisive influence on his actions) also the means that are indispensably necessary to his actions and that lie in his power. This proposition, as far as willing is concerned, is analytic. For in willing an object as my effect there is already thought the causality of myself as an acting cause, i.e., the use of means. The imperative derives the concept of actions necessary to this end from the concept of willing this end. (Synthetic propositions are indeed required for determining the means to a proposed end; but such propositions are concerned not with the ground, i.e., the act of the will, but only with the way to realize the object of the will.) Mathematics teaches by nothing but synthetic propositions that in order to bisect a line according to a sure principle I must from each of its extremities draw arcs such that they intersect. But when I know that the proposed result can come about only by means of such an action, then the proposition (if I fully will the

[2]The word "prudence" is used in a double sense: firstly, it can mean worldly wisdom, and, secondly, private wisdom. The former is the skill of someone in influencing others so as to use them for his own purposes. The latter is the sagacity to combine all these purposes for his own lasting advantage. The value of the former is properly reduced to the latter, and it might better be said of one who is prudent in the former sense but not in the latter that he is clever and cunning, but on the whole imprudent.

[3]It seems to me that the proper meaning of the word "pragmatic" could be defined most accurately in this way. For those sanctions are called pragmatic which properly flow not from the law of states as necessary enactments but from provision for the general welfare. A history is pragmatically written when it teaches prudence, i.e., instructs the world how it can provide for its interests better than, or at least as well as, has been done in former times.

[4][That is, why should one let his actions be determined at various times by one or the other of these three kinds of imperatives?]

effect, then I also will the action required for it) is analytic. For it is one and the same thing to conceive of something as an effect that is possible in a certain way through me and to conceive of myself as acting in the same way with regard to the aforesaid effect.

If it were only as easy to give a determinate concept of happiness, then the imperatives of prudence would exactly correspond to those of skill and would be likewise analytic. For there could be said in this case just as in the former that whoever wills the end also wills (necessarily according to reason) the sole means thereto which are in his power. But, unfortunately, the concept of happiness is such an indeterminate one that even though everyone wishes to attain happiness, yet he can never say definitely and consistently what it is that he really wishes and wills. The reason for this is that all the elements belonging to the concept of happiness are unexceptionally empirical, i.e., they must be borrowed from experience, while for the idea of happiness there is required an absolute whole, a maximum of well-being in my present and in every future condition. Now it is impossible for the most insightful and at the same time most powerful, but nonetheless finite, being to frame here a determinate concept of what it is that he really wills. Does he want riches? How much anxiety, envy, and intrigue might he not thereby bring down upon his own head! Or knowledge and insight? Perhaps these might only give him an eye that much sharper for revealing that much more dreadfully evils which are at present hidden but are yet unavoidable, or such an eye might burden him with still further needs for the desires which already concern him enough. Or long life? Who guarantees that it would not be a long misery? Or health at least? How often has infirmity of the body kept one from excesses into which perfect health would have allowed him to fall, and so on? In brief, he is not able on any principle to determine with complete certainty what will make him truly happy, because to do so would require omniscience. Therefore, one cannot act according to determinate principles in order to be happy, but only according to empirical counsels, e.g., of diet, frugality, politeness, reserve, etc., which are shown by experience to contribute on the average the most to well-being. There follows from this that imperatives of prudence, strictly speaking, cannot command at all, i.e., present actions objectively as practically necessary. They are to be taken as counsels (*consilia*) rather than as commands (*praecepta*) of reason. The problem of determining certainly and universally what action will promote the happiness of a rational being is completely insoluble. Therefore, regarding such action no imperative that in the strictest sense could command what is to be done to make one happy is possible, inasmuch as happiness is not an ideal of reason but of imagination. Such an ideal rests merely on empirical grounds; in vain can there be expected that such grounds should determine an action whereby the totality of an infinite series of consequences could be attained. This imperative of prudence would, nevertheless, be an analytic practical proposition if one assumes that the means to happiness could with certainty be assigned; for it differs from the imperative of skill only in that for it the end is given while for the latter the end is merely possible. Since both, however, command only the means to what is assumed to be willed as an end, the imperative commanding him who wills the end to will likewise the means thereto is in both cases analytic. Hence there is also no difficulty regarding the possibility of an imperative of prudence.

On the other hand, the question as to how the imperative of morality is possible is undoubtedly the only one requiring a solution. For it is not at all hypothetical; and hence the objective necessity which it presents cannot be based on any presupposition, as was the case with the hypothetical imperatives. Only there must never here be forgotten that no example can show, i.e., empirically, whether there is any such imperative at all. Rather, care must be taken lest all imperatives which are seemingly categorical may nevertheless be covertly hypothetical. For instance, when it is said that you should not make a false promise, the assumption is that the necessity of this avoidance is no mere advice for escaping some other evil, so that it might be said that you should not make a false promise lest you ruin your credit when the falsity comes to light. But when it is asserted that an action of this kind must be regarded as bad in itself, then the imperative of prohibition is therefore categorical.

Nevertheless, it cannot with certainty be shown by means of an example that the will is here determined solely by the law without any other incentive, even though such may seem to be the case. For it is always possible that secretly there is fear of disgrace and perhaps also obscure dread of other dangers; such fear and dread may have influenced the will. Who can prove by experience that a cause is not present? Experience only shows that a cause is not perceived. But in such a case the so-called moral imperative, which as such appears to be categorical and unconditioned, would actually be only a pragmatic precept which makes us pay attention to our own advantage and merely teaches us to take such advantage into consideration.

We shall, therefore, have to investigate the possibility of a categorical imperative entirely a priori, inasmuch as we do not here have the advantage of having its reality given in experience and consequently of thus being obligated merely to explain its possibility rather than to establish it. In the meantime so much can be seen for now: the categorical imperative alone purports to be a practical law, while all the others may be called principles of the will but not laws. The reason for this is that whatever is necessary merely in order to attain some arbitrary purpose can be regarded as in itself contingent, and the precept can always be ignored once the purpose is abandoned. Contrariwise, an unconditioned command does not leave the will free to choose the opposite at its own liking. Consequently, only such a command carries with it that necessity which is demanded from a law.

Secondly, in the case of this categorical imperative, or law of morality, the reason for the difficulty (of discerning its possibility) is quite serious. The categorical imperative is an a priori synthetic practical proposition;[5] and since discerning the possibility of propositions of this sort involves so much difficulty in theoretic knowledge, there may readily be gathered that there will be no less difficulty in practical knowledge.

In solving this problem, we want first to inquire whether perhaps the mere concept of a categorical imperative may not also supply us with the formula containing the proposition that can alone be a categorical imperative. For even when we know the purport of such an absolute command, the question as to how it is possible will still require a special and difficult effort. . . .

If I think of a hypothetical imperative in general, I do not know beforehand what it will contain until its condition is given. But if I think of a categorical imperative, I know immediately what it contains. For since, besides the law, the imperative contains only the necessity that the maxim[6] should accord with this law, while the law contains no condition to restrict it, there remains nothing but the universality of a law as such with which the maxim of the action should conform. This conformity alone is properly what is represented as necessary by the imperative.

Hence there is only one categorical imperative and it is this: Act only according to that maxim whereby you can at the same time will that it should become a universal law.[7] . . .

The will is thought of as a faculty of determining itself to action in accordance with the representation of certain laws, and such a faculty can be found only in rational beings. Now what serves the will as the objective ground of its self-determination is an end; and if this end is given by reason alone, then it must be equally valid for all rational beings. On the other hand, what contains merely the ground of the possibility of the action, whose effect is an end, is called the means. The subjective

[5]I connect a priori, and therefore necessarily, the act with the will without presupposing any condition taken from some inclination (though I make such a connection only objectively, i.e., under the idea of a reason having full power over all subjective motives). Hence this is a practical proposition which does not analytically derive the willing of an action from some other willing already presupposed (for we possess no such perfect will) but which connects the willing of an action immediately with the concept of the will of a rational being as something which is not contained in this concept.

[6]A maxim is the subjective principle of acting and must be distinguished from the objective principle, viz., the practical law. A maxim contains the practical rule which reason determines in accordance with the conditions of the subject (often his ignorance or his inclinations) and is thus the principle according to which the subject does act. But the law is the objective principle valid for every rational being, and it is the principle according to which he ought to act, i.e., an imperative.

[7][This formulation of the categorical imperative is often referred to as the formula of universal law.]

ground of desire is the incentive; the objective ground of volition is the motive. Hence there arises the distinction between subjective ends, which rest on incentives, and objective ends, which depend on motives valid for every rational being. Practical principles are formal when they abstract from all subjective ends; they are material, however, when they are founded upon subjective ends, and hence upon certain incentives. The ends which a rational being arbitrarily proposes to himself as effects of this action (material ends) are all merely relative, for only their relation to a specially constituted faculty of desire in the subject gives them their worth. Consequently, such worth cannot provide any universal principles, which are valid and necessary for all rational beings and, furthermore, are valid for every volition, i.e., cannot provide any practical laws. Therefore, all such relative ends can be grounds only for hypothetical imperatives.

But let us suppose that there were something whose existence has in itself an absolute worth, something which as an end in itself could be a ground of determinate laws. In it, and in it alone, would there be the ground of a possible categorical imperative, i.e., of a practical law.

Now I say that man, and in general every rational being, exists as an end in himself and not merely as a means to be arbitrarily used by this or that will. He must in all his actions, whether directed to himself or to other rational beings, always be regarded at the same time as an end. All the objects of inclinations have only a conditioned value; for if there were not these inclinations and the needs founded on them, then their object would be without value. But the inclinations themselves, being sources of needs, are so far from having an absolute value such as to render them desirable for their own sake that the universal wish of every rational being must be, rather, to be wholly free from them. Accordingly, the value of any object obtainable by our action is always conditioned. Beings whose existence depends not on our will but on nature have, nevertheless, if they are not rational beings, only a relative value as means and are therefore called things. On the other hand, rational beings are called persons inasmuch as their nature already marks them out as ends in themselves, i.e., as something which is not to be used merely as means and hence there is imposed thereby a limit on all arbitrary use of such beings, which are thus objects of respect. Persons are, therefore, not merely subjective ends, whose existence as an effect of our actions has a value for us; but such beings are objective ends, i.e., exist as ends in themselves. Such an end is one for which there can be substituted no other end to which such beings should serve merely as means, for otherwise nothing at all of absolute value would be found anywhere. But if all value were conditioned and hence contingent, then no supreme practical principle could be found for reason at all.

If then there is to be supreme practical principle and, as far as the human will is concerned, a categorical imperative, then it must be such that from the conception of what is necessarily an end for everyone because this end is an end in itself it constitutes an objective principle of the will and can hence serve as a practical law. The ground of such a principle is this: rational nature exists as an end in itself. In this way man necessarily thinks of his own existence; thus far is it a subjective principle of human actions. But in this way also does every other rational being think of his existence on the same rational ground that holds also for me;[8] hence it is at the same time an objective principle, from which, as a supreme practical ground, all laws of the will must be able to be derived. The practical imperative will therefore be the following: Act in such a way that you treat humanity, whether in your own person or in the person of another, always at the same time as an end and never simply as a means.[9] . . .

This principle of humanity and of every rational nature generally as an end in itself is the supreme limiting condition of every man's freedom of action. This principle is not borrowed from experience, first, because of its universality, inasmuch as it applies to all rational beings generally, and no experience is capable of determining anything about them; and, secondly, because in experience

[8]This proposition I here put forward as a postulate. The grounds for it will be found in the last section.

[9][This often-quoted version of the categorical imperative is usually referred to as the formula of the end in itself.]

(subjectively) humanity is not thought of as the end of men, i.e., as an object that we of ourselves actually make our end which as a law ought to constitute the supreme limiting condition of all subjective ends (whatever they may be); and hence this principle must arise from pure reason [and not from experience]. That is to say that the ground of all practical legislation lies objectively in the rule and in the form of universality, which (according to the first principle) makes the rule capable of being a law (say, for example, a law of nature). Subjectively, however, the ground of all practical legislation lies in the end; but (according to the second principle) the subject of all ends is every rational being as an end in himself. From this there now follows the third practical principle of the will as the supreme condition of the will's conformity with universal practical reason, viz., the idea of the will of every rational being as a will that legislates universal law.[10]

According to this principle all maxims are rejected which are not consistent with the will's own legislation of universal law. The will is thus not merely subject to the law but is subject to the law in such a way that it must be regarded also as legislating for itself and only on this account as being subject to the law (of which it can regard itself as the author).

In the previous formulations of imperatives, viz., that based on the conception of the conformity of actions to universal law in a way similar to a natural order and that based on the universal prerogative of rational beings as ends in themselves, these imperatives just because they were thought of as categorical excluded from their legislative authority all admixture of any interest as an incentive. They were, however, only assumed to be categorical because such an assumption had to be made if the concept of duty was to be explained. But that there were practical propositions which commanded categorically could not itself be proved, nor can it be proved anywhere in this section. But one thing could have been done, viz., to indicate that in willing from duty the renunciation of all interest is the specific mark distinguishing a categorical imperative from a hypothetical one and that such renunciation was expressed in the imperative itself by means of some determination contained in it. This is done in the present (third) formulation of the principle, namely, in the idea of the will of every rational being as a will that legislates universal law.

When such a will is thought of, then even though a will which is subject to law may be bound to this law by means of some interest, nevertheless a will that is itself a supreme lawgiver is not able as such to depend on any interest. For a will which is so dependent would itself require yet another law restricting the interest of its self-love to the condition that such interest should itself be valid as a universal law.

Thus the principle that every human will as a will that legislates universal law in all its maxims,[11] provided it is otherwise correct, would be well suited to being a categorical imperative in the following respect: just because of the idea of legislating universal law such an imperative is not based on any interest, and therefore it alone of all possible imperatives can be unconditional. Or still better, the proposition being converted, if there is a categorical imperative (i.e., a law for the will of every rational being), then it can only command that everything be done from the maxim of such a will as could at the same time have as its object only itself regarded as legislating universal law. For only then are the practical principle and the imperative which the will obeys unconditional, inasmuch as the will can be based on no interest at all.

When we look back upon all previous attempts that have been made to discover the principle of morality, there is no reason now to wonder why they one and all had to fail. Man was viewed as bound to laws by his duty; but it was not seen that man is subject only to his own, yet universal, legislation and that he is bound only to act in accordance with his own will, which is, however, a will purposed by nature to legislate universal laws. For when man is thought as being merely subject to a

[10][This is usually called the formula of autonomy.]

[11]I may here be excused from citing instances to elucidate this principle inasmuch as those which were first used to elucidate the categorical imperative and its formula can all serve the same purpose here.

law (whatever it might be), then the law had to carry with it some interest functioning as an attracting stimulus or as a constraining force for obedience, inasmuch as the law did not arise as a law from his own will. Rather, in order that his will conform with law, it had to be necessitated by something else to act in a certain way. By this absolutely necessary conclusion, however, all the labor spent in finding a supreme ground for duty was irretrievably lost; duty was never discovered, but only the necessity of acting from a certain interest. This might be either one's own interest or another's, but either way the imperative had to be always conditional and could never possibly serve as a moral command. I want, therefore, to call my principle the principle of the autonomy of the will, in contrast with every other principle, which I accordingly count under heteronomy.

The concept of every rational being as one who must regard himself as legislating universal law by all his will's maxims, so that he may judge himself and his actions from this point of view, leads to another very fruitful concept, which depends on the aforementioned one, viz., that of a kingdom of ends.

By "kingdom" I understand a systematic union of different rational beings through common laws. Now laws determine ends as regards their universal validity; therefore, if one abstracts from the personal differences of rational beings and also from all content of their private ends, then it will be possible to think of a whole of all ends in systematic connection (a whole both of rational being as ends in themselves and also of the particular ends which each may set for himself); that is, one can think of a kingdom of ends that is possible on the aforesaid principles.

For all rational beings stand under the law that each of them should treat himself and all others never merely as means but always at the same time as an end in himself. Hereby arises a systematic union of rational beings through common objective laws, i.e., a kingdom that may be called a kingdom of ends (certainly only an ideal), inasmuch as these laws have in view the very relation of such beings to one another as ends and means.[12]

A rational being belongs to the kingdom of ends as a member when he legislates in it universal laws while also being himself subject to these laws. He belongs to it as sovereign, when as legislator he is himself subject to the will of no other.

A rational being must always regard himself as legislator in a kingdom of ends rendered possible by freedom of the will, whether as member or as sovereign. The position of the latter can be maintained not merely through the maxims of his will but only if he is a completely independent being without needs and with unlimited power adequate to his will.

Hence morality consists in the relation of all action to that legislation whereby alone a kingdom of ends is possible. This legislation must be found in every rational being and must be able to arise from his will, whose principle then is never to act on any maxim except such as can also be a universal law and hence such as the will can thereby regard itself as at the same time the legislator of universal law. If now the maxims do not by their very nature already necessarily conform with this objective principle of rational beings as legislating universal laws, then the necessity of acting on that principle is called practical necessitation, i.e., duty. Duty does not apply to the sovereign in the kingdom of ends, but it does apply to every member and to each in the same degree.

The practical necessity of acting according to this principle, i.e., duty, does not rest at all on feelings, impulses, and inclinations, but only on the relation of rational beings to one another, a relation in which the will of a rational being must always be regarded at the same time as legislative, because otherwise he could not be thought of as an end in himself. Reason, therefore, relates every maxim of the will as legislating universal laws to every other will and also to every action toward oneself; it does so not on account of any other practical motive or future advantage but rather from the idea of the dignity of a rational being who obeys no law except what he at the same time enacts himself.

In the kingdom of ends everything has either a price or a dignity. Whatever has a price can be replaced by something else as its equivalent; on the other hand, whatever is above all price, and therefore admits of no equivalent, has a dignity.

[12][This is usually called the formula of the kingdom of ends.]

Whatever has reference to general human inclinations and needs has a market price; whatever, without presupposing any need, accords with a certain taste, i.e., a delight in the mere unpurposive play of our mental powers,[13] has an affective price; but that which constitutes the condition under which alone something can be an end in itself has not merely a relative worth, i.e., a price, but has an intrinsic worth, i.e., dignity.

Now morality is the condition under which alone a rational being can be an end in himself, for only thereby can he be a legislating member in the kingdom of ends. Hence morality and humanity, insofar as it is capable of morality, alone have dignity. Skill and diligence in work have a market price; wit, lively imagination, and humor have an affective price; but fidelity to promises and benevolence based on principles (not on instinct) have intrinsic worth. Neither nature nor art contain anything which in default of these could be put in their place; for their worth consists, not in the effects which arise from them, nor in the advantage and profit which they provide, but in mental dispositions, i.e., in the maxims of the will which are ready in this way to manifest themselves in action, even if they are not favored with success. Such actions also need no recommendation from any subjective disposition or taste so as to meet with immediate favor and delight; there is no need of any immediate propensity or feeling toward them. They exhibit the will performing them as an object of immediate respect; and nothing but reason is required to impose them upon the will, which is not to be cajoled into them, since in the case of duties such cajoling would be a contradiction. This estimation, therefore, lets the worth of such a disposition be recognized as dignity and puts it infinitely beyond all price, with which it cannot in the least be brought into competition or comparison without, as it were, violating its sanctity.

What then is it that entitles the morally good disposition, or virtue, to make such lofty claims? It is nothing less than the share which such a disposition affords the rational being of legislating universal laws, so that he is fit to be a member in a possible kingdom of ends, for which his own nature has already determined him as an end in himself and therefore as a legislator in the kingdom of ends. Thereby is he free as regards all laws of nature, and he obeys only those laws which he gives to himself. Accordingly, his maxims can belong to a universal legislation to which he at the same time subjects himself. For nothing can have any worth other than what the law determines. But the legislation itself which determines all worth must for that very reason have dignity, i.e., unconditional and incomparable worth; and the word "respect" alone provides a suitable expression for the esteem which a rational being must have for it. Hence autonomy is the ground of the dignity of human nature and of every rational nature. . . .

Study Questions

1. Explain why Kant thinks that the only thing that can be called good without qualification is a good will. Why does he hold that even happiness is not as high a good as a good will?

2. Why, according to Kant, does an action have moral worth only if it is done from duty? Why does he maintain that a kind or generous action has no moral worth if it is done by someone who acts that way because he or she finds satisfaction in spreading joy? Does he mean that such acts should not be praised or encouraged?

3. What does Kant mean by saying that the moral worth of an action done from duty does not lie in the *purpose* which is to be achieved through the action but in the *maxim* by which the action is determined?

[13][See Kant, *Critique of Aesthetic Judgment,* §'s 1–5.]

4. According to Kant, you could not be content to hold as a universal law the maxim that it is all right to extricate yourself from a difficulty by making a false promise. Why couldn't you be content to hold this maxim to be a universal law?
5. Explain the difference between hypothetical and categorical imperatives. Which of these, according to Kant, can command morally, and why?
6. Why, according to Kant, must we always act so that we treat rational beings always as ends and never as a means only?
7. What does Kant mean by a realm of ends?
8. "Autonomy is thus the basis of the dignity of both human nature and every rational nature." What does this mean?

The Utilitarians

Whereas Kant believed that the only thing that can be taken as good without qualification is a good will, the utilitarians, whose most famous exponents were Jeremy Bentham (1748–1832) and John Stuart Mill (1806–1873) said that the only thing that can be taken as good without qualification is happiness. The principle of utility, as explained by Bentham, is "the principle which approves or disapproves of every action whatsoever, according to the tendency which it appears to have to augment or diminish the happiness of the party whose interest is in question: . . . if that party be the community in general then the happiness of the community: if a particular individual, then the happiness of that individual."

But should we approve an action if it promotes an individual's happiness but not the community's (or does the reverse)? Bentham makes it clear elsewhere that it is primarily the happiness of the community that is to be promoted in accordance with the utility principle. Should we promote the average happiness or the total happiness of the community? This too is unclear. There is a difference: If by having a child a couple would raise the total happiness of the community (by adding another person to it) but would not increase the average happiness, does Bentham's principle tell them to have the child? And which is better, on Bentham's principle, a smaller community of very happy people or a larger community of less happy people?

What is not ambiguous about Bentham's utility principle is that intentions count for nothing, morally speaking. This is true of all forms of utilitarianism. What counts is results or consequences. (Utilitarianism is thus a type of *consequentialism.* Consequentialists evaluate the moral worth of actions on the basis of their consequences). Even a malicious or mean-spirited act, according to this philosophy, is morally better than a well-intentioned act if it happens to produce more happiness. In all cases, said Bentham, the morally best act is the one that produces, compared to all possible alternative acts, the greatest amount of happiness.

Utilitarianism may not seem to you to be a new philosophy, since the Epicureans and Stoics and even Aristotle, Augustine, and Aquinas all favored pursuing happiness. But when Bentham said that the best act is the one that produces the most happiness, he meant the most happiness *generally*, the most happiness *with everyone considered.* Thus utilitarianism is popularly, but unfortunately, described as the philosophy that "you should act so as to promote the greatest happiness of the greatest number." As we explained in Chapter 5, however, this catchy phrase is actually incoherent. It treats what in fact are two independent variables as if they were a single thing.

For Bentham, happiness consists entirely in *pleasure*, and *ought*, *right*, *good*, and similar terms have meaning only when they are defined in terms of pleasure. "Nature has placed mankind under the governance of two sovereign masters," he wrote, "*pain* and *pleasure.* It is for them alone to point out what we ought to do, as well as determine what we shall do."

Bentham also thought that to determine which of two or more acts is morally the best, you should consider only the *amount* of pleasure the acts will produce. He developed a "calculus" of pleasure and pain by which this might be done objectively. If a society gets even just a little bit more pleasure from reading gross pornography than from reading fine literature, then by all means, according to Bentham, let it have pornography.

Notice too that Bentham's utilitarianism is what in Chapter 5 we called act-utilitarianism: the rightness of an act is determined by its effect on the general happiness. In other words, by Bentham's principle we are to evaluate the moral correctness of actions by their effect on the general happiness.

John Stuart Mill, the other great classic utilitarian (and Bentham's godson) also subscribes to act-utilitarianism in some passages: "actions are right in proportion as they tend to promote happiness; wrong as they tend to produce the reverse of happiness." But in other passages, Mill seems to advocate what in Chapter 5 we called rule-utilitarianism, according to which we are to evaluate the moral correctness of an action, *not* with reference to its effect on the general happiness, but with reference to the effect on the general happiness of the rule or principle that the action exemplifies. In other words, the rule-utilitarian tries to determine the effect of rules of conduct on the general happiness and then act in accordance with the rules that would maximize the general happiness. Suppose, for instance, that by murdering Moore, Stewart increases the general happiness: Moore, we shall assume, is an obnoxious blight whose passing absolutely no one will regret. Act-utilitarianism would dictate that Stewart murder Moore. But if society were to accept murder as a rule of conduct, ultimately the general happiness would be diminished; therefore, rule-utilitarianism would not condone Stewart's action.

Mill also held, in contrast with Bentham, that some pleasures are *inherently* better than others. Such pleasures are to be preferred even over a greater amount of pleasure of a lower quality, according to Mill's version of utilitarianism. Which pleasures are the superior ones? Given two pleasures, if most of the people who have experienced both prefer one to the other, the first is of higher quality, Mill said.

Mill's conception of happiness is more sophisticated, or at least more complicated, than Bentham's. Happiness does not consist in ongoing rapture, according to Mill, but in "moments of such, in an existence made up of few and transitory pains, many and various pleasures, with a decided predominance of the active over the passive, and having as the foundation of the whole not to expect more from life than it is capable of bestowing."

The selections that follow are from Bentham's *Principles of Morals and Legislation* and Mill's *Utilitarianism.*

from *An Introduction to the Principles of Morals and Legislation*

Jeremy Bentham

Jeremy Bentham (1748–1832) devoted his life to reforming English law, and many important nineteenth-century legal and social reforms were due to his influence. Reprinted here are chapters I, III, IV, and X of the 1823 edition of his *Introduction to the Principles of Morals and Legislation*, first published in 1789. We have omitted some of Bentham's footnotes.

Chapter I
Of the Principle of Utility

I. Nature has placed mankind under the governance of two sovereign masters, *pain* and *pleasure*. It is for them alone to point out what we ought to do, as well as to determine what we shall do. On the one hand the standard of right and wrong, on the other chain of causes and effects, are fastened to their throne. They govern us in all we do, in all we say, in all we think: every effort we can make to throw off our subjection, will serve but to demonstrate and confirm it. In words a man may pretend to abjure their empire: but in reality he will remain subject to it all the while. The *principle of utility** recognizes this subjection, and assumes it for the foundation of that system, the object of which is to rear the fabric of felicity by the hands of reason and of law. Systems which attempt to question it, deal in sounds instead of sense, in caprice instead of reason, in darkness instead of light.

But enough of metaphor and declamation: it is not by such means that moral science is to be improved.

II. The principle of utility is the foundation of the present work: it will be proper therefore at the outset to given an explicit and determinate account of what is meant by it. By the principle of utility is meant that principle which approves or disapproves of every action whatsoever, according to the tendency which it appears to have to augment or diminish the happiness of the party whose interest is in question: or, what is the same thing in other words, to promote or to oppose that happiness. I say of every action whatsoever; and therefore not only of every action of a private individual, but of every measure of government.

III. By utility is meant that property in any object, whereby it tends to produce benefit, advantage, pleasure, good, or happiness, (all this in the present case comes to the same thing) or (what comes again to the same thing) to prevent the happening of mischief, pain, evil, or unhappiness to the party whose interest is considered: if that party be the community in general, then the happiness of the community: if a particular individual, then the happiness of that individual.

IV. The interest of the community is one of the most general expressions that can occur in the phraseology of morals: no wonder that the meaning of it is often lost. When it has a meaning, it is this. The community is a fictitious *body*, composed of the individual persons who are considered as constituting as it were its *members*. The interest of the community then is, what?—the sum of the interests of the several members who compose it.

*Note by the Author, July 1822.

To this denomination has of late been added, or substituted, the *greatest happiness or greatest felicity* principle: this for shortness, instead of saying at length *that principle* which states the greatest happiness of all those whose interest is in question, as being the right and proper, and only right and proper and universally desirable, end of human action: of human action in every situation, and in particular in that of a functionary or set of functionaries exercising the powers of Government. The word *utility* does not so clearly point to the ideas of *pleasure* and *pain* as the words *happiness* and *felicity* do: nor does it lead us to the consideration of the *number*, of the interests affected; to the number, as being the circumstance, which contributes, in the largest proportion, to the formation of the standard here in question; the *standard of right and wrong*, by which alone the propriety of human conduct, in every situation can with propriety be tried. This want of a sufficiently manifest connexion between the ideas of *happiness* and *pleasure* on the one hand, and the idea of *utility* on the other, I have every now and then found operating, and with but too much efficiency, as a bar to the acceptance, that might otherwise have been given, to this principle.

V. It is in vain to talk of the interest of the community, without understanding what is the interest of the individual.* A thing is said to promote the interest, or to be *for* the interest, of an individual, when it tends to add to the sum total of his pleasures: or, what comes to the same thing, to diminish the sum total of his pains.

VI. An action then may be said to be conformable to the principle of utility, or, for shortness sake, to utility, (meaning with respect to the community at large) when the tendency it has to augment the happiness of the community is greater than any which it has to diminish it.

VII. A measure of government (which is but a particular kind of action, performed by a particular person or persons) may be said to be conformable to or dictated by the principle of utility, when in like manner the tendency which it has to augment the happiness of the community is greater than any which it has to diminish it.

VIII. When an action, or in particular a measure of government, is supposed by a man to be conformable to the principle of utility, it may be convenient, for the purposes of discourse, to imagine a kind of law or dictate, called a law or dictate of utility: and to speak of the action in question, as being conformable to such law or dictate.

IX. A man may be said to be a partizan of the principle of utility, when the approbation or disapprobation he annexes to any action, or to any measure, is determined by and proportioned to the tendency which he conceive it to have to augment or to diminish the happiness of the community: or in other words, to its conformity or unconformity to the laws or dictates of utility.

X. Of an action that is conformable to the principle of utility one may always say either that it is one that ought to be done, or at least that it is not one that ought not to be done. One may say also, that it is right it should be done; at least that it is not wrong it should be done: that it is a right action; at least that it is not a wrong action. When thus interpreted, the words *ought*, and *right* and *wrong*, and others of that stamp, have a meaning: when otherwise, they have none.

*Interest is one of those words, which not having any superior *genus,* cannot in the ordinary way be defined.

XI. Has the rectitude of this principle been ever formally contested? It should seem that it had, by those who have not known what they have been meaning. Is it susceptible of any direct proof? It should seem not: for that which is used to prove every thing else, cannot itself be proved: a chain of proofs must have their commencement somewhere. To give such proof is as impossible as it is needless.

XII. Not that there is or ever has been that human creature breathing, however stupid or perverse, who has not on many, perhaps on most occasions of his life, deferred to it. By the natural constitution of the human frame, on most occasions of their lives men in general embrace this principle, without thinking of it: if not for the ordering of their own actions, yet for the trying of their own actions, as well as those of other men. There have been, at the same time, not many, perhaps, even of the most intelligent, who have been disposed to embrace it purely and without reserve. There are even few who have not taken some occasion or other to quarrel with it, either on account of their not understanding always how to apply it, or on account of some prejudice or other which they were afraid to examine into, or could not bear to part with. For such is the stuff that man is made of: in principle and in practice, in a right track and in a wrong one, the rarest of all human qualities is consistency.

XIII. When a man attempts to combat the principle of utility, it is with reasons drawn, without his being aware of it, from that very principle itself. His arguments, if they prove any thing, prove not that the principle is *wrong*, but that, according to the applications he supposes to be made of it, it is *misapplied.* Is it possible for a man to move the earth? Yes; but he must first find out another earth to stand upon.

XIV. To disprove the propriety of it by arguments is impossible; but, from the causes that have been mentioned, or from some confused or partial view of it, a man may happen to be disposed not to relish it. Where this is the case, if he thinks the settling of his opinions on such a subject worth the trouble, let him take the following steps, and at length, perhaps, he may come to reconcile himself to it.

1. Let him settle with himself, whether he would wish to discard this principle altogether; if so, let him consider what it is that all his reasonings (in matters of politics especially) can amount to?
2. If he would, let him settle with himself, whether he would judge and act without any principle, or whether there is any other he would judge and act by?
3. If there be, let him examine and satisfy himself whether the principle he thinks he has found is really any separate intelligible principle; or whether it be not a mere principle in words, a kind of phrase, which at bottom expresses neither more nor less than the mere averment of his own unfounded sentiments; that is, what in another person he might be apt to call caprice?
4. If he is inclined to think that his own approbation or disapprobation, annexed to the idea of an act, without any regard to its consequences, is a sufficient foundation for him to judge and act upon, let him ask himself whether his sentiment is to be a standard of right and wrong, with respect to every other man, or whether every man's sentiment has the same privilege of being a standard to itself?
5. In the first case, let him ask himself whether his principle is not despotical, and hostile to all the rest of the human race?
6. In the second case, whether it is not anarchical, and whether at this rate there are not as many different standards of right and wrong as there are men? and whether even to the same man, the same thing, which is right today, may not (without the least change in its nature) be wrong tomorrow? and whether the same thing is not right and wrong in the same place at the same time? and in either case, whether all argument is not at an end? and whether, when two men have said, "I like this," and "I don't like it," they can (upon such a principle) have any thing more to say?
7. If he should have said to himself, No: for that the sentiment which he proposes as a standard must be grounded on reflection, let him say on what particulars the reflection is to turn? if on particulars having relation to the utility of the act, then let him say whether this is not deserting his own principle, and borrowing assistance from that very one in opposition to which he sets it up: or if not on those particulars, on what other particulars?
8. If he should be for compounding the matter, and adopting his own principle in part, and the principle of utility in part, let him say how far he will adopt it?
9. When he has settled with himself where he will stop, then let him ask himself how he justifies to himself the adopting it so far? and why he will not adopt it any farther?
10. Admitting any other principle than the principle of utility to be a right principle, a principle that it is right for a man to pursue; admitting (what is not true) that the word *right* can have a meaning without reference to utility, let him say whether there is any such thing as a *motive* that a man can have to pursue the dictates of it: if there is, let him say what that motive is, and how it is to be distinguished from those which enforce the dictates of utility: if not, then lastly let him say what it is this other principle can be good for?

Chapter III Of the Four Sanctions or Sources of Pain and Pleasure

I. It has been shown that the happiness of the individuals, of whom a community is composed, that is their pleasures and their security, is the end and the sole end which the legislator ought to have in view: the sole standard, in conformity to which each individual ought, as far as depends upon the legislator, to be *made* to fashion his behaviour. But whether it be this or any thing else that is to be *done,* there is nothing by which a man can ultimately be *made* to do it, but either pain or pleasure. Having taken a general view of these two grand objects (viz. pleasure, and what comes to the same thing, immunity from pain) in the character of *final* causes; it will be necessary to take a view of pleasure and pain itself, in the character of *efficient* causes or means.

II. There are four distinguishable sources from which pleasure and pain are in use to flow: considered separately, they may be termed the *physical,* the *political,* the *moral,* and the *religious:* and inasmuch as the pleasures and pains belonging to each of them are capable of giving a binding force to any law or rule of conduct, they may all of them be termed sanctions.*

III. If it be in the present life, and from the ordinary course of nature, not purposely modified by the interposition of the will of any human being, nor by any extraordinary interposition of any superior invisible being, that the pleasure or the pain takes place or is expected, it may be said to issue from or to belong to the *physical sanction.*

IV. If at the hands of a *particular* person or set of persons in the community, who under names correspondent to that of *judge,* are chosen for the particular purpose of dispensing it, according to the will of the sovereign or supreme ruling power in the state, it may be said to issue from the *political sanction.*

V. If at the hands of such chance persons in the community, as the party in question may happen in the course of his life to have concerns with, according to each man's spontaneous disposition, and not according to any settled or concerted rule, it may be said to issue from the *moral* or *popular sanction.**

VI. If from the immediate hand of a superior invisible being, either in the present life, or in a future, it may be said to issue from the *religious sanction.*

VII. Pleasures or pains which may be expected to issue from the *physical, political,* or *moral* sanctions, must all of them be expected to be experienced, if ever, in the *present* life: those which may be expected to issue from the *religious* sanction, may be expected to be experienced either in the *present* life or in a *future.*

VIII. Those which can be experienced in the present life, can of course be no others than such as human nature in the course of the present life is susceptible of: and from each of these sources may flow all the pleasures or pains of which, in the course of the present life, human nature is susceptible. With regard to these then (with which alone we have in this place any concern) those of them which belong to any one of those sanctions, differ not ultimately in kind from those which belong to any one of the other three: the only difference there is among them lies in the circumstances that accompany their production. A suffering which befalls a man in the natural and spontaneous course of things, shall be styled, for instance, a *calamity;* in which case, if it be supposed to befall him through any imprudence of his, it may be styled a punishment issuing from the physical sanction. Now this same suffering, if inflicted by the law, will be what is commonly called a *punishment;* if incurred for want of any friendly assistance, which the misconduct, or supposed misconduct, of the sufferer has occasioned to be withholden, a punishment issuing from the *moral* sanction; if through the immediate interposition of a particular

*Sanctio, in Latin, was used to signify the *act of binding,* and, by a common grammatical transition, *any thing which serves to bind a man:* to wit, to the observance of such or such a mode of conduct. According to a Latin grammarian, the import of the word is derived by rather a far-fetched process (such as those commonly are, and in a great measure indeed must be, by which intellectual ideas are derived from sensible ones) from the word *sanguis,* blood: because, among the Romans, with a view to inculcate into the people a persuasion that such or such a mode of conduct would be rendered obligatory upon a man by the force of what I call the religious sanction (that is, that he would be made to suffer by the extraordinary interposition of some superior being, if he failed to observe the mode of conduct in question) certain ceremonies were contrived by the priests: in the course of which ceremonies the blood of victims was made use of.

A Sanction then is a source of obligatory powers or *motives:* that is, of *pains* and *pleasures;* which, according as they are connected with such or such modes of conduct, operate, and are indeed the only things which can operate, as *motives.*

*Better termed *popular,* as more directly indicative of its constituent cause; as likewise of its relation to the more common phrase *public opinion,* in French *opinion publique,* the name there given to that tutelary power, of which of late so much is said, and by which so much is done. The latter appellation is however unhappy and inexpressive; since if *opinion* is material, it is only in virtue of the influence it exercises over action, through the medium of the affections and the will.

providence, a punishment issuing from the religious sanction.

IX. A man's goods, or his person, are consumed by fire. If this happened to him by what is called an accident, it was a calamity; if by reason of his own imprudence (for instance, from his neglecting to put his candle out) it may be styled a punishment of the physical sanction: if it happened to him by the sentence of the political magistrate, a punishment belonging to the political sanction; that is, what is commonly called a punishment: if for want of any assistance which his *neighbour* withheld from him out of some dislike to his *moral* character, a punishment of the *moral* sanction: if by an immediate act of God's displeasure, manifested on account of some sin committed by him, or through any distraction of mind, occasioned by the dread of such displeasure, a punishment of the *religious* sanction.

X. As to such of the pleasures and pains belonging to the religious sanction, as regard a future life, of what kind these may be we cannot know. These lie not open to our observation. During the present life they are matter only of expectation: and, whether that expectation be derived from natural or revealed religion, the particular kind of pleasure or pain, if it be different from all those which lie open to our observation, is what we can have no idea of. The best ideas we can obtain of such pains and pleasures are altogether unliquidated in point of quality. In what other respects our ideas of them may be liquidated will be considered in another place.

XI. Of these four sanctions the physical is altogether, we may observe, the ground-work of the political and the moral: so is it also of the religious, in as far as the latter bears relation to the present life. It is included in each of those other three. This may operate in any case, (that is, any of the pains or pleasures belonging to it may operate) independently of *them:* none of *them* can operate but by means of this. In a word, the powers of nature may operate of themselves; but neither the magistrate, nor men at large, *can* operate, nor is God in the case in question *supposed* to operate, but through the powers of nature.

XII. For these four objects, which in their nature have so much in common, it seemed of use to find a common name. It seemed of use, in the first place, for the convenience of giving a name to certain pleasures and pains, for which a name equally characteristic could hardly otherwise have been found: in the second place, for the sake of holding up the efficacy of certain moral forces, the influence of which is apt not to be sufficiently attended to. Does the political sanction exert an influence over the conduct of mankind? The moral, the religious sanctions do so too. In every inch of his career are the operations of the political magistrate liable to be aided or impeded by these two foreign powers: who, one or other of them, or both, are sure to be either his rivals or his allies. Does it happen to him to leave them out in his calculations? he will be sure almost to find himself mistaken in the result. Of all this we shall find abundant proofs in the sequel of his work. It behooves him, therefore, to have them continually before his eyes; and that under such a name as exhibits the relation they bear to his own purposes and designs.

Chapter IV Value of a Lot of Pleasure or Pain, How To Be Measured

I. Pleasures then, and the avoidance of pains, are the *ends* which the legislator has in view: it behoves him therefore to understand their *value.* Pleasures and pains are the *instruments* he has to work with: it behoves him therefore to understand their force, which is again, in other words, their value.

II. To a person considered *by himself,* the value of a pleasure or pain considered *by itself,* will be greater or less, according to the four following circumstances:*

---

*These circumstances have since been denominated elements or dimensions of value in a pleasure or a pain.

Not long after the publication of the first edition, the following memoriter verses were framed, in the view of lodging more effectually, in the memory, these points, on which the whole fabric of morals and legislation may be seen to rest.

Intense, long, certain, speedy, fruitful, pure—
Such marks in *pleasures* and in *pains* endure.
Such pleasures seek, if *private* be thy end:
If it be *public,* wide let them *extend.*
Such *pains* avoid, whichever be thy view:
If pains *must* come, let them *extend* to few.

1. Its *intensity.*
2. Its *duration.*
3. Its *certainty* or *uncertainty.*
4. Its *propinquity* or *remoteness.*

III. These are the circumstances which are to be considered in estimating a pleasure or a pain considered each of them by itself. But when the value of any pleasure or pain is considered for the purpose of estimating the tendency of any act by which it is produced, there are two other circumstances to be taken into the account; these are,

5. Its *fecundity,* or the chance it has of being followed by sensations of the same kind: that is, pleasures, if it be a pleasure: pains, if it be a pain.
6. Its *purity,* or the chance it has of *not* being followed by sensations of the opposite kind: that is, pains, if it be a pleasure: pleasures, if it be a pain.

These two last, however, are in strictness scarcely to be deemed properties of the pleasure or the pain itself; they are not, therefore, in strictness to be taken into the account of the value of that pleasure or that pain. They are in strictness to be deemed properties only of the act, or other event, by which such pleasure or pain has been produced; and accordingly are only to be taken into the account of the tendency of such act or such event.

IV. To a *number* of persons, with reference to each of whom the value of a pleasure or a pain is considered, it will be greater or less, according to seven circumstances: to wit, the six preceding ones; viz.

1. Its *intensity.*
2. Its *duration.*
3. Its *certainty* or *uncertainty.*
4. Its *propinquity* or *remoteness.*
5. Its *fecundity.*
6. Its *purity.*

And one other; to wit:

7. Its *extent;* that is, the number of persons to whom it *extends;* or (in other words) who are affected by it.

V. To take an exact account then of the general tendency of any act, by which the interests of a community are affected, proceed as follows. Begin with any one person of those whose interests seem most immediately to be affected by it: and take an account.

1. Of the value of each distinguishable *pleasure* which appears to be produced by it in the *first* instance.
2. Of the value of each *pain* which appears to be produced by it in the first instance.
3. Of the value of each pleasure which appears to be produced by it *after* the first. This constitutes the *fecundity* of the first *pleasure* and the *impurity* of the first *pain.*
4. Of the value of each *pain* which appears to be produced by it after the first. This constitutes the *fecundity* of the first *pain,* and the *impurity* of the first *pleasure.*
5. Sum up all the values of all the *pleasures* on the one side, and those of all the *pains* on the other. The balance, if it be on the side of pleasure, will give the *good* tendency of the act upon the whole, with respect to the interests of that *individual* person; if on the side of pain, the *bad* tendency of it upon the whole.
6. Take an account of the *number* of persons whose interests appear to be concerned; and repeat the above process with respect to each. *Sum up* the numbers expressive of the degrees of good tendency which the act has, with respect to each individual, in regard to whom the tendency of it is *good* upon the whole: . . . do this again with respect to each individual, in regard to whom the tendency of it is *bad* upon the whole. Take the *balance;* which, if on the side of *pleasure,* will give the general *good tendency* of the act, with respect to the total number or community of indi-

viduals concerned; if on the side of pain, the general *evil tendency,* with respect to the same community.

VI. It is not to be expected that this process should be strictly pursued previously to every moral judgment, or to every legislative or judicial operation. It may, however, be always kept in view: and as near as the process actually pursued on these occasions approaches to it, so near will such process approach to the character of an exact one.

VII. The same process is alike applicable to pleasure and pain, in whatever shape they appear: and by whatever denomination they are distinguished: to pleasure, whether it be called *good* (which is properly the cause or instrument of pleasure) or *profit* (which is distant pleasure, or the cause or instrument of distant pleasure,) or *convenience,* or *advantage, benefit, emolument, happiness,* and so forth: to pain, whether it be called evil, (which corresponds to *good*) or *mischief,* or *inconvenience,* or *disadvantage,* or *loss,* or *unhappiness,* and so forth.

VIII. Nor is this a novel and unwarranted, any more than it is a useless theory. In all this there is nothing but what the practice of mankind, wheresoever they have a clear view of their own interest, is perfectly conformable to. An article of property, an estate in land, for instance, is valuable, on what account? On account of the pleasures of all kinds which it enables a man to produce, and what comes to the same thing the pains of all kinds which it enables him to avert. But the value of such an article of property is universally understood to rise or fall according to the length or shortness of the time which a man has in it: the certainty or uncertainty of its coming into possession: and the nearness or remoteness of the time at which, if at all, it is to come into possession. As to the *intensity* of the pleasures which a man may derive from it, this is never thought of, because it depends upon the use which each particular person may come to make of it; which cannot be estimated till the particular pleasures he may come to derive from it, or the particular pains he may come to exclude by means of it, are brought to view. For the same reason, neither does he think of the *fecundity* or *purity* of those pleasures.

Chapter 1 Of Motives

2. No motives either constantly good or constantly bad

IX. In all this chain of motives, the principal or original link seems to be the last internal motive in prospect: it is to this that all the other motives in prospect owe their materiality: and the immediately acting motive its existence. This motive in prospect, we see is always some pleasure, or some pain; some pleasure, which the act in question is expected to be a means of continuing or producing: some pain which it is expected to be a means of discontinuing or preventing. A motive is substantially nothing more than pleasure or pain, operating in a certain manner.

X. Now, pleasure is in *itself* a good: nay, even setting aside immunity from pain, the only good: pain is in itself an evil; and, indeed, without exception, the only evil; or else the words good and evil have no meaning. And this is alike true of every sort of pain, and of every sort of pleasure. It follows, therefore, immediately and incontestably, that *there is no such thing as any sort of motive that is in itself a bad one.*

XI. It is common, however, to speak of actions as proceeding from *good* or *bad* motives: in which case the motives meant are such as are internal. The expression is far from being an accurate one; and as it is apt to occur in the consideration of almost every kind of offence, it will be requisite to settle the precise meaning of it, and observe how far it quadrates with the truth of things.

XII. With respect to goodness and badness, as it is with everything else that is not itself either pain or pleasure, so is it with motives. If they are good or bad, it is only on account of their effects: good, on account of their tendency to produce pleasure, or avert pain: bad, on account of their tendency to produce pain, or avert pleasure. Now the case is, that from one and the same motive, and from every kind of motive, may proceed actions that are good, others that are bad, and others that are indifferent.

Study Questions

1. What is the principle of utility, and when may an action be said to be conformable to it?
2. Can the utility principle be directly proved, according to Bentham? If not, does he believe it necessary to give a proof? Why, or why not?
3. What is a sanction, according to Bentham? What are four sanctions of pain and pleasure, in his opinion? Why are sanctions important?
4. Describe how the value of an act is to be calculated, according to Bentham.
5. What does Bentham mean by saying that there is no such thing as any sort of motive that is in itself a bad one, and why does he say it?

Utilitarianism

John Stuart Mill

John Stuart Mill (1806–1873) was an important economist and social reformer as well as an influential philosopher. The following selection is the complete text of *Utilitarianism,* first published in 1863.

Chapter I
General Remarks

There are few circumstances among those which make up the present condition of human knowledge more unlike what might have been expected, or more significant of the backward state in which speculation on the most important subjects still lingers, than the little progress which has been made in the decision of the controversy respecting the criterion of right and wrong. From the dawn of philosophy, the question concerning the *summum bonum,* or, what is the same thing, concerning the foundation of morality, has been accounted the main problem in speculative thought, has occupied the most gifted intellects and divided them into sects and schools carrying on a vigorous warfare against one another. And after more than two thousand years the same discussions continue, philosophers are still ranged under the same contending banners, and neither thinkers nor mankind at large seem nearer to being unanimous on the subject than when the youth Socrates listened to the old Protagoras and asserted (if Plato's dialogue be grounded on a real conversation) the theory of utilitarianism against the popular morality of the so-called sophist.

It is true that similar confusion and uncertainty and, in some cases, similar discordance exist respecting the first principles of all the sciences, not excepting that which is deemed the most certain of them — mathematics, without much impairing, generally indeed without impairing at all, the trustworthiness of the conclusions of those sciences. An apparent anomaly, the explanation of which is that the detailed doctrines of a science are not usually deduced from, nor depend for their evidence upon, what are called its first principles. Were it not so, there would be no science more precarious, or whose conclusions were more insufficiently made out, than algebra, which derives none of its certainty from what are commonly taught to learners as its elements, since these, as laid down by some of its most eminent teachers, are as full of fictions as English law, and of mysteries as theology. The truths which are ultimately accepted as the first principles of a science are really the last results of metaphysical analysis practiced on the elementary notions with which the science is conversant; and their relation to the science is not that of foundations to an edifice, but of roots to a tree, which may perform their office equally well though they be never dug down to and exposed to light. But though in science the particular truths precede the general theory, the contrary might be expected to be the case with a practical art, such as morals or legislation. All action is for the sake of some end, and rules of action, it seems natural to suppose, must take their whole character and color from the end to which they are subservient. When we engage in a pursuit, a clear and precise conception of what we are pursuing would seem to be the first thing we need, instead of the last we are to look forward to. A test of right and wrong must be the means, one would think, of ascertaining what is right or wrong, and not a consequence of having already ascertained it.

The difficulty is not avoided by having recourse to the popular theory of a natural faculty, a sense of instinct, informing us of right and wrong. For—besides that the existence of such a moral instinct is itself one of the matters in dispute—those believers in it who have any pretensions to philosophy have been obliged to abandon the idea that it discerns what is right or wrong in the particular case in hand, as our other senses discern the sight or sound actually present. Our moral faculty, according to all those of its interpreters who are entitled to the name of thinkers, supplies us only with the general principles of moral judgments; it is a branch of our reason, not of our sensitive faculty, and must be looked to for the abstract doctrines of morality, not for perception of it in the concrete. The intuitive, no less than what may be termed the inductive, school of ethics insists on the necessity of general laws. They both agree that the morality of an individual action is not a question of direct perception, but of the application of a law to an individual case. They recognize also, to a great extent, the same moral laws, but differ as to their evidence and the source from which they derive their authority. According to the one opinion, the principles of morals are evident *a priori*, requiring nothing to command assent except that the meaning of the terms be understood. According to the other doctrine, right and wrong, as well as truth and falsehood, are questions of observation and experience. But both hold equally that morality must be deduced from principles; and the intuitive school affirm as strongly as the inductive that there is a science of morals. Yet they seldom attempt to make out a list of the *a priori* principles which are to serve as the premises of the science; still more rarely do they make any effort to reduce those various principles to one first principle or common ground of obligation. They either assume the ordinary precepts of morals as of *a priori* authority, or they lay down as the common groundwork of those maxims some generality much less obviously authoritative than the maxims themselves, and which has never succeeded in gaining popular acceptance. Yet to support their pretensions there ought either to be some one fundamental principle or law at the root of all morality, or, if there be several, there should be a determinate order of precedence among them; and the one principle, or the rule for deciding between the various principles when they conflict, ought to be self-evident.

To inquire how far the bad effects of this deficiency have been mitigated in practice, or to what extent the moral beliefs of mankind have been vitiated or made uncertain by the absence of any distinct recognition of an ultimate standard, would imply a complete survey and criticism of past and present ethical doctrine. It would, however, be easy to show that whatever steadiness or consistency these moral beliefs have attained has been mainly due to the tacit influence of a standard not recognized. Although the nonexistence of an acknowledged first principle has made ethics not so much a guide as a consecration of men's actual sentiments, still, as men's sentiments, both of favor and of aversion, are greatly influenced by what they suppose to be the effects of things upon their happiness, the principle of utility, or, as Bentham latterly called it, the greatest happiness principle, has had a large share in forming the moral doctrines even of those who most scornfully reject its authority. Nor is there any school of thought which refuses to admit that the influence of actions on happiness is a most material and even predominant consideration in many of the details of morals, however unwilling to acknowledge it as the fundamental principle of morality and the source of moral obligation. I might go much further and say that to all those *a priori* moralists who deem it necessary to argue at all, utilitarian arguments are indispensable. It is not my present purpose to criticize these thinkers; but I cannot help referring, for illustration, to a systematic treatise by one of the most illustrious of them, the *Metaphysics of Ethics* by Kant. This remarkable man, whose system of thought will long remain one of the landmarks in the history of philosophical speculation, does, in the treatise in question, lay down a universal first principle as the origin and ground of moral obligation; it is this: "So act that the rule on which thou actest would admit of being adopted as a law by all rational beings." But when he begins to deduce from this precept any of the actual duties of morality, he fails, almost grotesquely, to show that there would be any contradiction, any logical (not to say physical) impossibility, in the adoption by all rational beings of the most outrageously immoral rules of conduct. All he shows is that the *consequences* of their universal adoption would be such as no one would choose to incur.

On the present occasion, I shall, without further discussion of the other theories, attempt to contribute something toward the understanding and appreciation of the "utilitarian" or "happiness" theory, and toward such proof as it is susceptible of. It is evident that this cannot be proof in the ordinary and popular meaning of the term. Questions of ultimate ends are not amenable to direct proof. Whatever can be proved to be good must be so by being shown to be a means to something admitted to be good without proof. The medical art is proved to be good by its conducing to health; but how is it possible to prove that health is good? The art of music is good, for the reason, among others, that it produces pleasure; but what proof is it possible to give that pleasure is good? If, then, it is asserted that there is a comprehensive formula, including all things which are in themselves good, and that whatever else is good is not so as an end but as a means, the formula may be accepted or rejected, but is not a subject of what is commonly understood by proof. We are not, however, to infer that its acceptance or rejection must depend on blind impulse or arbitrary choice. There is a larger meaning of the word "proof," in which this question is as amenable to it as any other of the disputed questions of philosophy. The subject is within the cognizance of the rational faculty; and neither does that faculty deal with it solely in the way of intuition. Considerations may be presented capable of determining the intellect either to give or withhold its assent to the doctrine; and this is equivalent to proof.

We shall examine presently of what nature are these considerations; in what manner they apply to the case, and what rational grounds, therefore, can be given for accepting or rejecting the utilitarian formula. But it is a preliminary condition of rational acceptance or rejection that the formula should be correctly understood. I believe that the very imperfect notion ordinarily formed of its meaning is the chief obstacle which impedes its reception and that, could it be cleared even from only the grosser misconceptions, the question would be greatly simplified and a large proportion of its difficulties removed. Before, therefore, I attempt to enter into the philosophical grounds which can be given for assenting to the utilitarian standard, I shall offer some illustrations of the doctrine itself, with the view of showing more clearly what it is, distinguishing it from what it is not, and disposing of such of the practical objections to it as either originate in, or are closely connected with, mistaken interpretations of its meaning. Having thus prepared the ground, I shall afterwards endeavor to throw such light as I can call upon the question considered as one of philosophical theory.

Chapter II
What Utilitarianism Is

A passing remark is all that needs be given to the ignorant blunder of supposing that those who stand up for utility as the test of right and wrong use the term in that restricted and merely colloquial sense in which utility is opposed to pleasure. An apology is due to the philosophical opponents of utilitarianism for even the momentary appearance of confounding them with anyone capable of so absurd a misconception; which is the more extraordinary, inasmuch as the contrary accusation, of referring everything to pleasure, and that, too, in its grossest form, is another of the common charges against utilitarianism: and, as has been pointedly remarked by an able writer, the same sort of persons, and often the very same persons, denounce the theory "as impracticably dry when the word 'utility' precedes the word 'pleasure,' and as too practicably voluptuous when the word 'pleasure' precedes the word 'utility.'" Those who know anything about the matter are aware that every writer, from Epicurus to Bentham, who maintained the theory of utility meant by it, not something to be contradistinguished from pleasure, but pleasure itself, together with exemption from pain; and instead of opposing the useful to the agreeable or the ornamental, have always declared that the useful means these, among other things. Yet the common herd, including the herd of writers, not only in newspapers and periodicals, but in books of weight and pretension, are perpetually falling into this shallow mistake. Having caught up the word "utilitarian," while knowing nothing whatever about it but its sound, they habitually express by it the rejection or the neglect of pleasure in some of its forms: of beauty, of ornament, or of amusement. Nor is the term thus ignorantly misapplied solely in disparagement, but occasionally in compliment, as though it implied superiority to frivolity and the mere pleasures of the moment. And this perverted use is the only one in which the word is popularly known, and the one from which the new generation are acquiring their sole notion of its meaning. Those who introduced the word, but who had for many years discontinued it as a distinctive appellation, may well feel themselves called upon to resume it if by doing so they can hope to contribute anything toward rescuing it from this utter degradation.[1]

[1]The author of this essay has reason for believing himself to be the first person who brought the word "utilitarian" into use. He did not invent it, but adopted it from a passing expression in Mr. Galt's *Annals of the Parish.* After using it as a designation for several years, he and others abandoned it from a growing dislike to anything resembling a badge or watchword of sectarian distinction. But as a name for one single opinion, not a set of opinions—to denote the recognition of utility as a standard, not any particular way of applying it—the term supplies a want in the language, and offers, in many cases, a convenient mode of avoiding tiresome circumlocution.

The creed which accepts as the foundation of morals "utility" or the "greatest happiness principle" holds that actions are right in proportion as they tend to promote happiness; wrong as they tend to produce the reverse of happiness. By happiness is intended pleasure and the absence of pain; by unhappiness, pain and the privation of pleasure. To give a clear view of the moral standard set up by the theory, much more requires to be said; in particular, what things it includes in the ideas of pain and pleasure, and to what extent this is left an open question. But these supplementary explanations do not affect the theory of life on which this theory of morality is grounded—namely, that pleasure and freedom from pain are the only things desirable as ends; and that all desirable things (which are as numerous in the utilitarian as in any other scheme) are desirable either for pleasure inherent in themselves or as means to the promotion of pleasure and the prevention of pain.

Now such a theory of life excites in many minds, and among them in some of the most estimable in feeling and purpose, inveterate dislike. To suppose that life has (as they express it) no higher end than pleasure—no better and nobler object of desire and pursuit—they designate as utterly mean and groveling, as a doctrine worthy only of swine, to whom the followers of Epicurus were, at a very early period, contemptuously likened; and modern holders of the doctrine are occasionally made the subject of equally polite comparisons by its German, French, and English assailants.

When thus attacked, the Epicureans have always answered that it is not they, but their accusers, who represent human nature in a degrading light, since the accusation supposes human beings to be capable of no pleasures except those of which swine are capable. If this supposition were true, the charge could not be gainsaid, but would then be no longer an imputation; for if the sources of pleasure were precisely the same to human beings and to swine, the rule of life which is good enough for the one would be good enough for the other. The comparison of the Epicurean life to that of beasts is felt as degrading, precisely because a beast's pleasures do not satisfy a human being's conceptions of happiness. Human beings have faculties more elevated than the animal appetites and, when once made conscious of them, do not regard anything as happiness which does not include their gratification. I do not, indeed, consider the Epicureans to have been by any means faultless in drawing out their scheme of consequences from the utilitarian principle. To do this in any sufficient manner, many Stoic, as well as Christian, elements require to be included. But there is no known Epicurean theory of life which does not assign to the pleasures of the intellect, of the feelings and imagination, and of the moral sentiments a much higher value as pleasures than to those of mere sensation. It must be admitted, however, that utilitarian writers in general have placed the superiority of mental over bodily pleasures chiefly in the greater permanency, safety, uncostliness, etc., of the former — that is, in their circumstantial advantages rather than in their intrinsic nature. And on all these points utilitarians have fully proved their case; but they might have taken the other and, as it may be called, higher ground with entire consistency. It is quite compatible with the principle of utility to recognize the fact that some kinds of pleasure are more desirable and more valuable than others. It would be absurd that, while in estimating all other things quality is considered as well as quantity, the estimation of pleasure should be supposed to depend on quantity alone.

If I am asked what I mean by difference of quality in pleasures, or what makes one pleasure more valuable than another, merely as a pleasure, except its being greater in amount, there is but one possible answer. Of two pleasures, if there be one to which all or almost all who have experience of both give a decided preference, irrespective of any feeling of moral obligation to prefer it, that is the more desirable pleasure. If one of the two is, by those who are competently acquainted with both, placed so far above the other that they prefer it, even though knowing it to be attended with a greater amount of discontent, and would not resign it for any quantity of the other pleasure which their nature is capable of, we are justified in ascribing to the preferred enjoyment a superiority in quality so far outweighing quantity as to render it, in comparison, of small account.

Now it is an unquestionable fact that those who are equally acquainted with and equally capable of appreciating and enjoying both do give a most marked preference to the manner of existence which employs their higher faculties. Few human creatures would consent to be changed into any of the lower animals for a promise of the fullest allowance of a beast's pleasures; no intelligent human being would consent to be a fool, no instructed person would be an ignoramus, no person of feeling and conscience would be selfish and base, even though they should be persuaded that the fool, the dunce, or the rascal is better satisfied with his lot than they are with theirs. They would not resign what they possess more than he for the most complete satisfaction of all the desires which they have in common with him. If they ever fancy they would, it is only in cases of unhappiness so extreme that to escape from it they would exchange their lot for almost any other, however undesirable in their own eyes. A being of higher faculties requires more to make him happy, is capable probably of more acute suffering, and certainly accessible to it at more points, than one of an inferior type; but in spite of these liabilities, he can never really wish to sink into what he feels to be a lower grade of existence. We may give what explanation we please of this unwillingness; we may attribute it to pride, a name which is given indiscriminately to some of the most and to some of the least estimable feelings of which mankind are capable; we may refer it to the love of liberty and personal independence, an appeal to which was with the Stoics one of the most effective means for the inculcation of it; to the love of power or to the love of excitement, both of which do really enter into and contribute to it; but its most appropriate appellation is a sense of dignity, which all human beings possess in one form or other, and in some, though by no means in exact, proportion to their higher faculties, and which is so essential a part of the happiness of those in whom it is strong that nothing which conflicts with it could be otherwise than momentarily an object of desire to them. Whoever supposes that this preference takes place at a sacrifice of happiness — that the superior being, in anything like equal circumstances, is not happier than the inferior — confounds the two very different ideas of happiness and content. It is indisputable that the being whose capacities of enjoyment are low has the greatest chance of having them fully satisfied; and a highly endowed being will always feel that any happiness which he can look for, as the world is constituted, is imperfect. But he can learn to bear its imperfections, if they are at all bearable; and they will not make him envy the being who is indeed unconscious of the imperfections, but only because he feels not at all the good which those imperfections qualify. It is better to be a human being dissatisfied than a pig satisfied; better to be Socrates dissatisfied than a fool satisfied. And if the fool, or the pig, are of a different opinion, it is because they only know their own side of the question. The other party to the comparison knows both sides.

It may be objected that many who are capable of the higher pleasures occasionally, under the influence of temptation, postpone them to the lower. But this is quite compatible with a full appreciation of the intrinsic superiority of the higher. Men often, from infirmity of character, make their election for the nearer good, though they know it to be the less valuable; and this no less when the choice is between two bodily pleasures than when it is between bodily and mental. They pursue sensual indulgences to the injury of health, though perfectly aware that health is the greater good. It may be further objected that many who begin with youthful enthusiasm for everything noble, as they advance in years, sink into indolence and selfishness. But I do not believe that those who undergo this very common change voluntarily choose the lower description of pleasures in preference to the higher. I believe that, before they devote themselves exclusively to the one, they have already become incapable of the other. Capacity for the nobler feelings is in most natures a very tender plant, easily killed, not only by hostile influences, but by mere want of sustenance; and in the majority of young persons it speedily dies away if the occupations to which their position in life has devoted them, and the society into which it has thrown them, are not favorable to keeping that higher capacity in exercise. Men lose their high aspirations as they lose their intellectual tastes, because they have not time or opportunity for indulging them; and they addict themselves to inferior pleasures, not because they deliberately prefer them, but because they are either the only ones to which they have access or the only ones which they are any longer capable of enjoying. It may be questioned whether anyone who has remained equally susceptible to both classes of pleasures ever knowingly and calmly preferred the lower, though many, in all ages, have broken down in an ineffectual attempt to combine both.

From this verdict of the only competent judges, I apprehend there can be no appeal. On a question which is the best worth having of two pleasures, or which of two modes of existence is the most grateful to the feelings, apart from its moral attributes and from its consequences, the judgment of those who are qualified by knowledge of both, or, if they differ, that of the majority among them, must be admitted as final. And there needs be the less hesitation to accept this judgment respecting the quality of pleasures, since there is no other tribunal to be referred to even on the question of quantity. What means are there of determining which is the acutest of two pains, or the intensest of two pleasurable sensations, except the general suffrage of those who are familiar with both? Neither pains nor pleasures are homogeneous, and pain is always heterogeneous with pleasure. What is there to decide whether a particular pleasure is worth purchasing at the cost of a particular pain, except the feelings and judgment of the experienced? When, therefore, those feelings and judgment declare the pleasures derived from the higher faculties to be preferable *in kind*, apart from the question of intensity, to those of which the animal nature, disjoined from the higher faculties, is susceptible, they are entitled on this subject to the same regard.

I have dwelt on this point as being a necessary part of a perfectly just conception of utility or happiness considered as the directive rule of human conduct. But it is by no means an indispensable condition to the acceptance of the utilitarian standard; for that standard is not the agent's own greatest happiness, but the greatest amount of happiness altogether; and if it may possibly be doubted whether a noble character is always the happier for its nobleness, there can be no doubt that it makes other people happier, and that the world in general is immensely a gainer by it. Utilitarianism, therefore, could only attain its end by the general cultivation of nobleness of character, even if each individual were only benefited by the nobleness of others, and his own, so far as happiness is concerned, were a sheer deduction from the benefit. But the bare enunciation of such an absurdity as this last renders refutation superfluous.

According to the greatest happiness principle, as above explained, the ultimate end, with reference to and for the sake of which all other things are desirable—whether we are considering our own good or that of other people—is an existence exempt as far as possible from pain, and as rich as possible in enjoyments, both in point of quantity and quality; the test of quality and the rule for measuring it against quantity being the preference felt by those who, in their opportunities of experience, to which must be added their habits of self-consciousness and self-observation, are best furnished with the means of comparison. This, being according to the utilitarian opinion the end of human action, is necessarily also the standard of morality, which may accordingly be defined "the rules and precepts for human conduct," by the observance of which an existence such as has been described might be, to the greatest extent possible, secured to all mankind; and not to them only, but, so far as the nature of things admits, to the whole sentient creation.

Against this doctrine, however, arises another class of objectors who say that happiness, in any form, cannot be the rational purpose of human life and action; because, in the first place, it is unattainable; and they contemptuously ask, What right hast thou to be happy?—a question which Mr. Carlyle clinches by the addition, What right, a short time ago, hadst thou even *to be*? Next they say that men can do *without* happiness; that all noble human beings have felt this, and could not have become noble but by learning the lesson of *Entsagen,* or renunciation; which lesson, thoroughly learned and submitted to, they affirm to be the beginning and necessary condition of all virtue.

The first of these objections would go to the root of the matter were it well founded; for if no happiness is to be had at all by human beings, the attainment of it cannot be the end of morality or of any rational conduct. Though, even in that case, something might still be said for the utilitarian theory, since utility includes not solely the pursuit of happiness, but the prevention or mitigation of unhappiness; and if the former aim be chimerical, there will be all the greater scope and more imperative need for the latter, so long at least as mankind think fit to live and do not take refuge in the simultaneous act of suicide recommended under certain conditions by Novalis. When, however, it is thus positively asserted to be impossible that human life should be happy, the assertion, if not something like a verbal quibble, is at least an exaggeration. If by happiness be meant a continuity of highly pleasurable excitement, it is evident enough that this is impossible. A state of exalted pleasure lasts only moments or in some cases, and with some intermissions, hours or days, and is the occasional brilliant flash of enjoyment, not its permanent and steady flame. Of this the philosophers who have taught that happiness is the end of life were as fully aware as those who taunt them. The happiness which they meant was not a life of rapture, but moments of such, in an existence made up of few and transitory pains, many and various pleasures, with a decided predominance of the active over the passive, and having as the foundation of the whole not to expect more from life than it is capable of bestowing. A life thus composed, to those who have been fortunate enough to obtain it, has always appeared worthy of the name of happiness. And such an existence is even now the lot of many during some considerable portion of their lives. The present wretched education and wretched social arrangements are the only real hindrance to its being attainable by almost all.

The objectors perhaps may doubt whether human beings, if taught to consider happiness as the end of life, would be satisfied with such a moderate share of it. But great numbers of mankind have been satisfied with much less. The main constituents of a satisfied life appear to be two, either of which by itself is often found sufficient for the purpose: tranquillity and excitement. With much tranquillity, many find that they can be content with very little pleasure; with much excitement, many can reconcile themselves to a considerable quantity of pain. There is assuredly no inherent impossibility of enabling even the mass of mankind to unite both, since the two are so far from being incompatible that they are in natural alliance, the prolongation of either being a preparation for, and exciting a wish for, the other. It is only those in whom indolence amounts to a vice that do not desire excitement after an interval of repose; it is only those in whom the need of excitement is a disease that feel the tranquillity which follows excitement dull and insipid, instead of pleasurable in direct proportion to the excitement which preceded it. When people who are tolerably fortunate in their outward lot do not find in life sufficient enjoyment to make it valuable to them, the cause generally is caring for nobody but themselves. To those who have neither public nor private affections, the excitements of life are much curtailed, and in any case dwindle in value as the time approaches when all selfish interests must be terminated by death; while those who leave after them objects of personal affection, and especially those who have also cultivated a fellow-feeling with the collective interests of mankind, retain as lively an interest in life on the eve of death as in the vigor of youth and health. Next to selfishness, the principal cause which makes life unsatisfactory is want of mental cultivation. A cultivated mind—I do not mean that of a philosopher, but any mind to which the fountains of knowledge have been opened, and which has been taught, in any tolerable degree, to exercise its faculties—finds sources of inexhaustible interest in all that surrounds it: in the objects of nature, the achievements of art, the imaginations of poetry, the incidents of history, the ways of mankind, past and present, and their prospects in the future. It is possible, indeed, to become indifferent to all this, and that too without having exhausted a thousandth part of it, but only when one has had from the beginning no moral or human interest in these things and has sought in them only the gratification of curiosity.

Now there is absolutely no reason in the nature of things why an amount of mental culture sufficient to give an intelligent interest in these objects of contemplation should not be the inheritance of everyone born in a civilized country. As little is there an inherent necessity that any human being should be a selfish egotist, devoid of every feeling or care but those which center in his own miserable individuality. Something far superior to this is sufficiently common even now, to give ample earnest of what the human species may be made. Genuine private affections and a sincere interest in the public good are possible, though in unequal degrees, to every rightly brought up human being. In a world in which there is so much to interest, so much to enjoy, and so much also to correct and improve, everyone who has this moderate amount of moral and intellectual requisites is capable of an existence which may be called enviable; and unless such a person, through bad laws or subjection to the will of others, is denied the liberty to use the sources of happiness within his reach, he will not fail to find this enviable existence, if he escape the positive evils of life, the great sources of physical and mental suffering—such as indigence, disease, and the unkindness, worthlessness, or premature loss of objects of affection. The main stress of the problem lies, therefore, in the contest with these calamities from which it is a rare good fortune entirely to escape; which, as things now are, cannot be obviated, and often cannot be in any material degree mitigated. Yet no one whose opinion deserves a moment's consideration can doubt that most of the great positive evils of the world are in themselves removable, and will, if human affairs continue to improve, be in the end reduced within narrow limits. Poverty, in any sense implying suffering, may be completely extinguished by the wisdom of society combined with the good sense and providence of individuals. Even that most intractable of enemies, disease, may be indefinitely reduced in dimensions by good physical and moral education and proper control of noxious influences, while the progress of science holds out a promise for the future of still more direct conquests over this detestable foe. And every advance in that direction relieves us from some, not only of the chances which cut short our own lives, but, what concerns us still more, which deprive us of those in whom our happiness is wrapt up. As for vicissitudes of fortune and other disappointments connected with worldly circumstances, these are principally the effect either of gross imprudence, of ill-regulated desires, or of bad or imperfect social institutions. All the grand sources, in short, of human suffering are in a great degree, many of them almost entirely, conquerable by human care and effort; and though their removal is grievously slow—though a long succession of generations will perish in the breach before the conquest is completed, and this world becomes all that, if will and knowledge were not wanting, it might easily be made—yet every mind sufficiently intelligent and generous to bear a part, however small and inconspicuous, in the endeavor will draw a noble enjoyment from the contest itself, which he would not for any bribe in the form of selfish indulgence consent to be without.

And this leads to the true estimation of what is said by the objectors concerning the possibility and the obligation of learning to do without happiness. Unquestionably it is possible to do without happiness; it is done involuntarily by nineteen-twentieths of mankind, even in those parts of our present world which are least deep in barbarism; and it often has to be done voluntarily by the hero or the martyr, for the sake of something which he prizes more than his individual happiness. But this something, what is it, unless the happiness of others or some of the requisites of happiness? It is noble to be capable of resigning entirely one's own portion of happiness, or chances of it; but, after all, this self-sacrifice must be for some end; it is not its own end; and if we are told that its end is not happiness but virtue, which is better than happiness, I ask, would the sacrifice be made if the hero or martyr did not believe that it would earn for others immunity from similar sacrifices? Would it be made if he thought that his renunciation of happiness for himself would produce no fruit for any of his fellow creatures, but to make their lot like his and place them also in the condition of persons who have renounced happiness? All honor to those who can abnegate for themselves the personal enjoyment of life when by such renunciation they contribute worthily to increase the amount of happiness in the world; but he who does it or professes to do it for any other purpose is no more deserving of admiration than the ascetic mounted on his pillar. He may be an inspiriting proof of what men *can* do, but assuredly not an example of what they *should*.

Though it is only in a very imperfect state of the world's arrangements that anyone can best serve the happiness of others by the absolute sacrifice of his own, yet, so long as the world is in that imperfect state, I fully acknowledge that the readiness to make such a sacrifice is the highest virtue which can be found in man. I will add that in this condition of the world, paradoxical as the assertion may be, the conscious ability to do without happiness gives the best prospect of realizing such happiness as is attainable. For nothing except that consciousness can raise a person above the chances of life by making him feel that, let fate and fortune do their worst, they have not power to subdue him; which, once felt, frees him from excess of anxiety concerning the evils of life and enables him, like many a Stoic in the worst times of the Roman Empire, to cultivate in tranquillity the sources of satisfaction accessible to him, without concerning himself about the uncertainty of their duration any more than about their inevitable end.

Meanwhile, let utilitarians never cease to claim the morality of self-devotion as a possession which belongs by as good a right to them as either to the Stoic or to the Transcendentalist. The utilitarian morality does recognize in human beings the power of sacrificing their own greatest good for the good of others. It only refuses to admit that the sacrifice is itself a good. A sacrifice which does not increase or tend to increase the sum total of happiness, it considers as wasted. The only self-renunciation which it applauds is devotion to the happiness, or to some of the means of happiness, of others, either of mankind collectively or of individuals within the limits imposed by the collective interests of mankind.

I must again repeat what the assailants of utilitarianism seldom have the justice to acknowledge, that the happiness which forms the utilitarian standard of what is right in conduct is not the agent's own happiness but that of all concerned. As between his own happiness and that of others, utilitarianism requires him to be as strictly impartial as a disinterested and benevolent spectator. In the golden rule of Jesus of Nazareth, we read the complete spirit of the ethics of utility. "To do as you would be done by," and "to love your neighbor as yourself," constitute the ideal perfection of utilitarian morality. As the means of making the nearest approach to this ideal, utility would enjoin first, that laws and social arrangements should place the happiness or (as, speaking practically, it may be called) the interest of every individual as nearly as possible in harmony with the interest of the whole;

and, secondly, that education and opinion, which have so vast a power over human character, should so use that power as to establish in the mind of every individual an indissoluble association between his own happiness and the good of the whole, especially between his own happiness and the practice of such modes of conduct, negative and positive, as regard for the universal happiness prescribes; so that not only he may be unable to conceive the possibility of happiness to himself, consistently with conduct opposed to the general good, but also that a direct impulse to promote the general good may be in every individual one of the habitual motives of action, and the sentiments connected therewith may fill a large and prominent place in every human being's sentient existence. If the impugners of the utilitarian morality represented it to their own minds in this its true character, I know not what recommendation possessed by any other morality they could possibly affirm to be wanting to it; what more beautiful or more exalted developments of human nature any other ethical system can be supposed to foster, or what springs of action, not accessible to the utilitarian, such systems rely on for giving effect to their mandates.

The objectors to utilitarianism cannot always be charged with representing it in a discreditable light. On the contrary, those among them who entertain anything like a just idea of its disinterested character sometimes find fault with its standard as being too high for humanity. They say it is exacting too much to require that people shall always act from the inducement of promoting the general interests of society. But this is to mistake the very meaning of a standard of morals and confound the rule of action with the motive of it. It is the business of ethics to tell us what are our duties, or by what test we may know them; but no system of ethics requires that the sole motive of all we do shall be a feeling of duty; on the contrary, ninety-nine hundredths of all our actions are done from other motives, and rightly so done if the rule of duty does not condemn them. It is the more unjust to utilitarianism that this particular misapprehension should be made a ground of objection to it, inasmuch as utilitarian moralists have gone beyond almost all others in affirming that the motive has nothing to do with the morality of the action, though much with the worth of the agent. He who saves a fellow creature from drowning does what is morally right, whether his motive be duty or the hope of being paid for his trouble; he who betrays the friend that trusts him is guilty of a crime, even if his object be to serve another friend to whom he is under greater obligations.[2] But to speak only of actions done from the motive of duty, and in direct obedience to principle: it is a misapprehension of the utilitarian mode of thought to conceive it as implying that people should fix their minds upon so wide a generality as the world, or society at large. The great majority of good actions are intended not for the benefit of the world, but for that of individuals, of which the good of the world is made up; and the thoughts of the most virtuous man need not on these occa-

---

[2]An opponent, whose intellectual and moral fairness it is a pleasure to acknowledge (the Rev. J. Llewellyn Davies), has objected to this passage, saying, "Surely the rightness or wrongness of saving a man from drowning does depend very much upon the motive with which it is done. Suppose that a tyrant, when his enemy jumped into the sea to escape from him, saved him from drowning simply in order that he might inflict upon him more exquisite tortures, would it tend to clearness to speak of that rescue as 'a morally right action'? Or suppose again, according to one of the stock illustrations of ethical inquiries, that a man betrayed a trust received from a friend, because the discharge of it would fatally injure that friend himself or someone belonging to him, would utilitarianism compel one to call the betrayal 'a crime' as much as if it had been done from the meanest motive?"

I submit that he who saves another from drowning in order to kill him by torture afterwards does not differ only in motive from him who does the same thing from duty or benevolence; the act itself is different. The rescue of the man is, in the case supposed, only the necessary first step of an act far more atrocious than leaving him to drown would have been. Had Mr. Davies said, "The rightness or wrongness of saving a man from drowning does depend very much"—not upon the motive, but—"upon the *intention,*" no utilitarian would have differed from him. Mr. Davies, by an oversight too common not to be quite venial, has in this case confounded the very different ideas of Motive and Intention. There is no point which utilitarian thinkers (and Bentham preeminently) have taken more pains to illustrate than this. The morality of the action depends entirely upon the intention—that is, upon what the agent *wills* to do. But the motive, that is, the feeling which makes him will so to do, if it makes no difference in the act, makes none in the morality: though it makes a great difference in our moral estimation of the agent, especially if it indicates a good or a bad habitual *disposition*—a bent of character from which useful, or from which hurtful actions are likely to arise.

[The foregoing note appeared in the second (1864) edition of Utilitarianism *but was dropped in succeeding ones.]*

sions travel beyond the particular persons concerned, except so far as is necessary to assure himself that in benefiting them he is not violating the rights, that is, the legitimate and authorized expectations, of anyone else. The multiplication of happiness is, according to the utilitarian ethics, the object of virtue: the occasions on which any person (except one in a thousand) has it in his power to do this on an extended scale—in other words, to be a public benefactor—are but exceptional; and on these occasions alone is he called on to consider public utility; in every other case, private utility, the interest or happiness of some few persons, is all he has to attend to. Those alone the influence of whose actions extends to society in general need concern themselves habitually about so large an object. In the case of abstinences indeed—of things which people forbear to do from moral considerations, though the consequences in the particular case might be beneficial—it would be unworthy of an intelligent agent not to be consciously aware that the action is of a class which, if practiced generally, would be generally injurious, and that this is the ground of the obligation to abstain from it. The amount of regard for the public interest implied in this recognition is no greater than is demanded by every system of morals, for they all enjoin to abstain from whatever is manifestly pernicious to society.

The same considerations dispose of another reproach against the doctrine of utility, founded on a still grosser misconception of the purpose of a standard of morality and of the very meaning of the words "right" and "wrong." It is often affirmed that utilitarianism renders men cold and unsympathizing; that it chills their moral feelings toward individuals; that it makes them regard only the dry and hard consideration of the consequences of actions, not taking into their moral estimate the qualities from which those actions emanate. If the assertion means that they do not allow their judgment respecting the rightness or wrongness of an action to be influenced by their opinion of the qualities of the person who does it, this is a complaint not against utilitarianism, but against any standard of morality at all; for certainly no known ethical standard decides an action to be good or bad because it is done by a good or a bad man, still less because done by an amiable, a brave, or a benevolent man, or the contrary. These considerations are relevant, not to the estimation of actions, but of persons; and there is nothing in the utilitarian theory inconsistent with the fact that there are other things which interest us in persons besides the rightness and wrongness of their actions. The Stoics, indeed, with the paradoxical misuse of language which was part of their system, and by which they strove to raise themselves above all concern about anything but virtue, were fond of saying that he who has that has everything; that he, and only he, is rich, is beautiful, is a king. But no claim of this description is made for the virtuous man by the utilitarian doctrine. Utilitarians are quite aware that there are other desirable possessions and qualities besides virtue, and are perfectly willing to allow to all of them their full worth. They are also aware that a right action does not necessarily indicate a virtuous character, and that actions which are blamable often proceed from qualities entitled to praise. When this is apparent in any particular case, it modifies their estimation, not certainly of the act, but of the agent. I grant that they are, notwithstanding, of opinion that in the long run the best proof of a good character is good actions; and resolutely refuse to consider any mental disposition as good of which the predominant tendency is to produce bad conduct. This makes them unpopular with many people, but it is an unpopularity which they must share with everyone who regards the distinction between right and wrong in a serious light; and the reproach is not one which a conscientious utilitarian need be anxious to repel.

If no more be meant by the objection than that many utilitarians look on the morality of actions, as measured by the utilitarian standards, with too exclusive a regard, and do not lay sufficient stress upon the other beauties of character which go toward making a human being lovable or admirable, this may be admitted. Utilitarians who have cultivated their moral feelings, but not their sympathies, nor their artistic perceptions, do fall into this mistake; and so do all other moralists under the same conditions. What can be said in excuse for other moralists is equally available for them, namely, that, if there is to be any error, it is better that it should be on that side. As a matter of fact, we may affirm that among utilitarians, as among adherents of other systems, there is every imaginable degree of rigidity and of laxity in the application of their standard; some are even puritanically rigorous, while others are as indulgent as can possibly be desired by sinner or by sentimentalist. But on the whole, a doctrine which brings prominently forward the interest that mankind have in the repression and prevention of conduct which violates the moral law is likely to be inferior to no other in turning the sanctions of opinion against such violations. It is true, the question "What does violate the moral law?" is one on which those who recognize different standards of morality are likely now and then to differ. But difference of opinion on moral questions was not first introduced into the world by utilitarianism, while that doctrine does supply, if not always an easy, at all events a tangible and intelligible, mode of deciding such differences.

It may not be superfluous to notice a few more of the common misapprehensions of utilitarian ethics, even those which are so obvious and gross that it might appear impossible for any person of candor and intelligence to fall into them; since persons, even of considerable mental endowment, often give themselves so little trouble to understand the bearings of any opinion against which they entertain a prejudice, and men are in general so little conscious of this voluntary ignorance as a defect that the vulgarest misunderstandings of ethical doctrines are continually met with in the deliberate writings of persons of the greatest pretensions both to high principle and to philosophy. We not uncommonly hear the doctrine of utility inveighed against as a *godless* doctrine. If it be necessary to say anything at all against so mere an assumption, we may say that the question depends upon what idea we have formed of the moral character of the Deity. If it be a true belief that God desires, above all things, the happiness of his creatures, and that this was his purpose in their creation, utility is not only not a godless doctrine, but more profoundly religious than any other. If it be meant that utilitarianism does not recognize the revealed will of God as the supreme law of morals, I answer that a utilitarian who believes in the perfect goodness and wisdom of *God* necessarily believes that whatever God has thought fit to reveal on the subject of morals must fulfill the requirements of utility in a supreme degree. But others besides utilitarians have been of opinion that the Christian revelation was intended, and is fitted, to inform the hearts and minds of mankind with a spirit which should enable them to find for themselves what is right, and incline them to do it when found, rather than to tell them, except in a very general way, what it is; and that we need a doctrine of ethics, carefully followed out, to *interpret* to us the will of God. Whether this opinion is correct or not, it is superfluous here to discuss; since whatever aid religion, either natural or revealed, can afford to ethical investigation is as open to the utilitarian moralist as to any other. He can use it as the testimony of God to the usefulness or hurtfulness of any given course of action by as good a right as others can use it for the indication of a transcendental law having no connection with usefulness or with happiness.

Again, utility is often summarily stigmatized as an immoral doctrine by giving it the name of "expediency," and taking advantage of the popular use of that term to contrast it with principle. But the expedient, in the sense in which it is opposed to the right, generally means that which is expedient for the particular interest of the agent himself; as when a minister sacrifices the interests of his country to keep himself in place. When it means anything better than this, it means that which is expedient for some immediate object, some temporary purpose, but which violates a rule whose observance is expedient in a much higher degree. The expedient, in this sense, instead of being the same thing with the useful, is a branch of the hurtful. Thus it would often be expedient, for the purpose of getting over some momentary embarrassment, or attaining some object immediately useful to ourselves or others, to tell a lie. But inasmuch as the cultivation in ourselves of a sensitive feeling on the subject of veracity is one of the most useful, and the enfeeblement of that feeling one of the most hurtful, things to which our conduct can be instrumental; and inasmuch as any, even unintentional, deviation from truth does that much toward weakening the trustworthiness of human assertion, which is not only the principal support of all present social well-being, but the insufficiency of which does more than any one thing that can be named to keep back civilization, virtue, everything on which human happiness on the largest scale depends—we feel that the violation, for a present advantage, of a rule of such transcendent expediency is not expedient, and that he who, for the sake of convenience to himself or to some other individual, does what depends on him to deprive mankind of the good, and inflict upon them the evil, involved in the greater or less reliance which they can place in each other's word, acts the part of one of their worst enemies. Yet that even this rule, sacred as it is, admits of possible exceptions is acknowledged by all moralists; the chief of which is when the withholding of some fact (as of information from a malefactor, or of bad news from a person dangerously ill) would save an individual (especially an individual other than oneself) from great and unmerited evil, and when the withholding can only be effected by denial. But in order that the exception may not extend itself beyond the need, and may have the least possible effect in weakening reliance on veracity, it ought to be recognized and, if possible, its limits defined; and, if the principle of utility is good for anything, it must be good for weighing these conflicting utilities against one another and marking out the region within which one or the other preponderates.

Again, defenders of utility often find themselves called upon to reply to such objections as this—that there is not time, previous to action, for calculating and weighing the effects of any line of conduct on the general happiness. This is exactly as if anyone were to say that it is impossible to guide our conduct by Christianity because there is not time, on every occasion on which anything has to be done, to read through the Old and New Testaments. The answer to the objection is that there has been ample time, namely, the whole past duration of the human species. During all that time mankind have been learning by experience the tendencies of actions; on which experience all the prudence as well as all the morality of life are dependent. People talk as if the commencement of this course of experience had hitherto been put off, and as if, at the moment when some man feels tempted to meddle with the property or life of another, he had to begin considering for the first time whether murder and theft are injurious to human happiness. Even then I do not think that he would find the question very puzzling; but, at all events, the matter is now done to his hand. It is truly a whimsical supposition that, if mankind were agreed in considering utility to be the test of morality, they would remain without any agreement as to what *is* useful, and would take no measures for having their notions on the subject taught to the young and enforced by law and opinion. There is no difficulty in proving any ethical standard whatever to work ill if we suppose universal idiocy to be conjoined with it; but on any hypothesis short of that, mankind must by this time have acquired positive beliefs as to the effects of some actions on their happiness; and the beliefs which have thus come down are the rules of morality for the multitude, and for the philosopher until he has succeeded in finding better. That philosophers might easily do this, even now, on many subjects; that the received code of ethics is by no means of divine right; and that mankind have still much to learn as to the effects of actions on the general happiness, I admit or rather earnestly maintain. The corollaries from the principle of utility, like the precepts of every practical art, admit of indefinite improvement, and, in a progressive state of the human mind, their improvement is perpetually going on. But to consider the rules of morality as improvable is one thing; to pass over the intermediate generalization entirely and endeavor to test each individual action directly by the first principle is another. It is a strange notion that the acknowledgment of a first principle is inconsistent with the admission of secondary ones. To inform a traveler respecting the place of his ultimate destination is not to forbid the use of landmarks and direction-posts on the way. The proposition that happiness is the end and aim of morality does not mean that no road ought to be laid down to that goal, or that persons going thither should not be advised to take one direction rather than another. Men really ought to leave off talking a kind of nonsense on this subject, which they would neither talk nor listen to on other matters of practical concernment. Nobody argues that the art of navigation is not founded on astronomy because sailors cannot wait to calculate the Nautical Almanac. Being rational creatures, they go to sea with it ready calculated; and all rational creatures go out upon the sea of life with their minds made up on the common questions of right and wrong, as well as on many of the far more difficult questions of wise and foolish. And this, as long as foresight is a human quality, it is to be presumed they will continue to do. Whatever we adopt as the fundamental principle of morality, we require subordinate principles to apply it by; the impossibility of doing without them, being common to all systems, can afford no argument against any one in particular; but gravely to argue as if no such secondary principles could be had, and as if mankind had remained till now, and always must remain, without drawing any general conclusions from the experience of human life is as high a pitch, I think, as absurdity has ever reached in philosophical controversy.

The remainder of the stock arguments against utilitarianism mostly consist in laying to its charge the common infirmities of human nature, and the general difficulties which embarrass conscientious persons in shaping their course through life. We are told that a utilitarian will be apt to make his own particular case an exception to moral rules, and, when under temptation, will see a utility in the breach of a rule, greater than he will see in its observance. But is utility the only creed which is able to furnish us with excuses for evil-doing and means of cheating our own conscience? They are afforded in abundance by all doctrines which recognize as a fact in morals the existence of conflicting considerations, which all doctrines do that have been believed by sane persons. It is not the fault of any creed, but of the complicated nature of human affairs, that rules of conduct cannot be so framed as to require no exceptions, and that hardly any kind of action can safely be laid down as either always obligatory or always condemnable. There is no ethical creed which does not temper the rigidity of its laws by giving a certain latitude, under the moral responsibility of the agent, for accommodation to peculiarities of circumstances; and under every creed, at the opening thus made, self-deception and dishonest casuistry get in. There exists no moral system under which there do not arise unequivocal cases of conflicting obligation. These are the real difficulties, the knotty points both in the theory of ethics and in the conscientious guidance of personal conduct. They are overcome practically, with greater or with less success, according to the intellect and virtue of the individual; but it can hardly be pretended that anyone will be the less qualified for dealing with them, from possessing an ultimate standard to which conflicting rights and duties can be referred. If utility is the ultimate source of moral obligations, utility may be invoked to decide between them when their demands are incompatible. Though the application of the standard may be difficult, it is better than none at all; while in other systems, the moral laws all claiming independent authority, there is no common umpire entitled to interfere between them; their claims to precedence one over another rest on little better than sophistry, and, unless determined, as they generally are, by the unacknowledged influence of consideration of utility, afford a free scope for the action of personal desires and partialities. We must remember that only in these cases of conflict between secondary principles is it requisite that first principles should be appealed to. There is no case of moral obligation in which some secondary principle is not involved; and if only one, there can seldom be any real doubt which one it is, in the mind of any person by whom the principle itself is recognized.

Chapter III
Of the Ultimate Sanction of the Principle of Utility

The question is often asked, and properly so, in regard to any supposed moral standard—What is its sanction? what are the motives to obey? or, more specifically, what is the source of its obligation? whence does it derive its binding force? It is a necessary part of moral philosophy to provide the answer to this question, which, though frequently assuming the shape of an objection to the utilitarian morality, as if it had some special applicability to that above others, really arises in regard to all standards. It arises, in fact, whenever a person is called on to *adopt* a standard, or refer morality to any basis on which he has not been accustomed to rest it. For the customary morality, that which education and opinion have consecrated, is the only one which presents itself to the mind with the feeling of being *in itself* obligatory; and when a person is asked to believe that this morality *derives* its obligation from some general principle round which custom has not thrown the same halo, the assertion is to him a paradox; the supposed corollaries seem to have a more binding force than the original theorem; the superstructure seems to stand better without than with what is represented as its foundation. He says to himself, I feel that I am bound not to rob or murder, betray or deceive; but why am I bound to promote the general happiness? If my own happiness lies in something else, why may I not give that the preference?

If the view adopted by the utilitarian philosophy of the nature of the moral sense be correct, this difficulty will always present itself until the influences which form moral character have taken the same hold of the principle which they have taken of some of the consequences — until, by the improvement of education, the feeling of unity with our fellow creatures shall be (what it cannot be denied that Christ intended it to be) as deeply rooted in our character, and to our own consciousness as completely a part of our nature, as the horror of crime is in an ordinarily well-brought-up young person. In the meantime, however, the difficulty has no peculiar application to the doctrine of utility, but is inherent in every attempt to analyze morality and reduce it to principles; which, unless the principle is already in men's minds invested with as much sacredness as any of its applications, always seems to divest them of a part of their sanctity.

The principle of utility either has, or there is no reason why it might not have, all the sanctions which belong to any other system of morals. Those sanctions are either external or internal. Of the external sanctions it is not necessary to speak at any length. They are the hope of favor and the fear of displeasure from our fellow creatures or from the Ruler of the universe, along with whatever we may have of sympathy or affection for them, or of love and awe of Him, inclining us to do His will independently of selfish consequences. There is evidently no reason why all these motives for observance should not attach themselves to the utilitarian morality as completely and as powerfully as to any other. Indeed, those of them which refer to our fellow creatures are sure to do so, in proportion to the amount of general intelligence; for whether there be any other ground of moral obligation than the general happiness or not, men do desire happiness; and however imperfect may be their own practice, they desire and commend all conduct in others toward themselves by which they think their happiness is promoted. With regard to the religious motive, if men believe, as most profess to do, in the goodness of God, those who think that conduciveness to the general happiness is the essence or even only the criterion of good must necessarily believe that it is also that which God approves. The whole force therefore of external reward and punishment, whether physical or moral, and whether proceeding from God or from our fellow men, together with all that the capacities of human nature admit of disinterested devotion to either, become available to enforce the utilitarian morality, in proportion as that morality is recognized; and the more powerfully, the more the appliances of education and general cultivation are bent to the purpose.

So far as to external sanctions. The internal sanction of duty, whatever our standard of duty may be, is one and the same — a feeling in our own mind; a pain, more or less intense, attendant on violation of duty, which in properly cultivated moral natures rises, in the more serious cases, into shrinking from it as an impossibility. This feeling, when disinterested and connecting itself with the pure idea of duty, and not with some particular form of it, or with any of the merely accessory circumstances, is the essence of conscience; though in that complex phenomenon as it actually exists, the simple fact is in general all encrusted over with collateral associations derived from sympathy, from love, and still more from fear; from all the forms of religious feeling; from the recollections of childhood and of all our past life; from self-esteem, desire of the esteem of others, and occasionally even self-abasement. This extreme complication is, I apprehend, the origin of the sort of mystical character which, by a tendency of the human mind of which there are many other examples, is apt to be attributed to the idea of moral obligation, and which leads people to believe that the idea cannot possibly attach itself to any other objects than those which, by a supposed mysterious law, are found in our present experience to excite it. Its binding force, however, consists in the existence of a mass of feeling which must be broken through in order to do what violates our standard of right, and which, if we do nevertheless violate that standard, will probably have to be encountered afterwards in the form of remorse. Whatever theory we have of the nature or origin of conscience, this is what essentially constitutes it.

The ultimate sanction, therefore, of all morality (external motives apart) being a subjective feeling in our own minds, I see nothing embarrassing to those whose standard is utility in the question, What is the sanction of that particular standard? We may answer, the same as of all other moral standards—the conscientious feelings of mankind. Undoubtedly this sanction has no binding efficacy on those who do not possess the feelings it appeals to; but neither will these persons be more obedient to any other moral principle than to the utilitarian one. On them morality of any kind has no hold but through the external sanctions. Meanwhile the feelings exist, a fact in human nature, the reality of which, and the great power with which they are capable of acting on those in whom they have been duly cultivated, are proved by experience. No reason has ever been shown why they may not be cultivated to as great intensity in connection with the utilitarian as with any other rule of morals.

There is, I am aware, a disposition to believe that a person who sees in moral obligation a transcendental fact, an objective reality belonging to the province of "things in themselves," is likely to be more obedient to it than one who believes it to be entirely subjective, having its seat in human consciousness only. But whatever a person's opinion may be on this point of ontology, the force he is really urged by is his own subjective feeling, and is exactly measured by its strength. No one's belief that duty is an objective reality is stronger than the belief that God is so; yet the belief in God, apart from the expectation of actual reward and punishment, only operates on conduct through, and in proportion to, the subjective religious feeling. The sanction, so far as it is disinterested, is always in the mind itself; and the notion, therefore, of the transcendental moralists must be that this sanction will not exist *in* the mind unless it is believed to have its root out of the mind; and that if a person is able to say to himself, "That which is restraining me and which is called my conscience is only a feeling in my own mind," he may possibly draw the conclusion that when the feeling ceases the obligation ceases, and that if he find the feeling inconvenient, he may disregard it and endeavor to get rid of it. But is this danger confined to the utilitarian morality? Does the belief that moral obligation has its seat outside the mind make the feeling of it too strong to be got rid of? The fact is so far otherwise that all moralists admit and lament the ease with which, in the generality of minds, conscience can be silenced or stifled. The question, "Need I obey my conscience?" is quite as often put to themselves by persons who never heard of the principle of utility as by its adherents. Those whose conscientious feelings are so weak as to allow of their asking this question, if they answer it affirmatively, will not do so because they believe in the transcendental theory, but because of the external sanctions.

It is not necessary, for the present purpose, to decide whether the feeling of duty is innate or implanted. Assuming it to be innate, it is an open question to what objects it naturally attaches itself; for the philosophic supporters of that theory are now agreed that the intuitive perception is of principles of morality and not of the details. If there be anything innate in the matter, I see no reason why the feeling which is innate should not be that of regard to the pleasures and pains of others. If there is any principle of morals which is intuitively obligatory, I should say it must be that. If so, the intuitive ethics would coincide with the utilitarian, and there would be no further quarrel between them. Even as it is, the intuitive moralists, though they believe that there are other intuitive moral obligations, do already believe this to be one; for they unanimously hold that a large *portion* of morality turns upon the consideration due to the interests of our fellow creatures. Therefore, if the belief in the transcendental origin of moral obligation gives any additional efficacy to the internal sanction, it appears to me that the utilitarian principle has already the benefit of it.

On the other hand, if, as is my own belief, the moral feelings are not innate but acquired, they are not for that reason the less natural. It is natural to man to speak, to reason, to build cities, to cultivate the ground, though these are acquired faculties. The moral feelings are not indeed a part of our nature in the sense of being in any perceptible degree present in all of us; but this, unhappily, is a fact admitted by those who believe the most strenuously in their transcendental origin. Like the other acquired capacities above referred to, the moral faculty, if not a part of our nature, is a natural outgrowth from it; capable, like them, in a certain small degree, of springing up spontaneously; and susceptible of being brought by cultivation to a high degree of development. Unhappily it is also susceptible, by a sufficient use of the external sanctions and of the force of early impressions, of being cultivated in almost any direction, so that there is hardly anything so absurd or so mischievous that it may not, by means of these influences, be made to act on the human mind with all the authority of conscience. To doubt that the same potency might be given by the same means to the principle of utility, even if it had no foundation in human nature, would be flying in the face of all experience.

But moral associations which are wholly of artificial creation, when the intellectual culture goes on, yield by degrees to the dissolving force of analysis; and if the feeling of duty, when associated with utility, would appear equally arbitrary; if there were no leading department of our nature, no powerful class of sentiments, with which that association would harmonize, which would make us feel it congenial and incline us not only to foster it in others (for which we have abundant interested motives), but also to cherish it in ourselves—if there were not, in short, a natural basis of sentiment for utilitarian morality, it might well happen that this association also, even after it had been implanted by education, might be analyzed away.

But there is this basis of powerful natural sentiment; and this it is which, when once the general happiness *is* recognized as the ethical standard, will constitute the strength of the utilitarian morality. This firm foundation is that of the social feelings of mankind—the desire to be in unity with our fellow creatures, which is already a powerful principle in human nature, and happily one of those which tend to become stronger, even without express inculcation, from the influences of advancing civilization. The social state is at once so natural, so necessary, and so habitual to man, that, except in some unusual circumstances or by an effort of voluntary abstraction, he never conceives himself otherwise than as a member of a body; and this association is riveted more and more, as mankind are further removed from the state of savage independence. Any condition, therefore, which is essential to a state of society becomes more and more an inseparable part of every person's conception of the state of things which he is born into, and which is the destiny of a human being. Now society between human beings, except in the relation of master and slave, is manifestly impossible on any other footing than that the interests of all are to be consulted. Society between equals can only exist on the understanding that the interests of all are to be regarded equally. And since in all states of civilization, every person, except an absolute monarch, has equals, everyone is obliged to live on these terms with somebody; and in every age some advance is made toward a state in which it will be impossible to live permanently on other terms with anybody. In this way people grow up unable to conceive as possible to them a state of total disregard of other people's interests. They are under a necessity of conceiving themselves as at least abstaining from all the grosser injuries, and (if only for their own protection) living in a state of constant protest against them. They are also familiar with the fact of co-operating with others and proposing of themselves a collective, not an individual, interest as the aim (at least for the time being) of their actions. So long as they are co-operating, their ends are identified with those of others; there is at least a temporary feeling that the interests of others are their own interests. Not only does all strengthening of social ties, and all healthy growth of society, give to each individual a stronger personal interest in practically consulting the welfare of others, it also leads him to identify his *feelings* more and more with their good, or at least with an even greater degree of practical consideration for it. He comes, as though instinctively, to be conscious of himself as a being who *of course* pays regard to others. The good of others becomes to him a thing naturally and necessarily to be attended to, like any of the physical conditions of our existence. Now, whatever amount of this feeling a person has, he is urged by the strongest motives both of interest and of sympathy to demonstrate it, and to the utmost of his power encourage it in others; and even if he has none of it himself, he is as greatly interested as anyone else that others should have it. Consequently, the smallest germs of the feeling are laid hold of and nourished by the contagion of sympathy and the influences of education; and a complete web of corroborative association is woven round it by the powerful agency of the external sanctions. This mode of conceiving ourselves and human life, as civilization goes on, is felt to be more and more natural. Every step in political improvement renders it more so, by removing the sources of opposition of interest and leveling those inequalities of legal privilege between individuals or classes, owing to which there are large portions of mankind whose happiness it is still practicable to disregard. In an improving state of the human mind, the influences are constantly on the increase which tend to generate in each individual a feeling of unity with all the rest; which, if perfect, would make him never think of, or desire, any beneficial condition for himself in the benefits of which they are not included. If we now suppose this feeling of unity to be taught as a religion, and the whole force of education, of institutions, and of opinion directed, as it once was in the case of religion, to make every person grow up from infancy surrounded on all sides both by the profession and the practice of it, I think that no one who can realize this conception will feel any misgiving about the sufficiency of the ultimate sanction for the happiness morality. To any ethical student who finds the realization difficult, I recommend, as a means of facilitating it, the second of M. Comte's two principal works, the *Traité de politique positive.* I entertain the strongest objections to the system of politics and morals set forth in that treatise, but I think it has superabundantly shown the possibility of giving to the service of humanity, even without the aid of belief in a Providence, both the psychological power and the social efficacy of a religion, making it take hold of human life, and color all thought, feeling, and action in a manner of which the greatest ascendancy ever exercised by any religion may be but a type and foretaste; and of which the danger is, not that it should be insufficient, but that it should be so excessive as to interfere unduly with human freedom and individuality.

Neither is it necessary to the feeling which constitutes the binding force of the utilitarian morality on those who recognize it to wait for those social influences which would make its obligation felt by mankind at large. In the comparatively early state of human advancement in which we now live, a person cannot, indeed, feel that entireness of sympathy with all others which would make any real discordance in the general direction of their conduct in life impossible, but already a person in whom the social feeling is at all developed cannot bring himself to think of the rest of his fellow creatures as struggling rivals with him for the means of happiness, whom he must desire to see defeated in their object in order that he may succeed in his. The deeply rooted conception which every individual even now has of himself as a social being tends to make him feel it one of his natural wants that there should be harmony between his feelings and aims and those of his fellow creatures. If differences of opinion and of mental culture make it impossible for him to share many of their actual feelings—perhaps make him denounce and defy those feelings—he still needs to be conscious that his real aim and theirs do not conflict; that he is not opposing himself to what they really wish for, namely, their own good, but is, on the contrary, promoting it. This feeling in most individuals is much inferior in strength to their selfish feelings, and is often wanting altogether. But to those who have it, it possesses all the characters of a natural feeling. It does not present itself to their minds as a superstition of education or a law despotically imposed by the power of society, but as an attribute which it would not be well for them to be without. This conviction is the ultimate sanction of the greatest happiness morality. This it is which makes any mind of well-developed feelings work with, and not against, the outward motives to care for others, afforded by what I have called the external sanctions; and, when those sanctions are wanting or act in an opposite direction, constitutes in itself a powerful internal binding force, in proportion to the sensitiveness and thoughtfulness of the character, since few but those whose mind is a moral blank could bear to lay out their course of life on the plan of paying no regard to others except so far as their own private interest compels.

Chapter IV
Of What Sort of Proof the Principle of Utility is Susceptible

It has already been remarked that questions of ultimate ends do not admit of proof, in the ordinary acceptation of the term. To be incapable of proof by reasoning is common to all first principles, to the first premises of our knowledge, as well as to those of our conduct. But the former, being matters of fact, may be the subject of a direct appeal to the faculties which judge of fact—namely, our senses and our internal consciousness. Can an appeal be made to the same faculties on questions of practical ends? Or by what other faculty is cognizance taken of them?

Questions about ends are, in other words, questions what things are desirable. The utilitarian doctrine is that happiness is desirable, and the only thing desirable, as an end; all other things being only desirable as means to that end. What ought to be required of this doctrine, what conditions is it requisite that the doctrine should fulfill—to make good its claim to be believed?

The only proof capable of being given that an object is visible is that people actually see it. The only proof that a sound is audible is that people hear it; and so of the other sources of our experience. In like manner, I apprehend, the sole evidence it is possible to produce that anything is desirable is that people do actually desire it. If the end which the utilitarian doctrine proposes to itself were not, in theory and in practice, acknowledged to be an end, nothing could ever convince any person that it was so. No reason can be given why the general happiness is desirable, except that each person, so far as he believes it to be attainable, desires his own happiness. This, however, being a fact, we have not only all the proof which the case admits of, but all which it is possible to require, that happiness is a good, that each person's happiness is a good to that person, and the general happiness, therefore, a good to the aggregate of all persons. Happiness has made out its title as *one* of the ends of conduct and, consequently, one of the criteria of morality.

But it has not, by this alone, proved itself to be the sole criterion. To do that, it would seem, by the same rule, necessary to show, not only that people desire happiness, but that they never desire anything else. Now it is palpable that they do desire things which, in common language, are decidedly distinguished from happiness. They desire, for example, virtue and the absence of vice no less really than pleasure and the absence of pain. The desire of virtue is not as universal, but it is as authentic a fact as the desire of happiness. And hence the opponents of the utilitarian standard deem that they have a right to infer that there are other ends of human action besides happiness, and that happiness is not the standard of approbation and disapprobation.

But does the utilitarian doctrine deny that people desire virtue, or maintain that virtue is not a thing to be desired? The very reverse. It maintains not only that virtue is to be desired, but that it is to be desired disinterestedly, for itself. Whatever may be the opinion of utilitarian moralists as to the original conditions by which virtue is made virtue, however they may believe (as they do) that actions and dispositions are only virtuous because they promote another end than virtue, yet this being granted, and it having been decided, from considerations of this description, what *is* virtuous, they not only place virtue at the very head of the things which are good as means to the ultimate end, but they also recognize as a psychological fact the possibility of its being, to the individual, a good in itself, without looking to any end beyond it; and hold that the mind is not in a right state, not in a state conformable to utility, not in the state most conducive to the general happiness, unless it does love virtue in this manner—as a thing desirable in itself, even although, in the individual instance, it should not produce those other desirable consequences which it tends to produce, and on account of which it is held to be virtue. This opinion is not, in the smallest degree, a departure from the happiness principle. The ingredients of happiness are very various, and each of them is desirable in itself, and not merely when considered as swelling an aggregate. The principle of utility does not mean that any given pleasure, as music, for instance, or any given exemption from pain, as for example health, is to be looked upon as means to a collective something termed happiness, and to be desired on that account. They are desired and desirable in and for themselves; besides being means, they are a part of the end. Virtue, according to the utilitarian doctrine, is not naturally and originally part of the end, but it is capable of becoming so; and in those who live it disinterestedly it has become so, and is desired and cherished, not as a means to happiness, but as a part of their happiness.

To illustrate this further, we may remember that virtue is not the only thing originally a means, and which if it were not a means to anything else would be and remain indifferent, but which by association with what it is a means to comes to be desired for itself, and that too with the utmost intensity. What, for example, shall we say of the love of money? There is nothing originally more desirable about money than about any heap of glittering pebbles. Its worth is solely that of the things which it will buy; the desires for other things than itself, which it is a means of gratifying. Yet the love of money is not only one of the strongest moving forces of human life, but money is, in many cases, desired in and for itself; the desire to possess it is often stronger than the desire to use it, and goes on increasing when all the desires which point to ends beyond it, to be compassed by it, are falling off. It may, then, be said truly that money is desired not for the sake of an end, but as part of the end. From being a means to happiness, it has come to be itself a principal ingredient of the individual's conception of happiness. The same may be said of the majority of the great objects of human life: power, for example, or fame, except that to each of these there is a certain amount of immediate pleasure annexed, which has at least the semblance of being naturally inherent in them—a thing which cannot be said of money. Still, however, the strongest natural attraction, both of power and of fame, is the immense aid they give to the attainment of our other wishes; and it is the strong association thus generated between them and all our objects of desire which gives to the direct desire of them the intensity it often assumes, so as in some characters to surpass in strength all other desires. In these cases the means have become a part of the end, and a more important part of it than any of the things which they are means to. What was once desired as an instrument for the attainment of happiness has come to be desired for its own sake. In being desired for its own sake it is, however, desired as *part* of happiness. The person is made, or thinks he would be made, happy by its mere possession; and is made unhappy by failure to obtain it. The desire of it is not a different thing from the desire of happiness any more than the love of music or the desire of health. They are included in happiness. They are some of the elements of which the desire of happiness is made up. Happiness is not an abstract idea but a concrete whole; and these are some of its parts. And the utilitarian standard sanctions and approves their being so. Life would be a poor thing, very ill provided with sources of happiness, if there were not this provision of nature by which things originally indifferent, but conducive to, or otherwise associated with, the satisfaction of our primitive desires, become in themselves sources of pleasure more valuable than the primitive pleasures, both in permanency, in the space of human existence that they are capable of covering, and even in intensity.

Virtue, according to the utilitarian conception, is a good of this description. There was no original desire of it, or motive to it, save its conduciveness to pleasure, and especially to protection from pain. But through the association thus formed it may be felt a good in itself, and desired as such with as great intensity as any other good; and with this difference between it and the love of money, of power, or of fame—that all of these may, and often do, render the individual noxious to the other members of the society to which he belongs, whereas there is nothing which makes him so much a blessing to them as the cultivation of the disinterested love of virtue. And consequently, the utilitarian standard, while it tolerates and approves those other acquired desires, up to the point beyond which they would be more injurious to the general happiness than promotive to it, enjoins and requires the cultivation of the love of virtue up to the greatest strength possible, as being above all things important to the general happiness.

It results from the preceding considerations that there is in reality nothing desired except happiness. Whatever is desired otherwise than as a means to some end beyond itself, and ultimately to happiness, is desired as itself a part of happiness, and is not desired for itself until it has become so. Those who desire virtue for its own sake desire it either because the consciousness of it is a pleasure, or because the consciousness of being without it is a pain, or for both reasons united; as in truth the pleasure and pain seldom exist separately, but almost always together — the same person feeling pleasure in the degree of virtue attained, and pain in not having attained more. If one of these gave him no pleasure, and the other no pain, he would not love or desire virtue, or would desire it only for the other benefits which it might produce to himself or to persons whom he cared for.

We have now, then, an answer to the question, of what sort of proof the principle of utility is susceptible. If the opinion which I have now stated is psychologically true — if human nature is so constituted as to desire nothing which is not either a part of happiness or a means of happiness — we can have no other proof, and we require no other, that these are the only things desirable. If so, happiness is the sole end of human action, and the promotion of it the test by which to judge of all human conduct; from whence it necessarily follows that it must be the criterion of morality, since a part is included in the whole.

And now to decide whether this is really so, whether mankind do desire nothing for itself but that which is a pleasure to them, or of which the absence is a pain, we have evidently arrived at a question of fact and experience, dependent, like all similar questions, upon evidence. It can only be determined by practiced self-consciousness and self-observation, assisted by observation of others. I believe that these sources of evidence, impartially consulted, will declare that desiring a thing and finding it pleasant, aversion to it and thinking of it as painful, are phenomena entirely inseparable or, rather, two parts of the same phenomenon — in strictness of language, two different modes of naming the same psychological fact; that to think of an object as desirable (unless for the sake of its consequences) and to think of it as pleasant are one and the same thing; and that to desire anything except in proportion as the idea of it is pleasant is a physical and metaphysical impossibility.

So obvious does this appear to me that I expect it will hardly be disputed; and the objection made will be, not that desire can possibly be directed to anything ultimately except pleasure and exemption from pain, but that the will is a different thing from desire; that a person of confirmed virtue or any other person whose purposes are fixed carries out his purposes without any thought of the pleasure he has in contemplating them or expects to derive from their fulfillment, and persists in acting on them, even though these pleasures are much diminished by changes in his character or decay of his passive sensibilities, or are outweighed by the pains which the pursuit of the purposes may bring upon him. All this I fully admit and have stated it elsewhere as positively and emphatically as anyone. Will, the active phenomenon, is a different thing from desire, the state of passive sensibility, and, though originally an offshoot from it, may in time take root and detach itself from the parent stock, so much so that in the case of a habitual purpose, instead of willing the thing because we desire it, we often desire it only because we will it. This, however, is but an instance of that familiar fact, the power of habit, and is nowise confined to the case of virtuous actions. Many indifferent things which men originally did from a motive of some sort they continue to do from habit. Sometimes this is done unconsciously, the consciousness coming only after the action; at other times with conscious volition, but volition which has become habitual and is put in operation by the force of habit, in opposition perhaps to the deliberate preference, as often happens with those who have contracted habits of vicious or hurtful indulgence. Third and last comes the case in which the habitual act of will in the individual instance is not in contradiction to the general intention prevailing at other times, but in fulfillment of it, as in the case of the person of confirmed virtue and of all who pursue deliberately and consistently any determinate end. The distinction between will and desire thus understood is an authentic and highly important psychological fact; but the fact consists solely in this—that will, like all other parts of our constitution, is amenable to habit, and that we may will from habit what we no longer desire for itself, or desire only because we will it. It is not the less true that will, in the beginning, is entirely produced by desire, including in that term the repelling influence of pain as well as the attractive one of pleasure. Let us take into consideration no longer the person who has a confirmed will to do right, but him in whom that virtuous will is still feeble, conquerable by temptation, and not to be fully relied on; by what means can it be strengthened? How can the will to be virtuous, where it does not exist in sufficient force, be implanted or awakened? Only by making the person *desire* virtue—by making him think of it in a pleasurable light, or of its absence in a painful one. It is by associating the doing right with pleasure, or the wrong with pain, or by eliciting and impressing and bringing home to the person's experience the pleasure naturally involved in the one or the pain in the other, that it is possible to call forth that will to be virtuous which, when confirmed, acts without any thought of either pleasure or pain. Will is the child of desire, and passes out of the dominion of its parent only to come under that of habit. That which is the result of habit affords no presumption of being intrinsically good; and there would be no reason for wishing that the purpose of virtue should become independent of pleasure and pain were it not that the influence of the pleasurable and painful associations which prompt to virtue is not sufficiently to be depended on for unerring constancy of action until it has acquired the support of habit. Both in feeling and in conduct, habit is the only thing which imparts certainty; and it is because of the importance to others of being able to rely absolutely on one's feelings and conduct, and to oneself of being able to rely on one's own, that the will to do right ought to be cultivated into this habitual independence. In other words, this state of the will is a means to good, not intrinsically a good; and does not contradict the doctrine that nothing is a good to human beings but in so far as it is either itself pleasurable or a means of attaining pleasure or averting pain.

But if this doctrine be true, the principle of utility is proved. Whether it is so or not must now be left to the consideration of the thoughtful reader.

Chapter V
On the Connection between Justice and Utility

In all ages of speculation one of the strongest obstacles to the reception of the doctrine that utility or happiness is the criterion of right and wrong has been drawn from the idea of justice. The powerful sentiment and apparently clear perception which that word recalls with a rapidity and certainty resembling an instinct have seemed to the majority of thinkers to point to an inherent quality in things; to show that the just must have an existence in nature as something absolute, generically distinct from every variety of the expedient and, in idea, opposed to it, though (as is commonly acknowledged) never, in the long run, disjoined from it in fact.

In the case of this, as of our other moral sentiments, there is no necessary connection between the question of its origin and that of its binding force. That a feeling is bestowed on us by nature does not necessarily legitimate all its promptings. The feeling of justice might be a peculiar instinct, and might yet require, like our other instincts, to be controlled and enlightened by a higher reason. If we have intellectual instincts leading us to judge in a particular way, as well as animal instincts that prompt us to act in a particular way, there is no necessity that the former should be more infallible in their sphere than the latter in theirs; it may as well happen that wrong judgments are occasionally suggested by those, as wrong actions by these. But though it is one thing to believe that we have natural feelings of justice, and another to acknowledge them as an ultimate criterion of conduct, these two opinions are very closely connected in point of fact. Mankind are always predisposed to believe that any subjective feeling, not otherwise accounted for, is a revelation of some objective reality. Our present object is to determine whether the reality to which the feeling of justice corresponds is one which needs any such special revelation, whether the justice or injustice of an action is a thing intrinsically peculiar and distinct from all its other qualities or only a combination of certain of those qualities presented under a peculiar aspect. For the purpose of this inquiry it is practically important to consider whether the feeling itself, of justice and injustice, is *sui generis* like our sensations of color and taste or a derivative feeling formed by a combination of others. And this it is the more essential to examine, as people are in general willing enough to allow that objectively the dictates of justice coincide with a part of the field of general expediency; but inasmuch as the subjective mental feeling of justice is different from that which commonly attaches to simple expediency, and, except in the extreme cases of the latter, is far more imperative in its demands, people find it difficult to see in justice only a particular kind or branch of general utility, and think that its superior binding force requires a totally different origin.

To throw light upon this question, it is necessary to attempt to ascertain what is the distinguishing character of justice, or of injustice; what is the quality, or whether there is any quality, attributed in common to all modes of conduct designated as unjust (for justice, like many other moral attributes, is best defined by its opposite), and distinguishing them from such modes of conduct as are disapproved, but without having that particular epithet of disapprobation applied to them. If in everything which men are accustomed to characterize as just or unjust some one common attribute or collection of attributes is always present, we may judge whether this particular attribute or combination of attributes would be capable of gathering round it a sentiment of that peculiar character and intensity by virtue of the general laws of our emotional constitution, or whether the sentiment is inexplicable and requires to be regarded as a special provision of nature. If we find the former to be the case, we shall, in resolving this question, have resolved also the main problem; if the latter, we shall have to seek for some other mode of investigating it.

To find the common attributes of a variety of objects, it is necessary to begin by surveying the objects themselves in the concrete. Let us therefore advert successively to the various modes of action and arrangements of human affairs which are classed, by universal or widely spread opinion, as just or as unjust. The things well known to excite the sentiments associated with those names are of a very multifarious character. I shall pass them rapidly in review, without studying any particular arrangement.

In the first place, it is most considered unjust to deprive anyone of his personal liberty, his property, or any other thing which belongs to him by law. Here, therefore is one instance of the application of the terms "just" and "unjust" in a perfectly definite sense, namely, that it is just to respect, unjust to violate, the *legal rights* of anyone. But this judgment admits of several exceptions, arising from the other forms in which the notions of justice and injustice present themselves. For example, the person who suffers the deprivation may (as the phrase is) have *forfeited* the rights which he is so deprived of—a case to which we shall return presently. But also—

Secondly, the legal rights of which he is deprived may be rights which *ought* not to have belonged to him; in other words, the law which confers on him these rights may be a bad law. When it is so or when (which is the same thing for our purpose) it is supposed to be so, opinions will differ as to the justice or injustice of infringing it. Some maintain that no law, however bad, ought to be disobeyed by an individual citizen; that his opposition to it, if shown at all, should only be shown in endeavoring to get it altered by competent authority. This opinion (which condemns many of the most illustrious benefactors of mankind, and would often protect pernicious institutions against the only weapons which, in the state of things existing at the time, have any chance of succeeding against them) is defended by those who hold it on grounds of expediency, principally on that of the importance to the common interest of mankind, of maintaining inviolate the sentiment of submission to law. Other persons, again, hold the directly contrary opinion that any law, judged to be bad, may blamelessly be disobeyed, even though it be not judged to be unjust but only inexpedient, while others would confine the license of disobedience to the case of unjust laws; but, again, some say that all laws which are inexpedient are unjust, since every law imposes some restriction on the natural liberty of mankind, which restriction is an injustice unless legitimated by tending to their good. Among these diversities of opinion it seems to be universally admitted that there may be unjust laws, and that law, consequently, is not the ultimate criterion of justice, but may give to one person a benefit, or impose on another an evil, which justice condemns. When, however, a law is thought to be unjust, it seems always to be regarded as being so in the same way in which a breach of law is unjust, namely, by infringing somebody's right, which, as it cannot in this case be a legal right, receives a different appellation and is called a moral right. We may say, therefore, that a second case of injustice consists in taking or withholding from any person that to which he has a *moral right.*

Thirdly, it is universally considered just that each person should obtain that (whether good or evil) which he *deserves,* and unjust that he should obtain a good or be made to undergo an evil which he does not deserve. This is, perhaps, the clearest and most emphatic form in which the idea of justice is conceived by the general mind. As it involves the notion of desert, the question arises what constitutes desert? Speaking in a general way, a person is understood to deserve good if he does right, evil if he does wrong; and in a more particular sense, to deserve good from those to whom he does or has done good, and evil from those to whom he does or has done evil. The precept of returning good for evil has never been regarded as a case of the fulfillment of justice, but as one in which the claims of justice are waived, in obedience to other considerations.

Fourthly, it is confessedly unjust to *break faith* with anyone: to violate an engagement, either express or implied, or disappoint expectations raised by our own conduct, at least if we have raised those expectations knowingly and voluntarily. Like the other obligations of justice already spoken of, this one is not regarded as absolute, but as capable of being overruled by a stronger obligation of justice on the other side, or by such conduct on the part of the person concerned as is deemed to absolve us from our obligation to him and to constitute a *forfeiture* of the benefit which he has been led to expect.

Fifthly, it is, by universal admission, inconsistent with justice to be *partial*—to show favor or preference to one person over another in matters to which favor and preference do not properly apply. Impartiality, however, does not seem to be regarded as a duty in itself, but rather as instrumental to some other duty; for it is admitted that favor and preference are not always censurable, and, indeed, the cases in which they are condemned are rather the exception than the rule. A person would be more likely to be blamed than applauded for giving his family or friends no superiority in good offices over strangers when he could do so without violating any other duty; and no one thinks it unjust to seek one person in preference to another as a friend, connection, or companion. Impartiality where rights are concerned is of course obligatory, but this is involved in the more general obligations of giving to everyone his right. A tribunal, for example, must be impartial because it is bound to award, without regard to any other consideration, a disputed object to the one of two parties who has the right to it. There are other cases in which impartiality means being solely influenced by desert, as with those who, in the capacity of judges, preceptors, or parents, administer reward and punishment as such. There are cases, again, in which it means being solely influenced by considerations for the public interest, as in making a selection among candidates for a government employment. Impartiality, in short, as an obligation of justice, may be said to mean being exclusively influenced by the considerations which it is supposed ought to influence the particular case in hand, and resisting solicitation of any motives which prompt to conduct different from what those considerations would dictate.

Nearly allied to the idea of impartiality is that of *equality,* which often enters as a component part both into the conception of justice and into the practice of it, and, in the eyes of many persons, constitutes its essence. But in this, still more than in any other case, the notion of justice varies in different persons, and always conforms in its variations to their notion of utility. Each person maintains that equality is the dictate of justice, except where he thinks that expediency requires inequality. The justice of giving equal protection to the rights of all is maintained by those who support the most outrageous inequality in the rights themselves. Even in slave countries it is theoretically admitted that the rights of slave, such as they are, ought to be as sacred as those of the master, and that a tribunal which fails to enforce them with equal strictness is wanting in justice; while, at the same time, institutions which leave to the salve scarcely any rights to enforce are not deemed unjust because they are not deemed inexpedient. Those who think that utility requires distinctions of rank do not consider it unjust that riches and social privileges should be unequally dispensed; but those who think this inequality inexpedient think it unjust also. Whoever thinks that government is necessary sees no injustice in as much inequality as is constituted by giving to the magistrate powers not granted to other people. Even among those who hold leveling doctrines, there are differences of opinion about expediency. Some communists consider it unjust that the produce of the labor of the community should be shared on any other principle than that of exact equality; others think it just that those should receive most whose wants are greatest; while others hold that those who work harder, or who produce more, or whose services are more valuable to the community, may justly claim a larger quota in the division of the produce. And the sense of natural justice may be plausibly appealed to in behalf of every one of these opinions.

Among so many diverse applications of the term "justice," which yet is not regarded as ambiguous, it is a matter of some difficulty to seize the mental link which holds them together, and on which the moral sentiment adhering to the term essentially depends. Perhaps, in this embarrassment, some help may be derived from the history of the word, as indicated by its etymology.

In most if not all languages, the etymology of the word which corresponds to "just" points distinctly to an origin connected with the ordinances of law. *Justum* is a form of *jussum,* that which has been ordered. *Dikaion* comes directly from *dike,* a suit at law. *Recht,* from which came *right* and *righteous,* is synonymous with law. The courts of justice, the administration of justice, are the courts and the administration of law. *La justice,* in French, is the established term for judicature. I am not committing the fallacy, imputed with some show of truth to Horne Tooke, of assuming that a word must still continue to mean what it originally meant. Etymology is slight evidence of what the idea now signified is, but the very best evidence of how it sprang up. There can, I think, be no doubt that the *idée mère,* the primitive element, in the formation of the notion of justice was conformity to law. It constituted the entire idea among the Hebrews, up to the birth of Christianity; as might be expected in the case of a people whose laws attempted to embrace all subjects on which precepts were required, and who believed those laws to be a direct emanation from the Supreme Being. But other nations, and in particular the Greeks and Romans, who knew that their laws had been made originally, and still continued to be made, by men, were not afraid to admit that those men might make bad laws; might do, by law, the same things, and from the same motives, which if done by individuals without the sanction of law would be called unjust. And hence the sentiment of injustice came to be attached, not to all violations of law, but only to violations of such laws as *ought* to exist, including such as ought to exist but do not, and to laws themselves if supposed to be contrary to what ought to be law. In this manner the idea of law and of its injunctions was still predominant in the notion of justice, even when the laws actually in force ceased to be accepted as the standard of it.

It is true that mankind consider the idea of justice and its obligations as applicable to many things which neither are, nor is it desired that they should be, regulated by law. Nobody desires that laws should interfere with the whole detail of private life; yet everyone allows that in all daily conduct a person may and does show himself to be either just or unjust. But even here, the idea of the breach of what ought to be law still lingers in a modified shape. It would always give us pleasure, and chime in with our feelings of fitness, that acts which we deem unjust should be punished, though we do not always think it expedient that this should be done by the tribunals. We forego that gratification on account of incidental inconveniences. We should be glad to see just conduct enforced and injustice repressed, even in the minutest details, if we were not, with reason, afraid of trusting the magistrate with so unlimited an amount of power over individuals. When we think that a person is bound in justice to do a thing, it is an ordinary form of language to say that he ought to be compelled to do it. We should be gratified to see the obligation enforced by anybody who had the power. If we see that its enforcement by law would be inexpedient, we lament the impossibility, we consider the impunity given to injustice as an evil and strive to make amends for it by bringing a strong expression of our own and the public disapprobation to bear upon the offender. Thus the idea of legal constraint is still the generating idea of the notion of justice, though undergoing several transformations before that notion as it exists in an advanced state of society becomes complete.

The above is, I think, a true account, as far as it goes, of the origin and progressive growth of the idea of justice. But we must observe that it contains as yet nothing to distinguish that obligation from moral obligation in general. For the truth is that the idea of penal sanction, which is the essence of law, enters not only into the conception of injustice, but into that of any kind of wrong. We do not call anything wrong unless we mean to imply that a person ought to be punished in some way or other for doing it—if not by law, by the opinion of his fellow creatures; if not by opinion, by the reproaches of his own conscience. This seems the real turning point of the distinction between mortality and simple expediency. It is a part of the notion of duty in every one of its forms that a person may rightfully be compelled to fulfill it. Duty is a thing which may be *exacted* from a person, as one exacts a debt. Unless we think that it may be exacted from him, we do not call it his duty. Reasons of prudence, or the interest of other people, may militate against actually exacting it, but the person himself, it is clearly understood, would not be entitled to complain. There are other things, on the contrary, which we wish that people should do, which we like or admire them for doing, perhaps dislike or despise them for not doing, but yet admit that they are not bound to do; it is not a case of moral obligation; we do not blame them, that is, we do not think that they are proper objects of punishment. How we come by these ideas of deserving and not deserving punishment will appear, perhaps, in the sequel; but I think there is no doubt that this distinction lies at the bottom of the notions of right and wrong; that we call any conduct wrong, or employ, instead, some other term of dislike or disparagement, according as we think that the person ought, or ought not, to be punished for it; and we say it would be right to do so and so, or merely that it would be desirable or laudable, according as we would wish to see the person whom it concerns compelled, or only persuaded and exhorted, to act in that manner.[3]

This, therefore, being the characteristic difference which marks off, not justice, but morality in general from the remaining provinces of expediency and worthiness, the character is still to be sought which distinguishes justice from other branches of morality. Now it is known that ethical writers divide moral duties into two classes, denoted by the ill-chosen expressions, duties of perfect and of imperfect obligation; the latter being those in which, though the act is obligatory, the particular occasions of performing it are left to our choice, as in the case of charity or beneficence, which we are indeed bound to practice but not toward any definite person, nor at any prescribed time. In the more precise language of philosophic jurists, duties of perfect obligation, are those duties in virtue of which a correlative *right* resides in some person or persons; duties of imperfect obligation are those moral obligations which do not give birth to any right. I think it will be found that this distinction exactly coincides with that which exists between justice and the other obligations of morality. In our survey of the various popular acceptations of justice, the term appeared generally

---

[3]See this point enforced and illustrated by Professor Bain, in an admirable chapter (entitled "The Ethical Emotions, or the Moral Sense"), of the second of the two treatises composing his elaborate and profound work on the Mind [*The Emotions and the Will,* 1859].

to involve the idea of a personal right—a claim on the part of one or more individuals, like that which the law gives when it confers a proprietary or other legal right. Whether the injustice consists in depriving a person of a possession, or in breaking faith with him, or in treating him worse than he deserves, or worse than other people who have no greater claims—in each case the supposition implies two things: a wrong done, and some assignable person who is wronged. Injustice may also be done by treating a person better than others; but the wrong in this case is to his competitors, who are also assignable persons. It seems to me that this feature in the case—a right in some person, correlative to the moral obligation—constitutes the specific difference between justice and generosity or beneficence. Justice implies something which it is not only right to do, and wrong not to do, but which some individual person can claim from us as his moral right. No one has a moral right to our generosity or beneficence because we are not morally bound to practice those virtues toward any given individual. And it will be found with respect to this as to every correct definition that the instances which seem to conflict with it are those which most confirm it. For if a moralist attempts, as some have done, to make out that mankind generally, though not any given individual, have a right to all the good we can do them, he at once, by that thesis, including generosity and beneficence within the category of justice. He is obliged to say that our utmost exertions are *due* to our fellow creatures, thus assimilating them to a debt; or that nothing less can be a sufficient *return* for what society does for us, thus classing the case as one of gratitude; both of which are acknowledged cases of justice, and not of the virtue of beneficence; and whoever does not place the distinction between justice and morality in general, where we have now placed it, will be found to make no distinction between them at all, but to merge all morality in justice.

Having thus endeavored to determine the distinctive elements which enter into the composition of the idea of justice, we are ready to enter on the inquiry whether the feeling which accompanies the idea is attached to it by a special dispensation of nature, or whether it could have grown up, by any known laws, out of the idea itself; and, in particular, whether it can have originated in considerations of general expediency.

I conceive that the sentiment itself does not arise from anything which would commonly or correctly be termed an idea of expediency, but that, though the sentiment does not, whatever is moral in it does.

We have seen that the two essential ingredients in the sentiment of justice are the desire to punish a person who has done harm and the knowledge or belief that there is some definite individual or individuals to whom harm has been done.

Now it appears to me that the desire to punish a person who has done harm to some individual is a spontaneous outgrowth from two sentiments, both in the highest degree natural and which either are or resemble instincts: the impulse of self-defense and the feeling of sympathy.

It is natural to resent and to repel or retaliate any harm done or attempted against ourselves or against those with whom we sympathize. The origin of this sentiment it is not necessary here to discuss. Whether it be an instinct or a result of intelligence, it is, we know, common to all animal nature; for every animal tries to hurt those who have hurt, or who it thinks are about to hurt, itself or its young. Human beings, on this point, only differ from other animals in two particulars. First, in being capable of sympathizing, not solely with their offspring, or, like some of the more noble animals, with some superior animal who is kind to them, but with all human, and even with all sentient, beings; secondly, in having a more developed intelligence, which gives a wider range to the whole of their sentiments, whether self-regarding or sympathetic. By virtue of his superior intelligence, even apart from his superior range of sympathy, a human being is capable of apprehending a community of interest between himself and the human society of which he forms a part, such that any conduct which threatens the security of the society generally is threatening to his own, and calls forth his instinct (if instinct it be) of self-defense. The same superiority of intelligence, joined to the power of sympathizing with human beings generally, enables him to attach himself to the collective idea of his tribe, his country, or mankind in such a manner that any act hurtful to them raises his instinct of sympathy and urges him to resistance.

The sentiment of justice, in that one of its elements, which consists of the desire to punish, is thus, I conceive, the natural feeling of retaliation or vengeance, rendered by intellect and sympathy applicable to those injuries, that is, to those hurts, which wound us through, or in common with, society at large. This sentiment, in itself, has nothing moral in it; what is moral is the exclusive subordination of it to the social sympathies, so as to wait on and obey their call. For the natural feeling would make us resent indiscriminately whatever anyone does that is disagreeable to us; but, when moralized by the social feeling, it only acts in the directions conformable to the general good: just persons resenting a hurt to society, though not otherwise a hurt to themselves, and not resenting a hurt to themselves, however painful, unless it be of the kind which society has a common interest with them in the repression of.

It is no objection against this doctrine to say that, when we feel our sentiment of justice outraged, we are not thinking of society at large or of any collective interest, but only of the individual case. It is common enough, certainly, though the reverse of commendable, to feel resentment merely because we have suffered pain; but a person whose resentment is really a moral feeling, that is, who considers whether an act is blamable before he allows himself to resent it—such a person, though he may not say expressly to himself that he is standing up for the interest of society, certainly does feel that he is asserting a rule which is for the benefit of others as well as for his own. If he is not feeling this, if he is regarding the act solely as it affects him individually, he is not consciously just; he is not concerning himself about the justice of his actions. This is admitted even by anti-utilitarian moralists. When Kant (as before remarked) propounds as the fundamental principle of morals, "So act that thy rule of conduct might be adopted as a law by all rational beings," he virtually acknowledges that the interest of mankind collectively, or at least of mankind indiscriminately, must be in the mind of the agent when conscientiously deciding on the morality of the act. Otherwise he uses words without a meaning; for that a rule even of utter selfishness could not *possibly* be adopted by all rational beings—that there is any insuperable obstacle in the nature of things to its adoption—cannot be even plausibly maintained. To give any meaning to Kant's principle, the sense put upon it must be that we ought to shape our conduct by a rule which all rational beings might adopt *with benefit to their collective interest.*

To recapitulate: the idea of justice supposes two things—a rule of conduct and a sentiment which sanctions the rule. The first must be supposed common to all mankind and intended for their good. The other (the sentiment) is a desire that punishment may be suffered by those who infringe the rule. There is involved, in addition, the conception of some definite person who suffers by the infringement whose rights (to use the expression appropriated to the case) are violated by it. And the sentiment of justice appears to me to be the animal desire to repel or retaliate a hurt or damage to oneself or to those with whom one sympathizes, widened so as to include all persons, by the human capacity of enlarged sympathy and the human conception of intelligent self-interest. From the latter elements the feeling derives its morality; from the former, its peculiar impressiveness and energy of self-assertion.

I have, throughout, treated the idea of a *right* residing in the injured person and violated by the injury, not as a separate element in the composition of the idea and sentiment, but as one of the forms in which the other two elements clothe themselves. These elements are a hurt to some assignable person or persons on the one hand, and a demand for punishment on the other. An examination of our own minds, I think, will show that these two things include all that we mean when we speak of violation of a right. When we call anything a person's right, we mean that he has a valid claim on society to protect him in the possession of it, either by the force of law, or by that of education and opinion. If he has what we consider a sufficient claim, on whatever account, to have something guaranteed to him by society, we say that he has a right to it. If we desire to prove that anything does not belong to him by right, we think this done as soon as it is admitted that society ought not to take measures for securing it to him, but should leave him to chance, or to his own exertions. Thus, a person is said to have a right to what he can earn in fair professional competition; because society ought not to allow any other person to hinder him from endeavouring to earn in that manner as much as he can. But he has not a right to three hundred a-year, though he may happen to be earning it; because society is not called on to provide that he shall earn that sum. On the contrary, if he owns ten thousand pounds three per cent stock, he has a right to three hundred a-year; because society has come under an obligation to provide him with an income of that amount.

To have a right, then, is, I conceive, to have something which society ought to defend me in the possession of. If the objector goes on to ask, why it ought? I can give him no other reason than general utility. If that expression does not seem to convey a sufficient feeling of the strength of the obligation, nor to account for the peculiar energy of the feeling, it is because there goes to the composition of the sentiment, not a rational only but also an animal element, the thirst for retaliation; and this thirst derives its intensity, as well as its moral justification, from the extraordinarily important and impressive kind of utility which is concerned. The interest involved is that of security, to every one's feelings the most vital of all interests. All other earthly benefits are needed by one person, not needed by another; and many of them can, if necessary, be cheerfully foregone, or replaced by something else; but security no human being can possibly do without; on it we depend for all our immunity from evil, and for the whole value of all and every good, beyond the passing moment; since nothing but the gratification of the instant could be of any worth to us, if we could be deprived of everything the next instant by whoever was momentarily stronger than ourselves. Now this most indispensable of all necessaries, after physical nutriment, cannot be had, unless the machinery for providing it is kept unintermittedly in active play. Our notion, therefore, of the claim we have on our fellow creatures to join in making safe for us the very groundwork of our existence, gathers feelings around it so much more intense than those concerned in any of the more common cases of utility, that the difference in degree (as is often the case in psychology) becomes a real difference in kind. The claim assumes that character of absoluteness, that apparent infinity, and incommensurability with all other considerations, which constitute the distinction between the feeling of right and wrong and that of ordinary expediency and inexpediency. The feelings concerned are so powerful, and we count so positively on finding a responsive feeling in others (all being alike interested), that *ought* and *should* grow into *must,* and recognized indispensability becomes a moral necessity, analogous to physical, and often not inferior to it in binding force.

If the preceding analysis, or something resembling it, be not the correct account of the notion of justice — if justice be totally independent of utility, and be a standard *per se,* which the mind can recognize by simple introspection of itself — it is hard to understand why that internal oracle is so ambiguous, and why so many things appear either just or unjust, according to the light in which they are regarded.

We are continually informed that utility is an uncertain standard, which every different person interprets differently, and that there is no safety but in the immutable, ineffaceable, and unmistakable dictates of justice, which carry their evidence in themselves and are independent of the fluctuations of opinion. One would suppose from this that on questions of justice there could be no controversy; that, if we take that for our rule, its application to any given case could leave us in as little doubt as a mathematical demonstration. So far is this from being the fact that there is as much difference of opinion, and as much discussion, about what is just as about what is useful to society. Not only have different nations and individuals different notions of justice, but in the mind of one and the same individual, justice is not some one rule, principle, or maxim, but many which do not always coincide in their dictates, and, in choosing between which, he is guided either by some extraneous standard or by his own personal predilections.

For instance, there are some who say that it is unjust to punish anyone for the sake of example to others, that punishment is just only when intended for the good of the sufferer himself. Others maintain the extreme reverse, contending that to punish persons who have attained years of discretion, for their own benefit, is despotism and injustice, since, if the matter at issue is solely their own good, no one has a right to control their own judgment of it; but that they may justly be punished to prevent evil to others, this being the exercise of the legitimate right of self-defense. Mr. Owen, again, affirms that it is unjust to punish at all, for the criminal did not make his own character; his education and the circumstances which surrounded him have made him a criminal, and for these he is not responsible. All these opinions are extremely plausible; and so long as the question is argued as one of justice simply, without going down to the principles which lie under justice and are the source of its authority, I am unable to see how any of these reasoners can be refuted. For in truth every one of the three builds upon rules of justice confessedly true. The first appeals to the acknowledged injustice of singling out an individual and making him a sacrifice, without his consent, for other people's benefit. The second relies on the acknowledged justice of self-defense and the admitted injustice of forcing one person to conform to another's notions of what constitutes his good. The Owenite invokes the admitted principle that it is unjust to punish anyone for what he cannot help. Each is triumphant so long as he is not compelled to take into consideration any other maxims of justice than the one he has selected; but as soon as their several maxims are brought face to face, each disputant seems to have exactly as much to say for himself as the others. No one of them can carry out his own notion of justice without trampling upon another equally binding. These are difficulties; they have always been felt to be such; and many devices have been invented to turn rather than to overcome them. As a refuge from the last of the three, men imagined what they called the freedom of the will—fancying that they could not justify punishing a man whose will is in a thoroughly hateful state unless it be supposed to have come into that state through no influence of anterior circumstances. To escape from the other difficulties, a favorite contrivance has been the fiction of a contract whereby at some unknown period all the members of society engaged to obey the laws and consented to be punished for any disobedience to them, thereby giving to their legislators the right, which it is assumed they would not otherwise have had, of punishing them, either for their own good or for that of society. This happy thought was considered to get rid of the whole difficulty and to legitimate the infliction of punishment, in virtue of another received maxim of justice, *volenti non fit injuria*—that is not unjust which is done with the consent of the person who is supposed to be hurt by it. I need hardly remark that, even if the consent were not a mere fiction, this maxim is not superior in authority to the others which it is brought in to supersede. It is, on the contrary, an instructive specimen of the loose and irregular manner in which supposed principles of justice grow up. This particular one evidently came into use as a help to the coarse exigencies of courts of law, which are sometimes obliged to be content with very uncertain presumptions, on account of the greater evils which would often arise from any attempt on their part to cut finer. But even courts of law are not able to adhere consistently to the maxim, for they allow voluntary engagements to be set aside on the ground of fraud, and sometimes on that of mere mistake or misinformation.

Again, when the legitimacy of inflicting punishment is admitted, how many conflicting conceptions of justice come to light in discussing the proper apportionment of punishments to offenses. No rule on the subject recommends itself so strongly to the primitive and spontaneous sentiment of justice as the *lex talionis*, an eye for an eye and a tooth for a tooth. Though this principle of the Jewish and of the Mohammedan law has been generally abandoned in Europe as a practical maxim, there is, I suspect, in most minds, a secret hankering after it; and when retribution accidentally falls on an offender in that precise shape, the general feeling of satisfaction evinced bears witness how natural is the sentiment to which this repayment in kind is acceptable. With many, the test of justice in penal infliction is that the punishment should be proportioned to the offense, meaning that it should be exactly measured by the moral guilt of the culprit (whatever be their standard for measuring moral guilt), the consideration what amount of punishment is necessary to deter from the offense having nothing to do with the question of justice, in their estimation; while their are others to whom that consideration is all in all, who maintain that it is not just, at least for man, to inflict on a fellow creature, whatever may be his offenses, any amount of suffering beyond the least that will suffice to prevent him from repeating, and others from imitating, his misconduct.

To take another example from a subject already once referred to. In co-operative industrial association, is it just or not that talent or skill should give a title to superior remuneration? On the negative side of the question it is argued that whoever does the best he can deserves equally well, and ought not in justice to be put in a position of inferiority for no fault of his own; that superior abilities have already advantages more than enough, in the admiration they excite, the personal influence they command, and the internal sources of satisfaction attending them, without adding to these a superior share of the world's goods; and that society is bound in justice rather to make compensation to the less favored for this unmerited inequality of advantages than to aggravate it. On the contrary side it is contended that society receives more from the more efficient laborer; that, his services being more useful, society owes him a larger return for them; that a greater share of the joint result is actually his work, and not to allow his claim to it is a kind of robbery; that, if he is only to receive as much as others, he can only be justly required to produce as much, and to give a smaller amount of time and exertion, proportioned to his superior efficiency. Who shall decide between these appeals to conflicting principles of justice? Justice has in this case two sides to it, which it is impossible to bring into harmony, and the two disputants have chosen opposite sides; the one looks to what it is just that the individual should receive, the other to what it is just that the community should give. Each, from his own point of view, is unanswerable; and any choice between them, on grounds of justice, must be perfectly arbitrary. Social utility alone can decide the preference.

How many, again, and how irreconcilable are the standards of justice to which reference is made in discussing the repartition of taxation. One opinion is that payment to the state should be in numerical proportion to pecuniary means. Others think that justice dictates what they term graduated taxation—taking a higher percentage from those who have more to spare. In point of natural justice a strong case might be made for disregarding means altogether, and taking the same absolute sum (whenever it could be got) from everyone; as the subscribers to a mess or to a club all pay the same sum for the same privileges, whether they can all equally afford it or not. Since the protection (it might be said) of law and government is afforded to and is equally required by all, there is no injustice in making all buy it at the same price. It is reckoned justice, not injustice, that a dealer should charge to all customers the same price for the same article, not a price varying according to their means of payment. This doctrine, as applied to taxation, finds no advocates because it conflicts so strongly with man's feelings of humanity and of social expediency; but the principle of justice which it invokes is as true and as binding as those which can be appealed to against it. Accordingly it exerts a tacit influence on the line of defense employed for other modes of assessing taxation. People feel obliged to argue that the state does more for the rich man than for the poor, as a justification for its taking more from them, though this is in reality not true, for the rich would be far better able to protect themselves, in the absence of law or government, than the poor, and indeed would probably be successful in converting the poor into their slaves. Others, again, so far defer to the same conception of justice as to maintain that all should pay an equal capitation tax for the protection of their persons (these being of equal value to all), and an unequal tax for the protection of their property, which is unequal. To this others reply that the all of one man is as valuable to him as the all of another. From these confusions there is no other mode of extrication than the utilitarian.

Is, then, the difference between the just and the expedient a merely imaginary distinction? Have mankind been under a delusion in thinking that justice is a more sacred thing than policy, and that the latter ought only to be listened to after the former has been satisfied? By no means. The exposition we have given of the nature and origin of the sentiment recognizes a real distinction; and no one of those who profess the most sublime contempt for the consequences of actions as an element in their morality attaches more importance to the distinction than I do. While I dispute the pretensions of any theory which sets up an imaginary standard of justice not grounded on utility, I account the justice which is grounded on utility to be the chief part, and incomparably the most sacred and binding part, of all morality. Justice is a name for certain classes of moral rules which concern the essentials of human well-being more nearly, and are therefore of more absolute obligation, than any other rules for the guidance of life; and the notion which we have found to be of the essence of the idea of justice—that of a right residing in an individual—implies and testifies to this more binding obligation.

The moral rules which forbid mankind to hurt one another (in which we must never forget to include wrongful interference with each other's freedom) are more vital to human well-being than any maxims, however important, which only point out the best mode of managing some department of human affairs. They have also the peculiarity that they are the main element in determining the whole of the social feelings of mankind. It is their observance which alone preserves peace among human beings; if obedience to them were not the rule, and disobedience the exception, everyone would see in everyone else an enemy against whom he must be perpetually guarding himself. What is hardly less important, these are the precepts which mankind have the strongest and the most direct inducements for impressing upon one another. By merely giving to each other prudential instruction or exhortation, they may gain, or think they gain, nothing; in inculcating on each other the duty of positive beneficence, they have an unmistakable interest, but far less in degree; a person may possibly not need the benefits of others, but he always needs that they should not do him hurt. Thus the moralities which protect every individual from being harmed by others, either directly or by being hindered in his freedom of pursuing his own good, are at once those which he himself has most at heart and those which he has the strongest interest in publishing and enforcing by word and deed. It is by a person's observance of these that his fitness to exist as one of the fellowship of human beings is tested and decided; for on that depends his being a nuisance or not to those with whom he is in contact. Now it is these moralities primarily which compose the obligations of justice. The most marked cases of injustice, and those which give the tone to the feeling of repugnance which characterizes the sentiment, are acts of wrongful aggression or wrongful exercise of power over someone; the next are those which consist in wrongfully withholding from him something which is his due—in both cases inflicting on him a positive hurt, either in the form of direct suffering or of the privation of some good which he had reasonable ground, either of a physical or of a social kind, for counting upon.

The same powerful motives which command the observance of these primary moralities enjoin the punishment of those who violate them; and as the impulses of self-defense, of defense of others, and of vengeance are all called forth against such persons, retribution, or evil for evil, becomes closely connected with the sentiment of justice, and is universally included in the idea. Good for good is also one of the dictates of justice; and this, though its social utility is evident, and though it carries with it a natural human feeling, has not at first sight that obvious connection with hurt or injury which, existing in the most elementary cases of just and unjust, is the source of the characteristic intensity of the sentiment. But the connection, though less obvious, is not less real. He who accepts benefits and denies a return of them when needed inflicts a real hurt by disappointing one of the most natural and reasonable of expectations, and one which he must at least tacitly have encouraged, otherwise the benefits would seldom have been conferred. The important rank, among human evils and wrongs, of the disappointment of expectation is shown in the fact that it constitutes the principal criminality of two such highly immoral acts as a breach of friendship and a breach of promise. Few hurts which human beings can sustain are greater, and none wound more, than when that on which they habitually and with full assurance relied fails them in the hour of need; and few wrongs are greater than this mere withholding of good; none excite more resentment, either in the person suffering or in a sympathizing spectator. The principle, therefore, of giving to each what they deserve, that is, good for good as well as evil for evil, is not only included within the idea of justice as we have defined it, but is a proper object of that intensity of sentiment which places the just in human estimation above the simply expedient.

Most of the maxims of justice current in the world, and commonly appealed to in its transactions, are simply instrumental to carrying into effect the principles of justice which we have now spoken of. That a person is only responsible for what he has done voluntarily, or could voluntarily have avoided, that it is unjust to condemn any person unheard; that the punishment ought to be proportioned to the offense, and the like, are maxims intended to prevent the just principle of evil for evil from being perverted to the infliction of evil without that justification. The greater part of these common maxims have come into use from the practice of courts of justice, which have been naturally led to a more complete recognition and elaboration than was likely to suggest itself to others, of the rules necessary to enable them to fulfill their double function—of inflicting punishment when due, and of awarding to each person his right.

That first of judicial virtues, impartiality, is an obligation of justice, partly for the reason last mentioned, as being a necessary condition of the fulfillment of other obligations of justice. But this is not the only source of the exalted rank, among human obligations, of those maxims of equality and impartiality, which, both in popular estimation and in that of the most enlightened, are included among the precepts of justice. In one point of view, they may be considered as corollaries from the principles already laid down. If it is a duty to do to each according to his deserts, returning good for good, as well as repressing evil by evil, it necessarily follows that we should treat all equally well (when no higher duty forbids) who have deserved equally well of *us,* and that society should treat all equally well who have deserved equally well of *it,* that is, who have deserved equally well absolutely. This is the highest abstract standard of social and distributive justice, toward which all institutions and the efforts of all virtuous citizens should be made in the utmost possible degree to converge. But this great moral duty rests upon a still deeper foundation, being a direct emanation from the first principle of morals, and not a mere logical corollary from secondary or derivative doctrines. It is involved in the very meaning of utility, or the greatest happiness principle. That principle is a mere form of words without rational signification unless one person's happiness, supposed equal in degree (with the proper allowance made for kind), is counted for exactly as much as another's. Those conditions being supplied, Bentham's dictum, "everybody to count for one, nobody for more than one," might be written under the principle of utility as an explanatory commentary.[4] The equal claim of everybody to happiness, in the estimation of the moralist and of the legislator, involves an equal claim to all the means of happiness except in so far as the inevitable conditions of human life and the general interest in which that of every individual is included set limits to the maxim; and those limits ought to be strictly construed. As every other maxim of justice, so this is by no

---

[4]This implication, in the first principle of the utilitarian scheme, of perfect impartiality between persons is regarded by Mr. Herbert Spencer (in his *Social Statics*) as a disproof of the pretensions of utility to be a sufficient guide to right; since (he says) the principle of utility presupposes the anterior principle that everybody has an equal right to happiness. It may be more correctly described as supposing that equal amounts of happiness are equally desirable, whether felt by the same or different persons. This, however, is not a *pre*supposition, not a premise needful to support the principle of utility, but the very principle itself; for what is the principle of utility if it be not that "happiness" and "desirable" are synonymous terms? If there is any anterior principle implied, it can be no other than this, that the truths of arithmetic are applicable to the valuation of happiness, as of all other measurable quantities.

(Mr. Herbert Spencer, in a private communication on the subject of the preceding note, objects to being considered an opponent of utilitarianism and states that he regards happiness as the ultimate end of morality; but deems that end only partially attainable by empirical generalizations from the observed results of conduct, and completely attainable only by deducing, from the laws of life and the conditions of existence, what kinds of action necessarily tend to produce happiness, and what kinds to produce unhappiness. With the exception of the word "necessarily," I have no dissent to express from this doctrine; and (omitting that word) I am not aware that any modern advocate of utilitarianism is of a different opinion. Bentham, certainly, to whom in the *Social Statics* Mr. Spencer particularly referred, is, least of all writers, chargeable with unwillingness to deduce the effect of actions on happiness from the laws of human nature and the universal conditions of human life. The common charge against him is of relying too exclusively upon such deductions and declining altogether to be bound by the generalizations from specific experience which Mr. Spencer thinks that utilitarians generally confine themselves to. My own opinion (and, as I collect, Mr. Spencer's) is that in ethics, as in all other branches of scientific study, the consilience of the results of both these processes, each corroborating and verifying the other, is requisite to give to any general proposition the kind and degree of evidence which constitutes scientific proof.)

means applied or held applicable universally; on the contrary, as I have already remarked, it bends to every person's ideas of social expediency. But in whatever case it is deemed applicable at all, it is held to be the dictate of justice. All persons are deemed to have a *right* to equality of treatment, except when some recognized social expediency requires the reverse. And hence all social inequalities which have ceased to be considered expedient assume the character, not of simple inexpediency, but of injustice, and appear so tyrannical that people are apt to wonder how they ever could have been tolerated—forgetful that they themselves, perhaps, tolerate other inequalities under an equally mistaken notion of expediency, the correction of which would make that which they approve seem quite as monstrous as what they have at last learned to condemn. The entire history of social improvement has been a series of transitions by which one custom or institution after another, from being a supposed primary necessity of social existence, has passed into the rank of a universally stigmatized injustice and tyranny. So it has been with the distinctions of slaves and freemen, nobles and serfs, patricians and plebeians; and so it will be, and in part already is, with the aristocracies of color, race, and sex.

It appears from what has been said that justice is a name for certain moral requirements which, regarded collectively, stand higher in the scale of social utility, and are therefore of more paramount obligation, than any others, though particular cases may occur in which some other social duty is so important as to overrule any one of the general maxims of justice. Thus, to save a life, it may not only be allowable, but a duty, to steal or take by force the necessary food or medicine, or to kidnap and compel to officiate the only qualified medical practitioner. In such cases, as we do not call anything justice which is not a virtue, we usually say, not that justice must give way to some other moral principle, but that what is just in ordinary cases is, by reason of that other principle, not just in the particular case. By this useful accommodation of language, the character of indefeasibility attributed to justice is kept up, and we are saved from the necessity of maintaining that there can be laudable injustice.

The considerations which have now been adduced resolve, I conceive, the only real difficulty in the utilitarian theory of morals. It has always been evident that all cases of justice are also cases of expediency; the difference is in the peculiar sentiment which attaches to the former, as contradistinguished from the latter. If this characteristic sentiment has been sufficiently accounted for; if there is no necessity to assume for it any peculiarity of origin; if it is simply the natural feeling of resentment, moralized by being made co-existensive with the demands of social good; and if this feeling not only does but ought to exist in all the classes of cases to which the idea of justice corresponds—that idea no longer presents itself as a stumbling block to the utilitarian ethics. Justice remains the appropriate name for certain social utilities which are vastly more important, and therefore more absolute and imperative, than any others are as a class (though not more so than others may be in particular cases); and which, therefore, ought to be, as well as naturally are, guarded by a sentiment, not only different in degree, but also in kind; distinguished from the milder feeling which attaches to the mere idea of promoting human pleasure or convenience at once by the more definite nature of its commands and by the sterner character of its sanctions.

Study Questions

1. What does Mill mean by saying that questions of ultimate ends are not amenable to direct proof? Use examples as necessary.
2. What does Mill mean when he says that utility is the foundation of morals?

3. Does Mill believe that some kinds of pleasure are more desirable and more valuable than others? If so, what kinds? How do you tell which pleasures are more desirable?
4. Who, according to Mill, have the greatest chance of having their desires satisfied?
5. Which counts as higher for Mill, quantity or quality of pleasure? In other words, what is his rule for measuring quality as against quantity?
6. Sketch Mill's answer to the opponent who says that happiness cannot be the rational purpose of human life and action.
7. Whose happiness is more important, according to Mill, one's own or the happiness of others? Does Mill believe that people can best serve the happiness of others by an absolute sacrifice of their own? What does he think of social arrangements whereby that seems to be the case?
8. What is Mill's response to those who say that it is asking too much to require people always to act for the sake of promoting the general interests of society?
9. Suppose that in one particular instance a certain act might benefit society, but that this *type* of act if practiced as a general rule would have the opposite effect. Would Mill say that, in this instance, we ought to do the act?
10. Is an act a good act because it was done by a good person, according to Mill? Is it possible for a bad person to act rightly, according to him?
11. What is Mill's response to those who think utilitarianism is a godless doctrine?
12. Explain Mill's rejoinder to the objection that a person doesn't have time to calculate the effects of an act on the general happiness.
13. What, according to Mill, is the ultimate sanction of all moral standards? By the way, what is a sanction, according to Mill?
14. What, according to Mill, is the evidence that happiness is a good? Do people ever desire anything except happiness, in his opinion? Does he think that virtue, or money, or listening to music might be desired for their own sake?
15. According to Mill, the *idea* of justice supposes what two things? And what are the two essential ingredients in the *sentiment* of justice?
16. From what does the desire to punish a person who has done harm to some individual stem, according to Mill?
17. What is it, in Mill's opinion, to have a right?
18. What is Mill's response to objectors who claim that justice, not utility, should be the standard of morality because justice is less ambiguous than utility?
19. How are appeals to conflicting principles of justice to be resolved, according to Mill?
20. Does Mill believe that the distinction between justice and utility is merely imaginary? What *is* the connection between justice and utility? According to Mill, justice is really a name for what?

Nietzsche

As you will see when you read the essay that follows, Friedrich Nietzsche's style of philosophizing is a bit different from that of the other philosophers we've studied. For Nietzsche, apparently, there is no such thing as objective truth. Accordingly, Nietzsche does not proceed by dispassionate analysis; instead, he favors a style of philosophizing much more literary than that of the other philosophers in this book. Nietzsche is more apt simply to *express* his sentiments than to attempt to "prove" them by rational argument. Such "proof" as there might be for his views he communicates to his readers via the powerful imagery of his words.

In essence, Nietzsche's moral philosophy rests on the assumption that there are no objective standards of right and wrong, good and evil. Moral principles, in Nietzsche's view, are determined by human societies. Further, there are fundamentally just two moralities: master morality, the morality of the noble and aristocratic classes; and slave morality, the morality of the masses.

The noble human being honors himself, according to Nietzsche, and does not require the approval of others for his psychological comfort. He is hard and intolerant, accepting his own egoism without qualm. He despises the masses beneath him and can sacrifice their numbers without pity. He has a duty only to his own peers and understands the importance of honor. He reveres age and tradition and is disdainful of warmheartedness or altruism. He defines what is harmful entirely by what is harmful to him.

Slave morality, by contrast — the paradigm of which is Christian ethics — emphasizes compassion, the warm heart, patience, industry, humility, friendliness, and a longing for freedom.

Nietzsche made it clear that his preferences were for master morality. Every enhancement of the species as well as the individual is a by-product of aristocratic social structures, he maintained. If it is a good and healthy aristocracy, it experiences itself as — and indeed is — the meaning and highest justification of society. The herd-morality principle of refraining from injury, violence, and exploitation is really a principle of disintegration and decay, a denial of life.

Why is it a denial of life? Because for Nietzsche, life *is* the will to power. Its essence *is* the appropriation, overpowering, and suppression of the alien and weaker. It is from this conception of life that his distaste for slave morality and preference for master morality stems; it is the latter morality that is life-affirming in Nietzsche's sense.

The selection that follows is from *Beyond Good and Evil.* This title conveys the idea that the noble individual lives beyond slave morality.

from *Beyond Good and Evil*

Friedrich Nietzsche

When he was only twenty-five years old, Friedrich Nietzsche (1844–1900) was appointed to the chair of classical philology at Basel. His life was plagued by poor health and, ultimately, insanity. These selections are from part 9 of Helen Zimmern's 1885 translation of *Beyond Good and Evil.*

Ninth Chapter
What Is Noble?

257.

Every elevation of the type "man," has hitherto been the work of an aristocratic society—and so will it always be—a society believing in a long scale of gradations of rank and differences of worth among human beings, and requiring slavery in some form or other. Without the *pathos of distance,* such as grows out of the incarnated difference of classes, out of the constant outlooking and downlooking of the ruling caste on subordinates and instruments, and out of their equally constant practice of obeying and commanding, of keeping down and keeping at a distance—that other more mysterious pathos could never have arisen, the longing for an ever new widening of distance within the soul itself, the formation of ever higher, rarer, further, more extended, more comprehensive states, in short, just the elevation of the type "man," the continued "self-surmounting of man," to use a moral formula in a supermoral sense. To be sure, one must not resign oneself to any humanitarian illusions about the history of the origin of an aristocratic society (that is to say, of the preliminary condition for the elevation of the type "man"): the truth is hard. Let us acknowledge unprejudicedly how every higher civilisation hitherto has *originated!* Men with a still natural nature, barbarians in every terrible sense of the word, men of prey, still in possession of unbroken strength of will and desire for power, threw themselves upon weaker, more moral, more peaceful races (perhaps trading or cattle-rearing communities), or upon old mellow civilisations in which the final vital force was flickering out in brilliant fireworks of wit and depravity. At the commencement, the noble caste was always the barbarian caste: their superiority did not consist first of all in their physical, but in their psychical power—they were more *complete* men (which at every point also implies the same as "more complete beasts").

258.

Corruption—as the indication that anarchy threatens to break out among the instincts, and that the foundation of the emotions, called "life," is convulsed—is something radically different according to the organisation in which it manifests itself. When, for instance, an aristocracy like that of France at the beginning of the Revolution, flung away its privileges with sublime disgust and sacrificed itself to an excess of its moral sentiments, it was corruption:—it was really only the closing act of the corruption which had existed for centuries, by virtue of which that aristocracy had abdicated step by step its lordly prerogatives and lowered itself to a *function* of royalty (in the end even to its decoration and parade-dress). The essential thing, however, in a good and healthy aristocracy is that it should *not* regard itself as a function either of the kingship or the commonwealth, but as the *significance* and highest justification thereof—that it should therefore accept with a good conscience the sacrifice of a legion of individuals, who, *for its sake,* must be suppressed and reduced to imperfect men, to slaves and instruments. Its fundamental belief must be precisely that society is *not* allowed to exist for its own sake, but only as a foundation and scaffolding, by means of which a select class of beings may be able to elevate themselves to their higher duties, and in general to a higher *existence*:

like those sun-seeking climbing plants in Java—they are called *Sipo Matador,*—which encircle an oak so long and so often with their arms, until at last, high above it, but supported by it, they can unfold their tops in the open light, and exhibit their happiness.

259.

To refrain mutually from injury, from violence, from exploitation, and put one's will on a par with that of others: this may result in a certain rough sense in good conduct among individuals when the necessary conditions are given (namely, the actual similarity of the individuals in amount of force and degree of worth, and their co-relation within one organisation). As soon, however, as one wished to take this principle more generally, and if possible even as *the fundamental principle of society,* it would immediately disclose what it really is—namely, a Will to the *denial* of life, a principle of dissolution and decay. Here one must think profoundly to the very basis and resist all sentimental weakness: life itself is *essentially* appropriation, injury, conquest of the strange and weak, suppression, severity, obtrusion of peculiar forms, incorporation, and at the least, putting it mildest, exploitation;—but why should one for ever use precisely these words on which for ages a disparaging purpose has been stamped? Even the organisation within which, as was previously supposed, the individuals treat each other as equal—it takes place in every healthy aristocracy—must itself, if it be a living and not a dying organisation, do all that towards other bodies, which the individuals within it refrain from doing to each other: it will have to be the incarnated Will to Power, it will endeavour to grow, to gain ground, attract to itself and acquire ascendency—not owing to any morality or immorality, but because it *lives,* and because life *is* precisely Will to Power. On no point, however, is the ordinary consciousness of Europeans more unwilling to be corrected than on this matter; people now rave everywhere, even under the guise of science, about coming conditions of society in which "the exploiting character" is to be absent:—that sounds to my ears as if they promised to invent a mode of life which should refrain from all organic functions. "Exploitation" does not belong to a depraved, or imperfect and primitive society: it belongs to the *nature* of the living being as a primary organic function; it is a consequence of the intrinsic Will to Power, which is precisely the Will to Life.—Granting that as a theory this is a novelty—as a reality it is the *fundamental fact* of all history: let us be so far honest towards ourselves!

260.

In a tour through the many finer and coarser moralities which have hitherto prevailed or still prevail on the earth, I found certain traits recurring regularly together and connected with one another, until finally two primary types revealed themselves to me, and a radical distinction was brought to light. There is *master-morality* and *slave-morality;*—I would at once add, however, that in all higher and mixed civilisations, there are also attempts at the reconciliation of the two moralities; but one finds still oftener the confusion and mutual misunderstanding of them, indeed, sometimes their close juxtaposition—even in the same man, within one soul. The distinctions of moral values have either originated in a ruling caste, pleasantly conscious of being different from the ruled—or among the ruled class, the slaves and dependents of all sorts. In the first case, when it is the rulers who determine the conception "good," it is the exalted, proud disposition which is regarded as the distinguishing feature, and that which determines the order of rank. The noble type of man separates from himself the beings in whom the opposite of this exalted, proud disposition displays itself: he despises them. Let it at once be noted that in this first kind of morality the antithesis "good" and "bad" means practically the same as "noble" and "despicable";—the antithesis "good" and "*evil*" is of a different origin. The cowardly, the timid, the insignificant, and those thinking merely of narrow utility are despised; moreover, also, the distrustful, with their constrained glances, the self-abasing, the dog-like kind of men who let themselves be abused, the mendicant flatterers, and above all the liars:—it is a fundamental belief of all aristocrats that the common people are untruthful. "We truthful ones"—the nobility in ancient Greece called themselves. It is obvious that everywhere the designations of moral value were at first applied to *men*, and were only derivatively and at a later period applied to *actions*; it is a gross mistake, therefore, when historians of morals start with questions like, "Why have sympathetic actions been praised?" The noble type of man regards *himself* as a determiner of values; he does not require to be approved of; he passes the judgment: "What is injurious to me is injurious in itself"; he knows that it is he himself only who confers honour on things; he is a *creator of values*. He honours whatever he recognises in himself: such morality is self-glorification. In the foreground there is the feeling of plenitude, of power, which seeks to overflow, the happiness of high tension, the consciousness of a wealth which would fain give and bestow: — the noble man also helps the unfortunate, but not — or scarcely — out of pity, but rather from an impulse generated by the superabundance of power. The noble man honours in himself the powerful one, him also who has power over himself, who knows how to speak and how to keep silence, who takes pleasure in subjecting himself to severity and hardness, and has reverence for all that is severe and hard. "Wotan placed a hard heart in my breast," says an old Scandinavian Saga: it is thus rightly expressed from the soul of a proud Viking. Such a type of man is even proud of *not* being made for sympathy; the hero of the Saga therefore adds warningly: "He who has not a hard heart when young, will never have one." The noble and brave who think thus are the furthest removed from the morality which sees precisely in sympathy, or in acting for the good of others, or in *désintéressement*, the characteristic of the moral; faith in oneself, pride in oneself, a radical enmity and irony towards "selflessness," belongs as definitely to noble morality, as do a careless scorn and precaution in presence of sympathy and the "warm heart." — It is the powerful who *know* how to honour, it is their art, their domain for invention. The profound reverence for age and for tradition — all law rests on this double reverence, — the belief and prejudice in favour of ancestors and unfavourable to newcomers, is typical in the morality of the powerful; and if, reversely, men of "modern ideas" believe almost instinctively in "progress" and the "future," and are more and more lacking in respect for old age, the ignoble origin of these "ideas" has complacently betrayed itself thereby. A morality of the ruling class, however, is more especially foreign and irritating to present-day taste in the sternness of its principle that one has duties only to one's equals; that one may act towards beings of a lower rank, towards all that is foreign, just as seems good to one, or "as the heart desires," and in any case "beyond good and evil": it is here that sympathy and similar sentiments can have a place. The ability and obligation to exercise prolonged gratitude and prolonged revenge — both only within the circle of equals, — artfulness in retaliation, *raffinement* of the idea in friendship, a certain necessity to have enemies (as outlets for the emotions of envy, quarrelsomeness, arrogance — in fact, in order to be a good *friend*): all these are typical characteristics of the noble morality, which, as has been pointed out, is not the morality of "modern ideas," and is therefore at present difficult to realise, and also to unearth and disclose. — It is otherwise with the second type of morality, *slave-morality*. Supposing that the abused, the oppressed, the suffering, the unemancipated, the weary, and those uncertain of themselves, should moralise, what will be the common element in their moral estimates? Probably a pessimistic suspicion with regard to the entire situation of man will find expression, perhaps a condemnation of man, together with his situation. The slave has an unfavourable eye for the virtues of the powerful; has a scepticism and distrust, a *refinement* of distrust of everything "good" that is there honoured — he would fain persuade himself that the very happiness there is not genuine. On the other hand, *those* qualities which serve to alleviate the existence of sufferers are brought into prominence and flooded with light; it is here that sympathy, the kind, helping hand, the warm heart, patience, diligence, humility, and friendliness attain to honour; for here these are the most useful qualities, and almost the only means of supporting the burden of existence. Slave-morality is essentially the morality of utility. Here is the seat of the origin of the famous antithesis "good" and "*evil*": — power and dangerousness are assumed to reside in the evil, a certain dreadfulness, subtlety, and strength, which do not admit of being despised. According to slave-morality, therefore, the "evil" man arouses fear; according to master-morality, it is precisely the "good" man who arouses fear and seeks to arouse it, while the bad man is regarded as the despicable being. The contrast attains its maximum when, in accordance with the logical consequences of slave-morality, a shade of depreciation—it may be slight and well-intentioned—at last attaches itself even to the "good" man of this morality; because, according to the servile mode of thought, the good man must in any case be the *safe* man: he is good-natured, easily deceived, perhaps a little stupid, *un bonhomme.* Everywhere that slave-morality gains the ascendency, language shows a tendency to approximate the significations of the words "good" and "stupid."—A last fundamental difference: the desire for *freedom,* the instinct for happiness and the refinements of the feeling of liberty belong as necessarily to slave-morals and morality, as artifice and enthusiasm in reverence and devotion are the regular symptoms of an aristocratic mode of thinking and estimating.—Hence we can understand without further detail why love *as a passion*—it is our European specialty—must absolutely be of noble origin; as is well known, its invention is due to the Provençal poet-cavaliers, those brilliant ingenious men of the "*gai saber,*" to whom Europe owes so much, and almost owes itself.

261.

Vanity is one of the things which are perhaps most difficult for a noble man to understand: he will be tempted to deny it, where another kind of man thinks he sees it self-evidently. The problem for him is to represent to his mind beings who seek to arouse a good opinion of themselves which they themselves do not possess—and consequently also do not "deserve,"—and who yet *believe* in this good opinion afterwards. This seems to him on the one hand such bad taste and so self-disrespectful, and on the other hand so grotesquely unreasonable, that he would like to consider vanity an exception, and is doubtful about it in most cases when it is spoken of. He will say, for instance: "I may be mistaken about my value, and on the other hand may nevertheless demand that my value should be acknowledged by others precisely as I rate it:—that, however, is not vanity (but self-conceit, or, in most cases, that which is called 'humility,' and also 'modesty')." Or he will even say: "For many reasons I can delight in the good opinion of others, perhaps because I love and honour them, and rejoice in all their joys, perhaps also because their good opinion endorses and strengthens my belief in my own good opinion, perhaps because the good opinion of others, even in cases where I do not share it, is useful to me, or gives promise of usefulness:—all this, however, is not vanity." The man of noble character must first bring it home forcibly to his mind, especially with the aid of history, that, from time immemorial, in all social strata in any way dependent, the ordinary man *was* only that which he *passed for:*—not being at all accustomed to fix values, he did not assign even to himself any other value than that which his master assigned to him (it is the peculiar *right of masters* to create values). It may be looked upon as the result of an extraordinary atavism, that the ordinary man, even at present, is still always *waiting* for an opinion about himself, and then instinctively submitting himself to it; yet by no means only to a "good" opinion, but also to a bad and unjust one (think, for instance, of the greater part of the self-appreciations and self-depreciations which believing women learn from their confessors, and which in general the believing Christian learns from his Church). In fact, conformably to the slow rise of the democratic social order (and its cause, the blending of the blood of masters and slaves), the originally noble and rare impulse of the masters to assign a value to themselves and to "think well" of themselves, will now be more and more encouraged and extended; but it has at all times an older, ampler, and more radically ingrained propensity opposed to it—and in the phenomenon of "vanity" this older propensity overmasters the younger. The vain person rejoices over *every* good opinion which he hears about himself (quite apart from the point of view of its usefulness, and equally regardless of its truth or falsehood), just as he suffers from every bad opinion: for he subjects himself to both, he *feels* himself subjected to both, by that oldest instinct of subjection which breaks forth in him.—It is "the slave" in the vain man's blood, the remains of the slave's craftiness—and how much of the "slave" is still left in woman, for instance!—which seeks to *seduce* to good opinions of itself; it is the slave, too, who immediately afterwards falls prostrate himself before these opinions, as though he had not called them forth.—And to repeat it again: vanity is an atavism.

262.

A *species* originates, and a type becomes established and strong in the long struggle with essentially constant *unfavourable* conditions. On the other hand, it is known by the experience of breeders that species which receive superabundant nourishment, and in general a surplus of protection and care, immediately tend in the most marked way to develop variations, and are fertile in prodigies and monstrosities (also in monstrous vices). Now look at an aristocratic commonwealth, say an ancient Greek *polis*, or Venice, as a voluntary or involuntary contrivance for the purpose of *rearing* human beings; there are there men beside one another, thrown upon their own resources, who want to make their species prevail, chiefly because they *must* prevail, or else run the terrible danger of being exterminated. The favour, the superabundance, the protection are there lacking under which variations are fostered; the species needs itself as species, as something which, precisely by virtue of its hardness, its uniformity, and simplicity of structure, can in general prevail and make itself permanent in constant struggle with its neighbours, or with rebellious or rebellion-threatening vassals. The most varied experience teaches it what are the qualities to which it principally owes the fact that it still exists, in spite of all Gods and men, and has hitherto been victorious: these qualities it calls virtues, and these virtues along it develops to maturity. It does so with severity, indeed it desires severity; every aristocratic morality is intolerant in the education of youth, in the control of women, in the marriage customs, in the relations of old and young, in the penal laws (which have an eye only for the degenerating): it counts intolerance itself among the virtues, under the name of "justice." A type with few, but very few marked features, a species of severe, warlike, wisely silent, reserved and reticent men (and as such, with the most delicate sensibility for the charm and *nuances* of society) is thus established, unaffected by the vicissitudes of generations; the constant struggle with uniform *unfavourable* conditions is, as already remarked, the cause of a type becoming stable and hard. Finally, however, a happy state of things results, the enormous tension is relaxed; there are perhaps no more enemies among the neighbouring peoples, and the means of life, even the enjoyment of life, are present in superabundance. With one stroke the bond and constraint of the old discipline severs: it is no longer regarded as necessary, as a condition of existence—if it would continue, it can only do as a form of *luxury*, as an archaising *taste*. Variations, whether they be deviations (into the higher, finer, and rarer), or deteriorations and monstrosities, appear suddenly on the scene in the greater exuberance and splendour; the individual dares to be individual and detach himself. At this turning-point of history there manifest themselves, side by side, and often mixed and entangled together, a magnificent, manifold, virgin-forest-like upgrowth and up-striving, a kind of *tropical tempo* in the rivalry of growth, and an extraordinary decay and self-destruction, owing to the savagely opposing and seemingly exploding egoisms, which strive with one another "for sun and light," and can no longer assign any limit, restraint, or forbearance for themselves by means of the hitherto existing morality. It was this morality itself which piled up the strength so enormously, which bent the bow in so threatening a manner:—it is now "out of date," it is getting "out of date." The dangerous and disquieting point has been reached when the greater, more manifold, more comprehensive life *is lived beyond* the old morality; the "individual" stands out, and is obliged to have recourse to his own law-giving, his own arts and artifices for self-preservation, self-elevation, and self-deliverance. Nothing but new "Whys," nothing but new "Hows," no common formulas any longer, misunderstanding and disregard in league with each other, decay, deterioration, and the loftiest desires frightfully entangled, the genius of the race overflowing from all cornucopias of good and bad, a portentous simultaneousness of Spring and Autumn, full of new charms and mysteries peculiar to the fresh, still inexhausted, still unwearied corruption. Danger is again present, the mother of morality, great danger; this time shifted into the individual, into the neighbour and friend, into the street, into their own child, into their own heart, into all the most personal and secret recesses of their desires and volitions. What will the moral philosophers who appear at this time have to preach? They discover, these sharp onlookers and loafers, that the end is quickly approaching, that everything around them decays and produces decay, that nothing will endure until the day after tomorrow, except one species of man, the incurably *mediocre.* The mediocre alone have a prospect of continuing and propagating themselves — they will be the men of the future, the sole survivors; "be like them! become mediocre!" is now the only morality which has still a significance, which still obtains a hearing. — But it is difficult to preach this morality of mediocrity! it can never avow what it is and what it desires! it has to talk of moderation and dignity and duty and brotherly love — it will have difficulty *in concealing its irony!*

263.

There is an *instinct for rank,* which more than anything else is already the sign of a *high* rank; there is a *delight* in the *nuances* of reverence which leads one to infer noble origin and habits. The refinement, goodness, and loftiness of a soul are put to a perilous test when something passes by that is of the highest rank, but is not yet protected by the awe of authority from obtrusive touches and incivilities: something that goes its way like a living touchstone, undistinguished, undiscovered, and tentative, perhaps voluntarily veiled and disguised. He whose task and practice it is to investigate souls, will avail himself of many varieties of this very art to determine the ultimate value of a soul, the unalterable, innate order of rank to which it belongs: he will test it by its *instinct for reverence. Différence engendre haine*: the vulgarity of many a nature spurts up suddenly like dirty water, when any holy vessel, any jewel from closed shrines, any book bearing the marks of great destiny, is brought before it; while on the other hand, there is an involuntary silence, a hesitation of the eye, a cessation of all gestures, by which it is indicated that a soul *feels* the nearness of what is worthiest of respect. The way in which, on the whole, the reverence for the *Bible* has hitherto been maintained in Europe, is perhaps the best example of discipline and refinement of manners which Europe owes to Christianity: books of such profoundness and supreme significance require for their protection an external tyranny of authority, in order to acquire the *period* of thousands of years which is necessary to exhaust and unriddle them. Much has been achieved when the sentiment has been at last instilled into the masses (the shallow-pates and the boobies of every kind) that they are not allowed to touch everything, that there are holy experiences before which they must take off their shoes and keep away the unclean hand — it is almost their highest advance towards humanity. On the contrary, in the so-called cultured classes, the believers in "modern ideas," nothing is perhaps so repulsive as their lack of shame, the easy insolence of eye and hand with which they touch, taste, and finger everything; and it is possible that even yet there is more *relative* nobility of taste, and more tact for reverence among the people, among the lower classes of the people, especially among peasants, than among the newspaper-reading *demi-monde* of intellect, the cultured class.

264.

It cannot be effaced from a man's soul what his ancestors have preferably and most constantly done: whether they were perhaps diligent economisers attached to a desk and a cash-box, modest and citizen-like in their desires, modest also in their virtues; or whether they were accustomed to commanding from morning till night, fond of rude pleasures and probably of still ruder duties and reponsibilities; or whether, finally, at one time or another, they have sacrificed old privileges of birth and possession, in order to live wholly for their faith — for their "God," — as men of an inexorable and sensitive conscience, which blushes at every compromise. It is quite impossible for a man *not* to have the qualities and predilections of his parents and ancestors in his constitution, whatever appearances may suggest to the contrary. This is the problem of race. Granted that one knows something of the parents, it is admissible to draw a conclusion about the child: any kind of offensive incontinence, any kind of sordid envy, or of clumsy self-vaunting — the three things which together have constituted the genuine plebeian type in all times—such must pass over to the child, as surely as bad blood; and with the help of the best education and culture one will only succeed in *deceiving* with regard to such heredity.— And what else does education and culture try to do nowadays! In our very democratic, or rather, very plebeian age, "education" and "culture" *must* be essentially the art of deceiving—deceiving with regard to origin, with regard to the inherited plebeianism in body and soul. An educator who nowadays preached truthfulness above everything else, and called out constantly to his pupils: "Be true! Be natural! Show yourselves as you are!"—even such a virtuous and sincere ass would learn in a short time to have recourse to the *furca* of Horace, *naturam expellere*: with what results? "Plebeianism" *usque recurret.**

265.

At the risk of displeasing innocent ears, I submit that egoism belongs to the essence of a noble soul, I mean the unalterable belief that to a being such as "we," other beings must naturally be in subjection, and have to sacrifice themselves. The noble soul accepts the fact of his egoism without question, and also without consciousness of harshness, constraint, or arbitrariness therein, but rather as something that may have its basis in the primary law of things:—if he sought a designation for it he would say: "It is justice itself." He acknowledges under certain circumstances, which made him hesitate at first, that there are other equally privileged ones; as soon as he has settled this question of rank, he moves among those equals and equally privileged ones with the same assurance, as regards modesty and delicate respect, which he enjoys in intercourse with himself—in accordance with an innate heavenly mechanism which all the stars understand. It is an *additional* instance of his egoism, this artfulness and self-limitation in intercourse with his equals—every star is a similar egoist; he honours *himself* in them, and in the rights which he concedes to them, he has no doubt that the exchange of honours and rights, as the *essence* of all intercourse, belongs also to the natural condition of things. The noble soul gives as he takes, prompted by the passionate and sensitive instinct of requital, which is at the root of his nature. The notion of "favour" has, *inter pares*, neither significance nor good repute; there may be a sublime way of letting gifts as it were light upon one from above, and of drinking them thirstily like dewdrops; but for those arts and displays the noble soul has no aptitude. His egoism hinders him here: in general, he looks "aloft" unwillingly—he looks either *forward*, horizontally and deliberately, or downwards—*he knows that he is on a height.*

266.

"One can only truly esteem him who does not *look out for* himself."—Goethe to Rath Schlosser.

Study Questions

1. According to Nietzsche, every enhancement of the human species has been the result of what?
2. What, according to Nietzsche, is the essential characteristic of a good and healthy aristocracy? What does such a society therefore accept, in his opinion? What is a healthy aristocracy's fundamental faith?
3. What is Nietzsche's opinion of making the elimination of exploitation a fundamental goal of society? What is his opinion of exploitation generally?
4. Why does Nietzsche say that life is essentially appropriation, injury, overpowering of what is alien and weaker, and so on?

*Horace's "Epistles," I. x. 24.

5. In master morality, what do "good" and "bad" mean, according to Nietzsche? What do they mean in slave morality? What are those who inspire fear, according to slave morality? According to master morality?
6. Who determines moral values among the noble, according to Nietzsche?
7. Some people think that moral designations were first applied to actions and then derivatively to people. What does Nietzsche think?
8. Whose morality is forward-looking and lacks respect for tradition, in Nietzsche's opinion?
9. In what regard is master morality most offensive to present taste, according to Nietzsche?
10. Explain in what way slave morality is a morality of utility.
11. What happens to the words "good" and "stupid" when slave morality becomes preponderant, according to Nietzsche?
12. What does Nietzsche mean when he says "egoism belongs to the nature of a noble soul"?

C H A P T E R 1 1

Recent Moral Philosophy

Recent moral philosophy began largely as a discussion of some of the ideas presented in the book *Principia Ethica*, written by George Edward Moore (1873–1958). Shortly we will present an excerpt from this book.

Intuitionism

G. E. Moore

Moore, like many or most of his predecessors, wished to know what is good. His opinion on the subject was somewhat unusual when you remember the things other philosophers have listed as good, such as pleasure, serenity, divine love, a noble soul, and so on. Moore's opinion, by contrast, was that "Personal affection and aesthetic enjoyments include by far the greatest good with which we are acquainted."

However, as interesting as it was, it wasn't Moore's opinion about personal affection and aesthetic enjoyments that intrigued his contemporaries. Moore had spent a good deal of time in *Principia Ethica* on some preliminary matters, and it was this preliminary discussion that set the stage for contemporary moral philosophy.

In particular, Moore had devoted much time to (1) considering what the proper subject matter of moral philosophy is, (2) clarifying what the question "What is good?" means, (3) considering whether and how good is to be defined or analyzed, (4) determining what *sort* of property good or goodness is, (5) ascertaining what the logical relationship is between good things and right acts, and (6) diagnosing some of what he thought were mistakes and confusions in the assumptions and reasoning of past moral philosophers. As it turned out, these preliminary matters established the agenda for much of recent moral philosophy. Many of the issues moral philosophers have investigated in this century are either directly related to these matters, or at least cropped up in discussions connected to them.

The proper subject matter of moral philosophy, according to Moore, is to conduct a general inquiry into what is good. But because he thought the question "What is good?" can be construed in different ways, not all of them relevant to moral philosophy, Moore took some pains to clarify it. Indeed, according to Moore, a major mistake of other moral philosophers had been their failure to get clear on the very question—What is good?—that they were trying to answer. As a result, they had confused with one another two entirely different inquiries: one about what sorts of things are good, the other about what *good* means or how it is to be defined.

Because of this confusion, according to Moore, moral philosophers had failed to notice the fundamental truth of ethics—namely, that good cannot be defined at all! It cannot be defined, according to Moore, because it is a *simple property* of good things; it is not a compound consisting of yet simpler elements. It is not like, say, pleasant weather, which consists of ingredients including warm days, cool nights, sunshine, gentle breezes, and the like. It is more like, say, warmth, which is not a mixture of simpler constituents.

Further, according to Moore, good or goodness (which come to the same) is *not a natural property*. This means, roughly, that goodness is not a property investigated by the empirical sciences. We say "roughly," because Moore was unable to give an account of "natural property" that fully satisfied even him.

According to Moore, one of the main mistakes of earlier moral philosophers had been to treat good as if it were a natural or empirically detectable property, such as, for example, happiness or pleasure. Treating good in this way is equivalent, in Moore's view, to treating good as if it were something that it is not. "If I am asked 'What is good?' my answer is that good is good, and that is the end of the matter," he wrote.

But unlike *good*, according to Moore, *right* can be defined. The right course of action, he said, is simply the course of action that will produce the greatest amount of good.

H. A. Prichard

This last view of Moore's contrasts with that put forth in an influential paper, "Does Moral Philosophy Rest On A Mistake?" written by another early recent moral philosopher, Harold Arthur Prichard. Prichard's idea was that moral philosophy does indeed rest on a mistake, namely, the mistake of attempting to *justify* moral principles about how we behave. This idea—that moral philosophy rests on the mistake of attempting to justify moral principles about how we behave—if you think about it, is surprising. Most of us feel instinctively that a central task of moral philosophy just must be to provide justification for moral principles about behavior.

Prichard, however, argued that all such attempted justifications involve the fatal flaw of trying to derive the rightness of an act either from its intrinsic goodness or from the goodness it produces. The rightness of an act, he said, simply is not reducible to its goodness. Further, even if what it is my moral duty to do does produce good, *that* is not why I ought to do it. The only reason I should do something that I should do, he argued, is that I should do it. Our moral obligations, he said, are self-evident. If we really have some question as to whether we should do *A* in situation *B*, the remedy lies not in trying to prove we should do *A*, "but in getting face to face with a particular instance of the situation *B*, and then directly appreciating the obligation to originate *A* in that situation."

As you can see, Prichard disagrees completely with Moore's view that the rightness of an act derives from the goodness it produces. But notice that Moore and Prichard are not espousing a theory about what *is* good and right; instead, they are espousing a theory about *theories* about what is good and right. They are clarifying the enterprise of moral philosophy. Their theories are not ethical theories, but metaethical theories—theories about ethical theorizing. Much recent moral philosophy is of the metaethical variety.

Notice too that Moore and Prichard, despite their differences, both assumed that moral terms, terms such as *right* and *good*, are adjectives by means of which properties, albeit non-natural properties, are ascribed to actions or things. They are both cognitivists, in short (see Chapter 3). If I say that Ms. Farnsworth did a good thing, for example, I am attributing the moral property of goodness to whatever it was she did. Again, Moore and Prichard did not believe that moral properties are *natural* properties, nor did they believe that we ascertain the presence or absence of moral properties through *empirical* observation. Instead, we directly apprehend them, apparently through some sort of nonsensory, nonempirical faculty. For this reason, Moore and Prichard are called *intuitionists.* Both assumed that moral judgments attribute (non-natural) moral properties to things, and thus are a type of (nonempirical) factual judgment, judgments that are straightforwardly true or false.

from *Principia Ethica*

G. E. Moore

George Edward Moore (1873–1958) was a professor of philosophy at Cambridge University in England and editor of the philosophy journal *Mind.* Presented here is most of chapter I of his *Principia Ethica* (1903; Buffalo, N.Y.: Prometheus Books, 1988).

Chapter I. The Subject-Matter of Ethics.

1. It is very easy to point out some among our every-day judgments, with the truth of which Ethics is undoubtedly concerned. Whenever we say, "So and so is a good man," or "That fellow is a villain"; whenever we ask, "What ought I to do?" or "Is it wrong for me to do like this?"; whenever we hazard such remarks as "Temperance is a virtue and drunkenness a vice"—it is undoubtedly the business of Ethics to discuss such questions and such statements; to argue what is the true answer when we ask what it is right to do, and to give reasons for thinking that our statements about the character of persons or the morality of actions are true or false. In the vast majority of cases, where we make statements involving any of the terms "virtue," "vice," "duty," "right," "ought," "good," "bad," we are making ethical judgments; and if we wish to discuss their truth, we shall be discussing a point of Ethics.

So much as this is not disputed; but it falls very far short of defining the province of Ethics. That province may indeed be defined as the whole truth about that which is at the same time common to all such judgments and peculiar to them. But we have still to ask the question: What is it that is thus common and peculiar? And this is a question to which very different answers have been given by ethical philosophers of acknowledged reputation, and none of them, perhaps, completely satisfactory.

2. If we take such examples as those given above, we shall not be far wrong in saying that they are all of them concerned with the question of "conduct"—with the question, what, in the conduct of us, human beings, is good, and what is bad, what is right, and what is wrong. For when we say that a man is good, we commonly mean that he acts rightly; when we say that drunkenness is a vice, we commonly mean that to get drunk is a wrong or wicked action. And this discussion of human conduct is, in fact, that with which the name "Ethics" is most intimately associated. It is so associated by derivation; and conduct is undoubtedly by far the commonest and most generally interesting object of ethical judgments.

Accordingly, we find that many ethical philosophers are disposed to accept as an adequate definition of "Ethics" the statement that it deals with the question what is good or bad in human conduct. They hold that its enquiries are properly confined to "conduct" or to "practice"; they hold that the name "practical philosophy" covers all the matter with which it has to do. Now, without discussing the proper meaning of the word (for verbal questions are properly left to the writers of dictionaries and other persons interested in literature; philosophy, as we shall see, has no concern with them), I may say that I intend to use "Ethics" to cover more than this—a usage, for which there is, I think, quite sufficient authority. I am using it to cover an enquiry for which, at all events, there is no other word: the general enquiry into what is good.

Ethics is undoubtedly concerned with the question what good conduct is; but, being concerned with this, it obviously does not start at the beginning, unless it is prepared to tell us what is good as well as what is conduct. For "good conduct" is a complex notion: all conduct is not good; for some is certainly bad and some may be indifferent. And on the other hand, other things, beside conduct, may be good; and if they are so, then, "good" denotes some property, that is common to them and conduct; and if we examine good conduct alone of all good things, then we shall be in danger of mistaking for this property, some property which is not shared by those other things: and thus we shall have made a mistake about Ethics even in this limited sense; for we shall not know what good conduct really is. This is a mistake which many writers have actually made, from limiting their enquiry to conduct. And hence I shall try to avoid it by considering first what is good in general; hoping, that if we can arrive at any certainty about this, it will be much easier to settle the question of good conduct: for we all know pretty well what "conduct" is. This, then, is our first question: What is good? and What is bad? and to the discussion of this question (or these questions) I give the name of Ethics, since that science must, at all events, include it.

3. But this is a question which may have many meanings. If, for example, each of us were to say "I am doing good now" or "I had a good dinner yesterday," these statements would each of them be some sort of answer to our question, although perhaps a false one. So, too, when A asks B what school he ought to send his son to, B's answer will certainly be an ethical judgment. And similarly all distribution of praise or blame to any personage or thing that has existed, now exists, or will exist, does give some answer to the question "What is good?" In all such cases some particular thing is judged to be good or bad: the question "What?" is answered by "This." But this is not the sense in which a scientific Ethics asks the question. Not one, of all the many million answers of this kind, which must be true, can form a part of an ethical system; although that science must contain reasons and principles sufficient for deciding on the truth of all of them. There are far too many persons, things and events in the world, past, present, or to come, for a discussion of their individual merits to be embraced in any science. Ethics, therefore, does not deal at all with facts of this nature, facts that are unique, individual, absolutely particular; facts with which such studies as history, geography, astronomy, are compelled, in part at least, to deal. And, for this reason, it is not the business of the ethical philosopher to give personal advice or exhortation.

4. But there is another meaning which may be given to the question "What is good?" "Books are good" would be an answer to it, though an answer obviously false; for some books are very bad indeed. And ethical judgments of this kind do indeed belong to Ethics; though I shall not deal with many of them. Such is the judgment "Pleasure is good"—a judgment, of which Ethics should discuss the truth, although it is not nearly as important as that other judgment, with which we shall be much occupied presently—"Pleasure *alone* is good." It is judgments of this sort, which are made in such books on Ethics as contain a list of "virtues"—in Aristotle's "Ethics" for example. But it is judgments of precisely the same kind, which from the substance of what is commonly supposed to be a study different from Ethics, and one much less respectable—the study of Casuistry. We may be told that Casuistry differs from Ethics, in that it is much more detailed and particular, Ethics much more general. But it is most important to notice that Casuistry does not deal with anything that is absolutely particular—particular in the only sense in which a perfectly precise line can be drawn between it and what is general. It is not particular in the sense just noticed, the sense in which this book is a particular book, and A's friend's advice particular advice. Casuistry may indeed be *more* particular and Ethics *more* general; but that means that they differ only in degree and not in kind. And this is universally true of "particular" and "general," when used in this common, but inaccurate, sense. So far as Ethics allows itself to give lists of virtues or even to name constituents of the Ideal, it is indistinguishable from Casuistry. Both alike deal with what is general, in the sense in which physics and chemistry deal with what is general. Just as chemistry aims at discovering what are the properties of oxygen, *wherever it occurs*, and not only of this or that particular specimen of oxygen; so Casuistry aims at discovering what actions are good, *wherever they occur*. In this respect Ethics and Casuistry alike are to be classed with such sciences as physics, chemistry and physiology, in their absolute distinction from those of which history and geography are instances. And it is to be noted that, owing to their detailed nature, casuistical investigations are actually nearer to physics and to chemistry than are the investigations usually assigned to Ethics. For just as physics cannot rest content with the discovery that light is propagated by waves of ether, but must go on to discover the particular nature of the ether-waves corresponding to each several colour;

so Casuistry, not content with the general law that charity is a virtue must attempt to discover the relative merits of every different form of charity. Casuistry forms, therefore, part of the ideal of ethical science: Ethics cannot be complete without it. The defects of Casuistry are not defects of principle; no objection can be taken to its aim and object. It has failed only because it is far too difficult a subject to be treated adequately in our present state of knowledge. The casuist has been unable to distinguish, in the cases which he treats, those elements upon which their value depends. Hence he often thinks two cases to be alike in respect of value, when in reality they are alike only in some other respect. It is to mistakes of this kind that the pernicious influence of such investigations has been due. For Casuistry is the goal of ethical investigation. It cannot be safely attempted at the beginning of our studies, but only at the end.

5. But our question "What is good?" may have still another meaning. We may, in the third place, mean to ask, not what thing or things are good, but how "good" is to be defined. This is an enquiry which belongs only to Ethics, not to Casuistry; and this is the enquiry which will occupy us first.

It is an enquiry to which most special attention should be directed; since this question, how "good" is to be defined, is the most fundamental question in all Ethics. That which is meant by "good" is, in fact, except its converse "bad," the *only* simple object of thought which is peculiar to Ethics. Its definition is, therefore, the most essential point in the definition of Ethics; and moreover a mistake with regard to it entails a far larger number of erroneous ethical judgments than any other. Unless this first question be fully understood, and its true answer clearly recognised, the rest of Ethics is as good as useless from the point of view of systematic knowledge. True ethical judgments, of the two kinds last dealt with, may indeed be made by those who do not know the answer to this question as well as by those who do; and it goes without saying that the two classes of people may lead equally good lives. But it is extremely unlikely that the *most general* ethical judgments will be equally valid, in the absence of a true answer to this question: I shall presently try to shew that the gravest errors have been largely due to beliefs in a false answer. And, in any case, it is impossible that, till the answer to this question be known, any one should know *what is the evidence* for any ethical judgment whatsoever. But the main object of Ethics, as a systematic science, is to give correct *reasons* for thinking that this or that is good; and, unless this question be answered, such reasons cannot be given. Even, therefore, apart from the fact that a false answer leads to false conclusions, the present enquiry is a most necessary and important part of the science of Ethics.

6. What, then, is good? How is good to be defined? Now, it may be thought that this is a verbal question. A definition does indeed often mean the expressing of one word's meaning in other words. But this is not the sort of definition I am asking for. Such a definition can never be of ultimate importance in any study except lexicography. If I wanted that kind of definition I should have to consider in the first place how people generally used the word "good"; but my business is not with its proper usage, as established by custom. I should, indeed, be foolish, if I tried to use it for something which it did not usually denote: if, for instance, I were to announce that, whenever I used the word "good," I must be understood to be thinking of that object which is usually denoted by the word "table." I shall, therefore, use the word in the sense in which I think it is ordinarily used; but at the same time I am not anxious to discuss whether I am right in thinking that it is so used. My business is solely with that object or idea, which I hold, rightly or wrongly, that the word is generally used to stand for. What I want to discover is the nature of that object or idea, and about this I am extremely anxious to arrive at an agreement.

But, if we understand the question in this sense, my answer to it may seem a very disappointing one. If I am asked "What is good?" my answer is that good is good, and that is the end of the matter. Or if I am asked "How is good to be defined?" my answer is that it cannot be defined, and that is all I have to say about it. But disappointing as these answers may appear, they are of the very last importance. To readers who are familiar with philosophic terminology, I can express their importance by saying that they amount to this: That propositions about the good are all of them synthetic and never analytic; and that is plainly no trivial matter. And the same thing may be expressed more popularly, by saying that, if I am right, then nobody can foist upon us such an axiom as that "Pleasure is the only good" or that "The good is the desired" on the pretence that this is "the very meaning of the word."

7. Let us, then, consider this position. My point is that "good" is a simple notion, just as "yellow" is a simple notion; that, just as you cannot, by any manner of means, explain to any one who does not already know it, what yellow is, so you cannot explain what good is. Definitions of the kind that I was asking for, definitions which describe the real nature of the object or notion denoted by a word, and which do not merely tell us what the word is used to mean, are only possible when the object or notion in question is something complex. You can give a definition of a horse, because a horse has many different properties and qualities, all of which you can enumerate. But when you have enumerated them all, when you have reduced a horse to his simplest terms, then you can no longer define those terms. They are simply something which you think of or perceive, and to any one who cannot think of or perceive them, you can never, by any definition, make their nature known. It may perhaps be objected to this that we are able to describe to others, objects which they have never seen or thought of. We can, for instance, make a man understand what a chimaera is, although he has never heard of one or seen one. You can tell him that it is an animal with a lioness's head and body, with a goat's head growing from the middle of its back, and with a snake in place of a tail. But here the object which you are describing is a complex object; it is entirely composed of parts, with which we are all perfectly familiar—a snake, a goat, a lioness; and we know, too, the manner in which those parts are to be put together, because we know what is meant by the middle of a lioness's back, and where her tail is wont to grow. And so it is with all objects, not previously known, which we are able to define: they are all complex; all composed of parts, which may themselves, in the first instance, be capable of similar definition, but which must in the end be reducible to simplest parts, which can no longer be defined. But yellow and good, we say, are not complex: they are notions of that simple kind, out of which definitions are composed and with which the power of further defining ceases.

8. When we say, as Webster says, "The definition of horse is 'A hoofed quadruped of the genus Equus,'" we may, in fact, mean three different things. (1) We may mean merely: "When I say 'horse,' you are to understand that I am talking about a hoofed quadruped of the genus Equus." This might be called the arbitrary verbal definition: and I do not mean that good is indefinable in that sense. (2) We may mean, as Webster ought to mean: "When most English people say 'horse,' they mean a hoofed quadruped of the genus Equus." This may be called the verbal definition proper, and I do not say that good is indefinable in this sense either; for it is certainly possible to discover how people use a word: otherwise, we could never have known that "good" may be translated by "gut" in German and by "bon" in French. But (3) we may, when we define horse, mean something much more important. We may mean that a certain object, which we all of us know, is composed in a certain manner: that it has four legs, a head, a heart, a liver, etc., etc., all of them arranged in definite relations to one another. It is in this sense that I deny good to be definable. I say that it is not composed of any parts, which we can substitute for it in our minds when we are thinking of it. We might think just as clearly and correctly about a horse, if we thought of all its parts and their arrangement instead of thinking of the whole: we could, I say, think how a horse differed from a donkey just as well, just as truly, in this way, as now we do, only not so easily; but there is nothing whatsoever which we could so substitute for good; and that is what I mean, when I say that good is indefinable.

9. But I am afraid I have still not removed the chief difficulty which may prevent acceptance of the proposition that good is indefinable. I do not mean to say that *the* good, that which is good, is thus indefinable; if I did think so, I should not be writing on Ethics, for my main object is to help towards discovering that definition. It is just because I think there will be less risk of error in our

search for a definition of "the good," that I am now insisting that *good* is indefinable. I must try to explain the difference between these two. I suppose it may be granted that "good" is an adjective. Well "the good," "that which is good," must therefore be the substantive to which the adjective "good" will apply: it must be the whole of that to which the adjective will apply, and the adjective must *always* truly apply to it. But if it is that to which the adjective will apply, it must be something different from that adjective itself; and the whole of that something different, whatever it is, will be our definition of *the* good. Now it may be that this something will have other adjectives, beside "good," that will apply to it. It may be full of pleasure, for example; it may be intelligent: and if these two adjectives are really part of its definition, then it will certainly be true, that pleasure and intelligence are good. And many people appear to think that, if we say "Pleasure and intelligence are good," or if we say "Only pleasure and intelligence are good," we are defining "good." Well, I cannot deny that propositions of this nature may sometimes be called definitions; I do not know well enough how the word is generally used to decide upon this point. I only wish it to be understood that that is not what I mean when I say there is no possible definition of good, and that I shall not mean this if I use the word again. I do most fully believe that some true proposition of the form "Intelligence is good and intelligence alone is good" can be found; if none could be found, our definition of *the* good would be impossible. As it is, I believe *the* good to be definable; and yet I still say that good itself is indefinable.

10. "Good," then, if we mean by it that quality which we assert to belong to a thing, when we say that the thing is good, is incapable of any definition, in the most important sense of that word. The most important sense of "definition" is that in which a definition states what are the parts which invariably compose a certain whole; and in this sense "good" has no definition because it is simple and has no parts. It is one of those innumerable objects of thought which are themselves incapable of definition, because they are the ultimate terms by reference to which whatever *is* capable of definition must be defined. That there must be an indefinite number of such terms is obvious, on reflection; since we cannot define anything except by an analysis, which, when carried as far as it will go, refers us to something, which is simply different from anything else, and which by that ultimate difference explains the peculiarity of the whole which we are defining: for every whole contains some parts which are common to other wholes also. There is, therefore, no intrinsic difficulty in the contention that "good" denotes a simple and indefinable quality. There are many other instances of such qualities.

Consider yellow, for example. We may try to define it, by describing its physical equivalent; we may state what kind of light-vibrations must stimulate the normal eye, in order that we may perceive it. But a moment's reflection is sufficient to shew that those light-vibrations are not themselves what we mean by yellow. *They* are not what we perceive. Indeed we should never have been able to discover their existence, unless we had first been struck by the patent difference of quality between the different colours. The most we can be entitled to say of those vibrations is that they are what corresponds in space to the yellow which we actually perceive.

Yet a mistake of this simple kind has commonly been made about "good." It may be true that all things which are good are *also* something else, just as it is true that all things which are yellow produce a certain kind of vibration in the light. And it is a fact, that Ethics aims at discovering what are those other properties belonging to all things which are good. But far too many philosophers have thought that when they named those other properties they were actually defining good; that these properties, in fact, were simply not "other," but absolutely and entirely the same with goodness. This view I propose to call the "naturalistic fallacy" and of it I shall now endeavour to dispose.

11. Let us consider what it is such philosophers say. And first it is to be noticed that they do not agree among themselves. They not only say that they are right as to what good is, but they endeavour to prove that other people who say that it is something else, are wrong. One, for instance, will affirm that good is pleasure, another, perhaps, that good is that which is desired; and each of

these will argue eagerly to prove that the other is wrong. But how is that possible? One of them says that good is nothing but the object of desire, and at the same time tries to prove that it is not pleasure. But from his first assertion, that good just means the object of desire, one of two things must follow as regards his proof:

(1) He may be trying to prove that the object of desire is not pleasure. But, if this be all, where is his Ethics? The position he is maintaining is merely a psychological one. Desire is something which occurs in our minds, and pleasure is something else which so occurs; and our would-be ethical philosopher is merely holding that the latter is not the object of the former. But what has that to do with the question in dispute? His opponent held the ethical proposition that pleasure was the good, and although he should prove a million times over the psychological proposition that pleasure is not the object of desire, he is no nearer proving his opponent to be wrong. The position is like this. One man says a triangle is a circle: another replies "A triangle is a straight line, and I will prove to you that I am right: *for*" (this is the only argument) "a straight line is not a circle." "That is quite true," the other may reply; "but nevertheless a triangle is a circle, and you have said nothing whatever to prove the contrary. What is proved is that one of us is wrong, for we agree that a triangle cannot be both a straight line and a circle: but which is wrong, there can be no earthly means of proving, since you define triangle as straight line and I define it as circle."—Well, that is one alternative which any naturalistic Ethics has to face; if good is *defined* as something else, it is then impossible either to prove that any other definition is wrong or even to deny such definition.

(2) The other alternative will scarcely be more welcome. It is that the discussion is after all a verbal one. When A says "Good means pleasant" and B says "Good means desired," they may merely wish to assert that most people have used the word for what is pleasant and for what is desired respectively. And this is quite an interesting subject for discussion: only it is not a whit more an ethical discussion than the last was. Nor do I think that any exponent of naturalistic Ethics would be willing to allow that this was all he meant. They are all so anxious to persuade us that what they call the good is what we really ought to do. "Do, pray, act so, because the word 'good' is generally used to denote actions of this nature": such, on this view, would be the substance of their teaching. And in so far as they tell us how we ought to act, their teaching is truly ethical, as they mean it to be. But how perfectly absurd is the reason they would give for it! "You are to do this, because most people use a certain word to denote conduct such as this." "You are to say the thing which is not, because most people call it lying." That is an argument just as good!—My dear sirs, what we want to know from you as ethical teachers, is not how people use a word; it is not even, what kind of actions they approve, which the use of this word "good" may certainly imply: what we want to know is simply what *is* good. We may indeed agree that what most people do think good, is actually so; we shall at all events be glad to know their opinions: but when we say their opinions about what *is* good, we do mean what we say; we do not care whether they call that thing which they mean "horse" or "table" or "chair," "gut" or "bon" or "*αγαθός*"; we want to know what it is that they so call. When they say "Pleasure is good," we cannot believe that they merely mean "Pleasure is pleasure" and nothing more than that.

12. Suppose a man says "I am pleased"; and suppose that is not a lie or a mistake but the truth. Well, if it is true, what does that mean? It means that his mind, a certain definite mind, distinguished by certain definite marks from all others, has at this moment a certain definite feeling called pleasure. "Pleased" *means* nothing but having pleasure, and though we may be more pleased or less pleased, and even, we may admit for the present, have one or another kind of pleasure; yet in so far as it is pleasure we have, whether there be more or less of it, and whether it be of one kind or another, what we have is one definite thing, absolutely indefinable, some one thing that is the same in all the various degrees and in all the various kinds of it that there may be. We may be able to say how it is related to other things: that, for example, it is in the mind, that it causes desire, that we are conscious of it, etc., etc. We can, I say, describe its relations to other things, but define it we

can *not.* And if anybody tried to define pleasure for us as being any other natural object; if anybody were to say, for instance, that pleasure *means* the sensation of red, and were to proceed to deduce from that that pleasure is a colour, we should be entitled to laugh at him and to distrust his future statements about pleasure. Well, that would be the same fallacy which I have called the naturalistic fallacy. That "pleased" does not mean "having the sensation of red," or anything else whatever, does not prevent us from understanding what it does mean. It is enough for us to know that "pleased" does mean "having the sensation of pleasure," and though pleasure is absolutely indefinable, though pleasure is pleasure and nothing else whatever, yet we feel no difficulty in saying that we are pleased. The reason is, of course, that when I say "I am pleased," I do *not* mean that "I" am the same thing as "having pleasure." And similarly no difficulty need be found in my saying that "pleasure is good" and yet not meaning that "pleasure" is the same thing as "good," that pleasure *means* good, and that good *means* pleasure. If I were to imagine that when I said "I am pleased," I meant that I was exactly the same thing as "pleased," I should not indeed call that a naturalistic fallacy, although it would be the same fallacy as I have called naturalistic with reference to Ethics. The reason of this is obvious enough. When a man confuses two natural objects with one another, defining the one by the other, if for instance, he confuses himself, who is one natural object, with "pleased" or with "pleasure" which are others, then there is no reason to call the fallacy naturalistic. But if he confuses "good," which is not in the same sense a natural object, with any natural object whatever, then there is a reason for calling that a naturalistic fallacy; its being made with regard to "good" marks it as something quite specific, and this specific mistake deserves a name because it is so common. As for the reasons why good is not to be considered a natural object, they may be reserved for discussion in another place. But, for the present, it is sufficient to notice this: Even if it were a natural object, that would not alter the nature of the fallacy nor diminish its importance one whit. All that I have said about it would remain quite equally true: only the name which I have called it would not be so appropriate as I think it is. And I do not care about the name: what I do care about is the fallacy. It does not matter what we call it, provided we recognise it when we meet with it. It is to be met with in almost every book on Ethics; and yet it is not recognised: and that is why it is necessary to multiply illustrations of it, and convenient to give it a name. It is a very simple fallacy indeed. When we say that an orange is yellow, we do not think our statement binds us to hold that "orange" means nothing else than "yellow," or that nothing can be yellow but an orange. Supposing the orange is also sweet! Does that bind us to say that "sweet" is exactly the same thing as "yellow," that "sweet" must be defined as "yellow"? And supposing it be recognised that "yellow" just means "yellow" and nothing else whatever, does that make it any more difficult to hold that oranges are yellow? Most certainly it does not: on the contrary, it would be absolutely meaningless to say that oranges were yellow, unless yellow did in the end mean just "yellow" and nothing else whatever—unless it was absolutely indefinable. We should not get any very clear notion about things, which are yellow—we should not get very far with our science, if we were bound to hold that everything which was yellow, *meant* exactly the same thing as yellow. We should find we had to hold that an orange was exactly the same thing as a stool, a piece of paper, a lemon, anything you like. We could prove any number of absurdities; but should we be the nearer to the truth? Why, then, should it be different with "good"? Why, if good is good and indefinable, should I be held to deny that pleasure is good? Is there any difficulty in holding both to be true at once? On the contrary, there is no meaning in saying that pleasure is good, unless good is something different from pleasure. It is absolutely useless, so far as Ethics is concerned, to prove, as Mr. Spencer tries to do, that increase of pleasure coincides with increase of life, unless good *means* something different from either life or pleasure. He might just as well try to prove that an orange is yellow by shewing that it always is wrapped up in paper.

13. In fact, if it is not the case that "good" denotes something simple and indefinable, only two

alternatives are possible: either it is a complex, a given whole, about the correct analysis of which there may be disagreement; or else it means nothing at all, and there is no such subject as Ethics. In general, however, ethical philosophers have attempted to define good, without recognising what such an attempt must mean. They actually use arguments which involve one or both of the absurdities considered in § 11. We are, therefore, justified in concluding that the attempt to define good is chiefly due to want of clearness as to the possible nature of definition. There are, in fact, only two serious alternatives to be considered, in order to establish the conclusion that "good" does denote a simple and indefinable notion. It might possibly denote a complex, as "horse" does; or it might have no meaning at all. Neither of these possibilities has, however, been clearly conceived and seriously maintained, as such, by those who presume to define good; and both may be dismissed by a simple appeal to facts.

(1) The hypothesis that disagreement about the meaning of good is disagreement with regard to the correct analysis of a given whole, may be most plainly seen to be incorrect by consideration of the fact that, whatever definition be offered, it may be always asked, with significance, of the complex so defined, whether it is itself good. To take, for instance, one of the more plausible, because one of the more complicated, of such proposed definitions, it may easily be thought, at first sight, that to be good may mean to be that which we desire to desire. Thus if we apply this definition to a particular instance and say "When we think that A is good, we are thinking that A is one of the things which we desire to desire," our proposition may seem quite plausible. But, if we carry the investigation further, and ask ourselves "Is it good to desire to desire A?" it is apparent, on a little reflection, that this question is itself as intelligible, as the original question "Is A good?"—that we are, in fact, now asking for exactly the same information about the desire to desire A, for which we formerly asked with regard to A itself. But it is also apparent that the meaning of this second question cannot be correctly analysed into "Is the desire to desire A one of the things which we desire to desire?": we have not before our minds anything so complicated as the question "Do we desire to desire to desire to desire A?" Moreover any one can easily convince himself by inspection that the predicate of this proposition—"good"—is positively different from the notion of "desiring to desire" which enters into its subject: "That we should desire to desire A is good" is *not* merely equivalent to "That A should be good is good." It may indeed be true that what we desire to desire is always also good; perhaps, even the converse may be true: but it is very doubtful whether this is the case, and the mere fact that we understand very well what is meant by doubting it, shews clearly that we have two different notions before our minds.

(2) And the same consideration is sufficient to dismiss the hypothesis that "good" has no meaning whatsoever. It is very natural to make the mistake of supposing that what is universally true is of such a nature that its negation would be self-contradictory: the importance which has been assigned to analytic propositions in the history of philosophy shews how easy such a mistake is. And thus it is very easy to conclude that what seems to be a universal ethical principle is in fact an identical proposition; that, if, for example, whatever is called "good" seems to be pleasant, the proposition "Pleasure is the good" does not assert a connection between two different notions, but involves only one, that of pleasure, which is easily recognised as a distinct entity. But whoever will attentively consider with himself what is actually before his mind when he asks the question "Is pleasure (or whatever it may be) after all good?" can easily satisfy himself that he is not merely wondering whether pleasure is pleasant. And if he will try this experiment with each suggested definition in succession, he may become expert enough to recognise that in every case he has before his mind a unique object, with regard to the connection of which with any other object, a distinct question may be asked. Every one does in fact understand the question "Is this good?" When he thinks of it, his state of mind is different from what it would be, were he asked 'Is this pleasant, or desired, or approved?' It has a distinct meaning for him, even though he may not recognise in what respect it is distinct. Whenever

he thinks of "intrinsic value," or "intrinsic worth," or says that a thing "ought to exist," he has before his mind the unique object—the unique property of things—which I mean by "good." Everybody is constantly aware of this notion, although he may never become aware at all that it is different from other notions of which he is also aware. But, for correct ethical reasoning, it is extremely important that he should become aware of this fact; and, as soon as the nature of the problem is clearly understood, there should be little difficulty in advancing so far in analysis.

14. "Good," then, is indefinable; and yet, so far as I know, there is only one ethical writer, Prof. Henry Sidgwick, who has clearly recognised and stated this fact. We shall see, indeed, how far many of the most reputed ethical systems fall short of drawing the conclusions which follow from such a recognition. At present I will only quote one instance, which will serve to illustrate the meaning and importance of this principle that "good" is indefinable, or, as Prof. Sidgwick says, an "unanalysable notion." It is an instance to which Prof. Sidgwick himself refers in a note on the passage, in which he argues that "ought" is unanalysable.[1]

"Bentham," says Sidgwick, "explains that his fundamental principle 'states the greatest happiness of all those whose interest is in question as being the right and proper end of human action'"; and yet "his language in other passages of the same chapter would seem to imply" that he *means* by the word "right" "conducive to the general happiness." Prof. Sidgwick sees that, if you take these two statements together, you get the absurd result that "greatest happiness is the end of human action, which is conducive to the general happiness"; and so absurd does it seem to him to call this result, as Bentham calls it, "the fundamental principle of a moral system," that he suggests that Bentham cannot have meant it. Yet Prof. Sidgwick himself states elsewhere[2] that Psychological Hedonism is 'not seldom confounded with Egoistic Hedonism'; and that confusion, as we shall see, rests chiefly on that same fallacy, the naturalistic fallacy, which is implied in Bentham's statements. Prof. Sidgwick admits therefore that this fallacy is sometimes committed, absurd as it is; and I am inclined to think that Bentham may really have been one of those who committed it. Mill, as we shall see, certainly did commit it. In any case, whether Bentham committed it or not, his doctrine, as above quoted, will serve as a very good illustration of this fallacy, and of the importance of the contrary proposition that good is indefinable.

Let us consider this doctrine. Bentham seems to imply, so Prof. Sidgwick says, that the word "right" *means* "conducive to general happiness." Now this, by itself, need not necessarily involve the naturalistic fallacy. For the word "right" is very commonly appropriated to actions which lead to the attainment of what is good; which are regarded as *means* to the ideal and not as ends-in-themselves. This use of "right," as denoting what is good as a means, whether or not it be also good as an end, is indeed the use to which I shall confine the word. Had Bentham been using "right" in this sense, it might be perfectly consistent for him to *define* right as "conducive to the general happiness," *provided only* (and notice this proviso) he had already proved, or laid down as an axiom, that general happiness was *the* good, or (what is equivalent to this) that general happiness alone was good. For in that case he would have already defined *the* good as general happiness (a position perfectly consistent, as we have seen, with the contention that "good" is indefinable), and, since right was to be defined as "conducive to *the* good," it would actually *mean* "conducive to general happiness." But this method of escape from the charge of having committed the naturalistic fallacy has been closed by Bentham himself. For his fundamental principle is, we see, that the greatest happiness of all concerned is the *right* and proper *end* of human action. He applies the word "right," therefore, to the end, as such, not only to the means which are conducive to it; and, that being so, right can no longer be defined as "conducive to the general happiness," without involving the fallacy in question. For now it is obvious that the definition of right as conducive to general happiness can be used by him in support

[1] *Methods of Ethics,* Bk. 1, Chap. iii, § 1 (6th edition).
[2] *Methods of Ethics,* Bk. 1, Chap. iv, § 1.

of the fundamental principle that general happiness is the right end; instead of being itself derived from that principle. If right, by definition, means conducive to general happiness, then it is obvious that general happiness is the right end. It is not necessary now first to prove or assert that general happiness is the right end, before right is defined as conducive to general happiness—a perfectly valid procedure; but on the contrary the definition of right as conducive to general happiness proves general happiness to be the right end—a perfectly invalid procedure, since in this case the statement that 'general happiness is the right end of human action' is not an ethical principle at all, but either, as we have seen, a proposition about the meaning of words, or else a proposition about the *nature* of general happiness, not about its rightness or goodness.

Now, I do not wish the importance I assign to this fallacy to be misunderstood. The discovery of it does not at all refute Bentham's contention that greatest happiness is the proper end of human action, if that be understood as an ethical proposition, as he undoubtedly intended it. That principle may be true all the same; we shall consider whether it is so in succeeding chapters. Bentham might have maintained it, as Prof. Sidgwick does, even if the fallacy had been pointed out to him. What I am maintaining is that the *reasons* which he actually gives for his ethical proposition are fallacious ones so far as they consist in a definition of right. What I suggest is that he did not perceive them to be fallacious; that, if he had done so, he would have been led to seek for other reasons in support of his Utilitarianism; and that, had he sought for other reasons, he *might* have found none which he thought to be sufficient. In that case he would have changed his whole system—a most important consequence. It is undoubtedly also possible that he would have thought other reasons to be sufficient, and in that case his ethical system, in its main results, would still have stood. But, even in this latter case, his use of the fallacy would be a serious objection to him as an ethical philosopher. For it is the business of Ethics, I must insist, not only to obtain true results, but also to find valid reasons for them. The direct object of Ethics is knowledge and not practice; and any one who uses the naturalistic fallacy has certainly not fulfilled this first object, however correct his practical principles may be.

My objections to Naturalism are then, in the first place, that it offers no reason at all, far less any valid reason, for any ethical principle whatever; and in this it already fails to satisfy the requirements of Ethics, as a scientific study. But in the second place I contend that, though it gives a reason for no ethical principle, it is a *cause* of the acceptance of false principles—it deludes the mind into accepting ethical principles, which are false; and in this it is contrary to every aim of Ethics. It is easy to see that if we start with a definition of right conduct as conduct conducive to general happiness; then, knowing that right conduct is universally conduct conducive to the good, we very easily arrive at the result that the good is general happiness. If, on the other hand, we once recognise that we must start our Ethics without a definition, we shall be much more apt to look about us, before we adopt any ethical principle whatever; and the more we look about us, the less likely are we to adopt a false one. It may be replied to this: Yes, but we shall look about us just as much, before we settle on our definition, and are therefore just as likely to be right. But I will try to shew that this is not the case. If we start with the conviction that a definition of good can be found, we start with the conviction that good *can mean* nothing else than some one property of things; and our only business will then be to discover what that property is. But if we recognise that, so far as the meaning of good goes, anything whatever may be good, we start with a much more open mind. Moreover, apart from the fact that, when we think we have a definition, we cannot logically defend our ethical principles in any way whatever, we shall also be much less apt to defend them well, even if illogically. For we shall start with the conviction that good must mean so and so, and shall therefore be inclined either to misunderstand our opponent's arguments or to cut them short with the reply, "This is not an open question: the very meaning of the word decides it; no one can think otherwise except through confusion." . . .

Study Questions

1. According to Moore, with what is ethics primarily concerned?
2. What interpretation of the question "What is good?" is Moore concerned with?
3. What sort of definition of good does Moore say he wants to find?
4. Explain what Moore means by saying that "good" is a simple notion. Use an example if you want to.
5. What does Moore mean when he says that good is indefinable?
6. Does Moore think *the* good is indefinable? Explain.
7. What is the naturalistic fallacy?
8. Can disagreement about the meaning of good be a disagreement about the correct analysis of a given whole, according to Moore? Explain.

Does Moral Philosophy Rest on a Mistake?

H. A. Prichard

Harold Arthur Prichard (1871–1947) was White's Professor of Moral Philosophy at Oxford University, England. From *Mind* 21, no. 81 (January 1912): 21–37.

Probably to most students of Moral Philosophy there comes a time when they feel a vague sense of dissatisfaction with the whole subject. And the sense of dissatisfaction tends to grow rather than to diminish. It is not so much that the positions, and still more the arguments, of particular thinkers seem unconvincing, though this is true. It is rather that the aim of the subject becomes increasingly obscure. "What," it is asked, "are we really going to learn by Moral Philosophy?" "What are books on Moral Philosophy really trying to show, and when their aim is clear, why are they so unconvincing and artificial?" And again: "Why is it so difficult to substitute anything better?" Personally, I have been led by growing dissatisfaction of this kind to wonder whether the reason may not be that the subject, at any rate as usually understood, consists in the attempt to answer an improper question. And in this article I shall venture to contend that the existence of the whole subject, as usually understood, rests on a mistake, and on a mistake parallel to that on which rests, as I think, the subject usually called the Theory of Knowledge.

If we reflect on our own mental history or on the history of the subject, we feel no doubt about the nature of the demand which originates the subject. Any one who, stimulated by education, has come to feel the force of the various obligations in life, at some time or other comes to feel the irksomeness of carrying them out, and to recognize the sacrifice of interest involved; and if thoughtful, he inevitably puts to himself the question: "Is there really a reason why I should act in the ways in which hitherto I have thought I ought to act? May I not have been all the time under an illusion in so thinking? Should not I really be justified in simply trying to have a good time?" Yet, like Glaucon, feeling that somehow he ought after all to act in these ways, he asks for a *proof* that this feeling is justified. In other words, he asks "*Why* should I do these things?" and his and other people's moral philosophizing is an attempt to supply the answer, i.e. to supply by a process of reflection a proof of the truth of what he and they have prior to reflection believed immediately or without proof. This frame of mind seems to present a close parallel to the frame of mind which originates the Theory of Knowledge. Just as the recognition that the doing of our duty often vitally interferes with the satisfaction of our inclinations leads us to wonder whether we really ought to do what we usually call our duty, so the recognition that we and others are liable to mistakes in knowledge generally leads us, as it did Descartes, to wonder whether hitherto we may not have been always mistaken. And just as we try to find a proof, based on the general consideration of action and of human life, that we ought to act in the ways usually called moral, so we, like Descartes, propose by a process of reflection on our thinking to find a test of knowledge, i.e. a principle by applying which we can show that a certain condition of mind was really knowledge, a condition which *ex hypothesi* existed independently of the process of reflection.

Now, how has the moral question been answered? So far as I can see, the answers all fall, and fall from the necessities of the case, into one of two species. *Either* they state that we ought to do so and so, because, as we see when we fully apprehend the facts, doing so will be for our good, i.e. really, as I would rather say, for our advantage, or, better still, for our happiness; *or* they state that we ought to do so and so, because something realized either in or by the action is good. In other words, the reason "why" is stated in terms either of the agent's happiness or of the goodness of something involved in the action.

To see the prevalence of the former species of answer, we have only to consider the history of Moral Philosophy. To take obvious instances, Plato, Butler, Hutcheson, Paley, Mill, each in his own way seeks at bottom to convince the individual that he ought to act in so-called moral ways by showing that to do so will really be for his happiness. Plato is perhaps the most significant instance, because of all philosophers he is the one to whom we are least willing to ascribe a mistake on such matters, and a mistake on his part would be evidence of the deep-rootedness of the tendency to make it. To show that Plato really justifies morality by its profitableness, it is only necessary to point out (1) that the very formulation of the thesis to be met, viz. that justice is *ἀλλότριον ἀγαθόν* [someone else's good] implies that any refutation must consist in showing that justice is *οἰκεῖον ἀγαθόν* [one's own good], i.e., really, as the context shows, one's own advantage, and (2) that the term *λυσιτελεῖν* [to be profitable] supplies the key not only to the problem but also to its solution.

The tendency to justify acting on moral rules in this way is natural. For if, as often happens, we put to ourselves the question "Why should we do so and so?" we are satisfied by being convinced either that the doing so will lead to something which we want (e.g. that taking certain medicine will heal our disease), or that the doing so itself, as we see when we appreciate its nature, is something that we want or should like, e.g. playing golf. The formulation of the question implies a state of unwillingness or indifference towards the action, and we are brought into a condition of willingness by the answer. And this process seems to be precisely what we desire when we ask, e.g., "Why should we keep our engagements to our own loss?"; for it is just the fact that the keeping of our engagements runs counter to the satisfaction of our desires which produced the question.

The answer is, of course, not an answer, for it fails to convince us that we ought to keep our engagements; even if successful on its own lines, it only makes us *want* to keep them. And Kant was really only pointing out this fact when he distinguished hypothetical and categorical imperatives, even though he obscured the name of the fact by wrongly describing his so-called "hypothetical imperatives" as imperatives. But if this answer be no answer, what other can be offered? Only, it seems, an answer which bases the obligation to do something on the *goodness* either of something to which the act leads or of the act itself. Suppose, when wondering whether we really ought to act in the ways usually called moral, we are told as a means of resolving our doubt that those acts are right which produce happiness. We at once ask: "Whose happiness?" If we are told "Our own happiness," then, though we shall lose our hesitation to act in these ways, we shall not recover our sense that we ought to do so. But how can this result be avoided? Apparently, only by being told one of two things; *either* that anyone's happiness is a thing good in itself, and that *therefore* we ought to do whatever will produce it, *or* that working for happiness is itself good, and that the intrinsic goodness of such an action is the reason why we ought to do it. The advantage of this appeal to the goodness of something consists in the fact that it avoids reference to desire, and instead, refers to something impersonal and objective. In this way it seems possible to avoid the resolution of obligation into inclination. But just for this reason it is of the essence of the answer, that to be effective it must neither include nor involve the view that the apprehension of the goodness of anything necessarily arouses the desire for it. Otherwise the answer resolves itself into a form of the former answer by substituting desire or inclination for the sense of obligation, and in this way it loses what seems its special advantage.

Now it seems to me that both forms of this answer break down, though each for a different reason.

Consider the first form. It is what may be called Utilitarianism in the generic sense, in which what is good is not limited to pleasure. It takes its stand upon the distinction between something which is not itself an action, but which can be produced by an action, and the action which will produce it, and contends that if something which is not an action is good, then we *ought* to undertake the action which will, directly or indirectly, originate it.[1]

But this argument, if it is to restore the sense of obligation to act, must presuppose an intermediate link, viz. the further thesis that what is good ought to be.[2] The necessity of this link is obvious. An "ought," if it is to be derived at all, can only be derived from another "ought." Moreover, this link tacitly presupposes another, viz. that the apprehension that something good which is not an action ought to be involves just the feeling of imperativeness or obligation which is to be aroused by the thought of the action which will originate it. Otherwise the argument will not lead us to feel the obligation to produce it by the action. And, surely, both this link and its implication are false.[3] The word "ought" refers to actions and to actions alone. The proper language is never "So and so ought to be," but "I ought to do so and so." Even if we are sometimes moved to say that the world or something in it is not what it ought to be, what we really mean is that God or some human being has not made something what he ought to have made it. And it is merely stating another side of this fact to urge that we can only feel the imperativeness upon us of something which is in our power; for it is actions and actions alone which, directly at least, are in our power.

Perhaps, however, the best way to see the failure of this view is to see its failure to correspond to our actual moral convictions. Suppose we ask ourselves whether our sense that we ought to pay our debts or to tell the truth arises from our recognition that in doing so we should be originating something good, e.g. material comfort in *A* or true belief in *B*, i.e. suppose we ask ourselves whether it is this aspect of the action which leads to our recognition that we ought to do it. We at once and without hesitation answer "No." Again, if we take as our illustration our sense that we ought to act justly as between two parties, we have, if possible, even less hesitation in giving a similar answer; for the balance of resulting good may be, and often is, not on the side of justice.

At best it can only be maintained that there is this element of truth in the Utilitarian view, that unless we recognize that something which an act will originate is good, we should not recognize that we ought to do the action. Unless we thought knowledge a good thing, it may be urged, we should not think that we ought to tell the truth; unless we thought pain a bad thing, we should not think the infliction of it, without special reason, wrong. But this is not to imply that the badness of

---

[1]Cf. Dr. Rashdall's *Theory of Good and Evil,* Vol. I, p. 138.

[2]Dr. Rashdall, if I understand him rightly, supplies this link (cf. *ibid.,* pp. 135–136).

[3]When we speak of anything, e.g., of some emotion or of some quality of a human being, as good, we never dream in our ordinary consciousness of going on to say that therefore it ought to be.

error is the reason why it is wrong to lie, or the badness of pain the reason why we ought not to inflict it without special cause.[4]

It is, I think, just because this form of the view is so plainly at variance with our moral consciousness that we are driven to adopt the other form of the view, viz. that the act is good in itself and that its intrinsic goodness is the reason why it ought to be done. It is this form which has always made the most serious appeal; for the goodness of the act itself seems more closely related to the obligation to do it than that of its mere consequences or results, and therefore, if obligation is to be based on the goodness of something, it would seem that this goodness should be that of the act itself. Moreover, the view gains plausibility from the fact that moral actions are most conspicuously those to which the term 'intrinsically good' is applicable.

Nevertheless this view, though perhaps less superficial, is equally untenable. For it leads to precisely the dilemma which faces everyone who tries to solve the problem raised by Kant's theory of the good will. To see this, we need only consider the nature of the acts to which we apply the term "intrinsically good."

There is, of course, no doubt that we approve and even admire certain actions, and also that we should describe them as good, and as good in themselves. But it is, I think, equally unquestionable that our approval and our use of the term "good" is always in respect of the motive and refers to actions which have been actually done and of which we think we know the motive. Further, the actions of which we approve and which we should describe as intrinsically good are of two and only two kinds. They are either actions in which the agent did what he did because he thought he ought to do it, or actions of which the motive was a desire prompted by some good emotion, such as gratitude, affection, family feeling, or public spirit, the most prominent of such desires in books on Moral Philosophy being that ascribed to what is vaguely called benevolence. For the sake of simplicity I omit the case of actions done partly from some such desire and partly from a sense of duty; for even if all good actions are done from a combination of these motives, the argument will not be affected. The dilemma is this. If the motive in respect of which we think an action good is the sense of obligation, then so far from the sense that we ought to do it being derived from our apprehension of its goodness, our apprehension of its goodness will presuppose the sense that we ought to do it. In other words, in this case the recognition that the act is good will plainly *presuppose* the recognition that the act is right, whereas the view under consideration is that the recognition of the goodness of the act *gives rise* to the recognition of its rightness. On the other hand, if the motive in respect of which we think an action good is some intrinsically good desire, such as the desire to help a friend, the recognition of the goodness of the act will equally fail to give rise to the sense of obligation to do it. For we cannot feel that we ought to do that the doing of which is *ex hypothesi* prompted solely by the desire to do it.[5]

The fallacy underlying the view is that while to base the rightness of an act upon its intrinsic goodness implies that the goodness in question is that of the motive, in reality the rightness or wrongness of an act has nothing to do with any question of motives at all. For, as any instance will show, the rightness of an action concerns an action not in the fuller sense of the term in which we include the motive in the action, but in the narrower and commoner sense in which we distinguish an action from its motive and mean by an action merely the conscious origination of something, an origination which on different occasions or in different people may be prompted by different motives. The question "Ought I to pay my bills?" really means simply "Ought I to bring about my tradesmen's possession of what by my previous acts I explicitly or implicitly promised them?" There is, and can be, no question of whether I ought to pay my debts from a particular motive. No doubt we know that

[4]It may be noted that if the badness of pain were the reason why we ought not to inflict pain on another, it would equally be a reason why we ought not to inflict pain on ourselves; yet, though we should allow the wanton infliction of pain on ourselves to be foolish, we should not think of describing it as wrong.

[5]It is, I think, on this latter horn of the dilemma that Martineau's view falls; cf. *Types of Ethical Theory,* Part II, Book I.

if we pay our bills we shall pay them with a motive, but in considering whether we ought to pay them we inevitably think of the act in abstraction from the motive. Even if we knew what our motive would be if we did the act, we should not be any nearer an answer to the question.

Moreover, if we eventually pay our bills from fear of the county court, we shall still have done *what* we ought, even though we shall not have done it *as* we ought. The attempt to bring in the motive involves a mistake similar to that involved in supposing that we can will to will. To feel that I ought to pay my bills is to be *moved towards* paying them. But what I can be moved towards must always be an action and not an action in which I am moved in a particular way, i.e. an action from a particular motive; otherwise I should be moved towards being moved, which is impossible. Yet the view under consideration involves this impossibility, for it really resolves the sense that I ought to do so and so, into the sense that I ought to be moved to do it in a particular way.[6]

So far my contentions have been mainly negative, but they form, I think, a useful, if not a necessary, introduction to what I take to be the truth. This I will now endeavour to state, first formulating what, as I think, is the real nature of our apprehension or appreciation of moral obligations, and then applying the result to elucidate the question of the existence of Moral Philosophy.

The sense of obligation to do, or of the rightness of, an action of a particular kind is absolutely underivative or immediate. The rightness of an action consists in its being the origination of something of a certain kind *A* in a situation of a certain kind, a situation consisting in a certain relation *B* of the agent to others or to his own nature. To appreciate its rightness two preliminaries may be necessary. We may have to follow out the consequences of the proposed action more fully than we have hitherto done, in order to realize that in the action we should originate *A*. Thus we may not appreciate the wrongness of telling a certain story until we realize that we should thereby be hurting the feelings of one of our audience. Again, we may have to take into account the relation *B* involved in the situation, which we had hitherto failed to notice. For instance, we may not appreciate the obligation to give *X* a present, until we remember that he has done us an act of kindness. But, given that by a process which is, of course, merely a process of general and not of moral thinking we come to recognize that the proposed act is one by which we shall originate *A* in a relation *B*, then we appreciate the obligation immediately or directly, the appreciation being an activity of *moral* thinking. We recognize, for instance, that this performance of a service to *X*, who has done us a service, just in virtue of its being the performance of a service to one who has rendered a service to the would-be agent, ought to be done by us. This apprehension is immediate, in precisely the sense in which a mathematical apprehension is immediate, e.g. the apprehension that this three-sided figure, in virtue of its being three-sided, must have three angles. Both apprehensions are immediate in the sense that in both insight into the nature of the subject directly leads us to recognize its possession of the predicate; and it is only stating this fact from the other side to say that in both cases the fact apprehended is self-evident.

The plausibility of the view that obligations are not self-evident but need proof lies in the fact that an act which is referred to as an obligation may be incompletely stated, what I have called the preliminaries to appreciating the obligation being incomplete. If, e.g., we refer to the act of repaying *X* by a present merely as giving *X* a present, it appears, and indeed is, necessary to give a reason. In other words, wherever a moral act is regarded in this incomplete way the question "*Why* should I do it?" is perfectly legitimate. This fact suggests, but suggests wrongly, that even if the nature of the act is completely stated, it is still necessary to give a reason, or, in other words, to supply a proof.

The relations involved in obligations of various kinds are, of course, very different. The relation in certain cases is a relation to others due to a past act of theirs or ours. The obligation to repay a benefit involves a relation due to a past act of the benefactor. The obligation to pay a bill involves a relation due to a past act of ours in which we have either said or implied that we would make a certain re-

[6]It is of course not denied here that an action done from a particular motive be *good;* it is only denied that the *rightness* of an action depends on its being done with a particular motive.

turn for something which we have asked for and received. On the other hand, the obligation to speak the truth implies no such definite act; it involves a relation consisting in the fact that others are trusting us to speak the truth, a relation the apprehension of which gives rise to the sense that communication of the truth is something owing by us to them. Again, the obligation not to hurt the feelings of another involves no special relation of us to that other, i.e. no relation other than that involved in our both being men, and men in one and the same world. Moreover, it seems that the relation involved in an obligation need not be a relation to another at all. Thus we should admit that there is an obligation to overcome our natural timidity or greediness, and that this involves no relations to others. Still there is a relation involved, viz. a relation to our own disposition. It is simply because we can and because others cannot directly modify our disposition that it is our business to improve it, and that it is not theirs, or at least, not theirs to the same extent.

The negative side of this is, of course, that we do not come to appreciate an obligation by an *argument,* i.e. by a process of non-moral thinking, and that, in particular, we do not do so by an argument of which a premise is the ethical but not moral activity of appreciating the goodness either of the act or of a consequence of the act; i.e. that our sense of the rightness of an act is not a conclusion from our appreciation of the goodness either of it or of anything else.

It will probably be urged that on this view our various obligations form, like Aristotle's categories, an unrelated chaos in which it is impossible to acquiesce. For, according to it, the obligation to repay a benefit, or to pay a debt, or to keep a promise, presupposes a previous act of another; whereas the obligation to speak the truth or not to harm another does not; and, again, the obligation to remove our timidity involves no relations to others at all. Yet, at any rate, an effective *argumentum ad hominem* is at hand in the fact that the various qualities which we recognize as good are equally unrelated; e.g. courage, humility and interest in knowledge. If, as is plainly the case, *αγαθά* differ *ῇ αγαθά* [Goods differ *qua* goods], why should not obligations equally differ *qua* their obligatoriness? Moreover, if this were not so there could in the end be only one obligation, which is palpably contrary to fact.[7]

Certain observations will help to make the view clearer.

In the first place, it may seem that the view, being — as it is — avowedly put forward in opposition to the view that what is right is derived from what is good, must itself involve the opposite of this, viz. the Kantian position that what is good is based upon what is right, i.e. that an act, if it be good, is good because it is right. But this is not so. For, on the view put forward, the rightness of a right action lies solely in the origination in which the act consists, whereas the intrinsic goodness of an action lies solely in its motive; and this implies that a morally good action is morally good not simply because it is a right action but because it is a right action done because it is right, i.e. from a sense of obligation. And this implication, it may be remarked incidentally, seems plainly true.

In the second place, the view involves that when, or rather so far as, we act from a sense of obligation, we have no purpose or end. By a "purpose" or "end" we really mean something the existence of which we desire, and desire of the existence of which leads us to act. Usually our purpose is something which the act will originate, as when we turn round in order to look at a picture. But it may be the action itself, i.e. the origination of something, as when we hit a golf-ball into a hole

[7]Two other objections may be anticipated: (1) that obligations cannot be self-evident, since many actions regarded as obligations by some are not so regarded by others, and (2) that if obligations are self-evident, the problem of how we ought to act in the presence of conflicting obligations is insoluble.

To the first I should reply:

(*a*) That the appreciation of an obligation is, of course, only possible for a developed moral being, and that different degrees of development are possible.

(*b*) That the failure to recognize some particular obligation is usually due to the fact that, owing to a lack of thoughtfulness, what I have called the preliminaries to this recognition are incomplete.

(*c*) That the view put forward is consistent with the admission that, owing to a lack of thoughtfulness, even the best men are blind to many of their obligations, and that in the end our obligations are seen to be co-extensive with almost the whole of our life.

To the second objection I should reply that obligation admits of degrees, and that where obligations conflict, the decision of what we ought to do turns not on the question "Which of the alternative courses of action will originate the greater good?" but on the question "Which is the greater obligation?"

or kill someone out of revenge.[8] Now if by a purpose we mean something the existence of which we desire and desire for which leads us to act, then plainly, so far as we act from a sense of obligation, we have no purpose, consisting either in the action or in anything which it will produce. This is so obvious that it scarcely seems worth pointing out. But I do so for two reasons. (1) If we fail to scrutinize the meaning of the terms "end" and "purpose," we are apt to assume uncritically that all deliberate action, i.e. action proper, must have a purpose; we then become puzzled both when we look for the purpose of an action done from a sense of obligation, and also when we try to apply to such an action the distinction of means and end, the truth all the time being that since there is no end, there is no means either. (2) The attempt to base the sense of obligation on the recognition of the goodness of something is really an attempt to find a purpose in a moral action in the shape of something good which, as good, we want. And the expectation that the goodness of something underlies an obligation disappears as soon as we cease to look for a purpose.

The thesis, however, that, so far as we act from a sense of obligation, we have no purpose must not be misunderstood. It must not be taken either to mean or to imply that so far as we so act we have no *motive.* No doubt in ordinary speech the words "motive" and "purpose" are usually treated as correlatives, "motive" standing for the desire which induces us to act, and "purpose" standing for the object of this desire. But this is only because, when we are looking for the motive of the action, say, of some crime, we are usually presupposing that the act in question is prompted by a desire and not by the sense of obligation. At bottom, however, we mean by a motive what moves us to act; a sense of obligation does sometimes move us to act; and in our ordinary consciousness we should not hesitate to allow that the action we were considering might have had as its motive a sense of obligation. Desire and the sense of obligation are co-ordinate forms or species of motive.

In the third place, if the view put forward be right, we must sharply distinguish morality and virtue as independent, though related, species of goodness, neither being an aspect of something of which the other is an aspect, nor again a form or species of the other, nor again something deducible from the other: and we must at the same time allow that it is possible to do the same act either virtuously or morally or in both ways at once. And surely this is true. An act, to be virtuous, must, as Aristotle saw, be done willingly or with pleasure; as such it is just not done from a sense of obligation but from some desire which is intrinsically good, as arising from some intrinsically good emotion. Thus, in an act of generosity the motive is the desire to help another arising from sympathy with that other; in an act which is courageous and no more, i.e. in an act which is not at the same time an act of public spirit or family affection or the like, we prevent ourselves from being dominated by a feeling of terror, desiring to do so from a sense of shame at being terrified. The goodness of such an act is different from the goodness of an act to which we apply the term moral in the strict and narrow sense, viz. an act done from a sense of obligation. Its goodness lies in the intrinsic goodness of the emotion and of the consequent desire under which we act, the goodness of this motive being different from the goodness of the moral motive proper, viz. the sense of duty or obligation. Nevertheless, at any rate in certain cases, an act can be done either virtuously or morally or in both ways at once. It is possible to repay a benefit either from desire to repay it, or from the feeling that we ought to do so, or from both motives combined. A doctor may tend his patients either from a desire arising out of interest in his patients or in the exercise of skill, or from a sense of duty, or from a desire and a sense of duty combined. Further, although we recognize that in each case the act possesses an intrinsic goodness, we regard that action as the best in which both motives are combined; in other words, we regard as the really best man the man in whom virtue and morality are united.

It may be objected that the distinction between the two kinds of motive is untenable, on the

[8]It is no objection to urge that an action cannot be its own purpose, since the purpose of something cannot be the thing itself. For, speaking strictly, the purpose is not the *action's* purpose but *our* purpose, and there is no contradiction in holding that our purpose in acting may be the action.

ground that the *desire* to repay a benefit, for example, is only the manifestation of that which manifests itself as the *sense of obligation* to repay whenever we think of something in the action which is other than the repayment and which we should not like, such as the loss or pain involved. Yet the distinction can, I think, easily be shown to be tenable. For in the analogous case of revenge, the desire to return the injury and the sense that we ought not to do so, leading, as they do, in opposite directions, are plainly distinct; and the obviousness of the distinction here seems to remove any difficulty in admitting the existence of a parallel distinction between the desire to return a benefit and the sense that we ought to return it.[9]

Further, the view implies that an obligation can no more be based on or derived from a virtue than a virtue can be derived from an obligation, in which latter case a virtue would consist in carrying out an obligation. And the implication is surely true and important. Take the case of courage. It is untrue to urge that, since courage is a virtue, we ought to act courageously. It is and must be untrue, because, as we see in the end, to feel an obligation to act courageously would involve a contradiction. For, as I have urged before, we can only feel an obligation to *act;* we cannot feel an obligation to *act from a certain desire,* in this case the desire to conquer one's feelings of terror arising from the sense of shame which they arouse. Moreover, if the sense of obligation to act in a particular way leads to an action, the action will be an action done from a sense of obligation, and therefore not, if the above analysis of virtue be right, an act of courage.

The mistake of supposing that there can be an obligation to act courageously seems to arise from two causes. In the first place, there is often an obligation to do that which involves the conquering or controlling of our fear in the doing of it, e.g. the obligation to walk along the side of a precipice to fetch a doctor for a member of our family. Here the acting on the obligation is externally, though only externally, the same as an act of courage proper. In the second place there is an obligation to acquire courage, i.e. to do such things as will enable us afterwards to act courageously, and this may be mistaken for an obligation to act courageously. The same considerations can, of course, be applied, *mutatis mutandis,* to the other virtues.

The fact, if it be a fact, that virtue is no basis for morality will explain what otherwise it is difficult to account for, viz. the extreme sense of dissatisfaction produced by a close reading of Aristotle's *Ethics.* Why is the *Ethics* so disappointing? Not, I think, because it really answers two radically different questions as if they were one: (1) "What is the happy life?" (2) "What is the virtuous life?" It is, rather, because Aristotle does not do what we as moral philosophers want him to do, viz. to convince us that we really ought to do what in our nonreflective consciousness we have hitherto believed we ought to do, or if not, to tell us what, if any, are the other things which we really ought to do, and to prove to us that he is right. Now, if what I have just been contending is true, a systematic account of the virtuous character cannot possibly satisfy this demand. At best it can only make clear to us the details of one of our obligations, viz. the obligation to make ourselves better men; but the achievement of this does not help us to discover what we ought to do in life as a whole, and why; to think that it did would be to think that our only business in life was self-improvement. Hence it is not surprising that Aristotle's account of the good man strikes us as almost wholly of academic value, with little relation to our real demand, which is formulated in Plato's words: *ού γάρ περί τοῦ ἐπιτυχόντος ό λόγος, άλλάπερί τοῦ ὄντινα τ ρόπον χρῆ ζῆν*. [for no light matter is at stake, nothing less than the rule of human life].

I am not, of course, *criticizing* Aristotle for failing to satisfy this demand, except so far as here and there he leads us to think that he intends to satisfy it. For my main contention is that the demand cannot be satisfied, and cannot be satisfied

[9]This sharp distinction of virtue and morality as co-ordinate and independent forms of goodness will explain a fact which otherwise it is difficult to account for. If we turn from books on Moral Philosophy to any vivid account of human life and action such as we find in Shakespeare, nothing strikes us more than the comparative remoteness of the discussions of Moral Philosophy from the facts of actual life. Is not this largely because, while Moral Philosophy has, quite rightly, concentrated its attention on the fact of obligation, in the case of many of those whom we admire most and whose lives are of the greatest interest, the sense of obligation, though it may be an important, is not a dominating factor in their lives?

because it is illegitimate. Thus we are brought to the question: "Is there really such a thing as Moral Philosophy, and, if there is, in what sense?"

We should first consider the parallel case—as it appears to be—of the Theory of Knowledge. As I urged before, at some time or other in the history of all of us, if we are thoughtful, the frequency of our own and of others' mistakes is bound to lead to the reflection that possibly we and others have *always* been mistaken in consequence of some radical defect of our faculties. In consequence, certain things which previously we should have said without hesitation that we *knew,* as e.g. that 4 x 7 = 28, become subject to doubt; we become able only to say that we thought we knew these things. We inevitably go on to look for some general procedure by which we can ascertain that a given condition of mind is really one of knowledge. And this involves the search for a criterion of knowledge, i.e. for a principle by applying which we can settle that a given state of mind is really knowledge. The search for this criterion and the application of it, when found, is what is called the Theory of Knowledge. The search implies that instead of its being the fact that the knowledge that *A* is *B* is obtained directly by consideration of the nature of *A* and *B,* the knowledge that *A* is *B,* in the full or complete sense, can only be obtained by first knowing that *A* is *B,* and then knowing that we knew it by applying a criterion, such as Descartes's principle that what we clearly and distinctly conceive is true.

Now it is easy to show that the doubt whether *A* is *B,* based on this speculative or general ground, could, if genuine, never be set at rest. For if, in order really to know that *A* is *B,* we must first know that we knew it, then really, to know that we knew it, we must first know that we knew that we knew it. But—what is more important—it is also easy to show that this doubt is not a genuine doubt but rests on a confusion the exposure of which removes the doubt. For when we *say* we doubt whether our previous condition was one of knowledge, what we *mean,* if we mean anything at all, is that we doubt whether our previous *belief* was *true,* a belief which we should express as the *thinking* that *A* is *B.* For in order to doubt whether our previous condition was one of knowledge, we have to think of it not as knowledge but as only belief, and our only question can be "Was this belief true?" But as soon as we see that we are thinking of our previous condition as only one of belief, we see that what we are now doubting is not what we first *said* we were doubting, viz. whether a previous condition of knowledge was really knowledge. Hence, to remove the doubt, it is only necessary to appreciate the real nature of our consciousness in apprehending, e.g., that 7 x 4 = 28, and thereby see that it was no mere condition of believing but a condition of knowing, and then to notice that in our subsequent doubt what we are really doubting is not whether this consciousness was really knowledge, but whether a consciousness of another kind, viz. a belief that 7 x 4 = 28, was true. We thereby see that though a doubt based on speculative grounds is possible, it is not a doubt concerning what we believed the doubt concerned, and that a doubt concerning this latter is impossible.

Two results follow. In the first place, if, as is usually the case, we mean by the "Theory of Knowledge" the knowledge which supplies the answer to the question "Is what we have hitherto thought knowledge really knowledge?," there is and can be no such thing, and the supposition that there can is simply due to a confusion. There can be no answer to an illegitimate question, except that the question is illegitimate. Nevertheless the question is one which we continue to put until we realize the inevitable immediacy of knowledge. And it is positive knowledge that knowledge is immediate and neither can be, nor needs to be, improved or vindicated by the further knowledge that it was knowledge. This positive knowledge sets at rest the inevitable doubt, and, so far as by the "Theory of Knowledge" is meant this knowledge, then even though this knowledge be the knowledge that there is no Theory of Knowledge in the former sense, to that extent the Theory of Knowledge exists.

In the second place, suppose we come genuinely to doubt whether, e.g., 7 x 4 = 28 owing to a genuine doubt whether we were right in believing yesterday that 7 x 4 = 28, a doubt which can in fact only arise if we have lost our hold of, i.e. no longer remember, the real nature of our consciousness of yesterday, and so think of it as consisting in believing. Plainly, the only remedy is to do the sum again. Or, to put the matter generally, if we do come to doubt whether it is true that *A* is *B,* as we once thought, the remedy lies not in any process of reflection but in such a reconsideration of the nature of *A* and *B* as leads to the knowledge that *A* is *B*.

With these considerations in mind, consider the parallel which, as it seems to me, is presented—though with certain differences—by Moral Philosophy. The sense that we ought to do certain things arises in our unreflective consciousness, being an activity of moral thinking occasioned by the various situations in which we find ourselves. At this stage our attitude to these obligations is one of unquestioning confidence. But inevitably the appreciation of the degree to which the execution of these obligations is contrary to our interest raises the doubt whether after all these obligations are really obligatory, i.e. whether our sense that we ought not to do certain things is not illusion. We then want to have it *proved* to us that we ought to do so, i.e. to be convinced of this by a process which, as an argument, is different in kind from our original and unreflective appreciation of it. This demand is, as I have argued, illegitimate.

Hence, in the first place, if, as is almost universally the case, by Moral Philosophy is meant the knowledge which would satisfy this demand, there is no such knowledge, and all attempts to attain it are doomed to failure because they rest on a mistake, the mistake of supposing the possibility of proving what can only be apprehended directly by an act of moral thinking. Nevertheless the demand, though illegitimate, is inevitable until we have carried the process of reflection far enough to realize the self-evidence of our obligations, i.e. the immediacy of our apprehension of them. This realization of their self-evidence is positive knowledge, and so far, and so far only, as the term Moral Philosophy is confined to this knowledge and to the knowledge of the parallel immediacy of the apprehension of the goodness of the various virtues and of good dispositions generally, is there such a thing as Moral Philosophy. But since this knowledge may allay doubts which often affect the whole conduct of life, it is, though not extensive, important and even vitally important.

In the second place, suppose we come genuinely to doubt whether we ought, for example, to pay our debts, owing to a genuine doubt whether our previous conviction that we ought to do so is true, a doubt which can, in fact, only arise if we fail to remember the real nature of what we now call our past conviction. The only remedy lies in actually getting into a situation which occasions the obligation, or—if our imagination be strong enough—in imagining ourselves in that situation, and then letting our moral capacities of thinking do their work. Or, to put the matter generally, if we do doubt whether there is really an obligation to originate *A* in a situation *B*, the remedy lies not in any process of general thinking, but in getting face to face with a particular instance of the situation *B*, and then directly appreciating the obligation to originate *A* in that situation.

Study Questions

1. What are the two species of answer to the question "Why ought we do so and so?" according to Prichard?
2. Why does Prichard say that the rightness or wrongness of an act has nothing to do with any question of motives at all?
3. What mistake does moral philosophy rest on, according to Prichard?
4. Is the rightness of an act reducible to its goodness, according to Prichard? Explain.
5. What is the reason I should do something that I should do, according to Prichard?
6. If we question whether we should do something in a certain situation, how should we resolve the question? How should we *not* resolve it?

Emotivism and Prescriptivism

It certainly is possible to question this assumption made by Moore and Prichard that moral pronouncements attribute properties to things. One group of philosophers who did so were the *emotivists*, who were *noncognitivists* (again, see Chapter 3). Moral utterances, the emotivists said, largely serve to express emotions or attitudes. Some emotivists held, indeed, that moral pronouncements, such as "Ms. Farnsworth did a good thing," or "Ms. Farnsworth did a bad thing," are not even genuine propositions. What they really are, they said, are expressions of approval that are dressed up grammatically to look like propositions. As A. J. Ayer, an important exponent of emotivism, wrote in *Language, Truth, and Logic,*

> In saying that a certain type of action is right or wrong, I am not making any factual statement, not even a statement about my own state of mind: I am merely expressing certain moral sentiments. . . . in every case in which one would commonly be said to be making an ethical judgement, the function of the relevant ethical word is purely "emotive." It is used to express feeling about certain objects, but not to make any assertion about them.

C. L. Stevenson

One of the most sophisticated emotivist theorists was Charles Leslie Stevenson. Stevenson—to summarize his position—drew a distinction between beliefs and attitudes (a distinction you will read about in the selection below). He then suggested that the purpose of a moral judgment is not to convey beliefs but primarily to express and influence attitudes. It is because ethical disputes are in part disagreements in attitude that they cannot always be resolved using the scientific methods by which empirical disagreements (disagreements "in belief," in Stevenson's terminology) are resolved. It is not because they are disagreements over non-natural, nonempirical moral properties that are disclosed to us through some sort of mysterious faculty, as Moore and Prichard seemed to hold.

However, Stevenson (and other emotivists) and the intuitionists all agreed on one thing: that moral conclusions do not logically follow from empirical premises. The intuitionists held this on the ground that moral judgments are about nonempirical facts. Stevenson's explanation was different: He held that a moral judgment expresses an attitude *as a part of its meaning*, whereas empirical premises are purely descriptive and do not. This, according to Stevenson, is the explanation of why, as Hume noted, there is a problem about inferring an "ought" from an "is." The attitudinal component of the moral conclusion always "goes beyond" the empirical content of the empirical premises. (We'll return to this issue in a moment.)

In the selection below, Stevenson explains what he thinks is the nature of ethical disputes and why such disputes cannot logically be resolved by observation or other scientific means. Essentially, his main point is that if Stewart and Moore (or anyone else, of course) have an ethical disagreement, it will necessarily involve a disagreement in attitude; so, for Stewart to get Moore to agree with him, Stewart must change Moore's attitude.

R. M. Hare

Prescriptivism, another important noncognitivist theory, was proposed by Richard Mervyn Hare. Unlike the emotivists, who thought the function of moral discourse is primarily or even essentially to express and influence attitudes, Hare thinks its primary function is to *prescribe* a course of action. The difference may seem altogether too subtle to be worth mentioning, until you reflect a bit. The emotivists treat a moral judgment as something like a TV advertisement that seeks to influence your attitudes about, say, a brand of beer by portraying attractive young people having fun while drinking that beer. Such an ad is neither true nor false, nor reasonable nor unreasonable; likewise, on the emotivist theory, if Stewart advises Moore that something is the morally right thing to do, he is just seeking to influence Moore's attitudes.

Accordingly, it would seem, Stewart's judgment, like the TV ad, is not the sort of thing whose truth or reasonableness we might intelligibly discuss — like the ad, it doesn't really come under the categories of *true* or *reasonable* or their opposites and derivatives. But on Hare's understanding of moral discourse, Stewart is saying something whose truth and reasonableness it is intelligible to discuss. He is prescribing a course of action for Moore. And so, unlike the beer ad, Stewart's judgment is a judgment for which we could sensibly ask Stewart to supply supporting reasons. In other words, Hare's analysis of Stewart's claim as prescriptive seems to allow more room for rational deliberation as to its truth and merit, and this seems more in accord with our untutored feeling that reasoning has an important role to play in ethical discussions.

According to Hare also, a moral judgment is both overriding and universalizable. It is overriding in that it takes priority over other principles you hold. It is universalizable in that to judge that something is morally right or proper is to commit yourself to holding that it is right or proper for anyone in relevantly similar circumstances. As we observed in Chapter 2, Hare seems to hold that a principle's being both overriding and universalizable is a sufficient condition of the principle's being a moral principle; this means that, according to Hare, what makes a principle a moral one is not its *content* or *subject matter,* but certain logical features. Theoretically, a moral principle could be about *anything,* given Hare's view.

In the reading below, Hare endeavors to show how universalizability as a feature of moral judgment making supports a form of utilitarianism (discussed in Chapter 5). The article also addresses a concern that many educated laypersons have when they first encounter twentieth-century moral philosophy, a concern namely about the importance of metaethics — about the *value* of analyzing moral terminology and examining the logic of moral discourse. "Well," an educated layperson might wonder, "I suppose it is all very nice to consider what *good* and *right* and so forth mean and how logically they behave, but shouldn't moral philosophy ultimately tell us what we should *do*?" In his article, Hare tries to show that metaethics is not divorced from normative ethics and that, to the contrary, a proper understanding of the logic of moral discourse supports a form of utilitarianism.

The Nature of Ethical Disagreement

C. L. Stevenson

C. L. Stevenson (1908–1979) was professor of philosophy at the University of Michigan, Ann Arbor, for most of his career, having previously taught at Yale University. This selection is from his collection *Facts and Values: Studies in Ethical Analysis* (New Haven: Yale University Press, 1963). It originally appeared in the Italian journal *Sigma* (vols. 1–2, 1947–1948).

When people disagree about the value of something—one saying that it is good or right, and another that it is bad or wrong—by what methods of argument or inquiry can their disagreement be resolved? Can it be resolved by the methods of science, or does it require methods of some other kind, or is it open to no rational solution at all?

The question must be clarified before it can be answered. And the word that is particularly in need of clarification, as we shall see, is the word "disagreement."

Let us begin by noting that "disagreement" has two broad senses: In the first sense it refers to what I shall call "disagreement in belief." This occurs when Mr. A believes *p*, when Mr. B believes *not-p*, or something incompatible with *p*, and when neither is content to let the belief of the other remain unchallenged. Thus doctors may disagree in belief about the causes of an illness; and friends may disagree in belief about the exact date on which they last met.

In the second sense, the word refers to what I shall call "disagreement in attitude." This occurs when Mr. A has a favorable attitude to something, when Mr. B has an unfavorable or less favorable attitude to it, and when neither is content to let the other's attitude remain unchanged. The term "attitude" is here used in much the same sense that R. B. Perry uses "interest"; it designates any psychological disposition of being *for* or *against* something. Hence love and hate are relatively specific kinds of attitudes, as are approval and disapproval, and so on.

This second sense can be illustrated in this way: Two men are planning to have dinner together. One is particularly anxious to eat at a certain restaurant, but the other doesn't like it. Temporarily, then, the men cannot "agree" on where to dine. Their argument may be trivial, and perhaps only half serious; but in any case it represents a disagreement *in attitude*. The men have divergent preferences, and each is trying to redirect the preference of the other.

Further examples are readily found. Mrs. Smith wishes to cultivate only the four hundred; Mr. Smith is loyal to his old poker-playing friends. They accordingly disagree, in attitude, about whom to invite to their party. The progressive mayor wants modern school-buildings and large parks; the older citizens are against these "newfangled" ways; so they disagree on civic policy. These cases differ from the one about the restaurant only in that the clash of attitudes is more serious, and may lead to more vigorous argument.

The difference between the two senses of "disagreement" is essentially this: the first involves an opposition of beliefs, both of which cannot be true, and the second involves an opposition of attitudes, both of which cannot be satisfied.

Let us apply this distinction to a case that will sharpen it. Mr. A believes that most voters will favor a proposed tax, and Mr. B disagrees with him. The disagreement concerns attitudes—those of the voters—but note that A and B are *not* disagreeing in attitude. Their disagreement is *in belief about* attitudes. It is simply a special kind of disagreement in belief, differing from disagreement in belief about head colds only with regard to subject matter. It implies not an opposition of the actual attitudes of the speakers, but only of their beliefs about certain attitudes. Disagreement *in* attitude, on the other hand, implies that the very attitudes of the speakers are opposed. A and B may have opposed beliefs about attitudes without having opposed attitudes, just as they may have opposed beliefs about head colds without having opposed head colds. Hence we must not, from the fact that an argument is concerned with attitudes, infer that it necessarily involves disagreement *in* attitude.

We may now turn more directly to disagreement about values, with particular reference to normative ethics. When people argue about what is good, do they disagree in belief, or do they disagree in attitude? A long tradition of ethical theorists strongly suggest, whether they always intend to or not, that the disagreement is one *in belief.* Naturalistic theorists, for instance, identify an ethical judgment with some sort of scientific statement, and so make normative ethics a branch of science. Now a scientific argument typically exemplifies disagreement in belief, and if an ethical argument is simply a scientific one, then it too exemplifies disagreement in belief. The usual naturalistic theories of ethics that stress attitudes—such as those of Hume, Westermarck, Perry, Richards, and so many others—stress disagreement in belief no less than the rest. They imply, of course, that disagreement about what is good is disagreement *in belief* about attitudes; but we have seen that that is simply one sort of disagreement in belief, and by no means the same as disagreement *in* attitude. Analyses that stress disagreement *in* attitude are extremely rare.

If ethical arguments, as we encounter them in everyday life, involved disagreement in belief exclusively—whether the beliefs were about attitudes or about something else—then I should have no quarrel with the ordinary sort of naturalistic analysis. Normative judgments could be taken as scientific statements, and amenable to the usual scientific proof. But a moment's attention will readily show that disagreement in belief has not the exclusive role that theory has so repeatedly ascribed to it. It must be readily granted that ethical arguments usually involve disagreement in belief; but they *also* involve disagreement in attitude. And the conspicuous role of disagreement in attitude is what we usually take, whether we realize it nor not, as the distinguishing feature of ethical arguments. For example:

Suppose that the representative of a union urges that the wage level in a given company ought to be higher—that is only right that the workers receive more pay. The company representative urges in reply that the workers ought to receive no more than they get. Such an argument clearly represents a disagreement in attitude. The union is *for* higher wages; the company is *against* them, and neither is content to let the other's attitude remain unchanged. In *addition* to this disagreement in attitude, of course, the argument may represent no little disagreement in belief. Perhaps the parties disagree about how much the cost of living has risen, and how much the workers are suffering under the present wage scale. Or perhaps they disagree about the company's earnings, and the extent to which the company could raise wages and still operate at a profit. Like any typical ethical argument, then, this argument involves both disagreement in attitude and disagreement in belief.

It is easy to see, however, that the disagreement in attitude plays a unifying and predominating role in the argument. This is so in two ways:

In the first place, disagreement in attitude determines what beliefs are *relevant* to the argument. Suppose that the company affirms that the wage scale of fifty years ago was far lower than it is now. The union will immediately urge that this contention, even though true, is irrelevant. And it is irrelevant simply because information about the wage level of fifty years ago, maintained under totally different circumstances, is not likely to affect the present attitudes of either party. To be relevant, any belief that is introduced into the argument must be one that is likely to lead one side or the other to have a different attitude, and so reconcile disagreement in attitude. Attitudes are often functions of beliefs. We often change our attitudes to something when we change our beliefs about it; just as a child ceases to *want* to touch a live coal when he comes to *believe* that it will burn him. Thus in the present argument, any beliefs that are at all likely to alter attitudes, such as those about the increasing cost of living or the financial state of the company, will be considered by both sides to be relevant to the argument. Agreement in belief on these matters may lead to agreement in attitude toward the wage scale. But beliefs that are likely to alter the attitudes of neither side will be declared irrelevant. They will have no bearing on the disagreement in attitude, with which both parties are primarily concerned.

In the second place, ethical argument usually terminates when disagreement in attitude terminates, even though a certain amount of disagreement in belief remains. Suppose, for instance, that the company and the union continue to disagree in belief about the increasing cost of living, but that the company, even so, ends by favoring the higher wage scale. The union will then be content to end the argument, and will cease to press its point about living costs. It may bring up that point again, in some future argument of the same sort, or in urging the righteousness of its victory to the newspaper columnists; but for the moment the fact that the company has agreed in attitude is sufficient to terminate the argument. On the other hand: suppose that both parties agreed on all beliefs that were introduced into the argument, but even so continued to disagree in attitude. In that case neither party would feel that their dispute had been successfully terminated. They might look for other beliefs that could be introduced into the argument. They might use words to play on each other's emotions. They might agree (in attitude) to submit the case of arbitration, both feeling that a decision, even if strongly adverse to one party or the other, would be preferable to a continued impasse. Or, perhaps, they might abandon hope of settling their dispute by any peaceable means.

In many other cases, of course, men discuss ethical topics without having the strong, uncompromising attitudes that the present example has illustrated. They are often as much concerned with redirecting their own attitudes, in the light of greater knowledge, as with redirecting the attitudes of others. And the attitudes involved are often altruistic, rather than selfish. Yet the above example will serve, so long as that is understood, to suggest the nature of ethical disagreement. Both disagreement in attitude and disagreement in belief are involved, but the former predominates in that (1) it determines what sort of disagreement in belief is relevantly disputed in a given ethical argument, and (2) it determines, by its continued presence or its resolution, whether or not the argument has been settled. We may see further how intimately the two sorts of disagreement are related: since attitudes are often functions of beliefs, an agreement in belief may lead people, as a matter of psychological fact, to agree in attitude.

Having discussed disagreement, we may turn to the broad question that was first mentioned, namely: By what methods or argument or inquiry may disagreement about matters of value be resolved?

It will be obvious that to whatever extent an argument involves disagreement in belief, it is open to the usual methods of the sciences. If these methods are the *only* rational methods for supporting beliefs — as I believe to be so, but cannot now take time to discuss — then scientific methods are the only rational methods for resolving the disagreement in *belief* that arguments about values may include.

But if science is granted an undisputed sway in reconciling beliefs, it does not thereby acquire, without qualification, an undisputed sway in reconciling attitudes. We have seen that arguments about values include disagreement in attitude, no less than disagreement in belief, and that in certain ways the disagreement in attitude predominates. By what methods shall the latter sort of disagreement be resolved?

The methods of science are still available for that purpose, but only in an indirect way. Initially, these methods have only to do with establishing agreement in belief. If they serve further to establish agreement in attitude, that will be due simply to the psychological fact that altered beliefs may cause altered attitudes. Hence scientific methods are conclusive in ending arguments about values only to the extent that their success in obtaining agreement in belief will in turn lead to agreement in attitude.

In other words: the extent to which scientific methods can bring about agreement on values depends on the extent to which a commonly accepted body of scientific beliefs would cause us to have a commonly accepted set of attitudes.

How much is the development of science likely to achieve, then, with regard to values? To what extent *would* common beliefs lead to common attitudes? It is, perhaps, a pardonable enthusiasm to *hope* that science will do everything — to hope that in some rosy future, when all men know the consequences of their acts, they will all have common aspirations, and live peaceably in complete moral accord. But if we speak not from our enthusiastic hopes, but from our present knowledge, the answer must be far less exciting. We usually *do not know,* at the beginning of any argument about values, whether an agreement in belief, scientifically established, will lead to an agreement in attitude or not. It is logically possible, at least, that two men should continue to disagree in attitude even though they had all their beliefs in common, and even though neither had made any logical or inductive error, or omitted any relevant evidence. Differences in temperament, or in early training, or in social status, might make the men retain different attitudes even though both were possessed of the complete scientific truth. Whether this logical possibility is an empirical likelihood I shall not presume to say; but it is unquestionably a possibility that must not be left out of account.

To say that science can always settle arguments about value, we have seen, is to make this assumption: Agreement in attitude will always be consequent upon complete agreement in belief, and science can always bring about the latter. Taken as purely heuristic, this assumption has its usefulness. It leads people to discover the discrepancies in their beliefs, and to prolong enlightening argument that *may* lead, as a matter of fact, from commonly accepted beliefs to commonly accepted attitudes. It leads people to reconcile their attitudes in a rational, permanent way, rather than by rhapsody or exhortation. But the assumption is *nothing more*, for present knowledge, than a heuristic maxim. It is wholly without any proper foundation of probability. I conclude, therefore, that scientific methods cannot be guaranteed the definite rôle in the so-called "normative sciences" that they may have in the natural sciences. Apart from a heuristic assumption to the contrary, it is possible that the growth of scientific knowledge may leave many disputes about values permanently unsolved. Should these disputes persist, there are non-rational methods for dealing with them, of course, such as impassioned, moving oratory. But the purely intellectual methods of science, and, indeed, *all* methods of reasoning, may be insufficient to settle disputes about values, even though they may greatly help to do so.

For the same reasons, I conclude that normative ethics is not a branch of any science. It deliberately deals with a type of disagreement that science deliberately avoids. Ethics is not psychology, for instance; for although psychologists may, of course, agree or disagree in belief about attitudes, they need not, as psychologists, be concerned with whether they agree or disagree with one another in attitude. Insofar as normative ethics draws from the sciences, in order to change attitudes via changing people's beliefs, it *draws* from *all* the sciences; but a moralist's peculiar aim — that of *redirecting* attitudes — is a type of activity, rather than knowledge, and falls within no science. Science may study that activity, and may help indirectly to forward it; but it is not *identical* with that activity.

I have only a moment to explain why the ethical terms, such as "good," "wrong," "ought," and so on, are so habitually used to deal with disagreement in attitude. On account of their repeated occurrence in emotional situations they have acquired a strong emotive meaning. This emotive meaning makes them serviceable in initiating changes in a hearer's attitudes. Sheer emotive impact is not likely, under many circumstances, to change attitudes in any permanent way; but it *begins* a process that can then be supported by other means.

There is no occasion for saying that the meaning of ethical terms is *purely* emotive, like that of "alas" or "hurrah." We have seen that ethical *arguments* include many expressions of *belief;* and the rough rules of ordinary language permit us to say that some of these beliefs are expressed by an ethical judgment itself. But the beliefs so expressed are by no means always the same. Ethical terms are notable for their ambiguity, and opponents in an argument may use them in different senses.

Sometimes this leads to artificial issues; but it usually does not. So long as one person says "This is good" with emotive praise, and another says "No, it is bad," with emotive condemnation, a disagreement in attitude is manifest. Whether or not the beliefs that these statements express are logically incompatible may not be discovered until later in the argument; but even if they are actually compatible, disagreement in attitude will be preserved by emotive meaning; and this disagreement, so central to ethics, may lead to an argument that is certainly not artificial in its issues, so long as it is taken for what it is.

The many theorists who have refused to identify ethical statements with scientific ones have much to be said in their favor. They have seen that ethical judgments mold or alter attitudes, rather than describe them, and they have seen that ethical judgments can be guaranteed no definitive scientific support. But one need not, on that account, provide ethics with any extramundane, sui generis *subject matter*. The distinguishing features of an ethical judgment can be preserved by a recognition of emotive meaning and disagreement in attitude, rather than by some non-natural quality—and with far greater intelligibility. If an unique subject matter is *postulated,* as it usually is, to preserve the important distinction between normative ethics and science, it serves no purpose that is not served by the very simple analysis I have here suggested. Unless non-natural qualities can be defended by positive arguments, rather than as an "only resort" from the acknowledged weakness of ordinary forms of naturalism, they would seem nothing more than the invisible shadows cast by emotive meaning.

Study Questions

1. What, according to Stevenson, is the difference between a disagreement in belief and a disagreement in attitude? Use examples as necessary.
2. Naturalists would hold that which of these types of disagreement is involved in moral disputes?
3. What does Stevenson mean when he says that disagreements in attitude play a unifying and predominating role in ethical arguments? What are his reasons for saying this?
4. When, according to Stevenson, do we regard a consideration as relevant to a given ethical dispute? When, according to him, do we consider an ethical disagreement to be terminated?
5. Describe the proper role of scientific reasoning in ethical discussions, according to Stevenson.
6. Does Stevenson think the use of ethical language is helpful in dealing with disagreements in attitude? Explain.
7. Does Stevenson believe that the meaning of ethical terms is purely emotive?
8. What does Stevenson think about the idea that ethical judgments are about some non-natural quality? What does he think the non-natural qualities really are?

Ethical Theory and Utilitarianism

R. M. Hare

Richard M. Hare (b. 1919) is Professor of Philosophy at the University of Florida, Gainesville, and until recently was White's Professor of Moral Philosophy at Oxford University. The following selection is from *Contemporary British Philosophy,* 4th ed., edited by H. D. Lewis (London: Allen and Unwin, 1976).

Contemporary moral philosophy (and the British is no exception) is in a phase which must seem curious to anybody who has observed its course since, say, the 1940s. During all that time moral philosophers of the analytic tradition have devoted most of their work to fundamental questions about the analysis or the meaning of the moral words and the types of reasoning that are valid on moral questions. It may be that some of them were attracted by the intrinsic theoretical interest of this branch of philosophical logic; and indeed it is interesting. But it may surely be said that the greater part, like myself, studied these questions with an ulterior motive: they saw this study as the philosopher's main contribution to the solution of practical moral problems such as trouble most of us. For if we do not understand the very terms in which the problems are posed, how shall we ever get to the root of them? I, at least, gave evidence of this motive in my writings and am publishing many papers on practical questions.[1] But, now that philosophers in greater numbers have woken up to the need for such a contribution, and whole new journals are devoted to the practical applications of philosophy, what do we find the philosophers doing? In the main they proceed as if nothing had been learnt in the course of all that analytical enquiry—as if we had become no clearer now than in, say, 1936, or even 1903, how good moral arguments are to be distinguished from bad.

I cannot believe that we need be so pessimistic; nor that I am alone in thinking that logic can help with moral argument. But surprisingly many philosophers, as soon as they turn their hands to a practical question, forget all about their peculiar art, and think that the questions of the market place can be solved only by the methods of the market place—i.e. by a combination of prejudice (called intuition) and rhetoric. The philosopher's special contribution to such discussions lies in the ability that he ought to possess to clarify the concepts that are being employed (above all the moral concepts themselves) and thus, by revealing their logical properties, to expose fallacies and put valid arguments in their stead. This he cannot do unless he has an understanding (dare I say a theory?) of the moral concepts; and that is what we have been looking for all these years. And yet we find philosophers writing in such a way that it is entirely unclear what understanding they have of the moral concepts or of the rules of moral reasoning.[2] It is often hard to tell whether they are naturalists, relying on supposed equivalences between moral and non-moral concepts, or intuitionists, whose only appeal is to whatever moral sentiments they can get their readers to share with them. Most of them seem to be some sort of descriptivists; but as they retreat through an ever vaguer naturalism into a hardly avowed intuitionism, it becomes more and more obscure what, in their view, moral statements

[1]See, for example, my *Freedom and Reason* (*FR*) (Oxford, 1963), ch. 11; *Applications of Moral Philosophy* (London, 1972); "Rules of War and Moral Reasoning," *Ph. and Public Affairs,* 1 (1972); "Language and Moral Education," *New Essays in the Philosophy of Education,* G. Langford and D. J. O'Connor (eds) (London, 1973); "Abortion and the Golden Rule," *Ph. and Public Affairs,* 4 (1975); "Political Obligation," *Social Ends and Political Means,* T. Honderich (ed.) (forthcoming); and "Contrasting Methods of Environmental Planning," *Nature and Conduct,* R. S. Peters (ed.) (London, 1975).

[2]See the beginning of my paper "Abortion and the Golden Rule," cited in note 1.

say, and therefore how we could decide whether to accept them or not. Philosophy, as a rational discipline, has been left behind.

It is the object of this paper to show how a theory about the meanings of the moral words can be the foundation for a theory of normative moral reasoning. The conceptual theory is a non-descriptivist but nevertheless rationalist sort.[3] That this sort of theory could claim to provide the basis of an account of moral reasoning will seem paradoxical only to the prejudiced and to those who have not read Kant. It is precisely that sort of prejudice, which has led to the troubles I have been complaining of: the belief that only a descriptivist theory can provide a rational basis for morality, and that therefore it is better to explore any blind alley than expose oneself to the imputation of irrationalism and subjectivism by becoming a non-descriptivist.

The normative theory that I shall advocate has close analogies with utilitarianism, and I should not hesitate to call it utilitarian, were it not that this name covers a wide variety of views, all of which have been the victims of prejudices rightly excited by the cruder among them. In calling my own normative theory utilitarian, I beg the reader to look at the theory itself, and ask whether it cannot avoid the objections that have been made against other kinds of utilitarianism. I hope to show in this paper that it can avoid at least some of them. But if I escape calumny while remaining both a non-descriptivist and a utilitarian, it will be a marvel.

In my review of Professor Rawls's book[4] I said that there were close formal similarities between rational contractor theories such as Rawls's, ideal observer theories such as have been advocated by many writers[5] and my own universal prescriptivist theory. I also said that theories of this form can be made to lead very naturally to a kind of utilitarianism, and that Rawls avoided this outcome only by a very liberal use of intuitions to make his rational contractors come to a non-utilitarian contract. Rawls advocates his theory as an alternative to utilitarianism. Whether the system which I shall sketch is to be regarded as utilitarian or not is largely a matter of terminology. The form of argument which it employs is, as I have already said, formally extremely similar to Rawls's; the substantive conclusions are, however, markedly different. I should like to think of my view as, in Professor Brandt's expression, "a credible form of utilitarianism";[6] no doubt Rawls would classify it as an incredible form of utilitarianism; others might say that it is a compromise between his views and more ordinary kinds of utilitarianism. This does not much matter.

I try to base myself, unlike Rawls, entirely on the formal properties of the moral concepts as revealed by the logical study of moral language; and in particular on the features of prescriptivity and universalisability which I think moral judgments, in the central uses which we shall be considering, all have. These two features provide a framework for moral reasoning which is formally similar to Rawls's own more dramatic machinery. But, rather than put the argument in his way, I will do overtly what he does covertly—that is to say, I do not speculate about what some fictitious rational contractors *would* judge if they were put in a certain position subject to certain restrictions; rather, I subject myself to certain (formally analogous) restrictions and put myself (imaginatively) in this position, as Rawls in effect does,[7] and *do* some judging. Since the position and the restrictions are formally analogous, this ought to make no difference.

In this position, I am prescribing universally for all situations just like the one I am considering; and thus for all such situations, *whatever* role,

[3]It is substantially that set out in *FR*. For the distinction between non-descriptivism and subjectivisim, see my "Some Confusions about Subjectivity," Lindley Lecture, 1974, University of Kansas.

[4]*Ph.Q.*, 23 (1973); cf. my paper "Rules of War and Moral Reasoning," cited in note 1, and B. Barry, *The Liberal Theory of Justice* (Oxford, 1973), pp. 12–13.

[5]See, for example, the discussion between R. Firth and R. B. Brandt in *Ph. and Phen. Res.*, 12 (1952) and 15 (1955); also D. Haslett, *Moral Rightness* (The Hague, 1974).

[6]R. B. Brandt, "Towards a Credible Form of Utilitarianism," *Morality and the Language of Conduct*, H.-N. Castaneda and G. Nakhnikian (eds) (Detroit, 1963).

[7]See my review of Rawls, *Ph.Q.*, 23 (1973), p. 249.

among those in the situations, I might myself occupy. I shall therefore give equal weight to the equal interests of the occupants of all the roles in the situation; and, since any of these occupants might be myself, this weight will be positive. Thus the impartiality which is the purpose of Rawls's "veil of ignorance" is achieved by purely formal means; and so is the purpose of his insistence that his contractors be rational, i.e. prudent. We have therefore, by consideration of the logic of the moral concepts alone, put ourselves in as strong a position as Rawls hopes to put himself by his more elaborate, but at the same time, as I have claimed, less firmly based apparatus.

Let us now use these tools. Rawls himself says that an ideal observer theory leads to utilitarianism; and the same ought to be true of the formal apparatus which I have just sketched. How does giving equal weight to the equal interests of all the parties lead to utilitarianism? And to what kind of utilitarianism does it lead? If I am trying to give equal weight to the equal interests of all the parties in a situation, I must, it seems, regard a benefit or harm done to one party as of equal value or disvalue to an equal benefit or harm done to any other party. This seem to mean that I shall promote the interests of the parties most, while giving equal weight to them all, if I maximise the total benefits over the entire population; and this is the classical principle of utility. For fixed populations it is practically equivalent to the average utility principle which bids us maximise not total but average utility; when the size of the population is itself affected by a decision, the two principles diverge, and I have given reasons in my review of Rawls's book for preferring the classical or total utility principle. In these calculations, benefits are to be taken to include the reduction of harms.

I am not, however, going to put my theory in terms of benefits and the reduction of harms, because this leads to difficulties that I wish to avoid. Let us say, rather, that what the principle of utility requires of me is to do for each man affected by my actions what I wish were done for me in the hypothetical circumstances that I were in precisely his situation; and, if my actions affect more than one man (as they nearly always will) to do what I wish, all in all, to be done for me in the hypothetical circumstances that I occupied all their situations (not of course at the same time but, shall we say?, in random order). This way of putting the matter, which is due to C. I. Lewis,[8] emphasizes that I have to give the same weight to everybody's equal interests; and we must remember that, in so far as I am one of the people affected (as in nearly all cases I am) my own interests have to be given the same, and no more, weight—that is to say, my own actual situation is one of those that I have to suppose myself occupying in this random order.

Some further notes on this suggestion will be in place here. First, it is sometimes alleged that justice has to be at odds with utility. But if we ask how we are to be just between the competing interests of different people, it seems hard to give any other answer than that it is by giving equal weight, impartially, to the equal interests of everybody. And this is precisely what yields the utility principle. It does not necessarily yield equality in the resulting distribution. There are, certainly, very good utilitarian reasons for seeking equality in distribution too; but justice is something distinct. The utilitarian is sometimes said to be indifferent between equal and unequal distributions, provided that total utility is equal. This is so; but it conceals two important utilitarian grounds for a fairly high degree of equality of actual goods (tempered, of course, as in most systems including Rawls's, by various advantages that are secured by moderate inequalities). The first is the diminishing marginal utility of all commodities and of money, which means that approaches towards equality will tend to increase total utility. The second is that inequalities tend to produce, at any rate in educated societies, envy, hatred and malice, whose disutility needs no emphasising. I am convinced that when these two factors are taken into account, utilitarians have no need to fear the accusation that they could favour extreme inequalities of distribution in actual modern societies. Fantastic hypothetical cases can no doubt be invented in which they would have to favour them; but, as we shall see, this is an illegitimate form of argument.

---

[8]An *Analysis of Knowledge and Valuation* (La Salle, 1946), p. 547; see also Haslett, op. cit., ch. 3.

Secondly, the transition from a formulation in terms of interests to one in terms of desires or prescriptions, or vice versa, is far from plain sailing. Both formulations raise problems which are beyond the scope of this paper. If we formulate utilitarianism in terms of interests, we have the problem of determining what are someone's true interests. Even if we do not confuse the issue, as some do, by introducing moral considerations into this prudential question (i.e. by alleging that becoming morally better, or worse, in itself affects a man's interests),[9] we still have to find a way of cashing statements about interests in terms of such states of mind as likings, desires, etc., both actual and hypothetical. For this reason a formulation directly in terms of these states of mind ought to be more perspicuous. But two difficult problems remain: the first is that of how present desires and likings are to be balanced against future, and actual desires and likings against those which would be experienced if certain alternative actions were taken; the second is whether desires need to be mentioned at all in a formulation of utilitarianism, or whether likings by themselves will do. It would seem that if we arrive at utilitarianism via universal prescriptivism, as I am trying to do, we shall favour the former of the last pair of alternatives; for desires, in the required sense, are assents to prescriptions. All these are questions within the theory of prudence, with which, although it is an essential adjunct to normative moral theory, I do not hope to deal in this paper.[10]

I must mention, however, that when I said above that I have to do for each man affected by my actions what I wish were done for me, etc., I was speaking inaccurately. When I do the judging referred to on page 370, I have to do it as rationally as possible. This, if I am making a moral judgment, involves prescribing universally; but in prescribing (albeit universally) I cannot, if rational, ignore prudence altogether, but have to universalise this prudence. Put more clearly, this means that, whether I am prescribing in my own interest or in someone else's (see the next paragraph), I must ask, not what I or he does actually at present wish, but what, prudentially speaking, we should wish. It is from this rational point of view (in the prudential sense of "rational") that I have to give my universal prescriptions. In other words, it is *qua* rational that I have to judge; and this involves at least judging with a clear and unconfused idea of what I am saying and what the actual consequences of the prescription that I am issuing would be, for myself and others. It also involves, when I am considering the desires of others, considering what they would be if those others were perfectly prudent—i.e. desired what they would desire if they were fully informed and unconfused. Thus morality, at least for the utilitarian, can only be founded on prudence, which has then to be universalised. All this we shall have to leave undiscussed, remembering, however, that when, in what follows, I say "desire," "prescribe," etc., I mean "desire, prescribe, etc., from the point of view of one who is prudent so far as his own interest goes." It is important always to supply this qualification whether I am speaking of our own desires or those of others; but I shall omit it from now on because it would make my sentences intolerably cumbrous, and signalise the omission, in the next paragraph only, by adding the subscript "$_p$" to the words "desire," etc., as required, omitting even this subscript thereafter. I hope that one paragraph will suffice to familiarise the reader with this point.

Thirdly, when we speak of the "situations" of the various parties, we have to include in the situations all the desires$_p$, likings$_p$, etc., that the people have in them—that is to say, I am to do for the others what I wish$_p$ to be done for me were I to have their likings$_p$, etc., and not those which I now have. And, similarly, I am not to take into account (when I ask what I wish$_p$ should be done to me in a certain situation) my own present desires$_p$, likings$_p$, etc. There is one exception to this: I have said that one of the situations that I have to consider is my own present situation; I have to love$_p$ my neighbour *as,* but *no more than* and *no less than,* myself, and likewise to do to others *as* I wish$_p$ them to do to me. Therefore just as, when I am considering what I wish$_p$ to be done to me where I in *X*'s situation, where *X* is somebody else, I have to think of

[9] Cf. Plato, *Republic,* 335.

[10] The theory of prudence is ably handled in D. A. J. Richards, *A Theory of Reasons for Action* (Oxford, 1971); Haslett, op. cit.; and R. B. Brandt, John Locke Lectures (Oxford, forthcoming).

the situation as including *his* desires$_p$, likings$_p$, etc., and discount my own, so, in the single case where *X* is myself, I have to take into account *my* desires$_p$, likings$_p$, etc. In other words, *qua* author of the moral decision I have to discount my own desires$_p$, etc., and consider only the desires$_p$, etc., of the affected party; but where (as normally) I am one of the affected parties, I have to consider my own desires$_p$, etc., *qua* affected party, on equal terms with those of all the other affected parties.[11]

It will be asked: if we strip me, *qua* author of the moral decision, of all desires and likings, how is it determined what decision I shall come to? The answer is that it is determined by the desires and likings of those whom I take into account as affected parties (including, as I said, myself, but only *qua* affected party and not *qua* author). I am to ask, indeed, what I do wish should be done for me, were I in their situations; but were I in their situations, I should have their desires, etc., so I must forget about my own present desires (with the exception just made) and consider only the desires which *they* have; and if I do this, what I *do* wish for will be the satisfaction of *those* desires; that, therefore, is what I shall prescribe, so far as is possible.

I wish to point out that my present formulation enables me to deal in an agreeably clear way with the problem of the fanatic, who has given me so much trouble in the past.[12] In so far as, in order to prescribe universally, I have to strip away (*qua* author of the moral decision) all my present desires, etc., I shall have to strip away, among them, all the ideas that I have; for an ideal is a kind of desire or liking (in the generic sense in which I am using those terms); it is, to use Aristotle's word, an *orexis*.[13] This does not mean that I have to give up having ideals, nor even that I must stop giving any consideration to my ideals when I make my moral decisions; it means only that I am not allowed to take them into account *qua* author of the moral decision. I am, however, allowed to take them into account, along with the ideals of all the other parties affected, when I consider my own position, among others, as an affected party. This means that for the purposes of the moral decision it makes no difference *who has* the ideal. It means that we have to give impartial consideration to the ideals of ourselves and others. In cases, however, where the pursuit of our own ideals does not affect the ideals or the interests of others, we are allowed and indeed encouraged to pursue them.

All this being so, the only sort of fanatic that is going to bother us is the person whose ideals are so intensely pursued that the weight that has to be given to them, considered impartially, outbalances the combined weights of all the ideals, desires, likings, etc., that have to be frustrated in order to achieve them. For example, if the Nazi's desire not to have Jews around is intense enough to outweigh all the sufferings caused to Jews by arranging not to have them around, then, on this version of utilitarianism, as on any theory with the same formal structure, it ought to be satisfied. The problem is to be overcome by, first, pointing out that fanatics of this heroic stature are never likely to be encountered (that no *actual* Nazis had such intense desires is, I think, obvious); secondly, by remembering that, as I shall be showing in a moment, cases that are never likely to be actually encountered do not have to be squared with the thinking of the ordinary man, whose principles are not designed to cope with such cases. It is therefore illegitimate to attack such a theory as I have sketched by saying "You can't ask us to believe that it would be right to give this fantastic fanatical Nazi what he wanted"; this argument depends on appealing to the ordinary man's judgement about a case with which, as

---

[11]Professor Bernard Williams says, "It is absurd to demand of such a man, when the sums come in from the utility network which the projects of others have in part determined, that he should just step aside from his own project and decision and acknowledge the decision which utilitarian calculation requires." (J. J. C. Smart and B. A. O. Williams, *Utilitarianism: For and Against* (Cambridge, 1973), p. 116, and cf. p. 117n.) Christian humility and *agape* and their humanist counterparts are, then, according to Williams's standards, an absurd demand (which is hardly remarkable). What is more remarkable is the boldness of the persuasive definition by which he labels the self-centred pursuit of one's own projects "integrity" and accounts it a fault in utilitarianism that it could conflict with this.

[12]*FR*, ch. 9; "Wrongness and Harm," in my *Essays on the Moral Concepts* (London, 1972).

[13]*De Anima*, 433a 9ff.

we shall see, his intuitions were not designed to deal.

A similar move enables us to deal with another alleged difficulty (even if we do not, as we legitimately might, make use of the fact that all desires that come into our reasoning are desires$_p$, i.e. desires that a man will have after he has become perfectly prudent). It is sometimes said to be a fault in utilitarianism that it makes us give weight to bad desires (such as the desire of a sadist to torture his victim) solely in proportion to their intensity; received opinion, it is claimed, gives no weight at all, or even a negative weight, to such desires. But received opinion has grown up to deal with cases likely to be encountered; and we are most *un*likely, even if we give sadistic desires weight in accordance with their intensity, to encounter a case in which utility will be maximised by letting the sadist have his way. For first, the suffering of the victim will normally be more intense than the pleasure of the sadist. And, secondly, sadists can often be given substitute pleasures or even actually cured. And, thirdly, the side-effects of allowing the sadist to have what he wants are enormous. So it will be clear, when I have explained in more detail why fantastic cases in which these disutilities do not occur cannot legitimately be used in this kind of argument, why it is perfectly all right to allow weight to bad desires.

We have now, therefore, to make an important distinction between two kinds of "levels" of moral thinking. It has some affinities with a distinction made by Rawls in his article, "Two Concepts of Rules"[14] (in which he was by way of defending utilitarianism), though it is not the same; it also owes something to Sir David Ross,[15] and indeed to others. I call it the difference between level-1 and level-2 thinking, or between the principles employed at these two levels.[16] Level-1 principles are for use in practical moral thinking, especially under conditions of stress. They have to be general enough to be impartable by education (including self-education), and to be "of ready application in the emergency,"[17] but are not to be confused with rules of thumb (whose breach excites no compunction). Level-2 principles are what would be arrived at by leisured moral thought in completely adequate knowledge of the facts, as the right answer in a specific case.) They are universal but can be as specific (the opposite of "general," not of "universal"[18]) as needs be. Level-1 principles are inculcated in moral education; but the selection of the level-1 principles for this purpose should be guided by leisured thought, resulting in level-2 principles for specific considered situations, the object being to have those level-1 principles whose general acceptance will lead to actions in accord with the best level-2 principles in most situations that are actually encountered. Fantastic and highly unusual situations, therefore, need not be considered for this purpose.

I have set out this distinction in detail elsewhere;[19] here we only need to go into some particular points which are relevant. The thinking that I have been talking about so far in this paper, until the preceding paragraph, and indeed in most of my philosophical writings until recently, is level-2. It results in a kind of act-utilitarianism which, because of the universalisability of moral judgements, is practically equivalent to a rule-utilitarianism whose rules are allowed to be of any required degree of specificity. Such thinking is appropriate only to "a cool hour," in which there is time for unlimited investigation of the facts, and there is no temptation to special pleading. It can use hypothetical cases, even fantastic ones. In principles it can, given superhuman knowledge of the facts, yield answers as to what should be done in any cases one cares to describe.

The commonest trick of the opponents of utilitarianism is to take examples of such thinking, usually addressed to fantastic cases, and confront them with what the ordinary man would think. It makes the utilitarian look like a moral monster. The antiutilitarians have usually confined their own thought about moral reasoning (with fairly

[14] *Ph. Rev.*, 64 (1955).

[15] *The Right and the Good* (Oxford, 1930), pp. 19ff.

[16] See my review of Rawls, cited in note 4, p. 153; "Principles," *Proc. Arist. Soc.*, 72 (1972–3); "Rules of War and Moral Reasoning," cited in note 1; *FR*, pp. 43–5.

[17] Burke; see *FR*, p. 45.

[18] See "Principles," cited in note 16.

[19] See note 16.

infrequent lapses which often go unnoticed) to what I am calling level 1, the level of everyday moral thinking on ordinary, often stressful, occasions in which information is sparse. So they find it natural to take the side of the ordinary man in a supposed fight with the utilitarian whose views lead him to say, if put at the disconcertingly unfamiliar standpoint of the archangel Gabriel, such extraordinary things about these carefully contrived examples.

To argue in this way is entirely to neglect the importance for moral philosophy of a study of moral education. Let us suppose that a fully-informed archangelic act-utilitarian is thinking about how to bring up his children. He will obviously not bring them up to practise on every occasion on which they are confronted with a moral question the kind of archangelic thinking that he himself is capable of; if they are ordinary children, he knows that they will get it wrong. They will not have the time, or the information, or the self-mastery to avoid self-deception promoted by self-interest; this is the real, as opposed to the imagined, veil of ignorance which determines our moral principles.

So he will do two things. First, he will try to implant in them a set of good general principles. I advisedly use the word "implant"; these are not rules of thumb, but principles which they will not be able to break without the greatest repugnance, and whose breach by others will arouse in them the highest indignation. These will be the principles they will use in their ordinary level-1 moral thinking, especially in situations of stress. Secondly, since he is not always going to be with them, and since they will have to educate *their* children, and indeed continue to educate themselves, he will teach them, as far as they are able, to do the kind of thinking that he has been doing himself. This thinking will have three functions. First of all, it will be used when the good general principles conflict in particular cases. If the principles have been well chosen, this will happen rarely; but it will happen. Secondly, there will be cases (even rarer) in which, though there is no conflict between general principles, there is something highly unusual about the case which prompts the question whether the general principles are really fitted to deal with it. But thirdly, and much the most important, this level-2 thinking will be used to *select* the general principles to be taught both to this and to succeeding generations. The general principles may change, and should change (because the environment changes). And note that, if the educator were not (as we have supposed him to be) archangelic, we could not even assume that the best level-1 principles were imparted in the first place; perhaps they might be improved.

How will the selection be done? By using level-2 thinking to consider cases, both actual and hypothetical, which crucially illustrate, and help to adjudicate, disputes between rival general principles. But, because the general principles are being selected for use in actual situations, there will have to be a careful proportioning of the weight to be put upon a particular case to the probability of its actually occurring in the lives of the people who are to use the principles. So the fantastic cases that are so beloved of anti-utilitarians will have very little employment in this kind of thinking (except as a diversion for philosophers or to illustrate purely logical points, which is sometimes necessary). Fantastic unlikely cases will never be used to turn the scales as between rival general principles for practical use. The result will be a set of general principles, constantly evolving, but on the whole stable, such that their use in moral education, including self-education, and their consequent acceptance by the society at large, will lead to the nearest possible approximation to the prescriptions of archangelic thinking. They will be the set of principles with the highest acceptance-utility. They are likely to include principles of justice.

It is now necessary to introduce some further distinctions, all of which, fortunately, have already been made elsewhere, and can therefore be merely summarised. The first, alluded to already, is that between specific rule-utilitarianism (which is practically equivalent to universalistic act-utilitarianism) and general rule-utilitarianism.[20] Both are compatible with act-utilitarianism if their roles are carefully distinguished. Specific rule-utilitarianism is appropriate to level-2 thinking, general rule-utilitarianism to level-1 thinking; and therefore the rules of specific rule-utilitarianism can be of

[20]See "Principles," cited in note 16.

unlimited specificity, but those of general rule-utilitarianism have to be general enough for their role. The thinking of our archangel will thus be a specific rule-utilitarian sort; and the thinking of the ordinary people whom he has educated will be for the most part of a general rule-utilitarian sort, though they will supplement this, when they have to and when they dare, with such archangelic thinking as they are capable of.

The second distinction is that between what Professor Smart[21] calls (morally) "right" actions and (morally) "rational" actions. Although Smart's way of putting the distinction is not quite adequate, as he himself recognises, I shall, as he does, adopt it for the sake of brevity. Both here, and in connexion with the "acceptance-utility" mentioned above, somewhat more sophisticated calculations of probability are required than might at first be thought. But for simplicity let us say that an action is rational if it is the action (most likely) to be right, even if, when all the facts are known, as they were not when it was done, it turns out not to have been right. In such a society as we have described, the (morally) rational action will nearly always be that in accordance with the good general principles of level 1, because they have been selected precisely in order to make this the case. Such actions may not always turn out to have been (morally) right in Smart's sense when the cards are turned face upwards; but the agent is not to be blamed for this.

It is a difficult question, just how simple and general these level-1 principles ought to be. If we are speaking of the principles to be inculcated throughout the society, the answer will obviously vary with the extent to which the members of it are sophisticated and morally self-disciplined enough to grasp and apply relatively complex principles without running into the dangers we have mentioned. We might distinguish sub-groups within the society, and individuals within these sub-groups, and even the same individual at different stages, according to their ability to handle complex principles. Most people's level-1 principles become somewhat more complex as they gain experience of handling different situations, and they may well become so complex as to defy verbal formulation; but the value of the old simple maxims may also come to be appreciated. In any case, level-1 principles can never, because of the exigencies of their role, become as complex as level-2 principles are allowed to be.

A third distinction is that between good actions and the right action.[22] The latter is the action in accordance with level-2 principles arrived at by exhaustive, fully-informed and clear thinking about specific cases. A good action is what a good man would do, even if not right. In general this is the same as the morally rational action, but there may be complications, in that the motivation of the man has to be taken into account. The good (i.e. the morally well-educated) man, while he is sometimes able and willing to question and even to amend the principles he has been taught, will have acquired in his upbringing a set of motives and dispositions such that breaking these principles goes very much against the grain for him. The very goodness of his character will make him sometimes do actions which do not conform to archangelic prescriptions. This may be for one of at least two reasons. The first is that when he did them he was not fully informed and perhaps knew it, and knew also his own moral and intellectual weaknesses, and therefore (humbly and correctly) thought it morally rational to abide by his level-1 principles, and thus did something which turned out in the event not to be morally right. The second is that, although he could have known that the morally rational action was on this unusual occasion one in breach of his ingrained principles (it required him, say, to let down his closest friend), he found it so much against the grain that he just could not bring himself to do it. In the first case what he did was both rational and a morally good action. In the second case it was morally good but misguided—a wrong and indeed irrational act done from the best of motives. And no doubt there are other possibilities.

The situation I have been describing is a somewhat stylised model of our own, except that we

---

[21]Smart and Williams, op. cit., pp. 46f.

[22]See my *The Language of Morals,* p. 186.

have no archangel to educate us, but rely on the deliverances, not even of philosopher kings, but of Aristotelian *phronimoi* of very varying degrees of excellence. What will happen if a lot of moral philosophers are let loose on this situation? Level-1 thinking forms the greater part of the moral thinking of good men, and perhaps the whole of the moral thinking of good men who have nothing of the philosopher in them, including some of our philosophical colleagues. Such are the intuitionists, to whom their good ingrained principles seem to be sources of unquestionable knowledge. Others of a more enquiring bent will ask why they should accept these intuitions, and, getting no satisfactory answer, will come to the conclusion that the received principles have no ground at all and that the only way to decide what you ought to do is to reason it out on each occasion. Such people will at best become a crude kind of act-utilitarians. Between these two sets of philosophers there will be the sort of ludicrous battles that we have been witnessing so much of. The philosopher who understands the situation better will see that both are right about a great deal and that they really ought to make up their quarrel. They are talking about different levels of thought, both of which are necessary on appropriate occasions.

What kind of philosopher will this understanding person be? Will he be any kind of utilitarian? I see no reason why he should not be. For, first of all, level-2 thinking, which is necessary, is not only utilitarian but act-utilitarian (for, as we have seen, the specific rule-utilitarian thinking of this level and universalistic act-utilitarianism are practically equivalent). And there are excellent act-utilitarian reasons for an educator to bring up his charges to follow, on most occasions, level-1 thinking on the basis of a set of principles selected by high-quality level-2 thinking. This applies equally to self-education. So at any rate all acts that could be called educative or self-educative can have a solid act-utilitarian foundation. To educate oneself and other men in level-1 principles *is* for the best, and only the crudest of act-utilitarians fails to see this. There will also be good act-utilitarian reasons for *following* the good general principles in nearly all cases; for to do so will be rational, or most likely to be right; and even an act-utilitarian, when he comes to tell us how we should proceed when choosing what to do, can only tell us to do what is *most probably* right, because we do not know, when choosing, what is right.

There will be occasions, as I have said, when a man brought up (on good general principles) by a consistent act-utilitarian will do a rational act which turns out not to be right; and there will even be occasions on which he will do a good action which is neither rational nor right, because, although he could have known that it would be right on this unusual occasion to do an act contrary to the good general principles, he could not bring himself to contemplate it, because it went so much against the grain. And since one cannot pre-tune human nature all that finely, it may well be that act-utilitarian educator will have to put up with the possibility of such cases, in the assurance that, if his principles are well chosen, they will be rare. For if he attempted to educate people so that they would do the rational thing in these cases, it could only be by incorporating into their principles clauses which might lead them, in other more numerous cases, to do acts most likely to be wrong. Moral upbringing is a compromise imposed by the coarseness of the pupil's discrimination and the inability of his human educators to predict with any accuracy the scrapes he will get into.

The exclusion from the argument of highly unusual cases, which I hope I have now achieved, is the main move in my defence of this sort of utilitarianism. There are also some subsidiary moves, some of which I have already mentioned, and all of which will be familiar. It is no argument against act-utilitarianism that in some unusual cases it would take a bad man to do what according to the utilitarian is the morally right or even the morally rational thing; good men are those who are firmly wedded to the principles which *on nearly all actual occasions* will lead them to do the right thing, and it is inescapable that on unusual occasions moderately good men will do the wrong thing. The nearer they approach archangelic status, the more, on unusual occasions, they will be able to chance their arm and do what they think will be the right act in defiance of their principles; but most of us ordinary mortals will be wise to be fairly cautious. As Aristotle said, we have to incline towards the vice which is the lesser danger for *us*, and away from that extreme which is to *us* the greater temptation.[23] For some, in the present context, the greater danger may be too much rigidity in the application of level-1 principles; but perhaps for more (and I think that I am one of them) it is a too great readiness to let them slip. It is a matter of temperament; we have to know ourselves (empirically); the philosopher cannot tell each of us which is the greater danger for him.

The moves that I have already made will, I think, deal with some other cases which are well known from the literature. Such are the case of the man who is tempted, on utilitarian grounds, to use electricity during a power crisis, contrary to the government's instructions; and the case of the voter who abstains in the belief that enough others will vote. In both these cases it is alleged that some utility would be gained, and none lost, by these dastardly actions. These are not, on the face of it, fantastic or unusual cases, although the degree of knowledge stipulated as to what others will do is perhaps unusual. Yet it would be impolitic, in moral education, to bring up people to behave like this, if we were seeking level-1 principles with the highest acceptance-utility; if we tried, the result would be that nearly everyone would consume electricity under those conditions, and hardly anybody would vote. However, the chief answer to these cases is that which I have used elsewhere[24] to deal with car-pushing and death-bed promise cases which are also well canvassed. It is best approached by going back to the logical beginning and asking whether I am prepared to prescribe, or even permit, that others should (*a*) use electricity, thus taking advantage of my law-abidingness, when I am going without it; (*b*) abstain from voting when I do so at inconvenience to myself, thereby taking advantage of my public spirit; (*c*) only pretend to push the car when I am rupturing myself in the effort to get it started; (*d*) make death-bed promises to me (for example to look after my children) and then treat them as of no weight. I unhesitatingly answer "No" to all these questions; and I think that I should give the same answer even if I were perfectly prudent and were universalising my prescriptions to cover other perfectly prudent affected parties (see above, page 372). For it is not imprudent, but prudent rather, to seek the satisfaction of desires which are important to me, even if I am not going to know whether they have been satisfied or not. There is nothing in principle to prevent a fully informed and clear-headed person wanting above all that his children should not starve after his death; and if that is what he wants above all, it is prudent for him to seek what will achieve it, and therefore prescribe this.

Since the logical machinery on which my brand of utilitarianism is based yields these answers, so should the utilitarianism that is based on it; and it is worth while to ask, How? The clue lies in the observation that to frustrate a desire of mine is against my interest even if I do not know that it is being frustrated, or if I am dead. If anybody does not agree, I ask him to apply the logical apparatus direct and forget about interests. Here is a point at which, perhaps, some people will want to say that my Kantian or Christian variety of utilitarianism, based on giving equal weight to the prudent prescriptions or desires of all, diverges from the usual varieties so much that it does not deserve to be called a kind of utilitarianism at all. I am not much interested in that terminological question; but for what it is worth I will record my opinion that the dying man's interests *are* harmed if promises are made to him and then broken, and even more that mine are harmed if people are cheating me without my knowing it. In the latter case, they are harmed because I very much want this not to happen; and my desire that it should not happen is boosted by my level-1 sense of justice, which the utilitarian educators who brought me up wisely inculcated in me.

Whichever way we put it, whether in terms of what I am prepared to prescribe or permit universally (and therefore also for when I am the victim) or in terms of how to be fair as between the interests of all the affected parties, I conclude that the

[23] *Nicomachean Ethics,* 1109 b 1.

[24] See my paper "The Argument from Received Opinion" in my *Essays on Philosophical Method* (London, 1971), pp. 128ff.; *FR,* pp. 132ff.

acts I have listed will come out wrong on the act-utilitarian calculation, because of the harms done to the interests of those who are cheated, or the non-fulfilment of prescriptions to which, we may assume, they attach high importance. If we add to this move the preceding one which rules out fantastic cases, and are clear about the distinction between judgements about the character of the agent, judgements about the moral rationality of the action, and judgements about its moral rightness as shown by the outcome, I think that this form of utilitarianism can answer the objections I have mentioned. Much more needs to be said; the present paper is only a beginning, and is not very original.[25] I publish it only to give some indication of the way in which ethical theory can help with normative moral questions, and to try to get the discussion of utilitarianism centered round credible forms of it, rather than forms which we all know will not do.

[25]Among many others from whose ideas I have learnt, I should like in particular to mention Dr Lynda Sharp (Mrs Lynda Paine), in whose thesis *Forms and Criticisms of Utilitarianism* (deposited in the Bodleian Library at Oxford) some of the above topics are discussed in greater detail.

Study Questions

1. What does Hare think is the special contribution of philosophers to moral discussions?
2. What is the object of Hare's paper?
3. What does Hare mean when he says that he achieves impartiality by purely formal means?
4. Hare thinks that if you were to prescribe universally for all situations that are just like the situation you are considering, you would have to give equal weight to the equal interests of all parties. Giving equal weight to the equal interests of all the parties leads to utilitarianism, he says. Explain why it does.
5. How does Hare deal with the objection that the requirements of justice conflict with the requirements of utility?
6. How does Hare deal with the objection that utilitarians may have to endorse extreme inequalities in the distribution of goods?
7. What does Hare mean when he says that morality, at least for the utilitarian, can be founded only on prudence, which must then be universalized?
8. How does Hare deal with the objection that his position requires him to reward a fanatic whose desires are overwhelmingly intense?
9. How does Hare deal with the objection that he will have to give weight to bad desires solely in proportion to their intensity?
10. Describe the difference between Level-1 principles and Level-2 principles.
11. Hare discusses an objection based on four "highly unusual" cases. Describe the four cases.
12. Explain how Hare deals with the objection that is based on these four cases.

Ideal Rule Utilitarianism

The next selection, by Richard B. Brandt, is related in content to Hare's essay above, though in fact the Brandt essay predates the other. Brandt does not think that a correct analysis or understanding of moral concepts entails the truth of utilitarianism (though he does think that you cannot explain utilitarianism without making use of an analysis of the concept of morality). Having thus largely severed utilitarianism, as a normative ethical position, from metaethics, Brandt goes on to argue for a form of rule-utilitarianism. (Again, see Chapter 5 for a discussion of utilitarianism.) An "ideal" moral code, as Brandt defines it, is one whose acceptance by a society would produce at least as much good per person as would acceptance of any other moral code, and an act is right if and only if it wouldn't be prohibited by the moral code ideal for the society. He then discusses three further points: what it is for a moral code to be accepted, the difference between the rules of a society's moral code and the rules of its institutions, and how the relative utility of a moral code is to be estimated. He concludes by noting that despite the utilitarian nature of an ideal moral code, it will not itself contain the rule that a person ought always act so as to maximize utility. Nor, he says, need conflicts between rules in an ideal moral code always be resolved so as to maximize utility.

You may recall encountering Brandt in Chapter 3, in our discussion of epistemological issues in moral philosophy. (Epistemology, you may remember, is concerned with the sources, nature, and criteria of knowledge.) In Chapter 3 we treated two methods of moral inquiry: the method of reflective equilibrium of John Rawls and Brandt's theory that a person secures moral knowledge by considering the code the person would wish to have accepted in his or her own society were he or she fully aware of all the consequences of the society's accepting the moral code.

Some Merits of One Form of Rule-Utilitarianism

Richard B. Brandt

Richard B. Brandt (b. 1910) is Emeritus Professor of Philosophy at the University of Michigan, Ann Arbor. The following selection is an edited version of "Some Merits of One Form of Rule-Utilitarianism," from Brandt's *Morality, Utilitarianism, and Rights* (New York: Cambridge University Press, 1992).

1. Utilitarianism is the thesis that the moral predicates of an act—at least its objective rightness or wrongness, and sometimes also its moral praiseworthiness or blameworthiness—are functions in some way, direct or indirect, of consequences for the welfare of sentient creatures, and of nothing else. Utilitarians differ about what precise function they are; and they differ about what constitutes welfare and how it is to be measured. But they agree that all one needs to know, in order to make moral appraisals correctly, is the consequences of certain things for welfare.

Utilitarianism is thus a normative ethical thesis and not, at least not necessarily, a metaethical position—that is, a position about the meaning and justification of ethical statements. It is true that some utilitarians have declared that the truth of the normative thesis follows, given the ordinary, or proper, meaning of moral terms such as "right." I shall ignore this further, metaethical claim. More recently some writers have suggested something very similar, to the effect that our concept of "morality" is such that we could not call a system of rules a "moral system" unless it were utilitarian in some sense. . . .

In any case, even if "nonutilitarian morality" (or "right, but harmful") were a contradiction in terms, utilitarianism as a normative thesis would not yet be established, for it would be open to a nonutilitarian to advocate changing the meaning of "morality" (or "right") in order to allow for his normative views. There is, of course, the other face of the coin: Even if, as we actually use the term "morality" (or "right"), the above expressions are not contradictions in terms, it might be a good and justifiable thing for people to be taught to use words so that these expressions would become self-contradictory. But if there are good reasons for doing the last, presumably there are good and convincing reasons for adopting utilitarianism as a normative thesis, without undertaking such a roundabout route to the goal. I shall, therefore, discuss utilitarianism as a normative thesis, without supposing that it can be supported by arguing that a nonutilitarian morality is a contradiction in terms.

2. If an analysis of concepts like "morally wrong" and "morality" and "moral code" does not enable us to establish the truth of the utilitarian thesis, the question arises what standard a normative theory like utilitarianism has to meet in order for a reasonable presumption to be established in its favor. It is well known that the identity and justification of any such standard can be debated at length. In order to set bounds to the present discussion, I shall state briefly the standard I shall take for granted for purposes of the present discussion. Approximately this standard would be acceptable to a good many writers on normative ethics. However this may be, it would be agreed that it is worth knowing whether some form of utilitarianism meets this standard better than any other form of utilitarian theory, and it is this question which I shall discuss.

The standard that I suggest an acceptable normative moral theory has to meet is this: The theory must contain no unintelligible concepts or internal inconsistencies; it must not be inconsistent with known facts; it must be capable of precise formulation so that its implications for action can be determined; and—most important—its implications must be acceptable to thoughtful persons who have had reasonably wide experience, when taken in the light of supporting remarks that can be made, and when compared with the implications of other clearly statable normative theories. It is not required that the implications of a satisfactory theory be consonant with the uncriticized moral intuitions of intelligent and experienced people, but only with those intuitions which stand in the light of supporting remarks, etc. Furthermore, it is not required of an acceptable theory that the best consequences would be produced by people adopting that theory, in contrast to other theories by which they might be convinced. (The theory might be so complex that it would be a good thing if most people did not try their hand at applying it to concrete situations!) It may be a moving *ad hominem* argument, if one can persuade an act-utilitarian that it would have bad consequences for people to try to determine the right act according to that theory, and to live by their conclusions, but such a showing would not be a reasonable ground for rejecting that normative theory. . . .

4. The type of utilitarianism on which I wish to focus is a form of rule-utilitarianism, as contrasted with act-utilitarianism. According to the latter type of theory (espoused by Sidgwick and Moore), an act is objectively right if no other act the agent could perform would produce better consequences. (On this view, an act is blameworthy if and only if it is right to perform the act of blaming or condemning it; the principles of blameworthiness are a special case of the principle of objectively right actions.) Act-utilitarianism is hence a rather atomistic theory: The rightness of a single act is fixed by its effects on the world. Rule-utilitarianism, in contrast, is the view that the rightness of an act is fixed, not by its relative utility, but by the utility of having a relevant moral rule, or of most or all members of a certain class of acts being performed.

The implications of act-utilitarianism are seriously counterintuitive, and I shall ignore it except to consider whether some ostensibly different theories really are different.

5. Rule-utilitarianisms may be divided into two main groups, according as the rightness of a particular act is made a function of ideal rules in some sense, or of the actual and recognized rules of a society. The variety of theory I shall explain more fully is of the former type.

According to the latter type of theory, a person's moral duties or obligations in a particular situation are determined, with some exceptions, solely by the moral rules, or institutions, or practices prevalent in the society, and not by what rules (etc.) it would ideally be best to have in the society. (It is sometimes held that actual moral rules, practices, etc., are only a necessary condition of an act's being morally obligatory or wrong.) Views roughly of this sort have been held in recent years by A. MacBeath, Stephen Toulmin, John Rawls, P. F. Strawson, J. O. Urmson, and B. J. Diggs. Indeed, Strawson says in effect that for there to be a moral obligation on one is just for there to be a socially sanctioned demand on him, in a situation where he has an interest in the system of demands his society is wont to impose on its members, and where such demands are generally acknowledged and respected by members of his society.[1] And Toulmin asserts that when a person asks, "Is this the right to do?" what he is normally asking is whether a proposed action "conforms to the moral code" of his group, "whether the action in question belongs to a class of actions generally approved of in the agent's community." In deliberating about the question what is right to do, he says, "there is no more general 'reason' to be given beyond one which related the action . . . to an accepted social practice."[2]

So far the proposal does not appear to be a form of utilitarianism at all. The theory is utilitarian, however, in the following way: It is thought that what is relevant for a decision whether to try to change moral codes, institutions, etc., or for a justification of them, is the relative utility of the code, practice, etc. The recognized code or practice determines the individual's moral obligations in a particular case; utility of the code or practice determines

[1]P. F. Strawson, "Social Morality and Individual Ideal," *Philosophy* 36 (1961): 1–17.

[2]Stephen Toulmin, *An Examination of the Place of Reason in Ethics*, Cambridge University Press, 1950, pp. 144–5. See various acute criticisms, with which I mostly agree, in Rawls's review, *Philos. Rev.* 60 (1951): 572–80.

whether it is justified or ought to be changed. Furthermore, it is sometimes held that utilitarian considerations have some relevance to the rightness of a particular action. For instance, Toulmin thinks that in case the requirements of the recognized code or practice conflict in a particular case, the individual ought (although strictly, he is not morally obligated) to do what will maximize utility in the situation, and that in case an individual can relieve the distress of another, he ought (strictly, is not morally obligated) to do so, even if the recognized code does not require him to.[3]

This theory, at least in some of its forms or parts, has such conspicuously counterintuitive implications that it fails to meet the standard for a satisfactory normative theory. In general, we do not believe that an act's being prohibited by the moral code of one's society is sufficient to make it morally wrong. Moral codes have prohibited such things as work on the Sabbath, marriage to a divorced person, medically necessary abortion, and suicide; but we do not believe it was really wrong for persons living in a society with such prohibitions, to engage in these actions.[4]

Neither do we think it a necessary condition of an act's being wrong that it be prohibited by the code of the agent's society, or of it being obligatory that an act be required by the code of his society. A society may permit a man to have his wife put to death for infidelity, or to have a child put to death for almost any reason; but we still think such actions wrong. Moreover, a society may permit a man absolute freedom in divorcing his wife, and recognize no obligations on his part toward her; but we think, I believe, that a man has some obligations for the welfare of a wife of thirty years' standing (with some qualifications), whatever his society may think.[5]

Some parts of the theory in some of its forms, however, appear to be correct. In particular, the theory in some forms implies that, if a person has a certain recognized obligation in an institution or practice (for example, a child to support his aged parent, a citizen to pay his taxes), then he morally does have this obligation, with some exceptions, irrespective of whether in an ideal institution he would or would not have. This we do roughly believe, although we need not at the same time accept the reasoning that has been offered to explain how the fact of a practice or institution leads to the moral obligation. The fact that the theory seems right in this would be a strong point in its favor if charges were correct that "ideal" forms of rule-utilitarianism necessarily differ at this point. B. J. Diggs, for instance, has charged that the "ideal" theories imply that:

> one may freely disregard a rule if ever he discovers that action on the rule is not maximally felicific, and in this respect makes moral rules like "practical maxims". . . It deprives social and moral rules of their authority and naturally is in sharp conflict with practice. On this alternative rule utilitarianism collapses into act utilitarianism. Surely it is a mistake to maintain that a set of rules, thought to be ideally utilitarian or felicific, is the criterion of right action. . . . If we are presented with a list [of rules], but these are

[3]Toulmin and Rawls sometimes go further, and suggest that a person is morally free to do something the actual code or practice of his society prohibits, if he is convinced that the society would be better off if the code or practice were rewritten so as to permit that sort of thing, and he is prepared to live according to the ideally revised code. If their theory were developed in this direction, it need not be different from some "ideal" forms of rule-utilitarianism, although, as stated, the theory makes the recognized code the standard for moral obligations, with exceptions granted to individuals who hold certain moral opinions. See Toulmin, op. cit., pp. 151–2, and Rawls, "Two Concepts of Rules," *Philos. Rev.* 64 (1955), pp. 28–9, especially 25. It should be noticed that Rawls's proposal is different from Toulmin's in an important way. He is concerned with only a segment of the moral code, the part that can be viewed as the rules of practices. As he observes, this may be only a small part of the moral code.

[4]Does a stranger living in a society have a moral obligation to conform to its moral code? I suggest we think that he does not, unless it is the right moral code or perhaps at least he thinks it is, although we think that offense he might give to the feelings of others should be taken into account, as well as the result his nonconformity might have in weakening regard for moral rules in general.

[5]It is a different question whether we should hold offenders in such societies seriously morally blameworthy. People cannot be expected to rise much above the level of recognized morality, and we condemn them little when they do not.

> not rules in practice, the most one could reasonably do is to try to get them adopted.[6]

I believe, however, and shall explain in detail later that this charge is without foundation.

6. Let us turn now to "ideal" forms of rule-utilitarianism, which affirm that whether it is morally obligatory or morally right to do a certain thing in a particular situation is fixed, not by the actual code or practice of the society (these may be indirectly relevant, as forming part of the situation), but by some "ideal" rule—that is, by the utility of having a certain general moral rule, or by the utility of all or most actions being performed which are members of a relevant class of actions.

If the rightness of an act is fixed by the utility of a relevant rule (class), are we to say that the rule (class) that qualifies must be the optimific rule (class), the one which maximizes utility, or must the rule (class) meet only some less stringent requirement (for example, be better than the absence of any rule regulating the type of conduct in question)? And, if it is to be of the optimific type, are all utilities to be counted, or perhaps only "negative" utilities, as is done when it is suggested that the rule (class) must be the one which minimizes suffering?[7]

The simplest proposal—that the rule (class) which qualifies is the one that maximizes utility, with all utilities, whether "positive" or "negative," being counted—also seems to me to be the best, and it is the one I shall shortly explain more fully. . . .

7. I propose, then, that we tentatively opt for an "ideal" rule-utilitarianism, of the "maximizing utility" variety. This decision, however, leaves various choices still to be made, between theories better or worse fitted to meet various problems. Rather than attempt to list alternatives, and explain why one choice rather than another between them would work out better, I propose to describe in some detail the type of theory that seems most plausible. I shall later show how this theory meets the one problem to which the "actual rule" theories seemed to have a nice solution; and I shall discuss its merits, as compared with another quite similar type of theory suggested by Jonathan Harrison and others.

The theory I wish to describe is rather similar to one proposed by J. D. Mabbott in his 1953 British Academy lecture, "Moral Rules." It is also very similar to the view defended by J. S. Mill in *Utilitarianism*, although Mill's formulation is ambiguous at some points, and he apparently did not draw some distinctions he should have drawn (I shall revert to this historical point).

For convenience I shall refer to the theory as the "ideal moral code" theory. The essence of it is as follows. Let us first say that a moral code is "ideal" if its currency in a particular society would produce at least as much good per person (the total divided by the number of persons) as the currency of any other moral code. (Two different codes might meet this condition, but, in order to avoid complicated formulations, the following discussion will ignore this possibility.) Given this stipulation for the meaning of "ideal," the Ideal Moral Code theory consists in the assertion of the following thesis: *An act is right if and only if it would not be prohibited by the moral code ideal for the society; and an agent is morally blameworthy (praiseworthy) for an act if, and to the degree that, the moral code ideal in that society would condemn (praise) him for it.* It is a virtue of this theory that it is a theory both about objective rightness and about moral blameworthiness (praiseworthiness) of actions, but the assertion about blameworthiness will be virtually ignored in what follows.

8. In order to have a clear proposal before us, however, the foregoing summary statement must be filled out in three ways: (1) by explaining what it is for a moral code to have currency; (2) by making clear what is the difference between the rules of a society's moral code and the rules of its institutions; and (3) by describing how the relative utility of a moral code is to be estimated.

[6]"Rules and Utilitarianism," *Amer. Philos. Quarterly*, I (1964), 32–44.

[7]In a footnote to chapter 9 of *The Open Society*, Professor Popper suggested that utilitarianism would be more acceptable if its test were minimizing suffering rather than maximizing welfare, to which J. J. C. Smart replied (*Mind*, 1958, pp. 542–3) that the proposal implies that we ought to destroy all living beings, as the surest way to eliminate suffering. It appears, however, that Professor Popper does not seriously advocate what seemed to be the position of the earlier footnote (addendum to fourth edition, p. 386).

First, then, the notion of a moral code having currency in a society.

For a moral code to have currency in a society, two things must be true. First, a high proportion of the adults in the society must subscribe to the moral principles, or have the moral opinions, constitutive of the code. Exactly how high the proportion should be, we can hardly decide on the basis of the ordinary meaning of "the moral code"; but probably it would not be wrong to require at least 90 percent agreement. Thus, if at least 90 percent of the adults subscribe to principle *A*, and 90 percent to principle *B*, etc., we may say that a code consisting of *A* and *B* (etc.) has currency in the society, provided the second condition is met. Second, we want to say that certain principles *A, B*, etc. belong to the moral code of a society only if they are recognized as such. That is, it must be that a large proportion of the adults of the society would respond correctly if asked, with respect to *A* and *B*, whether most members of the society subscribed to them. (It need not be required that adults base their judgments on such good evidence as recollection of moral discussions; it is enough if for some reason the correct opinion about what is accepted is widespread.) It is of course possible for certain principles to constitute a moral code with currency in a society even if some persons in the society have no moral opinions at all, or if there is disagreement, for example, if everyone in the society disagrees with every other person with respect to at least one principle.

The more difficult question is what it is for an individual to subscribe to a moral principle or to have a moral opinion. What is it, then, for someone to think sincerely that any action of the kind *F* is wrong? (1) He is to some extent motivated to avoid actions he thinks are *F*, and often, if asked why he does not perform such an action when it appears to be to his advantage, offers, as one of his reasons, that it is *F*. In addition, the person's motivation to avoid *F*-actions does not derive entirely from his belief that *F*-actions on his part are likely to be harmful to him or to persons to whom he is somehow attached. (2) If he thinks he has just performed an *F*-action, he feels guilty or remorseful or uncomfortable about it, unless he thinks he has some excuse—unless, for instance, he knows that at the time of action he did not think his action would be an *F*-action. "Guilt" (etc.) is not to be understood as implying some special origin such as interiorization of parental prohibitions, or as being a vestige of anxiety about punishment. It is left open that it might be an unlearned emotional response to the thought of being the cause of the suffering of another person. Any feeling that must be viewed simply as anxiety about anticipated consequences, for one's self or a person to whom one is attached, is not, however, to count as a "guilt" feeling. (3) If he believes that someone has performed an *F*-action, he will tend to admire him less as a person, unless he thinks that the individual has a good excuse. He thinks that action of this sort, without excuse, reflects on character—this being spelled out, in part, by reference to traits like honesty, respect for the rights of others, and so on. (4) He thinks that these attitudes of his are correct or well justified, in some sense, but with one restriction: it is not enough if he thinks that what justifies them is simply the fact that they are shared by all or most members of his society. This restriction corresponds with our distinction between a moral conviction and something else. For instance, we are inclined to think no moral attitude is involved if an Englishman disapproves of something but says that his disapproval is justified by the fact that it is shared by "well-bred Englishmen." In such cases we are inclined to say that the individual subscribes only to a custom, or to a rule of etiquette or manners. On the other hand, if the individual thinks that what justifies his attitude unfavorable to *F*-actions is that *F*-actions are contrary to the will of God (and the individual's attitude is not merely a prudential one), or inconsistent with the welfare of mankind, or contrary to human nature, we are disposed to say the attitude is a moral attitude and the opinions expressed are moral ones. And the same if he thinks his attitude justified, but can give no reason. There are perhaps other restrictions we should make on acceptable justifications (perhaps to distinguish a moral code from a code of honor), and other types of justifications we should wish to list as clearly acceptable (perhaps an appeal to human equality).

9. It is important to distinguish between the moral code of a society and its institutions, or the

rules of its institutions. It is especially important for the Ideal Moral Code theory, for this theory involves the conception of a moral code ideal for a society in the context of its institutions, so that it is necessary to distinguish the moral code a society does or might have from its institutions and their rules. The distinction is also one we actually do make in our thinking, although it is blurred in some cases. (For instance, is "Honor thy father and thy mother" a moral rule, or a rule of the family institution, in our society?)[8]

An institution is a set of positions or statuses, with which certain privileges and jobs are associated. (We can speak of these as "rights and "duties" if we are careful to explain that we do not mean moral rights and duties.) That is, there are certain, usually nameable, positions that consist in the fact that anyone who is assigned to the position is expected to do certain things, and at the same time is expected to have certain things done for him. The individuals occupying these positions are a group of cooperating agents in a system that as a whole is thought to have the aim of serving certain ends. (For example, a university is thought to serve the ends of education, research, etc.) The rules of the system concern jobs that must be done in order that the goals of the institution be achieved; they allocate the necessary jobs to different positions. Take, for instance, a university. There are various positions in it: the presidency, the professional ranks, the registrars, librarians, etc. It is understood that one who occupies a certain post has certain duties, say teaching a specified number of classes or spending time working on research in the case of the instructing staff. Obviously the university cannot achieve its ends unless certain persons do the teaching, some tend to the administration, some do certain jobs in the library, and so on. Another such system is the family. We need not speculate on the "purpose" of the family, whether it is primarily a device for producing a new generation, etc. But it is clear that when a man enters marriage, he takes a position to which certain jobs are attached, such as providing support for the family to the best of his ability, and to which also certain rights are attached, such as exclusive sexual rights with his wife, and the right to be cared for should he become incapacited.

If an "institution" is defined in this way, it is clear that the moral code of a society cannot itself be construed as an institution, nor its rules as rules of an institution. The moral code is society-wide, so if we were to identify its rules as institutional rules, we should presumably have to say that everyone belongs to this institution. But what is the "purpose" of society as a whole? Are there any distinctions of status, with rights and duties attached, that we could identify as the "positions" in the moral system? Can we say that moral rules consist in the assignment of jobs in such a way that the aims of the institution may be achieved? It is true that there is a certain analogy: society as a whole might be said to be aiming at the good life for all, and the moral rules of the society might be viewed as the rules with which all must conform in order to achieve this end. But the analogy is feeble. Society as a whole is obviously not an organization like a university, an educational system, the church, General Motors, etc.; there is no specific goal in the achievement of which each position has a designated role to play. Our answer to the above questions must be in the negative: Morality is not an institution in the explained sense, nor are moral rules institutional expectations or rules.

The moral code of a society may, of course, have implications that bear on institutional rules. For one thing, the moral code may imply that an institutional system is morally wrong and ought to be changed. Moreover, the moral code may imply that a person has also a moral duty to do something that is his institutional job. For instance, it may be a moral rule that a person ought to do whatever he has undertaken to do, or that he ought not to accept the benefits of a position without performing its duties. Take for instance the rules, "A professor should meet his classes" or

[8]The confusion is compounded by the fact that terms like "obligation" and "duty" are used sometimes to speak about moral obligations and duties, and sometimes not. The fact that persons have a certain legal duty in certain situations is a rule of the legal institutions of the society; a person may not have a moral duty to do what is his legal duty. The fact that a person has an obligation to invite a certain individual to dinner is a matter of manners or etiquette, and at least may not be a matter of moral obligation. See R. B. Brandt, "The Concepts of Duty and Obligation," *Minds 73* (1964), especially pp. 380–4.

"Wives ought to make the beds." Since the professor has undertaken to do what pertains to his office, and the same for a wife, and since these tasks are known to pertain to the respective offices, the moral rule that a person is morally bound (with certain qualifications) to do what he has undertaken to do implies, in context, that the professor is morally bound to meet his classes and the wife to make the beds, other things being equal (that is, there being no contrary moral obligations in the situation). But these implications are not themselves part of the moral code. No one would say that a parent had neglected to teach his child the moral code of the society if he had neglected to teach him that professors must meet classes, and that wives must make the beds. A person becomes obligated to do these things only by participating in an institution, by taking on the status of professor or wife. Parents do not teach children to have guilt feelings about missing classes, or making beds. The moral code consists only of moral general rules, defining what is to be done in certain types of situations in which practically everyone will find himself. ("Do what you have promised!")

Admittedly some rules can be both moral and institutional: "Take care of your father in his old age" might be both an institutional rule of the family organization and also a part of the moral code of a society. (In this situation, one can still raise the question whether this moral rule is optimific in a society with that institutional rule; the answer could be negative.) . . .

10. It has been proposed above that an action is right if and only if it would not be prohibited by the moral code ideal for the society in which it occurs, where a moral code is taken to be "ideal" if and only if its currency would produce at least as much good per person as the currency of any other moral code.[9] We must now give more attention to the conception of an ideal moral code, and how it may be decided when a given moral code will produce as much good per person as any other. We may, however, reasonably bypass the familiar problems of judgments of comparative utilities, especially when different persons are involved, since these problems are faced by all moral theories that have any plausibility. We shall simply assume that rough judgments of this sort are made and can be justified.

(a) We should first notice that, as "currency" has been explained above, a moral code could not be current in a society if it were too complex to be learned or applied. We may therefore confine our consideration to codes simple enough to be absorbed by human beings, roughly in the way in which people learn actual moral codes.

(b) We have already distinguished the concept of an institution and its rules from the concept of a moral rule, or a rule of the moral code. (We have, however, pointed out that in some cases a moral rule may prescribe the same thing that is also an institutional expectation. But this is not a necessary situation, and a moral code could condemn an institutional expectation.) Therefore, in deciding how much good the currency of a specific moral system would do, we consider the institutional setting as it is, as part of the situation. We are asking which moral code would produce the most good in the long run in this setting. One good to be reckoned, of course, might be that the currency of a given moral code would tend to change the institutional system.

(c) In deciding which moral code will produce the most per person good, we must take into account the probability that certain types of situations will arise in the society. For instance, we must take for granted that people will make promises and subsequently want to break them, that people will sometimes assault other persons in order to achieve their own ends, that people will be in distress and the need the assistance of others, and so on. We may not suppose that, because an ideal moral code might have certain features, it need not have other features because they will not be required; for instance, we may not suppose, on the ground that an ideal moral system would forbid everyone to purchase a gun, that such a moral system needs no provisions about the possession and use of guns—just as our present moral and legal codes have provisions about self-defense,

[9]Some utilitarians have suggested that the right act is determined by the total net intrinsic good produced. This view can have embarrassing consequences for problems of population control. The view here advocated is that the right act is determined by the per person, average, net intrinsic good produced.

which would be unnecessary if everyone obeyed the provision never to assault anyone.

It is true that the currency of a moral code with certain provisions might bring about a reduction in certain types of situations, for example, the number of assaults or cases of dishonesty. And the reduction might be substantial, if the moral code were current which prohibited these offenses very strongly. (We must remember that an ideal moral code might differ from the actual one not only in what it prohibits or enjoins, but also in how strongly it prohibits or enjoins.) But it is consistent to suppose that a moral code prohibits a certain form of behavior very severely, and yet that the behavior will occur, since the "currency" of a moral code requires only 90 percent subscription to it, and a "strong" subscription, on the average, permits a great range from person to person. In any case there must be doubt whether the best moral code will prohibit many things very severely, since there are serious human costs in severe prohibitions: the burden of guilt feelings, the traumas caused by the severe criticism by others which is a part of having a strong injunction in a code, the risks of any training process that would succeed in interiorizing a severe prohibition, and so on.

(d) It would be a great oversimplification if, in assessing the comparative utility of various codes, we confined ourselves merely to counting the benefits of people doing (refraining from doing) certain things, as a result of subscribing to a certain code. To consider only this would be as absurd as estimating the utility of some feature of a legal system by attending only to the utility of people behaving in the way the law aims to make them behave—and overlooking the fact that the law only reduces and does not eliminate misbehavior, as well as the disutility of punishment to the convicted, and the cost of the administration of criminal law. In the case of morals, we must weigh the benefit of the improvement in behavior as a result of the restriction built into conscience, against the cost of the restriction—the burden of guilt feelings, the effects of the training process, etc. There is a further necessary refinement. In both law and morals we must adjust our estimates of utility by taking into account the envisaged system of excuses. That *mens rea* is required as a condition of guilt in the case of most legal offenses is most important; and it is highly important for the utility of a moral system whether accident, intent, and motives are taken into account in deciding a person's liability to moral criticism. A description of a moral code is incomplete until we have specified the severity of condemnation (by conscience or the criticism of others) to be attached to various actions, along with the excuses to be allowed as exculpating or mitigating. . . .

13. It is sometimes thought that a rule-utilitarianism rather like Mill's cannot differ in its implication about what is right or wrong from the act-utilitarian theory. This is a mistake.

The contention would be correct if two dubious assumptions happened to be true. The first is that one of the rules of an optimific moral code will be that a person ought always to do whatever will maximize utility. The second is that, when there is a conflict between the rules of an optimific code, what a person ought to do is to maximize utility. For then, either the utilitarian rule is the only one that applies (and it always will be relevant), in which case the person ought to do what the act-utilitarian directs; or if there is a conflict among the relevant rules, the conflict-resolving principle takes over, and this, of course, prescribes exactly what act-utilitarianism prescribes. Either way, we come out where the act-utilitarian comes out.

But there is no reason at all to suppose that there will be a utilitarian rule in an optimific moral code. In fact, obviously there will not be. It is true that there should be a directive to relieve the distress of others, when this can be done, say, at relatively low personal cost; and there should be a directive not to injure other persons, except in special situations. And so on. But none of this amounts to a straight directive to do the most good possible. Life would be chaotic if people tried to observe any such moral requirement.

The second assumption was apparently acceptable to Mill. But a utilitarian principle is by no means the only possible conflict-resolving principle. For if we say, with the Ideal Moral Code theory, that what is right is fixed by the content of the moral system with maximum utility, the possibility is open that the utility-maximizing moral system will contain some rather different device for resolving conflicts between lowest-level moral rules. The ideal system might contain several higher-level conflict-resolving principles, all different from Mill's. Or, if there is a single one, it could be a directive to maximize utility; it could be a directive to do what an intelligent person who had fully interiorized the rest of the ideal moral system would feel best satisfied with doing; and so on. But the final court of appeal need not be an appeal to direct utilities. Hence the argument that Mill-like rule-utilitarianism must collapse into direct utilitarianism is doubly at fault.[10]

In fact, far from "collapsing" into act-utilitarianism, the Ideal Moral Code theory appears to avoid the serious objections which have been leveled at direct utilitarianism. One objection to the latter view is that it implies that various immoral actions (murdering one's elderly father, breaking solemn promises) are right or even obligatory if only they can be kept secret. The Ideal Moral Code theory has no such implication. For it obviously would not maximize utility to have a moral code which condoned secret murders or breaches of promise. W. D. Ross criticized act-utilitarianism on the ground that it ignored the personal relations important in ordinary morality, and he listed a half-dozen types of moral rule which he thought captured the main themes of thoughtful morality: obligations of fidelity, obligations of gratitude, obligations to make restitution for injuries, obligations to help other persons, to avoid injuring them, to improve one's self, and to bring about a just distribution of good things in life. An ideal moral code, however, would presumably contain substantially such rules in any society, doubtless not precisely as Ross stated them. So the rule-utilitarian need not fail to recognize the personal character of morality. . . .

[10]Could some moral problems be so unique that they would not be provided for by the set of rules it is best for the society to have? If so, how should they be appraised morally? Must there be some appeal to rules covering cases most closely analogous, as seems to be the procedure in law? If so, should we say that an act is right if it is not prohibited, either explicitly or by close analogy, by an ideal moral code? I shall not attempt to answer these questions.

Study Questions

1. Does Brandt think that a correct understanding of moral concepts would enable us to establish utilitarianism?
2. Explain the standard which, according to Brandt, an acceptable normative moral theory must meet.
3. Explain the two forms of rule-utilitarianism Brandt discusses. With which form is he primarily concerned?
4. Explain the ideal moral code theory. When is an act right, according to this theory?
5. What must be true of a moral code if it's to have currency in a society?
6. What does it mean for a person to think that an action is wrong, according to Brandt?
7. Why is it important to distinguish the rules of a society's moral code from the rules of its institutions? Explain this distinction as Brandt sees it.
8. Explain the issues involved in establishing the utility of a moral code.
9. Why, according to Brandt, is it a mistake to think that rule-utilitarianism cannot differ from act-utilitarianism in its implication about what is right and wrong? Why does Brandt think that the ideal moral code theory does not collapse into act-utilitarianism?

Naturalism

According to Moore, it is a mistake, or "fallacy," to treat goodness as if it were a natural property. Moore called this mistake the *naturalistic fallacy.* Many early twentieth-century philosophers after Moore used this term, but unfortunately they did not all seem to have in mind the same thing. However, the naturalistic fallacy—if it is a fallacy—is basically the mistake of thinking that some set of purely descriptive or empirical (or "natural") premises entails a normative (prescriptive or evaluative) conclusion. Moore, Prichard, Stevenson and other emotivists, and perhaps indeed most philosophers of the first part of the twentieth century all maintained, either explicitly or implicitly, that descriptive statements on the one hand and statements of value (that is, normative statements) on the other are logically entirely different types of statements. There is therefore always a logical gap between descriptive premises and any normative conclusion they are said to support. Let's make this less abstract by giving an example.

Consider this argument: "Harold lied to his parents; therefore, Harold did something wrong." Does the premise entail the conclusion? To think that it does is to accept some form of naturalism and is a "fallacy," according to Moore, Prichard, the emotivists, and other antinaturalists. The premise, they would say, does not entail the conclusion: To get to the conclusion, you must add to the premise a gap-bridging normative principle to the effect that lying to one's parents is wrong. Such a principle welds the factual or "natural" phenomenon of lying to the moral quality of wrongness. The naturalistic fallacy basically consists in thinking that such arguments do *not* require a gap-bridging normative principle. Without bringing in some such principle to bridge the gap between fact and value, you cannot, the antinaturalists held, extract a normative conclusion from a descriptive premise. Their point of view is often expressed in Hume's maxim—a maxim we have encountered before—that you cannot derive an "ought" from an "is."

Moore, Prichard, and the emotivists were concerned with coming to a correct understanding or "analysis" of these gap-bridging principles. But is it really true that there is a gap to begin with? Is it really true that you cannot derive an "ought" from an "is," that a normative conclusion cannot be derived from purely descriptive premises? Is naturalism really a "fallacy"? For the first half of this century, many philosophers saw the rejection of naturalism as the most significant accomplishment of contemporary moral theory. But eventually philosophers began to see difficulties in antinaturalism, as you will see in the next two selections, one from John Searle and the other from Philippa Foot. Both Foot and Searle hold that there are empirical criteria for ascribing moral predicates to things; thus, in effect, Foot and Searle are *naturalists* (though they are not *reductivist* naturalists of the sort who maintain that moral properties just are or can be "reduced" to empirical properties).

John Searle

In the selection below, John Searle defines the naturalistic fallacy as the belief that some set of descriptive statements can entail an evaluative statement without the addition of at least one evaluative premise. He then offers and explains in detail what he thinks is a counterexample to the thesis that this belief is false. The counterexample is an argument that proceeds—without apparent help from any normative ("evaluative") premise—from the clearly descriptive assertion that Jones uttered the words "I hereby promise to pay you, Smith, five dollars," to the clearly normative or evaluative conclusion that Jones *ought* to pay Smith five dollars. Next, Searle discusses and attempts to discount three objections to his counterexample.

In the final section of his article, Searle discusses the traditional empiricist theory that there is a rigid distinction between the descriptive and the evaluative. In his opinion, this theory renders such concepts as commitment, responsibility, and obligation incoherent. His main point is that some descriptive statements presuppose the existence of certain rule-governed institutions whose constituent rules involve obligations, commitments, and responsibilities; within such systems of rules, we can derive an "ought" from an "is." More generally, Searle proposes that the alleged distinction between descriptive and evaluative statements consists in conflating two distinctions: (1) the distinction between the *acts* of describing something and evaluating something and (2) the distinction between *claims* that are objectively decidable as true or false and claims that are not objectively so decidable.

How to Derive "Ought" from "Is"[1]

John R. Searle

John Searle (b. 1932) is Mills Professor of Philosophy, University of California, Berkeley. The following selection is used by permission of Professor Searle. It originally appeared in *Philosophical Review* 73 (1964): 43–58.

I

It is often said that one cannot derive an "ought" from an "is." This thesis, which comes from a famous passage in Hume's *Treatise*, while not as clear as it might be, is at least clear in broad outline: there is a class of statements of fact which is locally distinct from a class of statements of value. No set of statements of fact by themselves entails any statement of value. Put in more contemporary terminology, no set of *descriptive* statements can entail an *evaluative* statement without the addition of at least one evaluative premise. To believe otherwise is to commit what has been called the naturalistic fallacy.

I shall attempt to demonstrate a counterexample to this thesis.[2] It is not of course to be supposed that a single counterexample can refute a philosophical thesis, but in the present instance if we can present a plausible counterexample and can in addition give some account or explanation of how and why it is a counterexample, and if we can further offer a theory to back up our counterexample—a theory which will generate an indefinite number of counterexamples—we may at the very least cast considerable light on the original thesis; and possibly, if we can do all these things, we may even incline ourselves to the view that the scope of that thesis was more restricted than we had originally supposed. A counterexample must proceed by taking a statement or statements which any proponent of the thesis would grant were purely factual or "descriptive" (they need not actually contain the word "is") and show how they are logically related to a statement which a proponent of the thesis would regard as clearly "evaluative." (In the present instance it will contain an "ought.")[3]

Consider the following series of statements:

1. Jones uttered the words "I hereby promise to pay you, Smith, five dollars."
2. Jones promised to pay Smith five dollars.
3. Jones placed himself under (undertook) an obligation to pay Smith five dollars.
4. Jones is under an obligation to pay Smith five dollars.
5. Jones ought to pay Smith five dollars.

I shall argue concerning this list that the relation between any statement and its successor, while not in every case one of "entailment," is nonetheless not just a contingent relation; and the additional statements necessary to make the relationship one of entailment do not need to involve any evaluative statements, moral principles, or anything of the sort.

Let us begin. How is (1) related to (2)? In certain circumstances, uttering the words in quota-

[1]Earlier versions of this paper were read before the Stanford Philosophy Colloqium and the Pacific Division of the American Philosophical Association. I am indebted to many people for helpful comments and criticisms, especially Hans Herzberger, Arnold Kaufmann, Benson Mates, A. I. Melden, and Dagmar Searle.

[2]In its modern version. I shall not be concerned with Hume's treatment of the problem.

[3]If this enterprise succeeds, we shall have bridged the gap between "evaluative" and "descriptive" and consequently have demonstrated a weakness in this very terminology. At present, however, my strategy is to play along with the terminology, pretending that the notions of evaluative and descriptive are fairly clear. At the end of the paper I shall state in what respects I think they embody a muddle.

tion marks in (1) is the act of making a promise. And it is a part of or a consequence of the meaning of the words in (1) that in those circumstances uttering them is promising. "I hereby promise" is a paradigm device in English for performing the act described in (2), promising.

Let us state this fact about English usage in the form of an extra premise:

(1a) Under certain conditions *C* anyone who utters the words (sentence) "I hereby promise to pay you, Smith, five dollars" promises to pay Smith five dollars.

What sorts of things are involved under the rubric "conditions *C*"? What is involved will be all those conditions, those states of affairs, which are necessary and sufficient conditions for the utterance of the words (sentence) to constitute the successful performance of the act of promising. The conditions will include such things as that the speaker is in the presence of the hearer Smith, they are both conscious, both speakers of English, speaking seriously. The speaker knows what he is doing, is not under the influence of drugs, not hypnotized or acting in a play, not telling a joke or reporting an event, and so forth. This list will no doubt be somewhat indefinite because the boundaries of the concept of a promise, like the boundaries of most concepts in a natural language, are a bit loose.[4] But one thing is clear; however loose the boundaries may be, and however difficult it may be to decide marginal cases, the conditions under which a man who utters "I hereby promise" can correctly be said to have made a promise are straightforwardly empirical conditions.

So let us add as an extra premise the empirical assumption that these conditions obtain.

(1b) Conditions *C* obtain.

From (1), (1a), and (1b) we derive (2). The argument is of the form: If *C* then (if *U* then *P*): *C* for conditions, *U* for utterance, *P* for promise. Adding the premises *U* and *C* to this hypothetical we derive (2). And as far as I can see, no moral premises are lurking in the logical woodpile. More needs to be said about the relation of (1) to (2), but I reserve that for later.

What is the relation between (2) and (3)? I take it that promising is, by definition, an act of placing oneself under an obligation. No analysis of the concept of promising will be complete which does not include the feature of the promiser placing himself under or undertaking or accepting or recognizing an obligation to the promisee, to perform some future course of action, normally for the benefit of the promisee. One may be tempted to think that promising can be analyzed in terms of creating expectations in one's hearers, or some such, but a little reflection will show that the crucial distinction between statements of intention on the one hand and the promises on the other lies in the nature and degree of commitment or obligation undertaken in promising.

I am therefore inclined to say that (2) entails (3) straight off, but I can have no objection if anyone wishes to add—for the purpose of formal neatness—the tautological premise:

(2a) All promises are acts of placing oneself under (undertaking) an obligation to do the thing promised.

How is (3) related to (4)? If one has placed oneself under an obligation, then, other things being equal, one is under an obligation. That I take it also is a tautology. Of course it is possible for all sorts of things to happen which will release one from obligations one has undertaken and hence the need for the *ceteris paribus* rider. To get an entailment between (3) and (4) we therefore need a qualifying statement to the effect that:

(3a) Other things are equal.

Formalists, as in the move from (2) to (3), may wish to add the tautological premise:

(3b) All those who place themselves under an obligation are, other things being equal, under an obligation.

The move from (3) to (4) is thus of the same form as the move from (1) to (2): If *E* then (if *PUO* then *UO*): *E* for other things are equal, *PUO* for place under obligation and *UO* for under obligation. Adding the two premises *E* and *PUO* we derive *UO*.

[4]In addition the concept of a promise is a member of a class of concepts which suffer from looseness of a peculiar kind, viz. defeasibility. Cf. H. L. A. Hart, "The Ascription of Responsibility and Rights," *Logic and Language*, First Series, ed. by A. Flew (Oxford, 1951).

Is (3a), the *ceteris paribus* clause, a concealed evaluative premise? It certainly looks as if it might be, especially in the formulation I have given it, but I think we can show that, though questions about whether other things are equal frequently involve evaluative considerations, it is not logically necessary that they should in every case. I shall postpone discussion of this until after the next step.

What is the relation between (4) and (5)? Analogous to the tautology which explicates the relation of (3) and (4) there is here the tautology that, other things being equal, one ought to do what one is under an obligation to do. And here, just as in the previous case, we need some premise of the form:

(4a) Other things are equal.

We need the *ceteris paribus* clause to eliminate the possibility that something extraneous to the relation of "obligation" to "ought" might interfere.[5] Here, as in the previous two steps, we eliminate the appearance of enthymeme by pointing out that the apparently suppressed premise is tautological and hence, though formally neat, it is redundant. If, however, we wish to state it formally, this argument is of the same form as the move from (3) to (4): If *E* then (if *UO* then *O*); *E* for other things are equal, *UO* for under obligation, *O* for ought. Adding the premises *E* and *UO* we derive *O*.

Now a word about the phrase "other things being equal" and how it functions in my attempted derivation. This topic and the closely related topic of defeasibility are extremely difficult and I shall not try to do more than justify my claim that the satisfaction of the condition does not necessarily involve anything evaluative. The force of the expression "other things being equal" in the present instance is roughly this. Unless we have some reason (that is, unless we are actually prepared to give some reason) for supposing the obligation is void (step 4) or the agent ought not to keep the promise (step 5), then the obligation holds and he ought to keep the promise. It is not part of the force of the phrase "other things being equal" that in order to satisfy it we need to establish a universal negative proposition to the effect that no reason could ever be given by anyone for supposing the agent is not under an obligation or ought not to keep the promise. That would be impossible and would render the phrase useless. It is sufficient to satisfy the condition that no reason to the contrary can in fact be given.

If a reason is given for supposing the obligation is void or that the promiser ought not to keep a promise, then characteristically a situation calling for an evaluation arises. Suppose, for example, we consider a promised act wrong, but we grant that the promiser did undertake an obligation. Ought he to keep the promise? There is no established procedure for objectively deciding such cases in advance, and an evaluation (if that is really the right word) is in order. But unless we have some reason to the contrary, the *ceteris paribus* condition is satisfied, no evaluation is necessary, and the question whether he ought to do it is settled by saying "he promised." It is always an open possibility that we may have to make an evaluation in order to derive "he ought" from "he promised," for we may have to evaluate a counterargument. But an evaluation is not logically necessary in every case, for there may as a matter of fact be no counterarguments. I am therefore inclined to think that there is nothing necessarily evaluative about the *ceteris paribus* condition, even though deciding whether it is satisfied will frequently involve evaluations.

But suppose I am wrong about this: would that salvage the belief in an unbridgeable logical gulf between "is" and "ought"? I think not, for we can always rewrite my steps (4) and (5) so that they include the *ceteris paribus* clause as part of the conclusion. Thus from our premises we would then have derived "Other things being equal Jones ought to pay Smith five dollars," and that would still be sufficient to refute the tradition, for we

[5]The *ceteris paribus* clause in this step excludes somewhat different sorts of cases from those excluded in the previous step. In general we say, "He undertook an obligation, but nonetheless he is not (now) under an obligation" when the obligation has been *removed*, e.g., if the promisee says, "I release you from your obligation." But we say, "He is under an obligation, but nonetheless ought not to fulfil it" in cases where the obligation is *overridden* by some other considerations, e.g., a prior obligation.

would still have shown a relation of entailment between descriptive and evaluative statements. It was not the fact that extenuating circumstances can void obligations that drove philosophers to the naturalistic fallacy fallacy; it was rather a theory of language, as we shall see later on.

We have thus derived (in as strict a sense of "derive" as natural languages will admit of) an "ought" from an "is." And the extra premises which were needed to make the derivation work were in no cause moral or evaluative in nature. They consisted of empirical assumptions, tautologies, and descriptions of word usage. It must be pointed out also that the "ought" is a "categorical" not a "hypothetical" ought. (5) does not say that Jones ought to pay up if he wants such and such. It says he ought to pay up, period. Note also that the steps of the derivation are carried on in the third person. We are not concluding "I ought" from "I said 'I promise,'" but "he ought" from "he said 'I promise.'"

The proof unfolds the connexion between the utterance of certain words and the speech act of promising and then in turn unfolds promising into obligation and moves from obligation to "ought." The step from (1) to (2) is radically different from the others and requires special comment. In (1) we construe "I hereby promise . . ." as an English phrase having a certain meaning. It is a consequence of that meaning that the utterance of that phrase under certain conditions is the act of promising. Thus by presenting the quoted expressions in (1) and by describing their use in (1a) we have as it were already invoked the institution of promising. We might have started with an even more ground-floor premise than (1) by saying:

(1b) Jones uttered the phonetic sequence: /ai + hirbai + pramis + təpei + yu + smiθ + faiv + dalərz/

We would then have needed extra empirical premises stating that this phonetic sequence was associated in certain ways with certain meaningful units relative to certain dialects.

The moves from (2) to (5) are relatively easy. We rely on definitional connexions between "promise," "obligate," and "ought," and the only problem which arises is that obligations can be overridden or removed in a variety of ways and we need to take account of that fact. We solve our difficulty by adding further premises to the effect that there are no contrary considerations, that other things are equal.

II

In this section I intend to discuss three possible objections to the derivation.

First Objection

Since the first premise is descriptive and the conclusion evaluative, there must be a concealed evaluative premise in the description of the conditions in (1b).

So far, this argument merely begs the question by assuming the logical gulf between descriptive and evaluative which the derivation is designed to challenge. To make the objection stick, the defender of the distinction would have to show how exactly (1b) must contain an evaluative premise and what sort of premise it might be. Uttering certain words in certain conditions just *is* promising and the description of these conditions needs no evaluative element. The essential thing is that in the transition from (1) to (2) we move from the specification of a certain utterance of words to the specification of a certain speech act. The move is achieved because the speech act is a conventional act; and the utterance of the words, according to the conventions, constitutes the performance of just that speech act.

A variant of this first objection is to say: all you have shown is that "promise" is an evaluative, not a descriptive, concept. But this objection again begs the question and in the end will prove disastrous to the original distinction between descriptive and evaluative. For that a man uttered certain words and that these words have the meaning they do are surely objective facts. And if the statement of these two objective facts plus a description of the conditions of the utterance is sufficient to entail the statement (2) which the objector alleges to be an evaluative statement (Jones promised to pay Smith five dollars), then an evaluative conclusion is derived from descriptive premises without even going through steps (3), (4), and (5).

Second Objection

Ultimately the derivation rests on the principle that one ought to keep one's promises and that is a moral principle, hence evaluative.

I don't know whether "one ought to keep one's promises" is a "moral" principle, but whether or not it is, it is also tautological; for it is nothing more than a derivation from the two tautologies:

All promises are (create, are undertakings of, are acceptances of) obligations,

and

One ought to keep (fulfil) one's obligations.

What needs to be explained is why so many philosophers have failed to see the tautological character of this principle. Three things I think have concealed its character from them.

The first is a failure to distinguish external questions about the institution of promising from internal questions asked within the framework of the institution. The questions "Why do we have such an institution as promising?" and "Ought we to have such institutionalized forms of obligation as promising?" are external questions asked about and not within the institution of promising. And the question "Ought one to keep one's promises?" can be confused with or can be taken as (and I think has often been taken as) an external question roughly expressible as "Ought one to accept the institution of promising?" But taken literally, as an internal question, as a question about promises and not about the institution of promising, the question "Ought one to keep one's promises?" is as empty as the question "Are triangles three-sided?" To recognize something as a promise is to grant that, other things being equal, it ought to be kept.

A second fact which has clouded the issue is this. There are many situations, both real and imaginable, where one ought not to keep a promise, where the obligation to keep a promise is overridden by some further considerations, and it was for this reason that we needed those clumsy *ceteris paribus* clauses in our derivation. But the fact that obligations can be overridden does not show that there were no obligations in the first place. On the contrary. And these original obligations are all that is needed to make the proof work.

Yet a third factor is the following. Many philosophers still fail to realize the full force of saying that "I hereby promise" is a performative expression. In uttering it one performs but does not describe the act of promising. Once promising is seen as a speech act of a kind different from describing, then it is easier to see that one of the features of the act is the undertaking of an obligation. But if one thinks the utterance of "I promise" or "I hereby promise" is a peculiar kind of description—for example, of one's mental state—then the relation between promising and obligation is going to seem very mysterious.

Third Objection

The derivation uses only a factual or inverted-commas sense of the evaluative terms employed. For example, an anthropologist observing the behaviour and attitudes of the Anglo-Saxons might well go through these derivations, but nothing evaluative would be included. Thus step (2) is equivalent to "He did what they call promising" and step (5) to "According to them he ought to pay Smith five dollars." But since all of the steps (2) to (5) are in *oratio obliqua* and hence disguised statements of fact, the fact-value distinction remains unaffected.

This objection fails to damage the derivation, for what it says is only that the steps *can* be reconstructed as in *oratio obliqua*, that we can construe them as a series of external statements, that we can construct a parallel (or at any rate related) proof about reported speech. But what I am arguing is that, taken quite literally, without any *oratio obliqua* additions or interpretations, the derivation is valid. That one can construct a similar argument which would fail to refute the fact-value distinction does not show that this proof fails to refute it. Indeed it is irrelevant.

III

So far I have presented a counterexample to the thesis that one cannot derive an "ought" from an "is" and considered three possible objections to it.

Even supposing what I have said so far is true, still one feels a certain uneasiness. One feels there must be some trick involved somewhere. We might state our uneasiness thus: How can my granting a mere fact about a man, such as the fact that he uttered certain words or that he made a promise, commit *me* to the view that *he* ought to do something? I now want briefly to discuss what broader philosophic significance my attempted derivation may have, in such a way as to give us the outlines of an answer to this question.

I shall begin by discussing the grounds for supposing that it cannot be answered at all.

The inclination to accept a rigid distinction between "is" and "ought," between descriptive and evaluative, rests on a certain picture of the way words relate to the world. It is a very attractive picture, so attractive (to me at least) that it is not entirely clear to what extent the mere presentation of counterexamples can challenge it. What is needed is an explanation of how and why this classical empiricist picture fails to deal with such counterexamples. Briefly, the picture is constructed something like this: first we present examples of so-called descriptive statements ("my car goes eighty miles an hour," "Jones is six feet tall," "Smith has brown hair"), and we constrast them with so-called evaluative statements ("my car is a good car," "Jones ought to pay Smith five dollars," "Smith is a nasty man"). Anyone can see that they are different. We articulate the difference by pointing out that for the descriptive statements the question of truth or falsity is objectively decidable, because to know the meaning of the descriptive expressions is to know under what objectively ascertainable conditions the statements which contain them are true or false. But in the case of evaluative statements the situation is quite different. To know the meaning of the evaluative expressions is not by itself sufficient for knowing under what conditions the statements containing them are true or false, because the meaning of the expressions is such that the statements are not capable of objective or factual truth or falsity at all. Any justification a speaker can give of one of his evaluative statements essentially involves some appeal to attitudes he holds, to criteria of assessment he has adopted, or to moral principles by which he has chosen to live and judge other people. Descriptive statements are thus objective, evaluative statements subjective, and the difference is a consequence of the different sorts of terms employed.

The underlying reason for these differences is that evaluative statements perform a completely different job from descriptive statements. Their job is not to describe any features of the world but to express the speaker's emotions, to express his attitudes, to praise or condemn, to laud or insult, to comment, to recommend, to advise, and so forth. Once we see the different jobs the two perform, we see that there must be a logical gulf between them. Evaluative statements must be different from descriptive statements in order to do their job, for if they were objective they could no longer function to evaluate. Put metaphysically, values cannot lie in the world, for if they did they would cease to be values and would just be another part of the world. Put in the formal mode, one cannot define an evaluative word in terms of descriptive words, for if one did, one would no longer be able to use the evaluative word to commend, but only to describe. Put yet another way, any effort to derive an "ought" from an "is" must be a waste of time, for all it could show even if it succeeded would be that the "is" was not a real "is" but only a disguised "ought" or, alternatively, that the "ought" was not a real "ought" but only a disguised "is."

This summary of the traditional empirical view has been very brief, but I hope it conveys something of the power of this picture. In the hands of certain modern authors, especially Hare and Nowell-Smith, the picture attains considerable subtlety and sophistication.

What is wrong with this picture? No doubt many things are wrong with it. In the end I am going to say that one of the things wrong with it is that it fails to give us any coherent account of such notions as commitment, responsibility, and obligation.

In order to work toward this conclusion I can begin by saying that the picture fails to account for the *different types* of "descriptive" statements. Its paradigms of descriptive statements are such utterances as "my car goes eighty miles an hour," "Jones is six feet tall," "Smith has brown hair," and the like. But it is forced by its own rigidity to construe

"Jones got married," "Smith made a promise," "Jackson has five dollars," and "Brown hit a home run" as descriptive statements as well. It is so forced, because whether or not someone got married, made a promise, has five dollars, or hit a home run is as much a matter of objective fact as whether he has red hair or brown eyes. Yet the former kind of statement (statements containing "married," "promise," and so forth) seem to be quite different from the simple empirical paradigms of descriptive statements. How are they different? Though both kinds of statements state matters of objective fact, the statements containing words such as "married," "promise," "home run," and "five dollars" state facts whose existence presupposes certain institutions: a man has five dollars, given the institution of money. Take away the institution and all he has is a rectangular bit of paper with green ink on it. A man hits a home run only given the institution of baseball; without the institution he only hits a sphere with a stick. Similarly, a man gets married or makes a promise only within the institutions of marriage and promising. Without them, all he does is utter words or makes gestures. We might characterize such facts as institutional facts, and contrast them with noninstitutional, or brute, facts: that a man has a bit of paper with green ink on it is a brute fact, that he has five dollars is an institutional fact.[6] The classical picture fails to account for the differences between statements of brute fact and statements of institutional fact.

The word "institution" sounds artificial here, so let us ask: what sorts of institutions are these? In order to answer that question I need to distinguish between two different kinds of rules or conventions. Some rules regulate antecedently existing forms of behaviour. For example, the rules of polite table behaviour regulate eating, but eating exists independently of these rules. Some rules, on the other hand, do not merely regulate but create or define new forms of behaviour: the rules of chess, for example, do not merely regulate an antecedently existing activity called playing chess; they, as it were, create the possibility of or define that activity. The activity of playing chess is constituted by action in accordance with these rules. Chess has no existence apart from these rules. The distinction I am trying to make was foreshadowed by Kant's distinction between regulative and constitutive principles, so let us adopt his terminology and describe our distinction as a distinction between regulative and constitutive rules. Regulative rules regulate activities whose existence is independent of the rules; constitutive rules constitute (and also regulate) forms of activity whose existence is logically dependent on the rules.[7]

Now the institutions that I have been talking about are systems of constitutive rules. The institutions of marriage, money, and promising are like the institutions of baseball or chess in that they are systems of such constitutive rules or conventions. What I have called institutional facts are facts which presuppose such institutions.

Once we recognize the existence of and begin to grasp the nature of such institutional facts, it is but a short step to see that many forms of obligations, commitments, rights, and responsibilities are similarly institutionalized. It is often a matter of fact that one has certain obligations, commitments, rights, and responsibilities, but it is a matter of institutional, not brute, fact. It is one such institutionalized form of obligation, promising, which I invoked above to derive an "ought" from an "is." I started with a brute fact, that a man uttered certain words, and then invoked the institution in such a way as to generate institutional facts by which we arrived at the institutional fact that the man ought to pay another man five dollars. The whole proof rests on an appeal to the constitutive rule that to make a promise is to undertake an obligation.

We are now in a position to see how we can generate an indefinite number of such proofs. Consider the following vastly different example. We are in our half of the seventh inning and I have a big lead off second base. The pitcher whirls, fires to the shortstop covering, and I am tagged out a

[6]For a discussion of this distinction see G. E. M. Anscombe, "Brute Facts," *Analysis* (1958).

[7]For a discussion of a related distinction see J. Rawls, "Two Concepts of Rules," *Philosophical Review*, LXIV (1955).

good ten feet down the line. The umpire shouts, "Out!" I, however, being a positivist, hold my ground. The umpire tells me to return to the dugout. I point out to him that you can't derive an "ought" from an "is." No set of descriptive statements describing matters of fact, I say, will entail any evaluative statements to the effect that I should or ought to leave the field. You just can't get orders or recommendations from facts alone. What is needed is an evaluative major premise. I therefore return to and stay on second base (until I am carried off the field). I think everyone feels my claims here to be preposterous, and preposterous in the sense of logically absurd. Of course you can derive an "ought" from an "is," and though to actually set out the derivation in this case would be vastly more complicated than in the case of promising, it is in principle no different. By undertaking to play baseball I have committed myself to the observation of certain constitutive rules.

We are now also in a position to see that the tautology that one ought to keep one's promises is only one of a class of similar tautologies concerning institutionalized forms of obligation. For example, "one ought not to steal" can be taken as saying that to recognize something as someone else's property necessarily involves recognizing his right to dispose of it. This is a constitutive rule of the institution of private property.[8] "One ought not to tell lies" can be taken as saying that to make an assertion necessarily involves undertaking an obligation to speak truthfully. Another constitutive rule. "One ought to pay one's debts" can be construed as saying that to recognize something as a debt is necessarily to recognize an obligation to pay it. It is easy to see how all these principles will generate counterexamples to the thesis that you cannot derive an "ought" from an "is."

My tentative conclusions, then, are as follows:

1. The classical picture fails to account for institutional facts.
2. Institutional facts exist within systems of constitutive rules.
3. Some systems of constitutive rules involve obligations, commitments, and responsibilities.
4. Within those systems we can derive "ought's" from "is's" on the model of the first derivation.

With these conclusions we now return to the question with which I began this section: How can my stating a fact about a man, such as the fact that he made a promise, commit me to a view about what he ought to do? One can begin to answer this question by saying that for me to state such an institutional fact is already to invoke the constitutive rules of the institution. It is those rules that give the word "promise" its meaning. But those rules are such that to commit myself to the view that Jones made a promise involves committing myself to what he ought to do (other things being equal).

If you like, then, we have shown that "promise" is an evaluative word, but since it is also purely descriptive, we have really shown that the whole distinction needs to be re-examined. The alleged distinction between descriptive and evaluative statements is really a conflation of at least two distinctions. On the one hand there is a distinction between different kinds of speech acts, one family of speech acts including evaluations, another family including descriptions. This is a distinction between different kinds of illocutionary force.[9] On the other hand there is a distinction between utterances which involve claims objectively decidable as true or false and those which involve claims not objectively decidable, but which are "matters of personal decision" or "matters of opinion." It has been assumed that the former distinction is (must

---

[8]Proudhon said: "Property is theft." If one tries to take this as an internal remark it makes no sense. It was intended as an external remark attacking and rejecting the institution of private property. It gets its air of paradox and its force by using terms which are internal to the institution in order to attack the institution.

Standing on the deck of some institutions one can tinker with constitutive rules and even throw some other institutions overboard. But could one throw all institutions overboard (in order perhaps to avoid ever having to derive an "ought" from an "is")? One could not and still engage in those forms of behaviour we consider characteristically human. Suppose Proudhon had added (and tried to live by): "Truth is a lie, marriage is infidelity, language is uncommunicative, law is a crime," and so on with every possible institution.

[9]See J. L. Austin, *How to Do Things with Words* (Cambridge, Mass., 1962), for an explanation of this notion.

be) a special case of the latter, that if something has the illocutionary force of an evaluation, it cannot be entailed by factual premises. Part of the point of my argument is to show that this contention is false, that factual premises can entail evaluative conclusions. If I am right, then the alleged distinction between descriptive and evaluative utterances is useful only as a distinction between two kinds of illocutionary force, describing and evaluating, and it is not even very useful there, since if we are to use these terms strictly, they are only two among hundreds of kinds of illocutionary force; and utterances of sentences of the form (5)—"Jones ought to pay Smith five dollars"—would not characteristically fall in either class.

Study Questions

1. What is it, according to Searle, to commit the naturalistic fallacy?
2. What is the *ceteris paribus* clause, and why does Searle add it to the move from (3) to (4) and from (4) to (5)?
3. What are Searle's reasons for saying that clause is not evaluative?
4. Explain the First Objection to Searle's derivation of an "ought" from an "is." How does he respond to the objection?
5. What is the difference between external questions and internal questions about the institution of promising?
6. What is the difference between an institutional fact and a brute fact?
7. Does Searle believe that an evaluative word can also be purely descriptive? Explain. Does he believe that there is a distinction between descriptive and evaluative statements? Explain.

Philippa Foot

Philippa Foot, as you may recall from Chapter 2, disagrees with an idea we associated with R. M. Hare: that it is not the content or subject matter of a judgment that makes it specifically a moral judgment. In the following essay, Foot wishes to criticize two assumptions on which, in her view, the rejction of naturalism had been founded. Thus, in effect, she calls into question the entire antinaturalism movement and its belief that evaluations are logically independent from the empirical statements on which they are often based.

The first assumption is that a person logically could rest his or her beliefs about a matter of value wholly on premises that nobody else would recognize as evidence at all. As she develops this assumption, it becomes the assumption that a person can call "good" (or commend or positively evaluate) just anything he or she pleases. The second assumption is that, given what other people regard as evidence for an evaluative conclusion, a person may logically refuse to draw this conclusion because the evidence does not count as evidence for *that person.*

In criticizing the first assumption, she points to — and analyzes in some detail — the absurdity of supposing that no background explanation is required to make sense of commending someone or calling that person "good" for clasping his or her hands three times an hour. To think that you could commend or call anything whatsoever "good" is like thinking, say, that you logically could hold anything whatsoever dangerous or injurious. "Good" and commending are not pieces of tape that can be affixed to anything at all. To suppose that they could is equivalent to thinking that "good" and commending have meanings independent of their objects. But there is no way of describing the evaluative meaning of "good" without specifying the object to which it is supposed to be attached. And that object must be the proper object of such a thing as evaluation.

In her discussion of the second assumption, Foot calls attention to Thrasymachus's argument in the first book of Plato's *Republic*: that since injustice is more profitable than justice, a person who can get away with injustice has a reason to be unjust. Contemporary moral philosophy, Foot says, sees no difficulty in saying that you could accept Thrasymachus's premise and not accept his conclusion; thus, contemporary moral philosophy in effect accepts the second assumption, she implies. But this, she argues, is a mistake: If justice is not profitable to the just man, then it cannot logically be commended as a virtue.

Moral Beliefs

Philippa Foot

Philippa Foot (b. 1920) is Emeritus Professor of Philosophy at the University of California, Los Angeles, and a fellow of Somerville College, Oxford University. The following selection appeared in *Proceedings of the Aristotelian Society* 59 (1958–1959): 83–104.

To many people it seems that the most notable advance in moral philosophy during the past fifty years or so has been the refutation of naturalism; and they are a little shocked that at this late date such an issue should be reopened. It is easy to understand their attitude: given certain apparently unquestionable assumptions, it would be about as sensible to try to reintroduce naturalism as to try to square the circle. Those who see it like this have satisfied themselves that they know in advance that any naturalistic theory must have a catch in it somewhere, and are put out at having to waste more time exposing an old fallacy. This paper is an attempt to persuade them to look critically at the premises on which their arguments are based.

It would not be an exaggeration to say that the whole of moral philosophy, as it is now widely taught, rests on a contrast between statements of fact and evaluations, which runs something like this: "The truth or falsity of statements of fact is shewn by means of evidence; and what counts as evidence is laid down in the meaning of the expressions occurring in the statement of fact. (For instance, the meaning of "round" and "flat" made Magellan's voyages evidence for the roundness rather than the flatness of the Earth; someone who went on questioning whether the evidence was evidence could eventually be shewn to have made some linguistic mistake.) It follows that no two people can make the same statement and count completely different things as evidence; in the end one at least of them could be convicted of linguistic ignorance. It also follows that if a man is given good evidence for a factual conclusion he cannot just refuse to accept the conclusion on the ground that in his scheme of things this evidence is not evidence at all. With evaluations, however, it is different. An evaluation is not connected logically with the factual statements on which it is based. One man may say that a thing is good because of some fact about it, and another may refuse to take the fact as any evidence at all, for nothing is laid down in the meaning of "good" which connects it with one piece of "evidence" rather than another. It follows that a moral eccentric could argue to moral conclusions from quite idiosyncratic premisses; he could say, for instance, that a man was a good man because he clasped and unclasped his hands, and never turned N.N.E. after turning S.S.W. He could also reject someone else's evaluation simply by denying that his evidence was evidence at all.

"The fact about 'good' which allows the eccentric still to use this term without falling into a morass of meaninglessness, is its 'action-guiding' or 'practical' function. This it retains; for like everyone else he considers himself bound to choose the things he calls 'good' rather than those he calls 'bad.' Like the rest of the world he uses 'good' in connexion only with a 'pro-attitude'; it is only that he has pro-attitudes to quite different hings, and therefore calls them good."

There are here two assumptions about "evaluations," which I will call assumption (1) and assumption (2).

Assumption (1) is that some individual may, without logical error, base his beliefs about matters of value entirely on premises which no one else would recognize as giving any evidence at all. Assumption (2) is that, given the kind of statement which other people regard as evidence for an evaluative conclusion, he may refuse to draw the conclusion because *this* does not count as evidence for *him*.

Let us consider assumption (1). We might say that this depends on the possibility of keeping the meaning of "good" steady through all changes in the facts about anything which are to count in favour of its goodness. (I do not mean, of course, that a man can make changes as fast as he chooses; only that, whatever he has chosen, it will not be possible to rule him out of order.) But there is a better formulation, which cuts out trivial disputes about the meaning which "good" happens to have in some section of the community. Let us say that the assumption is that the evaluative function of "good" can remain constant through changes in the evaluative principle; on this ground it could be said that even if no one can call a man *good* because he clasps and unclasps his hands, he can commend him or express his *pro-attitude* towards him, and if necessary can invent a new moral vocabulary to express his unusual moral code.

Those who hold such a theory will naturally add several qualifications. In the first place, most people now agree with Hare, against Stevenson, that such words as "good" only apply to individual cases through the application of general principles, so that even the extreme moral eccentric must accept principles of commendation. In the second place "commending," "having a pro-attitude," and so on, are supposed to be connected with doing and choosing, so that it would be impossible to say, e.g., that a man was a good man only if he lived for a thousand years. The range of evaluation is supposed to be restricted to the range of possible action and choice. I am not here concerned to question these supposed restrictions on the use of evaluative terms, but only to argue that they are not enough.

The crucial question is this. Is it possible to extract from the meaning of words such as "good" some element called "evaluative meaning" which we can think of as externally related to its objects? Such an element would be represented, for instance, in the rule that when any action was "commended" the speaker must hold himself bound to accept an imperative "let me do these things." This is externally related to its object because, within the limitation which we noticed earlier, to possible actions, it would make sense to think of anything as the subject of such "commendation." On this hypothesis a moral eccentric could be described as commending the clasping of hands as the action of a good man, and we should not have to look for some background to give the supposition sense. That is to say, on this hypothesis the clasping of hands could be commended without any explanation; it could be what those who hold such theories call "an ultimate moral principle."

I wish to say that this hypothesis is untenable, and that there is no describing the evaluative meaning of "good," evaluation, commending, or anything of the sort, without fixing the object to which they are supposed to be attached. Without first laying hands on the proper object of such things as evaluation, we shall catch in our net either something quite different such as accepting an order or making a resolution, or else nothing at all.

Before I consider this question, I shall first discuss some other mental attitudes and beliefs which have this internal relation to their object. By this I hope to clarify the concept of internal relation to an object, and incidentally, if my examples arouse resistance, but are eventually accepted, to show how easy it is to overlook an internal relation where it exists.

Consider, for instance, pride.

People are often surprised at the suggestion that there are limits to the things a man can be proud of, about which indeed he can feel pride. I do not know quite what account they want to give of pride; perhaps something to do with smiling and walking with a jaunty air, and holding an object up where other people can see it; or perhaps they think that pride is a kind of internal sensation, so that one might naturally beat one's breast and say "pride is something I feel *here*." The difficulties of the second view are well known; the logically private object cannot be what a name in the public language is the name of.[1] The first view is the more plausible, and it may seem reasonable to say that given certain behaviour a man can be described as showing that he is proud of something, whatever that something may be. In one sense this is true, and in another sense not. Given any description of an object, action, personal characteristic, etc., it is not possible to rule it out as an object of pride. Before we can do so we need to know what would be said about it by the man who is to be proud of it, or feels proud of it; but if he does not hold the

[1]See Wittgenstein, *Philosophical Investigations*, especially §§ 243–315.

right beliefs about it then whatever his attitude is it is not pride. Consider, for instance, the suggestion that someone might be proud of the sky or the sea: he looks at them and what he feels is *pride*, or he puffs out his chest and gestures with *pride* in their direction. This makes sense only if a special assumption is made about his beliefs, for instance that he is under some crazy delusion and believes that he has saved the sky from falling, or the sea from drying up. The characteristic object of pride is something seen (*a*) as in some way a man's own, and (*b*) as some sort of achievement or advantage; without this object pride cannot be described. To see that the second condition is necessary, one should try supposing that a man happens to feel proud because he has laid one of his hands on the other, three times in an hour. Here again the supposition that it is pride that he feels will make perfectly good sense if a special background is filled in. Perhaps he is ill, and it is an achievement even to do this; perhaps this gesture has some religious or political significance, and he is a brave man who will so defy the gods or the rulers. But with no special background there can be no pride, not because no one could psychologically speaking feel pride in such a case, but because whatever he did feel could not logically be pride. Of course, people can see strange things as achievements, though not just anything, and they can identify themselves with remote ancestors, and relations, and neighbours, and even on occasions with Mankind. I do not wish to deny there are many far-fetched and comic examples of pride.

We could have chosen many other examples of mental attitudes which are internally related to their object in a similar way. For instance, fear is not just trembling, and running, and turning pale; without the thought of some menacing evil no amount of this will add up to fear. Nor could anyone be said to feel dismay about something he did not see as bad; if his thoughts about it were that it was altogether a good thing, he could not say that (oddly enough) what he felt about it was dismay. "How odd, I feel dismayed when I ought to be pleased" is the prelude to a hunt for the adverse aspect of the thing, thought of as lurking behind the pleasant façade. But someone may object that pride and fear and dismay are feelings or emotions and therefore not a proper analogy for "commendation," and there will be an advantage in considering a different kind of example. We could discuss, for instance, the belief that a certain thing is dangerous, and ask whether this could logically be held about anything whatsoever. Like "this is good," "this is dangerous" is an assertion, which we should naturally accept or reject by speaking of its truth or falsity; we seem to support such statements with evidence, and moreover there may seem to be a "warning function" connected with the word "dangerous" as there is supposed to be a "commending function" connected with the word "good." For suppose that philosophers, puzzled about the property of dangerousness, decided that the word did not stand for a property at all, but was essentially a practical or action-guiding term, used for *warning*. Unless used in an "inverted comma sense" the word "dangerous" was used to warn, and this meant that anyone using it in such a sense committed himself to avoiding the things he called dangerous, to preventing other people from going near them, and perhaps to running in the opposite direction. If the conclusion were not obviously ridiculous, it would to easy to infer that a man whose application of the term was different from ours throughout might say that the oddest things were dangerous without fear of disproof; the idea would be that he could still be described as "thinking them dangerous," or at least as "warning," because by his attitude and actions he would have fulfilled the conditions for these things. This is nonsense because without its proper object *warning*, like *believing dangerous*, will not be there. It is logically impossible to warn about anything not thought of as threatening evil, and for danger we need a particular kind of serious evil such as injury or death.

There are, however, some differences between thinking a thing dangerous and feeling proud, frightened or dismayed. When a man says that something is dangerous he must support his statement with a special kind of evidence; but when he says that he feels proud or frightened or dismayed the description of the object of his pride or fright or dismay does not have quite this relation to his original statement. If he is shown that the thing he was proud of was not his after all, or was not after all anything very grand, he may have to say that his pride was not justified, but he will not have to take back the statement that he was proud. On the other hand, someone who says that a thing is dangerous, and later sees that he made a mistake in thinking that an injury might result from it, has to go back on his original statement and admit that he was wrong. In neither case, however, is the speaker able to go on as before. A man who discovered that it was not his pumpkin but someone else's which had won the prize could only say that he still felt proud, if he could produce some other ground for pride. It is in this way that even feelings are logically vulnerable to facts.

It will probably be objected against these examples that for part of the way at least they beg the question. It will be said that indeed a man can be proud only of something he thinks a good action, or an achievement, or a sign of noble birth; as he can feel dismay only about something which he sees as bad, frightened at some threatened evil; similarly he can warn only if he is also prepared to speak, for instance, of injury. But this will limit the range of possible objects of those attitudes and beliefs only if the range of these terms is limited to its turn. To meet this objection I shall discuss the meaning of "injury" because this is the simplest case. Anyone who feels inclined to say that anything could be counted as an achievement, or as the evil of which people were afraid, or about which they felt dismayed, should just try this out. I wish to consider the proposition that anything could be thought of as dangerous, because if it causes injury it is dangerous, and anything could be counted as an injury. I shall consider bodily injury because this is the injury connected with danger; it is not correct to put up a notice by the roadside reading "Danger!" on account of bushes which might scratch a car. Nor can a substance be labelled "dangerous" on the ground that it can injure delicate fabrics; although we can speak of the danger that it may do so, that is not the use of the word which I am considering here.

When a body is injured it is changed for the worse in a special way, and we want to know which changes count as injuries. First of all, it matters how an injury comes about; e.g., it cannot be caused by natural decay. Then it seems clear that not just any kind of thing will do, for instance, any unusual mark on the body, however much trouble a man might take to have it removed. By far the most important class of injuries are injuries to a part of the body, counting as injuries because there is interference with the function of that part; injury to a leg, an eye, an ear, a hand, a muscle, the heart, the brain, the spinal cord. An injury to an eye is one that affects, or is likely to affect, its sight; an injury to a hand one which makes it less well able to reach out and grasp, and perform other operations of this kind. A leg can be injured because its movements and supporting power can be affected; a lung because it can become too weak to draw in the proper amount of air. We are most ready to speak of an injury where the function of a part of the body is to perform a characteristic operation, as in these examples. We might hesitate to say that a skull can be injured, and might prefer to speak of damage to it, since although there is indeed a function (a protective function) there is no operation. But thinking of the protective function of the skull we may want to speak of injury here. In so far as the concept of *injury* depends on that of *function* it is narrowly limited, since not even every use to which a part of the body is put will count as its function. Why is it that, even if it is the means by which they earn their living, we would never consider the removal of the dwarf's hump or the bearded lady's beard as a bodily injury? It will be tempting to say that these things are disfigurements, but this is not the point; if we suppose that a man who had some invisible extra muscle made his living as a court jester by waggling his ears, the ear would not have been injured if this were made to disappear. If it were natural to men to communicate by movements of the ear, then ears would have the function of signalling (we have no word for this kind of "speaking") and an impairment of this function would be an injury; but things are not like this. This court jester would use his ears to make people laugh, but this is not the function of ears.

No doubt many people will feel impatient when such facts are mentioned, because they think that it is quite unimportant that this or that *happens* to be the case, and it seems to them arbitrary that the loss of the beard, the hump, or the ear muscle would not be called an injury. Isn't the loss of that by which one makes one's living a pretty catastrophic loss? Yet it seems quite natural that these are not counted as injuries if one thinks about the conditions of human life, and contrasts the loss of a special ability to make people gape or laugh with the ability to see, hear, walk, or pick things up. The first is only needed for one very special way of living; the other in any foreseeable future for any man. This restriction seems all the more natural when we observe that other threats besides that of injury can constitute danger: of death, for instance, or mental derangement. A shock which could cause mental instability or impairment of memory would be called dangerous, because a man needs such things as intelligence, memory, and concentration as he needs sight or hearing or the use of hands. Here we do not speak of injury unless it is possible to connect the impairment with some physical change, but we speak of danger because there is the same loss of a capacity which any man needs.

There can be injury outside the range we have been considering; for a man may sometimes be said to have received injuries where no part of his body has had its function interfered with. In general, I think that any blow which disarranged the body in such a way that there was lasting pain would inflict an injury, even if no other ill resulted, but I do not know of any other important extension of the concept.

It seems therefore that since the range of things which can be called injuries is quite narrowly restricted, the word "dangerous" is restricted in so far as it is connected with injury. We have the right to say that a man cannot decide to call just anything dangerous, however much he puts up fences and shakes his head.

So far I have been arguing that such things as pride, fear, dismay, and the thought that something is dangerous have an internal relation to their object, and hope that what I mean is becoming clear. Now we must consider whether those attitudes or beliefs which are the moral philosopher's study are similar, or whether such things as "evaluation" and "thinking something good" and "commendation" could logically be found in combination with any object whatsoever. All I can do here is to give an example which may make this suggestion seem implausible, and to knock away a few of its supports. The example will come from the range of trivial and pointless actions such as we were considering in speaking of the man who clasped his hands three times an hour, and we can point to the oddity of the suggestion that this can be called a good action. We are bound by the terms of our question to refrain from adding any special background, and it should be stated once more that the question is about what can count in favour of the goodness or badness of a man or an action, and not what could be, or be thought, good or bad with a special background. I believe that the view I am attacking often seems plausible only because the special background is surreptitiously introduced.

Someone who said that clasping the hands three times in an hour was a good action would first have to answer the question "How do you mean?" For the sentence "this is a good action" is not one which has a clear meaning. Presumably, since our subject is moral philosophy, it does not here mean "that was a good thing to do" as this might be said of a man who had done something sensible in the course of any enterprise whatever; we are to confine our attention to 'the moral use of "good."' I am not clear that it makes sense to speak of "a moral use of 'good,'" but we can pick out a number of cases which raise moral issues. It is because these are so diverse and because "this is a good action" does not pick out any one of them, that we must ask "How do you mean?" For instance, some things that are done fulfil a duty, such as the duty of parents to children or children to parents. I suppose that when philosophers speak of good actions they would include these. Some come under the heading of a virtue such as charity, and they will be included too. Others again are actions which require the virtues of courage or temperance, and here the moral aspect is due to the fact that they are done in spite of fear or the temptation of pleasure; they must indeed be done for the sake of some real or fancied good, but not necessarily what philosophers would want to call a moral good. Courage is not *particularly* concerned with saving other people's lives, or temperance with leaving them their share of the food and drink, and the goodness of *what is done* may here be all kinds of usefulness. It is because there are these very diverse cases included (I suppose) under the expression "a good action" that we should refuse to consider applying it without asking what is meant, and we should now ask what is intended when someone is supposed to say that "clasping the hands three times in an hour is a good action." Is it supposed that this action fulfils a duty? Then in virtue of what does a man have this duty, and to whom does he owe it? We have promised not to slip in a special background, but he cannot possibly have a *duty* to clasp his hands unless such a background exists. Nor could it be an act of charity, for it is not thought to do anyone any good, nor again a gesture of humility unless a special assumption turns it into this. The action could be courageous, but only if it were done both in the face of fear and for the sake of a good; and we are not allowed to put in special circumstances which could make this the case.

I am sure that the following objection will now be raised. "Of course clasping one's hands three times in an hour cannot be brought under one of the virtues which we recognize, but that is only to say that it is not a good action by our current moral code. It is logically possible that in a quite different moral code quite different virtues should be recognized, for which we have not even got a name." I cannot answer this objection properly, for that would need a satisfactory account of the concept of a virtue. But anyone who thinks it would be easy to describe a new virtue connected with clasping the hands three times in an hour should just try. I think he will find that he has to cheat, and suppose that in the community concerned the clasping of hands has been given some special significance, or is thought to have some special effect. The difficulty is obviously connected with the fact that without a special background there is no possibility of answering the question "What's the point?" It is no good saying that there would be a point in doing the action because the action was a morally good action: the question is how it can be given any such description if we cannot first speak about the point. And it is just as crazy to suppose that we can call *anything* the point of doing something without having to say what the point of *that* is. In clasping one's hands one may make a slight sucking noise, but what is the point of that? It is surely clear that moral virtues must be connected with human good and harm, and that it is quite impossible to call anything you like good or harm. Consider, for instance, the suggestion that a man might say he had been harmed because a bucket of water had been taken out of the sea. As usual it would be possible to think up circumstances in which this remark would make sense; for instance, when coupled with a belief in magical influences; but then the harm would consist in what was done by the evil spirits, not in the taking of the water from the sea. It would be just as odd if someone were supposed to say that harm had been done to him because the hairs of his head had been reduced to an even number.[2]

I conclude that assumption (1) is very dubious indeed, and that no one should be allowed to speak as if we can understand "evaluation," "commendation" or "pro-attitude," whatever the actions concerned.

II

I propose now to consider what was called Assumption (2), which said that a man might always refuse to accept the conclusion of an argument about values, because what counted as evidence for other people did not count for him. Assumption (2) could be true even if Assumption (1) were false, for it might be that once a particular question of values — say a moral question — had been accepted, any disputant was bound to accept particular pieces of evidence as relevant, the same pieces as everyone else, but that he could always refuse to draw any moral conclusions whatsoever or to discuss any questions which introduced moral terms. Nor do we mean "he might refuse to draw the conclusion" in the trivial sense in which anyone can perhaps refuse to draw *any* conclusion; the point is that any statement of value always

[2]In face of this sort of example many philosophers take refuge in the thicket of aesthetics. It would be interesting to know if they are willing to let their whole case rest on the possibility that there might be aesthetic objections to what was done.

seems to go beyond any statement of fact, so that he might have a reason for accepting the factual premises but refusing to accept the evaluative conclusion. That this is so seems to those who argue in this way to follow from the practical implication of evaluation. When a man uses a word such as "good" in an "evaluative" and not an "inverted comma" sense, he is supposed to commit his will. From this it has seemed to follow inevitably that there is a logical gap between fact and value; for is it not one thing to say that a thing is so, and another to have a particular attitude towards its being so; one thing to see that certain effects will follow from a given action, and another to care? Whatever account was offered of the essential feature of evaluation—whether in terms of feelings, attitudes, the acceptance of imperatives or what not—the fact remained that with an evaluation there was a committal in a new dimension, and that this was not guaranteed by any acceptance of facts.

I shall argue that this view is mistaken; that the practical implication of the use of moral terms has been put in the wrong place, and that if it is described correctly the logical gap between factual premises and moral conclusion disappears.

In this argument it will be useful to have as a pattern the practical or "action-guiding" force of the word "injury," which is in some, though not all, ways similar to that of moral terms. It is clear I think that an injury is necessarily something bad and therefore something which as such anyone always has a reason to avoid, and philosophers will therefore be tempted to say that anyone who uses "injury" in its full "action-guiding" sense commits himself to avoiding the things he calls injuries. They will then be in the usual difficulties about the man who says he knows he ought to do something but does not intend to do it; perhaps also about weakness of the will. Suppose that instead we look again at the kinds of things which count as injuries, to see if the connexion with the will does not start here. As has been shown, a man is injured whenever some part of his body, in being damaged, has become less well able to fulfil its ordinary function. It follows that he suffers a disability, or is liable to do so; with an injured hand he will be less well able to pick things up, hold on to them, tie them together or chop them up, and so on. With defective eyes there will be a thousand other things he is unable to do, and in both cases we should naturally say that he will often be unable to get what he wants to get or avoid what he wants to avoid.

Philosophers will no doubt seize on the word "want," and say that if we suppose that a man happens to want the things which an injury to his body prevents him from getting, we have slipped in a supposition about a "pro-attitude" already; and that anyone who does not happen to have these wants can still refuse to use "injury" in its prescriptive, or "action-guiding" sense. And so it may seem that the only way to make a *necessary* connexion between "injury" and the things that are to be avoided, is to say that it is used in an "action-guiding sense" only when applied to something the speaker intends to avoid. But we should look carefully at the crucial move in that argument, and query the suggestion that someone might happen not to want anything for which he would need the use of hands or eyes. Hands and eyes, like ears and legs, play a part in so many operations that a man could only be said not to need them if he had no wants at all. That such people exist, in asylums, is not to the present purpose at all; the proper use of his limbs is something a man has reason to want if he wants anything.

I do not know just what someone who denies this proposition could have in mind. Perhaps he is thinking of changing the facts of human existence, so that merely wishing, or the sound of the voice, will bring the world to heel? More likely he is proposing to rig the circumstances of some individual's existence within the framework of the ordinary world, by supposing for instance that he is a prince whose servant will sow and reap and fetch and carry for him, and so use their hands and eyes in his service that he will not need the use of his. Let us suppose that such a story could be told about a man's life; it is wildly implausible, but let us pretend that it is not. It is clear that in spite of this we could say that any man had a reason to shun injury; for even if at the end of his life it could be said that by a strange set of circumstances he had never needed the use of his eyes, or his hands, this could not possibly be foreseen. Only by once more changing the facts of human existence, and supposing every vicissitude foreseeable, could such a supposition be made.

This is not to say that an injury might not bring more incidental gain than necessary harm; one has only to think of times when the order has gone out that able-bodied men are to be put to the sword. Such a gain might even, in some peculiar circumstances, be reliably foreseen, so that a man would have even better reason for seeking than for avoiding injury. In this respect the word "injury" differs from terms such as "injustice"; the practical force of "injury" means only that anyone has *a* reason to avoid injuries, not that he has an overriding reason to do so.

It will be noticed that this account of the "action-guiding" force of "injury" links it with reasons for acting rather than with actually doing something. I do not think, however, that this makes it a less good pattern for the "action-guiding" force of moral terms. Philosophers who have supposed that actual action was required if "good" were to be used in a sincere evaluation have gone into difficulties over weakness of will, and they should surely agree that enough has been done if we can show that any mean has reason to aim at virtue and avoid vice. But is this impossibly difficult if we consider the kinds of things that count as virtue and vice? Consider, for instance, the cardinal virtues, prudence, temperance, courage and justice. Obviously any man needs prudence, but does he not also need to resist the temptation of pleasure when there is harm involved? And how could it be argued that he would never need to face what was fearful for the sake of some good? It is not obvious what someone would mean if he said that temperance or courage were not good qualities, and this not because of the "praising" sense of these *words*, but because of the things that courage and temperance are.

I should like to use these examples to show the artificiality of the notions of "commendation" and of "pro-attitudes" as these are commonly employed. Philosophers who talk about these things will say that after the facts have been accepted—say that X is the kind of man who will climb a dangerous mountain, beard an irascible employer for a rise in pay, and in general face the fearful for the sake of something he thinks worth while—there remains the question of "commendation" or "evaluation." If the word "courage" is used they will ask whether or not the man who speaks of another as having courage is supposed to have commended him. If we say "yes" they will insist that the judgement about courage *goes beyond the facts*, and might therefore be rejected by someone who refused to do so; if we say "no" they will argue that "courage" is being used in a purely descriptive or "inverted comma sense," and that we have not got an example of the evaluative use of language which is the moral philosopher's special study. What sense can be made, however, of the question "does he commend?" What is this extra element which is supposed to be present or absent after the facts have been settled? It is not a matter of liking the man who has courage, or of thinking him altogether good, but of "commending him for his courage." How are we supposed to do that? The answer that will be given is that we only commend someone else in speaking of him as courageous if we accept the imperative "let me be courageous" for ourselves. But this is quite unnecessary. I can speak of someone else as having the virtue of courage, and of course recognize it as a virtue in the proper sense, while knowing that I am a complete coward, and making no resolution to reform. I know that I should be better off if I were courageous, and so have a reason to cultivate courage but I may also know that I will do nothing of the kind.

If someone were to say that courage was not a virtue he would have to say that it was not a quality by which a man came to act well. Perhaps he would be thinking that someone might be worse off for his courage, which is true, but only because an incidental harm might arise. For instance, the courageous man might have underestimated a risk, and run into some disaster which a cowardly man would have avoided because he was not prepared to take any risk at all. And his courage, like any other virtue, could be the cause of harm to him because possessing it he fell into some disastrous state of pride.[3] Similarly, those who question the virtue of temperance are probably thinking not of

---

[3]Cp. Aquinas, *Summa Theologica*, 1–11, q. 55, Art. 4.

the virtue itself but of men whose temperance has consisted in resisting pleasure for the sake of some illusory good, or those who have made this virtue their pride.

But what, it will be asked, of justice? For while prudence, courage and temperance are qualities which benefit the man who has them, justice seems rather to benefit others, and to work to the disadvantage of the just man himself. Justice as it is treated here, as one of the cardinal virtues, covers all those things owed to other people: it is under injustice that murder, theft and lying come, as well as the withholding of what is owed for instance by parents to children and by children to parents, as well as the dealings which would be called unjust in everyday speech. So the man who avoids injustice will find himself in need of things he has returned to their owner, unable to obtain an advantage by cheating and lying; involved in all those difficulties painted by Thrasymachus in the first book of the Republic, in order to show that injustice is more profitable than justice to a man of strength and wit. We will be asked how, on our theory, justice can be a virtue and injustice a vice, since it will surely be difficult to show that any man whatsoever must need to be just as he needs the use of his hands and eyes, or needs prudence, courage and temperance?

Before answering this question I shall argue that if it cannot be answered, then justice can no longer be recommended as a virtue. The point of this is not to show that it must be answerable, since justice is a virtue, but rather to suggest that we should at least consider the possibility that justice is not a virtue. This suggestion was taken seriously by Socrates in the Republic, where it was assumed by everyone that if Thrasymachus could establish his premise—that injustice was more profitable than justice—his conclusion would follow: that a man who had the strength to get away with injustice had reason to follow this as the best way of life. It is a striking fact about modern moral philosophy that no one sees any difficulty in accepting Thrasymachus' premise and rejecting his conclusion, and it is because Nietzsche's position is at this point much closer to that of Plato that he is remote from academic moralists of the present day.

In the Republic it is assumed that if justice is not a good to the just man, moralists who recommend it as a virtue are perpetrating a fraud. Agreeing with this, I shall be asked where exactly the fraud comes in; where the untruth that justice is profitable to the individual is supposed to be told? As a preliminary answer we might ask how many people are prepared to say frankly that injustice is more profitable than justice? Leaving aside, as elsewhere in this paper, religious beliefs which might complicate the matter, we will suppose that some tough atheistical character has asked "Why should I be just?" (Those who believe that this question has something wrong with it can employ their favourite device for sieving out "evaluating meaning," and suppose that the question is "Why should I be 'just'?") Are we prepared to reply "As far as you are concerned you will be better off if you are unjust, but it matters to the rest of us that you should be just, so we are trying to get you to be just"? He would be likely to enquire into our methods, and then take care not to be found out, and I do not think that many of those who think that it is not necessary to show that justice is profitable to the just man would easily accept that there was nothing more they could say.

The crucial question is: "Can we give anyone, strong or weak, a reason why he should be just?"—and it is no help at all to say that since "just" and "unjust" are "action-guiding words" no one can even ask "Why should I be just?" Confronted with that argument the man who wants to do unjust things has only to be careful to avoid the *word*, and he has not been given a reason why he should not do the things which other people call "unjust." Probably it will be argued that he has been given a reason so far as anyone can ever be given a reason for doing or not doing anything, for the chain of reasons must always come to an end somewhere, and it may seem that one may always reject the reason which another man accepts. But this is a mistake; some answers to the question "why should I?" bring the series to a close and some do not. Hume showed how *one* answer closed the series in the following passage:

"Ask a man *why he uses exercise*; he will answer, *because he desires to keep his health.* If you then enquire, *why he desires health*, he will readily reply, *because sickness is painful.* If you push your enquiries farther, and desire a reason *why he hates pain*, it is impossible he can ever give any. This is an ultimate end, and is never referred to any other object." (*Enquiries*, Appendix I, V.) Hume might just as well have ended this series with boredom: sickness often brings boredom, and no one is required to give a reason why he does not want to be bored, any more than he has to give a reason why he does want to pursue what interests him. In general, anyone is given a reason for acting when he is shown the way to something he wants; but for some wants the question "Why do you want that?" will make sense, and for others it will not.[4] It seems clear that in this division justice falls on the opposite side from pleasure and interest and such things. "Why shouldn't I do that?" is not answered by the words "because it is unjust" as it is answered by showing that the action will bring boredom, loneliness, pain, discomfort or certain kinds of incapacity, and this is why it is not true to say that "it's unjust" gives a reason in so far as any reasons can ever be given. "It's unjust" gives a reason only if the nature of justice can be shown to be such that it is necessarily connected with what a man wants.

This shows why a great deal hangs on the question of whether justice is or is not a good to the just man, and why those who accept Thrasymachus' premise and reject his conclusion are in a dubious position. They recommend justice to each man, as something he has a reason to follow, but when challenged to show why he should do so they will not always be able to reply. This last assertion does not depend on any "selfish theory of human nature" in the philosophical sense. It is often possible to give a man a reason for acting by showing him that someone else will suffer if he does not; someone else's good may really be more to him than his own. But the affection which mothers feel for children, and lovers for each other, and friends for friends, will not take us far when we are asked for reasons why a man should be just; partly because it will not extend far enough, and partly because the actions dictated by benevolence and justice are not always the same. Suppose that I owe someone money; ". . . what if he be my enemy, and has given me just cause to hate him? What if he be a vicious man, and deserves the hatred of all mankind? What if he be a miser, and can make no use of what I would deprive him of? What if he be a profligate debauchee, and would rather receive harm than benefit from large possessions?"[5] Even if the general practice of justice could be brought under the motive of universal benevolence—the desire for the greatest happiness of the greatest number—many people certainly do not have any such desire. So that if justice is only to be recommended on these grounds a thousand tough characters will be able to say that they have been given no reason for practising justice, and many more would say the same if they were not too timid or too stupid to ask questions about the code of behaviour which they have been taught. Thus, given Thrasymachus' premise Thrasymachus' point of view is reasonable; we have no particular reason to admire those who practise justice through timidity or stupidity.

It seems to me, therefore, that if Thrasymachus' thesis is accepted things cannot go on as before; we shall have to admit that the belief on which the status of justice as a virtue was founded is mistaken, and if we still want to get people to be just we must recommend justice to them in a new way. We shall have to admit that injustice is more profitable than justice, at least for the strong, and then do our best to see that hardly anyone can get away with being unjust. We have, of course, the alternative of keeping quiet, hoping that for the most part people will follow convention into a kind of justice, and not ask awkward questions, but this policy might be overtaken by a vague scepticism even on the part of those who do not know just what is lacking; we should also be at the mercy of anyone who was able and willing to expose our fraud.

Is it true, however, to say that justice is not something a man needs in his dealings with his fellows, supposing only that he be strong? Those who think that he can get on perfectly well without being just should be asked to say exactly how such a man is supposed to live. We know that he is to practise injustice whenever the unjust act would

[4]For an excellent discussion of reasons for action, see G. E. M. Anscombe, *Intention* § 34–40.

[5]Hume, *Treatise* Book III, Part II, Sect. 1.

bring him advantage; but what is he to say? Does he admit that he does not recognize the rights of other people, or does he pretend? In the first case even those who combine with him will know that on a change of fortune, or a shift of affection, he may turn to plunder them, and he must be as wary of their treachery as they are of his. Presumably the happy unjust man is supposed, as in Book II of the Republic, to be a very cunning liar and actor, combining complete injustice with the appearance of justice: he is prepared to treat others ruthlessly, but pretends that nothing is further from his mind. Philosophers often speak as if a man could thus hide himself even from those around him, but the supposition is doubtful, and in any case the price in vigilance would be colossal. If he lets even a few people see his true attitude he must guard himself against them; if he lets no one into the secret he must always be careful in case the least spontaneity betray him. Such facts are important because the need a man has for justice in dealings with other men depends on the fact that they are men and not inanimate objects or animals. If a man only needed other men as he needs household objects, and if men could be manipulated like household objects, or beaten into a reliable submission like donkeys, the case would be different. As things are, the supposition that injustice is more profitable than justice is very dubious, although like cowardice and intemperance it might turn out incidentally to be profitable.

The reason why it seems to some people so impossibly difficult to show that justice is more profitable than injustice is that they consider in isolation particular just acts. It is perfectly true that if a man is just it follows that he will be prepared, in the event of very evil circumstances, even to face death rather than to act unjustly—for instance, in getting an innocent man convicted of a crime of which he has been accused. For him it turns out that his justice brings disaster on him, and yet like anyone else he had good reason to be a just and not an unjust man. He could not have it both ways and while possessing the virtue of justice hold himself ready to be unjust should any great advantage accrue. The man who has the virtue of justice is not ready to do certain things, and if he is too easily tempted we shall say that he was ready after all.

Study Questions

1. According to Foot, the whole of moral philosophy rests on a contrast between statements of fact and evaluations. Explain this contrast.
2. What two assumptions are made about evaluations, according to Foot?
3. Can a person feel pride about anything at all, according to Foot? Explain.
4. Can anything be counted as an injury, according to Foot? Explain.
5. Could it be an ultimate moral principle to say that a person was a good person because he clasped and unclasped his hands three times in an hour, according to Foot?
6. Why, according to Foot, has it seemed that any statement of value always seems to go beyond any statement of fact?
7. What was Thrasymachus's premise, and what was his conclusion?
8. According to Foot, does modern moral philosophy see any difficulty in accepting Thrasymachus's premise and in rejecting his conclusion? Does Foot see any difficulty in this? Explain.

Selected Recent Issues

Another naturalist position is ethical relativism, the theory that a moral fact is just simply a fact about the moral beliefs of an actual society, or—to offer a more guarded statement—the theory that moral facts ultimately are always determined by the norms and practices of actual societies. In Chapter 3, we discussed some of the difficulties involved in accepting relativism as well as the dubious logic of the idea that since values are relative, a person should be tolerant of the practices of others. Nevertheless, despite these difficulties, it's fair to say that some versions of ethical relativism are not clearly implausible. Ethical relativism has been rather widely discussed in recent years. In the next reading, Princeton philosopher Gilbert Harman puts forth a defense of one version of ethical relativism. Following that selection, we'll look at three other topics of recent interest: happiness, justice, and the question of the moral weight of numbers.

Relativism—Gilbert Harman

Since this is a difficult article, we'll provide you with a fairly detailed guide to it. The article will be much easier to understand if you keep in mind that for Harman, saying that *someone ought to do something* "means roughly" that *that person has a moral reason to do it.*

Harman begins by describing what he calls the naive view of morality, which has three provisos:

1. A nonrelativistic proviso: there are basic moral demands that everyone accepts (or at least has reason to accept)
2. A universalistic proviso: these demands are supposed to have universal application; that is, they are supposed to be binding on everyone
3. An agent-centered proviso: these demands are supposed to be the source of all moral reasons for agents to do things.

However, says Harman, there are no moral demands that everyone accepts or has reason to accept, even when the scope of "everyone" is restricted to people who are not irrational, stupid, or uninformed. In other words, the nonrelativism proviso of the naive view, proviso (1), is false.

He then goes on to discuss difficulties that the apparent falsity of (1) raises for R. M. Hare. According to Harman, Hare tries to abandon nonrelativism while attempting to retain the universality proviso; Hare tries, in other words, to abandon nonrelativism while attempting to retain the view that basic moral principles or demands are demands on everyone. Unfortunately, according to Harman, what Hare wants to do cannot be done because the falsity of nonrelativism implies the falsity of universality.

Harman then puts forth his own relativistic theory, called "morality as politics." On this theory, moral demands result from a tacit agreement among a "more or less well-defined" group of people as to what is in their own interest; consequently, there are various moralities, each postulating different basic demands. These demands are accepted by the members of a group as demands on themselves and other members of the group. Harman thinks that the fact that the members of a group agree on provisions thought to be in their own interest helps explain the utilitarian aspects of our own morality. Also, the fact that compromises are necessary among the members of the group explains why, in our morality, the duty to avoid harm to others is stronger than the duty to help those who need help. Harman then criticizes an alternative explanation of this ranking of duties, put forth by Richard L. Trammel.

Harman next explains that moral "ought" judgments are a type of "inner judgment"—judgments that are made only about those who are assumed to accept the moral demands on which the judgments are based. In other words, if Stewart judges that Moore morally ought to do something, Stewart assumes that Moore accepts the basic moral demands on which the judgment is based. However, according to Harman, not all moral judgments are inner judgments: just as you can judge that outsiders are friends or enemies, you can judge that outsiders are good or bad or evil from the point of view of your morality, even if the outsiders do not share your morality.

On Harman's relativism, a moral "ought" is not universalizable (because it applies only to those who accept the underlying morality). Nevertheless, if you judge that someone morally ought to do something, you are, at least, committed to the judgment that in similar circumstances *you* ought to do the same thing.

In the remainder of the essay, Harman contrasts his own relativism with other theories that, like his, are substitutions for naive morality or are derived from substitutions for naive morality. Included in the discussion are act utilitarianism, emotivism, a version of Kantian ethics, and rule utilitarianism. All of these, in Harman's eyes, are unrealistic as accounts of what morality requires.

Harman concludes the essay with a discussion of the implications for his theory of the fact that an individual is a member of different groups with different principles.

Relativistic Ethics: Morality as Politics

Gilbert Harman

Gilbert Harman (b. 1938) is a professor of philosophy at Princeton University. His specialities, besides ethics, include epistemology and the philosophy of language. This selection was originally published in *Midwest Studies in Philosophy* 3 (1978).

Let me begin by saying something about what I will call "the naïve view" of morality. In this view, morality involves one or more basic moral demands that everyone accepts, or has reasons to accept, as demands on everyone on which all moral reasons to do things depend. This view has three parts. First, it says that there are certain basic moral demands that everyone accepts or at least has reasons to accept; let one refer to this as the claim that morality is "nonrelative." Second, these demands are supposed to be accepted as demands on everyone; they are to have universal application. I will refer to this as the claim that morality is "universal." Third, these demands are supposed to be the source of all moral reasons for agents to do things; I will refer to this as the claim that morality is "agent centered" or, sometimes, that it "takes the point of view of an agent" rather than a critic. In the naïve view, then, morality is nonrelative, universal, and agent centered.

In this view, the basic moral demands are or ought to be accepted by *everyone*, as demands on *everyone*, providing reasons for *everyone*. Who is "everyone"? Kant included every rational being, not only human beings but also angels and rational inhabitants of other planets. A rational Martian would accept, or have reasons to accept, the basic demands of morality because, according to Kant, the basic moral demands are simply demands of rationality which follow from the nature of reason (which he took to be the same in all rational beings).

We need not be so strict, however. Some people who accept what I am calling the naïve view may not wish to commit themselves about Martians. They may see the source of moral demands in human nature, rather than in an absolutely universal reason. They may suppose, for example, that these demands derive from a natural human sympathy one feels for others or from some other presumed fact about "the human condition." They may therefore wish to restrict the range of "everyone," claiming only that every rational human being accepts or has reasons to accept the basic demands of morality. Some may even want to restrict the range of "everyone" even further to those who have been exposed to civilized morality, for they may not wish to claim that so-called ignorant savages have any reason to accept the basic demands of morality.

For my present purposes, it does not matter whether or not the range of "everyone" is restricted in one of these ways, for it seems to me highly probable that, whether or not the range of "everyone" is thus restricted, there are no substantive moral demands everyone has a reason to accept. I am inclined to believe that, for any such demand, someone might fail to accept it without being ignorant of relevant facts, without having miscalculated, without having failed to see the consequences of his or her opinions, and without being in any way irrational. You cannot always argue someone into being moral. Much depends on his or her antecedent interests and principles. If his or her principles and interests diverge sufficiently from yours, it may well happen that he or she has no reason to accept your morality.

Invaders from outer space who are unaffected by weapons we might use against them may have no reason to concern themselves with us. The fact that their actions are harmful to us may carry no weight at all with them, without their being in any way ignorant or irrational. Certain successful criminals seem to have no reason to be at all concerned about their victims; they simply do not care, seemingly without being irrational or ignorant in not caring. Cynical politicians who are interested only in acquiring and maintaining power will lie to the public without necessarily being uninformed, irrational, or stupid. In each of these cases someone would seem not to have reasons to accept moral demands most of us take to be important. Many other cases might also be cited, cases of commonplace amorality, other cases in which someone accepts a morality radically different from ours, and so forth.

Such cases obviously poses a problem for the naïve view. Various responses are possible. Consider for example R. M. Hare's theory. Recall that, in the naïve view, morality involves one or more basic demands that everyone accepts or ought to accept as demands on everyone on which all moral reasons to do things depend; morality is, in other words, nonrelative, universal, and agent centered. Hare is attracted to this naïve position but, like many people today, he also believes that there are no substantive moral demands that everyone has a reason to accept. His response is to abandon nonrelativism, while attempting to retain universality and the point of view of the agent. In his view, then, each person accepts certain basic demands as demands on everyone on which all moral reasons to do things depend, but the demands in question may vary from one person to another.

This means that Hare takes himself to accept certain moral demands as demands on everyone even though he also agrees that some people have no reason at all to act in accordance with those demands; but that is puzzling. To accept a demand as a moral demand on George, among others, would seem to involve the thought that George ought to act in accordance with that demand—that there are moral reasons for him to do so. How then can Hare also suppose that George may, after all, have no reasons to act in accordance with that demand?

The answer is that, in Hare's view, one can accept a moral demand as a demand on everyone without supposing that everyone now has a reason to act in accordance with that demand. It is enough if one intends to try to get everyone else to accept that demand as a demand on him or herself.

There are, however, two things wrong with this. First, it does not provide a reasonable interpretation of universality. Hare is only pretending to accept certain demands as demands on everyone. Rather, he accepts them merely as demands on himself that he intends to try to get everyone else to accept. Second, the intention to try to get everyone else to accept a given demand is itself quite unusual. Few people ever have intentions of this sort. So it is unlikely that many people would ever accept moral demands in the way that Hare's theory says they should.

A related difficulty arises for Hare's analysis of the moral *ought*. In Hare's view, *George ought not to eat meat* is roughly equivalent to *George's not eating meat is in accordance with the general imperatives I hereby accept.* This allows a vegetarian to judge that George ought not to eat meat even if the vegetarian also believes that George (who is not a vegetarian) has no reason not to eat meat. But this is surely to misuse the moral *ought*, which is normally used to speak of things an agent has moral reasons to do.

Indeed, in each of its uses, the word *ought* is used to speak of things for which someone has reasons. The epistemic *ought*, for example, is used to speak of things that there are reasons to expect, as when we say that the train ought to be here soon. The evaluative *ought* is used to speak of what there are reasons to hope or wish for or take some other positive attitude towards, as when we say that there ought to be more love in the world or that a knife ought to be sharp. The simple *ought* of rationality is used to speak of something for which an agent has reasons of any sort to do, as when we say that a burglar ought to wear gloves. And the moral *ought* is used to speak of things an agent has moral reasons to do, as when we say that a burglar ought to reform and go straight.

In elaborating this connection between the moral *ought* and talk of reasons, I do not mean that the fact that an agent morally ought to do something is itself a moral reason to do it. That would be open to the objection that such a fact gives an agent a reason to do something only if he or she has some reason to care about what he or she ought morally to do. Actually, the issue here is whether the fact that an agent has a reason to do something is itself a reason for him or her to do that thing. Similarly, we can easily imagine a dispute as to whether the fact that the train ought to be here soon is a reason to expect the train to be here soon, which is to dispute whether the fact that there is a reason to expect the train to be here soon is itself a reason to expect the train to be here soon. This sort of technical issue is, however, not directly relevant to our present concerns, and I will not try to resolve it.

Hare's problems result from his attempt to retain universality and the point of view of the agent while abandoning nonrelativism. Given the point of view of the agent, for any substantive moral demand D, there will be the following argument against the universality of D.

1. There is someone S who fails to adhere to D without being in any relevant way irrational, stupid, or uninformed.

So, 2. S has no reason to adhere to D.

So, 3. it is not true that S ought morally to adhere to D.

We have been discussing the move from (2), "S has no reason," to (3), "it is not true that S ought." To reject this step of the argument is, I think, to distort the meaning of the moral *ought.* Similarly, to reject the step from (1), "S can fail to adhere to D without being irrational, etc.," to (2), "S has no reason to adhere to D," is to break the connection between reasons and rationality, in my view thereby draining the term *reason* of its ordinary meaning.

Here it might be objected that, despite the truth of (1), S does have a reason to adhere to D, namely the fact that he or she ought morally to do so. But, first, as we have seen, it is obscure whether such a fact itself gives S a reason to adhere to D. And, anyway, it more than begs the question to assume that this is a fact, since the argument shows that it is not. To suppose that it is a fact that S ought morally to adhere to D is simply to suppose that S has a reason to adhere to D, but S has no such reason if he or she can fail to adhere to D without being in any way irrational, stupid, or uninformed.

A related objection to the argument (1)—(3) is that (2), "S has no reason to adhere to D," is ambiguous. According to this objection, *reason for* S *to adhere to* D might mean either *motivating reason for* S *to adhere to* D or *reason for* S *to think he or she ought to adhere to* D. The objection maintains that (2) follows from (1) only if *reason* means motivating reason, whereas (3) follows from (2) only if *reason* means reason for thinking one ought. Therefore, according to this objection, the argument depends upon an equivocation.[1]

But in fact the term *reason* is not ambiguous in this way and there is no equivocation in the argument.[2] *Reason for* S *to adhere to* D never means either *motivating reason or reason for* S *to think he or she ought to adhere to* D. The second interpretation gets things backwards, since S *ought to adhere to* D means roughly that S has a reason to adhere to D. A reason for S to think he or she ought to adhere to D is not directly a reason for S to adhere to D but only a reason for S to think he or she has a reason to adhere to D. The question whether this is indirectly a reason for S to adhere to D is the same obscure technical issue previously mentioned as not directly to the point. On the other hand, *reason for* S *to adhere to* D cannot ever mean *motivating reason,* since it is always consistent to suppose that such a reason is not a motivating reason because S is unaware of it, or is aware of it but is acting irrationally, and so on. So this objection is simply mistaken.

A different objection distinguishes S's having reasons to do D from there being reasons for S to do D. According to this objection, for it to be true that S ought to do D, it is enough that there be reasons for S to do D. It is not required that S actually have those reasons to do D. (S might be quite unaware of the reasons.) So (3), "It is not true that S ought," does not follow from (2), "S has no reason," according to this objection.

This raises a complex issue. For one thing, we must note an ambiguity in the remark that there are reasons for S to do D. This might refer to reasons for doing D that S has or would have if for example he or she was aware of them. It might also refer to reasons for our hoping or wanting S to do D. In this second sense, "there are reasons for S to do D" is clearly not equivalent to "S ought morally to do D" and is equivalent only to "S ought to do D" meaning "it ought to be the case that S does D." So only the first interpretation of "there are reasons for S to do D" is relevant to our present concerns.

Now, the distinction between there being reasons for S to do D, in this sense, and S's having reasons to do D is a subtle and difficult one. I am not exactly sure what the distinction rests on. It is not simply a question of whether S is aware of the reasons, since S may have a reason of which he or she is unaware. The distinction seems to have something to do with how easy it would be for S to become aware of relevant facts or do the relevant reasoning, etc. Perhaps, if this is relatively easy, we say S has reasons and, if it is less easy, we say only that there are reasons for S. I am not sure. In any event, the distinctions is obviously not crucial in the context of the argument (1)–(3), since in the first premise (1) we suppose that S is *fully informed*, etc. In this context, then, to speak of the reasons there are for S to do D is to speak of the reasons S has to do D. If S has no reasons to do D, then in the relevant sense there are no reasons for S to do D. So, one cannot escape the argument (1)–(3) by distinguishing reasons for S to do D from reasons S has to do D.

Let me consider one other objection. According to this objection, there are things S ought to care about whether or not he or she actually does care. For example, S ought to care about the welfare of other people, even if in fact S does not care. If S did care about others, that would give S a reason to treat others in certain ways. Since S does not care, S fails to have this reason to treat others in that way. But, S ought to treat others in that way, since S ought to care about their welfare, according to this objection. So, according to the objection, it can be true that S ought to do D even if S has no reason to do D.

This objection confuses different senses of *ought*. If S ought to care about the welfare of others in the sense that he or she has reasons to care, then these reasons are also reasons for S to act in the appropriate way towards others. But, if S ought to care only in the sense that it ought to be the case that S cared, in other words that it would be a good thing if S cared, all the follows is that S ought to act in the appropriate way in the sense: it ought to be the case that S acted in that way. It does not follow that S ought morally to act in that way. So this last objection fails too.

Since these objections do not go through, it seems that the argument (1)–(3) does show that, if nonrelativism is denied, universality must also be denied, given the point of view of the agent.

Now, there do not seem to be any very persuasive direct arguments in favor of nonrelativism. Someone might claim that it is part of the meaning of *rational*, as this term is ordinarily used, that someone is correctly called rational only if he or she accepts certain basic moral demands. But that seems clearly false as a piece of empirical linguistics. There is also Thomas Nagel's ingenious argument in *The Possibility of Altruism*, which seeks to show how the failure to accept certain moral demands involves a failure to appreciate the objective nature of reasons, a failure that amounts to "practical solipsism." But Nagel does not show that any mistake or irrationality is involved in not taking reasons to be objective, in his sense; he does not show that people have reasons to avoid "practical solipsism." So, he does not show that everyone has reasons to accept the relevant moral demands.

There is, however, a more promising indirect argument in favor of nonrelativism. For morality as it is ordinarily conceived does seem to involve universality; it presupposes that basic moral demands are demands on everyone. But we have seen in (1)–(3) that relativism implies the falsity of universality, given the point of view of the agent. Or, putting this the other way, from that point of view, universality implies nonrelativism. So, assuming the truth of universality, (1)–(3) can be used in reverse to argue for nonrelativism.

Rather, we should say this: Two plausible ideas are in conflict, relativism and universality. It is difficult to believe in nonrelativism, because it is difficult to believe that there are substantive moral demands that everyone has reasons to accept. But, if relativism is true, then universality is false, and that is hard to believe, because it is hard to believe that basic moral principles do not apply to everyone.

More precisely, if relativism is true, as seems likely, the ordinary notion of morality is based on a false presupposition and we find ourselves in the position of those who thought morality was the law of God and then began to suspect there was no God. Relativism implies that morality as we ordinarily understand it is a delusion, a vain and chimerical notion.

Fortunately, there is a reasonable substitute. We can have relativism and a good approximation of morality as it is ordinarily conceived if we modify the naïve view by relativising the range of "everyone" throughout to those who accept or have reasons to accept certain basic moral demands. In this relativistic view, there are various moralities, each involving different basic demands, demands which certain people accept or have reasons to accept as demands on those people—in other words on those people who accept or have reasons to accept those demands—demands on which depend all reasons arising from that morality for those people to do things.

This is a natural view of morality to take if one supposes that morality rests on a tacit agreement or convention among a group of people. Other things being equal, the existence of an agreement or convention gives someone a reason to act in accordance with it only if he or she accepts the agreement or has reasons to do so. Furthermore, the hypothesis that moral demands derive from conventions arrived at through implicit bargaining and mutual adjustment helps to account for the content of actual moralities. The fact that participants aim at provisions that are in their own interests helps to explain the rough utilitarian character of our own morality. The fact that compromises are necessary among people of different powers and resources accounts for the fact that the duty to avoid harm to others is much stronger in our morality than is the duty to help those who need help, even though these duties should have the same strength from a purely utilitarian point of view. Since everyone would benefit equally from a duty not to harm others, whereas the poor and weak would benefit much more from a duty of mutual aid than the rich and powerful would, the expected compromise is a fairly strong prohibition against harm and a weaker duty of mutual aid, which is what we have in our morality.[3] It is difficult to see how else the distinction we make might be explained.

Consider, for example, the suggestion made by Richard L. Trammel,[4] who argues that three factors are relevant.

1. You can avoid harming anyone but you cannot help all who would benefit from your help, since there are too many for you to help them all.
2. If you harm someone, that person is necessarily harmed; but, if you fail to help someone who needs help, that person is not necessarily unhelped, since someone else may help.
3. If you harm someone, you are necessarily responsible for that person's plight; but, if you fail to help someone who needs help, you are not necessarily responsible for that person's plight.

These three factors are real enough, but they fail to explain the moral distinction in question. For (1) and (3) presuppose that very distinction and (2) is a purely verbal point.

Let us begin with

(2) If you harm someone, that person is necessarily harmed; but, if you fail to help someone who needs help, that person is not necessarily unhelped, since someone else may help.

In order to see that this is a purely verbal point, it is sufficient to observe that, if you act so that a particular person will be harmed unless someone else intervenes to save that person, that person is not necessarily harmed, since someone else may intervene; on the other hand, if you fail to help a person needing help whom no one else is going to help, that person is necessarily unhelped. Now, almost any case in which someone violates the duty not to harm someone can be described either as a case of harming someone or as a case of acting in such a way that the person in question will be harmed unless someone intervenes to save that person. Given the one description, the person is necessarily harmed; given the other description of the same act, the person is not necessarily harmed. Similarly, almost any case in which someone violates what we take to be the weaker duty to help someone can be described either as a case of failing to help someone needing help or as a case of failing to help someone needing help whom no one else is going to help. Given the one description, the person is not necessarily unhelped; given the other description of the same act, the person is necessarily unhelped. We do not suppose, however, that the strength of these duties depends on how cases falling under them are described.

Let us now consider Trammel's

(1) You can avoid harming anyone but you cannot help all who would benefit from your help, since there are too many for you to help them all.

To see that this presupposes that we distinguish harming and not helping as we now do, consider what would be true in a society in which people were as strongly motivated morally to help each other as not to harm each other. Such a society would be much more egalitarian and altruistic than ours. There would not be the vast numbers of people needing help in such a society as there are in our society, because the members of the imagined society would be quick to provide help whenever they perceived a need for it. Therefore, (1) would no longer be true. In such a society you could help all who would benefit from your help to the same extent that you could avoid harming anyone. (1) is true of our society only because our recognition of a moral distinction between harming and not helping is responsible for there being vast numbers of people who need help who do not get it.

Let us turn now to Trammel's

(3) If you harm someone, you are necessarily responsible for that person's plight; but, if you fail to help someone who needs help, you are not necessarily responsible for that person's plight.

This is true of our society only because what someone is responsible for depends in part on that person's duties and obligations. In a more egalitarian and altruistic society, which did not recognize a moral distinction between harming and not helping, you would be considered responsible for a person's plight if you failed to give the person help when it was needed.

Trammel's account of our intuitive distinction is therefore no real alternative to a tacit agreement theory which explains the intuitive distinction as arising as a result of a compromise between people of varying powers and resources.

In my view, then, moral argument can involve not only argument over the consequences of basic demands but also bargaining over the basic demands themselves. Morality is therefore continuous with politics. Furthermore, a person may belong to a number of different groups with different moralities which may sometimes have conflicting implications. When that happens, a person must decide which side he or she is on.

As in Hare's analysis, a moral *ought* judgment will be made in relation to moral demands accepted by the person making the judgment. But, since such a judgment says that a certain agent has reasons to do something, the judgment presupposes that the agent also accepts the relevant moral demands or at least has reasons to accept them. *George morally ought not to eat meat* means, roughly, that George's not eating meat is in accordance with the moral demands that "we" accept, where "we" includes the speaker, George, and the intended audience, if any.

Moral *ought* judgments are therefore a species of what I call "inner judgments." Inner judgments are made only about those who are assumed to accept (or have reasons to accept) the moral demands on which the judgments are based. Inner moral judgments include not only moral *ought* judgments but also any other moral judgments that attribute moral reasons to someone—for example, the judgment that it was morally wrong of someone to have done a certain thing.

Although all moral judgments are, in this view, relative judgments made in relation to certain moral demands, not all moral judgments are inner judgments in this sense. One can judge that certain outsiders are good or bad or evil from the point of view of one's morality even if they do not share that morality, just as one can judge that outsiders are friends or enemies. Similarly, one can judge that certain situations are good or bad or right or wrong or that they ought or ought not to be the case, even if these situations involve agents that do not participate in the morality relative to which the judgment is made.

It is important to distinguish the moral *ought*, which is used to make inner moral judgments about agents, from the evaluative *ought*, which is used to make non-inner judgments about situations. The sentence *George ought not to eat meat* is ambiguous. It may be used to express an inner moral judgment of George, which presupposes that he accepts or has reasons to accept the relevant moral demands. It may also be used to express a favorable evaluation of the possible state of affairs in which George does not eat meat, an evaluation which does not imply or assume that George himself has any reason to avoid meat but implies only that we, with our standards, have a reason to hope or wish that George will not eat meat (and therefore perhaps a reason to try to bring it about that George does not eat meat). The first interpretation, as an inner judgment, is more natural if we say *George ought morally not to eat meat.* The second interpretation, as a non-inner evaluation, is more natural if we say *meat ought not to be eaten by George* or *it ought not to be the case that George eats meat.*[5]

Now, philosophers commonly say that moral *ought* judgments are "universalizable," by which they mean in part this:

> If you judge of someone that he or she ought morally to do a particular thing, then you are committed to the further judgment that anyone else in similar circumstances ought morally to do the same thing.

This does not hold in the relativistic conception of morality I have been describing, however, since a moral *ought* judgment about someone who accepts or has reasons to accept the relevant moral demands has no implications about anyone who neither accepts nor has reasons to accept those demands. A useful special case does hold, however:

> If you judge of someone that he or she ought morally to do a particular thing, then you are committed to the further judgment that in similar circumstances you ought to do the same thing.

This means, in particular, that you cannot complain about him or her unless you agree that if the situation were reversed, you ought not to act as he or she is acting.

Moral *ought* judgments are also often said to be universalizable in another respect, which is supposed to rule out arbitrary discrimination:

> If you ought to treat someone in a particular way, you ought to treat any other person in the same way unless there is a morally relevant difference between them.

This principle can be counted trivially true, since any difference in the way you ought morally to treat people can be counted as a "morally relevant" difference. Still, the spirit of the principle can be violated in a relativistic conception of morality if the distinction between "us" and "them" is taken to be "morally relevant." In fact, many moralities afford less protection for outsiders than for the primary members of the group, without basing this distinction on any further ground. A morality is, of course, not forced to discriminate in the particular way, but I suspect that almost every morality does so at least to some extent.

Of course, a morality may rest on a tacit convention or agreement without participants realizing it. Participants may in fact accept the naïve view, with its presupposition of nonrelativism. I do not wish to say that the relativistic theory I have been describing, morality as politics, captures everyone's conception of morality. I am inclined to believe, rather, that morality as conceived by the naïve view does not exist, that the moralities that do exist are based on convention or tacit agreement, and that morality as politics is an acceptable substitute for the naïve conception and indeed that it is the most acceptable substitute for that conception of morality.

Notice that in this conception of morality, which I am calling morality as politics, a morality is basically a group affair, depending on moral demands jointly accepted by several people after a certain amount of tacit bargaining and adjustment. We might allow also for a purely personal morality in which someone places demands only upon him or herself. But this is a special and limiting case.

There are other possible substitutes for naïve morality which take a morality to be essentially an individual personal matter, depending only on the moral demands accepted by a single person. These conceptions tend to be extremely agent centered, as in one form of existentialism, or extremely critic centered, as in R. M. Hare's theory and in one version of emotivism. In an extremely agent centered conception of morality, someone accepts moral demands only as demands on him or herself. He or she is therefore able to judge his or her own actions morally but not those of anyone else. In an extremely critic centered conception, like Hare's, someone accepts certain demands as demands that can be used in morally judging anyone's actions, including those who have no reasons to act in accordance with those demands. The same is true of that version of emotivism which takes moral *ought* judgments merely to express one's favorable approval of someone's doing something—obviously one can be in favor of someone's doing a particular thing without supposing that he or she has any reasons to do it. Such a conception of morality is best thought of as abandoning the moral *ought to do,* used to speak of an agent's reasons, in favor of the evaluative *ought to be,* used to evaluate possible states of affairs.

Now it matters a great deal in practice which substitute for naïve morality is adopted. The acceptance of an extremely agent centered conception of morality makes moral discourse among different people virtually impossible. The acceptance of an extremely critic centered conception, on the other hand, tends to lead to the acceptance of unrealistic normative theories like one or another version of utilitarianism or hypothetical contract theory.

Consider act utilitarianism, which says that everyone ought always to do whatever promises to have the best consequences; in other words, everyone ought always to act so as to maximize utility. This view has many implausible consequences. It would have you break your solemn promise whenever that would have better consequences than keeping your promise would. It forbids you to favor friends and relatives over perfect strangers in distributing the benefits of your actions. It implies that almost everything you do is morally wrong, since there is almost always an alternative action open to you that promises to have better consequences. It treats your failure to help someone as morally equivalent to actually harming someone.

One objection to act utilitarianism is that it has such implausible consequences. Another more revealing objection is that people are not only motivated to maximize utility but also have other motives which they take to be morally respectable, in some cases even morally required, without being irrational, stupid, or uninformed. Act utilitarianism is therefore quite unrealistic as a theory about the moral reasons people actually have, which means that it is unrealistic as an account of what people ought morally, to do. This lack of realism arises, I suggest, from a failure to distinguish the moral *ought to do* from the evaluative *ought to be.* Act utilitarianism makes sense as an account of what ought to be the case. Act utilitarianism makes no sense as an account of what people ought morally to do. It ought to be the case that any given person always acted so as to maximize expected utility; that would be wonderful! But it does not follow that each person has moral reasons only to maximize expected utility and nothing else.

Now, an extremely critic centered theory, like emotivism, can make an unrealistic moral theory like act utilitarianism seem quite plausible. For, it may well be that, as critics, we would always be in favor of a person's maximizing expected utility. This does not mean, however, that we suppose that a person always has moral reasons only to maximize utility.

Similar remarks apply to other versions of utilitarianism. Ideal rule utilitarianism, for example, says that you should always follow the best rules, namely the rules it would maximize utility for everyone to follow. Philosophers disagree as to whether this version has some plausible implications concerning what people ought to do than act utilitarianism does. But that disagreement is unimportant, since it is anyway obvious that no one has any reason to act as ideal rule utilitarianism recommends. To follow the best rules because it would maximize utility for everyone to follow them is to overlook the fact that other people will not in fact follow those rules. This is the fallacy of pacifism. Pacifism is the view that one should never use force against other people even to defend oneself against a direct attack, since (a) the world would be a much better place if no one ever used force against others and (b), if no one ever used force against other people, there would be no need to use force to defend oneself against a direct attack by someone else, since no such attack would ever occur. This is, however, to overlook the obvious point that in the real world people do sometimes attack other people and, in such a case, the person attacked often has a reason to use force to repel that attack. Ideal rule utilitarianism, which allows this sort of argument for pacificism confuses how one should act in an ideal world in which everyone followed the best rules with how one should act in the actual world in which people do not follow those rules.

There is a similar lack of realism in Kant's suggestion that you ought always to act as if you were a member of a kingdom of ends in which everyone always did the right thing. For the fact that people often do not do the right thing is something that you cannot ignore in deciding what you ought morally to do. The same point applies to hypothetical contract theories that say one ought to act in accordance with the rule that would be accepted under certain ideal conditions rather than the rules that have actually been accepted in the real world.

Like act utilitarianism, ideal rule utilitarianism is quite unrealistic as an account of what people ought morally to do—that is, as an account of what they have moral reasons to do—and is more plausible instead as an account of something that would be desirable—that is, as an account of what ought to be the case. No doubt, it would be wonderful if everyone always acted on the best set of rules—perhaps, it ought to be the case that everyone so acted. It does not follow that anyone now has any reason to act in that way.

Ideal rule utilitarianism, like act utilitarianism, is critic centered rather than agent centered, although there is a difference in what is being judged in the two cases. Whereas a simple form of emotivism can make act utilitarianism look plausible, Hare's theory, with its Kantian overtones, can make ideal rule utilitarianism look plausible. In the first view, what is taken to be relevant is one's attitude toward a particular agent's doing something given the actual circumstances of the case. In Hare's view, what is relevant is one's attitude toward universal adherence to one or another set of principles.

Philosophers have sometimes argued that act utilitarianism and ideal rule utilitarianism must coincide—that they are "extensionally equivalent." The point is that, if everyone were to follow the best set of rules, each person would presumably also always be acting so as to maximize expected utility. What that shows, however, is that act utilitarianism and ideal rule utilitarianism would be "extensionally equivalent" in an ideal world in which everyone acted on the best set of rules. It does not show that these views are "extensionally equivalent" in the actual world—and clearly they are not, since ideal rule utilitarianism recommends total pacifism, even in the real world, whereas act utilitarianism recommends against total pacificism in the real world on the grounds that there are times when using force has better consequences than not using it.

Other versions of utilitarianism can be mentioned. Actual rule utilitarianism says that a person ought to follow the actual rules accepted by the members of his or her group and that these rules are themselves to be assessed on utilitarian grounds. As an account of what people ought morally to do, this seems more realistic but not completely right, since you should sometimes not follow the rules everyone else follows. This suggests a variant of actual rule utilitarianism: a person ought to follow those actual rules which are justified on utilitarian grounds. This leaves a number of questions. What is it for a rule to be justified on utilitarian grounds? Different views are possible. It might be required that the rule have the best possible consequences or it ought be required only that its consequences be better than those of having no rule at all. What if the relevant actual rule fails this test? What should you do then? Again there is a range of options. You might be left free to do what you want. Or you might be required in this case to maximize expected utility. Or you might be required to act on the best rule, from a utilitarian point of view.

We might try to put various pieces together so as to obtain, almost by brute force, the utilitarian theory with the most plausible implications for what one ought morally to do. But this would hardly be an illuminating exercise. The complications in such a theory make it difficult to see what implications the theory really has concerning what people ought morally to do, so it is likely that the most that could really be said for such a theory would be that there were no clear counterexamples to it. Furthermore, the theory would almost certainly fail to say why anyone would have reasons to act in the way it said they had reasons to act.

Consider by contrast how easily the conception I have been calling morality as politics can account for utilitarian aspects of the moral reasons people actually have. As we have already noted, if a morality is based on a tacit agreement, it is to be expected that the rules of such a morality will be of some benefit to the people involved. Why else would they accept those rules? This, of course, does not mean that the rules actually accepted are ideal from a utilitarian point of view or even that all the rules accepted really do have good consequences.

Compare morality as politics with actual rule utilitarianism. Both say that moral reasons derive from actual rules or principles. But there are important differences. A number of difficulties facing actual rule utilitarianism are easily resolved in the conception of morality as politics. Actual rule utilitarianism says that you should follow the actual rules — the rules that people actually follow. But which people? Different people follow different rules. Which rules should you follow? It might be said that you should follow the principles of your society — not those of some other society. But what makes a society *your* society? Won't it turn out that there are a number of different groups to which you belong, with different principles? Should you adhere to all of these principles? What if they conflict? What rules do you follow then? And, anyway, why should you follow certain rules simply because other people do?

According to the conception of morality as politics, the principles that give you moral reasons to do things are the moral principles that you actually accept. You accept them as principles accepted by the members of some more or less well defined group. What makes a society your society is not, say, the proximity of its other members but rather that you accept the principles of that society as principles for you and other members of that society. You are indeed, in the relevant sense, a member of different groups with different principles: your family, friends, neighbors, colleagues at work, and so on. Since you accept all of the principles of all of these groups, all of the principles give you reasons to do things. This not to say that once you accept certain principles you must blindly adhere to them ever after. Your acceptance of certain principles can give you reasons to give up or modify other principles you accept. Your other goals and interests can have the same effect.

The principles you accept may conflict — in that case there is typically no easy answer as to what you ought to do; you will have to choose — reasoning somewhat as in any other case in which prior goals, intentions, or principles conflict, making a minimal change in your antecedent principles, etc., that will promote the coherence of your resulting overall view. What reason do you have to follow the relevant principles? You accept them; and your acceptance of them gives you reason to follow them. What reasons did you have to accept the principles in the first place? Reasons of various sorts, for example reasons of self interest: for, if you accept certain principles as governing your dealings with others, they will tend to accept the principles as governing their dealings with you. And, as previously mentioned, once you accept certain moral principles, that may give you reasons to accept other principles.

I conclude that morality as politics provides the most reasonable substitute for the naïve conception of morality. Recall that in what I am calling the naïve view morality is based on certain moral demands that everyone accepts, or at least has reasons to accept, as demands on everyone and on which all moral reasons depend. Although this seems to capture essential aspects of many people's conception of morality, I have suggested that it must almost certainly be rejected on the grounds that there are no substantive moral demands satisfying those conditions. Morality as politics retains much of the content of the naïve view but relativizes the references to "everyone" to the members of one or another group, all of whom accept certain moral demands as demands on themselves and other members of the group. I have argued that other conceptions of morality retain less of the content of the naïve view and tend toward unrealistic accounts of what morality requires. Extremely agent centered theories, as in certain forms of existentialism, practically abandon morality as a social enterprise. This is also though less obviously true of extremely critic centered theories, like certain forms of emotivism and like Hare's theory, which are best seen as rejecting the moral *ought* in favor of the *ought* of evaluation. This is, I have suggested, why these theories can make some very unrealistic accounts of what morality requires seem plausible, such as one or another form of utilitarianism.

Footnotes

1. W. K. Frankena, "Obligation and Motivation in Recent Moral Philosophy," *Essays in Moral Philosophy*, ed. A. I. Molden (Seattle, 1958), p. 43. Robert L. Holmes, "Is Morality a System of Hypothetical Imperatives?" *Analysis* 34 (1973–74): 98.
2. Philippa Foot, "'Is Morality a System of Hypothetical Imperatives?' A Reply to Mr. Holmes," *Analysis* 35 (1974–75): 53–56.
3. Gilbert Harman, "Moral Relativism Defended," *Philosophical Review* 84 (1975): 3–22. (I should note that in the present paper I am using the term "relativism" differently from the way I used it in "Moral Relativism Defended." There I used it to mean that certain moral judgments are "inner judgments" in a sense to be explained below.)
4. Richard L. Trammel, "Saving Life and Taking Life," *Journal of Philosophy* 72 (1975): 131–37.
5. See, I. L. Humberstone, "Two Sorts of 'Ought's,'" *Analysis* 32 (1971–72): 8–11.

Study Questions

1. Explain in your own words the three provisos of what Harman calls the naive view of morality.
2. Why does Harman reject the nonrelativism proviso?
3. According to Harman, could you accept the universalism proviso while rejecting the nonrelativism proviso? Explain.
4. Could you argue for nonrelativism on the grounds that someone is correctly called rational only if he or she accepts certain basic moral demands, according to Harman? Explain.
5. According to Harman, what does morality rest on? Can there be different moralities, each postulating different moral demands?
6. What does "George morally ought not to eat meat" mean, according to Harman? What does it mean according to Hare, in Harman's opinion?
7. Explain what Harman means when he calls a moral judgment an inner judgment. Are all moral judgments inner judgments, in his view?
8. In what sense, according to Harman, are moral judgments universalizable?
9. Could a moral theory whose moral reasons were different from the reasons people actually have be an acceptable account of what people ought morally to do, according to Harman? Explain.
10. Explain why Harman thinks that act-utilitarianism is unrealistic as a theory about the moral reasons people actually have.
11. Explain the fallacy of pacifism.
12. What is Harman's principal criticism of ideal rule-utilitarianism and Kantian ethics? Hint: They both rest on the same confusion.
13. On Harman's conception of morality, which principles are the ones that give you reasons to do things?

Happiness—Robert Nozick

As we pointed out in Chapter 4, the question of the nature of human well-being has attracted the attention of moral philosophers since before Socrates. Many philosophers, and many nonphilosophers too, have believed that human well-being consists entirely of happiness. Indeed, it may seem an obvious truism that the good life is the happy life and that the only issue we need to resolve is how we are to conceive of or define happiness. Consequently, throughout the history of Western ethics, moral philosophers have set forth various theories of the nature of happiness.

But is happiness the sole ingredient of the good life? The question has received some attention in the recent literature. The next article, by Robert Nozick of Harvard, answers the question in the negative. Nozick, who we discussed in Chapter 4, begins by noting that even if happiness were the only thing we cared about, we would not care solely about its total amount but would also care about how it was distributed within a lifetime, most of us preferring a life of increasing happiness. Indeed, Nozick says, most of us would be willing to give up some amount of happiness to achieve this objective. Further, he points out, a life that is filled with happiness but is otherwise empty is not one most people would desire.

At this point, Nozick considers pleasure, a feeling that is desired because of its own felt qualities. He notes that we care about things "in addition to how our lives *feel* to us from the inside." He then proposes a "thought experiment." Imagine, he says, an "experience machine" that you could connect up with and obtain any sequence of experiences you want for the rest of your life. Imagine further that once you are hooked up, you would not remember that the experiences are machine-produced and do not result from real-life events. Would you hook up for the rest of your life? Few people would, Nozick suspects. Most of us care more than just how things feel to us from the inside: what we value is an actual connection with reality, the ability to explore and alter it.

But, what, exactly, is the proper role of happiness, and what, exactly, is it? Nozick next considers types of "happiness emotions," especially (1) the feeling that our life is good now, and (2) being satisfied with our life as a whole. If we have the last kind of happiness, he notes, we want it to be *fitting*— that is, not based on a false evaluation: we want our life to have been a good one. The next question, therefore, is what makes a life a good life? Nozick notes that to answer "the presence of happiness" doesn't clarify anything: What we want to know is what to be happy *about.* In short, the desire for happiness, when understood properly, presupposes that things other than happiness are of value. What we want, he says, "is a life and a self that happiness is a fitting response to — and then to give it that response."

Happiness

Robert Nozick

Robert Nozick is Professor of Philosophy at Harvard University and the author of a number of works dealing with central problems of philosophy. The following selection is from Nozick's book *The Examined Life: Philosophical Meditations* (New York: Simon and Schuster, 1989).

Some theorists have claimed that happiness is the *only* important thing about life; all that should matter to a person—they say—is being happy; the sole standard for assessing a life is the amount or quantity of happiness it contains. It is ironic that making this exclusive claim for happiness distorts the flavor of what happy moments are like. For in these moments, almost everything seems wonderful: the way the sun shines, the way that person looks, the way water glistens on the river, the way the dogs play (yet not the way the murderer kills). This openness of happiness, its generosity of spirit and width of appreciation, gets warped and constricted by the claim—pretending to be its greatest friend—that only happiness matters, nothing else. That claim is begrudging, unlike happiness itself. Happiness can be precious, perhaps even preeminent, yet still be one important thing among others.

There are various ways to nibble away at the apparent obviousness of the view that happiness is the one thing that is important. First, even if happiness were the only thing we cared about, we would not care solely about its total amount. (When I use "we" in this way, I am inviting you to examine whether or not you agree. If you do, then I am elaborating and exploring our common view, but if after reflecting on the matter you find you do not agree, then I am traveling alone for a while.) We would care also about how that happiness was distributed within a lifetime. Imagine graphing someone's total happiness through life; the amount of happiness is represented on the vertical axis, time on the horizontal one. (If the phenomenon of happiness is extremely complicated and multidimensional, it is implausible that its amount could be graphed in this way—but in that case too the purported goal of maximizing our happiness becomes unclear.) If only the total amount of happiness mattered, we would be indifferent between a life of constantly increasing happiness and one of constant decrease, between an upward- and a downward-sloping curve, provided that the total amount of happiness, the total area under the curve, was the same in the two cases. Most of us, however, would prefer the upward-sloping line to the downward; we would prefer a life of increasing happiness to one of decrease. Part of the reason, but only a part, may be that since it makes us happy to look forward to greater happiness, doing so makes our current happiness score even higher. (Yet the person on the downward sloping curve alternatively can have the current Proustian pleasure of remembering past happiness.) Take the pleasure of anticipation into account, though, by building it into the curve whose height is therefore increased at certain places; still most of us would not care merely about the area under *this* enhanced curve, but about the curve's direction also. (Which life would you prefer your children to have, one of decline or of advance?)

We would be willing, moreover, to give up some amount of happiness to get our lives' narratives moving in the right direction, improving in general. Even if a downwardly sloping curve had slightly more area under it, we would prefer our own lives to slope upward. (If it encompassed vastly greater area, the choice might be different.) Therefore, the contour of the happiness has an independent weight, beyond breaking ties among lives whose total amounts of happiness are equal. In order to gain a more desirable narrative direction, we sometimes would choose *not* to maximize our total happiness. And if the factor of narrative direction might justify forgoing some amount of happiness, so other factors might also.*

Straight lines are not the only narrative curves. It would be silly, though, to try to pick the best happiness curve; diverse biographies can fit the very same curve, and we care also about the particular content of a life story. That thing we really want to slope upward might be our life's narrative story, not its amount of happiness. With these stories held constant, we might then care only about happiness's amount, not its slope. However, this too would support the general point that something matters—an upward slope, whether to the narrative line or to the happiness curve—besides the quantity of happiness.

We also can show that more matters than pleasure or happiness by considering a life that has these but otherwise is empty, a life of mindless pleasures or bovine contentment or frivolous amusements only, a happy life but a superficial one. "It is better," John Stuart Mill wrote, "to be a human being dissatisfied than a pig satisfied; better to be Socrates dissatisfied than a fool satisfied." And although it might be best of all to be Socrates satisfied, having both happiness and depth, we would give up some happiness in order to gain the depth.

We are not empty containers or buckets to be stuffed with good things, with pleasures or possessions or positive emotions or even with a rich and varied internal life. Such a bucket has no appropriate structure within; how the experiences fit together or are contoured over time is of no importance except insofar as some particular arrangements make further happy moments more probable. The view that only happiness matters ignores the question of what *we*—the very ones to be happy—are like. How could the most important thing about our life be what it *contains*, though? What makes the felt experiences of pleasure or happiness more important than what we ourselves are like?

Freud thought it a fundamental principle of behavior that we seek pleasure and try to avoid pain or unpleasure—he called this the pleasure principle. Sometimes one can more effectively secure pleasure by not proceeding to it directly; one countenances detours and postponements in immediate satisfaction, one even renounces particular sources of pleasure, due to the nature of the outside world. Freud called this acting in accordance with the reality principle. Freud's reality principle is subordinate to the pleasure principle: "Actually, the substitution of the reality principle for the pleasure principle implies no deposing of the pleasure principle but only a safeguarding of it. A momentary pleasure, uncertain in its results, is given

---

*It requires some care to accurately delineate the preference, all other things being equal, for the upward slope, to take into account the full complexities as one moves through life of anticipating and recollecting time intervals of changing lengths. However, the preference about the contour of one's children's lives avoids this problem, for you then are evaluating the life as a whole from a point outside it, and their anticipation and recollection will not enter if they do not know the life's contour. If anticipation of a future good pleases us more now than recollection of a past one, thereby affecting where the curves are placed, this fact itself might indicate a preference for the upward-sloping curve. (Similarly, people with amnesia might prefer that a given happiness were in their future rather than their past, even if the memory could be retrieved.) We also need to disentangle the preference for the upward slope from the preference for a happy ending which the upward slope might be taken to indicate. Consider one curve sloping upward until nearly the very end, and another curve sloping downward until nearly the every end, each having the same total area underneath; these two curves cross like an X. At nearly the very end, though, things are more complicated: For a person on each curve there is a half chance of staying at that level, and a half chance of immediately dropping or being raised to the level of the other curve, with life ending soon thereafter. The level of the end cannot be predicted from the course of the curve until then; if under these circumstances the upward slope still is preferred to the downward one, this preference concerns the course of the curves, not just their endings.

That we prefer the upward (and very much dislike the downward) slope might help explain other phenomena. Recently, two psychologists, Amos Tversky and Daniel Kahneman, have emphasized that in making choices people judge the outcomes of actions (contrary to the recommendations of existing normative theories) not by their absolute level but by whether they involve gains or losses as compared to some baseline or reference point, and that they weight losses more heavily than gains. (See Daniel Kahneman and Amos Tversky, "Prospect Theory," *Econometrica*, Vol. 47, 1979, pp. 263–291; "Rational Choice and the Framing of Decisions," in Robin Hogarth and Melvin Reder, eds., *Rational Choice* [Chicago: University of Chicago Press, 1987], pp. 67–94.) If people do prefer an upward-sloping curve, these two features are what one would expect: They will categorize outcomes as above or below a current or hypothetical reference point—are they gains or losses?—and they will give especially great weight to avoiding losses. (If, however, the preference for upward slope varies depending upon where the zero-level was, then that preference cannot be used to explain the two features; in any case, some might try to run the explanation in the other direction, seeing the preference for the upward slope as arising *from* the two features.)

up but only in order to gain along the new path an assured pleasure at a later time."*

These principles can be formulated more precisely, but technical refinements are not needed here.† Notice that there can be two different specifications of the pleasure to be maximized: the net immediate pleasure (that is, the total immediate pleasure minus the total immediate pain or unpleasure), or the total amount of net pleasure over a lifetime. (This latter goal might fully incorporate Freud's reality principle.) Since pleasure alone seemed too much tied to immediate sensation or excitement, some philosophers modulated the pleasure principle by distinguishing some kinds of pleasure as "higher." But even if this distinction between higher and lower pleasures were adequately formulated — something that hasn't yet been done — this would only add complications to the issue of choice: Can some amount of lower pleasure outweigh a higher pleasure? How much higher are the higher pleasures and do they too differ in their height? What is the overarching goal that incorporates this qualitative distinction? The distinction does not say that something different from pleasure also is important, just that the one thing that is important, pleasure, comes in different grades.

We can gain more precision about what pleasure is. By a pleasure or a pleasurable feeling I mean a feeling that is desired (partly) because of its own felt qualities. The feeling is not desired wholly because of what it leads to or enables you to do or because of some injunction it fulfills. If it is pleasurable, it is desired (in part at least) because of the felt qualities it has. I do not claim there is just one felt quality that always is present whenever pleasure occurs. Being pleasurable, as I use this term, is a function of being wanted partly for its own felt qualities, whatever these qualities may be. On this view, a masochist who desires pain for its own felt quality will find pain pleasurable. This is awkward, but no more so than masochism itself. If, however, the masochist desires pain because he (unconsciously) feels he desires to be punished, hurt, or humiliated, not desiring pain for its own felt qualities but for what that pain announces, then in that case the pain itself will not count as pleasurable. Someone *enjoys* an activity to the extent he engages in the activity because of its own intrinsic properties, not simply because of what it leads to or produces later. Its intrinsic properties are not limited to felt qualities, though; this leaves open the possibility that something is enjoyed yet not pleasurable. An example might be tennis played very forcefully; lunging for shots, scraping knees and elbows on the ground, you enjoy playing, but it is not exactly — not precisely — pleasurable.

From this definition of pleasure, it does not follow that there actually are any experiences that are wanted because of their own felt qualities; nor does it follow that we want there to be pleasurable experiences, ones we desire because of their felt qualities. What does follow from (my use of) the term is this: *If* experiences are pleasurable to us, then we do want them (to some extent). The term *pleasurable* just indicates that something is wanted because of its felt qualities. How much we want it, though, whether enough to sacrifice other things we hold good, and whether other things also are wanted, and wanted even more than pleasure, is left open. A person who wants to write a poem needn't want (primarily) the felt qualities of writing, or the felt qualities of being known to have written the poem. He may want, primarily, *to write* such a poem — for example, because he thinks *it* is valuable, or the activity of doing so is, with no special focus upon any felt qualities.

We care about things in addition to how our lives *feel* to us from the inside. This is shown by the following thought experiment. Imagine a machine that could give you any experience (or sequence of experiences) you might desire.* When

*"Formulations on the Two Principles of Mental Functioning," in James Strachey, ed., *The Standard Edition of the Complete Psychological Works of Sigmund Freud*, Vol. 12 (London: The Hogarth Press, 1958), p. 223.

†Behavioral psychologists offer more precise quantitative versions of the pleasure principle in statements of the law of effect; operations researchers and economists offer formal theories of the (reality) constraints on actions. The reality and pleasure principles together are mirrored in decision theory's dual structure, with its probabilities of alternative possible outcomes of feasible actions, and its utilities of these outcomes; as did Freud, decision theory maintains the priority of the pleasure principle in its own principle of maximizing expected utility.

*I first presented and discussed this experience-machine example in *Anarchy, State, and Utopia*, pp. 42–45.

connected to this experience machine, you can have the experience of writing a great poem or bringing about world peace or loving someone and being loved in return. You can experience the felt pleasures of these things, how they feel "from the inside." You can program your experiences for tomorrow, or this week, or this year, or even for the rest of your life. If your imagination is impoverished, you can use the library of suggestions extracted from biographies and enhanced by novelists and psychologists. You can live your fondest dreams "from the inside." Would you choose to do this for the rest of your life? If not, why not? (Other people also have the same option of using these machines which, let us suppose, are provided by friendly and trustworthy beings from another galaxy, so you need not refuse connecting in order to help others.) The question is not whether to try the machine temporarily, but whether to enter it for the rest of your life. Upon entering, you will not remember having done this; so no pleasures will get ruined by realizing they are machine-produced. Uncertainty too might be programmed by using the machine's optional random device (upon which various preselected alternatives can depend).

The question of whether to plug in to this experience machine is a question of value. (It differs from two related questions: an epistemological one — Can you know you are not already plugged in? — and a metaphysical one — Don't the machine experiences themselves constitute a real world?) The question is not whether plugging in is preferable to extremely dire alternatives — lives of torture, for instance — but whether plugging in would constitute the very best life, or tie for being best, because all that matters about a life is how it feels from the inside.

Notice that this is a *thought* experiment, designed to isolate one question: Do only our internal feelings matter to us? It would miss the point, then, to focus upon whether such a machine is technologically feasible. Also, the machine example must be looked at on its own; to answer the question by filtering it through a fixed view that internal experiences are the only things that *can* matter (so of course it would be all right to plug into the machine) would lose the opportunity to test that view independently. One way to determine if a view is inadequate is to check its consequences in particular cases, sometimes extreme ones, but if someone always decided what the result should be in any case by *applying* the given view itself, this would preclude discovering it did not correctly fit the case. Readers who hold they *would* plug in to the machine should notice whether their first impulse was *not* to do so, followed later by the thought that since only experiences could matter, the machine would be all right after all.

Few of us really think that only a person's experiences matter. We would not wish for our children a life of great satisfactions that all depended upon deceptions they would never detect: although they take pride in artistic accomplishments, the critics and their friends too are just pretending to admire their work yet snicker behind their backs; the apparently faithful mate carries on secret love affairs; their apparently loving children really detest them; and so on. Few of us upon hearing this description would exclaim, "What a wonderful life! It feels so happy and pleasurable from the inside." That person is living in a dream world, taking pleasure in things that aren't so. What he wants, though, is not merely to take pleasure in them; he wants *them to be so.* He values their being that way, and he takes pleasure in them because he thinks they *are* that way. He doesn't take pleasure merely in *thinking* they are.

We care about more than just how things feel to us from the inside; there is more to life than feeling happy. We care about what is actually the case. We want certain situations we value, prize, and think important to actually hold and be so. We want our beliefs, or certain of them, to be true and accurate; we want our emotions, or certain important ones, to be based upon facts that hold and to be fitting. We want to be importantly connected to reality, not to live in a delusion. We desire this not simply in order to more reliably acquire pleasures or other experiences, as Freud's reality principle dictates. Nor do we merely want the added pleasurable feeling of being connected to reality. Such an inner feeling, an illusory one, also can be provided by the experience machine.

What we want and value is an actual connection with reality. Call this the second reality principle (the first was Freud's): To focus on external reality, with your beliefs, evaluations, and emotions, is valuable *in itself,* not just as a means to more pleasure or happiness. And it is this connecting that is valuable, not simply having within ourselves true beliefs. Favoring truth introduces, in a subterranean fashion, the value of the connecting anyway—why else would true beliefs be (intrinsically) more valuable within us than false ones? And if we want to connect to reality by knowing it, and not simply to have true beliefs, then if knowledge involves tracking the facts—a view I have developed elsewhere—this involves a direct and explicit external connection. We do not, of course, simply want contact with reality; we want contact of certain kinds: exploring reality and responding, altering it and creating new actuality ourselves. Notice that I am not saying simply that since we desire connection to actuality the experience machine is defective because it does not give us whatever we desire—though the example is useful to show we *do* desire some things in addition to experiences—for that would make "getting whatever you desire" the primary standard. Rather, I am saying that the connection to actuality is important whether or not we desire it—that is *why* we desire it—and the experience machine is inadequate because it doesn't give us *that.**

*One psychologist, George Ainslie, offers an ingenious alternative explanation of our concern for contact with reality, one that sees this as a means, not as intrinsically valuable. According to Ainslie, to avoid satiation (and hence a diminution of pleasure) by *imagining* satisfactions, we need a clear line to limit pleasures to those less easily available, and reality provides that line; pleasures in reality are fewer and farther between (George Ainslie, "Beyond Microeconomics," in Jon Elster, ed., *The Multiple Self* [Cambridge, England: Cambridge University Press, 1986], pp. 133–175, especially pp. 149–157). Note that the phenomenon of satiation itself presumably has an evolutionary explanation. Organisms that don't get satiated in an activity (as in the experiments where apparatus enables rats to stimulate the pleasure centers in their brains) will stick to it to the exclusion of all else, and hence die of starvation or at any rate not go on to have or raise offspring. But in a reality framework too organisms will have to show some self-control, and not simply pursue easy pleasures even when they have not yet been satiated, so a reality principle would not completely fulfill the purpose Ainslie describes, and presumably other quite clear lines also could serve the purpose as well. One line might depend upon a division of the day according to biological rhythms—is sleep the time for easy pleasures and dreams the vehicle? Other lines might depend upon whether you were alone or accompanied, recently fed or not, close to a full moon, or whatever; these too could be used to restrict when the easy gain of pleasure was acceptable. Reality is not a unique means to this, nor is our concern with reality simply a means.

No doubt, too, we want a connection to actuality that we also share with other people. One of the distressing things about the experience machine, as described, is that you are alone in your particular illusion. (Is it more distressing that the others do not share your "world" or that you are cut off from the one they do share?) However, we can imagine that the experience machine provides the very same illusion to everyone (or to everyone you care about), giving each person a coordinate piece of it. When all are floating in the *same* tank, the experience machine may not be *as* objectionable, but it is objectionable nevertheless. Sharing coordinate perspectives might be one criterion of actuality, yet it does not guarantee that; and it is *both* that we want, the actuality *and* the sharing.

Notice that we have not said one should never plug in to such a machine, even temporarily. It might teach you things, or transform you in a way beneficial for your actual life later. It also might give pleasures that would be quite acceptable in limited doses. This is all quite different from spending the rest of your life on the machine; the internal contents of *that* life would be unconnected to actuality. It seems too that once on the machine a person would not make any choices, and certainly would not choose anything *freely.* One portion of what we want to be actual is our actually (and freely) choosing, not merely the appearance of that.

My reflections about happiness thus far have been about the *limits* of its role in life. What *is* its proper role, though, and what exactly is happiness; why has its role so often been exaggerated? A number of distinct emotions travel under the label of *happiness,* along with one thing that is more properly called a *mood* rather than an emotion. I want to consider three types of happiness emotion here: first, being happy that something or other is the case (or that many things are); second, feeling that your life is good now; and third, being satisfied with your life as a whole. Each of these three related happiness emotions will exhibit the general threefold structure that emotions have (described in the previous meditation): a belief, a positive evaluation, and a feeling based upon these. Where these three related emotions differ is in the object of the belief and evaluation, and perhaps also in the felt character of the associated feeling.*

The first type of happiness, being happy that some particular thing is the case, is reasonably familiar and clear, a straightforward instance of what has been said about emotion earlier. The second type — feeling that your life is good now — is more intricate. Recall those particular moments when you thought and felt, blissfully, that there was nothing else you wanted, your life was good then. Perhaps this occurred while walking alone in nature, or being with someone you loved. What marks these times is their completeness. There is something you have that you want, and no other wants come crowding in; there is nothing else that you think of wanting right then. I do not mean that if someone came up to you right then with a magic lamp, you would be at a loss to come up with a wish. But in the moments I am describing, these other desires — for more money or another job or another chocolate bar — simply are not operating. They are not felt, they are not lurking at the margins to enter. There is no additional thing you want right then, nothing feels lacking, your satisfaction is complete. The feeling that accompanies this is intense joy.

These moments are wonderful, and they are rare. Usually, additional wants are all too ready to introduce themselves. Some have suggested we reach this desirable state of not wanting anything else by the drastic route of eliminating *all* wants. But we don't find it helpful to be told to *first* get rid of our existing wants as a way of reaching the state of not wanting anything else. (And this is not simply because we doubt this route leads to an accompanying joy.) Rather, what we want is to be told of something so good, whose nature is so complete and satisfying, that reaching it will exclude any further wants from crowding in, *and* we want to be told how to reach this. Aristotle projected the quality of the feeling of not wanting anything additional out onto the world; he held that the complete good was such that nothing added to it could make it any better. I want to keep that quality within the feeling.

There are two conditions in which you feel that your life is good now, that there is nothing else you want: with the first a particular want already is satisfied; with the second you are embarked upon a process or path through which the other wants you have will be satisfied, and you have no *other* want than to be engaged in that process. Suppose someone wants nothing other than to go to the movies with friends, which he is doing. To be sure, he wants also to reach the movie theater, that it will not have burned down, that the projector will be operating, etc. However, these things all are included as parts of the process he is engaged in; they will come up in their appropriate turn. It would be different if instead he wanted to be going to a concert alone; then there *would* be something else he wanted. Since few goals are final and terminal — a point emphasized by John Dewey — the first mode of not wanting anything else usually will be found implicitly to involve the second mode, process. The fairy-tale Prince Charming wants nothing else once he has freed and married the princess because this means their living happily ever after.

One might worry that being happy all the time, in this second sense of the emotion of happiness, wanting nothing else, would eliminate all motivation for further activity or accomplishment. However, if what we want nothing other than is to be engaged in a process of living of a certain kind, for example, one involving exploring, responding, relating and creating — to be sure, we may want and expect this process also to include many moments of complete satisfaction of the first (nonprocess) type — then further activities and endeavors will be components of that very process.

When someone thinks, "My life now is good" the extent of time denoted by "now" is not fixed in advance. Hence, one can change its reference according to need. Even in a generally miserable period, you might narrow your gaze to a very particular moment, and want nothing else right then; alternatively, during a miserable moment you can recall that over a wider time period, one you also can call "now," your life is not miserable, and you might want nothing other than to be engaged in that life process, miserable moment and all. On the other hand, during moments of intense happiness we sometimes want to recall other kinds. For instance, within the Jewish tradition, at wed-

*There is a need for an accurate phenomenology of the specific character of these feelings.

dings one recalls and acknowledges the most bitter event, the destruction of the Temple; during school class reunions, one might pause in the celebrations to remember those who have died. We have not forgotten these events or people and even in our most intense happiness we pause to give them continuing due weight.

The third form taken by the emotion of happiness—satisfaction with one's life as a whole—has been explored by the Polish philosopher Wladyslaw Tatarkiewicz.* According to his account, happiness involves a complete, enduring, deep, and full satisfaction with the whole of one's life, a satisfaction whose component evaluation is true and justified. Tatarkiewicz builds so much into this notion—complete and total satisfaction, etc.—because he wants nothing to be superior to a happy life. But this makes it difficult for there to be two happy lives, one happier than the other. Here, we can be more relaxed about the fullness of the satisfaction, and about how high a degree of positiveness the evaluation involves. A happy life will be evaluated as good enough on the whole. A life can be a happy one in another sense, too, by containing many events of feeling happy about one thing or another—that was the first type of happiness emotion. Such a life might frequently feel happy, yet that person need not positively evaluate his life as a whole, even unconsciously. Indeed, he might make the opposite evaluation if he focused upon his life as a whole, perhaps because he thinks the constituent happy feelings not very important. Despite his frequent happy moments, then, he would not be happy in the third sense of being satisfied with his life as a whole.

We would be reluctant to term someone happy at a particular moment or in life in general if we thought the evaluations upon which his emotion was based were wildly wrong. Yet it would be too stringent simply to require that the evaluations be correct. Looking back upon earlier historical times, we may see people making evaluations which (by our lights) are incorrect yet which were understandable and not egregiously unjustified at that time; the incorrectness of the evaluation should not be an automatic bar to its composing happiness. (After all, we hope that recent gains in moral sensitivity to issues such as women's equality, homosexual rights, racial equality, and minority relations will not be the last.) Simply to substitute "jus-tified" (or "not unjustified") for "correct" would misclassify the person whose emotion is based upon correct but at that time, in that context, unjustified evaluations. Perhaps what serves is the weaker disjunction: true or at any rate justified (or not completely unjustified). Someone whose emotion is based upon completely and egregiously unjustified and false evaluations we will be reluctant to term happy, however he feels. He should have known better.*

*Wladyslaw Tatarkiewicz, *Analysis of Happiness* (The Hague: Martinus Nijhoff, 1976), pp. 8–16.

*Notice that an evaluation made now about your life during an earlier time period can differ from the evaluation you made then. The fact that different evaluations can be produced of that period of life—yours then, yours now, and also the evaluation that we, the observers, make—complicates the question of whether that period counts as happy. We are reluctant simply to treat its proper evaluation, for these purposes, as the one the person actually made then. For example, if you then evaluated your life positively and felt accordingly, but now in looking back you evaluate your overall life then in a negative way, were you happy then or not? At that earlier time you *felt* happy about your life then, but now you do not feel happy about your life then. Because of your current negative evaluation (especially if it is one we endorse), we would be reluctant to say, simply, that you were happy then. Consider the corresponding question on the other side. If you then negatively evaluated your life and felt accordingly, yet now in looking back you positively evaluate that time, were you happy then or not? Your negative feelings then mean that you, even in retrospect, were *not* happy then, unless you also had many happy feelings then and your overall negative evaluation then, producing no extensively lasting feelings of unhappiness, was based upon more abstract grounds, perhaps that you weren't an exemplary tragically suffering hero at that time. If you now come to evaluate that period positively, feeling accordingly about it, and it did not contain extensive negative feelings then even though it was then negatively evaluated, might we not conclude that it *was* a happy time then, after all? Such complications make it difficult to offer a sleek and straightforward view of happiness.

Notice also an ambiguity in the notion of one's life as a whole, the object that is evaluated. It might mean the *whole* time slice of your current life, including all its aspects, not just a few; or it might mean the whole of your life until now. (Does it include also the future that is expected?) A person might be happy now, and be a happy person now, because of her current life and how she (correctly) evaluates it, even if her past was unhappy enough to lead her not only to have evaluated it negatively then but to now evaluate all her life until now as (on balance) negative. The question of whether a life is a good one overall does not focus just upon an evaluation of the current time slice, nor does it simply average the contemporaneous evaluations of each time slice (even if these were accurate), for the answer might depend also upon the narrative contours of the life, upon how these different time slices fit together.

This third sense of happiness—satisfaction with one's life as a whole—makes it extremely easy to understand why we would want to be happy or to have a happy life. First, there is simply the pleasure of having that emotion. Feeling happy or satisfied about one's life as a whole is pleasurable in itself; it is something we want for its own felt qualities. (This feeling generally will not be as intense, though, as the joy which accompanies the second notion of happiness, wanting nothing else.) However, other emotions also can involve equally intense pleasurable feelings; why, then, has happiness loomed so central? We also want this emotion of happiness to be *fitting*. If the emotion does fit our life, then the component beliefs about our life as a whole will be true and the component positive evaluation will be correct. Hence, we *will* have a life that *is* valuable, one it is correct to evaluate positively.

The object of this third form of the emotion of happiness is one's life as a whole. That object—life as a whole—also is precisely what we are trying to evaluate when we try to discover what a very good life is, in order to decide how to live. What could be simpler than to focus upon an emotion that does the evaluating for us? Add that the emotion is fitting, and we therefore can be sure the life is a good one. (Add only that the evaluation was justified or not egregiously false, and it has a decent chance of being a good one.) However, for all we yet know, the reason a happy life must be a good one is not necessarily because of any feelings it contains but merely because if that evaluation was correct, the life has to be good. To think, because happiness certifies that a life is desirable, that happiness is supremely important in life is like thinking an accountant's positive statement is itself the most important fact in the operation of a firm. (Each statement, though, might produce further effects of its own.)

Another way to make this point: A life cannot just be happy while having nothing else valuable in it. Happiness rides piggyback on other things that are positively evaluated correctly. Without these, the happiness doesn't get started.

Happiness can occur at the metalevel as an evaluation *of* one's life, and at the object level as a feeling *within* the life; it can be in both places at once. No wonder happiness can seem to be the most important constituent of a life. For it *is* extremely important at the metalevel and it does occur (and can have some importance) at the object level too. The central importance of (this third notion of) happiness lies at the metalevel, though, as an evaluation of a life as a whole; hence, the crucial question is what in particular makes a life best. What characteristics must it have to be (correctly) evaluated in an extremely positive way? It is not very illuminating at this point simply to mention emotions of happiness once again.

This conclusion is reinforced if we ask what particular evaluation enters into this third emotion of happiness. Precisely which of the many different possible positive evaluations does happiness make of a life as a whole? Not that the life is a *moral* one, for that needn't make one happy; not that it is a happy one—that circle would not help; not simply that it is valuable that the life exist, that the universe is a better place for it, for someone might make that evaluation without being happy; not simply that the life is good, for you might grudgingly recognize that without thinking it fulfilled your major goals or that it was very good. Perhaps the evaluation of the life must be something like the following: that it is very good, also *for* the person living it, in whatever dimensions he considers most important and whatever dimensions *are* most important. This clearly leaves us with the question of which dimensions of a life *are* the important ones. What does make a life a good one? Once again, it is not illuminating simply to mention the emotion of happiness here. When we want to know what is important, we want to know what to be happy *about*.

There is another sense of the term *happiness*: having a happy mood or disposition. This is not itself an emotion but rather the proneness or tendency to have and feel the three types of happiness emotions just described. A mood is a tendency to make certain types of evaluations, to focus upon facts that can be evaluated that way, and to have the ensuing feelings. In a depressed mood, one is disposed to focus upon negative facts or upon the negative features of otherwise positive situations and hence to have the feelings appropriate to these. A happy person tends to look upon the bright side of things. (However, it would be foolish to want to do this in every situation.) A person's disposition, I think, is a tendency one level up, the tendency to be in certain moods. A person of happy disposition might be in a sad mood on occasion, because of specific factors, but that particular mood will not be an expression of his or her general tendency.

A happy disposition may be a more important determinant of happy feelings than any one of the person's true beliefs and positive evaluations, however large one of these may seem to loom for the moment; it may be more important than the specific character of the actual situation. For example, people frequently pursue goals that they think will make them happy (such as money, fame, power), yet achieving these produces happy feelings only temporarily. They do not linger longer in making positive evaluations of these changes, and so the attendant feelings do not last very long either. A *continuing* tendency to look upon positive features of situations and have the attendant feelings — a happy disposition, in other words — is far more likely to result in continuing feelings of happiness.

If there is any "secret of happiness," it resides in regularly choosing some baseline or benchmark or other against which features of the current situation can be evaluated as good or improving. The background it stands out from — hence, the evaluation we actually make — is constituted by our own expectations, levels of aspiration, standards, and demands. And these things are up to us, open to our control. One salient background against which to evaluate is the way things recently were. Perhaps the importance to our happiness of things improving, of some or another upward slope to our lives, is due not, then, to the intrinsic importance of a directional process but to the fact that such a process leads us to judge the present against the recent past, which, happily, it surpasses, rather than against some other baseline from which it might fall short. A person intent upon feeling happy will learn to choose suitable evaluative benchmarks, varying them from situation to situation — he might eventually even choose one that would diminish that very intentness.

Happiness can be served, then, by fiddling with our standards of evaluation — which ones we invoke and which benchmarks these utilize — and with the direction of our attention — which facts end up getting evaluated. The experience machine was objectionable because it completely cut us off from actuality. How much better, though, is aiming at happiness by such purposeful selectivity, which points us only toward some aspects of reality and toward some evaluative standards, omitting others? Wouldn't happiness gained thus be like being on a *partial* experience machine? In the next meditation I consider the issue of which facts to focus upon; while the correct evaluative principles that apply to these facts may not be up to us, the benchmarks and baselines we employ and when we are satisfied in comparison to what are a matter not of external actuality but of our stance toward it. No particular benchmark or baseline is written in the world; when we employ one, even when we select a particular one just in order to be happy, we need not be denying any portion of reality or disconnecting from it. It is in this sense that our happiness is within our own power. Yet just this fact, that happiness depends upon how we look upon things — to be sure, looking upon them in a certain way may be harder in some situations than in others — may make us wonder how important happiness itself can be, if it is that arbitrary. How someone looks upon things, however, might be an important fact about him; people who can never be satisfied, no matter what, may have not simply an unfortunate trait of temperament but a flaw of character. Yet to willfully and constantly shift baselines to suit various situations in order to feel happy in each seems flighty and arbitrary too. Perhaps, although the baselines are not fixed by anything external, we expect a person to show a certain congruence or consistency in these, with only smooth and gradual changes over time. Even so, a person could increase his happiness by setting his uniform sights accordingly.

Moods can affect one's feelings in various obvious ways: by directing attention toward positive (or negative) facts, by resisting dwelling on certain types of facts when they come to attention, by adjusting the benchmarks, by intensifying the degree of the evaluation, by intensifying the degree of the associated feeling by affecting the factor of proportionality, or by lengthening the feeling's duration. What determines the mood, though? Most obvious is the person's general disposition, which is just his tendency to be in certain moods. Another factor—more surprising—is a prediction of what the day's emotions will be. A person wakes up in the morning with some general idea of what emotions are in store for him that day, what events are likely to occur, and how these events will affect him. Of course, this prediction draws upon knowledge of yesterday's conditions and events and of today's likely ones, but it also is to some significant extent self-fulfilling. By setting his mood, the prediction affects what he will notice, how he will evaluate it, and what he will feel, and hence helps to make the prediction come true. A mood is like a weather prediction that could affect the weather. (Moreover, the prediction will not be independent of the first factor, the person's disposition.)

"Anticipation is better than realization," the saying goes. Here is one reason why this sometimes might be so. When we anticipate the occurrence of a likely future event, an event we desire, our current level of felt well-being already gets raised by the amount of that future utility (as the economists term it) we think is coming, discounted by the probability. To make the point clear, let us suppose or fantasize that units of happiness and probabilities can be measured exactly. Then, for example, an event that we initially estimate as bringing us ten units of happiness later and which we think will have a .7 probability of happening raises our level by seven units (.7 times 10) immediately. For that expectation, that expected value, is a current one. When the event itself finally occurs, then, there is room for a rise of only three more units. (This corresponds to the uncertainty that it would occur, the remaining probability of .3 times 10.) Hence the anticipation now might feel better, a rise of seven units' worth, than the realization, a rise of only the remaining three units, when it finally comes; this phenomenon will hold when the probability of that future satisfaction is greater than one half.*

*That this occurs when the probability is greater than one half is a frequent psychological phenomenon, not a law. Some people look ahead with a great fear to the possibility of the event's not occurring, and discount the future accordingly. When anticipation of a future good does add an amount to a person's current utility level, how will that person fare when the event doesn't occur?

We have found various reasons for thinking that happiness is not the only important thing in life: the contours of happiness over a lifetime, the importance of some contact with reality as shown by the experience machine example, the fact that other intense positive emotions have a similar status, the way evaluations built into the notion of happiness presuppose the other things too are of value. Still, we might grant that happiness is not the whole story yet wonder whether it isn't *most* of the story, the most important part. How can one try to estimate percentages on a question like this? Judging by happiness's small role in my own reflections—much of my thinking here was called forth by the weight others have given to it—it is only a small part of the *interesting* story.

Nevertheless, I want to recall near the close of this meditation how undeniably wonderful happiness, and a happy disposition, can be. How natural then that sometimes we think happiness is the most important thing in life. Those moments when we want to leap or run with exuberant energy, when our heart is light—how could we not want to have our life full of moments like these? Things feel just right, and with its optimism happiness expects this to continue and with its generosity, happiness wants to overflow.

Of course we wish people to have many such moments and days of happiness. (Is the proper unit of happiness the *day*?) Yet it is not clear that we want those moments constantly or want our lives to consist wholly and only of them. We want to experience other feelings too, ones with valuable aspects that happiness does not possess as strongly. And even the very feelings of happiness may want to direct themselves into other activities, such as helping others or artistic work, which then involve the predominance of different feelings. We want experiences, fitting ones, of profound connection with others, of deep understanding of natural phenomena, of love, of being profoundly moved by music or tragedy, or doing something new and innovative, experiences very different from the bounce and rosiness of the happy moments. What we want, in short, is a life and a self that happiness is a fitting response to—and then to give it that response.

Study Questions

1. Explain the first difficulty Nozick notes in the view that happiness is the only important thing in life.
2. Would most people prefer an empty life as long as it was filled with happiness, according to Nozick? What reasons does he give for his answer?
3. What is a pleasurable feeling, according to Nozick? Is there just one quality that always is present whenever pleasure occurs, in his view?
4. When would pain count as pleasure for a masochist, and when would it not, according to Nozick?
5. What does Nozick mean when he says that we care about things in addition to how our lives feel to us from the inside? Explain in your own words the thought experiment he uses to illustrate this idea.
6. Is being able to share happiness with other people an important component of happiness, according to Nozick? Explain.
7. In what way is freedom connected with happiness, according to Nozick?
8. What are the three types of happiness emotion that Nozick is concerned with?
9. What are the two conditions in which you feel that your life is good now, according to Nozick?
10. Is it possible during a miserable moment to believe that your life is now good, in Nozick's opinion?
11. Could a person who is satisfied with his or her life as a whole be happy if the evaluation of his or her life were false and unjustified, according to Nozick? Why?
12. What is it to have a happy disposition, according to Nozick?
13. Is there any secret of happiness, in Nozick's opinion? Explain.
14. Is it sufficient to say that the presence of happiness is what makes a life a good one, according to Nozick? Explain.

Justice — John Rawls

As we explained in Chapter 5, discussions of justice fall on the border between moral philosophy and political philosophy. Most basically, political philosophy is concerned with finding the best form of political arrangement; more specifically, political philosophy is concerned with the proper organization, function, and scope of the state. Plato defines political justice in terms of what he takes to be the proper organization of the state, whereas for Aristotle justice is a matter of according to people the benefits that are due to them. Our contemporary commonsense understanding of justice is much influenced by both the Platonic and the Aristotelian conceptions: We think of justice as the proper assignment, overseen by the state, of merited rewards and punishments. Philosophers generally distinguish distributive justice, the allocation of social benefits and burdens and the protection of liberties, rights, and opportunities from retributive justice, the rectification of wrongs.

For many contemporary philosophical discussions of distributive justice, the point of departure is the contractualist theory of John Rawls, the author of the next selection. As you'll see, Rawls's theory is very close to those presented by the other great contractarian theorists, Hobbes, Locke, and Rousseau. It is also very similar to Kant's moral philosophy in the equal respect it accords to each person.

According to Rawls, the members of a well-ordered, just society must determine by rational reflection what are the basic principles of distributive justice—the principles for assigning basic rights and duties and for determining the appropriate distribution of the benefits and burdens of society. If the determination of the principles is to be reasonable, the principles must be selected through a procedure that is *fair*, he says.

For the selection of the principles to be fair, we must select them as though we were ignorant of each other's, and our own, particular circumstances. In his most important book, *A Theory of Justice* (1971) Rawls argues that we must select the principles as though we were behind this *veil of ignorance* so that we won't be biased or tailor the principles to our own advantage. Of course, we never *actually* were or ever could be behind such a veil of ignorance. Rawls's veil of ignorance is simply a literary device intended "to make vivid to ourselves the restrictions that it seems reasonable to impose on arguments for principles of justice, and therefore on these principles themselves."

The principles we would select from behind the veil of ignorance—the principles, that is, that we would select if we are thinking rationally and attending to our own self-interest but are unbiased by knowledge of any details of our own actual circumstances—will be such that they will protect everyone. There are two fundamental principles, Rawls says. The first requires that each person has an equal right to the most extensive basic liberty compatible with a similar liberty for others. The second requires that inequalities be arranged so that they are both (a) reasonably expected to be to everyone's advantage and (b) attached to positions open to all people under conditions of fair equality of opportunity. If questions of priority arise between the two principles, the first takes precedence over the second, he argues. Because of this, someone's rights or liberty cannot be sacrificed for the common good, as some have argued could happen under a purely utilitarian conception of justice.

According to Rawls, these two principles are a special case of a more general conception of justice, according to which all social goods are to be distributed equally unless an unequal distribution is to everyone's advantage.

In the following article, Rawls first explains that the fundamental idea in the concept of justice is fairness. Second, he explains in some detail the two principles mentioned above. Third, he explains how self-interested and rational people could settle on these principles as fair (he does not use the idea of a veil of ignorance in this selection). Fourth, he argues that if the participants in a practice accept its rules as fair, they have a prima facie duty to comply with the practices; he also elaborates on the concept of the duty of fair play. Finally, he contrasts his conception of justice as fairness with a utilitarian conception of justice.

Justice as Fairness

John Rawls

John Rawls (b. 1921) is James Bryant Conant University Professor at Harvard University. The following selection first appeared in the *Philosophical Review* 67 (1958).

1. . . . In this paper I wish to show that the fundamental idea in the concept of justice is fairness; and I wish to offer an analysis of the concept of justice from this point of view. To bring out the force of this claim, and the analysis based upon it, I shall then argue that it is this aspect of justice for which ulititarianism, in its classical form, is unable to account, but which is expressed, even if misleadingly, by the idea of social contract.

To start with I shall develop a particular conception of justice by stating and commenting upon two principles which specify it, and by considering the circumstances and conditions under which they may be thought to arise. . . .

Throughout I consider justice only as a virtue of social institutions, or what I shall call practices. The principles of justice are regarded as formulating restrictions as to how practices may define positions and offices, and assign thereto powers and liabilities, rights and duties. Justice as a virtue of particular actions or of persons I do not take up at all. It is important to distinguish these various subjects of justice, since the meaning of the concept varies according to whether it is applied to practices, particular actions, or persons. These meanings are, indeed, connected, but they are not identical. I shall confine my discussion to the sense of justice as applied to practices, since this sense is the basic one. Once it is understood, the other senses should go quite easily.

Justice is to be understood in its customary sense as representing but *one* of the many virtues of social institutions, for these may be antiquated, inefficient, degrading, or any number of other things, without being unjust. Justice is not to be confused with an all-inclusive vision of a good society; it is only a part of any such conception. It is important, for example, to distinguish that sense of equality which is an aspect of the concept of justice from that sense of equality which belongs to a more comprehensive social ideal. There may well be inequalities which one concedes are just, or at least not unjust, but which, nevertheless, one wishes, on other grounds, to do away with. I shall focus attention, then, on the usual sense of justice in which it is essentially the elimination of arbitrary distinctions and the establishment, within the structure of a practice, of a proper balance between competing claims. . . .

2. The conception of justice which I want to develop may be stated in the form of two principles as follows: first, each person participating in a practice, or affected by it, has an equal right to the most extensive liberty compatible with a like liberty for all; and second, inequalities are arbitrary unless it is reasonable to expect that they will work out for everyone's advantage, and provided the positions and offices to which they attach, or from which they may be gained, are open to all. These principles express justice as a complex of three ideas: liberty, equality and reward for services contributing to the common good.

The term "person" is to be construed variously depending on the circumstances. On some occasions it will mean human individuals, but in others it may refer to nations, provinces, business firms, churches, teams, and so on. The principles of justice apply in all these instances, although there is a certain logical priority to the case of human individuals. As I shall use the term "person," it will be ambiguous in the manner indicated.

The first principle holds, of course, only if other things are equal: that is, while there must always be justification for departing from the initial position of equal liberty (which is defined by the pattern of rights and duties, powers and liabilities, established by a practice), and the burden of proof is placed on him who would depart from it, nevertheless, there can be, and often there is, a justification for doing so. Now, that similar particular cases, as defined by a practice, should be treated similarly as they arise, is part of the very concept of a practice; it is involved in the notion of an activity in accordance with rules. The first principle expresses an analogous conception, but as applied to the structure of practices themselves. It holds, for example, that there is a presumption against the distinctions and classifications made by legal systems and other practices to the extent that they infringe on the original and equal liberty of the persons participating in them. The second principle defines how this presumption may be rebutted.

It might be argued at this point that justice requires only an equal liberty. If, however, a greater liberty were possible for all without loss or conflict, then it would be irrational to settle on a lesser liberty. There is no reason for circumscribing rights unless their exercise would be incompatible, or would render the practice defining them less effective. Therefore no serious distortion of the concept of justice is likely to follow from including within it the greater concept of the greatest equal liberty.

The second principle defines what sorts of inequalities are permissible; it specifies how the presumption laid down by the first principle may be put aside. Now by inequalities it is best to understand not *any* differences between offices and positions, but differences in the benefits and burdens attached to them either directly or indirectly, such as prestige and wealth, or liability to taxation and compulsory services. Players in a game do not protest against there being different positions, such as batter, pitcher, catcher, and the like, nor to there being various privileges and powers as specified by the rules; nor do the citizens of a country object to there being the different offices of government such as president, senator, governor, judge, and so on, each with their special rights and duties. It is not differences of this kind that are normally thought of as inequalities, but differences in the resulting distribution established by a practice, or made possible by it, of the things that men strive to attain or avoid. Thus they may complain about the pattern of honors and rewards set up by a practice (e.g., the privileges and salaries of government officials) or they may object to the distribution of power and wealth which results from the various ways in which men avail themselves of the opportunities allowed by it (e.g., the concentration of wealth which may develop in a free price system allowing large entrepreneurial or speculative gains).

It should be noted that the second principle holds that an inequality is allowed only if there is reason to believe that the practice with the inequality, or resulting in it, will work for the advantage of *every* party engaging in it. Here it is important to stress that *every* party must gain from the inequality. Since the principle applies to practices, it implies that the representative man in every office or position defined by a practice, when he views it as a going concern, must find it reasonable to prefer his condition and prospects with the inequality to what they would be under the practice without it. The principle excludes, therefore, the justification of inequalities on the grounds that the disadvantages of those in one position are outweighed by the greater advantages of those in another position. This rather simple restriction is the main modification I wish to make in the utilitarian principle as usually understood. When coupled with the notion of a practice, it is a restriction of consequence, and one which some utilitarians, e.g., Hume and Mill, have used in their discussions of justice without realizing apparently its significance, or at least without calling attention to it. Why it is a significant modification of principle, changing one's conception of justice entirely, the whole of my argument will show.

Further, it is also necessary that the various offices to which special benefits or burdens attach are open to all. It may be, for example, to the common advantage, as just defined, to attach special benefits to certain offices. Perhaps by doing so the requisite talent can be attracted to them and encouraged to give its best efforts. But any offices having special benefits must be won in a fair competition in which contestants are judged on their merits. If some offices were not open, those excluded would normally be justified in feeling unjustly treated, even if they benefited from the greater efforts of those who were allowed to compete for them. Now if one can assume that offices are open, it is necessary only to consider the design of practices themselves and how they jointly, as a system, work together. It will be a mistake to focus attention on the varying relative positions of particular persons, who may be known to us by their proper names, and to require that each such change, as a once for all transaction viewed in isolation, must be in itself just. It is the system of practices which is to be judged, and judged from a general point of view: unless one is prepared to criticize it from the standpoint of a representative man holding some particular office, one has no complaint against it.

3. Given these principles one might try to derive them from a priori principles of reason, or claim that they were known by intuition. These are familiar enough steps and, at least in the case of the first principle, might be made with some success. Usually, however, such arguments, made at this point, are unconvincing. They are not likely to lead to an understanding of the basis of the principles of justice, not at least as principles of justice. I wish, therefore, to look at the principles in a different way.

Imagine a society of persons amongst whom a certain system of practices is *already* well established. Now suppose that by and large they are mutually self-interested; their allegiance to their established practices is normally founded on the prospect of self-advantage. One need not assume that, in all senses of the term "person," the persons in this society are mutually self-interested. If the characterization as mutually self-interested applies when the line of division is the family, it may still be true that members of families are bound by ties of sentiment and affection and willingly acknowledge duties in contradiction to self-interest. Mutual self-interestedness in the relations between families, nations, churches, and the like, is commonly associated with intense loyalty and devotion on the part of individual members. Therefore, one can form a more realistic conception of this society if one thinks of it as consisting of mutually self-interested families, or some other association. Further, it is not necessary to suppose that these persons are mutually self-interested under all circumstances, but only in the usual situations in which they participate in their common practices.

Now suppose also that these persons are rational: they know their own interests more or less accurately; they are capable of tracing out the likely consequences of adopting one practice rather than another; they are capable of adhering to a course of action once they have decided upon it; they can resist present temptations and the enticements of immediate gain; and the bare knowledge or perception of the difference between their condition and that of others is not, within certain limits and in itself, a source of great dissatisfaction. Only the last point adds anything to the usual definition of rationality. This definition should allow, I think, for the idea that a rational man would not be greatly downcast from knowing, or seeing, that others are in a better position than himself, unless he thought their being so was the result of injustice, or the consequence of letting chance work itself out for no useful common purpose, and so on. So if these persons strike us as unpleasantly egoistic, they are at least free in some degree from the fault of envy.

Finally, assume that these persons have roughly similar needs and interests, or needs and interests in various ways complementary, so that fruitful cooperation amongst them is possible; and suppose that they are sufficiently equal in power and ability to guarantee that in normal circumstances none is able to dominate the others. This condition (as well as the others) may seem excessively vague; but in view of the conception of justice to which the argument leads, there seems no reason for making it more exact here.

Since these persons are conceived as engaging in their common practices, which are already established, there is no question of our supposing them to come together to deliberate as to how they will set these practices up for the first time. Yet we can imagine that from time to time they discuss with one another whether any of them has a legitimate complaint against their established institutions. Such discussions are perfectly natural in any normal society. Now suppose that they have settled on doing this in the following way. They first try to arrive at the principles by which complaints, and so practices themselves, are to be judged. Their procedure for this is to let each person propose the principles upon which he wishes his complaints to be tried with the understanding that, if acknowledged, the complaints of others will be similarly tried, and that no complaints will be heard of until everyone is roughly of one mind as to how complaints are to be judged. They each understand further that the principles proposed and acknowledged on this occasion are binding on future occasions. Thus each will be wary of proposing a principle which would give him a peculiar advantage, in his present circumstances, supposing it to be accepted. Each person knows that he will be bound by it in future circumstances the peculiarities of which cannot be known, and which might well be such that the principle is then to his disadvantage. The idea is that everyone should be required to make *in advance* a firm commitment, which others also may reasonably be expected to make, and that no one be given the opportunity to tailor the canons of a legitimate complaint to fit his own special condition, and then to discard them when they no longer suit his purpose. Hence each person will propose principles of a general kind which will, to a large degree, gain their sense from the various applications to be made of them, the particular circumstances of which being as yet unknown. These principles will express the conditions in accordance with which each is the least unwilling to have his interests limited in the design of practices, given the competing interests of the others, on the supposition that the interests of others will be limited likewise. The restrictions which would so arise might be thought of as those a person would keep in mind if he were designing a practice in which his enemy were to assign him his place.

The two main parts of this conjectural account have a definite significance. The character and respective situations of the parties reflect the typical circumstances in which questions of justice arise. The procedure whereby principles are proposed and acknowledged represents constraints, analogous to those of having a morality, whereby rational and mutually self-interested persons are brought to act reasonably. Thus the first part reflects the fact that questions of justice arise when conflicting claims are made upon the design of a practice and where it is taken for granted that each person will insist, as far as possible, on what he considers his rights. It is typical of cases of justice to involve persons who are pressing on one another their claims, between which a fair balance or equilibrium must be found. On the other hand, as expressed by the second part, having a morality must at least imply the acknowledgment of principles as impartially applying to one's own conduct as well as another's, and moreover principles which may constitute a constraint, or limitation, upon the pursuit of one's own interests. There are, of course, other aspects of having a morality: the acknowledgment of moral principles must show itself in accepting a reference to them as reasons for limiting one's claims, in acknowledging the burden of providing a special explanation, or excuse, when one acts contrary to them, or else in showing shame and remorse and a desire to make amends and so on. It is sufficient to remark here that having a morality is analogous to having made a firm commitment in advance; for one must acknowledge the principles of morality even when to one's disadvantage. A man whose moral judgments always coincided with his interests could be suspected of having no morality at all.

Thus the first two parts of the foregoing account are intended to mirror the kinds of circumstances in which questions of justice arise and the constraints which having a morality would impose upon persons so situated. In this way one can see how the acceptance of the principles of justice might come about, for given all these conditions as described, it would be natural if the two principles of justice were to be acknowledged. Since there is no way for anyone to win special advantages for himself, each might consider it reasonable to acknowledge equality as an initial principle. There is, however, no reason why they should regard this position as final; for if there are inequalities which satisfy the second principle, the immediate gain which equality would allow can be considered as intelligently invested in view of its future return. If, as is quite likely, these inequalities work as incentives to draw out better efforts, the members of this society may look upon them as concessions to human nature: they, like us, may think that people ideally should want to serve one another. But as they are mutually self-interested, their acceptance of these inequalities is merely the acceptance of the relations in which they actually stand, and a recognition of the motives which lead them to engage in their common practices. *They* have no title to complain of one another. And so provided that the conditions of the principle are met, there is no reason why they should allow such inequalities. Indeed, it would be short-sighted of them to do so, and could result, in most cases, only from their being dejected by the bare knowledge, or perception, that others are better situated. Each person will, however, insist on an advantage to himself, and so on a common advantage, for none is willing to sacrifice anything for the others.

These remarks are not offered as a proof that persons so conceived and circumstanced would settle on the two principles, but only to show that these principles could have such a background, and so can be viewed as those principles which mutually self-interested and rational persons, when similarly situated and required to make in advance a firm commitment, could acknowledge as restrictions governing the assignment of rights and duties in their common practices, and thereby accept as limiting their rights against one another. The principles of justice may, then, be regarded as those principles which arise when the constraints of having a morality are imposed upon parties in their typical circumstances of justice. . . .

5. That the principles of justice may be regarded as arising in the manner described illustrates an important fact about them. Not only does it bring out the idea that justice is a primitive moral notion in that it arises once the concept of morality is imposed on mutually self-interested agents similarly circumstanced, but it emphasizes that, fundamental to justice, is the concept of fairness which relates to right dealing between persons who are cooperating with or competing against one another, as when one speaks of fair games, fair competition, and fair bargains, The question of fairness arises when free persons, who have no authority over one another, are engaging in a joint activity and amongst themselves settling or acknowledging the rules which define it and which determine the respective shares in its benefits and burdens. A practice will strike the parties as fair if none feels that, by participating in it, they or any of the others are taken advantage of, or forced to give in to claims which they do not regard as legitimate. This implies that each has a conception of legitimate claims which he thinks it reasonable for others as well as himself to acknowledge. If one thinks of the principles of justice as arising in the manner described, then they do define this sort of conception. A practice is just or fair, then, when it satisfies the principles which those who participate in it could propose to one another for mutual acceptance under the afore-mentioned circumstances. Persons engaged in a just, or fair, practice can face one another openly and support their respective positions, should they appear questionable, by reference to principles which it is reasonable to expect each to accept.

It is this notion of the possibility of mutual acknowledgment of principles by free persons who have no authority over one another which makes the concept of fairness fundamental to justice. Only if such acknowledgement is possible can there be true community between persons in their common practices; otherwise their relations will appear to them as founded to some extent on force. If, in ordinary speech, fairness applies more particularly to practices in which there is a choice whether to engage or not (e.g., in games, business competition), and justice to practices in which there is no choice (e.g., in slavery), the element of necessity does not render the conception of mutual acknowledgment inapplicable, although it may make it more urgent to change unjust than unfair institutions. For one activity in which one can always engage is that of proposing and acknowledging principles to one another supposing each to be similarly circumstanced; and to judge practices by the principles so arrived at is to apply the standard of fairness to them.

Now if the participants in a practice accept its rules as fair, and so have no complaint to lodge against it, there arises a prima facie duty (and a corresponding prima facie right) of the parties of each other to act in accordance with the practice when it falls upon them to comply. When any number of persons engage in a practice, or conduct a joint undertaking according to rules, and thus restrict their liberty, those who have submitted to these restrictions when required have the right to a similar acquiescence on the part of those who have benefited by their submission. These conditions will obtain if a practice is correctly acknowledged to be fair, for in this case all who participate in it will benefit from it. The rights and duties so arising are special rights and duties in that they depend on previous actions voluntarily undertaken, in this case on the parties having engaged in a common practice and knowingly accepted its benefits. It is not, however, an obligation which presupposes a deliberate performative act in the sense of a promise, or contract, and the like. An unfortunate mistake of proponents of the idea of the social contract was to suppose that political obligation does require some such act, or at least to use language which suggests it. It is sufficient that one has knowingly participated in and accepted the benefits of a practice acknowledged to be fair. This prima facie obligation may, of course, be overridden: it may happen, when it comes one's turn to follow a rule, that other considerations will justify not doing so. But one cannot, in general, be released from this obligation by denying the justice of the practice only when it falls on one to obey. If a person rejects a practice, he should, so far as possible, declare his intention in advance, and avoid participating in it or enjoying its benefits.

This duty I have called that of fair play, but it should be admitted that to refer to it in this way is, perhaps, to extend the ordinary notion of fairness. Usually acting unfairly is not so much the breaking of any particular rule, even if the infraction is difficult to detect (cheating), but taking advantage of loop-holes or ambiguities in rules, availing oneself of unexpected or special circumstances which make it impossible to enforce them, insisting that rules be enforced to one's advantage when they should be suspended, and more generally, acting contrary to the intention of a practice. It is for this reason that one speaks of the sense of fair play: acting fairly requires more than simply being able to follow rules; what is fair must often be felt, or perceived, one wants to say. It is not, however, an unnatural extension of the duty of fair play to have it include the obligation which participants who have knowingly accepted the benefits of their common practice owe to each other to act in accordance with it when their performace falls due; for it is usually considered unfair if someone accepts the benefits of a practice but refuses to do his part in maintaining it. Thus one might say of the tax-dodger that he violates the duty of fair play: he accepts the benefits of government but will not do his part in releasing resources to it; and members of labor unions often say that fellow workers who refuse to join are being unfair: they refer to them as "free riders," as persons who enjoy what are the supposed benefits of unionism, higher wages, shorter hours, job security, and the like, but who refuse to share in its burden in the form of paying dues, and so on.

The duty of fair play stands beside other prima facie duties such as fidelity and gratitude as a basic moral notion; yet it is not to be confused with them. These duties are all clearly distinct, as would be obvious from their definitions. As with any moral duty, that of fair play implies a constraint on self-interest in particular cases; on occasion it enjoins conduct which a rational egoist strictly defined would not decide upon. So while justice does not require of anyone that he sacrifice his interests in that *general position* and procedure whereby the principles of justice are proposed and acknowledged, it may happen that in particular situations, arising in the context of engaging in a practice, the duty of fair play will often cross his interests in the sense that he will be required to forego particular advantages which the peculiarities of his circumstances might permit him to take. There is, of course, nothing surprising in this. It is simply the consequence of the firm commitment which the parties may be supposed to have made, or which they would make, in the general position, together with the fact that they have participated in and accepted the benefits of a practice which they regard as fair. . . .

The acceptance of the duty of fair play by participants in a common practice is a reflection in each person of the recognition of the aspirations and interests of the others to be realized by their joint activity. Failing a special explanation, their acceptance of it is a necessary part of the criterion for their recognizing one another as persons with similar interests and capacities, as the conception of their relations in the general position supposes them to be. Otherwise they would show no recognition of one another as persons with similar capacities and interests, and indeed, in some cases perhaps hypothetical, they would not recognize one another as persons at all, but as complicated objects involved in a complicated activity. To recognize another as a person one must respond to him and act towards him in certain ways; and these ways are intimately connected with the various prima facie duties. Acknowledging these duties in *some* degree, and so having the elements of morality, is not a matter of choice, or of intuiting moral qualities, or a matter of the expression of feelings or attitudes (the three interpretations between which philosophical opinion frequently oscillates); it is simply the possession of one of the forms of conduct in which the recognition of others as persons is manifested. . . .

6. The discussion so far has been excessively abstract. While this is perhaps unavoidable, I should now like to bring out some of the features of the conception of justice as fairness by comparing it with the conception of justice in classical utilitarianism as represented by Bentham and Sidgwick, and its counterpart in welfare economics. This conception assimilates justice to benevolence and the latter in turn to the most efficient design of institutions to promote the general welfare. Justice is a kind of efficiency.

Now it is said occasionally that this form of utilitarianism puts no restrictions on what might be a just assignment of rights and duties in that there might be circumstances which, on utilitarian grounds, would justify institutions highly offensive to our ordinary sense of justice. But the classical utilitarian conception is not totally unprepared for this objection. Beginning with the notion that the general happiness can be represented by a social utility function consisting of a sum of individual utility functions with identical weights (this being the meaning of the maxim that each counts for one and no more than one), it is commonly assumed that the utility functions of individuals are similar in all essential respects. Differences between individuals are ascribed to accidents of education and upbringing, and they should not be taken into account. This assumption, coupled with that of diminishing marginal utility, results in a prima facie case for equality, e.g., of equality in the distribution of income during any given period of time, laying aside indirect effects on the future. But even if utilitarianism is interpreted as having such restrictions built into the utility function, and even if it is supposed that these restrictions have in practice much the same result as the application of the principles of justice (and appear, perhaps, to be ways of expressing these principles in the language of mathematics and psychology), the fundamental idea is very different from the conception of justice as fairness. For one thing, that the principles of justice should be accepted is interpreted as the contingent result of a higher administrative decision. The form of this decision is regarded as being similar to that of an entrepreneur deciding how much to produce of this or that commodity in view of its marginal revenue, or to that of someone distributing goods to needy persons according to the relative urgency of their wants. The choice between practices is thought of as being made on the basis of the allocation of benefits and burdens to individuals (these being measured by the present capitalized value of their utility over the full period of the practice's existence), which results from the distribution of rights and duties established by a practice.

Moreover, the individuals receiving these benefits are not conceived as being related in any way: they represent so many different directions in which limited resources may be allocated. The value of assigning resources to one direction rather than another depends solely on the preferences and interests of individuals as individuals. The satisfaction of desire has its value irrespective of the moral relations between persons, say as members of a joint undertaking, and the claims which, in the name of these interests, they are prepared to make on one another; and it is this value which is to be taken into account by the (ideal) legislator who is conceived as adjusting the rules of the system from the center so as to maximize the value of the social utility function.

It is thought that the principles of justice will not be violated by a legal system so conceived provided these executive decisions are correctly made. In this fact the principles of justice are said to have their derivation and explanation; they simply express the most important general features of social institutions in which the administrative problem is solved in the best way. These principles have, indeed, a special urgency because, given the facts of human nature, so much depends on them; and this explains the peculiar quality of the moral feelings associated with justice. This assimilation of justice to a higher order executive decision, certainly a striking conception, is central to classical utilitarianism; and it also brings out its profound individualism, in one sense of this ambiguous word. It regards persons as so many *separate* directions in which benefits and burdens may be assigned; and the value of the satisfaction or dissatisfaction of desire is not thought to depend in any way on the moral relations in which individuals stand, or on the kind of claims which they are willing, in the pursuit of their interests, to press on each other.

7. Many social decisions are, of course, of an administrative nature. Certainly this is so when it is a matter of social utility in what one may call its ordinary sense: that is, when it is a question of the efficient design of social institutions for the use of common means to achieve common ends. In this case either the benefits and burdens may be assumed to be impartially distributed, or the question of distribution is misplaced, as in the instance of maintaining public order and security or national defense. But as an interpretation of the basis of the principles of justice, classical utilitarianism is mistaken. It *permits* one to argue, for example, that slavery is unjust on the grounds that the advantages to the slaveholder as slaveholder do not counterbalance the disadvantages to the slave and to society at large burdened by a comparatively inefficient system of labor. Now the conception of justice as fairness, when applied to the practice of slavery with its offices of slaveholder and slave, would not allow one to consider the advantages of the slaveholder in the first place. As that office is not in accordance with principles which could be mutually acknowledged, the gains accruing to the slaveholder, assuming them to exist, cannot be counted as in *any* way mitigating the injustice of the practice. The question whether these gains outweigh the disadvantages to the slave and to society cannot arise, since in considering the justice of slavery these gains have no weight at all which requires that they be overridden. Where the conception of justice as fairness applies, slavery is *always* unjust.

I am not, of course, suggesting the absurdity that the classical utilitarians approved of slavery. I am only rejecting a type of argument which their view allows them to use in support of their disapproval of it. The conception of justice as derivative from efficiency implies that judging the justice of a practice is always, in principle at least, a matter of weighing up advantages and disadvantages, each having an intrinsic value or disvalue as the satisfaction of interests, irrespective of whether or not these interests necessarily involve acquiescence in principles which could not be mutually acknowledged. Utilitarianism cannot account for the fact that slavery is always unjust, nor for the fact that it would be recognized as irrelevant in defeating the accusation of injustice for one person to say to another, engaged with him in a common practice and debating its merits, that nevertheless it allowed of the greatest satisfaction of desire. The charge of injustice cannot be rebutted in this way. If justice were derivative from a higher order executive efficiency, this would not be so.

But now, even if it is taken as established that, so far as the ordinary conception of justice goes, slavery is always unjust (that is, slavery by definition violates commonly recognized principles of justice), the classical utilitarian would surely reply that these principles, as other moral principles subordinate to that of utility, are only generally correct. It is simply for the most part true that slavery is less efficient than other institutions; and while common sense may define the concept of justice so that slavery is unjust, nevertheless, where slavery would lead to the greatest satisfaction of desire, it is not wrong. Indeed, it is then right, and for the very same reason that justice, as ordinarily understood, is usually right. If, as ordinarily understood, slavery is always unjust, to this extent the utilitarian conception of justice might be admitted to differ from that of common moral opinion. Still the utilitarian would want to hold that, as a matter of moral principle, his view is correct in giving no special weight to considerations of justice beyond that allowed for by the general presumption of effectiveness. And this, he claims, is as it should it. The every day opinion is morally in error, although, indeed, it is a useful error, since it protects rules of generally high utility.

The question, then, relates not simply to the analysis of the concept of justice as common sense defines it, but the analysis of it in the wider sense as to how much weight considerations of justice, as defined, are to have when laid against other kinds of moral considerations. Here again I wish to argue that reasons of justice have a *special* weight for which only the conception of justice as fairness can account. Moreover, it belongs to the concept of justice that they do have this special weight. While Mill recognized that this was so, he thought that it could be accounted for by the special urgency of the moral feelings which naturally support principles of such high utility. But it is a mistake to resort to the urgency of feeling; as with the appeal to intuition, it manifests a failure to pursue the question far enough. The special weight of considerations of justice can be explained from the conception of justice as fairness. It is only necessary to elaborate a bit what has already been said as follows.

If one examines the circumstances in which a certain tolerance of slavery is justified, or perhaps better, excused, it turns out that these are of a rather special sort. Perhaps slavery exists as an inheritance from the past and it proves necessary to dismantle it piece by piece; at times slavery may conceivably be an advance on previous institutions. Now while there may be some excuse for slavery in special conditions, it is never an excuse for it that it is sufficiently advantageous to the slaveholder to outweigh the disadvantages to the slave and to society. A person who argues in this way is not perhaps making a wildly irrelevant remark; but he is guilty of a moral fallacy. There is disorder in his conception of the ranking of moral principles. For the slaveholder, by his own admission, has no moral title to the advantages which he receives as a slaveholder. He is no more prepared than the slave to acknowledge the principle upon which is founded the respective positions in which they both stand. Since slavery does not accord with principles which they could mutually acknowledge, they each may be supposed to agree that it is unjust: it grants claims which it ought not to grant and in doing so denies claims which it ought not to deny. Amongst persons in a general position who are debating the form of their common practices, it cannot, therefore, be offered as a reason for a practice that, in conceding these very claims that ought to be denied, it nevertheless meets existing interests more effectively. By their very nature the satisfaction of these claims is without weight and cannot enter into any tabulation of advantages and disadvantages.

Furthermore, it follows from the concept of morality that, to the extent that the slaveholder recognizes his position vis-a-vis the slave to be unjust, he would not choose to press his claims. His not wanting to receive his special advantages is one of the ways in which he shows that he thinks slavery is unjust. It would be fallacious for the legislator to suppose, then, that it is a ground for having a practice that it brings advantages greater than disadvantages, if those for whom the practice is designed, and to whom the advantages flow, acknowledge that they have no moral title to them and do not wish to receive them.

For these reasons the principles of justice have a special weight; and with respect to the principle of the greatest satisfaction of desire, as cited in the general position amongst those discussing the merits of their common practices, the principles of justice have an absolute weight. In this sense they are not contingent; and this is why their force is greater than can be accounted for by the general presumption (assuming that there is one) of the effectiveness, in the utilitarian sense, of practices which in fact satisfy them.

If one wants to continue using the concepts of classical utilitarianism, one will have to say, to meet this criticism, that at least the individual or social utility functions must be so defined that no value is given to the satisfaction of interests the representative claims of which violate the principles of justice. In this way it is no doubt possible to include these principles within the form of the utilitarian conception; but to do so is, of course, to change its inspiration altogether as a moral conception. For it is to incorporate within it principles which cannot be understood on the basis of a higher order executive decision aiming at the greatest satisfaction of desire. . . .

8. By way of conclusion I should like to make two remarks: first, the original modification of the utilitarian principle (that it require of practices that the offices and positions defined by them be equal unless it is reasonable to suppose that the representative man in *every* office would find the inequality to his advantage), slight as it may appear at first sight, actually has a different conception of justice standing behind it. I have tried to show how this is so by developing the concept of justice as fairness and by indicating how this notion

involves the mutual acceptance, from a general position, of the principles on which a practice is founded, and how this in turn requires the exclusion from consideration of claims violating the principles of justice. Thus the slight alteration of principle reveals another family of notions, another way of looking at the concept of justice.

Second, I should like to remark also that I have been dealing with the *concept* of justice. I have tried to set out the kinds of principles upon which judgments concerning the justice of practices may be said to stand. The analysis will be successful to the degree that it expresses the principles involved in these judgments when made by competent persons upon deliberation and reflection. Now every people may be supposed to have the concept of justice, since in the life of every society there must be at least some relations in which the parties consider themselves to be circumstanced and related as the concept of justice as fairness requires. Societies will differ from one another not in having or in failing to have this notion but in the range of cases to which they apply it and in the emphasis which they give to it as compared with other moral concepts. . . .

Study Questions

1. Explain in your own words the two principles that together set forth Rawls's conception of justice.
2. Explain the "rather simple modification" to utilitarianism that Rawls wishes to make.
3. What does Rawls mean by saying that the various *offices* to which special benefits belong must be open to all?
4. Describe the situation that Rawls invites us to imagine, in which people come together to discuss whether any of them have a legitimate complaint against their established institutions. What will these people first try to do?
5. Why will each of these people be reluctant to propose a principle that would give him or her an advantage if it were accepted by the rest?
6. Why does Rawls think that these people would naturally accept the two principles of justice mentioned in question 1? In particular, why would they allow the inequalities permitted by the second principle of justice?
7. What sort of practices will strike these people as fair, according to Rawls?
8. Explain why Rawls thinks the concept of fairness is fundamental to justice.
9. If the participants in a practice accept its rules as fair, then, according to Rawls, they have a duty to act according to the rules. Why?
10. What, according to Rawls, is the unfortunate mistake of social contract theorists?
11. According to Rawls, a participant in a common practice who accepts that he or she has a duty to play fair recognizes that each of the other participants is a person. Why does Rawls maintain this?
12. Rawls says that classical utilitarianism *permits* one to argue that slavery is unjust on the grounds that the advantages to the slaveholder as slaveholder do not counterbalance the disadvantages to the slave and to society. Explain why Rawls regards it as a deficiency in classical utilitarianism that it permits this argument against slavery.

The Weight of Numbers — John M. Taurek

If resources are limited, then it may be that we can bestow benefits on some people only by not bestowing them on others, and vice versa. In such trade-off situations, should the number of people in each group be a significant factor in our decision? Suppose, for example, that group A consists of one person, and group B consists of five. Suppose further that all six need to be treated with a certain drug that you have, or they will all die. Unfortunately, the one person needs all of the supply to live, but the other five require only one-fifth of the supply. You can save one, or you can save five, but you cannot save all six. Should you save the one, or should you save the five? Should you go with the larger group simply because it is larger?

In the following essay, John M. Taurek argues that the number of people involved is morally irrelevant to whether you should save the one or the five. He begins by supposing that the one person is someone you know and like and that the others are strangers to you. Taurek argues first that *if* you think it wouldn't be wrong to save your friend, then you must concede that the fact that there are five people on the one hand versus only one person on the other is morally irrelevant to the question of whom to save. Taurek next argues that it wouldn't be wrong for you to save your friend at the expense of the five; the conclusion, then, is that the relative number of people involved is indeed morally irrelevant to the question of whom you should save.

The alternative view, that you ought to save the many instead of the one, rests on the premise that, other things being equal, it is worse that the five should die rather than one. Taurek next argues against this premise by making a distinction between the loss *to an individual* or his or her life and the loss of an individual life: it is the loss to an individual of his or her life that counts to Taurek, not the loss of the individual's life. (Apparently — and strangely — the loss of an individual's life to *his or her friends and relatives* does not count for Taurek.) Five individuals each losing his or her life doesn't add up to anyone's experiencing a loss five times greater than the loss of any one of the five, just as five individuals each having a headache does not add up to anyone's having a superbad headache. So it is not a worse thing that the five should die rather than the one. The numbers "simply do not count."

In the remainder of the selection, Taurek analyzes and discounts some apparent absurdities in his view.

Should the Numbers Count?

John M. Taurek

John Taurek taught philosophy at the University of Southern California and Stanford University. The following was first published in *Philosophy and Public Affairs* 6, no. 4 (1977).

We have resources for bestowing benefits and for preventing harms. But there are limitations. There are many people we are not in a position to help at all. That is one kind of limitation. But there is another kind of limitation we encounter. Often we must choose between bestowing benefits on certain people, or preventing certain harms from befalling them, and bestowing benefits on or preventing harms from befalling certain others. We cannot do both. The general question discussed here is whether we should, in such trade-off situations, consider the relative numbers of people involved as something in itself of significance in determining our course of action.[1] The conclusion I reach is that we should not. I approach this general question by focusing on a particular hypothetical case in which we find ourselves in a position of being able to prevent a certain harm from befalling one person or to prevent a like harm from befalling each of five others, but unable to spare all six from harm.

The situation is that I have a supply of some life-saving drug.[2] Six people will all certainly die if they are not treated with the drug. But one of the six requires all of the drug if he is to survive. Each of the other five requires only one-fifth of the drug. What ought I do?

To many it seems obvious that in such cases, special considerations apart, one ought to save the greater number. I cannot accept this view. I believe that at least some of those who do accept it fail to appreciate the difficulty of reconciling their thinking here with other convictions they are inclined to hold with even greater tenacity. First, I want to delineate some of these difficulties. I hope that, in view of them, others might be brought to reflect more critically on the intuitions that underlie this position. I shall then present what seems to me a more appropriate and appealing way of viewing trade-off situations of the kind in question.

Those who think that I ought to distribute my drug in fifths to the five people usually qualify their position. They maintain that "other things being equal, or special considerations apart, one ought to save the greater number." What sort of special considerations to the contrary do they have in mind? What is being ruled out by the "other things being equal" clause?

One thing they have in mind, I think, is the possibility of special facts about the one person that would, in their view, make his death a far worse thing than one might otherwise have sup-

I owe a large debt to Rita V. Lewis, whose views on the issues dealt with in this paper have had a pervasive influence on both its content and style. I should also like to thank Herbert Morris for helpful comments made on an earlier version of this essay.

[1]The trade-off situations I am focusing on have relatively simple structures. They present us with three relevant options: (1) We may aid a certain person or group of persons. (2) We may aid an entirely different group of persons. (3) We may do nothing at all to aid anyone. (I exclude from consideration this last option, though I do not argue that doing nothing for anyone is impermissible. Whether, why or in what sense it is, are questions best left to another occasion.) Robert Schwartz has caused me some worries about trade-off situations that are as aptly styled as these simpler ones, and that involve different but overlapping groups of possible beneficiaries. For example, perhaps the exercise of one option would bring aid to *A* but none to either *B* or *C*. A second option might bring aid to both *A* or *B* but none to *C*. Yet a third option might be available that would bring aid to *C* but none to either *A* or *B*. It will be seen that it is not completely obvious how one holding the views I present on the simpler trade-off situations would deal with this case and with cases of still greater complexity. After having caused me the worries, Schwartz had the decency to think out an approach to these decision problems that would appear compatible with my thinking about the simpler ones. But I fear that a discussion of these complications would obscure my main argument here, so I have avoided it.

[2]This is the case described by Phillippa Foot in her paper on "Abortion and the Doctrine of Double Effect," in *Moral Problems*, ed. James Rachels (New York, 1971).

posed. Perhaps he is close to discovering some wonder drug or is on the verge of negotiating a lasting peace in the world's perennial trouble spot. The idea is that it could happen that this one person's continued existence is in some way crucial to the welfare of an unusually large number of people. This would make his death a far worse thing in the minds of some than it would otherwise be. Of course, they also have in mind the possibility that special facts about these five persons could make their deaths not nearly so bad a thing after all. They might be five driveling old people or five idiot infants, loved by no one. In light of such facts as these it may well be permissible, perhaps even obligatory in the view of some, to save the one wholesome person instead of the five others. So when people say, "other things being equal, one ought to save the greater number," they mean to rule out such special considerations as these. The thinking here is that, apart from some such considerations, the death of five innocent persons is a worse thing, a greater evil, a greater loss, than the death of one innocent person. Since I am in a position to prevent either of these bad things from happening, but not both, I am morally required to prevent the worst.

Such reasoning seems appealing to many. I find it difficult to understand and even more difficult to see how it is to be reconciled with certain other convictions widely shared by these same people. Suppose this one person, call him David, is someone I know and like, and the others are strangers to me. I might well give all of my drug to him. And I am inclined to think that were I to do so, I would not be acting immorally. I suspect that many share this view with me.

Of course, some people do think that I would be acting immorally. They think it would be wrong to give all the drug to David while the five others die just because David is someone I know and like. They may allow that this could make my action excusable, but on their view it would not make it right.

For the moment, I address myself to those who, while subscribing to the general position, nevertheless share my view that it would not be wrong for me to use my drug to save a person I know and like. They must deny that the original claim, together with the thinking that lies behind it, commits them to the view that I ought to save the five strangers in this case. Perhaps they will object that, in introducing David as someone I know and like, I have introduced another of those special considerations that were meant to be excluded by the "other things being equal" clause. But if this is one of the special considerations meant to be ruled out, it is of a different sort from the special considerations previously mentioned. These were facts about the five persons in light of which it was thought their deaths would not be so bad, after all; or facts about David that would make his death a worse thing than the death of a person of more ordinary credentials. The idea was that these considerations would make a difference to what I ought to do, because in light of them the death of the one person would in fact be a worse thing to have happen than would be the deaths of these five.

But I would not think that the fact that David happens to be someone I know and like would make his death a worse thing in comparison to the deaths of these others than it would be if, by chance, I didn't know him or knew him but happened not to like him. So it is not clear to me how this fact is to make a difference in what I am *morally required* to do in this situation. It is not clear to me how it is to make a difference in the view of those who think that, apart from it, I would have a moral obligation to save the five, an obligation deriving from the fact that it is a worse thing, other things being equal, that these five innocent persons should die than it is that this one should.

Perhaps there are special considerations of a kind different from those described thus far. Suppose that one person had contracted with me in advance to have just this quantity of the drug administered to him at this particular time. It could be thought that such a special obligation to the one party arising out of a contract would override the fact that I would be preventing a far worse thing from happening were I to give the drug to the five. An explicit contract or promise may not be the only source of such special obligations to another person. Perhaps a parent is thought to be thus specially obligated to his child, or a child to his parents. Perhaps a doctor has such a special obligation to his regular patients. Perhaps one might think one has such a special obligation to a benefactor, and so on. It seems reasonable to suppose that the existence of such special obligations to specific individuals involved were also meant to be excluded by the "other things being equal" clause. But can this be helpful to those who wish to reconcile their feeling that I do not do wrong when I give all my drug to a friend with an adherence to the original contention?

This does not seem to be a very promising line. Are we to suppose that I have in this situation an overriding obligation to save this one person, deriving from the fact that he is someone I know and like? Such a supposition does not appear to capture my thinking here at all. The fact is that I would act to save David's life because, knowing him and liking him, my concern for his well-being is simply greater than my concern for the well-being of those others, not because I recognize some overriding obligation to him. Imagine that the situation involved David and only one other person, a stranger. In the absence of any special claim of right possessed by the stranger, I would save David. If asked to explain or justify my choice, I would not think to say that I was *morally required* to give my drug to David in virtue of the fact that I happen to know and like him. The fact that David is a friend explains, naturally enough, my preference for saving him rather than this other person. It is the absence of any moral obligation to save this other person rather than David that makes my choice morally permissible. And, rightly or wrongly, that is how I think of my conduct in the situation under discussion. In securing David's survival I am acting on a purely personal preference. It is the absence of any moral requirement to save these others rather than David that makes my doing so morally permissible.

However, this talk of a special duty to the one person, arising not from any promise, contract or quasi-contractual relationship between us, but somehow from the mere fact that I know and like him, would appear to go too far. For, on such a view, it would be more than simply permissible for me to save David, it would be morally obligatory that I save him rather than these five others. And this is not the thinking of those who feel only that it would not be wrong of me to save David.

On the view in question, one is morally required to save the five instead of the one, other things being equal, because, other things being equal, it is a very much worse thing that these five innocent people should die than it is that this one should. But if this fact constitutes a compelling ground for a moral obligation to give the drug to these five rather than to this one, then I too shall have to acknowledge its moral force. The problem, then, is to explain, especially perhaps to these five people, how it is that merely because I know and like David and am unacquainted with them I can so easily escape the moral requirement to save their lives that would fall on most anyone else in my position. The only relevant consideration here is that I happen to like David more than I like any of them. Imagine my saying to them, "Admittedly, the facts are such that I would be morally obligated to give you this drug, if it didn't happen that I prefer to give it to him." The moral force of such facts must be feeble indeed to be overridden by an appeal as feeble as this.

Contrast this situation with almost any other in which we would be prepared to acknowledge the existence of grounds for a moral requirement to give the drug to these five people. Suppose, for example, that these five had contracted with me in advance to deliver this drug to them at this time and place. It would not seem likely that anyone would think that the fact that I would prefer to give it to someone else instead would alter in any way what I was morally required to do. But of course it might make it harder, psychologically, for me to do what I ought to do. Again, suppose that these five are American soldiers and I am an army doctor with what little is left of the issue of this drug. And let us suppose that this other person is someone I know and like but is a citizen of some other country. Would anyone imagine that the fact that I would prefer to use the drug to save this one person could someone nullify or lift my obligation to distribute the drug to the five soldiers?

The point is this. Generally, when the facts are such that any impartial person would recognize a moral obligation to do something as important to people as giving this drug to these five would be to them, then an appeal to the fact that one happens to be partial to the interests of some others would do nothing to override the moral obligation. Yet this is the position of those who maintain that in this situation any impartial person would be *morally required* to distribute his drug in fifths to the five. But because I, personally, would prefer to give it to someone else, it is permissible for me to do so.[3]

I am inclined to think, then, that we should either agree that it would be wrong for me to save David in this situation or admit that there are no grounds for a moral requirement on anyone, special obligations apart, to save the five instead of David. Now as I said earlier there are those who will take the view that I do wrong when I give preference to David in this situation. They may feel that what has been said so far only proves the point. So now I would like to say something in support of the opinion that it would be morally permissible for a person in such circumstances to save a friend rather than the five strangers.

Suppose the drug belongs to your friend David. It is his drug, his required dosage. Now there are these five strangers, strangers to David as well as to you. Would you try to persuade David to give his drug to these five people? Do you think you should? Suppose you were to try. How would you begin? You are asking him to give up his life so that each of the five others, all strangers to him, might continue to live.

Imagine trying to reason with David as you would, presumably, have reasoned with yourself were the drug yours. "David, to be sure it is a bad thing, a very bad thing, that you should die. But don't you see it is a far worse thing that these five people should die? Now you are in a position to prevent either of these bad things from happening. Unfortunately you cannot prevent them both. So you ought to insure that the worst thing doesn't happen."

Don't you think that David might demur? Isn't he likely to ask: "Worse for whom?" And it seems natural and relevant that he should continue to put his case in some such way as this: "It is a far worse thing for me that I should die than that they should. I allow that for each of them it would be a worse thing were they all to die while I continue to live than it would be were I to die and they to continue to live. Indeed I wouldn't ask, nor would I expect, any one of them to give up his life so that I, a perfect stranger, might continue to live mine. But why should you, or any one of them, expect me to give up my life so that each of them might continue to live his?"

I think David's question deserves an answer. What could there be about these strangers that might induce David to think it worth giving up his life so that they might continue to live theirs? The usual sort of utilitarian reasoning would be comical if it were not so outrageous. Imagine any one of these five entreating David, "Look here David. Here I am but one person. If you give me on-fifth of your drug I will continue to live. I am confident that I will garner over the long haul a net balance of pleasure over pain, happiness over misery. Admittedly, if this were all that would be realized by your death I should not expect that you would give up your life for it. I mean, it may not be unreasonable to think that you yourself, were you to continue to live, might succeed in realizing at least as favorable a balance of happiness. But here, don't you see, is a second person. If he continues to live he too will accumulate a nice balance of pleasure over pain. And here is yet a third, a fourth, and finally a fifth person. Now, we would not ask you to die to make possible the net happiness realized in the life of any one of us five. For you might well suppose that you could realize as much in your own lifetime. But it would be most unreasonable for you to think that you could realize in your one lifetime anything like as much happiness as we get when we add together our five distinct favorable balances."

Such reasoning coming from some disinterested outside party might be a little less contemptible, but surely not a bit less foolish. But if we recognize the absurdity of trying to sell David on the idea that it would be a worse thing were these five persons to die than it would be were he to die by suggesting he focus on the large sum of their added happinesses as compared to his own, just what kind of reasoning would sound less absurd? Is it less absurd to ask him to focus on the large sum of

[3]There are a number of possible contortions that one might go through in an attempt to reconcile these views. I cannot consider them all here. What I am chiefly interested in stressing is that there are serious difficulties involved in any attempt to reconcile these positions. My hope is that, in view of these difficulties, those who would maintain the original position might be brought to reconsider with an open mind the alleged grounds for the moral requirement to save the greater number in cases where one is in fact impartial in one's concern for those involved.

intrinsic value possessed by five human beings, quite apart from considerations of their happiness, as compared to the value of himself alone?

I cannot imagine that I could give David any reason why *he* should think it better that these five strangers should continue to live than that he should. In using his drug to preserve his own life he acts to preserve what is, understandably, more important to him. He values his own life more than he values any of theirs. This is, of course, not to say that he thinks he is more valuable, period, than any one of them, or than all of them taken together. (Whatever could such a remark mean?) Moreover, and this I would like to stress, in not giving his drug to these five people he does not wrong any of them. He violates no one's rights. None of these five has a legitimate claim on David's drug in this situation, and so the five together have no such claim. Were they to attack David and to take his drug, they would be murderers. Both you and David would be wholly within your rights to defend against any such attempt to deprive him of his drug.

Such, in any case, is my view. I hope that most people would agree with me. But if it is morally permissible for David in this situation to give himself all of his drug, why should it be morally impermissible for me to do the same? It is my drug. It is more important to me that David should continue to live than it is that these five strangers should. I value his life more than I value theirs. None of these five has any special claim to my drug in this situation. None of them can legitimately demand of me that I give him the drug instead of giving it to David. And so the five together have no such special claim. I violate no one's rights when I use my drug to save David's life. Were these five, realizing that I was about to give my drug to David, to attempt to take it from me, I would think myself wholly justified in resisting.

Thus far I have argued that, since it would not be morally impermissible for the one person, David, to use all of his drug to save himself instead of these five others, it cannot be morally impermissible for me, were the drug mine and given that I am under no special obligations to any of these five, to use it all to save David instead of these other five. In so arguing I have committed myself to a view that may strike some as counterintuitive. On my view, if one party, *A*, must decide whether to spare another party, *B*, some loss or harm *H*, or to spare a third party, *C*, some loss or harm *H′*, it cannot be *A*'s moral duty, special obligations apart, to spare *C* harm *H′* unless it would be *B*'s duty, in the absence of special obligations to the contrary, to spare *C* harm *H′* if he could, even at the expense of suffering *H* himself. To put it another way, my thinking here is simply this. If it would be morally permissible for *B* to choose to spare himself a certain loss, *H*, instead of sparing another person, *C*, a loss, *H′*, in a situation where he cannot spare *C* and himself as well, then it must be permissible for someone else, not under any relevant special obligations to the contrary, to take *B*'s perspective, that is, to choose to secure the outcome most favorable to *B* instead of the outcome most favorable to *C*, if he cannot secure what would be best for each.

The following kind of case might be raised as a counterexample. Many of us, perhaps most of us, might agree that were *B* somehow situated so that he could spare *C* the loss of his life, or spare himself the loss of an arm, but could not do both, it would not be morally required, special obligations apart, that he choose to spare *C* the loss of his life. "But," it will be asked, "suppose you are the one who must choose? You can either spare this person, *C*, the loss of his life, or spare *B* the loss of his arm. Even apart from any special obligations to *C*, wouldn't you acknowledge that you ought to spare *C* the loss of his life? Wouldn't it be wrong for you to spare *B* his loss and let *C* die?"

Well, I do not think it would be morally impermissible for me to spare *B* the loss of his arm in such a situation. What exactly would be the ground for such a moral requirement? I am to choose which of two possible outcomes is to be realized: in the one, *B* retains his arm intact and *C* dies; in the other, *B* loses his arm and *C* does not die. If the choice were *B*'s it would be permissible for him to choose the first outcome. But it is not permissible for me to make this same choice? Why exactly is this? By hypothesis, I am under no relevant special obligations in this situation. So what is the difference between *B* and me in virtue of which I am morally required to secure the outcome most favored by *C*, though *B* would not be? Unless it is for some reason morally impermissible for one person to take the same interest in another's welfare as he himself takes in it, it must be permissible for me, in the absence of special obligations to the contrary, to choose the outcome that is in *B*'s best interest. And, of course, this is what I would do if *B*'s welfare were more important to me than *C*'s.

There may well come a point, however, at which the difference between what *B* stands to lose and *C* stands to lose is such that I would spare *C* his loss. But in just these situations I am inclined to think that even if the choice were *B*'s he too should prefer that *C* be spared his loss. For some people such a point of difference may already have been reached in the case where *B* stands to lose an arm, while *C* stands to lose his life. There are profoundly important differences in attitude among people here that I do not know how to reconcile. I personally do not think that anyone should be moved, in the absence of special considerations, to spare me the loss of my life rather than sparing themselves the loss of an arm. Others seem to think that they should.

I suspect that many of those who see in the purported counterexample a forceful objection to my view are people who more than half believe that (ideally) they should be prepared to spare me the loss of my life even at the expense of losing their arms. Yet they are doubtful that they could bring themselves to make such a choice were it actually to come to that. Sensing this about themselves they are understandably reluctant to openly place such a demand on another. However when they imagine themselves in the role of a third party, who is not especially concerned about *B*, they feel less conflict about sparing *C* the loss of his life. They, after all, will not have to lose their arms. But if this is their thinking, then they are not raising a serious objection to the view I have taken.

Let me return now to a further discussion of the original trade-off situation. It is my conviction that were the drug David's to use, he would do nothing wrong, special obligations apart, were he to use it to save himself instead of giving it up to the five strangers. For the same reasons, I believe that were the drug mine and David someone I know and like, it would not be wrong of me, special obligations apart, to save him rather than the five strangers. And so I feel compelled to deny that any third party, relevant special obligations apart, would be *morally required* to save the five persons and let David die. So what do I think one should do in such a situation in the absence of any special concern for any of the parties involved?

First, let me suggest what I would do in many such cases. Here are six human beings. I can empathize with each of them. I would not like to see any of them die. But I cannot save everyone. Why not give each person an equal chance to survive? Perhaps I could flip a coin. Heads, I give my drug to these five. Tails, I give it to this one. In this way I give each of the six persons a fifty-fifty chance of surviving. Where such an option is open to me it would seem to best express my equal concern and respect for each person. Who among them could complain that I have done wrong? And on what grounds?[4]

The claim that one ought to save the many instead of the few was made to rest on the claim that, other things being equal, it is a worse thing that these five persons should die than that this one should. It is this evaluative judgment that I cannot accept. I do not wish to say in this situation that it is or would be a worse thing were these five persons to die and David to live than it is or would be were David to die and these five to continue to live. I do not wish to say this unless I am prepared to qualify it by explaining to whom or for whom or relative to what purpose it is or would be a worse thing.

I grant that for each one of the five persons, it would be worse were David to survive and they to die than it would be if David were to die and the five to survive. But, of course, from David's perspective the matter is otherwise. For him it would be a worse thing were he to die. From my perspective, I am supposing in this situation that it does not really matter who lives and who dies. My situation is not worsened or bettered by either outcome. No doubt others will be affected differently by what happens. For those who love or need David it would be a better thing were the others to

---

[4]After I had written this paper, my attention was called to Miss Anscombe's note of some years back on this case as put originally by Mrs. Foot. She too was impressed by the fact that in the event a person gave his drug to the one, none of the five others could complain that he had been wronged. Her note is entitled, "Who is Wronged?" *The Oxford Review*, no. 5, 1967.

die. But for those especially attached to or dependent on one or the other of these five, it would be better were David to die and these five to live.

Some will be impatient with all this. They will say it is true, no doubt, but irrelevant. They will insist that I say what would be a worse (or a better) thing, period. It seems obvious to them that from the moral point of view, since there is nothing special about any of these six persons, it is a worse thing that these five should die while this one continues to live than for this one to die while these five continue to live. It is a worse thing, not necessarily for anyone in particular, or relative to anyone's particular ends, but just a worse thing in itself.

I cannot give a satisfactory account of the meaning of judgments of this kind. But there are important differences between them and those judgments which relativize the value ascribed to some particular person or group, purpose or end. When I judge of two possible outcomes that the one would be worse (or better) for this person or this group, I do not, typically, thereby express a preference between these outcomes. Typically, I do not feel constrained to admit that I or anyone *should* prefer the one outcome to the other. But when I evaluate outcomes from an impersonal perspective (perhaps we may say from a moral perspective), matters are importantly different. When I judge that it would be a worse thing, period, were this to happen than were that to happen, then I do, typically, thereby express a preference between these outcomes. Moreover, at the very least, I feel constrained to admit that I *should* have a preference, even if I do not. It is a moral shortcoming not to prefer what is admittedly in itself a better thing to what is in itself a worse thing.

Hence, I cannot give such an impersonal evaluative judgment as the ground for a decision to give the drug to the five instead of to the one. I could not bring myself to say to this one person, "I give my drug to these five and let you die because, don't you see, it is a worse thing, a far worse thing, that they should die than that you should." I do not expect that David, or anyone in his position, should think it a better thing were he to die and these five others to survive than it would be were he to survive and they to die. I do not think him morally deficient in any way because he prefers the outcome in which he survives and the others die to the outcome in which they survive and he dies.

In a situation where the one person, David, is a friend of mine and the others strangers to me, I do have a preference for the one outcome as against the other, to me a natural and acceptable preference. But since I do not expect everyone to share such a preference I will not elevate its expression to the status of a universally binding evaluation. I do not say to the five strangers that I give all of my drug to my friend because it is a better thing in itself that he should survive than that they should. I do not believe any such thing. Rather, I simply explain that David is my friend. His survival is more important to me than theirs. I would expect them to understand this, provided they were members of a moral community acceptable to me, just as I would were our roles reversed. Further, in securing David's survival I violate no one's rights. No further justification of my action is needed, just as no further justification is needed in a situation where the drug belongs to the one person. He need not, and plainly should not, give as the ground for his decision to use his drug to secure his own survival the judgment that it is better in itself that he should survive than that they should. Who could expect any of them to accept that? He need only point out, as if this really needed remarking, that it is more important to him that he survive than it is to him that they should. Furthermore, in thus securing his own survival he violates none of their rights. What more need be said?

In the trade-off situation as presently conceived, all six persons are strangers to me. I have no special affection for any one of them, no greater concern for one than for any of the others. Further, by hypothesis, my situation will be made neither worse nor better by either outcome. Any preference I might show, therefore, if it is not to be thought arbitrary, would require grounding. Of course this is precisely what an impersonal evaluative judgment of the kind discussed would do. It would provide a reason for the preference I show should I give the drug to the five. But for the reasons given, I cannot subscribe to such an evaluation of these outcomes. Hence, in this situation I have absolutely no reason for showing preference to them as against him, and no reason for showing preference to him as against them. Thus I am inclined to treat each person equally by giving each an equal chance to survive.

Yet I can imagine it will still be said, despite everything, "But surely the numbers must count for something." I can hear the incredulous tones: "Would you flip a coin were it a question of saving fifty persons or saving one? Surely in situations where the numbers are this disproportionate you must admit that one ought to save the many rather than the few or the one."

I would flip a coin even in such a case, special considerations apart. I cannot see how or why the mere addition of numbers should change anything. It seems to me that those who, in situations of the kind in question, would have me count the relative numbers of people involved as something in itself of significance, would have me attach importance to human beings and what happens to them in merely the way I would to objects which I valued. If six objects are threatened by fire and I am in a position to retrieve the five in this room or the one in that room, but unable to get out all six, I would decide what to do in just the way I am told I should when it is human beings who are threatened. Each object will have a certain value in my eyes. If it happens that all six are of equal value, I will naturally preserve the many rather than the one. Why? Because the five objects are together five times more valuable in my eyes than the one.

But when I am moved to rescue human beings from harm in situations of the kind described, I cannot bring myself to think of them in just this way. I empathize with them. My concern for what happens to them is grounded chiefly in the realization that each of them is, as I would be in his place, terribly concerned about what happens to him. It is not my way to think of them as each having a certain *objective* value, determined however it is we determine the objective value of things, and then to make some estimate of the combined value of the five as against the one. If it were not for the fact that these objects were creatures much like me, for whom what happens to them is of great importance, I doubt that I would take much interest in their preservation. As merely intact objects they would mean very little to me, being, as such, nearly as common as toadstools. The loss of an arm of the *Pietà* means something to me not because the *Pietà* will miss it. But the loss of an arm of a creature like me means something to me only because I know he will miss it, just as I would miss mine. It is the loss *to this person* that I focus on. I lose nothing of value to me should he lose his arm. But if I have a concern for him, I shall wish he might be spared his loss.

And so it is in the original situation. I cannot but think of the situation in this way. For each of these six persons it is no doubt a terrible thing to die. Each faces the loss of something among the things he values most. His loss means something to me only, or chiefly, because of what it means to him. It is the loss to the individual that matters to me, not the loss of the individual. But should any one of these five lose his life, his loss is no greater a loss to him because, as it happens, four others (or forty-nine others) lose theirs as well. And neither he nor anyone else loses anything of greater value to him than does David, should David lose his life. Five individuals each losing his life does not add up to anyone's experiencing a loss five times greater than the loss suffered by any one of the five.

If I gave my drug to the five persons and let David die I cannot see that I would thereby have preserved anyone from suffering a loss greater than that I let David suffer. And, similarly, were I to give my drug to David and let the five die I cannot see that I would thereby have allowed anyone to suffer a loss greater than the loss I spared David. Each person's potential loss has the same significance to me, only as a loss to that person alone. Because, by hypothesis, I have an equal concern for each person involved, I am moved to give each of them an equal chance to be spared his loss.

My way of thinking about these trade-off situations consists, essentially, in seriously considering what will be lost or suffered by this one person if I do not prevent it, and in comparing the significance of that *for him* with what would be lost or suffered by anyone else if I do not prevent it. This reflects a refusal to take seriously in these situations any notion of the sum of two persons' separate losses. To me this appears a quite natural extension of the way in which most would view analogous trade-off situations involving differential losses to those involved, indeed even most of those who find my treatment of the cases thus far described paradoxical. Perhaps then, in one last effort to persuade them, it may be helpful to think about a trade-off situation of this kind.

Suppose I am told that if you, a stranger to me, agree to submit to some pain of significant intensity I will be spared a lesser one. Special circumstances apart, I can see no reason whatever why you should be willing to make such a sacrifice. It would be cowardly of me to ask it of you. Now add a second person, also a stranger to you. Again we are told that if you volunteer to undergo this same considerable pain each of us will be spared a lesser one. I feel it would be no less contemptible of me to ask you to make such a sacrifice in this situation. There is no reason you should be willing to undergo such a pain to spare me mine. There is no reason you should be willing to undergo such a pain to spare this other person his. And that is all there is to it.

Now, adding still others to our number, not one of whom will suffer as much as you are asked to bear, will not change things for me. It ought not to change things for any of us. If not one of us can give you a good reason why you should be willing to undergo a greater suffering so that he might be spared a lesser one, then there is simply no good reason why you should be asked to suffer so that the group may be spared. Suffering is not additive in this way. The discomfort of each of a large number of individuals experiencing a minor headache does not add up to anyone's experiencing a migraine. In such a trade-off situation as this we are to compare your pain or your loss, not to our collective or total pain, whatever exactly that is supposed to be, but to what will be suffered or lost by *any given single one of us.*

Perhaps it would not be unseemly for a stranger who will suffer some great agony or terrible loss unless you willingly submit to some relatively minor pain to ask you to consider this carefully, to ask you to empathize with him in what he will have to go through. But to my way of thinking it would be contemptible for any one of us in this crowd to ask you to consider carefully, "not, of course, what I personally will have to suffer. None of us is thinking of himself here! But contemplate, if you will, what *we* the group, will suffer. Think of the awful sum of pain that is in the balance here! There are so very many more of us." At best such thinking seems confused. Typically, I think, it is outrageous.

Yet, just such thinking is engaged in by those who, in situations of the kind described earlier, would be moved to a course of action by a *mere consideration* of the relative numbers of people involved. If the numbers should not be given any significance by those involved in these trade-off situations, why should they count for anyone? Suppose that I am in a position either to spare you your pain or to spare this large number of individuals each his lesser pain, but unable to spare both you and them. Why should I attach any significance to their numbers if none of those involved should? I cannot understand how I am supposed to add up their separate pains and attach significance to that alleged sum in a way that would be inappropriate were any of those involved to do it. If, by allowing you to suffer your pain, I do not see that I can thereby spare a single person any greater pain or, in this case, even as much pain, I do not see why calling my attention to the numbers should move me to spare them instead of you, any more than focusing on the numbers should move you to sacrifice for them collectively when you have no reason to sacrifice for them individually.

It is not my intention to argue that in this situation I ought to spare you rather than them because your pain is "greater" than would be the pain of any one of them. Rather, I want to make it clear that in reaching a decision in such a case it is natural to focus on a comparison of the pain you will suffer, if I do not prevent it, with the pain that would be suffered by any given individual in this group, if I do not prevent it. I want to stress that it does not seem natural in such a case to attempt to add up their separate pains. I would like to combat the apparent tendency of some people to react to the thought of each of fifty individuals suffering a pain of some given intensity in the same way as they might to the thought of some individual suffering a pain many or fifty times more intense. I cannot but think that some such tendency is at work in the minds of those who attribute significance to the numbers in these trade off situations.

In the original situation we were to imagine that I must choose between sparing David the loss of his life and sparing five others the loss of their lives. In making my decision I am not to compare his loss, on the one hand, to the collective or total loss to these five, on the other, whatever exactly that is supposed to be. Rather, I should compare what David stands to suffer or lose, if I do not prevent it, to what will be suffered or lost by any other person, if I do not prevent that. Calling my attention to the numbers should not move me to spare them instead of him, any more than focusing on the numbers should move him to sacrifice his life for the group when he has no reason to sacrifice for any individual in the group. The numbers, in themselves, simply do not count for me. I think they should not count for any of us.

I suppose that some will take the apparent absurdity of the following scene as constituting a formidable embarrassment to the opinions I have stated thus far. Volcanic eruptions have placed the lives of many in immediate jeopardy. A large number are gathered at the north end of the island, awaiting evacuation. A handful find themselves on the southern tip. Imagine the captain of the only Coast Guard evacuation ship in the area finding himself midway between. Where shall he head first? Having been persuaded by my argument, to the amazement of his crew and fellow officers, the consternation of the government, and the subsequent outrage in the press, he flips a coin and makes for the south.

Admittedly, it will seem obvious to many people in our moral culture that it is the captain's duty to direct his ship to the north end of the island straightaway with no preliminary coin toss. And I don't wish to deny that this may indeed be his duty. But we must ask what is the source or derivation of his duty? If it is said, simply, that it is the captain's duty to save the many rather than the few because, other things being equal, it is a worse thing that this handful should survive while the many perish than it would be were those few to die and these many to survive, then I would protest. I have said why I think such thinking is unreflective and unacceptable. But I doubt that it is the simple sort of thinking that lies behind the quick and certain judgments of most who, when presented with this case, declare that the captain would be in violation of his duty were he to flip a coin, and then, perhaps, proceed south.

This situation is different in certain important respects from the kind of case I've been discussing up to this point. In this situation, the captain is seen as deploying a resource that is not his own, not exclusively anyway. And though it is not made explicit in the description of the situation, I suspect that in the minds of those who are so quick to judge it is assumed that each of those in jeopardy has a citizen's equal claim to the use or benefit of that resource. For these reasons the Coast Guard captain is seen as *duty-bound* in the situation; duty-bound to behave in accordance with a policy for the use of that resource agreeable to those whose resource it is. Hence the considerations operative here are quite different from those relevant to the decision of a private citizen captaining his own ship or dispensing his own drug or reaching out his hand under no moral constraints but those that would fall on any man.

The recognition of these differences quite obviously colors the judgments of those to whom such a case is presented. Contrast, for example, the way in which most people would judge the Coast Guard captain's conduct with their judgment on the conduct of a private citizen. Were a private citizen to make first for the south end of the island because among the few are some dear to him while among the many are only strangers, most would not raise a hue and cry. Although some might urge that it would have a been a better thing had this person gone north to rescue a larger number, they are not likely to think of his action as a violation of his duty to these people. But even if, tragically enough, the Coast Guard captain had friends among the few and none among the many, it will be seen as a breach of his duty should he first see to the safety of his friends. Here it seems that people think of his action as a violation of the rights of those who have a legitimate claim on the resource. How could the Coast Guard captain justify his decision to go first to the south end of the island? How could he justify it to those many at the north end? A justification is owed to them in this case. Personal preferences won't do. For those in the north are seen as having each an equal claim on that resource.

So this case is different from those previously discussed. Still, it may be urged, the point is that the captain *is* thought to be required to secure the safety of the larger number first. It would be wrong of him to flip a coin to decide his course of action. And so isn't this a case of the numbers counting? For what other justification could be given to the handful left to die at the south end of the island except to say: "It would be a worse thing were those many in the north to perish than it would be should only the few of you die."

I think there is a possible alternative justification of the captain's action in this situation that involves no appeal to any such claim as that. It is a more attractive justification. I suspect it comes closer to what most people think (perhaps wrongly) is available in this sort of case. I believe we are inclined to think of the situation in this way. A number of people have joined to invest in a resource, the chief purpose of which is to serve the interests of those who have invested. Whether each has invested an absolutely equal amount, or whether individual investments are scaled to individual resources, is neither here nor there. Theoretically at least, each person's investment (or status) is seen as entitling him to an equal share, an equal claim on the use of that resource or on the benefits from its use. Now a policy for the employment of that resource in just such contingencies as this present trade-off situation must be adopted. And it must be a policy agreeable in advance to all those who are supposed to see their interests as equally served. The captain's duty, then, whatever it is, is seen as deriving from this agreement. Thus, to justify his action to those left behind we need only cite the policy to which they, along with the others, have agreed in advance (theoretically, anyway).

Into the formation of such an agreement or policy, a consideration of the relative numbers in possible future trade-off situations may enter in a way to which I would find no objection; in a way that commits no one to the impersonal, comparative evaluation of the outcomes appealed to in the previous justification of the captain's action. It could well be agreed to by all, in advance, that should a trade-off situation arise the resource is to be used to save the maximum number of those who have equal claims. For we may suppose that none of these people knows, at the time the resource is purchased in their collective name, where in the future he may find himself should a trade-off situation arise, whether among the few or among the many. Hence such a policy might be found acceptable to all these people simply on the ground that such a policy maximizes each individual's chances of benefiting from the resource.

Against the background supposition of such an agreement, a justification of the claim that it is the captain's duty to proceed straightway to the north end of the island could be given. It would be wholly compatible with my views on how the numbers should *not* count. For in such a justification no appeal is made to any claim that it is, or would be, in itself, a better thing that those few should die and these many survive than it would be were these few to survive and the many to perish. Such a justification requires no one to acknowledge that his life, or that he himself is, from some impersonal, objective (moral?) perspective, worth less than two or three or three hundred others.

I believe that most people would prefer to think that this sort of justification is available in most cases like the one under discussion. Unfortunately, in many cases it is not. For it may happen that the facts are such that a policy of using a resource to benefit the larger number when not all can be benefited could not plausibly be justified by an appeal to each claimant's desire to maximize his chances of benefiting—on the understanding, of course, that equal chances go to each other claim holder. Imagine, for example, that on this island the majority live around the north end while the southern portion is inhabited by relatively few. It is now proposed that everyone on the island invest in an evacuation ship. A policy of using the ship to save the larger number when not all can be saved could not easily be sold to those in the south on the ground that it provides each person with an equal and maximized chance of survival. It will be clear to them that with such a policy an equal investment does not purchase in the south a benefit equal to what it brings in the north. Still, of course, they might be induced to invest equally. Given their circumstances, it may be the best they can do for themselves. But they would not see this as a policy that gives equal weight to the interests of every would-be share holder.

If the bargaining position of the few were sufficiently strong, I believe these southerners might hold out for a more equitable policy, for genuinely equal shares in the benefits of the proposed resource, or for some reduction on their premiums, or for some compensating benefits from elsewhere. Now can we imagine those in the north at this point appealing to morality? "Look here, you are all decent people. Don't you see, if it comes down to it, that it would be a better thing if a larger number of us in the north survive while you perish than it would be were you relatively few to survive while we, the larger number, perish? So be sensible and faithful to the principles of true morality and let us agree that, should a trade-off situation arise, the evacuation ship will be used to save the larger number." Who could waste his time with such sophistries? It might be easier simply to compel the minority to go along with the policy. It would be less hypocritical anyway.[5]

[5]To be sure, matters may be far more complex than is supposed here. Perhaps this particular investment in an evacuation ship is but one of many investments made by the entire people of this island through their central government for, as it is commonly put, "the common good." Perhaps, then, it could be said to the southerners that although in this instance the proposed policy for the use of the evacuation ship does not accord to them an equal claim on its benefits, they should not complain. They may well have enjoyed advantages at the expense of the northerners in past instances of "social action," and may look forward, through the intrigues of legislative politics, to yet further advantages in the future. Perhaps it could be argued that somehow it all works out in the long run to everyone's advantage. Maybe even some version of the "majority-rule" principle for policy making could be trotted out in such a context. I despair of finding a clear line of argument in this mare's nest. But if one sets the problem against such a background, the search for a justification of the claim that it is the captain's duty to make straight for the north end of the island will lead back to the general moral underpinnings of government and its functions. And these issues, though related, go beyond the scope of this paper.

Thus far we have been thinking about a situation in which these people who live on this island have, or are proposing to invest in, an evacuation ship. Each person is supposed to see himself as having an equal claim on this resource, for whatever reasons, whether because he is asked to invest or because of his status as an inhabitant of this island. Since the resource is limited, a situation may develop in which not all of them can be served by it. Hence the need for a policy, some method for determining who will be benefited. Plainly there are many possible policies. But not every policy will allow these people to retain their sense of each having an equal claim on the resource. For example, imagine that it is suggested that medical researchers, high-powered managerial types, and people with IQs over 120, be given first priority. Such a policy, whatever the reasons for adopting it, manifestly does not treat everyone on the island equally. It does not reflect a genuinely equal concern for the survival of each person on this island. Thus, if equal concern is what the inhabitants think they are entitled to, they will reject such a policy.

But under certain conditions, they will reject the policy of using the ship to save the larger number in the event of a trade-off situation, and for the same reasons. The minority who live on the southern tip will not see such a policy as according to each islander an equal claim on the collective resource. Imagine that those in the south know that on the north end there are already more people than the evacuation ship can hold. It is proposed that in the event of a trade-off, the ship is to be used to secure the safety of the larger number. You could hardly expect to convince the southerners that such a policy reflects a genuinely equal concern for the survival of each person on the island, that it accords to them a genuinely equal claim on the resource. You may as well try to convince workers with IQs under 100 that the policy of giving priority to researchers, managers, and to people with IQs over 120 reflects an equal concern for their survival.

Now I think this is how most people will think about these matters when asked to judge a policy governing the use of a resource meant for their benefit. Yet it is curious that many of these same people will not think this way when setting out a policy for using their resource to benefit others. Suppose, for example, that the people on this island have purchased their evacuation ship. On a nearby island, also volcanic, lives another group of people. These people have no means of evacuation because they are too poor, perhaps. The islanders who own the ships are willing, when they themselves are in no danger, to extend aid to those on the other island. Again the question of policy arises. They could, of course, without violating anyone's rights, decide to rescue the other islanders in order of IQ or social importance. But perhaps they want a policy that will treat all equally, that will truly reflect their professedly equal concern for each person's survival. They will then reject a policy that gives preference to those who happen to have higher IQs or more prestigious social positions. It would be incompatible with their desire to show an equal concern for each person's survival. And yet if it happens that most of these inhabitants live around the north end, while a minority dwells in the south, our islanders, if they are like most of us, will adopt the policy of sending their mercy ship first to the north port to evacuate from among the many. True, those who live in the south cannot complain of any violation of their property rights in the vessel. But can such a policy be thought, any more in this case than in the former, to reflect an equal concern for the survival of each, northerner and southerner alike?

Study Questions

1. What does Taurek mean by a "trade-off" situation? Describe the hypothetical trade-off situation that Taurek examines.
2. If the single person in the situation in question 1 were a friend of Taurek's—let's call the friend David—what would Taurek do? Why would he do it? What does Taurek think this shows?
3. What, according to Taurek, would David say if Taurek were to try to persuade David to give his drug to the others?
4. Would Taurek agree with David? Why?
5. What would Taurek do if he had no special concern for any of the people who needed the drug? Would he accept the view that if it is a worse thing for the five persons to die and David to live than for David to die and the five to live? Why?
6. What would Taurek do if it were a question of saving fifty persons versus saving one? Explain why. What is it that matters to Taurek?
7. Explain the hypothetical situation involving the Coast Guard, and explain why Taurek thinks it is different from the original hypothetical situation.

Existentialism

We conclude Part II with a look at existentialist ethics. To this point, our discussion of twentieth-century moral philosophy has been directed at analytic ethics, the moral philosophy (primarily) of Anglo-American thinkers who are concerned mainly with the issues raised by G. E. Moore and his British contemporaries.

Let's clarify this further. Contemporary philosophy is largely a response to the towering metaphysical speculations of the absolute idealists, principally the theory of Georg Wilhelm Friedrich Hegel (1770–1831). Hegel held that all reality, which he called the Absolute, is the unfolding of infinite thought or reason, which he equated with "idea." This metaphysical position is therefore known as *idealism.* (Idealism in this sense is the opposite of *materialism,* the view that the basic reality of the world is physical matter. Hegel's idealism is not the idealism of the person who places ideals before practical considerations, although he may well have been this sort of idealist, too.)

There were basically two major responses to Hegel, one in the English-speaking world, the other principally on the European continent. In England, Hegel was ignored at first, but by the last part of the nineteenth century, a British version of Hegelianism had become very popular among British philosophers. (Perhaps the most influential British exponent of idealism was F. H. Bradley, 1846–1924.)

Among the British adherents of this neo-Hegelianism was Bertrand Russell (1872–1970), the most celebrated British philosopher of this century. Russell was a mathematician who became a philosopher in order to find, he said, some reason to believe in the truth of mathematics. He began his philosophizing as an idealist; after reading what Hegel said about mathematics, however, Russell concluded that it was "muddle-headed nonsense." Further, by degrees he came to believe that metaphysical idealism rested on errors in logic. His own metaphysical and epistemological theories, developed in reaction to British neo-Hegelianism, emphasized analysis as the proper method of philosophy.

Fundamentally, philosophical analysis resolves complex propositions or concepts into ones that are simpler and, presumably, less troubling philosophically. To take a very elementary example, consider the proposition "Unicorns don't exist." This proposition is troubling philosophically, because it seems to be about nonexisting things: If something doesn't exist, how can a proposition be about it? To put it another way, if the proposition is true, then its subject, "unicorns," fails to denote anything, and thus the proposition doesn't seem to be about anything. Such considerations might lead us to suppose that unicorns must therefore exist after all, in some secondary sense. However, by analysis the original proposition can be resolved into the proposition "There is nothing to which the symbol 'unicorn' applies." This proposition is about symbols, and not about things, so it does not raise perplexing questions about the metaphysical status of nonexisting things.

The idea that analysis is the proper method of philosophy came very quickly to dominate philosophical thought in Britain and, later, the United States and Canada. At the same time, philosophical analysis evolved into different things for different philosophers. Despite these differences, practitioners of analytic philosophy held in common the basic ideas that many or most traditional philosophical problems are generated through linguistic confusion and that therefore linguistic clarification is the best way to resolve them.

Russell's classmate at Cambridge was G. E. Moore (discussed earlier in this chapter), who, like Russell, began his philosophical thinking as an idealist. However, together with Russell, Moore too eventually came to abandon idealism and likewise applied techniques of analysis and linguistic clarification to philosophical questions. The result when he applied these techniques to questions of ethics was his *Principia Ethica.*

The second of the two major reactions to Hegel preceded Moore and Russell and was centered on the continent of Europe. Three philosophers in particular took great exception to the thoroughgoing rationalism of Hegel and the absolute idealists: Arthur Schopenhauer (1788–1860), Søren Kierkegaard (1813–1855), and Friedrich Nietzsche (1844–1900), whom we have already encountered.

Despite their differences, the writings of all three of these thinkers share common themes, among them that the world, in contrast with the Hegelian portrayal of it, is largely irrational and in any case beyond philosophy's ability to comprehend adequately or to conceptualize accurately or to explain why it is the way it is; that the human experience is one of emptiness, vacuity, despair, separation, and senselessness; and that the most important task that confronts the individual is to find how to live within a world that is irrational. These themes spread widely in the literature of the late nineteenth and early twentieth centuries and were reflected as well in such art movements as dadaism, surrealism, and expressionism. They also became the main themes of the existentialists, whose writings received worldwide attention just after World War II, itself an incontrovertible testimonial to the irrationality of the world and the apparent senselessness of much human activity.

Another theme common to Schopenhauer, Kierkegaard, Nietzsche, and later existentialist thinkers was that philosophy is sterile and remote from the concerns of real life. Existentialists therefore troubled themselves little with the philosophizing of the analytic philosophers, whose theorizing they would have found irrelevant to the human predicament. For their part, analytic philosophers, until recently, returned the favor and mostly ignored or discounted existentialism as a "literary movement." In short, there wasn't much dialogue between analytic philosophy, which was centered in English-speaking countries, and existentialism, which originated on the continent of Europe (but spread elsewhere, especially Latin America).

One of the most famous existentialist philosophers was Jean-Paul Sartre. Sartre's philosophy rests on the premise that there is no God and that, accordingly, "we do not find before us any values or orders which will justify our conduct":* because there is no God, there is no objective good or evil, right or wrong. Further, according to Sartre, because there is no God there is no ultimate reason why the world is the way it is; in other words, the world is irrational and absurd. And finally, according to Sartre, because there is no God humans experience themselves as *abandoned* and *forlorn*. The fundamental philosophical problem for Sartre, therefore, is how we are to live in an absurd and irrational world, a world without objective values and no guiding light.

According to Sartre, we must—and do—create our own values through our choices, decisions, and actions. But because we are adrift, because there is nothing objective to guide us, our choices are made in the anguished awareness of our total freedom to choose. We may attempt to escape anguish, Sartre says, by denying our responsibility or our freedom. But this attempt would be a pretense and a mark of self-deception and inauthenticity.

In final analysis, therefore, Sartre does not really deny the existence of values. Rather, he is a subjectivist, but not in the sense that he believes moral judgments are

*"Existentialism is a Humanism" (1946), in *Existentialism and Humanism*, trans. Philip Mairet (Brooklyn: Haskell House, 1977).

merely expressions of individual desires and attitudes. He is a subjectivist in the sense that he believes the subject creates his or her own values. But once they are created, these values are, for Sartre, absolute, and to act inconsistently relative to your own moral standards is, in his words, *bad faith.*

Another important existentialist writer is Albert Camus, who is the author of the selection below, from his work *The Myth of Sisyphus.* The themes presented in the selection are similar to those found in the philosophy of Sartre. Camus begins with the startling announcement that the only truly serious philosophical problem is that of suicide: Is life worth living, or is it not? The importance of this question, according to Camus, becomes evident when an individual confronts what he calls the "feeling of absurdity." The feeling of absurdity is the awareness that existence is utterly without meaning, or "absurd." (These come to the same thing for Camus.) Throughout this essay, when Camus refers to the "absurd man," he means the person who perceives the insignificance and pointlessness of life.

Camus acknowledges that many who have this understanding do not in fact commit suicide. Some do not because they are slaves to the habit of living, some because they hope eventually to find something that will give meaning to life. Such hope is a "fatal evasion," Camus says.

Camus then explains how the sense of life's meaninglessness may come to us during the daily routine, or while watching others and noting the insignificance of their activity, or when seeing ourselves in the mirror. Above all, it comes to us when we reflect on the certainty of our death and on the absolute indifference of the world to our deeds and aspirations.

The absurdity of existence is also apparent, Camus implies, in our inability to understand the world and in the world's indifference to our attempts to do so. Other living things, he says, cats for example, lack self-consciousness and thus are unaware of being different from the rest of the world. A person, by contrast, senses the separation between consciousness and the world out there: Here on the one hand am I, with a wild longing for clarity and understanding. There on the other is the world: cold, indifferent, unconscious, and "irrational." In the futility of our striving to gain understanding, the absurdity of life becomes apparent.

My anxiety that life is meaningless cannot be quieted through religion, Camus implies, though my temptation to reach out to religion and prophets may be great.

According to Camus, the "everyday man" (that is, one who has not become aware of the absurdity of existence) has certain aims and objectives; indeed, he will be a slave to them. After realizing the absurdity of existence, however, one gains freedom from the demands of one's objectives; but one also becomes indifferent to the future. This indifference absolutely undermines any set of values the individual might have had. Camus is saying, in other words, that since all activity is pointless and futile, what could be the difference between good and bad, right and wrong?

How does the individual who understands the absurdity of life respond, according to Camus? His answer is contained in the last part of the selection, in the form of a parable: Sisyphus must ceaselessly push a rock to the top of a mountain, from where it falls back down and must be pushed up again, over and over.

from *The Myth of Sisyphus*

Albert Camus

Albert Camus (1913–1960) was a journalist, playwright, novelist, social activist, and philosopher. The following selection is from *The Myth of Sisyphus*, translated from the French by Justin O'Brien (New York: Alfred A. Knopf, 1955).

Absurdity and Suicide

There is but one truly serious philosophical problem, and that is suicide. Judging whether life is or is not worth living amounts to answering the fundamental question of philosophy. All the rest—whether or not the world has three dimensions, whether the mind has nine or twelve categories—comes afterwards. These are games; one must first answer. And if it is true, as Nietzsche claims, that a philosopher, to deserve our respect, must preach by example, you can appreciate the importance of that reply, for it will precede the definitive act. These are facts the heart can feel; yet they call for careful study before they become clear to the intellect.

If I ask myself how to judge that this question is more urgent than that, I reply that one judges by the actions it entails. I have never seen anyone die for the ontological argument. Galileo, who held a scientific truth of great importance, abjured it with the greatest of ease as soon as it endangered his life. In a certain sense, he did right.[1] That truth was not worth the stake. Whether the earth or the sun revolves around the other is a matter of profound indifference. To tell the truth, it is a futile question. On the other hand, I see many people die because they judge that life is not worth living. I see others paradoxically getting killed for the ideas or illusions that give them a reason for living (what is called a reason for living is also an excellent reason for dying). I therefore conclude that the meaning of life is the most urgent of questions. How to answer it? On all essential problems (I mean thereby those that run the risk of leading to death or those that intensify the passion of living) there are probably but two methods of thought: the method of La Palisse and the method of Don Quixote. Solely the balance between evidence and lyricism can allow us to achieve simultaneously emotion and lucidity. In a subject at once so humble and so heavy with emotion, the learned and classical dialectic must yield, one can see, to a more modest attitude of mind deriving at one and the same time from common sense and understanding.

Suicide has never been dealt with except as a social phenomenon. On the contrary, we are concerned here, at the outset, with the relationship between individual thought and suicide. An act like this is prepared within the silence of the heart, as is a great work of art. The man himself is ignorant of it. One evening he pulls the trigger or jumps. Of an apartment-building manager who had killed himself I was told that he had lost his daughter five years before, that he had changed greatly since, and that that experience had "undermined" him. A more exact word cannot be imagined. Beginning to think is beginning to be undermined. Society has but little connection with such beginnings. The worm is in man's heart. That is where it must be sought. One must follow and understand this fatal game that leads from lucidity in the face of existence to flight from light. . . .

But if it is hard to fix the precise instant, the subtle step when the mind opted for death, it is easier to deduce from the act itself the consequences it implies. In a sense, and as in melodrama, killing yourself amounts to confessing. It is con-

[1] From the point of view of the relative value of truth. On the other hand, from the point of view of virile behavior, this scholar's fragility may well make us smile.

fessing that life is too much for you or that you do not understand it. Let's not go too far in such analogies, however, but rather return to everyday words. It is merely confessing that that "is not worth the trouble." Living, naturally, is never easy. You continue making the gestures commanded by existence for many reasons, the first of which is habit. Dying voluntarily implies that you have recognized, even instinctively, the ridiculous character of that habit, the absence of any profound reason for living, the insane character of that daily agitation, and the uselessness of suffering.

What, then, is that incalculable feeling that deprives the mind of the sleep necessary to life? A world that can be explained even with bad reasons is a familiar world. But, on the other hand, in a universe suddenly divested of illusions and lights, man feels an alien, a stranger. His exile is without remedy since he is deprived of the memory of a lost home or the hope of a promised land. This divorce between man and his life, the actor and his setting, is properly the feeling of absurdity. All healthy men having thought of their own suicide, it can be seen, without further explanation, that there is a direct connection between this feeling and the longing for death.

The subject of this essay is precisely this relationship between the absurd and suicide, the exact degree to which suicide is a solution to the absurd. The principle can be established that for a man who does not cheat, what he believes to be true must determine his action. Belief in the absurdity of existence must then dictate his conduct. It is legitimate to wonder, clearly and without false pathos, whether a conclusion of this importance requires forsaking as rapidly as possible an incomprehensible condition. I am speaking, of course, of men inclined to be in harmony with themselves.

Stated clearly, this problem may seem both simple and insoluble. But it is wrongly assumed that simple questions involve answers that are no less simple and that evidence implies evidence. *A priori* and reversing the terms of the problem, just as one does or does not kill oneself, it seems that there are but two philosophical solutions, either yes or no. This would be too easy. But allowance must be made for those who, without concluding, continue questioning. Here I am only slightly indulging in irony: this is the majority. I notice also that those who answer "no" act as if they thought "yes." As a matter of fact, I accept the Nietzschean criterion, they think "yes" in one way or another. On the other hand, it often happens that those who commit suicide were assured of the meaning of life. These contradictions are constant. It may even be said that they have never been so keen as on this point where, on the contrary, logic seems so desirable. It is a commonplace to compare philosophical theories and the behavior of those who profess them. . . . Schopenhauer is often cited, as a fit subject for laughter, because he praised suicide while seated at a well-set table. This is no subject for joking. That way of not taking the tragic seriously is not so grievous, but it helps to judge a man.

In the face of such contradictions and obscurities must we conclude that there is no relationship between the opinion one has about life and the act one commits to leave it? Let us not exaggerate in this direction. In a man's attachment to life there is something stronger than all the ills in the world. The body's judgment is as good as the mind's, and the body shrinks from annihilation. We get into the habit of living before acquiring the habit of thinking. In that race which daily hastens us toward death, the body maintains its irreparable lead. In short, the essence of that contradiction lies in what I shall call the act of eluding because it is both less and more than diversion in the Pascalian sense. Eluding is the invariable game. The typical act of eluding, the fatal evasion that constitutes the third theme of this essay, is hope. Hope for another life one must "deserve" or trickery of those who live not for life itself but for some great idea that will transcend it, refine it, give it meaning, and betray it. . . .

Absurdity and Meaning

All great deeds and all great thoughts have a ridiculous beginning. Great works are often born on a street-corner or in a restaurant's revolving door. So it is with absurdity. The absurd world more than others derives its nobility from that abject birth. In certain situations, replying "nothing" when asked what one is thinking about may be pretense in a man. Those who are loved are well aware of this. But if that reply is sincere, if it symbolizes that odd state of soul in which the void becomes eloquent, in which the chain of daily gestures is broken, in which the heart vainly seeks the link that will connect it again, then it is as if it were the first sign of absurdity.

It happens that the stage sets collapse. Rising, streetcar, four hours in the office or factory, meal, streetcar, four hours of work, meal, sleep, and Monday Tuesday Wednesday Thursday Friday and Saturday according to the same rhythm—this path is easily followed most of the time. But one day the "why" arises and everything begins in that weariness tinged with amazement. "Begins"—this is important. Weariness comes at the end of the acts of a mechanical life, but at the same time it inaugurates the impulse of consciousness. It awakens consciousness and provokes what follows. What follows is the gradual return into the chain or it is the definitive awakening. At the end of the awakening comes, in time, the consequence: suicide or recovery. In itself weariness has something sickening about it. Here, I must conclude that it is good. For everything begins with consciousness and noth-ing is worth anything except through it. . . .

At the heart of all beauty lies something inhuman, and these hills, the softness of the sky, the outline of these trees at this very minute lose the illusory meaning with which we had clothed them, henceforth more remote than a lost paradise. The primitive hostility of the world rises up to face us across millennia. For a second we cease to understand it because for centuries we have understood it in solely the images and designs that we had attributed to it beforehand, because henceforth we lack the power to make use of that artifice. The world evades us because it becomes itself again. That stage scenery masked by habit becomes again what it is. It withdraws at a distance from us. Just as there are days when under the familiar face of a woman, we see as a stranger her we had loved months or years ago, perhaps we shall come even to desire what suddenly leaves us so alone. But the time has not yet come. Just one thing: that denseness and that strangeness of the world is the absurd.

Men, too, secrete the inhuman. At certain moments of lucidity, the mechanical aspect of their gestures, their meaningless pantomime makes silly everything that surrounds them. A man is talking on the telephone behind a glass partition; you cannot hear him, but you see his incomprehensible dumb show: you wonder why he is alive. This discomfort in the face of man's own inhumanity, this incalculable tumble before the image of what we are, this "nausea," as a writer of today calls it, is also the absurd. Likewise, the stranger who at certain seconds comes to meet us in a mirror, the familiar and yet alarming brother we encounter in our own photographs is also the absurd.

I come at last to death and the attitude we have toward it. On this point everything has been said and it is only proper to avoid pathos. Yet one will never be sufficiently surprised that everyone lives as if no one "knew." This is because in reality there is no experience of death. Properly speaking, nothing has been experienced but what has been lived and made conscious. Here, it is barely possible to speak of the experience of others' deaths. It is a substitute, an illusion, and it never quite convinces us. That melancholy convention cannot be persuasive. The horror comes in reality from the mathematical aspect of the event. If time frightens us, this is because it works out the problem and the solution comes afterward. All the pretty speeches about the soul will have their contrary convincingly proved, at least for a time. From this inert body on which a slap makes no mark the soul has disappeared. This elementary and definitive aspect of the adventure constitutes the absurd feeling. Under the fatal lighting of that destiny, its uselessness becomes evident. No code of ethics and no effort are justifiable a priori in the face of the cruel mathematics that command our condition. . . .

Understanding the world for a man is reducing it to the human, stamping it with his seal. The cat's universe is not the universe of the anthill. The truism "All thought is anthropomorphic" has no other meaning. Likewise, the mind that aims to understand reality can consider itself satisfied only by reducing it to terms of thought. If man realized that the universe like him can love and suffer, he would be reconciled. If thought discovered in the shimmering mirrors of phenomena eternal relations capable of summing them up and summing themselves up in a single principle, then would be seen an intellectual joy of which the myth of the blessed would be but a ridiculous imitation. That nostalgia for unity, that appetite for the absolute illustrates the essential impulse of the human drama. But the fact of that nostalgia's existence does not imply that is it to be immediately satisfied. . . .

With the exception of professional rationalists, today people despair of true knowledge. If the only significant history of human thought were to be written, it would have to be the history of its successive regrets and its impotences.

Of whom and of what indeed can I say: "I know that!" This heart within me I can feel, and I judge that it exists. This world I can touch, and I likewise judge that it exists. There ends all my knowledge, and the rest is construction. For if I try to seize this self of which I feel sure, if I try to define and summarize it, it is nothing but water slipping through my fingers. I can sketch one by one all the aspects it is able to assume, all those likewise that have been attributed to is, this upbringing, this origin, this ardor of these silences, this nobility or this vileness. But aspects cannot be added up. This very heart which is mine will forever remain indefinable to me. Between the certainly I have of my existence and the content I try to give to that assurance, the gap will never be filled. Forever I shall be a stranger to myself. . . .

Hence the intelligence, too, tells me in its way that this world is absurd. . . . In this unintelligible and limited universe, man's fate henceforth assumes its meaning. A horde of irrationals has sprung up and surrounds him until his ultimate end. In his recovered and now studied lucidity, the feeling of the absurd becomes clear and definite. I said that the world is absurd, but I was too hasty. This world in itself is not reasonable, that is all that can be said. But what is absurd is the confrontation of this irrational and the wild longing for clarity whose call echoes in the human heart. The absurd depends as much on man as on the world. . . .

I don't know whether this world has a meaning that transcends it. But I know that I do not know that meaning and that it is impossible for me to just now to know it. What can a meaning outside my condition mean to me? I can understand only in human terms. What I touch, what resists me—that is what I understand. And these two certainties—my appetite for the absolute and for unity and the impossibility of reducing this world to a rational and reasonable principle—I also know that I cannot reconcile them. What other truth can I admit without lying, without bringing in a hope I lack and which means nothing within the limits of my condition?

If I were a tree among trees, a cat among animals, this life would have a meaning, or rather this problem would not rise, for I should belong to this world. I should *be* this world to which I am now opposed by my whole consciousness and my whole insistence upon familiarity. This ridiculous reason is what sets me in opposition to all creation. I cannot cross it out with a stroke of a pen. What I believe to be true I must therefore preserve. What seems to me so obvious, even against me, I must support. And what constitutes the basis of that conflict, of that break between the world and my mind, but the awareness of it? If therefore I want to preserve it, I can through a constant awareness, ever revived, ever alert. This is what, for the moment, I must remember. . . .

Let us insist again on the method: it is a matter of persisting. At a certain point on his path the absurd man is tempted. History is not lacking in either religions or prophets, even without gods. He is asked to leap. All he can reply is that he doesn't fully understand, that it is not obvious. Indeed, he does not want to do anything but what he fully understands. He is assured that this is the sin of pride, but he does not understand the notion of sin; that perhaps hell is in store, but he has not enough imagination to visualize that strange future; that he is losing immortal life, that seems to him an idle consideration. An attempt is made to get him to admit his guilt. He feels innocent. To tell the truth, that is all he feels—his irreparable innocence. This is what allows him everything. Hence, what he demands of himself is to live *solely* with what he knows, to accommodate himself to what is, and to bring in nothing that is not certain. He is told that nothing is. But this at least is a certainty. And it is with this that he is concerned: he wants to find out of it is possible to live *without appeal*. . . .

Before encountering the absurd, the everyday man lives with aims, a concern for the future or for justification (with regard to whom or what is not the question). He weighs his chances, he counts on "someday," his retirement or the labor of his sons. He still thinks that something in his life can be directed. In truth, he acts as if he were free, even if all the facts make a point of contradicting that liberty. But after the absurd, everything is upset. That idea that "I am," my way of acting as if everything has a meaning (even if, on occasion, I said that nothing has)—all that is given the lie in vertiginous fashion by the absurdity of a possible death. Thinking of the future, establishing aims for oneself, having preferences—all this presupposes a belief in freedom, even if one occasionally ascertains that one doesn't feel it. But at that moment I am well aware that that higher liberty, that freedom *to be*, which alone can serve as basis for a truth, does not exist. Death is there as the only reality. . . .

But at the same time the absurd man realizes that hitherto he was bound to that postulate of freedom on the illusion of which he was living. In a certain sense, that hampered him. To the extent to which he imagined a purpose to his life, he adapted himself to the demands of a purpose to be achieved and became the slave of his liberty. Thus I could not act otherwise than as the father (or the engineer or the leader of a nation, or the post-office subclerk) that I am preparing to be. . . .

The absurd enlightens me on this point: there is no future. Henceforth, this is the reason for my inner freedom. . . .

But what does life mean in such a universe? Nothing else for the moment but indifference to the future and a desire to use up everything that is given. Belief in the meaning of life always implies a scale of values, a choice, our preferences. Belief in the absurd, according to our definitions, teaches the contrary. But this is worth examining.

Knowing whether or not one can live *without appeal* is all that interests me. I do not want to get out of my depth. This aspect of life being given to me, can I adapt myself to it? Now, faced with this particular concern, belief in the absurd is tantamount to substituting the quantity of experiences for the quality. If I convince myself that this life has no other aspect than that of the absurd, if I feel that its whole equilibrium depends on that perpetual opposition between my conscious revolt and the darkness in which it struggles, if I admit that my freedom has no meaning except in relation to its limited fate, then I must say that what counts is not the best of living but the most living. . . .

On the one hand the absurd teaches that all experiences are unimportant, and on the other it urges toward the greatest quantity of experiences. How, then, can one fail to do as so many of those men I was speaking of earlier—choose the form of life that brings us the most possible of that human matter, thereby introducing a scale of values that on the other hand one claims to reject?

But again it is the absurd and its contradictory life that teaches us. For the mistake is thinking that that quantity of experiences depends on the circumstances of our life when it depends solely on us. Here we have to be over-simple. To two men living the same number of years, the world always provides the same sum of experiences. It is up to us to be conscious of them. Being aware of one's life, one's revolt, one's freedom, and to the maximum, is living, and to the maximum. Where lucidity dominates, the scale of values becomes useless. . . .

The Myth of Sisyphus

The gods had condemned Sisyphus to ceaselessly rolling a rock to the top of a mountain, whence the stone would fall back of its own weight. They had thought with some reason that there is no more dreadful punishment than futile and hopeless labor.

If one believes Homer, Sisyphus was the wisest and most prudent of mortals. According to another tradition, however, he was disposed to practice the profession of highwayman. I see no contradiction in this. Opinions differ as to the reasons why he became the futile laborer of the underworld. To begin with, he is accused of a certain levity in regard to the gods. He stole their secrets. Ægina, the daughter of Æsopus, was carried off by Jupiter. The father was shocked by that disappearance and complained to Sisyphus. He, who knew of the abduction, offered to tell about it on condition that Æsopus would give water to the citadel of Corinth. To the celestial thunderbolts he preferred the benediction of water. He was punished for this in the underworld. Homer tells us also that Sisyphus had put Death in chains. Pluto could not endure the sight of his deserted, silent empire. He dispatched the god of war, who liberated Death from the hands of her conqueror.

It is said also that Sisyphus, being near to death, rashly wanted to test his wife's love. He ordered her to cast his unburied body into the middle of the public square. Sisyphus woke up in the underworld. And there, annoyed by an obedience so contrary to human love, he obtained from Pluto permission to return to earth in order to chastise his wife. But when he had seen again the face of this world, enjoyed water and sun, warm stones and the sea, he no longer wanted to go back to the infernal darkness. Recalls, signs of anger, warnings were of no avail. Many years more he lived facing the curve of the gulf, the sparkling sea, and the smiles of earth. A decree of the gods was necessary. Mercury came and seized the impudent man by the collar and, snatching him from his joys, led him forcibly back to the underworld, where his rock was ready for him.

You have already grasped that Sisyphus is the absurd hero. He *is*, as much through his passions as through his torture. His scorn of the gods, his hatred of death, and his passion for life won him that unspeakable penalty in which the whole being is exerted toward accomplishing nothing. This is the price that must be paid for the passions of this earth. Nothing is told us about Sisyphus in the underworld. Myths are made for the imagination to breathe life into them. As for this myth, one sees merely the whole effort of a body straining to raise the huge stone, to roll it and push it up a slope a hundred times over; one sees the face screwed up, the cheek tight against the stone, the shoulder bracing the clay-covered mass, the foot wedging it, the fresh start with arms outstretched, the wholly human security of two earth-clotted hands. At the very end of his long effort measured by skyless space and time without depth, the purpose is achieved. Then Sisyphus watches the stone rush down in a few moments toward that lower world whence he will have to push it up again toward the summit. He goes back down to the plain.

It is during that return, that pause, that Sisyphus interests me. A face that toils so close to stones is already stone itself! I see that man going back down with a heavy yet measured step toward the torment of which he will never know the end. That hour like a breathing-space which returns as surely as his suffering, that is the hour of consciousness. At each of those moments when he leaves the heights and gradually sinks toward the lairs of the gods, he is superior to his fate. He is stronger than his rock.

If this myth is tragic, that is because its hero is conscious. Where would his torture be, indeed, if at every step the hope of succeeding upheld him? The workman of today works every day in his life at the same tasks, and this fate is no less absurd. But it is tragic only at the rare moments when it becomes conscious. Sisyphus, proletarian of the gods, powerless and rebellious, knows the whole extent of his wretched condition: it is what he thinks of during his descent. The lucidity that was to constitute his torture at the same time crowns his victory. There is no fate that cannot be surmounted by scorn.

If the descent is sometimes performed in sorrow, it can also take place in joy. This word is not too much. Again I fancy Sisyphus returning toward his rock, and the sorrow was in the beginning. When the images of earth cling too tightly to memory, when the call of happiness becomes too insistent, it happens that melancholy rises in man's heart: this is the rock's victory, this is the rock itself. The boundless grief is too heavy to bear. These are our nights of Gethsemane. But crushing truths perish from being acknowledged. Thus, Œdipus at the outset obeys fate without knowing it. But from the moment he knows, his tragedy begins. Yet at the same moment, blind and desperate, he realizes that the only bond linking him to the world is the cool hand of a girl. Then a tremendous remark rings out: "Despite so many ordeals, my advanced age and the nobility of my soul make me conclude that all is well." Sophocles' Œdipus, like Dostoevsky's Kirilov, thus gives the recipe for the absurd victory. Ancient wisdom confirms modern heroism.

One does not discover the absurd without being tempted to write a manual of happiness. "What! by such narrow ways—?" There is but one world, however. Happiness and the absurd are two sons of the same earth. They are inseparable. It would be a mistake to say that happiness necessarily springs from the absurd discovery. It happens as well that the feeling of the absurd springs from happiness. "I conclude that all is well," says Œdipus, and that remark is sacred. It echoes in the wild and limited universe of man. It teaches that all is not, has not been, exhausted. It drives out of this world a god who had come into it with dissatisfaction and a preference for futile sufferings. It makes of fate a human matter, which must be settled among men.

All Sisyphus' silent joy is contained therein. His fate belongs to him. His rock is his thing. Likewise, the absurd man, when he contemplates his torment, silences all the idols. In the universe suddenly restored to its silence, the myriad wondering little voices of the earth rise up. Unconscious, secret calls, invitations from all the faces, they are the necessary reverse and price of victory. There is no sun without shadow, and it is essential to know the night. The absurd man says yes and his effort will henceforth be unceasing. If there is a personal fate, there is no higher destiny, or at least there is but one which he concludes is inevitable and despicable. For the rest, he knows himself to be the master of his days. At that subtle moment when man glances backward over his life, Sisyphus returning toward his rock, in that slight pivoting he contemplates that series of unrelated actions which becomes his fate, created by him, combined under his memory's eye and soon sealed by his death. Thus, convinced of the wholly human origin of all that is human, a blind man eager to see who knows that the night has no end, he is still on the go. The rock is still rolling.

I leave Sisyphus at the foot of the mountain! One always finds one's burden again. But Sisyphus teaches the higher fidelity that negates the gods and raises rocks. He too concludes that all is well. This universe henceforth without a master seems to him neither sterile nor futile. Each atom of that stone, each mineral flake of that night-filled mountain, in itself forms a world. The struggle itself toward the heights is enough to fill a man's heart. One must imagine Sisyphus happy.

Study Questions

1. Explain what Camus means by saying that the only truly serious philosophical problem is that of suicide.
2. What is "the feeling of absurdity"?
3. Does Camus think that the question of suicide is important to everyone?
4. Does Camus think that everyone who has the feeling of absurdity commits suicide? Explain.
5. Describe some of the situations in which we might come to have the feeling of life's absurdity, according to Camus.
6. Does religion offer comfort against the feeling that life is absurd, according to Camus?
7. Does "the absurd man" have values, according to Camus? Explain.
8. Explain why Camus thinks of Sisyphus as "the absurd hero."
9. Why does Camus think that Sisyphus's consciousness is what makes Sisyphus tragic?
10. What does Camus mean by saying, "One must imagine Sisyphus happy"?

PART

APPLIED ETHICS

To beginners in philosophy, ethics sometimes seems sterile, abstract, and altogether too theoretical. Yet ethical theory always has been applied to concrete problems. This practice has been especially common in the past two decades or so, during which many moral philosophers have devoted their attention to specific moral issues of contemporary interest and importance. In Part III of this book, we give you a sampling of this recent literature in "applied ethics."

The issues you will find covered here fall under five topics: euthanasia, abortion, helping the needy, sexual morality, and preferential treatment (affirmative action). Each chapter of this part of the book consists of four recent essays pertaining to one or another of these issues.

CHAPTER 12

EUTHANASIA AND ABORTION

Euthanasia

The American Medical Association distinguishes two types of euthanasia: (1) active euthanasia, or mercy killing, and (2) passive euthanasia, that is, permitting a person to die by (for example) not employing life-sustaining measures. In the first reading in this chapter, James Rachels maintains that this distinction is without foundation. In fact, Rachels argues, from a moral point of view there is no relevant difference between so-called active and passive euthanasia.

Philippa Foot begins her essay by stipulating that to qualify as euthanasia, an act of killing or allowing to die must be for the good of the person who dies. She then considers what it is that can be for the good of someone, and especially considers the sense in which life itself is a good. The possibility of a conceptual linkage between *good* and *life-sustaining* are examined. In what way, Foot ponders, are the elements of good within our life relevant to the question of whether we benefit if our life is preserved?

Foot moves on to consider whether acts of euthanasia are ever morally permissible. Charity and justice make different moral demands on us in relation to killing (or allowing to die), she argues; James Rachels's idea that there is no relevant moral difference between active and passive euthanasia is seen to be false once we recognize this, she says.

Having clarified the distinction between the moral demands of justice and charity, Foot considers in some detail first the demands of justice relative to euthanasia, both active and passive, voluntary and nonvoluntary; and then the demands of charity. She concludes that nonvoluntary active euthanasia (killing someone against the person's will without his or her consent) is never justified but that the other combinations—voluntary active and passive euthanasia and nonvoluntary passive euthanasia—can at times be compatible with both justice and charity.

Finally, Foot considers our present practices in the light of these conclusions. She emphasizes some dangers in legalizing voluntary active euthanasia.

Active and Passive Euthanasia

James Rachels

James Rachels (b. 1941) is a Professor of Philosophy at the University of Alabama at Birmingham. The following selection appeared in *The New England Journal of Medicine* 292, no. 2 (January 9, 1975).

The distinction between active and passive euthanasia is thought to be crucial for medical ethics. The idea is that it is permissible, at least in some cases, to withhold treatment and allow a patient to die, but it is never permissible to take any direct action designed to kill the patient. This doctrine seems to be accepted by most doctors, and it was endorsed in a statement adopted by the House of Delegates of the American Medical Association on December 4, 1973:

> The intentional termination of the life of one human being by another—mercy killing—is contrary to that for which the medical profession stands and is contrary to the policy of the American Medical Association.
>
> The cessation of the employment of extraordinary means to prolong the life of the body when there is irrefutable evidence that biological death is imminent is the decision of the patient and/or his immediate family. The advice and judgment of the physician should be freely available to the patient and/or his immediate family.

However, a strong case can be made against this doctrine. In what follows I will set out some of the relevant arguments, and urge doctors to reconsider their views on this matter.

To begin with a familiar type of situation, a patient who is dying of incurable cancer of the throat is in terrible pain, which can no longer be satisfactorily alleviated. He is certain to die within a few days, even if present treatment is continued, but he does not want to go on living for those days since the pain is unbearable. So he asks the doctor for an end to it, and his family joins in the request.

Suppose the doctor agrees to withhold treatment, as the conventional doctrine says he may. The justification for his doing so is that the patient is in terrible agony, and since he is going to die anyway, it would be wrong to prolong his suffering needlessly. But now notice this. If one simply withholds treatment, it may take the patient longer to die, and so he may suffer more than he would if more direct action were taken and a lethal injection given. This fact provides strong reason for thinking that, once the initial decision not to prolong his agony has been made, active euthanasia is actually preferable to passive euthanasia, rather than the reverse. To say otherwise is to endorse the option that leads to more suffering rather than less, and is contrary to the humanitarian impulse that prompts the decision not to prolong his life in the first place.

Part of my point is that the process of being "allowed to die" can be relatively slow and painful, whereas being given a lethal injection is relatively quick and painless. Let me give a different sort of example. In the United States about one in 600 babies is born with Down's syndrome. Most of these babies are otherwise healthy—that is, with only the usual pediatric care, they will proceed to an otherwise normal infancy. Some, however, are born with congenital defects such as intestinal obstructions that require operations if they are to live. Sometimes, the parents and the doctor will decide not to operate, and let the infant die. Anthony Shaw describes what happens then.

> . . . When surgery is denied [the doctor] must try to keep the infant from suffering while natural forces sap the baby's life away. As a surgeon whose natural inclination is to use the scalpel to fight off death, standing by

> and watching a salvageable baby die is the most emotionally exhausting experience I know. It is easy at a conference, in a theoretical discussion, to decide that such infants should be allowed to die. It is altogether different to stand by in the nursery and watch as dehydration and infection wither a tiny being over hours and days. This is a terrible ordeal for me and the hospital staff—much more so than for the parents who never set foot in the nursery.[1]

I can understand why some people are opposed to all euthanasia, and insist that such infants must be allowed to live. I think I can also understand why other people favor destroying these babies quickly and painlessly. But why should anyone favor letting "dehydration and infection wither a tiny being over hours and days?" The doctrine that says that a baby may be allowed to dehydrate and wither, but may not be given an injection that would end its life without suffering, seems so patently cruel as to require no further refutation. The strong language is not intended to offend, but only to put the point in the clearest possible way.

My second argument is that the conventional doctrine leads to decisions concerning life and death made on irrelevant grounds.

Consider again the case of the infants with Down's syndrome who need operations for congenital defects unrelated to the syndrome to live. Sometimes there is no operation, and the baby dies, but when there is no such defect, the baby lives on. Now, an operation such as that to remove an intestinal obstruction is not prohibitively difficult. The reason why such operations are not performed in these cases is, clearly, that the child has Down's syndrome and the parents and doctor judge that because of that fact it is better for the child to die.

But notice that this situation is absurd, no matter what view one takes of the lives and potentials of such babies. If the life of such an infant is worth preserving, what does it matter if it needs a simple operation? Or, if one thinks it better that such a baby should not live on, what difference does it make that it happens to have an unobstructed intestinal tract? In either case, the matter of life and death is being decided on irrelevant grounds. It is the Down's syndrome, and not the intestines, that is the issue. The matter should be decided, if at all, on that basis, and not be allowed not depend on the essentially irrelevant question of whether the intestinal tract is blocked.

What makes this situation possible, of course, is the idea that when there is an intestinal blockage, one can "let the baby die," but when there is no such defect there is nothing that can be done, for one must not "kill" it. The fact that this idea leads to such results as deciding life or death on irrelevant grounds is another good reason why the doctrine should be rejected.

One reason why so many people think that there is an important moral difference between active and passive euthanasia is that they think killing someone is morally worse than letting someone die. But is it? Is killing, in itself, worse than letting die? To investigate this issue, two cases may be considered that are exactly alike except that one involves killing whereas the other involves letting someone die. Then, it can be asked whether this difference makes any difference to the moral assessments. It is important that the cases be exactly alike, except for this one difference, since otherwise one cannot be confident that it is this difference and not some other that accounts for any variation in the assessments of the two cases. So, let us consider this pair of cases:

In the first, Smith stands to gain a large inheritance if anything should happen to his six-year-old cousin. One evening while the child is taking his bath, Smith sneaks into the bathroom and drowns the child, and then arranges things so that it will look like an accident.

In the second, Jones also stands to gain if anything should happen to his six-year-old cousin. Like Smith, Jones sneaks in planning to drown the child in his bath. However, just as he enters the bathroom Jones sees the child slip and hit his head, and fall face down in the water. Jones is delighted; he stands by, ready to push the child's head back under if it is necessary, but it is not necessary. With only a little thrashing about the child drowns all by himself, "accidentally," as Jones watches and does nothing.

Now Smith killed the child, whereas Jones "merely" let the child die. That is the only difference between them. Did either man behave better, from a moral point of view? If the difference between killing and letting die were in itself a morally important matter, one should say that Jones's behavior was less reprehensible than Smith's. But does one really want to say that? I think not. In the first place, both men acted from the same motive, personal gain, and both had exactly the same end in view when they acted. It may be inferred from Smith's conduct that he is a bad man, although that judgment may be withdrawn or modified if certain further facts are learned about him—for example, that he is mentally deranged. But would not the very same thing be inferred about Jones from his conduct? And would not the same further considerations also be relevant to any modification of this judgment? Moreover, suppose Jones pleaded, in his own defense, "After all, I didn't do anything except just stand there and watch the child drown. I didn't kill him; I only let him die." Again, if letting die were in itself less bad than killing, this defense should have at least some weight. But it does not. Such a "defense" can only be regarded as a grotesque perversion of moral reasoning. Morally speaking, it is no defense at all.

Now it may be pointed out, quite properly, that the cases of euthanasia with which doctors are concerned are not like this at all. They do not involve personal gain or the destruction of normal healthy children. Doctors are concerned only with cases in which the patient's life is of no further use to him, or in which the patient's life has become or will soon become a terrible burden. However, the point is the same in these cases: the bare difference between killing and letting die does not, in itself, make a moral difference. If a doctor lets a patient die, for humane reasons, he is in the same moral position as if he had given the patient a lethal injection for humane reasons. If his decision was wrong—if, for example, the patient's illness was in fact curable—the decision would be equally regrettable no matter which method was used to carry it out. And if the doctor's decision was the right one, the method used is not in itself important.

The AMA policy statement isolates the crucial issue very well; the crucial issue is "the intentional termination of the life of one human being by another." But after identifying this issue, and forbidding "mercy killing," the statement goes on to deny that the cessation of treatment is the intentional termination of a life. This is where the mistake comes in, for what is the cessation of treatment, in these circumstances, if it is not "the intentional termination of the life of one human being by another?" Of course it is exactly that, and if it were not, there would be no point to it.

Many people will find this judgment hard to accept. One reason, I think, is that it is very easy to conflate the question of whether killing is, in itself, worse than letting die, with the very different question of whether most actual cases of killing are more reprehensible than most actual cases of letting die. Most actual cases of killing are clearly terrible (think, for example, of all the murders reported in the newspapers), and one hears of such cases every day. On the other hand, one hardly ever hears of a case of letting die, except for the actions of doctors who are motivated by humanitarian reasons. So one learns to think of killing in a much worse light than of letting die. But this does not mean that there is something about killing that makes it in itself worse than letting die, for it is not the bare difference between killing and letting die that makes the difference in these cases. Rather, the other factors—the murderer's motive of personal gain, for example, contrasted with the doctor's humanitarian motivation—account for different reactions to the different cases.

I have argued that killing is not in itself any worse than letting die; if my contention is right, it follows that active euthanasia is not any worse than passive euthanasia. What arguments can be given on the other side? The most common, I believe, is the following:

"The important difference between active and passive euthanasia is that, in passive euthanasia, the doctor does not do anything to bring about the patient's death. The doctor does nothing, and the patient dies of whatever ills already afflict him. In active euthanasia, however, the doctor does something to bring about the patient's death: he kills him. The doctor who gives the patient with cancer a lethal injection has himself caused his patient's death; whereas if he merely ceases treatment, the cancer is the cause of the death."

A number of points need to be made here. The first is that it is not exactly correct to say that in passive euthanasia the doctor does nothing, for he does do one thing that is very important: he lets the patient die. "Letting someone die" is certainly different, in some respects, from other types of action—mainly in that it is a kind of action that one may perform by way of not performing certain other actions. For example, one may let a patient die by way of not giving medication, just as one may insult someone by way of not shaking his hand. But for any purpose of moral assessment, it is a type of action nonetheless. The decision to let a patient die is subject to moral appraisal in the same way that a decision to kill him would be subject to moral appraisal: it may be assessed as wise or unwise, compassionate or sadistic, right or wrong. If a doctor deliberately let a patient die who was suffering from a routinely curable illness, the doctor would certainly be to blame for what he had done, just as he would be to blame if he had needlessly killed the patient. Charges against him would then be appropriate. If so, it would be no defense at all for him to insist that he didn't "do anything." He would have done something very serious indeed, for he let his patient die.

Fixing the cause of death may be very important from a legal point of view, for it may determine whether criminal charges are brought against the doctor. But I do not think that this notion can be used to show a moral difference between active and passive euthanasia. The reason why it is considered bad to be the cause of someone's death is that death is regarded as a great evil—and so it is. However, if it has been decided that euthanasia—even passive euthanasia—is desirable in a given case, it has also been decided that in this instance death is no greater an evil than the patient's continued existence. And if this is true, the usual reason for not wanting to be the cause of someone's death simply does not apply.

Finally, doctors may think that all of this is only of academic interest—the sort of thing that philosophers may worry about but that has no practical bearing on their own work. After all, doctors must be concerned about the legal consequences of what they do, and active euthanasia is clearly forbidden by the law. But even so, doctors should also be concerned with the fact that the law is forcing upon them a moral doctrine that may well be indefensible, and has a considerable effect on their practices. Of course, most doctors are not now in the position of being coerced in this matter, for they do not regard themselves as merely going along with what the law requires. Rather, in statements such as the AMA policy statement that I have quoted, they are endorsing this doctrine as a central point of medical ethics. In that statement, active euthanasia is condemned not merely as illegal but is "contrary to that for which the medical profession stands," whereas passive euthanasia is approved. However, the preceding considerations suggest that there is really no moral difference between the two considered in themselves (there may be important moral differences in some cases in their *consequences*, but, as I pointed out, these differences may make active euthanasia, and not passive euthanasia the morally preferable option). So, whereas doctors may have to discriminate between active and passive euthanasia to satisfy the law, they should not do any more than that. In particular, they should not give the distinction any added authority and weight by writing it into official statements of medical ethics.

Notes

1. A. Shaw, "Doctor, Do We Have a Choice?" *The New York Times Magazine*, January 30, 1972, p. 54.

Study Questions

1. Explain the difference between active and passive euthanasia.
2. Explain Rachels's reason for saying that killing a person is no worse than letting a person die.

3. Why do many people think that killing a person is worse than letting a person die, according to Rachels?
4. Explain the most common counterargument to Rachels's position.
5. What, according to Rachels, is wrong with that counterargument?

Euthanasia

Philippa Foot

Philippa Foot (b. 1920) is Professor Emeritus of Philosophy at the University of California at Los Angeles and a fellow of Somerville College, Oxford University. The following article appeared in *Philosophy and Public Affairs* 6, no. 2 (1977). This version has been abridged and revised by Professor Foot, and some footnotes have been omitted.

The widely used *Shorter Oxford English Dictionary* gives three meanings for the word "euthanasia": the first, "a quiet and easy death"; the second, "the means of procuring this"; and the third, "the action of inducing a quiet and easy death." It is a curious fact that no one of the three gives an adequate definition of the word as it is usually understood. For "euthanasia" means much more than a quiet and easy death, or the means of procuring it, or the action of inducing it. The definition specifies only the manner of the death, and if this were all that was implied a murderer, careful to drug his victim, could claim that his act was an act of euthanasia. We find this ridiculous because we take it for granted that in euthanasia it is death itself, not just the manner of death, that must be kind to the one who dies.

To see how important it is that "euthanasia" should not be used as the dictionary definition allows it to be used, merely to signify that a death was quiet and easy, one has only to remember that Hitler's "euthanasia" program traded on this ambiguity. Under this program, planned before the War but brought into full operation by a decree of 1 September 1939, some 275,000 people were gassed in centers which were to be a model for those in which Jews were later exterminated. Anyone in a state institution could be sent to the gas chambers if it was considered that he could not be "rehabilitated" for useful work. As Dr. Leo Alexander reports, relying on the testimony of a neuropathologist who received 500 brains from one of the killing centers,

> In Germany the exterminations included the mentally defective, psychotics (particularly schizophrenics), epileptics and patients suffering from infirmities of old age and from various organic neurological disorders such as infantile paralysis, Parkinsonism, multiple sclerosis and brain tumors. . . . In truth, all those unable to work and considered nonrehabilitable were killed.[1]

These people were killed because they were "useless" and "a burden on society"; only the manner of their deaths could be thought of as relatively easy and quiet.

Let us insist, then, that when we talk about euthanasia we are talking about a death understood as a good or happy event for the one who dies. This stipulation follows etymology, but is itself not

[1]Leo Alexander, "Medical Science under Dictatorship," *New England Journal of Medicine*, 14 July 1949, p. 40.

exactly in line with current usage, which would be captured by the condition that the death should *not* be an evil rather than that it *should* be a good. That this is how people talk is shown by the fact that the case of Karen Ann Quinlan and others in a state of permanent coma is often discussed under the heading of "euthanasia." Perhaps it is not too late to object to the use of the word "euthanasia" in this sense. Apart from the break with the Greek origins of the word there are other unfortunate aspects of this extension of the term. For if we say that the death must be supposed to be a good to the subject we can also specify that it shall be for his sake that an act of euthanasia is performed. If we say merely that death shall not be an evil to him, we cannot stipulate that benefiting him shall be the motive where euthanasia is in question. Given the importance of the question, For whose sake are we acting? it is good to have a definition of euthanasia which brings under this heading only cases of opting for death for the sake of the one who dies. Perhaps what is most important is to say either that euthanasia is to be for the good of the subject or at least that death is to be no evil to him, thus refusing to talk Hitler's language. However, in this paper it is the first condition that will be understood, with the additional proviso that by an act of euthanasia we mean one of inducing or otherwise opting for death for the sake of the one who is to die. . . .

. . . It is easy to say, as if this raised no problems, that an act of euthanasia is by definition one aiming at the *good* of the one whose death is in question, and that it is *for his sake* that his death is desired. But how is this to be explained? Presumably we are thinking of some evil already with him or to come on him if he continues to live, and death is thought of as a release from this evil. But this cannot be enough. Most people's lives contain evils such as grief or pain, but we do not therefore think that death would be a blessing to them. On the contrary life is generally supposed to be a good even for someone who is unusually unhappy or frustrated. How is it that one can ever wish for death for the sake of the one who is to die? This difficult question is central to the discussion of euthanasia, and we shall literally not know what we are talking about if we ask whether acts of euthanasia defined as we have defined them are ever morally permissible without first understanding better the reason for saying that life is a good, and the possibility that it is not always so.

If a man should save my life he would be my benefactor. In normal circumstances this is plainly true; but does one always benefit another in saving his life? It seems certain that he does not. Suppose, for instance, that a man were being tortured to death and was given a drug that lengthened his sufferings; this would not be a benefit but the reverse. Or suppose that in a ghetto in Nazi Germany a doctor saved the life of someone threatened by disease, but that the man once cured was transported to an extermination camp; the doctor might wish for the sake of the patient that he had died of the disease. Nor would a longer stretch of life always be a benefit to the person who was given it. Comparing Hitler's camps with those of Stalin, Dmitri Panin observes that in the latter the method of extermination was made worse by agonies that could stretch out over months.

> Death from a bullet would have been bliss compared with what many millions had to endure while dying of hunger. The kind of death to which they were condemned has nothing to equal it in treachery and sadism.[2]

These examples show that to save or prolong a man's life is not always to do him a service: it may be better for him if he dies earlier rather than later. It must therefore be agreed that while life is normally a benefit to the one who has it, this is not always so.

The judgment is often fairly easy to make—that life is or is not a good to someone—but the basis for it is very hard to find. When life is said to be a benefit or a good, on what grounds is the assertion made?

The difficulty is underestimated if it is supposed that the problem arises from the fact that

---

[2]Dmitri Panin, *The Notebooks of Sologdin* (London, 1976), pp. 66–67.

one who is dead has nothing, so that the good someone gets from being alive cannot be compared with the amount he would otherwise have had. For why should this particular comparison be necessary? Surely it would be enough if one could say whether or not someone whose life was prolonged had more good than evil in the extra stretch of time. Such estimates are not always possible, but frequently they are; we say, for example, "He was very happy in those last years," or, "He had little but unhappiness then." If the balance of good and evil determined whether life was a good to someone we would expect to find a correlation in the judgments. In fact, of course, we find nothing of the kind. First, a man who has no doubt that existence is a good to him may have no idea about the balance of happiness and unhappiness in his life, or of any other positive and negative factors that may be suggested. So the supposed criteria are not always operating where the judgment is made. And secondly the application of the criteria gives an answer that is often wrong. Many people have more evil than good in their lives; we do not, however, conclude that we would do these people no service by rescuing them from death.

To get around this last difficulty Thomas Nagel has suggested that experience itself is a good which must be brought in to balance accounts.

> . . . life is worth living even when the bad elements of experience are plentiful, and the good ones too meager to outweigh the bad ones on their own. The additional positive weight is supplied by experience itself, rather than by any of its contents.[3]

This seems implausible because if experience itself is a good it must be so even when what we experience is wholly bad, as in being tortured to death. How should one decide how much to count for this experiencing; and why count anything at all?

Others have tried to solve the problem by arguing that it is a man's desire for life that makes us call life a good: if he wants to live then anyone who prolongs his life does him a benefit. Yet someone may cling to life where we would say confidently that it would be better for him if he died, and he may admit it too. Speaking of those same conditions in which, as he said, a bullet would have been merciful, Panin writes,

> I should like to pass on my observations concerning the absence of suicides under the extremely severe conditions of our concentration camps. The more that life became desperate, the more a prisoner seemed determined to hold onto it.[4]

One might try to explain this by saying that hope was the ground of his wish to survive for further days and months in the camp. But there is nothing unintelligible in the idea that a man might cling to life though he knew those facts about his future which would make any charitable man wish that he might die.

The problem remains, and it is hard to know where to look for a solution. Is there a conceptual connection between *life* and *good*? Because life is not always a good we are apt to reject this idea, and to think that it must be a contingent fact that life is usually a good, as it is a contingent matter that legacies are usually a benefit, if they are. Yet it seems not to be a contingent matter that to save someone's life is ordinarily to benefit him. The problem is to find where the conceptual connection lies.

It may be good tactics to forget for a time that it is euthanasia we are discussing and to see how *life* and *good* are connected in the case of living beings other than men. Even plants have things done to them that are harmful or beneficial, and what does them good must be related in some way to their living and dying. Let us therefore consider plants and animals, and then come back to human beings. At least we shall get away from the temptation to think that the connection between life and benefit must everywhere be a matter of happiness and unhappiness or of pleasure and pain; the idea being absurd in the case of animals and impossible even to formulate for plants.

[3]Thomas Nagel, "Death," in James Rachels, ed., *Moral Problems* (New York, 1971), p. 362.

[4]Panin, *Sologdin*, p. 85.

In case anyone thinks that the concept of the beneficial applies only in a secondary or analogical way to plants, he should be reminded that we speak quite straightforwardly in saying, for instance, that a certain amount of sunlight is beneficial to most plants. What is in question here is the habitat in which plants of particular species flourish, but we can also talk, in a slightly different way, of what does them good, where there is some suggestion of improvement or remedy. What has the beneficial to do with sustaining life? It is tempting to answer, "everything," thinking that a healthy condition just is the one apt to secure survival. In fact, however, what is beneficial to a plant may have to do with reproduction rather than the survival of the individual members of the species. Nevertheless there is a plain connection between the beneficial and the life-sustaining even for the individual plant; if something makes it better able to survive in conditions normal for that species it is ipso facto good for it. We need go no further, and could go no further, in explaining why a certain environment or treatment is good for a plant than to show how it helps this plant to survive.[5]

This connection between the life-sustaining and the beneficial is reasonably unproblematic, and there is nothing fanciful or zoomorphic in speaking of benefiting or doing good to plants. A connection with its survival can make something beneficial to a plant. But this is not, of course, to say that we count life as a good to a plant. We may save its life by giving it what is beneficial; we do not benefit it by saving its life.

A more ramified concept of benefit is used in speaking of animal life. New things can be said, such as that an animal is better or worse off for something that happened, or that it was a good or bad thing for it that it did happen. And new things count as benefit. In the first place, there is comfort, which often is, but need not be, related to health. When loosening a collar which is too tight for a dog we can say, "That will be better for it." So we see that the words "better for it" have two different meanings which we mark when necessary by a difference of emphasis, saying "better *for* it" when health is involved. And secondly an animal can be benefited by having its life saved. "Could you do anything for it?" can be answered by, "Yes, I managed to save its life." Sometimes we may understand this, just as we would for a plant, to mean that we had checked some disease. But we can also do something for an animal by scaring away its predator. If we do this, it is a good thing for the animal that we did, unless of course it immediately meets a more unpleasant end by some other means. Similarly, on the bad side, an animal may be worse off for our intervention, and this not because it pines or suffers but simply because it gets killed.

The problem that vexes us when we think about euthanasia comes on the scene at this point. For if we can do something for an animal—can benefit it—by relieving its suffering but also by saving its life, where does the greater benefit come when only death will end pain? It seemed that life was a good in its own right; yet pain seemed to be an evil with equal status and could therefore make life not a good after all. Is it only life without pain that is a good when animals are concerned? This does not seem a crazy suggestion when we are thinking of animals, since unlike human beings they do not have suffering as part of their normal life. But it is perhaps the idea of ordinary life that matters here. We would not say that we had done anything for an animal if we had merely kept it alive, either in an unconscious state or in a condition where, though conscious, it was unable to operate in an ordinary way; and the fact is that animals in severe and continuous pain simply do no operate normally. So we do not, on the whole, have the option of doing the animal good by saving its life though the life would be a life of pain. No doubt there are borderline cases, but that is no problem. We are not trying to make new judgments possible, but rather to find the principle of the ones we do make.

When we reach human life the problems seem even more troublesome. For now we must take quite new things into account, such as the subject's own view of his life. It is arguable that this places

[5]Yet some detail needs to be filled in to explain why we should not say that a scarecrow is beneficial to the plants it protects. Perhaps what is beneficial must either be a feature of the plant itself, such as protective prickles, or else must work on the plant directly, such as a line of trees which give it shade.

extra constraints on the solution: might it not be counted as a necessary condition of life's being a good to a man that he should see it as such? Is there not some difficulty about the idea that a benefit might be done to him by the saving or prolonging of his life even though he himself wished for death? Of course he might have a quite mistaken view of his own prospects, but let us ignore this and think only of cases where it is life as he knows it that is in question. Can we think that the prolonging of this life would be a benefit to him even though he would rather have it end than continue? It seems that this cannot be ruled out. That there is no simple incompatibility between life as a good and the wish for death is shown by the possibility that a man should wish himself dead, not for his own sake, but for the sake of someone else. And if we try to amend the thesis to say that life cannot be a good to one who wishes *for his own sake* that he should die, we find the crucial concept slipping through our fingers. As Bishop Butler pointed out long ago not all ends are either benevolent or self-interested. Does a man wish for death for his own sake in the relevant sense if, for instance, he wishes to revenge himself on another by his death. Or what if he is proud and refuses to stomach dependence or incapacity even though there are many good things left in life for him? The truth seems to be that the wish for death is sometimes compatible with life's being a good and sometimes not, which is possible because the description "wishing for death" is one covering diverse states of mind from that of the determined suicide, pathologically depressed, to that of one who is surprised to find that the thought of a fatal accident is viewed with relief. On the one hand, a man may see his life as a burden but go about his business in a more or less ordinary way; on the other hand, the wish for death may take the form of a rejection of everything that is in life, as it does in severe depression. It seems reasonable to say that life is not a good to one permanently in the latter state, and we must return to this topic later on.

When are we to say that life is a good or a benefit to a man? The dilemma that faces us is this. If we say that life as such is a good we find ourselves refuted by the examples given at the beginning of this discussion. We therefore incline to think that it is as bringing good things that life is a good, where it is a good. But if life is a good only because it is the condition of good things why is it not equally an evil when it brings bad things? And how can it be a good even when it brings more evil than good?

It should be noted that the problem has here been formulated in terms of the balance of good and evil, not that of happiness and unhappiness, and that it is not to be solved by the denial (which may be reasonable enough) that unhappiness is the only evil or happiness the only good. In this paper no view has been expressed about the nature of goods other than life itself. The point is that on any view of the goods and evils that life can contain, it seems that a life with more evil than good could still itself be a good.

It may be useful to review the judgments with which our theory must square. Do we think that life can be a good to one who suffers a lot of pain? Clearly we do. What about severely handicapped people; can life be a good to them? Clearly it can be, for even if someone is almost completely paralyzed, perhaps living in an iron lung, perhaps able to move things only by means of a tube held between his lips, we do not rule him out of order if he says that some benefactor saved his life. Nor is it different with mental handicap. There are many fairly severely handicapped people—such as those with Down's Syndrome (Mongolism)—for whom a simple affectionate life is possible. What about senility? Does this break the normal connection between life and good? Here we must surely distinguish between forms of senility. Some forms leave a life which we count someone as better off having than not having, so that a doctor who prolonged it would benefit the person concerned. With some kinds of senility this is however no longer true. There are some in geriatric wards who are barely conscious, though they can move a little and swallow food put into their mouths. To prolong such a state, whether in the old or in the very severely mentally handicapped is not to do them a service or confer a benefit. But of course it need not be the reverse: only if there is suffering would one wish for the sake of the patient that he should die.

It seems, therefore, that merely being alive even without suffering is not a good, and that we must make a distinction similar to that which we made when animals were our topic. But how is the line to be drawn in the case of men? What is to count as ordinary human life in the relevant sense? If it were only the very senile or very ill who were to be said not to have this life it might seem right to describe it in terms of *operation.* But it will be hard to find the sense in which the men described by Panin were not operating, given that they dragged themselves out to the forest to work. What is it about the life that the prisoners were living that makes us put it on the other side of the dividing line from that of some severely ill or suffering patients, and from most of the physically or mentally handicapped? It is not that they were in captivity, for life in captivity can certainly be a good. Nor is it merely the unusual nature of their life. In some ways the prisoners were living more as other men do than the patient in an iron lung.

The suggested solution to the problem is, then, that there is a certain conceptual connection between *life* and *good* in the case of human beings as in that of animals and even plants. Here, as there, however, it is not the mere state of being alive that can determine, or itself count as, a good, but rather life coming up to some standard of normality. It was argued that it is as part of ordinary life that the elements of good that a man may have are relevant to the question of whether saving his life counts as benefiting him. Ordinary human lives, even very hard lives, contain a minimum of basic goods, but when these are absent the idea of life is no longer linked to that of good. And since it is in this way that the elements of good contained in a man's life are relevant to the question of whether he is benefited if his life is preserved, there is no reason why it should be the balance of good and evil that counts.

It should be added that evils are relevant in one way when, as in the examples discussed above, they destroy the possibility of ordinary goods, but in a different way when they invade a life from which the goods are already absent for a different reason. So, for instance, the connection between *life* and *good* may be broken because consciousness has sunk to a very low level, as in extreme senility or severe brain damage. In itself this kind of life seems to be neither good nor evil, but if suffering sets in one would hope for a speedy end.

The idea we need seems to be that of life which is ordinary human life in the following respect—that it contains a minimum of basic human goods. What is ordinary in human life—even in very hard lives—is that a man is not driven to work far beyond his capacity; that he has the support of a family or community; that he can more or less satisfy his hunger; that he has hopes for the future; that he can lie down to rest at night. Such things were denied to the men in the Vyatlag camps described by Panin; not even rest at night was allowed them when they were tormented by bedbugs, by noise and stench, and by routines such as body-searches and bath-parades—arranged for the night time so that work norms would not be reduced. Disease too can so take over a man's life that the normal human goods disappear. When a patient is so overwhelmed by pain or nausea that he cannot eat with pleasure, if he can eat at all, and is out of the reach of even the most loving voice, he no longer has ordinary human life in the sense in which the words are used here. And we may now pick up a thread from an earlier part of the discussion by remarking that crippling depression can destroy the enjoyment of ordinary goods as effectively as external circumstances can remove them.

This, admittedly inadequate, discussion of the sense in which life is normally a good, and of the reasons why it may not be so in some particular case, completes the account of what euthanasia is here taken to be. An act of euthanasia, whether literally act or rather omission, is attributed to an agent who opts for the death of another because in his case life seems to be an evil rather than a good. The question now to be asked is whether acts of euthanasia are ever justifiable. But there are two topics here rather than one. For it is one thing to say that some acts of euthanasia considered only in themselves and their results are morally unobjectionable, and another to say that it would be all right to legalize them. Perhaps the practice of euthanasia would allow too many abuses, and perhaps there would be too many mistakes. Moreover the practice might have very important and highly undesirable side effects, because it is unlikely that we could change our principles about the treatment of the old and the ill without changing fundamental emotional attitudes and social relations. The topics must, therefore, be treated separately. In the next part of the discussion, nothing will be said about the social consequences and possible abuses of the practice of euthanasia, but only about acts of euthanasia considered in themselves.

What we want to know is whether acts of euthanasia, defined as we have defined them, are ever morally permissible. To be more accurate, we want to know whether it is ever sufficient justification of the choice of death for another that death can be counted a benefit rather than harm, and that this is why the choice is made.

It will be impossible to get a clear view of the area to which this topic belongs without first marking the distinct grounds on which objection may lie when one man opts for the death of another. There are two different virtues whose requirements are, in general, contrary to such actions. An unjustified act of killing, or allowing to die, is contrary to justice or to charity, or to both virtues, and the moral failings are distinct. Justice has to do with what men *owe* each other in the way of noninterference and positive service. When used in this wide sense, which has its history in the doctrine of the cardinal virtues, justice is not especially connected with, for instance, law courts but with the whole area of rights, and duties corresponding to rights. Thus murder is one form of injustice, dishonesty another, and wrongful failure to keep contracts a third; chicanery in a law court or defrauding someone of his inheritance are simply other cases of injustice. Justice as such is not directly linked to the good of another, and may require that something be rendered to him even where it will do him harm, as Hume pointed out when he remarked that a debt must be paid even to a profligate debauchee who "would rather receive harm than benefit from large possessions."[6] Charity, on the other hand, is the virtue which attaches us to the good of others. An act of charity is in question only where something is not demanded by justice, but a lack of charity and of justice can be shown where a man is denied something which he both needs and has a right to; both charity and justice demand that widows and orphans are not defrauded, and the man who cheats them is neither charitable nor just.

It is easy to see that the two grounds of objection to inducing death are distinct. A murder is an act of injustice. A culpable failure to come to the aid of someone whose life is threatened is normally contrary, not to justice, but to charity. But where one man is under contract, explicit or implicit, to come to the aid of another injustice too will be shown. Thus injustice may be involved either in an act or an omission, and the same is true of a lack of charity; charity may demand that someone be aided, but also that an unkind word not be spoken.

The distinction between charity and justice will turn out to be of the first importance when voluntary and nonvoluntary euthanasia are distinguished later on. . . .

Let us now ask how the right to life affects the morality of acts of euthanasia. Are such acts sometimes or always ruled out by the right to life? This is certainly a possibility; for although an act of euthanasia is, by our definition, a matter of opting for death for the good of the one who is to die, there is, as we noted earlier, no direct connection between that to which a man has a right and that which is for his good. It is true that men have the right only to the kind of thing that is, in general, a good: we do not think that people have the right to garbage or polluted air. Nevertheless, a man may have the right to something which he himself would be better off without; where rights exist it is a man's will that counts not his or anyone else's estimate of benefit or harm. So the duties complementary to the right to life—the general duty of noninterference and the duty of service incurred by certain persons—are not affected by the quality of a man's life or by his prospects. Even if it is true that he would be, as we say, "better off dead," so long as he wants to live this does not justify us in killing him and may not justify us in deliberately allowing him to die. All of us have the duty of noninterference, and some of us may have the duty to sustain his life. Suppose, for example, that a retreating army has to leave behind wounded or exhausted soldiers in the wastes of an arid or snowbound lane where the only prospect is death by starvation or at the hands of an enemy notoriously cruel. It has often been the practice to accord a merciful bullet to men in such desperate straits. But suppose that one of them demands that he

[6] David Hume, *Treatise*, Book III, Part II, Section 1.

should be left alive? It seems clear that his comrades have no right to kill him, though it is a quite different question as to whether they should give him a life-prolonging drug. The right to life can sometimes give a duty of positive service, but does not do so here. What it does give is the right to be left alone.

Interesting enough we have arrived by way of a consideration of the right to life at the distinction normally labeled "active" versus "passive" euthanasia, and often thought to be irrelevant to the moral issue.[7] Once it is seen that the right to life is a distinct ground of objection to certain acts of euthanasia, and that this right creates a duty of non-interference more widespread than the duties of care there can be no doubt about the relevance of the distinction between passive and active euthanasia. Where everyone may have the duty to leave someone alone, it may be that no one has the duty to maintain his life, or that only some people do.

Where then do the boundaries of the "active" and "passive" lie? In some ways the words are themselves misleading, because they suggest the difference between act and omission which is not quite what we want. Certainly the act of shooting someone is the kind of thing we were talking about under the heading of "interference," and omitting to give him a drug a case of refusing care. But the act of turning off a respirator should surely be thought of as no different from the decision not to start it; if doctors had decided that a patient should be allowed to die, either course of action might follow, and both should be counted as passive rather than active euthanasia if euthanasia were in question. The point seems to be that interference in a course of treatment is not the same as other interference in a man's life, and particularly if the same body of people are responsible for the treatment and for its discontinuance. In such a case we could speak of the disconnecting of the apparatus as killing the man, or of the hospital as allowing him to die. By and large, it is the act of killing that is ruled out under the heading of non-interference, but not in every case.

Doctors commonly recognize this distinction, and the grounds on which some philosophers have denied it seem untenable. James Rachels, for instance, believes that if the difference between active and passive is relevant anywhere, it should be relevant everywhere, and he has pointed to an example in which it seems to make no difference which is done. If someone saw a child drowning in a bath it would seem just as bad to let it drown as to push its head under water.[8] If "it makes no difference" means that one act would be as iniquitous as the other this is true. It is not that killing is *worse* than allowing to die, but that the two are contrary to distinct virtues, which gives the possibility that in some circumstances one is impermissible and the other permissible. In the circumstances invented by Rachels, both are wicked: it is contrary to justice to push the child's head under the water—something one has no right to do. To leave it to drown is not contrary to justice, but it is a particularly glaring example of lack of charity. Here it makes no practical difference because the requirements of justice and charity coincide; but in the case of the retreating army they did not: charity would have required that the wounded soldier be killed had not justice required that he be left alive.[9] In such a case it makes all the difference whether a man opts for the death of another in a positive action, or whether he allows him to die. An analogy with the right to property will make the point clear. If a man owns something he has the right to it even when its possession does him harm, and we have no right to take it from him. But if one day it should blow away, maybe nothing requires us to get it back for him; we could not deprive him of it, but we may allow it to go. This is not to deny that it will often be an unfriendly act or one based on an arrogant judgment when we fuse to do what he wants. Nevertheless, we would be within our rights, and it might be that no moral objection of any kind would lie against our refusal. A more direct counter-example to Rachels' thesis lies in the *permissibility* of leaving one baby to

[7]See, for example, James Rachels, "Active and Passive Euthanasia," *New England Journal of Medicine* 292, no. 2 (9 Jan. 1975): 78–80.

[8]Ibid.

[9]It is not, however, that justice and charity conflict. A man does not lack charity because he refrains from an act of injustice which would have been for someone's good.

drown while hurrying to save five, as contrasted with the *impermissibility* of pushing the one under the water even if by this means five could be saved.

It is important to emphasize that a man's rights may stand between us and the action we would dearly like to take for his sake. They may, of course, also prevent action which we would like to take for the sake of others, as when it might be tempting to kill one man to save several. But it is interesting that the limits of allowable interference, however uncertain, seem stricter in the first case than the second. Perhaps there are no cases in which it would be all right to kill a man against his will *for his own sake* unless they could equally well be described as cases of allowing him to die, as in the example of turning off the respirator. However, there are circumstances, even if these are very rare, in which one man's life would justifiably be sacrificed to save others, and "killing" would be the only description of what was being done. For instance, a vehicle which had gone out of control might be steered from a path on which it would kill more than one man to a path on which it would kill one.[10] But it would not be permissible to steer a vehicle towards someone in order to kill him, against his will, for his own good. An analogy with property rights illustrates the point. One may not destroy a man's property against his will on the grounds that he would be better off without it; there are however circumstances in which it could be destroyed for the sake of others. If his house is liable to fall and kill him that is his affair; it might, however, without injustice be destroyed to stop the spread of a fire.

We see then that the distinction between active and passive, important as it is elsewhere, has a special importance in the area of euthanasia. It should also be clear why James Rachels' other argument, that it is often "more humane" to kill than to allow to die, does not show that the distinction between active and passive euthanasia is morally irrelevant. It might be "more humane" in this sense to deprive a man of the property that brings evils on him, or to refuse to pay what is owed to Hume's profligate debauchee; but if we say this we must admit that an act which is "more humane" than its alternative may be morally objectionable because it infringes rights.

So far we have said very little about the right to service as opposed to the right to noninterference, though it was agreed that both might be brought under the heading of "the right to life." What about the duty to preserve life that may belong to special classes of persons such as bodyguards, firemen, or doctors? Unlike the general public they are not within their rights if they merely refrain from interfering and do not try to sustain life. The subject's claim-rights are two-fold as far as they are concerned and passive as well as active euthanasia may be ruled out here if it is against his will. This is not to say that he has the right to any and every service needed to save or prolong his life; the rights of other people set limits to what may be demanded, both because they have the right not to be interfered with and because they may have a competing right to services. Furthermore one must enquire just what the contract or implicit agreement amounts to in each case. Firemen and bodyguards presumably have a duty which is simply to preserve life, within the limits of justice to others and of reasonableness to themselves. With doctors it may however be different, since their duty relates not only to preserving life but also to the relief of suffering. It is not clear what a doctor's duties are to his patient if life can be prolonged only at the cost of suffering or suffering relieved only by means that shorten life. George Fletcher has argued that what the doctor is under contract to do depends on what is generally done, because this is what a patient will reasonably expect.[11] This seems right. If procedures are part of normal medical practice then it seems that the patient can demand them however much it may be against his interest to do so. Once again it is not a matter of what is "most humane."

That the patient's right to life may set limits to permissible acts of euthanasia seems undeniable. If

---

[10]For a discussion of such questions, see my article "The Problem of Abortion and the Doctrine of Double Effect," *Oxford Review*, no. 5 (1967); reprinted in Rachels, *Moral Problems*, and Gorovitz, *Moral Problems in Medicine.*

[11]George Fletcher, "Legal Aspects of the Decision not to Prolong Life," *Journal of the American Medical Association* 203, no. 1 (1 Jan. 1968): 119–122. Reprinted in Gorovitz.

he does not want to die no one has the right to practice active euthanasia on him, and passive euthanasia may also be ruled out where he has a right to the services of doctors or others.

Perhaps few will deny what has so far been said about the impermissibility of acts of euthanasia simply because we have so far spoken about the case of one who positively wants to live, and about his rights, whereas those who advocate euthanasia are usually thinking either about those who wish to die or about those whose wishes cannot be ascertained either because they cannot properly be said to have wishes or because, for one reason or another, we are unable to form a reliable estimate of what they are. The question that must now be asked is whether the latter type of case, where euthanasia though not involuntary would again be nonvoluntary, is different from the one discussed so far. Would we have the right to kill someone for his own good so long as we had no idea that he positively wished to live? And what about the life-prolonging duties of doctors in the same circumstances? This is a very difficult problem. On the one hand, it seems ridiculous to suppose that a man's right to life is something which generates duties only where he has signaled that he wants to live; as a borrower does indeed have a duty to return something lent on indefinite loan only if the lender indicates that he wants it back. On the other hand, it might be argued that there is something illogical about the idea that a right has been infringed if someone incapable of saying whether he wants it or not is deprived of something that is doing him harm rather than good. Yet on the analogy of property we would say that a right has been infringed. Only if someone had earlier told us that in such circumstances he would not want to keep the thing could we think that his right had been waived. Perhaps if we could make confident judgments about what anyone in such circumstances would wish, or what he would have wished beforehand had he considered the matter, we could agree to consider the right to life as "dormant," needing to be asserted if the normal duties were to remain. But as things are we cannot make any such assumption; we simply do not know what most people would want, or would have wanted, us to do unless they tell us. This is certainly the case so far as active measures to end life are concerned. Possibly it is different, or will become different, in the matter of being kept alive, so general is the feeling against using sophisticated procedures on moribund patients, and so much is this dreaded by people who are old or terminally ill. Once again the distinction between active and passive euthanasia has come on the scene, but this time because most people's attitudes to the two are so different. It is just possible that we might presume, in the absence of specific evidence, that someone would not wish, beyond a certain point, to be kept alive; it is certainly not possible to assume that he would wish to be killed.

In the last paragraph we have begun to broach the topic of voluntary euthanasia, and this we must now discuss. What is to be said about the case in which there is no doubt about someone's wish to die: either he has told us beforehand that he would wish it in circumstances such as he is now in, and has shown no sign of a change of mind, or else he tells us now, being in possession of his faculties and of a steady mind. We should surely say that the objections previously urged against acts of euthanasia, which it must be remembered were all on the ground of rights, had disappeared. It does not seem that one would infringe someone's right to life in killing him with his permission and in fact at his request. Why should someone not be able to waive his right to life, or rather, as would be more likely to happen, to cancel some of the duties of noninterference that this right entails? (He is more likely to say that he should be killed by this man at this time in this manner, than to say that anyone may kill him at any time and in any way.) Similarly someone may give permission for the destruction of his property, and request it. The important thing is that he gives a critical permission, and it seems that this is enough to cancel the duty normally associated with the right. If someone gives you permission to destroy his property it can no longer be said that you have no right to do so, and I do not see why it should not be the case with taking a man's life. An objection might be made on the ground that only God has the right to take life, but in this paper religious as opposed to moral arguments are being left aside. Religion apart, there seems to be no case to be made out for an infringement of rights if a man who wishes to die is allowed to die or even killed. But of course it does not follow that there is no moral objection to it. Even with property, which is after all a relatively small matter, one might be wrong to destroy what one had the right to destroy. For, apart from its value to other people, it might be valuable to the man who wanted it destroyed, and charity might require us to hold our hand where justice did not.

Let us review the conclusion of this part of the argument, which has been about euthanasia and the right to life. It has been argued that from this side come stringent restrictions on the acts of euthanasia that could be morally permissible. Active nonvoluntary euthanasia is ruled out by that part of the right to life which creates the duty of noninterference though passive nonvoluntary euthanasia is not ruled out, except where the right to life-preserving action has been created by some special condition such as a contract between a man and his doctor, and it is not always certain just what such a contract involves. Voluntary euthanasia is another matter: as the preceding paragraph suggested, no right is infringed if a man is allowed to die or even killed at his own request.

Turning now to the other objection that normally holds against inducing the death of another, that it is against charity, or benevolence, we must tell a very different story. Charity is the virtue that gives attachment to the good of others, and because life is normally a good, charity normally demands that it should be saved or prolonged. But as we so defined an act of euthanasia that it seeks a man's death for his own sake—for his good—charity will normally speak in favor of it. This is not, of course, to say that charity can require an act of euthanasia which justice forbids, but if an act of euthanasia is not contrary to justice—that is, it does not infringe rights—charity will rather be in its favor against.

Once more the distinction between nonvoluntary and voluntary euthanasia must be considered. Could it ever be compatible with charity to seek a man's death although he wanted to live, or at least had not let us know that he wanted to die? It has been argued that in such circumstances active euthanasia would infringe his right to life, but passive euthanasia would not do so, unless he had some special right to life-preserving service from the one who allowed him to die. What would charity dictate? Obviously when a man wants to live there is a presumption that he will be benefited if his life is prolonged, and if it is so the question of euthanasia does not arise. But it is, on the other hand, possible that he wants to live where it would be better for him to die: perhaps he does not realize the desperate situation he is in, or perhaps he is afraid of dying. So, in spite of a very proper resistance to refusing to go along with a man's own wishes in the matter of life and death, someone might justifiably refuse to prolong the life even of someone who asked him to prolong it, as in the case of refusing to give the wounded soldier a drug that would keep him alive to meet a terrible end. And it is even more obvious that charity does not always dictate that life should be prolonged where a man's own wishes, hypothetical or actual, are not known.

So much for the relation of charity to nonvoluntary passive euthanasia, which was not, like nonvoluntary active euthanasia, ruled out by the right to life. Let us now ask what charity has to say about voluntary euthanasia both active and passive. It was suggested in the discussion of justice that if of sound mind and steady desire a man might give others the *right* to allow him to die or even to kill him, where otherwise this would be ruled out. But it was pointed out that this would not settle the question of whether the act was morally permissible, and it is this that we must now consider. Could not charity speak against what justice allowed? Indeed it might do so. For while the fact that a man wants to die suggests that his life is wretched, and while his rejection of life may itself tend to take the good out of the things he might have enjoyed, nevertheless his wish to die might here be opposed for his own sake just as it might be if suicide were in question. Perhaps there is hope that his mental condition will improve. Perhaps he is mistaken in thinking his disease incurable. Perhaps he wants to die for the sake of someone else on whom he feels he is a burden, and we are not ready to accept this sacrifice whether for ourselves or others. In such cases, and there will surely be many of them, it could not be for his own sake that we kill him or allow him to die, and therefore euthanasia as defined in this paper would not be in question. But this is not to deny that there could be acts of voluntary euthanasia both passive and active against which neither justice nor charity would speak.

We have now considered the morality of euthanasia both voluntary and nonvoluntary, and active and passive. The conclusion has been that nonvoluntary active euthanasia (roughly, killing a man against his will or without his consent) is never justified; that is to say, that a man's being killed for his own good never justifies the act unless he himself has consented to it. A man's rights are infringed by such an action, and it is therefore contrary to justice. However, all the other combinations, nonvoluntary passive euthanasia, voluntary active euthanasia, and voluntary passive euthanasia are sometimes compatible with both justice and charity. But the strong condition carried in the definition of euthanasia adopted in this paper must not be forgotten; an act of euthanasia as here understood is one whose purpose is to benefit the one who dies.

In the light of this discussion let us look at our present practices. Are they good or are they bad? And what changes might be made, thinking now not only of the morality of particular acts of euthanasia but also of the indirect effects of instituting different practices, of the abuses to which they might be subject and of the changes that might come about if euthanasia became a recognized part of the social scene.

The first thing to notice is that it is wrong to ask whether we should introduce the practice of euthanasia as if it were not something we already had. In fact we do have it. For instance it is common, where the medical prognosis is very bad, for doctors to recommend against measures to prolong life, and particularly where a process of degeneration producing one medical emergency after another has already set in. If these doctors are not certainly within their legal rights this is something that is apt to come as a surprise to them as to the general public. It is also obvious that euthanasia is often practiced where old people are concerned. If someone very old and soon to die is attacked by a disease that makes his life wretched, doctors do not always come in with life-prolonging drugs. Perhaps poor patients are more fortunate in this respect than rich patients, being more often left to die in peace; but it is in any case a well recognized piece of medical practice, which is a form of euthanasia.

No doubt the case of infants with mental or physical defects will be suggested as another example of the practice of euthanasia as we already have it, since such infants are sometimes deliberately allowed to die. That they are deliberately allowed to die is certain; children with severe spina bifida malformations are not always operated on even when it is thought that without the operation they will die; and even in the case of children with Down's Syndrome who have intestinal obstructions the relatively simple operation that would make it possible to feed them is sometimes not performed.[12] Whether this is euthanasia in our sense or only as the Nazis understood it is another matter. We must ask the crucial question, "Is it for the sake of the child himself that the doctors and parents choose his death?" In some cases the answer may really be yes, and what is more important it may really be true that the kind of life which is a good is not possible or likely for his child, and that there is little but suffering and frustration in store for him.[13] But this must presuppose that the medical prognosis is wretchedly bad, as it may be for some spina bifida children. With children who are born with Down's Syndrome it is, however, quite different. Most of these are able to live on for quite a time in a reasonably contented way, remaining like children all their lives but capable of affectionate relationships and able to play games and perform simple tasks. The fact is, of course, that the doctors who recommend against life-saving procedures for handicapped infants are usually thinking not of them but rather of their parents and of other children in the family or of the "burden on society" if the children survive. So it is not for their sake but to avoid trouble to others that they are allowed to die. When

[12] I have been told this by a pediatrician in a well-known medical center in the United States. It is confirmed by Anthony M. Shaw and Iris A. Shaw, "Dilemma of Informed Consent in Children," *The New England Journal of Medicine* 289, no. 17 (25 Oct. 1973): 885–890. Reprinted in Gorovitz.

[13] It must be remembered, however, that many of the social miseries of spina bifida children could be avoided. Professor R. B. Zachary is surely right to insist on this. See, for example, "Ethical and Social Aspects of Spina Bifida," *The Lancet*, 3 Aug. 1968, pp. 274–276. Reprinted in Gorovitz.

brought out into the open this seems unacceptable: at least we do not easily accept the principle that adults who need special care should be counted too burdensome to be kept alive. It must in any case be insisted that if children with Down's Syndrome are deliberately allowed to die this is not a matter of euthanasia except in Hitler's sense. And for our children, since we scruple to gas them, not even the manner of their death is "quiet and easy"; when not treated for an intestinal obstruction a baby simply starves to death. Perhaps some will take this as an argument for allowing active euthanasia, in which case they will be in the company of an S.S. man stationed in the Warthgenau who sent Eichmann a memorandum telling him that "Jews in the coming winter could not longer be fed" and submitting for his consideration a proposal as to whether "it would not be the most humane solution to kill those Jews who were incapable of work through some quicker means."[14] If we say we are *unable* to look after children with handicaps we are no more telling the truth than was the S.S. man who said that the Jews could not be fed.

Nevertheless if it is ever right to allow deformed children to die because life will be a misery to them, or not to take measures to prolong for a little the life of a newborn baby whose life cannot extend beyond a few months of intense medical intervention, there is a genuine problem about active as opposed to passive euthanasia. There are well-known cases in which the medical staff has looked on wretchedly while an infant died slowly from starvation and dehydration because they did not feel able to give a lethal injection. According to the principles discussed in the earlier part of this paper they would indeed have had no right to give it, since an infant cannot ask that it should be done. The only possible solution—supposing that voluntary active euthanasia were to be legalized—would be to appoint guardians to act on the infant's behalf. In a different climate of opinion this might not be dangerous, but at present, when people so readily assume that the life of a handicapped baby is of no value, one would be loath to support it.

[14]Quoted by Hannah Arendt, *Eichmann in Jerusalem* (London 1963), p. 90.

Finally, on the subject of handicapped children, another word should be said about those with severe mental defects. For them too it might sometimes be right to say that one would wish for death for their sake. But not even severe mental handicap automatically brings a child within the scope even of a possible act of euthanasia. If the level of consciousness is low enough it could not be said that life is a good to them, any more than in the case of those suffering from extreme senility. Nevertheless if they do not suffer it will not be an act of euthanasia by which someone opts for their death. Perhaps charity does not demand that strenuous measures are taken to keep people in this state alive, but euthanasia does not come into the matter, any more than it does when someone is, like Karen Ann Quinlan, in a state of permanent coma. Much could be said about this last case. It might even be suggested that in the case of unconsciousness this "life" is not the life to which "the right to life" refers. But that is not our topic here.

What we must consider, even if only briefly, is the possibility that euthanasia, genuine euthanasia, and not contrary to the requirements of justice or charity, should be legalized over a wider area. Here we are up against the really serious problem of abuse. Many people want, and want very badly, to be rid of their elderly relatives and even of their ailing husbands or wives. Would any safeguards ever be able to stop them describing as euthanasia what was really for their own benefit? And would it be possible to prevent the occurrence of acts which were genuinely acts of euthanasia but morally impermissible because infringing the rights of a patient who wished to live?

Perhaps the furthest we should go is to encourage patients to make their own contracts with a doctor by making it known whether they wish him to prolong their life in case of painful terminal illness or of incapacity. A document such as the Living Will seems eminently sensible, and should surely be allowed to give a doctor following the previously expressed wishes of the patient immunity from legal proceedings by relatives.[15] Legaliz-

[15]Details of this document are to be found in J. A. Behnke and Sissela Bok, eds., *The Dilemmas of Euthanasia* (New York, 1975), and in A. B. Downing, ed., *Euthanasia and the Right to Life: The Case for Voluntary Euthanasia* (London, 1969).

ing active euthanasia is, however, another matter. Apart from the special repugnance doctors feel towards the idea of a lethal injection, it may be of the very greatest importance to keep a psychological barrier up against killing. Moreover it is active euthanasia which is the most liable to abuse. Hitler would not have been able to kill 275,000 people in his "euthanasia" program if he had had to wait for them to need life-saving treatment. But there are other objections to active euthanasia, even voluntary active euthanasia. In the first place it would be hard to devise procedures that would protect people from being persuaded into giving their consent. And secondly the possibility of active voluntary euthanasia might change the social scene in ways that would be very bad. As things are, people do, by and large, expect to be looked after if they are old or ill. This is one of the good things that we have, but we might lose it, and be much worse off without it. It might come to be expected that someone likely to need a lot of looking after should call for the doctor and demand his own death. Something comparable could be good in an extremely poverty-stricken community where the children genuinely suffered from lack of food; but in rich societies such as ours it would surely be a spiritual disaster. Such possibilities should make us very wary of supporting large measures of euthanasia, even where moral principle applied to the individual act does not rule it out.

I would like to thank Derek Parfit and the editors of *Philosophy & Public Affairs* for their very helpful comments.

Study Questions

1. Does the balance of happiness and unhappiness in a person's life determine whether life is a good to him or her, according to Foot? Why?
2. Is it a person's desire for life that makes us call life a good, according to Foot? Explain.
3. Is it possible to benefit a person by saving his or her life even if he or she would rather it end than continue, according to Foot? Explain.
4. Does the mere state of being alive count as a good for Foot? If not, what else is required for life to count as a good? Under what conditions might life *not* be counted as a good?
5. Explain the differences between the virtues of justice and charity, as Foot sees them.
6. Is there a legitimate distinction between active and passive euthanasia, according to Foot? Explain.
7. Is nonvoluntary active or passive euthanasia a violation of a person's right to life, according to Foot?
8. Does voluntary active or passive euthanasia violate a person's right to life, in Foot's opinion?
9. Does Foot think that nonvoluntary active or passive euthanasia is a violation of the dictates of charity? Explain.
10. Is voluntary active or passive euthanasia a violation of the dictates of charity, according to Foot?
11. Could active or passive euthanasia of children who are deformed or who cannot live long ever be right, in Foot's view? Explain.
12. Explain the difficulties, as Foot sees them, involved in legalizing euthanasia, including even those cases that are not contrary to the requirements of justice or charity.

Abortion

Roger Wertheimer, in the first reading in this section, begins by delineating various positions on the abortion issues. The "extreme conservative" or "Catholic," according to Wertheimer, believes that the fetus, once conceived, may not be destroyed for any reason short of saving the mother's life. (He calls this view "Catholic" but emphasizes that it is by no means limited to Catholics.) The key premise of the Catholic position is that the human fetus is a full-fledged human being. Given that premise, Wertheimer says, nothing, short of the necessity of saving some other innocent person, could justify our destroying a human fetus. It is pointless, furthermore, for a liberal to object to antiabortion laws by citing all the terrible consequences they can have for women and children and society in general. Also, Wertheimer points out, given that premise, the Catholic cannot be expected to approve of abortion on the part of those who think the fetus is not a human being, any more than a liberal can be expected to approve of racial discrimination on the part of those who subscribe to racist beliefs.

Why are liberals so unable to respond to the Catholic premise? Wertheimer asks. Because they cannot even make sense of it. How can anyone who knows the facts about embryos believe they are human beings? liberals wonder. Yet in truth, Wertheimer notes, reasonable people can agree on every fact and still disagree on whether embryos are human beings.

Liberals emphasize the apparent vast differences between a fetus in its earliest stages and a human infant. The Catholic, by contrast, points to the similarities between each successive stage of fetal development: as you go back, stage by stage, from the infant to the zygote, the Catholic maintains, you don't find any differences between successive stages significant enough to prohibit abortion at one stage and permit it at the prior stage. The conservative's argument, Wertheimer notes, is the same kind of argument given by those who point to the similarities between blacks and whites, describe the differences, and then show that no difference justifies discriminating against a black.

The liberal argument stressing the difference between zygote and infant and the conservative argument stressing the resemblances between consecutive stages of fetal development are equally strong and equally weak, Wertheimer says. If you favor one over the other, you do so not because of logic, but because you respond in a certain way to the pertinent facts. Further, until there is a common response to these facts, the assertion that the fetus is a human being is neither true nor false, Wertheimer maintains: we are "stuck with the indeterminateness of the fetus' humanity."

Having come to this point, Wertheimer then considers what he calls the moderate position, which he implies is popular and which he says is as problematic as it is popular. Equally problematic, he argues, is a *Gedanken* experiment (thought experiment) that asks us to consider what we would say if, for example, the developing fetus somehow came to be in full public view. Any argument based on such a "sci-fi" fantasy would, in reality, merely be an imaginative restatement of the conservative's original argument.

Opponents of abortion often rest their case on the idea that the fetus is a human being, a person, and thus has a right to life. In the second essay following, Judith Thomson considers whether, even granting this idea, it follows that abortion is morally wrong. It does *not* follow, she says.

She begins by setting forth the standard antiabortion argument that a person's (the fetus's) right to life takes precedence over another person's (the mother's) right to do what she wants with her own body. Thomson then offers an analogy that suggests there is something wrong with this argument: Suppose that you were forced to allow your body to be used for a prolonged period to preserve the life of someone else (in Thomson's example, a famous violinist with a kidney ailment)? She refers to this analogy on several occasions throughout the essay.

Next, in section 1, Thomson criticizes the "extreme view" that abortion is impermissible even to save the mother's life. A woman morally can defend her life against the threat to it posed by an unborn child even if the defense involves the death of the child, she maintains. In section 2, she argues that it is also morally permissible for a third party to accede to a request for an abortion by the woman whose life is so threatened.

Then Thomson turns to the stickier issue of the rightfulness of abortion in cases where the mother's life is not at stake. In section 3, she argues that having a right to life does not guarantee having a right to use another person's body—even if one needs the body to sustain one's own life. In section 4, she argues that the right to life consists *not* in the right not to be killed, but rather in the right not to be killed *unjustly.* The most that can be said, she argues, is only that there are *some* cases in which abortion is unjust killing. In sections 5 and 6, Thomson develops the view that you are not morally required to make large sacrifices to sustain the life of another who has no right to demand them. In other words, we are not morally required to be "Very Good Samaritans." Thomson does leave open the possibility, however, that there may be cases in which an unborn person is entitled to such sacrifices (as when, perhaps, a woman has assumed responsibility for having a child).

In section 7, Thomson discusses an objection that might be raised by pro-life advocates: that a woman has a unique kind of relationship with the fetus. And in the last section of the essay, she discusses objections that might be raised by those who are pro-choice. Thomson makes it clear that she has argued for the permissibility of abortion in some cases, not for the right to secure the death of an unborn child.

Understanding the Abortion Argument

Roger Wertheimer

Roger Wertheimer (b. 1942) is Associate Professor of Philosophy at California State University, Long Beach. This article was published in *Philosophy and Public Affairs* 1, no. 1 (1971).

At what stage of fetal development, if any, and for what reasons, if any, is abortion justifiable? Each part of the question has received diverse answers, which in turn have been combined in various ways.

According to the liberal, the fetus should be disposable upon the mother's request until it is viable; thereafter it may be destroyed only to save the mother's life. To an extreme liberal the fetus is always like an appendix, and may be destroyed upon demand anytime before its birth. A moderate view is that until viability the fetus should be disposable if it is the result of felonious intercourse, or if the mother's or child's physical or mental health would probably be gravely impaired. This position is susceptible to wide variations. The conservative position is that the fetus may be aborted before quickening but not after, unless the mother's life is at stake. For the extreme conservative, the fetus, once conceived, may not be destroyed for any reason short of saving the mother's life.

This last might be called the Catholic view, but note that it, or some close variant of it, is shared by numerous Christian sects, and is or was maintained by Jews, by Indians of both hemispheres, by a variety of tribes of diverse geographical location and cultural level, and even by some contemporary atheistical biochemists who are political liberals. Much the same can be said of any of the listed positions. I call attention to such facts for two reasons. First, they suggest that the abortion issue is in some way special, since, given any position on abortion and any position on any other issue, you can probably find a substantial group of people who have simultaneously held both. Second, these facts are regularly denied or distorted by the disputants. Thus, liberals habitually argue as though extreme conservatism were an invention of contemporary scholasticism with a mere century of popish heritage behind it. This in the face of the fact that that position has had the force of law in most American states for more than a century, and continues to be law even in states where Catholicism is without influence. We shall see that these two points are not unrelated.

Now, it is commonly said that the crux of the controversy is a disagreement as to the *value* of fetal life in its various stages. But I submit that this subtly but seriously misdescribes the actual arguments, and, further, betrays a questionable understanding of morality and perhaps a questionable morality as well. Instead, I suggest, we had best take the fundamental question to be: When does a human life begin?

First off I should note that the expressions "a human life," "a human being," "a person" are virtually interchangeable in this context. As I use these expressions, except for monstrosities, every member of our species is indubitably a person, a human being at the very latest at birth. The question is whether we are human lives at any time before birth. Virtually everyone, at least every party to the current controversy, *actually* does agree to this. However, we should be aware that in this area both agreement and disagreement are often merely verbal and therefore only apparent. For example, many people will say that it takes a month or even more after birth for the infant to become a person, and they will explain themselves by saying that a human being must have self-consciousness, or a personality. But upon investigation this disagreement normally turns out to be almost wholly semantic, for we can agree on all the facts about child development, and furthermore we can agree, at least in a general way, in our moral judgments on the care to be accorded the child at various stages. Thus, though they deny that a day-old infant is a person, they admit that its life cannot be forfeited for any reason that would not equally apply to a two-year-old.

On the other hand, significant disagreements can be masked by a merely verbal agreement. Sometimes a liberal will grant that a previable fetus is a human being, but investigation reveals that he means only that the fetus is a potential human being. Or he may call it human to distinguish it from canine and feline fetuses, and call it alive or living in opposition to dead or inert. But the sum of these parts does not equal what he means when he uses the phrase "a human life" in connection with himself and his friends, for in that extended sense he could equally apply that expression to human terata, and, at least in extreme cases, he is inclined to deny that they are human lives, and to dispose of them accordingly.

Implicit in my remarks is the suggestion that one way to find out how someone uses the expression "human being" and related ones is by looking at his moral judgments. I am suggesting that this is a way, sometimes the only way, of learning both what someone means by such expressions and what his conception of a human being is. It seems clear enough that given that a man has a certain set of desires, we can discern his conception of something, X, by seeing what kinds of behavior he takes to be appropriate regarding X. I am saying that we may have to look at his *moral* beliefs regarding X, especially if X is a human being. And I want to say further that while some moral judgments are involved in determining whether the fetus is a human being, still, the crucial question about the fetus is not "How much is it worth?" but "What is it?"

The defense of the extreme conservative position runs as follows. The key premise is that a human fetus is a human being, not a partial or potential one, but a full-fledged, actualized human life. Given that premise, the entire conservative position unfolds with a simple, relentless logic, every principle of which would be endorsed by any sensible liberal. Suppose human embryos are human beings. Their innocence is beyond question, so nothing could justify our destroying them except, perhaps, the necessity of saving some other innocent human life. That is, since similar cases must be treated in similar ways, some consideration would justify the abortion of a prenatal child if and only if a comparable consideration would justify the killing of a postnatal child.

This is a serious and troubling argument posing an objection in principle to abortion. It is the *only* such argument. Nothing else could possibly justify the staggering social costs of the present abortion laws.

It should be unmistakably obvious what the Catholic position is. Yet, and this deserves heavy emphasis, liberals seem not to understand it, for their arguments are almost invariably infelicitous. The Catholic defense of the status quo is left unfazed, even untouched, by the standard liberal critique that consists of an inventory of the calamitous effects of our abortion laws on mother and child, on family, and on society in general. Of course, were it not for those effects we would feel no press to be rid of the laws—nor any *need* to retain them. That inventory does present a conclusive rebuttal of any of the piddling objections conservatives often toss in for good measure. But still, the precise, scientific tabulations of grief do not add up to an argument here, for sometimes pain, no matter how considerable and how undesirable, may not be avoidable, may not stem from some injustice. I do not intend to understate that pain; the tragedies brought on by unwanted children are plentiful and serious—but so too are those brought on by unwanted parents, yet few liberals would legalize parricide as the final solution to the massive social problem of the permanently visiting parent who drains his children's financial and emotional resources. In the Church's view, these cases are fully analogous: the fetus is as much a human life as is the parent; they share the same moral status. Either can be a source of abiding anguish and hardship for the other—and sometimes there may be no escape. In this, our world, some people get stuck with the care of others, and sometimes there may be no way of getting unstuck, at least no just and decent way. Taking the other person's life is not such a way.

The very elegance of the Catholic response is maddening. The ease with which it sweeps into irrelevance the whole catalogue of sorrow has incited many a liberal libel of the Catholic clergy as callous and unfeeling monsters, denied domestic empathy by their celibacy and the simplest human sympathies by their unnatural asceticism. Of course, slander is no substitute for argument—that's what the logic books say—and yet, we cast our aspersions with care, for they must deprive the audience of the *right* to believe the speaker. What wants explanation, then, is why the particular accusation of a *warped sensibility* seems, to the liberal, both just and pertinent. I shall come back to this. For the moment, it suffices to record that the liberal's accusation attests to a misunderstanding of the Catholic defense, for it is singularly inappropriate to label a man heartless who wants only to protect innocent human lives at all costs.

There is a subsidiary approach, a peculiarly liberal one, which seeks to disarm the Catholic position not by disputing it, but by conceding the Catholic's right to believe it and act accordingly. The liberal asks only that Catholics concede him the same freedom, and thus abandon support of abortion laws. The Catholic must retort that the issue is not, as the liberal supposes, one of religious ritual and self-regarding behavior, but of minority rights, the minority being not Catholics but the fetuses of all faiths, and the right being the right of an innocent human being to life itself. The liberal's proposal is predicated on abortion being a crime without a victim, but in the Catholic view the fetus is a full-scale victim and is so independent of the liberal's recognition of that fact. Catholics can no more think it wrong for themselves but permissible for Protestants to destroy a fetus than liberals can think it wrong for themselves but permissible for racists to victimize blacks. Given this premise, the Catholic is as justified in employing the power of the state to protect embryos as the liberal is to protect blacks. I shall be returning to this analogy, because the favored defense of slavery and discrimination takes the form of a claim that the subjugated creatures are by nature inferior to their masters, that they are *not fully human.*

Now, why do liberals, even the cleverest ones, so consistently fail to make contact with the Catholic challenge? After all, as I have made plain, once premised that the fetus is a person, the entire conservative position recites the common sense of any moral man. The liberal's failure is, I suggest, due to the premise. He doesn't know how to respond to the argument, because he cannot *make sense* of that premise. To him, it is not simply false, but wildly, madly false, it is nonsense, totally unintelligible, literally unbelievable. Just look at an embryo. It is an amorphous speck of apparently coagulated protoplasm. It has no eyes or ears, no head at all. It can't walk or talk; you can't dress it or wash it. Why, it doesn't even qualify as a Barbie doll, and yet millions of people call it a human being, just like one of us. It's as though someone were to look at an acorn and call it an oak tree, or, better, it's as though someone squirted a paint tube at a canvas and called the outcome a painting, a work of art—and people believed him. The whole thing is precisely that mad—and just that sane. The liberal is befuddled by the conservative's argument, just as Giotto would be were he to assess a Pollock production as a *painting.* If the premises make no sense, then neither will the rest of the argument, except as an exercise in abstract logic.

The Catholic claim would be a joke were it not that millions of people take it seriously, and millions more suffer for their solemnity. Liberals need an explanation of how it is possible for the conservatives to believe what they say, for after all, conservatives are not ignorant or misinformed about the facts here—I mean, for example, the facts of embryology. So the liberal asks, "How *can* they believe what they say? How *can* they even make sense of it?" The question is forced upon the liberal because his conception of rationality is jeopardized by the possibility that a normal, unbiased observer of the relevant facts could really accept the conservative claims. It is this question, I think, that drives the liberal to attribute the whole antiabortion movement to Catholicism and to the Roman clergy in particular. For it is comforting to suppose that the conservative beliefs could take root only in a mind that had been carefully cultivated since infancy to support every extravagant dogma of an arcane theology fathered by the victims of unnatural and unhealthy lives. But, discomforting though it may be, people, and not just Catholics, can and sometimes do agree on all the facts about embryos and still disagree as to whether they are persons. Indeed, apparently people can agree on *every* fact and still disagree on whether it is a fact that embryos are human beings. So now one might begin to wonder: What sort of fact is it?

I hasten to add that not only can both parties agree on the scientific facts, they need not disagree on any supernatural facts either. The conservative claim does not presuppose that we are invested with a soul, some sort of divine substance, at or shortly after our conception. No doubt it helps to have one's mind befogged by visions of holy hocus-pocus, but it's not necessary, since some unmuddled atheists endorse a demythologized Catholic view. Moreover, since ensoulment is an unverifiable occurrence, the theologian dates it either by means of some relevation—which, by the way, the Church does not (though some of its parishioners may accept the humanity of embryos on the Church's say-so)—or by means of the same scientifically acceptable data by which his atheistical counterpart gauges the emergence of an unbesouled human life (e.g., that at such and such a time the organism is capable of independent life, or is motile).

The religious position derives its plausibility from independent secular considerations. It serves as an expression of them, not as a substitute for them. In brief, here as elsewhere, talk about souls involves an unnecessary shuffle. Yet, though unnecessary, admittedly it is not without effect, for such conceptions color our perceptions and attitudes toward the world and thereby give sense and substance to certain arguments whose secular translations lack appeal. To take a pertinent instance, the official Church position (not the one believed by most of the laity or used against the liberals, but the official position) is that precisely because ensoulment is an unverifiable occurrence, we can't locate it with certainty, and hence abortion at any stage involves the *risk* of destroying a human life. But first off, it is doubtful whether this claim can support the practical conclusions the Catholic draws. For even if it is true, is abortion an *unwarrantable* risk? Always? Is it morally indefensible to fire a pistol into an uninspected barrel? After all, a child *might* be hiding in it. Secondly, though this argument has no attractive secular version, still, it derives its appeal from profane considerations. For what is it that so much as makes it seem that a blastocyst *might* be a person? If the conception of being besouled is cut loose from the conception of being human *sans* soul, then a human soul might reside in anything at all (or at least any living thing), and then the destruction of anything (or any living thing) would involve the risk of killing someone.

I have said that the argument from risk has no secular counterpart. But why not? Well, for example, what sense would it make to the liberal to suppose that an embryo *might* be a person? Are there any discoveries that are really (not just logically) possible which would lead him to admit he was mistaken? It is not a *hypothesis* for the liberal that embryos are not persons; *mutatis mutandis* for the conservative.

At this juncture of the argument, a liberal with a positivistic background will announce that it's just a matter of definition whether the fetus is a person. If by this the liberal means that the question "Is a fetus a person?" is equivalent to "Is it proper to call a fetus a person?"—that is, "Is it true to say of a fetus, 'It is a person'?"—then the liberal is quite right and quite unhelpful. But he is likely to add that we can define words any way we like. And that is either true and unhelpful or flatly false. For note, both liberals and conservatives think it wrong to kill an innocent person except when other human lives would be lost. So neither party will reform its speech habits regarding the fetus unless that moral principle is reworded in a way that vouchsafes its position on abortion. Any stipulated definition can be recommended only by appealing to the very matters under dispute. Any such definition will therefore fail of universal acceptance and thus only mask the real issues, unless it is a mere systematic symbol switch. In brief, agreement on a definition will be a consequence of, not a substitute for, agreement on the facts.

A more sophisticated liberal may suggest that fetuses are borderline cases. Asking whether fetuses are persons is like asking whether viruses are living creatures; the proper answer is that they are like them in some ways but not in others; the rules of the language don't dictate one way or the other, so you can say what you will. Yet this suggests that we share a single concept of a human being, one with a fuzzy or multifaceted boundary that would make any normal person feel indecision about whether a fetus is a human being, and would enable that person, however he decided, to understand readily how someone else might decide otherwise. But at best this describes only the minds of moderates. Liberals and conservatives suffer little indecision, and, further, they are enigmatic to one another, both intellectually and as whole persons. And finally, precisely because with the virus you can say what you will, it is unlike the fetus. As regards the virus, scientists can manage nicely while totally ignoring the issue. Not so with the fetus, because deciding what to call it is tantamount to a serious and unavoidable moral decision.

This last remark suggests that the fetus' humanity is really a moral issue, not a factual one at all. But I submit that if one insists on using that raggy fact—value distinction, then one ought to say that the dispute is over a matter of fact in the sense in which it is a fact that the Negro slaves were human beings. But it would be better to say that this dispute calls that distinction into question. To see this, let us look at how people actually argue about when a human life begins.

The liberal dates hominization from birth or viability. The choice of either stage is explicable by reference to some obvious considerations. At birth the child leaves its own private space and enters the public world. And he can be looked at and acted upon and interacted with. And so on. On the other hand, someone may say viability is the crucial point, because it is then that the child has the capacity to do all those things it does at birth; the sole difference is a quite inessential one of geography.

Now note about both of these sets of considerations that they are not used as proofs or parts of proofs that human life begins at birth or at viability. What would the major premise of such a proof be? The liberal does not—nor does anyone else—have a rule of the language or a definition of "human life" from which it follows that if the organism has such and such properties, then it is a human life. True, some people have tried to state the essence of human life and argue from that definition, but the correctness of any such definition must first be tested against our judgments of particular cases, and on some of those judgments people disagree; so the argument using such a definition which tries to settle that disagreement can only beg the question. Thus, it seems more accurate to say simply that the kinds of considerations I have mentioned explain why the liberal chooses to date human life in a certain way. More accurately still, I don't think the liberal chooses or decides at all; rather, he looks at certain facts and he responds in a particular way to those facts: he dates human life from birth or from viability—and he acts and feels accordingly. There is nothing surprising in such behavior, not anything irrational or illegitimate.

All this can be said of any of the considerations that have been used to mark the beginning of a human life.

Liberals always misplace the attractions of fertilization as the critical date when they try to argue that if you go back that far, you could just as well call the sperm or the egg a human being. But people call the zygote a human life not just because it contains the DNA blueprint which determines the physical development of the organism from then on, and not just because of the potential inherent in it, but also because it and it alone can claim to be the beginning of the spatio-temporal-causal chain of the physical object that is a human body. And though I think the abortion controversy throws doubt on the claim that bodily continuity is the *sole* criterion of personal identity, I think the attractions of that philosophical thesis are of a piece with the attractions of fertilization as the point marking the start of a person. Given our conceptual framework, one can't go back further. Neither the sperm nor the egg could be, by itself, a human being, any more than an atom of sodium or an atom of chlorine could by itself properly be called salt. One proof of this is that *no one* is in the least inclined to call a sperm or an egg a human life, a fact acknowledged by the liberal's very argument, which has the form of a *reductio ad absurdum.*

These are some of the considerations, but how are they actually presented? What, for example, does the liberal say and do? Note that his arguments are usually formulated as a series of rhetorical questions. He points to certain facts, and then, quite understandably, he expects his listeners to respond in a particular way—and when they don't, he finds their behavior incomprehensible. First he will point to an infant and say, "Look at it! Aren't you inclined to say that it is one of us?" And then he will describe an embryo as I did earlier, and say, "Look at the difference between it and us! Could you call that a human being?" All this is quite legitimate, but notice what the liberal is doing.

First, he has us focus our attention on the *earliest stages* of the fetus, where the contrast with us is greatest. He does not have us look at the fetus shortly before viability or birth, where the differences between it and what he is willing to call a human being are quite minimal. Still, this is not an unfair tactic when combating the view that the fertilized egg is a human life. The other side of this maneuver is that he has us compare the embryo with *us adults.* This seems fair in that we are our own best paradigms of a person. If you and I aren't to be called human beings, then what is? And yet the liberal would not say that a young child or a neonate or even a viable fetus is to be called a human life only in an extended sense. He wants to say that the infant at birth or the viable fetus is a one hundred percent human being, but, again, the differences between a neonate and aviable fetus or between a viable fetus and a soon-to-be-viable fetus are not impressive.

The liberal has one other arrow in his meager quiver. He will say that if you call an embryo a human life, then presumably you think it is a valuable entity. But, he adds, what does it have that is of any value? Its biochemical potential to become one of us doesn't ensure that it itself is of any real value, especially if neither the mother nor any other interested party wants it to fulfill that potential.

When liberals say that an embryo is of no value if no one has a good reason to want to do anything but destroy it, I think they are on firm ground. But the conservative is not saying that the embryo has some really nifty property, so precious that it's a horrid waste to destroy it. No, he is saying that the embryo is a human being and it is wrong to kill human beings, and that is why you must not destroy the embryo. The conservative realizes that, unless he uses religious premises, premises inadmissible in the court of common morality, he has no way of categorically condemning the killing of a fetus except by arguing that a fetus is a person. And he doesn't call it a human being because its properties are valuable. The properties it has which make it a human being may be valuable, but he does not claim that it is their value which makes it a human being. Rather, he argues that it is a human being by turning the liberal's argument inside out.

The conservative points, and keeps pointing, to the similarities between each set of successive stages of fetal development, instead of pointing, as the liberal does, to the gross differences between widely separated stages. Each step of his argument is persuasive, but if this were all there was to it, his total argument would be no more compelling than one which traded on the fuzziness of the boundaries of baldness and the arbitrariness of any sharp line of demarcation to conclude that Richard M. Nixon is glabrous. If this were the whole conservative argument, then it would be open to the liberal's *reductio* argument, which says that if you go back as far as the zygote, the sperm and the egg must also be called persons. But in fact the conservative can stop at the zygote; fertilization does seem to be a nonarbitrary point marking the inception of a particular object, a human body. That is, the conservative has independent reasons for picking the date of conception, just like the liberal who picks the date of conception, just like the liberal who picks the date of birth or viability, and unlike the sophist who concludes that Nixon is bald.

But we still don't have the whole conservative argument, for on the basis of what has been said so far the conservative should also call an acorn an oak tree, but he doesn't, and the reason he uses is that, as regards a human life, it would be *morally* arbitrary to use any date other than that of conception. That is, he can ask liberals to name the earliest stage at which they are willing to call the organism a human being, something which may not be killed for any reason short of saving some other human life. The conservative will then take the stage of development immediately preceding the one the liberals choose and challenge them to point to a difference between the two stages, a difference that is a morally relevant difference.

Suppose the liberal picks the date of birth. Yet a newborn infant is only a fetus that has suffered a change of address and some physiological changes like respiration. A neonate delivered in its twenty-fifth week lies in an incubator physically less well developed and no more independent than a normal fetus in its thirty-seventh week in the womb. What difference is there that can be used to justify killing the prenatal child where it would be wrong to kill the postnatal child?

Or suppose the liberal uses the date of viability. But the viability of a fetus is its capacity to survive outside the mother, and *that* is totally relative to the state of the available medical technology. In principle, eventually the fetus may be deliverable at any time, perhaps even at conception. The problems this poses for liberals are obvious, and in fact one finds that either a liberal doesn't understand what viability really is, so that he takes it to be necessarily linked to the later fetal stages; or he is an extreme liberal in disguise, who is playing along with the first kind of liberal for political purposes; or he has abandoned the viability criterion and is madly scurrying about in search of some other factor in the late fetal stages which might serve as a nonarbitrary cutoff point. But I am inclined to suppose that the conservative is right, that going back stage by stage from the infant to the zygote one will not find any differences between successive stages significant enough to bear the enormous moral burden of allowing wholesale slaughter at the earlier stage while categorically denying that permission at the next stage.

The full power and persuasiveness of the conservative argument is still not revealed until we uncover its similarities to and connections with any of the dialectical devices that have been used to widen a man's recognition of his fellowship with all the members of his biological species. It is a matter of record that men of good will have often failed to recognize that a certain class of fellow creatures were really human beings just like themselves.

To take but one example, the history of Negro slavery includes among the white oppressors men who were, in all other regards, essentially just and decent. Many such men sincerely defended their practice of slavery with the claim that the Negro was not a member of the moral community of men. Not only legally, but also conceptually, for the white master, the Negro was property, livestock. He would be inclined to, and actually did, simply point to the Negro and say: "Look at them! Can't you see the differences between them and us?" And the fact is that at one time that argument had an undeniable power, as undeniable as the perceptual differences it appealed to. Check your own perceptions. Ask yourself whether you really, in a purely phenomenological sense, *see* a member of another race in the same way you see a member of your own. Why is it that all Chinamen look alike and are so inscrutable? Add to the physiological facts the staggering cultural disparities dividing slave and master, and you may start to sense the force of the master's argument. What has been the rebuttal? We point to the similarities between Negro and white, and then step by step describe the differences and show about each one that it is not a morally relevant difference, not the kind of difference that warrants discriminating against a Negro.

The parallels with the abortion controversy are palpable. Let me extend them some more. First, sometimes a disagreement over a creature's humanity does turn on beliefs about subsidiary matters of fact—but it need not. Further, when it does not, when the disagreement develops from differing responses to the same data, the issue is still a factual one and not a matter of taste. It is not that one party prefers or approves of or has a favorable attitude or emotion toward some property, while the other party does not. Our response concerns what the thing is, not whether we like it or whether it is good. And when I say I don't *care* about the color of a man's skin, that it's not *important* to me, I am saying something quite different than when I say I don't care about the color of a woman's hair. I am saying that this property cannot be used to justify discriminatory behavior or social arrangements. It cannot be so used because it is irrelevant; neither black skin nor white skin is, in and of itself, of any value. The slaveholder's response is not that white skin is of intrinsic value. Rather, he replies that people with naturally black skin are niggers, and that is an inferior kind of creature. So too, the liberal does not claim that infants possess some intrinsically valuable attribute lacked by prenatal children. Rather, he says that a prenatal child is a fetus, not a human being.

In brief, when seen in its totality the conservative's argument *is* the liberal's argument turned completely inside out. While the liberal stresses the differences between disparate stages, the conservative stresses the resemblances between consecutive stages. The liberal asks, "What has a zygote got that is valuable?" and the conservative answers,

"Nothing, but it's a human being, so it is wrong to abort it." Then the conservative asks, "What does a fetus lack that an infant has that is so valuable?" and the liberal answers, "Nothing, but it's a fetus, not a human being, so it is all right to abort it." The arguments are equally strong and equally weak, for they are the *same* argument, an argument that can be pointed in either of two directions. The argument does not itself point in either direction: it is *we* who must point it, and we who are led by it. If you are led in one direction rather than the other, that is not because of logic, but because you respond in a certain way to certain facts.

Recall that the arguments are usually formulated in the interrogative, not the indicative, mood. Though the answers are supposed to be absolutely obvious, they are not comfortably assertible. Why? Because an assertion is a truth claim which invites a request for a proof, but here any assertible proof presupposes premises which beg the question. If one may speak of proof here, it can lie only in the audience's response, in their acceptance of the answer and of its obviousness. The questions convince by leading us to appreciate familiar facts. The conclusion is validated not through assertible presuppositions, but through our acknowledgment that the questions are *rhetorical.* You might say that the conclusion is our seeing a certain aspect: e.g., we see the embryo as a human being. But this seems an unduly provocative description of the situation, for what is at issue is whether such an aspect is there to be seen.

Evidently, we have here a paradigm of what Wittgenstein had in mind when he spoke of the possibility of two people agreeing on the application of a rule for a long period, and then, suddenly and quite inexplicably, diverging in what they call going on in the same way. This possibility led him to insist that linguistic communication presupposes not only agreement in definitions, but also agreement in judgments, in what he called forms of life—something that seems lacking in the case at hand. Apparently, the conclusion to draw is that it is not true that the fetus is a human being, but it is not false either. Without an agreement in judgments, without a common response to the pertinent data, the assertion that the fetus is a human being cannot be assigned a genuine truth-value.

Yet, we surely want to say that Negroes are and always have been full-fledged human beings, no matter what certain segments of mankind may have thought, and no matter how numerous or unanimous those segments were. The humanity of the slaves seems unlike that of the fetus, but not because by now a monolithic majority recognizes—however grudgingly—the full human status of Negroes, whereas no position regarding the fetus commands more than a plurality. The mere fact of disagreement in judgments or forms of life would not render unsettleable statements about the humanity of fetuses, otherwise the comparable statements about Negroes, or for that matter whites, would meet a similar fate. What seems special about the fetus is that, apparently, we have no vantage point from which to criticize opposing systems of belief.

It will be said by some that a form of life is something not really criticizable by or from an opposing form of life. In this instance the point is without practical relevance, since the differences between the disputants are not so systematic and entire as to block every avenue of rational discussion. Clearly, their communality is very great, their differences relatively isolated and free-floating.

At this stage of the dispute over a creature's humanity, I stand to the slaveholder in roughly the same relation I stand to the color-blind man who judges this sheet of paper to be gray. Our differing color judgments express our differing immediate responses to the same data. But his color judgment is mistaken because his vision is defective. I criticize his judgment by criticizing him, by showing him to be abnormal, deviant—which is not the same as being in the minority. In a like manner we criticize those basic beliefs and attitudes which sanction and are sustained by the slaveholder's form of life. We argue that his form of life is, so to speak, an accident of history, explicable by reference to special socio-psychological circumstances that are inessential to the nature of blacks and whites. The fact that Negroes *can* and, special circumstances aside, naturally *would* be regarded and treated no differently than Caucasians is at once a necessary and a sufficient condition for its being right to so regard and treat them. Thus, while we may in large measure understand the life-style of the slaveholder and perhaps without condemnation of the man, we need not and should not condone his behavior.

Liberals and conservatives rail at each other with this same canonical schema. And if, for example, antiabortionism required the perverting of natural reason and normal sensibilities by a system of superstitions, then the liberal could discredit it—but it doesn't, so he can't. As things stand, it is not at all clear what, if anything, is the normal or natural or healthy response toward the fetus; it is not clear what is to count as the special historical and social circumstances, which, if removed, would leave us with the appropriate way to regard and treat the fetus. And I think that the unlimited possibility of natural *responses* is simply the other side of the fact of severely limited possibilities of natural *relationships* with the fetus. After all, there isn't much we can do with a fetus; either we let it out or we do it in. I have little hope of seeing a justification for doing one thing or the other unless this situation changes. As things stand, the range of interactions is so minimal that we are not compelled to regard the fetus in any particular way. For example, respect for a fetus cannot be wrung from us as respect for a Negro can and is, unless we are irretrievably warped or stunted.

We seem to be stuck with the indeterminateness of the fetus' humanity. This does not mean that, whatever you believe, it is true or true for you if you believe it. Quite the contrary, it means that, whatever you believe, it's not true—but neither is it false. You believe it, and that's the end of the matter.

But obviously that's not the end of the matter; the same urgent moral and political decisions still confront us. But before we run off to make our existential leaps over the liberal-conservative impasse, we might meander through the moderate position. I'll shorten the trip by speaking only of features found throughout the spectrum of moderate views. For the moderate, the fetus is not a human being, but it's not a mere maternal appendage either; it's a human fetus, and it has a separate moral status just as animals do. A fetus is not an object that we can treat however we wish, neither is it a person whom we must treat as we would wish to be treated in return. Thus, *some* legal prohibitions on abortions *might* be justified in the name of the fetus *qua* human fetus, just as we accord some legal protection to animals, not for the sake of the owners, but for the benefit of the animals themselves.

Ultimately, most liberals and conservatives are, in a sense, only extreme moderates. Few liberals really regard abortion, at least in the later stages, as a bit of elective surgery. Suppose a woman had her fifth-month fetus aborted purely out of curiosity as to what it looked like, and perhaps then had it bronzed. Who among us would not deem both her and her actions reprehensible? One might refuse to outlaw the behavior, but still, clearly we do not respond to this case as we would to the removal of an appendix or a tooth. Similarly, in my experience few of even the staunchest conservatives consistently regard the fetus, at least in the earlier stages, in the same way as they do a fellow adult. When the cause of grief is a miscarriage, the object of grief is the mother; rarely does anyone feel pity or sorrow for the embryo itself. Nevertheless, enough people give enough substance to the liberal and conservative positions to justify describing them as I have done as views differing in kind rather than degree.

The moderate position is as problematic as it is popular. The moderate is driven in two directions, liberalism and conservatism, by the very same question: Why do you make these exceptions and not those?

The difficulty here is comparable to that regarding animals. There are dogs, pigs, mosquitoes, worms, bacteria, etc., and we kill them for food, clothing, ornamentation, sport, convenience, and out of simple irritation or unblinking inadvertence. We allow different animals to be killed for different reasons, and there are enormous differences between people on all of this. In general, for most of us, the higher the evolutionary stage of the species or the later the developmental stage of the fetus, the more restricted our permission to kill. But it is far more complicated than that, and anyone with a fully consistent, let alone principled, system of beliefs on these matters is usually thought fanatical by the rest of us.

To stabilize his position, the moderate would have to *invent* a new set of moral categories and principles. A happy amalgamation of the ones we have won't do, because our principles of justice apply solely to the relations between persons. But *how* is one to invent new categories and principles? I'm not sure it can be done, especially with the scanty building materials available. Again, our interactions with fetuses are extremely limited and peripheral, which is why our normative conceptual machinery in this area is so abbreviated, unformed, and up for grabs.

But perhaps this could be otherwise. Close your eyes for a moment and imagine that, due to advances in medical technology or mutation caused by a nuclear war, the relevant cutaneous and membranous shields became transparent from conception to parturition, so that when a mother put aside her modesty and her clothing the developing fetus would be in full public view. Or suppose instead, or in addition, that anyone could at any time pluck a fetus from its womb, air it, observe it, fondle it, and then stick it back in after a few minutes. And we could further suppose that this made for healthier babies, and so maybe laws would be passed requiring that it be done regularly. And we might also imagine that gestation took nine days rather than nine months. What then would we think of aborting a fetus? What would *you* think of aborting it? And what does that say about what you *now* think?

In my experience, when such imaginative exercises are properly presented, people are often, not always, moved by them, different people by different stories. They begin to talk about all of it somewhat differently than they had before, and less differently from each other. However, the role of such conjectures in or as arguments is far from clear. I don't think we discover the justifications for our beliefs by such a procedure. A liberal who is disturbed by the picture of a transparent womb may be acquiring some self-knowledge; he may come to realize how much power being visible and being hidden have for us and for him, and he may make a connection between this situation and the differing experiences of an infantryman and a bombardier. But surely the fetus' being hidden was not the liberal's *reason* for thinking it expendable.

Nor is it evident that such *Gedanken* experiments reveal the causes of our beliefs. Their results seem too unreliable to provide anything but the grossest projections as to how we would in fact react in the imagined situations. When I present myself with such science fiction fantasies, I am inclined to respond as I do to a question posed by Hilary Putnam[1]: If we build robots with a psychology isomorphic with ours and a physical structure comparable to ours, should we award them civil rights? In contrast to Putnam, who thinks we can now give a more disinterested and hence objective answer to this question, I would say that our present answer, whatever it is, is so disinterested as to count for nothing. It seems to me that such questions about the robot or the fetus can't be answered in advance. This seems so for much the same reason that some things, especially regarding moral matters, can't be told to a child. A child can of course hear the words and operate with them, but he will not really understand them without undergoing certain experiences, and maybe not even then. Odd as it may sound, I want to know exactly what the robot looks like and what it's like to live with it. I want to know how in fact we—how I—look at it, respond to it, and feel toward it. Hypothetical situations of this sort raise questions which seem answerable only when the situation is realized, and perhaps then there is no longer a real question.

I am suggesting that what our natural response to a thing is, how we naturally react to it cognitively, affectively, and behaviorally, is partly definitive of that thing, and is therefore partly definitive of how we ought to respond to that thing. Often only an actual confrontation will tell us what we need to know, and sometimes we may each respond differently, and thus have differing understandings.

Moreover, the relation of such hypothetical situations to our actual situation is problematic. My hunch is that if the fetal condition I described were realized, fewer of us would be liberals and more of us would be conservatives and moderates. But suppose that in fact we would all be hidebound conservatives and that we knew that now.

[1] Hilary Putnam, "Robots: Machines or Artificially Created Life?" *The Journal of Philosophy* 61, no. 21 (1964): 668–691.

Would a contemporary liberal be irrational, unjustified, or wicked if he remained adamant? Well, if a slaveholder with a conscience were shown why he feels about Negroes as he does, and that he would regard them as his equals if only he had not been reared to think otherwise, he might change his ways, and if he didn't I would unhesitatingly call him irrational and his behavior unjustified and wicked.

But now suppose that dogs or chimps could and did talk so that they entered our lives in more significant roles than those of experimental tools, friendly playthings, or faithful servants, and we enacted antivivisectionalist legislation. If we discovered all this now, the news might deeply stir us, but would we necessarily be wrong if we still used animals as we do? Here, so I am inclined to think, we might sensibly maintain that in the hypothetical case the animals and their relations with us are essentially and relevantly different from what they now are. The capacities may exist now, but their realization constitutes a crucial change like that from an infant to an adult, and unlike that from a slave to a citizen. We would no more need to revise our treatment of animals than we need to apply the same principles of reciprocity to children and adults.

In the abortion case my instincts are similar but shakier. Yet I think that the adamant liberal could reply that what is special about fetuses, what distinguishes them from babies, slaves, animals, robots, and the rest, is that they essentially are and relate to us as bundles of potentialities. So, obviously, if their potentialities were actualized, not singly or partially, but in sufficient number and degree, we would feel differently. But to make them and their situation in respect to us different enough so that we would naturally regard them as human beings, they would have to become what they can become: human beings. In the hypothetical situation, they are babies in a biological incubator, and therefore that situation is irrelevant to our situation. In brief, an argument based on such a situation only restates the conservative's original argument with imaginary changes instead of the actual set of changes which transforms the fetus into a human child.

Study Questions

1. What, according to Wertheimer, is the extreme conservative position, and what is its defense?
2. Why, according to Wertheimer, do liberals fail to respond to the conservative argument?
3. Is whether the fetus is a person just a matter of definition, according to Wertheimer? Explain.
4. What, according to Wertheimer, is the conservative response to the liberal argument that if you call an embryo a person, you are implying that it has certain properties that are valuable?
5. Characterize the conservative response, according to Wertheimer, to a liberal attempt to assign personhood to a fetus at the date of viability.
6. Does Wertheimer agree that going back stage by stage from the infant to the zygote will disclose no morally significant differences between successive stages? Explain.
7. What does Wertheimer mean that the conservative's argument is the liberal's argument turned completely inside out?
8. Compare the conservative argument to the argument of those who assign kinship to all members of the human species.
9. *Is* the fetus a human being, according to Wertheimer? Explain.
10. Describe the moderate position, according to Wertheimer, and why he thinks it is problematic.

A Defense of Abortion[1]

Judith Jarvis Thomson

Judith Jarvis Thomson (b. 1929) teaches philosophy at the Massachusetts Institute of Technology. This article appeared in *Philosophy and Public Affairs* 1, no. 1 (1971).

Most opposition to abortion relies on the premise that the fetus is a human being, a person, from the moment of conception. The premise is argued for, but, as I think, not well. Take, for example, the most common argument. We are asked to notice that the development of a human being from conception through birth into childhood is continuous; then it is said that to draw a line, to choose a point in this development and say 'before this point the thing is not a person, after this point it is a person" is to make an arbitrary choice, a choice for which in the nature of things no good reason can be given. It is concluded that the fetus is, or anyway that we had better say it is, a person from the moment of conception. But this conclusion does not follow. Similar things might be said about the development of an acorn into an oak tree, and it does not follow that acorns are oak trees, or that we had better say they are. Arguments of this form are sometimes called "slippery slope arguments"—the phrase is perhaps self-explanatory—and it is dismaying that opponents of abortion rely on them so heavily and uncritically.

I am inclined to agree, however, that the prospects for "drawing a line" in the development of the fetus look dim. I am inclined to think also that we shall probably have to agree that the fetus has already become a human person well before birth. Indeed, it comes as a surprise when one first learns how early in its life it begins to acquire human characteristics. By the tenth week, for example, it already has a face, arms and legs, fingers and toes; it has internal organs, and brain activity is detectable.[2] On the other hand, I think that the premise is false, that the fetus is not a person from the moment of conception. A newly fertilized ovum, a newly implanted clump of cells, is no more a person than an acorn is an oak tree. But I shall not discuss any of this. For it seems to me to be of great interest to ask what happens if, for the sake of argument, we allow the premise. How, precisely, are we supposed to get from there to the conclusion that abortion is morally impermissible? Opponents of abortion commonly spend most of their time establishing that the fetus is a person, and hardly any time explaining the step from there to the impermissibility of abortion. Perhaps they think the step too simple and obvious to require much comment. Or perhaps instead they are simply being economical in argument. Many of those who defend abortion rely on the premise that the fetus is not a person, but only a bit of tissue that will become a person at birth; and why pay out more arguments than you have to? Whatever the explanation, I suggest that the step they take is neither easy nor obvious, that it calls for closer examination than it is commonly given, and that when we do give it this closer examination we shall feel inclined to reject it.

I propose, then, that we grant that the fetus is a person from the moment of conception. How does the argument go from here? Something like this, I take it. Every person has a right to life. So the fetus has a right to life. No doubt the mother has a right to decide what shall happen in and to

[1]I am very much indebted to James Thomson for discussion, criticism, and many helpful suggestions.

[2]Daniel Callahan, *Abortion: Law, Choice and Morality* (New York, 1970), p. 373. This book gives a fascinating survey of the available information on abortion. The Jewish tradition is surveyed in David M. Feldman, *Birth Control in Jewish Law* (New York, 1968), Part 5, the Catholic tradition in John T. Noonan, Jr., "An Almost Absolute Value in History," in *The Morality of Abortion*, ed. John T. Noonan, Jr. (Cambridge, Mass., 1970).

her body; everyone would grant that. But surely a person's right to life is stronger and more stringent than the mother's right to decide what happens in and to her body, and so outweighs it. So the fetus may not be killed; an abortion may not be performed.

It sounds plausible. But now let me ask you to imagine this. You wake up in the morning and find yourself back to back in bed with an unconscious violinist. A famous unconscious violinist. He has been found to have a fatal kidney ailment, and the Society of Music Lovers has canvassed all the available medical records and found that you alone have the right blood type to help. They have therefore kidnapped you, and last night the violinist's circulatory system was plugged into yours, so that your kidneys can be used to extract poisons from his blood as well as your own. The direct of the hospital now tells you, "Look, we're sorry the Society of Music Lovers did this to you—we would never have permitted it if we had known. But still, they did it, and the violinist now is plugged into you. To unplug you would be to kill him. But never mind, it's only for nine months. By then he will have recovered from his ailment, and can safety be unplugged from you." Is it morally incumbent on you to accede to this situation? No doubt it would be very nice of you if you did, a great kindness. But do you *have* to accede to it? What if it were not nine months, but nine years? Or longer still? What if the director of the hospital says, "Tough luck, I agree, but you've now got to stay in bed, with the violinist plugged into you, for the rest of your life. Because remember this. All persons have a right to life, and violinists are persons. Granted you have a right to decide what happens in and to your body, but a person's right to life outweighs your right to decide what happens in and to your body. So you cannot ever be unplugged from him." I imagine you would regard this as outrageous, which suggests that something really is wrong with that plausible-sounding argument I mentioned a moment ago.

In this case, of course, you were kidnapped; you didn't volunteer for the operation that plugged the violinist into your kidneys. Can those who oppose abortion on the ground I mentioned make an exception for a pregnancy due to rape? Certainly. They can say that persons have a right to life only if they didn't come into existence because of rape; or they can say that all persons have a right to life, but that some have less of a right to life than others, in particular, that those who came into existence because of rape have less. But these statements have a rather unpleasant sound. Surely the question of whether you have a right to life at all, or how much of it you have, shouldn't turn on the question of whether or not you are the product of a rape. And in fact the people who oppose abortion on the ground I mentioned do not make this distinction, and hence do not make an exception in case of rape.

Nor do they make an exception for a case in which the mother has to spend the nine months of her pregnancy in bed. They would agree that would be a great pity, and hard on the mother; but all the same, all persons have a right to life, the fetus is a person, and so on. I suspect, in fact, that they would not make an exception for a case in which, miraculously enough, the pregnancy went on for nine years, or even the rest of the mother's life.

Some won't even make an exception for a case in which continuation of the pregnancy is likely to shorten the mother's life; they regard abortion as impermissible even to save the mother's life. Such cases are nowadays very rare, and many opponents of abortion do not accept this extreme view. All the same, it is a good place to begin: a number of points of interest come out in respect to it.

1. Let us call the view that abortion is impermissible even to save the mother's life "the extreme view." I want to suggest first that it does not issue from the argument I mentioned earlier without the addition of some fairly powerful premises. Suppose a woman has become pregnant, and now learns that she has a cardiac condition such that she will die if she carries the baby to term. What may be done for her? The fetus, being a person, has a right to life, but as the mother is a person too, so has she a right to life. Presumably they have an equal right to life. How is it supposed to come out that an abortion may not be performed? If mother and child have an equal right to life, shouldn't we per-

haps flip a coin? Or should we add to the mother's right to life her right to decide what happens in and to her body, which everybody seems to be ready to grant—the sum of her rights now outweighing the fetus' right to life?

The most familiar argument here is the following. We are told that performing the abortion would be directly killing[3] the child, whereas doing nothing would not be killing the mother, but only letting her die. Moreover, in killing the child, one would be killing an innocent person, for the child has committed no crime, and is not aiming at his mother's death. And then there are a variety of ways in which this might be continued. (1) But as directly killing an innocent person is always and absolutely impermissible, an abortion may not be performed. Or, (2) as directly killing an innocent person is murder, and murder is always and absolutely impermissible, an abortion may not be performed.[4] Or, (3) as one's duty to refrain from directly killing an innocent person is more stringent than one's duty to keep a person from dying, an abortion may not be performed. Or, (4) if one's only options are directly killing an innocent person or letting a person die, one must prefer letting the person die, and thus an abortion may not be performed.[5]

Some people seem to have thought that these are not further premises which must be added if the conclusion is to be reached, but that they follow from the very fact that an innocent person has a right to life.[6] But this seems to me to be a mistake, and perhaps the simplest way to show this is to bring out that while we must certainly grant that innocent persons have a right to life, the theses in (1) through (4) are all false. Take (2), for example. If directly killing an innocent person is murder, and thus is impermissible, then the mother's directly killing the innocent person inside her is murder, and thus is impermissible. But it cannot seriously be thought to be murder if the mother performs an abortion on herself to save her life. It cannot seriously be said that she *must* refrain, that she *must* sit passively by and wait for her death. Let us look again at the case of you and the violinist. There you are, in bed with the violinist, and the director of the hospital says to you, "It's all most distressing, and I deeply sympathize, but you see this is putting an additional strain on your kidneys, and you'll be dead within the month. But you *have* to stay where you are all the same. Because unplugging you would be directly killing an innocent violinist, and that's murder, and that's impermissible." If anything in the world is true, it is that you do not commit murder, you do not do what is impermissible, if you reach around to your back and unplug yourself from that violinist to save your life.

The main focus of attention in writings on abortion has been on what a third party may or may not do in answer to a request from a woman for an abortion. This is in a way understandable. Things being as they are, there isn't much a woman can safely do to abort herself. So the question asked is what a third party may do, and what the mother may do, if it is mentioned at all, is

---

[3]The term "direct" in the arguments I refer to is a technical one. Roughly, what is meant by "direct killing" is either killing as an end in itself, or killing as a means to some end, for example, the end of saving someone else's life. See note 6, below, for an example of its use.

[4]Cf. *Encyclical Letter of Pope Pius XI on Christian Marriage*, St. Paul Editions (Boston, n.d.), p. 32: "however much we may pity the mother whose health and even life is gravely imperiled in the performance of the duty allotted to her by nature, nevertheless what could ever be a sufficient reason for excusing in any way the direct murder of the innocent? This is precisely what we are dealing with here." Noonan (*The Morality of Abortion*, p. 43) reads this as follows: "What cause can ever avail to excuse in any way the direct killing of the innocent? For it is a question of that."

[5]The thesis in (4) is in an interesting way weaker than those in (1), (2), and (3): they rule out abortion even in cases in which both mother *and* child will die if the abortion is not performed. By contrast, one who held the view expressed in (4) could consistently say that one needn't prefer letting two persons die to killing one.

[6]Cf. the following passage from Pius XII, *Address to the Italian Catholic Society of Midwives*: "The baby in the maternal breast has the right to life immediately from God.—Hence there is no man, no human authority, no science, no medical, eugenic, social, economic or moral 'indication' which can establish or grant a valid juridical ground for a direct deliberate disposition of an innocent human life, that is a disposition which looks to its destruction either as an end or as a means to another end perhaps in itself not illicit.—The baby, still not born, is a man in the same degree and for the same reason as the mother" (quoted in Noonan, *The Morality of Abortion*, p. 45).

deduced, almost as an afterthought, from what it is concluded that third parties may do. But it seems to me that to treat the matter in this way is to refuse to grant to the mother that very status of person which is so firmly insisted on for the fetus. For we cannot simply read off what a person may do from what a third party may do. Suppose you find yourself trapped in a tiny house with a growing child. I mean a very tiny house, and a rapidly growing child—you are already up against the wall of the house and in a few minutes you'll be crushed to death. The child on the other hand won't be crushed to death; if nothing is done to stop him from growing he'll be hurt, but in the end he'll simply burst open the house and walk out a free man. Now I could well understand it if a bystander were to say, "There's nothing we can do for you. We cannot choose between your life and his, we cannot be the ones to decide who is to live, we cannot intervene." But it cannot be concluded that you too can do nothing, that you cannot attack it to save your life. However innocent the child may be, you do not have to wait passively while it crushes you to death. Perhaps a pregnant woman is vaguely felt to have the status of house, to which we don't allow the right of self-defense. But if the woman houses the child, it should be remembered that she is a person who houses it.

I should perhaps stop to say explicitly that I am not claiming that people have a right to do anything whatever to save their lives. I think, rather, that there are drastic limits to the right of self-defense. If someone threatens you with death unless you torture someone else to death, I think you have not the right, even to save your life, to do so. But the case under consideration here is very different. In our case there are only two people involved, one whose life is threatened, and one who threatens it. Both are innocent: the one who is threatened is not threatened because of any fault, the one who threatens does not threaten because of any fault. For this reason we may feel that we bystanders cannot intervene. But the person threatened can.

In sum, a woman surely can defend her life against the threat to it posed by the unborn child, even if doing so involves its death. And this shows not merely that the theses in (1) through (4) are false; it shows also that the extreme view of abortion is false, and so we need not canvass any other possible ways of arriving at it from the argument I mentioned at the outset.

2. The extreme view could of course be weakened to say that while abortion is permissible to save the mother's life, it may not be performed by a third party, but only by the mother herself. But this cannot be right either. For what we have to keep in mind is that the mother and the unborn child are not like two tenants in a small house which has, by an unfortunate mistake, been rented to both: the mother *owns* the house. The fact that she does adds to the offensiveness of deducing that the mother can do nothing from the supposition that third parties can do nothing. But it does more than this: it casts a bright light on the supposition that third parties can do nothing. Certainly it lets us see that a third party who says "I cannot choose between you" is fooling himself if he thinks this is impartiality. If Jones has found and fastened on a certain coat, which he needs to keep him from freezing, but which Smith also needs to keep him from freezing, then it is not impartiality that says "I cannot choose between you" when Smith owns the coat. Women have said again and again "This body is *my* body!" and they have reason to feel angry, reason to feel that it has been like shouting into the wind. Smith, after all, is hardly likely to bless us if we say to him, "Of course it's your coat, anybody would grant that it is. But no one may choose between you and Jones who is to have it."

We should really ask what it is that says "no one may choose" in the face of the fact that the body that houses the child is the mother's body. It may be simply a failure to appreciate this fact. But it may be something more interesting, namely the sense that one has a right to refuse to lay hands on people, even where it would be just and fair to do so, even where justice seems to require that somebody do so. Thus justice might call for somebody to get Smith's coat back from Jones, and yet you have a right to refuse to be the one to lay hands on Jones, a right to refuse to do physical violence to him. This, I think, must be granted. But then what should be said is not "no one may choose," but only "*I* cannot choose," and indeed not even this, but "*I* will not *act*," leaving it open that somebody else can or should, and in particular that anyone in a position of authority, with the job of securing people's rights, both can and should. So this is no difficulty. I have not been arguing that any given third party must accede to the mother's request that he perform an abortion to save her life, but only that he may.

I suppose that in some views of human life the mother's body is only on loan to her, the loan not being one which gives her any prior claim to it. One who held this view might well think it impartiality to say "I cannot choose." But I shall simply ignore this possibility. My own view is that if a human being has any just, prior claim to anything at all, he has a just, prior claim to his own body. And perhaps this needn't be argued for here anyway, since, as I mentioned, the arguments against abortion we are looking at do grant that the woman has a right to decide what happens in and to her body.

But although they do grant it, I have tried to show that they do not take seriously what is done in granting it. I suggest the same thing will reappear even more clearly when we turn away from cases in which the mother's life is at stake, and attend, as I propose we now do, to the vastly more common cases in which a woman wants an abortion for some less weighty reason than preserving her own life.

3. Where the mother's life is not at stake, the argument I mentioned at the outset seems to have a much stronger pull. "Everyone has a right to life, so the unborn person has a right to life." And isn't the child's right to life weightier than anything other than the mother's own right to life, which she might put forward as ground for an abortion?

This argument treats the right to life as if it were unproblematic. It is not, and this seems to me to be precisely the source of the mistake.

For we should now, at long last, ask what it comes to, to have a right to life. In some views having a right to life includes having a right to be given at least the bare minimum one needs for continued life. But suppose that what in fact *is* the bare minimum a man needs for continued life is something he has no right at all to be given? If I am sick unto death, and the only thing that will save my life is the touch of Henry Fonda's cool hand on my fevered brow, then all the same, I have no right to be given the touch of Henry Fonda's cool hand on my fevered brow. It would be frightfully nice of him to fly in from the West Coast to provide it. It would be less nice, though no doubt well meant, if my friends flew out to the West Coast and carried Henry Fonda back with them. But I have no right at all against anybody that he should do this for me. Or again, to return to the story I told earlier, the fact that for continued life that violinist needs the continued use of your kidneys does not establish that he has a right to be given the continued use of your kidneys. He certainly has no right against you that *you* should give him continued use of your kidneys. For nobody has any right to use your kidneys unless you give him such a right; and nobody has the right against you that you shall give him this right—if you do allow him to go on using your kidneys, this is a kindness on your part, and not something he can claim from you as his due. Nor has he any right against anybody else that *they* should give him continued use of your kidneys. Certainly he had no right against the Society of Music Lovers that they should plug him into you in the first place. And if you now start to unplug yourself, having learned that you will otherwise have to spend nine years in bed with him, there is nobody in the world who must try to prevent you, in order to see to it that he is given something he has a right to be given.

Some people are rather stricter about the right to life. In their view, it does not include the right to be given anything, but amounts to, and only to, the right not to be killed by anybody. But here a related difficulty arises. If everybody is to refrain from killing that violinist, then everybody must refrain from doing a great many different sorts of things. Everybody must refrain from slitting his throat, everybody must refrain from shooting him—and everybody must refrain from unplugging you from him. But does he have a right against everybody that they shall refrain from unplugging you from him? To refrain from doing this is to allow him to continue to use your kidneys. It could be argued that he has a right against us that *we* should allow him to continue to use your kidneys. That is, while he had no right against us that we should give him the use of your kidneys, it might be argued that he anyway has a right against us that we shall not now intervene and deprive him of the use of your kidneys. I shall come back to third-party interventions later. But certainly the violinist has no right against you that *you* shall allow him to continue to use your kidneys. As I said, if you do allow him to use them, it is a kindness on your part, and not something you owe him.

The difficulty I point to here is not peculiar to the right to life. It reappears in connection with all the other natural rights; and it is something which an adequate account of rights must deal with. For present purposes it is enough just to draw attention to it. But I would stress that I am not arguing that people do not have a right to life—quite to the contrary, it seems to me that the primary control we must place on the acceptability of an account of rights is that it should turn out in that account to be a truth that all persons have a right to life. I am arguing only that having a right to life does not guarantee having either a right to be given the use of or a right to be allowed continued use of another person's body—even if one needs it for life itself. So the right to life will not serve the opponents of abortion in the very simple and clear way in which they seem to have thought it would.

4. There is another way to bring out the difficulty. In the most ordinary sort of case, to deprive someone of what he has a right to is to treat him unjustly. Suppose a boy and his small brother are jointly given a box of chocolates for Christmas. If the older boy takes the box and refuses to give his brother any of the chocolates, he is unjust to him, for the brother has been given a right to half of them. But suppose that, having learned that otherwise it means nine years in bed with that violinist, you unplug yourself from him. You surely are not being unjust to him, for you gave him no right to use your kidneys, and no one else can have given him any such right. But we have to notice that in unplugging yourself, you are killing him; and violinists, like everybody else, have a right to life, and thus in the view we were considering just now, the right not to be killed. So here you do what he supposedly has a right you shall not do, but you do not act unjustly to him in doing it.

The emendation which may be made at this point is this: the right to life consists not in the right not to be killed, but rather in the right not to be killed unjustly. This runs a risk of circularity, but never mind: it would enable us to square the fact that the violinist has a right to life with the fact that you do not act unjustly toward him in unplugging yourself, thereby killing him. For if you do not kill him unjustly, you do not violate his right to life, and so it is no wonder you do him no injustice.

But if this emendation is accepted, the gap in the argument against abortion stares us plainly in the face: it is by no means enough to show that the fetus is a person, and to remind us that all persons have a right to life—we need to be shown also that killing the fetus violates its right to life, i.e., that abortion is unjust killing. And is it?

I suppose we may take it as a datum that in a case of pregnancy due to rape the mother has not given the unborn person a right to the use of her body for food and shelter. Indeed, in what pregnancy could it be supposed that the mother has given the unborn person such a right? It is not as if there were unborn persons drifting about the world, to whom a woman who wants a child says "I invite you in."

But it might be argued that there are other ways one can have acquired a right to the use of another person's body than by having been invited to use it by that person. Suppose a woman voluntarily indulges in intercourse, knowing of the chance it will issue in pregnancy, and then she does become pregnant; is she not in part responsible for the presence, in fact the very existence, of the unborn person inside her? No doubt she did not invite it. But doesn't her partial responsibility for its being there itself give it a right to the use of her body?[7] If so, then her aborting it would be more like the

[7]The need for a discussion of this argument was brought home to me by members of the Society for Ethical and Legal Philosophy, to whom this paper was originally presented.

boy's taking away the chocolates, and less like your unplugging yourself from the violinist—doing so would be depriving it of what it does have a right to, and thus would be doing it an injustice.

And then, too, it might be asked whether or not she can kill it even to save her own life: If she voluntarily called it into existence, how can she now kill it, even in self-defense?

The first thing to be said about this is that it is something new. Opponents of abortion have been so concerned to make out the independence of the fetus, in order to establish that it has a right to life, just as its mother does, that they have tended to overlook the possible support they might gain from making out that the fetus is *dependent* on the mother, in order to establish that she has a special kind of responsibility for it, a responsibility that gives it rights against her which are not possessed by any independent person—such as an ailing violinist who is a stranger to her.

On the other hand, this argument would give the unborn person a right to its mother's body only if her pregnancy resulted from a voluntary act, undertaken in full knowledge of the chance a pregnancy might result from it. It would leave out entirely the unborn person whose existence is due to rape. Pending the availability of some further argument, then, we would be left with the conclusion that unborn persons whose existence is due to rape have no right to the use of their mothers' bodies, and thus that aborting them is not depriving them of anything they have a right to and hence is not unjust killing.

And we should also notice that it is not at all plain that this argument really does go even as far as it purports to. For there are cases and cases, and the details make a difference. If the room is stuffy, and I therefore open a window to air it, and a burglar climbs in, it would be absurd to say, "Ah, now he can stay, she's given him a right to the use of her house—for she is partially responsible for his presence there, having voluntarily done what enabled him to get in, full knowledge that there are such things as burglars, and that burglars burgle." It would be still more absurd to say this if I had had bars installed outside my windows, precisely to prevent burglars from getting in, and a burglar got in only because of a defect in the bars. It remains equally absurd if we imagine it is not a burglar who climbs in, but an innocent person who blunders or falls in. Again, suppose it were like this: people-seeds drift about in the air like pollen, and if you open your windows, one may drift in and take root in your carpets or upholstery. You don't want children, so you fix up your windows with fine mesh screens, the very best you can buy. As can happen, however, and on very, very rare occasions does happen, one of the screens is defective; and a seed drifts in and takes root. Does the person-plant who now develops have a right to the use of your house? Surely not—despite the fact that you voluntarily opened your windows, you knowingly kept carpets and upholstered furniture, and you knew that screens were sometimes defective. Someone may argue that you are responsible for its rooting, that it does have a right to your house, because after all you *could* have lived out your life with bare floors and furniture, or with sealed windows and doors. But this won't do—for by the same token anyone can avoid a pregnancy due to rape by having a hysterectomy, or anyway by never leaving home without a (reliable!) army.

It seems to me that the argument we are looking at can establish at most that there are *some* cases in which the unborn person has a right to the use of its mother's body, and therefore *some* cases in which abortion is unjust killing. There is room for much discussion and argument as to precisely which, if any. But I think we should sidestep this issue and leave it open, for at any rate the argument certainly does not establish that all abortion is unjust killing.

5. There is room for yet another argument here, however. We surely must all grant that there may be cases in which it would be morally indecent to detach a person from your body at the cost of his life. Suppose you learn that what the violinist needs is not nine years of your life, but only one hour: all you need do to save his life is to spend one hour in that bed with him. Suppose also that letting him use your kidneys for that one hour would not affect your health in the slightest. Admittedly you were kidnapped. Admittedly you did not give anyone permission to plug him into you. Nevertheless it seems to me plain you *ought* to

allow him to use your kidneys for that hour—it would be indecent to refuse.

Again, suppose pregnancy lasted only an hour, and constituted no threat to life or health. And suppose that a woman becomes pregnant as a result of rape. Admittedly she did not voluntarily do anything to bring about the existence of a child. Admittedly she did nothing at all which would give the unborn person a right to the use of her body. All the same it might well be said, as in the newly emended violinist story, that she *ought* to allow it to remain for that hour—that it would be indecent in her to refuse.

Now some people are inclined to use the term "right" in such a way that it follows from the fact that you ought to allow a person to use your body for the hour he needs, that he has a right to use your body for the hour he needs, even though he has not been given that right by any person or act. They may say that it follows also that if you refuse, you act unjustly toward him. This use of the term is perhaps so common that it cannot be called wrong; nevertheless it seems to me to be an unfortunate loosening of what we would do better to keep a tight rein on. Suppose that box of chocolates I mentioned earlier had not been given to both boys jointly, but was given only to the older boy. There he sits, stolidly eating his way through the box, his small brother watching enviously. Here we are likely to say "You ought not to be so mean. You ought to give your brother some of those chocolates." My own view is that it just does not follow from the truth of this that the brother has any right to any of the chocolates. If the boy refuses to give his brother any, he is greedy, stingy, callous—but not unjust. I suppose that the people I have in mind will say it does follow that the brother has a right to some of the chocolates, and thus that the boy does act unjustly if he refuses to give his brother any. But the effect of saying this is to obscure what we should keep distinct, namely the difference between the boy's refusal in this case and the boy's refusal in the earlier case, in which the box was given to both boys jointly, and in which the small brother thus had what was from any point of view clear title to half.

A further objection to so using the term "right" that from the fact that A ought to do a thing for B, it follows that B has a right against A that A do it for him, is that it is going to make the question of whether or not a man has a right to a thing turn on how easy it is to provide him with it; and this seems not merely unfortunate, but morally unacceptable. Take the case of Henry Fonda again. I said earlier that I had no right to the touch of his cool hand on my fevered brow, even though I needed it to save my life. I said it would be frightfully nice of him to fly in from the West Coast to provide me with it, but that I had no right against him that he should do so. But suppose he isn't on the West Coast. Suppose he has only to walk across the room, place a hand briefly on my brow—and lo, my life is saved. Then surely he ought to do it, it would be indecent to refuse. Is it to be said "Ah, well, it follows that in this case she has a right to the touch of his hand on her brow, and so it would be an injustice in him to refuse"? So that I have a right to it when it is easy for him to provide it, though no right when it's hard? It's rather a shocking idea that anyone's rights should fade away and disappear as it gets harder and harder to accord them to him.

So my own view is that even though you ought to let the violinist use your kidneys for the one hour he needs, we should not conclude that he has a right to do so—we should say that if you refuse, you are, like the boy who owns all the chocolates and will give none away, self-centered and callous, indecent in fact, but not unjust. And similarly, that even supposing a case in which a woman pregnant due to rape ought to allow the unborn person to use her body for the hour he needs, we should not conclude that he has a right to do so; we should conclude that she is self-centered, callous, indecent, but not unjust, if she refuses. The complaints are no less grave; they are just different. However, there is no need to insist on this point. If anyone does wish to deduce "he has a right" from "you ought," then all the same he must surely grant that there are cases in which it is not morally required of you that you allow that violinist to use your kidneys, and in which he does not have a right to use them, and in which you do not do him an injustice if you refuse. And so also for mother and unborn child. Except in such cases as the unborn person has a right to demand it—and we were leaving open the possibility that there may be such cases—nobody is morally *required* to make large sacrifices, of health, of all other interests and concerns, of all other duties and commitments, for nine years, or even for nine months, in order to keep another person alive.

6. We have in fact to distinguish between two kinds of Samaritan: the Good Samaritan and what we might call the Minimally Decent Samaritan. The story of the Good Samaritan, you will remember, goes like this:

> A certain man went down from Jerusalem to Jericho, and fell among thieves, which stripped him of his raiment, and wounded him, and departed, leaving him half dead.
>
> And by chance there came down a certain priest that way; and when he saw him, he passed by on the other side.
>
> And likewise a Levite, when he was at the place, came and looked on him, and passed by on the other side.
>
> But a certain Samaritan, as he journeyed, came where he was; and when he saw him he had compassion on him.
>
> And went to him, and bound up his wounds, pouring in oil and wine, and set him on his own beast, and brought him to an inn, and took care of him.
>
> And on the morrow, when he departed, he took out two pence, and gave them to the host, and said unto him, "Take care of him; and whatsoever thou spendest more, when I come again, I will repay thee."
>
> (Luke 10:30-35)

The Good Samaritan went out of his way, at some cost to himself, to help one in need of it. We are not told what the options were, that is, whether or not the priest and the Levite could have helped by doing less than the Good Samaritan did, but assuming they could have, then the fact they did nothing at all shows they were not even Minimally Decent Samaritans, not because they were not Samaritans, but because they were not even minimally decent.

These things are a matter of degree, of course, but there is a difference, and it comes out perhaps most clearly in the story of Kitty Genovese, who, as you will remember, was murdered while thirty-eight people watched or listened, and did nothing at all to help her. A Good Samaritan would have rushed out to give direct assistance against the murderer. Or perhaps we had better allow that it would have been a Splendid Samaritan who did this, on the ground that it would have involved a risk of death for himself. But the thirty-eight not only did not do this, they did not even trouble to pick up a phone to call the police. Minimally Decent Samaritanism would call for doing at least that, and their not having done it was monstrous.

After telling the story of the Good Samaritan, Jesus said "Go, and do thou likewise." Perhaps he meant that we are morally required to act as the Good Samaritan did. Perhaps he was urging people to do more than is morally required of them. At all events it seems plain that it was not morally required of any of the thirty-eight that he rush out to give direct assistance at the risk of his own life, and that it is not morally required of anyone that he give long stretches of his life—nine years or nine months—to sustaining the life of a person who has no special right (we were leaving open the possibility of this) to demand it.

Indeed, with one rather striking class of exceptions, no one in any country in the world is *legally* required to do anywhere near as much as this for anyone else. The class of exceptions is obvious. My main concern here is not the state of the law in respect to abortion, but it is worth drawing attention to the fact that in no state in this country is any man compelled by law to be even a Minimally Decent Samaritan to any person; there is no law under which charges could be brought against the thirty-eight who stood by while Kitty Genovese died. By contrast, in most states in this country women are compelled by law to be not merely Minimally December Samaritans, but Good Samaritans to unborn persons inside them. This doesn't by itself settle anything one way or the other, because it may well be argued that there should be laws in this country—as there are in many European countries—compelling at least Minimally Decent Samaritanism.[8] But it does show that there is a gross injustice in the existing state of

[8]For a discussion of the difficulties involved, and a survey of the European experience with such laws, see *The Good Samaritan and the Law*, ed. James M. Ratcliffe (New York, 1966).

the law. And it shows also that the groups currently working against liberalization of abortion laws, in fact working toward having it declared unconstitutional for a state to permit abortion, had better start working for the adoption of Good Samaritan laws generally, or earn the charge that they are acting in bad faith.

I should think, myself, that Minimally Decent Samaritan laws would be one thing, Good Samaritan laws quite another, and in fact highly improper. But we are not here concerned with the law. What we should ask is not whether anybody should be compelled by law to be a Good Samaritan, but whether we must accede to a situation in which somebody is being compelled—by nature, perhaps—to be a Good Samaritan. We have, in other words, to look now at third-party interventions. I have been arguing that no person is morally required to make large sacrifices to sustain the life of another who has no right to demand them, and this even where the sacrifices do not include life itself; we are not morally required to be Good Samaritans or anyway Very Good Samaritans to one another. But what if a man cannot extricate himself from such a situation? What if he appeals to us to extricate him? It seems to me plain that there are cases in which we can, cases in which a Good Samaritan would extricate him. There you are, you were kidnapped, and nine years in bed with that violinist lie ahead of you. You have your own life to lead. You are sorry, but you simply cannot see giving up so much of your life to the sustaining of his. You cannot extricate yourself, and ask us to do so. I should have thought that—in light of his having no right to the use of your body—it was obvious that we do not have to accede to your being forced to give up so much. We can do what you ask. There is no injustice to the violinist in our doing so.

7. Following the lead of the opponents of abortion, I have throughout been speaking of the fetus merely as a person, and what I have been asking is whether or not the argument we began with, which proceeds only from the fetus' being a person, really does establish its conclusion. I have argued that it does not.

But of course there are arguments and arguments, and it may be said that I have simply fastened on the wrong one. It may be said that what is important is not merely the fact that the fetus is a person, but that it is a person for whom the woman has a special kind of responsibility issuing from the fact that she is its mother. And it might be argued that all my analogies are therefore irrelevant—for you do not have that special kind of responsibility for that violinist, Henry Fonda does not have that special kind of responsibility for me. And our attention might be drawn to the fact that men and women both *are* compelled by law to provide support for their children.

I have in effect dealt (briefly) with this argument in section 4 above; but a (still briefer) recapitulation now may be in order. Surely we do not have any such "special responsibility" for a person unless we have assumed it, explicitly or implicitly. If a set of parents do not try to prevent pregnancy, do not obtain an abortion, and then at the time of birth of the child do not put it out for adoption, but rather take it home with them, then they have assumed responsibility for it, they have given it rights, and they cannot *now* withdraw support from it at the cost of its life because they now find it difficult to go on providing for it. But if they have taken all reasonable precautions against having a child, they do not simply by virtue of their biological relationship to the child who comes into existence have a special responsibility for it. They may wish to assume responsibility for it, or they may not wish to. And I am suggesting that if assuming responsibility for it would require large sacrifices, then they may refuse. A Good Samaritan would not refuse—or anyway, a Splendid Samaritan, if the sacrifices that had to be made were enormous. But then so would a Good Samaritan assume responsibility for that violinist; so would Henry Fonda, if he is a Good Samaritan, fly in from the West Coast and assume responsibility for me.

8. My argument will be found unsatisfactory on two counts by many of those who want to regard abortion as morally permissible. First, while I do argue that abortion is not impermissible, I do not argue that it is always permissible. There may well be cases in which carrying the child to term requires only Minimally Decent Samaritanism of the mother, and this is a standard we must not fall

below. I am inclined to think it a merit of my account precisely that it does *not* give a general yes or a general no. It allows for and supports our sense that, for example, a sick and desperately frightened fourteen-year-old schoolgirl, pregnant due to rape, may *of course* choose abortion, and that any law which rules this out is an insane law. And it also allows for and supports our sense that in other cases resort to abortion is even positively indecent. It would be indecent in the woman to request an abortion, and indecent in a doctor to perform it, if she is in her seventh month, and wants the abortion just to avoid the nuisance of postponing a trip abroad. The very fact that the arguments I have been drawing attention to treat all cases of abortion, or even all cases of abortion in which the mother's life is not at stake, as morally on a par ought to have made them suspect at the outset.

Secondly, while I am arguing for the permissibility of abortion in some cases, I am not arguing for the right to secure the death of the unborn child. It is easy to confuse these two things in that up to a certain point in the life of the fetus it is not able to survive outside the mother's body; hence removing it from her body guarantees its death. But they are importantly different. I have argued that you are not morally required to spend nine months in bed, sustaining the life of that violinist; but to say this is by no means to say that if, when you unplug yourself, there is a miracle and he survives, you then have a right to turn round and slit his throat. You may detach yourself even if this costs him his life; you have no right to be guaranteed his death, by some other means, if unplugging yourself does not kill him. There are some people who will feel dissatisfied by this feature of my argument. A woman may be utterly devastated by the thought of a child, a bit of herself, put out for adoption and never seen or heard of again. She may therefore want not merely that the child be detached from her, but more, that it die. Some opponents of abortion are inclined to regard this as beneath contempt—thereby showing insensitivity to what is surely a powerful source of despair. All the same, I agree that the desire for the child's death is not one which anybody may gratify, should it turn out to be possible to detach the child alive.

At this place, however, it should be remembered that we have only been pretending throughout that the fetus is a human being from the moment of conception. A very early abortion is surely not the killing of a person, and so is not dealt with by anything I have said here.

Study Questions

1. Why, according to Thomson, is it morally permissible for a woman to defend her life against a threat to it posed by an unborn child, even if the defense involves abortion?
2. Is it morally permissible for a third party to accede to a request for an abortion by the woman whose life is so threatened, in Thomson's opinion? Explain why.
3. Does the right to life guarantee one the right to use another person's body if the other body is required to sustain one's own life, according to Thomson? Explain why or why not.
4. Are we morally required to make large sacrifices to sustain the life of someone who has no right to demand them, according to Thomson? Explain why she answers as she does.
5. Explain whether a mother always has a special responsibility for her child, in the opinion of Thomson.
6. Does Thomson argue that abortion is always morally permissible? Explain.

CHAPTER 13

HELPING OTHERS IN NEED

Supererogation

The first reading in this chapter, by J. O. Urmson, could easily have appeared in Part II, for it is largely an essay in metaethics. Nevertheless, we include it here, because this chapter is concerned with the issue of helping others in need, which is sometimes considered a supererogatory act. A supererogatory act, you'll recall, is an act that goes beyond the call of duty.

Human actions have traditionally been divided into duties, permissible actions, and wrong actions. Urmson, however, asserts that this threefold classification is inadequate to the facts of morality. In particular, it leaves unmentioned actions that go beyond the requirements of moral duty—actions, for example, of a saint or a hero. An action of this type is in fact optional from the standpoint of morality, although the "saint" or "hero" who performs it may not think it is optional. Accordingly, says Urmson, as moral theorists we need to discover some theory that will allow for such acts as these, acts which an agent may feel called upon to do but which can't be demanded and whose omission isn't a wrongdoing.

A morality or moral code, in Urmson's opinion, should serve human needs. He offers five reasons why, given that purpose, the moral code must make a distinction between the basic rules of duty and the higher or supererogatory acts that go beyond these rules. In the latter part of his essay, Urmson specifies these reasons. You may be uncertain exactly what Urmson is up to in this part of his essay: He is simply giving reasons why moral philosophers should theorize in such a way as not to deny the distinction between duties and acts that go beyond duties. You will note that Urmson views our duties as basic requirements that are to be universally demanded because they provide a tolerable basis for society, and he regards "the higher flights of morality" as "more positive contributions [to human needs] that go beyond" what is universally required. In other words, Urmson seems to be saying that the dictates of duty need extend only to what is required for people to live together in society: It need not be our *duty*, for example (and these are our examples and not Urmson's, for he doesn't give any), to help people in other societies or to prevent animal suffering.

Saints and Heroes

J. O. Urmson

J. O. Urmson (b. 1915) is Emeritus Henry Waldgrave Stuart Professor at Stanford University and a fellow of Corpus Christi College, Oxford. This article appeared in *Essays in Moral Philosophy*, ed. A. I. Meldon (Seattle: University of Washington Press, 1958).

Moral philosophers tend to discriminate, explicitly or implicitly, three types of action from the point of view of moral worth. First, they recognize actions that are a duty, or obligatory, or that we ought to perform, treating that terms as approximately synonymous; second, they recognize actions that are right in so far as they are permissible from a moral standpoint and not ruled out by moral considerations, but that are not morally required of us, like the lead of this or that card at bridge; third, they recognize actions that are wrong, that we ought not to do. Some moral philosophers, indeed, could hardly discriminate even these three types of action consistently with the rest of their philosophy. Moore, for example, could hardly recognize a class of morally indifferent actions, permissible but not enjoined, since it is to be presumed that good or ill of some sort will result from the moral trivial of our actions. But most moral philosophers recognize these three types of action and attempt to provide a moral theory that will make intelligible such a threefold classification.

To my mind this threefold classification, or any classification that is merely a variation on or elaboration of it, is totally inadequate to the facts of morality; any moral theory that leaves room only for such a classification will in consequence also be inadequate. My main task is this paper will be to show the inadequacy of such a classification by drawing attention to two of the types of action that most conspicuously lie outside such a classification; I shall go on to hazard some views on what sort of theory will most easily cope with the facts to which I draw attention, but the facts are here the primary interest.

We sometimes call a person a saint, or an action saintly, using the word "saintly" in a purely moral sense with no religious implications; also we sometimes call a person a hero or an action heroic. It is too clear to need argument that the words "saint" and "hero" are at least normally used in such a way as to be favorably evaluative; it would be impossible to claim that this evaluation is always moral, for clearly we sometimes call a person a saint when evaluating him religiously rather than morally and may call a person the hero of a game or athletic contest in which no moral qualities were displayed, but I shall take it that no formal argument is necessary to show that at least sometimes we use both words for moral evaluation.

If "hero" and "saint" can be words of moral evaluation, we may proceed to the attempt to make explicit the criteria that we implicitly employ for their use in moral contexts. It appears that we so use them in more than one type of situation, and that there is a close parallel between the ways in which the two terms "hero" and "saint" are used; we shall here notice three types of situation in which they are used which seem to be sufficiently different to merit distinction. As the first two types of situation to be noticed are ones that can be readily subsumed under the threefold classification mentioned above, it will be sufficient here to note them and pass on to the third type of situation, which, since it cannot be subsumed under that classification, is for the purposes of this paper the most interesting.

A person may be called a saint (1) if he does his duty regularly in contexts in which inclination, desire, or self-interest would lead most people not to do it, and does so as a result of exercising abnormal self-control; parallel to this a person may be called a hero (1) if he does his duty in contexts in which terror, fear, or a drive to self-preservation would lead most men not to do it, and does so by exercising abnormal self-control. Similarly for actions: an action may be called saintly (1) if it is a case of duty done by virtue of self-control in a context in which most men would be led astray by inclination or self-interest, and an action may be called heroic (1) if it is a case of duty done by virtue of self-control in a context in which most men would be led astray by fear or a drive for self-preservation. The only difference between the saintly and the heroic in this sort of situation is that the one involves resistance to desire and self-interest; the other, resistance to fear and self-preservation. This is quite a clear difference, though there may be marginal cases, or cases in which motives were mixed, in which it would be equally appropriate to call an action indifferently saintly or heroic. It is easy to give examples of both the heroic and the saintly as distinguished above: the unmarried daughter does the saintly deed of staying at home to tend her ailing and widowed father; the terrified doctor heroically stays by his patients in a plague-ridden city.

A person may be called a saint (2) if he does his duty in contexts in which inclination or self-interest would lead most men not to do it, not, as in the previous paragraph, by abnormal self-control, but without effort; parallel to this a person may be called a hero (2) if he does his duty in contexts in which fear would lead most men not to do it, and does so without effort. The corresponding accounts of a saintly (2) or heroic (2) action can easily be derived. Here we have the conspicuously virtuous deed, in the Aristotelian sense, as opposed to the conspicuously self-controlled, encratic deed of the previous paragraph. People thus purged of temptation or disciplined against fear may be rare, but Aristotle thought there could be such; there is a tendency today to think of such people as merely lucky or unimaginative, but Aristotle thought more highly of them than of people who need to exercise self-control.

It is clear that, in the two types of situation so far considered, we are dealing with actions that fall under the concept of duty. Roughly, we are calling a person saintly or heroic because he does his duty in such difficult contexts that most men would fail in them. Since for the purposes of this paper I am merely conceding that we do use the terms "saintly" and "heroic" in these ways, it is unnecessary here to spend time arguing that we do so use them or in illustrating such uses. So used, the threefold classification of actions whose adequacy I wish to deny can clearly embrace them. I shall therefore pass immediately to a third use of the terms "heroic" and "saintly," which I am not merely willing to concede but obliged to establish.

I contend, then, that we may also call a person a saint (3) if he does actions that are far beyond the limits of his duty, whether by control of contrary inclination and interest or without effort; parallel to this we may call a person a hero (3) if he does actions that are far beyond the bounds of his duty, whether by control of natural fear or without effort. Such actions are saintly (3) or heroic (3). Here, as it seems to me, we have the hero or saint, heroic or saintly deed, par excellence; until now we have been considering but minor saints and heroes. We have considered the, certainly, heroic action of the doctor who does his duty by sticking to his patients in a plague-stricken city; we have now to consider the case of the doctor, who, no differently situated from countless other doctors in other places, volunteers to join the depleted medical forces in that city. Previously we were considering the soldier who heroically does his duty in the face of such dangers as would cause most to shirk—the sort of man who is rightly awarded the Military Medal in the British Army; we have now to consider the case of the soldier who does more than his superior officers would never ask him to do—the man to whom, often posthumously, the Victoria Cross is awarded. Similarly, we have to turn from saintly self-discipline in the way of duty to the dedicated, self-effacing life in the service of others which is not even contemplated by the majority of upright, kind, and honest men, let alone expected of them.

Let us be clear that we are not now considering cases of natural affection, such as the sacrifice made by a mother for her child; such cases may be said with some justice not to fall under the concept of morality but to be admirable in some different way. Such cases as are here under consideration may be taken to be as little bound up with such emotions as affection as any moral action may be. We may consider an example of what is meant by "heroism" (3) in more detail to bring this out.

We may imagine a squad of soldiers to be practicing the throwing of live hand grenades; a grenade slips from the hand of one of them and rolls on the ground near the squad; one of them sacrifices his life by throwing himself on the grenade and protecting his comrades with his own body. It is quite unreasonable to suppose that such a man must be impelled by the sort of emotion that he might be impelled by if his best friend were in the squad; he might only just have joined the squad; it is clearly an action having moral status. But if the soldier had not thrown himself on the grenade would he have failed in his duty? Though clearly he is superior in some way to his comrades, can we possibly say that they failed in their duty by not trying to be the one who sacrificed himself? If he had not done so, could anyone have said to him, "You ought to have thrown yourself on that grenade"? Could a superior have decently ordered him to do it? The answer to all these questions is plainly negative. We clearly have here a case of a moral action, a heroic action, which cannot be subsumed under the classification whose inadequacy we are exposing.

But someone may not be happy with this conclusion, and for more respectable reasons than a desire to save the traditional doctrine. He may reason as follows: in so far as the soldier had time to feel or think at all, he presumably felt that he ought to do that deed; he considered it the proper thing to do; he, if no one else, might have reproached himself for failing to do his duty if he had shirked the deed. So, it may be argued, if an act presents itself to us in the way this act may be supposed to have presented itself to this soldier, then it is our duty to do it; we have no option. This objection to my thesis clearly has some substance, but it involves a misconception of what is at issue. I have no desire to present the act of heroism as one that is naturally regarded as optional by the hero, as something he might or might not do; I concede that he might regard himself as being obliged to act as he does. But if he were to survive the action only a modesty so excessive as to appear false could make him say, "I only did my duty," for we know and he knows, that he has done more than duty requires. Further, though he might say to himself that so to act was a duty, he could not say so even before hand to anyone else, and no one else could ever say it. Subjectively, we may say, at the time of action the deed presented itself as a duty, but it was not a duty.

Another illustration, this time of saintliness, may help. It is recorded by Bonaventura that after Francis of Assisi had finished preaching to the birds one celebrated occasion his companions gathered around him to praise and admire. But Francis himself was not a bit pleased; he was full of self-reproach that he had hitherto failed in what he now considered to be his duty to preach to the feathered world. There is indeed no degree of saintliness that a suitable person may not come to consider it to be his duty to achieve. Yet there is a world of difference between this failure to have preached hitherto to the birds and a case of straightforward breach of duty, however venial. First, Francis could without absurdity reproach himself for his failure to do his duty, but it would be quite ridiculous for anyone else to do so, as one could have done if he had failed to keep his vow, for example. Second, it is not recorded that Francis ever reproached anyone else for failure to preach to the birds as a breach of duty. He could claim this action for himself as a duty and could perhaps have exhorted others to preach to the birds; but there could be no question of reproaches for not so acting.

To sum up on this point, then, it seems clear that there is no action, however quixotic, heroic, or saintly, which the agent may not regard himself as obliged to perform, as much as he may feel himself obliged to tell the truth and to keep his promises. Such actions do not present themselves as optional to the agent when he is deliberating; but, since he alone can call such an action of his a duty, and then only from the deliberative viewpoint, only for himself and not for others, and not even for himself as a piece of objective reporting, and since nobody else can call on him to perform such an act as they can call on him to tell the truth and to keep his promises, there is here a most important difference from the rock-bottom duties which are duties for all and from every point of view, and to which anyone may draw attention. Thus we need not deny the points made by our imaginary objector in order to substantiate the point that some acts of heroism and saintliness cannot be adequately subsumed under the concept of duty.

Let us then take it as established that we have to deal in ethics not with a simple trichotomy of duties, permissible actions, and wrong actions, or any substantially similar conceptual scheme, but with something more complicated. We have to add at least the complication of actions that are certainly of moral worth but that fall outside the notion of a duty and seem to go beyond it, actions worthy of being called heroic or saintly. It should indeed be noted that heroic or saintly actions are not the sole, but merely conspicuous, cases of actions that exceed the basic demands of duty; there can be cases of disinterested kindness and generosity, for example, that are clearly more than basic duty requires and yet hardly ask for the high titles, "saintly" and "heroic." Indeed, every case of "going the second mile" is a case in point, for it cannot be one's duty to go the second mile in the same basic sense as it is to go the first—otherwise it could be argued first that it is one's duty to go two miles and therefore that the spirit of the rule of the second mile requires that one go altogether four miles, and by repetition one could establish the need to go every time on an infinite journey. It is possible to go just beyond one's duty by being a little more generous, forbearing, helpful, or forgiving than fair dealing demands, or to go a very long way beyond the basic code of duties with the saint or the hero. When I here draw attention to the heroic and saintly deed, I do so merely in order to have conspicuous cases of a whole realm of actions that lie outside the trichotomy I have criticized and therefore, as I believe, outside the purview of most ethical theories.

Before considering the implications for ethics of the facts we have up to now been concerned to note, it might be of value to draw attention to a less exalted parallel to these facts. If we belong to a club there will be rules of the club, written or unwritten, calling upon us to fulfill certain basic requirements that are a condition of membership, and that may be said to be the duties of membership. It may perhaps be such a basic requirement that we pay a subscription. It will probably be indifferent whether we pay this subscription by check or in cash—both procedures will be "right"—and almost certainly it will be quite indifferent what sort of hat we wear at the meetings. Here, then, we have conformity to rule which is the analogue of doing one's duty, breach of rule which is the analogue of wrongdoing, and a host of indifferent actions, in accordance with the traditional trichotomy. But among the rule-abiding members of such a club what differences there can be! It is very likely that there will be one, or perhaps two or three, to whose devotion and loyal service the success of the club is due far more than to the activities of all the other members together; these are the saints and the heroes of the clubs, who do more for them by far than any member could possibly be asked to do, whose many services could not possibly be demanded in the rules. Behind them come a motley selection, varying from the keen to the lukewarm, whose contributions vary in value and descend sometimes to almost nothing beyond what the rules demand. The moral contribution of people to society can vary in value in the same way.

So much, then, for the simple facts to which I have wished to draw attention. They are simple facts and, unless I have misrepresented them, they are facts of which we are all, in a way, perfectly well aware. It would be absurd to suggest that moral philosophers have hitherto been unaware of the existence of saints and heroes and have never even alluded to them in their works. But it does seem that these facts have been neglected in their general, systematic accounts of morality. It is indeed easy to see that on some of the best-known theories there is no room for such facts. If for Moore, and for most utilitarians, any action is a duty that will produce the greatest possible good in the circumstances, for them the most heroic self-sacrifice or saintly self-forgetfulness will be duties on all fours with truth-telling and promise-keeping. For Kant, beyond the counsels of prudence and the rules of skill, there is only the categorical imperative of duty, and every duty is equally and utterly binding on all men; it is true that he recognizes the limiting case of the holy will, but the holy will is not a will that goes beyond duty but a will that is beyond morality through being incapable of acting except in accordance with the imperative. The nearest to an equivalent to a holy will in the case we have been noting is the saintly will in the second sense we distinguished—the will that effortlessly does its duty when most would fail—but this is not a true parallel and in any case does not fall within the class of moral actions that go beyond duty to which our attention is primarily given. It is also true that Kant recognized virtues and talents as having conditional value, but not moral value, whereas the acts of heroism and saintliness we have considered have full moral worth, and their value is as unconditional as anyone could wish. Without committing ourselves to a scholarly examination of Kant's ethical works, it is surely evident that Kant could not consistently do justice to the facts before us. Intuitionism seems to me so obscurantist that I should not wish to prophesy what an intuitionist might feel himself entitled to say; but those intuitionists with whose works I am acquainted found their theories on an intuition of the fitting, the prima facie duty or the claim; the act that has this character to the highest degree at any time is a duty. While they recognize greater and lesser, stronger and weaker, claims, this is only in order to be able to deal with the problem of the conflict of duties; they assign no place to the act that, while not a duty, is of high moral importance.

Simple utilitarianism, Kantianism, and intuitionism, then, have no obvious theoretical niche for the saint and the hero. It is possible, no doubt, to revise these theories to accommodate the facts, but until so modified successfully they must surely be treated as unacceptable, and the modifications required might well detract from their plausibility. The intuitionists, for example, might lay claim to the intuition of a nonnatural characteristic of saintliness, of heroism, of decency, of sportingness, and so on, but this would give to their theory still more the appearance of utilizing the advantages of theft over honest toil.

Thus as moral theorists we need to discover some theory that will allow for both absolute duties, which in Mill's phrase, can be exacted from a man like a debt, to omit which is to do wrong and to deserve censure, and which may be embodied in formal rules or principles, and also for a range of actions which are of moral value and which an agent may feel called upon to perform, but which cannot be demanded and whose omission cannot be called wrongdoing. Traditional moral theories, I have suggested, fail to do this. It would be well beyond the scope of this paper and probably beyond my capacity, to produce here and now a full moral theory designed to accommodate all these facts, including the facts of saintliness and heroism. But I do think that of all traditional theories utilitarianism can be most easily modified to accommodate the facts, and would like before ending this paper to bring forward some considerations tending to support this point of view.

Moore went to great pains to determine exactly the nature of the intrinsically good, and Mill to discover the *summum bonum*, Moore's aim being to explain thereby directly the rightness and wrongness of particular actions and Mill's to justify a set of moral principles in the light of which the rightness or wrongness of particular actions can be decided. But, though there can be very tricky problems of duty, they do not naturally present themselves as problems whose solution depends upon an exact determination of an ultimate end; while the moral principles that come most readily to mind—truth telling; promise-keeping; abstinence from murder, theft, and violence; and the like—make a nice discrimination of the supreme good seem irrelevant. We do not need to debate whether it is Moore's string of intrinsic goods or Mill's happiness that is achieved by conformity to such principles; it is enough to see that without them social life would be impossible and any life would indeed be solitary, poor, nasty, brutish, and short. Even self-interest (which some have seen as the sole foundation of morality) is sufficient ground to render it wise to preach, if not to practice such principles. Such considerations as these, which are not novel, have led some utilitarians to treat avoidance of the *summum malum* rather than the achievement of the *summum bonum* as the foundation of morality. Yet to others this has seemed, with some justification, to assign to morality too ignoble a place.

But the facts we have been considering earlier in this paper are surely relevant at this point. It is absurd to ask just what ideal is being served by abstinence from murder; but on the other hand nobody could see in acts of heroism such as we have been considering a mere avoidance of antisocial behavior. Here we have something more gracious, actions that need to be inspired by a positive ideal. If duty can, as Mill said, be exacted from persons as a debt, it is because duty is a minimum requirement for living together; the positive contribution of actions that go beyond duty could not be so exacted.

It may, however, be objected that this is a glorification of the higher flights of morality at the expense of duty, toward which an unduly cynical attitude is being taken. In so far as the suggestion is that we are forgetting how hard the way of duty may be and that doing one's duty can at times deserve to be called heroic and saintly, the answer is that we have mentioned this and acknowledge it; it is not forgotten but irrelevant to the point at issue, which is the place of duty in a moral classification of actions, not the problem of the worth of moral agents. But I may be taken to be acquiescing in a low and circumscribed view of duty which I may be advised to enlarge. We should, it may be said, hitch our wagons to the stars and not to be content to say: you must do this and that as duties, and it would be very nice if you were to do these other things but we do not expect them of you. Is it perhaps only an imperfect conception of duty which finds it not to comprise the whole of morality? I want to examine this difficulty quite frankly, and to explain why I think that we properly recognize morality that goes beyond duty; for it seems to one incontestable that properly or improperly we do so.

No intelligent person will claim infallibility for his moral views. But allowing for this one must claim that one's moral code is ideal so far as one can see; or to say, "I recognize moral code A but see clearly that moral code B is superior to it," is but a way of saying that one recognizes moral code B but is only prepared to live up to moral code A. In some sense, then everybody must be prepared to justify his moral code as idea; but some philosophers have misunderstood this sense. Many philosophers have thought it necessary, if they were to defend their moral code as ideal, to try to show that it had a superhuman, a priori validity. Kant, for example, tried to show that the moral principles he accepted were such as any rational being, whether man or angel, must inevitably accept; the reputedly empiricist Locke thought that it must be possible to work out a deductive justification of moral laws. In making such claims such philosophers have unintentionally done morality a disservice; for their failure to show that the moral code was ideal in the sense of being a rationally justifiable system independent of time, place, circumstance, and human nature has led many to conclude that there can be no justification of a moral code, that moral codes are a matter of taste or convention.

But morality, I take it, is something that should serve human needs, not something that incidentally sweeps man up with itself, and to show that a morality was ideal would be to show that it best served man — man as he is and as he can be expected to become, not man as he would be if he were perfectly rational or an incorporeal angel. Just as it would be fatuous to build our machines so that they would give the best results according to an abstract conception of mechanical principles, and is much more desirable to design them to withstand to some extent our hamfistedness, ignorance, and carelessness, so our morality must be one that will work. In the only sense of "ideal" that is of importance in action, it is part of the ideal that a moral code should actually help to contribute to human well-being, and a moral code that would work only for angels (for whom it would in any case be unnecessary) would be a far from ideal moral code for human beings. There is, indeed, a place for ideals that are practically unworkable in human affairs, as there is a place for the blueprint of a machine that will never go into production; but it is not the place of such ideals to serve as a basic code of duties.

If, then, we are aiming at a moral code that will best serve human needs, a code that is ideal in the sense that a world in which such a code is acknowledged will be a better place than a world in which some other sort of moral code is acknowledged, it seems that there are ample grounds why our code should distinguish between basic rules, summarily set forth in simple rules and binding on all, and the higher flights of morality of which saintliness and heroism are outstanding examples. These grounds I shall enumerate at once.

1. It is important to give a special status of urgency, and to exert exceptional pressure, in those matters in which compliance with the demands of morality by all is indispensable. An army without men of heroic valor would be impoverished, but without general attention to the duties laid down in military law it would become a mere rabble. Similarly, while life in a world without its saints and heroes would be impoverished, it would only be poor and not necessarily brutish or short as when basic duties are neglected.

2. If we are to exact basic duties like debts, and censure failure, such duties must be, in ordinary circumstances, within the capacity of the ordinary man. It would be silly for us to say to ourselves, our children, and our fellow men, "This and that you and everyone else must do," if the acts in question are such that manifestly but few could bring themselves to do them, though we may ourselves resolve to try to be of that few. To take a parallel from positive law, the prohibition laws asked too much of the American people and were consequently broken systematically; and as people got used to breaking the law a general lowering of respect for the law naturally followed; it no longer seemed that a law was something that everybody could be expected to obey. Similarly in Britain the gambling laws, some of which are utterly unpractical, have fallen into contempt as a body. So, if we were to represent the heroic act of sacrificing one's life for one's comrades as a basic duty, the effect would be to lower the degree of urgency and stringency that the notion of duty does in fact possess. The basic moral code must not be in part too far beyond the capacity of the ordinary men on ordinary occasions, or a general breakdown of compliance with the moral code would be an inevitable consequence; duty would seem to be something high and unattainable, and not for "the likes of us." Admirers of the Sermon on the Mount do not in practice, and could not, treat failure to turn the other cheek and to give one's cloak also as being on all fours with breaches of the Ten Commandments, however earnestly they themselves try to live a Christian life.

3. A moral code, if it is to be a code, must be formulable, and if it is to be a code to be observed it must be formulable in rules of manageable complexity. The ordinary man has to apply and interpret this code without recourse to a Supreme Court or House of Lords. But one can have such rules only in cases in which a type of action that is reasonably easy to recognize is almost invariably desirable or undesirable, as killing is almost invariably undesirable and promise-keeping almost invariably desirable. Where no definite rule of manageable complexity can be justified, we cannot work on that moral plane on which types of action can be enjoined or condemned as duty or crime. It has no doubt often been the case that a person who has gone off to distant parts to nurse lepers has thereby done a deed of great moral worth. But such an action is not merely too far beyond average human capacity to be regarded as a duty, as was insisted in (2) above; it would be quite ridiculous for everyone, however circumstanced, to be expected to go off and nurse lepers. But it would be absurd to try to formulate complicated rules to determine in just what circumstance such an action is a duty. This same point can readily be applied to such less spectacular matters as excusing legitimate debts or nursing sick neighbors.

4. It is part of the notion of a duty that we have a right to demand compliance from others even when we are interested parties. I may demand that you keep your promises to me, tell me the truth, and do me no violence, and I may reproach you if you transgress. But however admirable the tending of strangers in sickness may be, it is not a basic duty, and we are not entitled to reproach those to whom we are strangers if they do not tend us in sickness; nor can I tell you, if you fail to give me a cigarette when I have run out, that you have failed in your duty to not, however much you may subsequently reproach your self for your meanness if you do so fail. A line may be drawn between what we can expect and demand from others and what we can merely hope for and receive with gratitude when we get it; duty falls on one side of this line, and other acts with moral value on the other, and rightly so.

5. In the case of basic moral duties we act to some extent under constraint. We have no choice but to apply pressure on each other to conform

in these fundamental matters; here moral principles are like public laws rather than like private ideals. But free choice of the better course of action is always preferable to action under pressure, even when the pressure is but moral. When possible, therefore, it is better that pressure should not be applied and that there should be encouragement and commendation for performance rather than outright demands and censure in the event of nonperformance. There are no doubt degrees in this matter. Some pressure may reasonably be brought to persuade a person to go some way beyond basic duty in the direction of kindliness and forbearance, to be not merely a just man but also not too hard a man. But, while there is nothing whatever objectionable in the idea of someone's being pressed to carry out such a basic duty as promise-keeping, there is something horrifying in the thought of pressure being brought on him to perform an act of heroism. Though the man might feel himself morally called upon to do the deed, it would be a moral outrage to apply pressure on him to do such a deed as sacrificing his life for others.

These five points make it clear why I do not think that the distinction of basic duty from other acts of moral worth, which I claim to detect in ordinary moral thought, is a sign of the inferiority of our everyday moral thinking to that of the general run of moral theorists. It in no way involves anyone in acquiescing in a second best. No doubt from the agent's point of view it is imperative that he should endeavor to live up to the highest ideals of behavior that he can think of, and if an action falls within the ideal it is for him irrelevant whether or not it is a duty or some more supererogatory act. But it simply does not follow that the distinction is in every way unimportant, for it is important that we should not demand ideal conduct from others in the way in which we must demand basic morality from them, or blame them equally for failures in all fields. It is not cynicism to make the minimum positive demands upon one's fellow men; but to characterize an act as a duty is so to demand it.

Thus we may regard the imperatives of duty as prohibiting behavior that is intolerable if men are to live together in society and demanding the minimum of cooperation toward the same end; that is why we have to treat compliance as compulsory and dereliction as liable to public censure. We do not need to ask with Bentham whether pushpin is as good as poetry, with Mill whether it is better to be Socrates dissatisfied or a fool satisfied, or with Moore whether a beautiful world with no one to see it would have intrinsic worth; what is and what is not tolerable in society depends on no such nice discrimination. Utilitarians, when attempting to justify the main rules of duty in terms of a *summum bonum*, have surely invoked many different types of utilitarian justification, ranging from the avoidance of the intolerable to the fulfillment of the last detail of a most rarefied ideal.

Thus I wish to suggest that utilitarianism can best accommodate the facts to which I have drawn attention; but I have not wished to support any particular view about the supreme good or the importance of pleasure. By utilitarianism I mean only a theory that moral justification of actions must be in terms of results. We can be content to say that duty is mainly concerned with the avoidance of intolerable results, while other forms of moral behavior have more positive aims.

To summarize, I have suggested that the trichotomy of duties, indifferent actions, and wrongdoing is inadequate. There are many kinds of action that involve going beyond duty proper, saintly and heroic actions being conspicuous examples of such kinds of action. It has been my main concern to note this point and to ask moral philosophers to theorize in a way that does not tacitly deny it, as most traditional theories have. But I have also been so rash as to suggest that we may look upon our duties as basic requirements to be universally demanded as providing the only tolerable basis of social life. The higher flights of morality can then be regarded as more positive contributions that go beyond what is universally to be exacted; but while not exacted publicly they are clearly equally pressing *in foro interno* on those who are not content merely to avoid the intolerable. Whether this should be called a version of utilitarianism, as I suggest, is a matter of small moment.

Study Questions

1. What are the three moral categories into which actions have traditionally been divided, according to Urmson?
2. Describe the three types of situations in which the terms *hero* and *saint* are used. With which type is Urmson concerned?
3. Do you agree with Urmson that the soldier who throws himself on the grenade goes beyond the requirements of duty?
4. What does Urmson mean when he says that simple utilitarianism, Kantianism, and intuitionism have no theoretical niche for the saint or the hero?
5. Which traditional moral theory can be most easily modified to accommodate moral behavior that goes beyond the call of duty, according to Urmson?
6. How does Urmson respond to the idea that a conception of duty that does not include saintly or heroic behavior is an improper or imperfect conception of duty?
7. Why, according to Urmson, would a moral code that will best serve human needs make a distinction between basic duty and "the higher flights of morality"? (He gives five reasons.)

Charity As a Moral Obligation

If you are like most people, and like Urmson, you make a distinction between duty and charity. You would probably say it *is* your duty not to let your parents starve to death, but it *isn't* your duty to prevent people on the other side of the world—Mauritanians, for instance—from starving to death. If someone wants to send food to Mauritania, well, that's just fine. But it's not wrong for a person not to do so. Charity is commendable, but morally optional. So runs the popular view, which we take the liberty to assign to you.

In the next essay, Peter Singer challenges this view. He begins with two assumptions: (1) Suffering and death from lack of food, shelter, and medical care are bad. (2) If it is in our power to prevent something bad from happening, without thereby sacrificing anything that's important morally speaking, we ought to do it. If you see a child drowning in a pond, for example, you ought to wade in and save the child even if doing so ruins your clothes.

Perhaps we can just agree with Singer on the first assumption and move on to the second. Do you agree with the second assumption? Be very careful, because if you do, then so-called charity is not morally optional, at least if Singer is right.

First of all, Singer says, principle (2) takes no account of proximity or distance. It doesn't matter whether a starving person is in your backyard or ten thousand miles away in Mauritania; if it is in your power to help the individual, you ought to do it. Secondly, it doesn't matter that there are millions of others who could and should help. Your obligation to help starving Mauritanians is not lessened by the fact that millions of Americans (and others) could help starving Mauritanians.

So, in short, given principle (2), what we normally call charity is not morally optional. People who spend money on new clothes or a larger TV set instead of giving to famine relief are doing something morally wrong. It is their moral *duty* to contribute to famine relief, argues Singer.

Urmson, as we have seen, would extend the dictates of duty only to what is required for people to function together in society. Singer explicitly rejects Urmson's view: "From the moral point of view, the prevention of the starvation of millions of people outside our society must be considered at least as pressing as the upholding of property norms without our society."

Urmson also argues, in the selection above, that moral duties should not go beyond the capacities of normal people to obey. This view too Singer rejects.

Having established to his satisfaction the position that we ought to do all we can to prevent starvation, Singer next criticizes selected popular notions about how we should deal with famine. Ought you to refuse to give to private charities on the grounds that famine relief should be a function of government? Not so, argues Singer. And what about the idea that until there is effective population control, relieving famine merely postpones starvation? Fine, says Singer: If the most effective means of combating starvation is population control, you ought to be doing all you can to promote population control.

But just how much ought we to be giving away? Even if you don't give to the point of reducing yourself nearly to starvation, Singer maintains, you and we and everyone else who is relatively affluent are morally obliged "to give away enough to ensure that the consumer society, dependent as it is on people spending on trivia rather than giving to famine relief, would slow down and perhaps disappear entirely." Moreover, this end (the termination of consumerism) is desirable in itself, Singer asserts.

Singer concludes his article with some comments about the responsibilities of philosophers.

Famine, Affluence, and Morality

Peter Singer

Peter Singer (b. 1946) is Professor of Philosophy and Director of the Centre for Human Bioethics at Monash University, Melbourne, Australia. The selection was published in *Philosophy and Public Affairs* 1, no. 3 (1972).

I begin with the assumption that suffering and death from lack of food, shelter, and medical care are bad. I think most people will agree about this, although one may reach the same view by different routes. I shall not argue for this view. People can hold all sorts of eccentric positions, and perhaps from some of them it would not follow that death by starvation is in itself bad. It is difficult, perhaps impossible, to refute such positions, and so for brevity I will henceforth take this assumption as accepted. Those who disagree need read no further.

My next point is this: if it is in our power to prevent something bad from happening, without thereby sacrificing anything of comparable moral importance, we ought, morally, to do it. By "without sacrificing anything of comparable moral importance" I mean without causing anything else comparably bad to happen, or doing something that is wrong in itself, or failing to promote some moral good, comparable in significance to the bad thing that we can prevent. This principle seems almost as uncontroversial as the last one. It requires us only to prevent what is bad, and not to promote what is good, and it requires this of us only when we can do it without sacrificing anything that is, from the moral point of view, comparably important. I could even, as far as the application of my argument to the Bengal emergency is concerned, qualify the point so as to make it: if it is in our power to prevent something very bad from happening, without thereby sacrificing anything morally significant, we ought, morally, to do it. An application of this principle would be as follows: if I am walking past a shallow pond and see a child drowning in it, I ought to wade in and pull the child out. This will mean getting my clothes muddy, but this is insignificant, while the death of the child would presumably be a very bad thing.

The uncontroversial appearance of the principle just stated is deceptive. If it were acted upon, even in its qualified form, our lives, our society, and our world would be fundamentally changed. For the principle takes, firstly, no account of proximity or distance. It makes no moral difference whether the person I can help is a neighbor's child ten yards from me or a Bengali whose name I shall never know, ten thousand miles away. Secondly, the principle makes no distinction between cases in which I am the only person who could possibly do anything and cases in which I am just one among millions in the same position.

I do not think I need to say much in defense of the refusal to take proximity and distance into account. The fact that a person is physically near to us, so that we have personal contact with him, may make it more likely that we *shall* assist him, but this does not show that we *ought* to help him rather than another who happens to be further away. If we accept any principle of impartiality, universalizability, equality, or whatever, we cannot discriminate against someone merely because he is far away from us (or we are far away from him). Admittedly, it is possible that we are in a better position to judge what needs to be done to help a person near to us than one far away, and perhaps also to provide the assistance we judge to be necessary. If this were the case, it would be a reason for helping those near to us first. This may once have been a justification for being more concerned with the poor in one's own town than with famine victims in India. Unfortunately for those who like to keep their moral responsibilities limited, instant communication and swift transportation have changed the situation. From the moral point of view, the development of the world into a "global village" has made an important, though still unrecognized, difference to our moral situation. Expert observers and supervisors, sent out by famine relief organizations or permanently stationed in famine-prone areas, can direct our aid to a refugee in Bengal almost as effectively as we could get it to someone in our own block. There would seem, therefore, to be no possible justification for discriminating on geographical grounds.

There may be a greater need to defend the second implication of my principle—that the fact that there are millions of other people in the same position, in respect to the Bengali refugees, as I am, does not make the situation significantly different from a situation in which I am the only person who can prevent something very bad from occurring. Again, of course, I admit that there is a psychological difference between the cases; one feels less guilty about doing nothing if one can point to others, similarly placed, who have also done nothing. Yet this can make no real difference to our moral obligations.[1] Should I consider that I am less obliged to pull the drowning child out of the pond if on looking around I see other people, no further away than I am, who have also noticed the child but are doing nothing? One has only to ask this question to see the absurdity of the view that numbers lessen obligation. It is a view that is an ideal excuse for inactivity; unfortunately most of the major evils—poverty, overpopulation, pollution—are problems in which everyone is almost equally involved.

The view that numbers do make a difference can be made plausible if stated in this way: if everyone in circumstances like mine gave £5 to the Bengali Relief Fund, there would be enough to provide food, shelter, and medical care for the refugees; there is no reason why I should give more than anyone else in the same circumstances as I am; therefore I have no obligation to give more than £5. Each premise in this argument is true, and the argument looks sound. It may convince us, unless we notice that it is based on a hypothetical premise, although the conclusion is not stated hypothetically. The argument would be sound if the conclusion were: if everyone in circumstances like mine were to give £5, I would have no obligation to give more than £5. If the conclusion were so stated, however, it would be obvious that the argument has no bearing on a situation in which it is not the case that everyone else gives £5. This, of course, is the actual situation. It is more or less certain that not everyone in circumstances like mine will give £5. So there will not be enough to provide the needed food, shelter, and medical care. Therefore by giving more than £5 I will prevent more suffering than I would if I gave just £5.

It might be thought that this argument has an absurd consequence. Since the situation appears to be that very few people are likely to give substantial amounts, it follows that I and everyone else in similar circumstances ought to give as much as possible, that is, at least up to the point at which by giving more one would begin to cause serious suffering for oneself and one's dependents—perhaps even beyond this point to the point of marginal utility, at which by giving more one would cause oneself and one's dependents as much suffering as one would prevent in Bengal. If everyone does this, however, there will be more than can be used for the benefit of the refugees, and some of the sacrifice will have been unnecessary. Thus, if everyone does what he ought to do, the result will not be as good as it would be if everyone did a little less than he ought to do, or if only some do all that they ought to do.

The paradox here arises only if we assume that the actions in question—sending money to the relief funds—are performed more or less simultaneously, and are also unexpected. For if it is to be expected that everyone is going to contribute something, then clearly each is not obliged to give as much as he would have been obliged to had others not been giving too. And if everyone is not acting more or less simultaneously, then those giv-

[1]In view of the special sense philosophers often give to the term, I should say that I use "obligation" simply as the abstract noun derived from "ought," so that "I have an obligation to" means no more, and no less, that "I ought to." This usage is in accordance with the definition of "ought" given by the *Shorter Oxford English Dictionary:* "the general verb to express duty or obligation." I do not think any issue of substance hangs on the way the term is used; sentences in which I use "obligation" could all be rewritten, although somewhat clumsily, as sentences in which a clause containing "ought" replaces the term "obligation."

ing later will know how much more is needed, and will have no obligation to give more than is necessary to reach this amount. To say this is not to deny the principle that people in the same circumstances have the same obligations, but to point out that the fact that others have given, or may be expected to give, is a relevant circumstance: those giving after it has become known that many others are giving and those giving before are not in the same circumstances. So the seemingly absurd consequence of the principle I have put forward can occur only if people are in error about the actual circumstances—that is, if they think they are giving when others are not, but in fact they are giving when others are. The result of everyone doing what he really ought to do cannot be worse than the result of everyone doing less than he ought to do, although the result of everyone doing what he reasonably believes he ought to do could be.

If my argument so far has been sound, neither our distance from a preventable evil nor the number of other people who, in respect to that evil, are in the same situation as we are, lessens our obligation to mitigate or prevent that evil. I shall therefore take as established the principle I asserted earlier. As I have already said, I need to assert it only in its qualified form: if it is in our power to prevent something very bad from happening, without thereby sacrificing anything else morally significant, we ought, morally, to do it.

The outcome of this argument is that our traditional moral categories are upset. The traditional distinction between duty and charity cannot be drawn, or at least, not in the place we normally draw it. Giving money to the Bengal Relief Fund is regarded as an act of charity in our society. The bodies which collect money are known as "charities." These organizations see themselves in this way—if you send them a check, you will be thanked for your "generosity." Because giving money is regarded as an act of charity, it is not thought that there is anything wrong with not giving. The charitable man may be praised, but the man who is not charitable is not condemned. People do not feel in any way ashamed or guilty about spending money on new clothes or a new car instead of giving it to famine relief. (Indeed, the alternative does not occur to them.) This way of looking at the matter cannot be justified. When we buy new clothes not to keep ourselves warm but to look "well-dressed" we are not providing for any important need. We would not be sacrificing anything significant if we were to continue to wear our old clothes, and give the money to famine relief. By doing so, we would be preventing another person from starving. It follows from what I have said earlier that we ought to give money away, rather than spend it on clothes which we do not need to keep us warm. To do so is not charitable, or generous. Nor is it the kind of act which philosophers and theologians have called "supererogatory"—an act which it would be good to do, but not wrong not to do. On the contrary, we ought to give the money away, and it is wrong not to do so.

I am not maintaining that there are no acts which are charitable, or that there are no acts which it would be good to do but not wrong not to do. It may be possible to redraw the distinction between duty and charity in some other place. All I am arguing here is that the present way of drawing the distinction, which makes it an act of charity for a man living at the level of affluence which most people in the "developed nations" enjoy to give money to save someone else from starvation, cannot be supported. It is beyond the scope of my argument to consider whether the distinction should be redrawn or abolished altogether. There would be many other possible ways of drawing the distinction—for instance, one might decide that it is good to make other people as happy as possible, but not wrong not to do so.

Despite the limited nature of the revision in our moral conceptual scheme which I am proposing, the revision would, given the extent of both affluence and famine in the world today, have radical implications. These implications may lead to further objections, distinct from those I have already considered. I shall discuss two of these.

One objection to the position I have taken might be simply that it is too drastic a revision of our moral scheme. People do not ordinarily judge in the way I have suggested they should. Most people reserve their moral condemnation for those who violate some moral norm, such as the norm against taking another person's property. They do not condemn those who indulge in luxury instead of giving to famine relief. But given that I did not set out to present a morally neutral description of the way people make moral judgments, the way people do in fact judge has nothing to do with the validity of my conclusion. My conclusion follows from the principle which I advanced earlier, and unless that principle is rejected, or the arguments shown to be unsound, I think the conclusion must stand, however strange it appears.

It might, nevertheless, be interesting to consider why our society, and most other societies, do judge differently from the way I have suggested they should. In a well-known article, J. O. Urmson suggests that the imperatives of duty, which tell us what we must do, as distinct from what it would be good to do but not wrong not to do, function so as to prohibit behavior that is intolerable if men are to live together in society.[2] This may explain the origin and continued existence of the present division between acts of duty and acts of charity. Moral attitudes are shaped by the needs of society, and no doubt society needs people who will observe the rules that make social existence tolerable. From the point of view of a particular society, it is essential to prevent violations of norms against killing, stealing, and so on. It is quite inessential, however, to help people outside one's own society.

If this is an explanation of our common distinction between duty and supererogation, however, it is not a justification of it. The moral point of view requires us to look beyond the interests of our own society. Previously, as I have already mentioned, this may hardly have been feasible, but it is quite feasible now. From the moral point of view, the prevention of the starvation of millions of people outside our society must be considered at least as pressing as the upholding of property norms within our society.

It has been argued by some writers, among them Sidgwick and Urmson, that we need to have a basic moral code which is not too far beyond the capacities of the ordinary man, for otherwise there will be a general breakdown of compliance with the moral code. Crudely stated, this argument suggests that if we tell people that they ought to refrain from murder and give everything they do not really need to famine relief, they will do neither, whereas if we tell them that they ought to refrain from murder and that it is good to give to famine relief but not wrong not to do so, they will at least refrain from murder. The issue here is: Where should we draw the line between conduct that is required and conduct that is good although not required, so as to get the best possible result? This would seem to be an empirical question, although a very difficult one. One objection to the Sidgwick-Urmson line of argument is that it takes insufficient account of the effect that moral standards can have on the decisions we make. Given a society in which a wealthy man who gives five percent of his income to famine relief is regarded as most generous, it is not surprising that a proposal that we all ought to give away half our incomes will be thought to be absurdly unrealistic. In a society which held that no man should have more than enough while others have less than they need, such a proposal might seem narrow-minded. What it is possible for a man to do and what he is likely to do are both, I think, very greatly influenced by what people around him are doing and expecting him to do. In any case, the possibility that by spreading the idea that we ought to be doing very much more than we are to relieve famine we shall bring about a general breakdown of moral behavior seems remote. If the stakes are an end to widespread starvation, it is worth the risk. Finally, it should be emphasized that these considerations are relevant only to the issue of what we should require from others, and not to what we ourselves ought to do.

The second objection to my attack on the present distinction between duty and charity is one which has from time to time been made against utilitarianism. It follows from some forms of utilitarian theory that we all ought, morally, to be working full time to increase the balance of happiness over misery. The position I have taken here would not lead to this conclusion in all circumstances, for if there were no bad occurrences that we could prevent without sacrificing something

---

[2] J.O. Urmson, "Saints and Heroes," in *Essays in Moral Philosophy*, ed. Abraham I. Melden (Seattle and London, 1958), p. 214. For a related but significantly different view see also Henry Sidgwick, *The Methods of Ethics*, 7th edn. (London, 1907), pp. 220–221, 492–493.

of comparable moral importance, my argument would have no application. Given the present conditions in many parts of the world, however, it does follow from my argument that we ought, morally, to be working full time to relieve great suffering of the sort that occurs as a result of famine or other disasters. Of course, mitigating circumstances can be adduced—for instance, that if we wear ourselves out through overwork, we shall be less effective than we would otherwise have been. Nevertheless, when all considerations of this sort have been taken into account, the conclusion remains: we ought to be preventing as much suffering as we can without sacrificing something else of comparable moral importance. This conclusion is one which we may be reluctant to face. I cannot see, though, why it should be regarded as a criticism of the position for which I have argued, rather than a criticism of our ordinary standards of behavior. Since most people are self-interested to some degree, very few of us are likely to do everything that we ought to do. It would, however, hardly be honest to take this as evidence that it is not the case that we ought to do it.

It may still be thought that my conclusions are so wildly out of line with what everyone else thinks and has always thought that there must be something wrong with the argument somewhere. In order to show that my conclusions, while certainly contrary to contemporary Western moral standards, would not have seemed so extraordinary at other times and in other places, I would like to quote a passage from a writer not normally thought of as a way-out radical, Thomas Aquinas.

> Now, according to the natural order instituted by divine providence, material goods are provided for the satisfaction of human needs. Therefore the division and appropriation of property, which proceeds from human law, must not hinder the satisfaction of man's necessity from such goods. Equally, whatever a man has in superabundance is owed, of natural right, to the poor for their sustenance. So Ambrosius says, and it is also to be found in the *Decretum Gratiani*: "The bread which you withhold belongs to the hungry; the clothing you shut away, to the naked; and the money you bury in the earth is the redemption and freedom of the penniless."[3]

I now want to consider a number of points, more practical than philosophical, which are relevant to the application of the moral conclusion we have reached. These points challenge not the idea that we ought to be doing all we can to prevent starvation, but the idea that giving away a great deal of money is the best means to this end.

It is sometimes said that overseas aid should be a government responsibility, and that therefore one ought not to give to privately run charities. Giving privately, it is said, allows the government and the noncontributing members of society to escape their responsibilities.

This argument seems to assume that the more people there are who give to privately organized famine relief funds, the less likely it is that the government will take over full responsibility for such aid. This assumption is unsupported, and does not strike me as at all plausible. The opposite view—that if no one gives voluntarily, a government will assume that its citizens are uninterested in famine relief and would not wish to be forced into giving aid—seems more plausible. In any case, unless there were a definite probability that by refusing to give one would be helping to bring about massive government assistance, people who do refuse to make voluntary contributions are refusing to prevent a certain amount of suffering without being able to point to any tangible beneficial consequence of their refusal. So the onus of showing how their refusal will bring about government action is on those who refuse to give.

I do not, of course, want to dispute the contention that governments of affluent nations should be giving many times the amount of genuine, no-strings-attached aid that they are giving now. I agree, too, that giving privately is not enough, and that we ought to be campaigning actively for entirely new standards for both public and private contributions to famine relief. Indeed, I would

[3] *Summa Theologica,* II–II, Question 66, Article 7, in *Aquinas, Selected Political Writings,* ed. A. P. d'Entreves, trans. J. G. Dawson (Oxford, 1948), p. 171.

sympathize with someone who thought that campaigning was more important than giving oneself, although I doubt whether preaching what one does not practice would be very effective. Unfortunately, for many people the idea that "it's the government's responsibility" is a reason for not giving which does not appear to entail any political action either.

Another, more serious reason for not giving to famine relief funds is that until there is effective population control, relieving famine merely postpones starvation. If we save the Bengal refugees now, others, perhaps the children of these refugees, will face starvation in a few years' time. In support of this, one may cite the now well-known facts about the population explosion and the relatively limited scope for expanded production.

This point, like the previous one, is an argument against relieving suffering that is happening now, because of a belief about what might happen in the future; it is unlike the previous point in that very good evidence can be adduced in support of this belief about the future. I will not go into the evidence here. I accept that the earth cannot support indefinitely a population rising at the present rate. This certainly poses a problem for anyone who thinks it important to prevent famine. Again, however, one could accept the argument without drawing the conclusion that it absolves one from any obligation to do anything to prevent famine. The conclusion that should be drawn is that the best means of preventing famine, in the long run, is population control. It would then follow from the position reached earlier that one ought to be doing all one can to promote population control (unless one held that all forms of population control were wrong in themselves, or would have significantly bad consequences). Since there are organizations working specifically for population control, one would then support them rather than more orthodox methods of preventing famine.

A third point raised by the conclusion reached earlier relates to the question of just how much we all ought to be giving away. One possibility, which has already been mentioned, is that we ought to give until we reach the level of marginal utility—that is, the level at which, by giving more, I would cause as much suffering to myself or my dependents as I would relieve by my gift. This would mean, of course, that one would reduce oneself to very near the material circumstances of a Bengali refugee. It will be recalled that earlier I put forward both a strong and a moderate version of the principle of preventing bad occurrences. The strong version, which required us to prevent bad things from happening unless in doing so we would be sacrificing something of comparable moral significance, does seem to require reducing ourselves to the level of marginal utility. I should also say that the strong version seems to me to be the correct one. I proposed the more moderate version—that we should prevent bad occurrences unless, to do so, we had to sacrifice something morally significant—only in order to show that even on this surely undeniable principle a great change in our way of life is required. On the more moderate principle, it may not follow that we ought to reduce ourselves to the level of marginal utility, for one might hold that to reduce oneself and one's family to this level is to cause something significantly bad to happen. Whether this is so I shall not discuss, since, as I have said, I can see no good reason for holding the moderate version of the principle rather than the strong version. Even if we accepted the principle only in its moderate form, however, it should be clear that we would have to give away enough to ensure that the consumer society, dependent as it is on people spending on trivia rather than giving to famine relief, would slow down and perhaps disappear entirely. There are several reasons why this would be desirable in itself. The value and necessity of economic growth are now being questioned not only by conservationists, but by economists as well.[4] There is no doubt, too, that the consumer society has had a distorting effect on the goals and purposes of its members. Yet looking at the matter purely from the point of view of overseas aid, there must be a limit to the extent to which we should deliberately slow down our economy; for it might be the case that if we gave away, say, forty percent of our Gross National Product,

---

[4]See, for instance, John Kenneth Galbraith, *The New Industrial State* (Boston, 1967); and E. J. Mishan, *The Costs of Economic Growth* (London, 1967).

we would slow down the economy so much that in absolute terms we would be giving less than if we gave twenty-five percent of the much larger GNP that we would have if we limited our contribution to this smaller percentage.

I mention this only as an indication of the sort of factor that one would have to take into account in working out an ideal. Since Western societies generally consider one percent of the GNP an acceptable level for overseas aid, the matter is entirely academic. Nor does it affect the question of how much an individual should give in a society in which very few are giving substantial amounts.

It is sometimes said, though less often now than it used to be, that philosophers have no special role to play in public affairs, since most public issues depend primarily on an assessment of facts. On questions of fact, it is said, philosophers as such have no special expertise, and so it has been possible to engage in philosophy without committing oneself to any position on major public issues. No doubt there are some issues of social policy and foreign policy about which it can truly be said that a really expert assessment of the facts is required before taking sides or acting, but the issue of famine is surely not one of these. The facts about the existence of suffering are beyond dispute. Nor, I think, is it disputed that we can do something about it, either through orthodox methods of famine relief or through population control or both. This is therefore an issue on which philosophers are competent to take a position. The issue is one which faces everyone who has more money than he needs to support himself and his dependents, or who is in a position to take some sort of political action. These categories must include practically every teacher and student of philosophy in the universities of the Western world. If philosophy is to deal with matters that are relevant to both teachers and students, this is an issue that philosophers should discuss.

Discussion, though, is not enough. What is the point of relating philosophy to public (and personal) affairs if we do not take our conclusions seriously? In this instance, taking our conclusion seriously means acting upon it. The philosopher will not find it any easier than anyone else to alter his attitudes and way of life to the extent that, if I am right, is involved in doing everything that we ought to be doing. At the very least, though, one can make a start. The philosopher who does so will have to sacrifice some of the benefits of the consumer society, but he can find compensation in the satisfaction of a way of life in which theory and practice, if not yet in harmony, are at least coming together.

Study Questions

1. Singer says that if it is in our power to prevent something bad from happening, "without thereby sacrificing anything of comparable moral importance," we ought to do it. What does he mean by that phrase?

2. Is the sacrifice we are morally required to do affected by proximity or distance, according to Singer? Why?

3. Is my moral obligation to help prevent something bad from happening lessened, according to Singer, if there are millions of other people who likewise could help prevent it? Explain.

4. Explain Singer's rejoinder to this argument: If everyone else gave £5 to the Bengal Relief Fund, there would be enough to care for the refugees; there is no reason why I should give more than anyone else; therefore I have no obligation to give more than £5. What implication of his rejoinder does Singer explicitly accept?

5. What becomes of the traditional distinction between duty and charity, according to Singer?

6. How does Singer respond to the objection that his position is too drastic a revision of our moral scheme?
7. What is Singer's rejoinder to Urmson's theory that there should be a distinction between duty and supererogation?
8. What is Singer's response to those who say that overseas aid should be a government responsibility and that therefore the individual ought not give to privately run charities?
9. What is Singer's response to the idea that relieving famine merely postpones starvation?

The Right Not to Give

The next essay, by John Arthur, is a reply to Singer and to Richard Watson, a philosopher who has taken a position similar to Singer's.

Arthur begins, in section 1, with a brief critical discussion of the idea that all human life is of equal value. He then moves on quickly to examine an important premise on which Singer's argument rests. This premise, which Arthur calls the principle of the greater moral evil, is that if we can prevent something bad without sacrificing anything of comparable moral value, we ought to do so.

This principle, Arthur notes at the beginning of section 2, is a part of a moral code. But our moral code also says, Arthur points out, that we are entitled to invoke our own *rights* as justification for not giving to distant strangers or when the cost to us is substantial. Our moral code further says that we are entitled to the *just deserts* of our efforts and do not automatically have to give them up to others in need. In short, our moral code gives weight to both Singer's greater moral evil principle and to "entitlements" (that is, our rights and deserts). Singer and Watson can thus be viewed as reformers who recommend that we drop that part of our code that permits us to invoke our rights and our just deserts as justification for not making large sacrifices for strangers.

So, in section 3, Arthur considers whether Singer's and Watson's recommendation can be justified by the Kantian idea that moral judgments must be universalizable. It cannot, Arthur finds.

But couldn't our moral code just simply be mistaken in holding that we can invoke our rights and just deserts as justification for not making large sacrifices for strangers? Arthur asks. Thus in section 4 he considers the purpose of a moral code. If our moral code doesn't serve its purpose in permitting us to invoke our rights and just deserts as justification for not making large sacrifices to strangers, then we should change our moral codes, as Singer and Watson recommend. But the purpose of a moral code, Arthur argues in this section, is to promote the general welfare. And to do that, it must be practical and not make unrealistic assumptions about human nature our knowledge. And, he says, given that the purpose of a moral code is to promote the general welfare and given that it must be practical and realistic, it follows that it should *not* ignore our entitlements and should permit us at least sometimes to invoke them as justification for not giving aid. In other words, our moral code should not be reformed along the lines recommended by Singer and Watson.

Equality, Entitlements, and the Distribution of Income

John Arthur

John Arthur (b. 1946) is an associate professor of philosophy at State University of New York, Binghamton. This selection is from *Applying Ethics*, ed. Vincent Barry (Belmont, Calif.: Wadsworth, 1981).

Introduction

My guess is that everyone who reads these words is wealthy by comparison with the poorest millions of people on our planet. Not only do we have plenty of money for food, clothing, housing, and other necessities, but a fair amount is left over for far less important purchases like phonograph records, fancy clothes, trips, intoxicants, movies, and so on. And what's more, we don't usually give thought to whether or not we ought to spend our money on such luxuries rather than to give it to those who need it more; we just assume it's ours to do with as we please.

Peter Singer, "Famine, Affluence, and Morality," and Richard Watson, "Reason and Morality in a World of Limited Food" argue that our assumption is wrong, that we should not buy luxuries when others are in severe need. But are they correct? In the first two sections of this paper my aim is to get into focus just what their arguments are, and to evaluate them. Both Singer and Watson, it seems to me, ignore an important feature of our moral code, namely that it allows people who deserve or have rights to their earnings to keep them.

But the fact that our code encourages a form of behavior is not a complete defense, for it is possible that our current moral attitudes are mistaken. Sections 3 and 4 consider this possibility from two angles: universalizability and the notion of an ideal moral code. Neither of these approaches, I argue, requires that desert and rights be sacrificed in the name of redistribution.

1. Equality and the Duty to Aid

What does our moral code have to say about helping people in need? Watson emphasizes what he calls the "principle of equity." Since "all human life is of equal value," and difference in treatment should be "based on freely chosen actions and not accidents of birth or environment," he thinks that we have "equal rights to the necessities of life." To distribute food unequally assumes that some lives are worth more than others, an assumption which, he says, we do not accept. Watson believes, in fact, that we put such importance on the "equity principle" that it should not be violated even if unequal distribution is the only way for anybody to survive. (Leaving aside for the moment whether or not he is correct about our code, it seems to me that if it really did require us to commit mass suicide rather than allow inequality in wealth, then we would want to abandon it for a more suitable set of rules. But more on that later.)

Is Watson correct in assuming that all life is of equal value? Did Adolph Hitler and Martin Luther King, for example, lead two such lives? Clearly one did far more good and less harm than the other. Nor are moral virtues like courage, kindness, and trustworthiness equally distributed among people. So there are at least two senses in which people are not morally equal.

Yet the phrase "All men are equal" has an almost platitudinous ring, and many of us would not hesitate to say that equality is a cornerstone of our morality. But what does it mean? It seems to me that we might have in mind one of two things. First is an idea that Thomas Jefferson expressed in the *Declaration of Independence.* "All men are created equal" meant, for him, that no man is the moral inferior of another, that, in other words, there are certain rights which all men share equally, including life and liberty. We are entitled to pursue our own lives with a minimum of interference from others, and no person is the natural slave of another. But, as Jefferson also knew, equality in that sense does not require equal distribution of the necessities of life, only that we not interfere with one another, allowing instead every person the liberty to pursue his own affairs, so long as he does not violate the rights of his fellows.

Others, however, have something different in mind when they speak of human equality. I want to develop this second idea by recounting briefly the details of Singer's argument in "Famine, Affluence, and Morality." He first argues that two general moral principles are widely accepted, and then that those principles imply an obligation to eliminate starvation.

The first principle is simply that "suffering and death from lack of food, shelter and medical care are bad." Some may be inclined to think that the mere existence of such an evil in itself places an obligation on others, but that is, of course, the problem which Singer addresses. I take it that he is not begging the question in this obvious way and will argue from the existence of evil to the obligation of others to eliminate it. But how, exactly, does he establish this? The second principle, he thinks, shows the connection, but it is here that controversy arises.

This principle, which I will call the greater moral evil rule, is as follows:

> If it is in our power to prevent something bad from happening, without thereby sacrificing anything of comparable moral importance, we ought, morally, to do it.[1]

In other words, people are entitled to keep their earnings only if there is no way for them to prevent a greater evil by giving them away. Providing others with food, clothing, and housing would generally be of more importance than buying luxuries, so the greater moral evil rule now requires substantial redistribution of wealth.

Certainly there are few, if any, of us who live by that rule, although that hardly shows we are *justified* in our way of life; we often fail to live up to our own standards. Why does Singer think our shared morality requires that we follow the greater moral evil rule? What arguments does he give for it?

He begins with an analogy. Suppose you came across a child drowning in a shallow pond. Certainly we feel it would be wrong not to help. Even if saving the child meant we must dirty our clothes, we would emphasize that those clothes are not of comparable significance to the child's life. The greater moral evil rule thus seems a natural way of capturing why we think it would be wrong not to help.

But the argument for the greater moral evil rule is not limited to Singer's claim that it explains our feelings about the drowning child or that it appears "uncontroversial." Moral equality also enters the picture. Besides the Jeffersonian idea that we share certain rights equally, most of us are also attracted to another type of equality, namely that like amounts of suffering (or happiness) are of equal significance, no matter who is experiencing them. I cannot reasonably say that, while my pain is no more severe than yours, I am somehow special and it's more important that mine be alleviated. Objectivity requires us to admit the opposite, that no one has a unique status which warrants such special pleading. So equality demands equal consideration of interests as well as respect for certain rights.

But if we fail to give to famine relief and instead purchase a new car when the old one will do, or buy fancy clothes for a friend when his or her old ones are perfectly good, are we not assuming that the relatively minor enjoyment we or our friends may get is as important as another person's life? And that is a form of prejudice; we are acting as if people were not equal in the sense that their interests deserve equal consideration. We are giving special consideration to ourselves or to our group, rather like a racist does. Equal consideration of interests thus leads naturally to the greater moral evil rule.

2. Rights and Desert

Equality, in the sense of giving equal consideration to equally serious needs, is part of our moral code.

And so we are led, quite rightly I think, to the conclusion that we should prevent harm to others if in doing so we do not sacrifice anything of comparable moral importance. But there is also another side to the coin, one which Singer and Watson ignore. This can be expressed rather awkwardly by the notion of entitlements. These fall into two broad categories, rights and desert. A few examples will show what I mean.

All of us could help others by giving away or allowing others to use our bodies. While your life may be shortened by the loss of a kidney or less enjoyable if lived with only one eye, those costs are probably not comparable to the loss experienced by a person who will die without any kidney or who is totally blind. We can even imagine persons who will actually be harmed in some way by your not granting sexual favors to them. Perhaps the absence of a sexual partner would cause psychological harm or even rape. Now suppose that you can prevent this evil without sacrificing anything of comparable importance. Obviously such relations may not be pleasant, but according to the greater moral evil rule, that is not enough; to be justified in refusing, you must show that the unpleasantness you would experience is of equal importance to the harm you are preventing. Otherwise, the rule says you must consent.

If anything is clear, however, it is that our code does not *require* such heroism; you are entitled to keep your second eye and kidney and not bestow sexual favors on anyone who may be harmed without them. The reason for this is often expressed in terms of rights; it's your body, you have a right to it, and that weighs against whatever duty you have to help. To sacrifice a kidney for a stranger is to do more than is required, it's heroic.

Moral rights are normally divided into two categories. Negative rights are rights of noninterference. The right to life, for example, is a right not to be killed. Property rights, the right to privacy, and the right to exercise religious freedom are also negative, requiring only that people leave others alone and not interfere.

Positive rights, however, are rights of recipience. By not putting their children up for adoption, parents give them various positive rights, including the rights to be fed, clothed, and housed. If I agree to share in a business venture, my promise creates a right of recipience, so that when I back out of the deal, I've violated your right.

Negative rights also differ from positive in that the former are natural; the ones you have depend on what you are. If lower animals lack rights to life or liberty it is because there is a relevant difference between them and us. But the positive rights you may have are not natural; they arise because others have promised, agreed, or contracted to give you something.

Normally, then, a duty to help a stranger in need is not the result of a right he has. Such a right would be positive, and since no contract or promise was made, no such right exists. An exception to this would be a lifeguard who contracts to watch out for someone's children. The parent whose child drowns would in this case be doubly wronged. First, the lifeguard should not have cruelly or thoughtlessly ignored the child's interests, and second, he ought not to have violated the rights of the parents that he help. Here, unlike Singer's case, we can say there are rights at stake. Other bystanders also act wrongly by cruelly ignoring the child, but unlike the lifeguard they do not violate anybody's rights. Moral rights are one factor to be weighed, but we also have other obligations; I am not claiming that rights are all we need to consider. That view, like the greater moral evil rule, trades simplicity for accuracy. In fact, our code expects us to help people in need as well as to respect negative and positive rights. But we are also entitled to invoke our own rights as justification for not giving to distant strangers or when the cost to us is substantial, as when we give up an eye or a kidney.

Rights come in a variety of shapes and sizes, and people often disagree about both their shape and size. Can a woman kill an unborn child because of her right to control her body? Does mere inheritance transfer rights to property? Do dolphins have a right to live? While some rights are widely accepted, others are controversial.

One more comment about rights, then we'll look at desert. Watson's position, which I criticized for other reasons earlier, is also mistaken because he ignores important rights. He claims that we must pay no attention to "accidents of birth and environment" and base our treatment of people on "what they freely choose." But think about how you will (or did) select a spouse or lover. Are you not entitled to consider such "accidents of birth and environment" as attractiveness, personality, and intelligence? It is, after all, your future, and it is certainly a part of our shared moral code that you have a right to use those (or whatever) criteria you wish in selecting a mate. It is at best an exaggeration to say we must always "ignore accidents of birth and environment" in our treatment of people.

Desert is a second form of entitlement. Suppose, for example, an industrious farmer manages through hard work to produce a surplus of food for the winter while a lazy neighbor spends his summer fishing. Must our industrious farmer ignore his hard work and give the surplus away because his neighbor or his family will suffer? What again seems clear is that we have more than one factor to weigh. Not only should we compare the consequences of his keeping it with his giving it away; we also should weigh the fact that one farmer deserves the food, he earned it through his hard work. Perhaps his deserving the product of his labor is outweighed by the greater need of his lazy neighbor, or perhaps it isn't, but being outweighed is in any case not the same as weighing nothing!

Desert can be negative, too. The fact that the Nazi war criminal did what he did means he deserves punishment, that we have a reason to send him to jail. Other considerations, for example the fact that nobody will be deterred by his suffering, or that he is old and harmless, may weigh against punishment and so we may let him go; but again that does not mean he doesn't still deserve to be punished.

Our moral code gives weight to both the greater moral evil principle and entitlements. The former emphasizes equality, claiming that from an objective point of view all comparable suffering, whoever its victim, is equally significant. It encourages us to take an impartial look at all the various effects of our actions; it is thus forward-looking. When we consider matters of entitlement, however, our attention is directed to the past. Whether we have rights to money, property, eyes, or whatever, depends on how we came to possess them. If they were acquired by theft rather than from birth or through gift exchange, then the right is suspect. Desert, like rights, is also backward-looking, emphasizing past effort or past transgressions which now warrant reward or punishment.

Our commonly shared morality thus requires that we ignore neither consequences nor entitlements, neither the future results of our action nor relevant events in the past. It encourages people to help others in need, especially when it's a friend or someone we are close to geographically, and when the cost is not significant. But it also gives weight to rights and desert, so that we are not usually obligated to give to strangers.

One path is still open as a defense of the greater moral evil rule, and it deserves comment. I have assumed throughout that Singer wants to emphasize the great disparity in the amount of enjoyment someone may get from, say, a new car, as compared with the misery that could be prevented by using the money to save another's life. The fact that the two are not comparable means that the money should not be spent on the car. It is possible to interpret the rule differently, however. By admitting that having rights and deserving things are also of moral significance, Singer could accept what I have said so that the greater moral evil rule would survive intact.

The problem with this response, however, is that the greater moral evil rule has now become an almost empty platitude, urging nothing more than that we should prevent something bad unless we have adequate moral reason not to do so. Since rights and desert often provide such reasons, the rule would say nothing useful about our obligation to help others, and it certainly would not require us to "reduce ourselves to the level of marginal utility" so that the "consumer society" would "slow down and perhaps disappear" as Singer claims. I will therefore assume he would not accept such an interpretation of his view, that entitlements are not among the sacrifices which could balance off the suffering caused by failing to help people in need.

But unless we are moral relativists, the mere fact that entitlements are an important part of our moral code does not in itself justify such a role.

Singer and Watson can perhaps best be seen as moral reformers, advocating the rejection of rules which provide for distribution according to rights and desert. Certainly the fact that in the past our moral code condemned suicide and racial mixing while condoning slavery should not convince us that a more enlightened moral code, one which we would want to support, would take such positions. Rules which define acceptable behavior are continually changing, and we must allow for the replacement of inferior ones.

Why should we not view entitlements as examples of inferior rules we are better off without? What could justify our practice of evaluating actions by looking backward to rights and desert instead of just to their consequences? One answer is that more fundamental values than rights and desert are at stake, namely fairness, justice, and respect. Failure to reward those who earn good grades or promotions is wrong because it's *unfair*; ignoring past guilt shows a lack of regard for *justice*; and failure to respect rights to life, privacy, or religious choice suggests a lack of *respect for other persons.*

Some people may be persuaded by those remarks, feeling that entitlements are now on an acceptably firm foundation. But an advocate of equality may well want to question why fairness, justice, and respect for persons should matter. But since it is no more obvious that preventing suffering matters than that fairness, respect, and justice do, we again seem to have reached an impasse.

3. Universalizability

It is sometimes thought that we can choose between competing moral rules by noting which ones are compatible with some more fundamental rule. One such fundamental standard is attributed to Kant, though it is also rooted in traditional Christian thought. "Do unto others as you would have them do unto you" and the Kantian categorical imperative, "Act only on maxims that you can will would become universal laws," express an idea some think is basic to *all* moral rules. The suggestion is that if you think what you're doing is right, then you have got to be willing to universalize your judgment, that is, to acknowledge that anyone in similar circumstances would be correct if he were to follow the same rule.

Such familiar reasoning can be taken in two very different ways. The first requires only that a person not make himself an exception, that he live up to his own standard. This type of universalizability, however, cannot help choose between the two rules. An advocate of rights and desert would surely agree that whether he were the deserving or undeserving one, whether he had the specific right or did not have it, entitlements still should not be ignored. Nothing about the position of those supporting rights and desert suggests that they must make exceptions for themselves; such rules are in that sense universalizable. But the advocate of the greater moral evil rule can also be counted on to claim that he too should not be made an exception, and that *ignoring* entitlements in favor of the greater moral evil rule is the proper course whether or not he would benefit from the policy. Both views, then, could be universalized in the first sense.

But if we understand universalizability in another sense, neither of the rules passes the test. If being "willing to universalize the judgment" means that a supporter of a particular moral rule would be equally happy with the result were the roles reversed, then there is doubt whether either is universalizable. The rights advocate cannot promise always to like the outcome; he probably would *prefer*, were the tables turned and his life depended on somebody not keeping his rightfully owned income, that entitlements be ignored in that instance. But his opponent cannot pass the test either, since he would likely prefer that rights and desert *not* be ignored were he in a position to benefit from them. But in any case it is not at all clear why we should expect people who make moral judgments to be neutral as to which position they occupy. Must a judge who thinks justice requires that a murderer go to jail agree that he would prefer jail if he were the murderer? It seems that all he must do to universalize his judgment is agree that it would be *right* that he go to jail if the tables were turned, that, in other words, he is not exempt from the rules. But that is a test, as I said, which supporters of entitlements can pass.

So the test of universalizability does not provide grounds for rejecting entitlement rules, and we are once again at an impasse. A second possibility is to view the egalitarian as a moral reformer. Then, perhaps, the criticism of entitlements can be defended as part of a more reasonable and effective moral system. In the final section I look in detail at the idea that rights and desert would not be part of a such ideal moral code, one which we would support if we were fully rational.

4. Entitlements and the Ideal Moral Code

The idea I want now to consider is that part of our code should be dropped, so that people could no longer invoke rights and desert as justification for not making large sacrifices for strangers. In place of entitlements would be a rule regarding that any time we can prevent something bad without sacrificing anything of comparable moral significance we ought to do it. Our current code, however, allows people to say that while they would do more good with their earnings, still they have rights to the earnings, the earnings are deserved, and so need not be given away. The crucial question is whether we want to have such entitlement rules in our code, or whether we should reject them in favor of the greater moral evil rule.

Universalizability, I argued, gives no clear answer to this. Each position also finds a certain amount of support within our code, either from the idea of equal consideration of interests or from our concerns about fairness, justice, and respect for other persons. The problem to be resolved, then, is whether there are other reasons to drop entitlement rules in favor of the greater moral evil rule.

I believe that our best procedure is not to think about this or that specific rules, drawing analogies, refining it, and giving counterexamples, but to focus instead on the nature of morality as a whole. What is a moral code? What do we want it to do? What type of code do we want to support? These questions will give us a fresh perspective from which to consider the merits of rules which allow people to appeal to rights and desert and to weigh the issue of whether our present code should be reformed.

We can began with the obvious: A moral code is a system of rules designed to guide people's conduct. As such, it has characteristics in common with other systems of rules. Virtually every organization has rules which govern the conduct of members; clubs, baseball leagues, corporations, bureaucracies, profession associations, even *The* Organization all have rules. Another obvious point is this: What the rules are depends on why the organization exists. Rules function to enable people to accomplish goals which lead them to organize in the first place. Some rules, for example, "Don't snitch on fellow mafioso," "Pay dues to the fraternity," and "Don't give away trade secrets to competing companies," serve in obvious ways. Other times the real purposes of rules are controversial, as when doctors do not allow advertising by fellow members of the AMA.

Frequently rules reach beyond members of a specific organization, obligating everyone who is capable of following them to do so. These include costs of civil and criminal law, etiquette, custom, and morality. But before discussing the specific purposes of moral rules, it will be helpful to look briefly at some of the similarities and differences between these more universal codes.

First, the sanctions imposed on rule violators vary among different types of codes. While in our legal code, transgressions are punished by fines, jail, or repayment of damages, informal sanctions of praise, blame, or guilt encourage conformity to the rules of morality and etiquette. Another difference is that while violation of a moral rule is always a serious affair, this need not be so for legal rules of etiquette and custom. Many of us think it unimportant whether a fork is on the left side of a plate or whether an outmoded and widely ignored Sunday closing law is violated, but violation of a moral rule is not ignored. Indeed, that a moral rule has lost its importance is often shown by its demotion to status of mere custom.

A third difference is that legal rules, unlike rules of morality, custom, and etiquette, provide for a specific person or procedure that is empowered to alter the rules. If Congress acts to change the tax laws, then as of the date stated in the statute the rules are changed. Similarly for the governing rules of social clubs, government bureaucracies, and the AMA. Rules of custom, morals, and etiquette also change, of course, but they do so in a less precise and much more gradual fashion, with no person or group specifically empowered to make changes.

This fact, that moral rules are *in a sense* beyond the power of individuals to change, does not show that rules of morality, any more than those of etiquette, are objective in the same sense that scientific laws are. All that needs to happen for etiquette or morality to change is for people to change certain practices, namely the character traits they praise and blame, or the actions they approve and disapprove. Scientific laws, however, are discovered, not invented by society, and so are beyond human control. The law that the boiling point of water increases as its pressure increases cannot be changed by humans, either individually or collectively. Such laws are a part of the fabric of nature.

But the fact that moral rules, like legal ones, are not objective in the same sense as scientific ones does not mean that there is no objective standard of right or wrong, that one code is as good as another, or even that the "right thing to do" is just what the moral code currently followed in our society teaches is right. Like the rules of a fraternity or corporation, legal and moral rules can serve their purposes either well or poorly, and whether they do is a matter of objective fact. Further, if a moral code doesn't serve its purpose, we have good reason to criticize all or part of it, to ignore it, and to think of a way to change it, just as its serving us well provides a good reason to obey. In important respects morality is not at all subjective.

Take, for example, a rule which prohibits homosexual behavior. Suppose it serves no useful purpose, but only increases the burdens of guilt, shame, and social rejection borne by 10% of our population. If this is so, we have good reason to ignore the rule. On the other hand, if rules against killing and lying help us to accomplish what we want from a moral code, we have good reason to support those rules. Morality is created, and as with other systems of rules which we devise, a particular rule may or may not further the shared human goals and interests which motivated its creation. There is thus a connection between what we ought to do and how well a code serves its purposes. If a rule serves well the general purposes of a moral code, then we have reason to support it, and if we have reason to support it, we also have reason to obey it. But if, on the other hand, a rule is useless, or if it frustrates the purposes of morality, we have reason neither to support nor to follow it. All of this suggests the following conception of a right action: Any action is right which is approved by an ideal moral code, one which it is rational for us to support. Which code we would want to support would depend, of course, on which one is able to accomplish the purposes of morality.

If we are to judge actions in this way, by reference to what an ideal moral code would require, we must first have a clear notion of just what purposes morality is meant to service. And here again the comparison between legal and moral rules is instructive. Both systems discourage certain types of behavior—killing, robbing, and beating—while encouraging others—repaying debts, keeping important agreements, and providing for one's children. The purpose which both have in discouraging various behaviors is obvious. Such negative rules help keep people from causing harm. Think, for example, of how we are first taught it is wrong to hit a baby brother or sister. Parents explain the rule by emphasizing that it hurts the infant when we hit him. Promoting the welfare of ourselves, our friends and family, and to a lesser degree all who have the capacity to be harmed is the primary purpose of negative moral rules. It's how we learn them as children and why we support them as adults.

The same can be said of positive rules, rules which encourage various types of behavior. Our own welfare, as well as that of friends, family, and others, depends on general acceptance of rules which encourage keeping promises, fulfilling contracts, and meeting the needs of our children. Just try to imagine a society in which promises or agreements mean nothing, or where family members took no concern for one another. A life without positive or negative rights would be as Thomas Hobbes long ago observed: nasty, brutish, and short.

Moral rules thus serve two purposes. They promote our own welfare by discouraging acts of violence and promoting social conventions like promising and paying debts, and second, they perform the same service for our family, friends, and others. We have reason to support a moral code because we care about our own welfare, and because we care about the well-being of others. For most of us the ideal moral code, the one we would support because it best fulfills these purposes, is the code which is most effective in promoting general welfare.

But can everyone be counted on to share these concerns? Think, for example, of an egoist, who only desires that *he* be happy. Such a person, if he existed, would obviously like a code which maximizes his own welfare. How can we hope to get agreement about which code it is rational to support, if different people expect different things from moral rules?[2]

Before considering these questions, I want to mention two preliminary points. First, the problem with egoism is that it tends to make morality relative. If we are going to decide moral disputes by considering what would be required by the code which it is rational for people to support, then we must reach agreement about what that code is. Otherwise the right action for an altruist, the one which is required by the code which it's rational for him to support, may be the wrong act for the egoist. Yet how can the very same act done in identical circumstances be wrong for one person yet right for another? Maybe morality is relative in that way, but if so the prospects for peaceful resolution of important disputes is lessened, a result not to be hoped for.

My second point is that while we certainly do not want to assume people are perfect altruists, we also do not want to give people less credit than they deserve. There is some evidence, for example, that concern for others in our species is part of our biological heritage. Some geneticists think that many animals, particularly higher ones, take an innate interest in the welfare of other members of their species.[3] Other researchers argue that feelings of benevolence originate naturally, through classical conditioning; we develop negative associations with our own pain behavior (since we are then in pain) and this attitude becomes generalized to the pain behavior of others.[4] If either of these is true, egoism might be far more unusual than is commonly supposed, perhaps rare enough that it can be safely ignored.

There is also a line of reasoning which suggests that disagreement about which moral code to support need not be as deep as is often thought. What sort of code in fact *would* a rational egoist support? He would first think of proposing one which allows him to do anything whatsoever that he desires, while requiring that others ignore their own happiness and do what is in his interests. But here enters a family of considerations which will bring us back to the merits of entitlements versus the greater moral evil rule. Our egoist is contemplating what code to *support*, which means going before the public and trying to win general acceptance of his proposed rules. Caring for nobody else, he might secretly prefer the code I mentioned, yet it would hardly make sense for him to work for its public adoption since others are unlikely to put his welfare above the happiness of themselves and their families. So it looks as if the code an egoist would actually support might not be all that different from the ideal (welfare maximizing) code; he would be wasting his time to advocate rules that serve only his own interests because they have no chance of public acceptance.

The lesson to be learned here is a general one: The moral code it is rational for us to support must be practical; it must actually work. This means, among other things, that it must be able to gain the support of almost everyone.

But the code must be practical in other respects as well. I have emphasized that it is wrong to ignore the possibilities of altruism, but it is also important that a code not assume people are more unselfish than they are. Rules that would work only for angels are not the ones it is rational to support for humans. Second, an ideal code cannot assume we are more objective than we are; we often tend to rationalize when our own interests are at stake, and a rational person will also keep that in mind when choosing a moral code. Finally, it is not rational to support a code which assumes we have perfect knowledge. We are often mistaken about the consequences of what we do, and a workable code must take that into account as well.

I want now to bring these various considerations together in order to decide whether or not to reject entitlements in favor of the greater moral evil rule. I will assume that the egoist is not a serious obstacle to acceptance of a welfare maximizing code, either because egoists are, like angels, merely imaginary, or because a practical egoist would only support a code which can be expected to gain wide support. We still have to ask whether entitlements would be included in a welfare maximizing code. The initial temptation is to substitute the greater moral evil rule for entitlements, requiring people to prevent something bad whenever the cost to them is less significant than the benefit to another. Surely, we might think, total welfare would be increased by a code requiring people to give up their savings if a greater evil can be prevented.

I think, however, that this is wrong, and that an ideal code would provide for rights and would encourage rewarding according to desert. My reasons for thinking this stem from the importance of insuring that a moral code really does, in fact, work. Each of the three practical considerations mentioned above now enters the picture. First, it will be quite difficult to get people to accept a code which requires that they give away their savings, extra organs, or anything else merely because they can avoid a greater evil for a stranger. Many people simply wouldn't do it: they aren't that altruistic. If the code attempts to require it anyway, two results would likely follow. First, because many would not live up to the rules, there would be a tendency to create feelings of guilt in those who keep their savings in spite of having been taught it is wrong, as well as conflict between those who meet their obligations and those who do not. And, second, a more realistic code, one which doesn't expect more than can be accomplished, may actually result in more giving. It's a bit like trying to influence how children spend their money. Often they will buy less candy if rules allow them to do so occasionally but they are praised for spending on other things than if its purchase is prohibited. We cannot assume that making a charitable act a requirement will always encourage such behavior. Impractical rules not only create guilt and social conflict, they often tend to encourage the opposite of the desired result. By giving people the right to use their savings for themselves, yet praising those who do not exercise the right but help others instead, we have struck a good balance; the rules are at once practical yet reasonably effective.

Similar practical considerations would also influence our decision to support rules that allow people to keep what they deserve. For most people, working is not their favorite activity. If we are to prosper, however, goods and services must be produced. Incentives are therefore an important motivation, and one such incentive for work is income. Our code encourages work by allowing people to keep a large part of what they earn, indeed that's much the point of entitlements. "I worked hard for it, so I can keep it" is an oft-heard expression. If we eliminate this rule from our code and ask people to follow the greater moral evil rule instead, the result would likely be less work done and so less total production. Given a choice between not working and continuing to work knowing the efforts should go to benefit others, many would choose not to work.

Moral rules should be practical in a third sense, too. They cannot assume people are either more unbiased or more knowledgeable than they are. This fact has many implications for the sorts of rules we would want to include in a welfare maximizing code. For example, we may be tempted to avoid slavish conformity to counterproductive rules by allowing people to break promises whenever they think doing so would increase total welfare. But again we must not ignore human nature, in this case our tendency to give special weight to our own welfare and our inability to be always objective in tracing the effects of our actions. While we would not want to teach that promises must never be broken no matter what the consequences, we also would not want to encourage breaking promises any time a person can convince himself the results of doing so would be better than if he kept his word.

Similar considerations apply to the greater moral evil rule. Imagine a situation where someone feels he can prevent an evil befalling himself by taking what he needs from a large store. The idea that he's preventing something bad from happening (to himself) without sacrificing anything of comparable moral significance (the store won't miss the goods) would justify robbery. Although sometimes a particular act of theft really is welfare maximizing, it does not follow that we should support a *rule* which allows theft whenever the robber is preventing a greater evil. Such a rule, to work, would require more objectivity and more knowledge of long-term consequences than we have. Here again, including rights in our moral code serves a useful role, discouraging the tendency to rationalize our behavior by underestimating the harm we may cause to others or exaggerating the benefits that may accrue to ourselves.

The first sections of this paper attempted to show that our moral code is a bit schizophrenic. It seems to pull us in opposite directions, sometimes toward helping people who are in need, other times toward the view that rights and desert justify keeping things we have even if greater evil could be avoided were we to give away our extra eye or our savings account. This apparent inconsistency led us to a further question: Is the emphasis on entitlements really defensible, or should we try to resolve the tension in our own code by adopting the greater moral evil rule and ignoring entitlements? In this section I considered the idea that we might choose between entitlements and the greater moral evil rule by paying attention to the general nature of a moral code; and in particular to the sort of code we might want to support. I argued that all of us, including egoists, have reason to support a code which promotes the welfare of everyone who lives under it. That idea, of an ideal moral code which it is rational for everyone to support, provides a criterion for deciding which rules are sound and which ones we should support.

My conclusion is a conservative one: Concern that our moral code encourages production and not fail because it unrealistically assumes people are more altruistic or objective than they are means that our rules giving people rights to their possessions and encouraging distribution according to desert should be part of an ideal moral code. And since this is so, it is not always wrong to invoke rights or claim that money is deserved as justification for not giving aid, even when something worse could be prevented by offering help. The welfare maximizing moral code would not require us to maximize welfare in each individual case.

I have not yet discussed just how much weight should be given to entitlements, only that they are important and should not be ignored as Singer and Watson suggest. Certainly an ideal moral code would not allow people to overlook those in desperate need by making entitlements absolute, any more than it would ignore entitlements. But where would it draw the line?

It's hard to know, of course, but the following seems to me to be a sensible stab at an answer. Concerns about discouraging production and the general adherence to the code argue strongly against expecting too much; yet on the other hand, to allow extreme wealth in the face of grinding poverty would seem to put too much weight on entitlements. It seems to me, then, that a reasonable code would require people to help when there is no substantial cost to themselves, that is, when what they are sacrificing would not mean *significant* reduction in their own or their families' level of happiness. Since most people's savings accounts and nearly everybody's second kidney are not insignificant, entitlements would in those cases outweigh another's need. But if what is at stake is trivial, as dirtying one's clothes would normally be, then an ideal moral code would not allow rights to override the greater evil that can be prevented. Despite our code's unclear and sometimes schizophrenic posture, it seems to me that these judgments are not that different from our current moral attitudes. We tend to blame people who waste money on trivia when they could help others in need, yet not to expect people to make large sacrifices to distant strangers. An ideal moral code thus might not be a great deal different from our own.

Notes

1. Singer also offers a "weak" version of this principle which, it seems to me, is *too* weak. It requires giving aid only if the gift is of *no* moral significance to the giver. But since even minor embarrassment or small amounts of happiness are not completely without moral importance, this weak principle implies little or no obligation to aid, even to the drowning child.
2. This difficult leads many to think the choice of a code should be made behind a "veil of ignorance" about one's particular station in life, talents, class, and religious or other moral values. The major proponent of this view is John Rawls, *A Theory of Justice* (Cambridge: Harvard University Press, 1971).
3. Stephen Jay Gould, "So Cleverly Kind an Animal" in *Ever Since Darwin* (New York: W. W. Norton Co., 1977).
4. Richard B. Brandt, *Theory of Right and Good* (New York: Oxford University Press, 1979).

Study Questions

1. What are the two things we might mean when we say that all people are created equal, according to Arthur?
2. What is the greater moral evil rule?
3. What is the difference between negative rights and positive rights?
4. Are we ever able to invoke our own rights as a justification for not giving to strangers, according to Arthur?
5. What does Arthur mean by saying that the principle of the greater moral evil is forward-looking, whereas entitlements are backward-looking?
6. Why, according to Arthur, are Singer and Watson best viewed as moral reformers?
7. Why, according to Arthur, does the Kantian idea that moral judgments must be universalizable not provide grounds for rejecting entitlement rules?
8. What definition of a right action does Arthur give in section 4?
9. What is the purpose of moral rules, according to Arthur, and what is the ideal moral code?
10. What does Arthur mean when he says that a moral code must be practical?
11. Why, according to Arthur, would an ideal moral code provide for rights and encourage rewarding according to desert?

Charity and Kantianism

Onora O'Neill, in the next selection, applies one version of Kant's categorical imperative to questions of how to act toward those who do or may suffer famine. Don't just yet flip to those sections of this book in which we discussed Kant's ethics, because O'Neill begins the article by reviewing Kantian moral philosophy (sections

22, 23, and 24). Kant's categorical imperative, in the version O'Neill is concerned with, requires us always to act so as never to use another person as a mere means to some end. This requires us never to involve others in some scheme of action to which they could not in principle consent, for example, involving someone in a criminal activity by deceiving them about what you're up to.

In section 25, O'Neill distinguishes Kantian duties of justice from Kantian duties of beneficence. In section 26, she compares Kantian moral theory to utilitarian moral theory. (Roughly: You need a lot more data to come to a precise evaluation of actions on utilitarian grounds than you do on Kantian grounds, though more types of action are subject to utilitarian evaluation than to Kantian evaluation.) Then, in section 27, O'Neill discusses Kantian duties of justice in times of famine, and in Section 28, she discusses Kantian duties of beneficence in times of famine.

It may seem to you, as you read this article, that Kantian ethics are limited in comparison to utilitarian ethics, because Kant would have us concentrate, not on the results of actions, but on the intentions on which the actions are based. In the final section of the article, O'Neill argues that Kantian ethics are less limited in this regard than you might expect.

Kantian Approaches to Some Famine Problems

Onora O'Neill

Onora O'Neill (b. 1941) is Professor of Philosophy at the University of Essex. This selection was published in *Matters of Life and Death*, ed. Tom Regan (New York: Random House, 1980).

§22 A Simplified Account of Kant's Ethics

Kant's moral theory has acquired the reputation of being forbiddingly difficult to understand and, once understood, excessively demanding in its requirements. I don't believe that this reputation has been wholly earned, and I am going to try to undermine it. In §§23–26 I shall try to reduce some of the difficulties, and in §§27–30 I shall try to show the implications of a Kantian moral theory for action toward those who do or may suffer famine. Finally, I shall compare Kantian and utilitarian approaches and assess their strengths and weaknesses.

The main method by which I propose to avoid some of the difficulties of Kant's moral theory is by explaining only one part of the theory. This does not seem to me to be an irresponsible approach in this case. One of the things that makes Kant's moral theory hard to understand is that he gives a number of different versions of the principle that he calls the Supreme Principle of Morality, and these different versions don't look at all like one another. They also don't look at all like the utilitarians' Greatest Happiness Principle. But the Kantian principle is supposed to play a similar role in arguments about what to do.

Kant calls his Supreme Principle the *Categorical Imperative*; its various versions also have sonorous names. One is called the Formula of Universal Law; another is the Formula of the Kingdom of Ends. The one on which I shall concentrate is known as the *Formula of the End in Itself*. To understand why Kant thinks that these picturesquely named principles are equivalent to one another takes quite a lot of close and detailed analysis of Kant's philosophy. I shall avoid this and concentrate on showing the implications of this version of the Categorical Imperative.

§23 The Formula of the End in Itself

Kant states the Formula of the End in Itself as follows:

> Act in such a way that you always treat humanity, whether in your own person or in the person of any other, never simply as a means but always at the same time as an end.

To understand this we need to know what it is to treat a person as a means or as an end. According to Kant, each of our acts reflects one or more *maxims*. The maxim of the act is the principle on which one sees oneself as acting. A maxim expresses a person's policy, or if he or she has no settled policy, the principle underlying the particular intention or decision on which he or she acts. Thus, a person who decides "This year I'll give 10 percent of my income to famine relief" has as a maxim the principle of tithing his or her income for famine relief. In practice, the difference between intentions and maxims is of little importance, for given any intention, we can formulate the corresponding maxim by deleting references to particular times, places, and persons. In what follows I shall take the terms 'maxim' and 'intention' as equivalent.

Whenever we act intentionally, we have at least one maxim and can, if we reflect, state what it is. (There is of course room for self-deception here— "I'm only keeping the wolf from the door" we may claim as we wolf down enough to keep ourselves overweight, or, more to the point, enough to feed someone else who hasn't enough food.)

When we want to work out whether an act we propose to do is right or wrong, according to Kant, we should look at our maxims and not at how much misery or happiness the act is likely to produce, and whether it does better at increasing happiness than other available acts. We just have to check that the act we have in mind will not use anyone as a mere means, and, if possible, that it will treat other persons as ends in themselves.

§24 Using Persons As Mere Means

To use someone as a *mere means* is to involve them in a scheme of action *to which they could not in principle consent.* Kant does not say that there is anything wrong about using someone as a means. Evidently we have to do so in any cooperative scheme of action. If I cash a check I use the teller as a means, without whom I could not lay my hands on the cash; the teller in turn uses me as a means to earn his or her living. But in this case, each party consents to her or his part in the transaction. Kant would say that though they use one another as means, they do not use one another as *mere* means. Each person assumes that the other has maxims of his or her own and is not just a thing or a prop to be manipulated.

But there are other situations where one person uses another in a way to which the other could not in principle consent. For example, one person may make a promise to another with every intention of breaking it. If the promise is accepted, then the person to whom it was given must be ignorant of what the promisor's intention (maxim) really is. If one knew that the promisor did not intend to do what he or she was promising, one would, after all, not accept or rely on the promise. It would be as though there had been no promise made. Successful false promising depends on deceiving the person to whom the promise is made about what one's real maxim is. And since the person who is deceived doesn't know that real maxim, he or she can't in principle consent to his or her part in the proposed scheme of action. The person who is deceived is, as it were, a prop or a tool—a mere means—in the false promisor's scheme. A person who promises falsely treats the acceptor of the promise as a prop or a thing and not as a person. In Kant's view, it is this that makes false promising wrong.

One standard way of using others as mere means is by deceiving them. By getting someone involved in a business scheme or a criminal activity on false pretenses, or by giving a misleading account of what one is about, or by making a false promise or a fraudulent contract, one involves another in something to which he or she in principle cannot consent, since the scheme requires that he or she doesn't know what is going on. Another standard way of using others as mere means is by coercing them. If a rich or powerful person threatens a debtor with bankruptcy unless he or she joins in some scheme, then the creditor's intention is to coerce; and the debtor, if coerced, cannot consent to his or her part in the creditor's scheme. To make the example more specific: If a moneylender in an Indian village threatens not to renew a vital loan unless he is given the debtor's land, then he uses the debtor as a mere means. He coerces the debtor, who cannot truly consent to this "offer he can't refuse." (Of course the outward forms of such transactions may look like ordinary commercial dealings, but we know very well that some offers and demands couched in that form as coercive.)

In Kant's view, acts that are done on maxims that require deception or coercion of others, and so cannot have the consent of those others (for consent precludes both deception and coercion), are wrong. When we act on such maxims, we treat others as mere means, as things rather than as ends in themselves. If we act on such maxims, our acts are not only wrong but unjust: such acts wrong the particular others who are deceived or coerced.

§25 Treating Persons As Ends in Themselves

Duties of justice are, in Kant's view (as in many others'), the most important of our duties. When we fail in these duties, we have used some other or others as mere means. But there are also cases where, though we do not use others as mere means, still we fail to use them as ends in themselves in the fullest possible way. To treat someone as an end in him or herself requires in the first place that one not use him or her as mere means, that one respect each as a rational person with his or her own maxims. But beyond that, one may also seek to foster others' plans and maxims by sharing some of their ends. To act beneficently is to seek others' happiness, therefore to intend to achieve some of the things that those others aim at with their maxims. If I want to make others happy, I will adopt maxims that not merely do not manipulate them but that foster some of their plans and activities. Beneficent acts try to achieve what others want. However, we cannot seek everything that others want; their wants are too numerous and diverse, and, of course, sometimes incompatible. It follows that beneficence has to be selective.

There is then quite a sharp distinction between the requirements of justice and of beneficence in Kantian ethics. Justice requires that we act on *no* maxims that use others as mere means. Beneficence requires that we act on *some* maxims that foster others' ends, though it is a matter for judgment and discretion which of their ends we foster. Some maxims no doubt ought not to be fostered because it would be unjust to do so. Kantians are not committed to working interminably through a list of happiness-producing and misery-reducing acts; but there are some acts whose obligatoriness utilitarians may need to debate as they try to compare total outcomes of different choices, to which Kantians are stringently bound. Kantians will claim that they have done nothing wrong if none of their acts is unjust, and that their duty is complete if in addition their life plans have in the circumstances been reasonably beneficent.

In making sure that they meet all the demands of justice, Kantians do not try to compare all available acts and see which has the best effects. They consider only the proposals for action that occur to them and check that these proposals use no other as mere means. If they do not, the act is permissible; if omitting the act would use another as mere means, the act is obligatory. Kant's theory has less scope than utilitarianism. Kantians do not claim to discover whether acts whose maxims they don't know fully are just. They may be reluctant to judge others' acts or policies that cannot be regarded as the maxim of any person or institution. They cannot rank acts in order of merit. Yet, the theory offers more precision than utilitarianism when data are scarce. One can usually tell whether one's act would use others as mere means, even when its impact on human happiness is thoroughly obscure.

§26 Kantian Deliberations on Famine Problems

The theory I have just sketched may seem to have little to say about famine problems. For it is a theory that forbids us to use others as mere means but does not require us to direct our benevolence first to those who suffer most. A conscientious Kantian, it seems, has only to avoid being unjust to those who suffer famine and can then be beneficent to those nearer home. He or she would not be obliged to help the starving, even if no others were equally distressed.

Kant's moral theory does make less massive demands on moral agents than utilitarian moral theory. On the other hand, it is somewhat clearer just what the more stringent demands are, and they are not negligible. We have here a contrast between a theory that makes massive but often indeterminate demands and a theory that makes fewer but less unambiguous demands and leaves other questions, in particular the allocation of beneficence, unresolved. We have also a contrast between a theory whose scope is comprehensive and one that is applicable only to persons acting intentionally and to those institutions that adopt policies, and so maxims. Kantian ethics is silent about the moral status of unintentional action; utilitarians seek to assess all consequences regardless of the intentions that led to them.

§27 Kantian Duties of Justice in Time of Famine

In famine situations, Kantian moral theory requires unambiguously that we do no injustice. We should not act on any maxim that uses another as mere means, so we should neither deceive nor coerce others. Such a requirement can become quite exacting when the means of life are scarce, when persons can more easily be coerced, and when the advantage of gaining more than what is justly due to one is great. I shall give a list of acts that on Kantian principles it would be unjust to do, but that one might be strongly tempted to do in famine conditions.

I will begin with a list of acts that one might be tempted to do as a member of a famine-stricken population. First, where there is a rationing scheme, one ought not to cheat and seek to get more than one's share—any scheme of cheating will use someone as mere means. Nor may one take advantage of others' desperation to profiteer or divert goods onto the black market or to accumulate a fortune out of others' misfortunes. Transactions that are outwardly sales and purchases can be coercive when one party is desperate. All the forms of corruption that deceive or put pressure on others are also wrong: hoarding unallocated food, diverting relief supplies for private use, corruptly using one's influence to others' disadvantage. Such requirements are far from trivial and frequently violated in hard times. In severe famines, refraining from coercing and deceiving may risk one's own life and require the greatest courage.

Second, justice requires that in famine situations one still try to fulfill one's duties to particular others. For example, even in times of famine, a person has duties to try to provide for dependents. These duties may, tragically, be unfulfillable. If they are, Kantian ethical theory would not judge wrong the acts of a person who had done her or his best. There have no doubt been times in human history where there was nothing to be done except abandon the weak and old or to leave children to fend for themselves as best they might. But providing the supporter of dependents acts on maxims of attempting to meet their claims, he or she uses no others as mere means to his or her own survival and is not unjust. A conscientious attempt to meet the particular obligations one has undertaken may also require of one many further maxims of self-restraint and of endeavor—for example, it may require a conscientious attempt to avoid having (further) children; it may require contributing one's time and effort to programs of economic development. Where there is no other means to fulfill particular obligations, Kantian principles may require a generation of sacrifice. They will not, however, require one to seek to maximize the happiness of later generations but only to establish the modest security and prosperity needed for meeting present obligations.

The obligations of those who live with or near famine are undoubtedly stringent and exacting; for those who live further off it is rather harder to see what a Kantian moral theory demands. Might it not, for example, be permissible to do nothing at all about those suffering famine? Might one not ensure that one does nothing unjust to the victims of famine by adopting no maxims whatsoever that mention them? To do so would, at the least, require one to refrain from certain deceptive and coercive practices frequently employed during the European exploration and economic penetration of the now underdeveloped world and still not unknown. For example, it would be unjust to "purchase" valuable lands and resources from persons who don't understand commercial transactions or exclusive property rights or mineral rights, so do not understand that their acceptance of trinkets destroys their traditional economic pattern and way of life. The old adage "trade follows the flag" reminds us to how great an extent the economic penetration of the less-developed countries involved elements of coercion and deception, so was on Kantian principles unjust (regardless of whether or not the net effect has benefited the citizens of those countries).

Few persons in the developed world today find themselves faced with the possibility of adopting on a grand scale maxims of deceiving or coercing persons living in poverty. But at least some people find that their jobs require them to make decisions about investment and aid policies that enormously affect the lives of those nearest to famine. What does a commitment to Kantian moral theory demand of such persons?

It has become common in writings in ethics and social policy to distinguish between one's *personal responsibilities* and one's *role responsibilities.* So a person may say, "As an individual I sympathize, but in my official capacity I can do nothing"; or we may excuse persons' acts of coercion because they are acting in some particular capacity—e.g., as a soldier or a jailer. On the other hand, this distinction isn't made or accepted by everyone. At the Nuremberg trials of war criminals, the defense "I was only doing my job" was disallowed, at least for those whose command position meant that they had some discretion in what they did. Kantians generally would play down any distinction between a person's own responsibilities and his or her role responsibilities. They would not deny that in any capacity one is accountable for certain things for which as a private person one is not accountable. For example, the treasurer of an organization is accountable to the board and has to present periodic reports and to keep specified records. But if she fails to do one of these things for which she is held accountable she will be held responsible for that failure — it will be imputable to her as an individual. When we take on positions, we *add* to our responsibilities those that the job requires; but we do not lose those that are already required of us. Our social role or job gives us, on Kant's view, no license to use others as mere means; even business executives and aid officials and social revolutionaries will act unjustly, so wrongly, if they deceive or coerce — however benevolent their motives.

If persons are responsible for all their acts, it follows that it would be unjust for aid officials to coerce persons into accepting sterilization, wrong for them to use coercive power to achieve political advantages (such as military bases) or commercial advantages (such as trade agreements that will harm the other country). It would be wrong for the executives of large corporations to extort too high a price for continued operation employment and normal trading. Where a less-developed country is pushed to exempt a multinational corporation from tax laws, or to construct out of its meager tax revenues the infrastructure of roads, harbors, or airports (not to mention executive mansions) that the corporation — but perhaps not the country — needs, then one suspects that some coercion has been involved.

The problem with such judgments — and it is an immense problem — is that it is hard to identify coercion and deception in complicated institutional settings. It is not hard to understand what is coercive about one person threatening another with serious injury if he won't comply with the first person's suggestion. But it is not at all easy to tell where the outward forms of political and commercial negotiation — which often involve an element of threat — have become coercive. I can't here explore this fascinating question. But I think it is at least fairly clear that the preservation of the outward forms of negotiation, bargaining, and voluntary consent do *not* demonstrate that there is no coercion, especially when one party is vastly more powerful or the other in dire need. Just as our judiciary has a long tradition of voiding contracts and agreements on grounds of duress or incompetence of one of the parties, so one can imagine a tribunal of an analogous sort rejecting at least some treaties and agreements as coercive, despite the fact that they were negotiated between "sovereign" powers or their representatives. In particular, where such agreements were negotiated with some of the cruder deceptions and coercion of the early days of European economic expansion or the subtler coercions and deceptions of contemporary superpowers, it seems doubtful that the justice of the agreement could be sustained.

Justice, of course, is not everything, even for Kantians. But its demands are ones that they can reasonably strive to fulfill. They may have some uncertain moments — for example, does advocating cheap raw materials mean advocating an international trade system in which the less developed will continue to suffer the pressures of the developed world — or is it a benevolent policy that will maximize world trade and benefit all parties, while doing no one an injustice? But for Kantians, the important moral choices are above all those in which one acts directly, not those in which one decides which patterns of actions to encourage in others or in those institutions that one can influence. And such moral decisions include decisions about the benevolent acts that one will or will not do.

§28 Kantian Duties of Beneficence in Times of Famine

The grounds of duties of beneficence are that such acts not merely don't use others as mere means but are acts that develop or promote others' ends and that, in particular, foster others' capacities to pursue ends, to be autonomous beings.

Clearly there are many opportunities for beneficence. But one area in which the *primary* task of developing others' capacity to pursue their own ends is particularly needed is in the parts of the world where extreme poverty and hunger leave people unable to pursue *any* of their other ends. Beneficence directed at putting people in a position to pursue whatever ends they may have has, for Kant, a stronger claim on us than beneficence directed at sharing ends with those who are already in a position to pursue varieties of ends. It would be nice if I bought a tennis racquet to play with my friend who is tennis mad and never has enough partners; but it is more important to make people able to plan their own lives to a minimal extent. It is nice to walk a second mile with someone who requests one's company; better to share a cloak with someone who may otherwise be too cold to make any journey. Though these suggestions are not a detailed set of instructions for the allocation of beneficence by Kantians, they show that relief of famine must stand very high among duties of beneficence.

§29 The Limits of Kantian Ethics: Intentions and Results

Kantian ethics differs from utilitarian ethics both in its scope and in the precision with which it guides action. Every action, whether of a person or of an agency, can be assessed by utilitarian methods, provided only that information is available about all the consequences of the act. The theory has unlimited scope, but, owing to lack of data, often lacks precision. Kantian ethics has a more restricted scope. Since it assesses actions by looking at the maxims of agents, it can only assess intentional acts. This means that it is most at home in assessing individuals' acts; but it can be extended to assess acts of agencies that (like corporations and governments and student unions) have decision-making procedures. It can do nothing to assess patterns of action that reflect no intention or policy, hence it cannot assess the acts of groups lacking decision-making procedures, such as the student movement, the women's movement, or the consumer movement.

It may seem a great limitation of Kantian ethics that it concentrates on intentions to the neglect of results. It might seem that all conscientious Kantians have to do is to make sure that they never intend to use others as mere means, and that they sometimes intend to foster others' ends. And, as we all know, good intentions sometimes lead to bad results, and correspondingly, bad intentions sometimes do no harm, or even produce good. If Hardin is right, the good intentions of those who feed the starving lead to dreadful results in the long run. If some traditional arguments in favor of capitalism are right, the greed and selfishness of the profit motive have produced unparalleled prosperity for many.

But such discrepancies between intentions and results are the exception and not the rule. For we cannot just *claim* that our intentions are good and do what we will. Our intentions reflect what we expect the immediate results of our actions to be. Nobody credits the "intentions" of a couple who practice neither celibacy nor contraception but still insist "we never meant to have (more) children." Conception is likely (and known to be likely) in such cases. Where people's expressed intentions ignore the normal and predictable results of what they do, we infer that (if they are not amazingly ignorant) their words do not express their true intentions. The Formula of the End in Itself applies to the intentions on which one acts — not to some prettified version that one may avow. Provided this intention — the agent's real intention — uses no other as mere means, he or she does nothing unjust. If some of his or her intentions foster others' ends, then he or she is sometimes beneficent. It is therefore possible for people to test their proposals by Kantian arguments even when they lack the comprehensive causal knowledge that utilitarianism requires. Conscientious Kantians can work out whether they will be doing wrong by some act even though they know that their foresight is limited and that they may cause some harm or fail to cause some benefit. But they will not cause harms that they can foresee without this being reflected in their intentions.

Study Questions

1. What version of Kantian ethics is O'Neill concerned with?
2. What, according to O'Neill, is a Kantian maxim, and what principle must our maxims not violate?
3. What is it, according to O'Neill, to use someone as a mere means? What are some ways of using people as a mere means?
4. What is the distinction between the requirements of justice and of beneficence in Kantian ethics, according to O'Neill?
5. What, according to O'Neill, are the principal differences between Kantian ethics and utilitarianism?
6. Explain what O'Neill means by saying that in famine situations Kantian moral theory requires that we do no injustice.
7. What is the difference between one's personal responsibilities and one's role responsibilities? What would Kantians say about this distinction, according to O'Neill?
8. Briefly explain what Kantian ethics requires of people who make decisions about investment and aid policies involving underdeveloped countries.
9. Briefly describe Kantian duties of beneficence in times of famine, according to O'Neill.
10. Why is it, according to O'Neill, that the apparent limitation of Kantian ethics in concentrating on intentions is less severe than one might expect?

CHAPTER 14

SEXUAL MORALITY

Adultery

In the first essay in this section, Richard Wasserstrom asks but does not actually answer the question "Is adultery immoral?" Instead, Wasserstrom critically examines several arguments to the effect that adultery is immoral. One argument is that adultery involves the breach of an important promise. Another argument—one that Wasserstrom spends more time with—is that adultery involves deception. Examining this argument leads Wasserstrom to consider the idea of sexual intercourse as affection, sharing, and intimate communication. This idea, on the one hand, leads to a possible rationale for the rules of conventional sexual morality. On the other hand, he points out, whether adultery involves deception with respect to feelings depends on the meaning the involved parties attach to sex. Further, is it really desirable in the first place for sexual intimacy to be perceived as the vehicle of the most intimate communication? he wonders. After all, some hold that sex should be separated from love and affection. Others deny that the love and affection sex conveys should be shared by only one other person at a time.

Wasserstrom then considers whether adultery is immoral in an open marriage, one in which the partners agree in advance that extramarital sex can be acceptable. In particular, Wasserstrom is concerned first of all with whether such agreements are consistent with the concept of marriage: they are, he concludes. He also addresses the argument that such agreements, and adultery in general, are wrong because they weaken the institutions of marriage and the nuclear family. This argument, he concludes, depends on certain assumptions that have not been clearly established.

Richard Taylor, too, addresses the issue of adultery. But unlike Wasserstrom, he is not concerned with its moral status. Taylor takes it as a given that adultery is a fact of life; his concern is how best to minimize the terrible destructiveness of people's reactions to it. He offers a series of principles to help married couples (and couples in marriage-like relationships) cope with the adultery of one of the partners. The article is long but easy to read. You won't need our help to get through it.

Is Adultery Immoral?

Richard Wasserstrom

Richard Wasserstrom (b. 1936) teaches philosophy at Stevenson College, University of California, Santa Cruz. The following selection was published in *Today's Moral Problems*, ed. Richard Wasserstrom (New York: Macmillan, 1985).

Many discussions of the enforcement of morality by the law take as illustrative of the problem under consideration the regulation of various types of sexual behavior by the criminal law. It was, for example, the Wolfenden Report's recommendations concerning homosexuality and prostitution that led Lord Devlin to compose his now famous lecture, "The Enforcement of Morals." And that lecture in turn provoked important philosophical responses from H. L. A. Hart, Ronald Dworkin, and others.

Much, if not all, of the recent philosophical literature on the enforcement of morals appears to take for granted the immorality of the sexual behavior in question. The focus of discussion, at least, is whether such things as homosexuality, prostitution, and adultery ought to be made illegal even if they are immoral, and not whether they are immoral.

I propose in this paper to think about the latter, more neglected topic, that of sexual morality, and to do so in the following fashion. I shall consider just one kind of behavior that is often taken to be a case of sexual immorality—adultery. I am interested in pursuing at least two questions. First, I want to explore the question of in what respects adulterous behavior falls within the domain of morality at all: For this surely is one of the puzzles one encounters when considering the topic of sexual morality. It is often hard to see on what grounds much of the behavior is deemed to be either moral or immoral, for example, private homosexual behavior between consenting adults. I have purposely selected adultery because it seems a more plausible candidate for moral assessment than many other kinds of sexual behavior.

The second question I want to examine is that of what is to be said about adultery, without being especially concerned to stay within the area of morality. I shall endeavor, in other words, to identify and to assess a number of the major arguments that might be advanced against adultery. I believe that they are the chief arguments that would be given in support of the view that adultery is immoral, but I think they are worth considering even if some of them turn out to be nonmoral arguments and considerations.

A number of the issues involved seem to me to be complicated and difficult. In a number of places I have at best indicated where further philosophical exploration is required without having successfully conducted the exploration myself. The paper may very well be more useful as an illustration of how one might begin to think about the subject of sexual morality than as an elucidation of important truths about the topic.

Before I turn to the arguments themselves there are two preliminary points that require some clarification. Throughout the paper I shall refer to the immorality of such things as breaking a promise, deceiving someone, etc. In a very rough way, I mean by this that there is something morally wrong that is done in doing the action in question. I mean that the action is, in a strong sense, of "*prima facie*" *prima facie* wrong or unjustified. I do not mean that it may never be right or justifiable to do the action; just that the fact that it is an action of this description always does count against the rightness of the action. I leave entirely open the question of what it is that makes actions of this kind immoral in this sense of "immoral."

The second preliminary point concerns what is meant or implied by the concept of adultery. I mean by "adultery" any case of extramarital sex, and I want to explore the arguments for and against extramarital sex, undertaken in a variety of morally relevant situations. Someone might claim that the concept of adultery is conceptually connected with the concept of immorality, and that to characterize behavior as adulterous is already to characterize it as immoral or unjustified in the sense described above. There may be something to this. Hence the importance of making it clear that I want to talk about extramarital sexual relations. If they are always immoral, this is something that must be shown by argument. If the concept of adultery does in some sense entail or imply immorality, I want to ask whether that connection is a rationally based one. If not all cases of extramarital sex are immoral (again, in the sense described above), then the concept of adultery should either be weakened accordingly or restricted to those classes of extramarital sex for which the predication of immorality is warranted.

One argument for the immorality of adultery might go something like this: what makes adultery immoral is that it involves the breaking of a promise, and what makes adultery seriously wrong is that it involves the breaking of an important promise. For, so the argument might continue, one of the things the two parties promise each other when they get married is that they will abstain from sexual relationships with third persons. Because of this promise both spouses quite reasonably entertain the expectation that the other will behave in conformity with it. Hence, when one of the parties has sexual intercourse with a third person he or she breaks that promise about sexual relationships which was made when the marriage was entered into, and defeats the reasonable expectations of exclusivity entertained by the spouse.

In many cases the immorality involved in breaching the promise relating to extramarital sex may be a good deal more serious than that involved in the breach of other promises. This is so because adherence to this promise may be of much greater importance to the parties than is adherence to many of the other promises given or received by them in their lifetime. The breaking of this promise may be much more hurtful and painful than is typically the case.

Why is this so? To begin with, it may have been difficult for the nonadulterous spouse to have kept the promise. Hence that spouse may feel the unfairness of having restrained himself or herself in the absence of reciprocal restraint having been exercised by the adulterous spouse. In addition, the spouse may perceive the breaking of the promise as an indication of a kind of indifference on the part of the adulterous spouse. If you really cared about me and my feelings — the spouse might say — you would not have done this to me. And third, and related to the above, the spouse may see the act of sexual intercourse with another as a sign of affection for the other person and as an additional rejection of the nonadulterous spouse as the one who is loved by the adulterous spouse. It is not just that the adulterous spouse does not take the feelings of the spouse sufficiently into account, the adulterous spouse also indicates through the act of adultery affection for someone other than the spouse. I will return to these points later. For the present, it is sufficient to note that a set of arguments can be developed in support of the proposition that certain kinds of adultery are wrong just because they involve that breach of a serious promise which, among other things, leads to the intentional infliction of substantial pain by one spouse upon the other.

Another argument for the immorality of adultery focuses not on the existence of a promise of sexual exclusivity but on the connection between adultery and deception. According to this argument, adultery involves deception. And because deception is wrong, so is adultery.

Although it is certainly not obviously so, I shall simply assume in this paper that deception is always immoral. Thus the crucial issue for my purposes is the asserted connection between extramarital sex and deception. Is it plausible to maintain, as this argument does, that adultery always does involve deception and is on that basis to be condemned?

The most obvious person on whom deceptions might be practiced is the nonparticipating spouse; and the most obvious thing about which the nonparticipating spouse can be deceived is the existence of the adulterous act. One clear case of deception is that of lying. Instead of saying that the afternoon was spent in bed with *A*, the adulterous spouse asserts that it was spent in the library with *B*, or on the golf course with *C*.

There can also be deception even when no lies are told. Suppose, for instance, that a person has sexual intercourse with someone other than his or her spouse and just does not tell the spouse about it. Is that deception? It may not be a case of lying if, for example, the spouse is never asked by the other about the situation. Still, we might say, it is surely deceptive because of the promises that were exchanged at marriage. As we saw earlier, these promises provide a foundation for the reasonable belief that neither spouse will engage in sexual relationships with any other persons. Hence the failure to bring the fact of extramarital sex to the attention of the other spouse deceives that spouse about the present state of the marital relationship.

Adultery, in other words, can involve both active and passive deception. An adulterous spouse may just keep silent or, as is often the fact, the spouse may engage in an increasingly complex way of life devoted to the concealment of the facts from the nonparticipating spouse. Lies, half-truths, clandestine meetings, and the like may become a central feature of the adulterous spouse's existence. These are things that can and do happen, and when they do they make the case against adultery an easy one. Still neither active nor passive deception is inevitably a feature of an extramarital relationship.

It is possible, though, that a more subtle but pervasive kind of deceptiveness is a feature of adultery. It comes about because of the connection in our culture between sexual intimacy and certain feelings of love and affection. The point can be made indirectly at first by seeing that one way in which we can, in our culture, mark off our close friends from our mere acquaintances is through the kinds of intimacies that we are prepared to share with them. I may, for instance, be willing to reveal my very private thoughts and emotions to my closest friends or to my wife, but to one else. My sharing of these intimate facts about myself is from one perspective a way of making a gift to those who mean the most to me. Revealing these things and sharing them with those who mean the most to me is one means by which I create, maintain, and confirm those interpersonal relationships that are of most importance to me.

Now in our culture, it might be claimed, sexual intimacy is one of the chief currencies through which gifts of this sort are exchanged. One way to tell someone — particularly someone of the opposite sex — that you have feelings of affection and love for them is by allowing to them or sharing with them sexual behaviors that one doesn't share with the rest of the world. This way of measuring affection was certainly very much a part of the culture in which I matured. It worked something like this. If you were a girl, you showed how much you liked someone by the degree of sexual intimacy you would allow. If you like a boy only a little, you never did more than kiss — and even the kiss was not very passionate. If you liked the boy a lot and if your feelings was reciprocated, necking, and possibly petting, was permissible. If the attachment was still stronger and you thought it might even become a permanent relationship, the sexual activity was correspondingly more intense and more intimate, although whether it would ever lead to sexual intercourse depended on whether the parties (and particularly the girl) accepted fully the prohibition on nonmarital sex. The situation for the boy was related, but not exactly the same. The assumption was that males did not naturally link sex with affection in the way in which females did. However, since women did, males had to take this into account. That is to say, because a woman would permit sexual intimacies only if she had feelings of affection for the male and only if those feelings were reciprocated, the male had to have and express those feelings, too, before sexual intimacies of any sort would occur.

The result was that the importance of a correlation between sexual intimacy and feelings of love and affection was taught by the culture and assimilated by those growing up in the culture. The scale of possible positive feelings toward persons of the other sex ran from casual liking at the one end to the love that was deemed essential to and characteristic of marriage at the other. The scale of possible sexual behavior ran from brief, passionless kissing or hand-holding at the one end to sexual intercourse at the other. And the correlation between the two scales was quite precise. As a result, any act of sexual intimacy carried substantial meaning with it, and no act of sexual intimacy was simply a pleasurable set of bodily sensations. Many such acts were, of course, more pleasurable to the participants because they were a way of saying what the participants' feelings were. And sometimes they were less pleasurable for the same reason. The point is, however, that in any event sexual activity was much more than mere bodily enjoyment. It was not like eating a good meal, listening to good music, lying in the sun, or getting a pleasant back rub. It was behavior that meant a great deal concerning one's feelings for persons of the opposite sex in whom one was most interested and with whom one was most involved. It was among the most authoritative ways in which one could communicate to another the nature and degree of one's affection.

If this sketch is even roughly right, then several things become somewhat clearer. To begin with, a possible rationale for many of the rules of conventional sexual morality can be developed. If, for example, sexual intercourse is associated with the kind of affection and commitment to another that is regarded as characteristic of the marriage relationship, then it is natural that sexual intercourse should be thought properly to take place between persons who are married to each other. And if it is thought that this kind of affection and commitment is only to be found within the marriage relationship, then it is not surprising that sexual intercourse should only be thought to be proper within marriage.

Related to what has just been said is the idea that sexual intercourse ought to be restricted to those who are married to each other as a means by which to confirm the very special feelings that the spouses have for each other. Because the culture teaches that sexual intercourse means that the strongest of all feelings for each other are shared by the lovers, it is natural that persons who are married to each other should be able to say this to each other in this way. Revealing and confirming verbally that these feelings are present is one thing that helps to sustain the relationship; engaging in sexual intercourse is another.

In addition, this account would help to provide a framework within which to make sense of the notion that some sex is better than other sex. As I indicated earlier, the fact that sexual intimacy can be meaningful in the sense described tends to make it also the case that sexual intercourse can sometimes be more enjoyable than at other times. On this view, sexual intercourse will typically be more enjoyable where the strong feelings of affection are present than it will be where it is merely "mechanical." This is so in part because people enjoy being loved, especially by those whom they love. Just as we like to hear words of affection, so we like to receive affectionate behavior. And the meaning enhances the independently pleasurable behavior.

More to the point, moreover, an additional rationale for the prohibition on extramarital sex can now be developed. For given this way of viewing the sexual world, extramarital sex will almost always involve deception of a deeper sort. If the adulterous spouse does not in fact have the appropriate feelings of affection for the extramarital partner, then the adulterous spouse is deceiving that person about the presence of such feelings. If, on the other hand, the adulterous spouse does have the corresponding feelings for the extramarital partner but not toward the nonparticipating spouse, the adulterous spouse is very probably deceiving the nonparticipating spouse about the presence of such feelings toward that spouse. Indeed, it might be argued, whenever there is no longer love between the two persons who are married to each other, there is deception just because being married implies both to the participants and to the world that such a bond exists. Deception is inevitable, the argument might conclude, because the feelings of affection that ought to accompany any act of sexual intercourse can only be held toward one other person at any given time in one's life. And if this is so, then the adulterous spouse always deceives either the partner in adultery or the nonparticipating spouse about the existence of such feelings. Thus extramarital sex involves deception of this sort and is for this reason immoral even if no deception vis-à-vis the occurrence of the act of adultery takes place.

What might be said in response to the foregoing arguments? The first thing that might be said is that the account of the connection between sexual intimacy and feelings of affection is inaccurate. Not inaccurate in the sense that no one thinks of things that way, but in the sense that there is substantially more divergence of opinion than that account suggests. For example, the view I have delineated may describe reasonably accurately the concept of the sexual world in which I grew up, but it does not capture the sexual *weltanschauung* of today's youth at all. Thus, whether or not adultery implies deception in respect to feelings depends very much on the persons who are involved and the way they look at the "meaning" of sexual intimacy.

Second, the argument leaves to be answered the question of whether it is desirable for sexual intimacy to carry the sorts of messages described above. For those persons for whom sex does have these implications, there are special feelings and sensibilities that must be taken into account. But it is another question entirely whether any valuable end—moral or otherwise—is served by investing sexual behavior with such significance. That is something that must be shown and not just assumed. It might, for instance, be the case that substantially more good than harm would come from a kind of demystification of sexual behavior: one that would encourage the enjoyment of sex more for its own sake and one that would reject the centrality both of the association of sex with love and of love with only one other person.

I regard these as two of the more difficult, unresolved issues that our culture faces today in respect to thinking sensibly about the attitudes toward sex and love that we should try to develop in ourselves and in our children. Much of the contemporary literature that advocates sexual liberation of one sort or another embraces one or the other of two different views about the relationship between sex and love.

One view holds that sex should be separated from love and affection. To be sure sex is probably better when the partners genuinely like and enjoy each other. But sex is basically an intensive, exciting sensuous activity that can be enjoyed in a variety of suitable settings with a variety of suitable partners. The situation in respect to sexual pleasure is no different from that of the person who knows and appreciates fine food and who can have a very satisfying meal in any number of good restaurants with any number of congenial companions. One question that must be settled here is whether sex can be so demystified; another, more important question is whether it would be desirable to do so. What would we gain and what might we lose if we all lived in a world in which an act of sexual intercourse was no more or less significant or enjoyable than having a delicious meal in a nice setting with a good friend? The answer to this question lies beyond the scope of this paper.

The second view seeks to drive the wedge in a different place. It is not the link between sex and love that needs to be broken; rather, on this view, it is the connection between love and exclusivity that ought to be severed. For a number of the reasons already given, it is desirable, so this argument goes, that sexual intimacy continue to be reserved to and shared with only those for whom one has very great affection. The mistake lies in thinking that any "normal" adult will only have those feelings toward one other adult during his or her lifetime—or even at any time in his or her life. It is the concept of adult love, not ideas about sex, that, on this view, needs demystification. What are thought to be both unrealistic and unfortunate are the notions of exclusivity and possessiveness that attach to the dominant conception of love between adults in our and other cultures. Parents of four, five, six, or even ten children can certainly claim and sometimes claim correctly that they love all of their children, that they love them all equally, and that it is simply untrue to their feelings to insist that the numbers involved diminish either the quantity or the quality of their love. If this is an idea that is readily understandable in the case of parents and children, there is no necessary reason why it is an impossible or undesirable ideal in the case of adults. To be sure, there is probably a limit to the number of intimate "primary" relationships that any person can maintain at any given time without the quality of the relationship being affected. But one adult ought surely be able to love two, three, or even six other adults at any one time without that love being different in kind or degree from that of the traditional, monogamous, lifetime marriage. And as between the individuals in these relationships, whether within a marriage or without, sexual intimacy is fitting and good.

The issues raised by a position such as this one are also surely worth exploring in detail and with care. Is there something to be called "sexual love" which is different from parental love or the nonsexual love of close friends? Is there something about love in general that links it naturally and appropriately with feelings of exclusivity and possession? Or is there something about sexual love, whatever that may be, that makes these feelings especially fitting here? Once again the issues are conceptual, empirical, and normative all at once: What is love? How could it be different? Would it be a good thing or a bad thing if it were different?

Suppose, though, that having delineated these problems we were now to pass them by. Suppose, moreover, we were to be persuaded of the possibility and the desirability of weakening substantially either the links between sex and love or the links between sexual love and exclusivity. Would it not then be the case that adultery could be free from all of the morally objectionable features described so far? To be more specific, let us imagine that a husband and wife have what is today sometimes characterized as an "open marriage." Suppose, that is, that they have agreed in advance that extramarital sex is—under certain circumstances—acceptable behavior for each to engage in. Suppose, that as a result there is no impulse to deceive each other about the occurrence or nature of any such relationships, and that no deception in fact occurs. Suppose, too, that there is no deception in respect to the feelings involved between the adulterous spouse and the extramarital partner. And suppose, finally, that one or the other or both of the spouses then have sexual intercourse in circumstances consistent with these understandings. Under this description, so the argument might conclude, adultery is simply not immoral. At a minimum, adultery cannot very plausibly be condemned either on the ground that it involves deception or on the ground that it requires the breaking of a promise.

At least two responses are worth considering. One calls attention to the connection between marriage and adultery; the other looks to more instrumental arguments for the immorality of adultery. Both issues deserve further exploration.

One way to deal with the case of the "open marriage" is to question whether the two persons involved are still properly to be described as being married to each other. Part of the meaning of what it is for two persons to be married to each other, so this argument would go, is to have committed oneself to have sexual relationships only with one's spouse. Of course, it would be added, we know that that commitment is not always honored. We know that persons who are married to each other often do commit adultery. But there is a difference between being willing to make a commitment to marital fidelity, even though one may fail to honor that commitment, and not making the commitment at all. Whatever the relationship may be between the two individuals in the case described above, the absence of any commitment to sexual exclusivity requires the conclusion that their relationship is not a marital one. For a commitment to sexual exclusivity is a necessary although not a sufficient condition for the existence of a marriage.

Although there may be something to this suggestion, as it is stated it is too strong to be acceptable. To begin with, I think it is very doubtful that there are many, if any, *necessary* conditions for marriage; but even if there are, a commitment to sexual exclusivity is not such a condition.

To see that this is so, consider what might be taken to be some of the essential characteristics of a marriage. We might be tempted to propose that the concept of marriage requires the following: a formal ceremony of some sort in which mutual obligations are undertaken between two persons of the opposite sex; the capacity on the part of the persons involved to have sexual intercourse with each other; the willingness to have sexual intercourse only with each other; and feelings of love and affection between the two persons. The problem is that we can imagine relationships that are clearly marital and yet lack one or more of these features. For example, in our own society, it is possible for two persons to be married without going through a formal ceremony, as in the commonlaw marriages recognized in some jurisdictions. It is also possible for two persons to get married even though one or both lacks the capacity to engage in sexual intercourse. Thus, two very elderly persons who have neither the desire nor the ability to have intercourse can, nonetheless, get married, as can persons whose sexual organs have been injured so that intercourse is not possible. And we certainly know of marriages in which love was not present at the time of the marriage, as, for instance, in marriages of state and marriages of convenience.

Counterexamples not satisfying the condition relating to the abstention from extramarital sex are even more easily produced. We certainly know of societies and cultures in which polygamy and polyandry are practiced, and we have no difficulty in recognizing these relationships as cases of marriages. It might be objected, though, that these are not counterexamples because they are plural marriages rather than marriages in which sex is permitted with someone other than with one of the persons to whom one is married. But we also know of societies in which it is permissible for married persons to have sexual relationships with persons to whom they were not married; for example, temple prostitutes, concubines, and homosexual lovers. And even if we knew of no such societies, the conceptual claim would still, I submit, not be well taken. For suppose all of the other indicia of marriage were present: suppose the two persons were of the opposite sex, suppose they participated in a formal ceremony in which they understood themselves voluntarily to be entering into a relationship with each other in which substantial mutual commitments were assumed. If all these conditions were satisfied, we would not be in any doubt about whether or not the two persons were married even though they had not taken on a commitment of sexual exclusivity and even though they had expressly agreed that extramarital sexual intercourse was a permissible behavior for each to engage in.

A commitment to sexual exclusivity is neither a necessary nor a sufficient condition for the existence of a marriage. It does, nonetheless, have this much to do with the nature of marriage: like the other indicia enumerated above, its presence tends to establish the existence of a marriage. Thus, in the absence of a formal ceremony of any sort, an explicit commitment to sexual exclusivity would count in favor of regarding the two persons as married. The conceptual role of the commitment to sexual exclusivity can, perhaps, be brought out through the following example. Suppose we found a tribe which had a practice in which all the other indicia of marriage were present but in which the two parties were *prohibited* ever from having sexual intercourse with each other. Moreover, suppose that sexual intercourse with others was clearly permitted. In such a case we would, I think, reject the idea that the two were married to each other and we would describe their relationship in other terms, for example, as some kind of formalized, special friendship relation—a kind of heterosexual "blood-brother" bond.

Compare that case with the following. Suppose again that the tribe had a practice in which all of the other indicia of marriage were present, but instead of a prohibition on sexual intercourse between the persons in the relationship there was no rule at all. Sexual intercourse was permissible with the person with whom one had this ceremonial relationship, but it was no more or less permissible than with a number of older persons to whom one was not so related (for instance, all consenting adults of the opposite sex). Although we might be in doubt as to whether we ought to describe the persons as married to each other, we would probably conclude that they were married and that they simply were members of a tribe whose views about sex were quite different from our own.

What all of this shows is that *a prohibition* on sexual intercourse between the two persons involved in a relationship is conceptually incompatible with the claim that the two of them are married. The *permissibility* of intramarital sex is a necessary part of the idea of marriage. But no such incompatibility follows simply from the added permissibility of extramarital sex.

These arguments do not, of course, exhaust the arguments for the prohibition on extramarital sexual relations. The remaining argument that I wish to consider—as I indicated earlier—is a more instrumental one. It seeks to justify the prohibition by virtue of the role that it plays in the development and maintenance of nuclear families. The argument, or set of arguments, might, I believe, go something like this.

Consider first a farfetched nonsexual example. Suppose a society were organized so that after some suitable age—say, 18, 19, or 20—persons were forbidden to eat anything but bread and water with anyone but their spouse. Persons might still choose in such a society not to get married. Good food just might not be very important to them because they have underdeveloped taste buds. Or good food might be bad for them because there is something wrong with their digestive system. Or good food might be important to them, but they might decide that the enjoyment of good food would get in the way of the attainment of other things that were more important. But most persons would, I think, be led to favor marriage in part because they preferred a richer, more varied, diet to one of bread and water. And they might remain married because the family was the only legitimate setting within which good food was obtainable. If it is important to have society organized so that persons will both get married and stay married, such an arrangement would be well suited to the preservation of the family, and the prohibitions relating to food consumption could be understood as fulfilling that function.

It is obvious that one of the more powerful human desires is the desire for sexual gratification. The desire is a natural one, like hunger and thirst, in the sense that it need not be learned in order to be present within us and operative upon us. But there is in addition much that we do learn about what the act of sexual intercourse is like. Once we experience sexual intercourse ourselves—and in particular once we experience orgasm—we discover that it is among the most intensive, short-term pleasures of the body.

Because this is so, it is easy to see how the prohibition upon extramarital sex helps to hold marriage together. At least during that period of life when the enjoyment of sexual intercourse is one of the desirable bodily pleasures, persons will wish to enjoy those pleasures. If one consequence of being married is that one is prohibited from having sexual intercourse with anyone but one's spouse, then the spouses in a marriage are in a position to provide an important source of pleasure for each other that is unavailable to them elsewhere in the society.

The point emerges still more clearly if this rule of sexual morality is seen as of a piece with the other rules of sexual morality. When this prohibition is coupled, for example, with the prohibition on nonmarital sexual intercourse, we are presented with the inducement both to get married and to stay married. For if sexual intercourse is only legitimate within marriage, then persons seeking that gratification which is a feature of sexual intercourse are furnished explicit social directions for its attainment; namely marriage.

Nor, to continue the argument, is it necessary to focus exclusively on the bodily enjoyment that is involved. Orgasm may be a significant part of what there is to sexual intercourse, but it is not the whole of it. We need only recall the earlier discussion of the meaning that sexual intimacy has in our own culture to begin to see some of the more intricate ways in which sexual exclusivity may be connected with the establishment and maintenance of marriage as the primary heterosexual, love relationships. Adultery is wrong, in other words, because a prohibition on extramarital sex is a way to help maintain the institutions of marriage and the nuclear family.

Now I am frankly not sure what we are to say about an argument such as this one. What I am convinced of is that, like the arguments discussed earlier, this one also reveals something of the difficulty and complexity of the issues that are involved. So, what I want now to do—in the brief and final portion of this paper—is to try to delineate with reasonable precision what I take several of the fundamental, unresolved issues to be.

The first is whether this last argument is an argument for the *immorality* of extramarital sexual intercourse. What does seem clear is that there are differences between this argument and the ones considered earlier. The earlier arguments condemned adulterous behavior because it was behavior that involved breaking of a promise, taking unfair advantage, or deceiving another. To the degree to which the prohibition on extramarital sex can be supported by arguments which invoke considerations such as these, there is little question but that violations of the prohibition are properly regarded as immoral. And such a claim could be defended on one or both of two distinct grounds. The first is that things like promise-breaking and deception are just wrong. The second is that adultery involving promise-breaking or deception is wrong because it involves the straightforward infliction of harm on another human being—typically the nonadulterous spouse—who has a strong claim not to have that harm so inflicted.

The argument that connects the prohibition on extramarital sex with the maintenance and preservation of the institution of marriage is an argument for the instrumental value of the prohibition. To some degree this counts, I think, against regarding all violations of the prohibition as obvious cases of immorality. This is so partly because hypothetical imperatives are less clearly within the domain of morality than are categorical ones, and even more because instrumental prohibitions are within the domain of morality only if the end they serve or the way they serve it is itself within the domain of morality.

What this should help us see, I think, is the fact that the argument that connects the prohibition on adultery with the preservation of marriage is at best seriously incomplete. Before we ought to be convinced by it, we ought to have reasons for believing that marriage is a morally desirable and just social institution. And this is not quite as easy or obvious a task as it may seem to be. For the concept of marriage is, as we have seen, both a loosely structured and a complicated one. There may be all sorts of intimate, interpersonal relationships which will resemble but not be identical with the typical marriage relationship presupposed by the traditional sexual morality. There may be a number of distinguishable sexual and loving arrangements which can all legitimately claim to be called *marriages.* The prohibitions of the traditional sexual morality may be effective ways to maintain some marriages and ineffective ways to promote and preserve others. The prohibitions of the traditional sexual morality may make good psychological sense if certain psychological theories are true, and they may be purveyors of immense psychological mischief if other psychological theories are true. The prohibitions of the traditional sexual morality may seem obviously correct if sexual intimacy carries the meaning that the dominant culture has often ascribed to it, and they may seem equally bizarre when sex is viewed through the perspective of the counterculture. Irrespective of whether instrumental arguments of this sort are properly deemed moral arguments, they ought not to fully convince anyone until questions like these are answered.

Study Questions

1. State two arguments given for the immorality of adultery, according to Wasserstrom.
2. Why is the breach of promise involved in adultery particularly hurtful, according to Wasserstrom?
3. How might adultery involve both active and passive deception, according to Wasserstrom?
4. In what way does sexual intimacy carry substantial meaning with it, according to Wasserstrom?
5. What are the two things wrong with the argument that adultery implies deception in respect to feelings, according to Wasserstrom?
6. Are there many necessary conditions for a relationship to be a marriage, according to Wasserstrom? Explain.
7. Is a commitment to sexual exclusivity a necessary or a sufficient condition for the existence of marriage, according to Wasserstrom? Explain.
8. How does the prohibition on extramarital sex help hold marriage together, according to Wasserstrom?
9. In what way is the argument that connects the prohibition of adultery to the preservation of marriage incomplete, according to Wasserstrom?

from *Having Love Affairs*

Richard Taylor

Richard Taylor (b. 1919) is Professor Emeritus of Philosophy at the University of Rochester. This selection is from his book *Having Love Affairs* (Buffalo, N.Y.: Prometheus Books, 1982).

Rules for Husbands, Wives, and Lovers

. . . What is needed, then, are rules that can serve as guides for persons married to or living with each other when one or the other is thought to be having an affair, and also rules for those involved in the affair. There is a need to cope with love affairs in ways that will at least improve upon the usual reactions of the sort just described and that will reduce the power of these reactions to destroy other precious relationships as well as individual personalities. The relationships and personalities so effected are not only their own, but often those of others, sometimes including children. It is not an easy task, but certainly we can improve upon the present practice of letting those who feel betrayed make up their own rules and then lash about with this immense destructive force.

* * *

We have to approach this goal by reaffirming a fundamental ethical principle. . . . namely, that every sane and mature person is ultimately responsible to himself, and that he cannot surrender this responsibility to anyone. Another way of expressing the same idea is that no one can assume the responsibility for another's behavior so as to be able to determine right and wrong for the other person. . . .

There are two obvious exceptions to all this; namely, children and the feeble-minded, who lack rationality and are rightly considered incompetent to decide many things for themselves, which includes matters of ultimate right and wrong. No one supposes, however, that people revert to the status of children or the feeble-minded just by getting married, though many husbands and wives treat their partners as if they assumed exactly that.

* * *

It is one of life's paradoxes that many people seem to assume the very opposite of what has just been said. That is, instead of assuming ultimate responsibility for their own conduct, which no one else may usurp, they seem to suppose that the first order of business in life is to shed it, to transfer to someone else the responsibility for their decisions and, oftentimes, their whole way of life. Thus there are people who will hardly take a step in the world without anxiously wondering how it will be viewed by others—by their church, for example, or by society as a whole, or by their neighbors. For most people, the mere admonition that an action is disapproved by the church, or frowned upon by one's community, is quite sufficient to justify the rejection of it; and in this unthinking rejection, which allows others to choose for them, they strangely suppose themselves to be following a path of morality. What they are actually doing is to remove their behavior from the realm of moral consideration altogether thus rendering themselves, in the strictest sense, irresponsible. . . .

It is in the light of all this that I am now going to propose rules or guidelines having to do with love affairs, considering first the rules for people who believe their partners are so involved, and then rules for those who are engaged in a love affair. The point of each proposed rule is exactly the same, namely, to reduce or eliminate the fiercely destructive power of these relationships, and to promote the love, kindness, and respect between people that is so vastly more precious than the kind of free-wheeling moralizing and condemnation that seems so appropriate to some individuals and groups.

Rule One: Do not spy or pry.

By spying I mean any devious effort to learn whether someone is having an affair, regardless of who initiates the probe: a husband, a wife, or the partner of a marriage relationship. Its worst form is to watch, or arrange for others to watch, someone's comings and goings; but of course it also includes surreptitious looking at mail, eavesdropping, poking through waste paper, and things of this sort.

That such behavior violates the principle enunciated above is obvious, as it betrays a total lack of confidence in another person's judgment and determination of his own conduct, thus amounting to a declaration that he or she cannot be trusted. But, in addition to this, it is degrading to the spying partner. To be reduced to fishing through wastebaskets or pockets, putting one's ear to doors or telephone receivers, or, worse yet, engaging an ally to watch and report, is inherently ignominious and degrading.

But, one is tempted to reply, he or she "has a right to know." Not quite. One has perhaps a keen desire to know, but a right only to ask. Asking is, with respect to matters of this sort, the only acceptable form of inquiry. A suspected wrong on the part of one person cannot justify a clear and incontestable wrong, such as spying would be, on the part of another.

Moreover, besides being inherently disgraceful, spying is a clear breach of faith, or infidelity, in the strictest sense. It is an injury to the person spied on, of a kind that needs no more to be tolerated within marriage or a marriage relationship than within any other. To spy on a friend would be equivalent to declaring that no friendship exists at all, and a lesser standard can hardly apply within the closest and most intimate kind of friendship. Just as a person forfeits a friendship by turning from friend into spy, so too does a wife or husband, for example, forfeit a marriage in its meaningful sense. . . .

Beyond the ethical objections already offered, there is another, purely practical matter of immense significance: A spying person risks forever losing the respect and with it the love of the person spied upon, and in so doing probably contributes more to the destruction of the relationship than any third person ever could. Consider, for example, a wife who confronts her husband with a tender note ferreted from a wastebasket, or a snapshot lifted from his wallet, or telltales dug out of his pockets. She *wins*, at one level; that is, she proves her point, and the more so if such things constitute proof that he has lied to her. But she also *loses* something less abstract, namely, her husband's respect, and she runs a great risk of losing him as well. She is then likely to lay the blame for this not on herself, where it belongs, but on the outsider who she considers to be behind it. No husband can abide being treated like a child or a fool, even when he may appear to be his wife to be acting like one; nor can he long feel affection for anyone who treats him so, or admire someone who debases herself by such spying behavior. The same, of course, follows for any wife. . . .

Rule Two: Do not confront or entrap.

The one who feels forsaken and deceived is sometimes tempted to walk right in on the partner, trapping her or him in circumstances with a third person where no out is available. Here the aim is not, of course, to find out what is going on, since this appears to be already known, but to humiliate in the most effective and devastating manner possible. Thus a husband or wife will return home a day earlier than announced, or turn up unexpectedly at some likely place such as a motel to which the partner has been followed. Certainly a more total victory cannot be imagined. There is nothing the "guilty" party can do when "caught" but collapse in total mortification, and to this is added the relish of a devastating humiliation delivered to the third person. . . .

. . . [T]he deliberate effort to entrap or confront is a blow that must not ever be delivered, for reasons that are already obvious. To entrap someone is not merely to treat him like a child or a nonperson, as spying does. Worse than this, it treats him as a foe, as someone to be injured in pride and self-respect in a singularly hideous way. Now, to be sure, someone might in fact feel exactly that way toward his partner. But then certainly the questions to be asked are: Who has been faithless to the promise of love? Who has withdrawn the respect and affection upon which any love must rest? Whose actions have actually destroyed the relationship?

* * *

Here, one is tempted to say that sexual infidelity by itself is the ultimate faithlessness, such that no response to it can be inappropriate, and that when it occurs the relationship is already bankrupt. The one who is forsaken might as well salvage his or her remaining pride by gaining the final satisfaction that possessing clear proof of infidelity brings, thereby rubbing the mate's nose in it for the sweet and final relish.

This is beyond a doubt the fundamental and most widespread error in people's thinking on these matters; namely, that infidelity is of necessity sexual, and that an adulterous partner in marriage, for example, proves by his or her very actions that love for the other is dead and that the marriage now exists in appearance and name only. People do think this way, but it is totally the result of cultural conditioning, besides being completely false.

A Moslem man believes that if his wife is raped, by enemy soldiers for example, then she is irrevocably defiled and no longer fit to live with, so she is simply discarded. We look upon such an attitude as heartless and primitive, as one that could not exist in any intelligent and enlightened mind. But our own attitude towards sexual inconstancy is no less mindless and irrational. Like that of the Moslem man, ours is the product of nothing more than religious and cultural conditioning. Our emotional reaction to it is likely to be intense, but it is no less irrational. Like the Moslem's, it is a dreadfully destructive reaction.

Nature did not make us monogamous, nor was it ever decreed that a man's or a woman's every need could be met, finally and always, by some one person. Sometimes sexual infidelity is a mere act of playfulness, without significance, and it should be treated as such by being completely ignored. Even to wonder or inquire about it is to go too far, by giving it an importance, however small, that it simply lacks. On the other hand, sexual intimacy can involve very deep feelings, and it can assume tremendous significance in a person's life. Married people can, in fact, fall in love with outsiders. To say they should not is beside the point, for they do. Nor is this any sign of weakness or moral laxity; on the contrary, weakness is far more apt to lie on the side of those law abiding and unimaginative persons who simply never expose themselves to temptation and who take a complacent, even sometimes a disgusting pride in their strict but fundamentally timid adherence to conventional standards.

People who are strong, good, even noble, and who are utterly devoted to their own partners, nevertheless occasionally become entangled in love affairs with others. No exhortations from pulpits, no reminders of vows or promises, no inner resolutions are going to change this fact. The terse "Thou shalt not" long ago ceased to deserve any but the most simple-minded tribute. To think that even the strictest ethic of marriage can consist of this command alone is to dishonor husbands and wives by supposing that they have little capacity for feeling and thought and are unable to rise to a higher standard of conduct than to be conditioned, like apes, to a largely groundless taboo.

It is also insufficiently appreciated that while a love affair is likely to have an intense impact upon the personalities of the two people immediately involved, it is apt to be temporary in the case of people who are married, and the feelings elicited are almost never as rich and meaningful as either partner already has for the husband or wife who is there in the background. Sometimes, to be sure, a wife or husband leaves to marry someone else, but, by the very nature of things, this happens only in those cases where profound needs were unmet in the original marriage. Shortly, we shall consider this type of situation. But for now consider the case of a perfectly happy marriage wherein one or the other partner becomes entangled in a love affair. This cannot happen, you say. But it does, and fairly often. Nothing on earth is perfect. Every man, for example, has a boundless ego, and even though he can imagine no woman more wonderful than the partner he has, he can easily imagine someone in addition to her, and often finds himself in the company of such women. Similarly, a woman may feel in every way blessed in the partner she has, but this does not mean that she will take no notice of someone who, for example, appreciates elements in her personality or talents to which her partner is somewhat insensitive. To suppose otherwise is to presume a kind of human nature that exists nowhere on earth. What, then, of a happily married wife and mother who becomes infatuated with her English professor? Or the sincerely devoted husband and father whose animal vigor seems to him suddenly and rather overwhelmingly evoked by his secretary? The mere description of such things suggests, in its banality, the proper assessment of them; namely, that love affairs arising from circumstances like these are destined to be temporary and probably brief if left to themselves. Not much can actually be made of someone's admiration of a poetic soul, or of a woman's apparent sense of collapse in the presence of sheer prowess in a man who impresses her. Very little indeed—but love affairs can be made of such things. And because the basis of these relationships is of such limited value, the affairs are likely to be of limited duration.

Putting all of this another way, we can say that a couple who have had a long and happy marriage have innumerable things holding them together, and the product of all these things is a sincere and meaningful devotion to each other. There are memories that stretch over years, many things have been undertaken together, the successes and the failures; there are likely to be children and all the memories and feelings associated with their upbringing, and so on endlessly. Such a marriage can withstand many assaults and buffetings and still remain, not wholly intact, but not really damaged either, so far as the relationship itself is concerned. If things are left to themselves, anyone having such a marriage will never abandon it in favor of a relationship that is likely to be based upon only one or two things of comparatively trivial value. The appreciation of a woman's poetic skill, her loveliness, or her felt need for more esteem than she has, may easily lead her to the singular thrill of forbidden and passionate love, but it will not by itself lead her to the destruction of a marriage that is, of inestimably greater worth to her. Similarly, the lure of sex, in and of itself, will easily lead almost any man into an affair, even at considerable risk, but he will never let that destroy the good marriage he already has. Not, that is, if things are left to take their course.

And that brings us to our next rule.

Rule Three: Stay out of it.

What, then, is to be done, when one is almost sure one's partner is having an affair? Nothing, really, except to try to cultivate a certain attitude of serene confidence which will serve to put things back in order more effectively than anything else. It is almost impossible not to feel jealousy and resentment, and sometimes an appalling sense of insecurity, but these should be concealed, or at least expressed to some sympathetic ear other than that of the wandering mate. Beyond that, the most effective instrument, both for the preservation of one's own self-respect and sense of balance and for putting things in their true perspective, is a sense of humor from which you are careful to exclude any bite or edge. A husband of middle age, for example, whose ego seems suddenly carried aloft by the blandishments of a young, shallow, and bosomy nurse—secretary, student, or whomever—can be fairly comical. He views everything with gravity, finds inestimable virtue and nobility where none was apparent before, is borne down by the tragic overtones of these overpowering circumstances, and solemnly plays out the comic role until, sooner or later, he sees these new things for what they are worth, which is very little—provided, however, that things are left to run their course, without wife and friends leaping into the act. A wayward wife, on the other hand, spellbound by the first man who has ever appreciated her as a person—in other words,he nourishes her vanity—is not so comical, because she is not driven by the boundless ego of most men. The watchword for her husband should be patience rather than amusement; for in her case, too, things will run their course. . . .

What most often happens, however, when a husband or a wife finds out about an affair of the other, is everything that should not happen. That is, he (or she) throws himself (herself) into the act, becoming deeply and emotionally involved in it, enlisting the support of friends, and commencing, perhaps with their help, endless remonstrations and accusations. This never has any good result, other than the temporary release of emotion, and in fact produces exactly the result that should be prevented at all cost. The partners in this love affair now feel themselves beleaguered, friendless except for each other, and thus driven to each other's arms. Foolish as this may be, it is nevertheless virtually inevitable the moment any one makes a great thing of their affair, for the needs that drew them together to begin with are now vastly increased in intensity, and the road to destruction has been made clear.

* * *

Of course there is still the real possibility that an affair can destroy a marriage relationship. Wives do leave husbands of long standing, and husbands leave wives, in favor of others who appear on the scene. Marriage relationships that have no legal protection are even more vulnerable to this threat, which can become overwhelming and can drive one to the brink of breakdown when, in addition to the threat to home and affection, there is also a threat to one's security. This is especially threatening to numerous women, who have formed an economic dependence upon their husbands. It is clearly not enough, then, to say that someone thus threatened should just disregard what is going on, as though it were of the least importance.

But here what needs to be said once more is that no good marriage relationship can be threatened by a love affair so long as others keep out of it. A bad relationship can be endangered, and many do come to exactly this end: one partner or the other yields easily to the solicitations of what certainly looks like something better. We have to add, however, that no one is obligated to maintain a bad marriage anyway, and promises spoken long ago cannot still have meaning under these circumstances.

What is a bad marriage? Simply one in which no love exists on one or both sides. Regardless of what else may be said for such a home, how good it may look to the world, that its partners present the appearance of constancy, conspicuously adhering to every conventional standard and upholding the values that are honored everywhere, however appealing they may perhaps appear in a setting which includes beautiful children, that marriage has already failed in case love is not abundant in either partner. And it is, indeed, vulnerable to destruction by the first person who shows the slightest sign of offering a love to one partner that the other has withheld.

Thus, though a wife may be ever so dutiful, faultless, and virtuous in every skill required for the making of a home, if she lacks passion, then in a very real sense she already is without a husband, or he, at least, is without a wife. Similarly, a husband who is preoccupied with himself and his work, who is oblivious to the needs of his wife and insensitive to her vanities, who takes for granted her unique talents—whether they are significant or not—and who goes about his own business more or less as though she did not exist, has already withdrawn as a husband, except in name. . . .

What must be remembered by those persons who wish to condemn adultery is that the primary vow of marriage is to love, and that vow is not fulfilled by the kind of endless busyness exemplified in the industrious and ever generous husband or the dedicated homemaking wife. It is true that one of the partners in marriage may well be awakened to the startling realization that the other partner has been engaged in a full-fledged affair. What has to be stressed, however, is that the first infidelity may not have been committed by the one who is having an affair. The first and ultimate infidelity is to withhold the love that was promised, and which was originally represented as the reason for marriage to begin with. In such cases adultery is not infidelity, but a natural response to it. . . .

Rules About Feelings

Rule Four: Stop being jealous.

Jealousy is the most wrenching and destructive of human passions. Not only is it painful, but the pain is self-inflicted; and unlike most other emotions, no good ever comes from it, not even the release of tension or the assuaging of pride on the part of the jealous person. On the contrary, this passion is as destructive of oneself as it is of others.

Other emotions, even painful ones, are usually redeemed in some way, but not jealousy. Anger, for example, though ugly, is sometimes justified, and may even produce some genuinely worthwhile result, even if it consists of no more than the salvaging of an angry person's pride. Anger is sometimes called "righteous," although jealousy can never be so described. Anxiety, although painful, is seldom self-inflicted, and sometimes has its place in warding off actual evils. Pity, though unpleasant, can sometimes be tender and even ennobling. And resentment, to take still another passion is sometimes a goad to the correction of evils, such as injustice.

Jealousy, however, is never good for anything at all. It is a pain that is unredeemed, self-imposed, debilitating, ugly, and utterly destructive in its inward and outward effects. Rather than providing a kind of outlet for bad feelings, it has an amazing capacity for feeding on itself, festering away, nourishing depression, and defeating every good and generous impulse that could make itself felt. It does not even protect the pride of its victim, but on the contrary makes him more and more shameful both to himself and in the eyes of everyone else. To be overpowered by jealousy is the ultimate self-defeat. . . .

* * *

Jealousy always has its source in something almost as ugly as itself; namely, in the attitude of possessiveness towards another person. A man is likely to look upon his wife as *his* in the sense of a personal possession, and with this starting point he feels quite justified in imposing rules and restrictions just as he would upon any other thing to which he claims ownership. Thus the marriage relationship, which is supposed to inspire the most exalted love and friendship, becomes instead debased, reducing a partner to a mere chattel, a *thing*, or worse than this, a thing *owned*. . . .

. . . No human being can be owned. Even children are not literally the property of their parents, however much some parents may wish to think otherwise. How much less so, then, is an adult an item of property. Furthermore, apart from property rights, this kind of possessiveness is inconsistent with the most basic requirement of ethics: that a person be treated, always and by everyone, as a person and not as an object. And it is likewise inconsistent with the fundamental ethical requirement of any marriage relationship, which is, very simply, that its partners love each other.

* * *

These last two points need to be considered separately.

A mere *object* is without mind or will, and can therefore be dealt with as we please — unless, of course, it is something owned by someone else. In this case the manner in which we treat it bears on its owner's mind and will, that is, upon the interests of another person. But considering a thing apart from its relationship to persons, it is immune to injury, and has neither rights nor interests that can be violated. A person, on the other hand, has both mind and will. He has thoughts, feelings, purposes, aspirations, and interests. This gives an individual moral significance, and it matters overwhelmingly how he is treated. Indeed, his most basic interest is in the very treatment he receives from others, for his pride, self-esteem, and everything that gives him worth depends on it.

Since, then, a person, unlike a thing, is possessed of both mind and will, the most fundamental injury to him is to treat him as though he had neither. Such treatment consists precisely in substituting your *own* mind and will for his, which is exactly what happens when anyone asserts any right of possession whatever over another person. Thus, if it is a wife's wish to do something — for instance, to paint, to write, to travel, to earn an income, to have times and places of absolute privacy, or to enjoy the company of whomever she chooses — and her husband vetoes or annuls this desire, then he quite clearly is substituting his mind and will for hers, and is treating her as though she had neither. He treats her, in short, as an object. And whatever might be said of the conventional rules of marriage and of fidelity in their narrowest sense, it is doubtful whether there can be any more degraded standard of ethics than this. To treat a person as a mere object is not just *an* abuse of that person, but *the ultimate* abuse.

Generalizing from this, it is worth nothing that public moralists, most often represented by clergymen, who make it their primary business to set forth rules of morality for *others*, and even to get these rules of theirs passed into law, are not at all acting in accordance with any acceptable moral standard. They are doing the very opposite, by treating persons as though they were not persons but mere objects to be used and controlled. No civilized ethic can stand which excludes the idea of responsibility, and no responsibility can exist in anyone for those actions of his which are chosen, not by him, but by others. Through fear, law, and manipulation a moralist can sometimes achieve conformity to a rule that seems important to him, but he cannot thereby achieve anything remotely resembling morality.

With respect to the second point, namely, the requirement of love, it is quite obvious that possessive love, as it might be called, is no real expression of love at all, but its perversion. Loving an *object* is not really loving *it* at all; instead, it is an expression of self-love. A person who takes pride in his possessions, who glories in them, quite clearly does not love them for their own sake, but for his. They are just ornaments. A man's relationship to fine cars, buildings, or whatever, is exactly that of a woman's relationship to her jewelry. These are loved because they enhance their owners. It is as simple as that. Hence, for someone to love another individual possessively is precisely *not* to love that other, but only to love oneself. What must be remembered, however, is that partners of any marriage relationship are expected to love *each other*, and that *this* is the fundamental ethical requirement. There really is no other, except what is implied by this one. No one is ever asked to pledge lasting love *for himself*. This would be absurd. Accordingly, the moment that any husband or wife asserts any right of ownership over the other, at that moment the fundamental vow of marriage has been violated by withdrawing the love each swore to give, and substituting in its place a grotesque love of *oneself*. Here, it must be stressed again, is the basic infidelity or breach of faith. Sexual infidelity, as it is generally called, is at worst the expression of this more serious infidelity, namely, the corruption of love itself, and it is not always even that.

Rule Five: Stop feeling guilty.

A sense of shame and guilt is thought by some people to be the appropriate accompaniment to a love affair or, as it should be called in this context, an adulterous relationship. The very word "adultery" has the connotation of sin and guilt. This is the view of those who enjoy analyzing everything in terms of morality rather than common sense. That such feelings of guilt produce nothing but harm, that they are often a screen for the infliction of cruelties, that they produce lasting dislocations in the relationships of husbands and wives, these things do not matter to such people. Adultery, it is thought, is shameful, and no adulterer should be satisfied or complacent for having sunk to it. He should feel guilty. His feelings of guilt should be deep and intense, to match the gravity of his wrongdoing.

The idea is seldom expressed in just those terms, but it is nevertheless a familiar one—so familiar, in fact, that a husband or wife who is "faithless" (another guilt word) is apt to lapse, even wallow, in guilt without even pausing to think about it. It seems to some that the stain of wrongdoing will somehow be wiped away by that reaction; if one feels sorry enough for what has been done, then this will in some way compensate for having done it. . . .

* * *

. . . [G]uilt in such matters is a purely conditioned response. It is not written in the heavens, nor in nature, that guilt must accompany adultery as thunder accompanies lightning. The association has been wrought by men, and the sense of guilt that human beings have cast upon someone can just as surely and effectively be cast off. The sense of guilt does not accompany sexual indulgence *per se*; normally, none exists between married partners. It arises only in connection with sexual intimacy outside marriage, which means, outside a relationship that is plainly of human origin and creation. Nothing more clearly indicates that the sense of guilt is itself a social fabrication transmitted by each generation to the next. Its purpose is obvious, important, and perhaps even essential for much of our history; namely, to secure obedience to the prohibition of adultery. For the most part this has been a prohibition against the misuse of another man's property. Consciously or otherwise it is still perceived as such by persons who give the matter very little thought. The idea is simply that if people are made to associate guilt with a forbidden act, then they will not be likely to do it. There are parts of the world today, parts which would otherwise be called civilized, where adulterers are publicly stoned, flogged, or beheaded. We look upon such practices — many of which come to our attention quite regularly from Moslem countries — with shock and horror. But our own ethical ideas and practices concerning the rigid exclusiveness of sexual intimacy are often no less absurd; they are only less severe.

Many people believe that a love affair, however sincere, tender, and even perhaps inspiring it may be to its partners, is in some vague sense wrong, and that lovers should not feel quite right about it. Or in other words, they should feel guilty. That such feelings are destructive of those very relationships that the prohibition is meant to protect (i.e., marriages) is not thought to be relevant nor even much considered. It is believed that something not quite right has been done, and therefore those who did it ought not to feel good about themselves. They should feel a sense of guilt. Morality requires this. It does not occur to these people to ask whether there is really anything wrong with a love affair, or why anyone should have such guilt feelings. If they did ask this, they would realize that nothing has made it wrong except the reiteration of a purely human declaration. But what one human being thus declares, inspired by nothing but his own feelings, another can just as easily reject; and if a thousand people unite in saying "Thou shalt not," or if several generations do so, then it is still open to a single individual, having the same intelligence and reason as they, to turn a deaf ear to them. *No* moral obligation or prohibition can be laid upon one person by another, nor by a thousand others, whether they speak in the name of religion, tradition, or whatever. To deny this is to deny the possibility of any morality at all. To do something, or to refrain from something, just because one has been told to do so is the abdication of responsibility, not the fulfillment of it. It is to take the easy way out.

With proper conditioning during childhood, a person can be made to feel guilty about anything. He can be made to feel guilty about his treatment of the symbols of whatever religion he has been taught to think of as "his," such as a book that has been described to him as sacred, special beads, holy water, or even the very words derived from such contexts. He can be made to feel guilty about eating pork, or beef, or raspberries; about what he does or even thinks in the privacy of his own home; about masturbating, or entertaining forbidden images; about valuing his own life when others declare he should be willing to give it up for his country to assure the security of things they value; and so on, without end. It should be added that a person can also be made to feel guilty about adultery, and many in fact do. The sense of guilt here is so avidly kindled by society, even today, that otherwise enlightened and intelligent people still take for granted that one *should*, after all, feel some guilt about this. They do not very often ask why. It is merely the mindless repetition of what they have been told . . .

Rule Six: Don't give it away.

There is on the part of some men a strange and perverse need to have their love affairs discovered, even when this means the almost certain ruination of the affair itself and severe damage to their marriage or marriage relationships. Women are less predisposed to do this, and are thus more discreet. Men sometimes, and at least half deliberately, leave tender notes where their wives will find them, or leave telltales, such as pictures, or perhaps an item of jewelry. Rarely do they come right out and tell their wives what has been going on, unless this has been discovered anyway, or unless they are prompted by disordered feelings akin to shame or guilt, as already discussed; but they sometimes seem to come as close as they can, as if courting the excitement of risk. In response to the same inner workings of their minds, many men feel an urge to do something even more strange; namely, to arrange encounters between wives and lovers. In my talks with male students, a constantly recurring description had to do with encounters between two girls with whom they were simultaneously involved. Sometimes these were even agreed to by the girls in question. The man suggests, for example, that they might all have dinner together, or he invites one of them to a party he knows the other will be attending, and tells her so. One might wonder why any woman would go along with such a suggestion, and the acute discomfort of the situation proposed, but there is perhaps a natural desire on her part to meet, and thereby size up, a rival. The man, for his part, is put in the deliciously exciting position of beholding *two* beautiful people competing for his affection and, most delicious of all, possibly falling into overt rivalry or even a veritable fight before his very eyes or, better yet, the eyes of his friends. A man's ego can hardly hope for more. . . .

What is the explanation of all this? It is the male ego, and nothing more mysterious. A love affair is the most powerful fuel for that ego. When a man is loved not only by his wife, a woman whose love can be more or less taken for granted anyway, but also by another woman whose love can by no means be taken for granted, it is almost like breathing the excitement of life twice over. And then somehow to be able to convey to your wife, as if by accident, that you have this enviable blessing, that you are loved not just by her but by another, seems to many men to be nothing short of an authentication of their power and glory. Leaving notes or telltales for a wife to discover, and the joint presence of both women, are like unspoken boasts. Of course, if a man reflects upon it, he does not really want the message to be received, knowing that this will mean the end of everything. Still, the temptation is there. And even if his wife remains blind to the messages, he is nevertheless able to display to *himself* these reminders of manly glory. It is this alone that explains the impulse and temptation many men have to bring lovers and wives together in their own presence. There are probably no normal men who have not, in fact, indulged the fantasy of being made love to by two women at once; but the world being what it is, this usually has to remain a fantasy. Men settle for much less, such as the somewhat silly and incongruous arrangements just described.

But behavior of this kind is not only silly, it is worse than pointless. It is destructive. No woman was ever moved to awe or admiration for her husband upon discovering that he has proved irresistible to someone else, nor does it occur to her to put that interpretation on things. All she sees is a kind of childish display of egoism, not unlike a fowl spreading himself before two or three hens at once. Besides that, she sees a total disregard for her and her feelings. If she already dislikes her husband as a person even if not as an essential part of her home, which may be precious to her, then she may use her discovery of artfully placed notes and telltales for subtle efforts at blackmail. She might, for example, exercise less restraint henceforth in her spending, knowing that any protest by him can be effortlessly silenced. If, on the other hand, she has adored her husband up to now, then the effect of such discoveries is simply the damage, or even the total destruction, of that feeling, along with the demolition of her own pride and sense of worth. To say that she feels betrayed is, usually, to say the very least.

* * *

Do women ever behave in a similar fashion? That is, do they leave notes and telltales? Certainly not from any similar motive. It is usually no part of a woman's proof of her femininity to be found to have many lovers, as it is, strangely, the proof of a man's masculinity, as he is apt to imagine. A woman's inclination to have but one lover is usually as strong as a man's inclination to have many, for reasons already explored, and this augments the very practical reasons she has for maintaining the strictest secrecy concerning any love affair. . . .

Yet a wife will sometimes quite deliberately let it be discovered that she has, or has had, an affair—typically for one of two motives. For one thing, she may use this means to express her resentment of her husband, for whatever reason, particularly if she can easily afford to lose him, and would like to. Such a discovery can be as severe a blow to a husband's ego as his similar behavior is a blow to his wife's vanity or, as it should perhaps be called, self-esteem. The other motive would be to even a score. That is, a wife whose husband has carried on an affair has a certain inducement to have one too, however briefly and casually, and to let it be known that she has, just in order to show that she can. Affairs of this sort, however, are not likely to be serious, and cannot even really be called love affairs, as we have been using the term.

In any case, the tendency of a wife to betray her own love affair is usually so minimal as to be almost nonexistent, arising only in special and more or less harmless circumstances. The similar tendency of a man, on the other hand, is strong and constant. The rule that emerges, therefore, really applies mostly to men, and consists simply in this: Do not tell, hint at, or in any way betray the fact of such a love affair; but on the contrary, scrupulously guard its secrecy, at least from your wife, until it has been buried in the past—and work to bring that ending about as gently and decorously as you can.

* * *

What then, of the requirement of truth? Is it not the first obligation of friends and, above all, of husbands and wives? Should they not, therefore, be open and candid, not merely conveying by hints and discoveries, but openly admitting any infidelity?

That kind of thinking, which is quite common among people who are intelligent, thoughtful, and reflective by nature, expresses the worst and most destructive kind of empty moralizing about marriage. For in the first place, candor is *not* the first obligation of husbands and wives. The first obligation is to love, and a direct consequence of that love is the desire not to injure. Quite apart from this, at a purely practical level, we are presupposing here a marriage that is good and should be kept together. It can hardly be a moral requirement to destroy the marriage.

To be sure, marriages and marriage relationships are sometimes not good. All are less than perfect, many are bad, and husbands and wives seem on the whole as capable of despising each other as they are of loving each other. If anyone wishes to further corrupt and perhaps even destroy such a marriage, he does have here, in the simple enunciation of truth, an effective tool. Before he uses it, however, he should know what he is doing. He should not pretend to himself or anyone else that he is somehow fulfilling some requirement of morality.

A fairly common way of thinking about this is to suppose that, if love flourishes between two partners, then no outside love affair should get started in the first place. But in case it does, through some moral weakness on the part of one or the other, then what is required is a complete and full confession, so that everything can be put back in order and the marriage relationship can be resumed with a clean slate. The requirement of honesty can be met by nothing less.

But see the absurdities thus exhibited under the label of morality. The first is to suppose that feelings are somehow chosen, that just as one chooses a wife or partner, he also, at that same moment, chooses to be something other than what nature has made him, namely, something other than a person with a vast capacity for loving other people and a strong inclination to do so. To be sure, one need not act on every impulse, but also we can hardly be expected never to act on them. People are not loveless machines. Second, it is supposed that a love affair is a sign of some kind of weakness, a view that is fairly characteristic of women, but less so of men. A fulfilled and happily married woman sometimes withstands temptations to other loves, for the temptations themselves are apt to be weak. It is not so with a happily married man. He may indeed withstand those temptations, but it is no sign of weakness if he does not. Weakness is more likely to be, in fact, on the other side, that is, with men who fear emotional involvement, are uncertain of themselves, dread scandal, and generally crave the security of safe or even sometimes boring conventional relationships. If some man were to resolve, for whatever whimsical reason, to go about for a whole year on only one foot, even though the other was perfectly healthy, then in a superficial sense he could be accused of weakness in case he gave up on this, finally yielding to the urge to use both feet. But he would more reasonably be accused of stupidity for having undertaken such a project.

The grossest absurdity in the view before us, however, is the supposition that some sort of moral slate is in some abstract way wiped clean by a confession of sin. The motives for confession, as we have noted, are self-serving and sometimes also malicious; they are never really moral, though morality is, as with so many things, a good camouflage to their true and unseemly nature. Moreover, whatever may be the effect on this nebulous moral slate, the effect of disclosing a love affair to someone you genuinely care for is a devastatingly cruel one, and the damage to the marriage relationship itself is often irreparable.

Perhaps the world would be good if everyone were unshakably monogamous, if every husband and every wife entirely fulfilled every need of the other, if other persons never appeared on the scene to disrupt these happy arrangements or, if they did, then no lasting disruptions ever occurred—though it is far from obvious that this would really be good. In fact, however, people are very complex, and we are all subject to drives of overwhelming power that we never chose for ourselves. There can be no blame in these, nor in us for having them. Sometimes it is the unexpected in life, the unforeseeable dramas, the involvements of feelings whose richness we may perhaps not even have suspected, the sudden coming to life of what were heretofore quiet dreams, sometimes it is these things that give our inner lives and emotions their special flavor and even, sometimes, quicken creative powers and enable us to see things in new lights that we did not know were real. All such departures from what is standard, allowable, conventional, and above all, safe, are filled with dangers to things in the world that we cherish, such as our fond preconceptions, even our homes and families. The solution is not to thrust our heads in the sand and pretend these things never happen, nor to embrace the standard and conventional, as though it were a great blessing to do so, nor, above all, to condemn all that lies outside that small circle as immoral. Instead, the right approach is to minimize destruction, not merely by avoiding risk, but by knowing why you do what you do, and anticipating the possible consequences.

Study Questions

1. What is the fundamental ethical principle that Taylor cites at the beginning of his essay? What exceptions to it does he mention? Do people tend to agree with this principle, according to Taylor?
2. Explain what Taylor means by saying, "Do not spy or pry." How does such activity violate the principle mentioned in question 1, according to Taylor?
3. Does an individual have the right to know whether his or her partner is unfaithful, according to Taylor? Explain.
4. What is Taylor's response to the idea that infidelity is the ultimate faithlessness?
5. Is infidelity first committed by the first partner to have an affair, according to Taylor? Explain.
6. What is wrong with jealousy, in Taylor's opinion?
7. Should the partner who has become involved in an affair feel guilty, according to Taylor? How does the feeling of guilt originate, in his opinion?
8. Explain why candor is not the first obligation of husbands and wives, in Taylor's estimation.

Pornography

In the next reading, Ann Garry addresses not only whether pornography should be censored but also whether its content is morally objectionable because it degrades women. (We are omitting section II of the paper, which discusses the empirical claim that viewing pornography increases the callousness of one's sexual attitudes and behavior.) After a few preliminary remarks in section I, Garry, in section III, finds that the content in some pornographic films in which women are treated as sex objects does indeed degrade women and is thus morally objectionable.

She then examines the connection between losing respect for a woman and treating her as a sex object. She calls attention to a "traditional" or "proper" view, according to which women are to be respected because they are more pure, delicate, and fragile than men; given this traditional view, pornography, which depicts women in general engaging in inappropriate behavior, can easily be viewed as disrespectful to women. But feminists, Garry maintains, believe that this traditional view assigns to all women a secondary status and, accordingly, reject this analysis of why pornography degrades women. The real reason pornography degrades women, Garry suggests (tangentially to discussing whether a person who objects to treating women as sex objects must believe that sex is dirty), is that in our culture we think of a sex object as a *harmed* object. Consequently, to treat a woman as a sex object is automatically to degrade her as less than fully human. This connection between sex and harm also makes clear, Garry explains, why it is worse to treat women as sex objects than to treat men as sex objects. Furthermore, the same connection can be used, Garry explains, to resolve a dispute about pornography and women; the dispute is between those who, like Susan Brownmiller, regard the purpose of pornography as to degrade women and those who maintain that pornography treats men as sex objects, too.

Finally, in section IV, Garry explains that it is possible for pornography to have a nonsexist, morally acceptable content—if important changes come about in our conceptions of gender roles and sex.

Pornography and Respect for Women

Ann Garry

Pornography, like rape, is a male invention, designed to dehumanize women, to reduce the female to an object of sexual access, not to free sensuality from moralistic or parental inhibition. . . . Pornography is the undiluted essence of anti-female propaganda.

—Susan Brownmiller, *Against Our Will: Men, Women and Rape*[1]

It is often asserted that a distinguishing characteristic of sexually explicit material is the degrading and demeaning portrayal of the role and status of the human female. It has been argued that erotic materials describe the female as a mere sexual object to be exploited and manipulated sexually. . . . A recent survey shows that 41 percent of American males and 46 percent of the females believe that "sexual materials lead people to lose respect for women." . . . Recent experiments suggest that such fears are probably unwarranted.

—Presidential Commission on Obscenity and Pornography[2]

Ann Garry (b. 1943) teaches philosophy at California State University, Los Angeles. The following selection is from *Philosophy and Women,* edited by Sharon Bishop and Marjorie Weinzweig. (Wadsworth: Belmont, CA, 1979.) Section II has been deleted.

The kind of apparent conflict illustrated in these passages is easy to find in one's own thinking as well. For example, I have been inclined to think that pornography is innocuous and to dismiss "moral" arguments for censoring it because many such arguments rest on an assumption I do not share—that sex is an evil to be controlled. At the same time I believe that it is wrong to exploit or degrade human beings, particularly women and others who are especially susceptible. So if pornography degrades human beings, then even if I would oppose its censorship I surely cannot find it morally innocuous.

In an attempt to resolve this apparent conflict I discuss three questions: does pornography degrade (or exploit or dehumanize) human beings? If so, does it degrade women in ways or to an extent that it does not degrade men? If so, must pornography degrade women, as Brownmiller thinks, or could genuinely innocuous, nonsexist pornography exist? Although much current pornography does degrade women, I will argue that it is possible to have non-degrading, nonsexist pornography. However, this possibility rests on our making certain fundamental changes in our conceptions of sex and sex roles.

I

First, some preliminary remarks: Many people now avoid using 'pornography' as a descriptive term and reserve 'obscenity' for use in legal contexts. Because 'pornography' is thought to be a judgmental word, it is replaced by 'explicit sexual material,' 'sexually oriented materials,' 'erotica,' and so on.[3] I use 'pornography' to label those explicit sexual materials intended to arouse the reader or viewer sexually. I seriously doubt whether there is a clearly defined class of cases that fits my characterization of pornography. This does not bother me, for I am interested here in obvious cases that would be uncontroversially pornographic—the worst, least artistic kind. The pornography I discuss is that which, taken as a whole, lacks "serious literary, artistic, political, or scientific merit."[4] I often use pornographic films as examples because they generate more concern today than do books or magazines.

What interests me is not whether pornography should be censored but whether one can object to it on moral grounds. The only moral ground I consider is whether pornography degrades people; obviously, other possible grounds exist, but I find this one to be the most plausible.[5] Of the many kinds of degradation and exploitation possible in the production of pornography, I focus only on the content of the pornographic work. I exclude from this discussion (i) the ways in which pornographic film makers might exploit people in making a film, distributing it, and charging too much to see it; (ii) the likelihood that actors, actresses, or technicians will be exploited, underpaid, or made to lose self-respect or self-esteem; and (iii) the exploitation and degradation surrounding the prostitution and crime that often accompany urban centers of pornography.[6] I want to determine whether pornography shows (expresses) and commends behavior or attitudes that exploit or degrade people. For example, if a pornographic film conveys that raping a woman is acceptable, then the content is degrading to women and might be called morally objectionable. Morally objectionable content is not peculiar to pornography; it can also be found in nonpornographic books, films, advertisements, and so on. The question is whether morally objectionable content is necessary to pornography. . . .

III

The . . . argument I will consider is that pornography is morally objectionable, not because it leads people to show disrespect for women, but because pornography itself exemplifies and recommends behavior that violates the moral principle to respect persons. The content of pornography is what one objects to. It treats women as mere sex objects "to be exploited and manipulated" and degrades the role and status of women. In order to evaluate this argument, I will first clarify what it would mean for pornography itself to treat someone as a sex object in a degrading manner. I will then deal with three issues central to the discussion of pornography and respect for women: how "losing respect" for a woman is connected with treating her as a sex object; what is wrong with treating someone as a sex object; and why it is worse to treat women rather than men as sex objects. I will argue that the current content of pornography sometimes violates the moral principle to respect persons. Then, in Part IV of this paper, I will suggest that pornography need not violate this principle if certain fundamental changes were to occur in attitudes about sex.

To many people, including Brownmiller and some other feminists, it appears to be an obvious truth that pornography treats people, especially women, as sex objects in a degrading manner. And if we omit 'in a degrading manner,' the statement seems hard to dispute: How could pornography *not* treat people as sex objects?

First, is it permissible to say that either the content of pornography or pornography itself degrades people or treats people as sex objects? It is not difficult to find examples of degrading content in which women are treated as sex objects. Some pornographic films convey the message that all women really want to be raped, that their resisting struggle is not to be believed. By portraying women in this manner, the content of the movie degrades women. Degrading women is morally objectionable. While seeing the movie need not cause anyone to imitate the behavior shown, we can call the content degrading to women because of the character of the behavior and attitudes it recommends. The same kind of point can be made about films (or books or TV commercials) with other kinds of degrading, thus morally objectionable, content—for example, racist messages.[7]

The next step in the argument is to infer that, because the content or message of pornography is morally objectionable, we can call pornography itself morally objectionable. Support for this step can be found in an analogy. If a person takes every opportunity to recommend that men rape women, we would think not only that his recommendation is immoral but that he is immoral too. In the case of pornography, the objection to making an inference from recommended behavior to the person who recommends is that we ascribe predicates such as 'immoral' differently to people than to films or books. A film vehicle for an objectionable message is still an object independent of its message, its director, its producer, those who act in it, and those who respond to it. Hence one cannot make an unsupported inference from "the content of the film is morally objectionable" to "the film is morally objectionable." Because the central points in this paper do not depend on whether pornography itself (in addition to its content) is morally objectionable, I will not try to support this inference. (The question about the relation of content to the work itself is, of course, extremely interesting; but in part because I cannot decide which side of the argument is more persuasive, I will pass.[8]) Certainly one appropriate way to evaluate pornography is in terms of the moral features of its content. If a pornographic film exemplifies and recommends morally objectionable attitudes or behavior, then its content is morally objectionable.

Let us now turn to the first of our three questions about respect and sex objects: What is the connection between losing respect for a woman and treating her as a sex object? Some people who have lived through the era in which women were taught to worry about men "losing respect" for them if they engaged in sex in inappropriate circumstances find it troublesome (or at least amusing) that feminists — supposedly "liberated" women — are outraged at being treated as sex objects, either by pornography or in any other way. The apparent alignment between feminists and traditionally "proper" women need not surprise us when we look at it more closely.

The "respect" that men have traditionally believed they have for women — hence a respect they can lose — is not a general respect for persons as autonomous beings; nor is it respect that is earned because of one's personal merits or achievements. It is respect that is an outgrowth of the "double standard." Women are to be respected because they are more pure, delicate, and fragile than men, have more refined sensibilities, and so on. Because some women clearly do not have these qualities, thus do not deserve respect, women must be divided into two groups — the good ones on the pedestal and the bad ones who have fallen from it. One's mother, grandmother, Sunday School teacher, and usually one's wife are "good" women. The appropriate behavior by which to express respect for good women would be, for example, not swearing or telling dirty jokes in front of them, giving them seats on buses, and other "chivalrous" acts. This kind of "respect" for good women is the same sort that adolescent boys in the back seats of cars used to "promise" not to lose. Note that men define, display, and lose this kind of respect. If women lose respect for women, it is not typically a loss of respect for (other) women as a class but a loss of self-respect.

It has now become commonplace to acknowledge that, although a place on the pedestal might have advantages over a place in the "gutter" beneath it, a place on the pedestal is not at all equal to the place occupied by other people (i.e., men). "Respect" for those on the pedestal was not respect for whole, full-fledged people but for a special class of inferior beings.

If a person makes two traditional assumptions — that (at least some) sex is dirty and that women fall into two classes, good and bad — it is easy to see how that person might think that pornography could lead people to lose respect for women or that pornography is itself disrespectful to women.[9] Pornography describes or shows women engaging in activities inappropriate for good women to engage in — or at least inappropriate for them to be seen by strangers engaging in. If one sees these women as symbolic representatives of all women, then all women fall from grace with these women. This fall is possible, I believe, because the traditional "respect" that men have had for women is not genuine, wholehearted respect for full-fledged human beings but half-hearted respect for lesser beings, some of whom they feel the need to glorify and purify.[10] It is easy to fall from a pedestal. Can we imagine 41 percent of men and 46 percent of women answering "yes" to the question, "Do movies showing men engaging in violent acts lead people to lose respect for men?"?

Two interesting asymmetries appear. The first is that losing respect for men as a class (men with power, typically Anglo men) is more difficult than losing respect for women or ethnic minorities as a class. Anglo men whose behavior warrants disrespect are more likely to be seen as exceptional cases than are women or minorities (whose "transgressions" may be far less serious). Think of the following: women are temptresses; Blacks cheat the welfare system; Italians are gangsters; but the men of the Nixon administration are exceptions—Anglo men as a class did not lose respect because of Watergate and related scandals.

The second asymmetry concerns the active and passive roles of the sexes. Men are seen in the active role. If men lose respect for women because of something "evil" done by women (such as appearing in pornography), the fear is that men will then do harm to women—not the women will do harm to men. Whereas if women lose respect for male politicians because of Watergate, the fear is still that male politicians will do harm, not that women will do harm to male politicians. This asymmetry might be a result of one way in which our society thinks of sex as bad—as harm that men do to women (or to the person playing a female role, as in homosexual rape). Robert Baker calls attention to this point in "'Pricks' and 'Chicks'; A Plea for 'Persons'."[11] Our slang words for sexual intercourse—'fuck,' 'screw,' or older words such as 'take' or 'have'—not only can mean harm but have traditionally taken a male subject and a female object. The active male screws (harms) the passive female. A "bad" woman only tempts men to hurt her further.

It is easy to understand why one's proper grandmother would not want men to see pornography or lose respect for women. But feminists reject these "proper" assumptions: good and bad classes of women do not exist; and sex is not dirty (though many people believe it is). Why then are feminists angry at the treatment of women as sex objects, and why are some feminists opposed to pornography?

The answer is that feminists as well as proper grandparents are concerned with respect. However, there are differences. A feminist's distinction between treating a woman as a full-fledged person and treating her as merely a sex object does not correspond to the good-bad woman distinction. In the latter distinction, "good" and "bad" are properties applicable to groups of women. In the feminist view, all women are full-fledged people—some, however, are treated as sex objects and perhaps think of themselves as sex objects. A further difference is that, although "bad" women correspond to those thought to deserve treatment as sex objects, good women have not corresponded to full-fledged people; only men have been full-fledged people. Given the feminist's distinction, she has no difficulty whatever in saying that pornography treats women as sex objects, not as full-fledged people. She can morally object to pornography or anything else that treats women as sex objects.

One might wonder whether any objection to treatment as a sex object implies that the person objecting still believes, deep down, that sex is dirty. I don't think so. Several other possibilities emerge. First, even if I believe intellectually and emotionally that sex is healthy, I might object to being treated *only* as a sex object. In the same spirit, I would object to being treated *only* as a maker of chocolate chip cookies or *only* as a tennis partner, because only one of my talents is being valued. Second, perhaps I feel that sex is healthy, but it is apparent to me that you think sex is dirty; so I don't want you to treat me as a sex object. Third, being treated as any kind of object, not just a sex object, is unappealing. I would rather be a partner (sexual or otherwise) than an object. Fourth, and more plausible than the first three possibilities, is Robert Baker's view mentioned above. Both (i) our traditional double standard of sexual behavior for men and women and (ii) the linguistic evidence that we connect the concept of sex with the concept of harm point to what is wrong with treating women as sex objects. As I said earlier, 'fuck' and 'screw,' in their traditional uses, have taken a male subject, a female object, and have had at least two meanings: harm and have sexual intercourse with. (In addition, a prick is a man who harms people ruthlessly; and a motherfucker is so low that he would do something very harmful to his own dear mother.)[12] Because in our culture we connect sex with harm that men do to women, and because we think of the female role in sex as that of harmed object, we can see that to treat a woman as a sex object is automatically to treat her as less than fully human. To say this does not imply that no healthy sexual relationships exist; nor does it say anything about individual men's conscious intentions to degrade women by desiring them sexually (though no doubt some men have these intentions). It is merely to make a point about the concepts embodied in our language.

Psychoanalytic support for the connection between sex and harm comes from Robert J. Stoller. Stoller thinks that sexual excitement is linked with a wish to harm someone (and with at least a whisper of hostility). The key process of sexual excitement can be seen as dehumanization (fetishization) in fantasy of the desired person. He speculates that this is true in some degree of everyone, both men and women, with "normal" or "perverted" activities and fantasies.[13]

Thinking of sex objects as harmed objects enables us to explain some of the first three reasons why one wouldn't want to be treated as a sex object: (1) I may object to being treated only as a tennis partner, but being a tennis partner is not connected in our culture with being a harmed object; and (2) I may not think that sex is dirty and that I would be a harmed object; I may not know what your view is; but what bothers me is that this is the view embodied in our language and culture.

Awareness of the connection between sex and harm helps explain other interesting points. Women are angry about being treated as sex objects in situations or roles in which they do not intend to be regarded in that manner—for example, while serving on a committee or attending a discussion. It is not merely that a sexual role is inappropriate for the circumstances, it is thought to be a less fully human role than the one in which they intended to function.

Finally, the sex-harm connection makes clear why it is worse to treat women as sex objects than to treat men as sex objects, and why some men have had difficulty understanding women's anger about the matter. It is more difficult for heterosexual men than for women to assume the role of "harmed object" in sex; for men have the self-concept of sexual agents, not of passive objects. This is also related to my earlier point concerning the difference in the solidity of respect for men and for women; respect for women is more fragile. Despite exceptions, it is generally harder for people to degrade men, either sexually or nonsexually, than to degrade women. Men and women have grown up with different patterns of self-respect and expectations regarding the extent to which they deserve and will receive respect or degradation. The man who doesn't understand why women do not want to be treated as sex objects (because he'd sure like to be) would not think of himself as being harmed by that treatment; a woman might.[14] Pornography, probably more than any other contemporary institution, succeeds in treating men as sex objects.

Having seen that the connection between sex and harm helps explain both what is wrong with treating someone as a sex object and why it is worse to treat a woman in this way, I want to use the sex-harm connection to try to resolve a dispute about pornography and women. Brownmiller's view, remember, was that pornography is "the undiluted essence of anti-female propaganda" whose purpose is to degrade women.[15] Some people object to Brownmiller's view by saying that, since pornography treats both men and women as sex objects for the purpose of arousing the viewer, it is neither sexist, anti-female, nor designed to degrade women; it just happens that degrading of women arouses some men. How can this dispute be resolved?

Suppose we were to rate the content of all pornography from most morally objectionable to least morally objectionable. Among the most objectionable would be the most degrading—for example, "snuff" films and movies which recommend that men rape women, molest children and puppies, and treat nonmasochists very sadistically.

Next we would find a large amount of material (probably most pornography) not quite so blatantly offensive. With this material it is relevant to use the analysis of sex objects given above. As long as sex is connected with harm done to women, it will be very difficult not to see pornography as degrading to women. We can agree with Brownmiller's opponent that pornography treats men as sex objects, too, but we maintain that this is only pseudoequality: such treatment is still more degrading to women.[16]

In addition, pornography often exemplifies the active/passive, harmer/harmed object roles in a very obvious way. Because pornography today is male-oriented and is supposed to make a profit, the content is designed to appeal to male fantasies. Judging from the content of the most popular legally available pornography, male fantasies still run along the lines of stereotypical sex roles—and, if Stoller is right, include elements of hostility. In much pornography the women's purpose is to cater to male desires, to service the man or men. Her own pleasure is rarely emphasized for its own sake; she is merely allowed a little heavy breathing, perhaps in order to show her dependence on the great male "lover" who produces her pleasure. In addition, women are clearly made into passive objects in still photographs showing only close-ups of their genitals. Even in movies marketed to appeal to heterosexual couples, such as *Behind the Green Door*, the woman is passive and undemanding (and in this case kidnapped and hypnotized as well). Although many kinds of specialty magazines and films are gauged for different sexual tastes, very little contemporary pornography goes against traditional sex roles. There is certainly no significant attempt to replace the harmer/harmed distinction with anything more positive and healthy. In some stag movies, of course, men are treated sadistically by women; but this is an attempt to turn the tables on degradation, not a positive improvement.

What would cases toward the least objectionable end of the spectrum be like? They would be increasingly less degrading and sexist. The genuinely nonobjectionable cases would be nonsexist and nondegrading; but commercial examples do not readily spring to mind.[17] The question is: Does or could any pornography have nonsexist, nondegrading content?

IV

I want to start with the easier question: Is it possible for pornography to have nonsexist, morally acceptable content? Then I will consider whether any pornography of this sort currently exists.

Imagine the following situation, which exists only rarely today: Two fairly conventional people who love each other enjoy playing tennis and bridge together, cooking good food together, and having sex together. In all these activities they are free from hang-ups, guilt, and tendencies to dominate or objectify each other. These two people like to watch tennis matches and old romantic movies on TV, like to watch Julia Child cook, like to read the bridge column in the newspaper, and like to watch pornographic movies. Imagine further that this couple is not at all uncommon in society and that nonsexist pornography is as common as this kind of nonsexist sexual relationship. This situation sounds fine and healthy to me. I see no reason to think that an interest in pornography would disappear in these circumstances.[18] People seem to enjoy watching others experience or do (especially do well) what they enjoy experiencing, doing, or wish they could do themselves. We do not morally object to people watching tennis on TV; why would we object to these hypothetical people watching pornography?

Can we go from the situation today to the situation just imagined? In much current pornography, people are treated in morally objectionable ways. In the scene just imagined, however, pornography would be nonsexist, nondegrading, morally acceptable. The key to making the change is to break the connection between sex and harm. If Stoller is right, this task may be impossible while changing the scenarios of our sexual lives—scenarios that we have been writing since early childhood. (Stoller does not indicate whether he thinks it possible for adults to rewrite their scenarios or for social change to bring about the possibility of new scenarios in future generations.) But even if we believe that people can change their sexual scenarios, the sex-harm connection is deeply entrenched and has widespread implications. What is needed is a thorough change in people's deep-seated attitudes and feelings about sex roles in sex (sexual roles). Although I cannot even sketch a general outline of such changes here, changes in pornography should be part of a comprehensive program. Television, children's educational material, and nonpornographic movies and novels may be far better avenues for attempting to change attitudes; but one does not want to take the chance that pornography is working against one.

What can be done about pornography in particular? If one wanted to work within the current institutions, one's attempt to use pornography as a tool for the education of male pornography audiences would have to be fairly subtle at first; nonsexist pornography must become familiar enough to sell and be watched. One should realize too that any positive educational value that nonsexist pornography might have may well be as short-lived as most of the effects of pornography. But given these limitations, what could one do?

Two kinds of films must be considered. First is the short film with no plot or character development, just depicted sexual activity in which nonsexist pornography would treat men and women as equal sex partners.[19] The man would not control the circumstances in which the partners had sex or the choice of positions or acts; the woman's preference would be counted equally. There would be no suggestion of a power play or conquest on the man's part, no suggestion that "she likes it when I hurt her." Sexual intercourse would not be portrayed as primarily for the purpose of male ejaculation—his orgasm is not "the best part" of the movie. In addition, both the man and woman would express their enjoyment; the man need not be cool and detached.

The film with a plot provides even more opportunity for nonsexist education. Today's pornography often portrays the female characters as playthings even when not engaging in sexual activity. Nonsexist pornography could show women and men in roles equally valued by society, and sex equality would amount to more than possession of equally functional genitalia. Characters would customarily treat each other with respect and consideration, with no attempt to treat men or women brutally or thoughtlessly. The local Pussycat Theater showed a film written and directed by a woman (*The Passions of Carol*), which exhibited a few of the features just mentioned. The main female character in it was the editor of a magazine parody of *Viva.* The fact that some of the characters treated each other very nicely, warmly, and tenderly did not detract from the pornographic features of the movie. This should not surprise us, for even in traditional male-oriented films, lesbian scenes usually exhibit tenderness and kindness.

Plots for nonsexist films could include women in traditionally male jobs (e.g., long-distance truckdriver) or in positions usually held in respect by pornography audiences. For example, a high-ranking female Army officer, treated with respect by men and women alike, could be shown not only in various sexual encounters with other people but also carrying out her job in a humane manner.[20] Or perhaps the main character could be a female urologist. She could interact with nurses and other medical personnel, diagnose illnesses brilliantly, and treat patients with great sympathy as well as have sex with them. When the Army officer or the urologist engage in sexual activities, they will treat their partners and be treated by them in some of the considerate ways described above.

In the circumstances we imagined at the beginning of Part IV of this paper, our nonsexist films could be appreciated in the proper spirit. Under these conditions the content of our new pornography would clearly be nonsexist and morally acceptable. But would the content of such a film be morally acceptable if shown to a typical pornography audience today? It might seem strange for us to change our moral evaluation of the content on the basis of a different audience, but an audience today is likely to see the "respected" urologist and Army officer as playthings or unusual prostitutes—even if our intention in showing the film is to counteract this view. The effect is that, although the content of the film seems morally acceptable and our intention in showing it is morally flawless, women are still degraded.[21] The fact that audience attitude is so important makes one wary of giving wholehearted approval to any pornography seen today.

The fact that good intentions and content are insufficient does not imply that one's efforts toward change would be entirely in vain. Of course, I could not deny that anyone who tries to change an institution from within faces serious difficulties. This is particularly evident when one is trying to change both pornography and a whole set of related attitudes, feelings, and institutions concerning sex and sex roles. But in conjunction with other attempts to change this set of attitudes, it seems preferable to try to change pornography instead of closing one's eyes in the hope that it will go away. For I suspect that pornography is here to stay.[22]

Notes

1. (New York: Simon and Schuster, 1975), p. 394.
2. *The Report of the Commission on Obscenity and Pornography* (Washington, D.C., 1970), p. 201. Hereinafter, *Report.*
3. *Report,* p. 3, n. 4; and p. 149.
4. Roth v. United states, 354 U.S. 476, 489 (1957).
5. To degrade someone in this situation is to lower her/his rank or status in humanity. This is morally objectionable because it is incompatible with showing respect for a person. Some of the other moral grounds for objecting to pornography have been considered by the Supreme Court: Pornography invades our privacy and hurts the moral tone of the community. See Paris Adult Theatre I v. Slaton, 413 U.S. 49 (1973). Even less plausible than the Court's position is to say that pornography is immoral because it depicts sex, depicts an immoral kind of sex, or caters to voyeuristic tendencies. I believe that even if moral objections to pornography exist, one must preclude any simple inference from "pornography is immoral" to "pornography should be censored" because of other important values and principles such as freedom of expression and self-determination.
6. See Gail Sheehy, *Hustling* (New York: Dell, 1971) for a good discussion of prostitution, crime, and pornography.
7. Two further points need to be mentioned here. Sharon Bishop pointed out to me one reason why we might object to either a racist or rapist mentality in film: it might be difficult for a Black or a woman not to identify with the degraded person. A second point concerns different uses of the phrase 'treats women as sex objects.' A film treats a subject—the meaninglessness of contemporary life, women as sex objects, and so on—and this use of 'treats' is unproblematic. But one should not suppose that this is the same use of 'treats women as sex objects' that is found in the sentence 'David treats women as sex objects'; David is not treating the *subject* of women as sex objects.
8. In order to help one determine which position one feels inclined to take, consider the following statement: It is morally objectionable to write, make, sell, act in, use and enjoy pornography, in addition, the content of pornography is immoral; however, pornography itself is not morally objectionable. If this statement seems extremely problematic, then one might well be satisfied with the claim that pornography is degrading because its content is.
9. The traditional meaning of "lose respect for women" was evidently the one assumed in the Abelson survey cited by the Presidential Commission. No explanation of its meaning is given in the report of the study. See H. Abelson et al., "National Survey of Public Attitudes Toward and Experience With Erotic Materials," *Tech. Report,* vol. 6, pp. 1–137.
10. Many feminists point this out. One of the most accessible references is Shulamith Firestone, *The Dialectic of Sex: The Case for the Feminist Revolution* (New York: Bantam, 1970), especially pp. 128–32.
11. In Richard Wasserstrom, ed., *Today's Moral Problems* (New York: Macmillan, 1975), pp. 152–71; see pp. 167–71. Also in Robert Baker and Frederick Elliston, eds., *Philosophy and Sex* (Buffalo, N.Y.: Prometheus Books, 1975).
12. Baker, in Wasserstrom, *Today's Moral Problems,* pp. 168–169.
13. "Sexual Excitement," *Archives of General Psychiatry* 33 (1976), 899–909, especially p. 903. The extent to which Stoller sees men and women in different positions with respect to harm and hostility is not clear. He often treats men and women alike, but in *Perversion: The Erotic Form of Hatred* (New York: Pantheon, 1975), pp. 89–91, he calls attention to differences between men and women especially regarding their responses to pornography and lack of understanding by men of women's sexuality. Given that Stoller finds hostility to be an essential element in male-oriented pornography, and given that women have not responded readily to such pornography, one can speculate about the possibilities for women's sexuality: their

hostility might follow a different scenario; they might not be as hostile, and so on.

14. Men seem to be developing more sensitivity to being treated as sex objects. Many homosexual men have long understood the problem. As women become more sexually aggressive, some heterosexual men I know are beginning to feel treated as sex objects. A man can feel that he is not being taken seriously if a woman looks lustfully at him while he is holding forth about the French judicial system or the failure of liberal politics. Some of his most important talents are not being properly valued.

15. Brownmiller, *Against Our Will*, p. 394.

16. I don't agree with Brownmiller that the purpose of pornography is to dehumanize women; rather it is to arouse the audience. The differences between our views can be explained, in part, by the points from which we begin. She is writing about rape; her views about pornography grow out of her views about rape. I begin by thinking of pornography as merely depicted sexual activity, though I am well aware of the male hostility and contempt for women that it often expresses. That pornography degrades women and excites men is an illustration of this contempt.

17. Virginia Wright Wexman uses the film *Group Marriage* (Stephanie Rothman, 1973) as an example of "more enlightened erotica." Wexman also asks the following questions in an attempt to point out sexism in pornographic films:

    > Does it [the film] portray rape as pleasurable to women? Does it consistently show females nude but present men fully clothed? Does it present women as childlike creatures whose sexual interests must be guided by knowing experienced men? Does it show sexually aggressive women as castrating viragos? Does it pretend that sex is exclusively the prerogative of women under twenty-five? Does it focus on the physical aspects of lovemaking rather than the emotional ones? Does it portray women as purely sexual beings? ("Sexism of X-rated Films," *Chicago Sun-Times*, 28 March 1976.)

18. One might think, as does Stoller, that since pornography today depends on hostility, voyeurism, and sadomasochism (*Perversion*, p. 87), that sexually healthy people would not enjoy it. Two points should be noticed here, however: (1) Stoller need not think that pornography will disappear because hostility is an element of sexual excitement generally; and (2) voyeurism, when it invades no one's privacy, need not be seen as immoral; so although enjoyment of pornography might not be an expression of sexual health, it need not be immoral either.

19. If it is a lesbian or male homosexual film, no one would play a caricatured male or female role. The reader has probably noticed that I have limited my discussion to heterosexual pornography, but there are many interesting analogies to be drawn with male homosexual pornography. Very little lesbian pornography exists, though lesbian scenes are commonly found in male-oriented pornography.

20. One should note that behavior of this kind is still considered unacceptable by the military. A female officer resigned from the U.S. Navy recently rather than be court-martialed for having sex with several enlisted men whom she met in a class on interpersonal relations.

21. The content may seem morally acceptable only if one disregards such questions as, "Should a doctor have sex with her patients during office hours?" More important is the propriety of evaluating content wholly apart from the attitudes and reactions of the audience; one might not find it strange to say that one film has morally unacceptable content when shown tonight at the Pussycat Theater but acceptable content when shown tomorrow at a feminist conference.

22. Three "final" points must be made:

    1. I have not seriously considered censorship as an alternative course of action. Both Brownmiller and Sheehy are not averse to it. But as I suggested in note 5, other principles seem too valuable to sacrifice when other options are available. In addition, before justifying censorship on moral grounds one would want to compare pornography to other possible offensive material: advertising using sex and racial stereotypes, violence in TV and films, and so on.
    2. If my nonsexist pornography succeeded in having much "educational value," it might no longer be pornography according to my definition. This possibility seems too remote to worry me, however.
    3. In discussing the audience for nonsexist pornography, I have focused on the male audience. But there is no reason why pornography could not educate and appeal to women as well.

Earlier versions of this paper have been discussed at a meeting of the Society for Women in Philosophy at Stanford University, California State University, Los Angeles, Claremont Graduate School, Western Area Meeting of Women in Psychology, UCLA Political Philosophy Discussion Group, and California State University, Fullerton Annual Philosophy Symposium. Among the many people who made helpful comments were Alan Garfinkel, Jackie Thomason, and Fred Berger. This paper grew out of "Pornography, Sex Roles, and Morality," presented as a responding paper to Fred Berger's "Strictly Peeking: Some Views on Pornography, Sex, and Censorship" in a Philosophy and Public Affairs Symposium at the American Philosophical Association, Pacific Division Meeting, March 1975.

Study Questions

1. From the fact that the content of a pornographic film is morally objectionable, can one automatically infer that the film is morally objectionable, according to Garry? Explain.
2. What is the respect that men have traditionally believed they have for women, and why is it an outgrowth of a double standard, according to Garry?
3. What are the two asymmetries between respect for women and men, according to Garry?
4. Why do feminists reject the traditional explanation of why pornography is degrading to women, according to Garry?
5. Can you object to treating women as a sex object without believing that sex is dirty, according to Garry?
6. What is the real reason pornography degrades women, according to Garry?
7. Why is it worse to treat women as sex objects than to treat men that way, according to Garry?
8. What is the dispute that Garry uses the sex–harm connection to resolve, and how does she resolve the dispute?
9. How might it be possible for pornography to have a nonsexist, morally acceptable content, according to Garry?

Moral Evaluations of Sex

Often people characterize sexual activity as good or bad, as when they say that natural sex is good sex and perversion is bad. In the next reading, Sara L. Ruddick is concerned, first, with the characteristics of allegedly good sex and, second, with the moral significance of evaluations of sex. Here is an overview of the essay.

Ruddick starts by asking whether there is a specific morality that pertains to sex, or whether sex is to be evaluated solely by reference to general moral principles. She suggests that general moral principles are not easily applied to sexual activity.

She then considers three features in virtue of which some sexual activity is said to be better than others: pleasure, completeness, and naturalness. In other words, she wants to understand the idea that good sex is pleasurable, "complete," and "natural."

The section on the characteristics of sexual pleasure is pretty straightforward. The next section, on completeness, is a bit more difficult, because the concept of completeness, as applied to sex, is subtle. Roughly, Ruddick's idea is that in complete sex, the participants are mutually "embodied," mutually active, and mutually responsive to each other's desire.

In the next section, Ruddick analyzes the idea that good sex is "natural" and not "perverted." She says, "among the variety of objects and aims of sexual desire, I can see no other ground for selecting some as natural, except that they are of the type that can lead to reproduction." By "of the type that can lead to reproduction," Ruddick means they are *of a type* that could lead to reproduction *in normal physiological circumstances*; she isn't claiming that safe sex is perverted sex, for example. She also does not mean that a sex act that is not *intended* to achieve reproduction is perverted. Natural sexual desire is for *heterosexual genital activity*, certainly, not for reproduction. But what makes that desire natural is that it is "organized" so that, in normal circumstances, it could lead to reproduction. In this section, she also criticizes the notion that sexual acts can be classified as natural or perverted on the basis of their completeness.

Having examined the three primary characteristics of good sex, Ruddick next considers the benefit of sexual pleasure and the connection of that benefit with morality. Then, in turn, she discusses the moral significance of perversion and of completeness. Her view is that there is next to no moral significance in the perversity of unnatural sexual acts: there is no connection, she writes, between what is natural and what is good. This is not to say, of course, that some perversions are not immoral on independent grounds.

The longest discussion in the essay is about the moral significance of completeness. Her view here is that complete sex acts are morally superior because they have a tendency to resolve tensions fundamental to moral life and to produce emotions that are conducive to love, and because they involve respect for persons.

A few passages in this selection are moderately difficult. You may need to reread these a few times.

Better Sex

Sara L. Ruddick

Sara L. Ruddick (b. 1935) teaches at the New School for Social Research in New York City. The article reprinted here appeared in *Philosophy and Sex*, revised edition, edited by Robert Baker and Frederick Elliston (Buffalo, N.Y.: Prometheus Books, 1984).

It might be argued that there is no specifically sexual morality. We have, of course, become accustomed to speaking of sexual morality, but the "morality" of which we speak has a good deal to do with property, the division of labor, and male power, and little to do with our sexual lives. Sexual experiences, like experiences in driving automobiles, render us liable to specific moral situations. As drivers we must guard against infantile desires for revenge and excitement. As lovers we must guard against cruelty and betrayal, for we know sexual experiences provide special opportunities for each. We drive soberly because, before we get into a car, we believe that it is wrong to be careless of life. We resist temptations to adultery because we believe it wrong to betray trust, whether it be a parent, a sexual partner, or a political colleague who is betrayed. As lovers and drivers we act on principles that are particular applications of general moral principles. Moreover, given the superstitions from which sexual experience has suffered, it is wise to free ourselves, as lovers, from any moral concerns, other than those we have as human beings. There is no specifically sexual morality, and none should be invented. Or so it might be argued.

When we examine our moral "intuitions," however, the analogy with driving fails us. Unburdened of *sexual* morality, we do not find it easy to apply general moral principles to our sexual lives. The "morally average" lover can be cruel, violate trust, and neglect social duties with less opprobrium precisely *because* he is a lover. Only political passions and psychological or physical deprivation serve as well as sexual desire to excuse what would otherwise be seriously and clearly immoral acts. (Occasionally, sexual desire is itself conceived of as a deprivation, an involuntary lust. And there is, of course, a tradition that sees sexual morality as a way of controlling those unable to be sexless: "It is better to marry than to burn.") Often, in our sexual lives, we neither flout nor simply apply general moral principles. Rather, the values of sexual experience themselves figure in the construction of moral dilemmas. The conflict between better sex (more complete, natural, and pleasurable sex acts) and, say, social duty is not seen as a conflict between the immoral and compulsive, on one hand, and the morally good, on the other, but as a conflict between alternative moral acts.

Our intuitions vary but at least they suggest we can use "good" sex as a positive weight on some moral balance. What is that weight? Why do we put it there? How do we, in the first place, evaluate sexual experiences? On reflection, should we endorse these evaluations? These are the questions whose answers should constitute a specifically sexual morality.

In answering them, I will first consider three characteristics that have been used to distinguish some sex acts as better than others—greater pleasure, completeness, and naturalness. Other characteristics may be relevant to evaluating sex acts, but these three are central. If they have *moral* significance, then the sex acts characterized by them will be better than others not so characterized.

After considering those characteristics in virtue of which some sex acts are allegedly better than others, I will ask whether the presence of those characteristics renders the acts *morally* superior. I will not consider here the unclear and overused distinction between the moral and amoral, nor the illegitimate but familiar distinction between the moral and the prudent. I hope it is sufficient to set out dogmatically and schematically the moral notions I will use. I am confident that better sex is morally preferable to other sex, but I am not at all happy with my characterization of its moral significance. Ultimately, sexual morality cannot be considered apart from a "prudential" morality in which it is shown that what is good is good for us and what is good for us makes us good. In such a morality, not only sex, but art, fantasy, love, and a host of other intellectual and emotional enterprises will regain old mortal significances and acquire new ones. My remarks here, then, are partial and provisional.

A characteristic renders a sex act morally preferable to one without that characteristic if it gives, increases, or is instrumental in increasing the "benefit" of the act for the person engaging in it. Benefits can be classified as peremptory or optional. Peremptory benefits are experiences, relations, or objects that anyone who is neither irrational nor anhedonic will want so long as s/he wants anything at all. Optional benefits are experiences, relations, or objects that anyone, neither irrational nor anhedonic, will want so long as s/he will not lose a peremptory benefit. There is widespread disagreement about which benefits are peremptory. Self-respect, love, and health are common examples of peremptory benefits. Arms, legs, and hands are probably optional benefits. A person still wanting a great deal might give up limbs, just as s/he would give up life, when mutilation or death is required by self-respect. As adults we are largely responsible for procuring our own benefits and greatly dependent on good fortune for success in doing so. However, the moral significance of benefits is most clearly seen not from the standpoint of the person procuring and enjoying them but from the standpoint of another *caring* person, for example, a lover, parent, or political leader responsible for procuring benefits for specific others. A benefit may then be described as an experience, relation, or object that anyone who properly cares for another is obliged to attempt to secure for him/her. Criteria for the virtue of care and for benefit are reciprocally determined, the virtue consisting in part in recognizing and attempting to secure benefits for the person cared for, the identification of benefit depending on its recognition by those already seen to be properly caring.

In talking of benefits I shall be looking at our sexual lives from the vantage point of hope, not of fear. The principal interlocutor may be considered to be a child asking what s/he should rightly and reasonably hope for in living, rather than a potential criminal questioning conventional restraints. The specific question the child may be imagined to ask can now be put: In what way is better sex beneficial or conducive to experiences or relations or objects that are beneficial?

A characteristic renders a sex act morally preferable to one without that characteristic if either the act is thereby more just or the act is thereby likely to make the person engaging in it more just. Justice includes giving others what is due them, taking no more than what is one's own, and giving and taking according to prevailing principles of fairness.

A characteristic renders a sex act morally preferable to one without that characteristic if because of the characteristic the act is more virtuous or more likely to lead to virtue. A virtue is a disposition to attempt, and an ability to succeed in, good acts—acts of justice, acts that express or produce excellence, and acts that yield benefits to oneself or others.

Sexual Pleasure

Sexual experiences give rise to sensations and experiences that are paradigms of what is pleasant. Hedonism, in both its psychological and ethical forms, has blinded us to the nature and to the benefits of sensual pleasure by overextending the word "pleasure" to cover anything enjoyable or even agreeable.[1] The paradigmatic type of pleasure is sensual. Pleasure is a temporally extended, more or less intense quality of particular experiences. Pleasure is enjoyable independent of any function pleasurable activity fulfills. The infant who continues to suck well after s/he is nourished, expressing evident plea-

[1]This may be a consequence of the tepidness of the English "pleasant." It would be better to speak of lust and its satisfaction if our suspicion of pleasure had not been written into that part of our language.

sure in doing so, gives us a demonstration of the nature of pleasure.[2]

As we learn more about pleasant experiences we not only apply but also extend and attenuate the primary notion of "pleasure." But if pleasure is to have any nonsophistical psychological or moral interest, it must retain its connections with those paradigm instances of sexual pleasure that gives rise to it. We may, for example, extend the notion of pleasure so that particular episodes in the care of children give great pleasure; but the long term caring for children, however intrinsically rewarding, is not an experience of pleasure or unpleasure.

Sexual pleasure is a species of sexual pleasure with its own conditions of arousal and satisfaction. Sexual acts vary considerably in pleasure, the limiting case being a sexual act where no one experiences pleasure even though someone may experience affection or "relief of tension" through orgasm. Sexual pleasure can be considered either in a context of deprivation and its relief or in a context of satisfaction. Psychological theories have tended to emphasize the frustrated state of sexual desire and to construe sexual pleasure as a relief from that state. There are, however, alternative accounts of sexual pleasure that correspond more closely with our experience. Sexual pleasure is "a primary distinctively poignant pleasure experience that manifests itself from early infancy on. . . . Once experienced it continues to be savored. . . ."[3] Sexual desire is not experienced as frustration but as part of sexual pleasure. Normally, sexual desire transforms itself gradually into the pleasure that appears, misleadingly, to be an aim extrinsic to it. The natural structure of desire, not an inherent quality of frustration, accounts for the pain of an aroused but unsatisfied desire.

Sexual pleasure, like addictive pleasure generally, does not, except very temporarily, result in satiety. Rather, it increases the demand for more of the same while sharply limiting the possibility of substitutes. The experience of sensual pleasures, and particularly of sexual pleasures, has a pervasive effect on our perceptions of the world. We find bodies inviting, social encounters alluring, and smells, tastes, and sights resonant because our perception of them includes their sexual significance. Merleau-Ponty has written of a patient for whom "perception had lost its erotic structure, both temporally and physically."[4] As the result of a brain injury the patient's capacity for sexual desire and pleasure (though not his capacity for performing sexual acts) was impaired. He no longer sought sexual intercourse of his own accord, was left indifferent by the sights and smells of available bodies, and if in the midst of sexual intercourse his partner turned away, he showed no signs of displeasure. The capacity for sexual pleasure, upon which the erotic structure of perception depends, can be accidentally damaged. The question that this case raises is whether it would be desirable to interfere with this capacity in a more systematic way than we now do. With greater biochemical and psychiatric knowledge we shall presumably be able to manipulate it at will.[5] And if that becomes possible, toward what end should we interfere? I shall return to this question after describing the other two characteristics of better sex—completeness and naturalness.

Complete Sex Acts

The completeness of a sexual act depends upon the *relation* of the participants to their own and each other's *desire.* A sex act is complete if each

[2]The example is from Sigmund Freud, *Three Essays on Sexuality,* standard ed., vol. 7 (London: Hogarth, 1963), p. 182. The concept of pleasure I urge here is narrower but also, I think, more useful than the popular one. It is a concept that, to paraphrase Wittgenstein, we (could) learn when we learn the language. The idea of paradigmatic uses and subsequent more-or-less-divergent, more-or-less "normal" uses also is derived from Wittgenstein.

[3]George Klein, "Freud's Two theories of Sexuality," in L. Berger, ed., *Clinical-Cognitive Psychology, Models and Integrations* (Englewood Cliffs, N.J.: Prentice-Hall, 1969, pp. 131–81. This essay gives a clear idea of alternative psychological accounts of sexual pleasure.

[4]Maurice Merleau-Ponty, *Phenomenology of Perception,* trans. Colin Smith (London: Routledge & Kegan Paul, 1962), p.156.

[5]See Kurt Vonnegut, Jr., "Welcome to the Monkey House," in *Welcome to the Monkey House* (New York: Dell 1968), which concerns both the manipulation and the benefit of sexual pleasure.

partner allows him/herself to be "taken over" by an active desire, which is desire not merely for the other's body but also for her/his active desire. Completeness is hard to characterize, though complete sex acts are at least as natural as any others—especially, it seems, among those people who take them casually and for granted. The notion of "completeness" (as I shall call it) has figured under various guises in the work of Sartre, Merleau-Ponty, and more recently Thomas Nagel. "The being which desires is consciousness making itself body."[6] "What we try to possess, then, is not just a body, but a body brought to life by consciousness."[7] "It is important that the partner be aroused, and not merely aroused, but aroused by the awareness of one's desire."[8]

The precondition of complete sex acts is the "embodiment" of the participants. Each participant submits to sexual desires that take over consciousness and direct action. It is sexual desire and not a separable satisfaction of it (for example, orgasm) that is important here. Indeed, Sartre finds pleasure external to the essence of desire, and Nagel gives an example of embodiment in which the partners do not touch each other. Desire is pervasive and "overwhelming," but does not make its subject its involuntary victim (as it did the Boston Strangler, we are told), nor does it, except at its climax, alter capacities for ordinary perceptions, memories, and inferences. Nagel's embodied partners can presumably get themselves from bar stools to bed while their consciousness is "clogged" with desire. With what, then, is embodiment contrasted?

Philosophers make statements that when intended literally are evidence of pathology: "Human beings are automata"; "I never really see physical objects"; "I can never know what another person is feeling." The clearest statement of disembodiment that I know of is W. T. Stace's claim: "I become aware of my body in the end chiefly because it insists on accompanying me wherever I go."[9] What "just accompanies me" can also stay away. "When my body leaves me / I'm lonesome for it. / . . . body / goes away I don't know where / and it's lonesome to drift / above the space it / fills when it's here."[10] If "the body is felt more as one object among other objects in the world than as the core of the individual's own being,"[11] then what appears to be bodily can be disassociated from the "real self." Both a generalized separation of "self" from body and particular disembodied experiences have had their advocates. The attempt at disembodiment has also been seen as conceptually confused and psychologically disastrous.

We may often experience ourselves as relatively disembodied, observing or "using" our bodies to fulfill our intentions. On some occasions, however, such as in physical combat, sport, physical suffering, or danger, we "become" our bodies; our consciousness becomes bodily experience of bodily activity.[12] Sexual acts are occasions for such embodiment; they may, however, fail for a variety of reasons, for example, because of pretense or an excessive need for self-control. If someone is embodied by sexual desire, s/he submits to its direction. Spontaneous impulses of desire become her/his movements—some involuntary, like gestures of "courting behavior" or physical expressions of intense pleasure, and some deliberate. Her/his consciousness, or "mind," is taken over by desire and the pursuit of its object, in the way that at other times it may be taken over by an intellectual prob-

---

[6]Jean-Paul Sartre, *Being and Nothingness,* trans. Hazel E. Barnes (New York: Philosophical Library, 1956), p. 39.

[7]Merleau-Ponty, *Phenomenology of Perception,* p. 167.

[8]Thomas Nagel, "Sexual Perversion," *The Journal of Philosophy,* 66, no. 1 (January 16, 1969):13. . . . My original discussion of completeness was both greatly indebted to and confused by Nagel's. I have tried here to dispel some of the confusion.

[9]W. T. Stace, "Solipsism," from *The Theory of Knowledge and Existence,* reprinted in Tillman, Berofsky, and O'Connor, eds. *Introductory Philosophy* (New York: Harper & Row, 1967), p. 113.

[10]Denise Levertov, "Gone Away," in *O Taste and See* (New York: New Directions, 1962), p. 59. Copyright by Denise Levertov Goodman, New Directions Publishing Corporation, New York.

[11]R. D. Laing, *The Divided Self* (Baltimore: Pelican Books, 1965), p. 69.

[12]We need not become our bodies on such occasions. Pains, muscular feelings, and emotions can be reduced to mere "sensations" that may impinge on "me" but that I attempt to keep at a distance. Laing describes the case of a man who when beaten up felt that any damage to his body could not really hurt *him.* See *The Divided Self,* p. 68.

lem or by obsessive fantasies. But unlike the latter takeovers, this one is bodily. A desiring consciousness is flooded with specifically sexual feelings that eroticize all perception and movement. Consciousness "becomes flesh."

Granted the precondition of embodiment, complete sex acts occur when each partner's embodying desire is active and actively responsive to the other's. This second aspect of complete sex constitutes a "reflexive mutual recognition" of desire by desire.

The partner *actively* desires another person's desire. Active desiring includes more than embodiment, which might be achieved in objectless masturbation. It is more, also, than merely being aroused by and then taken over by desire, though it may come about as a result of deliberate arousal. It commits the actively desiring person to her/his desire and requires her/him to identify with it—that is, to recognize him/herself as a sexual agent as well as respondent. (Active desiring is less encouraged in women, and probably more women than men feel threatened by it.)

The other recognizes and responds to the partner's desire. Merely to recognize the desire as desire, not to reduce it to an itch or to depersonalize it as a "demand," may be threatening. Imperviousness to desire is the deepest defense against it. We have learned from research on families whose members tend to become schizophrenic that such imperviousness, the refusal to recognize a feeling for what it is, can force a vulnerable person to deny or to obscure the real nature of her/his feelings. Imperviousness tends to deprive even a relatively invulnerable person of her/his efficacy. The demand that our feelings elicit a response appropriate to them is part of a general demand that *we* be recognized, that our feelings be allowed to make a difference.

There are many ways in which sexual desire may be recognized, countless forms of submission and resistance. In complete sex, desire is recognized by a responding and active desire that commits the other, as it committed the partner. Given responding desire, both people identify themselves as sexually desiring the other. They are neither seducer nor seduced, neither suppliant nor benefactress, neither sadist nor victim, but sexual agents acting sexually out of their recognized desire. Indeed, in complete sex one not only welcomes and recognizes active desire, one desires it. Returned and endorsed desire becomes one of the features of an erotically structured perception. Desiring becomes desirable. (Men are less encouraged to desire the other's active and demanding desire, and such desiring is probably threatening to more men than women.)

In sum, in complete sex two persons embodied by sexual desire actively desire and respond to each other's active desire. Although it is difficult to write of complete sex without suggesting that one of the partners is the initiator, while the other responds, complete sex is reciprocal sex. The partners, whatever the circumstances of the coming together, are equal in activity and responsiveness of desire.

Sexual acts can be partly incomplete. A necrophiliac may be taken over by desire, and one may respond to a partner's desire without being embodied by one's own. Partners whose sexual activities are accompanied by private fantasies engage in an incomplete sex act. Consciousness is used by desire but remains apart from it, providing it with stimulants and controls. Neither partner responds to the other's desire, though each may appear to. Sartre's "dishonest masturbator," for whom masturbation is the sex act of choice, engages in a paradigmatically incomplete sex act: "He asks only to be slightly distanced from his own body, only for there to be a light coating of otherness over his flesh and over his thoughts. His personae are melting sweets. . . . The masturbator is enchanted at never being able to feel himself sufficiently another, and at producing for himself alone the diabolic appearance of a couple that fades away when one touches it. . . . Masturbation is the derealisation of the world and of the masturbator himself."[13]

Completeness is more difficult to describe than incompleteness, for it turns on precise but subtle

[13]Jean-Paul Sartre, *Saint Genet* (New York: Braziller, 1963), p. 398; cited and translated by R. D. Laing, *Self and Others* (New York: Pantheon, 1969), pp. 39–40.

ways of responding to a particular person's desire with specific expressions of impulse that are both spontaneous and responsive.

There are many possible sex acts that are pleasurable but not complete. Sartre, Nagel, and Merleau-Ponty each suggest that the desire for the responsive desire of one's partner is the "central impulse" of sexual desire.[14] The desire for a sleeping woman, for example, is possible only "in so far as this sleep appears on the ground of consciousness."[15] This seems much too strong. Some lovers desire that their partners resist, others like them coolly controlled, others prefer them asleep. We would not say that there was anything abnormal or less fully sexual about desire. Whether or not complete sex is preferable to incomplete sex (the question to which I shall turn shortly), incompleteness does not disqualify a sex act from being fully sexual.

Sexual Perversion

The final characteristic of allegedly better sex acts is that they are "natural" rather than "perverted." The ground for classifying sexual acts as either natural or unnatural is that the former type serve or could serve the evolutionary and biological function of sexuality—namely, reproduction. "Natural" sexual desire has as its "object" living persons of the opposite sex, and in particular their postpuberial genitals. The "aim" of natural sexual desire—that is, the act that "naturally" completes it—is genital intercourse. Perverse sex acts are deviations from the natural object (for example, homosexuality, fetishism) or from the standard aim (for example, voyeurism, sadism). Among the variety of objects and aims of sexual desire, I can see no other ground for selecting some as natural, except that they are of the type that can lead to reproduction.[16]

The connection of sexual desire with reproduction gives us the criterion but not the motive of the classification. The concept of perversion depends on a disjointedness between our experience of sexual desire from infancy on and the function of sexual desire—reproduction. In our collective experience of sexuality, perverse desires are as natural as nonperverse ones. The sexual desire of the polymorphously perverse child has many objects—for example, breasts, anus, mouth, genitals—and many aims—for example, autoerotic or other-directed looking, smelling, touching, hurting. From the social and developmental point of view, natural sex is an achievement, partly biological, partly conventional, consisting in a dominant organization of sexual desires in which perverted aims or objects are subordinate to natural ones. The concept of perversion reflects the vulnerability as much as the evolutionary warrant of this organization.

The connection of sexual desire with reproduction is not sufficient to yield the concept of perversion, but it is surely necessary. Nagel, however, thinks otherwise. There are, he points out, many sexual acts that do not lead to reproduction but that we are not even inclined to call perverse—for example, sexual acts between partners who are sterile. Perversion, according to him, is a psychological concept while reproduction is (only?) a physiological one. (Incidentally, this view of reproduction seems to me the clearest instance of male bias in Nagel's paper.)

Nagel is right about our judgments of particular acts, but he draws the wrong conclusions from those judgments. The perversity of sex acts does not depend upon whether they are intended to achieve reproduction. "Natural sexual desire is for heterosexual genital activity, not for reproduction. The ground for classifying that desire as natural is that it is so organized that it *could* lead to reproduction in normal physiological circumstances. The reproductive organization of sexual desires gives us a *criterion* of naturalness, but the *virtue* of which it is a criterion is the "naturalness" itself, not reproduction. Our vacillating attitude toward the apparently perverse acts of animals reflects our shifting from criterion to virtue. If, when confronted with a perverse act of animals, we withdraw the label "perverted" from our own similar acts rather than extend it to theirs, we are relin-

[14]Ibid., p. 13.

[15]Sartre, *Being and Nothingness,* p. 386.

[16]See, in support of this point, Sigmund Freud, *Introductory Lectures on Psychoanalysis,* standard ed., vol. 26 (London: Hogarth, 1963), chaps. 20, 21.

quishing the reproductive criterion of naturalness, while retaining the virtue. Animals cannot be "unnatural." If, on the other hand, we "discover" that animals can be perverts too, we are maintaining our criterion, but giving a somewhat altered sense to the "naturalness" of which it is a criterion.

Nagel's alternative attempt to classify acts as natural or perverted on the basis of their completeness fails. "Perverted" and "complete" are evaluations of an entirely different order. The completeness of a sex act depends upon qualities of the participants' experience and upon qualities of their relation — qualities of which they are the best judge. To say a sex act is perverted is to pass a conventional judgment about characteristics of the act, which could be evident to any observer. As one can pretend to be angry but not to shout, one can pretend to a complete, but no to a natural, sex act (though one may, of course, conceal desires for perverse sex acts or shout in order to mask one's feelings). As Nagel himself sees, judgments about particular sex acts clearly differentiate between perversion and completeness. Unadorned heterosexual intercourse where each partner has private fantasies is clearly "natural" and clearly "incomplete," but there is nothing prima facie incomplete about exclusive oral-genital intercourse or homosexual acts. If many perverse acts are incomplete, as Nagel claims, this is an important fact *about* perversion, but it is not the basis upon which we judge its occurrence.

Is Better Sex Really Better?

Some sex acts are, allegedly, better than others insofar as they are more pleasurable, complete, and natural. What is the moral significance of this evaluation? In answering this question, official sexual morality sometimes appeals to the social consequences of particular types of better sex acts. For example, since dominantly perverse organizations of sexual impulses limit reproduction, the merits of perversion depend upon the need to limit or increase population. Experience of sexual pleasure may be desirable if it promotes relaxation and communication in an acquisitive society, undesirable if it limits the desire to work or, in armies, to kill. The social consequences of complete sex have not received particular attention, because the quality of sexual experience has been of little interest to moralists. It might be found that those who had complete sexual relations were more cooperative, less amenable to political revolt. If so, complete sexual acts would be desirable in just and peaceable societies, undesirable in unjust societies requiring revolution.

The social desirability of types of sexual acts depends on particular social conditions and independent criteria of social desirability. It may be interesting and important to assess particular claims about the social desirability of sex acts, but this is not my concern. What is my concern is the extent to which we will allow our judgments of sexual worth to be influenced by social considerations. But this issue cannot even be raised until we have a better sense of sexual worth.

The Benefit of Sexual Pleasure

To say that an experience is pleasant is to give a self-evident, terminal reason for seeking it. We can sometimes "see" that an experience is pleasant. When, for example, we observe someone's sensual delight in eating, her/his behavior can expressively characterize pleasure. We can only question the benefit of such an experience by referring to other goods with which it might conflict. Though sensual pleasures might not be sufficient to warrant giving birth or to deter suicide, so long as we live they are self-evidently benefits to us.

The most eloquent detractors of sexual experience have admitted that it provides sensual pleasures so poignant that once experienced they are repeatedly, almost addictively, sought. Yet, unlike other appetites, such as hunger, sexual desire can be permanently resisted, and resistance has been advocated. How can the prima facie benefits of sexual pleasure appear deceptive?

There are several grounds for complaint. Sexual pleasure is ineradicably mixed, frustration being part of every sexual life. The capacity for sexual pleasure is unevenly distributed, cannot be voluntarily acquired, and diminishes through no fault of its subject. If such a pleasure were an intrinsic benefit, benefit would in this case be independent of moral effort. Then again, sexual pleasures are not serious. Enjoyment of them is one of life's greatest recreations, but none of its business. And finally, sexual desire has the defects of its strengths. Before satisfaction, it is, at the least, distracting; in satisfaction, it "makes one little roome, an everywhere." Like psychosis, sexual desire turns us from "reality"—whether the real be God, social justice, children, or intellectual endeavor. This turning away is more than a social consequence of desire, though it is that. Lovers themselves feel that their sexual desires are separate from their "real" political, domestic, ambitious, social selves.

If the plaintiff is taken to argue that sensual pleasures are peremptory benefits s/he is probably right. We can still want a good deal and forego sexual pleasures. We often forego pleasure just because we want something incompatible with it, for example, a continuing marriage. We must distinguish between giving up some occasions for sexual pleasure and giving up sexual pleasure itself. If all circumstances of sexual pleasure . . . threaten a peremptory benefit, such as self-respect, then the hope and the possibility of sexual pleasure may be relinquished. Since sexual pleasure is such a great, though optional, benefit, its loss is a sad one.

In emphasizing the unsocial, private nature of sexual experiences, the plaintiff is emphasizing a morally important characteristic of them. But her/his case against desire, as I have sketched it, is surely overstated. The mixed, partly frustrated character of any desire is not particularly pronounced for sexual desire, which is in fact especially plastic, or adaptable to changes (provided perverse sex acts have not been ruled out). Inhibition, social deprivation, or disease make our sexual lives unpleasant, but that is because they interfere with sexual desire, not because the desire is by its nature frustrating. More than other well-known desires (for example, desire for knowledge, success, or power), sexual desire is simply and completely satisfied upon attaining its object. Partly for this reason, even if we are overtaken by desire during sexual experience, our sexual experiences do not overtake us. Lovers turn away from the world while loving, but return—sometimes all too easily—when loving is done. The moralist rightly perceives sexual pleasure as a recreation, and those who upon realizing its benefits make a business of its pursuit appear ludicrous. The capacity for recreation, however, is surely a benefit that any human being rightly hopes for who hopes for anything. Indeed, in present social and economic conditions we are more likely to lay waste our powers in work than in play. Thus, though priest, revolutionary, and parent are alike in fearing sexual pleasure, this fear should inspire us to psychological and sociological investigation of the fearing rather than a moral doubt about the benefit of sexual pleasure.

The Moral Significance of Perversion

What is the moral significance of the perversity of a sexual act? Next to none, so far as I can see. Though perverted sex may be "unnatural" both from an evolutionary and developmental perspective, there is no connection, inverse or correlative, between what is natural and what is good. Perverted sex is sometimes said to be less pleasurable than natural sex. We have little reason to believe that this claim is true and no clear idea of the kind of evidence on which it would be based. In any case, to condemn perverse acts for lack of pleasure is to recognize the worth of pleasure, not of naturalness.

There are many other claims about the nature and consequences of perversion. Some merely restate "scientific" facts in morally tinged terminology. Perverse acts are, by definition and according to psychiatric theory, "immature" and "abnormal" since natural sex acts are selected by criteria of "normal" sexual function and "normal" and "mature" psychological development. But there is no greater connection of virtue with maturity and normality than there is of virtue with nature. The elimination of a village by an invading army would be no less evil if it were the expression of controlled, normal, natural, and mature aggression.

Nagel claims that many perverted sex acts are incomplete, and in making his point, gives the most specific arguments that I have read for the inferiority of perverted sex. But as he points out, there is no reason to think an act consisting solely of oral-genital intercourse is incomplete; it is doubtful whether homosexual acts and acts of buggery are especially liable to be incomplete; and the incompleteness of sexual intercourse with animals is a relative matter depending upon their limited consciousness. And again, the alleged inferiority is not a consequence of perversion but of incompleteness which can afflict natural sex as well.

Perverted acts might be thought to be inferior because they cannot result in children. Whatever the benefits and moral significance of the procreation and care of children (and I believe they are extensive and complicated), the virtue of proper care for children neither requires nor follows from biological parenthood. Even if it did, only a sexual life consisting solely of perverse acts rules out conception.

If perverted sex acts did rule out normal sex acts, if one were *either* perverted *or* natural, then certain kinds of sexual relations would be denied some perverts — relations that are benefits to those who enjoy them. It seems that sexual relations with the living and the human would be of greater benefit than those with the dead or with animals. But there is no reason to think that heterosexual relations are of greater benefit than homosexual ones. It might be thought that children can only be raised by heterosexual couples who perform an abundance of natural sex acts. If true (though truth seems highly unlikely), perverts will be denied the happiness of parenthood. This deprivation would be an *indirect* consequence of perverted sex and might yield a moral dilemma: How is one to choose between the benefits of children and the benefits of more pleasurable, more complex sex acts?

Some perversions are immoral on independent grounds. Sadism is the obvious example, though sadism practiced with a consenting masochist is far less evil than other, more familiar forms of aggression. Voyeurism may seem immoral because, since it must be secret to be satisfying, it violates others' rights to privacy.[17] Various kinds of rape can constitute perversion if rape, rather than genital intercourse, is the aim of desire. Rape is always seriously immoral, a vivid violation of respect for persons. Sometimes doubly perverse rape is doubly evil (the rape of a child), but in other cases (the rape of a pig) its evil is halved. In any case, though rape is always *wrong*, it is only perverse when raping becomes the aim and not the means of desire.

Someone can be dissuaded from acting on her/his perverse desires either from moral qualms or from social fears. Although there may be ample basis for the latter, I can find none for the former except the possible indirect loss of the benefits of child care. I am puzzled about this since reflective people who do not usually attempt to legislate the preferences of others think differently. There is no doubt that beliefs in these matters involve deep emotions that should be respected. But for those who do in fact have perverted desires, the first concern will be to satisfy them, not to divert or to understand them. For sexual pleasure is intrinsically a benefit, and complete sex acts, which depend upon expressing the desires one in fact has, are both beneficial and conducive to virtue. Therefore, barring extrinsic moral or social considerations, perverted sex acts are preferable to natural ones if the latter are less pleasurable or less complete.

The Moral Significance of Completeness

Complete sex consists in mutually embodied, mutually active, responsive desire. Embodiment, activity, and mutual responsiveness are instrumentally beneficial because they are conducive to our psychological well-being, which is an intrinsic benefit. The alleged pathological consequences of disembodiment are more specific and better documented than those of perversity.[18] To dissociate oneself from one's

[17]I am indebted to Dr. Leo Goldberger for this example.

[18]See, for example, R. D. Laing, *The Divided Self;* D. W. Winnicott, "Transitional Objects and Transitional Phenomena," *International Journal of Psychoanalysis,* 34 (1953), 89–97; Paul Federn, *Ego Psychology and the Psychoses* (New York: Basic Books, 1952); Phyllis Greenacre, *Trauma, Growth, and Personality* (New York: International Universities Press, 1969); Paul Schilder, *The Image and Appearance of the Human Body* (New York: International Universities Press, 1950); Moses Laufer, "Body Image and Masturbation in Adolescence," *The Psychoanalytic Study of the Child* 23 (1968), 114–46. Laing's work is the most specific about the nature and consequences of disembodiment, but the works cited, and others similar to them, give the clinical evidence upon which much of Laing's work depends.

actual body, either by creating a delusory body or by rejecting the bodily, is to court a variety of ill effects, ranging from self-disgust to diseases of the will, to faulty mental development, to the destruction of a recognizable "self," and finally to madness. It is difficult to assess psychiatric claims outside their theoretical contexts, but in this case I believe that they are justified. Relative embodiment is a stable, *normal* condition that is not confined to cases of complete embodiment. But psychiatrists tell us that exceptional physical occasions of embodiment seem to be required in order to balance tendencies to reject or to falsify the body. Sexual acts are not the only such occasions, but they do provide an immersion of consciousness in the bodily, which is pleasurable and especially conducive to correcting experiences of shame and disgust that work toward disembodiment.

The mutual responsiveness of complete sex is also instrumentally beneficial. It satisfies a general desire to be recognized as a particular "real" person and to make a difference to other particular "real" people. The satisfaction of this desire in sexual experience is especially rewarding, its thwarting especially cruel. Vulnerability is increased in complete sex by the active desiring of the partners. When betrayal, or for that matter, tenderness or ecstasy, ensues, one cannot dissociate oneself from the desire with which one identified and out of which one acted. The psychic danger is real, as people who attempt to achieve a distance from their desires could tell us. But the cost of distance is as evident as its gains. Passivity in respect to one's own sexual desire not only limits sexual pleasure but, more seriously, limits the extent to which the experience of sexual pleasure can be included as an experience of a coherent person. With passivity comes a kind of irresponsibility in which one can hide from one's desire, even from one's pleasure, "playing" seducer or victim, tease or savior. Active sexual desiring in complete sex acts affords an especially threatening but also especially happy occasion to relinquish these and similar roles. To the extent that the roles confuse and confound our intimate relations, the benefit from relinquishing them in our sexual acts, or the loss from adhering to them then, is especially poignant.

In addition to being beneficial, complete sex acts are morally superior for three reasons. They tend to resolve tensions fundamental to moral life; they are conducive to emotions that, if they become stable and dominant, are in turn conducive to the virtue of loving; and they involve a preeminently moral virtue—respect for persons.

In one of its aspects, morality is opposed to the private and untamed. Morality is "civilization," social and regulating; desire is "discontent," resisting their regulation. Obligation, rather than benefit, is the notion central to morality so conceived, and the virtues required of a moral person are directed to preserving right relations and social order. Both the insistence on natural sex and the encouragement of complete sex can be looked upon as attempts to make sexual desire more amenable to regulation. But whereas the regulation of perverted desires is extrinsic to them, those of completeness modify the desires themselves. The desiring sensual body that in our social lives we may laugh away or disown becomes our "self" and enters into a social relation. Narcissism and altruism are satisfied in complete sex acts in which one gives what one receives by receiving it. Social and private "selves" are unified in an act in which impersonal, spontaneous impulses govern an action that is responsive to a particular person. For this to be true we must surmount our social "roles" as well as our sexual "techniques" though we incorporate rather than surmount our social selves. We must also surmount regulations imposed in the name of naturalness if our desires are to be spontaneously expressed. Honestly spontaneous first love gives us back our private desiring selves while allowing us to see the desiring self of another. Mutually responding partners confirm each other's desires and declare them good. Such occasions, when we are "moral" without cost, help reconcile us to our moral being and to the usual mutual exclusion between our social and private lives.

The connection between sex and certain emotions—particularly love, jealousy, fear, and anger—is as evident as it is obscure. Complete sex acts seem more likely than incomplete pleasurable ones to lead toward affection and away from fear and anger, since any guilt and shame will be extrinsic to the act and meliorated by it. It is clear that we need not feel for someone any affection beyond that required (if any is) simply to participate with him/her in a complete sex act. However, it is equally clear that sexual pleasure, especially as experienced in complete sex acts, is conducive to many feelings — gratitude, tenderness, pride, appreciation, dependency, and others. These feelings magnify their object who occasioned them. When these magnifying feelings become stable and habitual they are conducive to love — not universal love, of course, but love of a particular sexual partner. However, even "selfish" love is a virtue, a disposition to care for someone as her/his interests and demands would dictate. Neither the best sex nor the best love require each other, but they go together more often than reason would expect — often enough to count the virtue of loving as one of the rewards of the capacity for sexual pleasure exercised in complete sex acts.

It might be argued that the coincidence of sex acts and several valued emotions is a cultural matter. It is notoriously difficult to make judgments about the emotional and, particularly, the sexual lives of others, especially culturally alien others. There is, however, some anthropological evidence that at first glance relativizes the connection between good sex and valued emotion. For example, among the Manus of New Guinea, it seems that relations of affection and love are encouraged primarily among brother and sister, while easy familiarity, joking, and superficial sexual play is expected only between cross-cousins. Sexual intercourse is, however, forbidden between siblings and cross-cousins but required of married men and women, who are as apt to hate as to care for each other and often seem to consider each other strangers. It seems, however, that the Manus do not value or experience complete or even pleasurable sex. Both men and women are described as puritanical, and the sexual life of women seems blatantly unrewarding. Moreover, their emotional life is generally impoverished. This impoverishment, in conjunction with an unappreciated and unrewarding sexual life dissociated from love or affection, would argue for a *connection* between better sex and valued emotions. If, as Peter Winch suggests, cultures provide their members with particular possibilities of making sense of their lives, and thereby with possibilities of good and evil, the Manus might be said to deny themselves one possibility both of sense and of good — namely the coincidence of good sex and of affection and love. Other cultures, including our own, allow this possibility, whose realization is encouraged in varying degrees by particular groups and members of the culture.[19]

Finally, as Sartre has suggested, complete sex acts preserve a respect for persons. Each person remains conscious and responsible, a "subject" rather than a depersonalized, will-less, or manipulated "object." Each actively desires that the other likewise remain a "subject." Respect for persons is a central virtue when matters of justice and obligation are at issue. Insofar as we can speak of respect for persons in complete sex acts, there are different, often contrary requirements of respect. Respect for persons, typically and in sex acts, requires that *actual present* partners participate, partners whose desires are recognized and endorsed. Respected for persons typically requires taking a distance from both one's own demands and those of others. But in sex acts the demands of desire take over, and equal distance is replaced by mutual responsiveness. Respect typically requires refusing to treat another person merely as a means to fulfilling demands. In sex acts, another person is so clearly a means to satisfaction that s/he is always on the verge of becoming merely a means ("intercourse counterfeits masturbation"). In complete sex acts, instrumentality vanishes only because it is mutual and mutually desired. Respect requires encouraging, or at least protecting, the autonomy of another. In complete sex, autonomy of will is recruited by desire, and freedom from others is replaced by frank dependence on another person's desire. Again the respect consists in the reciprocity of desiring dependence, which bypasses rather than violates autonomy.

Despite the radical differences between respect for persons in the usual moral contexts and respect for persons in sex acts, it is not, I think, a mere play on words to talk of respect in the latter case. When, in any sort of intercourse, persons are respected, their desires are not only, in fair measure, *fulfilled.* In addition, their desires are *active* and determine, in fair measure, the form of intercourse

[19]The evidence about the life of the Manus comes from Margaret Mead, *Growing Up in New Guinea* (Harmondsworth, England: Penguin Books, 1942). Peter Winch's discussion can be found in his "Understanding a Primitive Society," *American Philosophical Quartery,* 1 (1964), 307–34.

and the *manner* and *condition* of desire's satisfaction. These conditions are not only met in sexual intercourse when it is characterized by completeness; they come close to defining completeness.

Sartre is not alone in believing that just because the condition of completeness involves respect for persons, complete sex is impossible. Completeness is surely threatened by pervasive tendencies to fantasy, to possessiveness, and to varieties of a sadomasochistic desire. But a complete sex act, as I see it, does not involve an heroic restraint on our sexual impulses. Rather, a complete sex act is a normal mode of sexual activity expressing the natural structure and impulses of sexual desire.

While complete sex is morally superior because it involves respect for persons, incomplete sex acts do not necessarily involve immoral disrespect for persons. Depending upon the desires and expectations of the partners, incompleteness may involve neither respect nor disrespect. Masturbation, for example, allows only the limited completeness of embodiment and often fails of that. But masturbation only rarely involves disrespect to anyone. Even the respect of Sartre's allegedly desirable sleeping woman may not be violated if she is unknowingly involved in a sex act. Disrespect, though, probable, may in some cases be obviated by her sensibilities and expectation that she has previously expressed and her partner has understood. Sex acts provide one context in which respect for persons can be expressed. That context is important both because our sexual lives are of such importance to us and because they are so liable to injury because of the experience and the fear of the experience of disrespect. But many complete sex acts in which respect is maintained make other casual and incomplete sex acts unthreatening. In this case a goodly number of swallows can make a summer.

In sum, then, complete sex acts are superior to incomplete ones. First, they are, whatever their effects, better than various kinds of incomplete sex acts because they involve a kind of "respect for persons" in acts that are otherwise prone to violation of respect for, and often to violence to, persons. Second, complete sex acts are good because they are good for us. They are conducive to some fairly clearly defined kinds of psychological well-being that are beneficial. They are conducive to moral well-being because they relieve tensions that arise in our attempts to be moral and because they encourage the development of particular virtues.

To say that complete sex acts are preferable to incomplete ones is not to court a new puritanism. There are many kinds and degrees of incompleteness. Incomplete sex acts may not involve a disrespect for persons. Complete sex acts only *tend* to be good for us, and the realization of these tendencies depends upon individual lives and circumstances of sexual activity. The proper object of sexual desire is sexual pleasure. It would be a foolish ambition indeed to limit one's sexual acts to those in which completeness was likely. Any sexual act that is pleasurable is prima facie good, though the more incomplete it is—the more private, essentially autoerotic, unresponsive, unembodied, passive, or imposed—the more likely it is to be harmful to someone.

On Sexual Morality: Concluding Remarks

There are many questions we have neglected to consider because we have not been sufficiently attentive to the quality of sexual lives. For example, we know little about the ways of achieving better sex. When we must choose between inferior sex and abstinence, how and when will our choice of inferior sex damage our capacity for better sex? Does, for example, the repeated experience of controlled sexual disembodiment ("desire which takes over will take you too far") that we urge (or used to urge) on adolescents damage their capacity for complete sex? The answers to this and similar questions are not obvious, though unfounded opinions are always ready at hand.

Some of the traditional sexual vices might be condemned on the ground that they are inimical to better sex. Obscenity, or repeated public exposure to sexual acts, might impair our capacity for pleasure or for response to desire. Promiscuity might undercut the tendency of complete sex acts to promote emotions that magnify their object. Other of the traditional sexual vices are neither inimical nor conducive to better sex, but are condemned because of conflicting nonsexual benefits and obligations. For example, infidelity qua infidelity neither secures nor prevents better sex.

The obligations of fidelity have many sources, one of which may be a past history of shared complete sex acts, a history that included promises of exclusive intimacy. Such past promises are apt to conflict with as to accord with a current demand for better sex. I have said nothing about how such a conflict would be settled. I hope I have shown that where the possibility of better sex conflicts with obligations and other benefits, we have a *moral dilemma*, not just an occasion for moral self-discipline.

The pursuit of more pleasurable and more complete sex acts is, among many moral activities, distinguished not for its exigencies but for its rewards. Since our sexual lives are so important to us, and since, whatever our history and our hopes, we are sexual beings, this pursuit rightly engages our moral reflection. It should not be relegated to the immoral, nor to the "merely" prudent.

Postscript

I wrote this essay fourteen years ago. Since that time my ideas about thinking and writing, as well as about sexual morality, have been transformed by feminist and anti-militarist politics. The tone and language of the essay, as well as certain basic presuppositions of its arguments, now ring strangely in my ears. Nonetheless, what has been made public belongs to the public and I am pleased if this early paper still proves useful. In one respect, however, the essay seems seriously insensitive and limited. In 1970 I was largely unaware of the deep and extensive pain suffered by those whose sexuality is labeled "abnormal," "perverted," or "immature." On a more theoretical level, since 1970 we have learned to see the connections between misogyny, homophobia, militarism, and racism. I would like here to acknowledge my debt to the work of the feminist and gay liberation movements, which has made these theoretical connections while fighting ignorant and arrogant sexual politics. As a result many people now lead more complete and pleasurable sexual lives.

AUTHOR'S NOTE: An earlier version of this paper was published in *Moral Problems*, edited by James Rachels (New York: Harper & Row, 1971). I am grateful to many friends and students for their comments on the earlier version, especially to Bernard Gert, Evelyn Fox Keller, and James Rachels.

Study Questions

1. What does Ruddick mean by a "specifically sexual morality," and what does that have to do with "good sex" (p. 589)?
2. Explain what Ruddick means by saying that a precondition of a complete sex act is the embodiment of the participants.
3. Explain what she means by saying that a precondition of a complete sex act is a partner's actively desiring another person's desire.
4. On what basis can we select a sexual act as a natural act, according to Ruddick?
5. For sex to be natural, must it lead to reproduction, in Ruddick's opinion?
6. Can an unnatural sex act be complete, according to Ruddick? Why or why not?
7. What are the grounds for arguing that the desire for sexual pleasure should be resisted?
8. Ruddick disagrees with the arguments for suppressing sexual desire. Explain why.
9. Explain why Ruddick believes there is no significance in the perversity of unnatural sexual acts.
10. Why is complete sex morally superior, according to Ruddick?
11. In what way might some of the traditional sexual vices be condemned morally, according to Ruddick?

CHAPTER 15

Preferential Treatment

Strong versus Weak Affirmative Action

Thomas Nagel believes that there are three grave objections to "strong affirmative action." Strong affirmative action consists in preferring women members of minorities over equally or even better qualified white male applicants, for such things as jobs or admission to educational institutions. Nagel concedes that strong affirmative action is intrinsically undesirable because of these three objections. However, he believes that, as applied to blacks, strong affirmative action is a legitimate method of pursing a goal that is essential to the national welfare. He concludes that strong affirmative action is justifiable as a temporary policy for blacks.

Nagel then addresses the three objections to strong affirmative action, namely, that it is inefficient, unfair, and damaging to self-esteem. These objections are so serious, he believes, that they imply we should undertake strong affirmative action only for the sake of an urgent social goal. The removal of "the stubborn residue of racial caste" is such a goal, he next argues. However, he finds that strong affirmative action is not warranted for women or for Asian Americans. Latinos, according to Nagel, occupy an intermediate position.

A Defense of Affirmative Action

Thomas Nagel

Thomas Nagel (b. 1937) is Professor of Philosophy at New York University. The article reprinted here was testimony before the Subcommittee on the Constitution of the Senate Judiciary Committee, June 18, 1981.

The term "affirmative action" has changed in meaning since it was first introduced. Originally it referred only to special efforts to ensure equal opportunity for members of groups that had been subject to discrimination. These efforts included public advertisement of positions to be filled, active recruitment of qualified applicants from the formerly excluded groups, and special training programs to help them meet the standards for admission or appointment. There was also close attention to procedures of appointment, and sometimes to the results, with a view to detecting continued discrimination, conscious or unconscious.

More recently the term has come to refer also to some degree of definite preference for members of these groups in determining access to positions from which they were formerly excluded. Such preference might be allowed to influence decisions only between candidates who are otherwise equally qualified, but usually it involves the selection of women or minority members over other candidates who are better qualified for the position.

Let me call the first sort of policy "weak affirmative action" and the second "strong affirmative action." It is important to distinguish them, because the distinction is sometimes blurred in practice. It is strong affirmative action—the policy of preference—that arouses controversy. Most people would agree that weak or precautionary affirmative action is a good thing, and worth its cost in time and energy. But this does not imply that strong affirmative action is also justified.

I shall claim that in the present state of things it is justified, most clearly with respect to blacks. But I also believe that a defender of the practice must acknowledge that there are serious arguments against it, and that it is defensible only because the arguments for it have great weight. Moral opinion in this country is sharply divided over the issue because significant values are involved on both sides. My own view is that while strong affirmative action is intrinsically undesirable, it is a legitimate and perhaps indispensable method of pursuing a goal so important to the national welfare that it can be justified as a temporary, though not short-term, policy for both public and private institutions. In this respect it is like other policies that impose burdens on some of the public good.

Three Objections

I shall begin with the argument against. There are three objections to strong affirmative action: that it is inefficient; that it is unfair; and that it damages self-esteem.

The degree of inefficiency depends on how strong a role racial or sexual preference plays in the process of selection. Among candidates meeting the basic qualifications for a position, those better qualified will on the average perform better, whether they are doctors, policemen, teachers or electricians. There may be some cases, as in preferential college admissions, where the immediate usefulness of making educational resources available to an individual is thought to be greater because of the use to which the education will be put or because of the internal effects on the institution itself. But by and large, policies of strong affirmative action must reckon with the costs of some lowering in performance level: the stronger the preference, the larger the cost to be justified. Since both the costs and the value of the results will vary from case to case, this suggests that no one policy of affirmative action is likely to be correct in all cases, and that the cost in performance level should be taken into account in the design of a legitimate policy.

The charge of unfairness arouses the deepest disagreements. To be passed over because of membership in a group one was born into, where this has nothing to do with one's individual qualifications for a position, can arouse strong feelings of resentment. It is a departure from the ideal—one of the values finally recognized in our society—that people should be judged so far as possible on the basis of individual characteristics rather than involuntary group membership.

This does not mean that strong affirmative action is morally repugnant in the manner of racial or sexual discrimination. It is nothing like those practices, for though like them it employs race and sex as criteria of selection, it does so for entirely different reasons. Racial and sexual discrimination are based on contempt or even loathing for the excluded group, a feeling that certain contacts with them are degrading to members of the dominant group, that they are fit only for subordinate positions or menial work. Strong affirmative action involves none of this: it is simply a means of increasing the social and economic strength of formerly victimized groups, and does not stigmatize others.

There is an element of individual unfairness here, but it is more like the unfairness of conscription in wartime, or of property condemnation under the right of eminent domain. Those who benefit or lose out because of their race or sex cannot be said to deserve their good or bad fortune.

It might be said on the other side that the beneficiaries of affirmative action deserve it as compensation for past discrimination, and that compensation is rightly exacted from the group that has benefited from discrimination in the past. But this is a bad argument, because as the practice usually works, no effort is made to give preference to those who have suffered most from discrimination, or to prefer them especially to those who have benefited most from it, or been guilty of it. Only candidates who in other qualifications fall on one or the other side of the margin of decision will directly benefit or lose from the policy, and these are not necessarily, or even probably, the ones who especially deserve it. Women or blacks who don't have the qualifications even to be considered are likely to have been handicapped more by the effects of discrimination than those who receive preference. And the marginal white male candidate who is turned down can evoke our sympathy if he asks, "Why me?" (A policy of explicitly *compensatory* preference, which took into account each individual's background of poverty and discrimination, would escape some of these objections, and it has its defenders, but it is not the policy I want to defend. Whatever its merits, it will not serve the same purpose as direct affirmative action.)

The third objection concerns self-esteem, and is particularly serious. While strong affirmative action is in effect, and generally known to be so, no one in an affirmative action category who gets a desirable job or is admitted to a selective university can be sure that he or she has not benefited from the policy. Even those who would have made it anyway fall under suspicion, from themselves and from others: it comes to be widely felt that success does not mean the same thing for women and minorities. This painful damage to esteem cannot be avoided. It should make any defender of strong affirmative action want the practice to end as soon as it has achieved its basic purpose.

Justifying Affirmative Action

I have examined these three objections and tried to assess their weight, in order to decide how strong a countervailing reason is needed to justify such a policy. In my view, taken together they imply that strong affirmative action involving significant preference should be undertaken only if it will substantially further a social goal of the first importance. While this condition is not met by all programs of affirmative action now in effect, it is met by those which address the most deep-seated, stubborn, and radically unhealthy divisions in the society, divisions whose removal is a condition of basic justice and social cohesion.

The situation of black people in our country is unique in this respect. For almost a century after the abolition of slavery we had a rigid racial caste system of the ugliest kind, and it only began to break up twenty-five years ago. In the South it was enforced by law, and in the North, in a somewhat less severe form, by social convention. Whites were thought to be defiled by social or residential proximity to blacks, intermarriage was taboo, blacks were denied the same level of public goods—education and legal protection—as whites, were restricted to the most menial occupations, and were barred from any positions of authority over whites. The visceral feelings of black inferiority and untouchability that this system expressed were deeply ingrained in the members of both races, and they continue, not surprisingly, to have their effect. Blacks still form, to a considerable extent, a hereditary social and economic community characterized by wide-spread poverty, unemployment, and social alienation.

When this society finally got around to moving against the caste system, it might have done no more than to enforce straight equality of opportunity, perhaps with the help of weak affirmative action, and then wait a few hundred years while things gradually got better. Fortunately it decided instead to accelerate the process by both public and private institutional action, because there was wide recognition of the intractable character of the problem posed by this insular minority and its place in the nation's history and collective consciousness. This has not been going on very long, but the results are already impressive, especially in speeding the advancement of blacks into the middle class. Affirmative action has not done much to improve the position of poor and unskilled blacks. That is the most serious part of the problem and it requires a more direct economic attack. But increased access to higher education and upper-level jobs is an essential part of what must be achieved to break the structure of drastic separation that was left largely undisturbed by the legal abolition of the caste system.

Changes of this kind require a generation or two. My guess is that strong affirmative action for blacks will continue to be justified into the early decades of the next century, but that by then it will have accomplished what it can and will no longer be worth the costs. One point deserves special emphasis. The goal to be pursued is the reduction of a great social injustice, not proportional representation of the races in all institutions and professions. Proportional racial representation is of no value itself. It is not a legitimate social goal, and it should certainly not be the aim of strong affirmative action, whose drawbacks make it worth adopting only against a serious and intractable social evil.

This implies that the justification for strong affirmative action is much weaker in the case of other racial and ethnic groups, and in the case of women. At least, the practice will be justified in a narrower range of circumstances and for a shorter span of time than it is for blacks. No other group has been treated quite like this, and no other group is in a comparable status. Hispanic-Americans occupy an intermediate position, but it seems to me frankly absurd to include persons of oriental descent as beneficiaries of affirmative action, strong or weak. They are not a severely deprived and excluded minority and their eligibility serves only to swell the numbers that can be included on affirmative action reports. It also suggests that there is a drift in the policy toward adopting the goal of racial proportional representation for its own sake. This is a foolish mistake, and should be resisted. The only legitimate goal of the policy is to reduce egregious racial stratification.

With respect to women, I believe that except over the short term, and in professions or institutions from which their absence is particularly marked, strong affirmative action is not warranted and weak affirmative action is enough. This is based simply on the expectation that the social and economic situation of women will improve quite rapidly under conditions of full equality of opportunity. Recent progress provides some evidence for this. Women do not form a separate hereditary community, characteristically poor and uneducated, and their position is not likely to be self-perpetuating in the same way as that of an outcast race. The process requires less artificial acceleration, and any need for strong affirmative action for women can be expected to end sooner than it ends for blacks.

I said at the outset that there was a tendency to blur the distinction between weak and strong affirmative action. This occurs especially in the use of numerical quotas, a topic on which I want to comment briefly.

A quota may be a method of either weak or strong affirmative action, depending on the circumstances. It amounts to weak affirmative action—a safeguard against discrimination—if, and only if, there is independent evidence that average qualifications for the positions being filled are no lower in the group to which a minimum quota is being assigned than in the applicant group as a whole. This can be presumed true of unskilled jobs that most people can do, but it becomes less likely, and harder to establish, the greater the skill and education required for the position. At these levels, a quota proportional to population, or even to representation of the group in the applicant pool, is almost certain to amount to strong affirmative action. Moreover it is strong affirmative action of a particularly crude and indiscriminate kind, because it permits no variation in the degree of preference on the basis of costs in efficiency, depending on the qualification gap. For this reason I should defend quotas only where they serve the purpose of weak affirmative action. On the whole, strong affirmative action is better implemented by including group preference as one factor in appointment or admission decisions, and letting the results depend on its interaction with other factors.

I have tried to show that the arguments against strong affirmative action are clearly outweighed at present by the need for exceptional measures to remove the stubborn residues of racial caste. But advocates of the policy should acknowledge the reasons against it, which will ensure its termination when it is no longer necessary. Affirmative action is not an end in itself, but a means of dealing with a social situation that should be intolerable to us all.

Study Questions

1. Define strong and weak affirmative action, according to Nagel.
2. Explain the three objections to strong affirmative action that Nagel discusses.
3. In what way is the situation of blacks in this country unique, according to Nagel? Why does he believe that the justification of strong affirmative action for other groups is much weaker than that for blacks?
4. Does Nagel believe the proportional representation of the races in all institutions and professions is an important goal? Explain.
5. Why does Nagel believe that, generally, strong affirmative action is not warranted for women?
6. Why does Nagel think that quotas should be used only if they serve the purpose of weak affirmative action?

Reverse Discrimination

Michael Levin opposes affirmative action policies that amount to reverse discrimination. Reverse discrimination includes such policies as hiring a preset number of blacks, regardless of the qualifications of competing whites and regardless of whether these particular blacks have been wronged and whether the competing whites have benefited from discrimination.

The only defense of reverse discrimination, Levin says, is that it attempts to make right the *consequences* of a past wrong—namely, past racial discrimination. But there is nothing morally special about racial discrimination that requires us to block its consequences, he argues. If we deny Mr. X a job simply because he is black, that is wrong, and we owe Mr. X compensation. But we don't owe Mr. X's *children* jobs for that reason, any more than we would owe them jobs if he were murdered or defrauded. Nor, for that matter, do we owe Mr. X's children jobs just because *other members* of their race are discriminated against, Levin argues.

Is racial discrimination a special case in that it is an instance of a pattern? Is it special because in this country it has included a history of terror and lynching? Is it special because it has been state-approved and sometimes state-mandated? To all questions, Levin's answer is no. Past discrimination no more deserves extraordinary compensation than do many other wrongs, he maintains.

Further, Levin argues, even if discrimination against Mr. X has cost him a job, it doesn't follow that proper compensation is a *job* for Mr. X. We just do not have a general obligation to rectify the consequences of past wrongs, Levin says, because it is impossible to do so. It is impossible to say where a person would be if his ancestors or other members of his racial group had not been wronged. "If you wanted to make up to me for the theft of my grandfather's watch in 1900, how on Earth do you propose to reckon the position I would have been in had my grandfather's watch not been stolen? . . . If each of us tried to put himself just where he would be if there had been no past wrongs, we would all be caught in a man whirl of exchanging positions and privileges with one another."

Is Racial Discrimination Special?

Michael E. Levin

Michael Levin (b. 1943) is Professor of Philosophy at City College, City University of New York. This selection was published in the *Journal of Value Inquiry* 15 (1981).

I take "reverse discrimination" to be the policy of favoring members of certain groups (usually racial), in situations in which merit has been at least ideally the criterion, on that grounds that *past* members of these groups have suffered discrimination. I do not include giving someone a job he was denied because *he* was discriminated against, since such redress is justified by ordinary canons of justice, in particular that of giving someone what he is owed. I am referring, rather, to the practice of hiring or admitting a preset number of (e.g.) blacks regardless of whether the blacks so hired have been wronged, and regardless of the qualifications of competing whites. The difference between the two policies is that between restoring a robbery victim's property to him, and hunting up the descendants of robbery victims and giving them goods at the expense of people who themselves robbed no one. I have no quarrel with the former, many quarrels with the latter: I believe reverse discrimination is as ill-advised a course of action as any undertaken by this country in at least a century. It cannot be justified by its social benefits, since experience suggests that the consequences of this policy are proving disastrous. It cannot be justified as giving particular members of the chosen group what they would have gotten if they had not been discriminated against, since by stipulation "affirmative action" goes beyond such an appeal to ordinary ideas of justice and compensation. It penalizes a group of present-day whites—those who are at least as well qualified but passed over—with out proof that they have discriminated or directly benefited from discrimination; whites no more responsible for past discrimination than anyone else.

But such frontal assaults on reverse discrimination (or "affirmative action," in bureaucratese) usually accomplish nothing, so I will not attempt one here. I will try instead to focus on a clear-cut issue which is central to the debate but which has, surprisingly, been almost completely ignored. It is this: what is so special about racial discrimination? Let me put the question more exactly. I will be arguing shortly that the only possible defense of reverse discrimination represents it as an attempt to rectify the consequences of past racial discrimination. But why has society selected one kind of wrong—discrimination—as particularly deserving or demanding rectification? Other past wrongs have left their traces—acts of theft, despoliation, fraud, anti-Semitism—yet society has no organized policy of rectifying those wrongs. It surely seems that if the consequences of one kind of wrong should not be allowed to unfold, neither should those of any other. And this is what I want to convince you of: acts of racial discrimination have no morally special status. Important consequences flow from this. For reasons I will propose, it seems to me clear that society—and in particular the employer—has no general standing obligation to block the consequences of past wrongs. So if discriminatory acts are no more deserving of rectification than wrong acts generally, no one is under any obligation at all to rectify them, or to be deprived so that these acts may be rectified.

With these preliminary points as background, let us look at the issue again. I noted that reverse discrimination discriminates against whites in a way which cannot be justified by ordinary notions of justice. Thus, if it is justifiable at all, it must be because we owe something to present-day blacks in some extraordinary sense. And the standard reason offered is that the blacks to be hired today bear the burdens of past discrimination. Had there been no racial discrimination, they would have been able to get those jobs; their qualifications would have been as good as those of the better-qualified whites they are displacing. (It is sometimes added that all whites benefit in some way from past discrimination, so all whites owe blacks something, namely a more advantageous position.) Affirmative action is supposed to rectify the consequences of past discrimination, to draw the sting from acts so bad that their consequences cannot be permitted to unfold.

But if our aim is to undo the consequences of past discrimination, the issue I raised becomes very pressing. If there is nothing morally special about discrimination, nothing which makes it especially deserving of rectification, any policy which treats discrimination as if it were morally special is arbitrary and irrational. Consider: Mr. X, a black of today, is supposedly owed special treatment. But surely if you owe Mr. X special treatment because his ancestors were the target of one wrong—discrimination—it would seem that you owe Mr. Y special treatment if his ancestors were the target of some other wrong—theft, say. Racial discrimination is not the *only* wrong that can be committed against someone, and indeed it is far from the worst. I would rather be denied a job because I am Jewish than be murdered. My murderer violates my rights and handicaps my children much more seriously than someone who keeps me out of medical school. So the question is: if I owe Mr. X a job because his ancestors were discriminated against, don't I owe Mr. Y the same if his ancestors were defrauded? I believe the answer must be yes: there is nothing special about acts of discrimination. And even if you think I have misrepresented affirmative action or its rationale, the question and its answer are important. Other justifications for reverse discrimination also tend to treat racial discrimination as somehow special. Indeed, a quarter-century's preoccupation with race has created a sense that racial prejudice is not just a wrong but a sin, an inexpungeable blot on the soul. Whether this attitude is rational is an issue worth considering.

Let me start with a truism. Discrimination deserves to be halted where it exists, and redressed where it can be, because it is *wrong*. Discrimination is worth doing something about because *wrongs* are worth doing something about and discrimination is wrong. Once we grant this, we start to see that there is nothing *sui generis* about discrimination. It competes with other wrongs for righting. And I take it as obvious that some wrongs demand righting more urgently than others. If I pass a negative comment on Jones's tie in private but defame Robinson's ancestry on national television, I had better apologize to Robinson before I do so to Jones. And if I have embezzled the funds of an orphanage, top priority goes to seeing that I give the money back. Finally, if Smith is destitute because I defrauded Smith's father, I had better make amends before I worry about the sons of men I insulted. So: denying a man a job on grounds of color is evidently just one among many ways of wronging him. It is far less egregious than assault or murder.

It is frequently but mistakenly claimed that racial discrimination is special because it involves a group. Certainly, an act of discrimination involves a whole group in the sense that it involves treating an individual not in his own right but insofar as he belongs to a group. But racial discrimination is not the only kind of act that is thus group-related. Many wrongs having nothing to do with race are discriminatory in the precise sense that they base the treatment of an individual on membership in a morally irrelevant group. Nepotism is discrimination against nonrelatives. When I make my lazy nephew district manager, I am disqualifying more able competitors because they belong to a group—nonfamily—membership in which should not count in the matter at hand. Discrimination need not be racial: any time you make a moral distinction on morally relevant grounds, you discriminate invidiously. In a society in which racial discrimination was unknown but capricious nepotism was the norm, denial of due process on grounds of family would provoke as much indignation as racial discrimination does now.

It would be sheer confusion to argue that acts of racial discrimination are special because they insult a whole race as well as wrong an individual. When I assault you, I assault no one else—and when I discriminate against you, I discriminate against no one else. True, my discrimination may indicate a readiness to discriminate against others and may create widespread anxiety—but my assaulting you may indicate a readiness to assault others and create even greater general anxiety. If I bypass Mr. X because he is black, only Mr. X and his dependents suffer thereby. Perhaps because color is so salient a trait, we tend in uncritical moments to think of the black race as an entity existing in and of itself, above and beyond the particular blacks who make it up. Philosophers call this "reificiation." We then think that an assault to this reified race is particularly malign, either in itself or because this entity somehow transmits to all blacks the harm done by single acts of discrimination. Some such reasoning must underlie the oft-heard ideas that the harm done to a single black man "hurts blacks everywhere" and that the appointment of a black to the Supreme Court is "a victory for blacks everywhere," remarks which make no literal sense. This tendency to reify is especially pernicious in the context of compensation. Why are we willing to contemplate special treatment for blacks now, when we would not contemplate special treatment for someone whose ancestors were defrauded by a man who left no descendants? Because, I suspect, we think that by benefiting today's black we will apologize for the long-ago insult to the race, and that this apology and benefit will somehow be transmitted back to the blacks who endured the original discrimination. Were this picture accurate, it might justify supposing that past discriminatory acts cast longer shadows than other wrongs. But it is just a myth. A racial grouping no more deserves reification than does the class of people whose ancestors were defrauded. We resist the impulse in the latter case only because the trait in question is not visually salient and has no especially coherent history.

(Some slight sense can be made of "injury to a group," as when we say that a traitor endangers the security of a nation. But even here the harm done is to individuals, the particular citizens. The traitor deserves punishment because of the harm he has done to each citizen, not to "the nation" as a thing apart.)

Perhaps the main reason for thinking of acts of racial discrimination as morally distinctive is that each is an instance of a pattern. My discriminating against Mr. X is part of a self-sustaining pattern of wrongs. And, indeed, we do find wrong acts that together form a pattern more disturbing than each wrong act taken singly: Jack the Ripper's legacy is more appalling than eleven isolated murders. Wrongs seem to be like notes, which have different musical values when part of a melody than when heard in isolation. But this intuition must be carefully assessed. A single wrong act cannot be made *more wrong* because there is some other wrong act which it resembles. If I discriminate against you, my act has a certain amount of wrongness. If I then discriminate against someone else, my previous act against you does not take on more wrongness. This is so even with Jack the Ripper. His murder of the first prostitute did not become *more wrong* when he murdered his second. If he had died before committing his second murder, his first murder would still have been as bad as it actually was. If, say, he owed the family of the first prostitute some compensation for his action, he did not suddenly owe them more after his second. So the fact that acts of discrimination come in groups does not show that a single act of discrimination is any worse, any more deserving of rectification, than it would have been had it occurred alone.

Two factors account for our feeling that patterned wrongs are worse than isolated ones. The first is that the *perpetrator* of a patterned wrong is worse. Jack the Ripper is worse than a man who kills once from passion. But this does not mean that what he did, in each case, is worse than a single act of murder. Similarly, the worst we can say of bigotry is that a habitual bigot is worse than a one-shot bigot, not that an act of bigotry is in itself worse than an act of caprice. The second reason patterned wrongs seem especially malign is that they create anxiety through their promise of repetition. Jack the Ripper's actions create more anxiety than eleven unconnected murders because we believe he will strike again. But this shows only that it is especially important to *halt patterns*, be they of murder or discrimination. It does not mean that a particular act in a discriminatory pattern is worse than it would have been in isolation. And it is worth repeating that antidiscrimination laws without benefit of affirmative action suffice to halt patterns of discrimination

Granted, racial wrongs have gone beyond discrimination in hiring or the use of public facilities, extending all the way to lynching. But to acknowledge this is to bring racial wrongs under independent headings—denial of due process, assault, murder. Lynching Emmet Till was wrong not because Emmet Till was black, but because lynching is murder. So if blacks deserve special treatment because of (say) this country's history of lynching, it is because descendants of murder victims deserve special treatment. But this concedes my point: what was wrong about especially egregious acts of racial discrimination is what is wrong about parallel nonracial acts; and if we treat the former as special, we must treat the latter as special as well. I also deny that past discriminations were special because they were state-approved and in some case state-mandated. State sanction in itself can make no difference. Even if "the state" is an entity over and above its citizens and their legal relations, the wrongness of an act (although not the blameworthiness of an agent) is independent of who performs it. So if discriminating is wrong, it is wrong, and to the same extent, no matter who performs it. Therefore, state-sanctioned past discrimination is no stronger a candidate for rectification than any other discrimination. In any case, even if we did consider state sanction to be morally significant, to be consistent we would have to apply this to all other state-sanctioned wrongs. We would have to say, for example, that we ought to give special treatment now to descendants of people who were harmed under the terms of a statute repealed decades ago. But I take it that no one would support affirmative action for the grandchildren of brewmasters bankrupted by the Volstead Act.

Finally, it has been suggested that grave discriminatory wrongs, such as the lynching of Negroes, were special because done with the intention of intimidating the other members of the terrorized group. Quite so: but again this makes my very point. To call an act of lynching wrong for this reason is to bring it under the umbrella of *intimidation*: a precisely parallel nonracial act of intimidation is just as wrong (although we might have reason to think the perpetrator is not as vicious). Many years ago, unions were in the habit of wrecking restaurants that refused to be unionized as a warning to other restaurants. Even today, Mob enforcers will kill an informer, or a retailer who refuses to pay protection, in order to intimidate other potential informers or defaulters. So if we treat blacks as special because they belong to a class other members of which were terrorized, so must we treat restauranteurs as special, and indeed all small businessmen in businesses once victimized by the protection racket. And I take it that no one would suggest affirmative action for restauranteurs. Nor will it do to say that this is because today no restauranteur is in danger from union or Mob goons. In fact, a restauranteur is in considerably more danger than a black. The last lynching occurred in 1954, while union vandalism and crim-inal extortion are the stuff of today's sensational press.

A subsidiary point. I have so far let pass one peculiarity of affirmative action programs: they award jobs (or placement) to rectify past wrongs. Yet normally when we compensate someone for wrongful deprivation, we give him the equivalent of what he lost, giving him the thing itself only when feasible. If a pianist loses his hands through your negligence, you are not obligated to hire him to do a concert. The whole thrust of his complaint, after all, is that he is no longer competent to undertake such an enterprise. You owe him the money he would have made from concertizing, plus some monetary equivalent of the satisfaction your negligence has cost him. So *even if* past racial discrimination has wrongfully cost Mr. X a job, it does not follow that proper compensation is a job. What he is owed is the job or the monetary equivalent thereof. If the job is unavailable—where this normally included Mr. X's not being the best-qualified applicant—all he is owed is its monetary equivalent. Why, then, is it assumed without question in so many quarters that if past discrimination has cost present-day blacks jobs, they deserve *jobs* rather than the monetary equivalent of the jobs they would have gotten? Only, I believe, because we think there is something *special* about discrimination, that its consequences deserve amelioration in a way that the consequences of other wrongs do not. Discrimination is so bad that not only must we compensate for it, we must so change the world that things will become as if the wrong had never been. Only by attributing such reasoning can I make sense of the special form "affirmative action" programs inevitably take. And if indeed racial discrimination is not especially wrong, such special compensation starts to appear morally arbitrary and bizarre.

It is obvious that no employer has a general obligation to rectify wrongful acts, to offer extraordinary compensation. I am not speaking, again, of righting wrongs he perpetrates or directly benefits from. I mean that if, as a result of some wrong once done—not necessarily to an ancestor—I am worse off than I would have been, you, an arbitrarily chosen employer, have no obligation whatever to neutralize the consequences of that wrong. No one has any obligation to make me as well off as I would have been had that wrong not been committed. Why? Basically because it is *impossible* to rectify the consequences of all past wrongs. Consider how we might decide on compensatory payments. We trace the world back to the moment at which the wrong was done, suppose the wrong not done, and hypothetically trace forward the history of the world. Where I end up under this hypothetical reconstruction is where I deserve to be. I am owed the net difference between where I am now and where I would have been had the wrong not been done. But for most wrongs, it would take omniscience to say how the world would have turned out had the wrong not been done. If you wanted to make up to me the theft of my grandfather's watch in 1900, how on Earth do you propose to reckon the position I would have been in had my grandfather's watch not been stolen? I might have been richer by a watch. I might have been poorer—since, being in fact deprived of my watch, I have worked harder than I otherwise would have. I might not have existed—if my grandfather met my grandmother while hunting for his stolen watch. Indeed, if you suppose yourself under a general ameliorative obligation, you would have to calculate simultaneously how well off each and every one of us would have been had all past wrongs not occurred. There is more: I am supposedly owed a certain something. but who owes it to me? Surely not you—you don't owe me *all* of it. Do all employers owe me an equal proportion? Or is their proportion dependent on how much they have benefited from the initial theft? If the latter, how is one to calculate their debt, if the theft was in another country and another century?

Suppose I take it on myself to yield to Mr. X if I am better off than he is because of some past wrong—not to him, necessarily, since I am offering extraordinary compensation. Now surely there is some *other* past wrong which has made *me* worse off than I would otherwise have been, worse off than (say) Mr. Y. So I must drop myself down to make way for Mr. X, but I also deserve a push up beyond Mr. Y. If each of us tried to put himself just where he would be if there had been no past wrongs, we would all be caught in a mad whirl of exchanging positions and privileges with one another. If a full reckoning were in, those who now seem as if they would end up in a better position might end up in a worse one. Take Mr. X, an American black who we think is worse off then he would have been had there been no slavery. Yet he may now be better off than he would have been had his African ancestors not conquered a neighboring tribe that was then raided by slave traders; had his ancestors respected territorial boundaries, Mr. X might now be a sickly native of Uganda. So unless we quite arbitrarily decide to rectify only some wrongs, we are undertaking a quite impossible task. What about limiting ourselves to rectifying wrongs we know about? But then we should surely try as hard as possible to find out about other wrongs and trace their consequences. Once again, if we set out on that path, we will find ourselves with obligations that cannot be discharged. And an undischargable obligation is no obligation at all. Indeed, it is far from obvious that the consequences of discrimination are easier to trace than those of other wrongs. I know victims of theft who have nothing to show for it. Why not benefit them? It is clearer that they are worse off from a past wrong than that an arbitrarily chosen black is.

We must remember that we are all where we are in the competitive and distributional scheme of things because of past wrongs. It may be that we got something in a wrongful way, but those from whom we got it may have gotten it wrongfully in turn. Who knows but that all of us are in this room because of some dirty Hellenic trick on the plains of Marathon. Perhaps we would award

Western Civilization to the descendants of Xerxes, or give them its dollar equivalent! Each of us lies on a "compensation curve," which graphs jobs against our chances of getting them. These curves are connected: I can't move to a better one without bumping someone else down to a worse. If we try to put each person on the curve he would have occupied had there been no relevant wrongdoing, we will be raising and lowering everybody, sometimes at the same time, with no end in sight. Perhaps God is sufficiently powerful, well-intentioned, and well-informed to put each of us on his proper curve. But no lesser power—not ITT and not HEW—can undertake the task without absurdity.

Since, then, no one has any general rectificatory obligation, and since—as I argued earlier—past discrimination does not stand out from other wrongs as especially demanding righting, I can see no justification at all for reverse discrimination.

I have embedded my main point in a somewhat complex argumentative context. Let me end by highlighting it. While racial discrimination is wrong, it is only one wrong among many and has no special claim on our moral attention. Past discrimination no more deserves extraordinary compensation than many other wrongs. And any employment policy which does treat racial discrimination as special is arbitrary and irrational.

Study Questions

1. What is reverse discrimination, according to Levin?
2. What, according to Levin, is the only possible defense of reverse discrimination?
3. What does Levin mean by saying that there is nothing "morally special" about discrimination?
4. Should discrimination be halted, according to Levin? Why?
5. Why, according to Levin, is it a mistake to claim that racial discrimination is morally special because it involves a whole race?
6. Why, according to Levin, is it a mistake to claim that racial discrimination is morally special because each act of racial discrimination is an instance of a pattern?
7. Why does Levin maintain that it is a mistake to claim that racial discrimination is morally special because past discriminations were approved by the state?
8. If racial discrimination has cost Mr. X a job, does it follow that proper compensation for Mr. X is to give him a job, according to Levin? Explain.
9. Why is it the case, according to Levin, that we have no general obligation to rectify the consequences of past wrongs?

The Case of Allan Bakke

The next selection, by Ronald Dworkin, was published before that of Michael Levin. Nevertheless, it contains something of a response to Levin, though it was not intended to do so. In the article, Dworkin comments on the issues involved in a celebrated affirmative action Supreme Court case, *The Regents of the University of California* v. *Allan Bakke.* Allan Bakke, who was not accepted for admission to the medical school at the University of California, Davis, believed he was denied his rights because of the school's affirmative action policies. He subsequently sued the university.

Dworkin begins by explaining the Bakke case. He then sets forth the long-range goal of affirmative action: to reduce the degree to which American society is racially conscious; that is, to lesson the importance of race in American social and professional life. Affirmative action, in Dworkin's view, is *not* intended to redress or make right the past wrongdoing of racial discrimination. Affirmative action programs do *not*, Dworkin maintains, rest on any assumptions about the guilt of individuals or society for past wrongdoings. Instead, affirmative action is a strategy aimed at achieving a worthwhile objective: that individuals not suffer because they are members of a group that is the object of prejudice.

The heart of Bakke's contention was that the Davis affirmative action program deprived him of his rights, namely (1) the right to be judged on his merit, (2) the right to be judged as an individual rather than as a member of a social group, and (3) the right not to be denied opportunity because of his race. Dworkin examines these three ideas, referring to them as "slogans" or "catch phrases," and finding that, in fact, the principle on which they rest is the very goal of affirmative action: namely, that nobody should suffer because he or she is a member of a group thought less worthy of respect than other groups. But Bakke was not kept out of medical school because his race was thought less worthy of respect; therefore, Bakke has no case, Dworkin contends. It is regrettable, in Dworkin's opinion, that Bakke's personal desires and expectations were dashed by a program aimed at the general good. Steps taken toward the general good often have unfortunate consequences for individuals, however. It is also regrettable to fail to get into medical school because your test scores are too low. But, to take another case, it is also regrettable to lose your old and established business because the opening of a better highway bypasses the business. Indeed, as the owner of the business you may have invested more than Bakke and may have had more reason to believe your business would continue than Bakke had reason to believe he would have gotten into Davis. The scarce resources of medical schools must be used to provide what the more general society needs, Dworkin contends, despite the disappointment this policy causes in individual cases.

Why Bakke Has No Case

Ronald Dworkin

Ronald Dworkin (b. 1931) is a Professor of Jurisprudence at Oxford University and a Professor of Law at New York University. This article was published in *The New York Review of Books*, November 10, 1977.

On October 12, 1977 the Supreme Court heard oral argument in the case of *The Regents of the University of California* v. *Allen Bakke.* No lawsuit has ever been more widely watched or more thoroughly debated in the national and international press before the Court's decision. Still, some of the most pertinent facts set before the Court have not been clearly summarized.

The medical school of the University of California at Davis has an affirmative action program (called the "task force program") designed to admit more black and other minority students. It sets sixteen places aside for which only members of "educationally and economically disadvantaged minorities" compete. Allan Bakke, white, applied for one of the remaining eighty-four places; he was rejected but, since his test scores were relatively high, the medical school has conceded that it could not prove that he would have been rejected if the sixteen places reserved had been open to him. Bakke sued, arguing that the task force program deprived him of his constitutional rights. The California Supreme Court agreed, and ordered the medical school to admit him. The university appealed to the Supreme Court.

The Davis program for minorities is in certain respects more forthright (some would say cruder) than similar plans now in force in many other American universities and professional schools. Such programs aim to increase the enrollment of black and other minority students by allowing the fact of their race to count affirmatively as part of the case for admitting them. Some schools set a "target" of a particular number of minority places instead of setting aside a flat number of places. But Davis would not fill the number of places set aside unless there were sixteen minority candidates it considered clearly qualified for medical education. The difference is therefore one of administrative strategy and not of principle.

So the constitutional question raised by *Bakke* is of capital importance for higher education in America, and a large number of universities and schools have entered briefs *amicus curiae* urging the Court to reverse the California decision. They believe that if the decision is affirmed then they will no longer be free to use explicit racial criteria in any part of their admissions programs, and that they will therefore be unable to fulfill what they take to be their responsibilities to the nation.

It is often said that affirmative action programs aim to achieve a racially conscious society divided into racial and ethnic groups, each entitled, as a group, to some proportionable share of resources, careers, or opportunities. That is a perverse description. American society is currently a racially conscious society; this is the inevitable and evident consequence of a history of slavery, repression, and prejudice. Black men and women, boys and girls, are not free to choose for themselves in what roles—or as members of which social groups—others will characterize them. They are black, and no other feature of personality or allegiance or ambition will so thoroughly influence how they will be perceived and treated by others, and the range and character of the lives that will be open to them.

The tiny number of black doctors and professionals is both a consequence and a continuing cause of American racial consciousness, one link in a long and self-fueling chain reaction. Affirmative action programs use racially explicit criteria because their immediate goal is to increase the number of members of certain races in these professions. But their long-term goal is to *reduce* the degree to which American society is overall a racially conscious society.

The programs rest on two judgments. The first is a judgment of social theory: that America will continue to be pervaded by racial divisions as long as the most lucrative, satisfying, and important careers remain mainly the prerogative of members of the white race, while others feel themselves systematically excluded from a professional and social elite. The second is a calculation of strategy: that increasing the number of blacks who are at work in the professions will, in the long run, reduce the sense of frustration and injustice and racial self-consciousness in the black community to the point at which blacks may begin to think of themselves as individuals who can succeed like others through talent and initiative. At that future point the consequences of nonracial admissions programs, whatever these consequences might be, could be accepted with no sense of racial barriers or injustice.

It is therefore the worst possible misunderstanding to suppose that affirmative action programs are designed to produce a balkanized America, divided into racial and ethnic subnations. They use strong measures because weaker ones will fail; but their ultimate goal is to lessen not to increase the importance of race in American social and professional life.

According to the 1970 census, only 2.1 percent of US doctors were black. Affirmative action programs aim to provide more black doctors to serve black patients. This is not because it is desirable that blacks treat blacks and whites treat whites, but because blacks, for no fault of their own, are now unlikely to be well served by whites, and because a failure to provide the doctors they trust will exacerbate rather than reduce the resentment that now leads them to trust only their own. Affirmative action tries to provide more blacks as classmates for white doctors, not because it is desirable that a medical school class reflect the racial makeup of the community as a whole, but because professional association between blacks and whites will decrease the degree to which whites think of blacks as a race rather than as people, and thus the degree to which blacks think of themselves that way. It tries to provide "role models" for future black doctors, not because it is desirable for a black boy or girl to find adult models only among blacks, but because our history has made them so conscious of their race that the success of whites, for now, is likely to mean little or nothing for them.

The history of the campaign against racial injustice since 1954, when the Supreme Court decided *Brown* v. *Board of Education*, is a history in large part of failure. We have not succeeded in reforming the racial consciousness of our society by racially neutral means. We are therefore obliged to look upon the arguments for affirmative action with sympathy and an open mind. Of course, if Bakke is right that such programs, no matter how effective they may be, violate his constitutional rights then they cannot be permitted to continue. But we must not forbid them in the name of some mindless maxim, like the maxim that it cannot be right to fight fire with fire, or that the end cannot justify the means. If the strategic claims for affirmative action are cogent, they cannot be dismissed simply on the ground that racially explicit tests are distasteful. If such tests are distasteful it can only be for reasons that make the underlying social realities the programs attack more distasteful still.

The New Republic, in a recent editorial opposing affirmative action, missed that point. "It is critical to the success of a liberal pluralism," it said, "that group membership itself is not among the permissible criteria of inclusion and exclusion." But group membership is in fact, as a matter of social reality rather than formal admissions standards, part of what determines inclusion or exclusion for us now. If we must choose between a society that is in fact liberal and an illiberal society that scrupulously avoids formal racial criteria, we can hardly appeal to the ideals of liberal pluralism to prefer the latter.

Professor Archibald Cox of Harvard Law School, speaking for the University of California in oral argument, told the Supreme Court that this is the choice the United States must make. As things stand, he said, affirmative action programs are the only effective means of increasing the absurdly small number of black doctors. The California Supreme Court, in approving Bakke's claim, had urged the university to pursue that goal by methods that do not explicitly take race into account.

But that is unrealistic. We must distinguish, as Cox said, between two interpretations of what the California court's recommendation means. It might mean that the university should aim at the same immediate goal, of increasing the proportion of black and other minority students in the medical school, by an admissions procedure that on the surface is not racially conscious.

That is a recommendation of hypocrisy. If those who administer the admissions standards, however these are phrased, understand that their immediate goal is to increase the number of blacks in the school, then they will use race as a criterion in making the various subjective judgments the explicit criteria will require, because that will be, given the goal, the only right way to make those judgments. The recommendation might mean, on the other hand, that the school should adopt some nonracially conscious goal, like increasing the number of disadvantaged students of all races, and then hope that that goal will produce an increase in the number of blacks as a by-product. But even if that strategy is less hypocritical (which is far from plain), it will almost certainly fail because no different goal, scrupulously administered in a nonracially conscious way, will in fact significantly increase the number of black medical students.

Cox offered powerful evidence for that conclusion, and it is supported by the recent and comprehensive report of the Carnegie Council on Policy Studies in Higher Education. Suppose, for example, that the medical school sets aside separate places for applicants "disadvantaged" on some racially neutral test, like poverty, allowing only those disadvantaged in that way to compete for these places. If the school selects these from that group who scored best on standard medical school aptitude tests, then it will take almost no blacks, because blacks score relatively low even among the economically disadvantaged. But if the school chooses among the disadvantaged on some basis other than test scores, just so that more blacks will succeed, then it will not be administering the special procedure in a nonracially conscious way.

So Cox was able to put his case in the form of two simple propositions. A racially conscious test for admission, even one that sets aside certain places for qualified minority applicants exclusively, serves goals that are in themselves unobjectionable and even urgent. Such programs are, moreover, the only means that offer any significant promise of achieving these goals. If these programs are halted, then no more than a trickle of black students will enter medical or other professional schools for another generation at least.

If these propositions are sound, then on what ground can it be thought that such programs are either wrong or unconstitutional? We must notice an important distinction between two different sorts of objections that might be made. These programs are intended, as I said, to decrease the importance of race in the United States in the long run. It may be objected, first, that the programs will in fact harm the goal more than they will advance it. There is no way now to prove that that is so. Cox conceded, in his argument, that there are costs and risks in these programs.

Affirmative action programs seem to encourage, for example, a popular misunderstanding, which is that they assume that racial or ethnic groups are entitled to proportionate shares of opportunities, so that Italian or Polish ethnic minorities are, in theory, as entitled to their proportionate shares as blacks or Chicanos or American Indians are entitled to the shares the present programs give them. That is a plain mistake: the programs are not based on the idea that those who are aided are entitled to aid, but only on the strategic hypothesis that helping them is now an effective way of attacking a national problem. Some medical schools may well make that judgment, under certain circumstances, about a white ethnic minority. Indeed it seems likely that some medical schools are even now attempting to help white Appalachian applicants, for example, under programs of regional distribution.

So the popular understanding is wrong, but so long as it persists it is a cost of the program because the attitudes it encourages tend to a degree to make people more rather than less conscious of race. There are other possible costs. It is said, for example, that some blacks find affirmative action degrading; they find that it makes them more rather than less conscious of prejudice against their race as such. This attitude is also based on a misperception, I think, but for a small minority of blacks at least it is a genuine cost.

In the view of the many important universities who have such programs, however, the gains will very probably exceed the losses in reducing racial consciousness over-all. This view is hardly so implausible that it is wrong for these universities to seek to acquire the experience that will allow us to judge whether they are right. It would be particularly silly to forbid these experiments if we know that the failure to try will mean, as the evidence shows, that the status quo will almost certainly continue. In any case, this first objection could provide no argument that would justify a decision by the Supreme Court holding the programs unconstitutional. The Court has no business substituting its speculative judgment about the probable consequences of educational policies for the judgment of professional educators.

So the acknowledged uncertainties about the long-term results of such programs could not justify a Supreme Court decision making them illegal. But there is a second and very different form of objection. It may be argued that even if the programs *are* effective in making our society less a society dominated by race, they are nevertheless unconstitutional because they violate the individual constitutional rights of those, like Allan Bakke, who lose places in consequence. In the oral argument Reynold H. Colvin of San Francisco, who is Bakke's lawyer, made plain that his objection takes this second form. Mr. Justice White asked him whether he accepted that the goals affirmative action programs seek are important goals. Mr. Colvin acknowledged that they were. Suppose, Justice White continued, that affirmative action programs are, as Cox had argued, the only effective means of seeking such goals. Would Mr. Colvin nevertheless maintain that the programs are unconstitutional? Yes, he insisted, they would be, because his client has a constitutional right that the programs be abandoned, no matter what the consequences.

Mr. Colvin was wise to put his objections on this second ground; he was wise to claim that his client has rights that do not depend on any judgment about the likely consequences of affirmative action for society as a whole, because if he makes out that claim then the Court must give him the relief he seeks.

But can he be right? If Allan Bakke has a constitutional right so important that the urgent goals of affirmative action must yield, then this must be because affirmative action violates some fundamental principle of political morality. This is not a case in which what might be called formal or technical law requires a decision one way or the other. There is no language in the Constitution whose plain meaning forbids affirmative action. Only the most naïve theories of statutory construction could argue that such a result is required by the language of any earlier Supreme Court decision or of the Civil Rights Act of 1964 or of any other congressional enactment. If Mr. Colvin is right it must be because Allan Bakke has not simply some technical legal right but an important moral right as well.

What could that right be? The popular argument frequently made on editorial pages is that Bakke has a right to be judged on his merit. Or that he has a right to be judged as an individual rather than as a member of a social group. Or that he has a right, as much as any black man, not to be sacrificed or excluded from any opportunity because of his race alone. But these catch phrases are deceptive here, because, as reflection demonstrates, the only genuine principle they describe is the principle that no one should suffer from the prejudice or contempt of others. And that principle is not at stake in this case at all. In spite of popular opinion, the idea that the *Bakke* case presents a conflict between a desirable social goal and important individual rights is a piece of intellectual confusion.

Consider, for example, the claim that individuals applying for places in medical school should be judged on merit, and merit alone. If that slogan means that admissions committees should take nothing into account but scores on some particular intelligence test, then it is arbitrary and, in any case, contradicted by the long-standing practice of every medical school. If it means, on the other hand, that a medical school should choose candidates that it supposes will make the most useful doctors, then everything turns on the judgment of what factors make different doctors useful. The Davis medical school assigned to each regular applicant, as well as to each minority applicant, what is called a "benchmark score." This reflected not only the results of aptitude tests and college grade averages, but a subjective evaluation of the applicant's chances of functioning as an effective doctor, in view of society's present needs for medical service. Presumably the qualities deemed important were different from the qualities that a law school or engineering school or business school would seek, just as the intelligence tests a medical school might use would be different from the tests these other schools would find appropriate.

There is no combination of abilities and skills and traits that constitutes "merit" in the abstract; if quick hands count as "merit" in the case of a prospective surgeon, this is because quick hands will enable him to serve the public better and for no other reason. If a black skin will, as a matter of regrettable fact, enable another doctor to do a different medical job better, then that black skin is by the same token "merit" as well. That argument may strike some as dangerous; but only because they confuse its conclusion — that black skin may be a socially useful trait in particular circumstances — with the very different and despicable idea that one race may be inherently more worthy than another.

Consider the second of the catch phrases I have mentioned. It is said that Bakke has a right to be judged as an "individual," in deciding whether he is to be admitted to medical school and thus to the medical profession, and not as a member of some group that is being judged as a whole. What can that mean? Any admissions procedure must rely on generalizations about groups that are justified only statistically. The regular admissions process at Davis, for example, set a cutoff figure for college grade-point averages. Applicants whose averages fell below that figure were not invited to any interview, and therefore rejected out of hand.

An applicant whose average fell one point below the cutoff might well have had personal qualities of dedication or sympathy that would have been revealed at an interview, and that would have made him or her a better doctor than some applicant whose average rose one point above the line. But the former is excluded from the process on the basis of a decision taken for administrative convenience and grounded in the generalization, unlikely to hold true for every individual, that those with grade averages below the cutoff will not have other qualities sufficiently persuasive. Indeed, even the use of standard Medical College Aptitude Tests (MCAT) as part of the admissions procedure requires judging people as part of groups because it assumes that test scores are a guide to medical intelligence which is in turn a guide to medical ability. Though this judgment is no doubt true statistically, it hardly holds true for every individual.

Allan Bakke was himself refused admission to two other medical schools, not because of his race but because of his age: these schools thought that a student entering medical school at the age of thirty-three was likely to make less of a contribution to medical care over his career than someone entering at the standard age of twenty-one. Suppose these schools relied, not on any detailed investigation of whether Bakke himself had abilities that would contradict the generalization in his specific case, but on a rule of thumb that allowed only the most cursory look at applicants over (say) the age of thirty. Did these two medical schools violate his right to be judged as an individual rather than as a member of a group?

The Davis Medical School permitted whites to apply for the sixteen places reserved for members of "educationally or economically disadvantaged minorities," a phrase whose meaning might well include white ethnic minorities. In fact several whites have applied, though none has been accepted, and the California Court found that the special committee charged with administering the program had decided, in advance, against admitting any. Suppose that decision had been based on the following administrative theory: it is so unlikely that any white doctor can do as much to counteract racial imbalance in the medical professions as a well-qualified and trained black doctor can do that the committee should for reasons of convenience proceed on the presumption no white doctor could. That presumption is, as a matter of fact, more plausible that the corresponding presumption about medical students over the age of thirty, or even the presumption about applicants whose grade-point averages fall below the cutoff line. If the latter presumptions do not deny the alleged right of individuals to be judged as individuals in an admissions procedure, then neither can the former.

Mr. Colvin, in oral argument, argued the third of the catch phrases I mentioned. He said that his client had a right not to be excluded from medical school because of his race alone, and this as a statement of constitutional right sounds more plausible than claims about the right to be judged on merit or as an individual. It sounds plausible, however, because it suggests the following more complex principle. Every citizen has a constitutional right that he not suffer disadvantage, at least in the competition for any public benefit, because the race or religion or sect or region or other natural or artificial group to which he belongs is the object of prejudice or contempt.

That is a fundamentally important constitutional right, and it is that right that was systematically violated for many years by racist exclusions and anti-Semitic quotas. Color bars and Jewish quotas were not unfair just because they made race or religion relevant or because they fixed on qualities beyond individual control. It is true that blacks or Jews do not choose to be blacks or Jews. But it is also true that those who score low in aptitude or admissions tests do not choose their levels of intelligence. Nor do those denied admission because they are too old, or because they do not come from a part of the country underrepresented in the school, or because they cannot play basketball well, choose not to have the qualities that made the difference.

Race seems different because exclusions based on race have historically been motivated not by some instrumental calculation, as in the case of intelligence or age or regional distribution or athletic ability, but because of contempt for the excluded race or religion as such. Exclusion by race was in itself an insult, because it was generated by and signaled contempt.

Bakke's claim, therefore, must be made more specific than it is. He says he was kept out of medical school because of his race. Does he mean that he was kept out because his race is the object of prejudice or contempt? That suggestion is absurd. A very high proportion of those who were accepted (and, presumably, of those who run the admissions program) were members of the same race. He therefore means simply that if he had been black he would have been accepted, with no suggestion that this would have been so because blacks are thought more worthy or honorable than whites.

That is true: no doubt he would have been accepted if he were black. But it is also true, and in exactly the same sense, that he would have been accepted if he had been more intelligent, or made a better impression in his interview, or, in the case of other schools, if he had been younger when he decided to become a doctor. Race is not, in *his* case, a different matter from these other factors equally beyond his control. It is not a different matter because in his case race is not distinguished by the special character of public insult. On the contrary the program presupposes that his race is still widely if wrongly thought to be superior to others.

In the past, it made sense to say that an excluded black or Jewish student was being sacrificed because of his race or religion; that meant that his or her exclusion was treated as desirable in itself, not because it contributed to any goal in which he as well as the rest of society might take pride. Allan Bakke is being "sacrificed" because of his race only in a very artificial sense of the word. He is being "sacrificed" in the same artificial sense because of his level of intelligence, since he would have been accepted if he were more clever than he is. In both cases he is being excluded not by prejudice but because of a rational calculation about the socially most beneficial use of limited resources for medical education.

It may now be said that this distinction is too subtle, and that if racial classifications have been and may still be used for malign purposes, then everyone has a flat right that racial classifications not be used at all. This is the familiar appeal to the lazy virtue of simplicity. It supposes that if a line is difficult to draw, or might be difficult to administer if drawn, then there is wisdom in not making the attempt to draw it. There may be cases in which that is wise, but those would be cases in which nothing of great value would as a consequence be lost. If racially conscious admissions policies now offer the only substantial hope for bringing more qualified black and other minority doctors into the profession, then a great loss is suffered if medical schools are not allowed voluntarily to pursue such programs. We should then be trading away a chance to attack certain and present injustice in order to gain protection we may not need against speculative abuses we have other means to prevent. And such abuses cannot, in any case, be worse than the injustice to which we would then surrender.

We have now considered three familiar slogans, each widely thought to name a constitutional right that enables Allan Bakke to stop programs of affirmative action no matter how effective or necessary these might be. When we inspect these slogans, we find that they can stand for no genuine principle except one. This is the important principle that no one in our society should suffer because he is a member of a group thought less worthy of respect, as a group, than other groups. We have different aspects of that principle in mind when we say that individuals should be judged on merit, that they should be judged as individuals, and that they should not suffer disadvantages because of their race. The spirit of that fundamental principle is the spirit of the goal that affirmative action is intended to serve. The principle furnishes no support for those who find, as Bakke does, that their own interests conflict with that goal.

It is of course regrettable when any citizen's expectations are defeated by new programs serving some more general concern. It is regrettable, for example, when established small businesses fail because new and superior roads are built; in that case people have invested more than Bakke has. And they have more reason to believe their businesses will continue than Bakke had to suppose he could have entered the Davis medical school at thirty-three even without a task force program.

There is, of course, no suggestion in that program that Bakke shares in any collective or individual guilt for racial injustice in America; or that he is any less entitled to concern or respect than any black student accepted in the program. He has been disappointed, and he must have the sympathy due that disappointment, just as any other disappointed applicant—even one with much worse test scores who would not have been accepted in any event—must have sympathy. Each is disappointed because places in medical schools are scarce resources and must be used to provide what the more general society most needs. It is hardly Bakke's fault that racial justice is now a special need—but he has no right to prevent the most effective measures of securing that justice from being used.

Study Questions

1. What is the long-term goal of affirmative action programs, according to Dworkin? On what two judgments do these programs rest?

2. According to Dworkin, does affirmative action try to increase the proportion of blacks in medical school so that the class reflects the racial makeup of the community as a whole? If not, then what is the purpose of increasing that number, in his opinion?

3. Why does affirmative action try to provide role models for future black doctors, according to Dworkin?

4. Why does Dworkin find fault with a medical school's setting aside separate places for disadvantaged applicants on some racially neutral test of "disadvantaged"?

5. Do affirmative action programs present a conflict between a desirable social goal and individual rights, according to Dworkin? Explain.
6. What is Dworkin's criticism of the idea that individuals applying to medical school should be judged on merit?
7. Some people might argue that having a black skin will enable a physician to do a certain kind of medical job better. Is this a dangerous argument, according to Dworkin? Why, or why not?
8. Explain Dworkin's objection to the idea that Bakke has a right to be judged as an individual rather than as a member of a social group.
9. Explain his objection to the idea that Bakke had the opportunity not to be excluded from medical school because of his race.
10. On what principle do the three slogans that Dworkin discusses rest?
11. Is it permissible for steps taken for the general good to have unfortunate consequences for individuals, according to Dworkin? Explain.

Logic and Affirmative Action

Nicholas Capaldi, the author of the next essay, criticizes what he calls "the argument for affirmative action." Please note as you read it that the argument consists of four key concepts. Capaldi's essay consists in a critical analysis of each of these four key concepts. This is a very difficult essay, and we will help you with it. The basic idea is that, according to Capaldi, affirmative action can be justified only (1) by conceiving of discrimination in terms of nonempirical and nontestable conceptions of human nature and the goals of human activity, (2) by distorting the notion of compensation, and (3) by requiring radical social engineering.

The first concept is discrimination, as expressed in the idea that the major reason why blacks are less able to compete in American society is the discrimination they have suffered. In the section called "Discrimination," Capaldi begins by distinguishing prejudice from discrimination. He then addresses discrimination in the form of public policies ("the old objective sense" of "discrimination"), noting that it is nearly impossible to measure how much of a black individual's impairment actually resulted from these policies. Next, he asserts that because of this difficulty, affirmative action advocates conceive of (or "subtly redefine") discrimination as a property suffered by groups, not individuals; that is, these advocates believe that discrimination consists not merely in overt public policies but in a whole web of social practices and attitudes. Because this second kind of "nonobjective" or "theoretical" discrimination is "collective," its remedy can bypass the measurement difficulty noted above.

Capaldi concludes this section with a summary, but don't be confused, because the content of the summary is quite different from the content of the section it supposedly summarizes. Indeed, this summary would be more appropriate at the end of the paper than at the end of this section of the paper. Keep in mind that Capaldi's main intention in this section is to suggest that the claim that American blacks have suffered a long history of being discriminated against is not the straightforward and unambiguous factual claim it appears to be.

The next section deals with the concept of potential, as expressed in the idea that because of their long history of being discriminated against, blacks have not been able to realize their full potential. To what extent does it make sense even to talk about individuals or groups as having a potential? asks Capaldi. It makes sense, he suggests, only if you have a teleological view of human nature—the view that there is some true end or objective or goal of human activity. But, he says, there is no consensus about human nature that makes it meaningful to talk about the true ends of human activity. There is a myriad of views about the true ends of human activity and thus about peoples' potential, as well. It follows, therefore, that we can't establish what is required or sufficient for achieving those ends of fulfilling someone's potential. Further, without knowledge of or agreement about the ends of human activity, we can't know when the obstacles (in particular, discrimination) to achieving those ends have been removed.

At this point, Capaldi begins a discussion of the relationship between teleology (the idea that there is some true end at which human activity aims) and determinism (the idea that what happens is determined by what happened earlier). Proponents of affirmative action, he says, must choose the third of three options and subscribe both to teleology and to determinism—and that, he maintains, is not very easy to do.

Having examined the concepts of discrimination and potential, Capaldi next discusses (in the subsequent section of the paper, "The Distribution of Talent") the idea that the potential ("talent") of blacks is roughly equivalent to that of whites. In the absence of discrimination one would therefore expect, for example, that if blacks are 11 percent of the population, then 11 percent of all physicians would be black. Capaldi points out an apparent problem for affirmative action advocates when they are asked for evidence that talent (that is, potential) is equally distributed among blacks and whites: If talent is the same among the black population and the white population, then why is achievement different? The advocates of affirmative action answer that the disparity in achievement is due to discrimination. But—and this is the problem—if the advocates of affirmative action are then asked to offer evidence that there is discrimination, the only answer they give is that there is a disparity in achievement. The fact is, Capaldi says, we don't know how talents are distributed except through actual achievement. The advocates of affirmative action, in his opinion, provide no objective way of measuring talent (potential, ability) apart from achievement, and thus they give us bizarre statistical arguments. For example, these advocates dismiss statistics that blacks' IQs are lower than whites', maintaining that these statistics don't show a difference in potential between blacks and whites; at the same time, however, they completely accept statistics that black incomes are less than whites, claiming that these show evidence of discrimination.

Near the end of this section, Capaldi discusses discrimination in the second sense—discrimination not as factual policies but as collective social forces. Those liberals who conceive of discrimination in this second sense are committed to the idea that society is not a simple collection of individual people, but an organic system whose individuals interact with one another in synergistic ways. Such liberals face two difficulties: (1) specifying which interactions are responsible for the problems allegedly caused by discrimination, and (2) showing why any prescribed remedy will not produce further problems for society.

The last section of the essay focuses on compensation. Normally, for compensation to be paid to the victims of discrimination, it is necessary both to identify the party at fault and also to show that the discrimination caused an impairment of function. When discrimination is treated not as a matter of specific public policies but rather as a theory of collective social forces, neither condition can be met. Advocates of affirmative action, however, abandon the concept of compensation in favor of "realignment," or restoring victims to the position they would have had prior to discrimination. Capaldi then explains how realignment requires creating a wholly new kind of society.

The Illogic of Affirmative Action

Nicholas Capaldi

> . . . endeavouring that they should all start fair, and not in hanging a weight upon the swift to diminish the distance between them and the slow . . . but if all were done which it would be in the power of a good government to do, by instruction and by legislation, to diminish this inequality of opportunities, the difference of fortune arising from people's own earnings could not justly give umbrage.
>
> —John Stuart Mill, *Principles of Political Economy*, II, chapter 1, paragraph 3.

Nicholas Capaldi: (b. 1939) chairs the Department of Philosophy at the University of Tulsa. This selection is from his book *Out of Order: Affirmative Action and the Crisis of Doctrinaire Liberalism* (Buffalo, N.Y.: Prometheus Books, 1985).

Introduction

It is impossible to take affirmative action at face value. Its advocates either do not understand it and its connection with prior social movements such as civil rights, or they are deliberately camouflaging the novel policy of affirmative action by ingenious attempts to argue that it is a continuation of past policies. . . . It is now time to cut through the rhetoric and to expose the underlying structure and purpose of the policy of affirmative action.

Affirmative action has been defined by its official advocates as the policy of placing minorities in the position that the "minority would have enjoyed if it had not been the victim of discrimination." We have called this *realignment*, in the context of the shackled runner. The policy of affirmative action is by definition linked with the concept of "discrimination." In examining the concept of "discrimination" . . . and how it functions as part of the larger argument, we are going to show that the concept has been subtly redefined to fit the new purposes of affirmative action. Our analysis will show . . . that the new concept of "discrimination": (1) is theoretically impossible to specify, (2) is practically dangerous to administer (requiring a new social order reminiscent of the corporate fascist state . . .), and (3) presupposes a teleological view of human nature that is just plain false.

The Argument for Affirmative Action

As a result of their long history of being discriminated against in American society, blacks have not been able to realize their full potential.[1] This, in turn, has led to their not being able to acquire the maximum amount of merit that accrues to those who live in a society where merit relates in some fashion to developed potential. If America were a truly just society, it would seek to provide for the full development of everyone's potential, and it would see to it that merit was fully equated with social roles (jobs, etc.). Thus, if blacks were allowed to develop their full potential, they would play an increasingly significant role in our society. Moreover, since the innate potential of blacks as a group is roughly proportionately equivalent to the potential of whites as a group, the merit of the groups is roughly proportional, and hence the roles of the respective groups should be roughly proportional. So, for example, if blacks are 11 percent of the total population, then roughly 11 percent of all doctors could be expected to be black. A just society is thus committed to eliminating discrimination and compensating those who have suffered from its effects. One form of compensation is to give to those individuals who have been denied full development of potential the roles they rightly would have had if they had not been the victims of discrimination. Affirmative action is just such a measure and therefore is a legitimate form of compensation in a just society. There are four key concepts in this argument, which we shall examine:

1. discrimination
2. potential
3. the distribution of talent
4. compensation

Discrimination

Let us begin by distinguishing discrimination from prejudice. Prejudice is a psychological attitude that characterizes individuals. Discrimination is a social policy of exclusion directed against members of some readily identifiable group. The existence of prejudice is not evidence of discrimination. The existence of prejudice is neither a necessary nor a sufficient condition of discrimination. Those who refuse to endorse the policy of affirmative action are not necessarily denying the existence of prejudice. Moreover, prejudiced individuals do not always practice discrimination. In fact, such individuals may sometimes grant preferential treatment to the very people against whom they are prejudiced. This they may do from guilt, shame, or self-protection.

Prejudice is a prejudgment presumably based on a *lack of experience*, and perhaps acts in a way that precludes the acquisition of the kinds of experience that would contravene it. On the other hand, it is certainly possible to acquire negative judgments from experience. For example, it is a fact that certain neighborhoods populated largely by lower-class blacks are high crime areas. It is not prudent to walk in such areas at night. However, we have no specific word for these prudential judgments. While discrimination based upon a false prejudgment is unfair, the acquisition of criteria from experience and their application to life is precisely what we think of as sound judgment.

Therefore, we must not only discriminate between prejudice and discrimination, we must discriminate between prejudice and ordinary prudence, prejudice and hasty generalization, prejudice and the fallacies of division and composition. We must also be alert to the fact that prejudice is used as a pejorative term to characterize those who refuse to interpret their experience along lines favored by doctrinaire liberals. The most powerful and persuasive subliminal argument used by advocates of affirmative action is the confusion in the minds of most people between prudence and discrimination.

In the context of U.S. history, discrimination can be factually identified with Jim Crow legislation, identifiable with segregated schools and separate facilities in general. If this is the definition of discrimination, then we can note that in the past not all blacks were subjected to this kind of discrimination. Moreover, this form of discrimination has been outlawed.[2]

The argument, of course, is more complex. Still keeping the definition of discrimination confined to purely factual states of affairs like Jim Crow legislation, it can be argued that such legislation produced specific long-term effects. This considerably broadens the scope of the term. To take an example, if having attended a segregated school or having been denied the opportunity to become an apprentice in a union prior to the 1964 Civil Rights Act impairs the capacity of a black to compete in today's economy, then it is plausible to suggest that discrimination and its effects have created a problem for us now. But if discrimination is broadened in this way, then we must establish that discrimination in this sense is the *sole or major cause of the impairment of capacity to compete.*

This is much more difficult thing to do than most people seem to realize.[3] First of all, one would need an independent measure of capacity or potential in order to determine when and by how much it had been impaired. Second, how can we rule out other hypotheses? Is it not just as plausible to argue that events prior to Jim Crow legislation — such as the institution of slavery — may have established patterns of behavior that are at the root of impaired capacity? If slavery is the culprit, then we should note that it was a practice in Africa before the colonies were established. How do we know that some ancestor perhaps of the Ayatollah Khomeni may not have been the ultimate source of our problem? How would all of this apply to blacks born after 1964, a considerably large percentage? Is there some way to trace an intergenerational impairment of capacity? Is it possible that government programs such as welfare may be a larger factor? How far back into the past are we to go in order to arrive at some estimation of what is equitable? It would seem that there is no rationale for stopping at one place rather than another. As Justice Powell put it, this concept is ageless.

If we must take into account events prior to the arrival of blacks in the United States as slaves, then we must also take into account the alleged oppression of European and Asian immigrants prior to their arrival in the United States. The concept is quickly getting out of hand. Notice as well the final absurdity of this direction. If the object of affirmative action is to restore blacks to the position they would have had before they were impaired, then it might follow that blacks are to be repatriated to Africa! Most blacks would reject this suggestion, and I think it tells us a lot more than affirmative action advocates want us to hear.

At this point a radical transformation takes place in the argument. *Discrimination ceases to refer to a purely factual state of affairs and becomes a theoretical term.* This transformation is already implicit in the notion of "discrimination and its effects." This transformation might even be more accurately described as a metamorphosis.

This new conception of discrimination can be called the collective-participation model of discrimination. Here discrimination is a property of groups, not individuals, who are prevented from participating fully in social life. Participation is understood much more broadly than simply in economic terms. Since the problem created by this kind of discrimination is collective, then the remedy can be collective and can effectively bypass providing empirical evidence on an individual basis.

Lest anyone think that the second conception of discrimination is purely hypothetical, let me quote one recent policy definition: "Discriminatory acts can be viewed as acts that have a negative impact on minorities and women."[4] What are the consequences of this definition? Perhaps the most important is that if a merit system should as a contingent matter of fact have negative impact, then a merit system would be a discriminatory system. Moreover, this definition precludes the possibility of certain people being discriminated against, specifically white males.

I think that enough has been said to indicate that the argument for affirmative action is not a straightforward argument that begins with facts and some consensual norms and then proceeds to make recommendations. On the contrary, the very meaning of concepts like "discrimination" has been transformed, and we have uncovered a potential conflict of norms that may be at the heart of this controversial issue.

To sum up, we must distinguish two conceptions of discrimination:

discrimination$_1$ — those past public policies that have impaired and continued to impair the functioning of blacks. The difficulties here are:

- a. How much impairment is there? It seems next to impossible to determine this. The most remarkable thing about this possibility is that, although it is the most popular one and the one most often invoked, no serious empirical support is ever provided for any of the contingent elements that compose it.
- b. Other than outlawing such practices, what should be done about this impairment?
    1. compensation, where applicable (see later section in this chapter).
    2. remediation
        - a — depends upon availability of resources
        - b — must be shared with all victims, not just blacks.
        - c — this is a negotiable political-economic matter, not a right.
    3. neither compensation (1) nor remediation (2) is realignment.[5]

discrimination$_2$—all practices, private or public, past, present, or future, that inhibit full participation.

a. Affirmative action as realignment is a policy for this alleged form of discrimination.
b. It requires not just a marginal adjustment of personnel but a change in the goals of our society.
c. Advocates of affirmative action as realignment frequently slur the distinction between discrimination$_1$ and discrimination$_2$.

Potential and Freedom

The second key concept in the argument for affirmative action is the concept of potential. This stage of the argument makes it clear that we are dealing with a new understanding of discrimination. Quite literally, the argument is committed to the view that someone is discriminated against *if and only if* he has not been allowed to develop his full potential. Part of what this means is that if you have not developed your full potential then you have been discriminated against. This changes the kind of evidence required to determine the existence of discrimination. Instead of establishing the existence of discrimination and then showing impairment of potential, we now find out if an individual or group has reached full potential.

Two general observations come immediately to mind. First, it is not clear that this definition of "discrimination" will apply only to blacks. If it applies to nonblacks as well, and possibly to every individual and group, then we are committed by the ultimate logic of the full argument to a massive and total restructuring of society.[6] This is another reason that the policy of affirmative action deserves careful attention, for its implications are far more radical than is routinely recognized.

The second general problem is to what extent does it make sense to talk about individuals or groups as having a potential?[7] Put another way, to what extent are we asserting psychological or sociological facts, and to what extent are we appealing to norms?

It is difficult to imagine anyone wanting to maintain that each and every individual has a specific potential, such as the potential to be a shoemaker or to be a third baseman for the Yankees. On a strictly empirical basis, I might imagine an infinite number of potentials for an individual and at the same time eliminate a myriad of others. For example, I might have such dexterity that I can be said to have the potential to become a great pickpocket or a great surgeon. I might also have potentials that are socially and economically irrelevant, such as the ability to spit farther than any other human being. Moreover, these potentials might conflict: the development of one might preclude the development of another.

The argument would seem to make sense best as a teleological theory about human nature. What it presumes is that some one or a selected few of these potentials are more truly me than the others and, further, that the successful development of these "true" potentials as opposed to others will bring me something like happiness or satisfaction or fulfillment.

I think it is safe to identify the norms of the argument for affirmative action as those of liberalism. Liberalism, as we have defined it, consists of a basic psychological theory and derivative theories of social structure and political organization. The basic psychology is teleological. Every human being is alleged to have built-in ends. These ends form some sort of homeostatic system such that there is no ultimate conflict. If we fail to achieve an end, it is because of external environmental constraints. The necessary conditions for full development are known as needs. Society, in turn, is the product of interacting individuals. Just as there is no ultimate conflict among the drives of an individual, so there is no necessary conflict among the members of society. Conflict is symptomatic of ignorance or external constraints. Equilibrium is guaranteed by the assumption that no individual can be fully developed unless all are. Given this implicit harmony, there must be an objective social good embracing all other goods. Given this social good we can theoretically construct or reconstruct a society along optimal lines so that not only has each and every individual his rightful place but the total social good is maximized. To the extent that individuals or institutions fail, the state may intervene to bring about the monolithic and collective good.

If such a teleological theory is at work in the argument for affirmative action, then a number of issues must be faced. First, what is the empirical evidence for the existence of such a fundamental thesis about human nature? Second, what concept of freedom is entailed by a teleological conception of human nature? It is here that we shall have to raise questions about the elements of choice and responsibility. Third, what is the relation of the theological theory here invoked to the issue of determinism, specifically, the causal factors that influence or determine the pursuit of ends?

We begin by noting that there is no consensus either inside or outside of philosophy on the nature of man, or even whether man has a nature. This is not just an academic point but bears directly upon the argument. In short, there is no consensual basis for establishing the true potential or end or ends of human activity. Failure to produce positive evidence by itself does not disqualify the premise, but I think it does put the premise in limbo. For all we know some teleological theory of human nature might be true, but then for all we know any one of a number of teleological theories might be true. The ambiguity of such a position is exactly what allows for a multiplicity of conflicting teleological views. It is because a vast variety of teleological views are widely held that a variety of conflicting positions on affirmative action have been taken by people, all of whom think that they are appealing to the same argument.

I specifically want to focus attention on what I take to be the inherent difficulty of any form of liberalism. The very reason that there are alternative versions of liberalism, potentially infinite in number, is that all liberals subscribe to a teleological theory for which there are no empirical parameters. In short, any liberal can claim anything to be or not to be an ultimate end without fear of refutation on empirical grounds. What the conflict over affirmative action reveals more than anything else is a conflict among such liberal alternatives.

Not only is the argument jeopardized by conflicting interpretations of human teleology, but, in the absence of a consensus or clear evidential support for any one conception of human ends, there can be no persuasive arguments for what stands in the way of achieving those ends. Since we cannot conclusively establish the ends, we cannot conclusively establish the conditions both necessary and sufficient for achieving the ends, and we cannot therefore propose remedies when the conditions are absent. Even if we had a consensus on the ends, we might still have no consensus on the means.

What possible meaning, then, can be given to freedom and bondage ("discrimination") in this context? The argument seems to presuppose the liberal notion of freedom, traditionally defined as the absence of arbitrary external constraints. Constraints are arbitrary if they interfere with the achievement of legitimate ends. In contemporary political jargon, we are not free if our "needs" are not met, specifically our "basic needs." Far from being redundant, a "basic" need is a necessary condition to a legitimate end.

What happens when this conception of freedom addresses itself to what is claimed to be a case of "discrimination?" For example, suppose a local law forcibly excludes me from schools and libraries. It may very well be that under these circumstances I cannot acquire sufficient literacy to pursue my career aims or even discover what careers are available. A good deal of social legislation of the civil rights variety has aimed at and succeeded in large part in removing barriers or external constraints such as those just described. This approach is necessarily limited to removing external constraints. But how do we know when all of the obstacles have been removed? All of the barriers are removed when the anticipated end is achieved. Since alternative teleological theories anticipate different things, they cannot agree that all of the barriers have been removed. It does not matter what is done, for it is always open to an alternative teleology to claim that there is a next hidden variable to be removed.

When confronted with the problem of choice—namely, to what extent individuals who are discriminated against are responsible for their own predicament or how they handle it—those theorists who subscribe to this conception of freedom seem to fall back onto something like Locke's *tabula rasa.* It seems that our choices or decisions are based upon the information available and how we interpret the information. Yet, how we interpret the information also seems to be something accounted for in crudely empiricist terms. Thus, in a special sense, no individual is really responsible for how he reacts to any situation. Any number of philosophers who support affirmative action can be cited as subscribing to such a view.[8]

Even those who wish to get away from conceiving of the social world as the product of isolable atomic individuals hardly fare any better. *That* social and moral phenomena are in some sense influenced by social structure is obvious enough. *How* this social influence affects the autonomy of individuals remains obscure. Despite attempts to detach themselves from naive atomistic individualism, relational social theorists still keep talking about individuals as if they were passive recipients. Nowhere do they deal seriously with how the social actor can mold the audience as well.[9] At least, they don't when they discuss or advocate affirmative action. Moreover, I cannot imagine a form of social discourse that merely reflects existing conditions without providing at the same time a structure for transforming those conditions.

The final philosophical problem raised by the concept of potential is the relationship between teleology and determinism. By appealing to the notion of human potential, the argument seems committed to some teleological theory of human nature. By its concern with factors that objectively deflect from the development of that potential, the argument seems committed to some form of causal determinism.

We are faced with three possibilities. The argument for affirmative action is either (a) teleological but not deterministic; (b) deterministic but not teleological; or (c) a form of teleology that is held along with determinism.

If we choose the first alternative, an autonomous teleology, then we can neither definitively specify those conditions that inhibit development of potential nor offer any remedy against them. The second alternative is even more unpalatable, for a deterministic theory renders the whole enterprise of affirmative action, and any other policy, unintelligible. It is a commonplace objection, for example, to Skinner's behaviorism that it makes social planning a mystery, precisely because it cannot account for or justify those values in terms of which we seek to condition people. No reason can be given for preferring one result to another. The second alternative excludes all consideration of values.

I believe that affirmative action supporters are saddled with the third possibility, an untenable combination of teleology and determinism. A large part of this argument is a blatant appeal to determinism. Although many may grant that past discrimination is a condition of underachievement, few outside of affirmative action circles will grant that it is a cause. Moreover, the belief in and the search for both the necessary and sufficient conditions of achievement presuppose a deterministic universe wherein individual choice and initiative are illusory.

The combination of teleology and determinism serves an important propaganda function. In explaining why people fail to achieve, there is an appeal to determinism. When dealing with complaints that past remediation programs have failed or with evidence counter to their favorite assumptions, affirmative action supporters state their theory in teleological terms. It is impossible to refute any teleological assertion. If most people do not behave as affirmative action supporters say they do, we must remember that they speak about people under ideal circumstances. Finally, they conveniently ignore determinism when they want to blame their critics.

Affirmative action must somehow make sense of itself as both teleological and deterministic. To my knowledge, no one has ever shown precisely how this applies in human social behavior. Unfortunately, what affirmative action and many other social policies offer is speculation in the absence of positive knowledge. It is in fact a crude appeal to ignorance. Finally, there is no guarantee that if we obtained the relevant knowledge it would entail or be compatible with the preferred values or results.

Let me make these points more technically but briefly. A combination of teleology and determinism is a dualism, a theory that human nature operates on two different but related levels at once. It is not logically impossible. But if it were the case, and no one has shown that it is the case, it would amount to a miraculous coincidence. Moreover, such a coincidence need not be positive. We could be determined at one level to seek self-destruction at another level. Finally, there is no guarantee that the same coincidence holds for everybody, that is, we could each be determined (physiologically, genetically, and so on) to pursue different or conflicting aims. The latter possibility has led some theorists to postulate a wider social net that permits a distinction between "normal" and "abnormal" combinations of determinism and teleology. By the time we arrive at this stage we are already flirting with philosophical theories of organic social structure and totalitarianism. There is no space to develop these views here, but the transition to such organic totalities was the path taken by Hegel, it was the origin of the totalitarian element in liberalism, which we shall mention in later chapters, and it foreshadows the egalitarian emphasis on organic participation with which we end this chapter.

The Distribution of Talent

The linchpin of the argument for affirmative action is the assumption that the potential of blacks is roughly equivalent to that of whites. That is, it is assumed that the distribution of talent is proportionately equal to the percentage of the population as a whole.[10]

There are two kinds of questions we must raise about this premise. First, what kind of talent is being discussed? Second, what is the empirical status of the claim?

Let us begin with the kind of talent in question. It is usually assumed in the contexts in which this argument is presented that the talents in question are those traditionally recognized in a modern technological society and culture such as our own. In succeeding paragraphs I shall make the same assumption. But we should note the possibility that the argument really wants to assert that there are other talents relevant to a different kind of social world and that we are being urged to change the fundamental values in our society. This is all well and good. But if that is the case, then affirmative action is a very different kind of policy from what we were led to believe. It would then be, to put it crudely, not a question of letting blacks into the game but a question of changing the nature of the game.

Unless otherwise indicated, I assume talents to be those generally agreed upon and conventionally recognized as such. Now, the question is, what sort of empirical evidence do we have for the distribution of talent? The answer is none!

I do not see how, given present knowledge, there can be any such evidence. Racial intelligence, for example, is a bogus issue introduced long ago to advance political programs. Strictly speaking, intelligence or skill would be a property of individuals, not of groups. There is no way in which one "race" can be superior or inferior to another.

A call for evidence is usually greeted with a circular argument. First it is concluded that uneven racial distribution of achievement is the result of discrimination, and then the evidence for discrimination is supposed to be the uneven distribution of achievement. Moreover, the more we argue that achievement is dependent upon the environment, the more plausible it becomes to argue that everyone's native talent is identical. Is this really less plausible than the assumption that talents are proportionately distributed by group? The fact is, and it is a most frustrating one, we do not know—short of actual achievement—how talents are distributed.

Given the traditional American value scheme, it is to be expected that each person be treated as an individual on his or her personal merit, not by reference to any group. There is no reason even to calculate composite scores of groups, for the mere recording is an invitation to invidious comparison and potential misuse. To judge the individual by the composite property of any group is to commit the fallacy of division. Even if it were the case that the composite group scores were not equivalent, it would still be irrelevant for social policy. Of course, if the disparity in composite scores was an effect of something, then such scores would be important. But the causal relation must be shown and cannot be assumed merely from the score itself.

What advocates of affirmative action need is a causal argument linking certain forms of discrimination with the impairment of function. They fail to do this on two counts. First, they provide no independent measurement of talent prior to discrimination and, second, they have not clarified the theoretical interpretation of discrimination to the point where it can be identified independently of the concept of talent.

Advocates of affirmative action act as if the burden of proof rests on their opponents, whereas the burden is really on the advocates. Precisely because there is no objective way to gauge ability apart from some performance, the onus is on those who suggest a remedy for the problem. Switching the onus is a rhetorical tactic designed to embarrass opponents of affirmative action by smearing them with the charge of racism. There is also a blatant inconsistency here. Advocates of affirmative action repeatedly charge that current criteria of academic admission—and in fact all objective criteria—are incapable of predicting future professional success. At the same time they are serenely confident about all retroactive estimations of what might have been (contrary-to-fact conditionals).

Even if one admits that without discrimination blacks would perform better, this alone implies very little. For the sake of argument, suppose that on a scale of 200 to 800 the composite score of blacks is about 300 and that without discrimination the score would be 600. This will still not allow large numbers of blacks to enter those elite institutions where a score of 700 is the floor. Moreover, if we eliminate discrimination for all groups, who is to say that the competition would not be tougher. In fact, this seems to have happened in a sense. Now that everybody knows about special preparation for LSAT and MSAT exams, the scores have risen dramatically over the last decade. A score that guaranteed admission ten years ago will not accomplish that end now. The women's liberation movement has encouraged a large shift in career goals, so that blacks must compete now with women in a way that white males did not have to consider ten or twenty years ago.

Would it be possible to design and perform a crucial experiment on this issue? That is, suppose a randomly selected group of black children are put through a special program in order to determine "what might have been." If all interested parties to this dispute could agree, we might have a crucial experiment. Another crucial experiment that has been proposed is that we practice affirmative action for one or two generations.

No doubt some parties would abide by the results of the crucial experiment, but I doubt all would. Just in case the results are not statistical parity, we can prepare in advance the reasons that will be given for disregarding the experiment:

a. we chose the wrong sample of children,
b. too much pressure was put on this group, because they knew they were part of a crucial experiment,
c. we gave them the wrong remediation (hidden variable argument).

In the absence of clearly defined and empirically correlated concepts, we are given a bizarre statistical argument. Bare statistics about I.Q. differences are rejected out of hand or explained away, but bare statistics about comparative group income are given a magisterial status. We should realize that every simple correlation between a set of social circumstances and the lack of achievement can be met with a known counterexample. In the past it made sense to say that particular individuals succeeded despite persecution and discrimination. Such individuals are our cultural heroes. The present line of argument contravenes a large part of our past thinking on this issue.

The statistical argument also overlooks those statistics that contravene the case. In some activities, like athletics, blacks are not only overrepresented statistically but dominate the activity. Again, is it meaningful to compare group incomes and positions without qualification? For example, the average age of the Jew in the U.S. is mid-forties. The average age of the black is late twenties. Given the fact that in some fields income and prestige have some correlation with age and experience, the disparity would have to be modified downward. Ironically, this would also imply that blacks, and especially Hispanics, are entitled to an even greater percentage of slots at the entry levels.

It is sometimes argued that access to some roles is by reference to test scores and other criteria that bear no relation to those talents actually relevant to later job success. We may be choosing the wrong people by looking at the wrong criteria. This is a very plausible argument and deserves to be developed independently of this context. Yet, the argument makes sense only if we can determine success on the job. If there is an objective measure of success, then why not look into the selection records of various members of selection committees and personnel officers, and if some are more likely to pick future successes than others, then we should rely more on their judgment and intuition. Of course, there is no reason to believe that such intuition will produce the balanced outcome that is at issue or that it will not reflect even more unfavorably on some statistical groups.

The other thing worth noting about the barrage of arguments on standards is that some conflict with others when brought together. Consider this argument complex:

A →	B
discrimination	impairs testing ability
C →	D
mysterious attributes	job success

If C is a mystery, and if C is not identical with B, how do we know that discrimination impaired precisely those real qualities that account for job success? The answer is that we do not. This reduces the evidence of discrimination to mere appeals to pity.

The latest study of standardized tests, a four-year study under the auspices of the National Academy of Sciences, concluded that such tests were not biased and that they did predict later performance. The panel warned against exclusive use of the test but nevertheless insisted that the tests reliably measured what they were supposed to measure.

It is now admitted that it is in fact impractical to take individual cases of "discrimination" and to seek redress for the individuals involved. That is why we supposedly need a policy directed toward minority groups as a whole.[11] If it is difficult to build a case around individuals, how did we arrive at the generalization without specific instances? Why is it practically impossible? It would not seem to be a matter of expense here any more than that consideration would apply to criminal offenses. The difficulty is in proving discrimination as intent and in proving how this alleged 'discrimination' has thwarted the development of innate potential. I suspect that the reason the case is not made is that it cannot be made, and that the inability to document the case is the explanation behind the suggested administrative arrangement, namely, affirmative action. 'Discrimination' is not a fact but a theory used to justify a policy.

As we have already discovered, the difficulty is in providing any clear connection between potential and discrimination. Part of the difficulty is in determining the meaning and extension of potential. Part of the difficulty, as we have also seen, is the ambiguity in the concept of 'discrimination.' There is, however, another interpretation of 'discrimination' that we have mentioned but have not so far discussed in any detail, and it is the version we have called discrimination$_2$ (collectivist-participation). I would now like to turn to this distinguishable version of the argument for affirmative action.

Let us begin by considering the claim that 'discrimination' is not a mere matter of consciously held policies but of cumulative and indirect social forces. It is argued that 'discrimination' is a whole web of social circumstances rather than something that we can isolate. This interpretation of 'discrimination' is an analysis of social life in terms of organic or functional wholes as opposed to atomistic individualism.[12] It is both a methodological thesis about how to understand the social world and a normative thesis about how the social world ought to function. Again, the connection is not arbitrary but follows a pattern similar to other forms of liberalism where alleged facts about human nature (goals) serve as criteria for evaluating social practices. If modern liberalism is seriously committed to an organic view of society, then it faces on its own account special difficulties. The general difficulty is that a practical decision has to be made about how to implement a change in an organic system. Since the system does not operate in such a way that it can be explained by reference to its constituents but must take into account how the constituents interact with each other, two issues must be faced. First, which interactions are in fact primarily responsible for the malfunction of the system? Second, we can focus on selected causal influences and ignore others in implementing change?

What reason is there to believe that focussing on employment and graduate admissions will set the system aright? Let us, for the sake of argument, entertain the counter hypothesis that the major cause of lessened participation is family life amongst blacks. If so, then increased or full participation would seem to require a social or political policy aimed at that relationship. I am not alleging that this is the correct hypothesis. I am suggesting that I have seen no evidence—in fact, not even an argument—to the effect that we know which causes are major. The doctrinaire liberal must present some argument. He doesn't.

The second special difficulty for doctrinaire liberalism under these circumstances is that, having committed itself to the assumption that we operate within an organic system, it must also show that any policy it advocates will not produce a serious disruption of the *entire* system. This issue must be squarely faced. We cannot assume that our remedy is without side effects and that it will operate only on the individual constituents we select.

Compensation

The fourth and final key concept in the argument for affirmative action is the concept of compensation. For the argument to work, it must somehow be shown that compensation is a form of remediation, and remediation is the same as realignment. The reason for this is the important insight that if there are long-term effects of some forms of discrimination, some of them may not be eliminated or eliminable when the original practice is eliminated.

Let us take as an example something not directly connected with discrimination. Someone who is maimed or paralyzed cannot be restored to his original condition. Analogously, a young man unjustly incarcerated at the age of eighteen for a period of thirty years cannot have time restored to him, nor can be pursue many of the careers when he is released that he might have pursued when he was eighteen. Certainly no medical school will admit him. In the same way, those who have suffered certain specific long-term forms of discrimination cannot simply pick up where they might have been. For some, it is literally too late; for others, there are formidable handicaps to overcome.

Is compensation applicable to cases of discrimination, and, if so, in what form? To determine this, let us take some noncontroversial instances of compensation. Let us say that a doctor is paralyzed in an automobile accident in which another identifiable party was at fault. The doctor is likely to receive monetary compensation awarded by the court on the basis of projected earnings. Projected or potential earnings are calculated on the basis of what the doctor was already earning. Next, let us imagine that the doctor is killed in the accident. The doctor cannot be restored to life; the members of his family cannot be compensated for the loss of love and companionship. Again, the only meaningful compensation is monetary, based upon actual earnings. It is inconceivable that the courts would guarantee the children of the doctor a seat in medical school as a form of compensation.

In order for compensation to be paid to the victims of 'discrimination' we would have to (a) identify the party at fault and (b) show that the discrimination caused impairment of function. As far as (a) is concerned, even our doctor could not collect if there were no party at fault or if the guilty party were not apprehended and in a position to pay (e.g., insurance).

Where discrimination is treated as a factual state of affairs victims have been compensated. For example, applicants for jobs as truck drivers were given the first available jobs after a company was convicted of employment discrimination. When 'discrimination' is treated as a theory, the perpetrators are either unavailable, unidentifiable, or nonexistent. Recall that the advocates of affirmative action who treat 'discrimination' as a theoretical term stressed the concatenation of unintentional social forces that produced discrimination. The price they must now pay for that move is to disqualify themselves from using the concept of compensation.

It is this technical requirement of the concept of compensation that critics of affirmative action have in mind when they point out that young white males will be victimized by such a policy. A rough analogy would be to have the doctors who acquired the deceased doctor's patients pay compensation even though they had nothing to do with the accident. This, of course, is not compensation, and it can hardly be mandatory. A more accurate analogy with affirmative action is a situation in which there is no way to trace where the patients went but several doctors are arbitrarily singled out to pay—even though there is no way to establish that they have benefitted personally.

The issue of harming the innocent has come up again and again. Giving preference necessarily denies positions to more qualified nonminority applicants who are not themselves the perpetrators of any of the alleged historical forms of oppression.

All of the responses made to this criticism indicate an appeal to the notion that the social world is an organic whole operating with an inherent teleology. One response is that the harm is only apparent and temporary, but that the system as a whole will benefit.[13] Another response is that although the white male applicant may be better qualified it is because he is the beneficiary of advantages from a previously unfair arrangement. That is, without the system's malfunctioning those white applicants would not be better qualified. Moreover, affirmative action restores the system to its natural state.[14] Finally, it is alleged that the handicapping of white males is not directed toward specific young white males but to the class as a whole. Just as blacks are a subset, so whites are a subset of the total system. Properties of the whole or the subset are not properties of the individual members.[15] In short, the charge of harming the innocent is met with the response that it is not a meaningful charge in a teleological system. If the end is known, and if the means lead to that end, then the means cannot be bad, cannot be counterproductive, cannot disturb the equilibrium, and cannot produce undesirable side effects.

More than anything, this kind of response shows the extent to which the argument for affirmative action appeals to a hidden functionalist analysis of social structure. What appears to its critics as a logical gap between the problem of 'discrimination' and the solution of affirmative action is not a gap once the solution is seen as addressing itself to a different conception of the problem. Belief in this structure also explains why the proposed remedy is political, rather than legal, moral, or economic. The argument presupposes that no meaningful change is possible without basic social restructuring. Hence, the argument for affirmative action is not simply a response to a perceived evil but a commitment to complete social restructuring.

Long ago, when Southern racists in particular used to argue that blacks were inferior and therefore had to be segregated, they would be met by the argument that there were obviously superior blacks. Their answer was that the few exceptions don't count. The only practical way to maintain segregation was to exclude everybody. I suspect that the current response to reverse discrimination by supporters of affirmative action is as disingenuous as the response of the old racists.

With regard to the second requirement in the concept of compensation, calculating the degree of damage, we must repeat that, short of actual achievement in individual cases, there is no empirically meaningful way to identify what someone might have achieved. Herein lies a second crucial difference. In our previous compensation cases there was some way of calculating because there had been some performance. In the case of 'discrimination' there is the absence of performance and hence no way of calculating. One might even question whether compensation would come up for consideration. For example, suppose an outstanding college athlete is drafted by a professional team, but before he signs a contract he is permanently paralyzed in an automobile accident. Establishing potential earnings would be difficult. College stars have sometimes been failures in the professional ranks, and the length of an athletic career is conjectural, given the prevalence of injuries. A high school star athlete would be in an even more difficult position. A person who had never been allowed to try out for the team would just be in a tragic situation.

Even the advocates of affirmative action realize the inappropriateness of the concept of compensation to convey what they have in mind. Hence they assert that to compensate someone is to treat him as if he had his merit intact. What is intended is the restoration of the individual or the group to its rightful position before the damage was done.

The final metamorphosis of the concept of compensation comes when it is further specified that compensation entails giving the victim the role he would have had. This is equating remediation with realignment. How far this is from the ordinary and legal meaning of compensation can be seen with a moment's reflection. The athlete who is paralyzed before he can play in the professional league is not put into the starting lineup. Even if he could play, he would not be permitted to take the place of another and better player. Nor would we routinely change the rules of the game to allow disabled players to participate. What advocates of affirmative action want is a kind of social reform for which there is no clear analogue or precedent. Thus, they utilize the concept of compensation and then jettison it for what appears to be an ad hoc recommendation. This does not of itself invalidate the recommendation, but it does show that an entirely different argument would be needed.

Advocates of affirmative action are not primarily interested in correcting past wrongs but in *creating a new kind of society.* This can be brought out by reexamining the assumption about the distribution of talent. We have already challenged that assumption, but let us for the sake of argument assume it. Let us grant that a cross section of the population has a certain property. How do we know which members of the class in particular have that property? Let us grant to blacks 11 percent of the entering class at medical schools. How do I know which from among the group should be selected? Surely, it cannot be argued that the ones who apply to medical school should be selected, since some of those who did not apply might be the relevantly more talented ones but fail to apply because of the continuing effects of earlier 'discrimination'. Surely, it cannot be argued that the ones with the highest scores in that group should be selected, since some blacks with lower scores even amongst the class of blacks may actually be more talented but are handicapped by past 'discrimination.' In effect, we face the same problem within any group that we face with society as a whole, and therefore all of the arguments propounded by advocates of affirmative action about why traditional standards should not apply also work against applying some version of those standards within any subgroup.

It has not been shown that the right individuals in the preferred group are going to get the compensation. At best, the individual who receives preference can know only that some member of his subgroup deserves the position, though not necessarily himself or herself.

There is, however, one way of salvaging the argument. The foregoing rebuttal rests upon the assumption that merit has some tie with excellence and excellence is identified by the possession and use of a developed talent. That is why, for example, the permanently disabled athlete is not compensated with a place on the team at the expense of a current better player. This assumption, in turn, presupposes some clear conception of the game of life that can be identified with classical liberalism, or even some nonliberal conceptions of social norms. But who says that the rules have to remain the same? Why not redefine the game so that disabled players are subpar only with respect to the old rules or standards; by the new standards they are not subpar. In short, if we redefine all social roles we can minimize the differences among the players and therefore minimize their differing merits. This redefinition proceeds in two steps. First, challenge the notion that most roles require skills that belong only to a few people.[16] Second, redefine merit explicitly to accommodate the *monistic social values that maximize participation.*[17]

Under these circumstances it will not matter very much which black gets the position: fundamentally all people are the same. This is the concept of generic man implicit in the naturalistic teleology behind affirmative action. How do we know what is fundamental and relevant? The answer is whatever produces the correct participatory mix.

What are the consequences of accepting the foregoing new norms? First, it makes 'collective discrimination' a meaningful term and defines a problem whose existence is otherwise difficult to establish. Second, we can now advocate collective remedies such as affirmative action. Finally, it will ease the burden of accepting such treatment, because if an individual benefits, either he deserves it on behalf of his group or in the long run it does not matter which individual gets it.

If I consider myself to be a member of the group-of-blacks, then even though I have not been discriminated against in the sense that my personal potential has not been stunted, and even though I may have benefitted personally from the guilt feelings of some whites, I can call up in my soul a wholly artificial rage about how the group has been short-changed.[18] In fact, it is quite possible that some day no living black will have been discriminated against in the old objective sense and still the group as a whole can feel discriminated against. Even whites who accept collectivist self-images can feel that blacks have been shortchanged. Of course, we may ask why do blacks-as-a-group deserve 11 percent of anything, and the answer will be that in a truly just society that has recaptured generic man there should be no statistical differences of any kind.

Conclusion

The question has never been whether discrimination took place. The question has always been whether the kind of discrimination that has taken place is the special kind required by the policy of affirmative action. Taken at face value, we have concluded, the case has not been made. It has never been shown that discrimination is the sole cause of statistical disparity; it has never been shown that statistical disparity is an acceptable criterion for defining the problem. It is an utter distortion to suggest realignment as a meaningful version of compensation. The view of society as an organic whole is a controversial thesis in social science — not an established fact.

At the same time, we have labored to present a logically coherent version of the argument. We have been able to do so by suggesting a view of society as an organic whole in which the teleological element is participatory. If this version is embraced, then we are talking about a total social restructuring.

Notes

1. The argument for affirmative action may be schematized as follows:

 * 1. *If* you are black, *then* you have been discriminated against.

 * 2. *If* you have been discriminated against, *then* you have not been allowed to develop your full potential. (*Revised*: you develop your full potential *if and only if* you have *not* been discriminated against.)

 * 3. *If* you have not been allowed to develop your full potential, *then* you were not able to acquire maximum merit. (*Revised*: you have full merit *if and only if* you have developed your full potential.)

 * 4. *If* a society aspires to be just *then* it allows for the full development of potential, *and* it sees to it that social roles are equivalent to merit.

 * 5. Our society does aspire to be just.

 6. *Therefore*, our society seeks to develop everyone's full potential (from 4 and 5).

 7. *Therefore*, our society seeks to equate social roles and merit (from 4 and 5).

 8. *If* anyone had maximum merit, *then* he would have his rightful role (from 7).

 9. *If* anyone develops his full potential, *then* he acquires maximum merit (from 3 only as revised).

 10. *Therefore, if* anyone develops his full potential, *then* he acquires his rightful role (from 8 and 9).

 * 11. The innate potential of blacks is roughly proportionately equal to that of whites.

 12. *If* the potential of blacks is equivalent to the potential of whites, *then* the potential merit of blacks is equivalent to the potential merit of whites (from 11 and 9).

 13. *If* the potential merit of blacks is equivalent to the potential merit of whites, *then* the roles of blacks should be proportionately equivalent to the roles of whites (from 12, 11, and 8).

 14. *If* a society is just, *then* it seeks to develop full potential (from 4).

 15. *If* a society is just, *then* it will also seek to eliminate discrimination (from 14, and 2 only as revised).

 * 16. But *if* it is not always possible for a just society to eradicate totally all of the effects of discrimination, *then* in those cases it should give compensation.

 * 17. One way of granting compensation is to treat the victim of discrimination as if he had full merit.

 * 18. *If* we treat a person *as if* he had his full merit, *then* we give him the role he would have had.

 19. *If* we grant compensation, *then* we give people their rightful role (from 15, 16, 5, 17, and 18).

 20. Since the role blacks should have is equivalent to the roles whites should have, to grant compensation is at present to adoptive affirmative action, that is, to equate the roles (from 10, 11, 13, and 19).

MAKING THE ARGUMENT VALID

The argument as stated and schematized is not quite a valid argument. For example, step 9 is not entailed by step 3. In its initial formulation it would involve the *fallacy of denying the antecedent.* If, however, we equate potential and merit, step 9 follows. The move from step 2 to step 15 presents us with the same problem. It is only by revising step 2 that we again avoid the fallacy of denying the antecedent. It is only by equating potential and lack of discrimination that the argument becomes valid. As we shall see below, this revised premise is crucial because it allows that if you are not a victim of discrimination you automatically develop your full potential. This revised premise also permits us to conclude that you have not developed your full potential, then we may conclude that you have been discriminated against without having to provide additional empirical evidence of the discrimination.

IS THE ARGUMENT SOUND?

In order to assess the soundness of the argument we must isolate the underived premises and examine each in turn. The underived premises are: 1, 2, 3, 4, 5, 11, 16, 17, and 18. These premises may be examined under five convenient headings. The first two premises concern the concept of discrimination. The second premise, in addition, involves questions of a fundamental nature about mankind such as potential, freedom, and responsibility. Premises 3, 4, and 5 invoke the norms of what I shall call the liberal-utilitarian paradigm. Premise 11 is by far the most important. Logically it will help to elucidate the first two premises, and it will serve as the explanatory link between the norms and the application of the policy of affirmative action. Put another way, it connects the diagnosis with the prescription. Philosophically it raises profound issues about the methodology of the social sciences. Finally, premises 16, 17, and 18 concern the concept of compensation.

(1) $B \rightarrow D$
(2) $D \rightarrow -P$ (*revised:* $P \equiv -D$) $\equiv [(P \rightarrow -D) \cdot (-D \rightarrow P)]$
(3) $-P \rightarrow -M$ (*revised:* $P \equiv M$)
(4) $J \rightarrow [P \cdot (M \equiv R)]$
(5) J
(6) $\therefore P$ (*from* steps 4 and 5)
(7) $\therefore (M \equiv R)$ (*from* steps 4, 5, and 6)
(8) $\therefore M \rightarrow R$ (*from* step 7)
(9) $\therefore P \rightarrow M$ (*from* step 3 as revised)
(10) $\therefore P \rightarrow R$ (*from* steps 9 and 8)
(11) $P_b \equiv P_w$
(12) $\therefore (P_b \equiv P_w) \rightarrow (M_b \equiv M_w)$ (*from* steps 11 and 9)
(13) $\therefore (M_b \equiv M_w) \rightarrow (R_b \equiv R_w)$ (*from* steps 11, 12 and 8)
(14) $\therefore J \rightarrow P$ (*from* steps 4 and 5)
(15) $\therefore J \rightarrow -D$ (*from* steps 14 and 2 as revised)
(16) $-D \rightarrow C$
(17) $C \rightarrow$ as-if M
(18) as-if $M \rightarrow R$
(19) $\therefore C \rightarrow R$ (*from* steps 15, 16, and 5, 17, and 18)
(20) $C \rightarrow (R_b \equiv R_w)$ (*from* steps 19 and 11, 12, and 13)

All of the premises are expressed by Bernard R. Boxill, "The Morality of Preferential Hiring," *Philosophy & Public Affairs* 7, no. 3, 1978, pp. 246–68.

2. "But among younger generation blacks and whites, by the late 1960s, individuals with similar home backgrounds and the same education had the same income—regardless of race. Gross black-white differences had not disappeared, but the reasons for the remaining differences between young whites and blacks were factors at work before they ever set foot in an employer's office." Thomas Sowell, *Inquiry*, August 21, 1978, p. 11.

3. "No reasonable person doubts that past immoral and illegal discrimination is largely responsible for the present underrepresentation of blacks and American Indians in desired positions." Kent Greenawalt, *Discrimination and Reverse Discrimination* (New York: Knopf, 1983), p. 54.

4. Joe R. Feagin and Clairece Booker Feagin, *Discrimination American Style: Institutional Racism and Sexism* (Englewood, N.J.: Prentice-Hall, 1978).

5. Advocates of affirmative action do not want compensation in the form of remediation but in the form of realignment. See Boxill, op. cit.

6. (revised 2) $P \equiv -D$
(3) $P \equiv M$
(3a) $\therefore M \equiv -D$ (*from* 2 and 3)
(3b) $\therefore -D \rightarrow M$ (*from* 3a)
(15) $J \rightarrow -D$
(15a) $J \rightarrow M$ (*from* 15 and 3b)
(8) $M \rightarrow R$
(15b) $\therefore J \rightarrow R$ (i.e., reassign everyone to his rightful role)

7. Participation as a goal was first suggested in the nineteenth century by T. H. Green. Green, however, was concerned with the individual. Participation for the group, even in the form of proxies, is a recent doctrinaire liberal development.

8. "No one deserves his greater natural capacity nor merits a more favorable starting place in society." John Rawls, *A Theory of Justice* (1971), p. 102.

   "Most of what are regarded as the decisive circumstances for higher education have a great deal to do with things over which the individual has neither control nor responsibility: such things as home environment, socio-economic class of parents, and, of course, the quality of primary and secondary schools attended. Since individuals do not deserve having had any of these things vis-á-vis other individuals, they do not, for the most part, deserve their qualifications. And since they do not deserve their abilities they do not in any strong sense deserve to be admitted because of their abilities." Richard Wasserstrom, "Racism, Sexism and Preferential Treatment: An Approach to the Topics," *U.C.L.A. Law Review* 24, no. 2 (February 1877), p. 620.

   "The Chancellor has identified the wrong offender. Failure to learn is the result of the failure of the teaching process. The system encourages the protection—sometimes deliberately, sometimes unwittingly—of teachers who don't teach and supervisors who don't supervise. . . . Perhaps if the chancellor proposed a plan to eliminate underachievers among the professional staff, he would eliminate the need for a plan to hold back underachieving students." Clinton Howze, Jr., Community Superintendent, District 3, N.Y.C. Letter to the editor of the *New York Times* (November 21, 1979).

9. See Wasserstrom, op. cit.

10. B. Boxill, op. cit., p. 253. The same point is explicitly made by Sara Ann Ketchum, "Evidence, Statistics, and Rights: A Reply to Simon," *Analysis* 39 (1979), pp. 150–51. See also a statement by the U.S. Department of Labor (1965): "Intelligence potential is distributed among Negro infants in the same proportion and pattern as among Icelanders or Chinese, or any other group. . . ."

11. "Decades of discrimination by public bodies and private persons may have far reaching effects that make it difficult for minority applicants to compete . . . on an equal basis. The consequences of discrimination are too complex to dissect case-by-case; the effects on aspirations alone may raise for minority applicants a hurdle that does not face white applicants . . . and a (school or employer) dealing with imponderables of this sort ought not to be confined to the choice of either ignoring the problem or attempting the Sisyphean task of discerning its importance on an individual basis." Brief for the United States (Justice Department) as *amicus curiae* at 56, Regents of the University of California v. Bakke, No. 76–811.

12. "Blacks are viewed as a group; they view themselves as a group; their identity is in large part determined by membership in the group; their social status is linked to the status of the group; and much of our action, institutional and personal, is based on these perspectives." Owen Fiss, "Groups and the Equal Protection Clause," *Philosophy & Public Affairs* (1976), p. 148.

    "In my judgment, there is in the United States enough mobility and interdependence so that it is proper to take a national view." Greenawalt, op. cit., p. 56.

13. "While it may give minorities a little edge in some instances, and you may run into a danger of what we now commonly call reverse discrimination, I think the educational system needs this. Society needs this as much as the people we are trying to help. . . . a society working toward affirmative action and inclusiveness is going to be a stronger and more relevant society than one that accepts the limited concepts of objectivity. . . . I would admit that it is perhaps an individual injustice. But it might be necessary in order to overcome a historic group injustice or series of group injustices." Andrew Young, *Atlanta Journal and Constitution*, September 22, 1974.

14. ". . . by refusing to allow him [white male applicant] to get the job because of an unfair advantage, preferential hiring makes the competition fairer." B. Boxill, op. cit., p. 266.

    "The use of minimum racial, ethnic, religious and sexual quotas as a technique for correcting a serious discrimination in employment is a justifiable means of offsetting past wrongs by temporarily recruiting people from a group which has been discriminated against. . . . the alleged discrimination experienced by the individual white applicant under a system of compensatory treatment is not the same as the discrimination previously suffered by blacks. The white applicant is not being barred from employment because of his race; rather his claim to a particular job is being deferred while a remedy is applied." Memorandum of the Equality Commission of the *American Civil Liberties Union*, November 29, 1972.

15. Lois Tuckerman Weinberg, "An Answer to the 'Liberal' Objection to Special Admissions," in *Educational Theory* 29 (1979), p. 28.

16. "With adequate education and training, most people might competently perform almost any job, or at least a very large range of jobs." Norman Daniels, "Merit and Meritocracy," *Philosophy & Public Affairs* (1978), p. 219.

17. "The idea of merit must today be broadened to include a variety of other measures of individual potential and ability. . . . it is time to modify our screening practices in employment so as to give greater attention to the capabilities and experience of minorities and women." Feagin and Feagin, op. cit., pp. 172–74.

    A similar point is made by R. Wasserstrom, "The University and the Case for Preferential Treatment," *American Philosophical Quarterly* (April 1976), p. 165.

18. It is interesting to note that in two studies it was a concern for potential discrimination, or discrimination against a third party, rather than actual discrimination against the person reporting which the researchers found.

    One survey of female employees finds that only 8.1 percent of all working women report discrimination on their job. Of that 8.1 percent, one-half indicated that they felt the discrimination to be slight. "Sex Differences in Compensation," *Journal of Human Resources* (Fall 1971), pp. 434–47.

    In the case of blacks, it has been noted: "Despite the fact that a relatively high proportion of (black) men felt that their progress had been equal to or greater than that of comparable whites, the majority of the respondents . . . thought that they did not have equal opportunity with whites in their firm." U.S. Department of Labor, "A Study of Black Male Professionals in Industry," *Manpower Res. Monograph* No. 26 (1973).

Study Questions

1. Explain the differences among discrimination, prejudice, and prudence, as Capaldi sets them forth.
2. Why is it difficult to establish that discriminatory policies are the major cause of blacks' impaired capacity to compete in today's economy, according to Capaldi?
3. What transformation takes place in the argument for affirmative action because of the difficulty mentioned in question 2, according to Capaldi?
4. What is the connection between potential and discrimination, as explained by Capaldi in the first paragraph of the "Potential and Freedom" section?
5. According to Capaldi, it makes sense to talk about individuals and groups as having potential only if you have a teleological view of human nature. Explain what this means.
6. Is there empirical evidence for teleological theories about human nature, according to Capaldi? Explain.
7. What follows from the fact that we cannot establish the ends of human activity, according to Capaldi?
8. Explain why proponents of affirmative action seem committed both to teleology and to determinism, and why that is troublesome, according to Capaldi.
9. Explain the difficulty in giving evidence for the claim that the talent or potential of blacks is roughly equivalent to that of whites. Why does Capaldi think the call for such evidence is greeted with a circular argument?
10. Explain why it is inappropriate to view affirmative action as compensation, according to Capaldi.
11. Explain why Capaldi thinks that advocates of affirmative action are primarily interested, not in correcting past wrongs, but in creating a new kind of society.

Suggested Further Reading

Subject Matter of Ethics

Brandt, Richard. *Ethical Theory: The Problems of Normative and Critical Ethics.* New York: Prentice-Hall, 1959.

Frankena, W. K. *Ethics.* 2d ed. Englewood Cliffs, N.J.: Prentice-Hall, 1973.

Hospers, John. *Human Conduct: Problems of Ethics.* 2d ed. New York: Harcourt Brace Jovanovich, 1982.

History of Ethics

Abelard, Peter. *Abelard's Ethics.* Edited and translated by J. R. McCallum. Merrick, N.Y.: Richwood, 1976.

Aristotle. *Nicomachean Ethics.* Translated by J. A. K. Thomson. Revised by Hugh Tredennick. Harmondsworth: Penguin, 1976.

Augustine. *Confessions.* Translated by John K. Ryan. Garden City, N.Y.: Image Books, 1962.

Bentham, Jeremy. *An Introduction to the Principles of Morals and Legislation.* Edited by J. H. Burns and H. L. A. Hart. London: Athlone Press, 1970.

Dewey, John, and James H. Tufts. *Ethics.* New York: Holt, Rinehart and Winston, 1908.

Epictetus. *The Discourses.* Translated by George Long. New York: A. L. Burt, n.d.

Epicurus. *Letters, Principal Doctrines, and Vatican Sayings.* Translated by Russell M. Geer. New York: Macmillan, 1985.

Hobbes, Thomas. *Leviathan.* 1651. Edited by J. P. Plamenatz. London: Collins, 1962.

Hudson, W. D. *Modern Moral Philosophy.* 2d ed. New York: St. Martin's Press, 1983.

Hume, David. *An Enquiry Concerning the Principles of Morals.* Edited by J. B. Schneewind. Indianapolis: Hackett Publishing Company, 1983.

______. *A Treatise of Human Nature.* Edited by L. A. Selby-Bigge and revised by P. H. Nidditch. 3d ed. New York: Oxford University Press, 1978.

Kant, Immanuel. *Foundations of the Metaphysics of Morals: Text and Critical Essays.* Edited by R. P. Wolff. Translated by Lewis White Beck. New York: Macmillan, 1985.

______. *Lectures on Ethics.* Translated by Louis Infield. Indianapolis: Hackett Publishing Company, 1980.

______. *The Metaphysics of Morals.* Translated by Mary Gregor. Indianapolis: Hackett Publishing Company, 1991.

Laertius, Diogenes. *The Lives of Eminent Philosophers.* Translated by R. D. Hicks. Cambridge, Mass: Harvard University Press, 1950.

MacIntyre, Alasdair. *A Short History of Ethics.* New York: Macmillan, 1966.

Mill, John Stuart. *Utilitarianism: Text and Criticism.* Edited by James M. Smith and Ernest Sosa. Belmont, Calif.: Wadsworth, 1969.

Moore, G. E. *Ethics.* London: Oxford University Press, 1912.

______. *Principia Ethica.* First published 1903. Buffalo, N.Y.: Prometheus Books, 1988.

Nietzsche, Friedrich. *Beyond Good and Evil: Prelude to a Philosophy of the Future.* Translated by Walter Kaufmann. New York: Vintage, 1966.

______. *On the Genealogy of Morals.* Translated by Walter Kaufmann and R. J. Hollingdale. New York: Vintage, 1969.

Plato. *Gorgias.* Translated by Terence Irwin. Oxford: Clarendon Press, 1979.

______. *The Republic.* Translated by Allan Bloom. 2d ed. New York: Basic Books, 1991.

Prichard, H. A. *Moral Obligation: Essays and Lectures.* Oxford: Clarendon Press, 1949.

Ross, W. D. *The Foundations of Ethics.* Oxford: Clarendon Press, 1939.

______. *The Right and the Good.* Oxford: Clarendon Press, 1930.

Sartre, Jean-Paul. "Existentialism Is a Humanism." First published 1946. In *Existentialism and Humanism.* Translated by Philip Mairet. Brooklyn: Haskell House, 1977.

Schopenhauer, Arthur. *The Will to Live: Selected Writings of Arthur Schopenhauer.* Edited by Richard Taylor. Translated by T. Bailey Saunders. New York: Ungar, 1967.

Sidgwick, Henry. *The Methods of Ethics.* 7th ed. First published 1907. New York: Dover, 1966.

______. *Outlines of the History of Ethics.* 6th ed. First published 1886. New York: St. Martin's Press, 1931.

Thomas Aquinas. *Summa Theologica.* Translated by the Fathers of the English Dominican Province. 5 vols. Westminster, Md.: Christian Classics, 1981.

Warnock, Mary. *Ethics Since 1900.* 2d ed. London: Oxford University Press, 1966.

Ethical Naturalism

Anscombe, G. E. M. "Modern Moral Philosophy." In *Ethics,* edited by Judith Jarvis Thomson and Gerald Dworkin. New York: Harper and Row, 1968.

______. "On Brute Facts." In *Ethics, Religion and Politics.* Vol. 3 of *Collected Papers.* Oxford: Basil Blackwell, 1981.

Clark, S. R. L. "The Lack of Gap Between Fact and Value." *Proceedings of the Aristotelian Society,* Supplementary Volume 54 (1980): 225–240.

Geach, P. T. "Good and Evil." In *Theories of Ethics,* edited by Philippa Foot. Oxford: Oxford University Press, 1967.

Hudson, W. D., ed. *The Is-Ought Question: A Collection of Papers on the Central Problem in Moral Philosophy.* London: Macmillan Co., 1969.

Milo, Ronald. *Immorality.* Princeton: Princeton University Press, 1984.

Warnock, G. J. *Contemporary Moral Philosophy.* New York: St. Martin's Press, 1967.

Ethical Relativism

Gibbard, Allan F. *Wise Choices, Apt Feelings.* Cambridge, Mass.: Harvard University Press, 1991.

Harman, Gilbert. "Moral Relativism Defended." *Philosophical Review* 84 (1975): 3–22.

Ladd, John, ed. *Ethical Relativism.* Belmont, Calif.: Wadsworth, 1973.

Stewart, Robert M., and Lynn L. Thomas. "Recent Work on Ethical Relativism." *American Philosophical Quarterly* 28 (1991): 85–100.

Stout, Jeffrey. *Ethics After Babel.* Boston: Beacon Press, 1988.

Williams, Bernard. *Ethics and the Limits of Philosophy.* Cambridge, Mass.: Harvard University Press, 1985.

Wong, David. *Moral Relativity.* Berkeley: University of California Press, 1985.

Ethical Subjectivism and Noncognitivism

Ayer, A. J. *Language, Truth, and Logic.* 2d ed. First published 1946. New York: Dover, 1952.

Dewey, John. *Theory of Valuation.* Chicago: University of Chicago Press, 1939.

Hare, R. M. *Freedom and Reason.* New York: Oxford University Press, 1963.

______. *The Language of Morals.* Oxford: Clarendon Press, 1952.

______. *Moral Thinking: Its Levels, Methods, and Point.* New York: Oxford University Press, 1981.

Mackie, J. L. *Ethics: Inventing Right and Wrong.* Harmondsworth: Penguin, 1977.

Stevenson, Charles L. *Ethics and Language.* New Haven: Yale University Press, 1944.

______. *Facts and Values: Studies in Ethical Analysis.* New Haven: Yale University Press, 1963.

Urmson, J. O. *The Emotive Theory of Ethics.* London: Hutchinson, 1968.

Law and Morality

d'Entreves, A. P. *Natural Law.* London: Hutchinson, 1970.

Finnis, John. *Natural Law and Natural Rights.* Oxford: Oxford University Press, 1980.

Greenawalt, Kent. *Conflicts of Law and Morality.* New York: Oxford University Press, 1989.

Grey, Thomas C. *The Legal Enforcement of Morality.* New York: Knopf, 1983.

Hart, H. L. A. *The Concept of Law.* Oxford: Clarendon Press, 1961.

Ross, J. F. "Justice is Reasonableness: Aquinas On Human Law and Morality." *Monist* 58 (1974): 86–103.

Tuck, Richard. *Natural Rights Theories: Their Origin and Development.* New York: Cambridge University Press, 1979.

Psychology, Gender, and Moral Development

Baier, Annette. "What Do Women Want in a Moral Theory?" *Noûs* (1985): 53–63.

Blum, Lawrence. "Gilligan and Kohlberg: Implications for Moral Theory." *Ethics* 98 (1988): 472–491.

Card, Claudia. "Women's Voices and Ethical Ideals: Must We Mean What We Say?" *Ethics* 99 (1988): 125–135.

Gilligan, Carol. *In a Different Voice: Psychological Theory and Women's Development.* Cambridge, Mass.: Harvard University Press, 1982.

Kohlberg, Lawrence. *Essays on Moral Development.* New York: Harper and Row, 1981.

Noddings, Nel. *Caring: A Feminine Approach To Ethics and Moral Education.* Berkeley: University of California Press, 1984.

Piaget, Jean. *The Essential Piaget.* Edited by Howard Gruber and J. Jacques Voneche. New York: Basic Books, 1977.

______. *The Moral Judgement of the Child.* Translated by Marjorie Gabain. New York: Free Press, 1966.

Thomas, Lawrence. *Living Morally: A Psychology of Moral Character.* Philadelphia: Temple University Press, 1989.

Religion and Ethics

Helm, Paul, ed. *Divine Commands and Morality.* Oxford: Oxford University Press, 1979.

Kant, Immanuel. *Religion Within the Limits of Reason Alone.* Translated by T. M. Greene and H. H. Hudson. New York: Harper and Row, 1960.

Kierkegaard, Søren. *Fear and Trembling.* Translated by Howard Hong and Edna Hong. Princeton: Princeton University Press, 1983.

Mitchell, Basil. *Morality: Religious and Secular.* Oxford: Oxford University Press, 1980.

Nielsen, Kai. *Ethics Without God.* Rev. ed. Buffalo, N.Y.: Prometheus Books, 1990.

Outka, Gene, and J. P. Reeder, eds. *Religion and Morality: A Collection of Essays.* New York: Anchor Books, 1973.

Plato. *Euthyphro.* In *Plato: The Last Days of Socrates.* Translated by Hugh Tredennick. Baltimore, Md.: Penguin, 1959.

Quinn, Philip L. *Divine Commands and Moral Requirements.* Oxford: Clarendon Press, 1978.

Science and Ethics

Dawkins, Richard. *The Selfish Gene.* 2d ed. Oxford: Oxford University Press, 1989.

Gewirth, Alan. "Positive 'Ethics' and Normative 'Science'." In *Ethics,* edited by Judith Jarvis Thomson and Gerald Dworkin. New York: Harper and Row, 1968.

Huxley, T. H. *Evolution and Ethics.* London: Pilot Press, 1947.

Murphy, J. G. *Evolution, Morality, and the Meaning of Life.* Totowa, N.J.: Rowman and Littlefield, 1982.

Russell, Bertrand. *The Impact of Science on Society.* New York: Columbia University Press, 1951.

Singer, Peter. *The Expanding Circle: Ethics and Sociobiology.* Oxford: Oxford University Press, 1983.

Spencer, Herbert. *The Data of Ethics.* New York: Collier, 1901.

Wilson, E. O. *On Human Nature.* Cambridge, Mass.: Harvard University Press, 1978.

The Concept of Morality

Baier, Kurt. *The Moral Point of View.* Ithaca, N.Y.: Cornell University Press, 1958.

Frankena, W. K. "The Concept of Morality." *Journal of Philosophy* 63 (1966): 688–696.

Singer, Peter. "The Triviality of the Debate Over 'Is'-'Ought' and the Definition of 'Moral'." *American Philosophical Quarterly* 10 (1973): 51–56.

Smith, Steven A. *Satisfaction of Interest and the Concept of Morality.* Lewisburg, Pa.: Bucknell University Press, 1975.

Stace, W. T. *The Concept of Morals.* New York: Macmillan, 1937.

Wallace, Gerald, and A. D. M. Walker, eds. *The Definition of Morality.* London: Methuen, 1970.

Supererogation, Moral Dilemmas, and Weakness of Will

Charlton, William. *Weakness of Will: A Philosophical Introduction.* Oxford: Basil Blackwell, 1987.

Gowans, Christopher W., ed. *Moral Dilemmas.* New York: Oxford University Press, 1987.

Heyd, David. *Supererogation: Its Status in Ethical Theory.* New York: Cambridge University Press, 1982.

Skepticism, Objectivity, and Moral Knowledge

Butchvarov, Panayot. *Skepticism in Ethics.* Indianapolis: University of Indiana Press, 1989.

Copp, David, and David Zimmerman, eds. *Morality, Reason and Truth.* Totowa, N.J.: Rowman and Allanheld, 1985.

Honderich, Ted, ed. *Morality and Objectivity.* London: Routledge and Kegan Paul, 1985.

Milo, Ronald. *Aristotle on Practical Knowledge and Weakness of Will.* The Hague: Mouton, 1966.

Quinn, Warren. "Reflection and the Loss of Moral Knowledge: Williams On Objectivity." *Philosophy and Public Affairs* 16 (1987): 195–209.

Sayre-McCord, Geoffrey, ed. *Essays on Moral Realism.* Ithaca, N.Y.: Cornell University Press, 1988.

Theories of Well-Being and Meaningful Life

Brandt, R. B. *A Theory of the Good and the Right.* Oxford: Clarendon Press, 1981.

Edwards, R. B. *Pleasures and Pains: A Theory of Qualitative Hedonism.* Ithaca, N.Y.: Cornell University Press, 1979.

Griffin, James. *Well-Being.* Oxford: Clarendon Press, 1986.

Klemke, E. D., ed. *The Meaning of Life.* New York: Oxford University Press, 1981.

Kraut, Richard. "Two Conceptions of Happiness." *Philosophical Review* 88 (1979): 167–197.

McFall, Lynne. *Happiness.* Berne: Peter Lang, 1991.

Nozick, Robert. *The Examined Life: Philosophical Meditations.* New York: Simon and Schuster, 1990.

______. *Philosophical Explanations.* Cambridge, Mass.: Harvard University Press, 1981.

Smith, Steve, ed. *Ways of Wisdom.* Lanham, Md.: University Press of America, 1983.

Telfer, Elizabeth. *Happiness.* New York: St. Martin's Press, 1980.

Egoism

Butler, Joseph. *Five Sermons.* Edited by Stephen Darwall. Indianapolis: Hackett Publishing Company, 1983.

Gauthier, David, ed. *Morality and Rational Self-Interest.* Englewood Cliffs, N.J.: Prentice-Hall, 1970.

Machan, Tibor. "Recent Work on Ethical Egoism." *American Philosophical Quarterly* 16 (1979): 1–15.

Mandeville, Bernard. *The Fable of the Bees, Or: Private Vices, Publick Benefits.* Oxford: Clarendon Press, 1924.

Milo, Ronald, ed. *Egoism and Altruism.* Belmont, Calif.: Wadsworth, 1973.

Nozick, Robert. "On the Randian Argument." *Personalist* 52 (1971): 282–304.

Quinn, Warren. "Egoism As an Ethical System." *Journal of Philosophy* 71 (1974): 456–472.

Rand, Ayn. *The Virtue of Selfishness.* New York: New American Library, 1964.

Regis, Edward, Jr. "What Is Ethical Egoism?" *Ethics* 91 (1980): 50–62.

Utilitarianism

Brandt, R. B. *Morality, Utilitarianism, and Rights.* Cambridge: Cambridge University Press, 1992.

______. *A Theory of the Good and the Right.* Oxford: Clarendon Press, 1981.

Lyons, David. *The Forms and Limits of Utilitarianism.* Oxford: Clarendon Press, 1965.

Quinton, Anthony. *Utilitarian Ethics.* New York: St. Martin's Press, 1973.

Scheffler, Samuel. *The Rejection of Consequentialism.* Oxford: Clarendon Press, 1982.

Scheffler, Samuel, ed. *Consequentialism and Its Critics.* Oxford: Clarendon Press, 1988.

Sen, Amartya, and Bernard Williams, eds. *Utilitarianism and Beyond.* Cambridge: Cambridge University Press, 1982.

Smart, J. J. C., and Bernard Williams. *Utilitarianism: For and Against.* Cambridge: Cambridge University Press, 1973.

Deontological and Contractarian Theories

Donagan, Alan. *The Theory of Morality.* Chicago: University of Chicago Press, 1977.

Gauthier, David. *Morals By Agreement.* Oxford: Oxford University Press, 1986.

Gewirth, Alan. *Human Rights: Essays on Justification and Applications.* Chicago: University of Chicago Press, 1982.

______. *Reason and Morality.* Chicago: University of Chicago Press, 1978.

Nagel, Thomas. *The View From Nowhere.* New York: Oxford University Press, 1986.

Nozick, Robert. *Anarchy, State, and Utopia.* New York: Basic Books, 1974.

Rawls, John. *Political Liberalism.* New York: Columbia University Press, 1993.

______. *A Theory of Justice.* Cambridge, Mass.: Harvard University Press, 1971.

Scanlon, T. M. "Contractualism and Utilitarianism." In *Utilitarianism and Beyond,* edited by Amartya Sen and Bernard Williams. Cambridge: Cambridge University Press, 1982.

Virtue Ethics

Dent, N. J. H. *The Moral Psychology of the Virtues.* Cambridge: Cambridge University Press, 1984.

Foot, Philippa. *Virtues and Vices.* Oxford: Basil Blackwell, 1978.

Geach, P. T. *The Virtues.* Cambridge: Cambridge University Press, 1977.

Kekes, John. *Moral Tradition and Individuality.* Princeton: Princeton University Press, 1989.

MacIntyre, Alasdair. *After Virtue.* 2d ed. Notre Dame, Ind.: University of Notre Dame Press, 1984.

Sherman, Nancy. *The Fabric of Character: Aristotle's Theory of Virtue.* Oxford: Clarendon Press, 1989.

Taylor, Gabriele. *Pride, Shame, and Guilt: Emotions of Self-Assessment.* New York: Oxford University Press, 1985.

Wallace, James. *Virtues and Vices.* Ithaca, N.Y.: Cornell University Press, 1978.

Warnock, G. J. *The Object of Morality.* London: Methuen, 1971.

Free Will

Dennett, Daniel. *Elbow Room: The Varieties of Free Will Worth Wanting.* Oxford: Clarendon Press, 1984.

Edwards, Paul. "Hard and Soft Determinism." In *Determinism and Freedom in the Age of Modern Science,* edited by S. Hook. New York: Collier Books, 1961.

Honderich, Ted. *A Theory of Determinism: The Mind, Neuroscience, and Life Hopes.* New York: Oxford University Press, 1988.

Slote, Michael. "Understanding Free Will." *Journal of Philosophy* 77 (1980): 136–151.

van Inwagen, Peter. *An Essay On Free Will.* Oxford: Clarendon Press, 1983.

Watson, Gary, ed. *Free Will.* Oxford: Oxford University Press, 1982.

Responsibility and Punishment

Austin, J. L. "Three Ways of Spilling Ink." In *Philosophical Papers.* Oxford: Clarendon Press, 1961.

Feinberg, Joel. *Doing and Deserving: Essays on the Theory of Responsibility.* Princeton: Princeton University Press, 1970.

French, Peter A. *Responsibility Matters.* Lawrence, Kans.: University Press of Kansas, 1992.

______, ed. *Individual and Collective Responsibility: Massacre at My Lai.* Cambridge, Mass.: Schenkman Publishing Co., 1972.

______, ed. *The Spectrum of Responsibility.* New York: St. Martin's Press, 1991.

Glover, Jonathan. *Responsibility.* London: Routledge and Kegan Paul, 1970.

Honderich, Ted. *Punishment: The Supposed Justifications.* Harmondsworth: Penguin, 1984.

Murphy, J. G., ed. *Punishment and Rehabilitation.* Belmont, Calif.: Wadsworth, 1973.

Schoeman, Ferdinand, ed. *Responsibility, Character, and the Emotions.* Cambridge: Cambridge University Press, 1987.

Ten, C. L. *Crime, Guilt, and Punishment: A Philosophical Introduction.* Oxford: Clarendon Press, 1987.

Williams, Bernard. *Moral Luck: Philosophical Papers 1973–1980.* New York: Cambridge University Press, 1981.

______. *Problems of the Self: Philosophical Papers 1956–1972.* Cambridge: Cambridge University Press, 1973.

Intentions, Acts, and Omissions

Foot, Philippa. "Abortion and the Doctrine of Double Effect." In *Virtues and Vices.* Oxford: Basil Blackwell, 1978.

______. "Morality, Action and Outcome." In *Morality and Objectivity,* edited by Ted Honderich. London: Routledge and Kegan Paul, 1985.

Steinbock, Bonnie, ed. *Killing and Letting Die.* Englewood Cliffs, N.J.: Prentice-Hall, 1983.

Thomson, Judith Jarvis. *The Realm of Rights.* Cambridge, Mass.: Harvard University Press, 1990.

______. *Right, Restitution and Risk: Essays in Moral Theory.* Edited by William Parent. Cambridge, Mass.: Harvard University Press, 1986.

Euthanasia and Abortion

Baird, Robert M., and Stuart E. Rosenbaum, eds. *The Ethics of Abortion: Pro-Life Vs. Pro-Choice.* Buffalo, N.Y.: Prometheus Books, 1989.

______. *Euthanasia: The Moral Issues.* Buffalo, N.Y.: Prometheus Books, 1989.

Brody, Baruch, ed. *Suicide and Euthanasia: Historical and Contemporary Themes.* Dordrecht, Holland: Kluwer, 1989.

Feinberg, Joel, ed. *The Problem of Abortion.* 2d ed. Belmont, Calif.: Wadsworth, 1984.

Kamm, Frances Myrna. *Creation and Abortion: A Study in Moral and Legal Philosophy.* New York: Oxford University Press, 1992.

Kass, Leon R. "Neither for Love Nor Money: Why Doctors Must Not Kill." *The Public Interest* 94 (1989): 25–46.

Kevorkian, Jack. "The Last Fearsome Taboo: Medical Aspects of Planned Death." *Medicine and Law* 7 (1988): 1–14.

Rachels, James. *The End of Life.* Oxford: Oxford University Press, 1986.

Rodman, Hyman, et al. *The Abortion Question.* New York: Columbia University Press, 1987.

Steinbock, Bonnie. *Life Before Birth: The Moral and Legal Status of Embryos and Fetuses.* New York: Oxford University Press, 1992.

Thomasma, David C., and Glenn C. Graber. *Euthanasia: Toward an Ethical Social Policy.* New York: Continuum, 1990.

Tooley, Michael. *Abortion and Infanticide.* New York: Oxford University Press, 1983.

Helping Others in Need

Aiken, William, and Hugh LaFollette, eds. *World Hunger and Moral Obligation.* Englewood Cliffs, N.J.: Prentice-Hall, 1977.

Bedau, Hugo. "Human Rights and Foreign Assistance Programs." In *Human Rights and U.S. Foreign Policy,* edited by Peter G. Brown and Douglas MacLean. Lexington, Mass.: D. C. Heath, 1977.

DeGeorge, Richard T. "Property and Global Justice." In *Social and Personal Ethics,* edited by William H. Shaw. Belmont, Calif.: Wadsworth, 1993.

Hardin, Garrett. "Lifeboat Ethics: The Case Against Helping the Poor." *Psychology Today,* September 1974.

Lucas, Jr., George R., and Thomas W. Ogletree, eds. *Lifeboat Ethics: The Moral Dilemmas of World Hunger.* New York: Harper and Row, 1976.

Nagel, Thomas. "Poverty and Food: Why Charity Is Not Enough." In *Food Policy: The Responsibility of the United States in Life and Death Choices,* edited by Peter G. Brown and Henry Shue. New York: Free Press, 1977.

O'Neill, Onora. *Faces of Hunger: An Essay on Poverty, Justice, and Development.* London: Allen and Unwin, 1986.

______. "Moral Perplexities of Famine Relief." In *Matters of Life and Death: New Introductory Essays in Moral Philosophy.* Edited by Tom Regan. New York: Random House, 1980.

Sen, Amartya K. *Poverty and Famines: An Essay On Entitlement and Deprivation.* Oxford: Clarendon Press, 1981.

______. "The Right Not To Be Hungry." In *The Right to Food,* edited by P. Alston and K. Tomasevski. The Hague: Martinus Nijhoff, 1984.

Shue, Henry. *Basic Rights: Subsistence, Affluence, and U.S. Foreign Policy.* Princeton: Princeton University Press, 1980.

Singer, Peter. *Practical Ethics.* 2d ed. Cambridge: Cambridge University Press, 1993.

Sexual Morality

Atkinson, R. F. *Sexual Morality.* New York: Harcourt, Brace & Co., 1965.

Baird, Robert M. and Stuart E. Rosenbaum, eds. *Pornography: Private Right Or Public Menace?* Buffalo, N.Y.: Prometheus Books, 1991.

Baker, Robert, and Frederick Elliston, eds. *Philosophy and Sex.* 2d ed. Buffalo, N.Y.: Prometheus Books, 1984.

Borowitz, Eugene B. *Choosing a Sex Ethic: A Jewish Inquiry.* New York: Schocken Books, 1969.

Copp, David, and Susan Wendell, eds. *Pornography and Censorship.* Buffalo, N.Y.: Prometheus Books, 1983.

Richards, David A. J. *Sex, Drugs, Death, and the Law.* Totowa, N.J.: Rowman and Littlefield, 1982.

Scruton, Roger. *Sexual Desire.* New York: Macmillan, 1986.

Soble, Alan, ed. *Philosophy of Sex.* 2d ed. Savage, Md.: Rowman and Littlefield, 1991.

Taylor, Richard. *Having Love Affairs.* Buffalo, N.Y.: Prometheus Books, 1982.

Vannoy, Russell. *Sex Without Love: A Philosophical Exploration.* Buffalo, N.Y.: Prometheus Books, 1980.

Verene, D. P., ed. *Sexual Love and Western Morality.* New York: Harper and Row, 1972.

Wilson, John. *Love, Sex and Feminism.* New York: Praeger, 1980.

Preferential Treatment

Capaldi, Nicholas. *Out of Order: Affirmative Action and the Crisis of Doctrinaire Liberalism.* Buffalo, N.Y.: Prometheus Books, 1985.

Ezorsky, Gertrude. *Racism and Justice: The Case For Affirmative Action.* Ithaca, N.Y.: Cornell University Press, 1991.

Fullinwider, Robert K. *The Reverse Discrimination Controversy: A Moral and Legal Analysis.* Savage, Md.: Rowman and Littlefield, 1980.

Goldman, Alan H. *Justice and Reverse Discrimination.* Princeton: Princeton University Press, 1979.

Greenawalt, Kent. *Discrimination and Reverse Discrimination.* New York: Knopf, 1983.

Gross, Barry R. *Discrimination in Reverse: Is Turnabout Fair Play?* New York: New York University Press, 1978.

______, ed. *Reverse Discrimination.* Buffalo, N.Y.: Prometheus Books, 1977.

Rosenfeld, Michel. *Affirmative Action and Justice.* New Haven: Yale University Press, 1991.

Sowell, Thomas. *Markets and Minorities.* New York: Basic Books, 1981.

______. *Preferential Politics: An International Perspective.* New York: William Morrow, 1990.

Steele, Shelby. *The Content of Our Character.* New York: St. Martin's Press, 1990.

Taylor, Bron R. *Affirmative Action At Work: Law, Politics, and Ethics.* Pittsburgh: University of Pittsburgh Press, 1991.

ACKNOWLEDGMENTS

Pages 107, 128 Selections from *The Republic of Plato* reprinted from *The Dialogues of Plato* translated by Benjamin Jowett (4th ed. 1953) by permission of Oxford University Press.

Page 166 "Epicurus to Menoeceus" from *Epicurus: The Extant Remains.* Translated by Cyril Bailey. Oxford: Oxford University Press, 1926. Reprinted by permission of Oxford University Press.

Page 169 "The Encheiridion" by Epictetus. Reprinted by permission of the publishers and the Loeb Classical Library from *Epictetus: The Discourses,* Volume II, translated by W. A. Oldfather, Cambridge, Mass.: Harvard University Press, 1966.

Page 191 Selection from Peter Abelard, *Ethics.* Translated by J. R. McCallum. Merrick, NY: Richwood, 1976. Used with permission of Richwood Publishing.

Page 197 Selections from *Summa Theologica* by Thomas Aquinas reprinted with the permission of the Benziger Publishing Company.

Page 271 Immanuel Kant, *Grounding for the Metaphysics of Morals,* translated by James W. Ellington, 1981, Hackett Publishing Co., Inc. Copyright © 1981 by Hackett Publishing Co., Inc. Used with permission of the publisher.

Page 342 Selections from *Principia Ethica* by G. E. Moore (Buffalo, NY: Prometheus Books, 1988) used with permission of the publisher.

Page 352 "Does Moral Philosophy Rest on a Mistake?" by Harold Arthur Prichard. From *Mind,* 21 (1912):21–37. Reprinted by permission of Oxford University Press.

Page 364 "The Nature of Ethical Disagreement" by C. L. Stevenson. First appeared in *Sigma,* Vols. 1–2, Nos. 8–9 (1947–48).

Page 369 "Ethical Theory and Utilitarianism" by R. M. Hare from *Contemporary British Philosophy 4th,* ed. H. D. Lewis (Allen and Unwin, 1976). Copyright © 1976 by R. M. Hare. Used with permission.

Page 381 "Some Merits of One Form of Rule-Utilitarianism" from *Morality, Utilitarianism, and Rights* by Richard B. Brandt. New York: Cambridge University Press, 1992, pp. 111–131. Copyright © 1992 by Cambridge University Press. Reprinted with the permission of Cambridge University Press.

Page 392 "How to Derive 'Ought' From 'Is'" by John Searle. *Philosophical Review,* 73 (1964): 43–58. Reprinted by permission of John R. Searle, Mills Professor of Philosophy, University of California, Berkeley, California.

Page 401 "Moral Beliefs" by Philippa Foot. *Proceedings of the Aristotelian Society,* 59 (1958–59): 83–104. Reprinted by courtesy of the Editor of the Aristotelian Society: Copyright © 1958–59, and of the author.

Page 415 "Relativistic Ethics: Morality as Politics" by Gilbert Harman. From *Midwest Studies in Philosophy,* III (1978): 109–121. Copyright © 1978 by the University of Minnesota, Morris. Reprinted by permission of Midwest Studies in Philosophy, Inc.

Page 427 Selection from *The Examined Life: Philosophical Meditations* by Robert Nozick. Copyright © 1989 by Robert Nozick. Reprinted by permission of Simon & Schuster, Inc.

Page 439 "Justice As Fairness" by John Rawls. *Philosophical Review,* 67 (1958): 164–194. Used by permission of the author.

Page 450 Taurek, John M. "Should the Numbers Count?" From *Philosophy and Public Affairs,* 6 (1977): 293–316. Copyright © 1977 by Princeton University Press. Reprinted by permission of Princeton University Press.

Page 466 "The Myth of Sisyphus" by Albert Camus. From *The Myth of Sisyphus and Other Essays* by Albert Camus, trans., Justin O'Brien. Copyright © 1955 by Alfred A. Knopf, Inc. Reprinted by permission of the publisher.

Page 476 "Active and Passive Euthanasia" by James Rachels. From *The New England Journal of Medicine,* 292 (Jan. 9, 1975): 78–80. Reprinted by permission of *The New England Journal of Medicine.*

Page 480 "Euthanasia" by Philippa Foot. From *Philosophy and Public Affairs,* 6 (1977): 85–112. Copyright © 1977 by Philippa Foot. Reprinted with the permission of the author.

Page 496 Wertheimer, Roger. "Understanding the Abortion Argument." From *Philosophy and Public Affairs,* 1 (1971): 67–95. Copyright © 1971 by Princeton University Press. Reprinted by permission of Princeton University Press.

Page 507 Thomson, Judith Jarvis. "A Defense of Abortion." From *Philosophy and Public Affairs,* 1 (1971): 46–66. Copyright © 1971 by Princeton University Press. Reprinted by permission of Princeton University Press.

Page 519 "Saints and Heroes" by J. O. Urmson. Reprinted with permission of University of Washington Press from *Essays in Moral Philosophy,* ed. by A. I. Meldon. Copyright © 1958 by University of Washington Press.

Page 529 Singer, Peter. "Famine, Affluence, and Morality." From *Philosophy and Public Affairs,* 1 (1972): 229–243. Copyright © 1972 by Princeton University Press. Reprinted by permission of Princeton University Press.

Page 537 "Equality, Entitlements, and the Distribution of Income" by John Arthur. Copyright © 1981 by John

Arthur. This essay was first published in Vincent Barry, *Applying Ethics* (Belmont, CA: Wadsworth Pub. Co., 1981). Reprinted by permission of the author.

Page 549 "Kantian Approaches to Some Famine Problems" by Onora O'Neill. From *Matters of Life and Death,* ed. by Tom Regan. Copyright © 1980 by Random House, Inc. This material is reproduced with the permission of McGraw-Hill, Inc.

Page 557 "Is Adultery Immoral?" by Richard Wasserstrom. Reprinted with permission of Macmillan Publishing Company from *Today's Moral Problems, Third Edition,* by Richard A. Wasserstrom. Copyright © 1985 by Macmillan Publishing Company.

Page 566 Selections from Richard Taylor, *Having Love Affairs* (Buffalo, NY: Prometheus Books, 1982). Copyright © 1982 by Richard Taylor. Reprinted by permission of the author and publisher.

Page 578 "Pornography and Respect for Women" by Ann Garry. From *Philosophy and Women,* ed. by Sharon Bishop and Marjorie Weinzweig. Belmont, CA: Wadsworth, 1979. Used by permission of the author.

Page 589 "Better Sex" by Sara L. Ruddick. From Robert Baker and Frederick Elliston (eds.), *Philosophy and Sex, revised edition* (Buffalo, NY: Prometheus Books). Copyright © 1984 by Robert Baker and Frederick Elliston. Reprinted by permission of the publisher.

Page 603 "A Defense of Affirmative Action" by Thomas Nagel. Reprinted with the permission of the author.

Page 608 "Is Racial Discrimination Special?" by Michael E. Levin. From the *Journal of Value Inquiry,* vol. 15 (1981), pp. 225–232. Copyright © 1981 Martinus Nijhoff Publishers, The Hague. Reprinted by permission of Kluwer Academic Publishers.

Page 615 "Why Bakke Has No Case" by Ronald Dworkin. Reprinted with permission from *The New York Review of Books.* Copyright © 1977 Nyrev, Inc.

Page 625 "The Illogic of Affirmative Action" by Nicholas Capaldi. From Nicholas Capaldi, *Out of Order: Affirmative Action and the Crisis of Doctrinaire Liberalism* (Buffalo, NY: Prometheus Books). Copyright © 1985 by Nicholas Capaldi. Reprinted by permission of the publisher.

INDEX

The numbers of pages on which articles or book excerpts appear have been boldfaced.